WOMEN'S HUMAN RIGHTS: LEADING INTERNATIONAL AND NATIONAL CASES

Published by the Commonwealth Secretariat

Prepared in collaboration with the Centre for Comparative and Public Law, University of Hong Kong

Edited by Robyn Emerton, Kirstine Adams, Andrew Byrnes and Jane Connors

April 2005

Cavendish
Publishing
Limited

London • Sydney • Portland, Oregon

First published in Great Britain 2005 by
Cavendish Publishing Limited, The Glass House,
Wharton Street, London WC1X 9PX, United Kingdom
Telephone: + 44 (0)20 7278 8000   Facsimile: + 44 (0)20 7278 8080
Email: info@cavendishpublishing.com
Website: www.cavendishpublishing.com

Published in the United States by Cavendish Publishing
c/o International Specialized Book Services,
5824 NE Hassalo Street, Portland,
Oregon 97213-3644, USA

Published in Australia by Cavendish Publishing (Australia) Pty Ltd
45 Beach Street, Coogee, NSW 2034, Australia
Telephone: + 61 (2)9664 0909   Facsimile: + 61 (2)9664 5420
Email: info@cavendishpublishing.com.au
Website: www.cavendishpublishing.com.au

British Library Cataloguing in Publication Data

A catalogue record for this book has been requested

Library of Congress Cataloguing in Publication Data
Data available

ISBN 13: 978-1-859-41906-9
ISBN 10: 1-859-41906-2

1 3 5 7 9 10 8 6 4 2

Printed and bound in Great Britain by Antony Rowe Ltd., Chippenham, Wiltshire

FOREWORD

This compilation of case law is based on materials originally prepared for a series of judicial colloquia[1] on the human rights of women and the girl-child, organised by the Commonwealth Secretariat.

The purpose of the compilation is to respond to a perceived need for a collection of significant cases from around the world in which international or national courts have drawn on international standards to enhance the enjoyment of women's human rights and which would be of use to judges, lawyers and others in jurisdictions around the Commonwealth.

The compilation comprises some 47 cases in full text or edited extracts, grouped under common themes. Given the amount of material that might have been included, our selection has necessarily been a partial one.[2] The *Introduction* follows the structure of the compilation and provides an overview of the cases. It also contains references to other relevant cases that could not be included due to space limitations, as well as references to some useful secondary sources.

Nearly all the cases in the compilation result in a successful outcome in whole or part for the woman concerned, or are in our view in some other way a positive contribution to the enhancement of legal protection of women's human rights (although in some cases the decisions may give rise to broader theoretical or strategic concerns). We have thus not included some major cases which represent setbacks for the full enjoyment of women's equality. We make no apologies for this – there are, after all, so many cases over the centuries that have stood in the way of women's human rights. Given that few of the cases will be formally binding within any particular national system, they are offered both as illustrations of the possibilities for using international standards and as evidence that judges in other countries have found arguments based on international law helpful, or even persuasive, in carrying out their tasks.

The national cases come from courts in both developed and developing countries.[3] Whether a court will be receptive to considering a case from a foreign jurisdiction or an international court is hard to predict – some courts and judges are demonstrably more receptive than others, and the matter certainly does not turn on where the court is located. We hope that the cases in this compilation come from a broad enough range of jurisdictions to show that international human rights norms not only have potential to inform judicial decision-making, but are also increasingly being drawn on by courts around the world.

---

1 These colloquia followed the format of a series of judicial colloquia organised by the Legal Division of the Commonwealth Secretariat which had focused on the use of international human rights law standards in domestic law more generally. The United Nations Division for the Advancement of Women has also convened several judicial colloquia following a similar format since 1998. We have selected cases from among those available to us as of early 2004. In the *Introduction* we have noted a number of significant later developments.

2 For a review of many relevant cases up until 1990, see Rebecca J Cook, "International Human Rights Law Concerning Women: Case Notes and Comments" (1990) 23 *Vanderbilt Journal of Transnational Law* 779-818 (1990), http://www.law-lib.utoronto.ca/Diana/fulltext/cook.pdf.

3 We have not included any US decisions in this compendium, although many US cases are referred to in the cases included. For a recent wide-ranging collection of materials with a US (as well as international) focus, see Catharine A MacKinnon, *Sex Equality* (New York, Foundation Press, 2001).

The compilation also includes many cases from international and regional courts and tribunals, since these have made a significant contribution to the development of international human rights law. In particular, decisions of the former European Commission of Human Rights and the European Court of Human Rights have been influential in many areas of human rights law; and decisions of the European Court of Justice – the highest court of the European Union – have been milestones in the development of gender equality in the field of employment law. The decisions of other international bodies, in particular of the Inter-American Commission on Human Rights and the Inter-American Court of Human Rights, and the United Nations human rights treaty bodies, have also become increasingly important.

The preparation of this compilation has taken place over a much longer period than was originally planned and we would like to thank our colleagues in the Commonwealth Secretariat who have shown considerable patience with the delays in the production of the manuscript and who have provided us with assistance in bringing the project to completion. These include present and past officials of the Commonwealth Secretariat, in particular Lucia Kiwala, Rupert Jones-Parry, Diane Stafford, Nancy Spence and Judith May-Parker. We also gratefully acknowledge the support of Cavendish Publications, in particular Cara Arnett, Jon Lloyd and Ewan Cooper.

The duration of this project has meant that the editors have moved on from the institutions where they worked at the time when the project was initiated; the research involved has been supported in different ways by their current and former institutions. Most of the work involved in the preparation of the compendium has taken place at the Centre for Comparative and Public Law, Faculty of Law, University of Hong Kong over the period 1996–2004 (where Kirstine Adams, Andrew Byrnes and Robyn Emerton were all working). In addition, significant amounts of work were undertaken by Jane Connors* while at the Department of Law, School of Oriental and African Studies, University of London, and by Andrew Byrnes at the Centre for International and Public Law, Faculty of Law, Australian National University from mid-2001 to early 2005, and then as a Visiting Fellow at the Faculty of Law, University of New South Wales (whose Faculty he joined permanently from May 2005).

A number of people have assisted us in the collection, typing and editing of the cases included in the compilation (as well as with related tasks) and we would like to thank them for their assistance. They include Victoria Medd (in London); Josiah Chan, Anthony Fung, Flora Leung, Veronica Yiu, Jogendra Ghimire, Lison Harris and Johannes Chan (in Hong Kong); and Angela Smith, Andrei Seeto and Phil Drury (in Canberra).

---

*   Jane Connors presently works in the Office of the United Nations High Commissioner for Human Rights. The views expressed in the compilation are those of the authors and do not necessarily reflect the views of the Office of the High Commissioner for Human Rights.

Financial and other support for the research work involved has been provided by the Commonwealth Secretariat, the Centre for Comparative and Public Law, at the Faculty of Law, University of Hong Kong; by that Faculty itself; and by the Faculty of Law, Australian National University. We would like to thank our colleagues in different parts of the world who have suggested cases for inclusion and provided us with copies of them. In particular, we would like to thank a number of Jane Connors' former colleagues at SOAS – in particular James Read, Peter Slinn and John Hatchard – who were instrumental in the identification of a number of cases, some of which are found in the *Law Reports of the Commonwealth*.

Kirstine Adams (London)
Andrew Byrnes (Canberra and Sydney)
Jane Connors (Geneva)
Robyn Emerton (Hong Kong)
May 2005

COPYRIGHT ACKNOWLEDGMENTS

TABLE OF CONTENTS

VIOLENCE AGAINST WOMEN AS TORTURE, OR CRUEL, INHUMAN OR DEGRADING TREATMENT

VIOLENCE BY PRIVATE ACTORS

INTRODUCTION

Over the past two decades courts around the world have made increasing use of international standards to inform and enrich their decision-making. In the field of human rights this has been contributed to by the rapid increase in the number of international instruments and the burgeoning of jurisprudence under them. The willingness of many national courts to look to comparative case law (especially from courts in closely related systems of law) has been gradually extended to these international sources. This can be attributed to the openness of many judges, the diligence of advocates in bringing these sources to the attention of the courts, and the work of international organisations and international and national NGOs in disseminating information about international human rights law. The increased ease of access to this material through electronic means has accelerated and encouraged these developments, even as it has permitted the formation of networks to share this information.

This has been true not only of human rights generally, but also increasingly of the human rights of women. The adoption of specific international instruments addressing discrimination against women (in particular the Convention on the Elimination of All Forms of Discrimination against Women [the CEDAW Convention]), as well as the use of what some call "mainstream" human rights instruments and institutions by women's human rights advocates,[1] has led to many positive developments in the international law of human rights and the use of that law at the national level to advance women's rights.[2]

This compilation brings together a range of cases from international and national courts dealing with issues of relevance to the human rights of women, broadly grouped according to subject-matter.[3]

A   USE OF INTERNATIONAL NORMS BY NATIONAL COURTS

The cases in the first part of the compilation deal with a number of general issues about the nature of international obligations assumed by States under human rights treaties, and the reception and use of international law by national courts. From the perspective of international law, courts are organs of the State, and their actions may give rise to liability of the State under international law. This means that where, as a result of a court's decision (or failure to act), a person is denied a right guaranteed by a treaty or a rule of customary international law which is binding on the State, the international responsibility of the State is engaged – even though the court may have been obliged to act as it did by the provisions of national law.

While courts in many countries have considerable freedom in the sources on which they may draw to inform their decision-making, ultimately their primary duty is to apply national law as laid down in their Constitution, legislation and other authoritative sources of national law. In some cases, these sources may include international standards

---

1   See, e.g., Jane Connors, "Using General Human Rights Instruments to Advance the Human Rights of Women" in Kirstine Adams and Andrew Byrnes (eds), *Gender Equality and the Judiciary: Using International Human Rights Standards to Promote the Human Rights of Women and the Girl-child at the National Level* (London: Commonwealth Secretariat, 1999) 37.

2   For a review of many relevant cases up until 1990, see Rebecca J Cook, "International Human Rights Law Concerning Women: Case Notes and Comments" (1990) 23 *Vanderbilt Journal of Transnational Law* 779-818 (1990), www.law-lib.utoronto.ca/Diana/fulltext/cook.pdf.

3   For the basis of the selection of the cases, see the *Foreword*, above. Since many of the cases deal with issues across a number of categories, readers are advised to refer to the subject-matter index at the end of the compilation in addition to the discussion in this *Introduction*.

– for example, in systems which are described as "monist", international treaties are directly incorporated into national law upon their ratification, by virtue of a constitutional or general statutory provision. However, most Commonwealth countries (like the majority of common law countries), tend to follow what is described as a "dualist" system in relation to treaties, whereby international treaty norms will not be binding on the courts unless they have been *expressly* incorporated into the national law by legislative means. This is relatively uncommon so far as human rights treaties are concerned.

Nevertheless, there are a number of ways in which courts in Commonwealth and common law countries have accepted that the use of international standards which have not been directly incorporated into domestic law by constitutional or legislative provisions is legitimate (indeed may even be mandatory).[4] In nearly all Commonwealth and common law countries[5] unincorporated treaties may not generally be relied upon before domestic courts to found a cause of action, but they may nevertheless have an indirect impact on the interpretation and application of law.[6] The presumption that the legislature does not intend to legislate in a manner that is inconsistent with international law is well-accepted in most common law (and civil law) jurisdictions, and has as its corollary a principle of statutory interpretation that, where reasonably possible, statutes should be interpreted in a manner which is consistent with international law.

Courts have used unincorporated treaties in various ways, for example:[7]

- as an aid to constitutional or statutory interpretation, either generally or in order to resolve an "ambiguity"[8]

- as a relevant consideration to be taken into account in the exercise of an administrative discretion by a decision-maker[9]

---

4   This section draws on Andrew Byrnes, "The Use of International Human Rights Instruments in Domestic Litigation", paper prepared for the *Judicial colloquium on the application of international human rights law at the domestic level* (Bangkok, Thailand, 4 – 6 November 2002), organised by the United Nations Division for the Advancement of Women.

5   Exceptions include the United States of America, Cyprus and Nepal, where ratified treaties form part of domestic law, while some other common law countries have incorporated specific human rights treaties at a constitutional level. Many civil law countries provide that treaties and rules of customary international law form part of national law without a further need for legislative transformation.

6   At the same time it is also generally accepted in common law countries that rules of customary international law which are binding on the State form a part of, or are a source of, the common law, though the practical impact of this doctrine in modern times has been limited.

7   For an endorsement by Commonwealth judges and the possibilities of drawing on international treaties (including the CEDAW Convention), see *Victoria Falls Declaration of Principles for Promoting the Human Rights of Women* (1994) and *Conclusions of the Asia/South Pacific Judicial Colloquium for Senior Judges on the Domestic Application of International Human Rights Norms Relevant to Women's Human Rights*, in Andrew Byrnes, Jane Connors and Lum Bik (eds), *Advancing the Human Rights of Women: Using International Instruments in Domestic Litigation: Papers and Statements from the Asia/South Pacific Regional Judicial Colloquium, Hong Kong 20-22 May 1996* (London: Commonwealth Secretariat, 1997) [hereinafter *Hong Kong Colloquium*], at 3-8. These statements built on the declarations of previous Commonwealth judicial colloquia relating to the use of international human rights norms generally at the national level: see P N Bhagwati, "Creating a Judicial Culture to Promote the Enforcement of Women's Human Rights" in *id* at 20-21.

8   See, for example, *Attorney-General of Botswana v Unity Dow* [1991] LRC (Const) 574 (High Court of Botswana); [1992] LRC (Const) 623 (Court of Appeal of Botswana) [Case No 37, p 572 below] (consideration of various international instruments, including the CEDAW Convention, in deciding whether the constitutional guarantee of equality included discrimination based on sex).

9   See, for example, *R v Director of Immigration, ex parte Simon Yin Xiang-jiang* (1994) 4 HKPLR 264 (Hong Kong Court of Appeal) (existence of treaty obligation not to expel a stateless person except on grounds of national security or public morals should be taken into account by decision-maker considering whether to expel such a person on other grounds), citing *Tavita v Minister of Immigration* [1994] NZAR 116 (New Zealand Court of Appeal).

- as giving rise to a *legitimate expectation* that the provisions of the treaty will be applied by a decision-maker unless a hearing is given to the person affected[10]
- as a relevant factor in the exercise of a discretion conferred by legislation on judges[11]
- as a factor that may be taken into consideration in the development of the common law, where the common law is unclear,[12] and
- as a factor that may be taken into account when identifying the demands of public policy.[13]

Courts may also draw on rules of customary international law for some of these purposes, as well as on non-binding instruments or "soft" law to inform the process of decision-making.[14] Of increasing importance is the jurisprudence of international bodies such as the United Nations human rights treaty bodies, comprising both the case law of these treaty committees decided under their optional complaints procedures, and the general comments and general recommendations they have adopted.[15]

Many national constitutions, certainly most in Commonwealth countries, contain general guarantees of equality and non-discrimination, and many explicitly prohibit discrimination on the basis of sex. Yet in some constitutions, an explicit ban on sex discrimination may not have been included, and in others the relationship of guarantees of equality on the basis of sex to other provisions of the constitution (such as religious freedom or the preservation of traditional or customary laws) may be unclear or may even involve a direct conflict.

Many national courts have accepted that international law standards are a legitimate aid to constitutional interpretation. A leading Commonwealth case is *Minister of Home Affairs v Fisher* (1979),[16] in which the Privy Council endorsed a broad purposive approach to constitutional rights interpretation and the avoidance of "the austerity of tabulated legalism". In that case the Privy Council had to decide whether the word "child" in the Bermudan Constitution included an illegitimate child. In concluding that it did, the Privy Council took into account the European Convention on Human Rights and the Universal Declaration on Human Rights (as well as the United Nations Declaration on the Rights of the Child), noting that these were of particular relevance to the Constitution given its origins. Other courts have recognised the relevance of

---

10 *Minister for Immigration and Ethnic Affairs v Ah Hin Teoh* (1994) 128 ALR 353 (High Court of Australia) [Case No 4, p 33 below] (relevance of guarantees in the Children's Convention to decision to deport a parent).

11 See the discussion in *R v Togias* [2001] NSW CCA 5222 (NSW Court of Criminal Appeal), available through www.austlii.edu.au.

12 *Rantzen v Mirror Newspapers* [1994] QB 670 (English Court of Appeal) (guarantee of freedom of expression and its relation to applicable standard for review of jury awards in defamation cases).

13 See, for example, *Canada Trust Co v Ontario Human Rights Commission* (1990) 69 DLR (4th) 321 (Ontario Court of Appeal) (international treaties on non-discrimination, including the CEDAW Convention, taken into account in determining whether a sexist, racist and classist charitable trust was against public policy).

14 See, for example, the reference to the Declaration on the Elimination of Discrimination against Women 1969 in *Attorney-General of Botswana v Dow* [Case No 37, p 572 below], to the Cairo Declaration on Human Rights in Islam in *Mehmood* [Case No 12, p 184 below]. See also the reference by Sachs J to the Declaration on the Elimination of Violence against Women 1993 (GA Res 48/104) in *S v Baloyi (Minister of Justice and Another Intervening)*, 2000 (2) SA 425 (South African Constitutional Court).

15 The jurisprudence of the committees can be found at www.unhchr.ch. Examples of the use of this jurisprudence in this compendium include *Vishaka v State of Rajasthan* [Case No 2, p 11 below]. See generally Committee on International Human Rights Law and Practice of the International Law Association, *Interim report on the impact of the work of the United Nations human rights treaty bodies on national courts and tribunals, Report of the Seventieth Conference*, New Delhi (2002) 507-555 and *Final Report*, Berlin Conference (2004).

16 Case No 1, p 3 below.

international standards to informing their interpretation of constitutional guarantees. Examples in this compilation include the decisions of the Supreme Court of India in *Vishaka v State of Rajasthan* (1997),[17] the High Court of Zambia in *Longwe v Intercontinental Hotels* (1992),[18] and the Court of Appeal of Botswana in *Attorney-General of Botswana v Dow* (1992).[19] In this last case, a majority of the Court concluded that the failure to list "sex" as one of the grounds of prohibited discrimination in the Constitution of Botswana did not mean that the Constitution permitted such discrimination. The judges were bolstered in their conclusion by reference to a number of international treaties and other instruments (some of which were binding on Botswana, some of which were not).

B   STATE RESPONSIBILITY UNDER INTERNATIONAL LAW FOR VIOLATIONS OF THE HUMAN RIGHTS OF WOMEN

Human rights guarantees in international and national law are of little practical worth unless they are effectively implemented by States. In the first place, this requires the State to ensure that State organs and agents do not themselves directly engage in acts which violate human rights. However, it is now well-accepted that international law requires the State to do more than simply refrain from direct violations (so-called negative obligations); States must also take appropriate *positive* steps to ensure that persons within their jurisdictions in practice enjoy the rights guaranteed.[20] This may involve the allocation of resources or the adoption of other measures (including legislative ones) that will permit individuals to enjoy their rights by gaining effective access to State institutions or being afforded legal protection of rights *de jure* (in law) and *de facto* (in fact).

Equally importantly, it is now widely accepted that the positive obligations of the State may also extend to taking appropriate measures to ensure that persons are protected against violations of rights by *private* individuals (the so-called horizontal or third-party effect of human rights obligations). These may include obligations to take reasonable steps to prevent, investigate and punish such violations and to provide for compensation for and rehabilitation of the victims of such violations (though the latter category of obligation is still evolving).

The evolution and importance of positive obligations is illustrated by a number of cases in the compilation. One of the leading cases is *Airey v Ireland* (1979),[21] in which the European Court of Human Rights held that because the applicant was unable to afford legal representation in an application for a judicial separation and there was no alternative state funding (e.g., legal aid), the State had failed to provide the applicant with effective access to court. This constituted a breach of the rights to a fair hearing and to respect for family and private life under articles 6 and 8 of the European Convention on Human Rights.

In another case, involving sexual violence, *X and Y v The Netherlands* (1985),[22] the European Court of Human Rights considered a case in which a gap in the law meant that there was no possibility of bringing a criminal action against the person who had allegedly sexually assaulted a 16 year-old girl with a mental disability. The only remedies available were civil and these were found to be inadequate. The Court held

---

17   Case No 2, p 11 below.
18   Case No 3, p 20 below.
19   Case No 37, p 572 below.
20   See generally *Social and Economic Rights Action Centre and the Center for Economic and Social Rights v Nigeria*, African Commission on Human and Peoples' Rights, Communication No 155/96 (2001), paras 43-48, available at www.achpr.org/html/communications.html.
21   Case No 5, p 67 below.
22   Case No 6, p 81 below.

that a State has a positive obligation to adopt measures that give effect to the right to protection of family and private life under article 8 of the European Convention on Human Rights, that these measures must be effective and appropriate, and that this required the possibility of criminal proceedings in a case of such seriousness.[23]

In relation to the development of the obligation of the State to investigate, punish and remedy violations of rights by non-State actors, the most significant international decision has been the judgment of the Inter-American Court of Human Rights in the case of *Velásquez Rodríguez v Honduras* (1988).[24] In that case the Court considered the responsibility of the State of Honduras in relation to the disappearance of a person which had been carried out by persons acting under cover of public authority. The Court held that this clearly involved the responsibility of the State, but went much further than this in explaining the nature of the obligation of a State to "respect and ensure" human rights contained in article 1 of the American Convention on Human Rights. In a passage which has proved to be of central importance to the protection of women's human rights, the Court held:[25]

> "172 An illegal act which violates human rights and which is initially not directly imputable to a State (for example, because it is the act of a private person or because the person responsible has not been identified) can lead to international responsibility of the State, not because of the act itself, but because of the lack of due diligence to prevent the violation or to respond to it as required by the Convention.
>
> 173   What is decisive is whether a violation of the rights recognized by the Convention has occurred with the support or the acquiescence of the government, or whether the State has allowed the act to take place without taking measures to prevent it or to punish those responsible. Thus, the Court's task is to determine whether the violation is the result of a State's failure to fulfill its duty to respect and guarantee those rights, as required by Article 1(1) of the Convention.
>
> 174   The State has a legal duty to take reasonable steps to prevent human rights violations and to use the means at its disposal to carry out a serious investigation of violations committed within its jurisdiction, to identify those responsible, to impose the appropriate punishment and to ensure the victim adequate compensation.
>
> 175   This duty to prevent includes all those means of a legal, political, administrative and cultural nature that promote the protection of human rights and ensure that any violations are considered and treated as illegal acts, which, as such, may lead to the punishment of those responsible and the obligation to indemnify the victims for damages....
>
> 176   The State is obligated to investigate every situation involving a violation of the rights protected by the Convention. If the State apparatus acts in such a way that the violation goes unpunished and the victim's full enjoyment of such rights is not restored as soon as possible, the State has failed to comply with its duty to ensure the free and full exercise of those rights to the persons within its jurisdiction. The same is true when the State allows private persons or groups to act freely and with impunity to the detriment of the rights recognized by the Convention."

---

23   See also *Whiteside v United Kingdom*, Application No 20357/92, European Commission of Human Rights, decision on admissibility, 7 March 1994, where the Commission held that threatening behaviour by the applicant's ex-partner was sufficient to place the state under a positive obligation to protect the applicant's rights under the European Convention on Human Rights. As to the rule on exhaustion of domestic remedies, the Court held that domestic remedies must provide effective and sufficient redress in practice, not just in theory.
24   Case No 7, p 91 below.
25   *Id* at paras 172-176.

This jurisprudence and the decision were followed by the Inter-American Commission on Human Rights in *Fernandes v Brazil* (2001),[26] in which the Commission held that the failure by a State to take appropriate steps to investigate and punish a man who had over a period of time physically and psychologically abused his wife meant that it had failed to carry out its obligations to respect and ensure the rights to life, personal integrity and equality before the law (among others) had been violated.[27]

The relevance of the application of human rights guarantees to the actions of private parties in a constitutional context is illustrated by *Longwe v Intercontinental Hotels* (1992).[28] In this case the High Court of Zambia held that the guarantee of freedom of movement in the Constitution made it unlawful for a hotel to exclude from the public bar a woman unaccompanied by a man.

C   CONCEPTS OF DISCRIMINATION

General

Central to remedying violations of women's human rights is an understanding of the concept of discrimination and its legal definition. International legal instruments and jurisprudence have formulated definitions of discrimination in various ways. The most common formulation is a notion of equality which starts from an assumption of identical treatment of women and men, unless there is some "objective and reasonable justification" for differential treatment. This approach has frequently been articulated in cases decided by the human rights institutions of the Council of Europe (the Strasbourg organs) and in some United Nations case law, where the explicit differential treatment of women and men in law or practice has been challenged. The limitation of this approach is that for the most part it embodies a notion of equality as women's entitlement to what men have (only a partial, though important, view of equality); the critical dimension of the inquiry is in determining what is an "objective and reasonable" justification for a difference in treatment.

In *Abdulaziz, Cabales and Balkandali v United Kingdom* (1985),[29] the Strasbourg organs stated that "equality of the sexes is today a major goal" of the Council of Europe and that this meant that "very weighty reasons would have to be advanced before a difference of treatment on the ground of sex could be regarded as compatible with the Convention".[30] In that case the European Court of Human Rights upheld a challenge to

---

26 Case No 47, p 740 below. See also Committee on the Elimination of Discrimination against Women, *Report on Mexico under Article 8 of the Optional Protocol to the Convention*, CEDAW/C/2005/OP.8/MEXICO (27 January 2005).

27 Given the extent of violations of women's human rights by non-State actors in the community and in the family, the obligation of the State to ensure that adequate protection and remedies are provided is fundamentally important. A number of other cases decided under different instruments further illustrate this expanded understanding of the obligation of the State. In *L K v The Netherlands* (Communication No 4/1991, views of 16 March 1993), the United Nations Committee on the Elimination of Racial Discrimination held that a State was obliged under the Racial Discrimination Convention to ensure that legislation providing protection against acts of racial discrimination was enforced with due diligence and in an expeditious manner. While the decision was based on the particular language of the Racial Discrimination Convention, similar language appears in most other treaties. (Article 6 of that Convention provides that "States parties shall assure to everyone within their jurisdiction effective protection and remedies, through competent tribunals and other State institutions, against any act of racial discrimination . . ."). See also *Yilmaz-Dogan v Netherlands*, Committee on the Elimination of Racial Discrimination, Communication No 1/1984, Opinion of 10 August 1988; UN Doc CERD/C/36/D/1/1984.

28 Case No 3, p 20 below.

29 Case No 39, p 618 below.

30 *Id* at para 78.

United Kingdom immigration law and practice which imposed more onerous conditions on foreign female nationals who wished to bring their husbands to the United Kingdom than it did on foreign male nationals. The Court rejected the justification offered by the United Kingdom that equal treatment would have an adverse impact on the labour market.

This "sameness/difference" approach has been developed internationally and also by some national courts. Under the United Nations conventions containing guarantees of equality and non-discrimination, it is accepted that what is guaranteed is not some formal notion of equality but a substantive one. This has two, related dimensions: first, that even where men and women are treated identically, if a "neutral" law or practice has a disproportionate impact on women, then it will constitute discrimination unless it can be objectively and reasonably justified. Secondly, that an analysis of equality must look to questions of substantive disadvantage and disempowerment. These dimensions can be seen in the definitions of "discrimination" in the CEDAW and CERD Conventions, which have also been incorporated in the jurisprudence of some of the other treaty bodies whose treaties do not expressly define "discrimination".[31]

An important illustration of a substantive approach to discrimination is the case of *Andrews v Law Society of British Columbia* (1989),[32] which involved a challenge to British Columbia provisions limiting the right of permanent residents who were not Canadian citizens to be admitted to the Bar of the province. In a wide-ranging review of concepts of discrimination, the Supreme Court of Canada considered the meaning of the term "discrimination" under section 15 of the Canadian Charter of Rights and Freedoms, and rejected the notion that "those similarly situated should be similarly treated" was an adequate test of what amounted to discrimination. McIntyre J (and Lamer J concurring) held that:

> "discrimination may be described as a distinction, whether intentional or not but based on grounds relating to personal characteristics of the individual or group, which has the effect of imposing burdens, obligations, or disadvantages on such individual or group not imposed upon others, or which withholds or limits access to opportunities, benefits, and advantages available to other members of society".[33]

Affirmative action

Related to the definition of discrimination is the permissibility of "affirmative action", "positive measures", or "temporary special measures", all of which refer to measures which take a normally prohibited ground of discrimination as the basis for differential treatment of individuals, with the intention of redressing past or continuing disadvantage or discrimination suffered by that group. Such measures may vary widely from strict quotas to programmes encouraging applications by members of protected groups, and their legality may depend on the particular legislative or constitutional provisions in question.

Under international human rights law, measures intended to redress the disadvantage suffered by a particular, disadvantaged group are permissible (indeed, arguably required in some circumstances), and States are afforded a reasonable amount

---

31 Human Rights Committee, *General Comment* 18(37), paras 6 and 7. Article 1 of the CEDAW Convention provides:
    "'discrimination against women' shall mean any distinction, exclusion or restriction made on the basis of sex which has the effect or purpose of impairing or nullifying the recognition, enjoyment or exercise by women irrespective of their marital status, on a basis of equality of men and women, of human rights and fundamental freedoms in the political, economic, social, cultural, civil or any other field."

32 Case No 8, p 121 below.

33 (1989) 56 DLR (4th) 1, at 18.

of flexibility in designing measures of this sort.[34] It is not always clear whether such measures are acceptable because they are not in themselves discriminatory (on the ground that treating members of disadvantaged groups more favourably has an objective and reasonable justification), or because they are an explicit exemption of what would otherwise have been unlawful discrimination. Under the UN human rights treaties, positive measures of this sort (described as "temporary special measures" in the CEDAW Convention, for example) are envisaged to be "temporary", to be applied only so long as the conditions of disadvantage persist.

Re Municipal Officers' Association of Australia (1991)[35] is illustrative of what may be acceptable special measures under the CEDAW Convention. The case involved an examination of proposed changes to the rules of a union in the lead-up to a merger between three unions, which were designed to increase the participation of women in union management, and which proposed the establishment in union branches of a position on the executive of Branch Vice-President (Women), for which only female members could be nominated and vote. A similar position, National Vice-President (Women), was proposed for the National Executive. The Australian Industrial Relations Commission considered whether this differential treatment of members on the ground of sex fell within section 33 of the Sex Discrimination Act (Cth), which was intended to give effect to article 4(1) of the CEDAW Convention and which provided that it was not unlawful "to do an act a purpose of which is to ensure that persons of a particular sex ... have equal opportunities with other persons in circumstances in relation to which provision is made by this Act."

The Commission held that the proposed rules were consistent with both section 33 of the Sex Discrimination Act and the CEDAW Convention. It considered that the goal was to promote *de facto* equality of women, which meant "representation by women in governing and policy-making bodies within an organisation broadly corresponding to the proportion of female members." Since women had been under-represented in the governance of the amalgamating organisations, the Commission accepted that rules which reserved positions for women on the executive of the branches and of the organisation could contribute to altering the perception of lack of encouragement by the union and therefore ameliorate the effect of past discrimination, and were therefore permissible.

Opinions on what types of positive measures are legitimate vary between legal systems. For example, under the law of the European Union regulating sex discrimination in employment, the range of measures open to a State may be less broad than under the UN human rights treaties. In *Kalanke v Freie Hansestadt Bremen* (1995),[36] the European Court of Justice considered the consistency with the Equal Treatment Directive of a law adopted by the City of Bremen, which provided that, when filling certain categories of job, women with qualifications equal to those held by men applying for the same position would be given priority if they were under-represented in the

---

34 CEDAW Convention, art 4; CERD Convention, art 1(4); Human Rights Committee, *General Comment* 18(37). Article 4 of the CEDAW Convention provides:

"4(1) Adoption by States Parties of temporary special measures aimed at accelerating *de facto* equality between men and women shall not be considered discrimination as defined in the present Convention, but shall in no way entail as a consequence the maintenance of unequal or separate standards; these measures shall be discontinued when the objectives of equality of opportunity and treatment have been achieved."

The CEDAW Committee has discussed in detail the nature and scope of "temporary special measures" under the CEDAW Convention: *General Recommendation 25* (2004).

35 Case No 9, p 148 below.
36 Case No 10, p 159 below.

relevant personnel group (shown by women constituting less than half of the staff in the pay bracket of the relevant personnel group within a department).

The Court noted that, as article 2(1) of the Directive stipulated that "the principle of equal treatment shall mean that there shall be no discrimination whatsoever on grounds of sex", a quota system of this sort was inconsistent with that provision. However, it then considered whether the measure was one permitted by article 2(4), which provided that the Directive "shall be without prejudice to measures to promote equal opportunity for men and women, in particular by removing existing inequalities which affect women's opportunities". The Court noted that this provision was:

> "specifically and exclusively designed to allow measures which, although discriminatory in appearance, are in fact intended to eliminate or reduce actual instances of inequality which may exist in the reality of social life. It thus permits national measures relating to access to employment, including promotion, which give a specific advantage to women with a view to improving their ability to compete in the labour market and to pursue a career on an equal footing with men."[37]

However, it concluded that rules of this sort, "which guarantee women absolute and unconditional priority for appointment and promotion, go beyond promoting equal opportunities and overstep the limits of the exception in article 2(4) of the Directive."[38]

This conclusion must be understood in the light of the opinion provided to the Court by the Advocate-General, which reviews the history of the equality provisions in European law and concepts of equality, and explores the various options for positive measures and affirmative action. In particular, the Advocate-General draws a distinction between measures designed to promote equality of opportunity (by removing conditions of disadvantage) and ones designed to produce equality of result or outcome (which he considered were not protected by article 2(4)). In the present case, given that the two candidates for a position were by definition equally qualified, he concluded that the goal of equal opportunity (by bringing women and men to an equal starting-point) had been achieved, and that automatically to prefer a woman at that stage was unjustifiable sex discrimination.[39]

D   RIGHTS RELATING TO MARRIAGE

Right freely to choose one's spouse

The right to choose one's spouse is a fundamental right guaranteed by a number of international treaties and national constitutions. However, in some countries, as the result of traditional, customary or religious practices, a woman may not be free to choose

---

37 *Id* at para 18.
38 *Id* at para 22.
39 See also *Calderón v President of the Republic and another* (*Vote no 716-98*) (1998) 6 BHRC 306, in which the Constitutional Chamber of the Supreme Court of Justice of Costa Rica held that the failure of the executive government to include any women in the list of candidates forwarded to the legislature for appointment to the Board of Directors of the Monitoring Body for Public Services (*Junta Directiva de la Autoridad Reguladora de los Servicios Públicos*) was inconsistent with both the guarantees of equality under national law and the obligation embodied in article 7 of the CEDAW Convention to take appropriate measures to ensure that women enjoyed equality in public life. The government had to take active steps to achieve this goal - and this included nominating a similar number of women and men to public posts (assuming that there were sufficient qualified candidates of each sex). The court ordered the government to ensure that future nominations contained a representative number of women. See now *Jacobs v Belgium*, Communication No 943/2000, views adopted on 7 July 2004, in which the Human Rights Committee rejected a complaint by a Belgian man that a requirement that there be at least four members of each sex on two groups of eleven non-justices of the High Council of State was discriminatory. The Committee held this was an objective, reasonable and proportionate way, in the context, of pursuing gender equality in the composition of public advisory bodies.

her spouse and may be subject to social or family sanctions where she seeks to exercise that choice in a manner which is not consistent with traditionally accepted or mandated ways of choosing a spouse.

This issue has been addressed indirectly in several international cases included in the compilation, as well as in the important national decision of *Humaira Mehmood* (1999) decided by the Lahore High Court in Pakistan.[40] In *Ghaled v United Arab Emirates*[41] the United Nations Working Group on Arbitrary Detention considered the case of a Christian Lebanese man who had married a Muslim woman of UAE nationality in Lebanon. The husband did not convert to Islam, as was required under Sharia law if a Muslim woman were to marry a non-Muslim man; and he was subsequently charged before a Sharia court in the UAE with fornication and sentenced to 99 lashes and one year's imprisonment. Noting that the marriage had been entered into on the basis of the free will of the spouses, the Working Group concluded that the criminalisation and punishment of a person for marrying a person of another religion was inconsistent with the right to equality, the right to choose one's spouse, and the right to respect for privacy guaranteed by the Universal Declaration of Human Rights (articles 2, 7, 12, 16 and 18), and that therefore his detention was "arbitrary".

In the case of *Humaira Mehmood v SHO PS North Cantt*,[42] Humaira had secretly married Mehmood Butt against the will of her parents, who had promised her in marriage to a cousin when she was a child. Humaira was beaten, tortured and detained for a month, before being forcibly married to her cousin, a marriage which was backdated in the marriage register, so as to appear to have taken place one month before her marriage to Mehmood. Fearing for their lives, Humaira and Mehmood fled to Karachi, where they were pursued, the cousin filing a case with the police that Humaira had been abducted by Mehmood and that she had committed adultery (*zina*), since she was at that time married to the complainant. Humaira brought a petition before the Lahore High Court, refuting the claim that she had been abducted, and requesting the court to quash the charges against herself and Mehmood. In allowing the petition, the Court declared that it was a settled proposition of law that in Islam a woman could contract marriage of her own free will, and further that a marriage performed under coercion was no marriage at law. The Court noted that this was supported both by the Constitution, which guaranteed that everybody should be treated strictly in accordance with the law and provided that the State should protect marriage, as well as by the CEDAW Convention, article 16 of which requires state parties to take appropriate measures to eliminate discrimination against women in all matters relating to marriage, including the right freely to choose a spouse and to enter into marriage only with their free and full consent.

In *A S v Sweden*,[43] the Committee against Torture considered a claim by an Iranian woman in Sweden that returning her to Iran would expose her to a substantial risk of torture, in violation of article 3 of the Torture Convention. The woman was the widow of a martyr and as such supported and supervised by the Committee of Martyrs. She claimed that she had been forced into a *sighe* or *mutah* marriage as the result of threats by a high-ranking ayatollah to harm her and her children. A *sighe* or *mutah* marriage is a short-term marriage, in the present case stipulated for a period of one and a half years, and recognised legally by Shia Islam. The author was not expected to live with her *sighe* husband, but to be available for sexual services whenever he required. Because of her

---

40 Case No 12, p 184 below.
41 Case No 11, p 179 below.
42 Case No 12, p 184 below.
43 Case No 13, p 203 below.

relationship with a Christian man, who she understood had been sentenced to stoning for adultery after she had left Iran, she claimed that if she returned to Iran it was likely that she would suffer a similar fate. The Committee concluded that, given the material before it, the Swedish government was obliged not to return the applicant to Iran.[44]

Right to equality in marriage and in the family

Laws which assign different rights and responsibilities to men and women in marriage and on its dissolution have come under increasing scrutiny before international tribunals. Since these frequently reflect roles traditionally assigned to men and women, they have been successfully challenged in a number of cases, with arguments about the protection of women and the desirability for legal certainty or family unity generally not prevailing against the guarantees of formal and substantive equality in international human rights instruments.

In *Ato del Avellanal v Peru* (1988),[45] for example, a woman challenged article 168 of the Peruvian Civil Code, which provided that when a women is married, only her husband is entitled to represent matrimonial property before the courts. Unsuccessful before the Peruvian courts, the complainant succeeded before the Human Rights Committee, which held that this differential treatment was discriminatory and violated articles 3, 14(1) and 26 of the ICCPR.

Similar provisions remain in the civil codes of a number of countries. More recently, in *Morales de Sierra v Guatemala* (2001),[46] a married woman challenged a number of provisions of the Guatemalan Civil Code providing for different rights and responsibilities for husbands and wives, on the ground that they violated a number of rights in the American Convention on Human Rights, as well as article 15 and 16 of the CEDAW Convention. These provisions included an article similar to that considered in *Ato del Avellanal*, which empowered the husband to administer marital property, and stipulated the "special right and obligation" of the wife to care for minor children and the home. They also provided that a married woman might only work outside the home if this did not prejudice her role as mother and homemaker, and that a husband might oppose this as long as he provided for his wife and had adequate reasons for his opposition (a judge having the power to decide in case of disagreement).

The Inter-American Commission on Human Rights concluded that each of these provisions was inconsistent with the guarantees of equality in the American Convention and the CEDAW Convention, as well as other rights, rejecting the justifications accepted by the national constitutional court of the need for legal certainty in the family and concluding that the provisions established a situation of *de jure* dependency for the wife, created an insurmountable disequilibrium in spousal authority within the marriage, applied stereotyped notions of the roles of women and men which perpetuated *de facto* discrimination against women in the family sphere, and impeded the ability of men to develop fully their roles within the marriage and family.[47]

Rights to maintenance on divorce

The relationship between religious beliefs and practices and guarantees of gender equality is often complex and contentious, but there has been relatively little case law directly addressing these issues at the international level, although the cases included in

---

44 *Id* at para 9.
45 Case No 14, p 217 below.
46 Case No 15, p 222 below.
47 See also *Hariharan v Reserve Bank of India* [1999] 1 LRI 353 (Supreme Court of India) (law providing that father was to be guardian in preference to mother in most circumstances held discriminatory).

this compilation which deal with the right to choose one's spouse[48] address them in that specific context.

The relationship between religious beliefs and guarantees of gender equality arose in an indirect manner before the Supreme Court of India in *Mohammed Ahmed Khan v Shah Bano* (1985),[49] involving a Muslim man and woman who had divorced. The former husband had paid his former wife a monthly sum during the period of *iddat*, as required by Muslim personal law, but she also sought an order for maintenance under section 125 of the Criminal Procedure Code, which conferred power on a magistrate to order a man to provide maintenance for his divorced wife. The question was whether this provision applied to a case in which the husband had already complied with the requirements of his personal law in relation to payments on the termination of marriage.

The Supreme Court of India held that section 125 was entirely secular in its operation and the Constitution did not preclude it from applying to parties governed by personal law. The Court also held that, in any event, there was no conflict between section 125 and the provisions of personal law, since the requirements of Muslim law were to maintain the woman during the period of *iddat*, and did not address the situation where the former wife was unable to provide for herself after that period (to which section 125 applied).

The decision was controversial and led to protests from sectors of the Muslim community in India. The passage of the Muslim Women (Protection of Rights on Divorce) Act 1986, which sought to reverse the effect of the judgment in *Shah Bano*, followed. The 1986 Act precluded Muslim women from seeking the protection of section 125 of the Code, and provided that a divorced Muslim woman is entitled to a "reasonable and fair provision" from her husband in addition to any maintenance payments, and also placed an obligation on the woman's relatives and the State Board to provide support. In a subsequent challenge to the constitutionality of the 1986 Act on the ground that it violated the constitutional guarantee of equality, the Supreme Court held the law constitutional, but interpreted it as meaning that the right of the woman to "reasonable and fair provision" was not time-limited and that the husband could be liable under the 1986 Act for alimony payments beyond the stipulated period for maintenance.[50]

E   RIGHTS AS A MEMBER OF A MINORITY

The rights of women to recognition of their cultural and ethnic identity and to the rights and privileges that derive from that identity are also protected by international law. In *Lovelace v Canada* (1981),[51] Sandra Lovelace, a Canadian citizen and Maliseet Indian, married a non-Indian and, pursuant to the provisions of the federal Indian Act, lost her Indian status, and with it the right to live on a reserve with her community. An Indian man who married a non-Indian woman did not lose his Indian status in this way; the legislative provisions were intended to protect the Indian minority and were based on traditional patrilineal family relationships. Lovelace's situation persisted even after she was divorced from her husband. Lovelace argued that various of her rights under the International Covenant on Civil and Political Rights (ICCPR) had been infringed, including her rights as a member of a minority under article 27, which guarantees that persons belonging to minorities "shall not be denied the right in community with the other members of their group, to enjoy their own culture, to profess and practise their own religion, or to use their own language."

---

48 See above.
49 Case No 16, p 245 below.
50 *Daniel Latifi v Union of India*, summary available at (2002) 3 CHRLD 258 and on-line at www.interights.org.
51 Case No 17, p 261 below.

Although article 27 did not explicitly guarantee the right to live on a reserve, the Committee held that in order for Lovelace to enjoy the rights specified it was necessary for her to be able to live on the reserve. Since her marriage had broken down, denying her the right to live on the reserve was not reasonable or necessary to preserve the identity of the tribe.

F   RIGHT TO RESPECT FOR FAMILY LIFE

The institution of the family is of critical importance to women's social and economic position in society. Particular forms of family are privileged in different societies, and family links recognised by law are frequently used as the basis for a whole array of rights relating to marriage and divorce, the rights of children, employment and related benefits, nationality and residence rights, inheritance and property rights, among others. In this context the right to respect for one's family and private life and the right to non-discrimination in the enjoyment of that right, guaranteed under all the major human rights instruments, have been of particular importance.

An important issue has been which relationships constitute a "family" for the purposes of the international human rights instruments.[52] It is clear that a *de jure* heterosexual marriage recognised under the laws of individual countries constitutes a "family" under international law, whether or not children are born to the couple.[53] (The concerns in this area tend to arise in relation to the free exercise of the right to choose one's spouse, and to the legal and social assignment of traditional roles to husbands and wives, discussed above.)[54] More problematic have been relationships which arise outside this privileged form of marriage, in particular in legal systems in which a distinction is still maintained between children born within a *de jure* marriage, and those born outside such a relationship.

The international decisions have contributed to the assimilation of the position of a child born outside a *de jure* marriage to that of a child born within a *de jure* marriage, so far as the child's legal bonds with its biological parents are concerned. Where spouses are concerned, there is no guarantee of a right to divorce under international law, nor any right to have a *de facto* marriage treated as identical to a *de jure* marriage. Further, little progress has occurred with respect to the recognition of same-sex relationships, creating similar rights to those created by heterosexual *de jure* or *de facto* relationships.[55]

In *Marckx v Belgium* (1979),[56] the European Court of Human Rights considered the Belgian law governing the establishment of maternity and legitimacy of a child, which laid down special procedures for the legal recognition by a mother of her child born outside wedlock. The court held that article 8 of the European Convention drew no distinction between a "legitimate" and "illegitimate" family, and that the relationship between a mother and child was sufficient to establish a family. It also found that the relationship between a child and its mother and the mother's family was an important

---

52   The Human Rights Committee has stated in relation to the right to respect for family life under article 17 of the ICCPR:

"Regarding the term 'family', the objectives of the Covenant require that for purposes of article 17 this term be given a broad interpretation to include all those comprising the family as understood in the society of the State party concerned."
General Comment 16(32) (1988), para 5

53   Both the United Nations Human Rights Committee and the European Court of Human Rights have found that marriage itself was sufficient to constitute a family (*Aumeeruddy-Cziffra and others v Mauritius* before the United Nations Human Rights Committee [Case No 38, p 608 below]; and *Abdulaziz, Cabales and Balkandali v United Kingdom* before the European Court of Human Rights [Case No 39, p 618 below]).

54   See above, Section D.

55   See note 62 below.

56   Case No 18, p 273 below.

family relationship, and that the differential treatment of a "legitimate" child and a child recognised under the relevant procedure in relation to the mother's family was a violation of article 8. The court also held that the different treatment of a "legitimate" child and an "illegitimate" child so far as the right of the child to inherit on the mother's intestacy and the right of the mother to give or bequeath property to her child was a violation of article 8 in conjunction with the right to non-discrimination in article 14.[57]

The European Court came to a similar conclusion about the need to equate the status of children born within and outside a *de jure* marriage in *Johnston v Ireland* (1986).[58] In that case Roy Johnston, who had separated from his wife some years earlier, had been living for a considerable period in a *de facto* relationship with another woman. They had a daughter who, due to the unavailability of divorce in Ireland, was "illegitimate" under Irish law, and it was not possible for her status to be legitimated by the marriage of her parents. The European Court rejected the arguments that the European Convention guaranteed a right to divorce (derived either from the rights to marry, to respect for private or family life, or to freedom of thought) and that article 8 of the Convention required a State to establish for unmarried couples a status analogous to that or married couples. However, it did conclude that the child's right to respect for family life required that she be placed in the same legal and social position as a "legitimate" child.

Courts have also addressed related issues arising out of difference between the legal presumptions surrounding marriage and social reality For example, in *Kroon v The Netherlands* (1994),[59] the European Court addressed a case in which Catharina Kroon, whose marriage had broken down in 1980, had a child with a man other than her husband in 1987. Kroon's husband, whose whereabouts had been unknown to her since 1986, had been registered as the father of the child. Kroon obtained a divorce from her husband which became effective in 1988, and then sought to have a statement included in the register of births to the effect that her former husband was not the father of the child, so that her current partner could take steps to recognise the child as his. The registrar refused this request on the ground that, since the child had been born while Kroon was still married to her former husband, it was not open to her to deny her former husband's paternity, except in relation to a child born after the dissolution of the marriage. Recognition by another man was impossible under Netherlands law as it stood, unless the former husband brought proceedings to deny paternity.

The Court followed its earlier case law that the notion of family was not confined to solely marriage-based relationships and may encompass other *de facto* "family ties" where parties are living together outside marriage. Although the parties were not living together in this case, there were other factors which demonstrated that the relationship had sufficient constancy to create *de facto* "family ties". In the Court's view, a child born of such a relationship was part of that "family unit" from the moment of its birth and by the very fact of it. Accordingly, the Court concluded that respect for family life required that biological and social reality prevailed over a legal presumption which, as in the present case, flew in the face of established fact and the wishes of those concerned without actually benefiting anyone, concluding that the State was obliged to "act in a manner calculated to enable that tie to be developed and legal safeguards must be established that render possible as from the moment of birth or as soon as practicable thereafter the child's integration in his family".[60]

---

57   The Court also held that there was a violation of the mother's right to peaceful enjoyment of her possessions (Article 1, Protocol No 1), in conjunction with article 14.
58   Case No 19, p 296 below.
59   Case No 20, p 324 below.
60   *Id* at para 32. Courts have also recognised that the circumstances of women and men may differ substantially in relation to the legal status of children. In *Rasmussen v Denmark*, Judgment of 22 October 1984, the European Court of Human Rights held that different time limits for men and women to institute paternity proceedings were not discriminatory.

Different issues arose in the Zambian case of *Nawakwi v Attorney-General*.[61] Nawakwi was a single mother of two children. The father of the first was not known, while the father of the second was a Tanzanian. In order to have the children endorsed on her passport, Nawakwi had to swear various affidavits and, in the case of the second child, obtain the consent of the father of the child. The High Court of Zambia accepted her argument that these procedures were discriminatory on the basis of sex and therefore unconstitutional, holding that a single parent family headed by a male or female was a recognised family unit in Zambian society and that every mother of a child, single or married, was entitled to the same powers that the father enjoyed.[62]

G   REPRODUCTIVE RIGHTS

The struggle for women to attain control over their own reproductive capacities has been waged at the international as well as national level. While there have been a number of important international treaty provisions as well as non-binding declarations on the issue, there have been relatively few international cases involving reproductive rights.[63] The cases included in this compilation include three relating to access to information

---

61   Case No 21, p 340 below.
62   We have not included in this compilation recent cases which deal with discrimination against individuals or couples involved in same-sex relationships. International courts have not generally accepted same-sex relationships as the same as or even as equivalent to marriage. See, e.g., *Grant v South-West Trains Ltd*, Case C-249/96 [1998] ICR 449 (European Court of Justice) (holding that refusal to extend employment benefits to unmarried same-sex partners while doing so for unmarried partners of the opposite sex was not discrimination on the basis of sex); and *Joslin v New Zealand*, Human Rights Committee, Communication No 902/1999, views adopted on 17 July 2002 (holding that non-recognition of the right of two persons of the same-sex to marry was not a violation of the ICCPR). However, some national courts have been prepared to go some way towards assimilating the position of same-sex partners to same-sex spouses. For example, in *Fitzpatrick (AP) v Sterling Housing Association Ltd* [2001] 1 AC 27 the House of Lords gave a broad definition to "family" in the interpretation of the Rent Act 1977 governing the transfer of secured tenancies. They held that a family was not necessarily a married couple and that the purpose of the Act could be satisfied by a same-sex couple so long as they lived together in a long-standing, close, loving and faithful, monogamous relationship. However, the House held that the partner could not be considered a "spouse" under the legislation. In *Mendoza v Ghaidan* [2002] EWCA Civ 1533 (English Court of Appeal), in direct reliance on the Human Rights Act 1998, the Court of Appeal held that to refuse to include a same-sex partner within the meaning of the term "spouse" in the Act was discriminatory. See also *Attorney-General (Ontario) v M and H* [1999] 2 SCR 3, in which the Supreme Court of Canada reached a similar conclusion, and *Young v Australia*, Human Rights Committee, Communication No 941/200, views of 6 August 2003 (holding refusal to grant war veteran's pension to same-sex partner discriminatory).
For information about developments in international law and national case law, see the website of the International Lesbian and Gay Association, www.ilga.org. For a review of the international authorities in relation to the rights of transsexuals to marry, see the landmark judgment of the European Court of Human Rights in *Goodwin v United Kingdom*, 11 July 2002, and judgment of the House of Lords in *Bellinger v Bellinger* [2003] UKHL 21.
63   For a review of the work of the UN human rights treaty bodies in this area, see Rebecca J Cook, Bernard M Dickens and Mahmoud F Fathalla, *Reproductive health and human rights: integrating medicine, ethics and law* (Oxford: Clarendon Press, 2003); Julie Stanchieri, Isfahan Merali and Rebecca J. Cook, *The Application of Human Rights to Reproductive and Sexual Health: A Compilation of the Work of International Human Rights Treaty Bodies* (November 2000), available at http://www.law-lib.utoronto.ca/Diana/compilation/comp.htm. For a similar review of the Council of Europe and European Union contributions (including relevant case law), see Julie Stanchieri, Isfahan Merali, Nell Rasmussen, Dina Bogecho, and Rebecca J Cook, *The Application of Human Rights to Reproductive and Sexual Health: A Compilation of the Work of the European Human Rights System* (March 2002), www.astra.org.pl/tor/index_1.html. See generally Rebecca J Cook, "International Protection of Women's Reproductive Rights", (1992) 24 *New York University Journal of International Law & Politics* 645-728, available at www.law-lib.utoronto.ca/diana/fulltext/cook2.pdf and Martin Scheinin, "Sexual Rights as Human Rights - Protected under Existing Human Rights Treaties?" (1998) 67 *Nordic Journal of International Law* 17-35.

about abortion and access to abortion services, but they are of broader relevance to women's rights to exercise choice in this area of their lives and to have access to the information which they need to make informed choices.

In *Paton v United Kingdom* (1980),[64] a man had unsuccessfully sought an injunction from the English courts to prevent the termination of his wife's pregnancy. He complained to the European Commission on Human Rights, arguing that this refusal and the legislation permitting abortions violated various rights guaranteed to him (and his unborn child). The Commission rejected his complaint, holding that, if the European Convention did confer a right to life on a foetus (which was far from clear), it was not absolute and that the right of the woman to life and health would prevail. It also held that the woman's decision to terminate her pregnancy in order to avert risk or injury to her physical or mental health, in so far as it interfered with the applicant's right to respect for his family life under article 8, was justified under article 8(2) as being necessary for the protection of the rights of another person.

In *Brüggeman and Scheuten v Federal Republic of Germany* (1977),[65] the European Commission on Human Rights considered a challenge to restrictions on access to abortion under German law. The German Federal Constitutional Court had held that, while in principle an abortion was a criminal offence, where a woman was in a situation of distress and an abortion was performed by a doctor with her consent, following consultation, this was not punishable. Two German women claimed that the German law restricting abortion interfered with the right to respect for their private lives under article 8 of the European Convention (among other rights), in particular because they would not be free to have an abortion in the case of an unwanted pregnancy. The Commission rejected the claim, a majority holding that the legal restrictions and criminal penalty did not involve an interference with the private life of a woman. A minority of the Commission adopted a more convincing analysis that German law did involve a restriction on the private life of a woman, and that this restriction needed to be justified under article 8(2) of the Convention (though they differed as to whether that justification had been made out).

In *Open Door Counselling Ltd and Dublin Well Woman Centre Ltd and others v Ireland* (1992),[66] two organisations which provided counselling to pregnant women in Ireland, as well as two counsellors employed by them and two women who joined the application as women of child-bearing age, challenged restrictions on the provision of information to women in Ireland about the availability of abortion services abroad (abortion was illegal in Ireland and women who wished to have an abortion had to travel out of the country, generally to the United Kingdom). Those restrictions had been imposed on the two corporate applicants by an injunction granted by the Irish courts in proceedings brought by the Society for the Protection of Unborn Children (Ireland) Ltd. The applicants complained that this restriction was an unjustified interference with their right to impart and receive information, as guaranteed by article 10 of the European Convention, as well as a violation of the rights of various of the applicants under article 8 (right to respect for private life) and the right to non-discrimination under article 14 in the enjoyment of their rights under articles 8 and 10.

The European Court of Human Rights held that the restrictions imposed by the injunction were an impermissible restriction on the right to freedom of expression and to receive and impart information, because it was a disproportionate measure, albeit in pursuit of legitimate objectives. In reaching these views, the Court took into account the absolute and continuing nature of the restriction, the non-directive nature of the

64 Case No 22, p 351 below.
65 Case No 23, p 361 below.
66 Case No 24, p 375 below.

counselling, the availability of information from other sources in Ireland, the failure of the injunction to prevent large number of Irish women from continuing to obtain abortions in Great Britain, and the creation of a risk to the health of women.

H   RIGHT TO EQUALITY AND NON-DISCRIMINATION IN EMPLOYMENT

Access to employment

Historically, few cases questioning restrictions on access to employment for women have come before international courts.[67] However, this issue has recently been considered by European Court of Justice in two cases where women were barred from certain jobs in the military, namely *Kreil v Bundesrepublik Deutschland* (2000)[68] and *Sirdar v The Army Board, Secretary of State for Defence* (1999).[69] Whilst the facts of both cases are fairly narrow, we have included one of the cases, *Kreil*, as an illustration of how the Court approaches the principle of equal treatment in employment (as enshrined in the EC Equal Treatment Directive) and the criteria for permitted exceptions to it.

Kreil had applied to join the weapons electronic maintenance service of the German army, but had been rejected on ground that the Basic Law of Germany barred women from taking up military service involving the use of arms, and allowed them access only to the medical and military music services. The Court held that whilst the Equal Treatment Directive provided an exception to the general principle of non-discrimination in respect of occupational activities for which the sex of the worker is a determining factor (article 2(2)), this exception must be interpreted strictly. In particular, for a discriminatory act to come within the exception it must satisfy the test of proportionality, that is, it must be appropriate and necessary to achieve a legitimate purpose. Notwithstanding the discretion granted to national authorities to adopt measures guaranteeing public security, the Court held that Germany could not assume the general position that all armed units in its army had to remain exclusively male, without contravening the principle of proportionality. Importantly, it also stated that the exception in the Equal Treatment Directive was intended to protect a woman's biological condition and the special relationship which exists between a woman and her child, and that as a general exclusion of women from the military did not relate to these specific needs of protection, it could not be justified.[70]

---

67 One early case was *Interpretation of the Convention of 1919 Concerning Employment of Women during the Night* (1932), Permanent Court of International Justice, Series A/B, No 50.
68 Case No 25, p 413 below.
69 *Sirdar v The Army Board, Secretary of State for Defence*, European Court of Justice, Case 273/97, 25 October 1999.
70 By way of contrast, in *Sirdar* the European Court of Justice held that a UK policy which barred women from all posts in the Royal Marines (including, in this case, as a cook) did constitute a valid exception to the principle of non-discrimination. This particular policy (which significantly did not apply generally to all units in the British military) was held to be proportionate to its aim. The rationale was that the Royal Marines was a special assault unit which required all its members to be trained and combat-ready and that the employment of women would not allow for "interoperability", namely the special principle of the Royal Marines that each member of the unit must be able to perform a series of specific tasks and fight as part of an infantry unit, independent of his specialisation. However, the Advocate-General in his advisory opinion to the Court had questioned the claim that a female cook could not work in the Royal Marines, and called for a rigorous evaluation of whether the special conditions under which the marines operate made the absolute exclusion of women necessary for safeguarding the military effectiveness of the unit.

Discrimination on the basis of pregnancy as sex discrimination

Many national courts have held that discrimination on the ground of pregnancy constitutes direct sex discrimination. The European Court of Justice has also held that the dismissal of a female employee on the grounds of pregnancy constitutes direct discrimination on the ground of sex, contrary to EC law.[71] For example, in *Brown v Rentokil* (1998),[72] the European Court of Justice was asked to determine whether the dismissal of a female worker for absences due to pregnancy-related illness constituted discrimination contrary to the Equal Treatment Directive. The question arose in relation to a female employee who, pursuant to her employment contract, had been dismissed for being continuously absent from work for more than 26 weeks due to illness. Her illness was in fact pregnancy-related. Although there were statutory provisions in place which protected women from dismissal during maternity leave, Mrs Brown had not worked for long enough before her pregnancy to be eligible to benefit from these. She had also been ill before her maternity leave commenced. The Court held that the Directive provided not only for protection against dismissal during maternity leave, but also similar protection throughout the period of pregnancy. Dismissal of a female worker during pregnancy for pregnancy-related absences was linked to the occurrence of risks inherent in pregnancy and therefore had to be regarded as essentially based on the fact of pregnancy. Such a dismissal could only affect women and therefore constituted direct discrimination on the grounds of sex. The fact that a female worker was dismissed on the basis of a contractual term which applied equally to men and women did not alter this conclusion, since it applied to different situations – the situation of a pregnant worker who was unfit for work due to pregnancy-related illness was not comparable to that of a male worker who was ill and absent through incapacity for work for the same length of time.

Entitlement to benefits

A more common problem to reach the courts is the discriminatory treatment of women *during* employment, including in the provision of employment-related benefits. The compendium includes two cases relating to benefits denied/granted to pregnant female employees. Since pregnancy-related discrimination is not invariably a prohibited ground of discrimination in itself, this raises the question whether it constitutes sex discrimination (where sex discrimination is such a prohibited ground).

In *Brooks v Canada Safeway Ltd* (1989),[73] the Supreme Court of Canada held that pregnancy-related discrimination did amount to sex discrimination. In doing so, it departed from its earlier decision in *Bliss v Attorney General of Canada*,[74] in which it had concluded that there had been no sex discrimination in depriving pregnant women of unemployment benefits on the questionable basis that "any inequality between the sexes in this area is not created by legislation but by nature".[75] In *Brooks* the Supreme Court held that *Bliss* had either been wrongly decided, or would not have been decided in the same way now (ten years later), when "combining paid work with motherhood and accommodating the childbearing needs of working are ever-increasing imperatives".[76]

---

71   See, e.g., *Dekker v Stichting Vormingscentrum voor Jong Volwassenen* [1990] ECR I-3841; *Handels-og Kontorfunktionoerenes Forbund i Danmark v Dansk Arbejdsgiverforening* [1990] ECR I-3979; *Habermann-Beltermann v Arbeiterwohlfahrt Bezirksverband* [1994] ECR 1-1657; *Webb v EMO Air Cargo* (Case C-32/93) [1994] ICR 770; and *Tele Danmark A/S v Handels- og Kontorfunktionærernes Forbund i Danmark (HK) (acting on behalf of Marianne Brandt-Nielsen)*, (Case C-109/00), 4 October 2001.
72   Case No 26, p 420 below.
73   Case No 27, p 428 below.
74   [1979] 1 SCR 183.
75   *Id* at 190.
76   (1989) 59 DLR (4th) 321, at 339

On the facts of the case, the Supreme Court came to the conclusion that the employer's insurance scheme, which provided benefits to those who could not work for health-related reasons, discriminated against pregnant employees in terms and conditions of work.[77] Under the employer's scheme, pregnant women were automatically barred from claiming benefits for 17 weeks (indeed regardless of whether their absence from work was in fact pregnancy-related) and although they could claim benefits under a statutory scheme, the eligibility requirements were more stringent and the benefits less generous than the employer's scheme. In distinguishing pregnancy from other health-related reasons for not working, the Court held that the scheme placed pregnant women at an unfair disadvantage.[78] Turning to the key question of whether such discrimination amounted to discrimination on the grounds of sex (this being a prohibited ground of discrimination under the human rights legislation in question), the Court noted that the less favourable treatment accorded to the complainants "flowed entirely from their state of pregnancy, a condition unique to women" and found it difficult to conceive that distinctions or discriminations based on pregnancy could ever be regarded as anything other than discrimination based on sex. It was not relevant that the less favourable treatment did not affect *all* women, but rather only those women who were pregnant (an issue which also arises in the context of sexual harassment, see below).

In *Abdoulaye v Régie Nationale des Usines Renault SA* (1999),[79] the European Court of Justice addressed a similar issue in a preliminary ruling on the interpretation of Article 119 of the EC Treaty, which lays down the principle of equal pay for equal work (and has long been held to cover employment-related benefits, as well as salary). A number of male employees of the French car manufacturer Renault had brought proceedings before an Industrial Tribunal on the basis that they were discriminated against under the employees' social benefits scheme, which provided a lump sump payment to female employees when they went on maternity leave (in addition to maternity leave coverage), but did not make any such provision for male employees on the birth of a child. Whilst recognising that certain types of discrimination, such as maternity leave, were justified because they were related to the physiological characteristics of one sex, the male employees argued that this did not apply to the payment in question, as the birth of a child was a social event which concerned the whole family, including the father, and to deny him the same allowance amounted to unlawful discrimination.

However, the Court was of the view that there were occupational disadvantages inherent in taking maternity leave, which meant that women were not in the same position as men. These disadvantages included the fact that a woman on maternity leave might not be proposed for promotion, claim performance-related salary increases or take part in training, and that on her return her period of service would be reduced by the length of her absence. She would also have to adapt to new technology introduced in her absence. The Court therefore held that the principle of equal pay did not preclude the making of a lump-sum payment exclusively to female workers who took maternity leave, if the payment was designed to offset the occupational disadvantages which arose for women as a result of being away from work.

---

77 As a useful guiding principle, the Supreme Court clearly stated that employee benefit plans are increasingly part of the terms and conditions of employment, and once an employer offers a benefit plan, it must be applied in a non-discriminatory manner.

78 Drawing on *Andrews v Law Society* [Case No 8, p 121 below], the Supreme Court noted that the purpose of anti-discrimination legislation was to remove unfair disadvantages which had been imposed on groups in society. In this case, it was unfair for all the costs of pregnancy to be imposed on one-half of the population, when procreation was of benefit to society as whole.

79 Case No 28, p 446 below.

Sexual harassment as sex discrimination

A different problem which workers, both women and men, may face in their workplace is sexual harassment by their employer or fellow employees. There is established jurisprudence in a number of jurisdictions that such sexual harassment constitutes discrimination on the grounds of sex, thereby circumventing the lack of express prohibition of sexual harassment in the relevant constitution or legislation. Two of the cases selected for the compendium, which come from Canada and New Zealand, were decided in the mid to late 1980s, when a large number of cases on the issue of sexual harassment came before the courts in different countries.[80] The third, *Vishaka v Rajasthan* (1997),[81] comes from the 1990s and shows the influence of international standards on the law in this area.

In *Janzen and Govereau v Platy Enterprises Ltd* (1989), the Supreme Court of Canada conducted a detailed review of the relevant authorities and academic writings on sexual harassment in the workplace. Broadly defining work-based sexual harassment as "unwelcome conduct of a sexual nature that detrimentally affects the work environment or leads to adverse job-related consequences for the victims of the harassment", the Supreme Court concluded that sexual harassment could amount to sex discrimination. In doing so, it overruled the decision of the lower court, which, despite an unbroken line of judicial opinion to the contrary, had expressed amazement that sexual harassment had previously been equated with sex discrimination, since in its view, it stemmed from the personal characteristics of the victim, in terms of their sexual attractiveness, rather than their gender, and moreover could not be discriminatory since it did not affect *all* women.

Although the Supreme Court recognised that both men and women could be perpetrators and victims of sexual harassment, the crucial factor in this case, where the perpetrator was a heterosexual male, was that it was only female employees who ran the risk of sexual harassment; a man would have not been subjected to the same treatment. It did not matter that gender was not the only factor in the equation. Further, applying the reasoning in *Brooks* (above), the Court rejected the argument that there was no sex discrimination because only some but not all female employees had been subjected to the harassment, stating that "while the concept of discrimination is rooted in the notion of treating an individual as part of a group, rather than on the basis of the individual's personal characteristics, discrimination does not require uniform treatment of all members of a particular group".[83] Rather it was sufficient that a group characteristic, here gender, had been ascribed to an individual and was one of the factors in her treatment. Indeed, the Court noted that there were few instances in which all the members of a group would be adversely affected by a discriminatory practice.

Finally, the Supreme Court held that an employer could be vicariously liable for sexual harassment conducted by its employee, pursuant to a provision in the relevant human rights legislation that rendered employers liable for any discriminatory acts of their employees which occurred "in the course of employment". Adopting a purposive interpretation of this phrase, the Court held that it covered any acts which were work-related, including work-based sexual harassment, and not only those which fell narrowly within the employee's job description. Since the employers in this case had failed to take any action to remedy the situation, even after specific complaints had been

---

80 This includes a line of authorities in the US starting with *Barnes v Costle*, 561 F 2d 983 (DC Cir 1977) and *Bundy v Jackson*, 641 F 2d (DC Cir 1981), and the Scottish case of *Porcelli v Strathclyde Regional Council* [1986] ICR 564.
81 Case No 2, p 11 below.
82 Case No 29, p 451 below.
83 (1989) 59 DLR (4th) 352, at 378.

made to them, the Court held them vicariously liable for the sexual harassment perpetrated by their employee.

In the earlier case of *H v E* (1985),[84] the Equal Opportunities Tribunal in New Zealand considered whether a provision in the national human rights legislation prohibiting employers from dismissing a person or otherwise subjecting them to any detriment "by reason of sex" of that person also outlawed sexual harassment. Whilst the female employee in this case had actually resigned, the Tribunal held that her resignation was in substance a dismissal, given that her employer had left her with no alternative but to resign (he being the perpetrator of the sexual harassment in this case). Having conducted a detailed review of the case law in the US, Canada and Australia, the Tribunal turned to New Zealand's international obligations. Of particular interest is its conclusion that a failure to provide protection against sexual harassment would contravene the obligation to provide "just and favourable conditions of work" and to "guarantee conditions of work not inferior to those enjoyed by men" as required by article 23 of the Universal Declaration of Human Rights and article 7 of the International Covenant on Economic, Social and Cultural Rights (ICESCR) (to which New Zealand was a party). Ultimately, the Tribunal adopted a purposive approach to the interpretation of the legislation and concluded that it covered sexual harassment.[85]

In a more recent case, *Vishaka v Rajasthan* (1997),[86] the Supreme Court of India drew on the CEDAW Convention, *General Recommendation No 19* and various other commitments India had made at the international level and laid down its own guidelines on sexual harassment in the workplace, which it held would apply until Parliament enacted law on the subject.

Age of retirement

One further type of sex discrimination which has been considered by the courts is the stipulation of different retirement ages for men and women in the same or comparable jobs. This issue has been particularly addressed in cases concerning female flight attendants, who have been required to retire earlier than their male counterparts, due to a perceived need for female, but not male flight attendants, to be young and attractive. In *Air India v Nergesh Meerza* (1981), the Supreme Court of India harshly criticised the stereotypical assumption that young and attractive women acting as "show-pieces" could better serve the needs of passengers than older women with greater experience and goodwill, declaring it to be "an open insult to the institution of our sacred womanhood".[87]

The Supreme Court of Nepal in *Rina Bajracharya v HM Government Secretariat* (2000)[88] more recently considered this issue in examining the constitutionality of the regulations of Royal Nepal Airlines, the state-owned airline, which stipulated a retirement age of 55 years for crew generally, but a retirement age of 30 years or alternatively 10 years' service for female flight attendants. Drawing on sources including the CEDAW Convention – which is directly incorporated into Nepal's domestic law – the Supreme Court held that the regulations were in violation of the right to equality in Nepal's Constitution, which expressly prohibits discrimination on the grounds of sex. The Court

---

84   Case No 30, p 475 below.
85   See also *Aldridge v Booth* (1988) 80 ALR 1 (Federal Court of Australia) (holding that sexual harassment is a form of discrimination against women under article 11 of the CEDAW Convention).
86   Case No 2, p 11 below.
87   *Air India v Nergesh Meerza*, AIR 1981 SC 1829 (Supreme Court of India, 28 August 1981).
88   Case No 31, p 492 below. See also *Helen Tsang v Cathay Pacific Airways*, [2001] HKCA 345 (Court of Appeal, Hong Kong), available through www.hklii.org.

considered that it was of no consequence that the women's contracts might be extended for a further three years at a time, since this was on a purely discretionary basis, and was also restricted to ground jobs (which might not be available or suitable). Further, the Supreme Court made it clear that whilst the Constitution expressly permitted derogation from the principle of equality to allow for the special protection of women, this provision could not be turned on its head to justify unequal treatment towards women which restricted, rather than uplifted them, as the respondents had contended.

I RIGHT TO EQUALITY AND NON-DISCRIMINATION IN THE ENJOYMENT OF OTHER ECONOMIC AND SOCIAL RIGHTS AND ACCESS TO ECONOMIC RESOURCES

Social security and other benefits

Critical to efforts to eliminate discrimination against women are steps to ensure that public authorities and others do not treat women on the basis of stereotyped assumptions about their capacities, characteristics or traditional roles.[89] These assumptions can deny to women access to the benefits that men in the same position receive, and may contribute to women's economic dependency. A number of international cases have addressed differential treatment based on traditional or stereotyped assumptions about the position of women, and have consistently held them to be discriminatory.

For example, in *Zwaan de Vries v The Netherlands* (1987),[90] the Human Rights Committee considered a complaint concerning access to unemployment benefits. Under the national legislation, in order to receive unemployment benefits, a married woman had to prove that she was a "breadwinner" – a condition that did not apply to married men. The Committee held that article 26 of the ICCPR applied to economic and social rights and, while that article did not require a State to provide social security benefits, it did oblige the State not to discriminate on the grounds of sex when it chose to provide such benefits. The Committee held that the differentiation between married women and married men was a distinction based on sex and that it was not reasonable – a conclusion not explained in any great detail, but presumably based on acceptance of the argument that the distinction was based on stereotypical assumptions that men would always be breadwinners, but women not necessarily so.[91]

The decision of the Committee in the later case, *Vos v The Netherlands* (1988),[92] is less satisfying. In that case, Hendrika Vos, a woman with disabilities who had been drawing a disability pension during the life of her husband (from whom she had separated before she became disabled) challenged provisions of Netherlands social security law governing disability and widows' pensions. The legislation provided that, where a woman is entitled to a widow's pension on the death of her husband, payment of a disability allowance was discontinued (men were not eligible for a widower's pension).

---

89 For example, article 5(a) of the CEDAW Convention provides:
   "States Parties shall take all appropriate measures:
   (a) To modify the social and cultural patterns of conduct of men and women, with a view to achieving the elimination of prejudices and customary and all other practices which are based on the idea of the inferiority or the superiority of either of the sexes or on stereotyped roles for men and women…".
90 Case No 32, p 501 below.
91 The Netherlands government referred to this in its submission and indeed the relevant provisions were amended in the early 1980s to remove the discrimination.
92 Case No 33, p 511 below.

As a result, Vos received 90 guilders per month less than she had been receiving previously. While accepting that article 26 of the ICCPR applied, a majority of the Committee held that "the unfavourable result complained of by Mrs Vos follows from the application of a uniform rule to avoid overlapping in the allocation of social security benefits. This rule is based on objective and reasonable criteria, especially bearing in mind that both statutes under which Mrs Vos qualified for benefits aim at ensuring to all persons falling thereunder subsistence level income."[93]

In their joint dissenting individual opinion, Messrs Aguilar Urbina and Wennergren held that the differentiation involved could be seen as differential treatment of disabled women on the basis of their marital status and that the case should not just be viewed as a policy affecting one woman (Vos), but "rather an indeterminate group of persons who fall in the category of disabled women entitled to full disability pensions." They concluded that to institute such an inflexible system was discriminatory. It should be noted that the legislation challenged was based at least in part on the assumption that men would be full-time breadwinners and that women, if they worked at all, would work part-time and be entitled therefore to less by way of disability benefit than they would have been from a widow's pension. Vos' case did not fit this pattern, as she had been fully supporting herself at the time she became disabled.

In *Schuler-Zgraggen v Switzerland* (1993)[94] the European Court of Human Rights addressed a similar stereotypical assumption in a case involving a claim for a disability pension. In that case, the applicant received a full state invalidity pension as a result of an illness which incapacitated her for work. After the birth of her child and a medical examination by the Invalidity Insurance Board, the applicant's pension was stopped on the basis that she was 60–70 per cent able to look after her home and child, although she was still deemed wholly unfit for clerical work. The Board reached this decision on the basis of the assumption that many women give up their jobs when their first child is born and resume it only later, an assumption relied on by the courts who heard her appeal against the decision.

The European Court held that the application of this assumption involved sex-based differential treatment. It noted that the advancement of the equality of the sexes was a major goal of the member States of the Council of Europe and very weighty reasons would have to be put forward before such a difference of treatment could be justified. The Court concluded that no such reasons had been put forward in this case, that the distinction lacked reasonable and objective justification, and that it therefore constituted discrimination in relation to the enjoyment of the right to a fair hearing (article 6(1) in conjunction with article 14 of the Convention).

Rights to land and inheritance rights

Traditional beliefs and customary and religious practices may pose challenges for the full realisation of women's human rights, as they often reflect stereotyped notions of the proper roles of men and women or exclude women from full participation in various activities. Not only is equality guaranteed under international law, but so are freedom of religion, freedom of association and rights to participate in cultural life generally and for members of national minorities to do so specifically. In this area there is a significant challenge to notions of the universality of human rights. A number of the cases in this compilation explore the relationship between guarantees of non-discrimination and traditional or customary laws and practices. In some cases customary law may be

---

93   *Id* at para 12.
94   Case No 34, p 521 below.

expressly preserved, while in others its operation may be expressly subordinated to other constitutional guarantees such as the guarantee of equality.

Some of the cases in this volume illustrate how various courts in developing countries have addressed customary laws governing land ownership. Customary land law often discriminates against women, frequently restricting the succession of land to male heirs in order to keep the land within one family unit or clan to ensure that the land continues to be a source of livelihood for family or clan members.

Some courts concluded that customary law that discriminates against women is unconstitutional.[95] In *Ephrahim v Pastory and Kaizilege* (1991),[96] the High Court of Tanzania considered a case in which a woman inherited land from her father bequeathed to her in his will. The land in question was clan land governed by Haya customary law, which she sold to a non-clan member. Her nephew challenged her capacity to sell the land, claiming that under Haya customary law a female heir did not inherit full ownership in clan land with a right to sell it, but had only a usufructary right entitling the use of land during her lifetime, a position with which the trial court agreed. However, the District Court held on appeal that the prohibition of discrimination on the grounds of sex contained in the Bill of Rights of 1987 grants equal rights to men and women and that this right overrides customary law. The High Court upheld this judgment, concluding that the Bill of Rights, which is incorporated into the Constitution, was in effect the "Grundnorm" for all other law. Thus, Haya customary law, in so far as it discriminated against women on the grounds of sex, was contrary to the Bill of Rights and therefore unconstitutional and void. In addition, the court stated that Haya customary law was clearly contrary to Tanzania's international obligations, which were also incorporated into the Constitution.[97] At the same time, the Court concluded that alienation of clan land by female or male heirs remained subject to clan members' right of redemption of the land by payment of the purchase price to the purchaser, and accordingly, set a six-month period during which the nephew could redeem the land.

These decisions may be contrasted with some of the Indian jurisprudence, in particular judgments of the Supreme Court of India, which has taken a more cautious approach, expressing its reluctance to be seen to make law in this area where it considers that it is the appropriate domain of the legislature. Nonetheless, the Supreme Court has been prepared to issue orders to government authorities to undertake reviews of the compatibility of such laws with constitutional guarantees.

In approaching the issue of customary law and constitutional guarantees, the Supreme Court has frequently referred to international standards (both treaty and non-binding instruments). For example, in *Masilamani Mudaliar and others v Idol of Sri Swaminathawami Swaminathaswami Thirukoil and others* (1996),[98] the Court considered the constitutionality of customary law governing the transfer of property inherited by a woman through her father's will. A dispute arose when a male relative challenged her right to sell the property, contending that under customary law and the Hindu

---

95 See also *Noel v Toto* (Civil Case No 18 of 1994) in which the Supreme Court of Vanuatu considered whether customary law which discriminates against married women in respect to rights to land was unconstitutional in light of a guarantee of non-discrimination contained in Article 5 of the Constitution. The Court found that there was no obstacle to prevent it from deciding that non-discrimination was a fundamental principle and that therefore customary law discriminating against women in land ownership was unconstitutional. See www.vanuatu.usp.ac.fj/Paclawmat/Vanuatu_cases/Volume_G-N/Noel_v_Toto.html.
96 Case No 35, p 538 below.
97 See also the decision of the Court of Appeal, Enugu, Nigeria in *Muojekwo v Ejikeme* [2000] 5 NWLR 402, digested at www.interights.org
98 AIR 1996 SC 1697

Succession Act 1956 a woman did not inherit a full property right and therefore could not sell the property. The Court held the Hindu Succession Act should be interpreted consistently with Parliament's intention to eliminate discrimination and protect a woman's right to property in order to help women realise their rights to economic development, including social and cultural rights. Article 21 of the Indian Constitution, which guarantees the right to life, should be interpreted as including the right to livelihood, for the enjoyment of which the right to property is essential.

In reaching this conclusion, the Court also considered India's international obligations to be relevant as interpretive guides, namely the international obligations contained in the CEDAW Convention, as embodied in the Indian Protection of Human Rights Act. The Court also referred to other international instruments, including the Universal Declaration of Human Rights and the Declaration on the Right to Development.[99]

In *Madhu Kishwar v State of Bihar*,[100] the Supreme Court of India again considered whether customary law governing the transfer of property to women (this time in intestate succession) was discriminatory on the basis of sex. In this case there was no relevant legislation governing the particular customary property. The Court stated that the principle of non-discrimination was a fundamental right under the Constitution and that fundamental rights were supreme. While customs had been elevated to the status of law by article 13 of the Constitution, pre-constitutional laws which were inconsistent with fundamental rights contained in the Constitution were void.

Again the Court stated that the intention to promote human rights as evidenced by the Constitution and international obligations were relevant, that the Constitution should be interpreted as intending to give effect to international obligations, and that international treaties should therefore be used as aids for interpretation of the Constitution and other national laws.

The Court observed that the right to life protected under article 21 of the Constitution necessarily included the right to livelihood. Consequently, land should not be transferred through intestate succession to male heirs where to do so would deny female heirs the right to life and livelihood. The Court went even further, recommending that the legislature of the State of Bihar examine the issue of intestate succession for scheduled tribes.[101]

---

99 AIR 1996 SC 1697, at 1700-1703 (paras 15-24). For reasons of space, we have not been able to include the judgments in *Masilamani Mudaliar and others v Idol of Sri Swaminathawami Swaminathaswami Thirukoil and others* or *Madhu Kishwar and others v State of Bihar and others* in this compilation.
100 AIR 1996 SC 1864.
101 Not all courts have been so progressive. In *Magaya v Magaya*, SC No. 210-98, 16 February 1999, the Supreme Court of Zimbabwe found that customary law which discriminated against women was not unconstitutional. It held that although the Constitution prohibited discrimination, it did not expressly prohibit discrimination on the grounds of sex. Moreover, the Constitution expressly excluded customary land law from its principle of non-discrimination and it was not necessary to consider international obligations when interpreting the Constitution. See David M Bigge and Amélie von Briesen, "Conflict in the Zimbabwean Courts: Women's Rights and Indigenous Self-Determination in *Magaya v Magaya*" (2000) 13 *Harvard Human Rights Journal* 289.

J   EQUALITY AND NON-DISCRIMINATION IN CITIZENSHIP, NATIONALITY AND IMMIGRATION

Immigration and nationality law are areas in which women frequently suffer violations of their human rights. Immigration law is often complex and typically governed by a labyrinth of regulations and policy as well as statutory law with which States keenly protect their sovereign power. Nonetheless some cases suggest that courts have interpreted immigration law consistently with international human rights norms.

Nationality

Nationality and citizenship laws have often been based on assumptions or policies which treat women differently from men, sometimes disadvantaging them, at other times seeking to redress existing disadvantage. Historically, women who married a foreign national often lost their citizenship automatically (a loss sometimes sought to be redressed by automatic or relatively easy acquisition of the husband's nationality). The doctrine of the unity of the family adopted by many legal systems – reflected in rules about the need to adopt a single family name for all members of the same family (normally in law or practice the husband's name)[102] – also played a role in nationality law, with States' desire to reduce dual nationality resulting in restrictions on women transmitting their nationality to their children. Not only have these types of discrimination been important symbolically (by failing to recognise women as full citizens), but they may have important practical effects in relation to rights to residence, domicile and other matters, in particular where a marriage ends in divorce. These forms of discriminatory treatment have been eroded over the last 50 years, but there are still a surprising number of countries in which they still exist (especially restrictions on the transmission of nationality to children).

There are a number of cases in which courts have held these forms of discrimination to be contrary to international and national guarantees of equality. In its Advisory Opinion on *Proposed Amendments to the Naturalization Provisions of the Constitution of Costa Rica* (1984)[104] the Inter-American Court of Human Rights considered whether provisions providing for more favourable conditions for the acquisition of Costa Rican nationality by foreign wives of Costa Rican nationals than for foreign husbands were discriminatory. While recognising that these types of provisions had their origins in historical notions of the need for unity of the family in nationality matters and the disadvantages that women had faced in this regard, the Court considered that such differential treatment could not be justified and was therefore discriminatory and a violation of articles 17(4) and 24 of the American Convention.

---

102 See *Burghartz v Switzerland*, Judgment of 24 January 1994, in which the European Court of Human Rights held that it was unacceptable discrimination to permit a wife to add her surname to her husband's name (chosen as the family name) but not to permit a husband to add his name to his wife's surname when her name was chosen as the family name. The Court does not seem to have been prepared to go so far as to hold that the requirement of a single family name might in itself involve discrimination in fact, if each spouse wished to retain his or her own surname. See also the decision of the Human Rights Committee in *Müller and Engelhard v Namibia*, Communication No 919/200, views adopted on 26 March 2002, in which the Committee held that differential treatment of men and women in relation to the assumption of their spouse's surname on marriage constituted discrimination in violation of article 26 of the ICCPR.

103 See generally Christine Chinkin and Karen Knop, "Remembering Chrystal Macmillan: Women's Equality and Nationality in International Law" (2001) *Michigan Journal of International Law* 523-85 and International Law Association Committee on Feminism and International Law, *Final Report on Women's Nationality in International Law* (London Conference, 2000).

104 Case No 36, p 553 below.

The availability of defences to crimes against women which are based on traditional or stereotyped notions of the appropriate roles and privileges of women and men also violates fundamental guarantees of equality. So-called "honour" crimes take place where a person, usually a male family member, kills a woman for having "dishonoured" her family by transgressing the moral strictures laid down by her community and may take advantage of a legal defence or ground of mitigation, or may in practice escape the full rigour of the law for what is no less than murder.[114] This type of case clearly engages the responsibility of the State, which is obliged to ensure equality before the law through laws which do not include defences or grounds of mitigation in such cases and to ensure the effective enforcement of the law by law enforcement agencies and the criminal justice system.

Inequality before the law may also result from rules of evidence or procedure, or from traditional attitudes which discount women's evidence or consider it to be less valuable than that of men.[115] Rules requiring corroboration of sexual offences are based on certain assumptions about the reliability of women's evidence that reflect discriminatory attitudes. The decision of the Supreme Court of Namibia in *State v D* (1991),[116] which held such a rule unconstitutional, is a clear riposte to those assumptions. On the other hand, courts have also been able to invoke evidentiary rules to ensure that women are not unjustly convicted of offences and that their testimony is given full weight. The decision of the Federal Shariat Court of Pakistan in *Safia Bibi v State* (1983)[117] illustrates how that court, working within the national legislation (including Islamic law), overturned a conviction for *zina* of a young woman who claimed to have been raped and who had given birth to a child as a result of the rape.[118]

Violence against women as torture, or cruel, inhuman or degrading treatment

Lobbying by the international human rights community has been most visibly effective in relation to violence against women in times of conflict or in situations of political repression. During the 1990s regional and international courts charged with considering human rights abuses began to hold explicitly that acts of rape could constitute "torture", redressing an earlier tendency to classify such violations as constituting either inhumane treatment[119] or a breach of the right to private life.[120] In 1997 in *Aydin v Turkey*,[121] the European Court of Human Rights found that the rape of a young detained woman constituted torture under article 3 of the European Convention on Human Rights. Earlier that year the Inter-American Commission on Human Rights, reviewing developments at the United Nations and regional levels, had similarly ruled that an act of rape amounted to an act of torture: *Mejía and another v Peru* (1996),[122] on the basis that acts of rape which were intentional acts of violence inflicted by a member of the government's security forces with the purpose of punishing and threatening the victim amounted to torture.

---

114 See generally CIMEL and Interights, '*Honour*' *crimes project*, www2.soas.ac.uk/honourcrimes/index.htm.
115 See generally *R v Ewanchuk* [1999] 1 SCR 330 (Supreme Court of Canada).
116 Case No 44, p 701 below.
117 Case No 45, p 707 below.
118 The Court was not required to address the issue of whether it was consistent with human rights standards to make it a criminal offence to engage in sexual relations outside of marriage, something which would be protected under international law as between adults of the same or opposite sexes.
119 *Cyprus v Turkey*, European Commission of Human Rights, Application Nos 6780/74 and 9650/75, (1976) 4 EHRR 482.
120 *X and Y v Netherlands* [Case No 7, p 91 below].
121 Judgment of 25 September 1997, 25 EHRR 251.
122 Case No 46, p 713 below.

The jurisprudence of the two *ad hoc* international criminal tribunals established by the United Nations Security Council after the conflict in Bosnia-Herzegovina in 1992–93 and the genocide in Rwanda during 1994 builds on these cases. Systematic sexual and other violence against women, as well as other gender-specific violations of human rights, were a notable feature of those conflicts and the tribunals have decided a number of cases dealing with these issues.

In the *Celebici* case (1998)[123] a Trial Chamber of the International Criminal Tribunal for the former Yugoslavia (ICTY) concluded that rape and other forms of sexual assault were expressly prohibited by international humanitarian law. In considering whether rape is a form of torture, the Trial Chamber established the necessary elements of torture in the context of armed conflict, drawing on article 1 of the 1984 Convention Against Torture and Other Cruel, Inhuman or Degrading Treatment or Punishment (Torture Convention), which incorporates a purposive approach to the definition of torture. For example, torture includes acts of intimidation, coercion and discrimination of any kind used for the purposes of eliciting a confession. The Trial Chamber recognised the opinion of, *inter alia*, the Committee on the Elimination of Discrimination against Women, that violence directed against a woman because she is a woman is a form of discrimination for the purposes of defining torture.[124]

The International Criminal Tribunal for Rwanda[125] and the ICTY[126] have also sought to define the crime of rape (and associated crimes of sexual violence) under international law, drawing on comparative national developments.

Violence by private actors

Violence against women perpetrated by non-State actors has been an important area of developing jurisprudence. The positive obligations on a State to ensure protection against violations of rights by non-State actors (or to exercise "due diligence" in this regard) has been outlined above, and the concept of due diligence has been of particular importance in relation to violence against women. *X and Y v The Netherlands* has already been mentioned as an example of steps which a State must take to prevent sexual (and other forms of) violence in the community. The case of *Fernandes v Brazil* (2001)[127] builds on the jurisprudence of the Inter-American Court in the *Velásquez Rodriguez* case in the context of a State failure to respond to extreme and continuing violence in the family.

---

123 *Prosecutor v Delalić et al (Celebići Case)*, Trial Chamber II, 16 November 1989, www.icty.org, paras 475–497.
124 *Id* at para 493.
125 *Prosecutor v Akayesu*, Case No. ICTR-96-4-T, Judgment of 2 September 1998, www.ictr.org, para 598.
126 See *Prosecutor v Furund ija*, Trial Chamber II, 10 December 1998, paras 165–186; *Prosecutor v Kunarac*, Trial Chamber II, 22 February 2001, paras 436–460; Appeals Chamber, 12 June 2002, at paras 127-133, at www.icty.org. See the views of the CEDAW Committee in AT v Hungary, Communication No 2/2003, views of 26 January 2005. In this case the Committee held that the failure by the Hungarian legal system and law enforcement agencies to protect a woman against ongoing violence at the hands of her former *de facto* husband involved a violation by the Government of its obligations under the Convention.
127 Case No 47, p 740 below.

CONCLUSION

The above survey and the compendium of case law itself shows the significant advances that have been made over the last decade or so in encouraging international and national jurisdictions to take greater account of the rights and expectations of women in giving effect of human rights guarantees, as well as the many challenges that still remain. The compendium contains only a selection of cases that help to advance the human rights of women,[128] and there are many other authoritative national decisions which promise women equality and the full enjoyment of human rights. In the past decade there have been many significant judicial decisions which reflect a vision of gender equality. We hope that this collection may encourage others to push the boundaries of the law to ensure that all come to enjoy the guarantees of human rights and fundamental freedoms that are promised by the international legal framework.

Kirstine Adams, Robyn Emerton, Andrew Byrnes and Jane Connors

---

128 For example, important cases in the field of education include *Student Representative Council of Molepolole College of Education v Attorney General* [1995] 3 LRC 447 (Court of Appeal of Bostwana) (holding temporary and, in case of a second pregnancy, permanent exclusion of students who became pregnant was a violation of the constitutional guarantee of equality); and *Equal Opportunities Commission v Director of Education* [2001] 2 HKLRD 690 (Court of First Instance, Hong Kong) (holding that different treatment of boys and girls in process of selection for streamed schools amounted to discrimination), available at www.hklii.org.

ON-LINE ACCESS TO HUMAN RIGHTS SOURCE MATERIALS

Introduction

Most of the cases included in this case compilation, as well as the additional materials referred to in the *Introduction*, can be found on-line through the Internet. This section indicates the internet addresses for the various international human rights materials, as well as pointing to some important on-line databases and starting points for research on international and national law relating to human rights.[1]

United Nations human rights treaty bodies

Most documents relating to the work of the United Nations human rights treaty bodies (including decisions of the committees on individual complaints and their general comments and recommendations) can be found at the website of the Office of the United Nations High Commissioner for Human Rights:

www.unhchr.ch/tbs/doc.nsf (*Treaty bodies database*)

Materials relating to the Convention on the Elimination of All Forms of Discrimination against Women can also be found on the website of the United Nations Division for the Advancement of Women:

www.un.org/womenwatch/daw/cedaw/

Other useful sources include the University of Minnesota Human Rights Library at www1.umn.edu/humanrts/ (select *Other United Nations Documents*) and Bayefsky.com at www.bayefsky.com/

Regional human rights bodies

The documents of the various regional human rights bodies can be found on their respective websites:

European Court of Human Rights (including the documents of the former European Commission on Human Rights): www.echr.coe.int/Eng/ Judgments.htm (select *Search the Case Law – HUDOC*)[2]

Inter-American Court of Human Rights: www.corteidh.or.cr/ index_ing.html (select *Jurisprudence*) and Inter-American Commission on Human Rights: www.cidh.oas.org (select *Cases Published by the IACHR*)

African Commission on Human and Peoples' Rights: www.achpr.org/ (select *Communications – Decisions*)[3]

---

1   The information is correct as at 1 February 2005.
2   For decisions of the European Commission on Human Rights, it is important to tick "reports" in the case law collections box (which otherwise defaults to "judgments" of the European Court of Human Rights).
3   As at 1 February 2005, this page was still under construction. An alternative source for decisions of the African Commission is at the University of Minnesota Human Rights Library, at www1.umn.edu/humanrts/africa/comcases/comcases.html.

The University of Minnesota Human Rights Library at www1.umn.edu/humanrts/index.html is a useful alternative source (select *Regional Materials*), particularly for materials in relation to the African system which otherwise might be hard to locate.

Other international bodies

Judgments of the European Court of Justice can be found at curia.eu.int/en/index.htm (select *Proceedings: Case Law*).

National case law

Many national court systems have their own websites. A particularly useful way of identifying these is via the *World Legal Information Institute* database:

> www.worldlii.org/ (select *Courts and Case Law* in the Catalog box on the right hand side)

Excellent databases with a great deal of international case law and case law from Commonwealth countries are maintained by Interights:

> www.interights.org/ccl/default.asp (*Commonwealth Human Rights Case Law database*)

> www.interights.org/icl/default.asp (*International Human Rights Law Database*)

Further research

There are many guides to international and comparative human rights research. Readers may find helpful the *Guide to International Human Rights Research: Selected Sources*, at www.hku.hk/ccpl/research_resources/humanrightsguide/index.html. See also the very useful collection of references to human rights bibliographies and guides at the University of Minnesota Human Rights Library: www1.umn.edu/humanrts/bibliog/biblios.htm. In addition, the *Women's Human Rights Resources Database*, maintained as part of the DIANA project by the Bora Laskin Law Library at the University of Toronto, at www.law-lib.utoronto.ca/diana, contains references to a wide range of relevant primary and secondary materials specifically on women's human rights, as does the *Women's Link Worldwide* network website at www.womenslinkworldwide.org/whoweare.html.

TABLE OF CASES

TABLE OF NATIONAL LEGISLATION BY COUNTRY

New Zealand

Nigeria

Pakistan

TABLE OF EUROPEAN COMMUNITY LEGISLATION

TABLE OF GENERAL RECOMMENDATIONS OF THE UN TREATY BODIES

TABLE OF TREATIES AND OTHER
INTERNATIONAL INSTRUMENTS

USE OF INTERNATIONAL NORMS BY NATIONAL COURTS

CASE NO 1

MINISTER OF HOME AFFAIRS AND ANOTHER v FISHER AND ANOTHER

PRIVY COUNCIL

(APPEAL FROM THE COURT OF APPEAL FOR BERMUDA)

Judgment: 14 May 1979

Panel: Lord Wilberforce, Lord Hailsham of St Marylebone, Lord Salmon, Lord Fraser of Tullybelton and Sir William Douglas.

Human rights — Equality and non-discrimination — Discrimination on the ground of birth (legitimacy) — Freedom of movement — Right to respect for family life — Whether illegitimate child deemed to belong to Bermuda — Whether denial of Bermudian residence to illegitimate stepchild of Bermudian citizen, or to illegitimate child of non-citizen mother married to Bermudian citizen, in breach of child's freedom of movement, taking into account right to respect for family life — Constitution of Bermuda, ss 11(1), 11(5)(d)

Constitutional law — Interpretation — Human rights guarantees — Freedom of movement guaranteed to child belonging to Bermuda — Whether "child" includes illegitimate child — Relevance of international human rights instruments — Constitution of Bermuda, s 11(5)(d) — United Nations Declaration on the Rights of the Child, principle 6 — International Covenant on Civil and Political Rights, art 24 — European Convention on the Protection of Human Rights and Fundamental Freedoms, art 8

BACKGROUND

In 1972 Ms Fisher, the Jamaican mother of four illegitimate children born in Jamaica, married a Bermudian, who from the date of the marriage accepted all four children as children of his family. In 1975 Ms Fisher and her children took up residence with her husband in Bermuda and soon afterwards all four children were placed in state schools. In October 1976, the Minister of Home Affairs refused permission for the children to reside in Bermuda and ordered that they should leave. Ms Fisher and her husband applied to quash the order and for a declaration that the four children were "deemed to belong to Bermuda" under Chapter I, s 11(5)(d) of the Constitution of Bermuda because they were each a "stepchild" of a person who possessed Bermudian status, and that the Minister had infringed their right of freedom of movement under s 11(1) of the Constitution. The Supreme Court of Bermuda refused the declaration sought, on the ground that the words "child" and "stepchild" in s 11(5) referred only to legitimate children. The Court of Appeal reversed that decision, holding that the children were deemed to belong to Bermuda within the meaning of s 11(5)(d). The Minister of Home Affairs and the Minister of Education appealed to the Privy Council.

HELD (dismissing the appeal)

1   The Constitution of Bermuda has certain special characteristics. It is, particularly in Chapter I, drafted in a broad and ample style which lays down principles of width and

generality. Chapter I is headed "Protection of Fundamental Rights and Freedoms of the Individual". This chapter was greatly influenced by the European Convention for the Protection of Human Rights and Fundamental Freedoms, to which the United Kingdom is a party and which it had applied to dependent territories including Bermuda. It was in turn influenced by the Universal Declaration of Human Rights. These antecedents, and the form of Chapter I itself, called for a generous interpretation avoiding what has been called "the austerity of tabulated legalism", suitable to give to individuals the full measure of the fundamental rights and freedoms referred to (p 8).

2   There were two possible answers to the question whether these provisions should be construed in the manner and according to the rules which apply to Acts of Parliament. The first would be to say that, recognising the status of the Constitution as, in effect, an Act of Parliament, there was room for interpreting it with less rigidity, and greater generosity, than other Acts, such as those which are concerned with property, or succession, or citizenship. This would require the court to accept as a starting point the general presumption that "child" means "legitimate child" but to recognise that this presumption might be more easily displaced. The second would be more radical: it would be to treat a constitutional instrument such as this as *sui generis*, calling for principles of interpretation of its own, suitable to its particular character, without necessary acceptance of all the presumptions that are relevant to legislation of private law. It was possible that, as regards the question for decision, either method would lead to the same result. But the second method was preferred (p 9).

3   A constitution was a legal instrument giving rise, amongst other things, to individual rights capable of enforcement in a court of law. Respect had to be paid to the language which had been used and to the traditions and usages which had given meaning to that language. It was quite consistent with this, and with the recognition that rules of interpretation might apply, to take as a point of departure for the process of interpretation a recognition of the character and origin of the instrument, and to be guided by the principle of giving full recognition and effect to those fundamental rights and freedoms with a statement of which the Constitution commences. This had to mean approaching the question what is meant by "child" with an open mind. Section 11 opens with a general declaration of the right of freedom of movement. Section 11(5)(d) amounted to a clear recognition of the unity of the family as a group and acceptance of the principle that young children should not be separated from a group which as a whole belongs to Bermuda. This was in line with the guarantees under article 8 of the European Convention on Human Rights, which provides for respect for private and family life, principle 6 of the United Nations Declaration on the Rights of the Child, which provides protection against the separation of a child from its parents, and article 24 of the International Covenant on Civil and Political Rights, which guarantees protection to every child without any discrimination as to birth. Though these instruments at the date of the Constitution had no legal force, they could certainly not be disregarded as influences on legislative policy. The force of this argument, based purely on the Constitution itself, was such as to come the conclusion that "child" bears an unrestricted meaning (pp 10, 11).

Treaties and other international instruments referred to

European Convention for the Protection of Human Rights and Fundamental Freedoms 1950, art 8

International Covenant on Civil and Political Rights 1966, art 24

Universal Declaration of Human Rights 1948

Declaration on the Rights of the Child 1959, principle 6

National legislation referred to

Bermuda

Constitution of Bermuda 1967, ss 1, 11(1), 11(2) and 11(5)(d)

Immigration and Protection Act 1956, ss 16(4) and 100(c)

Matrimonial Causes Act 1974, s 1(1)

Nigeria

Constitution of Nigeria 1960

United Kingdom

Bermuda Constitution Act 1967

Bermuda Constitution Order 1968, Sch 2

Cases referred to

Brule v Plummer [1979] 2 SCR 343; 94 DLR (3d) 481

Dickinson v North Eastern Railway Co (1863) 33 LJ Ex 91; 9 LT 299; 159 ER 304

Galloway v Galloway [1956] AC 299

R v Totley (Inhabitants) (1845) 7 QB 596; 115 ER 614

Sydall v Castings Ltd [1967] 1 QB 302

Woolwich Union v Fulham Union [1906] 2 KB 240

JUDGMENT

The judgment of their Lordships was delivered by Lord Wilberforce.

LORD WILBERFORCE: This is an appeal from a judgment of the Court of Appeal for Bermuda, which by a majority (Georges and Duffus JJA, Hogan P dissenting) allowed the appeal of the respondents from a judgment of the Supreme Court of Bermuda (Seaton J) dated 6 January 1977.

The proceedings relate to the status in Bermuda of four illegitimate children of Mrs Eunice Carmeta Fisher, all under the age of 18. They were born in Jamaica, as was Mrs Fisher herself. In May 1972 Mrs Fisher (then Robinson) married Mr Collins MacDonald Fisher who possessed Bermudian status. As from the date of the marriage Mr Fisher has accepted all four children as children of his family. On 31 July 1975 Mrs Fisher came with the four children to take up residence with Mr Fisher in Bermuda; they were admitted by the immigration authorities, and soon afterwards were placed in state schools. Following a routine check carried out in the school year 1976–77, Mr Fisher was informed that the Ministry of Labour and Immigration had refused permission for two of the children to remain at school, and on 22 October 1976 the Ministry informed Mrs Fisher that she and the four children must leave Bermuda by 30 October 1976.

Separate legal proceedings (later consolidated) were then started by both Mr Fisher and Mrs Fisher seeking to establish (i) under the Bermuda Immigration and Protection Act 1956, s 16(4), that the four children are "deemed to possess and enjoy Bermudian status" and (ii) under s 11(5)(d) of the Constitution of Bermuda that they "belong to Bermuda". The procedural details of these proceedings are no longer material. At the hearing the Minister of Education gave an undertaking to reinstate the children in recognised schools in Bermuda, and this undertaking has been honoured.

It was decided by Seaton J in the Supreme Court that: (i) the children were not entitled to Bermudian status because, although s 16(4) of the 1956 Act applied to stepchildren of persons enjoying Bermudian status, and Mr Fisher, whose stepchildren they were, enjoyed that status, the word "stepchild" did not include an illegitimate child; (ii) that they did not "belong to Bermuda" because the words "child" and "stepchild" in s 11(5) of the Constitution did not include persons who were illegitimate.

On appeal the Court of Appeal unanimously upheld the decision of Seaton J on point (i), namely that the children were not deemed to enjoy Bermudian status. On point (ii) the majority held, reversing Seaton J, that the children belonged to Bermuda. There is no appeal against the decision on point (i), and the only question left is whether the four children "belong to Bermuda" within the meaning of s 11 of the Constitution. The appellants have undertaken in any event to treat the children as if, under s 100(c) (as renumbered in 1971) of the 1956 Act, they enjoyed immunity from deportation. The question therefore for decision is whether the word "child" in s 11(5)(d) of the Constitution includes an illegitimate child. The clause must first be placed in its context.

The Bermuda Constitution was brought into existence by the Bermuda Constitution Order 1968 (SI 1968 No 182) made under the Bermuda Constitution Act 1967 of the United Kingdom. It opens with Chapter I headed "Protection of Fundamental Rights and Freedoms of the Individual". Section 1 reads as follows:

> Whereas every person in Bermuda is entitled to the fundamental rights and freedoms of the individual, that is to say, has the right, whatever his race, place of origin, political opinions, colour, creed or sex, but subject to respect for the rights and freedoms of others and for the public interest, to each and all of the following, namely: – (a) life, liberty, security of the person and the protection of the law; (b) freedom of conscience, of expression and of assembly and association; and (c) protection for the privacy of his home and other property and from deprivation of property without compensation, the subsequent provisions of this Chapter shall have effect for the purpose of affording protection to the aforesaid rights and freedoms subject to such limitations of that protection as are contained in those provisions, being limitations designed to ensure that the enjoyment of the said rights and freedoms by any individual does not prejudice the rights and freedoms of others or the public interest.

Section 11 deals with freedom of movement; the following subsections are relevant:

> (1) Except with his consent, no person shall be hindered in the enjoyment of his freedom of movement, that is to say, the right to move freely throughout Bermuda, the right to reside in any part thereof, the right to enter Bermuda and immunity from expulsion therefrom.

> (2) Nothing contained in or done under the authority of any laws shall be held to be inconsistent with or in contravention of this section to the extent that the law in question makes provision ... (d) for the imposition of restrictions on the movement or residence within Bermuda of any person who does not belong to Bermuda or the exclusion or expulsion therefrom of any such person ...

> (5) For the purposes of this section, a person shall be deemed to belong to Bermuda if that person – (a) possesses Bermudian status ... (c) is the wife of a person to whom either of the foregoing paragraphs of this subsection applies not living apart from such person under a decree of a court or a deed of separation; or (d) is under the age of eighteen years and is the child, stepchild or child adopted in a manner recognised by law of a person to whom any of the foregoing paragraphs of this subsection applies.

Thus fundamental rights and freedoms are stated as the right of every individual, and s 11 is a provision intended to afford protection to these rights and freedoms, subject to proper limitations. Section 11 states the general rule of freedom of movement, which is to include the right to enter and to reside in any part of Bermuda, but it allows, as a permissible derogation from this right, restrictions in the case of any person who does not "belong to Bermuda". Section 11(5) then defines the classes of persons who "belong to Bermuda". Among these is "the child ... of a person to whom any of the foregoing paragraphs of this subsection applies". One such person is the wife of a person who possesses Bermudian status. What is meant, in this context, by the word "child"?

The meaning to be given to the word "child" in Acts of Parliament has been the subject of consideration in many reported cases. One finds in them number of general statements:

> The law does not contemplate illegitimacy. The proper description of a legitimate child is "child": *R v Totley (Inhabitants)* (1845) 7 QB 596, 600 *per* Lord Denman CJ;
>
> ... the word "child" in the act means legitimate child: *Dickinson v North Eastern Railway Co* (1863) 33 LJ Ex 91 *per* Pollock CB, similarly in 2 H & C 735.

Then, as society and social legislation become more varied, qualifications come to be made:

> It is of course true that that is only *prima facie* the meaning to be given to the word, and that a wider meaning may, in the case of some statutes, be given to it, so as to include an illegitimate child or illegitimate children, where that meaning is more consonant with the object of the statute: *Woolwich Union v Fulham Union* [1906] 2 KB 240, 246–247, *per* Vaughan Williams LJ.
>
> I do not think it necessary to refer to the authorities which established beyond question that, *prima facie*, the words "child" or "children" in an Act of Parliament mean a legitimate child or legitimate children, and that illegitimate children can only be included by express words or necessary implication from the context: *Galloway v Galloway* [1956] AC 299, 323 *per* Lord Tucker.

Founding on these statements, learned counsel for the appellants took as his starting point the compound proposition: (a) that we are here concerned with the interpretation of an Act of Parliament; (b) that in all Acts of Parliament the word "child" *prima facie* means "legitimate child"; (c) that departure from this meaning is only possible on the basis indicated in the words used by Vaughan Williams LJ or on that indicated in other words by Lord Tucker. Thus they invited their Lordships to consider the merits of the two formulae, to prefer that of Lord Tucker, and in any event to say that the preferred test, or, in the last resort, either alternative test, was not satisfied as regards the Constitution of Bermuda.

Their Lordships approach this line of argument in two stages. In the first place they consider that it involves too great a degree of rigidity to place all Acts of Parliament in one single class or on the same level. Acts of Parliament, particularly those involving the use of the word "child" or "children", differ greatly in their nature and subject matter. Leaving aside those Acts which use the word "child" apart from any relationship to anyone (in which cases "child" means simply a young person) there is a great difference between Acts concerned with succession to property, with settlement for the purposes of the Poor Law, with nationality, or with family matters, such as custody of children.

In cases concerned with the administration of the Poor Law, recognition is given to the existence of illegitimate children and to their dependence on their mother. To this extent their Lordships respectfully think that Viscount Simonds may have gone too far when he described the common law of England as not contemplating illegitimacy and shutting its eyes to the facts of life: *Galloway v Galloway* [1956] AC 299, 310–311. Matrimonial law in England has increasingly diminished the separation of illegitimate from legitimate children by the adoption of the concept "child of the family". Indeed the Matrimonial Causes Act 1974 (Bermuda), as well as recognising the "child of the family", contains a definition of "child", in relation to one or both of the parties to a marriage, as including "an illegitimate or adopted child of that party or, as the case may be, of both parties": s 1(1). This is, it is true, by way of express statutory enactment, but the fact that the separation is, for many purposes, less sharp than it was in the last century enables and requires the courts to consider, in each context in which the distinction between legitimate and illegitimate is sought to be made, whether, in that context, policy requires its recognition.

In matters of succession, and the same applies to the interpretation of wills and trust instruments (see *Sydall v Castings Ltd* [1967] 1 QB 302 *per* Diplock LJ), the rule that "child" means legitimate child is firmly rooted in the common law and in the sources of the laws of property, so it has always been insisted that clear words are needed if illegitimate, or adopted, children are to be treated in the same way as legitimate children. Instances of such clear words are becoming more frequent in modern legislation. But even without such clear words in a statute, a movement towards a biological interpretation of the word "child", even in this context, is appearing (see *Brule v Plummer* [1979] 2 SCR 343; [1979] 94 DLR (3d) 481).

In nationality Acts, which provide for acquisition of nationality by descent, the assumption is a strong one that "child" means legitimate child; the fact that such Acts often contain a definition to this effect, and provide expressly for exceptions, for example in favouring legitimated, or illegitimate, children, does not detract from the strength of this rule. In Bermuda, the Immigration and Protection Act 1956 proceeds on this basis, referring in certain places (ss 16(4) and 100(c)) to legitimated or illegitimate children; and it was the existence of these express exceptions, coupled with the general rule, that led both courts below to conclude that "stepchild", in s 16(4)(b), did not include the illegitimate child of a Bermudian man's wife.

So far the discussion has been related to Acts of Parliament concerned with specific subjects. Here, however, we are concerned with a constitution, brought into force certainly by Act of the United Kingdom Parliament, the Bermuda Constitution Act 1967, but established by a self-contained document set out in Schedule 2 to the Bermuda Constitution Order 1968. It can be seen that this instrument has certain special characteristics. (1) It is, particularly in Chapter I, drafted in a broad and ample style which lays down principles of width and generality. (2) Chapter I is headed "Protection of Fundamental Rights and Freedoms of the Individual". It is known that this chapter, as similar portions of other constitutional instruments drafted in the post-colonial period, starting with the Constitution of Nigeria, and including the constitutions of most Caribbean territories, was greatly influenced by the European Convention for the Protection of Human Rights and Fundamental Freedoms (1953). That Convention was signed and ratified by the United Kingdom and applied to dependent territories including Bermuda. It was in turn influenced by the United Nations Universal Declaration of Human Rights (1948). These antecedents, and the form of Chapter I itself, call for a generous interpretation avoiding what has been called "the austerity of tabulated legalism", suitable to give to individuals the full measure of the fundamental rights and freedoms referred to. (3) Section 11 of the Constitution forms part of Chapter I. It is thus to "have effect for the purpose of affording protection to the aforesaid rights and freedoms" subject only to such limitations contained in it "being limitations designed to ensure that the enjoyment of the said rights and freedoms by any individual does not prejudice ... the public interest".

When therefore it becomes necessary to interpret "the subsequent provisions of" Chapter I – in this case, s 11 – the question must inevitably be asked whether the appellants' premise, fundamental to their argument, that these provisions are to be construed in the manner and according to the rules which apply to Acts of Parliament, is sound. In their Lordships' view there are two possible answers to this. The first would be to say that, recognising the status of the Constitution as, in effect, an Act of Parliament, there is room for interpreting it with less rigidity, and greater generosity, than other Acts, such as those which are concerned with property, or succession, or citizenship. On the particular question this would require the court to accept as a starting point the general presumption that "child" means "legitimate child" but to recognise that this presumption may be more easily displaced. The second would be more radical: it would be to treat a constitutional instrument such as this as *sui generis*, calling for principles of interpretation of its own, suitable to its character as already described, without necessary acceptance of all the presumptions that are relevant to legislation of private law.

It is possible that, as regards the question now for decision, either method would lead to the same result. But their Lordships prefer the second. This is in no way to say that there are no rules of law which should apply to the interpretation of a constitution. A constitution is a legal instrument giving rise, amongst other things, to individual rights capable of enforcement in a court of law. Respect must be paid to the language which has been used and to the traditions and usages which have given meaning to that language. It is quite consistent with this, and with the recognition that rules of interpretation may apply, to take as a point of departure for the process of interpretation a recognition of the character and origin of the instrument, and to be guided by the principle of giving full recognition and effect to those fundamental rights and freedoms with a statement of which the Constitution commences. In their Lordships' opinion this must mean approaching the question what is meant by "child" with an open mind.

Prima facie, the stated rights and freedoms are those of "every person in Bermuda". This generality underlies the whole of Chapter I, which, by contrast with the 1956 Act, contains no reference to legitimacy, or illegitimacy, anywhere in its provisions. When one is considering the permissible limitations on those rights in the public interest, the right question to ask is whether there is any reason to suppose that in this context, exceptionally, matters of birth, in the particular society of which Bermuda consists, are regarded as relevant.

Section 11 opens with a general declaration of the right of freedom of movement, including that of residence, entry and immunity from expulsion. These rights may be limited (s 11(2)(d)) in the case of persons "not [belonging] to Bermuda" – a test not identical with that of citizenship, but a social test. Then, among those deemed to belong to Bermuda are (s 11(5)) a person who:

(a) possesses Bermudian status; ... (c) is the wife of [such a person]; or (d) is under the age of eighteen years and is the child, stepchild, or child adopted in a manner recognised by law of a person to whom any of the foregoing paragraphs of this subsection applies.

In their Lordships' opinion, para (d) in its context amounts to a clear recognition of the unity of the family as a group and acceptance of the principle that young children should not be separated from a group which as a whole belongs to Bermuda. This would be fully in line with art 8 of the European Convention for the Protection of Human Rights and Fundamental Freedoms (respect for family life), decisions on which have recognised the family unit and the right to protection of illegitimate children. Moreover the draftsman of the Constitution must have had in mind (a) the United

Nations Declaration of the Rights of the Child adopted by resolution 1386 (xiv) on 29 November 1959, which contains the words, in principle 6:

> [the child] shall, wherever possible, grow up in the care and under the responsibility of his parents ... a child of tender years shall not, save in exceptional circumstances, be separated from his mother,

and (b) art 24 of the International Covenant on Civil and Political Rights 1966 which guarantees protection to every child without any discrimination as to birth. Though these instruments at the date of the Constitution had no legal force, they can certainly not be disregarded as influences on legislative policy. [HOLDING 3]

Their Lordships consider that the force of this argument, based purely on the Constitution itself, is such as to compel the conclusion that "child" bears an unrestricted meaning. In theory, the Constitution might contain express words forcing a contrary conclusion, though given the manner in which constitutions of this style were enacted and adopted, the possibility seems remote. But, in fact, their Lordships consider it most unlikely that the draftsman being aware, as he must have been, of the provisions of the 1956 Act could have intended a limitation of the word "child" to legitimate children. In the first place, if he had intended this limitation, he must surely, following the example of the 1956 Act, have felt it necessary to spell it out. In the second place the concept of "belonging" of itself suggests the inclusion of a wider class; yet if the appellants are right, those described under s 11(5)(d) of the Constitution would largely coincide with persons having, or deemed to have, Bermudian status. Thirdly, under s 100 of the 1956 Act, these illegitimate children would enjoy immunity from deportation until they were 21. It seems most unlikely that such children should not be treated as "belonging to Bermuda" or that a stricter test, in respect of their right to freedom of movement, should be imposed on such children under s 11 of the Constitution than is imposed under the earlier Act. Their Lordships fully agree with the majority of the Court of Appeal in regarding these points as significant although they prefer to base their judgment on wider grounds.

Their Lordships are therefore of opinion that the judgments of the majority of the Court of Appeal are right and accordingly they will humbly advise Her Majesty that the appeal be dismissed. The appellants must pay the respondents' costs of the appeal.

Appeal dismissed.

CASE NO 2

VISHAKA AND OTHERS v
STATE OF RAJASTHAN AND OTHERS

SUPREME COURT OF INDIA

Judgment: 13 August 1997

Panel: JS Verma CJI, Sujata v Manohar and BN Kirpal, JJ.

Human rights — Equality and non-discrimination — Sex discrimination — Sexual harassment — Constitutional guarantees of gender equality and right to life and liberty — Lack of domestic legislative measures against sexual harassment — Appropriateness of court guidelines to fill legislative gap and prevent continued violations of constitutional rights — Convention on the Elimination of All Forms of Discrimination against Women, arts 11 and 24 — Constitution of India, arts 14, 15, 19, 21, 32 and 141.

Constitutional law — Interpretation — Human rights guarantees — Relevance of international human rights instruments and governments' commitments in international fora — Convention on the Elimination of All Forms of Discrimination against Women, arts 11 and 24 — Commitments of Government of India at Fourth World Conference on Women — Constitution of India, arts 14, 15, 19 and 21.

BACKGROUND

Ms Vishaka, an employee of the State Women's Development Program, had been gang-raped in response to her work campaigning against child marriage in the State of Rajasthan. Before the rape, Ms Vishaka had complained of sexual harassment to her State employer. However, the State had no functional policy on sexual harassment and the authorities had failed to follow up on her complaints.

Whilst the rape was the subject of a separate criminal action, the applicants, a group of non-governmental organisations, filed a public interest petition against the State of Rajasthan and the Union of India before the Supreme Court of India, pursuant to article 32 of the Constitution, for the enforcement of the fundamental rights of women under articles 14 (equality before the law), 15 (prohibition of discrimination on the grounds of sex), 19 (the right to practice any profession or to carry out any occupation, trade or business) and 21 (protection of life and personal liberty) of the Constitution. The applicants requested the Court to lay down binding guidelines on the duties of employers to respond to sexual harassment of their employees.

HELD (allowing the petition)

1   Sexual harassment in the workplace was a violation of the fundamental rights of gender equality and the right to life and liberty, contrary to articles 14, 15 and 21 of the Constitution. The incident revealed the hazards to which a working woman might be exposed and the depravity to which sexual harassment could degenerate; and the urgency for safeguards by an alternative mechanism in the absence of legislative

measures. An effective redress under article 32 of the Constitution required that some guidelines should be laid down for the protection of these rights to fill the legislative vacuum (pp 13, 14).

2   In the absence of domestic law occupying the field, to formulate effective measures to check the evil of sexual harassment of working women at all workplaces, the contents of international conventions and norms were significant for the purpose of interpretation of the guarantee of gender equality and the right to work with human dignity in articles 14, 15, 19(1)(g) and 21 of the Constitution and the safeguards against sexual harassment implicit therein. Any international convention not inconsistent with the fundamental rights and in harmony with its spirit must be read into these provisions to enlarge the meaning and content thereof, to promote the object of the constitutional guarantee (p 15).

3   The Government of India had ratified the Convention on the Elimination of All Forms of Discrimination against Women on 25 June 1993. This requires states parties to take all appropriate measures to eliminate discrimination against women in the field of employment (article 11) and to adopt all necessary measures at the national level aimed at achieving the full realisation of the rights in the Convention (article 24). Further, in respect of article 11, General Recommendation No 19 states that equality in employment can be seriously impaired when women are subjected to gender specific violence, such as sexual harassment in the workplace. At the Fourth World Conference on Women in Beijing, the Government of India also made an official commitment, *inter alia*, to formulate and operationalise a national policy on women and to institutionalise a national level mechanism to monitor the implementation of the Beijing Platform for Action. The Court therefore had no hesitation in placing reliance on the above for the purpose of construing the nature and ambit of the constitutional guarantee of gender equality in the Constitution (pp 16, 17).

4   In the absence of enacted law to provide for the effective enforcement of the basic human right of gender equality and guarantee against sexual harassment and abuse, more particularly against sexual harassment at workplaces, the Court's guidelines and norms (as specified in the judgment) were to be duly observed at all workplaces or other institutions, until legislation was enacted for the purpose, in the exercise of the power available under article 32 of the Constitution for enforcement of the fundamental rights. This would be treated as the law declared by the Court under article 141 of the Constitution (p 17).

Treaties and other international instruments referred to

Convention on the Elimination of All Forms of Discrimination against Women 1979, arts 11 and 24

International Covenant on Civil and Political Rights 1966

General Recommendations of the UN treaty bodies referred to

Committee on the Elimination of Discrimination against Women, General Recommendation No 19 (*Violence against Women*) (eleventh session, 1992).

National legislation referred to

India

Constitution of India 1950, arts 14, 15, 19(1)(g), 21, 32, 42, 51(c), 51A, 73, 141 and 253; Schedule 7, Entry 14

Industrial Employment (Standing Orders) Act 1946

Protection of Human Rights Act 1993, s 2(d)

Other materials referred to

Beijing Statement of Principles of the Independence of the Judiciary in the LAWASIA region, adopted by the Chief Justices of the Asia and the Pacific, United Nations Fourth World Conference World Conference on Women, Beijing 1995

Cases referred to

Minister of State for Immigration and Ethnic Affairs v Teoh (1995) 128 ALR 353; 69 ALJR 423; 183 CLR 273; below (p 33).

Nilabati Behera v State of Orissa [1993] 2 SCC 746; [1993] 2 SCR 581; [1993] AJR SC 1960

JUDGMENT

VERMA CJI: This Writ Petition has been filed for the enforcement of the fundamental rights of working women under Articles 14, 19 and 21 of the Constitution of India in view of the prevailing climate in which the violation of these rights is not uncommon. With the increasing awareness and emphasis on gender justice, there is [an]* increase in the effort to guard against such violations; and the resentment towards incidents of sexual harassment is also increasing. The present petition has been brought as a class action by certain social activists and NGOs with the aim of focusing attention towards this societal aberration, and assisting in finding suitable methods for realisation of the true concept of "gender equality"; and to prevent sexual harassment of working women in all work places through judicial process, to fill the vacuum in existing legislation.

The immediate cause for the filing of this writ petition is an incident of alleged brutal gang rape of a social worker in a village of Rajasthan. That incident is the subject matter of a separate criminal action and no further mention of it, by us, is necessary. The incident reveals the hazards to which a working woman may be exposed and the depravity to which sexual harassment can degenerate; and the urgency for safeguards by an alternative mechanism in the absence of legislative measures. In the absence of legislative measures, the need is to find an effective alternative mechanism to fulfil this felt and urgent social need.

Each such incident results in violation of the fundamental rights of "Gender Equality" and the "Right to Life and Liberty". It is a clear violation of the rights under Articles 14, 15 and 21 of the Constitution. One of the logical consequences of such an incident is also the violation of the victim's fundamental right under Article 19(1)(g): "to practice any profession or to carry out any occupation, trade or business". Such violations, therefore, attract the remedy under Article 32 for the enforcement of these fundamental rights of women. This class action under Article 32 of the Constitution is for this reason. A writ of mandamus in such a situation, if it is to be effective, needs to be

---

*   *Eds:* some minor adjustments have been made to the text for grammatical purposes.

accompanied by directions for prevention; as the violation of fundamental rights of this kind is a recurring phenomenon. The fundamental right to carry on any occupation, trade or profession depends on the availability of a "safe" working environment. Right to life means life with dignity. The primary responsibility for ensuring such safety and dignity through suitable legislation, and the creation of a mechanism for its enforcement, is of the legislature and the executive. When, however, instances of sexual harassment resulting in violation of fundamental rights of women workers under Articles 14, 19 and 21 are brought before us for redress under Article 32, an effective redress requires that some guidelines should be laid down for the protection of these rights to fill the legislative vacuum.

The notice of the petition was given to the State of Rajasthan and the Union of India. The learned Solicitor General appeared for the Union of India and rendered valuable assistance in the true spirit of a Law Officer to help us find a proper solution to this social problem of considerable magnitude. In addition to Ms Meenakshi Arora and Ms Naina Kapur who assisted the Court with full commitment, Shri Fali S Nariman appeared as Amicus Curiae and rendered great assistance. We place on record our great appreciation for every counsel who appeared in the case and rendered the needed assistance to the Court which has enabled us to deal with this unusual matter in the manner considered appropriate for a cause of this nature.

Apart from Article 32 of the Constitution of India, we may refer to some other provisions which envisage judicial intervention for eradication of this social evil. Some provisions in the Constitution in addition to Articles 14, 19(1)(g) and 21, which have relevance are:

Article 15:

15   Prohibition of discrimination on grounds of religion, race, caste, sex or place of birth.

(1)   The State shall not discriminate against any citizen on grounds only of religion, race, caste, sex, place of birth or any of them.

(2)   ...

(3)   Nothing in this article shall prevent the State from making any special provision for women and children.

(4)   ...

Article 42:

42   Provision for just and humane conditions of work and maternity relief – The State shall make provision for securing just and humane conditions of work and for maternity relief.

Article 51A:

51A   Fundamental duties. It shall be the duty of every citizen of India:

(a)   to abide by the Constitution and respect its ideals and institutions ...

(e)   to promote harmony and the spirit of common brotherhood amongst all the people of India transcending religious, linguistic and regional or sectional diversities; to renounce practices derogatory to the dignity of women; ...

Before we refer to the international conventions and norms having relevance in this field and the manner in which they assume significance in application and judicial interpretation, we may aver to some other provisions in the Constitution which permit such use. These provisions are:

Article 51:

51 Promotion of international peace and security. The State shall endeavour to ...

    (c) foster respect for international law and treaty obligations in the dealings of organised people with one another; ...

Article 253:

253 Legislation for giving effect to international agreements – Notwithstanding anything in the foregoing provisions of this Chapter, Parliament has power to make any law for the whole or any part of the territory of India for implementing any treaty, agreement or convention with any other country or countries or any decision made at any international conference, association or other body.

Seventh Schedule:

List I: Union List:

14 Entering into treaties and agreements with foreign countries and implementing of treaties, agreements and conventions with foreign countries ...

In the absence of domestic law occupying the field, to formulate effective measures to check the evil of sexual harassment of working women at all work places, the contents of international conventions and norms are significant for the purpose of interpretation of the guarantee of gender equality [and the] right to work with human dignity in Article 14, 15, 19(1)(g) and 21 of the Constitution and the safeguards against sexual harassment implicit therein. Any international convention not inconsistent with the fundamental rights and in harmony with its spirit must be read into these provisions to enlarge the meaning and content thereof, to promote the object of the constitutional guarantee. This is implicit from Article 51(c) and the enabling power of the Parliament to enact laws for implementing the International Conventions and norms by virtue of Article 253 read with Entry 14 of the Union List in Seventh Schedule of the Constitution. Article 73 also is relevant. It provides that the executive power of the Union shall extend to the matters with respect to which Parliament has power to make laws. The executive power of the Union is, therefore, available until the Parliament enacts legislation to expressly provide measures needed to curb the evil.

Thus, the power of this Court under Article 32 for enforcement of the fundamental rights and the executive power of the Union have to meet the challenge to protect the working women from sexual harassment and to make their fundamental rights meaningful. Governance of the society by the rule of law mandates this requirement as a logical concomitant of the constitutional scheme. The exercise performed by the Court in this matter is with this common perception shared with the learned Solicitor General and other members of the Bar who rendered valuable assistance in the performance of this difficult task in public interest.

The progress made at each hearing culminated in the formulation of guidelines to which the Union of India gave its consent through the learned Solicitor General, indicating that these should be the guidelines and norms declared by this Court to govern the behaviour of the employers and all others at the work places to curb this social evil.

Gender equality includes protection from sexual harassment and the right to work with dignity, which is a universally recognised basic human right. The common minimum requirement of this right has received global acceptance. The International Conventions and norms are, therefore, of great significance in the formulation of the guidelines to achieve this purpose.

The obligation of this Court under Article 32 of the Constitution for the enforcement of these fundamental rights in the absence of legislation must be viewed along with the role of the judiciary envisaged in the Beijing Statement of Principles of the Independence of the Judiciary in the LAWASIA region. These principles were accepted by the Chief Justices of Asia and the Pacific at Beijing in 1995 as those represented the minimum standards necessary to be observed in order to maintain the independence and effective functioning of the judiciary. The objectives of the judiciary mentioned in the Beijing Statement are:

Objectives of the Judiciary:

10   The objectives and functions of the judiciary include the following:

  (a)   to ensure that all persons are able to live securely under the Rule of Law;

  (b)   to promote, within the proper limits of the judicial function, the observance and the attainment of human rights; and

  (c)   to administer the law impartially among persons and between persons and the State.

Some provisions in the Convention on the Elimination of All Forms of Discrimination against Women of significance in the present context are:

Article 11:

1   State Parties shall take all appropriate measures to eliminate discrimination against women in the field of employment in order to ensure, on a basis of equality of men and women, the same rights, in particular:

  (a)   The right to work as an inalienable right of all human beings;

  (f)   The right to protection of health and to safety in working conditions, including the safeguarding of the function of reproduction.

Article 24:

State Parties undertake to adopt all necessary measures at the national level aimed at achieving the full realization of the rights recognised in the present Convention.

The general recommendations of CEDAW in this context in respect of Article 11 are:

Violence and equality in employment:

17   Equality in employment can be seriously impaired when women are subjected to gender specific violence, such as sexual harassment in the work place.

18   Sexual harassment includes such unwelcome sexually determined behaviour as physical contact and advances, sexually coloured remarks, showing pornography and sexual demands, whether by words or actions. Such conduct can be humiliating and may constitute a health and safety problem; it is discriminatory when the woman has reasonable grounds to believe that her objection would disadvantage her in connection with her employment, including recruiting or promotion, or when it creates a hostile working environment.

24(i)   Effective complaints procedures and remedies, including compensation, should be provided.

24(j)   States should include in their reports information about sexual harassment, and on measures to protect women from sexual harassment and other forms of violence of coercion in the work place.

The Government of India has ratified the above Resolution on June 25, 1993 with some reservations which are not material in the present context. At the Fourth World Conference on Women in Beijing, the Government of India has also made an official commitment, *inter alia*, to formulate and operationalize a national policy on women which will continuously guide and inform action at every level and in every sector; to set up a Commission for Women's Rights to act as a public defender of women's human rights; to institutionalise a national level mechanism to monitor the implementation of the Platform for Action. We have therefore no hesitation in placing reliance on the above for the purpose of construing the nature and ambit of the constitutional guarantee of gender equality in our Constitution.

The meaning and content of the fundamental rights guaranteed in the Constitution of India are of sufficient amplitude to encompass all the facets of gender equality including prevention of sexual harassment or abuse. Independence of [the] judiciary forms a part of our constitutional scheme. The international conventions and norms are to be read into them in the absence of enacted domestic law occupying the field when there is no inconsistency between them. It is now an accepted rule of judicial construction that regard must be had to international conventions and norms for construing domestic law when there is no inconsistency between them and there is a void in the domestic law. The High Court of Australia in *Minister for Immigration and Ethnic Affairs v Teoh* (1995) 128 ALR 353, has recognised the concept of legitimate expectation of its observance in the absence of a contrary legislative provision, even in the absence of a Bill of Rights in the Constitution of Australia.

In *Nilabati Behera v State of Orissa*, [1993] 2 SCC 746, a provision in the ICCPR was referred to, to support the view taken that an enforceable right to compensation is not alien to the concept of enforcement of a guaranteed right, as [the] public has a remedy under Article 32, distinct from the private law remedy in torts. There is no reason why these international conventions and norms cannot, therefore, be used for construing the fundamental rights expressly guaranteed in the Constitution of India which embody the basic concept of gender equality in all spheres of human activity.

In view of the above, and the absence of enacted law to provide for the effective enforcement of the basic human right of gender equality and guarantee against sexual harassment and abuse, more particularly against sexual harassment at work places, we lay down the guidelines and norms specified hereinafter for due observance at all work places or other institutions, until a legislation is enacted for the purpose. This is done in exercise of the power available under Article 32 of the Constitution for enforcement of the fundamental rights and it is further emphasised that this would be treated as the law declared by this Court under Article 141 of the Constitution.

The guidelines and norms prescribed herein are as under:

HAVING REGARD to the definition of "human rights" in Section 2(d) of the Protection of Human Rights Act, 1993,

TAKING NOTE of the fact that the present civil and penal laws in India do not adequately provide for specific protection of women from sexual harassment in work places and that enactment of such legislation will take considerable time,

It is necessary and expedient for employers in work places as well as other responsible persons or institutions to observe certain guidelines to ensure the prevention of sexual harassment of women:

1   *Duty of the Employer or other responsible persons in work places and other institutions:*

It shall be the duty of the employer or other responsible persons in work places or other institutions to prevent or deter the commission of acts of sexual harassment and to provide the procedures for the resolution, settlement or prosecution of acts of sexual harassment by taking all steps required.

2   *Definition:*

For this purpose, sexual harassment includes such unwelcome sexually determined behaviour (whether directly or by implication) as:

a)   physical contact and advances;

b)   a demand or request for sexual favours;

c)   sexually coloured remarks;

d)   showing pornography;

e)   any other unwelcome physical, verbal or non-verbal conduct of sexual nature.

Where any of these acts is committed in circumstances whereunder the victim of such conduct has a reasonable apprehension that in relation to the victim's employment or work whether she is drawing salary, or honorarium or voluntary, whether in Government, public or private enterprise such conduct can be humiliating and may constitute a health and safety problem. It is discriminatory for instance when the woman has reasonable grounds to believe that her objection would disadvantage her in connection with her employment or work including recruiting or promotion or when it creates a hostile work environment. Adverse consequences might be visited if the victim does not consent to the conduct in question or raises any objection thereto.

3   *Preventive Steps*:

All employers or persons in charge of [a] work place whether in the public or private sector should take appropriate steps to prevent sexual harassment. Without prejudice to the generality of this obligation they should take the following steps:

(a)   Express prohibition of sexual harassment as defined above at the work place should be notified, published and circulated in appropriate ways.

(b)   The Rules/Regulations of Government and Public Sector bodies relating to conduct and discipline should include rules/regulations prohibiting sexual harassment and provide for appropriate penalties in such rules against the offender.

(c)   As regards private employers steps should be taken to include the aforesaid prohibitions in the standing orders under the Industrial Employment (Standing Orders) Acts, 1946.

(d)   Appropriate work conditions should be provided in respect of work, leisure, health and hygiene to further ensure that there is no hostile environment towards women at work places and no employee woman should have reasonable grounds to believe that she is disadvantaged in connection with her employment.

4   *Criminal Proceedings*:

Where such conduct amounts to a specific offence under the Indian Penal Code or under any other law, the employer shall initiate appropriate action in accordance with law by making a complaint with the appropriate authority.

In particular, it should ensure that victims, or witnesses are not victimized of discriminated against while dealing with complaints of sexual harassment. The victims of sexual harassment should have the option to seek transfer of the perpetrator or their own transfer.

5   *Disciplinary Action*:

Where such conduct amounts to misconduct in employment as defined by the relevant service rules, appropriate disciplinary action should be initiated by the employer in accordance with those rules.

6   *Complaint Mechanism*:

Whether or not such conduct constitutes an offence under law or a breach of the service rules, an appropriate complaint mechanism should be created in the employer's organization for redress of the complaint made by the victim. Such complaint mechanism should ensure time bound treatment of complaints.

7   *Complaints Committee*:

The complaint mechanism referred to in (6) above, should be adequate to provide, where necessary, a Complaints Committee, a special counsellor or other support service, including the maintenance of confidentiality.

The Complaints Committee should be headed by a woman and not less than half of its members should be women. Further, to prevent the possibility of any undue pressure or influence from senior levels such Complaints Committee should involve a third party, either NGO or other body who is familiar with the issue of sexual harassment.

The Complaints Committee must make an annual report to the Government department concerned of the complaints and action taken by them.

The employers and person in charge will also report on the compliance with the aforesaid guidelines including on the reports of the Complaints Committee to the Government department.

8   *Workers' Initiative*:

Employees should be allowed to raise issues of sexual harassment at workers' meeting and in other appropriate forums and it should be affirmatively discussed in Employer-Employee Meetings.

9   *Awareness*:

Awareness of rights of female employees in this regard should be created in particular by prominently notifying the guidelines (and appropriate legislation when enacted on the subject) in a suitable manner.

10   *Third Party Harassment*:

Where sexual harassment occurs as a result of an act or omission by any third party or outsider, the employer and person in charge will take all steps necessary and reasonable to assist the affected person in terms of support and preventive action.

11   The Central/State Governments are requested to consider adopting suitable measures including legislation to ensure that the guidelines laid down by this order are also observed by the employers in Private Sector.

12   These guidelines will not prejudice any rights available under the Protection of Human Rights Act, 1993.

Accordingly, we direct that the above guidelines and norms would be strictly observed in all work places for the preservation and enforcement of the right to gender equality of working women. These directions would be binding and enforceable in law until suitable legislation is enacted to occupy the field. These Writ Petitions are disposed of, accordingly.

Order accordingly.

CASE NO 3

LONGWE v INTERCONTINENTAL HOTELS

HIGH COURT OF ZAMBIA

Judgment: 4 November 1992

Panel: Musumali J

Human rights — Equality and non-discrimination — Sex discrimination — Freedom of movement — Freedom of association — Whether rule barring unaccompanied women from a public place a violation of freedom of movement or association — Obligations under international human rights instruments — Constitution of Zambia, arts 11, 21, 22 and 23 — Convention on the Elimination of All Forms of Discrimination against Women, arts 1, 2 and 3 — African Charter on Human and Peoples' Rights, arts 1, 2 and 3

Constitutional law — Whether constitutional guarantees enforceable against private persons

BACKGROUND

Ms Longwe was refused entry to a hotel bar on the grounds that no unaccompanied women could be permitted entry. The hotel management had introduced this rule in an attempt to stop frequent disturbances which they claimed were caused by women not accompanied by men and which had brought about a series of complaints by hotel residents and male patrons alleging that women were soliciting. Unaccompanied women were allowed in all other areas of the hotel.

Ms Longwe brought a petition claiming that the refusal to allow her to enter the bar, a public place, was a violation of her right to freedom of movement and her right to be free from sex and marital status discrimination under articles 22 and 23 of the Constitution of Zambia. The court also considered her case under article 21 (freedom of association). Ms Longwe argued that, even if the hotel were to be considered as being private premises, it was still required to observe these constitutional provisions. Ms Longwe claimed that her constitutional rights were also reinforced by Zambia's international obligations under the Convention on the Elimination of All Forms of Discrimination against Women and the African Charter on Human Rights and Peoples' Rights, as well as the 1988 Bangalore Principles.

HELD (allowing the petition)

1   Article 11 of the Constitution gives to everyone who is resident in Zambia, whether a citizen or not, a right to be protected by the law. Therefore a person who felt that his or her rights had been infringed was entitled to seek an appropriate order before the courts (p 28).

2   The provisions of the Constitution were intended to apply to everybody, public and private, unless the context dictated otherwise (p 30).

3   The petitioner was discriminated against because she was a female who was not accompanied by a male. On the other hand, a male who was not accompanied by a female was able to move around freely and enter the bar. This was very naked discrimination against females on the basis of their sex by the hotel (p 30).

4   Article 23 of the Constitution allows derogations from its provisions in respect of acts authorised by an Act of Parliament or principles of law or delegated legislation. The discriminatory rule in question was not such an Act of Parliament, statutory instrument or a rule of law. Therefore none of the permitted derogations applied and the discrimination in question did not fall under article 23. The hotel's rule breached article 21 concerning freedom of assembly and association, and article 22 concerning freedom of movement. The rule denied women the freedom to go wherever and to associate with whomever they wished. The complaints of customers did not call for the management to put in place a rule which contravened the Bill of Rights without permission from legislation to do so (p 31).

5   The ratification of international treaties and conventions by a nation state without reservations was a clear testimony of the willingness by a state to be bound by the provisions of those documents. Where there was such willingness, when a matter came before the court which would not be covered by local legislation but would be covered by an international document, judicial notice should be taken of it in reaching a decision (p 31).

6   A meeting of jurists in an international forum could not make resolutions which were binding in law on their respective states, and whilst it was not wrong to take note of resolutions such as the Bangalore Principles, they should not, as a general rule, be accorded the same status as treaties and conventions (p 31).

Treaties and other international instruments referred to

African Charter on Human and Peoples' Rights 1980, arts 1, 2, 3, 4 and 5

Bangalore Principles 1988

Convention on the Elimination of All Forms of Discrimination against Women 1979, arts 1, 2 and 3

National legislation referred to

Constitution of Zambia 1991, arts 11–15, 17–19, 21–24, 26, 28, 62, 78, 80 and 113

Constitution of Zambia Act 1991, s 2

Interpretation and General Provisions Act (Cap 2)

Cases referred to

Browne v Bramot [1902] 1 KB 696

R v Higgins [1948] 1 KB 165

Solomon v Solomon (1877) C 22

JUDGMENT

MUSUMALI J: The petitioner, Sarah Hlupekile Longwe, has sued the Intercontinental Hotels Corporation Limited, trading as Intercontinental Hotels Lusaka, "the respondent" seeking the following declarations against the said hotel:

(1) That she has been and is likely to continue to be unfairly discriminated against on the grounds of sex.

(2) That she and indeed any person, female or male, is entitled to human rights and that it is therefore unlawful for the hotel to refuse admission to public places on the grounds that a person is female or is a female not accompanied by a male.

(3) That the ministerial policy position and the Investigator General's ruling marked exhibit SHL5 and SHL6 attached to her affidavit (in support of the petition) be a pronouncement of the law which should be so observed and enforced by all hotels, motels and other institutions and persons, punishable for contempt if not observed.

(4) That all public institutions be open to all people irrespective of sex or other discriminatory attributes, provided they have not breached any written laws or regulations and that all institutions whose policies and regulations result in female harassment are against the law, against public policy or interests, and against international conventions to which Zambia is a party.

(5) That an injunction be issued restraining the respondent hotel whether by itself, its servants or agents, or otherwise from turning away any unaccompanied woman from its hotel or doing any other act which amounts to discrimination of people on the basis of sex or marital status.

(6) That ordinary and exemplary damages be awarded to the petitioner for the embarrassment and humiliation caused to her; and

(7) Costs.

The evidence in this case is all agreed: that on 1 February 1992, the petitioner was refused entry into the Luangwa Bar of the respondent hotel on the ground that she was an unaccompanied female, ie that she did not have male company, which was the requisite company for women wanting to go into that bar. In his evidence Mr Malimba Kanyanga, the only witness for the respondent, said that women not accompanied by a male who was patronising that bar before this rule came into force used to fight amongst themselves for men; and that as a result of that behaviour hotel residents and other male patrons were complaining to the hotel management and urging it to do something to bar unaccompanied women into that bar. The said witness did not, however, produce any documents supporting his evidence on this point. But this is not a serious flaw to his testimony given the fact, and this was not in dispute at all, that women without male company were allowed in all other places open to the public in that hotel. So I did accept this evidence that there were complaints against the behaviour of women without male company who were patronising the bar in question which led to this rule or regulation, now the subject of this case. These are the important facts of this case.

In her submission Mrs Mushota, for the petitioner, said that this petition has been brought to this court under the provision of arts 11 and 23 of the Constitution. She then quoted these articles, and argued that under the Constitution human rights are given and guaranteed to everybody irrespective of sex. Those rights, she went on, include the freedom of movement. The respondent's behaviour towards the petitioner on the date and time in issue was a violation of her rights given her by article 23, argued Mrs Mushota, as it was based on her sex and presumed marital status.

Next, the learned counsel for the petitioner submitted that a hotel such as the respondent hotel is a public place. This was because the government (1) can regulate them; (2) gives trading licences to the hotels; and (3) has shares in this and some other similarly placed hotels. In addition to these factors, the hotel is bound to receive people who approach it and request it for the use of its facilities such as beds, food, drink and are willing to pay for them. In support of this contention she referred to the English case of *Browne v Bramot* [1902] 1 KB 696. A hotel, she went on, may only refuse to supply its facilities to people who approach and ask it for them, if in the case of beds it is full and in the case of food and drink they have run out or have been reserved for other customers. The learned counsel also referred this court to *R v Higgins* [1947] 2 All ER 619, [1948] 1 KB 165 and to *Charlesworth's Mercantile Law* (12th edn, 1972), and submitted that in this case the respondent's bar was not full when the petitioner wanted to patronise it. She then submitted that the hotel's right of admission should only be reserved in respect of indecently dressed or otherwise unfit people regardless of sex.

Lastly on this line of argument, Mrs Mushota submitted that even if the respondent hotel is held by this court to be a private premises, it would still be required to observe article 23(2) of our Constitution in the light of the definition of "person" under article 11 3(1) of the Constitution. Further, she said, there are other laws of this country which adequately provide for the infraction of "soliciting" which can be used to deal with any person suspected of contravening that law.

After these submissions Mrs Mushota moved on to the international instruments. She started off here by stating that Zambia has ratified many international treaties and UN conventions; that it is party to the African Charter on Human and Peoples' Rights ("The African Charter") and the Convention on the Elimination of All Forms of Discrimination against Women ("The Convention"). She then quoted arts 1–5 of the African Charter, and arts 1–3 of the Convention. The learned counsel then moved to and quoted the Bangalore Principles of 1988 which were formulated by Commonwealth chief justices and endorsed by a subsequent colloquium of Commonwealth African jurists and judges including the Chief Justice of Zambia.

Finally she submitted that the petitioner is entitled to damages for the public embarrassment and injury to her reputation by being treated as a prostitute.

The respondent's submissions were that (and here the learned counsel repeated the undisputed facts of this case which have already been reproduced in this judgment) that this was the second such refusal to the petitioner, the first one having been in 1984; that this petition has been presented under arts 11 and 23 of the Constitution and that in fact the proper article should have been article 28(1).

Mr Malila next tackled the issue of "discrimination" as defined by article 23(3) of the Constitution. Under this definition, he went on, the discrimination has to be based on one of the eight grounds, namely race, tribe, sex, place of origin, marital status, political opinions, colour or creed. The question is whether the petitioner was discriminated against in the sense mentioned in the definition. It was his view that she was not so discriminated against but merely "denied access" to the said bar because she was a woman unaccompanied by a man. He went on and said that at no time did the respondent put the petitioner's marital status in issue; that marital status is an irrelevant issue in determining whether or not an unaccompanied woman should be allowed into the bar in question or not. The policy in issue would catch all unaccompanied women, married or not, he said. The learned counsel went on and submitted that the petitioner was not allowed access into the said bar not because she was a woman but because she was a woman without male company. The petitioner was therefore not discriminated against in the wording of the definition in the Constitution.

Mr Malila then argued that should this court find that the petitioner was discriminated against, this court has to interpret the provision of article 23(3) of the Constitution properly so that the true meaning of the legislature as evidenced by the language which has been used in that article and not what the legislature may have intended to say but did not say, can come out. In support of this he referred the court to *Basu's Commentary on the Constitution of India* (5th edn) vol 1, pp 34–35 and to *Solomon v Solomon* (1877) C 22 at 38. The wording of article 23 of the Constitution is certain, precise and unambiguous, he submitted.

The learned counsel went on and said that the petitioner bears the burden of proving that the respondent violated article 23. To do so she has to prove either that (1) the respondent made law that made provision that is discriminatory either itself or in its effect; or (2) she was discriminated against by the respondent's agents acting pursuant to "any written law or in the performance of the functions of any public office or any public authority". He then said that the respondent is a limited company which does not have any power to make law, ie an Act of Parliament or a statutory instrument, as *per* arts 62, 78 and 80 of the Constitution respectively. The respondent thus has only a policy and not a law, submitted the learned counsel. Also, it has not been shown that the respondent's agent acted in the performance of a public office or public authority. In the light of these facts the petitioner has failed to establish that her article 23 right has been violated, he submitted.

Next the learned counsel tackled the freedom of movement under article 22 of the Constitution. After quoting the relevant parts of that article, Mr Malila went on and submitted that this is not an absolute right as it is limited by the requirements of articles 17(1), 23(2) and (3) and the civil "non-constitutional" rights such as the right to exclude unwanted visitors from one's premises and the right to sue for trespass to mention but two. He then said that the petitioner was free to exercise her freedom of movement wherever she pleased, but if she decided to exercise it on the respondent's premises, she was required to abide by any reasonable conditions obtaining on that premises. One such condition was that she had to be in male company if or when she wanted to patronise the bar in question. It was his contention that it has not been the intention of the legislature through article 22 to give to individuals unrestricted entry into any place, private or public. He then submitted further that constitutions are meant to cover state actions or state agencies.

He went on and said that Zambia, being a signatory of the UN Convention on the Elimination of All Forms of Discrimination against Women, may unfortunately have failed to pass an implementing statute or to include the salient points in the Constitution and may thereby not be living up to her international commitments. That being the case, went on the learned counsel, women cannot get all their rights provided them by that convention by coming to courts when those rights are not reflected in the Republican Constitution. For these reasons, it was his submission that the petition be dismissed with costs to the respondent.

The starting point in my determination of this dispute is to state the provisions of arts 11, 21–23 and 28 of the Constitution. Articles 11 and 23 have been relied upon by the petitioner as being the basis of this petition. Article 28 has, on the other hand, been contended by the defence as being the basis of this petition. Article 21 deals with the freedom of assembly and association. Article 22 deals with the freedom of movement and is also in issue in this matter. Leaving out provisions not relevant to this case, those articles provide as follows:

11   It is recognised and declared that every person in Zambia has been and shall continue to be entitled to the fundamental rights and freedoms of the individual, that is to say, the right, whatever his race, place of origin, political opinions, colour, creed, sex or marital status, but subject to the limitations contained in this Part, to each and all of the following, namely;

(a)   ... the protection of the law.

(b)   freedom of ... assembly movement and association ...

and the provisions of this article shall have effect for the purpose of affording protection to those rights and freedoms subject to such limitations of that protection as are contained in this Part, being limitations designed to ensure that the enjoyment of the said rights and freedoms by any individual does not prejudice the rights and freedoms of others or the public interest.

21 (1) Except with his own consent, no person shall be hindered in the enjoyment of his freedom of assembly and association, that is to say, his right to assemble freely and associate with other persons ...

(2) Nothing contained in or done under the authority of any law shall be held to be inconsistent with or in contravention of this Article to the extent that it is shown that the law in question makes provision: –

(a)   that is reasonable required in the interests of ... public morality ...

(b)   that is reasonably required for the purpose of protecting the rights or freedoms of other persons ...

and except so far as that provision or, the thing done under the authority thereof as the case may be, is shown not to be reasonably justifiable in a democratic society.

22 (1) Subject to the other provisions of this Article and except in accordance with any other written law, no citizen shall be deprived of his freedom of movement, and for the purposes of this Article freedom of movement means –

(a)   the right to move freely throughout Zambia ...

23 (1) Subject to clauses (4) (5) and (7) no law shall make any provision that is discriminatory either of itself or in its effect.

(2) Subject to clauses (6), (7) and (8), no person shall be treated in a discriminatory manner by any person acting by virtue of any written law or in the performance of the functions of any public office or any public authority.

(3) In this Article the expression "discriminatory" means, affording different treatment to different persons attributable, wholly or mainly to their respective descriptions by ... sex ... marital status ... whereby persons of one such description are subjected to disabilities or restrictions to which persons of another such description are not made subject or are accorded privileges or advantages which are not accorded to persons of another such description.

(4) Clause (1) shall not apply to any law so far as that law makes provision –

...

(e)   whereby persons of any such description as is mentioned in Clause (3) may be subjected to any disability or restriction or may be accorded any privilege or advantage which, having regard to its nature and the special circumstances pertaining to those persons or to persons of any other description, is reasonably justifiable in a democratic society ...

(6) Clause (2) shall not apply to anything which is expressly or by necessary implication authorised to be done by any such provision or law as is referred to in Clause (4) or (5).

(7) Nothing contained in or done under the authority of any law shall be held to be inconsistent with or in contravention of this Article to the extent that it is shown that the law in question makes provision whereby persons of any such description as in mentioned in Clause (3) may be subjected to any restriction on the rights and freedoms guaranteed by Articles 21 and 22, being such a restriction as is authorised by Clause (2) of Article 21 or Clause (3) of Article 22, as the case may be …

28 (1) Subject to Clause (5), if any person alleges that any of the provisions of Articles 11 to 26 inclusive has been, is being or is likely to be contravened in relation to him, then, without prejudice to any other action with respect to the same matter which is lawfully available, that person may apply for redress to the High Court which shall –

(a) hear and determine any such application …

and which may, make such order, issue such writs and give such directions as it may consider appropriate for the purpose of enforcing, or securing the enforcement of, any of the provisions of Article 11 to 26 inclusive

…

(3) No application shall be brought under Clause (1) on the grounds that the provisions of Articles 11 to 26 (inclusive) are likely to be contravened by reason of the proposals contained in any bill which, at the date of the application has not become a law.

The African Charter

Article 1

The member states of the Organisation of African Unity parties to the present Charter shall recognise the rights, duties and freedoms enshrined in this Charter and shall undertake to adopt legislative or other measures to give effect to them.

Article 2

Every individual shall be entitled to the enjoyment of the rights and freedoms recognised and guaranteed in the present Charter without distinction of any kind such as … sex … or other status.

Article 3

1   Every individual shall be equal before the law.

2   Every individual shall be entitled to equal protection of the law.

Article 4 talks about the inviolability of human beings. I will not reproduce it here as that principle is not in issue in this matter. Article 5 is also not in this matter.

*The Convention on The Elimination of All Forms of Discrimination against Women**

Article 1

Discrimination is any distinction, exclusion or restriction made on the basis of sex which has the effect or purpose of impairing or nullifying the recognition, enjoyment or exercise by women, irrespective of their marital status, on a basis of equality of men and women, of human rights and fundamental freedoms in the political, economic, social, cultural, civil or any other field.

Eds: the judge has paraphrased some of the following articles of the Convention (rather than reproduced them *verbatim*).

Article 2

Discrimination against women in all its forms is condemned and the states parties agree to undertake:

...

To ensure that public authorities and institutions shall refrain from engaging in any act or practice of discrimination against women.

To ensure that all acts of discrimination against women by persons, organisations or enterprises are eliminated.

Article 3

States parties agree to take all appropriate measures including legislation, in all fields in order to guarantee women their basic human rights and fundamental freedoms on the same basis as men.

Lastly Mrs Mushota referred to the Bangalore Principles of 1988 which have been brought into being by Commonwealth jurists and chief justices. That document provides as follows:

1   Fundamental human rights and freedoms are inherent in all humankind and find expression in constitutions and legal systems throughout the world and in the international human rights instruments.

2   These international human rights instruments provide important guidance in cases concerning fundamental human rights and freedoms.

3   There is an impressive body or jurisprudence, both international and national, concerning the interpretation of particular human rights and freedoms and their application. This body of jurisprudence is of practical relevance and value to the judges and lawyers generally.

4   In most countries whose legal systems are based upon the common law, international conventions are not directly enforceable in national courts unless their provisions have been incorporated by legislation into domestic law. However, there is a growing tendency for national courts to have regard to these international norms for the purpose of deciding cases where the domestic law – whether constitutional, statute or common law – is uncertain or incomplete.

5   This tendency is entirely welcome because it respects the universality of fundamental human rights and freedoms and the vital role of an independent judiciary in reconciling the competing claims of individuals and groups of persons with the general interests of the community.

6   While it is desirable for the norms contained in the international human rights instruments to be still more widely recognised and applied by national courts, this process must take fully into account local laws, traditions, circumstances and needs.

7   It is within the proper nature of the judicial process and well-established judicial functions for national courts to have regard to international obligations which a country undertakes – whether or not they have been incorporated into domestic law – for the purpose of removing ambiguity or uncertainty from national constitutions, legislation or common law.

8   However, where national law is clear and inconsistent with the international obligations of the state concerned, in common law countries the national court is obliged to give effect to national law. In such cases the court should draw such inconsistency to the attention of the appropriate authorities since the supremacy of

national law in no way mitigates a breach of an international legal obligation which is undertaken by a country.

9   It is essential to redress a situation where, by reason of traditional legal training which has tended to ignore the international dimension, judges and practising lawyers are often unaware of the remarkable and comprehensive developments of statements of international human rights norms. For the practical implementation of these views it is desirable to make provision for appropriate courses in universities and colleges, and for lawyers and law enforcement officials; provision in libraries of relevant materials; promotion of expert information to judges, lawyers and law enforcement officials; and meetings for exchanges of relevant information and experience.

10   These views are expressed in recognition of the fact that judges and lawyers have a special contribution to make in the administration of justice in fostering universal respect for fundamental human rights and freedoms.

My next task is the resolution of the issues which have been raised in this matter. In that exercise I feel compelled to start with the issue of whether or not this petition is well grounded on arts 11 and 23 of the Constitution on which it has been brought to this court. My answer is in the affirmative. This is because it is my considered view that article 11(a), as quoted already in this judgment, gives to every individual who is resident in this country, citizen or not, a right to be protected by the law. A person who therefore feels that his human right or rights, let alone any other provision of the law, is/are infringed is entitled to come to these courts and seek an appropriate order in his favour, on the basis of this article. Such a person is also in order to seek such redress on the basis of a specific provision of Part III of our Constitution even in the absence of arts 11 and 28. This is because each such article gives jurisdiction to this court to determine any complaint brought before it alleging a specific breach. Articles 12 – 24 inclusive and article 26 provide for such breaches, and anybody alleging such a breach or breaches, as the case may be, has locus on the basis of such allegation. But in our Constitution, the legislature thought it wise to further provide under article 28 for the different categories of aggrieved persons who have locus in these kind of matters. Those are people whose rights: (1) have already been breached; (2) are being breached and (3) in danger of being breached in the future. Thus a litigant alleging the breach of his human rights is able to base his action on either article 11 alone, or article 11 and other relevant articles of Part III or indeed article 28 and the relevant other article(s) of Part III. This action is therefore properly before this court.

Next is the issue that the incident complained of in this matter was not the first such occurrence in respect of the same person and in respect of the same bar. I got the impression that this issue was canvassed by the learned respondent's advocate to try and suggest that the petitioner should therefore have known better the second time. My view is that the petitioner was entitled to institute these kind of proceedings any time she was treated in the way she was on those two occasions, ie either on the first occasion or indeed on the second time, as she has decided to do this time. As to whether she should have known better the second time or not that is the very core of the case. So the answer will become obvious in the remaining part of this judgment.

The next issue is the contention by Mr Malila that constitutional provisions are meant to cover State actions or public bodies or public officers. The necessary amplification of this argument is that human rights observances are necessary only in matter of the State and/or public bodies and/or public officers; that other categories of people or institutions in a country are exempt from such observances altogether. At this juncture we need to know what is meant by human rights. The definition of Professor Louis Henkin in his article in (1981) 81 *Columbia LR* at 1582 succinctly answers this question. He defined human rights as:

> ... claims which every individual has or should have upon the society in which she or he lives. To call them human rights suggests that they are universal; they are the due of every human being in every human society. They do not differ with geography or history, culture or ideology, political or development. They do not depend on gender or race, class or status. To call them "rights" implies that they are claims "as of right" and not merely appeals to grace or charity or brotherhood or love; they need not be earned or deserved but are claims of entitlement and corresponding obligation, in some political order under some applicable law ...

I totally agree with this definition.

At this juncture I would like to explain the evolution of constitutions. This explanation applies to both unwritten and written constitutions in principle. But in practice it is more relevant to a state or states with a written constitution or constitutions. A constitution is a product of the surrender by the citizenry of their individual rights to their rulers (governments) in order for those rulers to distribute and supervise the enjoyment of those rights in an atmosphere of peaceful co-existence by all. Breaches of that enjoyment of the rights attracts certain sanctions so that normalcy is restored. Now the surrender of peoples' rights to the ruler inevitably has made the rulers very powerful *vis-à-vis* the individual citizenry. Since power corrupts and absolute power corrupts absolutely, there is a danger of abuse of those powers by the rulers against the very people who have reposed it in them on their behalf. So to try to control such abuse the people through their elected representatives have laid down certain rules of conduct of business by the rulers. With the passage of time it was recognised that those rules needed to apply to all organs of the state and public institutions or persons. Since those rules come from the collective will of the citizenry, it is felt that they form the basis of all the regulations that are passed to regulate the conduct of the citizenry and that to change them needs an absolute majority of the citizenry in favour. This is how difficult provisions of amending or repealing constitutional provisions have come into being. That majority is sometimes two-thirds or three-quarters of all the members of a given legislature or state if the arrangement is a federation. Thus human rights are almost always written into a country's constitution. This is in order to give them the requisite constitutional powers they deserve, as I have just explained. But what started as regulations to control the powers of the rulers have with the passage of time, in my considered view, come to cover the activities of even private individuals or institutions. This has come about, in my view, upon a realisation that there are certain activities by the individual citizens which would offend against the peaceful co-existential tenets of today's civilised living standards of man unless they are controlled by the supreme law of the land. And so present day provisions of human rights in constitutions command both the rulers and the ruled alike to observe certain standards. This feature is very easily noticed in our constitutions, ie the past and present ones. For example the right to life under article 12(1) and (2) of our Constitution is a command to everybody, ruler or ruled, to respect it. So are the rights: of personal liberty (article 13(1)); to freedom from slavery and forced labour (arts 14(1) and (2)); to freedom from torture (article 15); to privacy of home and other property (article 17(1)); and to freedom of conscience (article

19(1) – (4)). I could go on but these will support what I have just said. This is the same approach taken by even many, if not all international treaties. There may, of course, be some human rights which can only be accorded to the citizenry by a government department or some such public institution or a public servant. It is only ordinary common sense that in the wording of such a right, the appeal should be to the public institution(s) or public person. This is the category where the right to protection of the law under article 18 of our present Constitution falls. Whilst still on this issue it is pertinent also to say that under our Constitution the word "person" has been defined under article 113 as including:

any company or association or body of persons, corporate or unincorporated.

This shows that the constitutional provisions in this country are intended to apply to everybody: public or private persons unless the context otherwise dictates.

I must also state that it is true that most, if not all the rights, which have been provided for by the Bill of Rights are also covered by personal or private law such as the law of torts or criminal law. But that state of affairs does not deprive an aggrieved person of his choice of whether to proceed under the Bill of Rights or under another branch of the law. The golden choice in this regard is the aggrieved person's.

I then move on to the determination of the petitioner's right which was infringed by the respondent hotel, if any was so infringed at all. The starting point here is the determination of the issue whether or not the petitioner was discriminated against in her pursuit of life by being refused entry into the Luangwa Bar on the basis of her sex. I must here say that it was quite amusing reading the arguments put forth by Mr Malila for the respondent hotel, to try and persuade me to find in the respondent's favour that the petitioner was not so discriminated against. I have to say, on this question, that I have been more than satisfied that the petitioner was discriminated against in the manner she was treated in 1984 and this year (1992) when she tried to enter the Luangwa Bar. The reason for the discrimination was because she was a female who did not have male company at the material times. Now if that is not discrimination on the basis of sex or gender, what else is it, looking at the matter in a reasonable ordinary person's perspective? I have not been able to find any reasonable argument to persuade me into holding that this was not based on the fact that at the material time this female (the petitioner) because she was a female, and nothing else, was commanded by the hotel to be accompanied by another human being, but who must be a male, in order for her to be allowed by the hotel to patronise this bar. On the other hand, an unaccompanied male ie a male who was not in the company of a female, was free to patronise the same bar. This was very naked discrimination against the females on the basis of their gender or sex, by the respondent hotel.

Now was this discrimination allowed by the Constitution? Starting with the contentions by the respondent, this discrimination came into being because patrons of that bar, mostly male I think, had been complaining to the hotel management about the behaviour of unaccompanied women who used to patronise the bar in issue. Those women used to fight over men in that bar. Now reading the derogations allowed for under the Constitution they are in respect of acts authorised by an Act or Acts of Parliament or principles of law or delegated legislation. This is what arts 21(2), 22(3) and 23(4)–(7), to mention only these provisions, say. Now was this discriminatory rule by the respondent hotel a law in the context of the constitutional provisions that are in place in this country? The starting point in this regard is the definition of the word "law" which is in the Constitution itself. Browsing through it I found the definition of the term "existing law" under s 2 of the Constitution of Zambia Act 1991. It reads as follows:

> "Existing Law" means all law, whether a rule of law or a provision of an Act of Parliament or any other enactment or instrument whatsoever (including any Act of Parliament of the United Kingdom or Order of Her Majesty in Council). Having effect as part of the Law of Zambia or part thereof immediately before the commencement of this Act, and includes any Act of Parliament or statutory instrument made before such commencement and coming into force, on such commencement or thereafter.

The Interpretation and General Provisions Act (Cap 2) of the Laws of Zambia does not define the word "law". So the foregoing definition must rule.

My understanding of the word "law" as used in the context of the Bill of Rights is that it means an Act of Parliament or statutory instrument or a rule of law. The discriminatory regulation which is the subject of this litigation was thus not a law in the meaning of "law" in our Constitution. This is because only Parliament has power to make such laws. This means that (1) none of the permitted derogations of our Constitution applies now and applied at the material time to the regulation in question; and (2) the discrimination in question does not and did not fall under the provisions of article 23. But that regulation did breach arts 21 (freedom of assembly and association) and 22 (freedom of movement) in respect of the petitioner, and indeed all those women who have been refused entry into the Luangwa Bar of the respondent hotel over the years. This is because they were denied their choices of where to go and who to associate with by that regulation. The complaints by the patrons against the behaviour of women who were not being accompanied by men in that bar did not call for the putting in force of a rule or regulation which contravened the Bill of Rights, without the permission of, or authority from, the legislature to do so. The "fights over men" problem ought to have been taken care of by the use of the public law and order laws of this country.

Before I end, I have to say something about the effect of international treaties and conventions which the Republic of Zambia enters into and ratifies. The African Charter and the Convention, *supra* are two such examples. It is my considered view that ratification of such documents by a nation state without reservations is a clear testimony of the willingness by that state to be bound by the provisions of such a document. Since there is that willingness, if an issue comes before this court which would not be covered by local legislation but would be covered by such international document, I would take judicial notice of that treaty or convention in my resolution of the dispute.

As for documents such as the Bangalore Principles, I am of the view that they do not enjoy the same status as treaties and conventions. This is because it is my very considered view that in the separation of powers principle, I do not think that a meeting of jurists in an international forum can make resolutions which are binding on their respective states in law. I am of the strong view that such powers are entrusted in the executive wing of the state. So whilst it is not wrong to take note of such resolutions I think it is a misdirection in law to treat them as standing at par with treaties and conventions entered into and ratified by the executive wing. This is the general principle. There may be some exceptions, as is generally the case with general principles. But those exceptions would have to be decided upon if or when they occur. The Bangalore Principles do not appear to be exceptions to this general rule.

When all is said, therefore, since the regulation or rule in issue contravened the human rights provisions of our Constitution, as already explained, I order and direct that it be scrapped forthwith.

Mrs Mushota asked this court to grant her client ordinary and exemplary damages against the respondent hotel. I have to say that I did not receive any evidence which would support an award of exemplary damages. So that prayer is not granted.

Coming to ordinary damages, I did not also receive any evidence to show the degree of ordinary damages the petitioner suffered. I am therefore of the considered view that I can only award her a token amount. I accordingly award her a sum of five hundred kwacha (K500.00). I also award her the costs of this action.

CASE NO 4

MINISTER OF STATE FOR IMMIGRATION AND ETHNIC AFFAIRS v AH HIN TEOH

HIGH COURT OF AUSTRALIA

Judgment: 7 April 1995

Panel: Mason CJ; Deane, Toohey, Gaudron and McHugh JJ

Statutes — Interpretation — Relationship between international law and domestic law (law of Australia) — Unincorporated treaties — Whether administrative decision-makers required to take unincorporated treaties into account in interpreting domestic law — Doctrine of legitimate expectation — Immigration — Application by parent for permanent resident status — Convention on the Rights of the Child, art 3(1) — Migration Act 1958

Human Rights — Rights of the child — Immigration — Parent's application for permanent residence denied although child permanent resident — Judicial review — Unincorporated treaties — Doctrine of legitimate expectation — Whether legitimate expectation that best interests of child would be primary consideration of administrative decision-maker in reviewing parent's application for permanent residence — Convention on the Rights of the Child, art 3(1) — Migration Act 1958 — Administrative Decisions (Judicial Review) Act 1977

BACKGROUND

The respondent, Mr Teoh, was a citizen of Malaysia who had come to Australia on 8 May 1988 and had been granted a temporary entry visa. On 9 July 1988 he married an Australian citizen. Ms Teoh had four children from her earlier relationships, and had another three children with Mr Teoh.

In February 1989 Mr Teoh applied for permanent resident status. His application included a bail recognisance for his appearance at court on charges of dangerous driving and driving without a licence. He was convicted of driving without a licence and fined $200. On 16 November 1989 while his application for permanent resident status was still pending, Mr Teoh was arrested and charged with a number of drug offences, for which he was convicted and sentenced to 6 years' imprisonment. Around the same time, Mr Teoh pleaded guilty to charges relating to heroin and was given a suspended sentence of 18 months.

On 2 January 1991, the Department of Immigration informed Mr Teoh that his application for grant of resident status had been refused on the grounds that he was not of good character given his criminal record. On 29 and 30 January 1991 Mr Teoh and his wife applied for reconsideration of his application by the Immigration Review Panel. He was unsuccessful before the Panel, and a delegate of the Minister for Immigration accepted the recommendation of the Panel not to reconsider his application.

Mr Teoh unsuccessfully challenged this refusal before a single judge of the Federal Court, but succeeded before the Full Court of the Federal Court, which held, *inter alia*, that the Minister for Immigration's delegate had not properly taken into account the effect of the break-up of the family if Mr Teoh was not granted residence. It found that there was a legitimate expectation that the principles guaranteed in the Convention on the Rights of the Child (the Children's Convention), which had been ratified by Australia but not incorporated into Australian law, would be adhered to, including that contained in article 3(1) that "… in all actions concerning children … the best interests of the child shall be the primary consideration". The Minister appealed to the High Court of Australia.

HELD (dismissing the appeal (McHugh J dissenting))

Scope of statutory discretion

1   There was no provision in the Migration Act 1958 (on which the statutory discretion to grant residency was based) which made provisions of the Children's Convention extraneous to a decision-maker's consideration of an application for resident status and for review of a refusal of such an application. Nor had it been suggested that there was anything in the scope and purpose of the statute which would have that effect. It followed that the Immigration Review Panel and the Minister's delegate who accepted the recommendation of the Panel were entitled to have regard to the provisions of the Children's Convention so long as they were a legitimate subject-matter for consideration and were relevant to the issues for determination. (*Per* Mason CJ and Deane J, para 22.)

Status of the Children's Convention in Australian law

2   A treaty which had not been incorporated into Australian municipal law could not operate as a direct source of individual rights and obligations under that law. However, the fact that the Children's Convention had not been incorporated into Australian law did not mean that its ratification held no significance for Australian law. Where a statute or subordinate legislation is ambiguous, the courts should favour that construction which accords with Australia's obligations under a treaty or international convention to which Australia is a party, at least in those cases in which the legislation was enacted after or in contemplation of, entry into or ratification of the relevant international instrument. That was because Parliament, *prima facie*, intended to give effect to Australia's obligations under international law. (*Per* Mason CJ and Deane J, para 25, 26; see also Toohey J, para 20ff.)

3   The provisions of an international convention to which Australia is a party, especially one which declares universal fundamental rights, might be used by the courts as a legitimate guide in developing the common law. But the courts should act in this fashion with due circumspection when the Parliament itself had not seen fit to incorporate the provisions of a convention into domestic law. Judicial development of the common law should not to be seen as a backdoor means of importing an unincorporated convention into Australian law. (*Per* Mason CJ and Deane J, para 28.)

4   This case did not involve the resolution of an ambiguity in a statute, or the development of some existing principle of common law. The critical questions to be resolved were whether the provisions of the Children's Convention were relevant to the exercise of statutory discretion, and if so, whether Australia's ratification of the Children's Convention could give rise to a legitimate expectation that the decision-maker would exercise that discretion in conformity with the terms of the Children's

Convention. There was no intrinsic reason for excluding the provisions of the Children's Convention from consideration by the decision-maker in the exercise of his or her statutory discretion simply because it had not been incorporated into Australian municipal law. (*Per* Mason CJ and Deane J, para 29.)

Relevance of the Children's Convention

5   The crucial question was whether the decision to deport the respondent was an "action concerning children" for the purposes of article 3 of the Children's Convention. A broad reading and application of the provisions in article 3, one which gave the word "concerning" a wide-ranging application, was more likely to achieve the objects of the Children's Convention. (*Per* Mason CJ and Deane J, para 30.)

Doctrine of legitimate expectation

6   Ratification by Australia of an international convention was not to be dismissed as a merely platitudinous or ineffectual act, particularly when the instrument evidences internationally accepted standards to be applied by the courts and administrative authorities in dealing with the basic human rights affecting the family and children. Rather, ratification of a convention was a positive statement by the executive government of Australia to the world and to the Australian people that the executive government and its agencies would act in accordance with the convention. That positive statement was an adequate foundation for a legitimate expectation, absent statutory or executive indications to the contrary, that administrative decision-makers would act in conformity with the Children's Convention and treat the best interests of the children as "a primary consideration", and that, if they intended not to do so, they would give the persons affected an opportunity to argue against such a course. (*Per* Mason CJ and Deane J, para 34: *per* Toohey J, para 32.)

Other relevant factors

7   In other respects, there was not any failure to take relevant matters into account. It could not be said that the delegate either failed to turn her mind to the hardship the family would face or failed to have regard to the consequences of the break-up of the family unit. (*Per* Mason CJ and Deane J, para 41.)

Per McHugh J (dissenting)

Doctrine of legitimate expectation

1   It was not reasonable to expect that public officials would comply with the terms of conventions which they had no obligation to apply or consider merely because the federal government had ratified them. There could be no reasonable expectation that state government officials would comply with the terms of a convention merely because the executive government of the Commonwealth had ratified it. Members of the Australian community could not hold a reasonable expectation that, upon the ratification of a convention, its provisions would thereafter be applied to any decision falling within the scope of the convention. Unless a Minister or his or her officials had given an indication that the provisions of a convention would henceforth be applied to decisions affecting that ministry, it was not reasonable to expect that the provisions of that convention applied to those decisions. (*Per* Mc Hugh J, para 39.)

Relevance of the Children's Convention

2   Article 3 of the Children's Convention was not intended to apply to an action that has consequences for a child, but is not directed at the child, such as an application by an adult for resident status as in this case. Article 3 did not require the Minister's delegate to make the best interests of the children a primary consideration in deciding Mr Teoh's application any more than that article required the judge who sentenced him to make the best interest of the children a primary consideration in the sentencing process. (*Per* Mc Hugh J, paras 43 and 44.)

Treaties and other international instruments referred to

Declaration on the Rights of Mentally Retarded Persons 1971

Geneva Convention relating to the Status of Refugees 1951

Hague Convention on the Civil Aspects of International Child Abduction 1980

New York Protocol relating to the Status of Refugees 1967

United Nations Convention on the Rights of the Child 1989, arts 3, 5, 9, 43 and 44

National legislation referred to

Australia

Administrative Decisions (Judicial Review) Act 1977, ss 5(1)(e) and 5(2)(g)

Family Law Act 1975 (Cth), s 64(1)(a)

Family Law (Child Abduction Convention) Regulations 1986

Human Rights and Equal Opportunity Commission Act 1986, ss 3(1), 11(1) and 47(1); Schedule 4

Migration Act 1958, ss 5, 6(2) & 6, 6A, 7(3), 16(1)(c) and 60

Cases referred to

Ainsworth v Criminal Justice Commission (1992) 175 CLR 564

Akers v Minister for Immigration and Ethnic Affairs (1988) 20 FCR 363

Annetts v McCann (1990) 170 CLR 596

Attorney-General (NSW) v Quin (1990) 170 CLR 1

Attorney-General of Hong Kong v Ng Yuen Shiu [1983] 2 AC 629

Ballina Shire Council v Ringland (1994) 33 NSWLR 680

Haoucher v Minister for Immigration and Ethnic Affairs (1990) 169 CLR 648

In the Marriage of Murray and Tam (1993) 16 Fam LR 982

Kioa v West (1985) 159 CLR 550

Lek v Minister for Immigration, Local Government and Ethnic Affairs (1993) 117 ALR 455

Luu v Renevier (1989) 91 ALR 39

Minister for Aboriginal Affairs v Peko-Wallsend Ltd (1986) 162 CLR 24

Minister for Foreign Affairs and Trade v Magno (1992) 112 ALR 529; 37 FCR 298

Prasad v Minister for Immigration and Ethnic Affairs (1985) 65 ALR 549

Re Marion (1990) 14 Fam LR 427

Reference re Canada Assistance Plan (BC) (1991) 2 SCR 525; (1991) 83 DLR (4th) 297

Reg v Chief Immigration Officer [1976] 1 WLR 979

Reg v Home Secretary ex parte Brind (1991) 1 AC 696

Reg v Sandford (1994) 33 NSWLR 172

Schmidt v Secretary of State for Home Affairs [1969] 2 Ch 149

Secretary, Department of Health and Community Services v JWB and SMB (1992) 175 CLR 218

Singh v Minister for Immigration and Ethnic Affairs (1987) 15 FCR 4

Tavita v Minister of Immigration [1994] 2 NZLR 257

Tickner v Bropho (1993) 114 ALR 409; 40 FCR 183

Videto v Minister for Immigration and Ethnic Affairs (1985) 69 ALR 342

Water Conservation and Irrigation Commission (NSW) v Browning (1947) 74 CLR 492

Young v Registrar, Court of Appeal (No 3) (1993) 32 NSWLR 262

JUDGMENT

MASON CJ AND DEANE J:

1   This appeal, which is brought by the Minister from a unanimous decision of the Full Federal Court (Black CJ, Lee and Carr JJ) allowing an appeal by the respondent from a decision of French J, raises an important question concerning the relationship between international law and Australian law.

Factual background

2   The respondent, Mr Teoh, a Malaysian citizen, came to Australia on 5 May 1988 and was granted a temporary entry permit. On 9 July he married Jean Helen Lim, an Australian citizen, who had been the *de facto* spouse of his deceased brother. At the time of the marriage Mrs Teoh had four children, the eldest being the child of her first marriage, the other three being children of her *de facto* relationship with the respondent's brother. There are, in addition, three children of the marriage.

3   In October 1988 the respondent applied for and was granted a further temporary entry permit which allowed him to remain in Australia until 5 February 1989. Before that permit had expired the respondent applied for a permanent entry permit, otherwise referred to as a grant of resident status. In November 1990, when his application for resident status was still pending, the respondent was convicted of six counts of being knowingly concerned in the importation of heroin and of three counts of being in possession of heroin. He was sentenced to six years' imprisonment with a non-parole period of two years and eight months. The sentencing judge accepted that Mrs Teoh's addiction to heroin played a part in the respondent's actions.

4   In January 1991, the respondent received a letter informing him that an officer authorised under the Migration Act 1958 (Cth) ("the Act") had refused his application for the grant of resident status. The application was refused for the following reasons:

1.1   It is a policy requirement for grant of resident status that applicants be of good character.

1.2   Amongst other points, one of the bases of assessment is whether the applicant has a criminal record.

1.3   All applicants aged 16 years or over are subject to the character requirement.

In this case [the respondent] cannot meet the character requirement as he has a criminal record. [He] is currently serving 6 years' imprisonment with a 2 year 8 month non-parole period.

The reasons given reflected policy instructions issued by the Department to decision-makers, to which we shall refer later.

5   The Act (as it then stood) provided that, upon the expiration of a temporary entry permit, the holder became a prohibited non-citizen unless a further entry permit came into force.[1] The respondent was therefore told that he was an "illegal entrant" but that he could apply for a review of the decision refusing his application for resident status.

6   The respondent made such an application under reg 173A of the regulations made under the Act in 1989. His wife supported this application. A number of documents were annexed to the application. Among the documents was a copy of a character reference from the respondent's former employer, Mr R Deng. That reference included the following observations:

Since knowing [the respondent] and his family, I found he is a good father and very responsible family man. Despite his many hardships, he always placed his wife and children before his own interests. He cares for them and provides for their needs.

Also among the documents was a handwritten testimonial from Mrs P D Grant, the respondent's mother-in-law, which referred to the respondent as a concerned father and a great help to his wife who was a drug addict. According to Mrs Grant, the respondent was hardworking, had tried very hard to keep his wife out of trouble and to care for his children, and only wanted what was best for his family. She added that it would be a "great tragedy for the whole family" if he were to be deported, noting that he was the only person who could keep them together. The respondent's wife also included a letter in support of the application, stressing the need that the family had for the respondent's continued presence. At that time Mrs Teoh had six children living with her. They were all under ten years old. The youngest child was born later on 20 March 1992.

7   On 25 July 1991, the Immigration Review Panel recommended that the respondent's application for reconsideration be rejected. The Panel noted that Mrs Teoh, Mrs Grant and Mr Deng had made claims on compassionate grounds that the respondent's application be approved. The Panel referred specifically to the respondent's statement that his wife and children would suffer great financial and emotional hardship if he were deported. The Panel went on to make its recommendation for the following reasons:

---

1   Section 7(3).

All the evidence for this Application has been carefully examined, including the claims of Ms Teoh. It is realised that Ms Teoh and family are facing a very bleak and difficult future and will be deprived of a possible breadwinner as well as a father and husband if resident status is not granted. However, the applicant has committed a very serious crime and failed to meet the character requirements for the granting of Permanent Residency. The compassionate claims are not considered to be compelling enough for the waiver of policy in view of [Mr Teoh's] criminal record.

8   A delegate of the Minister accepted this recommendation on 26 July 1991 and on 17 February 1992, another delegate of the Minister made an order under section 60 of the Act that the respondent be deported. The respondent applied to the Federal Court to have these two decisions reviewed.

The decision at first instance

9   The respondent challenged the delegate's decision to refuse reconsideration of the refusal of the grant of resident status on three broad grounds:

(1) the delegate had failed to comply with the rules of procedural fairness because the respondent was not given an opportunity to contradict or otherwise deal with the finding that he was not of good character;

(2) the decision involved an improper exercise of power in that the delegate had failed to take relevant considerations into account; and

(3) the decision involved an improper exercise of power in that the delegate exercised her discretionary power in accordance with a policy without regard to the merits of the respondent's case.

10   French J rejected the challenge on these grounds. As the application to review the decision to deport was inextricably linked with the challenge to the decision refusing resident status, the respondent's application for review of the two decisions was dismissed.

The decision on appeal

11   At the hearing of the appeal to the Full Court of the Federal Court, the respondent sought leave to amend the grounds stated in his application for judicial review of the decision refusing resident status by adding the following further particular of procedural unfairness:

[T]he [Minister's delegate] failed to make appropriate investigations into the hardship to the [respondent's] wife and her children were the [respondent] refused resident status.

The respondent also sought leave to amend his notice of appeal by adding the following additional ground:

The Court erred in fact and in law in finding that the hardship to the [respondent's] wife and her children had been taken into relevant consideration.

The Full Court unanimously allowed both amendments notwithstanding the fact that, as Carr J pointed out, the respondent's counsel at first instance had expressly abandoned the ground that the Minister's delegate failed to take into account the hardship to the respondent's wife and her children were he refused resident status.

12   Black CJ concluded that the Minister's delegate did not properly consider the effect of the break-up of the family when she made her decision to refuse the grant of resident status to the respondent. Counsel for the Minister having conceded that the effect of the break-up of the family was a matter that the delegate was bound to take into account, her failure to do so involved an error of law.

13 Lee J considered that the Executive's ratification of the United Nations Convention on the Rights of the Child ("the Convention") was a statement to the national and international community that the Commonwealth recognised and accepted the principles of the Convention. Article 3.1 of the Convention provides that "[i]n all actions concerning children the best interests of the child shall be a primary consideration". Although noting that the Convention had not been incorporated into Australian law, his Honour stated that its ratification provided parents and children, whose interests could be affected by actions of the Commonwealth which concerned children, with a legitimate expectation that such actions would be conducted in a manner which adhered to the relevant principles of the Convention. This meant that, in such a context, the parents and children who might be affected by a relevant decision had a legitimate expectation that the Commonwealth decision-maker would act on the basis that the "best interests" of the children would be treated as "a primary consideration". His Honour held that the delegate had not exercised her power consistently with that expectation because she failed to initiate appropriate inquiries and obtain appropriate reports as to the future welfare of the children in the event that the respondent were deported. That failure involved an error of law.

14 Carr J's approach was similar to that adopted by Lee J. Carr J also considered that, although the Convention was not part of Australian municipal law, the children in this case had a legitimate expectation that their father's application would be treated by the Minister in a manner consistent with its terms.

15 In the result, the Court ordered that the delegate's decision of 26 July 1991 to refuse the respondent's application for the grant of resident status be set aside and that the application be referred to the Minister for reconsideration according to law. The Court also ordered that the other delegate's decision to deport the respondent be stayed until the Minister reconsidered and determined that application.

16 The Minister contends that the Full Court's decision is wrong on a number of grounds. It is only necessary to outline three of them for the purposes of this appeal:

(1) Lee and Carr JJ erred in holding that Australia's ratification of the Convention created a legitimate expectation in parents or children that any action or decision by the Commonwealth would be conducted or made in accordance with the principles of the Convention;

(2) even if ratification of the Convention created such an expectation, Lee and Carr JJ erred in holding that, in the circumstances of this case, procedural fairness required the Minister's delegate to initiate appropriate inquiries and obtain appropriate reports concerning the children; and

(3) Black CJ erred in holding that the Minister's delegate did not properly consider the break-up of the family when she made her decision to refuse the grant of resident status to the respondent.

The relevant statutory provisions

17 The respondent's application for a permanent entry permit was governed by the provisions of the Act as it stood before it was amended in 1989, as was the respondent's application for reconsideration of the refusal of a permanent entry permit. Section 6(2) then provided:

> An officer may, ... at the request or with the consent of a non-citizen, grant to the non-citizen an entry permit.

An entry permit might be temporary or permanent.[2] The word "officer" was defined by section 5 of the Act so as to include a person authorised by the Minister to discharge certain functions.

18 In order to qualify for the grant of a permanent entry permit conferring resident status, the respondent was required to satisfy one of the conditions set out in section 6A. So far as it is relevant, that section provided:

> (1) An entry permit shall not be granted to a non-citizen after his entry into Australia unless one or more of the following conditions is fulfilled in respect of him, that is to say ...
> (b) he is the spouse, child or aged parent of an Australian citizen or of the holder of an entry permit; ...
> (e) he is the holder of a temporary entry permit which is in force and there are strong compassionate or humanitarian grounds for the grant of an entry permit to him.

In his application for resident status, the respondent had relied on satisfaction of condition (b) alone even though, at the time of the application, he also clearly satisfied condition (e). It has not, however, been suggested that anything turns upon that for the purposes of the present case since it is common ground that the "strong compassionate or humanitarian grounds" which were required to satisfy condition (e) were a relevant consideration supporting a grant of resident status based on satisfaction of condition (b). In these circumstances, it is unnecessary to consider whether the fact that the respondent's temporary entry permit expired during the period between the time when his application for resident status was made and the time when it was dealt with would have precluded reliance upon satisfaction of condition (e) as an independent ground. As it was, satisfaction of condition (b) enabled the delegate to grant resident status in the exercise of a statutory discretion to grant or refuse the respondent's application.

19 It is convenient to refer now to section 16(1)(c) of the Act and to a policy requirement of good character contained in departmental instructions entitled "Integrated Departmental Instructions Manual, Grant of resident status, Number 17". Section 16(1)(c) provided:

> (1) Where ... a person who enters or entered Australia is not, or was not, at the time of that entry, an Australian citizen and who: ...
> (c) at the time of entry is or was a person of any of the following descriptions, namely: ...
> (ii) a person who has been convicted of a crime and sentenced to death, to imprisonment for life or to imprisonment for a period of not less than 1 year;
> (iii) a person who has been convicted of 2 or more crimes and sentenced to imprisonment for periods aggregating not less than 1 year; ... that person shall, notwithstanding section 10, be deemed to be a prohibited non-citizen unless he is the holder of an entry permit endorsed with a statement that the person granting that permit recognises him to be a person referred to in this sub-section.

Because the respondent sustained his convictions after his entry into Australia, section 16(1)(c) had no direct application.

20 However, paragraph 1.1 of the Departmental Instructions Manual, to which we have referred, stated: "It is a policy requirement for grant of resident status that applicants be of good character." Paragraph 1.2 specifically indicated that one of the bases of assessment was "whether the applicant has a criminal record". Paragraph 3.2 stated that

---

2   See s 6(6).

applicants who come within section 16(1)(c) do not meet the good character requirement and their applications would normally be refused unless they could show "strong cause why policy should be waived in their case". Paragraph 3.3 stated:

> Applicants who do not come within section 16(1)(c) of the Act may also fail to meet this good character requirement. The nature, number or recency of the offences or activities concerned and the potential for continuance or recidivism may be such as to warrant refusal on the overall merits of the case.

21 As understood in the light of the reasons stated by the chairperson, the recommendation of the Immigration Review Panel that the respondent's application for reconsideration be rejected was based on an acceptance of the Department's character objections, presumably grounded on paragraphs 1.1, 1.2 and 3.3 of the departmental instructions, and on a conclusion that the serious nature of the respondent's offences outweighed the compassionate factors on which he relied. This recommendation, as stated above, was accepted by the Minister's delegate.

The scope of the statutory discretion

22 Apart from the prescription by section 6A that one of the conditions shall be satisfied and the restriction arising from section 16(1)(c), the statutory discretion to grant or refuse resident status is "unconfined except in so far as the subject matter and the scope and purpose of the statutory enactments may enable the Court to pronounce given reasons to be definitely extraneous to any objects the legislature could have had in view", to use the words of Dixon J in *Water Conservation and Irrigation Commission (NSW) v Browning*.[3] There is no provision in the Act which makes the provisions of the Convention, assuming them to be otherwise relevant, extraneous to a decision-maker's considerations of an application for resident status and for review of a refusal of such an application. Nor has it been suggested that there is anything in the scope and purpose of the statute which would have that effect. It follows that the Immigration Review Panel and the Minister's delegate who accepted the recommendation of the Panel were entitled to have regard to the provisions of the Convention so long as they were a legitimate subject-matter for consideration and were relevant to the issues for determination.

The Convention

23 The Convention was ratified by the Commonwealth Executive on 17 December 1990 and it entered into force for Australia on 16 January 1991. These events occurred before the rejection of the respondent's application for reconsideration of the decision refusing resident status and before the Minister's delegate made the decision to deport him. On 22 December 1992, after those decisions had been made, the Attorney-General declared the Convention to be an international instrument relating to human rights and freedoms. This declaration was made pursuant to section 47(1) of the Human Rights and Equal Opportunity Commission Act 1986 (Cth).

24 Articles 3 and 9 of the Convention provide as follows:

Article 3

1　In all actions concerning children, whether undertaken by public or private social welfare institutions, courts of law, administrative authorities or legislative bodies, the best interests of the child shall be a primary consideration.

3　(1947) 74 CLR 492 at 505.

2   States Parties undertake to ensure the child such protection and care as is necessary for his or her well-being, taking into account the rights and duties of his or her parents, legal guardians, or other individuals legally responsible for him or her, and, to this end, shall take all appropriate legislative and administrative measures.

3   States Parties shall ensure that the institutions, services and facilities responsible for the care or protection of children shall conform with the standards established by competent authorities, particularly in the areas of safety, health, in the number and suitability of their staff, as well as competent supervision.

Article 9

1   States Parties shall ensure that a child shall not be separated from his or her parents against their will, except when competent authorities subject to judicial review determine, in accordance with applicable law and procedures, that such separation is necessary for the best interests of the child. Such determination may be necessary in a particular case such as one involving abuse or neglect of the child by the parents, or one where the parents are living separately and a decision must be made as to the child's place of residence.

2   In any proceedings pursuant to paragraph 1 of the present article, all interested parties shall be given an opportunity to participate in the proceedings and make their views known.

3   States Parties shall respect the right of the child who is separated from one or both parents to maintain personal relations and direct contact with both parents on a regular basis, except if it is contrary to the child's best interests.

4   Where such separation results from any action initiated by a State Party, such as the detention, imprisonment, exile, deportation or death (including death arising from any cause while the person is in the custody of the State) of one or both parents or of the child, that State Party shall, upon request, provide the parents, the child or, if appropriate, another member of the family with the essential information concerning the whereabouts of the absent member(s) of the family unless the provision of the information would be detrimental to the well-being of the child. States Parties shall further ensure that the submission of such a request shall of itself entail no adverse consequences for the person(s) concerned.

The status of the Convention in Australian law

25   It is well established that the provisions of an international treaty to which Australia is a party do not form part of Australian law unless those provisions have been validly incorporated into our municipal law by statute.[4] This principle has its foundation in the proposition that in our constitutional system the making and ratification of treaties fall within the province of the Executive in the exercise of its prerogative power whereas the making and the alteration of the law fall within the province of Parliament, not the Executive.[5] So, a treaty which has not been incorporated into our municipal law cannot operate as a direct source of individual rights and obligations under that law. In this case, it is common ground that the provisions of the Convention have not been incorporated in this way. It is not suggested that the declaration made pursuant to section 47(1) of the Human Rights and Equal Opportunity Commission Act has this effect.

4   *Chow Hung Ching v The King* (1948) 77 CLR 449 at 478; *Bradley v The Commonwealth* (1973) 128 CLR 557 at 582; *Simsek v Macphee* (1982) 148 CLR 636 at 641-642; *Koowarta v Bjelke-Petersen* (1982) 153 CLR 168 at 211-212, 224-225; *Kioa v West* (1985) 159 CLR 550 at 570; *Dietrich v The Queen* (1992) 177 CLR 292 at 305; *JH Rayner Ltd v Dept of Trade* [1990] 2 AC 418 at 500.

5   *Simsek v Macphee* (1982) 148 CLR at 641-642.

26 But the fact that the Convention has not been incorporated into Australian law does not mean that its ratification holds no significance for Australian law. Where a statute or subordinate legislation is ambiguous, the courts should favour that construction which accords with Australia's obligations under a treaty or international convention to which Australia is a party,[6] at least in those cases in which the legislation is enacted after, or in contemplation of, entry into, or ratification of, the relevant international instrument. That is because Parliament, *prima facie*, intends to give effect to Australia's obligations under international law.

27 It is accepted that a statute is to be interpreted and applied, as far as its language permits, so that it is in conformity and not in conflict with the established rules of international law.[7] The form in which this principle has been expressed might be thought to lend support to the view that the proposition enunciated in the preceding paragraph should be stated so as to require the courts to favour a construction, as far as the language of the legislation permits, that is in conformity and not in conflict with Australia's international obligations. That indeed is how we would regard the proposition as stated in the preceding paragraph. In this context, there are strong reasons for rejecting a narrow conception of ambiguity. If the language of the legislation is susceptible of a construction which is consistent with the terms of the international instrument and the obligations which it imposes on Australia, then that construction should prevail. So expressed, the principle is no more than a canon of construction and does not import the terms of the treaty or convention into our municipal law as a source of individual rights and obligations.[8]

28 Apart from influencing the construction of a statute or subordinate legislation, an international convention may play a part in the development by the courts of the common law. The provisions of an international convention to which Australia is a party, especially one which declares universal fundamental rights, may be used by the courts as a legitimate guide in developing the common law.[9] But the courts should act in this fashion with due circumspection when the Parliament itself has not seen fit to incorporate the provisions of a convention into our domestic law. Judicial development of the common law must not be seen as a backdoor means of importing an unincorporated convention into Australian law. A cautious approach to the development of the common law by reference to international conventions would be consistent with the approach which the courts have hitherto adopted to the development of the common law by reference to statutory policy and statutory materials.[10] Much will depend upon the nature of the relevant provision, the extent to which it has been accepted by the international community, the purpose which it is intended to serve and its relationship to the existing principles of our domestic law.

29 In the present case, however, we are not concerned with the resolution of an ambiguity in a statute. Nor are we concerned with the development of some existing principle of the common law. The critical questions to be resolved are whether the provisions of the Convention are relevant to the exercise of the statutory discretion and, if so, whether Australia's ratification of the Convention can give rise to a legitimate expectation that the decision-maker will exercise that discretion in conformity with the

6   *Chu Kheng Lim v Minister for Immigration* (1992) 176 CLR 1 at 38.

7   *Polites v The Commonwealth* (1945) 70 CLR 60 at 68-69, 77, 80-81.

8   *Reg v Home Secretary; Ex parte Brind* [1991] 1 AC 696 at 748.

9   *Mabo v Queensland* (No.2) (1992) 175 CLR 1 at 42 *per* Brennan J (with whom Mason CJ and McHugh J agreed); *Dietrich v The Queen* (1992) 177 CLR at 321 *per* Brennan J, 360 *per* Toohey J; *Jago v District Court of New South Wales* (1988) 12 NSWLR 558 at 569 *per* Kirby P; *Derbyshire County Council v Times Newspapers Ltd* [1992] QB 770.

10   *Lamb v Cotogno* (1987) 164 CLR at 11-12.

terms of the Convention. The foregoing discussion of the status of the Convention in Australian law reveals no intrinsic reason for excluding its provisions from consideration by the decision-maker simply because it has not been incorporated into our municipal law.

The relevance of the Convention

30 Lee and Carr JJ evidently considered that Article 3 of the Convention had an application to the exercise of the discretion, though their Honours did not express any cogent reasons for that conclusion. The respondent did not rely on Article 9, no doubt because it does not seem to address decisions to deport or, for that matter, decisions to refuse permanent entry. The crucial question is whether the decision was an "action concerning children". It is clear enough that the decision was an "action" in the relevant sense of that term, but was the decision an action "concerning children"? The ordinary meaning of "concerning" is "regarding, touching, in reference or relation to; about".[11] The appellant argues that the decision, though it affects the children, does not touch or relate to them. That, in our view, is an unduly narrow reading of the provision, particularly when regard is had to the grounds advanced in support of the application and the reasons given for its rejection, namely that the respondent's bad character outweighed the compassionate considerations arising from the effect that separation would have on the family unit, notably the young children. A broad reading and application of the provisions in Article 3, one which gives to the word "concerning" a wide-ranging application, is more likely to achieve the objects of the Convention.

31 One other aspect of Article 3 merits attention. The concluding words of Article 3.1 are "the best interests of the child shall be *a* primary consideration" (our emphasis). The article is careful to avoid putting the best interests of the child as *the* primary consideration; it does no more than give those interests first importance along with such other considerations as may, in the circumstances of a given case, require equal, but not paramount, weight. The impact of Article 3.1 in the present case is a matter to be dealt with later in these reasons.

The Full Court's use of the Convention as a foundation for a legitimate expectation and the creation of an obligation to initiate inquiries and reports in conjunction with procedural fairness

32 What is significant about the reasoning of Lee and Carr JJ is that, having used the Convention as a foundation for generating an expectation that its provisions would be implemented, their Honours held that, in the light of the Convention, procedural fairness required the initiation of appropriate inquiries and the obtaining of appropriate reports as to the future welfare of the children in the event that the respondent were deported. In taking this approach, Lee and Carr JJ acted in accordance with views expressed by some judges of the Federal Court in earlier cases. In *Videto v Minister for Immigration and Ethnic Affairs*,[12] Toohey J, after observing that "[a]s a broad proposition, I do not think that the Act imposes an obligation on a decision-maker to initiate inquiries", went on to indicate that in some situations such an obligation might arise. In *Prasad v Minister for Immigration and Ethnic Affairs*,[13] Wilcox J, with reference to section 5(2)(g) of the Administrative Decisions (Judicial Review) Act 1977 (Cth), said:[14]

---

11   The New Shorter Oxford English Dictionary on Historical Principles, 3rd ed (1993) at 467.

12   (1985) 69 ALR 342 at 353.

13   (1985) 65 ALR 549.

14   *Ibid* at 562.

The most restrictive view is that paragraph (g) applies only to a case in which the court is able to hold that, upon the material actually or constructively before the decision-maker, the decision was unreasonable. At the opposite extreme it is arguable that the question is whether, upon the evidence before the court as to the facts at the date of decision, and whether or not all of those facts were known to, or reasonably ascertainable by, the decision-maker, his decision, objectively considered, was unreasonable. An intermediate position is that the court is entitled to consider those facts which were known to the decision-maker, actually or constructively, together only with such additional facts as the decision-maker would have learned but for any unreasonable conduct by him.

His Honour went on to express a tentative preference for the intermediate position, based on the view that under section 5(1)(e) and section 5(2)(g) the court is concerned with the manner of exercise of the power. Just as a power is exercised in an improper manner if it is, upon the material before the decision-maker, a decision to which no reasonable person could come, so it is exercised in an improper manner if the decision-maker makes his or her decision in a manner so devoid of plausible justification that no reasonable person could have taken that course.

33 Accepting the correctness of this approach in an appropriate case, it does not seem to us that the present case was argued on the ground of section 5(2)(g) or on the basis of "Wednesbury" unreasonableness. And we do not see how the suggested failure to initiate inquiries can be supported on the footing that there was some departure from the common law standards of natural justice or procedural fairness. Nothing in the two cases to which we have referred, or in *Luu v Renevier*[15] or in *Lek v Minister for Immigration, Local Government and Ethnic Affairs*,[16] the other cases mentioned by Lee J, supports that view. Another difficulty with the approach taken by Lee and Carr JJ is that the requirement that the Minister's delegate initiate inquiries and obtain reports as to the future welfare of the children appears to stem from an assumption that the Minister's delegate was bound to exercise the statutory discretion in conformity with the Convention as if its provisions formed part of our municipal law. That assumption appears to have arisen from the finding that ratification of the Convention generated a legitimate expectation that its provisions would be applied.

34 Junior counsel for the appellant contended that a convention ratified by Australia but not incorporated into our law could never give rise to a legitimate expectation. No persuasive reason was offered to support this far-reaching proposition. The fact that the provisions of the Convention do not form part of our law are a less than compelling reason – legitimate expectations are not equated to rules or principles of law. Moreover, ratification by Australia of an international convention is not to be dismissed as a merely platitudinous or ineffectual act,[17] particularly when the instrument evidences internationally accepted standards to be applied by courts and administrative authorities in dealing with basic human rights affecting the family and children. Rather, ratification of a convention is a positive statement by the executive government of this country to the world and to the Australian people that the executive government and its agencies will act in accordance with the Convention. That positive statement is an adequate foundation for a legitimate expectation, absent statutory or executive indications to the contrary, that administrative decision-makers will act in conformity with the Convention[18] and treat the best interests of the children as "a primary

---

15 (1989) 91 ALR 39 at 45.

16 (1993) 117 ALR 455 at 474.

17 See *Minister for Foreign Affairs and Trade v Magno* (1992) 37 FCR 298 at 343; *Tavita v Minister of Immigration* [1994] 2 NZLR 257 at 266.

18 cf *Simsek v Macphee* (1982) 148 CLR at 644.

consideration". It is not necessary that a person seeking to set up such a legitimate expectation should be aware of the Convention or should personally entertain the expectation; it is enough that the expectation is reasonable in the sense that there are adequate materials to support it.

35 But, in the present case, who is entitled to claim that the expectation was legitimate? Lee J held that "parents and children" affected could do so, whereas Carr J held that only the children could make such a claim. Although it would be preferable for the children to make the claim directly, we can see no objection to a parent or guardian making the claim on behalf of a child. It seems that the present case has been conducted on the footing that the respondent, with the mother's support, has been asserting the children's claim.

36 The existence of a legitimate expectation that a decision-maker will act in a particular way does not necessarily compel him or her to act in that way. That is the difference between a legitimate expectation and a binding rule of law. To regard a legitimate expectation as requiring the decision-maker to act in a particular way is tantamount to treating it as a rule of law. It incorporates the provisions of the unincorporated convention into our municipal law by the back door. And that, as we have already said, is what Lee and Carr JJ seem to have done because the obligation to initiate inquiries and reports appears to stem from a view that the Minister's delegate was bound to apply Article 3.1.

37 But, if a decision-maker proposes to make a decision inconsistent with a legitimate expectation, procedural fairness requires that the persons affected should be given notice and an adequate opportunity of presenting a case against the taking of such a course. So, here, if the delegate proposed to give a decision which did not accord with the principle that the best interests of the children were to be a primary consideration, procedural fairness called for the delegate to take the steps just indicated.

Did the Minister's delegate comply with the Convention?

38 The question which then arises is whether the delegate made her decision without treating the best interests of the child as a primary consideration. There is nothing to indicate that the Panel or the Minister's delegate had regard to the terms of the Convention. That would not matter if it appears from the delegate's acceptance of the Panel's recommendation that the principle enshrined in Article 3.1 was applied. If that were the case, the legitimate expectation was fulfilled and no case of procedural unfairness could arise.

39 It can be said that the delegate carried out a balancing exercise in which she considered the plight of Mrs Teoh and the children and recognised that they would face a "very difficult and bleak future" if the respondent were deported. On the other hand, she considered that the respondent had been convicted of very serious offences and this factor outweighed the "compassionate claims". However, it does not seem to us that the Panel or the delegate regarded the best interests of the children as a primary consideration. The last sentence in the recommendation of the Panel reveals that, in conformity with the departmental instructions, it was treating the good character requirement as the primary consideration. The Panel said: "The compassionate claims are not considered to be compelling enough for *the waiver of policy* in view of Mr Teoh's criminal record" (emphasis added). The language of that sentence treats the policy requirement as paramount unless it can be displaced by other considerations. There is no indication that the best interests of the children are to be treated as a primary consideration. A decision-maker with an eye to the principle enshrined in the

Convention would be looking to the best interests of the children as a primary consideration, asking whether the force of any other consideration outweighed it. The decision necessarily reflected the difference between the principle and the instruction.

40 That view entails the conclusion that there was a want of procedural fairness. It may also entail, though this was not argued, a failure to apply a relevant principle in that the principle enshrined in Article 3.1 may possibly have a counterpart in the common law as it applies to cases where the welfare of a child is a matter relevant to the determination to be made.

41 In other respects, we do not consider that there was any failure to take relevant matters into account. It cannot be said that the delegate either failed to turn her mind to the hardship the family would face or failed to have regard to the consequences of the break-up of the family unit. She had a considerable amount of detailed information about the respondent's wife and children before her. As Carr J noted, her assessment of their plight was very gloomy indeed.

Conclusion

42 In the result the appeal should be dismissed though for reasons which differ from those given by the Full Court of the Federal Court. The appellant should pay the costs of the respondent.

TOOHEY J:

[...]*

The role of the Convention

20 It being common ground that the Convention is not part of Australian municipal law, what role should it have played in the decisions which have given rise to this appeal? In posing the question in this way, there is an underlying assumption that if the Convention were part of municipal law Articles 3 and 5 would indeed have an impact on the decisions that were made.

21 The appellant said that it was axiomatic that treaties (other than treaties terminating a state of war) do not impose obligations on individuals or invest individuals with additional rights or otherwise affect the rights of individuals under Australian law except in so far as the treaty is effectuated by statute. There is an abundance of authority to this effect.[14]

22 But it does not follow that the Convention has no role in the present case. It is important to see the way in which the respondent relied upon the Convention. It played no part in the hearing before French J. It is not mentioned in the notice of appeal to the Full Court. It seems to have surfaced during the hearing of the appeal to the Full Court and was relied upon by the respondent as an aspect of natural justice, in particular as giving rise to a legitimate expectation that the Panel would act consistently with the

---

*   **Eds:** In paragraphs 1–19 of his judgment (omitted here, together with footnotes 1–13), Toohey J repeats the background to the case and the judgments of the courts below. The full text of the judgment is available at (1995) 128 ALR 353; (1995) 69 ALJR 423 and (1995) CLR 273.

14   *Chow Hung Ching v R* (1948) 77 CLR 449 at 478 *per* Dixon J; *Bradley v Commonwealth* (1973) 128 CLR 557 at 582 *per* Barwick CJ and Gibbs J; *Simsek v MacPhee* (1982) 148 CLR 636 at 641–2 *per* Stephen J; *Koowarta v Bjelke-Petersen* (1982) 153 CLR 168 at 193 *per* Gibbs CJ; *Dietrich v R* (1992) 177 CLR 292 at 305 *per* Mason CJ and McHugh J, 359–60 *per* Toohey J. See also *Minister for Foreign Affairs and Trade v Magno* (1992) 112 ALR 529; *R v Sandford* (1994) 33 NSWLR 172 at 177 *per* Hunt CJ; *JH Rayner (Mincing Lane) Ltd v Department of Trade and Industry* [1990] 2 AC 418 at 500 *per* Lord Oliver.

Convention and, in particular, not act in a manner inconsistent with Australia's obligations under the Convention without giving the respondent an opportunity to be heard. Coupled with this expectation was an obligation to provide procedural fairness to the respondent, an obligation which required the decision-maker to obtain further information about the respondent's family before making a decision.

23   If the matter is approached in terms of legitimate expectation, it is no answer for the appellant to argue that the Convention does not give rise to individual rights and obligations in municipal law. The question rather is whether Australia's ratification of the Convention results in an expectation that those making administrative decisions under the aegis of the executive government of the Commonwealth will act in accordance with the Convention wherever it is relevant to the decision to be made.

24   In the appellant's submission the Convention had no bearing on and was irrelevant to the rights of the respondent and the obligations of the appellant. Ratification did not amount to adoption or incorporation of the Convention in the municipal law of Australia. Declaration for the purposes of the HREOC Act did no more than identify an international instrument as a guide to the Human Rights and Equal Opportunity Commission in fulfilling its functions of inquiring into and reporting on any act or practice that may be inconsistent with or contrary to human rights declared in the instrument. The appellant drew attention to the fact that the Convention receives no mention in the Migration Act 1958. By way of contrast, section 6A(1)(c) of that Act (now repealed) referred specifically to the 1951 Geneva Convention relating to the Status of Refugees and the 1967 New York Protocol relating to the Status of Refugees.

25   Concepts such as natural justice, procedural fairness and legitimate expectation are sometimes applied as if they were labels, somehow determining the outcome of a particular matter. But they have to be seen for what they are, in their particular context. It is one thing to say that natural justice demanded that the respondent be given every opportunity to present his case; certainly natural justice demanded that much. It is another thing to say that procedural fairness dictated that no decision adverse to his application be made without pursuing further the implications of deportation for his family. It is another thing again to say that the respondent had a legitimate expectation that the decision-maker would act in accordance with the Convention.

26   It was not part of the respondent's case that he was denied an opportunity to present the case in support of his application for resident status. The Department gave him the opportunity to provide whatever material he wished in support of his original application and his application for reconsideration. I shall defer the question of whether the delegate should have made further inquiries until I have dealt with the matter of the Convention and legitimate expectation. In doing this I recognise that legitimate expectation is often treated as an aspect of procedural fairness, though generally in the context of an expectation that a decision-maker should afford a person the opportunity to be heard on a particular matter.[15] As has been observed:[16] "The two broad categories into which the content of a legitimate expectation can be divided are those related to a benefit and those expressly directed to a hearing." In the present case the respondent contends for an expectation that the delegate would deal with his application in light of the criteria to be found in the Convention, particularly the principle that "the best interests of the child shall be a primary consideration". Accordingly, it was submitted,

---

15   See for instance *Haoucher v Minister for Immigration and Ethnic Affairs* (1990) 169 CLR 648 at 655, 670-671, 679-680, 684-685.

16   Tate, "The Coherence of 'Legitimate Expectations' and the Foundations of Natural Justice", (1988) 14 *Monash University Law Review* 15 at 50.

procedural fairness required that if the delegate proposed to act inconsistently with Australia's obligations under Articles 3 and 5 of the Convention, she should first have afforded the respondent the opportunity of persuading her that she should act consistently with its terms.

27 In *Reg v Home Secretary; Ex parte Brind*[17] the House of Lords rejected the broad proposition that the Secretary of State should exercise a statutory discretion in accordance with the terms of the European Convention for the Protection of Human Rights and Fundamental Freedoms, which was not part of English domestic law. That decision was considered by the New Zealand Court of Appeal in *Tavita v Minister of Immigration*[18] where a deportee argued that those concerned with ordering his deportation were bound to take into account the Convention and the International Covenant on Civil and Political Rights, both of which had been ratified by New Zealand. In the end the Court did not have to determine the point. But it said of the contrary proposition:[19]

> That is an unattractive argument, apparently implying that New Zealand's adherence to the international instruments has been at least partly window-dressing ... there must at least be hesitation about accepting it.

28 In *Minister for Foreign Affairs and Trade v Magno*[20] Gummow J essayed an analysis of the relationship between an instrument embodying an international obligation of Australia and a municipal statute dealing with that subject matter. His Honour looked at various aspects of that relationship, concluding that: "difficult questions of administrative law and of judicial review arise where, whilst the international obligation ... is not in terms imported into municipal law and the municipal law is not ambiguous, nevertheless, upon the proper construction of the municipal law, regard may be had by a decision maker exercising a discretion under that law to the international agreement or obligation".[21] In *In the Marriage of Murray and Tam*[22] Nicholson CJ and Fogarty J referred to Gummow J's analysis. The Family Court of Australia was concerned with an appeal from orders made pursuant to the Family Law (Child Abduction Convention) Regulations which in turn derived from the Hague Convention which Australia had ratified. Their Honours noted what Nicholson CJ had said earlier in his dissenting judgment in *Re Marion*[23] in relation to the Declaration on the Rights of Mentally Retarded Persons, incorporated as Schedule 4 to the HREOC Act, namely, that:

> it [is] strongly arguable that the existence of the human rights set out in the relevant instrument ... have been recognised by the parliament as a source of Australian domestic law by reason of this legislation.

Whether this is so is a matter which does not arise in the present case.

29 Returning to what was said in *Tavita*, certainly a submission by a decision-maker that no regard at all need be paid to Australia's acceptance of international obligations by virtue of ratification of a convention is unattractive. What is the next step? Ratification of itself does not make the obligations enforceable in the courts; legislation, not executive act, is required. But the assumption of such an obligation may give rise to legitimate expectations in the minds of those who are affected by administrative

---

17 [1991] 1 AC 696.
18 [1994] 2 NZLR 257.
19 *Ibid* at 266.
20 (1992) 112 ALR 529.
21 *Ibid* at 535.
22 (1993) 16 Fam LR 982.
23 (1990) 14 Fam LR 427 at 451.

decisions on which the obligation has some bearing. It is not necessary for a person in the position of the respondent to show that he was aware of the ratification of the Convention; legitimate expectation in this context does not depend upon the knowledge and state of mind of the individual concerned.[24] The matter is to be assessed objectively, in terms of what expectation might reasonably be engendered by any undertaking that the authority in question has given, whether itself or, as in the present case, by the government of which it is a part.[25] A subjective test is particularly inappropriate when the legitimate expectation is said to derive from something as general as the ratification of the Convention. For, by ratifying the Convention Australia has given a solemn undertaking to the world at large that it will: "in all actions concerning children, whether undertaken by public or private social welfare institutions, courts of law, administrative authorities or legislative bodies" make "the best interests of the child a primary consideration".

30 The appellant complained that the proliferation of conventions which Australia had ratified would impose an impossible task on decision-makers if they were to be the basis for legitimate expectations. But particular conventions will generally have an impact on particular decision-makers and often no great practical difficulties will arise in giving effect to the principles which they acknowledge. In any event it is not that decision-makers must give effect to the precept that "the best interests of the child shall be a primary consideration".[26] There may be other interests carrying equal weight. Rather, a decision-maker who does not intend to treat the best interests of a child as a primary consideration must give the person affected by the decision an opportunity to argue that the decision-maker should do so.

31 The touchstone in Article 3 is "actions concerning children". The scope of the provision can be gauged if the word "concerning" is given its ordinary meaning of "relating to; regarding; about"[27] or "regarding, touching, in reference or relation to; about".[28] The refusal of an application for resident status to a parent of dependent children living in Australia, with the direct consequence of deportation for the parent and the breaking up of the family, is an action concerning children.

32 It follows that while Australia's ratification of the Convention does not go so far as to incorporate it into domestic law, it does have consequences for agencies of the executive government of the Commonwealth. It results in an expectation that those making administrative decisions in actions concerning children will take into account as a primary consideration the best interests of the children and that, if they intend not to do so, they will give the persons affected an opportunity to argue against such a course. It may be said that such a view of ratification will have undue consequences for decision-makers. But it is important to bear in mind that we are not concerned with enforceable obligations, but with legitimate expectations, and that there can be no legitimate expectation if the actions of the legislature or the executive are inconsistent with such an expectation.

---

24 *Haoucher v Minister for Immigration and Ethnic Affairs* (1990) 169 CLR at 670.

25 Cf *A-G of Hong Kong v Ng Yuen Shiu* [1983] 2 AC 629 at 638 where the Privy Council said that "when a public authority has promised to follow a certain procedure, it is in the interests of good administration that it should act fairly and implement its promise, so long as implementation does not interfere with its statutory duty".

26 Cf Family Law Act 1975 (Cth), s 64(1)(a): "the court must regard the welfare of the child as the paramount consideration".

27 *The Macquarie Dictionary*, 2nd ed (1991) at 373.

28 *The New Shorter Oxford English Dictionary on Historical Principles*, 3rd ed (1993) at 467.

33 It was argued that proper consideration of the respondent's application necessitated further inquiries by the delegate. Indeed, a failure to make such inquiries underlies the judgments of Lee J and Carr J. Generally speaking, it is not the decision-maker's duty to initiate inquiries.[29] But in endorsing the Panel's recommendation, the delegate must be taken to have accepted that "Ms Teoh and family are facing a very bleak and difficult future". Before deciding that these considerations did not warrant "the waiver of policy in view of Mr Teoh's criminal record", inquiries could have been made at least of Parkerville Children's Home which had the children in its care and the Department of Community Welfare which had an ongoing involvement with them. The point is not that the delegate was obliged by the Convention to do so but that, had she done so, she might have been in a better position to meet the legitimate expectation to which the Convention gave rise. It is apparent that the delegate did not approach the matter on the footing that the interests of the children were a primary consideration. Instead, she appears to have treated the policy requirement that applicants for the grant of resident status be of good character as the primary consideration. It need hardly be said that the decision-maker might treat the best interests of the children as a primary consideration yet, in all the circumstances, refuse the application for resident status.

Conclusion

34 Before allowing the scales to come down against the respondent by reason of his criminal record, some more detailed assessment of the position of his family could have been undertaken. However, I would dismiss the appeal, not by reason of any failure by the delegate to initiate inquiries and obtain reports, but rather because she did not meet the respondent's legitimate expectation that she would give the best interests of the children the consideration required by the Convention or inform the respondent of her intention not to do so in order that he might argue against that course.

35 Accordingly, I would dismiss the appeal.

GAUDRON J:

1   The facts, the issues and the relevant legislative provisions are set out in the judgments of Mason CJ and Deane J and of Toohey J. It is necessary only to emphasise the consequence to the seven young children who constituted Mr Teoh's immediate family ("the children") of a decision refusing or confirming the refusal of his application for resident status. In that event, Mr Teoh would be required to leave the country and the children would be placed in a position where they grew up either fatherless or in another country, denied an upbringing in the country of which they are citizens.

2   As appears from the judgment of Mason CJ and Deane J, the case was argued in this Court primarily by reference to Article 3.1 of the United Nations Convention on the Rights of the Child ("the Convention") which provides that "(i)n all actions concerning children ... the best interests of the child shall be a primary consideration". It was argued for the appellant that, although his delegate was bound to have regard to the interests of the children, she was neither bound to proceed on the basis that their best interests were a primary consideration nor obliged as a matter of procedural fairness to give Mr Teoh an opportunity to persuade her of that course if she were minded to proceed on some other basis. In particular, it was argued that the Convention did not give rise to an obligation on the part of the delegate to act in accordance with its terms nor a legitimate expectation that she would act in that way. The argument emphasised that the Convention formed no part of municipal law at the time the decisions were made.

---

29 *Videto v Minister* (1985) 69 ALR 342 at 353.

3   I agree with Mason CJ and Deane J as to the status of the Convention in Australian law. However, I consider that the Convention is only of subsidiary significance in this case. What is significant is the status of the children as Australian citizens. Citizenship involves more than obligations on the part of the individual to the community constituting the body politic of which he or she is a member. It involves obligations on the part of the body politic to the individual, especially if the individual is in a position of vulnerability. And there are particular obligations to the child citizen in need of protection. So much was recognised as the duty of kings,[1] which gave rise to the *parens patriae* jurisdiction of the courts. No less is required of the government and the courts of a civilized democratic society.

4   In my view, it is arguable that citizenship carries with it a common law right on the part of children and their parents to have a child's best interests taken into account, at least as a primary consideration, in all discretionary decisions by governments and government agencies which directly affect that child's individual welfare, particularly decisions which affect children as dramatically and as fundamentally as those involved in this case. And it may be that, if there is a right of that kind, a decision-maker is required, at least in some circumstances, to initiate appropriate inquiries, as Carr and Lee JJ held should have happened in this case. However, it was not argued that there is any such right and, thus, the case falls to be decided by reference to the requirements of natural justice.

5   Quite apart from the Convention or its ratification, any reasonable person who considered the matter would, in my view, assume that the best interests of the child would be a primary consideration in all administrative decisions which directly affect children as individuals and which have consequences for their future welfare. Further, they would assume or expect that the interests of the child would be taken into account in that way as a matter of course and without any need for the issue to be raised with the decision-maker. They would make that assumption or have that expectation because of the special vulnerability of children, particularly where the break-up of the family unit is, or may be, involved, and because of their expectation that a civilized society would be alert to its responsibilities to children who are, or may be, in need of protection.

6   The significance of the Convention, in my view, is that it gives expression to a fundamental human right which is taken for granted by Australian society, in the sense that it is valued and respected here as in other civilized countries. And if there were any doubt whether that were so, ratification would tend to confirm the significance of the right within our society. Given that the Convention gives expression to an important right valued by the Australian community, it is reasonable to speak of an expectation that the Convention would be given effect. However, that may not be so in the case of a treaty or convention that is not in harmony with community values and expectations.

7   There is a want of procedural fairness if there is no opportunity to be heard on matters in issue. And there is no opportunity to be heard if the person concerned neither knows nor is in a position to anticipate what the issues are. That is also the case if it is assumed that a particular matter is not in issue and the assumption is reasonable in the circumstances. In my view and for the reasons already given, it is reasonable to assume that, in a case such as the present, the best interests of the children would be taken into

---

1   See, in relation to the "direct responsibility of the crown" which founds the "*parens patriae*" jurisdiction originally conferred on the English Court of Chancery, *Secretary, Department of Health and Community Services v JWB and SMB ("Marion's Case")* (1992) 175 CLR 218 at 258-259 and the cases there cited; cf at 279-280. See, in relation to the paramountcy of the child's welfare in the exercise of that jurisdiction, *Marion's Case* at 292-293 and the cases there cited.

account as a primary consideration and as a matter of course. That being so, procedural fairness required that, if the delegate were considering proceeding on some other basis, she should inform Mr Teoh in that regard and give him an opportunity to persuade her otherwise. It did not, however, require her to initiate inquiries and obtain reports about the future welfare of the children and, in this respect, I agree with the judgment of Mason CJ and Deane J.

8   I also agree with Mason CJ and Deane J, for the reasons that their Honours give, that the delegate did not proceed on the basis that she was to take the interests of the children into account as a primary consideration. There was, thus, a want of procedural fairness. The appeal should be dismissed.

MCHUGH J (dissenting):

1   The principal question in this appeal from an order of the Full Court of the Federal Court is whether Australia's ratification of the Convention on the Rights of the Child gave rise to a legitimate expectation on the part of the respondent or his children that a decision made under the Migration Act 1958 (Cth) concerning the grant of resident status to him would be made in accordance with Article 3 of the Convention. That Article requires that, in "all actions" concerning children, their "best interests" shall be a primary consideration.

2   If the principal question is answered in the negative, a further question arises as to whether, in the circumstances of this case, the decision-maker was under an obligation to make further inquiries about the future of the children if the respondent was refused resident status.

3   In my opinion, no legitimate expectation arose in this case because: (1) the doctrine of legitimate expectations is concerned with procedural fairness and imposes no obligation on a decision-maker to give substantive protection to any right, benefit, privilege or matter that is the subject of a legitimate expectation; (2) the doctrine of legitimate expectations does not require a decision-maker to inform a person affected by a decision that he or she will not apply a rule when the decision-maker is not bound and has given no undertaking to apply that rule; (3) the ratification of the Convention did not give rise to any legitimate expectation that an application for resident status would be decided in accordance with Article 3.

4   Accordingly, the appeal should be allowed because the judgment under appeal held that the respondent had a legitimate expectation that Article 3 would be applied.

5   In addition, the appeal should be allowed because the decision-maker did regard the best interests of the children as a primary consideration in determining the application for resident status and the circumstances did not give rise to any duty to make further inquiries about the welfare of the children.

The Convention on the Rights of the Child

6   The instrument ratifying the Convention on the Rights of the Child was deposited for Australia on 17 December 1990. The Convention entered into force generally on 2 September 1990 and for Australia on 16 January 1991.[1]

---

1   See Australian Treaty Series 1991 No 4.

Article 3 provides

1   In all actions concerning children, whether undertaken by public or private social welfare institutions, courts of law, administrative authorities or legislative bodies, the best interests of the child shall be a primary consideration.

2   States Parties undertake to ensure the child such protection and care as is necessary for his or her well-being, taking into account the rights and duties of his or her parents, legal guardians, or other individuals legally responsible for him or her, and, to this end, shall take all appropriate legislative and administrative measures.

3   States Parties shall ensure that the institutions, services and facilities responsible for the care or protection of children shall conform with the standards established by competent authorities, particularly in the areas of safety, health, in the number and suitability of their staff, as well as competent supervision.

7   The implementation of the Convention is dealt with in Part II of the Convention[2]. Article 43 establishes a Committee on the Rights of the Child made up of "ten experts of high moral standing and recognised competence" in the field covered by the Convention. Article 44 provides that parties undertake to submit to the Committee, through the Secretary-General of the United Nations, reports on the measures they have adopted to give effect to the rights recognised in the Convention and any difficulties "affecting the degree of fulfilment of the obligations" under the Convention. This must be done within two years of the entry into force of the Convention and thereafter every five years.

[...]*

The doctrine of legitimate expectations

22 For over 25 years, the courts have held that the rules of natural justice protect the legitimate expectations as well as the rights of persons affected by the exercise of power invested in a public official. The doctrine of legitimate expectations was invented by Lord Denning MR in *Schmidt v Secretary of State for Home Affairs*.[3] In its original form, it was a device that permitted the courts to invalidate decisions made without hearing a person who had a reasonable expectation, but no legal right, to the continuation of a benefit, privilege or state of affairs. It therefore helped to protect a person from the disappointment and often the injustice that arises from the unexpected termination by a government official of a state of affairs that otherwise seemed likely to continue. In *Attorney-General of Hong Kong v Ng Yuen Shiu*,[4] the Judicial Committee of the Privy Council extended the application of the doctrine of legitimate expectations to cases where a public official had undertaken that he or she would act in a certain way in making a decision. So in *Haoucher v Minister for Immigration and Ethnic Affairs*,[5] this Court held that, if a public official had undertaken to exercise a power only when certain conditions existed, a person affected by the exercise of the power had a right to be informed of the matters that called for the exercise of the power.

---

2   Arts 42-45.
*   **Eds:** in paragraphs 8-21 of his judgment (not included here), McHugh J describes the background to the case and the judgments of the courts below.
3   [1969] 2 Ch 149 at 170-171.
4   [1983] 2 AC 629.
5   (1990) 169 CLR 648.

23 After this Court's decisions in *Kioa v West*[6] and *Annetts v McCann*[7], however, a question must arise as to whether the doctrine of legitimate expectations still has a useful role to play. Those cases decided that, where a statute empowers a public official or tribunal to make an administrative decision that affects a person, then, in the absence of a contrary legislative indication, the critical question is not whether the doctrine of natural justice applies but "what does the duty to act fairly require in the circumstances of the particular case?".[8] In *Haoucher*,[9] Deane J expressed the view that the law seemed "to be moving towards a conceptually more satisfying position where common law requirements of procedural fairness will, in the absence of a clear contrary legislative intent, be recognised as applying generally to governmental executive decision-making".

24 I think that the rational development of this branch of the law requires acceptance of the view that the rules of procedural fairness are presumptively applicable to administrative and similar decisions made by public tribunals and officials. In the absence of a clear contrary legislative intention, those rules require a decision-maker "to bring to a person's attention the critical issue or factor on which the administrative decision is likely to turn so that he may have an opportunity of dealing with it".[10] If that approach is adopted, there is no need for any doctrine of legitimate expectations. The question becomes, what does fairness require in all the circumstances of the case?

25 Since *Kioa*, however, cases in this Court[11] have continued to use the concept of legitimate expectation to enliven the rules of procedural fairness. Furthermore, both in this Court and in the Full Court of the Federal Court, the argument in the present case proceeded upon the basis that, in so far as the right to procedural fairness depended upon Article 3 of the Convention, it was necessary to establish that the terms of the Convention gave rise to a legitimate expectation that the Minister's delegate would comply with the requirements of Article 3 in reaching a decision concerning the residential status of Mr Teoh. Accordingly, I will deal with the appeal on the basis that the respondent must establish that the terms of the Convention gave rise to a legitimate expectation that the Minister's delegate would comply with the terms of the Convention.

26 Hitherto, the view has been taken that circumstances do not give rise to a legitimate expectation sufficient to enliven the rules of procedural fairness unless the decision-maker has given an express or implied undertaking to persons such as the person affected or unless that person enjoys a benefit, privilege or state of affairs that seems likely to continue in the absence of special or unusual circumstances.[12] In 1988, one writer summarised the cases in which legitimate expectations have been held to arise as follows:[13]

---

6   (1985) 159 CLR 550.

7   (1990) 170 CLR 596.

8   *Kioa* (1985) 159 CLR at 585.

9   (1990) 169 CLR at 653.

10 *Kioa* (1985) 159 CLR at 587.

11 See, for example, *Haoucher* (1990) 169 CLR 648; *Attorney-General (NSW) v Quin* (1990) 170 CLR 1; *Ainsworth v Criminal Justice Commission* (1992) 175 CLR 564; and indeed *Kioa* (1985) 159 CLR 550 and *Annetts* (1990) 170 CLR 596 themselves.

12 *Kioa* (1985) 159 CLR at 583; *Haoucher* (1990) 169 CLR at 682.

13 Tate, "The Coherence of 'Legitimate Expectations' and the Foundations of Natural Justice", (1988) 14 *Monash University Law Review* 15 at 48-49.

[F]or an expectation to be "legitimate" in the required sense there must be positive grounds which are sufficient to render it objectively justifiable ...

Our analysis of the cases suggests that there are four principal sources which the courts recognise as capable of rendering expectations legitimate or reasonable; (1) a regular course of conduct which has not been altered by the adoption of a new policy; (2) express or implied assurances made clearly on behalf of the decision-making authority within the limits of the power exercised; (3) the possible consequences or effects of the expectation being defeated especially where those consequences include economic loss and damage to reputation, providing that the severity of the consequences are a function of justified reliance generated from substantial continuity in the possession of the benefit or a failure to be told that renewal cannot be expected; and (4) the satisfaction of statutory criteria." (footnotes omitted)

27 Prior to the present case, that summary seemed an accurate statement of the circumstances that could give rise to a legitimate expectation sufficient to enliven the rules of procedural fairness. None of them is present in this case. If Mr Teoh is to succeed, the doctrine of legitimate expectations will have to be extended. The Convention was not an instrument that the delegate was required to consider. Nor had the delegate undertaken to consider or apply its provisions. Moreover, neither Mr Teoh nor any member of his family had asked the delegate to take the provisions of Article 3 into account. It is only too obvious that they were oblivious of its existence.

28 A legitimate expectation may give rise to a requirement of procedural fairness but it does not give substantive protection to any right, benefit or privilege that is the subject of the expectation.[14] So even if the respondents had a legitimate expectation concerning the Convention, the delegate was not obliged to apply the Convention.

29 The next question is whether the rules of procedural fairness required the delegate to inform the respondents that Article 3 would not be applied even though reasonable persons would expect it to be applied. In my opinion, the delegate was not required to notify the respondents that Article 3 would not be applied. As long as a decision-maker has done nothing to lead a person to believe that a rule will be applied in making a decision, the rules of procedural fairness do not require the decision-maker to inform that person that the rule will not be applied. Fairness does not require that a decision-maker should invite a person to make submissions about a rule that the decision-maker is not bound, and has not undertaken or been asked, to apply. Indeed, in those circumstances, a person cannot have a reasonable expectation that the rule will be applied.

30 If a person asks a decision-maker to apply a rule which the decision-maker is not bound to apply, the rules of procedural fairness do not require the person affected to be informed that that rule will not be applied. It seems anomalous, therefore, to insist that a decision-maker must inform a person that a rule will not be applied merely because, objectively, reasonable persons have an expectation that such a rule would be applied. It seems even more anomalous that a person should have to be notified that a rule will not be applied if he or she is not even aware of the rule's existence. In my opinion, neither fairness nor good administration requires a decision-maker to inform a person that a rule will not be applied when the decision-maker has not led that person to believe that it would be applied.

---

14 See, for example, *Quin* (1990) 170 CLR at 21-22 *per* Mason CJ, 39-41 *per* Brennan J; *Haoucher* (1990) 169 CLR at 651-652 *per* Deane J; see also *Reference re Canada Assistance Plan (BC)* [1991] 2 SCR 525 at 557-558; (1991) 83 DLR (4th) 297 at 319.

31 Furthermore, the doctrine of procedural fairness is concerned with giving persons the opportunity to protect their rights, interests and reasonable expectations from the adverse effect of administrative and similar decisions. If the doctrine of legitimate expectations were now extended to matters about which the person affected has no knowledge, the term "expectation" would be a fiction so far as such persons were concerned. It is true that an expectation can only give rise to the right of procedural fairness if it is based on reasonable grounds.[15] It must be an expectation that is objectively reasonable for a person in the position of the claimant. But that does not mean that the state of mind of the person concerned is irrelevant. If the statement of Toohey J in *Haoucher*[16] that "[l]egitimate expectation does not depend upon the knowledge and state of mind of the individual concerned" is meant to maintain the contrary proposition, I am unable to agree with it. If a person does not have an expectation that he or she will enjoy a benefit or privilege or that a particular state of affairs will continue, no disappointment or injustice is suffered by that person if that benefit or privilege is discontinued. A person cannot lose an expectation that he or she does not hold. Fairness does not require that a person be informed about something to which the person has no right or about which that person has no expectation.

32 Even if a legitimate expectation did arise in a case such as the present, all that procedural fairness would require would be for the decision-maker to inform the person affected that the decision-maker would not be acting in the manner expected. As I have indicated, a legitimate expectation gives rise to a requirement of procedural fairness but it does not give substantive protection to any right, benefit or privilege that is the subject of the expectation.[17] Once the person was notified, the decision-maker would seem to have discharged his or her duty of procedural fairness. It may be that procedural fairness would also require the decision-maker to consider any subsequent submission that the rule should be applied. If it does, it merely shows how artificial is the doctrine of legitimate expectations in cases such as the present. Since the decision-maker is under no obligation to apply the rule, he or she would be at liberty to act in disregard of any subsequent submission that the rule should be applied.

33 It seems a strange, almost comic, consequence if procedural fairness requires a decision-maker to inform the person affected that he or she does not intend to apply a rule that the decision-maker cannot be required to apply, has not been asked or given an undertaking to apply, and of which the person affected by the decision has no knowledge.

The terms of the Convention did not give rise to a legitimate expectation in this case

34 However, if, contrary to my opinion, the doctrine of legitimate expectations is to be extended to cases where a person has no actual expectation that a particular course will be followed or a state of affairs continued, the terms of the Convention did not give rise to any legitimate expectation that the Minister or his delegate would exercise their powers under the Act in accordance with Australia's obligations under the Convention.

---

15 *Ng Yuen Shiu* [1983] 2 AC at 636.

16 (1990) 169 CLR at 670.

17 See, for example, *Quin* (1990) 170 CLR at 21-22 *per* Mason CJ, 39-41 *per* Brennan J; *Haoucher* [1990] 169 CLR at 651-652 *per* Deane J; see also *Reference re Canada Assistance Plan (BC)* [1991] 2 SCR at 557-558; [1991] 83 DLR (4th) 297 at 319.

35 Conventions entered into by the federal government do not form part of Australia's domestic law unless they have been incorporated by way of statute.[18] They may, of course, affect the interpretation or development of the law of Australia. Thus, in interpreting statutory provisions that are ambiguous, the courts will "favour a construction of a Commonwealth statute which accords with the obligations of Australia under an international treaty".[19] In that respect, conventions are in the same position as the rules of customary international law.[20] International conventions may also play a part in the development of the common law.[21] The question in this case, however, is not concerned with the interpretation of a statute or with the development of the common law. It is whether the ratification of the Convention on the Rights of the Child gave rise to a legitimate expectation that its terms would be implemented by the decision-maker in this case.

36 In exercising the discretion under the Migration Act in circumstances such as the present case, the terms of the Convention were matters which the Minister or his delegate could take into account.[22] Nothing in the Act indicates that the terms of the Convention were outside the range of matters that a decision-maker could properly take into account. Furthermore, the Minister conceded that, in the circumstances of this case, the break up of the family unit was a matter of major significance. But that does not mean that the residents of Australia had a legitimate expectation that, upon the ratification of the Convention, federal officials and statutory office holders would act in accordance with the Convention.

37 In international law, conventions are agreements between States. Australia's ratification of the Convention is a positive statement to other signatory nations that it intends to fulfil its obligations under that convention. If it does not do so, it is required to disclose its failure in its reports to the Committee on the Rights of the Child.[23] I am unable to agree with the view expressed by Lee J in the Full Court that the "ratification of the Convention by the Executive was a statement to the *national* and international community that the Commonwealth recognised and accepted the principles of the Convention"[24] (my emphasis). The ratification of a treaty is not a statement to the national community. It is, by its very nature, a statement to the international community. The people of Australia may note the commitments of Australia in international law, but, by ratifying the Convention, the Executive government does not give undertakings to its citizens or residents. The undertakings in the Convention are given to the other parties to the Convention. How, when or where those undertakings will be given force in Australia is a matter for the federal Parliament. This is a basic consequence of the fact that conventions do not have the force of law within Australia.

---

18 *Chow Hung Ching v The King* (1948) 77 CLR 449 at 478; *Bradley v The Commonwealth* (1973) 128 CLR 557 at 582; *Simsek v Macphee* (1982) 148 CLR 636 at 641-642; *Koowarta v Bjelke-Petersen* (1982) 153 CLR 168 at 193, 212, 224, 253; *Kioa* (1985) 159 CLR at 570-571, 604; *Dietrich v The Queen* (1992) 177 CLR 292 at 305-306, 321, 348-349, 359-360; *JH Rayner (Mincing Lane) Ltd v Department of Trade and Industry* [1990] 2 AC 418 at 476-477, 500; *Young v Registrar, Court of Appeal (No3)* (1993) 32 NSWLR 262 at 272-274; *In the Marriage of Murray and Tam* (1993) 16 Fam LR 982 at 997-998.

19 *Chu Kheng Lim v Minister for Immigration* (1992) 176 CLR 1 at 38.

20 *Polites v The Commonwealth* (1945) 70 CLR 60 at 68-69, 77, 80-81.

21 *Mabo v Queensland* (No.2) (1992) 175 CLR 1 at 42; *Dietrich* (1992) 177 CLR at 321, 360; *Jago v District Court of NSW* (1988) 12 NSWLR 558 at 569; *Ballina Shire Council v Ringland* (1994) 33 NSWLR 680 at 709-710.

22 *Minister for Aboriginal Affairs v Peko-Wallsend Ltd* (1986) 162 CLR 24 at 40.

23 See Arts 43-44.

24 *Teoh v Minister* (1994) 121 ALR 436 at 449; 49 FCR 409 at 420.

38 If the result of ratifying an international convention was to give rise to a legitimate expectation that that convention would be applied in Australia, the Executive government of the Commonwealth would have effectively amended the law of this country. It would follow that the convention would apply to every decision made by a federal official unless the official stated that he or she would not comply with the convention. If the expectation were held to apply to decisions made by State officials, it would mean that the Executive government's action in ratifying a convention had also altered the duties of State government officials. The consequences for administrative decision-making in this country would be enormous. Junior counsel for the Minister informed the Court that Australia is a party to about 900 treaties. Only a small percentage of them has been enacted into law. Administrative decision-makers would have to ensure that their decision-making complied with every relevant convention or inform a person affected that they would not be complying with those conventions.

39 I do not think that it is reasonable to expect that public officials will comply with the terms of conventions which they have no obligation to apply or consider merely because the federal government has ratified them. There can be no reasonable expectation that State government officials will comply with the terms of a convention merely because the Executive government of the Commonwealth has ratified it. In many cases, State governments will be strongly opposed to the federal government's ratification of an international convention. Further, many federal administrative decisions are made by public officials and tribunals that are independent of the Executive government of the Commonwealth. I do not think that there can be a reasonable expectation that these officials and tribunals will necessarily act in accordance with the terms of a convention which does not have the force of law. Even in the case of decisions made by officers employed in federal government departments, it seems difficult, if not impossible, to conclude that there is a reasonable expectation that the terms of a convention will be complied with forthwith upon ratification. The nature of the obligations undertaken may make it impracticable to implement them forthwith. Total compliance with the terms of a convention may require many years of effort, education and expenditure of resources. For these and similar reasons, the parties to a convention will often regard its provisions as goals to be implemented over a period of time rather than mandates calling for immediate compliance. That being so, I do not think that members of the Australian community can hold a reasonable expectation that, upon the ratification of a convention, its provisions will thereafter be applied to any decision falling within the scope of the convention. Unless a Minister or his or her officials have given an indication that the provisions of a convention will henceforth be applied to decisions affecting that ministry, it is not reasonable to expect that the provisions of that convention apply to those decisions.

40 Even when federal statute law recognises, or provides the means for recognising, an international convention, I do not think that a legitimate expectation arises that federal officials will apply the terms of the convention. The mechanism by which the federal government has chosen to implement many conventions relating to human rights including the present Convention, for example, is through the Human Rights and Equal Opportunity Commission Act 1986 (Cth) ("the HREOC Act"). Upon a convention being declared an "international instrument relating to human rights and freedoms" under section 47(1) of that Act, the convention becomes a "relevant international instrument".[25] Consequently, the rights outlined in the convention become "human rights" for the

25 Section 3(1).

purposes of the Act.[26] This enlivens those provisions of the Act concerning human rights and allows the Commission to examine enactments or proposed enactments to ascertain whether they are, or would be, inconsistent with or contrary to any human right;[27] to inquire into acts or practices that may be inconsistent with any human right;[28] to report to the Minister as to the action that needs to be taken by Australia in order to comply with the convention;[29] to prepare and publish guidelines for the avoidance of acts or practices that may be inconsistent with or contrary to the rights in the convention;[30] and to intervene (as the Commission did in this case) in proceedings that involve human rights issues.[31] The HREOC Act recognises that there may exist acts and practices that are inconsistent with or contrary to Australia's human rights obligations as defined by the Act.[32] The mechanisms for remedying those inconsistencies are those provided in the Act. I find it difficult to accept that Parliament intended that there should be remedies in the ordinary courts for breaches of an instrument declared for the purpose of section 47 of the HREOC Act when such remedies are not provided for by the Act.

41   At the relevant times in the present case, the Convention had not been declared to be an international instrument under the HREOC Act or otherwise been acted on or been recognised by the Parliament. In January 1993, however, the Convention was declared to be an international instrument for the purposes of that Act.[33] Thus, if the decision affecting Mr Teoh and his family had occurred after the Convention was declared to be an international instrument, either he or someone on behalf of his children could have made a complaint to the Commission that the Minister was in breach of the Convention. They would be entitled to seek redress through the mechanism of the HREOC Act for breach of the Convention. If, after due inquiry under Part II, Division 3 of the Act, the Commission considered that the complaint was made out, it could take steps to have the matter settled or report the breach to the Minister. But I do not think that they could contend that the decision of the Minister and his delegate was void. That is because neither the ratification of the Convention nor its declaration under section 47 gave rise to any legitimate expectation that the Minister or his delegates would comply with the Convention. There is no legitimate expectation that a federal official will act in accordance with a rule that that official is at liberty to disobey and about which the official has given no promise or undertaking.

42   Furthermore, the terms of the departmental policy referred to above leave little room for a reasonable expectation that the best interests of an applicant's children would be a primary consideration in an application for resident status. Paragraph 3.2 of the policy, although not directly applicable in this case, makes it plain that an application by a person who falls within section 16(1)(c) of the Act will "normally be refused unless they could show strong cause why [the] policy should be waived in their case". This strong and specific statement leaves no room for a reasonable expectation that the best interests of an applicant's children will be a primary consideration in determining an application. Other provisions of the policy make it plain that an applicant's involvement in violence, espionage, sabotage, general criminal or anti-social behaviour will ordinarily result in

---

26   Section 3(1).
27   Section 11(1)(e).
28   Section 11(1)(f).
29   Section 11(1)(k).
30   Section 11(1)(n).
31   Section 11(1)(o).
32   See Pt II, Div 3 of the HREOC Act.
33   See Commonwealth of Australia, Gazette GN 1, 13 January 1993 at 85.

the rejection of an application. There is, therefore, little, if any ground, in the policy for a reasonable expectation that the best interests of an applicant's child will always be a primary consideration in the decision-making process. Its terms are not consistent with the alleged legitimate expectation.

43   Even if Article 3 is generally applicable to actions under the Migration Act, I do not think that Article 3 was intended to apply to an action that has consequences for a child but is not directed at the child. Article 3 will have enormous consequences for decision-making in this country if it applies to actions that are not directed at but merely have consequences for children. It seems unlikely, for example, that it was the intention of the article that a court must make the best interests of a child a primary consideration in sentencing a parent. And there are many other areas of administration where it could hardly have been intended that the best interests of the child were to be a primary consideration in actions that have consequences for a child. Must a public authority make the best interests of a child a primary consideration in determining whether to acquire compulsorily the property of a parent? Must the Commissioner of Taxation make the best interests of a child a primary consideration in exercising his powers under the Income Tax Assessment Act 1936 (Cth)? Questions of this sort make it likely that the provisions of Article 3 were intended to apply to "actions" that were directed at children and not those that merely have consequences for children.

44   In my opinion, therefore, Article 3 was not intended to apply to an application by an adult person for resident status. Here the action was directed at Mr Teoh. It was not directed at the children. I do not think that Article 3 required the Minister's delegate to make the best interests of the children a primary consideration in deciding Mr Teoh's application any more than that article required the judge who sentenced him to make the best interests of the children a primary consideration in the sentencing process.

45   In my view, neither Mr Teoh nor the members of his family had any legitimate expectation that his application for resident status would be decided by reference to what were the best interests of the children as stipulated in Article 3 of the Convention. But in any event, even if, contrary to my view, such an expectation did arise, I think that only a very literal reading of Article 3, the decision of the delegate and the departmental documents would require a conclusion that the best interests of the children were not a primary consideration in the decision to refuse Mr Teoh resident status.

Did the delegate fail to act in accordance with the principle in Article 3?

46   The exact application of Article 3 is far from clear. What Lord Denning M.R. said in *Reg v Chief Immigration Officer*[34] concerning the European Convention for the Protection of Human Rights and Fundamental Freedoms applies to the Convention and its provisions. His Lordship said:

> The Convention is drafted in a style very different from the way which we are used to in legislation. It contains wide general statements of principle.

47   Article 3(1) insists that "[i]n all actions concerning children, whether undertaken by public or private social welfare institutions, courts of law, administrative authorities or legislative bodies, the best interests of the child shall be a primary consideration". But no guidance is given as to what weight is to be given to those interests in an "action". In the context of an application for resident status, it cannot require any more than that the delegate recognise that the interests of the children are best served by granting the

---

34   [1976] 1 WLR 979 at 985.

parent resident status. But that does not mean that those interests must be given the same weight as the bad character of the applicant. The use of the word "a" indicates that the best interests of the children need not be the primary consideration. And, as Carr J recognised, a primary consideration may have to accommodate itself to other overriding interests.[35]

48 On the evidence, the future of the family and the children was a primary consideration of the delegate. Both in the recommendation of the Immigration Review Panel and the departmental document prepared for the Panel, the welfare of the children and the break up of the family were regarded as constituting the compassionate grounds which could justify the grant of resident status, notwithstanding the bad character of Mr Teoh. In addition, those making decisions had before them letters from the applicant's wife arguing that a refusal of resident status would have a devastating effect on the children. I find it difficult to accept that the delegate in considering the compassionate grounds did not consider what the best interests of the child required. The effect that refusal of the application would have on the family was the principal matter relied on in support of the application after the application was initially refused on 2 January 1991. The whole case for the respondent was that the interests of the children and Mrs Teoh required the grant of the application. I cannot accept that the delegate did not consider the application with that in mind. On the assumption that there was a legitimate expectation of compliance with the terms of the Convention, the substance of the expectation was not denied. Accordingly, no denial of procedural fairness occurred.

Obligation for further inquiries

49 It therefore becomes necessary to examine the other question raised in this appeal – whether "the proper consideration of the break-up of the family unit as a relevant matter that the decision-maker was bound to take into account necessarily involved the making of further inquiry into the facts by the decision-maker".

50 In a number of cases, the Federal Court has found that a failure to make further inquiries constituted an improper exercise of the power granted by the statute or a failure to take into account a relevant consideration in exercising that power. In those cases, the Federal Court has held that further inquiries should have been made because (1) a specific matter was raised by an applicant or was within the knowledge of the Minister and that matter could not be properly considered without further inquiry,[36] (2) the information before the Minister was not up to date[37] or (3) the absence of information before the Minister resulted from the Minister's officers misleading the applicant.[38] This case does not fit into any of those categories.

51 The impact of the deportation on the family of Mr Teoh was fully considered by the Minister's delegate. Indeed, apart from Mr Teoh's criminal convictions, his ties to the family and his role in supporting his and his wife's children were the principal issues in the application. There is no ground for concluding that the delegate failed to consider the matter properly. It may be that further inquiries about the plight of the family may have led the delegate to place more weight on what would happen to the children if the application were refused. But this is a matter of weight. The weight that is given to a

---

35   *Teoh v Minister* (1994) 121 ALR at 467; 49 FCR at 438.
36   For example, *Lek v Minister for Immigration and Ethnic Affairs* (1993) 117 ALR 455; 45 FCR 418; *Akers v Minister for Immigration and Ethnic Affairs* (1988) 20 FCR 363; cf *Singh v Minister for Immigration and Ethnic Affairs* (1987) 15 FCR 4.
37   For example, *Tickner v Bropho* (1993) 114 ALR 409; 40 FCR 183.
38   For example, *Videto v Minister* (1985) 69 ALR 342; 8 FCR 167.

particular consideration is a matter for the decision-maker, not for the courts in an application for judicial review. This is not a case where the Minister's delegate simply discounted the assertions of hardship to the family. The delegate was asked to consider the position of the family, had information about the family, and made her decision on that basis. That she gave greater weight to the requirement of good character than to the welfare of the children is irrelevant for present purposes. The Migration Act entrusts the weighing of such considerations to administrative officials. It is a consequence of the doctrine of separation of powers that the decisions of administrative officials acting within their powers must be accepted by the courts of law whatever the courts may think of the merits of particular administrative decisions.

52 For these reasons, further inquiries were not required to fulfil any of the delegate's statutory or common law obligations.

Conclusion*

53 The appeal should be allowed. The decision of the Full Federal Court should be set aside. There should be no order as to the costs of the proceedings in this Court or the Federal Court.

---

*   **Eds:** In *Re Minister for Immigration and Multicultural Affairs; Ex parte Lam* [2003] HCA 6 (12 February 2003), available at www.austlii.edu.au, a number of members of the present High Court of Australia (McHugh, Gummow, Hayne and Callinan JJ) indicated their concerns about the doctrine of legitimate expectation developed in *Teoh*. Earlier, on 25 February 1997, the Minister for Foreign Affairs, Attorney-General and Minister for Justice (Australia) issued a Joint Statement responding to address the consequences of the *Teoh* decision, entitled *The Effect of Treaties in Administrative Decision-Making*, the purpose of which was "to ensure that the executive act of entry into a treaty does not give rise to legitimate expectations in administrative law".

STATE RESPONSIBILITY UNDER INTERNATIONAL LAW FOR VIOLATIONS OF THE HUMAN RIGHTS OF WOMEN

CASE NO 5

AIREY v IRELAND

EUROPEAN COURT OF HUMAN RIGHTS

Application No: 6289/73

Judgment: 9 October 1979

Panel: *Judges*: Wiarda (*President*), O'Donoghue, Vilhjálmsson, Ganshof van der Meersch, Evrigenis, Liesch and Gölcüklü.

Human rights — Positive obligations — Right to a fair hearing — Right to respect for family and private life — Right to effective remedy before national authority — Judicial separation — Lack of legal aid — Positive obligations of Contracting States — Whether prohibitive costs of court hearing violated right to a fair hearing or right to respect for family or private life — Whether state obliged to provide legal aid in civil cases — European Convention for the Protection of Human Rights and Fundamental Freedoms, arts 6(1), 8, 13 and 14

Human rights — Property — Equality and non-discrimination — Judicial separation — Lack of legal aid — Whether discrimination in favour of those with means to pay for legal representation

BACKGROUND

The applicant, Ms Airey, wished to petition for judicial separation from her husband in the Irish High Court. However, she lacked the financial means to employ a lawyer, and legal aid for civil proceedings was not available. In an application to the European Commission of Human Rights, the applicant alleged that these facts constituted violations of the European Convention on Human Rights, in particular article 6 (right to a fair hearing in the determination of civil rights), article 8 (right to respect for private and family life) by reason of the State's failure to provide an accessible legal procedure for the determination of rights and obligations created by Irish family law, and article 13 (right to an effective remedy before a national authority). She further claimed that there had been a violation of article 14 (non-discrimination on the grounds of property) which should be considered in conjunction with article 6, in that judicial separation was more easily available to those who could afford to pay.

The Commission found unanimously that the failure of the State to ensure the applicant's effective access to court to obtain a judicial separation constituted a violation of article 6(1), and therefore examination under articles 8, 13 and 14 was unnecessary. It referred the case to the European Court of Human Rights.

The Government of Ireland claimed that the case was inadmissible before the Court on the grounds, *inter alia*, that the application was manifestly ill-founded and that the applicant had failed to exhaust domestic remedies under article 26 of the Convention.

HELD (finding a violation of articles 6 and 8 of the Convention)

Article 6(1) alone (right to a fair hearing in the determination of civil rights)

1   Article 6(1) secures to everyone the right to have any claim relating to his civil rights and obligations brought before a court or tribunal. Article 6(1) accordingly comprised a right for Ms Airey to have access to the High Court in order to petition for judicial separation. (Para 22)

2   The Convention was intended to guarantee not rights that were theoretical or illusory but rights that were practical and effective. This was particularly so of the right of access to the courts in view of the prominent place held in a democratic society by the right to a fair trial. It was most improbable that a person in Ms Airey's position could effectively present his or her own case. Therefore the possibility to appear in person before the High Court did not provide the applicant with an effective right of access to the courts and, hence, also did not constitute a domestic remedy whose use was demanded by article 26. (Para 24)

3   Fulfilment of a duty under the Convention on occasion necessitates some positive action on the part of the State; in such circumstances, the State could not simply remain passive. The obligation to secure an effective right of access to the court fell into this category of duty. (Para 25)

4   In certain eventualities, the possibility of appearing before a court in person, even without a lawyer's assistance, would meet the requirements of article 6(1). In addition, whilst article 6(1) guaranteed to litigants an effective right of access to the courts for the determination of their "civil rights and obligations", it left to the State a free choice of the means to be used towards the end. The institution of a legal aid scheme constituted one of those means, but there were others such as, for example, a simplification of procedure. In any event, it was not the Court's function to indicate, let alone dictate, which measures should be taken; all that the Convention required was that an individual should enjoy his effective right of access to the courts in conditions not at variance with article 6(1). The Court's conclusion did not therefore imply that the State must provide free legal aid for every dispute relating to a "civil right". (Para 26)

Article 14 in conjunction with article 6(1)

5   There was no reason to examine the case under article 14 given that there had been a violation of article 6 of the Convention when taken alone. (Para 30)

Article 8 (right to respect for family and private life)

6   Ireland could not be said to have "interfered" with Ms Airey's private or family life: the substance of her complaint was not that the State had acted but that it had failed to act. However, although the object of article 8 was essentially that of protecting the individual against arbitrary interference by the public authorities, it did not merely compel the State to abstain from such interference: in addition to this primarily negative undertaking, there might be positive obligations inherent in an effective respect for private or family life.

7   Effective respect for private or family life obliged Ireland to make judicial separation effectively accessible, when appropriate, to anyone who might wish to have recourse thereto. However, it was not effectively accessible to the applicant; not having been put

in a position in which she could apply to the High Court, she was unable to seek recognition in law of her *de facto* separation from her husband. She had therefore been the victim of a violation of article 8. (Paras 32 & 33)

Article 13 (right to an effective remedy before a national authority)

8   Since articles 13 and 6(1) overlapped in this particular case, it was not necessary to determine whether there had been a failure to observe the requirements of article 13: these requirements were less strict than, and were entirely absorbed by, those of article 6(1). (Para 35)

Treaties and other international instruments referred to

European Convention for the Protection of Human Rights and Fundamental Freedoms 1950, arts (4), 6(1), 6(3)(c), 8, 13, 14, 26, 27(2), 31, 39(1), 50, 52 and 53

Rules of the European Court of Human Rights, rules 47, 50(3) and 50(3)

Committee of Ministers of the Council of Europe, Resolution 78(8) of March 1978

National legislation referred to

Republic of Ireland

Constitution of the Republic of Ireland 1937, art 41.3.2

Succession Act 1965, s 120(2)

Family Law (Maintenance of Spouses and Children) Act 1976, s 22

Cases referred to

Belgian Linguistic Case (Merits), ECHR, judgment of 23 July 1968, Series A, No 6; 1 EHRR 252

De Wilde, Ooms and Versyp v Belgium, ECHR, judgment of 18 June 1971, Series A, No 12; 1 EHRR 373

De Wilde, Ooms and Versyp v Belgium (No 2), ECHR, judgment of 10 March 1972, Series A, No 14; 1 EHRR 438

Delcourt v Belgium, ECHR, judgment of 17 January 1970, Series A, No 11; 1 EHRR 355

Golder v UK, ECHR, judgment of 21 February 1975, Series A, No 18; 1 EHRR 524

Klass v Federal Republic of Germany, ECHR, judgment of 6 September 1978, Series A, No 28; 2 EHRR 214

König v Federal Republic of Germany, ECHR, judgment of 28 June 1978, Series A, No 27; 2 EHRR 170

Luedicke, Belkacem and Koc v Federal Republic of Germany, ECHR, judgment of 28 November 1978, Series A, No 29; 2 EHRR 149

Marckx v Belgium, ECHR, judgment of 13 June 1979, Series A, No 31; 2 EHRR 330, below, p273

National Union of Belgium Police v Belgium, ECHR, judgment of 27 October 1975, Series A, No 19

JUDGMENT[*]

PROCEDURE[**]

AS TO THE FACTS

I   Particular facts of the case

8   Mrs Johanna Airey, an Irish national born in 1932, lives in Cork. She comes from a humble family background and went to work at a young age as a shop assistant. She married in 1953 and has four children, the youngest of whom is still dependent on her. At the time of the adoption of the Commission's report, Mrs Airey was in receipt of unemployment benefit from the State, but since July 1978, she has been employed. Her net weekly wage in December 1978 was £39.99. In 1974, she obtained a court order against her husband for payment of maintenance of £20 per week, which was increased in 1977 to £27 and in 1978 to £32. However, Mr Airey, who had previously been working as a lorry driver but was subsequently unemployed, ceased paying such maintenance in May 1978.

Mrs Airey alleges that her husband is an alcoholic and that, before 1972, he frequently threatened her with, and occasionally subjected her to, physical violence. In January 1972, in proceedings instituted by the applicant, Mr Airey was convicted by the District Court of Cork City of assaulting her and fined. In the following June he left the matrimonial home; he has never returned there to live, although Mrs Airey now fears that he may seek to do so.

9   For about eight years prior to 1972, Mrs Airey tried in vain to conclude a separation agreement with her husband. In 1971, he declined to sign a deed prepared by her solicitor for the purpose and her later attempts to obtain his co-operation were also unsuccessful.

Since June 1972, she had been endeavouring to obtain a decree of judicial separation on the grounds of Mr Airey's alleged physical and mental cruelty to her and their children, and has consulted several solicitors in this connection. However, she has been unable, in the absence of legal aid and not being in a financial position to meet herself the costs involved, to find a solicitor willing to act for her.

In 1976, Mrs Airey applied to an ecclesiastical tribunal for annulment of her marriage. Her application is still under investigation; if successful, it will not affect her civil status.

II   Domestic Law

10   In Ireland, although it is possible to obtain under certain conditions a decree of nullity – a declaration by the High Court that a marriage was null and void *ab initio* – divorce in the sense of dissolution of a marriage does not exist. In fact, Article 41.3.2 of the Constitution provides: "No law shall be enacted providing for the grant of a dissolution of marriage".

---

[*]   *Eds:* due to space constraints, the dissenting opinions of Judges O'Donoghue, Vilhjálmsson and Evrigenis have not been included. The full text of the judgment is available at the website of the European Court of Human Rights (see *On-Line Access to Human Rights Source Materials, supra* (p xlv)); EHRR 305 and 58 ILR 624.

[**]   *Eds:* paras 1–7, which relate to procedural matters, have not been included.

However, spouses may be relieved from the duty of cohabiting either by a legally binding deed of separation concluded between them or by a court decree of judicial separation (also known as a divorce *a mensa et thoro*). Such a decree has no effect on the existence of the marriage in law. It can be granted only if the petitioner furnishes evidence proving one of three specified matrimonial offences, namely, adultery, cruelty or unnatural practices. The parties will call and examine witnesses on this point.

By virtue of section 120(2) of the Succession Act 1965, an individual against whom a decree of judicial separation is granted forfeits certain succession rights over his or her spouse's estate.

11 Decrees of judicial separation are obtainable only in the High Court. The parties may conduct their case in person. However, the Government's replies to questions put by the Court reveal that in each of the 255 separation proceedings initiated in Ireland in the period from January 1972 to December 1978, without exception, the petitioner was represented by a lawyer.

In its report of 9 March 1978, the Commission noted that the approximate range of the costs incurred by a legally represented petitioner was £500–£700 in an uncontested action and £800–£1,200 in a contested action, the exact amount depending on such factors as the number of witnesses and the complexity of the issues involved. In the case of a successful petition by a wife, the general rule is that the husband will be ordered to pay all costs reasonably and properly incurred by her, the precise figure being fixed by a Taxing Master.

Legal aid is not at present available in Ireland for the purpose of seeking a judicial separation, nor indeed for any civil matters. In 1974, a Committee on Civil Legal Aid and Advice was established under the chairmanship of Mr Justice Pringle. It reported to the Government in December 1977, recommending the introduction of a comprehensive scheme of legal aid and advice in this area. At the hearings on 22 February 1979, counsel for the Government informed the Court that the Government had decided in principle to introduce legal aid in family law matters and that it was hoped to have the necessary measures taken before the end of 1979.

12 Since Mrs Airey's application to the Commission, the Family Law (Maintenance of Spouses and Children) Act 1976 has come into force. Section 22(1) of the Act provides:

> On application to it by either spouse, the court may, if it is of the opinion that there are reasonable grounds for believing that the safety or welfare of that spouse or of any dependent child of the family requires it, order the other spouse, if he is residing at a place where the applicant spouse or that child resides, to leave that place, and whether the other spouse is or is not residing at that place, prohibit him from entering that place until further order by the court or until such other time as the court shall specify.

Such an order – commonly known as a barring order – is not permanent and application may be made at any time for its discharge (section 22(2)). Furthermore, the maximum duration of an order given in the District Court – as opposed to the Circuit Court or the High Court – is three months, although provision is made for renewal.

A wife who has been assaulted by her husband may also institute summary criminal proceedings.

PROCEEDINGS BEFORE THE COMMISSION

13 In her application of 14 June 1973 to the Commission, Mrs Airey made various complaints in connection with the 1972 proceedings against her husband, with a claimed assault on her by the police in 1973 and with the unlawful detention she affirms she

underwent in 1973. Her main complaint was that the State failed to protect her against physical and mental cruelty from her allegedly violent and alcoholic husband:

- by not detaining him for treatment as an alcoholic;
- by not ensuring that he paid maintenance to her regularly;
- in that, because of the prohibitive cost of proceedings, she could not obtain a judicial separation.

As regards to the last item, the applicant maintained that there had been violations of the following:

- Article 6(1) of the Convention, by reason of the fact that her right of access to a court was effectively denied;
- Article 8, by reason of the failure of the State to ensure that there is an accessible legal procedure to determine rights and obligations which have been created by legislation regulating family matters;
- Article 13, in that she was deprived of an effective remedy before a national authority for the violations complained of;
- Article 14 in conjunction with article 6(1), in that judicial separation is more easily available to those who can afford to pay than to those without financial resources.

14 On 7 July 1977, the Commission accepted the application in so far as Mrs Airey complained of the inaccessibility of the remedy of a judicial separation and declared inadmissible the remainder of the application.

In its report of 9 March 1978, the Commission expresses the opinion:

- unanimously, that the failure of the State to ensure the applicant's effective access to court to enable her to obtain a judicial separation amounts to a breach of article 6(1);
- that, in view of the preceding conclusion, there is no need for it to examine the case under articles 13 and 14 (unanimously) or under article 8 (12 votes to one, with one abstention).

FINAL SUBMISSIONS AND OBSERVATIONS MADE TO THE COURT

15 At the hearings on 22 February 1979, the Government maintained the following submissions made in the memorial:

The Court is asked to find that the Commission should not have declared this application admissible.

The Court is asked to find that even if the case was correctly admitted by the Commission, it should have been dismissed on the merits.

The respondent Government is not in breach of its obligations under the European Convention on Human Rights.

On the same occasion, counsel for Mrs Airey resumed her client's position as follows:

The applicant claims that the total inaccessibility and exclusiveness of the remedy of a judicial separation in the High Court is a breach of her right of access to the civil courts which the Irish Government must secure under Article 6 para. 1; she submits that the absence of a modern, effective and accessible remedy for marriage breakdown under Irish law is a failure to respect her family life under Article 8; she submits that the exorbitantly high cost of obtaining a decree of judicial separation, which results in fewer than a dozen decrees in any year, constitutes a discrimination on the ground of property in violation of

Article 14; and she submits that she lacks an effective remedy under Irish law for her marriage breakdown and that this in itself is a breach of Article 13.

AS TO THE LAW

I   Preliminary Issues

16   The Government plead that Mrs Airey's application was inadmissible on the ground, first, that it was manifestly ill-founded and, secondly, that she had not exhausted domestic remedies.

According to the Commission, whilst the Court undoubtedly has jurisdiction to determine all issues of fact or of law arising in the course of the proceedings, it is not within the Court's competence to hold that the Commission erred in declaring an application admissible. At the hearings, the Principal Delegate expressed the opinion that issues related to the admissibility decision are examined by the Court as questions going to the merits of the case and not in the capacity of a court of appeal.

17   The Court has established two principles in this area. One is that the Commission's decisions by which applications are accepted are without appeal; the other is that, once a case is referred to it, the Court is endowed with full jurisdiction and may determine questions as to admissibility previously raised before the Commission (see *inter alia*, *Klass v Federal Republic of Germany* (1978), European Court of Human Rights, judgment of 6 September 1978, Series A, No 28, para 32). A combination of these principles shows that, when considering such questions, the Court is not acting as a court of appeal but is simply ascertaining whether the conditions allowing it to deal with the merits of the case are satisfied.

18   A submission by a government to the Court that an application is manifestly ill-founded does not in reality raise an issue concerning those conditions. It amounts to pleading that there is not even a *prima facie* case against the respondent State. A plea to this effect is an objection of which the Commission must take cognisance before ruling on admissibility (article 27(2) of the Convention); once it has been dismissed any such objection, the Commission is normally required, after examining the merits of the case, to state an opinion as to whether or not there has been a breach (article 31). On the other hand, the distinction between finding an allegation manifestly ill-founded and finding no violation is devoid of interest for the Court, whose task is to hold in a final judgment that the State concerned has observed or, on the contrary, infringed the Convention (articles 50, 52 and 53).

The same does not apply to a submission that domestic remedies have not been exhausted. The rule embodied in article 26 "dispenses States from answering before an international body for their acts before they have had an opportunity to put matters right through their own legal system" (*De Wilde, Ooms and Versyp v Belgium*, European Court of Human Rights, judgment of 18 June 1971, Series A, No 12, para 50); it concerns the possibility in law of bringing into play a State's responsibility under the Convention. It is thus clear that such a submission may well raise issues distinguishable from those relating to the merits of the allegation of a violation.

Accordingly, the Court does not have to rule on the first of the preliminary pleas relied on by the Government but must do so on the second; this latter plea was, moreover, raised by the Government before the Commission so that there is no question of estoppel (see *De Wilde, Ooms and Versyp v Belgium*, European Court of Human Rights, judgment of 18 June 1971, Series A, No 12, para 54).

19 The Government maintain that the applicant failed to exhaust domestic remedies in various respects:

(a) In the first place, they contend that she could have entered into a separation deed with her husband or could have applied for a barring order or for maintenance under the 1976 Act (see paras 10 and 12 above).

The Court emphasises that the only remedies which article 26 of the Convention requires to be exercised are remedies in respect of the violation complained of. The violation alleged by Mrs Airey is that in her case the State failed to secure access to court for the purpose of petitioning for judicial separation. However, neither the conclusion of a separation deed nor the grant of a barring or a maintenance order provides such access. Accordingly, the Court cannot accept the first limb of this plea.

(b) In the second place, the Government lay stress on the fact that the applicant could have appeared before the High Court without the assistance of a lawyer. They also contend that she has nothing to gain from a judicial separation.

The Court recalls that international law, to which article 26 makes express reference, demands recourse solely to such remedies as are both "available to the persons concerned and ... sufficient, that is to say, capable of providing redress for their complaints" (*De Wilde, Ooms and Versyp v Belgium*, European Court of Human Rights, judgment of 18 June 1971 Series A, No 12, para 60). However, the Court would not be able to decide whether the possibility open to Mrs Airey of conducting her case herself amounts to a "domestic remedy", in the above sense, without at the same time ruling on merits of her complaint under article 6(1), namely, the alleged lack of effective access to the High Court. Similarly, the argument that a judicial separation would be of no benefit to the applicant appears intimately connected with another aspect of this complaint, namely, whether any real prejudice was occasioned. The Court therefore joins to the merits the remainder of the pleas.

II Article 6 (1) taken alone

20 Article 6 (1) reads as follows:

> In the determination of his civil rights and obligations or of any criminal charge against him, everyone is entitled to a fair and public hearing within a reasonable time by an independent and impartial tribunal established by law. Judgment shall be pronounced publicly but the press and public may be excluded from all or part of the trial in the interests of morals, public order or national security in a democratic society, where the interest of juveniles or the protection of the private life of the parties so require, or to the extent strictly necessary in the opinion of the court in special circumstances where publicity would prejudice the interests of justice.

Mrs Airey cites *Golder v UK*, judgment of 21 February 1975, Series A, No 18, where the Court held that this paragraph embodies the right of access to a court for the determination of civil rights and obligations; she maintains that, since the prohibitive cost of litigation prevented her from bringing proceedings before the High Court for the purpose of petitioning for judicial separation, there has been a violation of the above-mentioned provision.

This contention is unanimously accepted in substance by the Commission but disputed by the Government.

21 The applicant wishes to obtain a decree of judicial separation. There can be no doubt that the outcome of separation proceedings is "decisive for private rights and obligations" and hence, *a fortiori*, for "civil rights and obligations" within the meaning of

article 6(1); this being so, article 6(1) is applicable in the present case (see *König v Federal Republic of Germany*, European Court of Human Rights, judgment of 18 June 1978, Series A, No 27, paras 90 and 95). Besides, the point was not contested before the Court.

22 "Article 6(1) secures to everyone the right to have any claim relating to his civil rights and obligations brought before a court or tribunal" (*Golder v UK*, European Court of Human Rights, judgment of 21 February 1975, Series A, No 18, para 36). Article 6 (1) accordingly comprises a right for Mrs Airey to have access to the High Court in order to petition for judicial separation.

23 It is convenient at this juncture to consider the Government's claim that the applicant has nothing to gain from a judicial separation (see para 19(b) above).

The Court rejects this line of reasoning. Judicial separation is a remedy provided for by Irish law and, as such, it should be available to anyone who satisfies the conditions prescribed thereby. It is for the individual to select which legal remedy to pursue; consequently, even if it were correct that Mrs Airey's choice has fallen on a remedy less suited than others to her particular circumstances, this would be of no moment.

24 The Government contend that the applicant does enjoy access to the High Court, since she is free to go before that court without the assistance of a lawyer.

The Court does not regard this possibility, of itself, as conclusive of the matter. The Convention is intended to guarantee not rights that are theoretical or illusory but rights that are practical and effective (see, *mutatis mutandis*, *the Belgian Linguistic Case (Merits)*, European Court of Human Rights, judgment of 23 July 1968, Series A, No 6, paras 3 *in fine* and 4; *Golder v UK*, European Court of Human Rights, judgment of 21 February 1975, Series A, No 18, para 35 *in fine*; *Luedicke, Belkacem and Koc v Federal Republic Of Germany*, European Court of Human Rights, judgment of 28 November 1978, Series A, No 29, para 42; and *Marckx v Belgium*, European Court of Human Rights, judgment of 13 June 1979, Series A, No 31, para 31). This is particularly so of the right of access of the courts in view of the prominent place held in a democratic society by the right to a fair trial (see, *mutatis mutandis*, *Delcourt v Belgium*, European Court of Human Rights, judgment of 17 January 1970, Series A, No 11, para 25). It must therefore be ascertained whether Mrs Airey's appearance before the High Court without the assistance of a lawyer would be effective, in the sense of whether she would be able to present her case properly and satisfactorily.

Contradictory views on this question were expressed by the Government and the Commission during the oral hearings. It seems certain to the Court that the applicant would be at a disadvantage if her husband were represented by a lawyer and she were not. Quite apart from this eventuality, it is not realistic, in the Court's opinion, to suppose that, in litigation of this nature, the applicant could effectively conduct her own case, despite the assistance which, as was stressed by the Government, the judge affords to parties acting in person.

In Ireland, a decree of judicial separation is not obtainable in a District Court, where the procedure is relatively simple, but only in the High Court. A specialist in Irish family law, Mr Alan J Shatter, regards the High Court as the least accessible court not only because "fees payable for representation before it are very high" but also by reason of the fact that "the procedure for instituting proceedings ... is complex particularly in the case of those proceedings which must be commenced by a petition", such as those for separation (*Family Law in the Republic of Ireland* (Dublin, 1977), p 21).

Furthermore, litigation of this kind, in addition to involving complicated points of law, necessitates proof of adultery, unnatural practices or, as in the present case, cruelty;

to establish the facts, expert evidence may have to be tendered and witnesses may have to be found, called and examined. What is more, marital disputes often entail an emotional involvement that is scarcely compatible with the degree of objectivity required by advocacy in court.

For these reasons, the Court considers it most improbable that a person in Mrs Airey's position (see para 8 above) can effectively present his or her own case. This view is corroborated by the Government's replies to the questions put by the Court, replies which reveal that in each of the 255 judicial separation proceedings initiated in Ireland in the period of January 1972 to December 1978, without exception, the petitioner was represented by a Lawyer (see para 11 above).

The Court concludes from the foregoing that the possibility to appear in person before the High Court does not provide the applicant with an effective right of access and, hence, that it also does not constitute a domestic remedy whose use is demanded by article 26 (see para 19(b) above).

25 The Government seek to distinguish the *Golder* case on the ground that, the applicant had been prevented from having access to court by reason of the positive obstacle placed in his way by the State in the shape of the Home Secretary's prohibition on his consulting a solicitor. The Government maintain that, in contrast, in the present case there is no positive obstacle emanating from the State and no deliberate attempt by the State to impede access: the alleged lack of access to court stems not from any act on the part of the authorities but solely from Mrs Airey's personal circumstances, a matter for which Ireland cannot be held responsible under the Convention.

Although this difference between the facts of the two cases is certainly correct, the Court does not agree with the conclusion which the Government draw therefrom. In the first place, hindrance in fact can contravene the Convention just like a legal impediment (*Golder v UK*, European Court of Human Rights, judgment of 21 February 1975, Series A, No 18, para 26). Furthermore, fulfilment of a duty under the Convention on occasion necessitates some positive action on the part of the State; in such circumstances, the State cannot simply remain passive, and "there is ... no room to distinguish between acts and omissions" (see, *mutatis mutandis, Marckx v Belgium*, European Court of Human Rights, judgment of 13 June 1979, Series A, No 31, para 31 and *De Wilde, Ooms and Versyp v Belgium* (No 2), European Court of Human Rights, judgment of 10 March 1972, Series A, No 14, p 10, para 22). The obligation to secure an effective right of access to the court falls into this category of duty.

26 The Government's principal argument rests on what they see as the consequence of the Commission's opinion, namely, that, in all cases concerning the determination of a "civil right", the State would have to provide free legal aid. In fact, the Convention's only express provision on free legal aid is article 6(3)(c) which relates to criminal proceedings and is itself subject to limitations; what is more, according to the Commission's established case law, article 6(1) does not guarantee any right to free legal aid as such. The Government add that since Ireland, when ratifying the Convention, made a reservation to article 6(3)(c) with the intention of limiting its obligations in the realm of criminal legal aid, *a fortiori* it cannot be said to have implicitly agreed to provide unlimited civil legal aid. Finally, in their submission, the Convention should not be interpreted so as to achieve social and economic developments in a Contracting State; such developments can only be progressive.

The Court is aware that the further realisation of social and economic rights is largely dependent on the situation – notably financial – reigning in the State in question. On the other hand, the Convention must be interpreted in the light of present-day conditions (*Marckx v Belgium*, European Court of Human Rights, judgment of 13 June 1979, Series A, No 31, 346, para 41), and it is designed to safeguard the individuals in a real and practical way as regards those areas with which it deals (see para 24 above). Whilst the Convention sets forth what are essentially civil and political rights, many of them have implications of a social or economic nature. The Court therefore considers, like the Commission, that the mere fact that an interpretation of the Convention may extend into the sphere of social and economic rights should not be a decisive factor against such an interpretation; there is no water-tight division separating that sphere from the field covered by the Convention.

The Court does not, moreover, share the Government's view as to the consequence of the Commission's opinion.

It would be erroneous to generalise the conclusion that the possibility to appear in person before the High Court does not provide Mrs Airey with an effective right of access; that conclusion does not hold good for all cases concerning "civil rights and obligations" or for everyone involved therein. In certain eventualities, the possibility of appearing before a court in person, even without a lawyer's assistance, will meet the requirements of article 6(1); there may be occasions when such a possibility secures adequate access even to the High Court. Indeed, much must depend on the particular circumstances.

In addition, whilst article 6(1) guarantees to litigants an effective right of access to the courts for the determination of their "civil rights and obligations", it leaves to the State a free choice of the means to be used towards the end. The institution of a legal aid scheme – which Ireland now envisages in family law matters (see para 11 above) – constitutes one of those means but there are others such as, for example, a simplification of procedure. In any event, it is not the Court's function to indicate, let alone dictate, which measures should be taken; all that the Convention requires is that an individual should enjoy his effective right of access to the courts in conditions not at variance with article 6(1) (see, *mutatis mutandis, National Union of Belgian Police v Belgium*, European Court of Human Rights, judgment of 27 October 1975, Series A, No 19, para 39 and *Marckx v Belgium*, European Court of Human Rights, judgment of 13 June 1979, Series A, No 19, para 31.)

The conclusion appearing at the end of paragraph 24 above does not therefore imply that the State must provide free legal aid for every dispute relating to a "civil right".

To hold that so far-reaching an obligation exists would, the Court agrees, sit ill with the facts that the Convention contains no provision on legal aid for those disputes, article 6(3)(c) dealing only with criminal proceedings. However, despite the absence of a similar clause for civil litigation, article 6(1) may sometimes compel the State to provide for the assistance of a lawyer when such assistance proves indispensable for an effective access to court either because legal representation is rendered compulsory, as is done by the domestic law of certain Contracting States for various types of litigation, or by reason of the complexity of the procedure or of the case.

As regards the Irish reservation to article 6(3)(c), it cannot be interpreted as affecting the obligations under article 6(1); accordingly, it is not relevant in the present context.

27 The applicant was unable to find a solicitor willing to act on her behalf in judicial separation proceedings. The Commission inferred that the reason why the solicitors she consulted were not prepared to act was that she would have been unable to meet the costs involved. The Government question this opinion but the Court finds it plausible and has been presented with no evidence which could invalidate it.

28 Having regard to all the circumstances of the case, the Court finds that Mrs Airey did not enjoy an effective right of access to the High Court for the purpose of petitioning for a decree of judicial separation. There has accordingly been a breach of article 6(1).

III On Article 14 taken in conjunction with Article 6(1)

29 The applicant maintains that, since the remedy of judicial separation is more easily available to those with than to those without financial resources, she is the victim of discrimination on the ground of "property" in breach of article 14 taken in conjunction with article 6(1).

The Commission was of the opinion that, in view of its conclusion concerning article 6(1), there was no need for it to consider the applicant under article 14. The Government made no submissions on this point.

30 Article 14 has no independent existence; it constitutes one particular element (non-discrimination) of each of the rights safeguarded by the Convention (see, *inter alia*, *Marckx v Belgium*, European Court of Human Rights, judgment of 13 June 1979, Series A, No 31, para 32). The articles enshrining those rights may be violated alone and/or in conjunction with article 14. If the Court does not find a separate breach of one of those articles that has been invoked both on its own and together with article 14, it must also examine the case under the latter article [article 14]. On the other hand, such an examination is not generally required when the Court finds a violation of the former article taken alone. The position is otherwise if a clear inequality of treatment in the enjoyment of the right in question is a fundamental aspect of the case, but this does not apply to the breach of article 6(1) found in the present proceedings; accordingly, the Court does not deem it necessary also to examine the case under article 14.

IV On Article 8

31 Mrs Airey argues that, by not ensuring that there is an accessible legal procedure in family law matters, Ireland has failed to respect her family life, thereby violating article 8, which provides:

> 1   Everyone has the right to respect for his private and family life, his home and his correspondence.
>
> 2   There shall be no interference by public authority with the exercise of this right except such as is in accordance with the law and is necessary in a democratic society in the interests of national security, public safety or the economic well-being of the country, for the prevention of disorder or crime, for the protection of health or morals, or for the protection of the rights and freedoms of others.

In its report, the Commission expressed the opinion that, in view of its conclusion concerning article 6(1) there was no need for it to consider the application under article 8. However, during the oral hearings the Principal Delegate submitted that there had also been a breach of this article. The contention is disputed by the Government.

32 The Court does not consider that Ireland can be said to have "interfered" with Mrs Airey's private or family life: the substance of her complaint is not that the State has acted but that it has failed to act. However, although the object of article 8 is essentially that of protecting the individual against arbitrary interference by the public authorities, it does not merely compel the State to abstain from such interference: in addition to this primarily negative undertaking, there may be positive obligations inherent in an effective respect for private or family life (see *Marckx v Belgium*, European Court of Human Rights, judgment of 13 June 1979, Series A, No 31, para 31).

33 In Ireland, many aspects of private or family life are regulated by law. As regards marriage, husband and wife are in principle under a duty to cohabit but are entitled, in certain cases, to petition for a decree of judicial separation; this amounts to recognition of the fact that the protection of their private or family life may sometimes necessitate their being relieved from the duty to live together.

Effective respect for private or family life obliges Ireland to make this means of protection effectively accessible, when appropriate, to anyone who may wish to have recourse thereto. However, it was not effectively accessible to the applicant: not having been put in a position in which she could apply to the High Court (see paras 20–28 above), she was unable to seek recognition in law of her de facto separation from her husband. She has therefore been the victim of a violation of article 8.

V On Article 13

34 Alleging that she was deprived of an effective remedy before a national authority for the violations complained of, Mrs Airey finally invokes article 13, which provides:

> Everyone whose rights and freedom as set forth in this Convention are violated shall have an effective remedy before a national authority notwithstanding that the violation has been committed by persons acting in an official capacity.

The Commission was of the opinion that, in view of its conclusion concerning article 6(1), there was no need for it to consider the application under article 13. The Government made no submissions on this point.

35 Mrs Airey wishes to exercise her right under Irish law to institute proceedings for judicial separation. The Court has already held that such proceedings concern a "civil right" within the meaning of article 6(1) (see para 21 above) and, further, that Ireland is obliged under article 8 to make the possibility of instituting them effectively available to Mrs Airey so that she may organise her private life (see para 33 above). Since article 13 and 6(1) overlap in this particular case, the Court does not deem it necessary to determine whether there has been a failure to observe the requirements of the former article [article 13]: these requirements are less strict than, and are entirely absorbed by, those of the latter article [article 6(1)] (see, *mutatis mutandis, De Wilde, Ooms and Versyp v Belgium*, European Court of Human Rights, judgment of 18 June 1971, Series A, No 12, para 95).

VI On Article 50

36 At the hearings, the applicant's counsel informed the Court that, should it find a breach of the Convention, her client would seek just satisfaction under article 50 under three headings: effective access to a remedy for breakdown of marriage; monetary compensation for her pain, suffering and mental anguish; and monetary compensation for costs incurred, mainly ancillary expenses, fees for lawyers and other special fees. The last two items were not quantified. The Government made no observations on the question of the application of article 50.

37 Accordingly, although it was raised under Rule 47 *bis* of the Rules of Court, the said question is not ready for decision. The Court is therefore obliged to reserve the question and to fix the further procedure, taking due account of the possibility of an agreement between the respondent State and the applicant (Rules of Court, r 50 (3) and (5)).

For these reasons, **THE COURT:**

On the Government's preliminary pleas:

1 *Rejects* unanimously the plea based by the Government on the application's manifest lack of foundation;

2 *Rejects* by six votes to one the first limb of the Government's plea that domestic remedies have not been exhausted (see para 19(a) above).

3 *Joins* to the merits, unanimously, the second limb of the last-mentioned plea (see para 19(b) above), but rejects it by six votes to one after an examination on the merits.

On the merits of the case, holds:

4 by five votes to two, that there has been a breach of article 6(1) of the Convention, taken alone;

5 by four votes to three, that it is not necessary also to examine the case under article 14 taken in conjunction with article 6(1);

6 by four votes to three, that there has been a breach of article 8;

7 by four votes to three, that it is not necessary also to examine the case under article 13;

8 unanimously, that the question of the application of article 50 is not ready for decision;

accordingly,

(a) reserves the whole of the said question;

(b) invites the Commission to submit to the Court within two months from the delivery of this Judgment, the Commission's observations on this question, including notification of any settlement at which the Government and the applicant may have arrived; and

(c) reserves the further procedure.

CASE NO 6

X AND Y v THE NETHERLANDS

EUROPEAN COURT OF HUMAN RIGHTS

Application No: 8978/80

Judgment: 26 March 1985

Panel: *Judges*: Ryssdal (*President*), Wiarda, Walsh, Sir Vincent Evans, Russo, Bernhardt and Gersing.

Human rights — Right to respect for private life — Right to respect for physical and moral integrity — Protection of physical integrity of person with an intellectual disability — Right not to be subjected to inhuman or degrading treatment — Right to effective remedy — Equality and non–discrimination — Discrimination on the grounds of disability — Violations by private actors — Whether impossibility of victim of sexual assault who had an intellectual disability, or non–victim, to bring criminal proceedings against perpetrator violated Convention rights — European Convention for the Protection of Human Rights and Fundamental Freedoms, arts 3, 8, 13 and 14

International law — State responsibility — Human rights — Positive obligations of Contracting States — Right to respect for private life — Violations by private actors — Measures to secure respect for private life as between individuals — Margin of appreciation — European Convention for the Protection of Human Rights and Fundamental Freedoms, art 8

BACKGROUND

Mr X complained to the police about a sexual assault by the accused on his daughter Ms Y, who had an intellectual disability. The prosecutor's office decided not to prosecute provided the accused did not repeat the offence. Mr X appealed against this decision and requested the court to direct that proceedings be brought. The appeal was dismissed, partly on the ground that although Ms Y was incapable of making the complaint herself, no-one else was legally entitled to complain on her behalf.

Mr X and Ms Y, the applicants, complained to the European Commission on Human Rights of violations of articles 3 (inhuman or degrading treatment), 8 (respect for private life), 13 (effective remedy before a national authority) and 14 (non-discrimination) of the European Convention on Human Rights. They claimed that the impossibility of having criminal proceedings instituted against the accused violated Ms Y's right to private life under article 8 of the Convention, specifically her right to physical and moral integrity.

The applicants also claimed that Ms Y had suffered "inhuman and degrading treatment" at the hands of the accused contrary to article 3 of the Convention. They argued that the State was in certain circumstances responsible for the acts of third parties and that the chronic psychological trauma caused to Ms Y was of a level that fell within article 3.

The applicants further argued that the difference of treatment established by the legislature between the categories of persons deserving special protection against sexual assaults constituted discrimination contrary to article 14 of the Convention, taken in conjunction with both articles 3 and 8.

The Commission found a violation of article 8 but not of article 3, and did not consider the applicability of articles 13 and 14. The Commission referred the case to the European Court of Human Rights.

HELD (finding a violation of article 8 of the Convention)

Article 8, taken alone, as regards Y (right to respect for private life)

1   Although the object of article 8 was essentially that of protecting the individual against arbitrary interference by the public authorities, it did not merely compel the State to abstain from such interference; there might be positive obligations inherent in an effective respect for private or family life. These obligations might involve the adoption of measures designed to secure respect for private life even in the sphere of the relations of individuals between themselves. (Para 23)

2   The protection afforded by the civil law in the case of wrongdoing of the kind inflicted on Ms Y was insufficient. This was a case where fundamental values and essential aspects of private life were at stake. Effective deterrence was indispensable in this area and it could be achieved only by criminal law provisions; indeed, it was by such provisions that the matter is normally regulated. Moreover, this was in fact an area in which the Netherlands had generally opted for a system of protection based on the criminal law. The only gap was as regards persons in the situation of Ms Y; in such cases, this system met a procedural obstacle which the Dutch legislature had apparently not foreseen. (Para 27)

3   Article 248*ter* of the Dutch Criminal Code requires a complaint by the actual victim before criminal proceedings can be instituted. The Arnhem Court of Appeal held that, in the case of an individual like Ms Y, the legal representative could not act on the victim's behalf for this purpose. It was not the task of the European Court of Human Rights to take the place of the competent national courts in the interpretation of domestic law, and therefore it should not be taken as established that in the case in question criminal proceedings could not be instituted on the basis of article 248*ter*. (Para 29)

4   Although the Government argued that article 239(2) of the Criminal Code could be used to institute a criminal case on behalf of Ms Y, this was apparently designed to penalise indecent exposure and not indecent assault, and was not clearly applicable to the present case. Thus, neither article 248*ter* nor article 239(2) of the Criminal Code provided Ms Y with practical and effective protection. It therefore had to be concluded, taking account of the nature of the wrongdoing in question, that Ms Y was the victim of a violation of article 8 of the Convention. (Paras 29 and 30)

Alleged violation of article 14 (right to non-discrimination), taken in conjunction with articles 8 (right to respect for private life) and 3 (right to protection from inhumane or degrading treatment)

5   It was not necessary to examine the case separately under article 14, either in conjunction with article 8 or with article 3 (Paras 32 and 34)

Alleged violation of article 13 (right to effective remedy before a national authority)

6   As the Court had already concluded in the context of article 8 that the lack of an adequate means of obtaining a remedy was one of the factors leading to the conclusion that article 8 had been violated, it was not necessary to examine the same issue under article 13. (Paras 36 and 37)

Treaties and other international instruments referred to

European Convention for the Protection of Human Rights and Fundamental Freedoms 1950, arts 3, 8, 13, 14 and 50

National legislation referred to

Netherlands

Code of Criminal Procedure, arts 12, 163, 164 and 445

Criminal Code, arts 64(1), 242, 246, 244, 245, 247, 243, 249, 239 and 248*ter*

Civil Code, art 378, Book 1; arts 1401 and 1407

Cases referred to

Airey v Ireland, ECHR, judgment of 9 October 1979, Series A, No. 32; 2 EHRR 305; *supra*, p 67.

Handyside v United Kingdom, ECHR, judgment of 7 December 1976, Series A, No 24; 1 EHRR 737

JUDGMENT

PROCEDURE [...]*

AS TO THE FACTS

I   The particular circumstances of the case

7   Mr X and his daughter Y were born in 1929 and on 13 December 1961 respectively. The daughter, who is mentally handicapped, had been living since 1970 in a privately-run home for mentally handicapped children.

8   During the night of 14 to 15 December 1977, Miss Y was woken up by a certain Mr B, the son-in-law of the directress; he lived with his wife on the premises of the institution although he was not employed there. Mr B forced the girl to follow him to his room, to undress and to have sexual intercourse with him. This incident, which occurred on the day after Miss Y's sixteenth birthday, had traumatic consequences for her, causing her major mental disturbance.

---

*   *Eds:* paras 1 to 6, which relate to procedural matters, have not been included.

9 On 16 December 1977, Mr X went to the local police station to file a complaint and to ask for criminal proceedings to be instituted. The police officer said that since Mr X considered his daughter unable to sign the complaint because of her mental condition, he could do so himself. The statement lodged by Mr X read as follows:

> In my capacity as father I denounce the offences committed by Mr B on the person of my daughter. I am doing this because she cannot do so herself, since, although 16 years of age, she is mentally and intellectually still a child.

10 The police officer drew up a report and it was signed by Mr X (articles 163 and 164 Code of Criminal Procedure). The officer subsequently informed the public prosecutor's office that in the light of the father's statement and of his own observations concerning the girl's mental condition, she did not seem to him capable of filing a complaint herself. According to the headmaster of the school she was attending and another teacher there, she was unable to express her wishes concerning the institution of proceedings.

11 On 29 May 1978, the public prosecutor's office provisionally decided not to open proceedings against Mr B, provided that he did not commit a similar offence within the next two years. The official in charge of the case so informed Mr X at a meeting on 27 September 1978.

12 On 4 December 1978, Mr X appealed against the decision of the public prosecutor's office to the Arnhem Court of Appeal, under article 12 of the Code of Criminal Procedure; he requested the court to direct that criminal proceedings be instituted.

In a supplementary memorial of 10 January 1979, he pointed out that subject to an exhaustive list of exceptions, none of which applied in the instant case, a legal representative was entitled to act on behalf of the complainant.

The Court of Appeal dismissed the appeal on 12 July 1979. In fact, it considered it doubtful whether a charge of rape (article 242 of Criminal Code; see para 14 below) could be proved. As for article 248*ter* (see para 16 below), it would have been applicable in the instant case, but only if the victim herself had taken action. In the Court of Appeal's view, the father's complaint (article 64(1) of the Criminal Code; see para 16 below) could not be regarded as a substitute for the complaint which the girl, being over the age of sixteen, should have lodged herself, although the police had regarded her as incapable of doing so; since in the instant case no one was legally empowered to file a complaint, there was on this point a gap in the law, but it could not be filled by means of a broad interpretation to the detriment of Mr B.

13 By virtue of article 445 of the Code of Criminal Procedure, there was no possibility of appealing on a point of law to the Supreme Court (*Hoge Raad*) against this decision.

II   Relevant domestic law

14 As regards sexual offences, the Netherlands Criminal Code makes a distinction between rape (article 242) and indecent assault (article 246), recourse to physical violence also being a constituent element of the latter offence.

15 Other more specific provisions afford in this area protection to certain categories of persons whose age, position of dependence or physical incapability renders it difficult or impossible for them to determine or impose their wishes.

Articles 244 and 245, respectively, make it a criminal offence to have sexual intercourse with a girl under the age of twelve or with a girl between the ages of twelve and sixteen, and under article 247 it is a criminal offence to commit an indecent assault on boys or girls under the age of sixteen. Articles 243 and 247 concern, respectively, sexual intercourse with, and indecent assault on, a woman known to the offender to be unconscious or helpless. According to the Supreme Court, however, the word "helpless" refers only to physical incapacity. Article 249 relates to indecent acts committed with a minor who is in a position of dependence *vis-à-vis* the perpetrator. Finally, article 239 concerns indecency, either in public or while another person is present against his will. Save for article 245, none of these provisions makes the institution of criminal proceedings conditional on the filing of a complaint by the victim.

16 The same does not apply to article 248*ter*, whereby a sentence of not more than four years' imprisonment may be imposed on any person who, "through gifts or promises ... through abuse of a dominant position resulting from factual circumstances, or through deceit, deliberately causes a minor of blameless conduct to commit indecent acts with him or to suffer such acts from him": in a case of this kind, the offender can be prosecuted only on complaint by the actual victim.

Under article 64(1), however, the legal representative may lodge the complaint on behalf of the victim if the latter is under the age of sixteen or is placed under guardianship (*curateele*): this latter institution exists only for persons who have reached the age of majority, namely twenty-one (article 378, Book 1, Civil Code).

17 At the hearings, counsel for the Government informed the Court that the Ministry of Justice had prepared a Bill modifying the provisions of the Criminal Code that related to sexual offences. Under the Bill, it would be an offence to make sexual advances to a mentally handicapped person.

PROCEEDINGS BEFORE THE COMMISSION

18 Mr X applied to the Commission on 10 January 1980 (App No 8978/80). He claimed that his daughter had been subject to inhuman and degrading treatment, within the meaning of article 3 of the Convention, and that the right of both his daughter and himself to respect for their private life, guaranteed by article 8, had been infringed. He further maintained that the right to respect for family life, also guaranteed by the same article, meant that parents must be able to have recourse to remedies in the event of their children being the victims of sexual abuse, particularly if the children were minors and if the father was their legal representative. In addition, Mr X claimed that he and his daughter had not had an effective remedy before a national authority as required by article 13, and that the situation complained of was discriminatory and contrary to article 14.

19 The Commission declared the application admissible on 17 December 1981. In its report of 5 July 1983 (article 31), it expressed the opinion:

– as regards Miss Y, that there had been a breach of article 8 of the Convention (unanimously), but not of article 3 (fifteen votes against one);

– that it was not necessary to examine the application either under article 14 taken in conjunction with article 8 or article 3, or under article 13;

– as regards Mr X, that no separate issue arose concerning his right to respect for family life.

FINAL SUBMISSION MADE TO THE COURT BY THE GOVERNMENT

20 In their memorial of 18 June 1984, the Government "respectfully request the Court to hold that there has been no violation of the Convention in the present case."

AS TO THE LAW

I　　　Alleged violation of Article 8, taken alone, as regards Miss Y

21 According to the applicants, the impossibility of having criminal proceedings instituted against Mr B violated article 8 of the Convention, which reads:

1　Everyone has the right to respect for his private and family life, his home and his correspondence.

2　There shall be no interference by a public authority with the exercise of this right except such as is in accordance with the law and is necessary in a democratic society in the interests of national security, public safety or the economic well-being of the country, for the prevention of disorder or crime, for the protection of health or morals, or for the protection of the rights and freedoms of others.

The Government contested this claim; the Commission, on the other hand, agreed with it in its essentials.

22 There was no dispute as to the applicability of article 8: the facts underlying the application to the Commission concern a matter of "private life", a concept which covers the physical and moral integrity of the person, including his or her sexual life.

23 The Court recalls that although the object of article 8 is essentially that of protecting the individual against arbitrary interference by the public authorities, it does not merely compel the State to abstain from such interference: in addition to this primarily negative undertaking, there may be positive obligations inherent in an effective respect for private or family life (*Airey v Ireland*, European Court of Human Rights, judgment of 9 October 1979, Series A, No 32, para 32). These obligations may involve the adoption of measures designed to secure respect for private life even in the sphere of the relations of individuals between themselves.

1　　Necessity for criminal-law provisions

24 The applicants argued that, for a young girl like Miss Y, the requisite degree of protection against the wrongdoing in question would have been provided only by means of the criminal law. In the Government's view, the Convention left it to each State to decide upon the means to be utilised and did not prevent it from opting for civil-law provisions.

The Court, which on this point agrees in substance with the opinion of the Commission, observes that the choice of the means calculated to secure compliance with article 8 in the sphere of the relations of individuals between themselves is in principle a matter that falls within the Contracting States' margin of appreciation. In this connection, there are different ways of ensuring "respect for private life", and the nature of the State's obligation will depend on the particular aspect of private life that is at issue. Recourse to the criminal law is not necessarily the only answer.

25 The Government cited the difficulty encountered by the legislature in laying down criminal law provisions calculated to afford the best possible protection of the physical integrity of the mentally handicapped: to go too far in this direction might lead to

unacceptable paternalism and occasion an inadmissible interference by the State with the individual's right to respect for his or her sexual life.

The Government stated that under article 1401 of the Civil Code, taken together with Article 1407, it would have been possible to bring before or file with the Netherlands courts, on behalf of Miss Y:

- an action for damages against Mr B for pecuniary or non-pecuniary damage;
- an application for an injunction against Mr B, to prevent repetition of the offence;
- a similar action or application against the directress of the children's home.

The applicants considered that these civil law remedies were unsuitable. They submitted that, amongst other things, the absence of any criminal investigation made it harder to furnish evidence on the four matters that had to be established under article 1401, namely a wrongful act, fault, damage and a causal link between the act and the damage. Furthermore, such proceedings were lengthy and involved difficulties of an emotional nature for the victim, since he or she had to play an active part therein.

26 At the hearings, the Commission's Delegate adopted the applicants' submissions in their essentials; he also doubted whether article 1401 could provide a proper basis for an award of compensation for non-pecuniary damage. He added that the need for protection existed *erga omnes*, whilst an injunction could only be directed to a limited circle of persons. Finally, the civil law lacked the deterrent effect that was inherent in the criminal law.

27 The Court finds that the protection afforded by the civil law in the case of wrongdoing of the kind inflicted on Miss Y is insufficient. This is a case where fundamental values and essential aspects of private life are at stake. Effective deterrence is indispensable in this area and it can be achieved only by criminal law provisions; indeed, it is by such provisions that the matter is normally regulated.

Moreover, as was pointed out by the Commission, this is in fact an area in which the Netherlands has generally opted for a system of protection based on the criminal law. The only gap, so far as the Commission and the Court have been made aware, is as regards persons in the situation of Miss Y; in such cases, this system meets a procedural obstacle which the Dutch legislature had apparently not foreseen.

2 Compatibility of the Dutch legislation with Article 8

28 According to the Government, it was the exceptional nature of the facts of the case which disclosed the gap in the law and it could not be said that there had been any failure on the part of the legislature. The Criminal Code admittedly contained no specific provision to the effect that it was an offence to make sexual advances to the mentally handicapped. However, criminal proceedings could in certain circumstances be instituted on the basis of article 239(2) of the Criminal Code, with or without a complaint by the victim, against anyone who violated the sexual integrity of a mentally handicapped person. Under this article it was an offence to commit an act of indecency "while another person is present against his will", a phrase which the Supreme Court had interpreted as also covering a person who was the actual victim of an indecent act.

According to the applicants, on the other hand, the current Criminal Code offered insufficient protection (see paras 41–43 of the Commission's Report; (1984) 6 EHRR, 311).

29 Two provisions of the Criminal Code are relevant to the present case, namely article 248*ter* and article 239(2).

Article 248*ter* requires a complaint by the actual victim before criminal proceedings can be instituted against someone who has contravened this provision (see para 16 above). The Arnhem Court of Appeal held that, in the case of an individual like Miss Y, the legal representative could not act on the victim's behalf for this purpose. The Court of Appeal did not feel able to fill this gap in the law by means of a broad interpretation to the detriment of Mr B. It is in no way the task of the European Court of Human Rights to take the place of the competent national courts in the interpretation of domestic law (see *Handyside v UK*, European Court of Human Rights, judgment of 7 December 1976, Series A, No 24, para 50), it regards it as established that in the case in question criminal proceedings could not be instituted on the basis of article 248*ter*.

As for article 239(2) (see para 15 above), this is apparently designed to penalise indecent exposure and not indecent assault, and was not clearly applicable to the present case. Indeed, no-one, even the public prosecutor's office, seems to have considered utilising this provision at the time, or even referring to it at the outset of the Strasbourg proceedings.

30 Thus, neither article 248*ter* nor article 239(2) of the Criminal Code provided Miss Y with practical and effective protection. It must therefore be concluded, taking account of the nature of the wrongdoing in question, that she was the victim of a violation of Article 8 of the Convention.

II   Alleged violation of Article 14, taken in conjunction with Article 8, as regards Miss Y

31 The applicants contended that the difference of treatment established by the legislature between the various categories of persons deserving of special protection against sexual assaults amounted to discrimination contrary to article 14 of the Convention, which reads as follows:

> The enjoyment of the rights and freedoms set forth in this Convention shall be secured without discrimination on any ground such as sex, race, colour, language, religion, political or other opinion, national or social origin, association with a national minority, property, birth or other status.

The Government disputed this contention. The Commission considered that no separate issue arose.

32 Article 14 has no independent existence; it constitutes one particular element (non-discrimination) of each of the rights safeguarded by the Convention. The articles enshrining those rights may be violated alone or in conjunction with article 14. An examination of the case under article 14 is not generally required when the Court finds a violation of one of the former articles taken alone. The position is otherwise if a clear inequality of treatment in the enjoyment of the right in question is a fundamental aspect of the case, but this does not apply to the breach of Article 8 found in the present proceedings (see *mutatis mutandis, Airey v Ireland*, European Court of Human Rights, judgment of 9 October 1979, Series A, No 32, para 30).

The Court accordingly does not deem it necessary to examine the case under article 14 as well.

III   Alleged violation of Article 3, taken alone or in conjunction with Article 14, as regards Miss Y

33 According to the applicants, Miss Y suffered at the hands of Mr B "inhuman and degrading treatment" contrary to article 3 of the Convention. They maintained that, for the purposes of this provision, the State was in certain circumstances responsible for the acts of third parties and that the chronic psychological trauma caused to Miss Y had attained such a level as to fall within the ambit of that article.

34 According to the Commission, article 3 had not been violated since there was no close and direct link between the gap in the Dutch law and "the field of protection covered" by the Article. At the hearings, the Government adopted this opinion and submitted that they were not answerable for the treatment inflicted on Miss Y. Having found that article 8 was violated, the Court does not consider that it has also to examine the case under article 3, taken alone or in conjunction with article 14.

IV   Alleged violation of Article 13 as regards Miss Y

35 The applicants alleged that they had had no effective remedy in the Netherlands for Miss Y's complaints. On this account they invoked article 13, which reads:

> Everyone whose rights and freedoms as set forth in this Convention are violated shall have an effective remedy before a national authority notwithstanding that the violation has been committed by persons acting in an official capacity.

They maintained, in particular, that the possibility of appealing, under article 12 of the Code of Criminal Procedure, to the Arnhem Court of Appeal did not constitute a remedy of this description. For the Government, on the other hand, this was a procedure designed to ensure that the criminal law was being correctly applied. The fact that the procedure did not serve the particular purpose did not mean that it did not exist.

The Commission expressed the opinion that it could not be deduced from article 13 that there had to be a remedy against legislation as such which was considered not to be in conformity with the Convention.

36 The Court has already considered, in the context of article 8, whether an adequate means of obtaining a remedy was available to Miss Y. Its finding that there was no such means was one of the factors which led it to conclude that article 8 had been violated. This being so, the Court does not have to examine the same issue under article 13.

V   The complaints of Mr X

37 Initially, Mr X also alleged that the gap in the Dutch law had violated his own rights under articles 8 and 13 of the Convention. The Commission considered that no separate issue arose in this respect. Counsel for the applicants did not revert to this aspect of the case at the hearings. The Court therefore sees no necessity to give a decision thereon.

VI   Article 50

38 Under Article 50 of the Convention,

> If the Court finds that a decision or a measure taken by a legal authority or any other authority of a High Contracting Party is completely or partially in conflict with the obligations arising from the ... Convention, and if the internal law of the said Party allows only partial reparation to be made for the consequences of this decision or measure, the decision of the Court shall, if necessary, afford just satisfaction to the injured party.

In her letter of 27 August 1984, Ms van Westerlaak explained that "approximately seven years after the event, the girl in question is still experiencing daily the consequences of the indecent assault of which she was the 'victim' and that 'this is the source of much tension within the family'". Ms van Westerlaak stated at the hearings that non-pecuniary damage was still being suffered. The Commission did not comment on these allegations. The Government also did not challenge the allegations as such, but they argued that the suffering was the result of the act committed by Mr B and not of the violation of the Convention. Accordingly, there was no reason to afford just satisfaction.

39 The Court notes that the claim is confined to non-pecuniary damage and does not relate to the costs of the proceedings.

40 No-one contests that Miss Y suffered damage. In addition, it is hardly deniable that the Dutch authorities have a degree of responsibility resulting from the deficiency in the legislation which gave rise to the violation of article 8. The applicants left it to the Court's discretion to determine a standard for compensation. The damage in question does not lend itself even to an approximate process of calculation. Assessing it on an equitable basis, as is required by article 50, the Court considers that Miss Y should be afforded just satisfaction which it fixes at 3,000 Dutch Guilders.

For these reasons, **THE COURT** unanimously:

1   *Holds* that there has been a violation of Article 8 as regards Miss Y;

2   *Holds* that it is not necessary to give a separate decision:

     (a) on her other complaints;

     (b) on the complaints of Mr X;

3   *Holds* that the respondent State is to pay to Miss Y three thousand (3,000) Dutch Guilders under article 50.

CASE NO 7

VELÁSQUEZ RODRÍGUEZ v HONDURAS

INTER-AMERICAN COURT OF HUMAN RIGHTS

Judgment: 29 July 1988

Panel: *Judges*: Nieto-Navia (*President*), Gros Espiell (*Vice President*), Piza, Buergenthal, Nikken, Fix-Zamudio; Espinal Irias (*Judge ad hoc*).

Human rights — Right to life — Right to integrity of the person — Right to personal liberty — Right of detainee to be taken without delay before a judge — Disappearance of individuals — Kidnapping — Arbitrary deprivation of liberty — Secret execution without trial — Prolonged isolation and deprivation of communication — State responsibility — Private actors — American Convention on Human Rights, arts 4, 5 and 7

International law — State responsibility — Disappearance of individuals — Exhaustion of domestic remedies — Burden of proof — Adequate and effective remedies — Positive obligations of state — Duty of due diligence — Duty to prevent and investigate human rights violations — American Convention on Human Rights

BACKGROUND

It was alleged that on 12 September 1981, Mr Manfredo Velásquez, a Honduran university student, was detained without a warrant for his arrest, along with others, by members of the National Office of Investigations (DNI) and members of G-2 of the armed forces of Honduras. It was reported that several eyewitnesses saw the detainees taken to the cells of a public security station in Tegucigalpa, where they were accused of political crimes and subjected to interrogation and torture. It was further alleged that on 17 September 1981, Mr Velásquez was moved to another army location where his interrogation continued. Police and security forces denied that he had been detained. His whereabouts were unknown. A petition was lodged on his behalf before the Inter-American Commission on Human Rights. After lengthy proceedings before the Commission, the matter was referred to the Inter-American Court of Human Rights.

HELD (finding various violations of the Convention)

Exhaustion of domestic remedies

1   A State claiming non-exhaustion of domestic remedies had the burden of proving that domestic remedies remained to be exhausted and that they were effective. (Para 59)

2   The rule of prior exhaustion of domestic remedies was a generally recognised principle of international law, which demands not only the formal existence of remedies, but also remedies which are effective and adequate. Adequate domestic remedies were those which were suitable to address an infringement of a legal right. If a remedy was not adequate in a specific case, it obviously need not be exhausted. (Paras 63 and 64)

3   Although there might have been legal remedies in Honduras that theoretically allowed a person detained by the authorities to be found, those remedies were ineffective in cases of disappearances. (Paras 68 and 80)

Burden and standard of proof in international jurisprudence

4   Because the Commission was accusing the Government of the disappearance of Manfredo Velásquez, it, in principle, should bear the burden of proving the facts underlying its petition. If it could be shown that there was an official practice of disappearances in Honduras, carried out by the Government or at least tolerated by it, and if the disappearance of Manfredo Velásquez could be linked to that practice, the Commission's allegations would have been proven to the Court's satisfaction, so long as the evidence presented on both points met the standard of proof required in cases such as this. (Paras 123 and 126)

5   The standards of proof were less formal in an international legal proceeding than in a domestic one. International jurisprudence had recognised the power of the courts to weigh the evidence freely, and had always avoided a rigid rule regarding the amount of proof necessary to support the judgment. Direct evidence, whether testimonial or documentary, was not the only type of evidence that might be legitimately considered in reaching a decision. (Paras 127, 128) Circumstantial evidence, indicia, and presumptions might be considered, so long as they led to conclusions consistent with the facts. Circumstantial or presumptive evidence was especially important in allegations of disappearances, because this type of repression was characterised by an attempt to suppress all information about the kidnapping or the whereabouts and fate of the victim. (Paras 130 and 131)

Forced disappearances

6   The phenomenon of disappearances was a complex form of human rights violation that must be understood and confronted in an integral fashion. (Para 150) The kidnapping of a person was an arbitrary deprivation of liberty, an infringement of a detainee's right to be taken without delay before a judge and to invoke the appropriate procedures to review the legality of the arrest, all in violation of article 7 of the Convention which recognises the right to personal liberty. (Para 155) It might also involve a violation of the right of any detainee to respect for his inherent dignity as a human being. Such treatment, therefore, violated article 5 of the Convention, which recognises the right to the integrity of the person. (Para 156) As the practice of disappearances often involved secret execution without trial, followed by concealment of the body to eliminate any material evidence of the crime and to ensure the impunity of those responsible, the practice constituted a flagrant violation of the right to life, recognised in article 4 of the Convention. The existence of the practice of disappearances, moreover, evinced a disregard of the duty to organise the State in such a manner as to guarantee the rights recognised in the Convention. (Paras 157–158)

State responsibility under the Convention

7   States Parties are obligated under article 1(1) of the Convention "to respect the rights and freedoms" recognised by the Convention. Therefore, the protection of human rights should necessarily comprise the concept of the restriction of the exercise of state power. (Para 165)

8   The second obligation of the States Parties under article 1(1) of the Convention is to "ensure" the free and full exercise of the rights recognised by the Convention to every person subject to its jurisdiction. This obligation implied the duty of the States Parties to organise the governmental apparatus and, in general, all the structures through which public power is exercised, so that they were capable of juridically ensuring the free and full enjoyment of human rights. As a consequence of this obligation, the States had to prevent, investigate and punish any violation of the rights recognised by the Convention and, moreover, if possible attempt to restore the right violated and provide compensation as warranted for damages resulting from the violation. (Para 166)

9   The obligation, under article 1 of the Convention, to ensure the free and full exercise of human rights was not fulfilled simply by the existence of a legal system designed to make it possible to comply with this obligation – it also required the Government to conduct itself so as to effectively ensure the free and full exercise of human rights. (Para 167)

10   Any exercise of public power that violated the rights recognised by the Convention was illegal. Regardless of whether the organ or official had contravened provisions of municipal law or overstepped the limits of his authority, under international law, a State was responsible for the acts of its agents undertaken in their official capacity and for their omissions, even when those agents acted outside the sphere of their authority or violated internal law. (Paras 169 and 170)

Duty to prevent and duty to investigate human rights violations by private actors

11   In principle, any violation of rights recognised by the Convention carried out by an act of public authority or by persons who use their position of authority was imputable to the State. However, an illegal act which violated human rights and which was initially not directly imputable to a State (for example, because it was the act of a private person or because the person responsible has not been identified) could lead to international responsibility of the State, not because of the act itself, but because of the lack of due diligence to prevent the violation or to respond to it as required by the Convention. (Para 172)

12   A violation of human rights could be established even if the identity of the individual perpetrator was unknown. What was decisive was whether a violation of the rights recognised by the Convention had occurred with the support or the acquiescence of the Government, or whether the State had allowed the act to take place without taking measures to prevent it or to punish those responsible. (Para 173)

13   The State had a legal duty to take reasonable steps to prevent human rights violations and to use the means at its disposal to carry out a serious investigation of violations committed within its jurisdiction, to identify those responsible, to impose the appropriate punishment and to ensure the victim adequate compensation. This duty to prevent included all those means of a legal, political, administrative and cultural nature that promote the protection of human rights and ensure that any violations are

considered and treated as illegal acts, which, as such, might lead to the punishment of those responsible and the obligation to indemnify the victims for damages. (Paras 174 and 175)

14 The State was obligated to investigate every situation involving a violation of the rights protected by the Convention. If the State apparatus acted in such a way that the violation went unpunished and the victim's full enjoyment of such rights was not restored as soon as possible, the State had failed to comply with its duty to ensure the free and full exercise of those rights to the persons within its jurisdiction. The same was true when the State allowed private persons or groups to act freely and with impunity to the detriment of the rights recognised by the Convention. (Para 176)

15 In certain circumstances, it might be difficult to investigate acts that violate an individual's rights. Nevertheless, it must be undertaken in a serious manner and not as a mere formality preordained to be ineffective. Where the acts of private parties that violated the Convention were not seriously investigated, those parties were aided in a sense by the government, thereby making the State responsible under international law. (Para 177)

16 According to the principle of the continuity of the State in international law, responsibility exists both independently of changes of government over a period of time and continuously from the time of the act that creates responsibility to the time when the act is declared illegal. (Para 184)

The involuntary disappearance of Manfredo Velásquez

17 In the present case, the evidence showed a complete inability of the procedures of the State of Honduras, which were theoretically adequate, to carry out an investigation into the disappearance of Manfredo Velásquez, and of the fulfillment of its duties to pay compensation and punish those responsible, as set out in article 1(1) of the Convention. (para 178) The fact that the legal order of Honduras did not authorise disappearances and that internal law defined them as crimes was irrelevant for the purposes of establishing whether Honduras was responsible under international law for the violations of human rights perpetrated within the practice of disappearances. (Para 183)

18 The facts found in this proceeding showed that the State of Honduras was responsible for the involuntary disappearance of Manfredo Velásquez. Thus, Honduras had violated articles 7, 5 and 4 of the Convention. (Para 185)

Treaties and other international instruments referred to

Statute of the Inter-American Court of Human Rights 1979, arts 1, 2, 10(3), 19(2), 25 and 28

American Declaration of the Rights and Duties of Man 1948

American Convention on Human Rights 1969, arts 1(1), 2, 4, 5, 7, 8(1), 25, 33, 44, 45, 46(1)(a), 46(2), 48, 50, 51, 57, 61, 62, 63(1), 63(2) and 68(2)

Rules of Procedure of the Inter-American Court of Human Rights, arts 23, 26(1), 27(3), 30(3), 33, 37, 42, 43, 44(1), 44(2) and 45

Inter-American Commission on Human Rights Regulations, arts 19(b), 34(5), 42, 45, 50(1) and 50(2)

Cases referred to

Corfu Channel (Merits, Judgment), ICJ, judgment of 9 April 1949, ICJ Reports 1949, p 4

Handyside v United Kingdom, ECHR, judgment of 7 December 1976, Series A, No 24; 1 EHRR 737

The Case of the SS "Lotus", PCIJ, judgment No 9 of 7 September 1927, Series A, No 10

Military and Paramilitary Activities in and against Nicaragua (Nicaragua v United States of America) (Merits, Judgment), ICJ, judgment of 26 November 1984, ICJ Reports 1986, p 14

The word "laws" in Article 30 of the American Convention on Human Rights, IACHR, Advisory Opinion OC-6/86 of 9 May 1986, Series A, No 6

Velásquez Rodríguez v Honduras (Preliminary Objections), IACHR, judgment of 26 July 1987, Series C, No 1 (1987)

OPINION

The Inter-American Court of Human Rights delivers the following judgment pursuant to Article 44(1) of its Rules of Procedure (hereinafter "the Rules of Procedure") in the instant case submitted by the Inter-American Commission on Human Rights against the State of Honduras.

[Procedure]*

1   The Inter-American Commission on Human Rights (hereinafter "the Commission") submitted the instant case to the Inter-American Court of Human Rights (hereinafter the "Court") on 24 April 1986. It originated in a petition (No 7920) against the State of Honduras (hereinafter "Honduras" or "the Government"), which the Secretariat of the Commission received on 7 October 1981.

2   In submitting the case, the Commission invoked Articles 50 and 51 of the American Convention on Human Rights (hereinafter "the Convention" or "the American Convention") and requested that the Court determine whether the State in question had violated Articles 4 (Right to Life), 5 (Right to Humane Treatment) and 7 (Right to Personal Liberty) of the Convention in the case of Angel Manfredo Velásquez Rodríguez (also known as Manfredo Velásquez). In addition, the Commission asked the Court to rule that "the consequences of the situation that constituted the breach of such right or freedom be remedied and that fair compensation be paid to the injured party or parties."

3   According to the petition filed with the Commission, and the supplementary information received subsequently, Manfredo Velásquez, a student at the National Autonomous University of Honduras, "was violently detained without a warrant for his arrest by members of the National Office of Investigations (DNI) and G-2 of the Armed Forces of Honduras." The detention took place in Tegucigalpa on the afternoon of 12 September 1981. According to the petitioners, several eyewitnesses reported that Manfredo Velásquez and others were detained and taken to the cells of Public Security Forces Station No 2 located in the Barrio E1 Manchen of Tegucigalpa, where he was "accused of alleged political crimes and subjected to harsh interrogation and cruel

---

*   *Eds:* headings (in square brackets) have been added by the editors for the convenience of readers.

torture." The petition added that on 17 September 1981, Manfredo Velásquez was moved to the First Infantry Battalion, where the interrogation continued, but that the police and security forces denied that he had been detained.

4   After transmitting the relevant parts of the petition to the Government, the Commission, on various occasions, requested information on the matter. Since the Commission received no reply, it applied Article 42 (formerly 39) of its Regulations and presumed "as true the allegations contained in the communication of 7 October 1981, concerning the detention and disappearance of Angel Manfredo Velásquez Rodríguez in the Republic of Honduras" and pointed out to the Government that such acts are most serious violations of the right to life (Art 4) and the right to personal liberty (Art 7) of the American Convention" (Resolution 30/83 of 4 October 1983).

5   On 18 November 1983, the Government requested the reconsideration of Resolution 30/83 on the grounds that domestic remedies had not been exhausted, that the National Office of Investigations had no knowledge of the whereabouts of Manfredo Velásquez, that the Government was making every effort to find him, and that there were rumors that Manfredo Velásquez was "with Salvadoran guerrilla groups."

6   On 30 May 1984, the Commission informed the Government that it had decided, "in light of the information submitted by the Honorable Government, to reconsider Resolution 30/83 and to continue its study of the case". The Commission also asked the Government to provide information on the exhaustion of domestic legal remedies.

7   On 29 January 1985, the Commission repeated its request of 30 May 1984 and notified the Government that it would render a final decision on the case at its meeting in March 1985. On 1 March of that year, the Government asked for a postponement of the final decision and reported that it had set up an Investigatory Commission to study the matter. The Commission agreed to the Government's request on 11 March, granting it thirty days in which to present the information requested.

8   On 17 October 1985, the Government presented to the Commission the Report of the Investigatory Commission.

9   On 7 April 1986, the Government provided information about the outcome of the proceeding brought in the First Criminal Court against those persons supposedly responsible for the disappearance of Manfredo Velásquez and others. That Court dismissed the complaints "except as they applied to General Gustavo Alvarez Martínez, because he had left the country and had not given testimony." This decision was later affirmed by the First Court Of Appeals.

10 By Resolution 22/86 of 18 April 1986, the Commission deemed the new information presented by the Government insufficient to warrant reconsideration of Resolution 30/83 and found, to the contrary, that "all evidence shows that Angel Manfredo Velásquez Rodríguez is still missing and that the Government of Honduras... has not offered convincing proof that would allow the Commission to determine that the allegations are not true". In that same Resolution, the Commission confirmed Resolution 30/83 and referred the matter to the Court.

11 The Court has jurisdiction to hear the instant case. Honduras ratified the Convention on 8 September 1977 and recognized the contentious jurisdiction of the Court, as set out in Article 62 of the Convention, on 9 September 1981. The case was submitted to the Court by the Commission pursuant to Article 61 of the Convention and Article 50(1) and 50(2) of the Regulations of the Commission.

12 The instant case was submitted to the Court on 24 April 1986. On 13 May 1986, the Secretariat of the Court transmitted the application to the Government, pursuant to Article 26(1) of the Rules of Procedure.

[...]*

16 In its submissions of 31 October 1986, the Government objected to the admissibility of the application filed by the Commission.

23 On 26 June 1987, the Court delivered its judgment on the preliminary objections. In this unanimous decision, the Court:

> 1   Reject[ed] the preliminary objections interposed by the Government of Honduras, except for the issues relating to the exhaustion of the domestic legal remedies, which (were) ordered joined to the merits of the case.
>
> 2   Decide[d] to proceed with the consideration of the instant case ...

28 The Court held hearings on the merits and heard the final arguments of the parties from 30 September to 7 October 1987.

38 The following non-governmental organizations submitted briefs as *amici curiae*: Amnesty International, Association of the Bar of the City of New York, Lawyers Committee for Human Rights and Minnesota Lawyers International Human Rights Committee.

39 By note of 4 November 1987, addressed to the President of the Court, the Commission asked the Court to take provisional measures under Article 63(2) of the Convention in view of the threats against the witnesses Milton Jiménez Puerto and Ramón Custodio López. ... By communications of 11 and 18 November 1987, the Agent of the Government informed the Court that the Honduran government would guarantee Ramón Custodio and Milton Jimenez "the respect of their physical and moral integrity ... and the faithful compliance with the Convention ..."

40 By note of 11 January 1988, the Commission informed the Court of the death of Jose Isaías Vilorio, which occurred on 5 January 1988 at 7.15 am. The Court had summoned him to appear as a witness on 18 January 1988. He was killed "on a public thoroughfare in Colonia San Miguel, Comayaguela, Tegucigalpa, by a group of armed men who placed the insignia of a Honduran guerrilla movement known as Cinchonero on his body and fled in a vehicle at high speed".

41 On 15 January 1988, the Court was informed of the assassinations of Moisés Landaverde and Miguel Angel Pavón which had occurred the previous evening in San Pedro Sula. Mr Pavón had testified before the Court on 30 September 1987 as a witness in this case. Also on 15 January, the Court adopted the following provisional measures under Article 63(2) of the Convention:

> 1   That the Government of Honduras adopt, without delay, such measures as are necessary to prevent further infringements of the basic rights of those who have appeared or have been summoned to do so before this Court in the *Velasquez Rodríguez, Fairén Garbi* and *Solís Corrales* and *Godínez Cruz* cases, in strict compliance with the obligation of respect for and observance of human rights, under the terms of Article 1(1) of the Convention.

---

*   **Eds:** only selected paragraphs from paras 13 to 49, which relate to further procedural issues, have been included below. The full text of the judgment is available at IACHR, Series C, No 4 (1989); 95 ILR 232; 28 ILM 291; and the websites of the IACHR and University of Minnesota Human Rights Library (see *On-Line Access to Human Rights Source Materials, supra,* p xlv).

2   That the Government of Honduras also employ all means within its power to investigate these reprehensible crimes, to identify the perpetrators and to impose the punishment provided for by the domestic law of Honduras.

[...]*

[Exhaustion of domestic remedies]

50   The Government raised several preliminary objections that the Court ruled upon in its Judgment of 26 June 1987 (see para 23 above). There the Court ordered the joining of the merits and the preliminary objection regarding the failure to exhaust domestic remedies, and gave the Government and the Commission another opportunity to "substantiate their contentions" on the matter (*Velásquez Rodríguez* Case, Preliminary Objections, see para 23, para 90).

51   The Court will first rule upon this preliminary objection. In so doing, it will make use of all the evidence before it, including that presented during the proceedings on the merits.

52   The Commission presented witnesses and documentary evidence on this point. The Government, in turn, submitted some documentary evidence, including examples of writs of *habeas corpus* successfully brought on behalf of some individuals (see para 120(c) below). The Government also stated that this remedy requires identification of the place of detention and of the authority under which the person is detained.

53   In addition to the writ of *habeas corpus*, the Government mentioned various remedies that might possibly be invoked, such as appeal, cassation, extraordinary writ of *amparo, ad effectum videndi*, criminal complaints against those ultimately responsible and a presumptive finding of death.

55   The Commission argued that the remedies mentioned by the Government were ineffective because of the internal conditions in the country during that period. It presented documentation of three writs of *habeas corpus* brought on behalf of Manfredo Velásquez that did not produce results. It also cited two criminal complaints that failed to lead to the identification and punishment of those responsible. In the Commission's opinion, those legal proceedings exhausted domestic remedies as required by Article 46(1)(a) of the Convention.

56   The Court will first consider the legal arguments relevant to the question of exhaustion of domestic remedies and then apply them to the case.

57   Article 46(1)(a) of the Convention provides that, in order for a petition or communication lodged with the Commission in accordance with Articles 44 or 45 to be admissible, it is necessary "that the remedies under domestic law have been pursued and exhausted in accordance with generally recognized principles of international law".

58   The same article, in the second paragraph, provides that this requirement shall not be applicable when:

(a)   the domestic legislation of the state concerned does not afford due process of law for the protection of the right or rights that have allegedly been violated;

---

*   **Eds:** paras 42 to 49 relate to the Court's Order of 19 January 1988 on additional measures regarding the protection of witnesses and the investigations of the assassinations mentioned above.

(b) the party alleging violation of his rights has been denied access to the remedies under domestic law or has been prevented from exhausting them; or

(c) there has been unwarranted delay in rendering a final judgment under the aforementioned remedies.

59 In its Judgment of 26 June 1987, the Court decided, *inter alia*, that "the State claiming non-exhaustion has an obligation to prove that domestic remedies remain to be exhausted and that they are effective" (*Velásquez Rodríguez* Case, Preliminary Objections, see para 23 above, para 88).

60 Concerning the burden of proof, the Court did not go beyond the conclusion cited in the preceding paragraph. The Court now affirms that if a State which alleges non-exhaustion proves the existence of specific domestic remedies that should have been utilized, the opposing party has the burden of showing that those remedies were exhausted or that the case comes within the exceptions of Article 46(2). It must not be rashly presumed that a State Party to the Convention has failed to comply with its obligation to provide effective domestic remedies.

61 The rule of prior exhaustion of domestic remedies allows the State to resolve the problem under its internal law before being confronted with an international proceeding. This is particularly true in the international jurisdiction of human rights, because the latter reinforces or complements the domestic jurisdiction (American Convention, Preamble).

62 It is a legal duty of the States to provide such remedies, as this Court indicated in its Judgment of 26 June 1987, when it stated:

> The rule of prior exhaustion of domestic remedies under the international law of human rights has certain implications that are present in the Convention. Under the Convention, States Parties have an obligation to provide effective judicial remedies to victims of human rights violations (Art. 25), remedies that must be substantiated in accordance with the rules of due process of law (Art. 8(1)), all in keeping with the general obligation of such States to guarantee the free and full exercise of the rights recognized by the Convention to all persons subject to their jurisdiction (Art. 1). (*Velásquez Rodríguez* Case, Preliminary Objections, see para 23 above, para. 91).

63 Article 46(1)(a) of the Convention speaks of "generally recognized principles of international law". Those principles refer not only to the formal existence of such remedies, but also to their adequacy and effectiveness, as shown by the exceptions set out in Article 46(2).

64 Adequate domestic remedies are those which are suitable to address an infringement of a legal right. A number of remedies exist in the legal system of every country, but not all are applicable in every circumstance. If a remedy is not adequate in a specific case, it obviously need not be exhausted. A norm is meant to have an effect and should not be interpreted in such a way as to negate its effect or lead to a result that is manifestly absurd or unreasonable. For example, a civil proceeding specifically cited by the Government, such as a presumptive finding of death based on disappearance, the purpose of which is to allow heirs to dispose of the estate of the person presumed deceased or to allow the spouse to remarry, is not an adequate remedy for finding a person or for obtaining his liberty.

65 Of the remedies cited by the Government, *habeas corpus* would be the normal means of finding a person presumably detained by the authorities, of ascertaining whether he is legally detained and, given the case, of obtaining his liberty. The other remedies cited by

the Government are either for reviewing a decision within an inchoate proceeding (such as those of appeal or cassation) or are addressed to other objectives. If, however, as the Government has stated, the writ of *habeas corpus* requires the identification of the place of detention and the authority ordering the detention, it would not be adequate for finding a person clandestinely held by State officials, since in such cases there is only hearsay evidence of the detention, and the whereabouts of the victim is unknown.

66 A remedy must also be effective – that is, capable of producing the result for which it was designed. Procedural requirements can make the remedy of *habeas corpus* ineffective: if it is powerless to compel the authorities; if it presents a danger to those who invoke it; or if it is not impartially applied.

67 On the other hand, contrary to the Commission's argument, the mere fact that a domestic remedy does not produce a result favorable to the petitioner does not in and of itself demonstrate the inexistence or exhaustion of all effective domestic remedies. For example, the petitioner may not have invoked the appropriate remedy in a timely fashion.

68 It is a different matter, however, when it is shown that remedies are denied for trivial reasons or without an examination of the merits, or if there is proof of the existence of a practice or policy ordered or tolerated by the government, the effect of which is to impede certain persons from invoking internal remedies that would normally be available to others. In such cases, resort to those remedies becomes a senseless formality. The exceptions of Article 46(2) would be fully applicable in those situations and would discharge the obligation to exhaust internal remedies since they cannot fulfill their objective in that case.

69 In the Government's opinion, a writ of *habeas corpus* does not exhaust the remedies of the Honduran legal system because there are other remedies, both ordinary and extraordinary, such as appeal, cassation, and extraordinary writ of *amparo*, as well as the civil remedy of a presumptive finding of death. In addition, in criminal procedures parties may use whatever evidence they choose. With respect to the cases of disappearances mentioned by the Commission, the Government stated that it had initiated some investigations and had opened others on the basis of complaints, and that the proceedings remain pending until those presumed responsible, either as principals or accomplices, are identified or apprehended.

70 In its conclusions, the Government stated that some writs of *habeas corpus* were granted from 1981 to 1984, which would prove that this remedy was not ineffective during that period. It submitted various documents to support its argument.

71 In response, the Commission argued that the practice of disappearances made exhaustion of domestic remedies impossible because such remedies were ineffective in correcting abuses imputed to the authorities or in causing kidnapped persons to reappear.

72 The Commission maintained that, in cases of disappearances, the fact that a writ of *habeas corpus* or *amparo* has been brought without success is sufficient to support a finding of exhaustion of domestic remedies as long as the person does not appear, because that is the most appropriate remedy in such a situation. It emphasized that neither writs of *habeas corpus* nor criminal complaints were effective in the case of Manfredo Velásquez. The Commission maintained that exhaustion should not be understood to require mechanical attempts at formal procedures; but rather to require a case-by-case analysis of the reasonable possibility of obtaining a remedy.

73 The Commission asserted that, because of the structure of the international system for the protection of human rights, the Government bears the burden of proof with respect to the exhaustion of domestic remedies. The objection of failure to exhaust presupposes the existence of an effective remedy. It stated that a criminal complaint is not an effective means to find a disappeared person, but only serves to establish individual responsibility.

74 The record before the Court shows that the following remedies were pursued on behalf of Manfredo Velásquez:

(a) Habeas Corpus

    (i) Brought by Zenaida Velásquez against the Public Security Forces on 17 September 1981. No result.

    (ii) Brought by Zenaida Velásquez on 6 February 1982. No result.

    (iii) Brought by various relatives of disappeared persons on behalf of Manfredo Velásquez and others on 4 July 1983. Denied on 11 September 1984.

(b) Criminal Complaints

    (i) Brought by the father and sister of Manfredo Velásquez before the First Criminal Court of Tegucigalpa on 9 November 1982. No result.

    (ii) Brought by Gertrudis Lanza González, joined by Zenaida Velásquez, before the First Criminal Court of Tegucigalpa against various members of the Armed Forces on 5 April 1984. The Court dismissed this proceeding and the First Court of Appeals affirmed on 16 January 1986, although it left open the complaint with regard to General Gustavo Alvarez Martínez, who was declared a defendant in absence. (see para 9 above)

75 Although the Government did not dispute that the above remedies had been brought, it maintained that the Commission should not have found the petition admissible, much less submitted it to the Court, because of the failure to exhaust the remedies provided by Honduran law, given that there are no final decisions in the record that show the contrary. It stated that the first writ of *habeas corpus* was declared void because the person bringing it did not follow through; regarding the second and third, the Government explained that additional writs cannot be brought on the same subject, the same facts, and based on the same legal provisions. As to the criminal complaints, the Government stated that no evidence had been submitted and, although presumptions had been raised, no proof had been offered and that the proceeding was still before Honduran courts until those guilty were specifically identified. It stated that one of the proceedings was dismissed for lack of evidence with respect to those accused who appeared before the court, but not with regard to General Alvarez Martínez, who was out of the country. Moreover, the Government maintained that dismissal does not exhaust domestic remedies because the extraordinary remedies of *amparo*, rehearing and cassation may be invoked and, in the instant case, the statute of limitations has not yet run, so the proceeding is pending.

76 The record (*infra* Chapter V) contains testimony of members of the Legislative Assembly of Honduras, Honduran lawyers, persons who were at one time disappeared, and relatives of disappeared persons, which purports to show that in the period in which the events took place, the legal remedies in Honduras were ineffective in obtaining the liberty of victims of a practice of enforced or involuntary disappearances (hereinafter "disappearance" or "disappearances"), ordered or tolerated by the Government. The record also contains dozens of newspaper clippings which allude to the same practice. According to that evidence, from 1981 to 1984 more than one hundred persons were illegally detained, many of whom never reappeared, and, in general, the

legal remedies which the Government claimed were available to the victims were ineffective.

77 That evidence also shows that some individuals were captured and detained without due process and subsequently reappeared. However, in some of those cases, the reappearances were not the result of any of the legal remedies which, according to the Government, would have been effective, but rather the result of other circumstances, such as the intervention of diplomatic missions or actions of human rights organizations.

78 The evidence offered shows that lawyers who filed writs of *habeas corpus* were intimidated, that those who were responsible for executing the writs were frequently prevented from entering or inspecting the places of detention, and that occasional criminal complaints against military or police officials were ineffective, either because certain procedural steps were not taken or because the complaints were dismissed without further proceedings.

79 The Government had the opportunity to call its own witnesses to refute the evidence presented by the Commission, but failed to do so. Although the Government's attorneys contested some of the points urged by the Commission, they did not offer convincing evidence to support their arguments. The Court summoned as witnesses some members of the armed forces mentioned during the proceeding, but their testimony was insufficient to overcome the weight of the evidence offered by the Commission to show that the judicial and governmental authorities did not act with due diligence in cases of disappearances. The instant case is such an example.

80 The testimony and other evidence received and not refuted leads to the conclusion that, during the period under consideration, although there may have been legal remedies in Honduras that theoretically allowed a person detained by the authorities to be found, those remedies were ineffective in cases of disappearances because the imprisonment was clandestine; formal requirements made them inapplicable in practice; the authorities against whom they were brought simply ignored them, or because attorneys and judges were threatened and intimidated by those authorities.

81 Aside from the question of whether between 1981 and 1984 there was a governmental policy of carrying out or tolerating the disappearance of certain persons, the Commission has shown that although writs of *habeas corpus* and criminal complaints were filed, they were ineffective or were mere formalities. The evidence offered by the Commission was not refuted and is sufficient to reject the Government's preliminary objection that the case is inadmissible because domestic remedies were not exhausted.

82 The Commission presented testimony and documentary evidence to show that there were many kidnappings and disappearances in Honduras from 1981 to 1984 and that those acts were attributable to the Armed Forces of Honduras (hereinafter "Armed Forces"), which was able to rely at least on the tolerance of the Government. Three officers of the Armed Forces testified on this subject at the request of the Court.

[...]*

---

*   **Eds:** paragraphs 83 to 106 set out the testimony of various witnesses as to the manner in which they had been kidnapped, imprisoned in clandestine jails and tortured, the fact that somewhere between 112 and 130 individuals were disappeared from 1981 to 1984, the existence of a special unit within the Armed Forces which carried out disappearances, the existence of secret jails and specially chosen places for the burial of those executed, and the *modus operandi* of the practice of disappearances. The Government either denied the truth of the relevant testimony, or sought to discredit it on the basis of alleged incompetency or lack of impartiality.

107 According to the testimony of his sister, eyewitnesses to the kidnapping of Manfredo Velásquez told her that he was detained on 12 September 1981, between 4:30 and 5:00 p.m., in a parking lot in downtown Tegucigalpa by seven heavily-armed men dressed in civilian clothes (one of them being First Sgt. José Isaías Vilorio), who used a white Ford without license plates (testimony of Zenaida Velásquez. See also testimony of Ramón Custodio López).

108 This witness informed the Court that Col Leonidas Torres Arias, who had been head of Honduran military intelligence, announced in a press conference in Mexico City that Manfredo Velásquez was kidnapped by a special squadron commanded by Capt Alexander Hernández, who was carrying out the direct orders of General Gustavo Alvarez Martínez (testimony of Zenaida Velásquez).

109 Lt Col Hernández testified that he never received any order to detain Manfredo Velásquez and had never worked in police operations (testimony of Alexander Hernández).

110 The Government objected, under Article 37 of the Rules of Procedure, to the testimony of Zenaida Velásquez because, as sister of the victim, she was a party interested in the outcome of the case.

111 The Court unanimously rejected the objection because it considered the fact that the witness was the victim's sister to be insufficient to disqualify her. The Court reserved the right to consider her testimony.

112 The Government asserted that her testimony was irrelevant because it did not refer to the case before the Court and that what she related about the kidnapping of her brother was not her personal knowledge but rather hearsay.

113 The former member of the Armed Forces who claimed to have belonged to the group that carried out kidnappings told the Court that, although he did not take part in the kidnapping of Manfredo Velásquez, Lt Flores Murillo had told him what had happened. According to this testimony, Manfredo Velásquez was kidnapped in downtown Tegucigalpa in an operation in which Sgt José Isaías Vilorio, men using the pseudonyms Ezequiel and Titanio, and Lt Flores Murillo himself, took part. The Lieutenant told him that during the struggle Ezequiel's gun went off and wounded Manfredo in the leg. They took the victim to INDUMIL (Military Industries) where they tortured him. They then turned him over to those in charge of carrying out executions who, at the orders of General Alvarez, Chief of the Armed Forces, took him out of Tegucigalpa and killed him with a knife and machete. They dismembered his body and buried the remains in different places (testimony of Florencio Caballero).

114 The current Director of Intelligence testified that Jose Isaías Vilorio was a file clerk of the DNI. He said he did not know Lt Flores Murillo and stated that INDUMIL had never been used as a detention center (testimony of Roberto Núñez Montes).

115 One witness testified that he was taken prisoner on 29 September 1981 by five or six persons who identified themselves as members of the Armed Forces and took him to the offices of DNI. They blindfolded him and took him in a car to an unknown place, where they tortured him. On 1 October 1981, while he was being held, he heard a moaning and pained voice through a hole in the door to an adjoining room. The person identified himself as Manfredo Velásquez and asked for help. According to the testimony of the witness, at that moment Lt Ramón Mejía came in and hit him because he found him standing up, although the witness told the Lieutenant that he had gotten up because he was tired. He added that, subsequently, Sgt Carlos Alfredo Martínez, whom he had met

at the bar where he worked, told him they had turned Manfredo Velásquez over to members of Battalion 316 (testimony of Leopoldo Aguilar Villalobos).

116 The Government asserted that the testimony of this witness "is not completely trustworthy because of discrepancies that should not be overlooked, such as the fact that he had testified that he had only been arrested once, in 1981, for trafficking in arms and hijacking a plane, when the truth was that Honduran police had arrested him on several occasions because of his unenviable record."

117 The Commission also presented evidence to show that from 1981 to 1984 domestic judicial remedies in Honduras were ineffective in protecting human rights, especially the rights of disappeared persons to life, liberty and personal integrity.

118 The Court heard the following testimony with respect to this point:

(a) The legal procedures of Honduras were ineffective in ascertaining the whereabouts of detainees and ensuring respect for their physical and moral integrity. When writs of *habeas corpus* were brought, the courts were slow to name judges to execute them and, once named, those judges were often ignored by police authorities. On several occasions, the authorities denied the detentions, even in cases in which the prisoners were later released. There were no judicial orders for the arrests and the places of detention were unknown. When writs of *habeas corpus* were formalized, the police authorities did not present the persons named in the writs (testimony of Miguel Angel Pavón Salazar, Ramón Custodio López, Milton Jiménez Puerto and Efraín Díaz Arrivillaga).

(b) The judges named by the Courts of Justice to execute the writs did not enjoy all the necessary guarantees. Moreover, they feared reprisals because they were often threatened. Judges were imprisoned on more than one occasion and some of them were physically mistreated by the authorities. Law professors and lawyers who defended political prisoners were pressured not to act in cases of human rights violations. Only two dared bring writs of *habeas corpus* on behalf of disappeared persons and one of those was arrested while he was filing a writ (testimony of Milton Jiménez Puerto, Miguel Angel Pavón Salazar, Ramón Custodio López, Cesar Augusto Murillo, René Velásquez Díaz and Zenaida Velásquez).

(c) In no case between 1981 and 1984 did a writ of *habeas corpus* on behalf of a disappeared person prove effective. If some individuals did reappear, this was not the result of such a legal remedy (testimony of Miguel Angel Pavón Salazar, Inés Consuelo Murillo, Cesar Augusto Murillo, Milton Jiménez Puerto, René Velásquez Díaz and Virgilio Carías).

119 The testimony and documentary evidence, corroborated by press clippings, presented by the Commission, tend to show:

(a) That there existed in Honduras from 1981 to 1984 a systematic and selective practice of disappearances carried out with the assistance or tolerance of the Government;

(b) That Manfredo Velásquez was a victim of that practice and was kidnapped and presumably tortured, executed and clandestinely buried by agents of the Armed Forces of Honduras; and

(c) That in the period in which those acts occurred, the legal remedies available in Honduras were not appropriate or effective to guarantee his rights to life, liberty and personal integrity.

120 The Government, in turn, submitted documents and based its argument on the testimony of three members of the Honduran Armed Forces, two of whom were summoned by the Court because they had been identified in the proceedings as directly involved in the general practice referred to and in the disappearance of Manfredo Velásquez. This evidence may be summarized as follows:

(a) The testimony purports to explain the organization and functioning of the security forces accused of carrying out the specific acts and denies any knowledge of or personal involvement in the acts of the officers who testified;

(b) Some documents purport to show that no civil suit had been brought to establish a presumption of the death of Manfredo Velásquez; and

(c) Other documents purport to prove that the Supreme Court of Honduras received and acted upon some writs of *habeas corpus* and that some of those writs resulted in the release of the persons on whose behalf they were brought.

121 The record contains no other direct evidence, such as expert opinion, inspections or reports.

[Standard of proof in international jurisprudence]

122 Before weighing the evidence, the Court must address some questions regarding the burden of proof and the general criteria considered in its evaluation and finding of the facts in the instant proceeding.

123 Because the Commission is accusing the Government of the disappearance of Manfredo Velásquez, it, in principle, should bear the burden of proving the facts underlying its petition.

124 The Commission's argument relies upon the proposition that the policy of disappearances, supported or tolerated by the Government, is designed to conceal and destroy evidence of disappearances. When the existence of such a policy or practice has been shown, the disappearance of a particular individual may be proved through circumstantial or indirect evidence or by logical inference. Otherwise, it would be impossible to prove that an individual has been disappeared.

125 The Government did not object to the Commission's approach. Nevertheless, it argued that neither the existence of a practice of disappearances in Honduras nor the participation of Honduran officials in the alleged disappearance of Manfredo Velásquez had been proven.

126 The Court finds no reason to consider the Commission's argument inadmissible. If it can be shown that there was an official practice of disappearances in Honduras, carried out by the Government or at least tolerated by it, and if the disappearance of Manfredo Velásquez can be linked to that practice, the Commission's allegations will have been proven to the Court's satisfaction, so long as the evidence presented on both points meets the standard of proof required in cases such as this.

127 The Court must determine what the standards of proof should be in the instant case. Neither the Convention, the Statute of the Court, nor its Rules of Procedure speak to this matter. Nevertheless, international jurisprudence has recognized the power of the courts to weigh the evidence freely, although it has always avoided a rigid rule regarding the amount of proof necessary to support the judgment (See *Corfu Channel*, Merits, Judgment, ICJ Reports 1949; *Military and Paramilitary Activities in and against Nicaragua (Nicaragua v United States of America)*, Merits, Judgment, ICJ Reports 1986, paras 29–30 and 59–60).

128 The standards of proof are less formal in an international legal proceeding than in a domestic one. The latter recognize different burdens of proof, depending upon the nature, character and seriousness of the case.

129 The Court cannot ignore the special seriousness of finding that a State Party to the Convention has carried out or has tolerated a practice of disappearances in its territory. This requires the Court to apply a standard of proof which considers the seriousness of the charge and which, notwithstanding what has already been said, is capable of establishing the truth of the allegations in a convincing manner.

130 The practice of international and domestic courts shows that direct evidence, whether testimonial or documentary, is not the only type of evidence that may be legitimately considered in reaching a decision. Circumstantial evidence, indicia, and presumptions may be considered, so long as they lead to conclusions consistent with the facts.

131 Circumstantial or presumptive evidence is especially important in allegations of disappearances, because this type of repression is characterized by an attempt to suppress all information about the kidnapping or the whereabouts and fate of the victim.

132 Since this Court is an international tribunal, it has its own specialized procedures. All the elements of domestic legal procedures are therefore not automatically applicable.

133 The above principle is generally valid in international proceedings, but is particularly applicable in human rights cases.

134 The international protection of human rights should not be confused with criminal justice. States do not appear before the Court as defendants in a criminal action. The objective of international human rights law is not to punish those individuals who are guilty of violations, but rather to protect the victims and to provide for the reparation of damages resulting from the acts of the States responsible.

135 In contrast to domestic criminal law, in proceedings to determine human rights violations the State cannot rely on the defense that the complainant has failed to present evidence when it cannot be obtained without the State's cooperation.

136 The State controls the means to verify acts occurring within its territory. Although the Commission has investigatory powers, it cannot exercise them within a State's jurisdiction unless it has the cooperation of that State.

137 Since the Government only offered some documentary evidence in support of its preliminary objections, but none on the merits, the Court must reach its decision without the valuable assistance of a more active participation by Honduras, which might otherwise have resulted in a more adequate presentation of its case.

138 The manner in which the Government conducted its defense would have sufficed to prove many of the Commission's allegations by virtue of the principle that the silence of the accused or elusive or ambiguous answers on its part may be interpreted as an acknowledgment of the truth of the allegations, so long as the contrary is not indicated by the record or is not compelled as a matter of law. This result would not hold under criminal law, which does not apply in the instant case (see paras 134 and 135 above). The Court tried to compensate for this procedural principle by admitting all the evidence offered, even if it was untimely, and by ordering the presentation of additional evidence. This was done, of course, without prejudice to its discretion to consider the silence or inaction of Honduras or to its duty to evaluate the evidence as a whole.

139 In its own proceedings and without prejudice to its having considered other elements of proof, the Commission invoked Article 42 of its Regulations, which reads as follows:

> The facts reported in the petition whose pertinent parts have been transmitted to the Government of the State in reference shall be presumed to be true if, during the maximum period set by the Commission under the provisions of Article 34 paragraph 5, the Government has not provided the pertinent information, as long as other evidence does not lead to a different conclusion.

Because the Government did not object here to the use of this legal presumption in the proceedings before the Commission and since the Government fully participated in these proceedings, Article 42 is irrelevant here.

140 In the instant case, the Court accepts the validity of the documents presented by the Commission and by Honduras, particularly because the parties did not oppose or object to those documents nor did they question their authenticity or veracity.

141 During the hearings, the Government objected, under Article 37 of the Rules of Procedure, to the testimony of witnesses called by the Commission. By decision of 6 October, 1987, the Court rejected the challenge, holding as follows:

> b   The objection refers to circumstances under which, according to the Government, the testimony of these witnesses might not be objective.
>
> c   It is within the Court's discretion, when rendering judgment, to weigh the evidence.
>
> d   A violation of the human rights set out in the Convention is established by facts found by the Court, not by the method of proof.
>
> ...
>
> f   When testimony is questioned, the challenging party has the burden of refuting that testimony.

142 During cross-examination, the Government's attorneys attempted to show that some witnesses were not impartial because of ideological reasons, origin or nationality, family relations, or a desire to discredit Honduras. They even insinuated that testifying against the State in these proceedings was disloyal to the nation. Likewise, they cited criminal records or pending charges to show that some witnesses were not competent to testify (see paras 86, 88, 90, 92, 101, 110 and 116 above).

143 It is true, of course, that certain factors may clearly influence a witness' truthfulness. However, the Government did not present any concrete evidence to show that the witnesses had not told the truth, but rather limited itself to making general observations regarding their alleged incompetency or lack of impartiality. This is insufficient to rebut testimony which is fundamentally consistent with that of other witnesses. The Court cannot ignore such testimony.

144 Moreover, some of the Government's arguments are unfounded within the context of human rights law. The insinuation that persons who, for any reason, resort to the Inter-American system for the protection of human rights are disloyal to their country is unacceptable and cannot constitute a basis for any penalty or negative consequence. Human rights are higher values that "are not derived from the fact that (an individual) is a national of a certain state, but are based upon attributes of his human personality"(American Declaration of the Rights and Duties of Man, Whereas clauses, and American Convention, Preamble).

145 Neither is it sustainable that having a criminal record or charges pending is sufficient in and of itself to find that a witness is not competent to testify in Court. As the Court ruled, in its decision of 6 October 1987, in the instant case:

> under the American Convention on Human Rights, it is impermissible to deny a witness, *a priori*, the possibility of testifying to facts relevant to a matter before the Court, even if he has an interest in that proceeding, because he has been prosecuted or even convicted under internal laws.

146 Many of the press clippings offered by the Commission cannot be considered as documentary evidence as such. However, many of them contain public and well-known facts which, as such, do not require proof; others are of evidentiary value, as has been recognized in international jurisprudence (*Military and Paramilitary Activities in and against Nicaragua*, see para 127 and paras 62–64 above), insofar as they textually reproduce public statements, especially those of high-ranking members of the Armed Forces, of the Government, or even of the Supreme Court of Honduras, such as some of those made by the President of the latter. Finally, others are important as a whole insofar as they corroborate testimony regarding the responsibility of the Honduran military and police for disappearances.

[Forced disappearances]

147 The Court now turns to the relevant facts that it finds to have been proven. They are as follows:

(a) During the period 1981 to 1984, 100 to 150 persons disappeared in the Republic of Honduras, and many were never heard from again (testimony of Miguel Angel Pavón Salazar, Ramón Custodio López, Efraín Díaz Arrivillaga, Florencio Caballero and press clippings).

(b) Those disappearances followed a similar pattern, beginning with the kidnapping of the victims by force, often in broad daylight and in public places, by armed men in civilian clothes and disguises, who acted with apparent impunity and who used vehicles without any official identification, with tinted windows and with false license plates or no plates (testimony of Miguel Angel Pavón Salazar, Ramón Custodio López, Efraín Díaz Arrivillaga, Florencio Caballero and press clippings).

(c) It was public and notorious knowledge in Honduras that the kidnappings were carried out by military personnel or the police, or persons acting under their orders (testimony of Miguel Angel Pavón Salazar, Ramón Custodio López, Efraín Díaz Arrivillaga, Florencio Caballero and press clippings).

(d) The disappearances were carried out in a systematic manner, regarding which the Court considers the following circumstances particularly relevant:

   (i) The victims were usually persons whom Honduran officials considered dangerous to State security (testimony of Miguel Angel Pavón Salazar, Ramón Custodio López, Efraín Díaz Arrivillaga, Florencio Caballero, Virgilio Carías, Milton Jiménez Puerto, René Velásquez Díaz, Inés Consuelo Murillo, José Gonzalo Flores Trejo, Zenaida Velásquez, Cesar Augusto Murillo and press clippings). In addition, the victims had usually been under surveillance for long periods of time (testimony of Ramón Custodio López and Florencio Caballero);

   (ii) The arms employed were reserved for the official use of the military and police, and the vehicles used had tinted glass, which requires special official authorization. In some cases, Government agents carried out the detentions openly and without any pretense or disguise; in others, Government agents had cleared the areas where the kidnappings were to take place and, on at least one occasion, when Government agents stopped the kidnappers they were allowed to continue freely on their way after showing their identification (testimony of Miguel Angel Pavón Salazar, Ramón Custodio López and Florencio Caballero);

(iii) The kidnappers blindfolded the victims, took them to secret, unofficial detention centers and moved them from one center to another. They interrogated the victims and subjected them to cruel and humiliating treatment and torture. Some were ultimately murdered and their bodies were buried in clandestine cemeteries (testimony of Miguel Angel Pavón Salazar, Ramón Custodio López, Florencio Caballero, René Velásquez Díaz, Inés Consuelo Murillo and José Gonzalo Flores Trejo);

(iv) When queried by relatives, lawyers and persons or entities interested in the protection of human rights, or by judges charged with executing writs of *habeas corpus*, the authorities systematically denied any knowledge of the detentions or the whereabouts or fate of the victims. That attitude was seen even in the cases of persons who later reappeared in the hands of the same authorities who had systematically denied holding them or knowing their fate (testimony of Inés Consuelo Murillo, José Gonzalo Flores Trejo, Efraín Díaz Arrivillaga, Florencio Caballero, Virgilio Carías, Milton Jiménez Puerto, René Velásquez Diaz, Zenaida Velásquez, Cesar Augusto Murillo and press clippings);

(v) Military and police officials as well as those from the Executive and Judicial Branches either denied the disappearances or were incapable of preventing or investigating them, punishing those responsible, or helping those interested discover the whereabouts and fate of the victims or the location of their remains. The investigative committees created by the Government and the Armed Forces did not produce any results. The judicial proceedings brought were processed slowly with a clear lack of interest and some were ultimately dismissed (testimony of Inés Consuelo Murillo, José Gonzalo Flores Trejo, Efraín Díaz Arrivillaga, Florencio Caballero, Virgilio Carías, Milton Jiménez Puerto, René Velásquez Díaz, Zenaida Velásquez, César Augusto Murillo and press clippings);

(e) On 12 September 1981, between 4:30 and 5:00 pm, several heavily-armed men in civilian clothes driving a white Ford without license plates kidnapped Manfredo Velásquez from a parking lot in downtown Tegucigalpa. Today, nearly seven years later, he remains disappeared, which creates a reasonable presumption that he is dead (testimony of Miguel Angel Pavón Salazar, Ramón Custodio López, Zenaida Velásquez, Florencio Caballero, Leopoldo Aguilar Villalobos and press clippings).

(f) Persons connected with the Armed Forces or under its direction carried out that kidnapping (testimony of Ramón Custodio López, Zenaida Velásquez, Florencio Caballero, Leopoldo Aguilar Villalobos and press clippings).

(g) The kidnapping and disappearance of Manfredo Velásquez falls within the systematic practice of disappearances referred to by the facts deemed proved in paragraphs (a) to (d). To wit:

(i) Manfredo Velásquez was a student who was involved in activities the authorities considered "dangerous" to national security (testimony of Miguel Angel Pavón Salazar, Ramón Custodio López and Zenaida Velásquez).

(ii) The kidnapping of Manfredo Velásquez was carried out in broad daylight by men in civilian clothes who used a vehicle without license plates.

(iii) In the case of Manfredo Velásquez, there were the same type of denials by his captors and the Armed Forces, the same omissions of the latter and of the Government in investigating and revealing his whereabouts, and the same ineffectiveness of the courts where three writs of *habeas corpus* and two criminal complaints were brought (testimony of Miguel Angel Pavón Salazar, Ramón Custodio López, Zenaida Velásquez, press clippings and documentary evidence).

(h) There is no evidence in the record that Manfredo Velásquez had disappeared in order to join subversive groups, other than a letter from the Mayor of Langue, which contained rumors to that effect. The letter itself shows that the Government associated him with activities it considered a threat to national security. However, the Government did not corroborate the view expressed in the letter with any other evidence. Nor is there any evidence that he was kidnapped by common criminals or other persons unrelated to the practice of disappearances existing at that time.

148 Based upon the above, the Court finds that the following facts have been proven in this proceeding: (1) a practice of disappearances carried out or tolerated by Honduran officials existed between 1981 and 1984; (2) Manfredo Velásquez disappeared at the hands of, or with the acquiescence of those officials within the framework of that practice; and (3) the Government of Honduras failed to guarantee the human rights affected by that practice.

149 Disappearances are not new in the history of human rights violations. However, their systematic and repeated nature and their use not only for causing certain individuals to disappear, either briefly or permanently, but also as a means of creating a general state of anguish, insecurity and fear, is a recent phenomenon. Although this practice exists virtually worldwide, it has occurred with exceptional intensity in Latin America in the last few years.

150 The phenomenon of disappearances is a complex form of human rights violation that must be understood and confronted in an integral fashion.

151 The establishment of a Working Group on Enforced or Involuntary Disappearances of the United Nations Commission on Human Rights, by Resolution 20 (XXXVI) of 29 February, 1980, is a clear demonstration of general censure and repudiation of the practice of disappearances, which had already received world attention at the UN General Assembly (Resolution 33/173 of 20 December 1978), the Economic and Social Council (Resolution 1979/38 of 10 May 1979) and the Subcommission for the Prevention of Discrimination and Protection of Minorities (Resolution 5B (XXXII) of 5 September 1979). The reports of the rapporteurs or special envoys of the Commission on Human Rights show concern that the practice of disappearances be stopped, the victims reappear and that those responsible be punished.

152 Within the Inter-American system, the General Assembly of the Organization of American States (OAS) and the Commission have repeatedly referred to the practice of disappearances and have urged that disappearances be investigated and that the practice be stopped (AG/RES 443 (IX-0/79) of 31 October 1979; AG/RES 510 (X-0/80) of 27 November 1980; AG/RES 618 (XII-0/82) of 20 November 1982; AG/RES 666 (XIII-0/83) of 18 November 1983; AG/RES 742 (XIV-0/84) of 17 November 1984 and AG/RES 890 (XVII-0/87) of 14 November 1987; Inter-American Commission on Human Rights: Annual Report 1978, pp 24–27; Annual Report, 1980–1981, pp 113–114; Annual Report, 1982–1983, pp 46–47; Annual Report, 1985–1986, pp 37–40; Annual Report, 1986–1987, pp 277–284 and in many of its Country Reports, such as OEA/Ser L/V/II.49, doc 19, 1980 (Argentina); OEA/Ser L/V/II.66, doc 17, 1985 (Chile) and OEA/Ser L/V/II.66, doc 16, 1985 (Guatemala)).

153 International practice and doctrine have often categorized disappearances as a crime against humanity, although there is no treaty in force which is applicable to the States Parties to the Convention and which uses this terminology (Inter-American Yearbook on Human Rights, 1985, pp. 368, 686 and 1102). The General Assembly of the OAS has

resolved that it "is an affront to the conscience of the hemisphere and constitutes a crime against humanity"(AG/RES 666, *supra*) and that "this practice is cruel and inhuman, mocks the rule of law, and undermines those norms which guarantee protection against arbitrary detention and the right to personal security and safety"(AG/RES 742, *supra*).

154 Without question, the State has the right and duty to guarantee its security. It is also indisputable that all societies suffer some deficiencies in their legal orders. However, regardless of the seriousness of certain actions and the culpability of the perpetrators of certain crimes, the power of the State is not unlimited, nor may the State resort to any means to attain its ends. The State is subject to law and morality. Disrespect for human dignity cannot serve as the basis for any State action.

155 The forced disappearance of human beings is a multiple and continuous violation of many rights under the Convention that the States Parties are obligated to respect and guarantee. The kidnapping of a person is an arbitrary deprivation of liberty, an infringement of a detainee's right to be taken without delay before a judge and to invoke the appropriate procedures to review the legality of the arrest, all in violation of Article 7 of the Convention which recognizes the right to personal liberty by providing that:

1   Every person has the right to personal liberty and security.

2   No one shall be deprived of his physical liberty except for the reasons and under the conditions established beforehand by the constitution of the State Party concerned or by a law established pursuant thereto.

3   No one shall be subject to arbitrary arrest or imprisonment.

4   Anyone who is detained shall be informed of the reasons for his detention and shall be promptly notified of the charge or charges against him.

5   Any person detained shall be brought promptly before a judge or other officer authorized by law to exercise judicial power and shall be entitled to trial within a reasonable time or to be released without prejudice to the continuation of the proceedings. His release may be subject to guarantees to assure his appearance for trial.

6   Anyone who is deprived of his liberty shall be entitled to recourse to a competent court, in order that the court may decide without delay on the lawfulness of his arrest or detention and order his release if the arrest or detention is unlawful. In States Parties whose laws provide that anyone who believes himself to be threatened with deprivation of his liberty is entitled to recourse to a competent court in order that it may decide on the lawfulness of such threat, this remedy may not be restricted or abolished. The interested party or another person in his behalf is entitled to seek these remedies.

156 Moreover, prolonged isolation and deprivation of communication are in themselves cruel and inhuman treatment, harmful to the psychological and moral integrity of the person and a violation of the right of any detainee to respect for his inherent dignity as a human being. Such treatment, therefore, violates Article 5 of the Convention, which recognizes the right to the integrity of the person by providing that:

1   Every person has the right to have his physical, mental, and moral integrity respected.

2   No-one shall be subjected to torture or to cruel inhuman, or degrading punishment or treatment. All persons deprived of their liberty shall be treated with respect for the inherent dignity of the human person.

In addition, investigations into the practice of disappearances and the testimony of victims who have regained their liberty show that those who are disappeared are often subjected to merciless treatment, including all types of indignities, torture and other cruel, inhuman and degrading treatment, in violation of the right to physical integrity recognized in Article 5 of the Convention.

157 The practice of disappearances often involves secret execution without trial, followed by concealment of the body to eliminate any material evidence of the crime and to ensure the impunity of those responsible. This is a flagrant violation of the right to life, recognized in Article 4 of the Convention, the first clause of which reads as follows:

1   Every person has the right to have his life respected. This right shall be protected by law and, in general, from the moment of conception. No one shall be arbitrarily deprived of his life.

158 The practice of disappearances, in addition to directly violating many provisions of the Convention, such as those noted above, constitutes a radical breach of the treaty in that it shows a crass abandonment of the values which emanate from the concept of human dignity and of the most basic principles of the Inter-American system and the Convention. The existence of this practice, moreover, evinces a disregard of the duty to organize the State in such a manner as to guarantee the rights recognized in the Convention, as set out below.

[State responsibility]

159 The Commission has asked the Court to find that Honduras has violated the rights guaranteed to Manfredo Velasquez by Articles 4, 5 and 7 of the Convention. The Government has denied the charges and seeks to be absolved.

160 This requires the Court to examine the conditions under which a particular act, which violates one of the rights recognized by the Convention, can be imputed to a State Party thereby establishing its international responsibility.

161 Article 1(1) of the Convention provides:

Article 1. Obligation to Respect Rights

1   The States Parties to this Convention undertake to respect the rights and freedoms recognized herein and to ensure to all persons subject to their jurisdiction the free and full exercise of those rights and freedoms, without any discrimination for reasons of race, color, sex, language, religion, political or other opinion, national or social origin, economic status, birth, or any other social condition.

162 This article specifies the obligation assumed by the States Parties in relation to each of the rights protected. Each claim alleging that one of those rights has been infringed necessarily implies that Article 1(1) of the Convention has also been violated.

163 The Commission did not specifically allege the violation of Article 1(1) of the Convention, but that does not preclude the Court from applying it. The precept contained therein constitutes the generic basis of the protection of the rights recognized by the Convention and would be applicable, in any case, by virtue of a general principle of law, *iura novit curia*, on which international jurisprudence has repeatedly relied and under which a court has the power and the duty to apply the juridical provisions relevant to a proceeding, even when the parties do not expressly invoke them ("*Lotus*" judgment No 9, 1927, PCIJ, Series A, No 10, p 31 and Eur Court HR, *Handyside* case, judgment of 7 December 1976, Series A, No 24, para 41).

164 Article 1(1) is essential in determining whether a violation of the human rights recognized by the Convention can be imputed to a State Party. In effect, that article

charges the States Parties with the fundamental duty to respect and guarantee the rights recognized in the Convention. Any impairment of those rights which can be attributed under the rules of international law to the action or omission of any public authority constitutes an act imputable to the State, which assumes responsibility in the terms provided by the Convention.

165 The first obligation assumed by the States Parties under Article 1(1) is "to respect the rights and freedoms" recognized by the Convention. The exercise of public authority has certain limits which derive from the fact that human rights are inherent attributes of human dignity and are, therefore, superior to the power of the State. On another occasion, this Court stated:

> The protection of human rights, particularly the civil and political rights set forth in the Convention, is in effect based on the affirmation of the existence of certain inviolable attributes of the individual that cannot be legitimately restricted through the exercise of governmental power. These are individual domains that are beyond the reach of the State or to which the State has but limited access. Thus, the protection of human rights must necessarily comprise the concept of the restriction of the exercise of state power (*The word "laws" in Article 30 of the American Convention on Human Rights*, Advisory Opinion OC-6/86 of 9 May 1986, Series A, No 6, para 21).

166 The second obligation of the States Parties is to "ensure" the free and full exercise of the rights recognized by the Convention to every person subject to its jurisdiction. This obligation implies the duty of the States Parties to organize the governmental apparatus and, in general, all the structures through which public power is exercised, so that they are capable of juridically ensuring the free and full enjoyment of human rights. As a consequence of this obligation, the States must prevent, investigate and punish any violation of the rights recognized by the Convention and, moreover, if possible attempt to restore the right violated and provide compensation as warranted for damages resulting from the violation.

167 The obligation to ensure the free and full exercise of human rights is not fulfilled by the existence of a legal system designed to make it possible to comply with this obligation – it also requires the government to conduct itself so as to effectively ensure the free and full exercise of human rights.

168 The obligation of the States is, thus, much more direct than that contained in Article 2, which reads:

> Article 2. Domestic Legal Effects

> Where the exercise of any of the rights or freedoms referred to in Article 1 is not already ensured by legislative or other provisions, the States Parties undertake to adopt, in accordance with their constitutional processes and the provisions of this Convention, such legislative or other measures as may be necessary to give effect to those rights or freedoms.

169 According to Article 1(1), any exercise of public power that violates the rights recognized by the Convention is illegal. Whenever a State organ, official or public entity violates one of those rights, this constitutes a failure of the duty to respect the rights and freedoms set forth in the Convention.

170 This conclusion is independent of whether the organ or official has contravened provisions of internal law or overstepped the limits of his authority: under international law a State is responsible for the acts of its agents undertaken in their official capacity and for their omissions, even when those agents act outside the sphere of their authority or violate internal law.

171 This principle suits perfectly the nature of the Convention, which is violated whenever public power is used to infringe the rights recognized therein. If acts of public power that exceed the State's authority or are illegal under its own laws were not considered to compromise that State's obligation under the treaty, the system of protection provided for in the Convention would be illusory.

172 Thus, in principle, any violation of rights recognized by the Convention carried out by an act of public authority or by persons who use their position of authority is imputable to the State. However, this does not define all the circumstances in which a State is obligated to prevent, investigate and punish human rights violations, nor all the cases in which the State might be found responsible for an infringement of those rights. An illegal act which violates human rights and which is initially not directly imputable to a State (for example, because it is the act of a private person or because the person responsible has not been identified) can lead to international responsibility of the State, not because of the act itself, but because of the lack of due diligence to prevent the violation or to respond to it as required by the Convention.

173 Violations of the Convention cannot be founded upon rules that take psychological factors into account in establishing individual culpability. For the purposes of analysis, the intent or motivation of the agent who has violated the rights recognized by the Convention is irrelevant – the violation can be established even if the identity of the individual perpetrator is unknown. What is decisive is whether a violation of the rights recognized by the Convention has occurred with the support or the acquiescence of the government, or whether the State has allowed the act to take place without taking measures to prevent it or to punish those responsible. Thus, the Court's task is to determine whether the violation is the result of a State's failure to fulfill its duty to respect and guarantee those rights, as required by Article 1(1) of the Convention.

174 The State has a legal duty to take reasonable steps to prevent human rights violations and to use the means at its disposal to carry out a serious investigation of violations committed within its jurisdiction, to identify those responsible, to impose the appropriate punishment and to ensure the victim adequate compensation.

175 This duty to prevent includes all those means of a legal, political, administrative and cultural nature that promote the protection of human rights and ensure that any violations are considered and treated as illegal acts, which, as such, may lead to the punishment of those responsible and the obligation to indemnify the victims for damages. It is not possible to make a detailed list of all such measures, since they vary with the law and the conditions of each State Party. Of course, while the State is obligated to prevent human rights abuses, the existence of a particular violation does not, in itself, prove the failure to take preventive measures. On the other hand, subjecting a person to official, repressive bodies that practice torture and assassination with impunity is itself a breach of the duty to prevent violations of the rights to life and physical integrity of the person, even if that particular person is not tortured or assassinated, or if those facts cannot be proven in a concrete case.

176 The State is obligated to investigate every situation involving a violation of the rights protected by the Convention. If the State apparatus acts in such a way that the violation goes unpunished and the victim's full enjoyment of such rights is not restored as soon as possible, the State has failed to comply with its duty to ensure the free and full exercise of those rights to the persons within its jurisdiction. The same is true when the State allows private persons or groups to act freely and with impunity to the detriment of the rights recognized by the Convention.

177 In certain circumstances, it may be difficult to investigate acts that violate an individual's rights. The duty to investigate, like the duty to prevent, is not breached merely because the investigation does not produce a satisfactory result. Nevertheless, it must be undertaken in a serious manner and not as a mere formality preordained to be ineffective. An investigation must have an objective and be assumed by the State as its own legal duty, not as a step taken by private interests that depends upon the initiative of the victim or his family or upon their offer of proof, without an effective search for the truth by the government. This is true regardless of what agent is eventually found responsible for the violation. Where the acts of private parties that violate the Convention are not seriously investigated, those parties are aided in a sense by the government, thereby making the State responsible on the international plane.

[Involuntary disappearance of Manfred Velásquez]

178 In the instant case, the evidence shows a complete inability of the procedures of the State of Honduras, which were theoretically adequate, to carry out an investigation into the disappearance of Manfredo Velásquez, and of the fulfillment of its duties to pay compensation and punish those responsible, as set out in Article 1(1) of the Convention.

179 As the Court has verified above, the failure of the judicial system to act upon the writs brought before various tribunals in the instant case has been proven. Not one writ of *habeas corpus* was processed. No judge had access to the places where Manfredo Velásquez might have been detained. The criminal complaint was dismissed.

180 Nor did the organs of the Executive Branch carry out a serious investigation to establish the fate of Manfredo Velásquez. There was no investigation of public allegations of a practice of disappearances nor a determination of whether Manfredo Velásquez had been a victim of that practice. The Commission's requests for information were ignored to the point that the Commission had to presume, under Article 42 of its Regulations, that the allegations were true. The offer of an investigation in accord with Resolution 30/83 of the Commission resulted in an investigation by the Armed Forces, the same body accused of direct responsibility for the disappearances. This raises grave questions regarding the seriousness of the investigation. The Government often resorted to asking relatives of the victims to present conclusive proof of their allegations even though those allegations, because they involved crimes against the person, should have been investigated on the Government's own initiative in fulfillment of the State's duty to ensure public order. This is especially true when the allegations refer to a practice carried out within the Armed Forces, which, because of its nature, is not subject to private investigations. No proceeding was initiated to establish responsibility for the disappearance of Manfredo Velásquez and apply punishment under internal law. All of the above leads to the conclusion that the Honduran authorities did not take effective action to ensure respect for human rights within the jurisdiction of that State as required by Article 1(1) of the Convention.

181 The duty to investigate facts of this type continues as long as there is uncertainty about the fate of the person who has disappeared. Even in the hypothetical case that those individually responsible for crimes of this type cannot be legally punished under certain circumstances, the State is obligated to use the means at its disposal to inform the relatives of the fate of the victims and, if they have been killed, the location of their remains.

182 The Court is convinced, and has so found, that the disappearance of Manfredo Velásquez was carried out by agents who acted under cover of public authority.

However, even had that fact not been proven, the failure of the State apparatus to act, which is clearly proven, is a failure on the part of Honduras to fulfill the duties it assumed under Article 1(1) of the Convention, which obligated it to ensure Manfredo Velásquez the free and full exercise of his human rights.

183 The Court notes that the legal order of Honduras does not authorize such acts and that internal law defines them as crimes. The Court also recognizes that not all levels of the Government of Honduras were necessarily aware of those acts, nor is there any evidence that such acts were the result of official orders. Nevertheless, those circumstances are irrelevant for the purposes of establishing whether Honduras is responsible under international law for the violations of human rights perpetrated within the practice of disappearances.

184 According to the principle of the continuity of the State in international law, responsibility exists both independently of changes of government over a period of time and continuously from the time of the act that creates responsibility to the time when the act is declared illegal. The foregoing is also valid in the area of human rights although, from an ethical or political point of view, the attitude of the new government may be much more respectful of those rights than that of the government in power when the violations occurred.

185 The Court, therefore, concludes that the facts found in this proceeding show that the State of Honduras is responsible for the involuntary disappearance of Angel Manfredo Velásquez Rodríguez. Thus, Honduras has violated Articles 7, 5 and 4 of the Convention.

186 As a result of the disappearance, Manfredo Velásquez was the victim of an arbitrary detention, which deprived him of his physical liberty without legal cause and without a determination of the lawfulness of his detention by a judge or competent tribunal. Those acts directly violate the right to personal liberty recognized by Article 7 of the Convention (see para 155 above) and are a violation imputable to Honduras of the duties to respect and ensure that right under Article 1(1).

187 The disappearance of Manfredo Velásquez violates the right to personal integrity recognized by Article 5 of the Convention (see para 156 above). First, the mere subjection of an individual to prolonged isolation and deprivation of communication is in itself cruel and inhuman treatment which harms the psychological and moral integrity of the person, and violates the right of every detainee under Article 5(1) and 5(2) to treatment respectful of his dignity. Second, although it has not been directly shown that Manfredo Velásquez was physically tortured, his kidnapping and imprisonment by governmental authorities, who have been shown to subject detainees to indignities, cruelty and torture, constitute a failure of Honduras to fulfill the duty imposed by Article 1(1) to ensure the rights under Article 5(1) and 5(2) of the Convention. The guarantee of physical integrity and the right of detainees to treatment respectful of their human dignity require States Parties to take reasonable steps to prevent situations which are truly harmful to the rights protected.

188 The above reasoning is applicable to the right to life recognized by Article 4 of the Convention (see para 157 above). The context in which the disappearance of Manfredo Velasquez occurred and the lack of knowledge seven years later about his fate create a reasonable presumption that he was killed. Even if there is a minimal margin of doubt in this respect, it must be presumed that his fate was decided by authorities who systematically executed detainees without trial and concealed their bodies in order to avoid punishment. This, together with the failure to investigate, is a violation by Honduras of a legal duty under Article 1(1) of the Convention to ensure the rights

recognized by Article 4(1). That duty is to ensure to every person subject to its jurisdiction the inviolability of the right to life and the right not to have one's life taken arbitrarily. These rights imply an obligation on the part of States Parties to take reasonable steps to prevent situations that could result in the violation of that right.

[Remedies]

189 Article 63(1) of the Convention provides:

> If the Court finds that there has been a violation of a right or freedom protected by this Convention, the Court shall rule that the injured party be ensured the enjoyment of his right or freedom that was violated. It shall also rule, if appropriate, that the consequences of the measure or situation that constituted the breach of such right or freedom be remedied and that fair compensation be paid to the injured party.

Clearly, in the instant case the Court cannot order that the victim be guaranteed the enjoyment of the rights or freedoms violated. The Court, however, can rule that the consequences of the breach of the rights be remedied and that just compensation be paid.

190 During this proceeding the Commission requested the payment of compensation, but did not offer evidence regarding the amount of damages or the manner of payment. Neither did the parties discuss these matters.

191 The Court believes that the parties can agree on the damages. If an agreement cannot be reached, the Court shall award an amount. The case shall, therefore, remain open for that purpose. The Court reserves the right to approve the agreement and, in the event no agreement is reached, to set the amount and order the manner of payment.

192 The Rules of Procedure establish the legal procedural relations among the Commission, the State or States Parties in the case and the Court itself, which continue in effect until the case is no longer before the Court. As the case is still before the Court, the Government and the Commission should negotiate the agreement referred to in the preceding paragraph. The recipients of the award of damages will be the next-of-kin of the victim. This does not in any way imply a ruling on the meaning of the word "parties" in any other context under the Convention or the rules pursuant thereto.

193 With no pleading to support an award of costs, it is not proper for the Court to rule on them (Art. 45(1), Rules of Procedure).

194 Therefore, **THE COURT:**

Unanimously

1   Rejects the preliminary objection interposed by the Government of Honduras alleging the inadmissibility of the case for the failure to exhaust domestic legal remedies.

Unanimously

2   Declares that Honduras has violated, in the case of Angel Manfredo Velásquez Rodríguez, its obligations to respect and to ensure the right to personal liberty set forth in Article 7 of the Convention, read in conjunction with Article 1(1) thereof.

Unanimously

3   Declares that Honduras has violated, in the case of Angel Manfredo Velásquez Rodríguez, its obligations to respect and to ensure the right to humane treatment set forth in Article 5 of the Convention, read in conjunction with Article 1(1) thereof.

Unanimously

4   Declares that Honduras has violated, in the case of Angel Manfredo Velásquez Rodríguez, its obligation to ensure the right to life set forth in Article 4 of the Convention, read in conjunction with Article 1(1) thereof.

Unanimously

5   Decides that Honduras is hereby required to pay fair compensation to the next-of-kin of the victim.

By six votes to one (Judge Rodolfo E Piza E dissenting)*

6   Decides that the form and amount of such compensation, failing agreement between Honduras and the Commission within six months of the date of this judgment, shall be settled by the Court and, for that purpose, retains jurisdiction of the case.

Unanimously

7   Decides that the agreement on the form and amount of the compensation shall be approved by the Court.

Unanimously

8   Does not find it necessary to render a decision concerning costs.

CONCEPTS OF DISCRIMINATION

CASE NO 8

ANDREWS v LAW SOCIETY OF BRITISH COLUMBIA

SUPREME COURT OF CANADA

Judgment: 2 February 1989

Panel: Dickson CJC, McIntyre, Lamer, Wilson, Le Dain,[1] La Forest and L'Heureux-Dubé JJ

Human rights — Equality and non-discrimination — Nationality — Citizenship — Discrimination against non-citizens — Proportionality — Citizenship required for admission to the practice of law — Whether the requirement was discriminatory with respect to qualified Canadian residents who were not citizens — Whether or not discriminatory requirement justified — Canadian Charter of Rights and Freedoms, ss 1 and 15(1) — Barristers and Solicitors Act, RSBC 1979, c 26, s 42

Human rights — Equality and non-discrimination — Discrimination based on personal characteristics — Equality before and under the law and equal protection and benefit of the law — Concept of equality — "Similarly situated" v "substantive disadvantage" approaches — Whether similarly situated should be similarly treated — Differential treatment of citizens and non-citizens

BACKGROUND

The respondent, Mr Andrews, was a British citizen permanently resident in Canada. He met all the requirements for admission to the British Columbia Bar required by section 42 of the Barristers and Solicitors Act 1979, except that of Canadian citizenship. Section 42 distinguished between permanent residents who were citizens and those who were non-citizens. Non-citizens were required to wait three years from the date of establishing their permanent residence to become citizens, and only after that time could they be considered for admission.

Mr Andrews sought a declaration that section 42 of the 1979 Act violated section 15(1) of the Canadian Charter of Rights and Freedoms. The action was dismissed by the trial court, but accepted by the British Columbia Court of Appeal. The Law Society of British Columbia appealed to the Supreme Court of Canada.

---

1   Le Dain J took no part in the judgment.

*   *Eds:* due to space constraints, the concurring judgment of La Forest J has not been included. The full text of the judgment is available at the website of the Supreme Court of Canada at http://www.lexum.umontreal.ca/csc-scc/en/; [1989] 1 SCR 143; [1989] 22 WWR 289; and (1989) 56 DLR (4th) 1.

HELD (dismissing the appeal)

Section 15(1) of the Canadian Charter of Rights and Freedoms

1   Section 42 of the Barristers and Solicitors Act 1979 infringed the equality rights guaranteed by section 15 of the Charter because it barred an entire class of persons from certain forms of employment, solely on the ground of a personal characteristic, ie their non-citizen status and without consideration of educational and professional qualifications or the other attributes or merits of individuals in the group (pp 125, 135).

2   Section 15(1) of the Charter provided a broader definition of the principle of equality than the Canadian Bill of Rights and was intended to remedy some of the shortcomings of the latter. Whereas the Bill of Rights spoke only of equality before the law, section 15(1) of the Charter spelled out four basic rights: (1) equality before the law; (2) equality under the law; (3) the right to equal protection of the law; and (4) the right to equal benefit of the law. This was not a general guarantee of equality within society. It did not place an obligation on individuals or groups to treat each other equally. Rather it was concerned with the application of the law (pp 132, 135).

3   The application of equality to similarly situated groups or individuals, that is the "similarly situated should be similarly treated" approach, did not afford a realistic test for a violation of equality rights. This approach might in fact result in inequality. A bad law would not be saved merely because it operates equally upon those to whom it has application. Nor would a law necessarily be bad because it made distinctions between individuals or groups. A central concern for the application of equality had to be the impact of the law on the individual or group concerned, and on those individuals or groups it might exclude. The ideal was that a law intended to bind all should not because of irrelevant personal differences have a more burdensome impact on one group than on another (pp 133, 134).

4   The words "without discrimination" in section 15 of the Charter were crucial. Discrimination was a distinction based on grounds relating to personal characteristics of the individual or group and, whether intentional or not, has an effect which imposes disadvantages not imposed upon others or which withholds or limits access to advantages available to other members of society. Distinctions based on personal characteristics attributed to an individual solely on the basis of association with a group would rarely escape the charge of discrimination, while those based on an individual's merits and capacities would rarely be so classed (p 138).

5   The words "without discrimination" required more than a mere finding of differentiation in the treatment of groups or individuals. Distinctions which involve prejudice or disadvantage are forbidden by section 15(1). The effect of the distinction or classification on the complainant had to be considered. A complainant under section 15(1) had to show not only that he or she is not receiving equal treatment before and under the law, or that the law has a differential impact on him or her in the protection or benefit of the law, but also, in addition, that the law is discriminatory (p 141).

6   The grounds of discrimination enumerated in section 15(1) were not exhaustive and the limits, if any, on grounds for discrimination which may be established in future cases awaited definition. Both the enumerated grounds themselves and other possible grounds of discrimination recognised under section 15(1) should be interpreted in a broad and generous manner reflecting the fact that they are constitutional provisions (p 138).

Section 1 of the Canadian Charter of Rights and Freedoms

Per Dickson CJC, Wilson, l'Heureux-Dubé J and La Forest JJ

7   The legislation at issue was not justified under section 1 of the Charter (p 129).

8   In order to override a guarantee in the Charter, the objective sought had to be pressing and substantial in a free and democratic society. The objective of the legislation was not sufficiently pressing and substantial. Given that section 15 was designed to protect those groups who suffer social, political and legal disadvantage in Canadian society, the burden resting on government to justify the type of discrimination against such groups was appropriately an onerous one (pp 126, 127).

9   The proportionality test was not met. The requirement of citizenship was not carefully tailored to achieve the objective that lawyers be familiar with Canadian institutions and customs, and might not even be rationally connected to it. Most citizens, natural-born or otherwise, were committed to Canadian society but that commitment was not ensured by citizenship. Conversely, non-citizens might be deeply committed to the country. Even if lawyers did perform a governmental function, citizenship did not guarantee that they would honourably and conscientiously carry out their public duties: that was a function of their being good lawyers, not of citizenship (p 128).

Per McIntyre and Lamer JJ dissenting in part

10   Whilst section 42 of the Barristers and Solicitors Act did make a legislative distinction between citizens and non-citizens, that distinction was reasonable and sustainable under section 1. It was chosen for the achievement of a desirable social goal: one aspect of the due regulation and qualification of the legal profession. This was an objective of importance and the measure was not disproportionate to the object to be attained. It was reasonable to expect that the newcomer who seeks to gain the privileges and status within the land and the right to exercise the great powers that admission to the practice of law would give should accept citizenship and its obligations as well as its advantages and benefits (pp 142, 146).

Treaties and other international instruments referred to

European Convention for the Protection of Human Rights and Fundamental Freedoms 1950, art 14

National legislation referred to

Canada

Barristers and Solicitors Act, RSBC 1979, c 26, s 42

Canadian Bill of Rights RSC 1960, App III, s 1(b)

Canadian Charter of Rights and Freedoms, Constitution Act 1982, Part I, ss 1, 2(b), 6, 7, 15, and 32

Canadian Citizenship Act, SC 1946, c 15

Canadian Human Rights Act, SC 1976–77, c 33, s 10

Constitution Act 1982, s 52

Human Rights Act, SM 1974, c 65, s 6(7)

Human Rights Code 1981, SO 1981, c 53, s 17

Human Rights Code, RSBC 1979, c 186, ss 1 and 22

Immigration Act, SC 1910, c 27

Indian Act, RSC 1970, c I-6, s 12(1)(b)

Individual's Rights Protection Act, RSA 1980, c I-2, s 38

Racial Discrimination Act 1944, SO 1944, c 51.

Saskatchewan Bill of Rights Act 1947, SS 1947, c 35

Unemployment Insurance Act 1971, SC 1970–71–72, c 48

United Kingdom

Solicitors (Amendment) Act 1974, c 26, s 1

USA

Constitution of the United States of America, 14th Amendment (1868)

Cases referred to

Attorney-General of Canada v Lavell; Issac et al v Bedard [1974] SCR 1349; (1974) 38 DLR (3d) 481

Case "Relating to Certain Aspects of the Laws on the Use of Languages in Education in Belgium" v Belgium (Merits) ("Belgian Linguistics Case No 2"), ECHR, judgment of 23 July 1968, Series A, No 6; 1 EHRR 252

Bhinder v Canadian National Railway Co [1985] 2 SCR 561; (1986) 23 DLR (4th) 481

Bliss v Attorney-General of Canada [1979] 1 SCR 183; (1978) 92 DLR (3d) 417

Canadian National Railway Co v Canada (Canadian Human Rights Commission) [1987] 1 SCR 1114; (1988) 40 DLR (4th) 193

Dennis v United States, 339 US 162 (1950); 94 L Ed 743

Fontiero v Richardson 411 US 677 (1973); 36 L Ed 2d 583

Graham v Richardson 403 US 365 (1971); 29 L Ed 2d 534

Hunter v Southam Inc [1984] 2 SCR 145; (1984) 11 DLR (4th) 641

MacKay v The Queen [1980] 2 SCR 370; (1981) 114 DLR (3d) 393

Mahe v Alta (Gov't) [1987] 6 WWR 331; (1988) 42 DLR (4th) 514

Ontario Human Rights Commission and O'Malley v Simpsons-Sears Ltd [1985] 2 SCR 536; (1985) 23 DLR (4th) 321

Plessy v Ferguson 163 US 537 (1896); 41 L Ed 256

R v Big M Drug Mart Ltd [1986] LRC (Const) 332; [1985] 1 SCR 295; (1985) 18 DLR (4th) 321

R v Drybones [1970] SCR 282; (1970) 9 DLR (3d) 473

R v Edwards Books and Art Ltd [1986] 2 SCR 713; (1987) 35 DLR (4th) 1

R v Ertel (1988) 35 CCC (3d) 398

R v Gonzales (1962) 37 WWR 257; (1962) 32 DLR (2d) 290

R v Oakes [1986] 1 SCR 103; (1986) 26 DLR (4th) 200

Re Dickenson and Law Society of Alberta (1978) 84 DLR (3d) 189

Reference re an Act to Amend the Education Act (1986) 53 OR (2d) 513; (1986) 25 DLR (4th) 1

Reference re Family Benefits Act (1986) 26 CRR 336

Reference re Public Service Employee Relations Act (Alta) [1987] 1 SCR 313; (1987) 38 DLR (4th) 161

Reference re Use of French in Criminal Proceedings in Saskatchewan [1987] 5 WWR 577; (1988) 44 DLR (4th) 16

Smith, Kline & French Laboratories Ltd v Canada (Attorney-General) [1987] 2 FC 359; (1987) 34 DLR (4th) 584

United States v Carolene Products Co 304 US 144 (1938); 82 L Ed 1234

JUDGMENT

The judgment of Dickson CJC and Wilson and L'Heureux-Dubé JJ was delivered by:

WILSON J: I have had the benefit of the reasons of my colleague, Justice McIntyre, and I am in complete agreement with him as to the way in which section 15(1) of the Canadian Charter of Rights and Freedoms should be interpreted and applied. I also agree with my colleague as to the way in which section 15(1) and section 1 of the Charter interact. I differ from him, however, on the application of section 1 to this particular case.

As my colleague points out, section 42 of the Barristers and Solicitors Act, RSBC 1979, c 26, differentiates between citizens and non-citizens with respect to admission to the practice of law. The distinction denies admission to non-citizens who are in all other respects qualified. While the citizenship requirement applies only to those non-citizens who are permanent residents, it has the effect of requiring those permanent residents to wait for a minimum of three years from the date of establishing their permanent residence before they can be considered for admission to the Bar. It imposes a burden, in the form of some delay in obtaining admission, on permanent residents who have acquired all or some of their legal training abroad.

I agree with my colleague that a rule which bars an entire class of persons from certain forms of employment solely on the ground that they are not Canadian citizens violates the equality rights of that class. I agree with him also that it discriminates against them on the ground of their personal characteristics, ie, their non-citizen status. I believe, therefore, that they are entitled to the protection of section 15.

Before turning to section 1, I would like to add a brief comment to what my colleague has said concerning non-citizens permanently resident in Canada forming the kind of "discrete and insular minority" to which the Supreme Court of the United States referred in *United States v Carolene Products Co* 304 US 144 (1938), at pp 152–53, n 4.

Relative to citizens, non-citizens are a group lacking in political power and as such are vulnerable to having their interests overlooked and their rights to equal concern and respect violated. They are among "those groups in society to whose needs and wishes elected officials have no apparent interest in attending": see J H Ely, *Democracy and Distrust* (1980), at p 151. Non-citizens, to take only the most obvious example, do not have the right to vote. Their vulnerability to becoming a disadvantaged group in our society is captured by John Stuart Mill's observation in Book III of *Considerations on Representative Government* that "in the absence of its natural defenders, the interests of the excluded is always in danger of being overlooked ... ." I would conclude therefore that non-citizens fall into an analogous category to those specifically enumerated in section 15. I emphasize, moreover, that this is a determination which is not to be made only in the context of the law which is subject to challenge but rather in the context of the place of the group in the entire social, political and legal fabric of our society. While legislatures must inevitably draw distinctions among the governed, such distinctions should not bring about or reinforce the disadvantage of certain groups and individuals by denying them the rights freely accorded to others.

I believe also that it is important to note that the range of discrete and insular minorities has changed and will continue to change with changing political and social circumstances. For example, Stone J writing in 1938, was concerned with religious, national and racial minorities. In enumerating the specific grounds in section 15, the framers of the Charter embraced these concerns in 1982 but also addressed themselves to the difficulties experienced by the disadvantaged on the grounds of ethnic origin, colour, sex, age and physical and mental disability. It can be anticipated that the discrete and insular minorities of tomorrow will include groups not recognized as such today. It is consistent with the constitutional status of section 15 that it be interpreted with sufficient flexibility to ensure the "unremitting protection" of equality rights in the years to come.

While I have emphasized that non-citizens are, in my view, an analogous group to those specifically enumerated in section 15 and, as such, are entitled to the protection of the section, I agree with my colleague that it is not necessary in this case to determine what limit, if any, there is on the grounds covered by section 15 and I do not do so.

Section 1

Having found an infringement of section 15 of the Charter, I turn now to the question whether the citizenship requirement for entry into the legal profession in British Columbia constitutes a reasonable limit which can be "demonstrably justified in a free and democratic society" under section 1.

As my colleague has pointed out, the onus of justifying the infringement rests upon those seeking to uphold the legislation, in this case the Attorney General of British Columbia and the Law Society of British Columbia, and the analysis to be conducted is that set forth by Chief Justice Dickson in *R v Oakes* [1986] 1 SCR 103.

The first hurdle to be crossed in order to override a right guaranteed in the Charter is that the objective sought to be achieved by the impugned law must relate to concerns which are "pressing and substantial" in a free and democratic society. The Chief Justice stated at pp 138–39:

> To establish that a limit is reasonable and demonstrably justified in a free and democratic society, two central criteria must be satisfied. First, the objective, which the measures responsible for a limit on a Charter right or freedom are designed to serve, must be "of sufficient importance to warrant overriding a constitutionally protected right or freedom": *R v Big M Drug Mart Ltd., supra*, at p. 352. The standard must be high in order to ensure that objectives which are trivial or discordant with the principles integral to a free and democratic society do not gain section 1 protection. It is necessary, at a minimum, that an objective relate to concerns which are pressing and substantial in a free and democratic society before it can be characterized as sufficiently important.

This, in my view, remains an appropriate standard when it is recognized that not every distinction between individuals and groups will violate section 15. If every distinction between individuals and groups gave rise to a violation of section 15, then this standard might well be too stringent for application in all cases and might deny the community at large the benefits associated with sound and desirable social and economic legislation. This is not a concern, however, once the position that every distinction drawn by law constitutes discrimination is rejected as indeed it is in the judgment of my colleague, McIntyre J. Given that section 15 is designed to protect those groups who suffer social, political and legal disadvantage in our society, the burden resting on government to justify the type of discrimination against such groups is appropriately an onerous one.

The second step in a section 1 inquiry involves the application of a proportionality test which requires the Court to balance a number of factors. The Court must consider the nature of the right, the extent of its infringement, and the degree to which the limitation furthers the attainment of the legitimate goal reflected in the legislation. As the Chief Justice stated in *R v Edwards Books and Art Ltd* [1986] 2 SCR 713, at p 768:

> Second, the means chosen to attain those objectives must be proportional or appropriate to the ends. The proportionality requirement, in turn, normally has three aspects: the limiting measures must be carefully designed, or rationally connected, to the objective; they must impair the right as little as possible; and their effects must not so severely trench on individual or group rights that the legislative objective, albeit important, is nevertheless outweighed by the abridgment of rights.

The appellant Law Society submitted that the Court of Appeal erred in its consideration of the citizenship requirement by failing to accord proper recognition to the role of the legal profession in the governmental process of the country and in failing to consider that Canadian citizenship could reasonably be regarded by the legislature as a requirement for the practice of law. The respondents, on the other hand, argued that the Court of Appeal was right in concluding that there was not a sufficiently rational connection between the required personal characteristic of citizenship and the governmental interest in ensuring that lawyers in British Columbia are familiar with Canadian institutions, are committed to Canadian society, and are capable of playing a role in our system of democratic government. I am in general agreement with the reasoning of the Court of Appeal on this aspect of the case for the following reasons.

The trial judge in this case concluded that the discrimination against non-citizens in section 42 of the Barristers and Solicitors Act was justified under section 1 of the Charter. He said ((1985) 22 DLR (4th) 9) at p 21:

> I find citizenship to be a personal characteristic which is relevant to the practice of law on account of the special commitment to the community which citizenship involves and not merely because the practical familiarity with the country necessary for that occupation can generally be expected in the case of citizens.

On appeal McLachlin JA, as she then was, found that the exclusion of non-citizens was not rationally connected to the governmental interest in ensuring that lawyers had a sufficient knowledge of local affairs and institutions for the competent practice of law. She stated ((1986) 27 DLR (4th) 600) at p 612:

> Citizenship does not ensure familiarity with Canadian institutions and customs. Only citizens who are not natural-born Canadians are required to have resided in Canada for a period of time. Natural-born Canadians may reside in whatever country they wish and still retain their citizenship. In short, citizenship offers no assurance that a person is conscious of the fundamental traditions and rights of our society. The requirement of citizenship is not an effective means of ensuring that the persons admitted to the bar are familiar with this country's institutions and customs: see *Re Dickenson and Law Society of Alberta* (1978), 84 D.L.R. (3d) 189 at p. 195, 5 Alta. L.R. (2d) 136, 10 A.R. 120.

I appreciate the desirability of lawyers being familiar with Canadian institutions and customs but I agree with McLachlin JA that the requirement of citizenship is not carefully tailored to achieve that objective and may not even be rationally connected to it. McDonald J pointed out in *Re Dickenson and Law Society of Alberta* (1978) 84 DLR (3d) 189, at p 195 that such a requirement affords no assurance that citizens who want to become lawyers are sufficiently familiar with Canadian institutions and "it could be better achieved by an examination of the particular qualifications of the applicant, whether he is a Canadian citizen, a British subject, or something else".

The second justification advanced by the appellants in support of the citizenship requirement is that citizenship evidences a real attachment to Canada. Once again I find myself in agreement with the following observations of McLachlin JA, at pp 612–13:

> The second reason for the distinction – that citizenship implies a commitment to Canadian society – fares little better upon close examination. Only those citizens who are not natural-born Canadians can be said to have made a conscious choice to establish themselves here permanently and to opt for full participation in the Canadian social process, including the right to vote and run for public office. While no doubt most citizens, natural-born or otherwise, are committed to Canadian society, citizenship does not ensure that that is the case. Conversely, non-citizens may be deeply committed to our country.

The third ground advanced to justify the requirement relates to the role lawyers are said to play in the governance of our country. McLachlin JA disputed the extent to which the practice of law involves the performance of a governmental function. She stated at p 614:

> While lawyers clearly play an important role in our society, it cannot be contended that the practice of law involves performing a state or government function. In this respect, the role of lawyers may be distinguished from that of legislators, judges, civil servants and policemen. The practice of law is first and foremost a private profession. Some lawyers work in the courts, some do not. Those who work in the courts may represent the Crown or act against it. It is true that all lawyers are officers of the court. That term, in my mind, implies allegiance and certain responsibilities to the institution of the court. But it does not mean that lawyers are part of the process of government.

Although I am in general agreement with her characterization of the role of lawyers *qua* lawyers in our society, my problem with this basis of justification is more fundamental. To my mind, even if lawyers do perform a governmental function, I do not think the requirement that they be citizens provides any guarantee that they will honourably and conscientiously carry out their public duties. They will carry them out, I believe, because they are good lawyers and not because they are Canadian citizens.

In my view, the reasoning advanced in support of the citizenship requirement simply does not meet the tests in *Oakes* for overriding a constitutional right particularly, as in this case, a right designed to protect "discrete and insular minorities" in our society. I would respectfully concur in the view expressed by McLachlin JA at p 617 that the citizenship requirement does not "appear to relate closely to those ends, much less to have been carefully designed to achieve them with minimum impairment of individual rights".

Disposition

I would dismiss the appeal with costs. I would answer the constitutional questions as follows:

Q(1) Does the Canadian citizenship requirement to be a lawyer in the Province of British Columbia as set out in section 42 of the Barristers and Solicitors Act, RSBC 1979, c 26 infringe or deny the rights guaranteed by section 15(1) of the Canadian Charter of Rights and Freedoms?

A Yes.

Q(2) If the Canadian citizenship requirement to be a lawyer in the Province of British Columbia as set out in section 42 of the Barristers and Solicitors Act, RSBC 1979, c 26 infringes or denies the rights guaranteed by section 15(1) of the Canadian Charter of Rights and Freedoms, is it justified by section 1 of the Canadian Charter of Rights and Freedoms?

A No.

The reasons of McIntyre and Lamer JJ were delivered by:

MCINTYRE J (DISSENTING IN PART): This appeal raises only one question. Does the citizenship requirement for entry into the legal profession contained in section 42 of the Barristers and Solicitors Act, RSBC 1979, c 26, (the "Act") contravene section 15(1) of the Canadian Charter of Rights and Freedoms? Section 42 provides:

42 The benchers may call to the Bar of the Province and admit as a solicitor of the Supreme Court

(a) a Canadian citizen with respect to whom they are satisfied that he …

and section 15 of the Charter states:

15(1) Every individual is equal before and under the law and has the right to the equal protection and equal benefit of the law without discrimination and, in particular, without discrimination based on race, national or ethnic origin, colour, religion, sex, age or mental or physical disability.

(2) Subsection (1) does not preclude any law, program or activity that has as its object the amelioration of conditions of disadvantaged individuals or groups including those that are disadvantaged because of race, national or ethnic origin, colour, religion, sex, age or mental or physical disability.

The respondent, Andrews, was a British subject permanently resident in Canada at the time these proceedings were commenced. He had taken law degrees at Oxford and had fulfilled all the requirements for admission to the practice of law in British Columbia, except that of Canadian citizenship. He commenced proceedings for a declaration that section 42 of the Act violates the Charter. He also sought an order in the nature of mandamus requiring the benchers of the Law Society of British Columbia to consider his application for call to the Bar and admission as a solicitor. His action was dismissed at trial before Taylor J in the Supreme Court of British Columbia in a judgment reported at (1985) 22 DLR (4th) 9. An appeal was allowed in the Court of Appeal (Hinkson, Craig and McLachlin JJA, at (1986) 27 DLR (4th) 600), and this appeal is taken by the Law Society of British Columbia, by leave granted 27 November 1986. Pursuant to an order of this Court on 28 January 1987, Gorel Elizabeth Kinersly, an American citizen who was at the time a permanent resident of Canada articling in the Province of British Columbia, was added as a co-respondent in this appeal. On 28 January 1987, the Chief Justice stated constitutional questions in the following terms:

(1) Does the Canadian citizenship requirement to be a lawyer in the Province of British Columbia as set out in section 42 of the Barristers and Solicitors Act, RSBC 1979, c 26 infringe or deny the rights guaranteed by section 15(1) of the Canadian Charter of Rights and Freedoms?

(2) If the Canadian citizenship requirement to be a lawyer in the Province of British Columbia as set out in section 42 of the Barristers and Solicitors Act, RSBC 1979, c 26 infringes or denies the rights guaranteed by section 15(1) of the Canadian Charter of Rights and Freedoms, is it justified by section 1 of the Canadian Charter of Rights and Freedoms?

Following the judgment in his favour, the respondent Andrews was called to the Bar and admitted as a solicitor in the Province of British Columbia and is now a Canadian citizen. The co-respondent, Kinersly, who had expressed an intention to become a Canadian citizen, became eligible to do so on 15 March 1988.

Disposition in the Courts Below

Taylor J, at trial, defined discrimination under section 15(1) of the Charter as the drawing of an irrational distinction between people based on some irrelevant personal characteristic for the purpose, or having the effect, of imposing upon the victim of the discrimination some penalty, disadvantage or indignity, or denying some advantage. He did not consider that the enumerated heads of discrimination in section 15(1), race, national or ethnic origin, colour, religion, sex, age or mental or physical disability, were a complete listing of the proscribed bases of discrimination, and said, at p 16:

Thus, in order to amount to discrimination under section 15(1), the personal characteristic on which a distinction is based must either be one which is entirely irrelevant in the context in which the distinction is made or one which is given a significance clearly beyond that which could reasonably be justified in such a context – the distinction must in this sense be irrational.

He said that the test would be the same whether or not the discrimination was on the basis of a characteristic enumerated in section 15(1) of the Charter. Citizenship, in his view, while not within the term, national origin, is nonetheless a characteristic which could form a basis for discrimination under section 15(1). He adopted a broad view of the concept of citizenship. He said, at p 20:

Citizenship is, I think, a privilege which is understood to carry with it commitments to promote the security and welfare of the country, and to protect the way of life in which Canadians have come to believe, which are not expected of a permanent resident, even a resident sworn to allegiance. A citizen is a part of the country, a resident non-citizen never really more than an attachment to it.

In determining the relevance of citizenship to entry into the legal profession, he referred to the wide powers accorded to lawyers in the administration of justice and the judicial process which give rise to a duty to protect the system from abuse and to respect the laws of the land. He said, at pp 20–21:

It cannot in my view be said that there is anything irrational in the view which has been taken by the Legislature that only Canadian citizens ought to exercise such powers in this province and be entrusted with such responsibilities.

He did not consider that any burden imposed on non-citizens by the citizenship requirement was disproportionate to the relevance of citizenship in view of the nature of the duties and responsibilities of members of the legal profession. He concluded that neither section 15(1) nor section 7 of the Charter were infringed by the Canadian citizenship requirement in section 42 of the Act.

McLachlin JA wrote the judgment for a unanimous Court of Appeal. She expressed the view, at p 605, that the real meaning of the concept of equal protection and benefit before and under the law is that:

> ... persons who are "similarly situated be similarly treated" and conversely, that persons who are "differently situated be differently treated".

She referred to two competing approaches which have been adopted in dealing with discrimination under section 15(1). One view is that any distinction is sufficient to establish discrimination, and when discrimination is found the courts should immediately turn to section 1 of the Charter for a determination of its constitutional validity. The other view is that discrimination under section 15(1) must be "invidious or pejorative" in nature, in that it must result from an unreasonable classification or unjustifiable differentiation. The second view, then, incorporates principles of justification and reasonableness into section 15(1) independently of section 1. She adopted essentially the second view rejecting the proposition that any differentiation would result in a resort to section 1 of the Charter, arguing that it could not have been intended to give a guarantee in section 15(1) against every legislative classification. To do so, she asserted, would be to trivialize the fundamental rights guaranteed by the Charter and deprive the words "without discrimination" in section 15(1) of any content and, in effect, to replace section 15(1) with section 1. This approach, in her opinion, would mean that many important and socially accepted distinctions, such as restrictions on drunken driving and special provisions for the care, protection, and education of children, would be subject to automatic review under section 1. To equate the provisions of section 15(1) with a guarantee against all distinction would, in effect, "elevate section 15 to the position of subsuming the other rights and freedoms defined by the Charter". She said that there must be an initial determination of the reasonableness and fairness of the impugned legislation under section 15(1). Therefore, she saw two questions emerge: what degree of evaluation of the legislation should be done under section 15(1), and what role, if any, remained for section 1 when legislation is attacked under section 15(1)?

In dealing with the first question, she said that the court should determine whether the impugned distinction is reasonable or fair, having regard to its purposes and aims and to its effect on the person concerned. She said, at pp 609–10:

> My response to the first question is that the question to be answered under section 15 should be whether the impugned distinction is reasonable or fair, having regard to the purposes and aims and its effect on persons adversely affected. I include the word "fair" as well as "reasonable" to emphasize that the test is not one of pure rationality but one connoting the treatment of persons in ways which are not unduly prejudicial to them. The test must be objective, and the discrimination must be proved on a balance of probabilities: *R v Oakes, supra,* (applying this test to section 1). The ultimate question is whether a fair-minded person, weighing the purposes of legislation against its effects on the individuals adversely affected, and giving due weight to the right of the Legislature to pass laws for the good of all, would conclude that the legislative means adopted are unreasonable or unfair.

She went on to state that section 1 would apply to permit discrimination in extraordinary circumstances, such as the internment of enemy aliens in wartime which would create discrimination not to be tolerated in peacetime.

She concluded that the citizenship requirement in the Act discriminated against the respondent. She rejected the Law Society's argument that the importance of the legal profession in the general scheme of the administration of the legal system justified the citizenship requirement. She reached the conclusion that the distinction deprived the respondent of the equal benefit of the law guaranteed under section 15, and she concluded on this point by saying, at p 616:

> In summary, none of the reasons offered for the requirement of citizenship for the practice of law offer a convincing justification for it. On the other hand, the requirement is clearly prejudicial to the appellant and those similarly placed. Having met all the other requirements for the admission to the bar, the appellant is nevertheless unable to gain admission to practise because he is not yet a Canadian citizen. I find that the appellant has discharged the onus upon him of showing that the requirement of citizenship for admission to the practice of law is unreasonable or unfair.

The Concept of Equality

Section 15(1) of the Charter provides for every individual a guarantee of equality before and under the law, as well as the equal protection and equal benefit of the law without discrimination. This is not a general guarantee of equality; it does not provide for equality between individuals or groups within society in a general or abstract sense, nor does it impose on individuals or groups an obligation to accord equal treatment to others. It is concerned with the application of the law. No problem regarding the scope of the word "law", as employed in section 15(1), can arise in this case because it is an Act of the Legislature which is under attack. Whether other governmental or quasi-governmental regulations, rules, or requirements may be termed laws under section 15(1) should be left for cases in which the issue arises.

The concept of equality has long been a feature of Western thought. As embodied in section 15(1) of the Charter, it is an elusive concept and, more than any of the other rights and freedoms guaranteed in the Charter, it lacks precise definition. As has been stated by John H Schaar, "Equality of Opportunity and Beyond", in *Nomos IX: Equality*, ed J Roland Pennock and John W Chapman (1967), at p 228:

> Equality is a protean word. It is one of those political symbols – liberty and fraternity are others – into which men have poured the deepest urgings of their heart. Every strongly held theory or conception of equality is at once a psychology, an ethic, a theory of social relations, and a vision of the good society.

It is a comparative concept, the condition of which may only be attained or discerned by comparison with the condition of others in the social and political setting in which the question arises. It must be recognized at once, however, that every difference in treatment between individuals under the law will not necessarily result in inequality and, as well, that identical treatment may frequently produce serious inequality. This proposition has found frequent expression in the literature on the subject but, as I have noted on a previous occasion, nowhere more aptly than in the well-known words of Frankfurter J in *Dennis v United States* 339 US 162 (1950), at p 184:

> It was a wise man who said that there is no greater inequality than the equal treatment of unequals.

The same thought has been expressed in this Court in the context of section 2(b) of the Charter in *R v Big M Drug Mart Ltd* [1985] 1 SCR 295, where Dickson CJ said at p 347:

The equality necessary to support religious freedom does not require identical treatment of all religions. In fact, the interests of true equality may well require differentiation in treatment.

In simple terms, then, it may be said that a law which treats all identically and which provides equality of treatment between "A" and "B" might well cause inequality for "C", depending on differences in personal characteristics and situations. To approach the ideal of full equality before and under the law – and in human affairs an approach is all that can be expected – the main consideration must be the impact of the law on the individual or the group concerned. Recognizing that there will always be an infinite variety of personal characteristics, capacities, entitlements and merits among those subject to a law, there must be accorded, as nearly as may be possible, an equality of benefit and protection and no more of the restrictions, penalties or burdens imposed upon one than another. In other words, the admittedly unattainable ideal should be that a law expressed to bind all should not because of irrelevant personal differences have a more burdensome or less beneficial impact on one than another.

McLachlin JA in the Court of Appeal expressed the view, at p 605, that:

> ... the essential meaning of the constitutional requirement of equal protection and equal benefit is that persons who are "similarly situated be similarly treated" and conversely, that persons who are "differently situated be differently treated" ...

In this, she was adopting and applying as a test a proposition which seems to have been widely accepted with some modifications in both trial and appeal court decisions throughout the country on section 15(1) of the Charter. See, for example, *Reference Re Family Benefits Act* (1986) 75 NSR (2d) 338 (NSSCAD), at p 351; *Reference Re Use of French in Criminal Proceedings in Saskatchewan* (1987) 44 DLR (4th) 16 (Sask CA), at p 46; *Smith, Kline & French Laboratories Ltd v Canada (Attorney General)* [1987] 2 FC 359, at p 366; *R v Ertel* (1987) 35 CCC (3d) 398, at p 419. The reliance on this concept appears to have derived, at least in recent times, from J T Tussman and J tenBroek, "The Equal Protection of Laws" (1949) 37 *Calif L Rev* 341. The similarly situated test is a restatement of the Aristotelian principle of formal equality – that "things that are alike should be treated alike, while things that are unalike should be treated unalike in proportion to their unalikeness" (*Ethica Nichomacea*, trans W Ross, Book V3, at p 1131a-6 (1925)).

The test as stated, however, is seriously deficient in that it excludes any consideration of the nature of the law. If it were to be applied literally, it could be used to justify the Nuremberg laws of Adolf Hitler. Similar treatment was contemplated for all Jews. The similarly situated test would have justified the formalistic separate but equal doctrine of *Plessy v Ferguson*, 163 US 537 (1896), a doctrine that incidentally was still the law in the United States at the time that Professor Tussman and J tenBroek wrote their much cited article: see M David Lepofsky and H Schwartz "Case Note" (1988) 67 *Can Bar Rev* 115, at pp 119–20. The test, somewhat differently phrased, was applied in the British Columbia Court of Appeal in *R v Gonzales* (1962) 132 CCC 237. The Court upheld, under section 1(b) of the Canadian Bill of Rights, RSC 1970, App III, a section of the Indian Act, RSC 1970, c I-6, which made it an offence for an Indian to have intoxicants in his possession off a reserve. In his locality there were no reserves. Tysoe JA said that equality before the law could not mean "the same laws for all persons", and defined the right in these words, at p 243:

> ... in its context s. 1(b) means in a general sense that there has existed and there shall continue to exist in Canada a right in every person to whom a particular law relates or extends no matter what may be a person's race, national origin, colour, religion or sex to stand on an equal footing with every other person to whom that particular law relates or extends and a right to the protection of the law.

This approach was rejected in this Court by Ritchie J in *R v Drybones* [1970] SCR 282, in a similar case involving a provision of the Indian Act making it an offence for an Indian to be intoxicated off a reserve. He said, at p 297:

> ... I cannot agree with this interpretation pursuant to which it seems to me that the most glaring discriminatory legislation against a racial group would have to be construed as recognizing the right of each of its individual members "to equality before the law", so long as all the other members are being discriminated against in the same way.

Thus, mere equality of application to similarly situated groups or individuals does not afford a realistic test for a violation of equality rights. For, as has been said, a bad law will not be saved merely because it operates equally upon those to whom it has application. Nor will a law necessarily be bad because it makes distinctions.

A similarly situated test focussing on the equal application of the law to those to whom it has application could lead to results akin to those in *Bliss v Attorney General of Canada* [1979] 1 SCR 183. In *Bliss*, a pregnant woman was denied unemployment benefits to which she would have been entitled had she not been pregnant. She claimed that the Unemployment Insurance Act, 1971, violated the equality guarantees of the Canadian Bill of Rights because it discriminated against her on the basis of her sex. Her claim was dismissed by this Court on the grounds that there was no discrimination on the basis of sex, since the class into which she fell under the Act was that of pregnant persons, and within that class, all persons were treated equally. This case, of course, was decided before the advent of the Charter.

I would also agree with the following criticism of the similarly situated test made by Kerans JA in *Mahe v Alta (Gov't)* (1987) 54 Alta LR (2d) 212, at p 244:

> ... the test accepts an idea of equality which is almost mechanical, with no scope for considering the reason for the distinction. In consequence, subtleties are found to justify a finding of dissimilarity which reduces the test to a categorization game. Moreover, the test is not helpful. After all, most laws are enacted for the specific purpose of offering a benefit or imposing a burden on some persons and not on others. The test catches every conceivable difference in legal treatment.

For the reasons outlined above, the test cannot be accepted as a fixed rule or formula for the resolution of equality questions arising under the Charter. Consideration must be given to the content of the law, to its purpose, and its impact upon those to whom it applies, and also upon those whom it excludes from its application. The issues which will arise from case to case are such that it would be wrong to attempt to confine these considerations within such a fixed and limited formula.

It is not every distinction or differentiation in treatment at law which will transgress the equality guarantees of section 15 of the Charter. It is, of course, obvious that legislatures may – and to govern effectively – must treat different individuals and groups in different ways. Indeed, such distinctions are one of the main preoccupations of legislatures. The classifying of individuals and groups, the making of different provisions respecting such groups, the application of different rules, regulations, requirements and qualifications to different persons is necessary for the governance of modern society. As noted above, for the accommodation of differences, which is the essence of true equality, it will frequently be necessary to make distinctions. What kinds of distinctions will be acceptable under section 15(1) and what kinds will violate its provisions?

In seeking an answer to these questions, the provisions of the Charter must have their full effect. In *R v Big M Drug Mart Ltd*, this Court emphasized this point at p 344, where Dickson CJ stated:

> This Court has already, in some measure, set out the basic approach to be taken in interpreting the Charter. In *Hunter v. Southam Inc.*, [1984] 2 S.C.R. 145, this Court expressed the view that the proper approach to the definition of the rights and freedoms guaranteed by the Charter was a purposive one. The meaning of a right or freedom guaranteed by the Charter was to be ascertained by an analysis of the *purpose* of such a guarantee; it was to be understood, in other words, in the light of the interests it was meant to protect.
>
> In my view this analysis is to be undertaken, and the purpose of the right or freedom in question is to be sought by reference to the character and the larger objects of the Charter itself, to the language chosen to articulate the specific right or freedom, to the historical origins of the concepts enshrined, and where applicable, to the meaning and purpose of the other specific rights and freedoms with which it is associated within the text of the Charter. The interpretation should be, as the judgment in *Southam* emphasizes, a generous rather than a legalistic one, aimed at fulfilling the purpose of the guarantee and securing for individuals the full benefit of the Charter's protection. At the same time it is important not to overshoot the actual purpose of the right or freedom in question, but to recall that the Charter was not enacted in a vacuum, and must therefore, as this Court's decision in *Law Society of Upper Canada v. Skapinker*, [1984] 1 S.C.R. 357, illustrates, be placed in its proper linguistic, philosophic and historical contexts. [Emphasis in original.]

These words are not inconsistent with the view I expressed in *Reference re Public Service Employee Relations Act (Alta)* [1987] 1 SCR 313.

The principle of equality before the law has long been recognized as a feature of our constitutional tradition and it found statutory recognition in the Canadian Bill of Rights. However, unlike the Canadian Bill of Rights, which spoke only of equality before the law, section 15(1) of the Charter provides a much broader protection. Section 15 spells out four basic rights: (1) the right to equality before the law; (2) the right to equality under the law; (3) the right to equal protection of the law; and (4) the right to equal benefit of the law. The inclusion of these last three additional rights in section 15 of the Charter was an attempt to remedy some of the shortcomings of the right to equality in the Canadian Bill of Rights. It also reflected the expanded concept of discrimination being developed under the various Human Rights Codes since the enactment of the Canadian Bill of Rights. The shortcomings of the Canadian Bill of Rights as far as the right to equality is concerned are well known. In *Attorney General of Canada v Lavell* [1974] SCR 1349, for example, this Court upheld section 12(1)(b) of the Indian Act which deprived women, but not men, of their membership in Indian Bands if they married non-Indians. The provision was held not to violate equality *before* the law although it might, the Court said, violate equality *under* the law if such were protected. In *Bliss, supra*, this Court held that the denial of unemployment insurance benefits to women because they were pregnant did not violate the guarantee of equality before the law, because any inequality in the protection and benefit of the law was "not created by legislation but by nature" (p 190). The case was distinguished from the Court's earlier decision in *Drybones, supra*, as not involving (pp 191–92) the imposition of a penalty on a racial group to which other citizens are not subjected, but as involving rather "a definition of the qualifications required for entitlement to benefits". It is readily apparent that the language of section 15 was deliberately chosen in order to remedy some of the perceived defects under the Canadian Bill of Rights. The antecedent statute is part of the "linguistic, philosophic and historical context" of section 15 of the Charter.

It is clear that the purpose of section 15 is to ensure equality in the formulation and application of the law. The promotion of equality entails the promotion of a society in which all are secure in the knowledge that they are recognized at law as human beings equally deserving of concern, respect and consideration. It has a large remedial component. Howland CJ and Robins JA (dissenting in the result but not with respect to this comment) in *Reference re an Act to Amend the Education Act* (1986) 53 OR (2d) 513, attempt to articulate the broad range of values embraced by section 15. They state at p 554:

> In our view, section 15(1) read as a whole constitutes a compendious expression of a positive right to equality in both the substance and the administration of the law. It is an all-encompassing right governing all legislative action. Like the ideals of "equal justice" and "equal access to the law", the right to equal protection and equal benefit of the law now enshrined in the Charter rests on the moral and ethical principle fundamental to a truly free and democratic society that all persons should be treated by the law on a footing of equality with equal concern and respect.

> It must be recognized, however, as well that the promotion of equality under section 15 has a much more specific goal than the mere elimination of distinctions. If the Charter was intended to eliminate all distinctions, then there would be no place for sections such as 27 (multicultural heritage); 2(a) (freedom of conscience and religion); 25 (aboriginal rights and freedoms); and other such provisions designed to safeguard certain distinctions. Moreover, the fact that identical treatment may frequently produce serious inequality is recognized in section 15(2), which states that the equality rights in section 15(1) do "not preclude any law, program or activity that has as its object the amelioration of conditions of disadvantaged individuals or groups ...

Discrimination

The right to equality before and under the law, and the rights to the equal protection and benefit of the law contained in section 15, are granted with the direction contained in section 15 itself that they be without discrimination. Discrimination is unacceptable in a democratic society because it epitomizes the worst effects of the denial of equality, and discrimination reinforced by law is particularly repugnant. The worst oppression will result from discriminatory measures having the force of law. It is against this evil that section 15 provides a guarantee.

Discrimination as referred to in section 15 of the Charter must be understood in the context of pre-Charter history. Prior to the enactment of section 15(1), the Legislatures of the various provinces and the federal Parliament had passed during the previous fifty years what may be generally referred to as Human Rights Acts. With the steady increase in population from the earliest days of European emigration into Canada and with the consequential growth of industry, agriculture and commerce and the vast increase in national wealth which followed, many social problems developed. The contact of the European immigrant with the indigenous population, the steady increase in immigration bringing those of neither French nor British background, and in more recent years the greatly expanded role of women in all forms of industrial, commercial and professional activity led to much inequality and many forms of discrimination. In great part these developments, in the absence of any significant legislative protection for the victims of discrimination, called into being the Human Rights Acts. In 1944, the Racial Discrimination Act, 1944, SO 1944, c 51, was passed, to be followed in 1947 by the Saskatchewan Bill of Rights Act, 1947, SS 1947, c 35, and in 1960 by the Canadian Bill of Rights. Since then every jurisdiction in Canada has enacted broad-ranging Human Rights Acts which have attacked most of the more common forms of discrimination found in society. This development has been recorded and discussed by Walter Tarnopolsky, now Tarnopolsky JA, in *Discrimination and the Law* (2nd ed 1985).

What does discrimination mean? The question has arisen most commonly in a consideration of the Human Rights Acts and the general concept of discrimination under those enactments has been fairly well settled. There is little difficulty, drawing upon the cases in this Court, in isolating an acceptable definition. In *Ontario Human Rights Commission and O'Malley v Simpsons-Sears Ltd* [1985] 2 SCR 536, at p 551, discrimination (in that case adverse effect discrimination) was described in these terms:

> It arises where an employer ... adopts a rule or standard ... which has a discriminatory effect upon a prohibited ground on one employee or group of employees in that it imposes, because of some special characteristic of the employee or group, obligations, penalties, or restrictive conditions not imposed on other members of the work force.

It was held in that case, as well, that no intent was required as an element of discrimination, for it is in essence the impact of the discriminatory act or provision upon the person affected which is decisive in considering any complaint. At p 547, this proposition was expressed in these terms:

> The Code aims at the removal of discrimination. This is to state the obvious. Its main approach, however, is not to punish the discriminator, but rather to provide relief for the victims of discrimination. It is the result or the effect of the action complained of which is significant. If it does, in fact, cause discrimination; if its effect is to impose on one person or group of persons obligations, penalties, or restrictive conditions not imposed on other members of the community, it is discriminatory.

In *Canadian National Railway Co v Canada (Canadian Human Rights Commission)* [1987] 1 SCR 1114, better known as the *Action Travail des Femmes* case, where it was alleged that the Canadian National Railway was guilty of discriminatory hiring and promotion practices contrary to section 10 of the Canadian Human Rights Act, SC 1976–77, c 33, in denying employment to women in certain unskilled positions, Dickson CJ in giving the judgment of the Court said, at pp 1138–39:

> A thorough study of "systemic discrimination" in Canada is to be found in the Abella Report on equality in employment. The terms of reference of the Royal Commission instructed it "to inquire into the most efficient, effective and equitable means of promoting employment opportunities, eliminating systemic discrimination and assisting individuals to compete for employment opportunities on an equal basis". (Order in Council P.C. 1983–1924 of 24 June 1983). Although Judge Abella chose not to offer a precise definition of systemic discrimination, the essentials may be gleaned from the following comments, found at p. 2 of the Abella Report.
>
> Discrimination ... means practices or attitudes that have, whether by design or impact, the effect of limiting an individual's or a group's right to the opportunities generally available because of attributed rather than actual characteristics ...
>
> It is not a question of whether this discrimination is motivated by an intentional desire to obstruct someone's potential, or whether it is the accidental by-product of innocently motivated practices or systems. If the barrier is affecting certain groups in a disproportionately negative way, it is a signal that the practices that lead to this adverse impact may be discriminatory.

There are many other statements which have aimed at a short definition of the term discrimination. In general, they are in accord with the statements referred to above. I would say then that discrimination may be described as a distinction, whether intentional or not but based on grounds relating to personal characteristics of the individual or group, which has the effect of imposing burdens, obligations, or disadvantages on such individual or group not imposed upon others, or which withholds or limits access to opportunities, benefits, and advantages available to other members of society. Distinctions based on personal characteristics attributed to an individual solely on the basis of association with a group will rarely escape the charge of discrimination, while those based on an individual's merits and capacities will rarely be so classed.

The Court in the case at bar must address the issue of discrimination as the term is used in section 15(1) of the Charter. In general, it may be said that the principles which have been applied under the Human Rights Acts are equally applicable in considering questions of discrimination under section 15(1). Certain differences arising from the difference between the Charter and the Human Rights Acts must, however, be considered. To begin with, discrimination in section 15(1) is limited to discrimination caused by the application or operation of law, whereas the Human Rights Acts apply also to private activities. Furthermore, and this is a distinction of more importance, all the Human Rights Acts passed in Canada specifically designate a certain limited number of grounds upon which discrimination is forbidden. Section 15(1) of the Charter is not so limited. The enumerated grounds in section 15(1) are not exclusive and the limits, if any, on grounds for discrimination which may be established in future cases await definition. The enumerated grounds do, however, reflect the most common and probably the most socially destructive and historically practised bases of discrimination and must, in the words of section 15(1), receive particular attention. Both the enumerated grounds themselves and other possible grounds of discrimination recognized under section 15(1) must be interpreted in a broad and generous manner, reflecting the fact that they are constitutional provisions not easily repealed or amended but intended to provide a "continuing framework for the legitimate exercise of governmental power" and, at the same time, for "the unremitting protection" of equality rights: see *Hunter v Southam Inc* [1984] 2 SCR 145, at p 155.

It should be noted as well that when the Human Rights Acts create exemptions or defences, such as a *bona fide* occupational requirement, an exemption for religious and political organizations, or definitional limits on age discrimination, these generally have the effect of completely removing the conduct complained of from the reach of the Act. See, for example, exemptions for special interest organizations contained in the Human Rights Code, RSBC 1979, c 186, as amended, section 22; the Human Rights Act, SM 1974, c 65, as amended, section 6(7); and the Human Rights Code, 1981, SO 1981, c 53, section 17. "Age" is often restrictively defined in the Human Rights Acts; in British Columbia, it is defined in section 1 of the Code to mean an age between 45 and 65; in section 38 of the Individual's Rights Protection Act, RSA 1980, c I-2, it is defined as eighteen and over. For an example of the application of a *bona fide* occupational requirement, see *Bhinder v Canadian National Railway Co* [1985] 2 SCR 561. Where discrimination is forbidden in the Human Rights Acts it is done in absolute terms, and where a defence or exception is allowed it, too, speaks in absolute terms and the discrimination is excused. There is, in this sense, no middle ground. In the Charter, however, while section 15(1), subject always to subs (2), expresses its prohibition of discrimination in absolute terms, section 1 makes allowance for a reasonable limit upon the operation of section 15(1). A different approach under section 15(1) is therefore required. While discrimination under section 15(1) will be of the same nature and in descriptive terms will fit the concept of discrimination developed under the Human Rights Acts, a further step will be required in order to decide whether discriminatory laws can be justified under section 1. The onus will be on the state to establish this. This is a distinct step called for under the Charter which is not found in most Human Rights Acts, because in those Acts justification for or defence to discrimination is generally found in specific exceptions to the substantive rights.

Relationship between section 15(1) and section 1 of the Charter

In determining the extent of the guarantee of equality in section 15(1) of the Charter, special consideration must be given to the relationship between section 15(1) and section 1. It is indeed the presence of section 1 in the Charter and the interaction between these sections which has led to the differing approaches to a definition of the section 15(1) right, and which has made necessary a judicial approach differing from that employed under the Canadian Bill of Rights. Under the Canadian Bill of Rights, a test was developed to distinguish between justified and unjustified legislative distinctions within the concept of equality before the law itself in the absence of anything equivalent to the section 1 limit: see *MacKay v The Queen* [1980] 2 SCR 370, where it was said, at p 407:

> ... and whether it is a necessary departure from the general principle of universal application of the law for the attainment of some necessary and desirable social objective. Inequalities created for such purposes may well be acceptable under the Canadian Bill of Rights.

It may be noted as well that the 14th Amendment to the American Constitution, which provides that no state shall deny to any person within its jurisdiction the "equal protection of the laws", contains no limiting provisions similar to section 1 of the Charter. As a result, judicial consideration has led to the development of varying standards of scrutiny of alleged violations of the equal protection provision which restrict or limit the equality guarantee within the concept of equal protection itself. Again, article 14 of the European Convention on Human Rights, 23 UNTS 222, which secures the rights guaranteed therein without discrimination, lacks a section 1 or its equivalent and has also developed a limit within the concept itself. In the *Belgian Linguistic Case (No 2)* (1968) 1 EHRR 252, at p 284, the court enunciated the following test:

> ... the principle of equality of treatment is violated if the distinction has no objective and reasonable justification. The existence of such a justification must be assessed in relation to the aim and effects of the measure under consideration, regard being had to principles which normally prevail in democratic societies. A difference in treatment in the exercise of a right laid down in the Convention must not only pursue a legitimate aim: Article 14 is likewise violated when it is clearly established that there is no reasonable relationship of proportionality between the means employed and the aim sought to be realised.

The distinguishing feature of the Charter, unlike the other enactments, is that consideration of such limiting factors is made under section 1. This Court has described the analytical approach to the Charter in *R v Oakes* [1986] 1 SCR 103; *R v Edwards Books and Art Ltd* [1986] 2 SCR 713, and other cases, the essential feature of which is that the right guaranteeing sections be kept analytically separate from section 1. In other words, when confronted with a problem under the Charter, the first question which must be answered will be whether or not an infringement of a guaranteed right has occurred. Any justification of an infringement which is found to have occurred must be made, if at all, under the broad provisions of section 1. It must be admitted at once that the relationship between these two sections may well be difficult to determine on a wholly satisfactory basis. It is, however, important to keep them analytically distinct if for no other reason than the different attribution of the burden of proof. It is for the citizen to establish that his or her Charter right has been infringed and for the state to justify the infringement.

Approaches to section 15(1)

Three main approaches have been adopted in determining the role of section 15(1), the meaning of discrimination set out in that section, and the relationship of section 15(1) and section 1. The first one, which was advanced by Professor Peter Hogg in *Constitutional Law of Canada* (2nd ed 1985) would treat every distinction drawn by law as discrimination under section 15(1). There would then follow a consideration of the distinction under the provisions of section 1 of the Charter. He said, at pp 800–801:

> I conclude that section 15 should be interpreted as providing for the universal application of every law. When a law draws a distinction between individuals, on any ground, that distinction is sufficient to constitute a breach of section 15, and to move the constitutional issue to section 1. The test of validity is that stipulated by section 1, namely, whether the law comes within the phrase "such reasonable limits prescribed by law as can be demonstrably justified in a free and democratic society".

He reached this conclusion on the basis that, where the Charter right is expressed in unqualified terms, section 1 supplies the standard of justification for any abridgment of the right. He argued that the word "discrimination" in section 15(1) could be read as introducing a qualification in the section itself, but he preferred to read the word in a neutral sense because this reading would immediately send the matter to section 1, which was included in the Charter for this purpose.

The second approach put forward by McLachlin JA in the Court of Appeal involved a consideration of the reasonableness and fairness of the impugned legislation under section 15(1). She stated, as has been noted above, at p 610:

> The ultimate question is whether a fair-minded person, weighing the purposes of legislation against its effects on the individuals adversely affected, and giving due weight to the right of the Legislature to pass laws for the good of all, would conclude that the legislative means adopted are unreasonable or unfair.

She assigned a very minor role to section 1 which would, it appears, be limited to allowing in times of emergency, war, or other crises the passage of discriminatory legislation which would normally be impermissible.

A third approach, sometimes described as an "enumerated or analogous grounds" approach, adopts the concept that discrimination is generally expressed by the enumerated grounds. Section 15(1) is designed to prevent discrimination based on these and analogous grounds. The approach is similar to that found in human rights and civil rights statutes which have been enacted throughout Canada in recent times. The following excerpts from the judgment of Hugessen JA in *Smith, Kline & French Laboratories v Canada (Attorney General)*, supra, at pp 367–69, illustrate this approach:

> The rights which it [section 15] guarantees are not based on any concept of strict, numerical equality amongst all human beings. If they were, virtually all legislation, whose function it is, after all, to define, distinguish and make categories, would be in *prima facie* breach of section 15 and would require justification under section 1. This would be to turn the exception into the rule. Since courts would be obliged to look for and find section 1 justification for most legislation, the alternative being anarchy, there is a real risk of paradox: the broader the reach given to section 15 the more likely it is that it will be deprived of any real content.

> The answer, in my view, is that the text of the section itself contains its own limitations. It only proscribes discrimination amongst the members of categories which are themselves similar. Thus the issue, for each case, will be to know which categories are permissible in determining similarity of situation and which are not. It is only in those cases where the categories themselves are not permissible, where equals are not treated equally, that there will be a breach of equality rights.

> As far as the text of section 15 itself is concerned, one may look to whether or not there is "discrimination", in the pejorative sense of that word, and as to whether the categories are based upon the grounds enumerated or grounds analogous to them. The inquiry, in effect,

concentrates upon the personal characteristics of those who claim to have been unequally treated. Questions of stereotyping, of historical disadvantagement, in a word, of prejudice, are the focus and there may even be a recognition that for some people equality has a different meaning than for others.

The analysis of discrimination in this approach must take place within the context of the enumerated grounds and those analogous to them. The words "without discrimination" require more than a mere finding of distinction between the treatment of groups or individuals. Those words are a form of qualifier built into section 15 itself and limit those distinctions which are forbidden by the section to those which involve prejudice or disadvantage.

I would accept the criticisms of the first approach made by McLachlin JA in the Court of Appeal. She noted that the labelling of every legislative distinction as an infringement of section 15(1) trivializes the fundamental rights guaranteed by the Charter and, secondly, that to interpret "without discrimination" as "without distinction" deprives the notion of discrimination of content. She continued, at p 607:

> Third, it cannot have been the intention of Parliament that the government be put to the requirement of establishing under section 1 that all laws which draw distinction between people are "demonstrably justified in a free and democratic society". If weighing of the justifiability of unequal treatment is neither required or permitted under section 15, the result will be that such universally accepted and manifestly desirable legal distinctions as those prohibiting children or drunk persons from driving motor vehicles will be viewed as violations of fundamental rights and be required to run the gauntlet of section 1.

> Finally, it may further be contended that to define discrimination under section 15 as synonymous with unequal treatment on the basis of personal classification will be to elevate section 15 to the position of subsuming the other rights and freedoms defined by the Charter.

In rejecting the Hogg approach, I would say that it draws a straight line from the finding of a distinction to a determination of its validity under section 1, but my objection would be that it virtually denies any role for section 15(1).

I would reject, as well, the approach adopted by McLachlin JA where she seeks to define discrimination under section 15(1) as an unjustifiable or unreasonable distinction. In so doing she avoids the mere distinction test but also makes a radical departure from the analytical approach to the Charter which has been approved by this Court. In the result, the determination would be made under section 15(1) and virtually no role would be left for section 1.

The third or "enumerated and analogous grounds" approach most closely accords with the purposes of section 15 and the definition of discrimination outlined above and leaves questions of justification to section 1. However, in assessing whether a complainant's rights have been infringed under section 15(1), it is not enough to focus only on the alleged ground of discrimination and decide whether or not it is an enumerated or analogous ground. The effect of the impugned distinction or classification on the complainant must be considered. Once it is accepted that not all distinctions and differentiations created by law are discriminatory, then a role must be assigned to section 15(1) which goes beyond the mere recognition of a legal distinction. A complainant under section 15(1) must show not only that he or she is not receiving equal treatment before and under the law or that the law has a differential impact on him or her in the protection or benefit accorded by law but, in addition, must show that the legislative impact of the law is discriminatory.

Where discrimination is found a breach of section 15(1) has occurred and – where section 15(2) is not applicable – any justification, any consideration of the reasonableness of the enactment; indeed, any consideration of factors which could justify the discrimination and support the constitutionality of the impugned enactment would take place under section 1. This approach would conform with the directions of this Court in earlier decisions concerning the application of section 1 and at the same time would allow for the screening out of the obviously trivial and vexatious claim. In this, it would provide a workable approach to the problem.

It would seem to me apparent that a legislative distinction has been made by section 42 of the Barristers and Solicitors Act between citizens and non-citizens with respect to the practice of law. The distinction would deny admission to the practice of law to non-citizens who in all other respects are qualified. Have the respondents, because of section 42 of the Act, been denied equality before and under the law or the equal protection of the law? In practical terms it should be noted that the citizenship requirement affects only those non-citizens who are permanent residents. The permanent resident must wait for a minimum of three years from the date of establishing permanent residence status before citizenship may be acquired. The distinction therefore imposes a burden in the form of some delay on permanent residents who have acquired all or some of their legal training abroad and is, therefore, discriminatory.

The rights guaranteed in section 15(1) apply to all persons whether citizens or not. A rule which bars an entire class of persons from certain forms of employment, solely on the grounds of a lack of citizenship status and without consideration of educational and professional qualifications or the other attributes or merits of individuals in the group, would, in my view, infringe section 15 equality rights. Non-citizens, lawfully permanent residents of Canada, are – in the words of the US Supreme Court in *United States v Carolene Products Co* 304 US 144 (1938), at pp 152–53, n 4, subsequently affirmed in *Graham v Richardson* 403 US 365 (1971), at p 372 – a good example of a "discrete and insular minority" who come within the protection of section 15.

Section 1

Having accepted the proposition that section 42 has infringed the right to equality guaranteed in section 15, it remains to consider whether, under the provisions of section 1 of the Charter, the citizenship requirement which is clearly prescribed by law is a reasonable limit which can be "demonstrably justified in a free and democratic society".

The onus of justifying the infringement of a guaranteed Charter right must, of course, rest upon the parties seeking to uphold the limitation, in this case, the Attorney General of British Columbia and the Law Society of British Columbia. As is evident from the decisions of this Court, there are two steps involved in the section 1 inquiry. First, the importance of the objective underlying the impugned law must be assessed. In *Oakes*, it was held that to override a Charter guaranteed right the objective must relate to concerns which are "pressing and substantial" in a free and democratic society. However, given the broad ambit of legislation which must be enacted to cover various aspects of the civil law dealing largely with administrative and regulatory matters and the necessity for the Legislature to make many distinctions between individuals and groups for such purposes, the standard of "pressing and substantial" may be too stringent for application in all cases. To hold otherwise would frequently deny the community-at-large the benefits associated with sound social and economic legislation. In my opinion, in approaching a case such as the one before us, the first question the Court should ask must relate to the nature and the purpose of the enactment, with a view to deciding whether the limitation represents a legitimate exercise of the legislative power for the attainment of a desirable social objective which would warrant overriding constitutionally protected rights. The second step in a section 1 inquiry involves a proportionality test whereby the Court must attempt to balance a number of factors. The Court must examine the nature of the right, the extent of its infringement, and the degree to which the limitation furthers the attainment of the desirable goal embodied in the legislation. Also involved in the inquiry will be the importance of the right to the individual or group concerned, and the broader social impact of both the impugned law and its alternatives. As the Chief Justice has stated in *R v Edwards Books and Art Ltd*, *supra*, at pp 768–69:

> Both in articulating the standard of proof and in describing the criteria comprising the proportionality requirement the Court has been careful to avoid rigid and inflexible standards.

I agree with this statement. There is no single test under section 1; rather, the Court must carefully engage in the balancing of many factors in determining whether an infringement is reasonable and demonstrably justified.

The section 15(1) guarantee is the broadest of all guarantees. It applies to and supports all other rights guaranteed by the Charter. However, it must be recognized that Parliament and the Legislatures have a right and a duty to make laws for the whole community: in this process, they must make innumerable legislative distinctions and categorizations in the pursuit of the role of government. When making distinctions between groups and individuals to achieve desirable social goals, it will rarely be possible to say of any legislative distinction that it is clearly the right legislative choice or that it is clearly a wrong one. As stated by the Chief Justice in *R v Edwards Books and Art Ltd*, at pp 781–82:

> A "reasonable limit" is one which, having regard to the principles enunciated in *Oakes*, it was reasonable for the legislature to impose. The courts are not called upon to substitute judicial opinions for legislative ones as to the place at which to draw a precise line.

In dealing with the many problems that arise legislatures must not be held to the standard of perfection, for in such matters perfection is unattainable. I would repeat the words of my colleague, La Forest J, in *R v Edwards Books and Art Ltd*, at p 795:

> By the foregoing, I do not mean to suggest that this Court should, as a general rule, defer to legislative judgments when those judgments trench upon rights considered fundamental in a free and democratic society. Quite the contrary, I would have thought the Charter established the opposite regime. On the other hand, having accepted the importance of the legislative objective, one must in the present context recognize that if the legislative goal is to be achieved, it will inevitably be achieved to the detriment of some. Moreover, attempts to protect the rights of one group will also inevitably impose burdens on the rights of other groups. There is no perfect scenario in which the rights of all can be equally protected.

> In seeking to achieve a goal that is demonstrably justified in a free and democratic society, therefore, a legislature must be given reasonable room to manoeuvre to meet these conflicting pressures.

Disposition

I now turn to the case at bar. The appellant Law Society in oral argument stressed three points. It argued that the Court of Appeal was correct in its analysis of the relationship between section 15(1) and section 1 of the Charter but that it erred in applying criteria properly to be considered in section 1, in deciding whether there was a breach of section 15(1). This argument has been discussed and disposed of above. It was further argued that the Court of Appeal erred in its consideration of the citizenship requirement in section 42 of the Barristers and Solicitors Act, in failing to give proper weight to the importance of the role of the legal profession in the legal and governmental processes of the country and in failing to consider that Canadian citizenship could reasonably be regarded by the Legislature as a requirement for the practice of law. The Law Society argued as well that because of the important duties and powers accorded to lawyers, they do indeed play a vital role in the governmental processes of the country and that, while generally citizenship requirements are discriminatory in nature, the involvement of lawyers in the administration of justice justified the citizenship requirement. The Attorney General of British Columbia supported these arguments and, as well, argued that for the Court to intervene and strike down the citizenship requirement would exceed the proper limits of judicial review.

The respondents in general supported the judgment of the Court of Appeal. They argued that citizenship bears no clear relationship to an individual's personal and professional characteristics, and questioned the classification of lawyers as significant actors in the State, or governmental process. While conceding that a citizenship requirement for many intimately concerned with the governing processes of the country would be proper and sustainable, it was argued that the relationship of the legal profession to government and the administration of justice was not such that the citizenship requirement could be considered as a reasonable requirement and that any "general helpfulness" of the citizenship requirement, in attaining the objectives of the Barristers and Solicitors Act, could not suffice to justify this form of discrimination against an individual. In essence, the difference between the parties centred on the question of the importance of the legal profession in the government of the country.

There is no difficulty in determining that in general terms the Barristers and Solicitors Act of British Columbia is a statute enacted for a valid and desirable social purpose, the creation and regulation of the legal profession and the practice of law. The narrower question, however, is whether the requirement that only citizens be admitted to the practice of law in British Columbia serves a desirable social purpose of sufficient importance to warrant overriding the equality guarantee. It is incontestable that the legal profession plays a very significant – in fact, a fundamentally important – role in the administration of justice, both in the criminal and the civil law. I would not attempt to answer the question arising from the judgments below as to whether the function of the profession may be termed judicial or quasi-judicial, but I would observe that in the absence of an independent legal profession, skilled and qualified to play its part in the administration of justice and the judicial process, the whole legal system would be in a parlous state. In the performance of what may be called his private function, that is, in advising on legal matters and in representing clients before the courts and other tribunals, the lawyer is accorded great powers not permitted to other professionals. As pointed out by Taylor J at first instance, by the use of the subpoena which he alone can procure on behalf of another, he can compel attendance upon examinations before trial and at trial upon pain of legal sanction for refusal. He may, as well, require the production of documents and records for examination and use in the proceedings. He may in some cases require the summoning of jurors, the sittings of courts and, in addition, he may make the fullest inquiry into the matters before the court with a full privilege against actions for slander arising out of his conduct in the court. The solicitor is also bound by the solicitor and client privilege against the disclosure of communications with his client concerning legal matters. This is said to be the only absolute privilege known to the law. Not only may the solicitor decline to disclose solicitor and client communications, the courts will not permit him to do so. This is a privilege against all comers, including the Crown, save where the disclosure of a crime would be involved. The responsibilities involved in its maintenance and in its breach where crimes are concerned are such that citizenship with its commitment to the welfare of the whole community is not an unreasonable requirement for the practice of law. While it may be arguable whether the lawyer exercises a judicial, quasi-judicial, or governmental role, it is clear that at his own discretion he can invoke the full force and authority of the State in procuring and enforcing judgments or other remedial measures which may be obtained. It is equally true that in defending an action he has the burden of protecting his client from the imposition of such state authority and power. By any standard, these powers and duties are vital to the maintenance of order in our society and the due administration of the law in the interest of the whole community.

The lawyer has, as well, what may be termed a public function. Governments at all levels, federal, provincial and municipal, rely extensively upon lawyers, both in technical and policy matters. In the drafting of legislation, regulations, treaties, agreements and other governmental documents and papers lawyers play a major role. In various aspects of this work they are called upon to advise upon legal and constitutional questions which frequently go to the very heart of the governmental role. To discharge these duties, familiarity is required with Canadian history, constitutional law, regional differences and concerns within the country and, in fact, with the whole Canadian governmental and political process. It is entirely reasonable, then, that legislators consider and adopt measures designed to maintain within the legal profession a body of qualified professionals with a commitment to the country and to the fulfilment of the important tasks which fall to it.

McLachlin JA was of the view that the citizenship requirement would not ensure familiarity with Canadian institutions and customs, nor would it ensure a commitment to Canada going beyond one involved in the concept of allegiance, as recognized by the taking of an oath of allegiance. I would agree with her that the desired results would not be ensured by the citizenship requirement but I would observe, at the same time, that no law will ever ensure anything. To abolish the requirement of citizenship on the basis that it would fail to ensure the attainment of its objectives would, in my view, be akin to abolishing the law against theft, for it has certainly not ensured the elimination of that crime. Citizenship, however, which requires the taking on of obligations and commitments to the community, difficult sometimes to describe but felt and understood by most citizens, as well as the rejection of past loyalties may reasonably be said to conduce to the desired result.

I would observe, as well, that the comment of McLachlin JA that the citizenship requirement was first adopted in British Columbia in 1971 requires some explanation. I do not think that the historical argument should be pushed too far: things need not always remain as once they were although, as noted in *R v Big M Drug Mart Ltd* and *Reference re Public Service Employee Relations Act (Alta)*, *supra*, Charter construction should be consistent with the history, traditions and social philosophies of our society. The concept of citizenship has been a requirement for entry into the legal profession in British Columbia from its earliest days. When the Law Society was formed in 1874 the profession was open to British subjects. At that time, the idea of a separate Canadian citizenship, as distinct from the general classification of British subject which included Canadians, was scarcely known – though as early as 1910, Immigration Act, SC 1910, c 27, the term "Canadian citizen" was defined for the purposes of the Immigration Act as a "British subject who has Canadian domicile". The concept of citizenship in those early days was embodied in the expression, British subject, and thus it was recognized as a requirement for entry into the legal profession in British Columbia. As Canada moved away from its colonial past, a separate identity for Canadians emerged and in 1946 with the passage of the Canadian Citizenship Act, SC 1946, c 15, the term, Canadian citizen, was formally recognized, giving effect to what had long been felt and accepted by most Canadians. In adopting the term as a qualification for entry into the legal profession in British Columbia, the Legislature was merely continuing its earlier requirement that the concept of citizenship, as then recognized in the term "British subject", be necessary for entry into the profession.

Public policy, of which the citizenship requirement in the Barristers and Solicitors Act is an element, is for the Legislature to establish. The role of the Charter, as applied by the courts, is to ensure that in applying public policy the Legislature does not adopt measures which are not sustainable under the Charter. It is not, however, for the courts to legislate or to substitute their views on public policy for those of the Legislature. I would repeat for ease of reference the words of the Chief Justice in *R v Edwards Books and Art Ltd, supra,* at pp 781–82:

> A "reasonable limit" is one which having regard to the principles enunciated in *Oakes,* it was reasonable for the legislature to impose. The courts are not called upon to substitute judicial opinions for legislative ones as to the place at which to draw a precise line.

The function of the Court is to measure the legislative enactment against the requirements of the Charter and where the enactment infringes the Charter, in this case the provisions of section 15(1), and is not sustainable under section 1, the remedial power of the Court is set out in section 52 of the Constitution Act, 1982: "any law that is inconsistent with the provisions of the Constitution is, to the extent of the inconsistency, of no force or effect".

The essence of section 1 is found in the expression "reasonable" and it is for the Court to decide if section 42 of the Barristers and Solicitors Act of British Columbia is a reasonable limit. In reaching the conclusion that it is, I would say that the legislative choice in this regard is not one between an answer that is clearly right and one that is clearly wrong. Either position may well be sustainable and, as noted by the Chief Justice, *supra,* the Court is not called upon to substitute its opinion as to where to draw the line. The Legislature in fixing public policy has chosen the citizenship requirement and, unless the Court can find that choice unreasonable, it has no power under the Charter to strike it down or, as has been said, no power to invade the legislative field and substitute its views for that of the Legislature. In my view, the citizenship requirement is reasonable and sustainable under section 1. It is chosen for the achievement of a desirable social goal: one aspect of the due regulation and qualification of the legal profession. This is an objective of importance and the measure is not disproportionate to the object to be attained. The maximum delay imposed upon the non-citizen from the date of acquisition of permanent resident status is three years. It will frequently be less. No impediment is put in the way of obtaining citizenship. In fact, the policy of the Canadian government is to encourage the newcomer to become a citizen. It is reasonable, in my view, to expect that the newcomer who seeks to gain the privileges and status within the land and the right to exercise the great powers that admission to the practice of law will give should accept citizenship and its obligations as well as its advantages and benefits. I would therefore allow the appeal and restore the judgment at trial. I would answer the constitutional questions as follows:

Q(1) Does the Canadian citizenship requirement to be a lawyer in the Province of British Columbia as set out in section 42 of the Barristers and Solicitors Act, RSBC 1979, c 26 infringe or deny the rights guaranteed by section 15(1) of the Canadian Charter of Rights and Freedoms?

A   Yes.

Q(2) If the Canadian citizenship requirement to be a lawyer in the Province of British Columbia as set out in section 42 of the Barristers and Solicitors Act, RSBC 1979, c 26 infringes or denies the rights guaranteed by section 15(1) of the Canadian Charter of Rights and Freedoms, is it justified by section 1 of the Canadian Charter of Rights and Freedoms?

A   Yes.

Appeal dismissed.

CASE NO 9

RE MUNICIPAL OFFICERS' ASSOCIATION OF AUSTRALIA AND ANOTHER

AUSTRALIAN INDUSTRIAL RELATIONS COMMISSION

Judgment: 6 February 1991

Panel: Moore DP

Human rights — Equality and non-discrimination — Sex discrimination — Affirmative action — Positive discrimination — Whether union rules reserving certain executive positions for women, and limiting elections for such positions to women, discriminatory — Whether rules covered by exception for positive discrimination — Industrial Relations Act 1988, s 252(1)(d) — Sex Discrimination Act 1984 (Cth), ss 19 and 33 — Convention on the Elimination of All Forms of Discrimination against Women, art 4

BACKGROUND

Three trade unions, the Municipal Officers' Association of Australia ("MOA"), the Australian Transport Officers' Federation ("ATOF") and the Technical Service Guild of Australia ("TSG"), were planning to amalgamate. In September 1990, they lodged an application to the Industrial Relations Commission (the "Commission") under section 235 of the Industrial Relations Act 1988 ("IR Act") for approval of a ballot on the proposed amalgamation. Under the IR Act, an amalgamation was not permitted to result in alterations to the rules of the host organisation (that is, the organisation whose registration was to continue after the amalgamation), which were contrary to the IR Act or otherwise "contrary to law". In this case, the host organisation was the MOA.

The proposed alterations to the rules of the MOA created a new branch structure within the organisation. Each branch was to have a branch executive, and on each of these, it was proposed to introduce a position designated Branch Vice-President (women). Only female members could be nominated for this position, and only female members of the branch would be entitled to vote in the election for this position. A similar position, National Vice President (women) was proposed on the National Executive.

The Commission considered whether the proposed rules contravened section 19 of the Sex Discrimination Act (Cth) ("SDA"), which makes it unlawful for an organisation to discriminate against its members on the ground of sex, and if so, whether they fell within the exception permitted by section 33 which covers acts intended to ensure equal opportunities for persons of a particular sex or marital status, or for pregnant women.

HELD (finding that the proposed amendments were not contrary to the SDA)

1   The SDA was remedial legislation and should be construed beneficially. Its operation should therefore be as wide as the terms of the legislation reasonably permitted and s 19 (which makes it unlawful for an organisation to discriminate against its members on the ground of sex) should be interpreted as being directed not only to the conduct of organisations, but also their rules (p 154).

2   One of the objects of the SDA, expressed in section 3(a), was to give effect to the Convention on the Elimination of All Forms of Discrimination against Women. Section 33 of the SDA appeared to reflect article 4 of the Convention, which provides that "temporary special measures aimed at accelerating *de facto* equality between men and women shall not be considered discrimination". In the context of trade union governance, *de facto* equality meant representation by women in governing and policy-making bodies within an organisation broadly corresponding to the proportion of female members. Women were underrepresented in the governance of the amalgamating organisations. Rules which reserved positions for women on the executive of the branches and of the organisation could contribute to altering the perception of lack of encouragement by the union and therefore ameliorate the effect of past discrimination (pp 155, 157).

3   The proposed rules would deny male union members access to a benefit provided by the organisation on the grounds of their sex (s 19(2)(a) of the SDA), as by virtue of their sex, they would not be able to participate in an election relating to a position within the organisation, nor to stand for election for that position. However, having regard to the possibility, if not likelihood, that s 33 SDA permitted rules of the type proposed, the proposed alterations to the rules were not contrary to the SDA (p 154).

Treaties and other international instruments referred to

Convention on the Elimination of All Forms of Discrimination against Women 1979, art 4(1)

International Convention on the Elimination of all Forms of Racial Discrimination 1965, art 1(4)

National legislation referred to

Australia

Anti-Discrimination Act 1977 (NSW)

Equal Opportunity Act 1984 (Vic), ss 25 and 31

Equal Opportunity Act 1984 (SA), ss 35, 35a, 47, 57 and 72

Equal Opportunity Act 1984 (WA), ss 15, 22, 31, 41, 48, 58, 64, 66F, 66M and 66R

Human Rights and Equal Opportunity Commission Act 1986 (Cth)

Industrial Relations Act 1988 (Cth), ss 196, 208(1), 233(b), 235 and 252(1)(d)

Industrial Relations Legislation Amendment Act 1990 (Cth), s18

Racial Discrimination Act 1975 (Cth), s 8(1)

Sex Discrimination Act 1989 (Cth), ss 5, 19, 25 and 33

United Kingdom

Sex Discrimination Act 1975, ss 12 and 49

Cases referred to

Corry v Keperra Country Golf Club (1985) 64 ALR 556

Doyle v Australian Workers' Union (1986) 68 ALR 591; (1986) 12 FLR 197

Gerhardy v Brown (1985) 159 CLR 70; (1985) 57 ALR 472

Lawley & Others v Transport Workers' Union of Australia, unreported, 18 September 1987

Leves v Haines (1986) EOC ¶92–167

Lowen v Ivanov (1986) EOC ¶92–169

Municipal Officers Association v Lancaster (1981) 54 FLR 129; (1981) 37 ALR 559

R v Equal Opportunity Board, ex parte Burns (1984) EOC ¶92–112

Re Australian Journalists' Association (1988) EOC ¶92–224

Stoker v Kellogg (Aust) Pty Ltd (1984) EOC ¶92–021

Tullamore Bowling and Citizens Club v Lander (1984) 2 NSWLR 32

Victorian Equal Opportunity Board in Ross v University of Melbourne (1990) EOC ¶92–290

Wardley v Ansett Transport Industries (Operations) Pty Ltd (1984) EOC ¶92–002

Worrel v Belconnen Community Youth Support Scheme (1986) EOC ¶92–151

Wright v McLeod (1983) 74 FLR 146; (1983) 51 ALR 483

DECISION

MOORE, DEPUTY PRESIDENT: In September 1990 an application was lodged under s 235 of the Industrial Relations Act 1988 ("IR Act") for the approval of a designated Presidential Member for the submission to ballot of an amalgamation between The Municipal Officers Association of Australia ("MOA"), The Australian Transport Officers Federation ("ATOF") and The Technical Service Guild of Australia ("TSG").

Since the application was lodged the provisions of the IR Act concerning amalgamations have been substantially amended by the Industrial Relations Legislation Amendment Act 1990. By operation of s 18 of that Act I am to deal with the application, from 1 February 1991, under the IR Act as amended. The statutory provisions concerning the issue I deal with in this decision have not, in substance, altered since submissions were made in December 1990. I will refer to the IR Act in its amended form.

One of the matters that must be considered before an amalgamation can be submitted to ballot is whether any proposed alterations of the rules of the host organisation (being the organisation whose registration is to continue) comply with, and are not contrary to, the IR Act and awards, and are not otherwise contrary to law (s 252(1)(d)). In the present case I have to consider certain of the proposed alterations to the rules of the MOA (which is the host organisation) as they may be contrary to the provisions of the Sex Discrimination Act 1984 (Cth) ("SDA").

I should, at this stage, indicate what I perceive to be the role of a designated Presidential Member in considering proposed alterations under s 252(1)(d).

[Roles of Industrial Relations Commission and Federal Court]*

The role of the Commission is, in some respects, the same as that of the Federal Court, which can be called upon to decide whether a rule or the rules of an organisation contravene s 196. This may involve a consideration of whether a rule or the rules are contrary to the IR Act or otherwise contrary to law. The Court's jurisdiction arises when an application is made by a member of an organisation under s 208(1) and, as far as I am aware, such applications are mostly contested by the organisation concerned. In such matters the Court has adopted the approach that the contents of the rules of registered organisations are primarily a matter for the organisations themselves.[1]

Further, as Gray J explained in *Lawley & Others v Transport Workers' Union of Australia*:[2]

> As was pointed out in *Doyle v. Australian Workers' Union* (1986) 68 A.L.R. 591 at pp. 599–600, the primary justification for a provision in the rules of an organisation is that the organisation has chosen to adopt it. The onus lies on an applicant for orders under s.140 to make out the defect in a rule or the rules.

Moreover, a decision of the Court under s 208 is authoritative in the sense that it determines, in a final and binding manner, whether the rule contravenes s 196 (though subject to any relevant changes to the factual background against which the rule was considered).

While the Commission is required to consider the same general issue that arises under s 208, it does so in a quite different context. Its decision is not authoritative in that a rule thought by the Commission to comply with s 252(1)(d) may later be held by the Court to contravene s 196. While the circumstances in which the Court would consider the rule in this latter situation are likely to arise infrequently, it has jurisdiction to do so.[3]

The role of the Commission under s 252(1)(d) is to scrutinise the proposed alterations to the rules to ensure they meet the requirements of the IR Act and are not contrary to awards or contrary to law. While this occurs in the context of a hearing (see s 250(a)(i)) the proceedings are ordinarily uncontested. It is likely that the amalgamating organisations would be the only parties represented at that hearing who would make submissions on the validity of the rules under s 252(1)(d) and they would support their validity. No question of onus would therefore arise. Section 252(1)(d) requires that a designated Presidential Member be satisfied, in a positive sense, that the proposed alterations confirm to the statutory requirements. However, it would be wrong, in my view, for the proposed alterations (which have been agreed upon by the amalgamating organisations) to be rejected other than in a clear case of non-conformity with those requirements.

Such an approach would give effect to the provisions of s 233(b) which require:

> (b) that this Act should be applied in relation to the amalgamation of organisations in a way that, to the greatest extent that is consistent with the attainment of the object mentioned in paragraph 3(g) (Democratic control of, and membership participation in affairs of, organisations), is fair, practical, quick and non-legalistic.

---

*   *Eds:* headings (in square brackets) have been added for the convenience of readers.
1   (1983) 74 FLR 147, see also *Municipal Officers Association v Lancaster* (1981) 54 FLR 129 and *Doyle v Australian Workers Union* (1986) 12 FLR 197.
2   Unreported, 18 September 1987.
3   (1979) 40 FLR 462.

To do otherwise would, in practice, mean an organisation would have to justify its adoption of a rule before the Commission when, before the Court, a member attacking the validity of a rule would bear the burden of establishing its invalidity. To do otherwise would also pay only limited regard to the principles discussed in *Wright v McLeod*.[4]

[Proposed alterations to rules of MOA]

The proposed alterations to the rules of MOA are, in substance, a new set of rules with new branch structures within the organisation. Each branch is to have a branch executive. The rules contemplate that on branch executives there will be a position designated Branch Vice President (women). That position can be filled only by a member who is a woman. Only members of the branch who are women may vote in the election for that position. A position with similar characteristics, National Vice President (women), is proposed on the National Executive.

The SDA provides:

19(1) It is unlawful for a registered organisation, the committee of management of a registered organisation or a member of the committee of management of a registered organisation to discriminate against a person on the ground of the person's sex, marital status or pregnancy:

(a) by refusing or failing to accept the person's application for membership; or

(b) in the terms or conditions on which the organisation is prepared to admit the person to membership.

(2) It is unlawful for a registered organisation, the committee of management of a registered organisation or a member of the committee of management of a registered organisation to discriminate against a person who is a member of the registered organisation, on the ground of the member's sex, marital status or pregnancy:

(a) by denying the member access, or limiting the member's access, to any benefit provided by the organisation;

(b) by depriving the member of membership or varying the terms of membership; or

(c) by subjecting the member to any other detriment.

Section 19 is in substantially the same terms as s 25[5] of the SDA which renders unlawful certain conduct of clubs and their committees.

Provisions similar to both s 19 and s 25 are found in the Anti-Discrimination Act 1977 (NSW) (see ss 11, 20A, 28, 34A, 43, 48A, 49F, 49LA, 49U, 49ZB, 49ZC and 49ZR), the Equal Opportunity Act 1984 (Vic) (see ss 25 and 31), the Equal Opportunity Act 1984 (SA) (see ss 35, 35a, 47, 57 and 72) and the Equal Opportunity Act (WA) (see ss 15, 22, 31, 41, 48, 58, 64, 66F, 66M and 66R).

Surprisingly these provisions have received only limited consideration by the various equal opportunity tribunals and the courts.

The language of s 19 of the SDA (and the equivalent provisions in state legislation) appears to have its genesis in the Sex Discrimination Act 1975 (UK), which contains a provision, s 12, in almost identical terms. The scope of s 12, of the UK Act, for present purposes, is apparent from another provision of the Act, s 49, which limits the operation of s 12 so as not to render unlawful provisions (presumably this is a reference to rules)

4   (1983) 74 FLR 147.
5   See *Corry v Keperra Country Golf Club* (1985) 64 ALR 556.

which reserve positions for some members of one sex on elected bodies. Section 49 appears not to save provisions which discriminate in relation to voting and may also not save provisions restricting, in a way that discriminates, rights to nominate candidates (see s 49(2)).

Before considering the proposed alterations and the SDA in detail I should mention that the applicant organisations have consulted the Human Rights and Equal Opportunity Commission which has indicated in correspondence with MOA that rules such as those I am considering are not contrary to the SDA. Its views must be given weight in proceedings such as these.

Against that background I have to consider the proposed alterations to the rules and s 19 of the SDA. Section 19 must be read in conjunction with s 5 which provides:

> 5(1) For the purposes of this Act, a person (in this sub-section referred to as the "discriminator") discriminates against another person (in this sub-section referred to as the "aggrieved person") on the ground of the sex of the aggrieved person if, by reason of:
>
> > (a) the sex of the aggrieved person;
> >
> > (b) a characteristic that appertains generally to persons of the sex of the aggrieved person; or
> >
> > (c) a characteristic that is generally imputed to persons of the sex of the aggrieved person,
>
> the discriminator treats the aggrieved person less favourably than, in circumstances that are the same or are not materially different, the discriminator treats or would treat a person of the opposite sex.
>
> (2) For the purposes of this Act, a person (in this sub-section referred to as the "discriminator") discriminates against another person (in this sub-section referred to as the "aggrieved person") on the ground of the sex of the aggrieved person if the discriminator requires the aggrieved person to comply with a requirement or condition:
>
> > (a) with which a substantially higher proportion of persons of the opposite sex to the aggrieved person comply or are able to comply;
> >
> > (b) which is not reasonable having regard to the circumstances of the case; and
> >
> > (c) with which the aggrieved person does not or is not able to comply.

Section 19 is framed in a way that renders unlawful acts of an organisation, the committee of management of the organisation or members of the committee. It is not, in terms, directed to rules of an organisation which have or may have a discriminatory effect.

However, the discriminatory acts referred to in s 19 include acts that would normally result from the operation of the rules of the organisation. Section 19(1)(b) refers to "the terms or conditions on which the organisation is prepared to admit the person to membership" and s 19(2)(b) refers to "varying the terms of membership". Both concern matters that the rules of a registered organisation would ordinarily deal with.

The Sex Discrimination Act 1975 (UK) provides a guide to the scope of s 19. Section 49 of the UK Act allows positions on governing bodies of trade unions to be reserved (presumably by the rules of the trade unions) for persons of one sex. It is apparent from s 49 that it does so because s 12 (which is in almost identical terms as s 19 of the SDA) would otherwise make unlawful a rule which reserved such positions. It is clear that the

SDA is remedial legislation and it should be construed beneficially.[6] Its operation should therefore be as wide as the terms of the legislation reasonably permit and I believe I should proceed on the basis that s 19 is directed not only to the conduct of organisations (through officers, employees and agents) but also their rules.

The question that then arises is whether the proposed alterations themselves contravene s 19 without regard to s 33 of the SDA and if so whether s 33 preserves their operation. It is first necessary to consider what is the effect of the proposed alterations. The provisions in the rules which identify the various positions of Vice President (women) have no substantive effect without the rules which provide the mechanism by which a person is elected to those positions. Those rules have two features. The first is that only a woman may be nominated as a candidate for the position and the second is that only women may vote in the election for the position.

The rules grant these rights to female members and do not accord those rights to male members. Does this constitute discrimination (as defined) whereby male members suffer one of the disabilities referred to in paragraphs (a), (b) or (c) of s 19(2)? It may be thought that in relation to existing members of MOA who are male what is proposed constitutes a variation of the terms of their membership, which is of the type comprehended by the language of s 19(2)(b). However, it is not necessary to consider this matter at length as the proposed rules, in my view, will deny male members a benefit provided by the organisation on the ground of their sex (s 19(2)(a)). If s 19(2)(2)(a) applies then it seems that s 19(2)(c) has no operation as it relates to "any other detriment" which appears to be a reference to a detriment other than those referred to in s 19(2)(a) or (b).

It is probably unnecessary to explain in detail why I have reached this conclusion as I am satisfied that s 33 most likely operates to nullify the effect s 19 would otherwise have. The benefits that the male members are denied are the right to stand and vote for a position on the Executive (either Branch or National). The expression "... or limiting ... access to a benefit" in State anti-discrimination legislation has been liberally construed.[7] I see no reason why this expression should not also be given a broad meaning as it appears in s 19 of the SDA. By virtue of their sex, male members cannot participate in an election relating to a position within the organisation. It is a position which forms part of a body that can determine matters of policy concerning the organisation or a branch (and therefore policy affecting male members). Even though male members may participate in the election of all other members of that body, their rights are more limited than those of female members in determining who sits on that body. Further, their rights to be elected to sit on the body are also more limited. In those circumstances it seems to me that male members are, on the grounds of their sex, denied access to a benefit in relation to the particular position, or expressing it slightly differently, their access to a benefit is limited if one looks at the election of the body as a whole. The relevant benefit is the right to stand and to vote which is provided by the organisation through its rules.

It is now necessary to consider s 33, which provides:

> 33 Nothing in Division 1 or 2 renders it unlawful to do an act a purpose of which is to ensure that persons of a particular sex or marital status or persons who are pregnant have

---

6   See *Wardley v Ansett Transport Industries (Operations) Pty Ltd* (1984) EOC 92-002, cf *Tullamore Bowling and Citizens Club v Lander* (1984) 2 NSWLR 32 at 52.

7   *R v Equal Opportunity Board; Ex parte Burns* (1984) EOC 92-112 at 76.11, *Stoker v Kellogg (Aust) Pty Ltd* (1984) EOC 92-021, *Leves v Haines* (1986) EOC 92-167 and *Lowen v Ivanov* (1986) EOC 92-169.

equal opportunities with other persons in circumstances in relation to which provision is made by this Act.

As far as I am aware this section has not been judicially considered (except by Boulton J of this Commission) and its meaning and scope is far from clear. I was referred to one case concerning s 33, *Worrell v Belconnen Community Youth Support Scheme*,[8] but that decision really throws little light on the meaning and scope of the section. It is, in any event, to be contrasted with the decision of the Victorian Equal Opportunity Board in *Ross v University of Melbourne*.[9]

The application of this section can be approached in at least two ways in the present circumstances. The first is to examine whether under the existing rules of MOA women enjoy equal opportunities to stand and vote for the executives of the organisation and branches. If it appears they do, then rules that give preferential treatment to women could not have, as a purpose, ensuring that women secure that which they already have, namely equal opportunities. This broadly was the approach of Boulton J in *Re The Australian Journalists' Association*.[10] In the present case it is clear that the rules contain no barriers to female members standing or voting in any election within the organisation and accordingly, approached this way, s 33 would not preserve the operation of rules which gave preferential treatment to female members.

However I am inclined to think that such an approach involves an unnecessarily narrow construction of s 33.

As a matter of fact women have been underrepresented on governing bodies within the amalgamating organisations. The proportion of women in governing bodies is significantly smaller than the proportion of women who are members. Does s 33 protect rules which have as a purpose to ensure that, at least to an extent, this will alter? Section 33 appears to reflect certain provisions in the Convention on the Elimination of All Forms of Discrimination Against Women.

The SDA has, as one of its objects:

3(a) to give effect to certain provisions of the Convention on the Elimination of All Forms of Discrimination against Women.

The Convention is a schedule to the SDA. Article 4 of Part l of that Convention provides:

4(1) Adoption by States Parties of temporary special measures aimed at accelerating *de facto* equality between men and women shall not be considered discrimination as defined in the present Convention, but shall in no way entail as a consequence the maintenance of unequal or separate standards; these measures shall be discontinued when the objectives of equality of opportunity and treatment have been achieved.

The Convention speaks of "*de facto*" equality. In the context of trade union government, I take that to mean representation by women in governing and policy making bodies within an organisation that broadly corresponds to the proportion of female members in the organisation itself.

The High Court has recently considered, in *Gerhardy v Brown*[11] the scope of s 8(1) of the Racial Discrimination Act 1975 (Cth) which gives operative effect to Article 1(4) of the International Convention on the Elimination of All Forms of Racial Discrimination. Article 1(4) permits special measures to be taken to advance the interests of racially or

---

8   (1986) EOC 92-151.
9   (1990) EOC 92-290.
10   (1988) EOC 92-224
11   (1985) 159 CLR 70.

ethnically disadvantaged groups or persons. The effect of Article 1(4) of that Convention appears to be the same as, or at least similar to, Article 4 of Part 1 of the Convention on the Elimination of All Forms of Discrimination Against Women.

In *Gerhardy v Brown* Brennan J discussed at length the concept of equality and measures designed to secure equality. He said:

> But it has long been recognised that formal equality before the law is insufficient to eliminate all forms of racial discrimination. In its Advisory Opinion on Minority Schools in Albania, ((1935) Ser A/B No 64 at p 19) the Permanent Court of International Justice noted the need for equality in fact as well as in law, saying:
>
>> "Equality in law precludes discrimination of any kind; whereas equality in fact may involve the necessity of different treatment in order to attain a result which establishes an equilibrium between different situations.
>>
>> It is easy to imagine cases in which equality of treatment of the majority and of the minority, whose situation and requirements are different, would result in equality in fact ..."
>
> As Mathew J said in the Supreme Court of India in *Kerala v Thomas* ((1976) 1 SCR 906 at p 951), quoting from a joint judgment of Chandrachud J and himself:
>
>> "Is of this that equality in law precludes discrimination of any kind; whereas equality in fact may involve the necessity of differential treatment in order to attain a result which establishes an equilibrium between different situations."
>
> In the same case, Ray CJ pithily observed ((1976) SCR at p 933):
>
>> "Equality of opportunity for unequals can only mean aggravation of inequality."
>
> The validity of these observations is manifest. Human rights and fundamental freedoms may be nullified or impaired by political, economic, social, cultural or religious influences in a society as well as by the formal operation of its laws. Formal equality before the law is an engine of oppression destructive of human dignity if the law entrenches inequalities "in the political, economic, social, cultural or any field of public life".

He later said:

> Formal equality must yield on occasions to achieve what the Permanent Court in the *Minority Schools of Albania Opinion* ((1935) Ser A/B No 64 at p 19) called "effective, genuine equality".
>
> A means by which the injustice or unreasonableness of formal equality can be diminished or avoided is the taking of special measures. A special measure is, ex hypothesis, discriminatory in character; it denies formal equality before the law in order to achieve effective and genuine equality. As Vierdag in *The Concept of Discrimination in International Law* (1973), p 136 says:
>
>> "The seeming, formal equality that in a way may appear from equal treatment is replaced by an apparent inequality of treatment that is aimed at achieving 'real', material equality somewhere in the future. And this inequality of treatment is accorded precisely on the basis of the characteristics that made it necessary to grant it: race, religion, social origin, and so on."
>
> A legally required distinction, exclusion, restriction or preference based on race nullifies or impairs formal equality in the enjoyment of human rights and fundamental freedoms, but it may advance effective and genuine equality.

His Honour goes on to consider, in the context of the Racial Discrimination Act 1975, what are special measures.[12] It would be consistent with some of His Honour's more general observations and the judgments of other members of the Court to treat s 33 of the SDA as permitting the creation of *de facto* equality (to adopt the language of the Convention). If this is its intended effect then measures which discriminate for the purpose of creating equality (*viz* proportional participation in union government) are protected by s 33. Such measures, however, would cease to be so protected when equality was achieved or where it was clear that constraints which operated, in fact, to limit female participation had been removed.

Precisely why women are underrepresented in the government of the amalgamating organisations is unclear. The rules create no barriers. Research in this area appears to be limited though there is at least one empirical study[13] (of MOA membership) which has concluded that two factors were perceived by women members as providing barriers to participation in union activities *viz* lack of child care and lack of encouragement by their union. It also concluded that female members were more likely to perceive lack of encouragement by the union as a significant barrier than male members.

The precise bases for this perception were not identified. It may be only a perception reflecting a subjective view of the members concerned. It may, however, be a response to past conduct by the organisation including its officers and employees. It may therefore be the result of past discriminatory conduct. Rules which reserve positions for women on the executives of branches and of the organisation could contribute to altering that perception and therefore ameliorate the effect of past discrimination. This may have the consequence of increasing the participation of female members in the government and administration of the amalgamated organisation. This may occur not only because women, of necessity, will occupy the positions reserved for female members but also because the organisation, by adopting the rules, would be seen by female members to be encouraging their participation in the government of the union.

A liberal construction of s 33 is consistent with the terms of the Convention and the observations of Brennan J. It is also a construction adopted by the Human Rights and Equal Opportunity Commission itself. Not only has it expressed its view that rules of the type I am considering are protected by s 33, but it indicated formally, when considering an application by the Australian Journalists' Association for an exemption under s 44 of the SDA following the decision of Boulton J, that "it does not necessarily agree with the interpretation of the Sex Discrimination Act 1984 which was expressed in the decision of Boulton J". In correspondence tendered in these proceedings the Secretary of the Commission says:

> The Commission does not agree with Boulton J's reasoning in this matter as it is of the view that the special measures provision, s 33 of the Sex Discrimination Act, operates to render elections conducted pursuant to the proposed rule changes not unlawful under that Act.

It is not clear whether this letter is intended to convey a formal view of the Commission.

---

12 For a critical analysis of *Gerhardy v Brown* see: D Wood "Positive Discrimination and the High Court", 17 *UNWA Law Review* (June 1987) 128 and W Sadurski, "*Gerhardy v Brown* v The Concept of Discrimination", 11 SU Law Review (March 1986) 5.

13 Gerard Griffin and John Benson: "Barriers to female membership participation in trade union activities", The University of Melbourne. The various assumptions I have just made, if correct, would justify the inclusion of rules of the type I am considering as a measure which has as a purpose ensuring equal opportunities. If s 33 is liberally construed, they are measures protected by that section.

Having regard to the possibility, if not likelihood, that s 33 permits rules of the type proposed, I cannot be satisfied that the proposed alterations are contrary to the SDA. Having regard to what, as I discussed earlier, I see as my function under s 252(1)(d), I believe I should therefore not require the applicant organisations to alter the proposed rules where there is only doubt as to their validity and when those rules have been regularly adopted by one of the organisations concerned in the amalgamation and agreed to by the others.

However it is plainly undesirable that organisations wishing to adopt rules of this type have to run the risk of the Registrar, the Australian Industrial Relations Commission or the Federal Court declaring invalid rules which the statutory authority responsible for the administration of the SDA, the Human Rights and Equal Opportunity Commission, believes conform with its provisions. While it is clearly a matter for that Commission whether to pursue the issue raised in these proceedings, I note that s 11(1)(j) of the Human Rights and Equal Opportunity Commission Act 1986 empowers the Commission:

> on its own initiative or when requested by the Minister, to report to the Minister as to the laws that should be made by the Parliament or action that should be taken by the Commonwealth, on matters relating to human rights.

It would be open to the legislature to either incorporate into the SDA provisions such as those in the UK legislation or make clear that rules of the type I am considering are proscribed.

ADDENDUM TO DECISION

The preceding decision was prepared for publication on 6 February 1991. On that day I received detailed written submissions from the Human Rights and Equal Opportunity Commission. Those written submissions indicated clearly that it viewed the proposed alterations as conforming to the SDA. There are matters of emphasis in the written submissions that I do not deal with in this decision. My conclusion, however, remains the same.

CASE NO 10

KALANKE v FREIE HANSESTADT BREMEN

EUROPEAN COURT OF JUSTICE

Case No: C-450/93

Judgment: 17 October 1995

Panel: *Judges:* Rodríguez Iglesias (*Presiding*), Kakouris, Edward, Puissochet (*President of Chambers*), Hirsch (*President of Chambers*), Mancini, Shockweiler, Moitinho de Almeida, Kapteyn (*Rapporteur*), Gulmann and Murray

Human rights — Equality and non-discrimination — Sex discrimination — Affirmative action — Positive discrimination — Whether a national law which guaranteed women absolute and unconditional priority over equally qualified men for appointment or promotion in certain sectors where women were under-represented was compatible with the principle of equal treatment for men and women under European Community law — Act on Equal Treatment of Men and Women in the Public Service of the Land of Bremen of 20 November 1990, s 4 — European Community Council Directive on Equal Treatment, Council Directive 76/207/EEC of 9 February 1976, arts 2(1) and 2(4)

BACKGROUND

The City of Bremen employed Mr Eckhard Kalanke and Ms Heike Glißmann as gardeners in the Parks Department. Both applied and were shortlisted for the position of section manager. Since they were equally qualified, preference had to be given to Ms Glißmann under the positive action provisions of the Bremen Law on Equal Treatment for Men and Women in Public Service. This law provided that when a position in a higher pay bracket was being considered, women with qualifications equal to those held by men applying for the same position would be given priority if women were under-represented. Women were deemed to be under-represented if they did not make up at least half of the staff in the pay bracket of the relevant personnel group within a department. Mr Kalanke brought proceedings before the Federal Labour Court, which found that the quota system was lawful under German constitutional and civil law. However, it considered that the Bremen Law was possibly incompatible with the European Community Council Directive on Equal Treatment, Council Directive 76/207/EEC of 9 February 1976 ("Equal Treatment Directive"). It therefore referred the case to the European Court of Justice for a preliminary ruling on the interpretation of articles 2(1) and 2(4) of the Directive.

HELD

1 The purpose of the Equal Treatment Directive, as stated in article 1(1), is to give effect in Member States to the principle of equal treatment for men and women as regards access to employment, including promotion. Article 2(1) states that "the principle of equal treatment shall mean that there shall be no discrimination whatsoever on grounds of sex". Article 2(1) precluded the application of a national rule providing

that, where men and women who are candidates for the same promotion are equally qualified, women are automatically to be given priority in sectors where they are under-represented. This involved discrimination on grounds of sex. (Paras 15–17)

2   However, article 2(4) provides that the Equal Treatment Directive "shall be without prejudice to measures to promote equal opportunity for men and women, in particular by removing existing inequalities which affect women's opportunities". That provision was specifically and exclusively designed to allow measures which, although discriminatory in appearance, are in fact intended to eliminate or reduce actual instances of inequality which may exist in the reality of social life. It thus permitted national measures relating to access to employment, including promotion, which give a specific advantage to women with a view to improving their ability to compete on the labour market and to pursue a career on an equal footing with men. National rules which guaranteed women absolute and unconditional priority for appointment and promotion, went beyond promoting equal opportunities and overstepped the limits of the exception in article 2(4) of the Directive. (Paras 17 – 19 and 22)

Treaties and other international instruments referred to

Treaty on European Union (the Maastricht Treaty), Annex 14, Agreement on Social Policy, art 6(3)

European Community law referred to

Council Directive 76/207/EEC of 9 February 1976 on the implementation of the principle of equal treatment for men and women as regards access to employment, vocational training and promotion, and working conditions (OJ 1976 L 39, p 40), arts 1(1), 1(2), 2(1), 2(3) and 2(4)

Council Recommendation 84/635 of 13 December 1984 on the promotion of positive action for women, preamble (OJ 1984 L331, p34)

National legislation referred to

Germany

Act on Equal Treatment of Men and Women in the Public Service of the Land of Bremen of 20 November 1990, s 4

Basic Law, arts 3(2), 3(3) and 33(2)

Constitution of the Land, art 2(2)

Civil Code, s 611

Cases referred to

City of Richmond v Croson 488 US 469 (1989); 102 L Ed 2d 854

Defrenne v Sabena, ECJ Case 149/77, 15 June 1978: [1978] ECR 1365; [1978] 3 CMLR 312

Re Protection of Women: EC Commission v France, ECJ Case 312/86, 25 October 1988: [1988] ECR 6315; [1989] 1 CMLR 408

Grimaldi v Fonds de Maladies Professionnelles, ECJ Case C-322/88, 13 December 1989: [1989] ECR I-4407, [1991] 2 CMLR 265; [1990] IRLR 400

Habermann-Beltermann v Arbeiterwohlfahrt, Bezirksverband Ndb/oPF eV, ECJ Case C-421/92, 5 May 1994: [1994] ECR I-1657; [1994] 2 CMLR 681

Hofmann v Barmer Ersatzkasse, ECJ Case 184/83, 12 July 1984: [1984] ECR 3047; [1986] 1 CMLR 242; [1985] ICR 731

Johnston v Chief Constable of the Royal Ulster Constabulary, ECJ Case 222/84, 15 May 1986: [1987] QB 129; [1986] 3 WLR 1038; [1986] 3 All ER 135; [1986] ECR 1651, [1986] 3 CMLR 240; [1987] ICR 83; [1986] IRLR 263

Regents of the University of California v Bakke 438 US 265 (1978); 57 L Ed 2d 750

Speybrouck v European Parliament, ECJ (Court of First Instance) Case T-45/90, 28 January 1992: [1992] II ECR 33

United Steelworkers of America AFL-CIO-CLC v Webster 443 US 193 (1979); 61 L Ed 2d 480

JUDGMENT

1   By order of 22 June 1993, received at the Court on 23 November 1993, the *Bundesarbeitsgericht* (Federal Labour Court) referred to the Court for a preliminary ruling under Article 177 EEC two questions on the interpretation of Article 2(1) and (4) of Council Directive 76/207 on the implementation of the principle of equal treatment for men and women as regards access to employment, vocational training and promotion, and working conditions (hereinafter "the Directive").[1]

2   Those questions were raised in proceedings between Mr Kalanke and *Freie Hansestadt Bremen* (City of Bremen).

3   Paragraph 4 of the *Landesgleichstellungsgesetz* of 20 November 1990 (Bremen Act on Equal Treatment for Men and Women in the Public Services, hereinafter the "LGG")[2] provides:

Appointment, assignment to an official post and promotion

1   In the case of an appointment (including establishment as a civil servant or judge) which is not made for training purposes, women who have the same qualifications as men applying for the same post are to be given priority in sectors where they are underrepresented.

2   In the case of an assignment to a position in a higher pay, remuneration and salary bracket, women who have the same qualifications as men applying for the same post are to be given priority if they are underrepresented. This also applies in the case of assignment to a different official post and promotion.

3   ...

4   Qualifications are to be evaluated exclusively in accordance with the requirements of the occupation, post to be filled or career bracket. Specific experience and capabilities, such as those acquired as a result of family work, social commitment or unpaid activity, are part of the qualifications within the meanings of subparagraphs (1) and (2) if they are of use in performing the duties of the position in question.

---

1   [1976] OJ L39/40.
2   *Bremisches Gesetzblatt*, at p 433.

5   There is underrepresentation if women do not make up at least half of the staff in the individual pay, remuneration and salary brackets in the relevant personnel group within a department. This also applies to the function levels provided for in the organisation chart.

4   It appears from the order for reference that, at the final stage of recruitment to a post of Section Manager in the Bremen Parks Department, two candidates, both in BAT pay bracket III, were shortlisted:

–   Mr Kalanke, the plaintiff in the main proceedings, holder of a diploma in horticulture and landscape gardening, who had worked since 1973 as a horticultural employee in the Parks Department and acted as permanent assistant to the Section Manager; and

–   Ms Glißmann, holder of a diploma in landscape gardening since 1983 and also employed, since 1975, as a horticultural employee in the Parks Department.

5   The Staff Committee refused to give its consent to Mr Kalanke's promotion, proposed by the Parks Department management. Reference to arbitration resulted in a recommendation in favour of Mr Kalanke. The Staff Committee then stated that the arbitration had failed and appealed to the Conciliation Board which, in a decision binding on the employer, considered that the two candidates were equally qualified and that priority should therefore be given, in accordance with the LGG, to the woman.

6   Before the *Arbeitsgericht* (Labour Court), Mr Kalanke claimed that he was better qualified than Ms Glißmann, a fact which the conciliation board had failed to recognise. He argued that, by reason of its quota system, the LGG was incompatible with the Bremen Constitution, with the *Grundgesetz* (German Basic Law) and with section 611a of the BGB (German Civil Code). His application was dismissed, however, by the *Arbeitsgericht* and again, on appeal, by the *Landesarbeitsgericht* (Regional Labour Court).

7   The First Chamber of the *Bundesarbeitsgericht*, hearing the plaintiff's application for review on a point of law, considers that resolution of the dispute depends essentially on the applicability of the LGG. It points out that if the Conciliation Board was wrong in applying that act, its decision would be unlawful because it gave an advantage, solely on the ground of sex, to an equally qualified female candidate. The *Bundesarbeitsgericht* accepts the *Landesarbeitsgericht's* finding that the two applicants were equally qualified for the post. Considering itself bound also by that court's finding that women are under-represented in the Parks Department, it holds that the Conciliation Board was obliged, under section 4(2) of the LGG, to refuse to agree to the plaintiff's appointment to the vacant post.

8   The *Bundesarbeitsgericht* points out that the case does not involve a system of strict quotas reserving a certain proportion of posts for women, regardless of their qualifications, but rather a system of quotas dependent on candidates' abilities. Women enjoy no priority unless the candidates of both sexes are equally qualified.

9   The national court considers that the quota system is compatible with the German constitutional and statutory provisions referred to in paragraph 6 above. More specifically, it points out that section 4 of the LGG must be interpreted in accordance with the *Grundgesetz* with the effect that, even if priority for promotion is to be given in principle to women, exceptions must be made in appropriate cases.

10   It notes a number of factors suggesting that such a system is not incompatible with the Directive.

11 Considering, however, that doubts remain in that regard, the *Bundesarbeitsgericht* has stayed the proceedings and sought a preliminary ruling from the Court on the following questions:

1　Must Article 2(4) of Council Directive 76/207 on the implementation of the principle of equal treatment for men and women as regards access to employment, vocational training and promotion, and working conditions, be interpreted as also covering statutory provisions under which, when a position in a higher pay bracket is being assigned, women with the same qualifications as men applying for the same position are to be given priority if women are under-represented, there being deemed to be under-representation if women do not make up at least half of the staff in the individual pay brackets in the relevant personnel group within a department, which also applies to the function levels provided for in the organisation chart?

2　If Question 1 is answered in the negative:

Must Article 2(1) of Council Directive 76/207 be interpreted, having regard to the principle of proportionality, as meaning that it is not permissible to apply statutory provisions under which, when a position in a higher pay bracket is being assigned, women with the same qualifications as men applying for the same position are to be given priority if women are under-represented, there being deemed to be under-representation if women do not make up at least half of the staff in the individual pay brackets in the relevant personnel group within a department, which also applies to the function levels provided for in the organisation chart?

12　Both questions seek to clarify the scope of the derogation from the principle of equal treatment allowed by Article 2(4) of the Directive and should therefore be examined together.

13　The national court asks, essentially, whether Article 2(1) and (4) of the Directive precludes national rules such as those in the present case which, where candidates of different sexes shortlisted for promotion are equally qualified, automatically give priority to women in sectors where they are under-represented, under-representation being deemed to exist when women do not make up at least half of the staff in the individual pay brackets in the relevant personnel group or in the function levels provided for in the organisation chart.

14　In its order for reference, the national court points out that a quota system such as that in issue may help to overcome in the future the disadvantages which women currently face and which perpetuate past inequalities, inasmuch as it accustoms people to seeing women also filling certain more senior posts. The traditional assignment of certain tasks to women and the concentration of women at the lower end of the scale are contrary to the equal rights criteria applicable today. In that connection, the national court cites figures illustrating the low proportion of women in the higher career brackets among city employees in Bremen, particularly if sectors, such as education, where the presence of women in higher posts is now established are excluded.

15　The purpose of the Directive is, as stated in Article 1(1), to put into effect in the Member States the principle of equal treatment for men and women as regards, *inter alia*, access to employment, including promotion. Article 2(1) states that the principle of equal treatment means that "there shall be no discrimination whatsoever on grounds of sex either directly or indirectly".

16 A national rule that, where men and women who are candidates for the same promotion are equally qualified, women are automatically to be given priority in sectors where they are under-represented, involves discrimination on grounds of sex.

17 It must, however, be considered whether such a national rule is permissible under Article 2(4), which provides that the Directive "shall be without prejudice to measures to promote equal opportunity for men and women, in particular by removing existing inequalities which affect women's opportunities".

18 That provision is specifically and exclusively designed to allow measures which, although discriminatory in appearance, are in fact intended to eliminate or reduce actual instances of inequality which may exist in the reality of social life (see Case 312/86, *EC Commission v France* ([1988] ECR 6315, [1989] 1 CMLR 408).

19 It thus permits national measures relating to access to employment, including promotion, which give a specific advantage to women with a view to improving their ability to compete on the labour market and to pursue a career on an equal footing with men.

20 As the Council considered in the third recital in the preamble to Recommendation 84/635 on the promotion of positive action for women ([1984] OJ L331, p 34), "existing legal provisions on equal treatment, which are designed to afford rights to individuals, are inadequate for the elimination of all existing inequalities unless parallel action is taken by governments, both sides of industry and other bodies concerned, to counteract the prejudicial effects on women in employment which arise from social attitudes, behaviour and structures".

21 Nevertheless, as a derogation from an individual right laid down in the Directive, Article 2(4) must be interpreted strictly (see Case 222/84, *Johnston v Chief Constable of the Royal Ulster Constabulary* ([1986] ECR 1651, [1986] 3 CMLR 240).

22 National rules which guarantee women absolute and unconditional priority for appointment or promotion go beyond promoting equal opportunities and overstep the limits of the exception in Article 2(4) of the Directive.

23 Furthermore, in so far as it seeks to achieve equal representation of men and women in all grades and levels within a department, such a system substitutes for equality of opportunity as envisaged in Article 2(4) the result which is only to be arrived at by providing such equality of opportunity.

24 The answer to the national court's questions must therefore be that Article 2(1) and (4) of the Directive precludes national rules such as those in the present case which, where candidates of different sexes shortlisted for promotion are equally qualified, automatically give priority to women in sectors where they are under-represented, under-representation being deemed to exist when women do not make up at least half of the staff in the individual pay brackets in the relevant personnel group or in the function levels provided for in the organisation chart.

Costs

25 The costs incurred by the United Kingdom and the Commission of the European Communities, which have submitted observations to the Court, are not recoverable. Since these proceedings are, for the parties to the main proceedings, a step in the action pending before the national court, the decision on costs is a matter for that court.

On those grounds, **THE COURT**, in answer to the questions referred to it by the *Bundesarbeitsgericht* by order of 22 June 1993, **HEREBY RULES**:

Article 2(1) and (4) of Council Directive 76/207 on the implementation of the principle of equal treatment for men and women as regards access to employment, vocational training and promotion, and working conditions precludes national rules such as those in the present case which, where candidates of different sexes shortlisted for promotion are equally qualified, automatically give priority to women in sectors where they are under-represented, under-representation being deemed to exist when women do not make up at least half of the staff in the individual pay brackets in the relevant personnel group or in the function levels provided for in the organisation chart.

ADVOCATE-GENERAL'S OPINION*

1   Is national legislation under which women are given priority in recruitment and/or in obtaining promotion provided that they have the same qualifications as the male applicants and that women are under-represented – in so far as they do not constitute one half of the personnel – in the individual remuneration brackets in the relevant personnel group, compatible with the principle of equal treatment for men and women laid down by the relevant Community legislation? In other words, does a system of quotas in favour of women, even if it is dependent on the conditions which I have just described, embody sex discrimination contrary to Community law or does it constitute permitted positive action inasmuch as it is designed to promote effective equal opportunities in the world of work?

That is, in essence, the purport of the questions referred to the Court for a preliminary ruling by the *Bundesarbeitsgericht* (Federal Labour Court) concerning, more particularly, the interpretation of Article 2(1) and (4) of Council Directive 76/207 on the implementation of the principle of equal treatment for men and women as regards access to employment, vocational training and promotion, and working conditions[1] (hereinafter "the Directive").

2   The purpose of the Directive, as set out in Article 1(1), is to "put into effect in the Member States the principle of equal treatment for men and women as regards access to employment, including promotion, and to vocational training and as regards working conditions and, on the conditions referred to in paragraph 2, social security". Article 2(1) then states that "the principle of equal treatment shall mean that there shall be no discrimination whatsoever on grounds of sex either directly or indirectly by reference in particular to marital or family status". However, Article 2(4), whose interpretation is sought, authorises the Member States to adopt and/or maintain in force "measures to promote equal opportunity for men and women, in particular by removing existing inequalities which affect women's opportunities in the areas referred to in Article 1(1)".

Express reference is made to Article 2(4) in the preamble to Council Recommendation 84/635 on the promotion of positive action for women,[2] which stresses the need for parallel action "to counteract the prejudicial effects on women in employment which arise from social attitudes, behaviour and structures" on the ground that existing legal provisions on equal treatment are "inadequate for the elimination of all existing inequalities".[3] The recommendation therefore calls on the Member States to "adopt a positive action policy designed to eliminate existing inequalities affecting women in

---

*   ***Eds:*** the Advocate-General's Opinion has been included in this case as it contains a very useful discussion of the concept and models of affirmative/ positive action, which was not explored in the judgment itself.
1   [1976] OJ L39/40.
2   [1984] OJ L331/34.
3   See the third recital in the preamble.

working life and to promote a better balance between the sexes in employment" (point 1) and, in particular, to take steps to ensure that positive action includes as far as possible actions having a bearing on "encouraging women candidates and the recruitment and promotion of women in sectors and professions and at levels where they are under-represented, particularly as regards positions of responsibility"(sixth indent point of 4). In sum, in the face of existing inequalities, Member States are recommended to encourage women candidates and the recruitment and promotion of women.

Lastly, it should be observed that a provision with substantially similar scope to Article 2(4) is contained in Article 6(3) of the agreement on social policy concluded between the Member States of the European Community with the exception of the United Kingdom of Great Britain and Northern Ireland annexed to the Maastricht Treaty with Protocol No 14. According to that provision, the principle of equal pay affirmed by the agreement "shall not prevent any Member State from maintaining or adopting measures providing for specific advantages in order to make it easier for women to pursue a vocational activity or to prevent or compensate for disadvantages in their professional careers".

3   To turn to the relevant national legislation, this is the *Gesetz zur Gleichstellung von Frau und Mann im öffentlichen Dienst des Landes Bremen*[4] (Act on Equal Treatment of Men and Women in the Public Service of the Land of Bremen, hereinafter referred to as the "LGG") of 20 November 1990, section 4 of which provides as follows:

Appointment, assignment to an official post and promotion

1   In the case of an appointment (including establishment of the status of official or judge) which is not made for training purposes, women who have qualifications equal to those of their male co-applicants shall be given priority in sectors where they are under-represented.

2   In the case of an assignment of an activity in a higher pay, remuneration and salary bracket, women who have qualifications equal to those of their male co-applicants shall be given priority if they are under-represented. This shall also apply in the case of assignment of a different official post and promotion.

3   ...

4   Qualifications shall be evaluated exclusively in accordance with the requirements of the profession, post to be occupied or career. Specific experience and capabilities, such as those acquired as a result of family work, social commitment or unpaid activity, are part of the qualifications within the meaning of subparagraphs (1) and (2) if they are of use in performing the activity in question.

5   There is under-representation if women do not represent at least one half of the persons in the individual pay, remuneration and salary brackets in the relevant personnel group of an official body. This also applies to the function levels provided for under the schedule of allocation of responsibilities.

4   I shall now turn to the facts which gave rise to these proceedings. In July 1990 the city of Bremen published a vacancy notice for the post of section manager of Section 21 of the City's Parks Department, a post in BAT[5] remuneration bracket IIa/Ib. In particular, the candidatures of Mr Kalanke and Mrs Glißmann, technical staff in BAT remuneration bracket III since 1973 and 1975 respectively. Mr Kalanke, the holder of a diploma in horticulture and landscape gardening, was the section manager's deputy at

---

4   *Bremisches Gesetzblatt*, at p 433.
5   BAT stands for *Bundesangestelltentarifvertrag*, that is to say, the collective pay agreement for clerical staff in the public sector.

the material time. Mrs Glißmann, who completed her studies as a horticultural scientist in 1967, had been the holder of a diploma in landscape gardening since 1983, when she passed the relevant State examination.

The departmental management of the Parks Department suggested that Mr Kalanke should be promoted, but this was opposed by the Personnel Committee. The subsequent arbitration, which resulted in a recommendation in favour of Mr Kalanke, was regarded as a failure by the Personnel Committee, which asked for the matter to be referred to the Conciliation Board. The Board ruled on 20 February 1991 that "both candidates possess the same qualifications for this post and the female candidate should therefore be given priority, *inter alia* on the basis of the *Landgleichstellungsgesetz* (Land Law on Equal Treatment)".

5   Mr Kalanke brought an action against that decision in the *Arbeitsgericht* (Labour Court) Bremen in which he argued that the Conciliation Board had failed to take account of the fact that he was better qualified and that, in any event, section 4 of the LGG conflicted with Article 3(2) and (3) and Article 33(2) of the *Grundgesetz* (Basic Law), Article 2(2) of the Constitution of the Land and section 611 of the *Bürgerliches Gesetzbuch* (Civil Code). The Arbeitsgericht dismissed the case; an appeal brought in the *Landesarbeitsgericht* (Regional Labour Court) was also unsuccessful.

Mr Kalanke therefore brought an appeal on points of law ("Revision") in the *Bundesarbeitsgericht*. That court pointed out first that the decision in the case depended essentially on the applicability of section 4 of the LGG in so far as the decision taken by the Conciliation Board would be unlawful only if the Board had wrongly applied the relevant law: if that were to be the case, Mrs Glißmann would have been given an unjustified advantage inasmuch as it was based solely on sex. Given that, as the appeal court had found, the Conciliation Board's decision as to the candidates having equal qualifications did not contravene any legal provision and that women were in fact under-represented in the sector in question,[6] the *Bundesarbeitsgericht* reached the conclusion that, under section 4 of the LGG, the Conciliation Board had rightly refused to agree to the appointment of Mr Kalanke. Lastly, it held that the quota rules set out in section 4 of the LGG were consistent with the national provisions which Mr Kalanke had argued had been infringed.

6   The *Bundesarbeitsgericht*, however, also considered it appropriate to assess section 4 of the LGG in the light of the principle of equal treatment as enshrined in Community provisions, in particular Article 2(1) and (4) of the Directive. It therefore requested the Court to give a preliminary ruling on: (a) whether Article 2(4) of the Directive should be interpreted as covering national provisions such as the ones described above; and (b), if not, whether, having regard to the principle of proportionality, Article 2(1) of the Directive means that such national provisions should be disapplied.

In fact, the two questions are closely linked and, as will become clearer subsequently, they do not call for two separate answers. Since Article 2(1) lays down the principle of equal treatment of men and women in general, peremptory terms and Article 2(4) constitutes a derogation to that principle, it follows that the interpretation of Article 2(4)

---

6   It appears from the order for reference that the administration of the city of Bremen employs on aggregate 49% men and 51% women. However, if the distribution of the sexes is broken down according to career brackets, the picture is different, with the proportion of women in the various classes being as follows: sub-clerical class 75%, clerical class 52%, executive class 50%, administrative class 30%.

cannot but take account of the principle set out in Article 2(1); consideration of the question of proportionality will be necessary in any event.

7   Having said that, it is a question first of establishing whether the quota system set up by section 4 of the LGG falls within the scope of Article 2(4) of the directive.

This is the first occasion on which the Court has been asked to rule on the interpretation of Article 2(4) of the directive in relation to a quota system in favour of women and, more generally, to positive action. The question is therefore certainly not a trivial one, quite the contrary. Although the derogation set out in Article 2(4) is in issue here, what is under discussion above all is the significance of the principle of equal treatment, the contrast between formal equality, in the sense of equal treatment as between individuals belonging to different groups, and substantive equality, in the sense of equal treatment as between groups. In the final analysis, must each individual's right not to be discriminated against on grounds of sex – which the Court itself has held is a fundamental right the observance of which it ensures[7] – yield to the rights of the disadvantaged group, in this case, women, in order to compensate for the discrimination suffered by that group in the past?

8   Before turning to the merits of the question, I consider that it is worth making a few observations on the idea of positive action.

Positive, or affirmative, action stems from the requirement to eliminate the existing obstacles affecting particular categories or groups of persons who are disadvantaged at work as a result. Positive action is, in particular, a means of achieving equal opportunities for minority or, in any event, disadvantaged groups, which generally takes place through the granting of preferential treatment to the groups in question.[8] In taking the group as such into consideration, positive action moreover marks a transition from the individual vision to the collective vision of equality.[9]

9   Positive action may assume several forms. A first model aims to remove, not discrimination in the legal sense, but a condition of disadvantage which characterises women's presence on the employment market. In this case, the objective is to eliminate the causes of the fewer employment and career opportunities which (still) beset female

---

7   Case 149/77, *Defrenne ii* [1978] ECR 1365, [1978] 3 CMLR 312, para 27; See also Case T-45/90, *Speybrouck* [1992] II ECR 33, in which the Court of First Instance reaffirmed that "the principle of equal treatment for men and women in matters of employment and, at the same time, the principle of the prohibition of any direct or indirect discrimination on grounds of sex form part of the fundamental rights the observance of which the Court of Justice and the Court of First Instance must ensure pursuant to Article 164 EEC" (para 47).

8   "Affirmative action" received its name in the United States from the Democratic administrations of the 1960s, which utilised a typical judicial measure (until then affirmative action had been imposed by the courts on employers responsible for discriminatory conduct) and made it into an administrative instrument. It arises in particular with the obligation of undertakings with government contracts to carry out action plans for the benefit of the black population, failing which they lose the contracts which they have obtained. On the basis of those conceptual precepts, the transition was made to affirmative action in favour of other ethic minorities or, in any event, weak strata of society, such as women. In the name of fairness, plans for preferential treatment were therefore planned and implemented, especially in the fields of access to higher education and recruitment.

9   Indeed, it is the use of the concept of the group which does not find unequivocal favour. In this regard, there is in fact a tendency to assert that preferential treatment in favour of certain groups will end up by increasing the feeling of inferiority *vis-à-vis* the majority, thus triggering a definitive marginalisation of those in whose favour it is done within rigid social cages. Another accusation levelled against preferential treatment in favour of disadvantaged groups is that it lowers the rate of efficiency of the system by jeopardising the social commitment of the rest.

employment, by taking action with respect, among other things, to vocational guidance and training.

A second model of positive action may be discerned in actions designed to foster balance between family and career responsibilities and a better distribution of those responsibilities between the two sexes. In that case, priority is given to measures relating to the arrangement of working hours, the development of child-care structures, the return to work of women who have devoted themselves to bringing up their children, and social security and fiscal offsetting policies which take account of family duties. In both those cases, positive action, albeit entailing the adoption of specific measures for women alone, designed in particular to foster the employment of women, has the aim of achieving equal opportunities and, in the final analysis, the attainment of substantive equality. However, the results will certainly not be immediate in terms of a quantitative increase in female employment.

A third model of positive action is that of action as a remedy for the persistent effects of historical discrimination of legal significance; in this case, the action takes on a compensatory nature, with the result that preferential treatment in favour of disadvantaged categories is legitimised, in particular through systems of quotas and goals.[10] Ultimately that model took hold or, at any event, came to be regarded as a panacea for eliminating existing inequalities in the reality of social life: in that way, an effective situation of equal opportunities comes to be equated with equal results. The measure consisting of the imposition of quotas has come up for much discussion, in particular from the point of view of its constitutionality: whilst it is true that it is an instrument which is certainly suitable for bringing about a quantitative increase in female employment, it is also true that it is the one which most affects the principle of equality as between individuals, a principle which is safeguarded constitutionally in most of the Member States' legal systems.

10 The strictness of quotas may vary. In the instant case, as has already been mentioned, the quotas concerned are not strict (that is to say, quotas laying down a target percentage of posts which must be attained regardless of the merits of the persons affected by the procedure) and neither do they fix mandatory minimum requirements. Rather, the quotas provide for preferential treatment for women only if they have equivalent qualifications to the male candidates.

---

10 In fact, quotas and goals are the two systems which have been used in the United States since the late 1960s to pursue the objective of eliminating existing inequalities. The quotas are used to reserve a number of posts for the most disadvantaged categories with a view to rebalancing their representation; the system of goals, on the other hand, is used to give higher points to members of the category in question, but without compromising every candidate's entitlement to compete for all available posts. The case law of the Supreme Court has consistently been particularly hostile to the criterion of strict quotas (see *Regents of the University of California v Bakke* 438 US 265 (1978)) and, while accepting the criterion of goals, it has specified forms and conditions for them. In short, the plan of affirmative action must first be transitional in nature: it serves in fact to correct situations of imbalance by restoring equality at the starting point and does not set out to reproduce them artificially even when the effects of past discrimination have been wiped out (see *United Steelworkers of America, AFL-CIO-CLC v Webster* 443 US 193 (1979)). Secondly, the plan must be justified by a number of objectively verifiable factual preconditions: for example, a manifest discrepancy between the racial breakdown of the civil community and that of the world of the university; or between the number of women occupying higher posts in relation to the female population as a whole. In Europe, positive action has begun to take hold or, at any event, to become the object of attention at the very time when affirmative action seems to be in a state of crisis in its country of origin. Indeed, in the United States, recourse is now had to the criterion of strict scrutiny, whereby rules affecting a fundamental right can be justified only if they satisfy a compelling government interest (see, for example, *City of Richmond v Croson* 488 US 469 (1989)).

This having been said, it is only too obvious that even in this case there is discrimination on grounds of sex.

11 It is true that any specific action in favour of a minority or, in any event, weak category conflicts with the principle of equality in the formal sense. It therefore is a question of establishing whether it is nevertheless conceivable that, in clearly defined circumstances, provisions may be adopted that conflict with that principle yet are nevertheless permitted by law in order to achieve an objective corresponding to a social choice, which, in turn, is calculated to cancel out the inequalities caused by past prejudice.

More specifically for the purposes of the instant case, matters turn on whether Article 2(4) of the Directive constitutes a proper legal basis for that purpose, that is to say, whether actions of the type in question are covered by the derogation laid down in that provision.

12 Article 2(4), as I have already mentioned, authorises Member States to adopt and/or maintain in force "measures to *promote equal opportunity* for men and women, in particular by removing *existing inequalities which affect women's opportunities* in the areas referred to in Article 1(1)".[11]

It is evident in the first place from the wording of the provision in question that, alongside negative measures, such as the prohibition of direct and covert (hence indirect) discrimination, the Directive provides – still with a view to guaranteeing effective equal treatment – for the adoption of measures requiring some action in order to implement them. This means that Article 2(4) of the Directive does indeed authorise the Member States to implement positive actions, but, as Article 2(4) itself specifies, only to the extent to which those actions are designed to promote and achieve equal opportunities for men and women, in particular by removing the existing inequalities which affect women's opportunities in the field of employment.

13 Next, in order to establish what positive actions are authorised by Article 2(4), it is necessary to define the concept of equal opportunities, more specifically in order to clarify whether that expression means equality with respect to starting points or with respect to points of arrival. To my mind, giving equal opportunities can only mean putting people in a position to attain equal results and hence restoring conditions of equality as between members of the two sexes as regards starting points. In order to achieve such a result, it is obviously necessary to removing the existing barriers standing in the way of the attainment of equal opportunities as between men and women in the field of employment: it will therefore be necessary first to identify the barriers and then remove them, using the most suitable instruments for the purpose.

It seems to me to be all too obvious that the national legislation at issue in this case it not designed to guarantee equality as regards starting points. The very fact that two candidates of different sex have equivalent qualifications implies in fact by definition that the two candidates have had and continue to have equal opportunities: they are therefore on an equal footing at the starting block. By giving priority to women, the national legislation at issue therefore aims to achieve equality as regards the result or, better, fair job distribution simply in numerical terms between men and women. This does not seem to me to fall within either the scope or the rationale of Article 2(4) of the Directive.

---

11   My emphasis.

14 That having been said, it should not be overlooked that the ultimate objective of equal opportunities is to promote the employment of women and attain substantive equality, and that equality as regards starting points alone will not in itself guarantee equal results, which, apart from depending on the merits of the persons concerned and the individual efforts which they make,[12] may also be influenced by a particular social structure which penalises women, in particular because of their dual role, on account of past discrimination, which causes their presence in some sectors, particularly at management level, to be marginal.

Accordingly, it remains to be considered whether Article 2(4) of the Directive can be interpreted in such a way as to encompass also actions entailing the predetermination of "results" through the imposition of quotas, be they strict or, as in this case, dependent on the fulfilment of specific conditions.

15 On the only occasion on which the Court has ruled on the interpretation of Article 2(4), it held that the exception provided for in that provision is "specifically and exclusively designed to allow measures which, although discriminatory in appearance, are in fact intended to eliminate or reduce actual instances of inequality which may exist in the reality of social life".[13] As a result, the Court held that the derogating provision contained in Article 2(4) did not cover special rights for women, such as shortening of working hours, advancement of the retirement age, obtaining leave when a child is ill, granting additional days of annual leave in respect of each child, payment of an allowance to mothers who have to meet the cost of nurseries and the like, and so on.

The Court therefore considered that Article 2(4) authorises treatment which is only discriminatory in appearance but designed in practice to remove existing obstacles standing in the way of equal opportunities for women.[14] This confirms that the objective is substantive equality; but, in my view, it also confirms that that objective may be pursued only through measures designed to achieve an actual situation of equal opportunities, with the result that the only inequalities authorised are those necessary to eliminate the obstacles or inequalities which prevent women from pursuing the same results as men on equal terms. Indeed, it is from that point of view that the measures specifically intended for women are only discriminatory in appearance; and it is only in this way that real and effective substantive equality will be achieved.

16 The principle of substantive equality necessitates taking account of the existing inequalities which arise because a person belongs to a particular class of persons or to a particular social group; it enables and requires the unequal, detrimental effects which those inequalities have on the members of the group in question to be eliminated or, in any event, neutralised by means of specific measures.

---

12 It further goes without saying that, in so far as the method employed to assess candidates' merits indirectly discriminated against women, the terms of the problem would change completely: what would then be involved is actual – albeit indirect – discrimination, against which action could be taken pursuant to specific provisions of the directive.

13 Case 312/86, *EC Commission v France* [1988] ECR 6315, [1989] 1 CMLR 408, para 15.

14 Existing inequalities affecting women may ensue, for instance, also from the conditions, organisation and distribution of work, which have differing effects on the sexes vis-à-vis employees, resulting in women being adversely affected in their occupational training and advancement and careers. From this perspective, in order to be effective, positive action should instead bear upon educational and vocational guidance so as to promote the employment of women in sectors where they are under-represented. At the same time, it should be observed that some of the French measures referred to above (in particular, flexible working hours and allowances for nurseries) are definitely discriminatory only in appearance, in so far as they are specifically designed to eliminate the existing obstacles standing in the way of the achievement of equal opportunities.

Unlike the principle of formal equality, which precludes basing unequal treatment of individuals on certain differentiating factors, such as sex, the principle of substantive equality refers to a positive concept by basing itself precisely on the relevance of those different factors themselves in order to legitimise an unequal right, which is to be used in order to achieve equality as between persons who are regarded not as neutral but having regard to their differences. In the final analysis, the principal of substantive equality complements the principle of formal equality and authorises only such deviations from that principle as are justified by the end which they seek to achieve, that of securing actual equality. The ultimate objective is therefore the same: securing equality as between persons.

17 Moreover, this is the very logic underlying the derogations from the principle of equal treatment. Rather than being genuine derogations from the prohibition of discrimination on grounds of sex, those provisions aim at ensuring that the principle of equal treatment is effective by authorising such inequalities as are necessary in order to achieve it. In the final analysis, what is involved is only discrimination in appearance in so far as it authorises or requires different treatment in favour of women and in order to protect them with a view to attaining substantive and not formal equality, which would in contrast be the negation of equality.

It is precisely in this light that the Court's case law on the derogation set out in Article 2(3)[15] should be read, where it held, in particular, that: "the Directive leaves Member States with a discretion as to the social measures which must be adopted in order to guarantee, within the framework laid down by the directive, the protection of women in connection with pregnancy and maternity and to offset the disadvantages which women, by comparison with men, suffer with regard to the retention of employment".[16]

Essentially, the derogation in question enables Member States to adopt measures designed to eliminate the unfavourable consequences for women of their biological condition. Consequently, the differentiated treatment reserved for women in particular situations, such as pregnancy, is only discriminatory in appearance: in actual fact, it aims to neutralise the effects of specific male/female differences and thereby to secure substantive equality. Accordingly, it is the *difference* which legitimises the deviations from formal equality, the specific measures conferring unequal entitlements: the law has regard to the existing difference in order to promote substantive equality as between persons.

18 In the case of the derogation set out in Article 2(4), the differentiated treatment is not linked with any specific condition of women but relates to all women as such. The rationale for the preferential treatment given to women lies in the general situation of disadvantage caused by past discrimination and the existing difficulties concerned with playing a dual role.

It is only too obvious that such difficulties will certainly not be resolved by means of quota systems and the like, which are even irrelevant to that end. Instead, what is required are measures relating to the organisation of work, in particular working hours, and structures for small children and other measures which will enable family and work commitments to be reconciled with each other. Moreover, as I have already observed, the

---

15 That provision authorises the Member States to adopt and/or maintain in force "provisions concerning the protection of women, particularly as regards pregnancy and maternity".

16 Case C-421/92, *Habermann-Beltermann* [1994] I ECR 1657, [1994] 2 CMLR 681, para 22. The same wording was used in the earlier judgment in Case 184/83, *Hofmann* [1984] ECR 3047, [1986] 1 CMLR 242, para 27.

Court has held, to my mind, however, with excessive severity, that even national measures of that type do not fall within the derogation set out in Article 2(4) of the Directive and are therefore incompatible with the principle of equal treatment.[17]

19 Next, as regards past discrimination against women, it is certainly undeniable that its effects are still felt today. The existence of a different (historical) social and cultural condition (for instance, the disparity in education and vocational training) continues to marginalise women on the employment markets. There is no doubt in fact that that condition constitutes existing inequality and a disadvantage which should be eliminated.

With respect to a situation of that type, however, Article 2(4) of the Directive does enable intervention by means of positive action, but, as I have already said, only so as to raise the starting threshold of the disadvantaged category in order to secure an effective situation of equal opportunity. Positive action must therefore be directed at removing the obstacles preventing women from having equal opportunities by tackling, for example, educational guidance and vocational training. In contrast, positive action may not be directed towards guaranteeing women equal results from occupying a job, that is to say, at points of arrival, by way of compensation for historical discrimination. In sum, positive action may not be regarded, even less employed, as a means of remedying, through discriminatory measures, a situation of impaired inequality in the past.

20 No different conclusion may be reached on the basis of a reading of the provision in question in the light of the aforementioned recommendation on the promotion of positive action. Although a recommendation is not a legally binding instrument, it may, as the Court has held, certainly be used as an aid for interpreting other Community provisions which it is intended to complement.[18]

However, the recommendation in question, whose preamble refers expressly to Article 2(4) of the Directive, contains no definition of positive action, but only a list of possible aims for such action. Yet it is clear from the listed aims that it equates positive action with measures designed to abolish existing barriers and/or inequalities affecting women, together, more generally, with measures calculated to eliminate the situation of disadvantage in which women find themselves *vis-a-vis* the world of work. The actual *promotion* of women's presence and involvement in all sectors and professions and at all levels of responsibility is defined in terms of encouragement, certainly not of mechanical preference. Positive action is therefore based on two premises: the presence of existing obstacles which stand in the way of the *achievement of equal opportunities* as between men and women and the (implicitly) temporary nature of positive action, whose legitimacy therefore depends on the continuance of the existing obstacles which are to be removed.

21 In the final analysis, the recommendation, too, classes positive action as an instrument of a policy of equal opportunities; in contrast, there is no mention of giving women the advantage in order to foster female employment, with the result that it cannot be interpreted as authorising sex discrimination which is not designed to remove the obstacles adversely affecting women's opportunities and hence, ultimately, the achievement of substantive equality.

This conclusion is not altered by the fact that the ideas of advantage and compensation for disadvantages are embodied in Article 6(3) of the abovementioned agreement on social policy, which prescribes equal pay for men and women. In fact, to my mind,

---

17 *EC Commission v France*, cited above, paras 15-16.
18 See Case C-322/88, *Grimaldi* [1989] I ECR 4407, [1991] 2 CMLR 265, paras 18-19.

specific advantages in the matter of pay, such as to compensate for career disadvantages and/or facilitate the exercise of an occupation, may consist at most in allowances for mothers who have to pay nursery charges and relate to other similar contingencies, and certainly not consist of discriminatory measures based on sex which are not designed to remove any obstacle. Once again, therefore, what is being contemplated is the elimination of the unfavourable consequences for women of their specific condition; the objective is still that of attaining an actual situation of equal opportunities for men and woman.

22 The foregoing observations definitely confirm that Article 2(4) of the Directive only enables existing inequalities affecting women to be eliminated, but certainly not through pure and simple reverse discrimination, that is to say, through measures not in fact designed to remove the obstacles preventing women from pursuing the same results on equal terms, but to confer the results on them directly or, in any event, to grant them priority in attaining those results *simply because they are women.*

In the final analysis, measures based on sex and not intended to eliminate an obstacle – to remove a situation of disadvantage – are, in their discriminatory aspect, as unlawful today for the purposes of promotion as they were in the past.

23 This conclusion cannot be regarded as conflicting with the discretion which the Directive leaves to the Member States as regards the social provisions which they adopt with a view to guaranteeing equal opportunities for women, since, as the Court has explained with regard to the derogation set out in Article 2(3), that discretion must be exercised within the confines laid down by the Directive itself.[19]

Moreover, with regard to the derogation contained in Article 2(2), the Court has specifically held that "it should first be observed that that provision, being a derogation from an individual right laid down in the Directive, must be interpreted strictly".[20] It then went on to hold that "in determining the scope of any derogation from an individual right such as the equal treatment of men and women provided for by the Directive, the principle of proportionality, one of the general principles of law underlying the Community legal order, must be observed".[21] Consequently, the national measure in question must not exceed that which is appropriate and necessary to achieve the intended aim.

24 The national measure at issue requires priority to be given to women in recruitment and/or promotion, provided only that they have the same qualifications as male candidates and are under-represented in the wage bracket in the relevant personnel group, that is to say, where they do not amount to half the staff. That measure, I would recall, applies solely to employment in the public service, consequently in the sector in which equal treatment of the two sexes is by definition – or, at least, ought to be – effectively guaranteed. By contrast, Article 2(4) of the Directive, as I have already mentioned, requires there to be obstacles to be removed and the measure taken to be temporary, inasmuch as it is lawful only so long as conditions of disadvantage exist and persist.

---

19 See most recently the judgment in *Habermann-Beltermann*, cited above, para 22.
20 Case 222/84, *Johnston v Chief Constable of the Royal Ulster Constabulary* [1986] ECR 1651, [1986] 3 CMLR 240, para 36. Similar considerations are also set out in para 44 of that judgment with regard to the derogation set out in Art 2(3).
21 Judgment in *Johnston*, cited above, para 38.

The national legislation at issue is temporary – albeit long-term – in so far as it will cease to have any *raison d'être* once women account for one half of the persons in each remuneration bracket in each personnel group. It is not clear, however, whether it will be repealed on the day when the fateful figure of 50% is reached or whether it will continue to be triggered whenever the number of women falls below the prescribed level: in any case, it is reasonable to suppose that very long time-scales will be involved. As for the obstacles which it sets out to remove, they are manifestly identified with under-representation. If it is assumed that under-representation of women in a given sector reflects existing inequality, such a measure tends merely to rebalance the numbers of men and women, but it will not remove the obstacles which brought about that situation. In other words, the obstacles are not removed but constitute the cause which purportedly renders the differentiated – on grounds of sex – legislative treatment lawful.

In this connection, however, it may be observed that under-representation of women in a given segment of the employment market, albeit indicative of inequality, is not necessarily attributable to a consummate determination to marginalise women. Hence the element of arbitrariness inherent in any preferential treatment which is mechanically confined to the under-represented group and based solely on that ground.

25 It is clear from the foregoing observations that a measure of the kind at issue is definitely disproportionate in relation to the aim pursued or, in any event, pursuable under Article 2(4) of the Directive, since that aim remains that of achieving equal opportunities for men and women and not of guaranteeing women the result where conditions are equal.

In the final analysis, whilst the national measure in question manifestly and unquestionably conflicts with the principle of equal treatment as defined in Article 2(1), it is not caught by the exception contained in Article 2(4) of the Directive, since, far from fostering equal opportunities for women, it aims to confer the results on them directly.

26 I am fully aware that the considerations set out above and the conclusion which I have reached are not consonant with the positions adopted by numerous authorities which have, directly or indirectly, considered this issue. I refer, among other things, to a number of stands taken by the European Parliament even recently and also to some of the literature, not only in the legal field. I am also conscious that a position different from the one which I regard as the correct one would be supported, not only by the legislation which is the subject of the main proceedings, but also by a number of measures adopted in Member States of the Community and in non-member countries in order to guarantee, for their part too, not equal opportunities but an equal share of jobs.

27 Nevertheless, I consider that I can and must resist the temptation to follow the trend, convinced as I am – and firmly so – that I would have to follow it, and propose that the Court should follow it, only if I agreed that that were the right direction to take.

This is not the case here in so far as I believe that the fundamental, inviolable objective of equality – the real equality not that equality which is only called for – may only be pursued in compliance with the law, in this case with a fundamental principle.

28 Moreover, in saying this I am not referring only to the limits of the law. I am convinced that women do not merit the attainment of numerical – and hence only formal – equality – moreover at the cost of an incontestable violation of a fundamental value of every civil society: equal rights, equal treatment for all. Formal, numerical equality is an objective which may salve some consciences, but it will remain illusory and devoid of all substance unless it goes together with measures which are genuinely destined to achieve equality, which was not the case in this instance and, in any event, it

was not claimed that any such measures were significant. In the final analysis, that which is necessary above all is a substantial change in the economic, social and cultural model which is at the root of the inequalities, a change which will certainly not be brought about by numbers and dialectical battles which are now on the defensive.

29   In the light of the foregoing considerations, I therefore propose that the Court should reply to the questions referred by the *Bundesarbeitsgericht* in the following terms:

Article 2(1) and (4) of Council Directive 76/207/EEC of 9 February 1976 precludes the application of national legislation under which women are given priority in recruitment and/or in promotion provided only that they have the same qualifications as male applicants, simply because they are under-represented in a remuneration bracket in the relevant personnel group, that is to say, where they do not account for one half of the personnel.

RIGHTS RELATING TO MARRIAGE

CASE NO 11

GHALED v UNITED ARAB EMIRATES

WORKING GROUP ON ARBITRARY DETENTION OF THE
UNITED NATIONS COMMISSION ON HUMAN RIGHTS

Opinion No 2/1998

Opinion adopted: 13 May 1998

Human rights — Right to marry — Equality and non-discrimination — Discrimination on grounds of religion — Spouses of different religions — Lawful marriage in country in which it took place (Lebanon) — Whether prosecution of spouses in United Arab Emirates for having contracted illegal marriage, and declaration that marriage was null and void under domestic law, was discriminatory on grounds of religion — Right to privacy — Whether prosecution of spouses of different religions for fornication constituted arbitrary interference with right to privacy — Universal Declaration of Human Rights, arts 2(1), 7, 12, 16(1) and 18

Human rights — Deprivation of liberty — Whether legal basis for detention — Arbitrary detention — Universal Declaration of Human Rights, art 9

BACKGROUND

It was reported that Mr Elie Dib Ghaled, a Christian Lebanese national, had been arrested and detained on 5 December 1995 whilst working in Abu Dhabi, United Arab Emirates (UAE). He had been arrested on account of his marriage to Ms Muna Salih Muhammed, a Muslim woman who was a national of the UAE. Under Shari'a law a Muslim woman is not allowed to marry a non-Muslim man unless he converts to Islam. Mr Ghaled was detained until 29 October 1996, when a Shari'a court tried and sentenced him to 99 lashes and one year's imprisonment for fornication. Although his year of detention ended on 5 December 1996, he was not released from detention until 31 July 1997. On 11 July 1997 Mr Ghaled's case was communicated to the Working Group on Arbitrary Detention of the United Nations Commission on Human Rights.

HELD (finding Mr Ghaled to have been arbitrarily detained)

1   Under article 2(1) of the Universal Declaration of Human Rights everyone is entitled to all the rights and freedoms set forth therein, without distinction of any kind such as sex or religion. Article 16 guarantees the right of adult individuals to marry without any limitation as to race, nationality or religion. The judicial prosecution of an individual for fornication and for having contracted matrimony with another person of a different religion, and for having concluded a marriage deemed null and void under domestic law was contrary to the principles enshrined in articles 2(1) and 16(1) of the Declaration. It was also contrary to article 18 of the Declaration, to the extent that the spouses had invoked the religious character of their marriage. (Para 10)

2   Article 7 of the Universal Declaration guarantees equality before the law without any discrimination, as well as equal protection before the law against any discrimination. In the present case, the differentiation between the legal status of

individuals and the application of different standards of legal protection for adults of different religions who married of their own free will amounted to a violation of article 7. (Para 12)

3   The indictment and prosecution of Mr Ghaled and his spouse for fornication, independently of the charge that they contracted an illegal marriage, represented an arbitrary interference with the right to privacy of the individuals concerned, and amounted to a violation of article 12 of the Universal Declaration. (Para 13)

4   The detention of Mr Ghaled after 5 December 1996 was clearly devoid of any legal basis. As such it was arbitrary and in violation of article 9 of the Universal Declaration of Human Rights. (Para 15)

Treaties and other international instruments referred to

International Covenant on Civil on Political Rights 1966

Universal Declaration of Human Rights 1948, arts 2(1), 5, 7, 9, 12, 16(1) and 18

National legislation referred to

United Arab Emirates

Code of Criminal Procedure, promulgated by Federal Act No 35 of 1992

OPINION

Communication addressed to the Government on 11 July 1997

Concerning: Elie Dib Ghaled

The State is not a party to the International Covenant on Civil and Political Rights

1   The Working Group on Arbitrary Detention was established pursuant to resolution 1991/42 of the Commission on Human Rights. The mandate of the Working Group was clarified and extended pursuant to resolution 1997/50. Acting in accordance with its methods of work, the Working Group forwarded the above-mentioned communication to the Government.

2   The Working Group conveys its appreciation to the Government for having forwarded the requisite information in good time.

3   The Working Group regards deprivation of liberty as arbitrary in the following cases:

(i)   When it manifestly cannot be justified on any legal basis (such as continued detention after the sentence has been served or despite an applicable amnesty act) (Category I);

(ii) When the deprivation or liberty is the result of a judgment or sentence for the exercise of the rights and freedoms proclaimed in articles 7, 13, 14, 18, 19, 20 and 21 of the Universal Declaration of Human Rights (Category II);

(iii) When the complete or partial non-observance of international standards relating to the right to a fair trial, as set forth in the Universal Declaration of Human Rights and in the relevant international instruments accepted by the States concerned, is of such gravity as to confer on the deprivation of liberty, of whatever kind, an arbitrary character (Category III).

4   In the light of the allegations made the Working Group welcomes the cooperation of the Government. The Working Group transmitted the reply provided by the Government to the source and received its comments. The Working Group believes that it is in a position to render an opinion on the facts and circumstances of the case, in the context of the allegations made and the response of the Government thereto, as well as the observations made by the source.

5   The communication, of which a summary was addressed to the Government, concerns Elie Dib Ghaled, a Christian Lebanese national. He was reportedly arrested and detained on 5 December 1995 by United Arab Emirates (UAE) law-enforcement officials at the Intercontinental Hotel in al-'Ain in Abu Dhabi, where he worked as a restaurant manager. The source reports that UAE law-enforcement officials took Elie Dib Ghaleb to his residence and searched for his marriage certificate. Reportedly, when they found it, they arrested him. He was then detained until 29 October 1996 when a Shari'a court in al-'Ain tried and sentenced him, allegedly because of his marriage, as a Christian, to a Muslim woman from the UAE. In fact, under Shari'a law, a Muslim woman is not allowed to marry a non-Muslim man unless he converts to Islam, therefore such marriage is considered null and void and Elie Dib Ghaleb was sentenced to 99 lashes and one year imprisonment for fornication.

6   In its reply dated 4 September 1997, the Government notes that the provisions of the Shari'a, the Constitution and the law apply to all offences committed in the territory of the UAE; no distinction is made between accused persons on the grounds of their religion or their nationality. In the present case, the Department of Public Prosecutions referred the two accused persons, Ms Muna Salih Muhammed (a UAE national, 23 years old) and Mr Elie Dib Ghaled (a Lebanese national, 28 years old), to the Shari'a Criminal Court at al-'Ain, pursuant to the provisions of Federal Act No 35 of 1992 promulgating the Code of Criminal Procedure, on the charge of committing the punishable offence of fornication. The Court examined the facts of the case, heard the statements and the representatives of the defendant and, after carefully weighing the evidence, found him guilty as charged. However, the sentence was remitted by the Court in view of Elie Dib Ghaled's recent conversion to Islam. But for having contracted an invalid marriage, another punishable offence, he was sentenced to one year in prison and 99 lashes; moreover, the contract of marriage with the first defendant (Muna Salih Muhammed) was declared null and void. The proceedings against the latter were suspended until her arrest. According to the Government, Elie Dib Ghaled was also found guilty of having violated the personal rights of the guardian (the father) of the first defendant, by inciting his Muslim daughter to contract an invalid marriage. The Court annulled the marriage owing to Mr Ghaled's failure to obtain the guardian's approval thereof.

7   The Government's reply does not indicate the date of conviction, whether the sentence was appealed, whether Ms Muna Salih Muhammed was eventually arrested, whether Mr Ghaled was released or whether corporal punishment was carried out on him. Nor does the Government's reply solve the contradiction between the imposition of a one-year prison term as of 5 December 1995 and his continued detention at the time of the Government's reply, dated 4 September 1997.

8   The comments of the source indicate that the judgment of the Shari'a Court at al-'Ain was pronounced on 28 October 1996 and that Elie Dib Ghaled was released on 31 July 1997. According to the source, the continued detention of Mr Ghaled between 5 December 1996, the date on which he completed his year of detention, and 31 July 1997, the date of his eventual release, had no basis in law.

9   As Mr Elie Dib Ghaled has been released and the Working Group does not have any information on the possible detention of Ms Muna Salih Muhammed, it could, in accordance with [its] working methods, file the case without pronouncing itself on the arbitrary character of the detention of the released individual. But the Working Group deems it appropriate to make a finding on the arbitrary or non-arbitrary character of Mr Ghaled's detention.

10 The Government emphasizes that in the case of Mr Elie Dib Ghaled and all other cases of individuals brought before the courts, the Shari'a, the Constitution and other applicable laws are applied on the territory of the UAE, without distinction as to religion or nationality of the accused. Article 2(1) of the Universal Declaration of Human Rights lays down that everyone is entitled to all the rights and freedoms set forth therein, without distinction of any kind such as, *inter alia*, sex or religion. One of the rights guaranteed by the Declaration is the right of adult individuals, under article 16(1), to marry without any limitation as to race, nationality or religion. The judicial prosecution of an individual for fornication and for having contracted matrimony with another person of a different religion, and for having concluded a marriage deemed null and void under domestic law is, in the Working Group's opinion, contrary to the principles enshrined in articles 2(1) and 16(1) of the Declaration. It is also contrary to article 18 of the Declaration, to the extent that the spouses have invoked the religious character of their marriage.

11 In other words, the marriage concluded in the present case was based on the free will of the two spouses. The case of Elie Dib Ghaled is all the more serious given that he married in Lebanon, where the marriage of persons of different belief and faith is entirely compatible with domestic legislation.

12 Article 7 of the Declaration guarantees equality before the law without any discrimination, as well as equal protection before the law against any discrimination. In the present case, the differentiation between the legal status of individuals and the application of different standards of legal protection for adults of different religions who married of their own free will amounts to a violation of article 7.

13 Lastly, the Working Group considers that the indictment and prosecution of Elie Dib Ghaled and his spouse for fornication, independently of the charge that they contracted an illegal marriage, represents an arbitrary interference with the right to privacy of the individuals concerned, and amounts to a violation of article 12 of the Universal Declaration of Human Rights.

14 In the case of Elie Dib Ghaled, who was sentenced to a one-year prison term, the violation of articles 7 and 12 of the Declaration entails a further violation of article 9 thereof, pursuant to which no one shall be subjected to arbitrary arrest or detention.

15 Elie Dib Ghaled was released on 31 July 1997. His detention after 5 December 1996, date on which his prison term of one year was fully served, until 31 July 1997 was clearly devoid of any legal basis. The Government itself concedes that the pre-trial detention of Elie Dib Ghaled was set off against the prison term to which he was sentenced on 28 October 1996.

16 In the light of the above, the Working Group renders the following opinion:

The deprivation of the liberty of Elie Dib Ghaled from 5 December 1995 to 5 December 1996 is arbitrary, as it contravenes articles 2(1), 5, 7, 9, 12, 16 and 18 of the Universal Declaration of Human Rights, and falls within Category II of the categories applicable to the consideration of cases submitted to the Working Group.

The deprivation of the liberty of Elie Dib Ghaled from 5 December 1996 to 31 July 1997 is arbitrary because it is in violation of article 9 of the Universal Declaration of Human Rights, manifestly cannot be justified on any legal basis and falls within Category I of the categories applicable to the consideration of cases submitted to the Working Group.

Insofar as the corporal punishment to which Mr Ghaled was sentenced is concerned, the Working Group refers the matter to the Special Rapporteur on Torture of the Commission on Human Rights.

17   As a consequence of the above opinion, the Working Group requests the Government of the United Arab Emirates to take the necessary steps to remedy the situation of Elie Dib Ghaled and his wife, to study the possibility of amending its legislation so as to bring it into line with the provisions of the Universal Declaration and to take appropriate initiatives with a view to becoming a party to the International Covenant on Civil and Political Rights.

Adopted on 13 May 1998.

CASE NO 12

HUMAIRA MEHMOOD v SHO NORTH CANTT LAHORE AND OTHERS

HIGH COURT PAKISTAN

Judgment: 18 February 1999

Panel: Tassaduq Hussain Jilani J

Human rights — Right to family life — Right to marry — Right freely to choose a spouse and to enter into marriage only with free and full consent — Validity of marriage (Nikah) — Need for consent — Meaning of consent — Determination of validity of marriage in case of conflicting marriage certificates (Nikah Namas) — Mohammadan Law, s 268(c) — Constitution of Pakistan, art 35 — Convention on the Elimination of All Forms of Discrimination against Women, art 16 — Cairo Declaration on Human Rights in Islam, arts 5 and 6

BACKGROUND

Ms Humaira Mehmood secretly married Mehmood Butt on 16 May 1997 and the marriage was registered the same day. Her parents, who had promised her in marriage to her cousin Moazzam Ghayas Khokhar when she was a child, were strongly opposed to her marrying Mehmood. When they found out that the marriage had taken place, they went to extreme lengths to enforce their will on their daughter. First, Humaira was beaten, tortured and taken to a hospital, where she was tightly bandaged up so as to immobilize her and detained for a month. On 3 July 1998, she was forcibly married to her cousin. The marriage was backdated in the marriage register as having taken place on 14 April 1997, ie one month before her marriage to Mehmood. In November 1998, fearing for their lives, Humaira and Mehmood fled to Karachi, where Humaira sought protection in a woman's shelter and Mehmood went into hiding. On 4 November 1998, Nazir Ahmad (a friend of Humaira's brother) registered a case with the police, claiming that Mehmood had abducted his niece (FIR [First Information Report] 524/98). This FIR was later cancelled by the police, when it was found to be false. On the basis of a further false complaint, this time made by Humaira's brother, that Humaira had left home after a quarrel with her mother and that he needed assistance to recover her, the Punjab police raided the shelter and turned Humaira over to her brother's custody. After a women's rights activist intervened, Humaira was released from her brother's custody and the matter was taken up before the Sindh High Court Karachi, which ordered the police not to arrest Humaira on any charges.

Then, on 25 December 1998, Moazzam Ghayas filed a case with the police that his alleged wife Humaira had been abducted by Mehmood and others on 29 October 1998 and that Humaira had committed adultery (*zina*) with Mehmood, as she was married to Moazzam (FIR 601/98). In January 1999, despite the earlier Sindh High Court order, as well as a pre-arrest bail order by the Lahore High Court in relation to the later charges, Punjab police and CIA staff arrested Humaira, Mehmood and his mother at Karachi airport, beat them, restrained them and detained them at separate police stations. Their arrests did not appear in the police case diary. Humaira brought a petition before the Lahore High Court, refuting the fact that she had been abducted, and requesting the court to quash the charges against herself, her husband and her mother-in-law, which had been brought by Moazzam Ghayas.

HELD (allowing the petitions)*

1   The Court had ample powers in the constitutional jurisdiction to interfere in an investigation where there was material on record to show that the investigation involved malice in law or fact. The High Court would not have ordinarily exercised jurisdiction under article 199 of the Constitution to quash the criminal proceedings initiated pursuant to registration of the case but in the face of the bias and the *mala fides* shown by police officials who handled this case, any restraint at this stage from the High Court would not only be unjust but would be tantamount to abdication of the powers vested in the High Court to put a check on state functionaries who abuse their lawful duty to help a particular individual and promote their personal interests. (Paras 14, 17 and 19)

2   Articles 4 and 25 of the Constitution guarantee that everybody shall be treated strictly in accordance with the law and article 35 provides that the State shall protect the marriage, the family, the mother and the child. The Court had also to respect the international human rights instruments to which Pakistan was a party. These included the Convention on Elimination of All Forms of Discrimination against Women, article 16 of which requires state parties to take appropriate measures to eliminate discrimination against women in all matters relating to marriage, including *inter alia* the right freely to choose a spouse and to enter into marriage only with their free and full consent. It was also party to the Cairo Declaration on Human Rights in Islam, which calls for the protection of marriage and the family. (Para 18)

3   It was a settled proposition of law that in Islam a *sui juris* woman can contract *Nikah* (marriage) of her own free will and *Nikah* performed under coercion is no *Nikah* in law. Where consent to a marriage is in dispute and a challenge made to a *Nikah Nama* (marriage certificate) which relates to a man and a woman who claim to be husband and wife, then the presumption of truth attaches to the *Nikah Nama* which is acknowledged by both the spouses and not by the intervener. Marriage with a woman during the subsistence of her earlier marriage with some other man is illegal and void. *Prima facie* the *Nikah* of Humaira with Mehmood was valid and no prosecution under the Hudood Laws could be initiated without a conclusive finding of a Family Court against the *Nikah* in question. The case registered and proceedings initiated pursuant to it reflected *mala fides*, had no legal effect and were quashed. (Paras 9, 10 and 22)

4   *Per curiam:* As Muslims we loudly proclaim our commitment to the lofty ideals of an Islamic Ideology. The advent of Islam was a milestone in human civilization. It came at a time when women were treated as serfs and chattel. It was Islam which declared equality between a man and a woman. In matters of marriage a woman was given equal right to choose her life partner. After attaining the age of puberty she could exercise her option and choice. Unfortunately, in our practical lives we are influenced by a host of other prejudices bequeathed by history, tradition and feudalism. Male chauvinism, feudal bias and compulsions of a conceited ego should not be confused with Islamic values. An enlightened approach is called for otherwise obscurantism in this field may break the social fabric. (Paras 21 and 22)

---

*   *Eds:* for the court's orders in relation to the police officers and others involved in the case, see para 23 below.

Treaties and other international instruments referred to

Convention on the Elimination of All Forms of Discrimination against Women 1979, art 16

Cairo Declaration on Human Rights in Islam 1990, arts 5 and 6

National legislation referred to

Pakistan

Code of Muslim Personal Law, s 34

Constitution of Pakistan, 1973, arts 4, 25, 35, 199 and 203-GG

Constitution of Pakistan, 1962, art 98

Contempt of Courts Act, s 3

Criminal Procedure Code, ss 161, 491 and 561-A

Mohammadan Law, s 268(c)

Offence of Zina (Enforcement of Hudood) Ordinance VII of 1979 North Cantt Lahore, s 16

PPC PS North Cantt Lahore s 380

Cases referred to

Ahmad Saeed v State 1996 SCMR 186

Anwar Ahmad Khan v The State and another 1996 SCMR 24

Arif Hussain & Mst Azra Perveen v The State PLD 1982 FSC 42

Asif Saigol and 2 others v Federation of Pakistan through the Interior Secretary, Pakistan Secretariat, Islamabad and 2 others PLD 1998 Lahore 287

Byram D Auari etc v The State NLR 1989 Criminal 460

Emperor v Kh Nazir Ahmad AIR 1945 PC 18

Haji Imam Din v SHO and 4 others 1989 PCrL J 2016

Hafiz Abdul Waheed v Miss Asma Jahangir and another PLD 1997 Lahore 3012

Haji Wali Muhwnmad v MBR PLJ 1984 Quetta 102

Jairam and Others v Jagdish and another 1980 PCrLJ 243

Lubna and another v Government of Punjab through Chief Secretary, Lahore and another PLD 1997 Lahore 186

Mahmood v Muhammad Shaft and another PLD 1998 Lahore 72

Mokayuddin v Khadija Bibi 41 Bombay LR 1020

Mst Abida Perveen and another v The State and 2 others 1997 PCrLJ 880

Mst Ishrat Bibi v SHO 1996 PCrLJ 1019

Mst Naseer Khatoon v The SHO Police Station City Mianwali and another 1994 PCrLJ 1111

Mst Nasreen Akhtar v The State 1994 PCrLJ 2016

Ms Sabai and Muhammad-Sher v The State NLR 1988 Criminal 274

Syed Fayyaz Hussain Hamdani v The State NLR 1982 19

Mst Totem Khatoon v SHO Factory Area, Sargodha 1998 PCrLJ 1029

Muhammad Arshad v Station House Officer and others (PLJ 1997 Lahore 869)

Muhammad Azam v Muhammad Iqbal and others PLD 1984 Supreme Court 95

Muhammad Bashir v The State 1983 NLR Criminal 501

Muhammad Hanif and others v Mukarram Khan and others PLD 1906 Lahore 58

Muhammad Rashid v Collector etc PLD 1978 Lahore 1370

Muhammad Sharif and 8 others v The State and another 1997 SCMR 304

Qaisar Mahmood v Muhammad Shaft and another PLD 1998 Lahore 72

Shahnaz Begum v The Hon'ble Judges of the High Court of Sindh and Baluchistan and another PLD 1971 SC 677

Wahiduddin Khan v Deputy Commissioner PLD 1964 Peshawar 104

Zamir Hussain v Badshak and 2 others 1998 PCrLJ 883

JUDGMENT*

1   This judgment shall dispose of Writ Petitions No 1472 of 1999 and No 420 of 1999. The former petition was filed for production of Ms Humaira, who was granted pre-arrest bail by this Court, but was arrested by respondents Nos 1 and 1A from Karachi. She was not produced before any Magistrate, and it was alleged that her life was in danger. In Writ Petition No 420 of 1999 filed by Ms Humaira, it is prayed that as nobody had abducted her and as she is not the wife of Malik Moazzam Ghayas Khokhar (respondent) the case registered FIR [First Information Report] No 601/98 dated 25 December 1998 under s 16 Offence of *Zina* (Enforcement of Hudood) Ordinance VII of 1979 PS North Cantt Lahore on the statement of respondent Malik Moazzam Ghayas Khokhar be quashed, wherein it is alleged that about two months prior to the registration of the case on 29 October 1998 at 8 pm, complainant's wife Ms Humaira (petitioner) was abducted from Fortress Stadium Lahore by Mehmood Butt, his mother Ms Zeb Naseem and two unknown persons who were armed with firearms; that the complainant made an abortive attempt to chase them but it was of no avail. It was further alleged that while leaving the house Ms Humaira had taken away rupees two lac and jewelry weighing thirty tolas.

2   In support of the afore-referred petitions Ms Hina Jilani, learned counsel for Ms Humaira (petitioner), has made the following submissions:

---

*   ***Eds:*** some minor typographical errors in the judgment have been corrected by the editors.

(i) that the incident alleged in the FIR [First Information Report] is dated 29 October
     1995, whereas the FIR was lodged on 25 December 1998. It is repellent to common
     sense that Malik Moazzam Ghayas Khokhar would wait for two months to report
     the abduction of his alleged wife Humaira who happens to be the only daughter of a
     sitting Member of the Provincial Assembly in the ruling party. The story itself,
     according to the learned counsel, is unnatural as nobody can abduct a thirty year old
     woman from a busy shopping area of the Fortress Stadium Lahore;

(ii) that Humaira petitioner has herself disowned her marriage with Malik Moazzam
     Ghayas Khokhar and the story of abduction;

(iii) that another case was registered as FIR No 524/98 on 4 November 1998 on the
     statement of one Nazir Ahmad wherein the place of incidence is the same and
     Mehmood Butt who is accused in the instant case is also an accused in the said case
     and the allegation in the said FIR was that on 2 November 1998 at about 6 pm
     complainant Nazir Ahmad's niece named Rabia *alias* Nanni aged 18/19 years was
     abducted by Mehmood Butt and his brother Naeem Butt in a Pajero bearing
     No LHY-8301 (the same vehicle as in FIR No 601/98). The FIR has been found to be
     false and Abdul Rauf Dogar SP CIA Lahore has conceded that the case was
     registered to arrest Mehmood Butt and Humaira both. Huimaira's name was not
     mentioned in this FIR because they wanted to hide the fact of afore-referred *Nikah*.
     The cancellation of this FIR proves beyond doubt that the whole subsequent story of
     abduction and the registration of case FIR No 601/98 quashment of which is sought,
     is also false and product of *mala fides*;

(iv) that the petitioner married Mehmood against the wishes of parents who were after
     her on that account. Apprehending danger to her life and the life of Mehmood Butt
     (her husband) they fled away to Karachi and sought protection in the Edhi Center in
     November, 1998. Brother of Humaira, Ali Abbas Khokhar, chased her there and
     made a Report No 23 dated 1 December1998 at PS Nazimabad Karachi to the effect
     that his sister Humaira after having a row with her mother left the house, was
     residing at Edhi Center and that he be helped to recover her. There was no mention
     in the said report about her alleged *Nikah* with Malik Moazzam Ghayas or about her
     abduction by Mehmood Butt. This is further endorsed by a letter dated 1 December
     1998 written by DSP Nazzmabad Karachi to the person in charge at the Edhi Center,
     wherein he requested that "possession" of Humaira be handed over to her brother
     Ali Abbas. Even in this letter there is no reference to Humaira's *Nikah* with Malik
     Moazzam Ghayas. These documents, according to the learned counsel, clearly
     indicate that whatsoever the nature of the alleged *Nikah* of Moazzam Ghayas she in
     fact was not his wife, the registration of case FIR No 601/98 in the afore-referred
     circumstances is clearly malicious;

(v) that the so called *Nikah* of Humaira with Moazzam Ghayas was not *Nikah* in the eyes
     of law as she was already married to Mehmood and that her thumb-impressions
     were obtained through force; that she never consented to it; that the *Nikah Khawan*
     [the celebrant] shown in the video of the *Nikah* ceremony is Nazir Ahmad whereas
     on the *Nikah Nama*, *Nikah Khawan* is Maulvi Noor Muhammad; that as *per* the
     statement of Humaira *Nikah* ceremony was held somewhere in September 1997
     whereas *Nikah Nama* has been ante-dated and it was shown that the *Nikah* was
     performed on 14 April 1997; that the said *Nikah* was registered in the Union Council
     on 28 July 1998 which proves that it was ante-dated with a view to make this *Nikah*
     prior in time to Humaira's genuine *Nikah* with Mehmood Butt to which she was a
     consenting party;

(vi) that Humaira's *Nikah* with Mehmood Butt was voluntarily performed and its date of
     performance and entry in the register is the same. The *Nikah Khawan* and the

witnesses have made statements not only before this Court but also before the Investigating Officer about the veracity of the said *Nikah*, therefore, it has greater credence than the Nikah Nama on which the prosecution wishes to rely; and

(vii) in support of the afore-referred submissions learned counsel for Humaira relied on the judgments reported as *Muhammad Arshad v Station House Officer and others* (PLJ 1997 Lahore 869), *Muhammad Sharifand 8 others v The State and another* (1997 SCMR 304), *Jairam and Bothers v Jagdish and another* (1980 PCrLJ 243), *Muhammad Bashir v The State* (1983 NLR Criminal 501) and *Haji Imam Din v SHO and 4 others* (1989 PCrL J 2016).

3   Pressing her prayer in Writ Petition No 1472/99 (wherein petitioner is Ms Shahtaj Qaziibash, a human right activist), learned counsel for the petitioner prayed that the manner in which Humaira was arrested from Karachi by the Punjab Police despite the interim pre-arrest bail granted by this Court reflects *mala fides* on the part of Respondents Nos 1 and 1 A ie Malik Muhammad Ashraf Inspector/SHO and Subah Sadiq SI PS North Cantt Lahore, who have thereby committed gross contempt of this Court which warrants an action against them.

4   Ch Muhammad Hussain Chhachhar Advocate, learned counsel for respondent Malik Moazzam Ghayas, filed no written statement either in Writ Petition No 1472/99 (contempt of court) or Writ Petition No 420/99 (wherein quashment of the FIR was sought) while opposing the prayer for quashment of the FIR submitted as follows:

(i)   that Humaira (petitioner) by contracting second *Nikah* with Mehmood Butt in the presence of her earlier *Nikah* with Malik Moazzam Ghayas and having eloped with the former has crossed the limits of God, is guilty of offence under the Hudood Laws and, therefore, is not entitled to indulgence by this Court in extraordinary writ jurisdiction; and

(ii) that the police did not go beyond the mandate of law as it merely investigated a case registered against Mehmood Butt and others who have been charged with serious offences. This Court, according to him, has jurisdiction to quash criminal proceedings but it has to be guided by certain broad principles laid down by this Court as also by the Honourable Supreme Court. The quashment can only be made if there is no evidence on record connecting the accused with the alleged offence or the prosecution launched is tainted with malice. The registration of a case is the first step whereby the machinery of law is set into motion, and if the story of abduction as contained in the FIR is not proved the police is well within its right to challenge the accused in other offences which come to light. Humaira having contracted second *Nikah* with Mehmood Butt in the presence of the earlier *Nikah*, is guilty of an offence under the Hudood Laws and *prima facie* a case is made out against her and others. Learned counsel however, conceded to a Court query that only the Family Court can give a conclusive finding *qua* the validity of the conflicting *Nikah Namas* and not the police.

In support of the afore-referred submissions, learned counsel for the respondent relied on the judgments reported as *Asif Saigol and 2 others v Federation of Pakistan through the Interior Secretary, Pakistan Secretariat, Islamabad and 2 others* (PLD 1998 Lahore 287), Mst Ishrat Bibi v SHO (1996 PCrLJ 1019), *Mst Labida Perucen and another v The State and 2 others* (1997 PCrLJ 880), *Mst Totem Khatoon v SHO Factory Area, Sargodha* (1998 PCrLJ 1029), *Qaisar Mahmood v Muhammad Shaft and another* (PLD 1998 Lahore 72) and *Lubna and another v Government of Punjab through Chief Secretary, Lahore and another* (PLD 1997 Lahore 186).

5   Ch Ali Muhammad Advocate, learned counsel appearing for Malik Abbas Khokhar (father of Humaira), adopted the arguments of Ch Muhammad Hussain Chhachhar

Advocate and added that there is no chance of compromise as she has crossed the limits of God.

6   Mr Ashtar Ausaf Ali, the learned Advocate General Punjab who appeared on Court call, submitted that in cases where disputed questions of fact are involved which warrant recording of evidence, this Court may not give a conclusive finding on the issues raised. He, however, added that this Court can give a tentative finding *qua* the validity of conflicting *Nikah Namas*. In this regard he relied on the judgments reported in *Hafiz Abdul Waheed v Miss Asma Jahangir and another* (PLD 1997 Lahore 301) and *Muhammad Azam v Muhammad Iqbal and others* (PLD 1984 Supreme Court 95). On the Court query as to whether in the instant case the Investigating Officer can give a finding *qua* the validity or otherwise of the conflicting *Nikah Namas*, learned Advocate General conceded that the Investigating Officer cannot and it is only the Family Court which has the conclusive jurisdiction. He, however, added that the police on the basis of allegations levelled and the material produced can challenge the accused. Coming to the question of pre-arrest bail and the manner in which Humaira was apprehended from Karachi, he submitted that Humaira had misused the concession of bail as she was fleeing abroad and although he would not defend the police officer who conducted the raid to apprehend her, yet he would not attribute *mala fides* to him. On a Court query the Investigating Officer (Abdul Haul Dogar SP CIA) after some hesitation conceded that as *per* his investigation, the story of abduction as alleged in FIR No 601/98 is false. He further conceded that *Nikah* of Humaira with Mehmood Butt was registered in the relevant register the same day when the *Nikah* was performed, ie on 16 May 1997, whereas in case of Malik Moazzam Ghayas's *Nikah* with Humaira, it was performed on 14 April 1997 and was entered in the relevant register maintained by the concerned union council on 3 July 1998, ie after the lapse of more than one year and two months. The Court further asked him as to whether he has made any entry of his opinion that the allegation of abduction as given in the FIR is false, the answer was in the negative and he gave no reason for not entering that finding in the case diary. The Court also asked him as to why the earlier case registered against Mehmood Butt in FIR No 524/98 PS North Cantt Lahore was cancelled. He replied that the said case was cancelled as false on 29 December 1998 as during the course of investigation it came to light that no girl by the name of Rabia was ever abducted and in fact it was Humaira who was abducted and that since the complainant Nazir Ahmad was a friend of Malik Ali Abbas, a brother of Humaira, he got the case registered by mentioning a fake name of Rabia.

7   Having heard learned counsel for the parties and having gone through the precedent case law relied upon, I am of the view that following questions have been mooted in these petitions:

(i)   Can this Court give a finding conclusive or interim *qua* the conflicting *Nikah Namas* relied upon by the parties, if so, to what extent?

(ii) Whether Ms Humaira was abducted as alleged in the FIR 601/98 PS North Cantt Lahore, if not, can this Court decide this question in these proceedings and quash the case registered in the FIR referred to above?

(iii) Did Respondents Nos 1 and 1A ie Malik Muhammad Ashraf Inspector/SHO and Subafi Sadiq SI PS North Cantt Lahore acted *malafidely* in chasing and apprehending Humaira, Mehmood Butt and his mother, and, if so, are they liable to any action by this Court in these proceedings?

8   Learned counsel for Humaira has disputed the factum of her *Nikah* with Moazzam Ghayas by stressing that her *Nikah* with Mehmood Butt was earlier in time; that the second *Nikah* with Moazzam was void *ab initio*; that the thumb-impressions were obtained through coercion and the video prepared purported to be a *Nikah* ceremony

was actually an attempt to fabricate evidence against the earlier *Nikah* and there being no date or *Rukksati* in it, it does not in any manner advance the case of respondent Moazzam Ghayas *qua* his claim of earlier *Nikah* with Humaira. However, before entering into the said controversy it would be pertinent to understand the concept of "consent" and the Institution of Marriage in Islam.

9   It is a settled proposition of law that in Islam a *sui juris* woman can contract *Nikah* of her own free will and *Nikah* performed under coercion is no *Nikah* in law. Instances are not lacking from Hadith and the Islamic history that the consent of a *sui juris* woman was held to be a *sine qua non* for a valid marriage in absence of which marriage was declared void. In *Tesrul Bari Sharah Sahi Bokhari* by Allama Waheeduz Zaman, published by Amjad Academy Lahore, at page 119, a case is quoted wherein a woman appearing before the Holy Prophet Muhammad (Peace be upon him) complained that her marriage (*Nikah*) had been performed against her consent. The Holy Prophet (Peace be upon him) annulled the marriage. The ratio laid down in *Mokayuddin v Khadija Bibi* (41 Bombay LR 1020) is based on the afore-referred command of the Holy Prophet (Peace be upon him). Syed Ameer Ali, a celebrated Islamic Jurist in his book *The Spirit of Islam* goes onto say that even a King cannot marry his daughter without her consent.

Another Muslim Scholar Nawab AMF Abdur Rehman in his book *Institutes of Mussalman Law* which is based on Qadri Pasha Mussalman Codes, refers to article 53, wherein mode of obtaining consent has been highlighted and it stipulates that when a girl weeps with sobs at the time of marriage it reflects lack of consent.

Dr Tanzil-ur-Rehman in his book *A Code of Muslim Personal Law* at page 67 says that "the second condition for constituting a marriage contract is the consent of the parties to the marriage contract. Marriage contract without the consent of parties is not valid".

The term "consent" means a conscious expression of one's desire without any external intimidation or coercion. In Jowitt's *Dictionary of English Law* consent has been defined as "consent supposes three things—a physical power, a mental power, and a free and serious use of them". Similarly in Stroud's *Judicial Dictionary* (5th edition, volume 1) consent has been defined as "consent is an act of reason, accompanied with deliberation, the mind weighing, as in a balance, the good and evil on each side". In the same dictionary it is defined as "it seems to be clear, that approbation subsequent to a marriage is not, in general, a sufficient compliance with a condition requiring 'consent', but Lord Hardwick, in *Burleton v Humfrey*, Amb 256, took a distinction between the words 'consent' and 'approbation', holding the latter to admit subsequent approval, where coupled with the former disjunctively; but he decided the case principally on another ground and in regard to the admission of subsequent consent the authority of the case has been questioned".

10   In situations where consent to a marriage is in dispute and a challenge is thrown to a *Nikah Nama* which is being owned by a man and a woman who claim to be husband and a wife then the presumption of truth attaches to the *Nikah Nama* which is being acknowledged by both the spouses and not by the intervener. In *Arif Hussain & Mst Azra Perveen v The State* (PLD 1982 FSC 42) the Court acquitted man and a woman who claimed to be husband and a wife and the only evidence led by them was their own statements and the statement of *Nikah Khawan*. The complainant in that case was the father of the girl. Similarly in *Mst Nasreen Akhtar v The State* (1994 PCrLJ 2016) the claim of a man and a woman being husband and wife and the *Nikah Nama* on the police file was found to be a complete defence and both were acquitted. In *Hafiz Abdul Waheed v Ms Asma Jahangir and another* (PLD 1997 Lahore 3021) a Full Bench of this Court allowed a

sui juris girl to go with the husband of her choice notwithstanding the fact that the father was complainant.

Marriage with a woman during the subsistence of her earlier marriage with some other man is illegal and void. Section 34 of the "Code of Muslim Personal Law" specifically caters to this situation. In a judgment report in ILR 15 Allahabad page 396, a *Nikah* during the subsistence of an earlier *Nikah* was declared as void.

11 The material brought on record if examined in the light of the afore-referred principles of the Islamic jurisprudence and the precedent case law would *prima facie* indicate as follows:

(a) That as *per* the *Parat Nikah* (the document which is prepared when marriage takes place) and the register maintained for registration of *Nikahs*, the *Nikah* of Humaira with Mehmood Butt was performed on 16 May 1997 and is entered the same day at Serial No 414 of Register *Nikah* Halqa No 72 Model Town Lahore. Witnesses to the said *Nikah* including the *Nikah Khawan* have not only testified to the said fact before this Court but also before the Investigating Officer. As against the afore-referred *Nikah Nama* which admittedly is being owned by Ms Humaira and Mehmood Butt, the counter *Nikah* evidencing Moazzam Ghayas's *Nikah* with Ms Humaira has following aspects which *prima facie* create a doubt in its authenticity of being prior in time or having been performed with Ms Humaira's consent:

   (i)   this *Nikah* as claimed by Moazzam Ghayas complainant was performed on 14 April 1997 but there is no corresponding entry in the *Nikah* Register of the said Union Council on the said date. In fact the, registration of *Nikah* is one year and two months later in time, ie 3 July 1998 at Serial No 122 Union Council Piplipahar;

   (ii) a video film of the afore-referred ceremony was produced by Ch Muhammad-Hussain Chhachhar Advocate and on his request it was seen in the Chamber in the presence of learned counsel for both the parties, Humaira and the Investigating Officer. Humaira was seen weeping and sobbing during the ceremony and as *per* his statement before this Court her sobs and cries could be heard by the persons sitting around her. On a Court query she explained that her cries and sobs were manifestation of her lack of consent in the performance of *Nikah*. This aspect of her statement was not challenged by the learned counsel for the respondent. When a woman cries and sobs as *per* article 53 of the Institutes of Mussalman Law referred to above, it reflects lack of consent on her part. She was not wearing any bridal jewelry and Moazzam Ghayas also appeared to be tense and without head-cover (Shera) which is generally worn by bridegrooms. The person who is shown to be performing *Nikah* is admittedly Maulvi Nazir Ahmad, whereas in *Nikah* Register, the *Nikah* is supposed to have been performed by Qari Noor Muhammad whose signature is there on the *Nikah* Register. This fact was admitted even by the Investigating Officer present in Court. The *Nikah Khawan* in the video never signed the *Nikah Nama*;

   (iii) there is no scene in the video showing Humaira putting her thumb-impressions in token of her consent;

   (iv) according to Humaira her thumb-impressions were forcibly obtained prior to the ceremony under threat and coercion and she never signed the *Nikah Nama*. But the prosecution claims that the *Nikah Nama* which has been placed on record bears her signatures. According to the Investigating Officer he obtained her twenty-seven specimen signatures and a copy of which has been on record as Mark-A. This Court also directed her to give her specimen signatures which she did, which have been placed on record as Mark-B. On a perusal of her specimen signatures with those of the signatures on the *Nikah Nama* there is apparent dissimilarity not only in spelling but also otherwise. This question was specifically put to Mr M Iqbal Khichi, Assistant Advocate General who conceded about the apparent dissimilarity but suggested that the matter may be referred to the Handwriting Expert;

(v) there is no scene in the video of her departure from her parents' house indicating "*Rukhsati*"; no bridal room is shown to show husband and wife sitting together. This *prima facie* endorses her contention that no "*Rukhsati*" took place as they could not persuade her to do that. According to her she had told her parents in clear terms that she was already married to Mehmood Butt and that even a copy of the *Nikak Nama* dated 16 May 1997 was given to her father through one of his friends named Azam but despite that, according to her, a drama was arranged to show her *Nikah* with Moazzam Ghayas and when at a latter stage she was being forced for a formal ceremony of "*Rukhsati*" she left the house and joined her husband Mehmood Butt, whereafter she was chased and a case was registered, quashment of which is sought;

(vi) during the video screening she had challenged Ch Muhammad Hussain Chhachhar Advocate/learned counsel for Moazzam Ghayas to produce any Invitation Card to show any reception held by the bridegroom (Valima Reception) to which learned counsel had no answer. *Prima facie*, it does not appeal to reason that the marriage of the only daughter of a Member of the Provincial Assembly who is a local landlord should be held in such simple manner without any invitation card, without the bride wearing any bridal dress or jewelry, a bridegroom without head-cover (*Sebra*) and a tension writ-large on his face and again it is surprising that the entry of the *Nikah* the daughter of such a local political high up should not be entered in the relevant register for a period of one year and two months.

(b) As Ms Humaira and Mehmood Butt have owned *Nikah Nama* dated 16 May 1997, a presumption of valid marriage would arise in their favour in view of section 268(c) of Mohammadan Law (by DF Mulla) as also in view of the law laid down by the Federal Sharia Court in *Arif Hussain & Azra Perueen v The State* (PID 1982 FSG 42) which in terms of article 203-GG of the Constitution is binding. If Moazzam Ghayas wishes to throw a challenge he has to go to the Court of plenary jurisdiction, ie the Family Court, to have a conclusive finding.

(c) Writ Petition No420/99 was admitted to regular hearing and learned counsel for Moazzam Ghayas, while accepting its notice, undertook to file written statement/reply. In response to a challenge thrown by Ms Humaira that Moazzam should appear to vouchsafe for his claim to be her husband, his learned counsel agreed that he would appear on the next date, but neither a written statement was filed nor did Moazzam Ghayas ever appear to testify on Oath about the fact of the *Nikah*. Learned counsel for the respondent even went to the extent of saying that he was present in Court premises but he prayed that he be excused from his appearance in Court. I was surprised at the stand taken by the learned counsel. However, as the learned counsel had not even filed a written statement, this Court was of the view that let the law take its own course. If a party chooses not to file a written statement then the averments made in the petition are admitted to be true.

In *Muhammad Rashid v Collector etc* (PLD 1978 Lahore 1370) arguments of the counsel for the respondent were not even entertained in absence of a written statement or a counter affidavit and the writ was allowed. The *ratio* laid down in the following case law is to the same effect:

(i) *Haji Wali Muhwnmad v MBR* (PLJ 1984 Quetta 102) a Division Bench judgment, and

(ii) *Wahiduddin Khan v Deputy Commissioner* (PLD 1964 Peshawar 104) a Division Bench judgment.

In the instant case the non-submission of the written statement and a counter affidavit would mean that the averments made in the petition stand *prima facie* proved.

12 Coming to the question of quotient of the FIR, this Court is of the view that there is no cavil to the proposition that the function of Court and police are complementary and are not overlapping and that each Institution should ordinarily remain within the parameters of its own domain. However, in *Shahnaz Begum v The Hon'ble Judges of the High Court of Sindh and Baluchistan and another* (PLD 1971 SC 677) which was in fact reiteration of the ratio laid down in *Emperor v Kh Nazir Ahmad* (AIR 1945 PC 18), at page 692, it was observed that "if an investigation is launched *mala fide* or is clearly beyond the jurisdiction of the Investigating Agencies concerned then it may be possible for the action of the Investigating Agencies to be corrected by a proper proceeding either under article 98 of the Constitution of 1962 or under the provisions of section 491 CrPC [Criminal Procedure Code], if the applicant is in the latter case in detention, but not by invoking the inherent power under section 561-A of the CrPC."

In *Muhammad Hanif and others v Mukarram Khan and others* (PLD 1906 Lahore 58) which is a Division Bench judgment of this Court in which it was laid down that "High Court proceeding under article 199 of the Constitution or under section 561-A CrPC should ordinarily not pass orders in matter exclusively preserved for the Police Department".

The *ratio* laid down in the afore-referred judgment is that the High Court, while proceeding under section 561-A CrPC, can only quash proceedings in a Court of law and would not ordinarily interfere in the police investigation. However, sitting in the Constitutional jurisdiction, this Court has power to interfere where the *mala fide* is apparent on record or where there is total lack of jurisdiction to proceed. The precedent case law relied upon by the learned counsel for the respondent Ch Muhammad Hussaia Chhachhar Advocate is distinguishable. In *Mst Tahira Khatoon v SHO Factory Area Sargodha* (1998 PCrLJ 1029) the observation made was "hence simply on the statement of the petitioner that the FIR No 173 of 1997 is *mala fide* and collusive, the same cannot be quashed at this stage". Reliance in this judgment was placed on *Ahmad Saeed v State* (1996 SCMR 186), in which case the moot point was whether the High Court could quash FIR on the ground of *mala fide* under section 561-A CrPC, and it was laid down that "we are afraid that the High Court under section 561-A CrPC could not quash FIR on the ground of *mala fide* or on the ground that the FIR discloses civil liability."

In *Mst Abida Perveen and another v The State and 2 others* (1997 PCrLJ 880) this Court did not quash FIR under article 199 of the Constitution because, firstly, there was no allegation of *mala fide* and secondly it was observed "the *Nikah Nama* produced as Annexure-B along with this petition shows the age of the bride as 20 years whereas the age of the bridegroom is not given at all. Likewise there was no witness or *Wakil* from the side of the bride as would appear from Columns Nos 7 and 8 of the *Nikah Nama* which have been left blank".

Yet another judgment of this Court relied upon by respondent's learned counsel is *Qaisar Mahmood v Muhammad Shaft and another* (PLD 1998 Lahore 72) in which quashment in a Hudood case was refused where petitioner husband had claimed valid marriage as a defence. In the said case the Court, while taking note of certain infirmities in *Nikah Nama*, was persuaded not to grant relief in the discretionary jurisdiction of this Court and it was observed that "it is not unknown that no Muslim marriage is valid without at least two persons witnessing the same but Column No 11, which is meant for the witnesses of the marriage, lies blank meaning thereby that there were no witnesses of this alleged marriage".

Zamir Hussain v Badshak and 2 others (1998 PCrLJ 883) would also not be relevant, as in the said case, the main consideration which weighed with the Court in refusing quashment was that no material was brought on record contrary to the prosecution story as given in the FIR to indicate that the FIR was registered for *mala fide* reasons.

In *Muhammad Azam v Muhammad Iqbal* (PLD 1984 SC 95) the facts were distinguishable. In that case the accused allegedly abducted the complainant's 14 year old daughter and committed rape with her. During trial he pleaded valid *Nikah* as defence. The victim girl did not support him and stated that *Nikah* was under coercion. The Trial Court convicted the accused, the Federal Shariat Court acquitted him and the Hon'ble Supreme Court remanded the case with the observation to record the statements of the *Nikah Khawan* and other witnesses who were not examined by the trial Court earlier.

13 However, this Court as also the Hon'ble Supreme Court have always interfered even at the investigation stage to promote the ends of justice where *mala fide* is manifest on record and there is material on record to suggest that the offence alleged is *prima facie* not attracted.

In *Syed Fayyaz Hussain Hamdani v The State* (NLR 1982 19) this Court quashed the criminal proceedings when there were documents brought on record to suggest that the case registered was not tenable in law.

In *Ms Sabai and Muhammad-Sher v The State* (NLR 1988 Criminal 274) FIR was quashed when there was strong material on record to indicate that the petitioners were husband and wife and in the said case the statement of the alleged wife and the affidavit of *Nikah* Registrar were found sufficient to quash the case registered.

In *Mst Naseer Khatoon v The SHO Police Station City Mianwali and another* (1994 PCrLJ 1111) the FIR in *Hudood* case was quashed as the SHO stated that the petitioners were husband and wife.

In *Byram D Auari etc v The State* (NLR 1989 Criminal 460), a Division Bench judgment of the Peshawar High Court, FIR was quashed as it was found that "in other words the Officer in charge of the Police Station was to apply his mind to the facts narrated to him and in case he finds that such a narration discloses an offence only then he shall register a case. The investigation which follows the registration of the case must have its roots in the alleged commission of an offence. The police report and the subsequent investigation launched thereto without the commission of an offence would obviously fall outside the competence of the authorities concerned. In the given circumstances, as in this case, it may obviously smack of *mala fides* as well. In such, the case registered against the petitioners and the subsequent warrant of arrest issued by Respondent No 4 are beyond the competence of the authorities concerned and *mala fides* in law as stated above."

In *Muhammad Arshad v Station House Officer and others* (1997 PCrLJ 928) FIR was quashed as it was found that the petitioners were husband and wife. At page 932 it was observed "according to Mulla a boy or girl who had attained puberty is at liberty to marry anyone he or she likes and the guardian has no right to interfere. Further, according to presumption of marriage detailed in s 268(c) of the Mohammadan Law, the fact of acknowledgment by the man or the woman as his wife is accepted as valid marriage".

In *Anwar Ahmad Khan v The State and another* (1996 SCMR 24) while dilating the powers of this Court under article 199 of the Constitution of the Islamic Republic of Pakistan the Hon'ble Supreme Court, at page 36, observed "it is well-settled principle that where investigation is *mala fide* or without jurisdiction, the High Court in exercise of its Constitutional jurisdiction under article 199 is competent to correct such proceedings and make necessary orders to ensure justice and fair play. The Investigating Authorities do not have the entire and total authority of running investigations according to their whims".

14 The afore-referred resumé of the precedent case law would show this Court has ample powers in the Constitutional jurisdiction to interfere where there is material on record to show that the investigation reached demonstrates either malice in law or fact. In the instant case there are the following features which lend strong credence to the allegations of *mala fides* levelled against the police and State functionaries:

(i) the police had acted beyond its lawful mandate in its drive to exert pressure on Mehmood Butt, his mother and his brother, so that he is separated from Humaira with whom there was a *Nikah* on record. Initially a case FIR No 524/98 was registered on 4 November 1998 at Police Station North Cantt Lahore though, on the statement of one Nazir Ahmad, who alleged that Mehmood Butt and Naeem Butt had abducted his niece Ms Rabia *alias* Nanni aged 18 years from Fortress Stadium Lahore on the evening of 2 November 1998 in a Pajero vehicle bearing registration number LHT 8301. This case was found to be false and it is conceded before this Court that it was registered to arrest Humaira and Mehmood;

(ii) a perusal of the case diary of FIR No 524/98 indicates that Subah Sadiq of PS North Cantt Lahore secured permission from his higher officers to visit Karachi on 28 November 1998 to affect the arrest of "Rabia". On 7 November 1998, SP Cantt Lahore wrote a letter to SSP Lahore to bring the names of Mehmood Butt, Ms Zeb Naseem (mother of Mehmood Butt), Naeem Butt and Naseem Butt on the Exit Control List as it was alleged that they had abducted complainant's niece Rabia and they were planning to flee abroad. The SSP Lahore in turn wrote a letter to the District Magistrate Lahore with the same request (No 20825 dated 7 November 1998) and the District Magistrate, it seems, wrote a letter to the Secretary Interior, but the final order passed by the Secretary Interior has not been produced before this Court. Statements of complainant Nazir Ahmad's wife and two other witnesses were also recorded about the abduction of Rabia under s 161 CrPC. On 29 November 1998 a police party headed by SI Subah Sadiq of PS North Cantt Lahore went to Karachi and the case diary indicated that Ali Abbas, a brother of Humaira, was also accompanying him and they were supposedly in search of the abductee, namely, Rabia *alias* Nanni. Raids were conducted by the police on Mehmood Butt's house. Edhi Center was contacted. On 7 November 1998 there is an entry in the case diary that SI Subah Sadiq came to know through the Press that the real name of Rabia *alias* Nanni was Humaira and on 17 December 1998 there is an entry that as *per* the newspaper report the abductee is Humaira Abbas and Muhammad Abbas Khokhar MPA is to be contacted and that despite efforts made he could not be contacted. The afore-referred entries were a dishonest attempt to camouflage the action taken by the local police in going all the way to Karachi and in raiding the Edhi Center where Humaira had got shelter. It was widely reported in the Press and never denied by the Punjab Police. A news clipping of the "Daily Dawn" Karachi dated 1 December 1998 (Annexure-A) reads as follows:

A heavy contingent of police, headed by a DSP and also comprising officials of the Punjab Police, on Tuesday stormed into the Edhi Home at Sohrab Goth, and took away a young married woman who had taken refuge there, Edhi sources said.

Humaira Mehmood, 28 year old daughter of a ruling PML, MPA from Okara, Abbas Khokhar, who had taken shelter in the Edhi's Home on November 27 apprehending that her family would kill her.

She is believed to have been flown to Lahore in the evening by a PIA flight by her brother, Ali Abbas, who also accompanied the police party during the raid on the Edhi's Home around 2.15 pm.

The Edhi sources said Humaira, who had married Mehmood Butt, had approached the Home on the advice of her husband who was in hiding since they left Lahore about a month ago.

Eye-witnesses said several dozens of passers-by crowded the Edhi's Home as the policemen, who had come in at least eight mobiles, dragged out the woman who besought the policemen not to take her away. "They will kill me", she continued to cry hysterically till she was thrown into a mobile van, they said.

When contacted, the DIG of Karachi told Dawn that the raid was conducted in accordance with the law and the woman had left her house officer estranged relations with her parents.

Prior to the raid Ali Abbas made an entry in the Police Station Nazimabad Karachi (Report No 23 dated 1 December 1998) that his sister Humaira Abbas had left the house after having a quarrel with her mother, that she is lodged in Edhi Center and that he be given assistance to recover her. A similar request was made by DSP Nazimabad in his letter addressed to the person in charge at the Edhi Center. Meanwhile a women's rights activist took up the matter with the Governor Sindh who intervened in the matter, Humaira was released from Ali Abbas, her brother, and she was lodged in Darul Amaan [a government run shelter] by police. The matter was taken up before the Hon'ble Sindh High Court Karachi in CP No 2003/98 and Humaira was allowed to remain in Darul Amaan until further orders. In the report submitted by DSP Nazimabad, the petitioner's story stands endorsed but the said police officer has given a twisted version. In paragraph 4 he submitted that "Ali Abbas, the real brother of noted missing girl, submitted copy of Station Diary Entry No 23 of PS Nazimabad, letter of undersigned noted above to the In-Charge Edhi Home Karachi and also introduced himself where In-Charge Edhi Home allowed to meet him with his noted sister (Humaira). After proceeding all formalities, authorities of Edhi Home Karachi handed over the possession of Ms Humaira to her real brother Ali Abbas. Ali Abbas filled the requisite form of Edhi Home, and also deposited his NIC (photo-copy) with In-Charge Edhi Home". In para 6 he stated "Ali Abbas the real brother noted missing girl taken over the possession of his sister Humiaira from Edhi Home but due to non-compromise between both the noted brother and sister (Ali Abbas and Humaira) the SDM Central Karachi recorded her statement and allowed her to stay at Darul Amaan Karachi.

(iii) A petition for pre-arrest bail was moved (Crl Misc No40-B/99), and this Court by order dated 5 January 1999 allowed her interim pre-arrest bail, her appearance before the Court dispensed with until the next date as it was submitted by the learned counsel that her custody being regulated by an order of the Division Bench of Sindh High Court Karachi in the afore-referred case. In the meanwhile, the Sindh High Court on an application made by Ms Humaira allowed her to leave Darul Amaan and live at a place of her choice and to appear before this Court on 3

February 1999 for which date Crl Misc No 40-B/99 was fixed before this Court. However, notwithstanding the bail granting order, Ms Humaira and Mehmood Butt were arrested from Karachi Airport whereafter a women's rights activist filed WP No 1472/99 wherein it was apprehended that Humaira's life was in danger and this Court directed the Inspector General of Punjab Police to ensure that Humaira Mehmood is produced before this Court on 1 February 1999. It was further directed that the Inspector General of Punjab Police shall be personally responsible for her safety. On the said date Ms Humaira appeared and narrated the whole story about her forcible abduction from Edhi Center, about intervention by the Governor Sindh, about Sindh High Court's order, about her subsequent arrest, the beating given to her and Mehmood Butt in front of several people at the Karachi Airport, the manner in which they were dragged and were taken in a van to an unknown destination followed by her real brother Ali Abbas. In the statement made before this Court Ms Humaira and Mehmood Butt both apprehended danger to their lives. Statement of SI Subah Sadiq was also recorded and in flagrant attempt to conceal the facts he stated "I did go to Edhi Center to inquire about Rabia *alias* Nanni but not to arrest Humaira. I did not even see Ms Humaira there. This was on 1 December 1998". His close liaison with Humaira's brother is manifest from his answer made to a Court query when he said "I was carrying a mobile telephone of Ali Abbas, a brother of Ms Humaira on which I received a call form CIA Staff Karachi that Ms Humaira Mehmood and Mehmood Butt were planning to leave country. Pursuant to the afore-referred call I reached Karachi Airport and found a DSP of CIA Staff and an Inspector, namely, Raza Hussain already present there. I affected the arrest of Ms Humaira Mehmood and Mehmood Butt and her mother Ms Zeb Naseem who is about fifty years age. I made an entry *qua* the arrest of the afore-referred persons in the Daily Diary of Police Station Karachi Airport, however, I had made no entry about their arrest in the case diary of the case registered FIR No 601/98 dated 25 December 1998 PS North Cantt Lahore. During the period that the afore-referred accused persons remained in my custody I did not record statement of any one of them. When I went to Karachi to appear before the Sindh High Court it was in my knowledge that this Court had granted pre-arrest bail to Humaira in Crl Misc No 40-B/99".

15 The afore-referred narration of events would show that SI Subali Sadiq of Punjab Police had gone twice to Karachi to effect Humaira's arrest, in the company of her brother Ali Abbas. On 30 November 1998 they raided Edhi Center Karachi, forcibly took her out at a time when no case *qua* her abduction had been registered, and it was under the garb of FIR No 524/98 dated 4 November 1998 PS North Cantt Lahore [reporting the abduction of Rabias *alias* Nanni] that the entire action was taken. However, when they were exposed at Karachi, a case was registered on 25 December 1998 in the same police station on the statement of Moazzam Ghayas who claimed to be the husband of Humaira and who until 25 December 1998 did not figure anywhere in the proceedings initiated by the local police to affect the arrest of Mehmood Butt and Humaira, as FIR No 601/98 dated 25 December 1998. The case registered as FIR No 524/08 was cancelled on 19 December 1998 as it was found that Nazir Ahmad complainant had falsely reported about the abduction of Rabia *alias* Nanni as his niece and in fact he wanted to help his friend Malik Abbas Khokhar whose daughter had been abducted.

16 The case registered as FIR No 601/98 dated 25 December 1998 PS North Cantt Lahore is *mala fide* on the face of it as it was registered after a delay of two months of the alleged occurrence of abduction. How can a husband keep quiet for two months over abduction of his wife particularly when the said wife (Humaira) happens to be the only daughter of a sitting MPA belonging to the ruling party and is the real cousin of

Moazzam Ghayas. The Investigating Officer (Abdul Rauf Dogar SP CIA Lahore) gave no finding about the veracity of the story given in FIR No 601/98 and it was only on the query made by this Court that he gave his finding in Court on 10 February 1999 that the version given in the FIR *qua* abduction of Humaira was false and that Humaira as a matter of fact had left her house of her own choice. Humaira alleged in open Court that the Investigating Officer had told him that if she were his daughter he would have killed her. Her learned counsel Miss Hina Jilani Advocate alleged that the statements of *Nikah* witnesses were not recorded correctly. On a direction of this Court, the Investigating Officer was made to read out the statement under section 161 CrPC of Shahbaz who was a witness of the *Nikah* and who was present in Court. The witness alleged that this was not his correct version and there had been interpolations in the statement. When I directed him to record his statement afresh, learned counsel for the respondent Ch Muhammad Hussais Chhachhar Advocate objected that the Court cannot direct the Investigating Officer to record the statement of a witness afresh. I overruled the objection. However, to allay the apprehension of the witness I directed him to place on record his affidavit and give a copy of the same to the Investigating Officer. On the following day the *Nikah Khawan* appeared and stated on Oath that he had been threatened by the police not to bring out the correct version and not to state that he had performed the *Nikah* of Humaira with Mehmood Butt. This witness apprehended danger to his life. His statement was recorded in Court and the Investigating Officer was directed to record the statement outside the Court as well. The Investigating Officer appeared before this Court on 3, 8, 9, 10 and 12 February 1999 but expressed his inability to trace out either *Nikah Khawan* or the Registrar. It was only on the direction of this Court that the learned Advocate General Punjab after efforts produced the *Nikah* Registrar along with the *Nikah* Register evidencing the *Nikah* of Humaira with Mehmood Butt which indicated that the *Nikah* was performed the same day as it was entered in the relevant register at Serial No 414 on 16 May 1997 whereas the alleged *Nikah* of Moazzam Ghayas (complainant-respondent) with Humaira was purported to have been performed on 14 April 1997, but his entry in the register is after one year and two months.

17 This Court would not have ordinarily exercised jurisdiction under article 199 of the Constitution to quash the criminal proceedings initiated pursuant to the registration of the afore-referred case but in the face of the bias and the *mala fide* shown by the police officials who handled this case not only at the SI/SHO level but at the SSP level and the SP CIA level, I am of the view that any restraint at this stage would not only be unjust but would tantamount to abdication of the powers vested in this Court to put a check on the State functionaries who abuse their lawful duty to help a particular individual and promote their personal interests. Beside the *mala fides* referred to above it has clearly been brought on record, rather conceded by the police, that the occurrence alleged in FIR No 601/98 PS North Cantt Lahore is false. Even on the question of conflicting *Nikahs* the weight of material brought on record tilts in favour of Humaira and Mehmood Butt and in absence of a conclusive finding of a Family Court against his marriage no prosecution can be launched in the peculiar facts of this case.

18 Coming to the role of the State functionaries in this case I find that the police officials who handled this case passed orders and acted in a manner which betrayed total disregard of law of the land and mandate of their calling. Articles 4 and 25 of the Constitution of Islamic Republic of Pakistan guarantee that everybody shall be treated strictly in accordance with law. Article 35 of the Constitution provides that the State shall protect the marriage, the family, the mother and the child. As a Member of the

International Comity of Nations we must respect the International Instruments of Human Rights to which we are a party.

Pakistan is a Member of United Nations and is signatory to the Convention on the Elimination of All Forms of Discrimination against Women which in its article 16 enjoins all the member states as follows:

1   States Parties shall take all appropriate measures to eliminate discrimination against women in all matters relating to marriage and family relations and in particular shall ensure, on a basis of equality of men and women:

   (a) the same right to enter into marriage;

   (b) the same right freely to choose a spouse and to enter into marriage only with their free and full consent;

   (c) the same rights and responsibilities during marriage and at its dissolution.

At a Conference attended by representatives of all the Islamic countries, including Pakistan, a Resolution was adopted which is known as the "Cairo Declaration on Human Rights in Islam" dated 5 August 1990. *Encyclopedia of Human Rights* by Edward Lawson (2nd Edition) at page 175 stipulates as follows:

Article 5(a)   The family is the foundation of society, and marriage is the basis of making a family. Men and women have the right to marriage, and no restrictions stemming from race, colour or nationality shall prevent them from enjoying this right.

   (b) Society and the State shall remove all obstacles to marriage and shall facilitate marital procedure. They shall ensure family protection and welfare.

Article 6(a)   Woman is equal to man in human dignity, and has rights to enjoy as well as duties to perform; she has her own civil entity and financial independence, and the right to retain her name and lineage.

   (b) The husband is responsible for the support and welfare of the family.

19 The police officials are guardians of the lives, liberties and the honour of the citizens. They owe their place in society to the taxes which are paid by the citizens. If these guards become poachers then no society and no States can have even a semblance of human rights and rule of law. It is not possible for this Court to enter into a detailed inquiry or fix liability of the wrong done and violations made. However, SI Subah Sadiq has confessed before this Court that he went to Karachi to arrest Rabia *alias* Nanni (a fake and non-existent person) though he tried to hide the real purpose that it was Ms Humaira whom he wanted to arrest on 30 November 1998, but the case diary and the Press clipping belie his stand. He conceded that he arrested Humaira and Mehmood on 20 January 1999 and brought them to Lahore and that he was aware that Humaira was on pre-arrest bail granted by this Court. He was party to the manner in which both of them were beaten at the Karachi Airport, they were put under a restraint and were being taken to an unknown place, their arrest was not shown even in the case which lends credence to the allegations levelled by Humaira and Mehmood Butt that they could have been done to death had this Court not intervened.

20 At a socio-moral plane the case had certain disconcerting overtones. Humaira was to be given in marriage to Moazzam in exchange of the latter's sister who was married to Humaira's brother. On the one hand there was anguish and pain of a father whose daughter had rebelled and refused to marry a person of his choice and had left her hearth and home to join someone with whom she had contracted marriage. The father called it a sinful act and was not prepared to accept her under any circumstances. On the other hand there was a girl in distress, who lost the prime of her youth waiting for a

parental permission to join a husband of her choice. She was in a critical dilemma ie of facing the social consequence of going back to a family fold where she stood eternally stigmatized or to go back with Mehmood whom she stood married to. The former course was full of tension, uncertainty and carried a death threat whereas in the latter course although there was a death threat yet it meant a fulfilment her desire, where she dreamt of security and if she survived the death threat she hoped for an ultimate release from the high walls of a feudal bondage. She chose the latter course and wanted the society to accept it. Perhaps she was not asking for too much at this age of her life but she was refused. On disclosure of her marriage she was beaten up, taken to the Surgical Theater of a Governmental run hospital, her entire body was bandaged and she was detained there for a month but she persevered. As *per* her perception a mock drama of her marriage with Moazzam Ghayas was arranged where she cried and sobbed but the parents could not persuade her to join him. No *Rukhsati* was performed and when they tried to force her she left the house. She was chased, harassed, abused, beaten and disgraced. This treatment was meted out to the only daughter of a father and at latter's behest and the real brother spearheaded it.

21 As Muslims we loudly proclaim our commitment to the lofty ideals of an Islamic Ideology. The advent of Islam was a milestone in human civilization. It came at a time when women were treated as serfs and chattel. Instances were not lacking when men used to bury their daughters alive. It was Islam which declared equality between a man and a woman. In matters of marriage a woman was given equal right to choose her life partner. After attaining the age of puberty she could exercise her option and choice. Unfortunately, in our practical lives we are influenced by a host of other prejudices bequeathed by history, tradition and feudalism. The self righteousness demonstrated by the respondents in calling her "adulterous", the manner in which she was hunted like a prey and the way the State functionaries become partners in a feudal vendetta notwithstanding the mandate of their office in getting their pound of flesh, reminded the Court of George Bernard Shaw's criticism of Englishmen in his Drama *The Man of Destiny*, he said:

> There is nothing so bad or so good that you will not find Englishman doing; but you will never find an Englishman in the wrong. He does everything on principle. He fights you on patriotic principles; he robs you on business principles; he enslaves you on imperial principles.

22 Behind the evangelistic facade there was a certain culture at play. It is that culture which needs to be tamed by law and an objective understanding of the Islamic values. Let us do a little self accountability and a little soul searching both individually and collectively. Let there be no contradiction in our thoughts and actions. Male chauvinism, feudal bias and compulsions of a conceited ego should not be confused with Islamic values. An enlightened approach is called for otherwise obscurantism in this field may break the social fabric.

23 For what has been discussed above I hold and direct as follows:

(i) that the material brought on record shows that the case registered FIR No 601/98 dated 25 December 1998 under s 16 Offence of Zina (Enforcement of Hudood) Ordinance VII of 1979 and 380 PPC PS North Cantt Lahore is false as no occurrence of the kind alleged ever took place. *Prima facie* the *Nikah* of Humaira with Mehmood is valid and no prosecution under the Hudood Laws can be initiated without a conclusive finding of a Family Court against the *Nikah* in question. The case registered and the proceedings initiated pursuant thereto reflect *mala fides*; those are, therefore, of no legal effect and are hereby quashed;

(ii) the documents placed on record, the statements of petitioner Humaira and the witnesses of *Nikah* including the *Nikah Khawan*, the entries made in the *Nikah* registers and the video film produced before this Court on behalf of the complainant *prima facie* lead to the conclusion that Humaira's *Nikah* with Mehmood was prior in time. The latter *Nikah*, during the subsistence of the earlier one and lacking her consent is void in Islam. Even otherwise as both the spouses have acknowledged the *Nikah* dated 16 May 1997 a presumption of truth is attached to it under the law;

(iii) by lying before this Court that he had gone to Karachi to affect the arrest of Rabias *alias* Nanni (a fake person) and not Humaira in the last week of November 1998 and by making a confession before this Court that in the first week of January 1999 he arrested Humaira from Karachi notwithstanding the pre-arrest bail granted to her by this Court, Subah Sadiq SI obstructed the process of justice and thereby committed a gross contempt of this Court. He is, therefore, convicted under s 8 of the Contempt of Courts Act and sentenced to one month SI on two counts and a fine of Rs 5,000/- (Rupees five thousand only) on two counts in default whereof he shall further undergo SI for fifteen days on each count. The sentences shall run concurrently. He shall be lodged in District Jail Lahore to serve the sentence;

(iv) the conduct of some of the police officials connected with the case including the present Investigating Officer needs scrutiny. The Inspector General of Police Punjab shall depute an officer not below the rank of a DIG to proceed against them departmentally;

(v) in view of the serious allegations levelled by Ms Humaira that when her *Nikah* with Mehmood Butt was brought to light she was beaten, tortured and taken to the Services Hospital Lahore, bandaged and kept there in confinement for a period of one month the Medical Superintendent of Services Hospital Lahore is directed to inquire in to the matter and proceed against the delinquent officials in accordance with law …

24 Writ Petitions Nos 1472 of 1999 and 420 of 1999 are allowed in the above-noted terms.

Petitions allowed.

CASE NO 13

AS v SWEDEN

UNITED NATIONS COMMITTEE AGAINST TORTURE

Communication No: 149/1999

Views adopted: 15 February 2001

Torture — Duty of state not to expel or return person to another state where substantial grounds exist for believing person would be in danger of being subjected to torture — Evidentiary requirements — Burden of proof — Right to choose one's spouse — Forced marriage — Subsequent relationship with person of one's own choosing — Whether substantial grounds existed for believing person would be in danger of being subjected to torture (stoning to death for adultery) if returned — Hudud Law, Chapter 1 — Convention against Torture and Other Cruel, Inhuman or Degrading Treatment or Punishment, art 3(1)

BACKGROUND

AS, the author of the communication, was an Iranian citizen, who was seeking refugee status in Sweden. In 1991, the Government of the Islamic Republic of Iran had declared AS's late husband a martyr. She was subsequently supported and supervised by a foundation, the Bonyad-e Shahid (or Committee of Martyrs), which was a powerful authority in Iranian society. She was required to follow the strict rules of Islamic society even more conscientiously than before. One of the aims of the Bonyad-e Shahid was to convince martyrs' widows to remarry, but AS resisted this. Nevertheless, in 1996, one of the leaders of the Bonyad-e Shahid forced AS into a *sighe* or *mutah* marriage, that is, a short term marriage, stipulated for one and a half years. AS was not expected to live with her *sighe* husband, but to be at his disposal for sexual services whenever required.

In 1997, AS fell in love with a Christian man. The two met in secret, since in Iran, Muslim women were not permitted to have relationships with Christians. One night they were caught and arrested. AS was taken to her *sighe* husband's home, where she was severely beaten by him. She was told that her case had been referred to the Revolutionary Court, but her *sighe* husband intervened to prevent this. After several days she left the country with her son, using a visa she had already acquired to visit her sister-in-law in Sweden. Shortly after arrival, she applied for asylum. AS later heard that, in her absence, she had been sentenced to death by stoning for adultery by the Revolutionary Court (as had her lover).

AS's asylum claim was rejected by the Swedish Immigration Board and, on appeal, by the Aliens Appeal Board. She then brought the case before the Committee against Torture, under article 22 of the Convention against Torture, claiming that she risked torture and execution upon return to Iran and that her forced return to that country would therefore constitute a violation by Sweden of article 3 of the Convention, which provides that State parties shall not expel or to return a person to another state where there are substantial grounds for believing that he or she would be in danger of being subjected to torture.

DECIDED (in favour of the author of the communication)

1   In determining whether there were substantial grounds for believing that the author would be in danger of being subjected to torture upon return to Iran, all relevant considerations had to be taken into account, including the existence of a consistent pattern of gross, flagrant or mass violations of human rights. The aim of the determination, however, was to establish whether the individual concerned would be personally at risk of being subjected to torture in the country to which she would return. It followed that the existence of a consistent pattern of gross, flagrant or mass violations of human rights in a country did not as such constitute a sufficient ground for determining that a particular person would be in danger of being subjected to torture upon his return to that country; additional grounds had to exist to show that the individual concerned would be personally at risk. (Para 8.3)

2   The author of a communication bears the burden of presenting an arguable case. The author had submitted sufficient details regarding her *sighe* or *mutah* marriage and alleged arrest that could have, and to a certain extent had been, verified by the Swedish immigration authorities, to shift the burden of proof. In this context, the State party had not made sufficient efforts to determine whether there were substantial grounds for believing that the author would be in danger of being subjected to torture. (Para 8.6)

3   Considering that the author's account of events was consistent with the Committee's knowledge about the present human rights situation in Iran, and that the author had given plausible explanations for her failure or inability to provide certain details which might have been of relevance to the case, the State party had an obligation, in accordance with article 3 of the Convention, to refrain from forcibly returning the author to Iran or to any other country where she ran a risk of being expelled or returned to Iran. (Para 9)

Treaties and other international instruments referred to

Committee against Torture, Rules of Procedure, rules 108(9) and 111(5)

Convention against Torture and other Cruel, Inhuman or Degrading Treatment or Punishment 1984, arts 3 and 22

General Comments of the UN Treaty Bodies referred to

Committee against Torture, General Comment on the Implementation of Article 3 in the context of Article 22 of the Convention against Torture (1997)

National legislation referred to

Iran

Hudud Law, Chapter 1

Sweden

Aliens Act 1989

Cases referred to

Jabari v Turkey, ECHR, judgment of 11 July 2000, 9 BHRC 1; 12(4) *International Journal of Refugee Law* 597

VIEWS

THE COMMITTEE AGAINST TORTURE, established under article 17 of the Convention against Torture and Other Cruel, Inhuman or Degrading Treatment or Punishment,

Meeting on 24 November 2000,

Having concluded its consideration of communication No 149/1999, submitted to the Committee against Torture under article 22 of the Convention against Torture and Other Cruel, Inhuman or Degrading Treatment or Punishment,

Having taken into account all information made available to it by the author of the communication, his counsel and the State party,

ADOPTS ITS VIEWS under article 22(7) of the Convention.

1.1   The author of the communication is AS, an Iranian citizen currently residing with her son in Sweden, where she is seeking refugee status. The author and her son arrived in Sweden on 23 December 1997 and applied for asylum on 29 December 1997. Ms S claims that she would risk torture and execution upon return to the Islamic Republic of Iran and that her forced return to that country would therefore constitute a violation by Sweden of article 3 of the Convention. The author is represented by counsel.

1.2   In accordance with article 22(3) of the Convention, the Committee transmitted communication No 149/1999 to the State party on 12 November 1999. Pursuant to rule 108(9) of the Committee's rules of procedure, the State party was requested not to expel the author to Iran pending the consideration of her case by the Committee. In a submission dated 12 January 2000 the State party informed the Committee that the author would not be expelled to her country of origin while her communication was under consideration by the Committee.

The facts as presented by the author

2.1   The author submits that she has never been politically active in Iran. In 1981, her husband, who was a high-ranking officer in the Iranian Air Force, was killed during training in circumstances that remain unclear; it has never been possible to determine whether his death was an accident. According to the author, she and her husband belonged to secular-minded families opposed to the regime of the mullahs.

2.2   In 1991, the Government of the Islamic Republic of Iran declared the author's late husband a martyr. The author states that martyrdom is an issue of utmost importance for the Shia Muslims in Iran. All families of martyrs are supported and supervised by a foundation, the Bonyad-e Shahid, the Committee of Martyrs, which constitutes a powerful authority in Iranian society. Thus, while the author and her two sons' material living conditions and status rose considerably, she had to submit to the rigid rules of Islamic society even more conscientiously than before. One of the aims of Bonyad-e Shahid was to convince the martyrs' widows to remarry, which the author refused to do.

2.3 At the end of 1996 one of the leaders of the Bonyad-e Shahid, the high-ranking Ayatollah Rahimian, finally forced the author to marry him by threatening to harm her and her children, the younger of whom is handicapped. The Ayatollah was a powerful man with the law on his side. The author claims that she was forced into a so-called *sighe* or *mutah* marriage, which is a short-term marriage, in the present case stipulated for a period of one and a half years, and is recognized legally only by Shia Muslims. The author was not expected to live with her *sighe* husband, but to be at his disposal for sexual services whenever required.

2.4 In 1997, the author met and fell in love with a Christian man. The two met in secret, since Muslim women are not allowed to have relationships with Christians. One night, when the author could not find a taxi, the man drove her home in his car. At a roadblock they were stopped by the Pasdaran (Iranian Revolutionary Guards), who searched the car. When it became clear that the man was Christian and the author a martyr's widow, both were taken into custody at Ozghol police station in the Lavison district of Tehran. According to the author, she has not seen the man since, but claims that since her arrival in Sweden she has learned that he confessed under torture to adultery and was imprisoned and sentenced to death by stoning.

2.5 The author says that she was harshly questioned by the Zeinab sisters, the female equivalents of the Pasdaran who investigate women suspected of "un-Islamic behaviour", and was informed that her case had been transmitted to the Revolutionary Court. When it was discovered that the author was not only a martyr's widow but also the *sighe* wife of a powerful ayatollah, the Pasdaran contacted him. The author was taken to the ayatollah's home where she was severely beaten by him for five or six hours. After two days the author was allowed to leave and the ayatollah used his influence to stop the case being sent to the Revolutionary Court.

2.6 The author states that prior to these events she had, after certain difficulties obtained a visa to visit her sister-in-law in Sweden. The trip was to take place the day after she left the home of the ayatollah. According to the information submitted, the author had planned to continue from Sweden to Canada where she and her lover hoped to be able to emigrate since he had family there, including a son. She left Iran with her younger son on a valid passport and the visa previously obtained, without difficulty.

2.7 The author and her son arrived in Sweden on 23 December 1997 and applied for asylum on 29 December 1997. The Swedish Immigration Board rejected the author's asylum claim on 13 July 1998. On 29 October 1999, the Aliens Appeal Board dismissed her appeal.

2.8 The author submits that since her departure from Iran she has been sentenced to death by stoning for adultery. Her sister-in-law in Sweden has been contacted by the ayatollah who told her that the author had been convicted. She was also told that the authorities had found films and photographs of the couple in the Christian man's apartment, which had been used as evidence.

2.9 The author draws the attention of the Committee to a report from the Swedish Embassy in Iran which states that Chapter I of the Iranian Hudud Law "deals with adultery, including whoring, and incest, satisfactory evidence of which is a confession repeated four times or testimony by four righteous men with the alternative of three men and two women, all of whom must be eyewitnesses. Capital punishment follows in cases of incest and other specified cases, eg when the adulterer is a non-Muslim and the abused a Muslim woman. Stoning is called for when the adulterer is married". The report further underlines that even if these strict rules of evidence are not met, the author can still be sentenced to death under the criminal law, where the rules of evidence are more flexible.

2.10 The author further draws the attention of the Committee to documentation submitted to the Swedish immigration authorities to support her claim, including a certificate testifying to her status as the wife of a martyr. She also includes a medical certificate from Kungälvs Psychiatric Hospital indicating that she suffers from anxiety, insomnia, suicidal thoughts and a strong fear for her personal safety if she were returned to Iran. The certificate states that the author has symptoms of post-traumatic stress syndrome combined with clinical depression.

The complaint

3.1 The author claims that there exist substantial grounds to believe that she would be subjected to torture if she were returned to Iran. Her forced return would therefore constitute a violation by Sweden of article 3 of the Convention. Furthermore, the author submits that there is a consistent pattern of gross human rights violations in Iran, circumstances that should be taken into account when deciding on expulsion.

The State party's observations on admissibility and merits

4.1 In its submission of 24 January 2000, the State party submits that it is not aware of the present matter having been or being the object of any other procedure of international investigation or settlement. As to the admissibility of the communication, the State party further explains that according to the Swedish Aliens Act, the author may at any time lodge a new application for a residence permit with the Aliens Appeal Board, based on new factual circumstances which have not previously been examined. Finally, the State party contends that the communication is inadmissible as incompatible with the provisions of the Convention, and lacking the necessary substantiation.

4.2 As to the merits of the communication, the State party explains that when determining whether article 3 of the Convention applies, the following considerations are relevant; (a) the general situation of human rights in the receiving country, although the existence of a consistent pattern of gross, flagrant or mass violations of human rights is not in itself determinative; and (b) the personal risk of the individual concerned of being subjected to torture in the country to which he/she would be returned.

4.3 The State party is aware of human rights violations taking place in Iran, including extrajudicial and summary executions, disappearances, as well as widespread use of torture and other degrading treatment.

4.4 As regards its assessment of whether or not the author would be personally at risk of being subjected to torture if returned to Iran, the State party draws the attention of the Committee to the fact that several of the provisions of the Swedish Aliens Act reflect the same principle as the one laid down in article 3(1) of the Convention. The State party recalls the jurisprudence of the Committee according to which, for the purposes of article 3, the individual concerned must face a foreseeable, real and personal risk of being tortured in the country to which he or she is returned. The State party further refers to the Committee's General Comment on the implementation of article 3 of the Convention which states that the risk of torture must be assessed on grounds that go beyond mere theory or suspicion, although the risk does not have to meet the test of being highly probable.

4.5 The State party recalls that the author of the present communication has not belonged to any political organization and has not been politically active in her home country. The author asserts that she has been sentenced to stoning by a Revolutionary Court in Iran, a judgment which she maintains would be enforced if she were to be sent back there. The State party states that it relies on the evaluation of the facts and evidence and the assessment of the author's credibility made by the Swedish Immigration Board and the Aliens Appeal Board upon their examination of the author's claim.

4.6 In its decision of 13 July 1998, the Swedish Immigration Board noted that apart from giving the names of her *sighe* husband and her Christian friend, the author had in several respects failed to submit verifiable information such as telephone numbers, addresses and names of her Christian friend's family members. The Immigration Board found it unlikely that the author claimed to have no knowledge of her Christian friend's exact home address and noted in this context that the author did not even want to submit her own home address in Iran.

4.7 The Immigration Board further noted that the author during the initial inquiry had stated that a Pasdaran friend had given her photographs of people in the Evin prison who had been tortured, which she had requested "out of curiosity" and which she gave to her Christian friend although she "didn't know" what he wanted them for. The Immigration Board judged that the information provided by the author in relation to this incident lacked credibility and seemed tailored so as not to reveal verifiable details.

4.8 Finally, the Immigration Board questioned the credibility of the author's account of her marriage to the ayatollah, her relationship with the Christian man and the problems that had emerged as a result of it.

4.9 In its decision of 29 October 1999, the Aliens Appeal Board agreed with the assessment of the Immigration Board. The Board further referred to the *travaux préparatoires* of the 1989 Aliens Act which state that the assessment of an asylum-seeker's claim should be based on the applicant's statements if his/her assertions of persecution seem plausible and the actual facts cannot be elucidated. The Board noted that the author had chosen to base her application for asylum on her own statements only and that she had not submitted any written evidence in support of her claim, despite the fact that she had been told of the importance of doing so.

4.10 In addition to the decisions of the Immigration Board and the Aliens Appeal Board, the State party refers to the UNHCR Handbook on Procedures and Criteria for Determining Refugee Status, according to which "the applicant should: (i) (t)ell the truth and assist the examiner to the full in establishing the facts of his case, [and] (ii) (m)ake an effort to support his statements by any available evidence and give a satisfactory explanation for any lack of evidence. If necessary he must make an effort to procure additional evidence". According to the UNHCR Handbook, the applicant should be given the benefit of the doubt, but only when all available evidence has been obtained and checked and when the examiner is satisfied as to the applicant's general credibility.

4.11 In the present case, the State party first reminds the Committee that the author has refused to provide verifiable information and that her reasons for doing so, ie that she was forbidden by her friend to do so and that new tenants are now occupying her apartment in Tehran, are not plausible.

4.12 Second, the State party maintains that it seems unlikely that the author, solely out of curiosity, would want to have photographs of tortured people in her possession. It seems even more unlikely that she would hand over such photographs to someone she had known only for a few months. Further, the State party notes that although the author claims that the authorities in Iran are in possession of a film showing her last meeting with her friend, no additional information has been provided by the author on this issue.

4.13 A third reason for doubting the author's credibility is that the author has not submitted any judgment or other evidence to support her claim that she has been sentenced for adultery by a Revolutionary Court. In addition, the author has not given any explanation as to why her sister-in-law was not able to obtain a copy of the Revolutionary Court's judgment when she visited Iran. Further, the State party notes that according to information available to it, the Revolutionary Courts in Iran have jurisdiction over political and religious crimes, but not over crimes such as adultery. Hudud crimes, ie crimes against God, including adultery, are dealt with by ordinary courts.

4.14 The State party further draws to the attention of the Committee that the author left Tehran without any problems only a few days after the incident which allegedly led to her detention, which would indicate that she was of no interest to the Iranian authorities at the moment of her departure. In addition, the author has claimed that she handed over her passport to her brother-in-law upon arrival in Sweden. However, the State party notes that her passport number is indicated on her asylum application which she submitted six days later. The explanation for this given by the author's counsel during the national asylum procedure, ie that the number might have been available from an earlier visit in Sweden by the author in 1996, is unlikely. There is nothing in the author's file that indicates that documents concerning her earlier visit to Sweden were available during the asylum application procedure.

4.15 The State party also draws the Committee's attention to the fact that the author has not cited any medical report in support of her statement that she was severely beaten by Ayatollah Rahimian only a few days before her arrival in Sweden. In addition, according to information received by the State party, the head of the Bonyad-e Shahid was, until April 1999, Hojatolleslam Mohammad Rahimian, but he does not hold the title of ayatollah.

4.16 Finally, the State party adds that when the author's sister-in-law applied for asylum in Sweden in 1987, she stated that her brother, the author's late husband, had died in a flying accident in 1981 caused by a technical fault. Ten years later, the author's brother-in-law and his family also applied for asylum and claimed that the author's husband had been killed for being critical of the regime and that he and his family would therefore be in danger of persecution if returned to Iran. The brother-in-law and his family were returned to Iran in November 1999 and the State party submits that it has not received any information indicating that they have been mistreated.

4.17 On the basis of the above, the State party maintains that the author's credibility can be questioned, that she has not presented any evidence in support of her claim and that she should therefore not be given the benefit of the doubt. In conclusion, the State party considers that the enforcement of the expulsion order to Iran would, under the present circumstances, not constitute a violation of article 3 of the Convention.

Counsel's comments

5.1 In her submissions dated 4 February and 6 March 2000, counsel disputes the arguments of the State party regarding the failure of the author to submit written evidence. Counsel states that the author has provided the only written evidence she could possibly obtain, ie her identity papers and documentation showing that she is the widow of a martyr. Counsel states that the ayatollah conducted the *sighe* or *mutah* wedding himself with no witnesses or written contract. As to her failure to provide the immigration authorities with a written court verdict, counsel submits that the author only has second-hand information about the verdict, as it was passed after her departure from Iran. She cannot, therefore, submit a written verdict. Counsel further disputes that the author's sister-in-law should have been able to obtain a copy of the verdict while visiting Iran. She further states that the author's sister-in-law long ago ended all contacts with the author because she strongly resents the fact that the author has had a relationship with any man after the death of her husband.

5.2 Counsel acknowledges that crimes such as adultery are handled by ordinary courts. However, she draws the attention of the Committee to the fact that the jurisdictional rules are not as strict in Iran as for example in the State party and that the prosecuting judge can choose the court. In addition, for a martyr's widow to ride alone with a Christian man in his car would probably fall under the heading of "un-islamic behaviour" and as such come under the jurisdiction of the Revolutionary Court. Even if this were not the case, counsel reminds the Committee that the author has only been informed that she has been sentenced to death by stoning by a court. Not being a lawyer, and in view of what she was told during her interrogation by the Zeinab sisters, the author assumes that the sentence was handed down by the Revolutionary Court and this assumption should not be taken as a reason for questioning the general veracity of her claim.

5.3 Counsel states that the author has given credible explanations for not being able or not wishing to provide the Swedish authorities with certain addresses and telephone numbers. Firstly, she had promised for the sake of security not to give her lover's telephone number to anyone and does not wish to break her promise even at the request of the immigration authorities. The Christian man always contacted the author on her mobile phone which he had given her for that purpose alone. The author left the mobile phone in Iran when she departed and as she never called her number herself or gave it to anyone, she cannot remember it. Further, counsel states that the address which is indicated on the author's visa application used to be her home address, but the author has repeatedly explained that new tenants are now living there and that she does not want to subject them to any difficulties caused by inquiries from the Swedish authorities. Finally, counsel stresses that the author has given detailed information about the neighbourhood, Aghdasiye, where her lover lived and that she has repeatedly underlined that she never knew the exact address since she always went to her secret meetings first by taxi to Meydon-e-Nobonyad where she was picked up by a car that brought her to the Christian man's home. Finally, all the author ever knew about the Christian man's relatives was that he had one sister and one brother living in United Kingdom and a son from a previous marriage living in Canada. She never met them and never asked their names.

5.4 Counsel underlines that the fact that the Swedish authorities do not find the author's explanations credible is a result of speculation based on the supposition that all people behave and think according to Swedish or Western standards. The authorities do not take into account the prevailing cautiousness in Iran with respect to giving personal information, particularly to public officials.

5.5 With reference to the photographs of victims of torture which the author claims to have handed over to her lover, counsel submits that this fact in no way diminishes the author's credibility. The couple were engaged in a serious relationship and intended to marry and there was no reason for the author not to pass on such photos to a man in whom she had total confidence. Further, counsel underlines that the author has never argued that her handling of the photographs in question supports or has anything to do with her asylum claim.

5.6 Counsel notes that the State party observes that the author has not cited any medical certificate attesting to injuries resulting from the beatings she was subjected to by her *sighe* husband. Counsel reminds the Committee that the author left Iran the following day and that her main preoccupation was to arrive safely in Sweden. Counsel further states that most Iranian women are used to violence by men and they do not or cannot expect the legal system to protect them, despite the positive changes which have recently taken place in Iran in this respect. As an example, counsel states that an Iranian woman wishing to report a rape must be examined by the courts' own doctors, as certificates by general doctors are not accepted by courts.

5.7 With reference to the fact that the author's passport number was given in her asylum application although she had claimed to have disposed of her passport upon arrival in Sweden, counsel states that there is no indication on the asylum application that the author's passport has been seized by the Immigration Board officer, which is the rule in order to secure enforcement of possible expulsion; this fact seems to support the author's version of events. In addition, the author has maintained that when filing her application she merely had to state her name, all other necessary details having appeared on a computer screen. This information has been corroborated by the Immigration Board registration officer who received the author's asylum application and who told counsel that, in recent years, a person granted a tourist visa is registered in a computer database, containing all available information, including passport numbers. The author had been granted a tourist visa for Sweden twice in recent years, so her account was absolutely correct.

5.8 Counsel notes that the State party has confirmed that the author's *sighe* husband was the head of the Bonyad-e Shahid, which should support the author's claim; he was generally referred to as "Ayatollah" even though his title was "Hojatolleslam". Counsel reminds the Committee that there are only some 10 real ayatollahs in Iran. The great majority of mullahs are of the rank of hojatolleslam. However, mullahs who have gained power, particularly political power, are often referred to as Ayatollah out of courtesy, an illustrative example being Ayatollah Khamenei whose office demanded the rank of an ayatollah but who was in fact only hojatolleslam when he was appointed.

5.9 With reference to the State party's argument that the author left Iran without difficulty, counsel points out that this is consistent with the author's version of the events leading to her flight. She has maintained that at the time of her departure she was not yet of interest to the Iranian authorities since her *sighe* husband had suppressed the Pasdaran report to the Revolutionary Court.

5.10 Finally, counsel states that what the author's dead husband's relatives have stated about the circumstances surrounding his death has no impact on the author's case or her credibility. It should be noted that the author herself has never stated that her husband was assassinated by the regime, but only that she had doubts about the circumstances pertaining to his death.

5.11 In support of counsel's arguments she submits a medical certificate dated 22 November 1999 from a senior psychiatrist at Sahlgrenska Hospital, where the author was taken after an attempted suicide. The attempt was made after the Swedish police had taken her and her son from a reception centre for asylum-seekers to a detention centre to ensure the execution of her expulsion. The diagnosis made was deep depression combined with contemplation of suicide.

5.12 Counsel further encloses a letter dated 27 December 1999 from the leading Swedish expert on Islam, Professor Jan Hjärpe, who confirms the author's account concerning the institution of *sighe* or *mutah* marriages and the legal sanctions provided for in cases of adultery.

5.13 Counsel draws the attention of the Committee to the fact that the immigration authorities in examining the author's case have not considered the situation of women in Iran, existing legislation and its application, or the values of the Iranian society. Counsel states that the argumentation of the authorities, based almost exclusively on the author's failure to submit certain verifiable information, seems to be a pretext for refusing the author's application. In conclusion, counsel submits that according to the information provided by the author, there exist substantial grounds to believe that the author would be subjected to torture if returned to Iran and that the author has provided reasonable explanations for why she has not been able to or not wished to furnish certain details.

Additional comments submitted by the State party

6.1 In its submission dated 2 May 2000, the State party contends that the Swedish Immigration Board and the Aliens Appeal Board have ensured a thorough investigation of the author's case. It reminds the Committee that during the asylum procedure, the author has been repeatedly reminded of the importance of submitting verifiable information, but that she has chosen not to do so. The State party does not find the explanations given hereto convincing, reiterates that the burden of proof in principle rests with the author and maintains that the author's credibility can be questioned.

6.2 Finally, the State party draws the attention of the Committee to the fact that the author first alleged that she had been sentenced to death for adultery during an initial interview held with her in May 1998. The State party submits that the author thus has had ample time to present a written judgment or other evidence to support that claim.

Additional information from the State party and counsel, requested by the Committee

7.1 Having taken note of the submissions made by both the author and the State party regarding the merits of the case, the Committee, on 19 and 20 June 2000, requested further information from the two parties.

Submissions by counsel

7.2 In her submission of 1 September 2000, counsel confirms previous information given regarding: (a) the nature of *sighe* or *mutah* marriages and the fact that witnesses are not necessary, nor registration before a judge if the partners themselves are capable of conducting the ceremony correctly; (b) the activities of Bonyad-e Shahid, affirming that martyrs' widows are presented, in listings and photo albums, for temporary marriages to its employees and directors. Counsel supports the information given with letters from, *inter alia*, the Association of Iranian Political Prisoners in Exile (AIPP), the Support Committee for Women in Iran and Professor Said Mahmoodi, Professor of International Law at the University of Stockholm.

7.3 With regard to the alleged death sentence against the author, counsel submits that despite attempts by AIPP, it has not been possible to find any evidence that the author's Christian lover had been imprisoned and that they both have been sentenced to death by stoning for adultery. AIPP, as well as other sources, maintain that such information is not possible to get if the prison, the court or the case numbers is not known.

7.4 Counsel submits letters and information given by experts in Islamic law confirming that a *sighe* wife is bound by the rules regarding adultery and that she is prohibited from having a sexual relationship with any man other than her *sighe* husband. Adultery with a Christian man bears the sanction of stoning to death. Counsel further submits that the law in theory requires either four righteous witnesses or a confession to the sexual act for stoning to be ordered, but that the author's *sighe* husband, being a powerful man in society, would not have difficulties finding persons willing to testify. According to international human rights organizations, the eye witness condition is rarely respected and stoning for adultery is still frequently practised in Iran, despite recent reforms in the country.

7.5 Reference and further clarifications were made with regard to telephone calls received by the author's sister-in-law (see para 2.8 above). The author's previous lawyer had told Swedish authorities that the sister-in-law in Sweden had been contacted by Hojatolleslam Rahimian who told her that the author had been found guilty. Counsel has since been in contact with the sister-in-law directly and states that the correct version of events was that the sister-in-law, shortly after the author's arrival in Sweden, was contacted by a man in rage who did not give his name but wanted to know the author's whereabouts in Sweden. The man was aggressive and knew all the details of the author's past and said that she had no right to leave Iran. The sister-in-law further states that she never attempted to verify the existence of a court judgment when she visited Iran.

7.6 With reference to the Committee's request for additional information, counsel states that the author's older son, born in 1980, tried to seek asylum in Sweden from Denmark in March 2000. In accordance with the Dublin Convention, after a short interview, he was sent back to Denmark where he is still waiting to be interrogated by Danish immigration authorities. Since his case had not yet been examined by the Danish authorities, counsel requested Amnesty International to interview him.

7.7 The records of the interview confirm statements made by the author regarding her *sighe* marriage and of her being called to the Bonyad-e Shahid office several times a week. The son also states that when his mother left she had told him that he had to leave school and hide with close relatives of hers in Baghistan. He received private teaching to become a veterinary surgeon and subsequently enrolled in University. On 25 January 2000 he was summoned to the university information office by the intelligence service, Harasar, from where two men took him to the Bonyad-e Shahid office in Tehran where he was detained, interrogated, threatened and beaten. He claims that the interrogators wanted to know his mother's whereabouts and that they threatened to keep him and beat him until his mother came "crawling on all fours" and then they would "carry out her sentence". The author's son claims that it was during the interrogation that he fully realized his mother's situation, although he had not spoken to her since she left the country.

7.8 In conclusion, counsel maintains that although it has not been possible to obtain direct written evidence, for the reasons given above, the chain of circumstantial evidence is of such a nature that there can be no reason to doubt the author's credibility. Reference is further made to a recent judgment of the European Court of Human Rights dated 11 July 2000, regarding an Iranian woman asylum-seeker who allegedly had committed adultery and who feared death by stoning, whipping or flogging if returned. As in the case of the author no written evidence existed in the form of a court judgment, but the Court stated that it "is not persuaded that the situation in the applicant's country of origin has evolved to the extent that adulterous behaviour is no longer considered a reprehensible affront to Islamic law. It has taken judicial notice of recent surveys of the current situation in Iran and notes that punishment of adultery by stoning still remains on the statute book and may be resorted to by authorities." (*Jabari v Turkey* (para 40), European Court of Human Rights, 11 July 2000). The Court ruled that to expel the applicant would be a violation of the European Convention for the Protection of Human Rights and Fundamental Freedoms.

Submissions by the State party

7.9   The State party made additional submissions on 19 September and 19 October 2000. With reference to the Committee's request for additional information, the State party reiterates its view that the burden is on the author to present an arguable case. It maintains that the author has not given any evidence in support of her claim and therefore there are serious reasons to doubt the veracity of those claims.

7.10 With regard to the author's alleged *sighe* marriage, the State party confirms that the law in Iran allows for such temporary forms of marriage. It further argues that although *sighe* marriages are not recorded on identification documents, such contracts should, according to reliable sources, contain a precise statement of the time-period involved and be registered by a competent authority. In practice, a religious authority may approve the marriage and issue a certificate. Given that the author claims that her *sighe* or *mutah* marriage was conducted by Hojatolleslam Rahimian himself and that no contract was signed, the State party has doubts as to whether the author entered into a legally valid marriage.

7.11 The State party points out that counsel in her last submissions to the Committee has included certificates and other information which have not previously been presented to the Swedish immigration authorities. As the new information seems to be invoked in order to prove the existence of *sighe* marriages in Iran, the State party emphasizes that it does not question this fact, nor the existence of the Bonyad-e Shahid, but, *inter alia*, the author's credibility in respect of her personal claims of having entered in such a marriage. The author's credibility is further diminished by the inconsistent information given relating to phone calls received by the author's sister-in-law.

7.12 In addition, even if the Committee does accept that the author has entered into such a marriage, the State party asserts that this in itself would not constitute substantial grounds for believing that the author would be in danger of being tortured or killed if returned to Iran.

7.13 It is further submitted that according to the Swedish Embassy in Tehran, it is not possible for the Embassy to inquire whether a competent family court, rather than the Revolutionary Court, has issued a judgment regarding the author. However, the author should, according to the Embassy, by proxy be able to obtain a copy of the judgment if it exists, or at least obtain the name of the court and the case number. The State party further submits that only a married person can be convicted of adultery; it therefore seems unlikely that the author's lover would have been sentenced to death as claimed.

7.14 In addition, the State party claims that neither reports from the United States Department of State nor from Amnesty International confirm the assertion by counsel that stoning is frequently practised in Iran.

7.15 With regard to the judgment by the European Court referred to by counsel, the State party points out that in that case the applicant had been granted refugee status by UNHCR and the European Court had relied on UNHCR's conclusions as to the credibility of the applicant and the veracity of her account. In the present case, two competent national authorities have scrutinized the author's case and found it not to be credible.

7.16 Finally, with regard to the information given by the author's son, currently residing in Denmark where he is seeking asylum, the State party underlines that this information is new and has not been presented to the national authorities. According to the State party, information submitted at a very late stage of the proceedings should be treated with the greatest caution. It further emphasizes a number of contradictory points in the newly submitted evidence: (a) during the son's interrogation by the Swedish Board of Immigration no mention was made of any court judgment or death sentence, information which, in the State party's view, would have been relevant in the circumstances; (b) the son gave contradictory answers to the question of whether he possessed a passport. The State party also finds it unlikely that the author was not aware of, and has never invoked, the harassment to which her son was allegedly subjected after her departure from Iran.

Issues and proceedings before the Committee

8.1 Before considering any claims contained in a communication, the Committee against Torture must decide whether or not it is admissible under article 22 of the Convention. The Committee has ascertained, as it is required to do under article 22(5)(a) of the Convention, that the same matter has not been and is not being examined under another procedure of international investigation or settlement. The Committee is further of the opinion that all available domestic remedies have been exhausted. The Committee finds that no further obstacles to the admissibility of the communication exist. Since both the State party and the author have provided observations on the merits of the communication, the Committee proceeds immediately with the considerations of those merits.

8.2 The issue before the Committee is whether the forced return of the author to the Islamic Republic of Iran would violate the obligation of Sweden under article 3 of the Convention not to expel or to return a person to another State where there are substantial grounds for believing that he or she would be in danger of being subjected to torture.

8.3 The Committee must decide, pursuant to article 3(1) of the Convention, whether there are substantial grounds for believing that the author would be in danger of being subjected to torture upon return to Iran. In reaching this decision, the Committee must take into account all relevant considerations, pursuant to article 3(2) of the Convention, including the existence of a consistent pattern of gross, flagrant or mass violations of human rights. The aim of the determination, however, is to establish whether the individual concerned would be personally at risk of being subjected to torture in the country to which she would return. It follows that the existence of a consistent pattern of gross, flagrant or mass violations of human rights in a country does not as such constitute a sufficient ground for determining that a particular person would be in danger of being subjected to torture upon his return to that country; additional grounds must exist to show that the individual concerned would be personally at risk. Similarly, the absence of a consistent pattern of gross violations of human rights does not mean that a person cannot be considered to be in danger of being subjected to torture in his or her specific circumstances.

8.4 From the information submitted by the author, the Committee notes that she is the widow of a martyr and as such supported and supervised by the Bonyad-e Shahid Committee of Martyrs. It is also noted that the author claims that she was forced into a *sighe* or *mutah* marriage and to have committed and been sentenced to stoning for adultery. Although treating the recent testimony of the author's son, seeking asylum in Denmark, with utmost caution, the Committee is nevertheless of the view that the information given further corroborates the account given by the author.

8.5 The Committee notes that the State party questions the author's credibility primarily because of her failure to submit verifiable information and refers in this context to international standards, ie the UNHCR Handbook on Procedures and Criteria for Determining Refugee Status, according to which an asylum-seeker has an obligation to make an effort to support his/her statements by any available evidence and to give a satisfactory explanation for any lack of evidence.

8.6 The Committee draws the attention of the parties to its General Comment on the implementation of article 3 of the Convention in the context of article 22, adopted on 21 November 1997, according to which the burden to present an arguable case is on the author of a communication. The Committee notes the State party's position that the author has not fulfilled her obligation to submit the verifiable information that would enable her to enjoy the benefit of the doubt. However, the Committee is of the view that the author has submitted sufficient details regarding her *sighe* or *mutah* marriage and alleged arrest, such as names of persons, their positions, dates, addresses, name of police station, etc, that could have, and to a certain extent have been, verified by the Swedish immigration authorities, to shift the burden of proof. In this context the Committee is of the view that the State party has not made sufficient efforts to determine whether there are substantial grounds for believing that the author would be in danger of being subjected to torture.

8.7 The State party does not dispute that gross, flagrant or mass violations of human rights have been committed in Iran. The Committee notes, *inter alia*, the report of the Special Representative of the Commission on Human Rights on the situation of human rights in Iran (E/CN.4/2000/35) of 18 January 2000, which indicates that although significant progress is being made in Iran with regard to the status of women in sectors like education and training, "little progress is being made with regard to remaining systematic barriers to equality" and for "the removal of patriarchal attitudes in society". It is further noted that the report, and numerous reports of non-governmental organizations, confirm that married women have recently been sentenced to death by stoning for adultery.

9   Considering that the author's account of events is consistent with the Committee's knowledge about the present human rights situation in Iran, and that the author has given plausible explanations for her failure or inability to provide certain details which might have been of relevance to the case, the Committee is of the view that, in the prevailing circumstances, the State party has an obligation, in accordance with article 3 of the Convention, to refrain from forcibly returning the author to Iran or to any other country where she runs a risk of being expelled or returned to Iran.

10   Pursuant to rule 111(5) of its Rules of Procedure, the Committee would wish to receive, within 90 days, information on any relevant measures taken by the State party in accordance with the Committee's present views.

CASE NO 14

ATO DEL AVELLANAL v PERU

UNITED NATIONS HUMAN RIGHTS COMMITTEE

Communication No: 202/1986

Views adopted: 28 October 1988

Human rights — Equality and non-discrimination — Sex discrimination — Equality before the law and the courts — Legal capacity of wife — Whether a law providing that where a woman is married, only her husband is entitled to represent matrimonial property issues before the courts was discriminatory on the ground of sex and in violation of the right to equality — Peruvian Civil Code, art 168 — International Covenant on Civil and Political Rights, arts 2, 3, 14, 16 and 26

BACKGROUND

The author of the communication, Ms Graciela Ato del Avellanal, was a Peruvian citizen, married and resident in Peru. She was the owner of two apartment blocks. When she acquired the properties in 1974, a number of tenants ceased paying rent. After unsuccessful attempts to collect the unpaid rent, she sued the tenants on 13 September 1978. The Court of First Instance found in her favour and ordered that the tenants pay the rent overdue since 1974. In 1980 the Superior Court reversed the decision, on the ground that the applicant was not entitled to sue because article 168 of the Peruvian Civil Code provided that when a women is married, only her husband is entitled to represent matrimonial property before the courts. On 10 December 1980, she appealed to the Supreme Court of Peru claiming, *inter alia*, that article 2(2) of the Peruvian Constitution, which provides that "the law grants rights to women which are not less than those granted to men", had abolished discrimination against women. The Supreme Court dismissed her appeal and upheld the decision of the Superior Court.

Ms Ato del Avellanal sought the recourse of *amparo* on 6 May 1984, claiming that denial of her right to litigate because she was a woman denied her rights under article 2(2) of the Constitution. The Supreme Court rejected her application on 10 April 1985. Ms Ato del Avellanal then submitted a communication to the Human Rights Committee under the Optional Protocol to the International Covenant on Civil and Political Rights, claiming Peru had violated her rights under articles 2(1) and (3), 16, 23(4) and 26 of the Covenant. The Optional Protocol had entered into force in respect of Peru on 3 January 1981.

DECIDED (finding violations of arts 3, 14(1) and 26 of the Covenant)

1   Article 14(1) of the ICCPR guarantees that "all persons shall be equal before the courts and tribunals". The Superior Court reversed the decision of the court of first instance on the sole ground that according to article 168 of the Peruvian Civil Code only the husband is entitled to represent matrimonial property, ie, that the wife was not equal to her husband for purposes of suing in court. Under article 3 of the ICCPR, State parties

undertake "to ensure the equal right of men and women to the enjoyment of all civil and political rights set forth in the present Covenant". Article 26 provides that all persons are equal before the law and are entitled to the equal protection of the law. The application of article 168 of the Peruvian Civil Code to the author resulted in denying her equality before the courts and constituted discrimination on the ground of sex. (Paras 10.1 and 10.2)

2   The events of this case, in so far as they continued or occurred after 3 January 1981 (the date of entry into force of the Optional Protocol to the ICCPR for Peru), disclosed violations of articles 3, 14(1) and 26 of the Covenant. The State party was under an obligation, in accordance with the provisions of article 2 of the Covenant, to take effective measures to remedy the violations suffered by the victim. (Paras 11 and 12)

Treaties and other international instruments referred to

International Covenant on Civil and Political Rights 1966, arts 2(1), 2(3), 3, 14(1), 16, 23(4) and 26

(First) Optional Protocol to the International Covenant on Civil and Political Rights 1966, arts 4(2), 5(1), 5(2)(a), 5(2)(b) and 5(4)

National legislation referred to

Peru

Peruvian Civil Code, art 168

Constitution of Peru, art 2(2)

Peruvian Law No 23156, art 41

Peruvian Law No 23506, arts 39 and 40

Peruvian Act No 23385, art 42

Peruvian Magna Carta, art 2(2)

VIEWS UNDER ARTICLE 5(4) OF THE OPTIONAL PROTOCOL

1   The author of the communication (initial letter dated 13 January 1986 and a subsequent letter dated 11 February 1987) is Graciela Ato del Avellanal, a Peruvian citizen born in 1934, employed as professor of music and married to Guillenno Burneo, currently residing in Peru. She is represented by counsel. It is claimed that the Government of Peru has violated articles 2(1), 2(3), 16, 23(4) and 26 of the Covenant, because the author has been allegedly discriminated against only because she is a woman.

2.1   The author is the owner of two apartment buildings in Lima, which she acquired in 1974. It appears that a number of tenants took advantage of the change in ownership to cease paying rent for their apartments. After unsuccessful attempts to collect the overdue rent, the author sued the tenants on 13 September 1978. The court of first instance found in her favour and ordered the tenants to pay her the rent due since 1974.

The Superior Court reversed the judgment on 21 November 1980 on the procedural ground that the author was not entitled to sue, because, according to article 168 of the Peruvian Civil Code, when a woman is married only the husband is entitled to represent matrimonial property before the Courts (*El marido es el representante de la sociedad conyugal*). On 10 December 1980, the author appealed to the Peruvian Supreme Court, submitting, *inter alia*, that the Peruvian Constitution now in force abolished discrimination against women and that article 2(2) of the Peruvian Magna Carta provides that "the law grants rights to women which are not less than those granted to men". However, on 15 February 1984 the Supreme Court upheld the decision of the Superior Court. Thereupon, the author interposed the recourse of *amparo* on 6 May 1984, claiming that in her case article 2(2) of the Constitution had been violated denying her the right to litigate before the courts only because she is a woman. The Supreme Court rejected the recourse of *amparo* on 10 April 1985.

2.2 Having thus exhausted domestic remedies in Peru, and pursuant to article 39 of the Peruvian Law No 23506, which specifically provides that a Peruvian citizen who considers that his or her constitutional rights have been violated may appeal to the Human Rights Committee of the United Nations, the author seeks United Nations assistance in vindicating her right to equality before the Peruvian courts.

3   By its decision of 19 March 1986, the Working Group of the Human Rights Committee transmitted the communication under rule 91 of the provisional rule of procedure to the State party concerned, requesting information and observations relevant to the question of the admissibility of the communication in so far as it may raise issues under articles 14(1), 16 and 26 in conjunction with articles 2 and 3 of the Covenant. The Working Group also requested the State party to provide the Committee with (a) the text of the decision of the Supreme Court of 10 April 1985; (b) any other relevant court orders or decisions not already provided by the author; and (c) the text of the relevant provisions of the domestic law, including those of the Peruvian Civil Code and Constitution.

4.1 By its submission dated 20 November 1986, the State party noted that "in the action brought by Mrs Graciela to del Avellanal and one other, the decision of the Supreme Court dated 10 April 1985 was deemed accepted, since no appeal was made against it under article 42 of Act No 23385".

4.2 The decision of the Supreme Court, dated 10 April 1985, "declares valid the ruling set out on 12 sheets, dated 24 July 1984, declaring inadmissible the application for *amparo* submitted on 2 sheets by Mrs Graciela Ato del Avellanal de Burneo and one other against the First Civil Section of the Supreme Court; [and] orders that the present decision, whether accepted or enforceable, be published in the *Diario Oficial, El Peruano* within the time-limit laid down in article 41 of Law No 23156".

5.1 Commenting on the State party's submission under rule 91, the author, in a submission dated 11 February 1987 contends that:

1   It is untrue that the ruling of 10 April 1985, of which I was notified on 5 August 1985, was accepted. As shown by the attached copy of the original application, my attorneys appealed against the decision in the petition of 6 August 1985, which was stamped as received by the Second Civil Section of the Supreme Court on 7 August 1985.

2   The Supreme Court has never notified my attorneys of the decision which it had handed down on the appeal of 6 August 1985.

5.2 The author also encloses a copy of a further application, stamped as received by the Second Civil Section of the Supreme Court on 3 October 1985 and reiterating the request that the appeal lodged should be upheld. She adds that "once again, the Supreme Court failed to notify my attorneys of the decision which it had handed down on this further petition".

6.1 Before considering any claims contained in a communication, the Human Rights Committee must, in accordance with rule 87 of its provisional rules of procedure, decide whether or not it is admissible under the Optional Protocol to the Covenant.

6.2 With regard to article 5(2)(a) of the Optional Protocol, the Committee observed that the matter complained of by the author was not being examined and had not been examined under another procedure of international investigation or settlement.

6.3 With regard to article 5(2)(b) of the Optional Protocol, the Committee noted the State party's contention that the author has failed to appeal the decision of the Peruvian Supreme Court of 10 April 1985. However, in the light of the author's submission of 11 February 1987 the Committee found that the communication satisfied the requirements of article 5(2)(b) of the Optional Protocol. The Committee further observed that this issue could be reviewed in the light of any further explanations or statements received from the State party under article 4(2) of the Optional Protocol.

7   On 9 July 1987, the Human Rights Committee therefore decided that the communication was admissible, in so far as it raised issues under articles 14(1), and 16 in conjunction with articles 2, 3 and 26 of the Covenant.

8.   The time-limit for the State party's submission under article 4(2) of the Optional Protocol expired on 6 February 1988. No submission has been received from the State party, despite a reminder sent to the State party on 17 May 1988.

9.1 The Human Rights Committee, having considered the present communication in the light of all the information made available to it, as provided in article 5(1) of the Optional Protocol, notes that the facts of the case, as submitted by the author, have not been contested by the State party.

9.2 In formulating its views, the Committee takes into account the failure of the State party to furnish certain information and clarifications, in particular with regard to the allegations of discrimination of which the author has complained. It is not sufficient to forward the text of the relevant laws and decisions, without specifically addressing the issues raised in the communication. It is implicit in article 4(2) of the Optional Protocol that the State party has the duty to investigate in good faith all allegations of violation of the Covenant made against it and its authorities, and to furnish to the Committee all relevant information. In the circumstances, due weight must be given to the author's allegations.

10.1 With respect to the requirement set forth in article 14(1) of the Covenant that "all persons shall be equal before the courts and tribunals", the Committee notes that the court of first instance decided in favour of the author, but the Superior Court reversed that decision on the sole ground that according to article 168 of the Peruvian Civil Code only the husband is entitled to represent matrimonial property, ie that the wife was not equal to her husband for purposes of suing in Court.

10.2 With regard to discrimination on the ground of sex, the Committee notes further that under article 3 of the Covenant States parties undertake "to ensure the equal right of men and women to the enjoyment of all civil and political rights set forth in the present

Covenant" and that article 26 provides that all persons are equal before the law and are entitled to the equal protection of the law. The Committee finds that the facts before it reveal that the application of article 168 of the Peruvian Civil Code to the author resulted in denying her equality before the courts and constituted discrimination on the ground of sex.

11   The Human Rights Committee, acting under article 5(4) of the Optional Protocol to the International Covenant on Civil and Political Rights, is of the view that the events of this case, in so far as they continued or occurred after 3 January 1981 (the date of entry into force of the Optional Protocol for Peru), disclose violations of articles 3, 14(1), and 26 of the Covenant.

12   The Committee, accordingly, is of the view that the State party is under an obligation, in accordance with the provisions of article 2 of the Covenant, to take effective measures to remedy the violations suffered by the victim. In this connection the Committee welcomes the State party's commitment, expressed in articles 39 and 40 of Law No 23506, to cooperate with the Human Rights Committee, and to implement its recommendation.

CASE NO 15

MORALES DE SIERRA v GUATEMALA

INTER-AMERICAN COMMISSION ON HUMAN RIGHTS

Case No: 11.625

Report No: 04/01

Date: 19 January 2001

Panel: Bicudo (*Chairman*): Grossman (*First Vice-Chairman*); Méndez, (*Second Vice-Chairman*); Goldman, Laurie and Prado Vallejo (*Commissioners*)[i]

Human rights — Equality and non-discrimination — Sex discrimination — Equality before the law — Equality before the courts — Equality of rights and balancing of responsibilities in marriage — Right to respect for private life — Legal capacity of wife — Whether laws reflecting traditional divisions of roles in marriage consistent with human rights — Guatemalan Civil Code, arts 109, 110, 113, 114, 115, 131, 133, 255 and 317 — Universal Declaration of Human Rights, art 16 — Convention on the Elimination of All Forms of Discrimination against Women, arts 1, 15 and 16 — American Convention on Human Rights, arts 1(1), 2, 17 and 24

BACKGROUND

The Center for Justice and International Law and Ms María Eugenia Morales de Sierra lodged a petition with the Inter-American Commission on Human Rights, challenging various provisions of the Guatemalan Civil Code, on the ground that their differential treatment of husbands and wives, and of married and single women, violated various rights guaranteed by the American Convention on Human Rights.

The relevant provisions of the Civil Code were:

 (i) Article 109, which conferred the power to represent the marital union on the husband;

 (ii) Article 131, which empowered the husband to administer marital property;

 (iii) Article 110, which conferred on the wife the "special right and obligation" to care for minor children and the home;

 (iv) Articles 113 and 114, which provided that a married woman may only work outside the home if this did not prejudice her role as mother and homemaker and that a husband may oppose his wife's activities outside the home as long as he provides for her and has adequate reasons for his opposition (a judge having the power to decide in case of disagreement);

 (v) Article 255, which conferred primary responsibility on the husband to represent the children of the union and to administer their property; and

---

i Commission member Marta Altolaguirre, national of Guatemala, did not participate in the discussion or vote on this Report, pursuant to Article 19(2) of the IACHR's Regulations.

(vi) Article 317, which provided that women could be excused from exercising certain forms of guardianship.

The Constitutional Court of Guatemala upheld the challenged provisions as constitutional on the grounds that they provided juridical certainty in the allocation of roles in marriage. When the case came before the Commission, the Guatemalan government pointed to a number of proposed reforms (none of which had been enacted by then). The Commission adopted a report on 1 October 1998, setting out its conclusions on the petitioners' claim. Subsequently, amendments to 7 of the 9 challenged provisions were made.

HELD (finding various violations of the Convention)

Right to equal protection of and before the law (article 24 of the Convention)

1   Differences in treatment in otherwise similar circumstances were not necessarily discriminatory. A distinction would not be discriminatory if it was based on reasonable and objective criteria, pursued a legitimate aim and employed means which were proportionate to the end sought. The Guatemalan Constitutional Court had upheld the various distinctions on the basis that they responded to a need for certainty and juridical security, to protect the marital home and children, respect for traditional Guatemalan values and, in certain cases, the need to protect women in their capacities as wives and mothers. The Court had made no effort to probe the validity of these assertions or to weigh alternative positions. The effect of the Civil Code was to mandate a system in which the ability of approximately half the married population to act on a range of essential matters was subordinated to the will of the other; the overarching effect of the challenged provisions was to deny married women legal autonomy, in violation of article 24. (Paras 31 and 38)

Equality of rights and balancing of responsibilities in marriage (article 17 of the Convention)

2   Far from ensuring the equality of rights and adequate balancing of responsibilities in marriage provided for in article 17 of the Convention, the challenged provisions institutionalised imbalances in the rights and duties of the spouses. The provisions established a situation of *de jure* dependency for the wife and created an insurmountable disequilibrium in the spousal authority within the marriage. Moreover the provisions applied stereotyped notions of the roles of women and men which perpetuated *de facto* discrimination against women in the family sphere, and which had the further effect of impeding the ability of men to fully develop their roles within the marriage and family. The legal regime was therefore incompatible with article 17(4) of the American Convention, read with reference to the requirements of article 16(1) of CEDAW. (Paras 44 and 45)

Right to privacy (article 11 of the Convention)

3   The challenged provisions, insofar as they restricted the complainant's ability to exercise her profession and dispose of her property, constituted an arbitrary interference with her right to have her private life respected. In mandating these and other forms of subordination of a wife's role, the State deprived married women of their autonomy to select and pursue options for their personal development and support, and denied

women the equal right to seek employment and benefit from the increased self-determination this affords. (Paras 48 and 49)

Obligation to respect and ensure rights and to adopt domestic legal measures (articles 1 and 2 of the Convention)

4   The failure of the State to respect and ensure the rights of the complainant under the Convention and other relevant treaties generated liability for all acts, public and private, committed pursuant to the discrimination effectuated against the victim in violation of those rights. In addition, the State was obliged to repair the consequence of the violations, including through measures to restore the rights of the victim to the full extent possible and to provide a just indemnity for the harm she had sustained. (Para 54)

Treaties and other international instruments referred to

American Convention on Human Rights 1969, arts 1(1), 2, 17, 24, 29, 41, 48, 50 and 61

American Declaration of the Rights and Duties of Man 1948

Convention on the Elimination of All Forms of Discrimination against Women 1979, arts 1, 15 and 16

Inter-American Convention on the Prevention, Punishment, and Eradication of Violence against Women ("Convention of Belém do Pará") 1994, art 6(b)

Universal Declaration of Human Rights 1948, art 16

General Comments and General Recommendations of the UN Treaty Bodies referred to

Committee on the Elimination of Discrimination against Women, General Recommendation 19 (*Violence against women*) (Eleventh session, 1992)

Committee on the Elimination of Discrimination against Women, General Recommendation 21 (*Equality in marriage and family relations*) (Thirteenth session, 1992)

Human Rights Committee, General Comment 16 (*Article 17*) (Thirty-second session, 1988)

National legislation referred to

Guatemala

Civil Code, arts 109, 110, 113, 114, 115, 131, 133, 255 and 317

Decree 80–98, arts 1, 2, 4, 5 and 8

Decree 27–99, art 1

Cases referred to

Ato del Avellanal v Peru, UN Human Rights Committee, Communication No 202/1986, views adopted 28 October 1998, *supra*, p 217

Belgian Linguistic Case (Merits), ECHR, judgment of 23 July 1968, Series A, No 6; 1 EHRR 252

Broeks v Netherlands, UN Human Rights Committee, Communication No 172/1984, views adopted 9 April 1987

Burghartz v Switzerland, ECHR, judgment of 22 February 1994, Series A, No 280-B; 18 EHRR 101

Gallardo v Mexico, IACommHR, Case 11.430, Report No 43/96, OEA/Ser.L/V/II.95, Doc 7 rev at 485 (1996)

Gaskin v United Kingdom, ECHR, judgment of 7 July 1989, Series A, No 160; 12 EHRR 36

Godínez Cruz Case, IACHR, judgment of 20 January 1989, Series C, No 5 (1989)

González v Costa Rica, IACommHR, Case 11.553, Report No 48/96, IACHR OEA/Ser.L/V/II.95, Doc 7 rev at 119 (1996)

International Responsibility for the Promulgation and Enforcement of Laws in violation of the Convention (Arts 1 and 2 of the American Convention on Human Rights), IACHR, Advisory Opinion OC-14/94 of 9 December 1994, Series A, No 14 (1994)

Kroon v Netherlands, ECHR, judgment of 27 October 1994, Series A, No 297-C; 19 EHRR 263; below, p 324

Niemetz v Germany, ECHR, judgment of 16 December 1992, Series A, No 251-B; 16 EHRR 97

"Other Treaties" Subject to the Advisory Jurisdiction of the Court (Art 64 American Convention on Human Rights), IACHR, Advisory Opinion OC-1/82 of 24 September 1982; 67 ILR 594; 22 ILM 51

Proposed Amendments to the Naturalization Provisions of the Constitution of Costa Rica, IACHR, Advisory Opinion OC-4/84 of 19 January 1984; below, p 553

Rees v United Kingdom, ECHR, judgment of 17 October 1986, Series A, No 106; 9 EHRR 56

Schmidt v Germany, ECHR, judgment of 18 July 1994, Series A, No 291-B

Schuler-Zgraggen v Switzerland, ECHR, judgment of 24 June 1993, Series A, No 263; 16 EHRR 405

Toonen v Australia, UN Human Rights Committee, Communication No 488/1992, views adopted 31 March 1994

Velásquez Rodríguez v Honduras, IACHR, judgment of 29 July 1988, Series C, No 4 (1988); supra, p 91

Velásquez Rodríguez v Honduras (Interpretation of the Compensatory Damages Judgment), IACHR, judgment of 17 August 1990, Series C, No 9 (1990)

Zwaan de Vries v Netherlands, UN Human Rights Committee, Communication No 182/1984, Views adopted 9 April 1987; below, p 501

REPORT

I   CLAIMS PRESENTED

1   On 22 February 1995, the Inter-American Commission on Human Rights (hereinafter "Commission") received a petition dated 8 February 1995, alleging that Articles 109, 110,

113, 114, 115, 131, 133, 255, and 317 of the Civil Code of the Republic of Guatemala (hereinafter "Civil Code"), which define the role of each spouse within the institution of marriage, create distinctions between men and women which are discriminatory and violate Articles 1(1), 2, 17 and 24 of the American Convention on Human Rights (hereinafter "American Convention").

2   The petitioners, the Center for Justice and International Law and María Eugenia Morales de Sierra, indicated that Article 109 of the Civil Code confers the power to represent the marital union upon the husband, while Article 115 sets forth the exceptional instances when this authority may be exercised by the wife. Article 131 empowers the husband to administer marital property, while Article 133 provides for limited exceptions to that rule. Article 110 addresses responsibilities within the marriage, conferring upon the wife the special "right and obligation" to care for minor children and the home. Article 113 provides that a married woman may only exercise a profession or maintain employment where this does not prejudice her role as mother and homemaker. They stated that, according to Article 114, a husband may oppose his wife's activities outside the home, as long as he provides for her and has justified reasons. In the case of a controversy with respect to the foregoing, a judge shall decide. Article 255 confers primary responsibility on the husband to represent the children of the union and to administer their property. Article 317 provides that, by virtue of her sex, a woman may be excused from exercising certain forms of guardianship.

3   The petitioners reported that the constitutionality of these legal provisions had been challenged before the Guatemalan Court of Constitutionality in Case 84–92. In response, the Court had ruled that the distinctions were constitutional, as, *inter alia*, they provided juridical certainty in the allocation of roles within marriage. The petitioners requested that the Commission find the foregoing provisions of the Civil Code incompatible *in abstracto* with the guarantees set forth in Articles 1(1), 2, 17 and 24 of the American Convention.

4   The Commission indicated to the petitioners the need to identify concrete victims, as this was a requirement under its case system. On 23 April 1997, the petitioners submitted their written presentation of María Eugenia Morales de Sierra as the concrete victim in the case.

II   PROCESSING BY THE COMMISSION

[...]*

III   THE POSITIONS OF THE PARTIES

The position of the petitioners

20   From the initiation of this matter, the petitioners have maintained that the challenged articles of the Civil Code of Guatemala establish distinctions between men and women which are discriminatory and therefore violate the terms of the American Convention. Pursuant to their designation of María Eugenia Morales de Sierra as the named victim, the petitioners asserted that these articles place her in a position of juridical subordination to her husband, and prevent her from exercising control over important aspects of her life. They indicate that the cited provisions discriminate against the victim in a manner which is immediate, direct and continuing, in violation of the

---

*   *Eds:* Paras 5-20, which relate to procedural matters, have not been included.

rights established in Articles 1(1), 2, 17, and 24 of the American Convention. Pursuant to their arguments submitted after Commission's adoption of Report 28/98 admitting the case, they further allege that this discrimination infringes upon the private and family life of the victim in contravention of Article 11(2) of the Convention.

21 The petitioners contend that Articles 109, 110, 113, 114, 115, 131, 133, 255 and 317 of the Civil Code create distinctions between married women, single women and married men, with the result that María Eugenia Morales is prohibited from exercising rights to which those other groups are entitled. Citing international human rights jurisprudence, including that of the Inter-American Court, they assert that, while a difference in treatment is not necessarily discriminatory, any such distinction must be objectively justified in the pursuit of a legitimate end, and the means employed must be proportionate to that end. The distinctions at issue in this case, they maintain, are illegitimate and unjustified.

22 The petitioners allege that, as a married woman living in Guatemala, a mother, a working professional, and the owner of property acquired jointly with her husband during their marriage, Ms Morales de Sierra is subject to the immediate effects of this legal regime by virtue of her sex and civil status, and the mere fact that the challenged provisions are in force. By virtue of Article 109, representation of the marital unit corresponds to the husband, and by virtue of Article 131, he administers the marital property. Articles 115 and 133 provide respective exceptions to these general rules only where the husband is essentially absent. By virtue of Article 255, the husband represents and administers the property of minors or incapacitated persons. A wife, in contrast, may be excused from exercising custody over such persons by virtue of her sex and the terms of Article 317. These articles prevent Ms Morales de Sierra from legally representing her own interests and those of her family, and require that she depend on her husband to do so.

23 Further, her right to work is conditioned on what the petitioners characterize as the anachronistic legislative division of duties within marriage, with Article 110 providing that care of the home and children corresponds to the wife and mother, and Articles 113 and 114 providing that a wife may pursue activities outside the home only to the extent that these do not prejudice her role within it. Although the victim's husband has never opposed her exercise of her profession, by law he could do so at any moment, and in the case of a dispute, a judge would decide. The petitioners refer to the *dicta* of the Inter-American Court in Advisory Opinion OC-14 in submitting that a norm which deprives a group within a population of certain rights, for example on the basis of a factor such as race or sex, automatically injures all the members of the group thus affected.

24 The petitioners dispute the finding of the Court of Constitutionality of Guatemala that the challenged provisions are justified as a form of protection for women, and as a means of establishing juridical certainty in the allocation of rights and responsibilities within marriage. They assert that the means employed are disproportionate and the resulting discrimination in treatment is unreasonable. These provisions, they argue, are contrary to the principle of equality between the spouses, and nullify the juridical capacity of a married woman within the domestic legal order, thereby controverting the protections set forth in Articles 17 and 24 of the American Convention, as well as the obligations set forth in Articles 1(1) and 2. Further, they argue that the manner in which the provisions impede the ability of the victim to exercise her rights, in limiting, for example, her right to work or to dispose of her property, constitutes an unjustified interference in her private life in contravention of Article 11(2).

25 Finally, the petitioners note that the challenged provisions contravene Articles 15 and 16 of the Convention on the Elimination of All Forms of Discrimination against Women, provisions to which the Commission may refer in formulating its decision. They further note that the recognized relationship between inequality in gender relations and the prevalence of violence against women may also serve to guide the Commission's findings.

The position of the State

26 The State does not controvert the substance of the claims raised by the petitioners. Rather, it maintains that it is continuing to take steps to modify the challenged articles of the Civil Code to bring them into conformity with the norms of the American Convention and the Convention on the Elimination of All Forms of Discrimination against Women. In proceedings before the Commission prior to the adoption of Report 28/98, the State acknowledged that the cited provisions are "out of date" and give rise to concerns with respect to the obligation of nondiscrimination. It further noted that efforts in favor of reform of the articles had been based on the fact that they contravene Article 46 of the Constitution, as well as provisions of the American Convention and the Convention on the Elimination of All Forms of Discrimination against Women. The Government emphasized that it had demonstrated its interest in derogating or reforming certain articles of the Civil Code, both through supporting initiatives in favor of legislative changes, and through a constitutional challenge to Articles 113 and 114 presented by the Attorney General in 1996.

27 It was principally on the basis of pending initiatives in favor of reform that the State had challenged the admissibility of the case, contending that domestic mechanisms continued to offer available and effective relief for the situation denounced, and that the petitioners had accordingly failed to satisfy the requirement of exhausting internal remedies.[1] Following the adoption of the Commission's report on admissibility, the State indicated that the Congress was continuing to pursue the objective of modifying certain articles of the Civil Code in order to bring them into conformity with the Convention on the Elimination of All Forms of Discrimination against Women. As of the State's 22 June 1998 submission, those reforms were still under discussion in the Congress. The State maintains that the measures undertaken in favor of reform of the challenged articles demonstrate its commitment to upholding the guarantees set forth in the Constitution, and in the American Convention on Human Rights and other applicable international law.

IV   CONSIDERATIONS REGARDING THE MERITS

Initial considerations

28 At the outset, it is pertinent to note that, notwithstanding the presentation of various draft reform projects before the Guatemalan congressional commissions charged with pronouncing on such initiatives, as of the date of the present report, the relevant articles of the Civil Code continue in force as the law of the Republic of Guatemala. In brief, Article 109 provides that representation of the marital union corresponds to the

---

1   See generally, *Morales de Sierra v Guatemala*, IACommHR, Case 11.625, Report No 28/98, IACHR OEA/Ser.L/V/II.98, Doc 6, rev at p 144 (1998) "Report", paras 23, 27 and 20.

husband, although both spouses have equal authority within the home.[2] Article 110 stipulates that the husband owes certain duties of protection and assistance to the wife, while the latter has the special right and duty to care for minor children and the home.[3] Article 113 sets forth that the wife may exercise a profession or pursue other responsibilities outside the home only insofar as this does not prejudice her responsibilities within it.[4] Article 114 establishes that the husband may oppose the pursuit of his wife's activities outside the home where he provides adequately for maintenance of the home and has "sufficiently justified reasons". Where necessary, a judge shall resolve disputes in this regard.[5] Article 115 states that representation of the marital union may be exercised by the wife where the husband fails to do so, particularly where he abandons the home, is imprisoned, or is otherwise absent.[6] Article 131 states that the husband shall administer the marital property.[7] Article 133 establishes exceptions to this rule on the same basis set forth in Article 115.[8] Article 255 states that, where husband and wife exercise parental authority over minor children, the husband shall represent the latter and administer their goods.[9] Article 317 establishes that specific

---

2   Article 109 of the Civil Code establishes: "(Representation of the marital union) The husband shall represent the marital union, but both spouses shall enjoy equal authority and considerations in the home; they shall establish their place of residence by common agreement and shall arrange everything concerning the education and establishment of their children, as well as the family budget."

3   Article 110 of the Civil Code establishes: "(Protection of the wife) The husband must provide protection and assistance to his wife and is obliged to supply everything needed to sustain the home in accordance with his economic means. The wife has the special right and duty to attend to and look after her children while they are minors and to manage the household chores."

4   Article 113 of the Civil Code establishes: "(Wife employed outside the home) The wife may perform work, (38) exercise a profession, business, occupation, or trade, (39) provided that her activity does not prejudice the interests and care of the children or other responsibilities in the home."[Notes 38 and 39 refer to articles of the Constitution and Commercial Code].

5   Article 114 of the Civil Code establishes: "The husband may object to his wife pursuing activities outside the home, so long as he provides adequately for maintenance of the home and has sufficiently justified grounds for objection. The judge shall rule outright on the issue."

6   Article 115 of the Civil Code establishes: "(Representation by the wife) Representation of the marital union shall be exercised by the wife should the husband fail to do so for any reason and particularly when: 1) If the husband is legally deprived of that right; 2) If the husband abandons the home of his own free will, or is declared to be absent; and 3) If the husband is sentenced to imprisonment and for the duration of such imprisonment."

7   Article 131 of the Civil Code establishes: "Under the system of absolute joint ownership [*comunidad absoluta*] by husband and wife or community of property acquired during marriage [*comunidad de gananciales*], the husband shall administer the marital property, exercising powers that shall not exceed the limits of normal administration. Each spouse or common-law spouse shall dispose freely of goods registered under his or her name in the public registries, without prejudice to the obligation to account to the other for any disposal of common property."

8   Article 133 of the Civil Code establishes: "(Administration by the wife) Administration of the marital property shall be transferred to the wife in the instances set forth in Article 115, with the same powers, restrictions, and responsibilities as those established in the foregoing articles."

9   Article 255 of the Civil Code establishes: "Where husband and wife, or common-law spouses, jointly exercise parental authority over minor children, the husband shall represent the minor or incompetent children and administer their goods."

classes of persons may be excused from exercising certain forms of custody, including, *inter alia*, women.[10]

29 The Commission received information about two initiatives in favor of reform of those articles during the on-site visit it carried out in Guatemala from 6 to 11 August 1998, but has yet to receive information as to corresponding action by the plenary of the Congress. Nor has it received information as to the outcome, if any, of the constitutional challenge against Articles 113 and 114 which was presented by the Attorney General before the Court of Constitutionality in 1996. While the State appears to link the continuation of efforts in favor of reform to its willingness to explore the option of friendly settlement, the petitioners have indicated that they consider the possibility of entering into friendly settlement negotiations to have been explored and exhausted.

30 Paragraphs 28 and 29 refer to a general situation which the Commission examined during its recent on-site visit to Guatemala, and to which it made reference in its Report on the Situation of Women in the Americas. (See references, *infra*.) In the concrete case of María Eugenia Morales de Sierra, the Commission explicitly addressed its competence *ratione personae* in its Report 28/98 on admissibility:

> With respect to the question of jurisdiction *ratione personae*, the Commission has previously explained that, in general, its competence under the individual case process pertains to facts involving the rights of a specific individual or individuals. See generally, IACHR, *Case of Emérita Montoya González*, Report 48/96, Case 11.553 (Costa Rica), in Annual Report of the IACHR 1996, OEA/Ser.L/V/II.95, Doc 7 rev, 14 March 1997, paras 28, 31. The Commission entertains a broader competence under Article 41.b of the Convention to address recommendations to member states for the adoption of progressive measures in favor of the protection of human rights.

Pursuant to their original petition for a decision *in abstracto*, which appeared to rely on the Commission's competence under Article 41.b of the American Convention rather than that under Article 41.f, the petitioners modified their petition and named María Eugenia Morales de Sierra as an individual victim, as previously noted, in their communication of 23 April 1997. With the identification of an individual victim, the Commission may advance with its decision on admissibility in the present case. As the Honorable Court has explained, in order to initiate the procedures established in Articles 48 and 50 of the American Convention, the Commission requires a petition denouncing a concrete violation with respect to a specific individual. IACHR, Advisory Opinion OC-14/94, "International Responsibility for the Promulgation and Enforcement of Laws in Violation of the Convention (Arts. 1 and 2 of the American Convention)", of 9 December 1994, para 45, see also, paras 46–47. With respect to the other contentious mechanisms of the system, Article 61.2 of the Convention establishes, further, that "[i]n order for the Court to hear a case, it is necessary that the procedures set forth in ... [those Articles] shall have been completed". "The contentious jurisdiction of the Court is intended to protect the rights and freedoms of specific individuals, not to resolve abstract questions." *Id* para 49.[11]

---

10 Article 317 of the Civil Code establishes: "(Exemption) The following may be excused from exercising custody and guardianship: 1) Those already exercising another custody or guardianship; 2) Persons over sixty years of age; 3) Those who have three or more children under their parental authority; 4) Women; 5) Persons of low-income for whom this responsibility would threaten their means of subsistence; 6) Persons prevented from exercising this responsibility due to chronic illness; and 7) Those who have to be absent from the country for over one year."

11 Report 28/98, *supra*, paras 30, 31.

The right of María Eugenia Morales de Sierra to equal protection of and before the law

31 The right to equal protection of the law set forth in Article 24 of the American Convention requires that national legislation accord its protections without discrimination. Differences in treatment in otherwise similar circumstances are not necessarily discriminatory.[12] A distinction which is based on "reasonable and objective criteria" may serve a legitimate state interest in conformity with the terms of Article 24.[13] It may, in fact, be required to achieve justice or to protect persons requiring the application of special measures.[14] A distinction based on reasonable and objective criteria (1) pursues a legitimate aim and (2) employs means which are proportional to the end sought.[15]

32 Pursuant to the status of Guatemala as a State Party to the Convention on the Elimination of All Forms of Discrimination against Women,[16] and the terms of Article 29 of the American Convention,[17] it must be noted that Article 15.1 of the former requires that States Parties shall ensure that women are accorded equality with men before the law. Article 15(2) specifies that women must be accorded the same legal capacity as men in civil matters, particularly with respect to concluding contracts and administering property, and the same opportunities to exercise that capacity. Discrimination against women as defined in this Convention is:

> any distinction, exclusion or restriction made on the basis of sex which has the effect or purpose of impairing or nullifying the recognition, enjoyment or exercise by women, irrespective of their marital status, on a basis of equality of men and women, of human rights and fundamental freedoms in the political, economic, social, cultural, civil or any other field.

This definition, responding as it does to the specific causes and consequences of gender discrimination, covers forms of systemic disadvantage affecting women that prior standards may not have contemplated.

33 In the proceedings before the Commission, the State has not controverted that Articles 109, 110, 113, 114, 115, 131, 133, 255 and 317 of the Civil Code create distinctions between married women and married men which are based on sex. In fact, it has acknowledged that aspects of the challenged provisions are inconsistent with the equality and non-discrimination provisions of the Constitution, the American Convention and the Convention on the Elimination of All Forms of Discrimination against Women.

34 Notwithstanding that recognition, however, the 24 June 1993 decision of the Court of Constitutionality on the validity of the cited articles remains the authoritative application and interpretation of national law. That decision bases itself on the fact that the Constitution establishes that men and women are entitled to equality of

---

12 See eg, ECHR, *Belgian Linguistics Case*, Series A, No 6, p 34, para 10.

13 See generally, *id*; UNHR Committee, *Broeks v The Netherlands*, Communication No 172/1984, para 13; *Zwaan de Vries v The Netherlands*, Communication No 182/1984, para 13.

14 See eg, IACHR, Advisory Opinion OC-4/84, "Proposed Amendments to the Naturalization Provisions of the Constitution of Costa Rica", 19 January 1984, para 56.

15 See eg, *Belgian Linguistics Case, supra*.

16 Guatemala ratified the Convention on 12 August 1982.

17 See IACHR, "Other Treaties" Subject to the Advisory Jurisdiction of the Court (Art 64 American Convention on Human Rights), Advisory Opinion OC-1/82 of 24 September 1982, Series A, No 1.

opportunities and responsibilities, whatever their civil status, as well as to equality of rights within marriage. It notes that certain human rights treaties, including the Convention on the Elimination of All Forms of Discrimination against Women, form part of internal law. In its analysis of Article 109, the Court indicates that the legal attribution of representation of the marital unit to the husband is justified by reason of "certainty and juridical security." This does not give rise to discrimination against the wife, the Court continues, as she is free to dispose of her own goods, and both spouses are attributed with equal authority within the home. The Court validates Article 115 on the same basis. With respect to Article 131, which vests authority in the husband to administer jointly held property, the Court recalls that, pursuant to Article 109, both spouses shall decide on matters concerning the family economy, including whether property shall be held separately or jointly. In the absence of such a decision, reasons of certainty and juridical security justify the application of Article 131. The Court finds Article 133 valid on the same basis.

35 In analyzing Article 110, which attributes responsibility for sustaining the home to the husband, and responsibility for caring for minor children and the home to the wife, the Court emphasizes the mutual support spouses must provide each other and the need to protect the marital home and any children. The division of roles is not aimed at discriminating, the Court finds, but at protecting the wife in her role as mother, and at protecting the children. The woman is not prejudiced; rather, the provisions enhance her authority. In analyzing Articles 113 and 114, which permit a woman to pursue work outside the home to the extent this does not conflict with her duties within it, the Court states that these contain no prohibition on the rights of the woman. As no right is absolute, the Articles contain limitations aimed primarily at protecting the children of the union. Consistent with the duties of each spouse, the husband may oppose his wife's activities outside the home only if he offers adequate sustenance and has justified reasons. The disposition that a judge shall decide in the event of a disagreement protects against the possibility of arbitrary action, as it ensures that the husband's reasons refer to the legally defined role of the wife and the protection of the children.

36 The Commission observes that the guarantees of equality and non-discrimination underpinning the American Convention and American Declaration of the Rights and Duties of Man reflect essential bases for the very concept of human rights. As the Inter-American Court has stated, these principles "are inherent in the idea of the oneness in dignity and worth of all human beings".[18] Statutory distinctions based on status criteria, such as, for example, race or sex, therefore necessarily give rise to heightened scrutiny. What the European Court and Commission have stated is also true for the Americas, that as "the advancement of the equality of the sexes is today a major goal," ... "very weighty reasons would have to be put forward" to justify a distinction based solely on the ground of sex.[19]

37 The gender-based distinctions under study have been upheld as a matter of domestic law essentially on the basis of the need for certainty and juridical security, the need to protect the marital home and children, respect for traditional Guatemalan values, and in certain cases, the need to protect women in their capacity as wives and mothers. However, the Court of Constitutionality made no effort to probe the validity of these assertions or to weigh alternative positions, and the Commission is not persuaded

---

18   Advisory Opinion OC-4, *supra*, para 55.
19   See eg, ECHR, *Karlheinz Schmidt v Germany*, Series A, No 291-B, 18 July 1994, para 24, citing, *Schuler-Zgraggen v Switzerland*, Series A, No 263, 24 June 1993, para 67, *Burghartz v Switzerland*, Series A, No 280-B, 22 February 1994, para 27.

that the distinctions cited are even consistent with the aims articulated. For example, the fact that Article 109 excludes a married woman from representing the marital union, except in extreme circumstances, neither contributes to the orderly administration of justice, nor does it favor her protection or that of the home or children. To the contrary, it deprives a married woman of the legal capacity necessary to invoke the judicial protection which the orderly administration of justice and the American Convention require be made available to every person.

38   By requiring married women to depend on their husbands to represent the union – in this case María Eugenia Morales de Sierra – the terms of the Civil Code mandate a system in which the ability of approximately half the married population to act on a range of essential matters is subordinated to the will of the other half. The overarching effect of the challenged provisions is to deny married women legal autonomy.[20] The fact that the Civil Code deprives María Eugenia Morales de Sierra, as a married woman, of legal capacities to which other Guatemalans are entitled leaves her rights vulnerable to violation without recourse.[21]

39   In the instant case the Commission finds that the gender-based distinctions established in the challenged articles cannot be justified, and contravene the rights of María Eugenia Morales de Sierra set forth in Article 24. These restrictions are of immediate effect, arising simply by virtue of the fact that the cited provisions are in force. As a married woman, she is denied protections on the basis of her sex which married men and other Guatemalans are accorded. The provisions she challenges restrict, *inter alia*, her legal capacity, her access to resources, her ability to enter into certain kinds of contracts (relating, for example, to property held jointly with her husband), to administer such property, and to invoke administrative or judicial recourse. They have the further effect of reinforcing systemic disadvantages which impede the ability of the victim to exercise a host of other rights and freedoms.

The case of María Eugenia Morales de Sierra and rights of the family: equality of rights and balancing of responsibilities in marriage

40   Article 17(1) of the American Convention establishes rights pertaining to family life pursuant to the disposition that, as "the natural and fundamental group unit of society", the family "is entitled to protection by society and the state". The right to marry and found a family is subject to certain conditions of national law, although the limitations thereby introduced must not be so restrictive "that the very essence of the right is impaired".[22] Article 17(4), which derives from Article 16(1) of the Universal Declaration of Human Rights, specifies that "States Parties shall take appropriate steps to ensure the equality of rights and the adequate balancing of responsibilities" in marriage and its dissolution. In this regard, Article 17(4) is the "concrete application" of the general principle of equal protection and non-discrimination of Article 24 to marriage.[23]

---

20   See generally, Committee on the Elimination of Discrimination against Women (CEDAW), General Recommendation 21, "Equality in marriage and family relations," UN Doc HRI/GEN/1/Rev1 at 90 (1994).
21   See generally, UNHR Committee, *Ato del Avellanal v Peru*, Communication No 202/1986, para 10.2.
22   ECHR, *Rees v United Kingdom*, Series A, No 106, 17 October 1986, para 50.
23   See OC-4/84, para 66.

41   In the case of Guatemala and other States Parties, the Convention on the Elimination of All Forms of Discrimination against Women specifies steps that must be taken to ensure substantive equality in family law and family relations. Pursuant to Article 16 of that Convention, States Parties are required to ensure, *inter alia*, "on the basis of equality between men and women," the same rights and duties with respect to the exercise of custody or other types of guardianship of children; the "same personal rights ... to choose a family name, a profession and an occupation"; and the same rights with respect to the ownership, administration and disposition of property.

42   The petitioners have indicated that the cited articles of the Civil Code impede the ability of wife and husband to equally exercise their rights and fulfill their responsibilities in marriage. María Eugenia Morales de Sierra alleges that, although her family life is based on the principle of reciprocal respect, the fact that the law vests exclusive authority in her husband to represent the marital union and their minor child creates a disequilibrium in the weight of the authority exercised by each spouse within their marriage – an imbalance which may be perceived within the family, community and society. While the victim, as a parent, has the right and duty to protect the best interests of her minor child, the law strips her of the legal capacity she requires to do that.

43   As discussed above, the challenged articles of the Civil Code establish distinct roles for each spouse. The husband is responsible for sustaining the home financially, and the wife is responsible for caring for the home and children (Article 110). The wife may work outside the home only to the extent this does not prejudice her legally defined role within it (Article 113), in which case her husband has the right to oppose such activities (Article 114). The husband represents the marital union (Article 109), controls jointly held property (Article 131), represents the minor children, and administers their property (Article 255). The Court of Constitutionality characterized the State's regulation of matrimony as providing certainty and juridical security to each spouse, and defended the disposition of roles on the basis that the norms set forth preferences which are not discriminatory, but protective.

44   The Commission finds that, far from ensuring the "equality of rights and adequate balancing of responsibilities" within marriage, the cited provisions institutionalize imbalances in the rights and duties of the spouses. While Article 110 suggests a division of labor between a husband's financial responsibilities and the wife's domestic responsibilities, it must be noted that, pursuant to Article 111, a wife with a separate source of income is required to contribute to the maintenance of the household, or to fully support it if her husband is unable to do so. The fact that the law vests a series of legal capacities exclusively in the husband establishes a situation of *de jure* dependency for the wife and creates an insurmountable disequilibrium in the spousal authority within the marriage. Moreover, the dispositions of the Civil Code apply stereotyped notions of the roles of women and men which perpetuate *de facto* discrimination against women in the family sphere, and which have the further effect of impeding the ability of men to fully develop their roles within the marriage and family. The articles at issue create imbalances in family life, inhibiting the role of men with respect to the home and children, and in that sense depriving children of the full and equal attention of both parents. "A stable family is one which is based on principles of equity, justice and individual fulfillment for each member."[24]

---

24   CEDAW, General Recommendation 21, *supra*, para 24.

45 In the case of Ms Morales de Sierra, the Commission concludes that the challenged articles controvert the duty of the State to protect the family by mandating a regime which prevents the victim from exercising her rights and responsibilities within marriage on an equal footing with her spouse. The State has failed to take steps to ensure the equality of rights and balancing of responsibilities within marriage. Accordingly, in this case, the marital regime in effect is incompatible with the terms of Article 17(4) of the American Convention, read with reference to the requirements of Article 16(1) of the Convention on the Elimination of All Forms of Discrimination Against Women.

The right to privacy and the present case

46 Article 11(1) of the American Convention sets forth that every person has the right to have his or her honor and dignity recognized. Pursuant to Article 11(2): "No one may be the object of arbitrary or abusive interference with his private life, his family, his home, or his correspondence, or of unlawful attacks on his honor or reputation". Article 11(3) provides that this right is to be protected by law. The requirements of Article 11 encompass a range of factors pertaining to the dignity of the individual, including, for example, the ability to pursue the development of one's personality and aspirations, determine one's identity, and define one's personal relationships.[25]

47 A principal objective of Article 11 is to protect individuals from arbitrary action by State authorities which infringes in the private sphere.[26] Of course, where State regulation of matters within that sphere is necessary to protect the rights of others, it may not only be justified, but required. The guarantee against arbitrariness is intended to ensure that any such regulation (or other action) comports with the norms and objectives of the Convention, and is reasonable under the circumstances.[27]

48 The petitioners claim that the cited articles of the Civil Code, particularly as they restrict María Eugenia Morales de Sierra's ability to exercise her profession and dispose of her property, constitute an arbitrary interference with her right to have her private life respected. In the proceedings generally, the victim has indicated that the cited provisions prevent her from exercising authority over basic aspects of her day-to-day life concerning her marriage, home, children and property. While she and her husband organize their home on the basis of mutual respect, her status in the family, community and society is conditioned by the attribution of authority to her husband to represent the marital union and their minor child. While their jointly held property has been obtained through mutual sacrifice, the law prevents her from administering it. Further, while her husband has never opposed her pursuit of her profession, the law authorizes him to do so at any moment. She notes that, although there are increasing opportunities for women to more fully incorporate themselves into the processes of national life and development, married women such as herself are continuously impeded by the fact that the law does not recognize them as having legal status equivalent to that enjoyed by other citizens.

---

25 See, *inter alia*, ECHR, *Gaskin v United Kingdom*, Series A, No 160 (addressing interest of applicant in accessing records concerning childhood and early development); *Niemetz v Germany*, Series A, No 251-B, para 29 (noting that respect for private life includes right to "establish and develop relationships," both personal and professional).

26 See generally, ECHR, *Kroon v The Netherlands*, Series A, No 297-C, para 31 (1994).

27 See UNHR Committee, *Toonen v Australia*, Communication No 488/1992, para 8.3, citing General Comment 16[32] on Article 17 of the ICCPR, Doc CCPR/C/21/Rev.1 (19 May 1989).

49 The provisions in question have been upheld as a matter of domestic law on the basis that they serve to protect the family, in particular the children. However, no link has been shown between the conditioning of the right of married women to work on spousal approval, or the subordination of a wife's control of jointly held property to that of her husband and the effective protection of the family or children. In mandating these and other forms of subordination of a wife's role, the State deprives married women of their autonomy to select and pursue options for their personal development and support. This legislation, most specifically in the way it makes a woman's right to work dependent on the consent of her husband, denies women the equal right to seek employment and benefit from the increased self-determination this affords.

50 Whether or not the husband of the victim – in this case María Eugenia Morales de Sierra – opposes her exercise of her profession[28] is not decisive in this regard. The analysis turns on the fact that the legislation infringes on the victim's personal sphere in a manner which cannot be justified. The mere fact that the husband of María Eugenia Morales de Sierra may oppose that she works, while she does not have the right to oppose this in his case, implies a discrimination. This discrimination has consequences from the point of view of her position in Guatemalan society, and reinforces cultural habits with respect to which the Commission has commented in its Report on the Status of Women in the Americas.[29] As a married woman, the law does not accord her the same rights or recognition as other citizens, and she cannot exercise the same freedoms they do in pursuing their aspirations. This situation has a harmful effect on public opinion in Guatemala, and on María Eugenia Morales de Sierra's position and status within her family, community and society.

The obligation of the State to respect and guarantee the rights of María Eugenia Morales de Sierra without discrimination, and to adopt domestic legal measures

51 As is demonstrated in the foregoing analysis, the State of Guatemala has failed to fulfill its obligations under Article 1(1) of the American Convention to "respect the rights and freedoms recognized [t]herein and to ensure to all persons subject to [its] jurisdiction the free and full exercise of those rights and freedoms, without any discrimination for reasons of ... [*inter alia*] sex ..." "Any impairment of those rights which can be attributed under the rules of international law to the action or omission of any public authority constitutes an act imputable to the State, which assumes responsibility in the terms provided by the Convention."[30] Article 1 imposes both negative and positive obligations on the State in pursuing the objective of guaranteeing rights which are practical and effective.

52 Articles 109, 110, 113, 114, 115, 131, 133, 255 and 317 have a continuous and direct effect on the victim in this case, in contravening her right to equal protection and to be free from discrimination, in failing to provide protections to ensure that her rights and responsibilities in marriage are equal to and balanced with those of her spouse, and in failing to uphold her right to respect for her dignity and private life. A person who enjoys the equal protection of and recognition before the law is empowered to act to ensure other rights in the face of public or private acts. Conversely, gender-

---

28 As noted above, in the present case the victim's husband has not opposed the exercise of her profession.

29 Published in Report of the IACHR 1997, OEA/Ser.L/V/II.98 doc 7 rev, 13 April 1998.

30 *Velásquez Rodríguez Case*, para 164; *Godínez Cruz Case*, para 173.

discrimination operates to impair or nullify the ability of women to freely and fully exercise their rights, and gives rise to an array of consequences.[31] The inter-American system has recognized, for example, that gender violence is "a manifestation of the historically unequal power relations between women and men".[32] "Traditional attitudes by which women are regarded as subordinate to men or as having stereotyped roles perpetuate widespread practices involving violence or coercion, such as family violence and abuse ..."[33] *De jure* or *de facto* economic subordination, in turn, "forces many women to stay in violent relationships".[34]

53 Recognizing that the defense and protection of human rights necessarily rests first and foremost with the domestic system, Article 2 of the Convention provides that States Parties shall adopt the legislative and other measures necessary to give effect to any right or freedom not already ensured as a matter of domestic law and practice. In the instant case, the State has failed to take the legislative action necessary to modify, repeal or definitively leave without effect Articles 109, 110, 113, 114, 115, 131, 133, 255 and 317 which discriminate against the victim and other married women in violation of Articles 24, 17 and 11 of the American Convention. When the articles at issue were challenged as unconstitutional, the State, acting through its Court of Constitutionality, failed to respond in conformity with the norms of the American Convention.[35] Although relevant national and international authorities have identified these articles as incompatible with the State's obligations under national and international law, they remain the law of the land.[36]

54 The obligation to respect and ensure the rights of the Convention requires the adoption of all the means necessary to assure María Eugenia Morales de Sierra the enjoyment of rights which are effective. The failure of the State to honor the obligations set forth in Articles 1 and 2 of the Convention generates liability, pursuant to the principles of international responsibility, for all acts, public and private, committed pursuant to the discrimination effectuated against the victim in violation of the rights recognized in the American Convention and other applicable treaties. Pursuant to those same principles, the State of Guatemala is obliged to repair the consequences of the violations established, including through measures to restore the rights of María Eugenia Morales de Sierra to the full extent possible, and to provide a just indemnity for the harm she has sustained. Measures of reparation are meant to provide a victim with an effective remedy, with the essential objective of providing full restitution for the injury suffered.[37]

---

31 See generally, Report on the Status of Women, *supra*, at p 1018-1020.

32 See, Inter-American Convention on the Prevention, Punishment and Eradication of Violence against Women (Convention of Belém do Pará), preamble, Art 7.e (ratified by Guatemala on 4 April 1995).

33 CEDAW, General Recommendation 19, "Violence against women," UN Doc HRI/GEN/1/Rev 1, p 84, at para 11 (1994); see generally, Convention of Belém do Pará, Art 6(b).

34 General Recommendation 19, *supra*, para 23.

35 See, Report No 43/96, Case 11.430, Mexico, OEA/Ser.L/V/II.95, Doc 7 rev, 14 March 1997, para 102.

36 See Report No 28/98, *supra*, paras 6, 7-23 (recording position of State itself that articles in question were not in conformity with national and international obligations); CEDAW, Thirteenth Sess, A/49/38, Sessional/Annual Report [consideration of report on Guatemala], paras 44, 48, 70-71, 78-79, 81 (expressing Committee's concern with respect to "highly discriminatory provisions" of Code restricting or violating fundamental rights).

37 *Velásquez Rodríguez Case*, Interpretation of the Compensatory Damages Judgment, Judgment of 17 August 1990, Series C, No 9, para 27.

V   ACTIONS SUBSEQUENT TO REPORT NO 86/98

55 Pursuant to the terms of Article 50 of the Convention, the Commission adopted Report N°86/98 on 1 October 1998. That Report set forth the Commission's analysis (contained in sections I – V) and finding that the State of Guatemala was responsible for having violated the rights of María Eugenia Morales de Sierra to equal protection, respect for family life, and respect for private life established in Articles 24, 17 and 11 of the American Convention on Human Rights. The Commission accordingly found the State responsible for having failed to uphold its Article 1 obligation to respect and ensure those rights under the Convention, as well as its Article 2 obligation to adopt the legislative and other measures necessary to give effect to those rights of the victim. Further, the Commission indicated that the conduct at issue also constituted violations of the obligations set forth in the Convention on the Elimination of All Forms of Discrimination against Women, most specifically, in Articles 15 and 16. Consequently, the Commission recommended (1) that the State take the legislative and other measures necessary to amend, repeal or definitively leave without effect Articles 109, 110, 113, 114, 115, 131, 133, 255 and 317 of the Civil Code so as to bring national law into conformity with the norms of the American Convention and give full effect to the rights and freedoms guaranteed to María Eugenia Morales de Sierra therein; and, (2) that it redress and adequately compensate María Eugenia Morales de Sierra for the violations established.

56 The Report was transmitted to the State of Guatemala on 6 November 1998. Pursuant to the terms set forth, the State was given two months from the date of that transmission to comply with the recommendations issued and report to the Commission on the measures taken for that purpose. By a note of the same date, the Commission informed the petitioners that a report on the case had been adopted pursuant to the terms of Article 50 and transmitted to the State ...

57 The State transmitted its response to Report 86/98 by note dated 7 December 1998. In that response, the State emphasized its acceptance of the need to address certain norms in the Civil Code that were out of date and discriminatory toward married women. However, it reiterated its position that the victim had not been personally prejudiced by the challenged norms, as her family life and professional career had not been harmed. In line with its recognition of the need to reform the provisions as a general matter, the State informed the Commission that the Congress had on 19 November 1998 approved Decree Number 80–98, enacting reforms to the Civil Code. The attached text reflected reforms to Articles 109, 110, 115, 131 and 255, and the derogation of Articles 114 and 133. The State further informed the Commission that the reforms would enter into force pursuant to their sanction, promulgation and publication.

58 On 28 December 1998, the Commission addressed the State to request that it supply information as soon as possible on the time required to accomplish the actions necessary for the reforms to enter into force. By a note of 12 January 1999, the State reported that the text of Decree 80–98 had been published in the *Diario de Centro América* on 23 December 1998. The modifications had entered into force eight days after publication. The State indicated that it considered that it had fully complied with the recommendations issued by the Commission in Report 86/98.

59 Having analyzed the reforms indicated, and having noted that they addressed seven of the nine provisions challenged by the petitioner, the Commission addressed the State on 25 January 1999, to request information as to any measures taken with respect to Articles 113 and 317, which were not addressed in Decree 80–98, and to ask for

additional information about the language of Article 131 as published, which appeared to be inconsistent with the explanation of the reform.[38] In view of the fact that the three month period provided in Article 51 was set to expire on 6 February 1999, the Commission requested a response within 7 days, and indicated that a request for an extension could only be considered if accompanied by an express manifestation by the State that this would suspend that time period.

60 By a note of that same date, the Commission transmitted a copy of the text of Decree 80–98 to the petitioners with a request for observations as to whether the reforms set forth satisfied in whole or in part the claims presented. A response was requested within 7 days.

61 On 25 January 1999, the petitioners submitted a request that the Commission schedule a hearing on this matter during its next period of sessions. The Commission acknowledged receipt on 29 January, and requested information as to the proposed purpose of such a hearing.

62 On 1 February 1999, the petitioners presented a communication setting forth their view as to why the reforms did not completely resolve the discrimination denounced or fully repair the violations suffered by the victim.

63 On 4 February 1999, the State presented information indicating that no measures had been taken with respect to Articles 113 and 317, and reiterating the reforms reported with respect to Article 131.

64 By a note of 5 February 1999, the State requested an extension of 60 days to present additional information concerning the case, with the express understanding that this would suspend the three-month time period provided in Article 51 of the Convention. That request was accepted, subject to that understanding, by a note of the same date, which indicated that the extension would expire on 7 April 1999.

65 By a note of that same date, the Commission informed the parties that it had granted a hearing concerning the case, scheduled for 5 March 1999. On 17 February 1999, the parties were informed that the date had been changed to 4 March 1999.

66 During that hearing the petitioners expressed their view that the State had yet to recognize a violation in the particular case, had made no measures of reparation, and had not addressed Articles 113 and 317, which formed an important part of their complaint. They also pointed out that the reformed text of Article 131 was unclear. Further, they indicated that what was required with respect to Articles 109 and 131 was that decisions on the representation of the marital union and marital property be taken jointly, rather than jointly or separately as the reforms provide.

67 The State, for its part, presented arguments as to why it considered that Article 317 did not require reform. Its position was that the Article permits women to request to be excused from exercising certain forms of custody; accordingly, it provides a privilege that can be invoked by choice and imposes no discrimination. The State indicated that a draft reform to derogate Article 113 had been elaborated in February, but that additional time would be required to work toward its adoption. With respect to Article 131, the State indicated that there had been a mistake in the transmission of the text when

---

38 According to Article 5 of Decree 80-98, "Article 131, paragraph 2 is amended to read as follows: 'Under the system of absolute joint ownership [*comunidad absoluta*] by husband and wife or that of community of property acquired during the marriage [*comunidad de gananciales*], both spouses shall administer the marital property, either jointly or separately.'"

published, and that this would be corrected. The State indicated that it wished to have an additional extension of one year to accomplish the measures indicated, with the understanding that this suspended the period referred to in Article 51 of the Convention.

68 On 10 and 11 March 1999, the petitioners submitted communications as to why they considered that an additional extension should not be granted. They indicated that the State had indicated no intention to derogate Article 317, or to amend Articles 109 or 131 to require joint decision making, and that there were no guarantees that Article 113 would in fact be derogated.

69 Pursuant to that hearing, by note of 24 March 1999, the State requested an additional one-year extension, again, with the express understanding that this interrupted the running of the three-month time period provided in Article 51. That communication was transmitted to the petitioners for their information on 31 March 1999. In the interim, on 29 March 1999, the petitioners had submitted an additional communication on these points, asking that the case be placed before the Inter-American Court of Human Rights without delay, or, if an extension were granted, that it be limited to three months.

70 On 7 April 1999, the Commission granted the requested extension of one year, with the understanding that this suspended the period referred to in Article 51, and under the condition that the State present significant advances toward full compliance with the recommendations in meetings to be convoked by the Commission during its next two periods of sessions.

71 By notes of 7 and 8 April 1999, the Commission convened the parties for a working meeting on 7 May 1999, during its 103rd period of sessions, to discuss the status of the recommendations issued in Report 86/98 and the measures of compliance that remained pending, particularly those concerning Articles 113, 131 and 317. By means of a note of 15 April 1999, the Commission informed the petitioners of the extension and the express conditions under which it had been granted.

72 As a follow-up to the 7 May 1999 meeting, the Commission addressed the State on 23 August 1999, with a request that it supply information within 30 days on the measures adopted to effectuate the recommendations issued in Report 86/98. On 31 August 1999, the Commission convened the parties for a hearing to be held on 5 October 1999, during its 104th period of sessions.

73 On 2 September 1999, the State informed the Commission that it had complied with the recommendations issued in Report 86/98 through the adoption of Decree 29–99, reforming Article 131 and derogating Article 113. A copy of the decree was attached, with the information that it had entered into force as of the date of the letter. Given this compliance, the State asked that the case be archived. This information was transmitted to the petitioners on 13 September 1999, with observations in response requested within 21 days.

74 In the course of the 5 October 1999 hearing, the petitioners presented a communication requesting that, in view of the reform of Article 131 and derogation of Article 113, the Commission issue a final report setting forth the partial compliance of the State. The petitioners congratulated the State for having reformed the majority of the discriminatory provisions challenged in the case, recognizing in particular the derogation of Articles 113 and 114, and reform to Article 110, establishing that spouses have an equal responsibility to care for the children and home. The petitioners asked that the final report expressly indicate the State's failure to derogate the challenged provision of Article 317. Further, they asked that it reflect that, by allowing either spouse to exercise authority autonomously, the reforms to Articles 109, 115, 131 and 255 do not

guarantee María Eugenia Morales de Sierra effective participation in decision making. They maintain that this may only be done by requiring joint consent in such decisions.

75 The State, for its part, reiterated the importance it attaches to having carried out the reforms in question. It also reiterated its view that Article 317 constitutes a privilege, a special consideration which may be invoked, rather than a form of discrimination which is imposed. The State indicated that it would submit the legislative history of the Article as well as opinions on the question by the Attorney General and President of the Congressional Commission of Women and the Family in support of its position. The petitioner's communication was formally transmitted to the State on 13 October 1999, with a request that any further information on the case be submitted within 30 days.

76 On 17 December 1999, the State submitted a response indicating its view that the reforms adopted had accomplished what was required, and reiterating its views with respect to Article 317. This information was transmitted to the petitioners on 21 December 1999, with any observations requested within 30 days.

77 The above proceedings having been carried out, and certain articles having been reformed pursuant to Decrees 80–98 and 27–99, the Commission wishes to briefly summarize the status of the legislation at issue in the present case. Articles 113, 114 and 133 have been derogated. Article 109 has been reformed to provide that representation of the marital union corresponds equally to both spouses, who shall have equal authority in the home and decide jointly on household and family matters. In the case of disagreement, a family court judge will decide who prevails.[39] Article 110 maintains its original heading, "protection of the wife", and first paragraph, stipulating that the husband owes certain duties of protection and assistance to the wife.[40] It has been modified with respect to its second paragraph to reflect that both spouses have the duty to care for minor children.[41] Article 115 has been modified to provide that in case of a disagreement between spouses as to representation of the marital union, a family judge will decide to whom it shall correspond on the basis of the conduct of each.[42] Article 131

---

39 According to Article 1 of Decree 80-98:
  Article 109 is amended to read as follows: "Article 109. Marital representation. Representation of the marital union shall correspond equally to both spouses, who shall have equal authority and considerations in the home; they shall establish their place of residence by common agreement, and shall arrange everything concerning the education and establishment of their children, as well as the family budget. In the event of disagreement between the spouses, a family court judge shall decide who prevails."

40 The non-amended part states: "Article 110. (Protection of the wife). The husband must provide protection and assistance to his wife and is obliged to supply everything needed to sustain the home in accordance with his economic means."

41 According to Article 2 of Decree 80-98, Article 110, paragraph 2 is amended to read as follows: "Both spouses shall have the obligation to attend to and care for their children while they are minors."

42 According to Article 4 of Decree 80-98:
  Article 115. In the event of disagreement between the spouses with regard to representation of the marital union, a family court judge will decide to whom it shall correspond on the basis of the conduct of each both inside and outside the home. The judge shall also indicate how long that spouse will exercise representation and the conditions that the other spouse must fulfill to recover the chance to represent the union once again.
  In any event, administration shall be exercised individually, without the need for a court order to that effect, in the following cases:
  1   If one of the spouses is prohibited from exercising administration by court order;
  2   Voluntary abandonment of the home or declaration of absence; and
  3   Pursuant to a sentence of imprisonment, and for its full duration.

has been amended to read that both spouses may administer marital property, either jointly or separately.[43] Article 255 has been modified to provide that both spouses shall represent children and administer their property, either jointly or separately.[44] Article 317, which allows certain classes of persons to be excused from exercising certain types of custody remains in its original form.[45]

78   The Commission fully recognizes and values the reforms enacted by the State of Guatemala in response to the recommendations set forth in Report 86/98. As the parties have recognized, these constitute a significant advance in the protection of the fundamental rights of the victim and of women in Guatemala. The reforms represent a substantial measure of compliance with the Commission's recommendations, and are consistent with the State's obligations as a Party to the American Convention.

79   The Commission is not, however, in a position to conclude that the State has fully complied with the recommendations. The original heading and first paragraph of Article 110, which remain in force, refer to the duty of the husband to protect and assist his wife within the marriage, a duty that, in and of itself, is consistent with the nature of the marital relationship. For its part, Article 111 of the Code establishes the obligation of the wife to contribute equitably to maintenance of the home to the extent that she can,[46] a duty that is also consistent with the relationship between spouses. While neither of these duties gives rise, in itself, to a situation of incompatibility, they continue to reflect an imbalance in that the legislation recognizes that the wife is the beneficiary of the husband's duty to protect and assist her, while the law does not impose the same duty on her with regard to her husband. Article 17(4) of the American Convention requires the State to "ensure the equality of rights and the adequate balancing of responsibilities of the spouses as to marriage".

80   With regard to Article 317, the decisive factor is not whether it is viewed as referring to a privilege or an obligation; what is dispositive is the nature of the distinction made in the provision and the justification offered for it. Essentially, the terms of Article 317 identify categories of persons who may be excused from custody or guardianship due to limitations, for example, economic or health reasons. It is not evident, nor has the State explained what limitation justifies including "women" in these categories. According to Article 17 of the American Convention, and as expressly stipulated in Article 16 of the

---

43   According to Article 1 of Decree 27-99:

Article 131. Under the system of absolute joint ownership [*comunidad absoluta*] by husband and wife or community of property acquired during marriage [*comunidad de gananciales*], both spouses shall administer the marital property, either jointly or separately.

Each spouse or common-law spouse shall dispose freely of goods registered under his or her name in the public registries, without prejudice to the obligation to account to the other for any disposal of common property.

44   According to Article 8 of Decree 80-98:

Article 255. For the duration of the marital union or common-law marriage, the father and mother shall jointly exercise parental authority. Both parents shall also, jointly or separately, represent and administer the property of minor or incompetent children, except in cases governed by Article 115, or in cases of separation or divorce, in which representation and administration shall be exercised by the spouse who has custody of the minor or incompetent child.

45   See notes 3-11, *supra*.

46   Article 111 of the Civil Code: "(Obligation of the wife to contribute to maintenance of the household). The wife shall also contribute equitably to maintenance of the household if she has property of her own or performs a job, profession, trade, or business; however, if the husband is unable to work and has no property of his own, the wife shall cover all the expenses out of her income."

Convention on the Elimination of All Forms of Discrimination against Women, States Parties must guarantee equal rights and duties with regard to exercising custody and other forms of guardianship of children.

81 In this sense, both Article 317 and the title and first paragraph of Article 110 suggest, expressly or implicitly, that women are characterized by inherent weaknesses that limit their capacity as compared to men. This affects María Eugenia Morales de Sierra in her right to equal protection of the law, in accordance with Article 24 of the American Convention, and to respect for her human dignity, pursuant to Article 11 of that Convention. Additionally, as stated in paragraph 44 above, these norms apply stereotyped notions about gender roles, thereby perpetuating *de facto* discrimination against women in the family sphere. Further, with regard to the question of compliance with the recommendations, the State has provided no measures of reparation to the victim in response to the findings and recommendations of the Commission.

82 The petitioners have responded to the modification of Articles 109, 115, 131 and 255 by contending that the Convention requires that the decisions at issue be taken by both spouses jointly, rather than autonomously as the reforms permit. Because this position was not developed in the proceedings prior to Report 86/98, and because it has not been sufficiently sustained subsequently in relation to the facts of the particular case and the experience of the victim, or the normative content or jurisprudence of the system, the Commission finds that the question has not been sufficiently defined in the case, and cannot conclude that the reforms fail to satisfy the recommendations for this reason.

VI   CONCLUSIONS

83 On the basis of the foregoing analysis and conclusions, the Commission finds that the recommendations issued in Report 86/98 have been complied with in important measure. It reiterates its conclusion that the State of Guatemala has not discharged its responsibility for having violated the rights of María Eugenia Morales de Sierra to equal protection, respect for family life, and respect for private life established in Articles 24, 17, and 11 of the American Convention on Human Rights in relation to the heading and paragraph one of Article 110 and paragraph four of Article 317. The Commission accordingly finds the State responsible for having failed to uphold its Article 1 obligation to respect and ensure those rights under the Convention, as well as its Article 2 obligation to adopt the legislative and other measures necessary to give effect to those rights of the victim.

VII   RECOMMENDATIONS

84   On the basis of the analysis and conclusions set forth in the present report,

THE INTER-AMERICAN COMMISSION ON HUMAN RIGHTS DECIDES:

To reiterate its recommendations to the State of Guatemala that it:

1   Adapt the pertinent provisions of the Civil Code to balance the legal recognition of the reciprocal duties of women and men in marriage and take the legislative and other measures necessary to amend Article 317 of the Civil Code so as to bring national law into conformity with the norms of the American Convention and give full effect to the rights and freedoms guaranteed to María Eugenia Morales de Sierra therein.

2   Redress and adequately compensate María Eugenia Morales de Sierra for the harm
       done by the violations established in this Report.

VIII   PUBLICATION

85 On 7 November 2000, the Commission transmitted Report No 92/00 – the text of
which is reproduced above – to the State of Guatemala and to the petitioners, pursuant
to Article 51(2) of the American Convention, and granted the State one month to comply
with the foregoing recommendations. In accordance with the aforementioned Article
51(2), at this stage in the proceedings the Commission shall restrict itself to evaluating
the measures taken by the Guatemalan State to comply with the recommendations and
remedy the situation examined. The Guatemalan State did not submit observations on
Report 92/00.

86 In view of the foregoing considerations and the provisions of Article 51(3) of the
American Convention and Article 48 of the Regulations of the Commission, the
Commission decides to reiterate the conclusions and recommendations contained,
respectively, in Chapters VI and VII *supra*, to publish this report; and to include it in its
Annual Report to the General Assembly of the OAS. Pursuant to the provisions
contained in the instruments governing its mandate, the IACHR will continue to
evaluate the measures taken by the State of Guatemala with respect to those
recommendations, until the State has fully complied with them.

Approved by the Inter-American Commission on Human Rights on 19 January 2001.

CASE NO 16

MOHAMMAD AHMED KHAN v SHAH BANO

SUPREME COURT OF INDIA

Judgment: 23 April 1985

Panel: Chandrachud CJ, Desai, Reddy, Venkataramiah and Misra JJ

Human rights — Divorce — Maintenance — Muslim Personal Law — Duty of husband to pay maintenance after the period of iddat to a divorced wife who is unable to maintain herself — Whether a conflict between Muslim Personal Law and right to maintenance — Payment of Mahr (dowry) — Whether Mahr is an amount payable on the occurrence of divorce, so as to cancel the husband's obligation to pay maintenance — Criminal Procedure Code 1973, ss 125, 127(3)(b)

BACKGROUND

The appellant, Mr Mohammad Ahmed Khan, divorced his wife, Ms Shah Bano, on 6 November 1978. Ms Shah Bano brought a petition for maintenance. Mr Khan claimed that he was under no duty to pay maintenance to her because he had already paid her a monthly sum during the period of *iddat* as required under Muslim personal law, but in August 1979 he was ordered to pay maintenance to her under section 125 of the Criminal Procedure Code.

Mr Khan appealed to the Supreme Court, arguing that section 125 of the Criminal Procedure Code was inapplicable to him. Section 125 provides that a person with sufficient means who neglects or refuses to maintain his wife, including a divorced wife who has not remarried, may be ordered by the court to pay monthly maintenance. Mr Khan argued that the applicable law was Muslim personal law, under which he had no duty to pay further maintenance to his former wife beyond the period of *iddat*. He further argued that the maintenance order should be dismissed because he had paid the sum of *Mahr* (dowry) in full pursuant to section 127(3)(b) of the Criminal Procedure Code, which provides that an order can be dismissed where the wife has received "the whole sum which, under any customary or personal law applicable to the parties, was payable on such divorce".

HELD (dismissing the appeal)

1   Section 125 of the Criminal Procedure Code was entirely secular in its application. The purpose of s 125 of the Criminal Procedure Code was to provide a quick and summary remedy to persons unable to maintain themselves. While s 125 did not supplant the personal law of the parties, equally, the religion professed by the parties or the personal law by which they were governed could not limit its applicability unless, within the framework of the Constitution, its application was restricted to a defined category of religious groups or classes (which was not the case in respect of s 125). (Para 7).

2   There was no conflict between s 125 of the Criminal Procedure Code and the requirements of Muslim Personal Law on the liability of the Muslim husband to provide for the maintenance of his divorced wife who was unable to maintain herself. Section 125 deals with cases in which a person who is possessed of sufficient means neglects or refuses to maintain, amongst others, his wife who is unable to maintain herself. Since the Muslim Personal Law, which limits the duty of the Muslim man to provide for the maintenance of the divorced wife to the period of *iddat*, did not contemplate or countenance the situation envisaged by s 125, it would be wrong to hold that the Muslim, according to his personal law, was not under an obligation to provide maintenance beyond the period of *iddat* to his divorced wife who was unable to maintain herself. The true position was that if the divorced wife was able to maintain herself, the husband's liability to provide maintenance for her would cease with the expiration of *iddat*. If his wife could not maintain herself, she was entitled to have recourse to s 125. This was in accordance with the Quran, which imposes an obligation on the Muslim husband to provide maintenance for his divorced wife. (Paras 14 and 20)

3   Section 127(3)(b) provides that a Magistrate shall cancel an order of maintenance on divorce if the wife has received "the whole of the sum which, under any customary or personal law applicable to the parties, was payable on such divorce". The payment of *Mahr* (dowry) was not payment of a sum payable "on divorce" for these purposes. (Para 22)

National legislation referred to

India

Code of Civil Procedure

Constitution of India, art 44

Criminal Procedure Code 1973, ss 125 and 127(3)(b)

Criminal Procedure Code 1898, s 488

Shariat Act, XXVI of 1937

Cases referred to

Bai Tahira v Ali Hussain Fidalli Chothia (1979) 2 SCR 75

Fazlunbi v K Kader Vali (1980) 3 SCR 1127

Hamira Bibi v Zubaide Bibi 43 Ind App 294; AIR 1916 PC 46

Jagir Kaur v Jaswant Singh (1964) 2 SCR 83, 84; (1964) 1 SCJ 386

Nanak Chand v Shri Chandra Kishore Agarwala (1970) 1 SCR 565; (1970) 1 SCJ 176

Syed Sabir Husain v Farzand Hasen, 65 Ind App 119; AIR 1938 PC 80

JUDGMENT

CHANDRACHUD, CJ:

1   This appeal does not involve any question of constitutional importance but that is not to say that it does not involve any question of importance. Some questions which arise under the ordinary civil and criminal law are of a far-reaching significance to large

segments of society – which have been traditionally subjected to unjust treatment. Women are one such segment. "Na stree swatantramarhati" said Manu, the Law giver: The woman does not deserve independence. And, it is alleged that the "fatal point in Islam is the degradation of woman". (*Selections from Kuran*, Edward William Lane 1843, Reprint 1982, page xc (Introduction)). To the Prophet is ascribed the statement, hopefully wrongly, that "Woman was made from a crooked rib, and if you try to bend it straight, it will break; therefore treat your wives kindly".

2   This appeal, arising out of an application filed by a divorced Muslim woman for maintenance under section 125 of the Code of Criminal Procedure, raises a straightforward issue which is of common interest not only to Muslim women, not only to women generally but, to all those who, aspiring to create an equal society of men and women, lure themselves into the belief that mankind has achieved a remarkable degree of progress in that direction. The appellant, who is an advocate by profession, was married to the respondent in 1932. Three sons and two daughters were born of that marriage. In 1975, the appellant drove the respondent out of the matrimonial home. In April 1978, the respondent filed a petition against the appellant under section 125 of the Code in the court of the learned Judicial Magistrate (First Class), Indore, asking for maintenance at the rate of Rs 500/ - per month. On 6 November 1978 the appellant divorced the respondent by an irrevocable *talaq*. His defence to the respondent's petition for maintenance was that she had ceased to be his wife by reason of the divorce granted by him, that he was therefore under no obligation to provide maintenance for her, that he had already paid maintenance to her at the rate of Rs200/ - per month for about two years and that he had deposited a sum of 3,000/ - in the court by way of dower during the period of *iddat*. In August 1979 the learned Magistrate directed the appellant to pay a princely sum of Rs25 - per month to the respondent by way of maintenance. It may be mentioned that the respondent had alleged that the appellant earns a professional income of about Rs60,000/ - per year. In July 1980, in a revisional application filed by the respondent, the High Court of Madhya Pradesh enhanced the amount of maintenance to Rs179.20 per month. The husband is before us by special leave.

3   Does the Muslim Personal Law impose no obligation upon the husband to provide for the maintenance of his divorced wife? Undoubtedly, the Muslim husband enjoys the privilege of being able to discard his wife whenever he chooses to do so, for reasons good, bad or indifferent. Indeed, for no reason at all. But, is the only price of that privilege the dole of a pittance during the period of *iddat*? And, is the law so ruthless in its inequality that, no matter how much the husband pays for the maintenance of his divorced wife during the period of *iddat*, the mere fact that he has paid something, no matter how little, absolves him for ever from the duty of paying adequately so as to enable her to keep her body and soul together? Then again, is there any provisions in the Muslim Personal Law under which a sum is payable to the wife "on divorce"? These are some of the important, though agonising, questions which arise for our decision.

4   The question as to whether section 125 of the Code applies to Muslims also is concluded by two decisions of this Court which are reported in *Bai Tahira v Ali Hussain Fidaalli Chothia* and *Fazlumbi v K Khader Vali*.[1] Those decisions took the view that the divorced Muslim wife is entitled to apply for maintenance under section 125. But, a Bench consisting of our learned Brethren, Murtaza Fazal Ali and A Varadarajan, JJ, were inclined to the view that those cases are not correctly decided. Therefore, they referred this appeal to a large Bench by an order dated 3 February 1981, which reads thus:

---

1   1979 (2) SCR 75.

As this case involves substantial questions of law of far-reaching consequences, we feel that the decisions of this Court in *Bai Tahira v Ali Hussain Fidaalli Chothia & Anr* and *Fuzlubi v K, Khader Vali & Anr*, require reconsideration because, in our opinion, they are not only in direct contravention of the plain and unambiguous language of section 127(3) (b) of the Code of Criminal Procedure, 1973 which far from overriding the Muslim Law on the subject protects and applies the same in cases where a wife has been divorced by the husband the dower specified has been paid and the period of *iddat* has been observed. The decision also appear to us to be against the fundamental concept of divorce by the husband and its consequences under the Muslim law which has been expressly protected by section 2 of the Muslim Personal Law (Shariat) Application Act, 1937 – an Act which was not noticed by the aforesaid decisions. We, therefore, direct that the matter may be placed before the Hon'ble Chief Justice for being heard by a larger Bench consisting of more than three Judges.

5   Section 125 of the Code of Criminal Procedure which deals with the right of maintenance reads thus:

125 Order for maintenance of wives, children and parent:

If any person having sufficient means neglects or refuses to maintain –

his wife, unable to maintain herself,

a Magistrate of the first class may, upon proof of such neglect or refusal, order such person to make a monthly allowance for the maintenance of his wife ... at such monthly rate not exceeding five hundred rupees in the whole, as such Magistrate thinks fit.

Explanation – For the purposes of this Chapter, –

"Wife" includes a woman who has been divorced by, or has obtained a divorce from, her husband and has not remarried.

If any person so ordered fails without sufficient cause to comply with the order, any such Magistrate may, for every breach of the order, issue a warrant for levying the amount due in the manner provided for levying fines, and may sentence such person, for the whole or any part of each month's allowance remaining unpaid after the execution of the warrant, to imprisonment for a term which may extend to one month or until payment if sooner made:

Provided ...

Provided further that if such person offers to maintain his wife on condition of her living with him, and she refuses to live with him, such Magistrate may consider any grounds of refusal stated by her, and may make an order under this section notwithstanding such offer, if he is satisfied that there is just ground for so doing.

Explanation – If a husband has contracted marriage with another woman or keeps a mistress, it shall be considered to be just ground for his wife's refusal to live with him.

6   Section 127(3)(b), on which the appellant has built up the edifice of his defence reads thus:

127 Alteration in allowance:

Where any order has been made under section 125 in favour of a woman who has been divorced by, or has obtained a divorce from, her husband, the Magistrate shall, if he is satisfied that –

(a) ...

(b) the woman has been divorced by her husband and that she has received, whether before or after the date of the said order, the whole of the sum which, under any customary or personal law applicable to the parties, was payable on such divorce, cancel such order, in the case where such sum was paid before such order, from the date on which such order was made,

in any other case, from the date of expiry of the period, if any, for which maintenance has been actually paid by the husband to the woman.

7   Under Section 125(1)(a), a person who, having sufficient means, neglects or refuses to maintain his wife who is unable to maintain herself, can be asked by the court to pay a monthly maintenance to her at a rate not exceeding Five Hundred rupees. By clause (b) of the Explanation to section 125(1) "wife" includes a divorced woman who has not remarried. These provisions are too clear and precise to admit of any doubt or refinement. The religion professed by a spouse or by the spouses has no place in the scheme of these provisions. Whether the spouses are Hindus or Muslims, Christians or parsis, pagans or heathens, is wholly irrelevant in the application of these provisions. The reason for this is axiomatic, in the sense that section 125 is a part of the Code of Criminal Procedure, not of the Civil Laws which define and govern the rights and obligations of the parties belonging to particular religions, like the Hindu Adoptions and Maintenance Act, the Shariat, or the Parsi Matrimonial Act. Section 125 was enacted in order to provide a quick and summary remedy to a class of persons who are unable to maintain themselves. What difference would it then make as to what is the religion professed by the neglected wife, child or parent? Neglect by a person of sufficient means to maintain these and the inability of these persons to maintain themselves are the objective criteria which determine the applicability of section 125. Such provisions, which are essentially of a prophylactic nature, cut across the barriers of religion. True, that they do not supplant the personal law of the parties but, equally, the religion professed by the parties or the state of the personal law by which they are governed, cannot have any repercussion on the applicability of such laws unless, within the framework of the Constitution, their application is restricted to a defined category of religious groups or classes. The liability imposed by section 125 to maintain close relatives who are indigent is founded upon the individual's obligation to the society to prevent vagrancy and destitution. That is the moral edict of the law and morality cannot be clubbed with religion. Clause (b) of the Explanation to section 125(1), which defines "wife" as including a divorced wife, contains no words of limitation to justify the exclusion of Muslim women from its scope. Section 125 is truly secular in character.

8   Sir James Fitzjames Stephen who piloted the Code of Criminal Procedure, 1872 as a Legal Member of the Viceroy's Council, described the precursor of Chapter IX of the Code in which section 125 occurs, as "a mode of preventing vagrancy or at least of preventing its consequences". In *Jagir Kaur v Jaswant Singh,* Subba Rao, J speaking for the Court said that Chapter XXXVI of the Code of 1898 which contained section 488, corresponding to section 125, "intends to serve a social purpose". In *Nanak Chand v Shri Chandra Kishore Agarwala,* Sikri, J, while pointing out that the scope of the Hindu Adoptions and Maintenance Act, 1956 and that of section 488 was different, said that section 488 was "applicable to all persons belonging to all religions and has no relationship with the personal law of the parties".

9   Under section 488 of the Code of 1898, the wife's right to maintenance depended upon the continuance of her married status. Therefore, that right could be defeated by the husband by divorcing her unilaterally as under the Muslim Personal Law, or by obtaining a decree of divorce against her under the other systems of law. It was in order to remove this hardship that the Joint Committee recommended that the benefit of the provisions regarding maintenance should be extended to a divorced woman, so long as she has not remarried after the divorce. That is the genesis of clause (b) of the Explanation to section 125(1), which provides that "wife" includes a woman who has

been divorced by, or has obtained a divorce from her husband and has not remarried. Even in the absence of this provision, the courts had held under the Code of 1898 that the provisions regarding maintenance were independent of the personal law governing the parties. The induction of the definition of "wife" so as to include a divorced woman lends even greater weight to that conclusion. "Wife" means a wife as defined, irrespective of the religion professed by her or by her husband. Therefore, a divorced Muslim woman, so long as she has not remarried, is a "wife" for the purpose of section 125. The statutory right available to her under that section is unaffected by the provisions of the personal law applicable to her.

10 The conclusion that the right conferred by section 125 can be exercised irrespective of the personal law of the parties is fortified, especially in regard to Muslims, by the provision contained in the Explanation to the second proviso to section 125(3) of the Code. That proviso says that if the husband offers to maintain his wife on condition that she should live with him, and she refuses to live with him, the Magistrate may consider any grounds of refusal stated by her, and may make an order of maintenance notwithstanding the offer of the husband, if he is satisfied that there is a just ground for passing such an order. According to the Explanation to the proviso:

> If a husband has contracted marriage with another woman or keeps a mistress, it shall be considered to be just ground for his wife's refusal to live with him.

It is too well-known that "A Mahomedan may have as many as four wives at the same time but not more. If he marries a fifth wife when he has already four, the marriage is not void, but merely irregular". (See Mulla's Digest of Moohummundan Law, 18th Edition, (18th ed), paragraph 255, page 285; and, Ameer Ali's Mahomedan Law, 5th Edition, Vol II, page 280). The explanation confers upon the wife the right to refuse to live with her husband if he contracts another marriage, leave alone 3 or 4 other marriages. It shows, unmistakably, that section 125 overrides the personal law, if there is any conflict between the two.

11 The whole of this discussion as to whether the right conferred by section 125 prevails over the personal law of the parties, has proceeded on the assumption that there is a conflict between the provisions of that section and those of the Muslim Personal Law. The argument that by reason of section 2 of the Shariat Act, XXVI of 1937, the rule of decision in matters relating, inter alia, to maintenance "shall be the Muslim Personal Law" also proceeds upon a similar assumption. We embarked upon the decision of the question of priority between the Code and the Muslim Personal Law on the assumption that there was a conflict between the two because, in so far as it lies in our power, we wanted to set to rest, once for all, the question whether section 125 would prevail over the personal law of the parties, in cases where they are in conflict.

12 The next logical step to take is to examine the question, on which considerable argument has been advanced before us, whether there is any conflict between the provisions of section 125 and those of the Muslim Personal Law on the liability of the Muslim husband to provide for the maintenance of his divorced wife.

13 The contention of the husband and of the interveners who support him is that under the Muslim Personal Law, the liability of the husband to maintain a divorced wife is limited to the period of iddat. In support of this proposition, they rely upon the statement of law on the point contained in certain text books. In Mulla's Mahomedan Law (18th Edition, para 279, page 301), there is a statement to the effect that, "After divorce, the wife is entitled to maintenance during the period of iddat". At page 302, the learned author says:

Where an order is made for the maintenance of a wife under section 488 of the Criminal Procedure Code and the wife is afterwards divorced, the order ceases to operate on the expiration of the period of *iddat*. The result is that a Mahomedan may defeat an order made against him under section 488 by divorcing his wife immediately after the order is made. His obligation to maintain his wife will cease in that case on the completion of her *iddat*.

Tyabji's *Muslim Law* (4th Edition, para 304, pages 268–269), contains the statement that:

On the expiration of the *iddat* after talaq, the wife's right to maintenance ceases, whether based on the Muslim Law, or on an order under the Criminal Procedure Code.

According to Dr Paras Diwan:

when a marriage is dissolved by divorce the wife is entitled to maintenance during the period of *iddat*. ... On the expiration of the period of *iddat*, the wife is not entitled to any maintenance under any circumstances. Muslim law does not recognise any obligation on the part of a man to maintain a wife whom he had divorced.

(*Muslim Law in Modern India*, 1982 Edition, page 130).

14 These statements in the text books are inadequate to establish the proposition that the Muslim husband is not under an obligation to provide for the maintenance of his divorced wife, who is unable to maintain herself. One must have regard to the entire conspectus of the Muslim Personal Law in order to determine the extent, both in quantum and in duration, of the husband's liability to provide for the maintenance of an indigent wife who has been divorced by him. Under that law, the husband is bound to pay *Mahr* to the wife as a mark of respect to her. True, that he may settle any amount he likes by way of dower upon his wife, which cannot be less than 10 Dirhams, which is equivalent to three or four rupees (*Mulla's Mahomedan Law*, 18th Edition, para 286, page 308). But, one must have regard to the realities of life. *Mahr* is a mark of respect to the wife. The sum settled by way of *Mahr* is generally expected to take care of the ordinary requirements of the wife, during the marriages and after. But these provisions of the Muslim Personal Law do not countenance cases in which the wife is unable to maintain herself after the divorce. We consider it not only incorrect but unjust, to extend the scope of the statements extracted above to cases in which a divorced wife is unable to maintain herself. We are of the opinion that the application of those statements of law must be restricted to that class of cases, in which there is no possibility of vagrancy or destitution arising out of the indigence of the divorced wife. We are not concerned here with the broad and general question whether husband is liable to maintain his wife, which includes a divorced wife, in all circumstances and at all events. That is not the subject matter of section 125. That sections deals with cases in which, a person who is possessed of sufficient means neglects or refuses to maintain, amongst others, his wife who is unable to maintain herself. Since the Muslim Personal Law, which limits the husband's liability to provide for the maintenance of the divorced wife to the period of *iddat*, does not contemplate or countenance the situation envisaged by section 125, it would be wrong to hold that the Muslim, according to his personal law, is not under an obligation to provide maintenance, beyond the period of *iddat*, to his divorced wife who is unable to maintain herself. The argument of the appellant that according to the Muslim Personal Law, his liability to provide for the maintenance of his divorced wife is limited to the period of *iddat*, despite the fact that she is unable to maintain herself, has therefore to be rejected. The true position is that, if the divorced wife is able to maintain herself, the husband's liability to provide maintenance for her ceases with the expiration of the period of *iddat*. If she is unable to maintain herself, she is entitled to take recourse to section 125 of the Code. The outcome of this discussion is that there is no conflict

between the provisions of section 125 and those of the Muslim Personal Law on the question of the Muslim husband's obligation to provide maintenance for a divorced wife who is unable to maintain herself.

15 There can be no greater authority on this question than the Holy Quran. "The Quran" the Sacred Book of Islam, comprises in its 114 Suras, or chapters the total of revelations believed to have been communicated to Prophet Muhammed, as a final expression of God's will. (*The Quran-Interpreted* by Arthur J Arberry). Verses (Aiyats) 241 and 242 of the Quran show that there is an obligation on Muslim husbands to provide for their divorced wives. The Arabic version of those Aiyats and their English translation are reproduced below:

Arabic version	English version
Ayat No 241	
WA LIL MOTALLAQATAY NTA UN	for divorced women maintenance (should be provided)
BILL MAROOFAY	on a reasonable scale
HAYQAN	This is duty
ALAL MUTAQUEENA	on the righteous
Avat No. 242	
KAZALEKA YABAIYYANULLAHO	Thus doth God
LAKUM AYATEHEE LA ALLA KUM TAQELOON	Make clear his signs to you: in order that you may understand

(See *The Holy Quran* by Yusuf Ali, page 96)

The correctness of the translation of these Aiyats is not in dispute except that, the contention of the appellant is that the word "Mata" in Aiyat No 241 means "provision" and not "maintenance". That is a distinction without a difference. Nor are we impressed by the shuffling plea of the All India Muslim Personal Law Board that, in Aiyat 241, the exhortation is to the "Muta Queena" that is, to the more pious and the more God-fearing not to the general run of the Muslims, the "Muslmini". In Aiyat 242, the Quran says: "It is expected that you will use your commonsense".

16 The English version of the two Aiyat in Muhammed Zafarullah Khan's *The Quran* (page 38) reads thus:

> For divorced women also there shall be provision according to what is fair. This is an obligation binding on the righteous. Thus does Allah make His commandments clear to you that you may understand.

17 The translation of Aiyats 240 to 242 in *The meaning of the Quran* (Vol 1, published by the Board of Islamic Publications, Delhi) reads thus:

240–241

Those of you, who shall die and leave wives behind them, should make a will to the effect that they should be provided with a year's maintenance and should not be turned out of their homes. But if they leave their homes of their own accord, you shall not be answerable for whatever they choose for themselves in a fair way: Allah is All-Powerful, All-wise. Likewise, the divorced women should also be given something in accordance with the known fair standard. This obligation upon the God-fearing people.

242

Thus Allah makes clear His commandments for you: It is expected that you will use your commonsense.

18 In *The Running Commentary of The Holy Quran* (1964 Edition) by Dr Allamah Khadim Rahmani Nuri, Aiyat No 241 is translated thus:

241

And for the divorced woman (also) a provision (should be made) with fairness (in addition to her dower); (This is) a duty (incumbent) on the reverent.

19 In *The meaning of the Glorious Quran, Text and Explanatory Translation*, by Marmaduke Pickthall, (Taj Company Ltd, Karachi), Aiyat 241 is translated thus:

241

For divorced women a provision in kindness: A duty for those who ward off (evil).

20 Finally, in *The Quran Interpreted* by Arthur, J Arberry, Aiyat 241 is translated thus:

241

There shall be for divorced women provision honourable an obligation on the godfearing.

So God makes clear His signs for you: Happily you will understand.

21 Dr KR Nuri in his book quoted above: *The Running Commentary of The Holy Quran*, says in the preface:

Belief in Islam does not mean mere confession of the existence of something. It really means the translation of the faith into action. Words without deeds carry no meaning in Islam. Therefore the term "believe and do good" has been used like a phrase all over the Quran. Belief in something means that man should inculcate the qualities or carry out the promptings or guidance of that thing in his action. Belief in Allah means that besides acknowledging the existence of the Author of the Universe, we are to show obedience to His Commandments ...

22 These Aiyats leave no doubt that the Quran imposes an obligation on the Muslim husband to make provision for or to provide maintenance to the divorced wife. The contrary argument does less than justice to the teachings of the Quran. As observed by Mr M Hidayatullah in his introduction to *Mulla's Mohmedan Law*, the Quran is Al-furqan, that is, one showing truth from falsehood and right from wrong.

23 The second plank of the appellant's argument is that the respondent's application under section 125 is liable to be dismissed because of the provision contained in section 127(3)(b). That section provides, to the extent material, that the Magistrate shall cancel the order of maintenance, if the wife is divorced by the husband and, she has received "the whole of the sum which, under any customary or personal law applicable to the parties, was payable on such divorce". That raises the question as to whether, under the Muslim Personal Law, any sum is payable to the wife "on divorce". We do not have to grope in the dark and speculate as to which kind of a sum this can be because,

the only argument advanced before us on behalf of the appellant and by the interveners supporting him, is that *Mahr* is the amount payable by the husband to the wife on divorce. We find it impossible to accept this argument.

24 In Mulla's *Principles of Mahomedan Law* (18th Edition, page 308), *Mahr* or Dower is defined in paragraph 285 as "a sum of money or other property which the wife is entitled to receive from the husband in consideration of the marriage". Dr Paras Diwan in his book, *Muslim Law in Modern India* (1982 Edition, page 60), criticises this definition on the ground that *Mahr* is not payable "in consideration of marriage" but is an obligation imposed by law on the husband as a mark of respect for the wife, as is evident from the fact that non-specification of *Mahr* at the time of marriage does not affect the validity of the marriage. We need not enter into this controversy and indeed, Mulla's book itself contains the further statement at page 308 that the word "consideration" is not used in the sense in which it is used in the Contract Act and that under the Mohammedan Law, Dower is an obligation imposed upon the husband as a mark of respect for the wife. We are concerned to find whether *Mahr* is an amount payable by the husband to the wife on divorce. Some confusion is caused by the fact that, under the Muslim Personal Law, the amount of *Mahr* is usually split into two parts, one of which is called "prompt" which is payable on demand, and the other is called "deferred", which is payable on the dissolution of the marriage by death or by divorce. But, the fact that deferred *Mahr* is payable at the time of the dissolution of marriage, cannot justify the conclusion that is then payable "on divorce". Even assuming that, in a given case, the entire amount of *Mahr* is of the deferred variety payable on the dissolution of marriage by divorce, it cannot be said that it is an amount which is payable on divorce. Divorce may be a convenient or identifiable point of time at which the deferred amount has to be paid by the husband to the wife. But, the payment of the amount is not occasioned by the divorce, which is what is meant by the expression "on divorce", which occurs in section 127(3)(b) of the Code. If *Mahr* is an amount which the wife is entitled to receive from the husband in consideration of the marriage, that is the very opposite of the amount being payable in consideration of divorce. Divorce dissolves the marriage. Therefore, no amount which is payable in consideration of the marriage can possibly be described as an amount payable in consideration of divorce. The alternative premise that *Mahr* is an obligation imposed upon the husband as a mark of respect for the wife, is wholly detrimental to the stance that it is an amount payable to the wife on divorced. A man may marry a woman for love, looks, learning or nothing at all. And, he may settle a sum upon her as a mark of respect for her. But he does not divorce her as a mark of respect. Therefore, a sum payable to the wife out of respect cannot be a sum payable "on divorce".

25 In an appeal from a Full Bench decision of the Allahabad High Court, the Privy Council in *Hamira Bibi v Zubaide Bibi* summed up the nature and character of *Mahr* in these words:

> Dower is an essential incident under the Mussulman law to the status of marriage; to such an extent that is so that when it is unspecified at the time the marriage is contracted, the law declares that it must be adjudged on definite principles. Regarded as a consideration for the marriage, it is, in theory, payable before consummation; but the law allows its division into two parts, one of which is called "prompt" payable before the wife can be called upon to enter the conjugal domicile; the other "deferred", payable on the dissolution of the contract by the death of either of the parties or by divorce. (Page 300–301)

26 This statement of law was adopted in another decision of the Privy Council in *Sayed Sabir Husain v Farzand Hasan*. It is not quite appropriate and seems invidious to describe any particular Bench of a court as "strong" but, we cannot resist the temptation of

mentioning that Mr Syed Ameer Ali was a party to the decision in *Hamira Bibi* while Sir Shadi Lal was a party to the decision in *Syed Sabir Husain*. These decisions show that the payment of dower may be deferred to a further date as, for example, death or divorce. But that does not mean that the payment of the deferred dower is occasioned by these events.

27 It is contended on behalf of the appellant that the proceedings of the Rajya Sabha dated December 18, 1973 (volume 86, column 186), when the bill which led to the Code of 1973 was on the anvil, would show that the intention of the Parliament was to leave the provisions of the Muslim Personal Law untouched. In this behalf, reliance is placed on the following statement made by Shri Ram Niwas Mirdha, the then Minister of State, Home Affairs:

> Dr Vyas very learnedly made certain observations that a divorced wife under the Muslim law deserves to be treated justly and she should get what is her equitable or legal due. Well, I will not go into this, but say that we would not like to interfere with the customary law of the Muslims through the Criminal Procedure Code. If there is a demand for change in the Muslim Personal Law it should actually come from the Muslim Community itself and we should wait for the Muslim public opinion on these matters to crystalise before we try to change this customary right make change in their personal law. Above all this is partly the place where we could do so. But as I tried to explain, the provision in the Bill is an adverse over the previous situation. Divorced woman have been included and brought within the ambit of clause 125, but a limitation is being imposed by this amendment to clause 127, namely, that the maintenance orders would cease to operate after the amounts due to her under the personal law are paid to her. This is a healthy compromise between that has been termed a conservative interpretation of law or a concession to conservative public opinion and liberal approach to the problem. We have made an advance and not tried to transgress what are the personal rights of Muslim woman. So this, I think, should satisfy non-members that whatever advance we have made is in the right direction and it should be welcomed.

28 It does appear from this speech that the Government did not desire to interfere with the personal law of the Muslims through the Criminal Procedure Code. It wanted the Muslim community to take the load and the Muslim public opinion to crystalise on the reforms in their personal law. However, we are not concerned with the question whether the Government did or did not desire to being about changes in the Muslim Personal Law by enacting sections 125 and 127 of the Code. As we have said earlier and, as admitted by the Minister, the Government did introduce such a change by defining the expression "wife" to include a divorced wife. It also introduced another significant change by providing that the fact that the husband has contracted marriage with another woman is a just ground for the wife's refusal to live with him. The provision contained in section 127(3)(b) may have been introduced because of the misconception that dower is an amount payable "on divorce". But, that cannot convert an amount payable as a mark of respect for the wife into an amount payable on divorce.

29 It must follow from this discussion, unavoidably a little too long, that the judgments of this Court in *Bai Tahire* (Krishna Iyer J, Tulzapurkar J and Pathak J) and *Fazlunbi* (Krishna Iyer J, one of us, Chinnappa Reddy J and A P Sen J) are correct. Justice Krishna Iyer who spoke for the Court in both these cases, relied greatly on the teleological and schematic method of interpretation so as to advance the purpose of the law. These constructional techniques have their own importance in the interpretation of statutes meant to ameliorate the conditions of suffering sections of the society. We have attempted to show that taking the language of the statute as one finds it, there is no escape from the conclusion that a divorced Muslim wife is entitled to apply for

maintenance under section 125 and that, *Mahr* is not a sum which, under the Muslim Personal Law, is payable on divorce.

30 Though *Bai Tahira* was correctly decided, we would like, respectfully, to draw attention to an error which has crept in the judgment. There is a statement at page 80 of the Report [(1979) SCR], in the context of section 127(3)(b) that "payment of *Mahr* money, as a customary discharge, is within the cognizance of that provision". We have taken the view that *Mahr*, not being payable on divorce, does not fall within the meaning of that provision.

31 It is a matter of deep regret that some of the interveners who supported the appellant, took up an extreme position by displaying an unwarranted zeal to defeat the right to maintenance of women who are unable to maintain themselves. The written submissions of the All India Muslim Personal Law Board have gone to the length of asserting that it is irrelevant to inquire as to how a Muslim divorcee should maintain herself. The facile answer of the Board is that the Personal Law has devised the system of *Mahr* to meet the requirements of women and if a woman is indigent, she must look to her relations, including nephews and cousins, to support her. This is a most unreasonable view of law as well as life. We appreciate that Begum Temur Jehan, a social worker who has been working in association with the Delhi City Women's Association for the uplift of Muslim women, intervened to support Mr Daniel Latifi who appeared on behalf of the wife.

32 It is also a matter of regret that Article 44 of our Constitution has remained a dead letter. It provides that "The State shall endeavour to secure for the citizens a uniform civil code throughout the territory of India". There is no evidence of any official activity for framing a common civil code for the country. A belief seems to have gained ground that it is for the Muslim community to take a lead in the matter of reforms of their personal law. A common Civil Code will help the cause of national integration by removing disparate loyalties to laws which have conflicting ideologies. No community is likely to bell the cat by making gratuitous concessions on this issue. It is the State which is charged with the duty of securing a uniform civil code for the citizens of the country and, unquestionably, it has the legislative competence to do so. A counsel in the case whispered, somewhat audibly, that legislative competence is one thing, the political courage to use that competence is quite another. We understand that difficulties involved in bringing persons of different faiths and persuasions on a common platform. But, a beginning has to be made if the Constitution is to have any meaning. Inevitably, the role of the reformer has to be assumed by the courts because, it is beyond the endurance of sensitive minds to allow injustice to be suffered when it is so palpable. But piecemeal attempts of courts to bridge the gap between personal laws cannot take the place of a common Civil Code. Justice to all is a far more satisfactory way of dispensing justice than justice from case to case.

33 Dr Tahir Mahmood in his book *Muslim Personal Law* (1977 Edition), pages 200–202), has made a powerful plea for framing a uniform Civil Code for all citizens of India. He says: "In pursuance of the goal of secularism, the State must stop administering religion-based personal laws". He wants the lead to come from the majority community but, we should have thought that, lead or no lead, the State must act. It would be useful to quote the appeal made by the author to the Muslim community:

Instead of wasting their energies in exerting theological and political pressure in order to secure an "immunity" for their traditional personal law from the state's legislative jurisdiction, the Muslims will do well to begin exploring and demonstrating how the true Islamic laws, purged of their time-worn and anachronistic interpretations, can enrich the common civil code of India.

At a Seminar held on 18 October 1980 under the auspices of the Department of Islamic and Comparative Law, Indian Institute of Islamic Studies, New Delhi, he also made an appeal to the Muslim community to display by their conduct a correct understanding of Islamic concepts on marriage and divorce (See *Islam and Comparative Law Quarterly*, April-June, 1981, page 146).

34 Before we conclude, we would like to draw attention to the *Report of the Commission on Marriage and Family Laws*, which was appointed by the Government of Pakistan by a Resolution dated August 4, 1955. The answer of the Commission to Question No 5 (page 1215 of the Report) is that:

a large number of middle-aged women who are being divorced without rhyme or reason should not be thrown on the streets without a roof over their heads and without any means of sustaining themselves and their children.

The Report concludes thus:

In the words of Allama Iqbal, "the question which is likely to confront Muslim countries in the near future, is whether the law of Islam is capable of evolution – a question which will require great intellectual effort, and is sure to be answered in the affirmative".

35 For those reasons, we dismiss the appeal and confirm the judgment of the High Court. The appellant will pay the costs of the appeal to respondent 1, which we quantify at rupees ten thousand. It is needless to add that it would be open to the respondent to make an application under section 127(1) of the Code for increasing the allowance of maintenance granted to her on proof of a change in the circumstances as envisaged by that section.

*Appeal dismissed.**

---

*   *Eds:* the Supreme Court's decision was controversial and led to protests from sectors of the Muslim community in India. The passage of the Muslim Women (Protection of Rights on Divorce) Act 1986, which sought to reverse the effect of the judgment in *Shah Bano*, followed. See further *Introduction, supra*, p xxiv.

RIGHTS AS A MEMBER OF A MINORITY

CASE NO 17

LOVELACE v CANADA

UNITED NATIONS HUMAN RIGHTS COMMITTEE

Communication No: 24/1977

Views adopted: 30 July 1981

Human rights — Equality and non-discrimination — Minorities — Sex discrimination — Right to marry and right to protection of family life and children — Right to choose one's residence — Right to enjoy cultural life — Preservation of Indian reserve and ethnic group — Indian women married to non-Indian men denied right to live on Indian reserve — Whether different treatment of Indian women married to non-Indian men vis-à-vis Indian men married to non-Indian women amounted to discrimination on the ground of sex — Whether woman who had lost her legal status as an Indian through marriage to a non-Indian was still a "person belonging" to a minority — Indian Act, ss 12 and 28(1) — International Covenant on Civil and Political Rights, arts 2, 3, 12, 17, 23, 24, 26 and 27

BACKGROUND

The author of the communication, Ms Sandra Lovelace, was a Canadian citizen of Indian origin living in Canada. She was born and registered as Maliseet Indian, but lost her rights and status as an Indian in accordance with section 12(1) of the Indian Act after marrying a non-Indian on 23 May 1970. Consequently she was denied the legal right to reside with her children in the Tobique Reserve. This continued to apply even after she divorced her husband. Under the Indian Act, an Indian man could marry a non-Indian woman without losing his Indian status. Ms Lovelace complained that the Indian Act was discriminatory on the grounds of sex contrary to the Canadian Bill of Rights and Canada's international obligations under articles 2, 3 and 26 of the International Covenant on Civil and Political Rights. She also claimed that her right to choose her residence (article 12) her right to protection of family life and children (articles 23 and 24) and protection of her rights as a member of an ethnic minority (article 27) of the Covenant had been denied.

The Government of Canada admitted that many provisions of the Indian Act, including section 12(1), were in need of reform. However, it said that the Indian Act was necessary to define the Indian ethnic group to ensure the protection of the Indian minority in accordance with article 27 of the Covenant. Furthermore, the definition was based on traditional patrilineal family relationships, which best served to protect Indian society from non-Indians, given that land in Indian reserves was under greater threat from non-Indian men rather than non-Indian women. While the Government was committed to changing the law, any changes could only be made with the consent of the community, which was itself divided over the matter. Therefore no immediate legislative reform could be expected.

HELD (finding a breach of article 27 of the Covenant)

Competence of Committee to examine communication

1   The Committee was not competent, as a rule, to examine allegations relating to events that took place before the Covenant came into force in Canada on 19 August 1976, namely the initial cause of Ms Lovelace's loss of Indian status on 23 May 1970. It was competent, however, to consider the consequences of earlier events which continued to constitute violations of the Covenant after the date the Covenant came into force in Canada. (Para 10)

Right to enjoy own culture and language with other members of one's ethnic group (article 27)

2   Whilst at present, Ms Lovelace did not qualify as an Indian under Canadian legislation, since she was ethnically a Maliseet Indian and had only been absent from her home reserve for a few years during the existence of her marriage, she was entitled to be regarded as "belonging" to this minority and to claim the benefits of article 27 of the Covenant. (Para 14)

3   The Indian Act dealt with many privileges that did not come within the scope of the Covenant, for example the right to live on a reserve was not guaranteed under article 27, nor did the Indian Act expressly interfere with the rights guaranteed under article 27. However, in order to achieve her right to live with the community to which she belonged, as guaranteed under article 27, Ms Lovelace would have had to live on the Tobique Reserve. There was no other place outside the Reserve where she could have had access to her native culture and language in community with the other members of her group. (Paras 14–15)

4   Statutory measures affecting the right to residence on a reserve of a person belonging to a minority should have both a reasonable and objective justification and should be consistent with the other provisions of the Covenant, read as a whole. This case should be considered in the light of the fact that Ms Lovelace's marriage to a non-Indian had broken up. It was natural in such a situation that she wished to return to the environment in which she was born, particularly as after the dissolution of her marriage her main cultural attachment was to the Maliseet band. Denying Ms Lovelace the right to reside on the reserve was not reasonable or necessary to preserve the identity of the tribe. To prevent her recognition as belonging to the band was an unjustifiable denial of her rights under article 26 of the Covenant, read in the context of the other provisions. (Paras 15 and 16)

Right to choose one's residence (article 12), the right to protection of family life and children (articles 17, 23 and 24) and the right protection against discrimination (articles 2, 3 and 26)

8   In view of the finding of breach of article 27, there was no need to consider on the facts whether there had been a breach of the rights concerning the protection of family life and children (articles 17, 23 and 24) and the general provision against discrimination (articles 2, 3, and 26). (Para 18)

Treaties and international instruments referred to

International Covenant on Civil and Political Rights 1966, arts 2, 3, 12(1), 12(3), 17(1), 23, 24, 26 and 27

Optional Protocol to the International Covenant on Civil and Political Rights 1966, arts 4(2) and 5(4)

National legislation referred to

Canada

Canadian Bill of Rights Act 1970

Consolidated Regulations of Canada 1978, c 949

Indian Timber Regulations, c 961, s 4

Indian Act, ss 12(1)(b), 14, 15, 16, 25, 28(1), 30, 31, 70, 71, 73(1)(g) and 87

Cases referred to

Attorney-General of Canada v Lavell, Isaac et al v Bedard [1974] SCR 1349; (1974) 38 DLR (3d) 481

VIEWS UNDER ARTICLE 5(4) OF THE OPTIONAL PROTOCOL[1]

1   The author of the communication dated 29 December 1977 and supplemented by letters of 17 April 1978, 28 November 1979 and 20 June 1980, is a 32 year old woman, living in Canada. She was born and registered as "Maliseet Indian" but has lost her rights and status as an Indian in accordance with section 12(1)(b) of the Indian Act, after having married a non-Indian on 23 May 1970. Pointing out that an Indian man who marries a non-Indian woman does not lose his Indian status, she claims that the Act is discriminatory on the grounds of sex and contrary to articles 2(1), 3, 23(1) and (4), 26 and 27 of the Covenant. As to the admissibility of the communication, she contends that she was not required to exhaust local remedies since the Supreme Court of Canada, in the *Attorney-General of Canada v Lavell, Isaac et al v Bedard* [1974] SCR 1349, held that section 12(1)(b) was fully operative, irrespective of its inconsistency with the Canadian Bill of Rights on account of discrimination based on sex.

2   By its decision of 18 July 1978 the Human Rights Committee transmitted the communication, under rule 91 of the provisional rules of procedure, to the State party concerned, requesting information and observations relevant to the question of admissibility of the communication. This request for information and observations was reiterated by a decision of the Committee's Working Group, dated 6 April 1979.

3   By its decision of 14 August 1979 the Human Rights Committee declared the communication admissible and requested the author of the communication to submit additional information concerning her age and her marriage, which had not been

---

1   Pursuant to rule 85 of the provisional rules of procedure, Mr Walter Surma Tarnopolsky did not participate in the consideration of this communication or in the adoption of the views of the Committee under article 5(4) of the Optional Protocol in this matter. The text of an individual opinion submitted by a Committee member is appended to these views.

indicated in the original submission. At that time no information or observations had been received from the State party concerning the question of admissibility of the communication.

4   In its submission dated 26 September 1979 relating to the admissibility of the communication, the State party informed the Committee that it had no comments on that point to make. This fact, however, should not be considered as an admission of the merits of the allegations or the arguments of the author of the communication.

5   In its submission under article 4(2) of the Optional Protocol concerning the merits of the case, dated 4 April 1980, the State party recognized that "many of the provisions of the Indian Act, including section 12(1)(b), require serious reconsideration and reform". The Government further referred to an earlier public declaration to the effect that it intended to put a reform bill before the Canadian Parliament. It nonetheless stressed the necessity of the Indian Act as an instrument designed to protect the Indian minority in accordance with article 27 of the Covenant. A definition of the Indian was inevitable in view of the special privileges granted to the Indian communities, in particular their right to occupy reserve lands. Traditionally, patrilineal family relationships were taken into account for determining legal claims. Since, additionally, in the farming societies of the nineteenth century, reserve land was felt to be more threatened by non-Indian men than by non-Indian women, legal enactments as from 1869 provided that an Indian woman who married a non-Indian man would lose her status as an Indian. These reasons were still valid. A change in the law could only be sought in consultation with the Indians themselves who, however, were divided on the issue of equal rights. The Indian community should not be endangered by legislative changes. Therefore, although the Government was in principle committed to amending section 12(l)(b) of the Indian Act, no quick and immediate legislative action could be expected.

6   The author of the communication, in her submission of 20 June 1980, disputes the contention that legal relationships within Indian families were traditionally patrilineal in nature. Her view is that the reasons put forward by the Canadian Government do not justify the discrimination against Indian women in section 12(1)(b) of the Indian Act. She concludes that the Human Rights Committee should recommend the State party to amend the provisions in question.

7.1 In an interim decision, adopted on 31 July 1980, the Human Rights Committee set out the issues of the case in the following considerations.

7.2 The Human Rights Committee recognized that the relevant provision of the Indian Act, although not legally restricting the right to marry as laid down in article 23(2) of the Covenant, entails serious disadvantages on the part of the Indian woman who wants to marry a non-Indian man and may in fact cause her to live with her fiancé in an unmarried relationship. There is thus a question as to whether the obligation of the State party under article 23 of the Covenant with regard to the protection of the family is complied with. Moreover, since only Indian women and not Indian men are subject to these disadvantages under the Act, the question arises whether Canada complies with its commitment under articles 2 and 3 to secure the rights under the Covenant without discrimination as to sex. On the other hand, article 27 of the Covenant requires States parties to accord protection to ethnic and linguistic minorities and the Committee must give due weight to this obligation. To enable it to form an opinion on these issues, it would assist the Committee to have certain additional observations and information.

7.3 In regard to the present communication, however, the Human Rights Committee must also take into account that the Covenant entered into force in respect of Canada on

19 August 1976, several years after the marriage of Mrs Lovelace. She consequently lost her status as an Indian at a time when Canada was not bound by the Covenant. The Human Rights Committee has held that it is empowered to consider a communication when the measures complained of, although they occurred before the entry into force of the Covenant, continued to have effects which themselves constitute a violation of the Covenant after that date. It is therefore relevant for the Committee to know whether the marriage of Mrs Lovelace in 1970 has had any such effects.

7.4 Since the author of the communication is ethnically an Indian, some persisting effects of her loss of legal status as an Indian may, as from the entry into force of the Covenant for Canada, amount to a violation of rights protected by the Covenant. The Human Rights Committee has been informed that persons in her situation are denied the right to live on an Indian reserve with resultant separation from the Indian community and members of their families. Such prohibition may affect rights which the Covenant guarantees in articles 12(1), 17, 23(1), 24 and 27. There may be other such effects of her loss of status.

8   The Human Rights Committee invited the parties to submit their observations on the above considerations and, as appropriate, to furnish replies to the following questions:

(a) How many Indian women marry non-Indian men on an average each year? Statistical data for the last 20 years should be provided.

(b) What is the legal basis of a prohibition to live on a reserve? Is it a direct result of the loss of Indian status or does it derive from a discretionary decision of the Council of the community concerned?

(c) What reasons are adduced to justify the denial of the right of abode on a reserve?

(d) What legislative proposals are under consideration for ensuring full equality between the sexes with regard to Indian status? How would they affect the position of Mrs Lovelace? How soon can it be expected that legislation will be introduced?

(e) What was Mrs Lovelace's place of abode prior to her marriage? Was she at that time living with other members of her family? Was she denied the right to reside on a reserve in consequence of her marriage?

(f) What other persisting effects of Mrs Lovelace's loss of status are there which may be relevant to any of the rights protected by the Covenant?

9.1 In submissions dated 22 October and 2 December 1980 the State party and the author, respectively, commented on the Committee's considerations and furnished replies to the questions asked.

9.2 It emerges from statistics provided by the State party that from 1965 to 1978, on an average, 510 Indian women married non-Indian men each year. Marriages between Indian women and Indian men of the same band during that period were 590 on the average each year; between Indian women and Indian men of a different band 422 on the average each year; and between Indian men and non-Indian women 448 on the average each year.

9.3 As to the legal basis of a prohibition to live on a reserve, the State party offers the following explanations:

Section 14 of the Indian Act provides that "[an Indian] woman who is a member of a band ceases to be a member of that band if she marries a person who is not a member of that band".[2] As such, she loses the right to the use and benefits, in common with other members of the band, of the land allotted to the band.[3] It should, however, be noted that "when [an Indian woman] marries a member of another band, she thereupon becomes a member of the band of which her husband is a member". As such, she is entitled to the use and benefit of lands allotted to her husband's band.

An Indian (including a woman) who ceases to be a member of a band ceases to be entitled to reside by right on a reserve. None the less it is possible for an individual to reside on a reserve if his or her presence thereon is tolerated by a band or its members. It should be noted that under section 30 of the Indian Act, any person who trespasses on a reserve is guilty of an offence. In addition, section 31 of the Act provides that an Indian or a band (and of course its agent, the Band Council) may seek relief or remedy against any person, other than an Indian, who is or has been:

(a) unlawfully in occupation or possession of;

(b) claiming adversely the right to occupation or possession of; or

(c) trespassing upon a reserve or part thereof.

9.4 As to the reasons adduced to justify the denial of the right of abode on a reserve, the State party states that the provisions of the Indian Act which govern the right to reside on a reserve have been enacted to give effect to various treaty obligations reserving to the Indians exclusive use of certain lands.

9.5 With regard to the legislative proposals under consideration, the State party offers the following information:

Legislative proposals are being considered which would ensure that no Indian person, male or female, would lose his or her status under any circumstances other than his or her own personal desire to renounce it.

In addition, changes to the present sections under which the status of the Indian woman and minor children is dependent upon the status of her spouse are also being considered.

Further recommendations are being considered which would give Band Councils powers to pass by-laws concerning membership in the band; such by-laws, however, would be required to be non-discriminatory in the areas of sex, religion and family affiliation.

In the case of Mrs Lovelace, when such new legislation is enacted, she would then be entitled to be registered as an Indian.

Legislative recommendations are being prepared for presentation to Cabinet for approval and placement on the Parliamentary Calendar for introduction before the House by mid-1981.

9.6 As to Mrs Lovelace's place of abode prior to her marriage, both parties confirm that she was at that time living on the Tobique Reserve with her parents. Sandra Lovelace adds that as a result of her marriage, she was denied the right to live on an Indian reserve. As to her abode since then the State party observes:

---

2   Mrs Lovelace married a non-Indian. As such, she ceased to be a member of the Tobique band. In addition, by the application of sub-paragraph 12(1)(b) of the Indian Act, she lost her Indian status.

3   It should be noted that when an Indian ceases to be a member of a band, he is entitled, if he meets the conditions set out in sections 15 and 16 of the Indian Act, to compensation from Her Majesty for this loss of membership.

Since her marriage and following her divorce, Mrs Lovelace has, from time to time lived on the reserve in the home of her parents, and the Band Council has made no move to prevent her from doing so. However, Mrs Lovelace wishes to live permanently on the reserve and to obtain a new house. To do so, she has to apply to the Band Council. Housing on reserves is provided with money set aside by Parliament for the benefit of registered Indians. The Council has not agreed to provide Mrs Lovelace with a new house. It considers that in the provision of such housing, priority is to be given to registered Indians.

9.7 In this connection the following additional information has been submitted on behalf of Mrs Lovelace:

At the present time, Sandra Lovelace is living on the Tobique Indian Reserve, although she has no right to remain there. She has returned to the Reserve with her children because her marriage has broken up and she has no other place to reside. She is able to remain on the reserve in violation of the law of the local Band Council because dissident members of the tribe who support her cause have threatened to resort to physical violence in her defence should the authorities attempt to remove her.

9.8 As to the other persisting effects of Mrs Lovelace's loss of Indian status the State party submits the following:

When Mrs Lovelace lost her Indian status through marriage to a non-Indian, she also lost access to federal government programs for Indian people in areas such as education, housing, social assistance, etc. At the same time, however, she and her children became eligible to receive similar benefits from programs the provincial government provides for all residents of the province.

Mrs Lovelace is no longer a member of the Tobique band and no longer an Indian under the terms of the Indian Act. She however is enjoying all the rights recognized in the Covenant, in the same way as any other individual within the territory of Canada and subject to its jurisdiction.

9.9 On behalf of Sandra Lovelace the following is submitted in this connection:

All the consequences of loss of status persist in that they are permanent and continue to deny the complainant rights she was born with.

A person who ceases to be an Indian under the Indian Act suffers the following consequences:

(1) Loss of the right to possess or reside on lands on a reserve (sections 25 and 28(1)). This includes loss of the right to return to the reserve after leaving, the right to inherit possessory interest in land from parents or others, and the right to be buried on a reserve;

(2) An Indian without status cannot receive loans from the Consolidated Revenue Fund for the purposes set out in section 70;

(3) An Indian without status cannot benefit from instruction in farming and cannot receive seed without charge from the Minister (see section 71);

(4) An Indian without status cannot benefit from medical treatment and health services provided under section 73(1)(g);

(5) An Indian without status cannot reside on tax exempt lands (section 87);

(6) A person ceasing to be an Indian loses the right to borrow money for housing from the Band Council (Consolidated Regulations of Canada, 1978, c 949);

(7) A person ceasing to be an Indian loses the right to cut timber free of dues on an Indian reserve (section 4, Indian Timber Regulations, c 961, 1978 Consolidated Regulations of Canada);

(8) A person ceasing to be an Indian loses additional hunting and fishing rights that may exist;

(9) The major loss to a person ceasing to be an Indian is the loss of the cultural benefits of living in an Indian community, the emotional ties to home, family, friends and neighbours, and the loss or identity.

10   The Human Rights Committee, in the examination of the communication before it, has to proceed from the basic fact that Sandra Lovelace married a non-Indian on 23 May 1970 and consequently lost her status as a Maliseet Indian under section 12(1)(b) of the Indian Act. This provision was – and still is – based on a distinction *de jure* on the ground of sex. However, neither its application to her marriage as the cause of her loss of Indian status nor its effects could at that time amount to a violation of the Covenant, because this instrument did not come into force for Canada until 19 August 1976. Moreover, the Committee is not competent, as a rule, to examine allegations relating to events having taken place before the entry into force of the Covenant and the Optional Protocol. Therefore as regards Canada it can only consider alleged violations of human rights occurring on or after 19 August 1976. In the case of a particular individual claiming to be a victim of a violation, it cannot express its view on the law in the abstract, without regard to the date on which this law was applied to the alleged victim. In the case of Sandra Lovelace it follows that the Committee is not competent to express any view on the original cause of her loss of Indian status, ie the Indian Act as applied to her at the time of her marriage in 1970.

11   The Committee recognizes, however, that the situation may be different if the alleged violations, although relating to events occurring before 19 August 1976, continue, or have effects which themselves constitute violations, after that date. In examining the situation of Sandra Lovelace in this respect, the Committee must have regard to all relevant provisions of the Covenant. It has considered, in particular, the extent to which the general provisions in articles 2 and 3, as well as the rights in articles 12(1), 17(1), 23(1), 24, 26 and 27, may be applicable to the facts of her present situation.

12   The Committee first observes that from 19 August 1976 Canada had undertaken under article 2(1) and (2) of the Covenant to respect and ensure to all individuals within its territory and subject to its jurisdiction, the rights recognized in the Covenant without distinction of any kind such as sex, and to adopt the necessary measures to give effect to these rights. Further, under article 3, Canada undertook to ensure the equal right of men and women to the enjoyment of these rights. These undertakings apply also to the position of Sandra Lovelace. The Committee considers, however, that it is not necessary for the purposes of her communication to decide their extent in all respects. The full scope of the obligation of Canada to remove the effects or inequalities caused by the application of existing laws to past events, in particular as regards such matters as civil or personal status, does not have to be examined in the present case, for the reasons set out below.

13.1 The Committee considers that the essence of the present complaint concerns the continuing effect of the Indian Act, in denying Sandra Lovelace legal status as an Indian, in particular because she cannot for this reason claim a legal right to reside where she wishes to, on the Tobique Reserve. This fact persists after the entry into force of the Covenant, and its effects have to be examined, without regard to their original cause. Among the effects referred to on behalf of the author (see para 9.9 above), the greater number, ((1) to (8)), relate to the Indian Act and other Canadian rules in fields which do not necessarily adversely affect the enjoyment of rights protected by the Covenant. In this respect the significant matter is her last claim, that "the major loss to a person ceasing to be an Indian is the loss of the cultural benefits of living in an Indian community, the emotional ties to home, family, friends and neighbours, and the loss of identity."

13.2 Although a number of provisions of the Covenant have been invoked by Sandra Lovelace, the Committee considers that the one which is most directly applicable to this complaint is article 27, which reads as follows:

> In those States in which ethnic, religious or linguistic minorities exist, persons belonging to such minorities shall not be denied the right in community with the other members of their group, to enjoy their own culture, to profess and practise their own religion, or to use their own language.

It has to be considered whether Sandra Lovelace, because she is denied the legal right to reside on the Tobique Reserve, has by that fact been denied the right guaranteed by article 27 to persons belonging to minorities, to enjoy their own culture and to use their own language in community with other members of their group.

14 The rights under article 27 of the Covenant have to be secured to "persons belonging" to the minority. At present Sandra Lovelace does not qualify as an Indian under Canadian legislation. However, the Indian Act deals primarily with a number of privileges which, as stated above, do not as such come within the scope of the Covenant. Protection under the Indian Act and protection under article 27 of the Covenant therefore have to be distinguished. Persons who are born and brought up on a reserve, who have kept ties with their community and wish to maintain these ties, must normally be considered as belonging to that minority within the meaning of the Covenant. Since Sandra Lovelace is ethnically a Maliseet Indian and has only been absent from her home reserve for a few years during the existence of her marriage, she is, in the opinion of the Committee, entitled to be regarded as "belonging" to this minority and to claim the benefits of article 27 of the Covenant. The question whether these benefits have been denied to her, depends on how far they extend.

15 The right to live on a reserve is not as such guaranteed by article 27 of the Covenant. Moreover, the Indian Act does not interfere directly with the functions which are expressly mentioned in that article. However, in the opinion of the Committee the right of Sandra Lovelace to access to her native culture and language "in community with the other members" of her group, has in fact been, and continues to be interfered with, because there is no place outside the Tobique Reserve where such a community exists. On the other hand, not every interference can be regarded as a denial of rights within the meaning of article 27. Restrictions on the right to residence, by way of national legislation, cannot be ruled out under article 27 of the Covenant. This also follows from the restrictions to article 12(1) of the Covenant set out in article 12(3). The Committee recognizes the need to define the category of persons entitled to live on a reserve, for such purposes as those explained by the Government regarding protection of its resources and preservation of the identity of its people. However, the obligations which the Government has since undertaken under the Covenant must also be taken into account.

16 In this respect, the Committee is of the view that statutory restrictions affecting the right to residence on a reserve of a person belonging to the minority concerned, must have both a reasonable and objective justification and be consistent with the other

provisions of the Covenant, read as a whole. Article 27 must be construed and applied in the light of the other provisions mentioned above, such as articles 12, 17 and 23 in so far as they may be relevant to the particular case, and also the provisions against discrimination, such as articles 2, 3 and 26, as the case may be. It is not necessary, however, to determine in any general manner which restrictions may be justified under the Covenant, in particular as a result of marriage, because the circumstances are special in the present case.

17 The case of Sandra Lovelace should be considered in the light of the fact that her marriage to a non-Indian has broken up. It is natural that in such a situation she wishes to return to the environment in which she was born, particularly as after the dissolution of her marriage her main cultural attachment again was to the Maliseet band. Whatever may be the merits of the Indian Act in other respects, it does not seem to the Committee that to deny Sandra Lovelace the right to reside on the reserve is reasonable, or necessary to preserve the identity of the tribe. The Committee therefore concludes that to prevent her recognition as belonging to the band is an unjustifiable denial of her rights under article 27 of the Covenant, read in the context of the other provisions referred to.

18 In view of this finding, the Committee does not consider it necessary to examine whether the same facts also show separate breaches of the other rights invoked. The specific rights most directly applicable to her situation are those under article 27 of the Covenant. The rights to choose one's residence (article 12), and the rights aimed at protecting family life and children (articles 17, 23 and 24) are only indirectly at stake in the present case. The facts of the case do not seem to require further examination under those articles. The Committee's finding of a lack of a reasonable justification for the interference with Sandra Lovelace's rights under article 27 of the Covenant also makes it unnecessary, as suggested above (para 12), to examine the general provisions against discrimination (articles 2, 3 and 26) in the context of the present case, and in particular to determine their bearing upon inequalities predating the coming into force of the Covenant for Canada.

19 Accordingly, the Human Rights Committee, acting under article 5(4) of the Optional Protocol to the International Covenant on Civil and Political Rights, is of the view that the facts of the present case, which establish that Sandra Lovelace has been denied the legal right to reside on the Tobique Reserve, disclose a breach by Canada of article 27 of the Covenant.

APPENDIX

Individual opinion submitted by a member of the Human Rights Committee under rule 94 (3) of the Committee's provisional rules of procedure

Individual opinion appended to the Committee's views at the request of Mr Nejib Bouziri

In the Lovelace case, not only article 27 but also articles 2(1), 3, 13(1) and (4) and 26 of the Covenant have been breached, for some of the provisions of the Indian Act are discriminatory, particularly as between men and women. The Act is still in force and, even though the Lovelace case arose before the date on which the Covenant became applicable in Canada, Mrs Lovelace is still suffering from the adverse discriminatory effects of the Act in matters other than that covered by article 27.

RIGHT TO RESPECT FOR FAMILY LIFE

CASE NO 18

MARCKX v BELGIUM

EUROPEAN COURT OF HUMAN RIGHTS

Application No: 6833/74

Judgment: 13 June 1979

Panel: *Judges*: Balladore Pallieri (*President*), Wiarda, Zekia, O'Donoghue, Pedersen, Vilhjálmsson, Ganshof van der Meersch, Fitzmaurice, Bindschedler-Robert, Evrigenis, Lagergren, Gölcüklü, Matscher, Pinheiro Farinha, Garcia de Enterría.

Human rights — Right to respect for family life — Right to marry and found a family — Discrimination on grounds of illegitimacy — Discrimination on the ground of being an unmarried mother — Whether the requirement that the maternal affiliation of an illegitimate child could only be established in Belgian law by a formal act of recognition, which then had effect only as between the mother and child and not the mother's family and child, is consistent with Convention rights — Whether "family" includes "illegitimate" family — Whether bond between a mother and child is sufficient to establish a "family" — Whether "family" extends to family of mother, including grandparents — Belgian Civil Code, art 756 — European Convention for the Protection of Human Rights and Fundamental Freedoms, arts 3, 8, 12 and 14

Human rights — Right to peaceful enjoyment of possessions — Inheritance — Property — Successions "irrégulières" — Right to respect for family life — Whether restrictions on illegitimate child's rights of inheritance regarding mother's and mother's family's property violated Convention rights — Belgian Civil Code, art 756 — European Convention for the Protection of Human Rights and Fundamental Freedoms, arts 8 and 14 — Protocol No 1, art 1

BACKGROUND

Following the birth and registration of her daughter Alexandra (the second applicant), Ms Paula Marckx (the first applicant) was required, as an unmarried mother, to appear before the District Judge on 26 October 1973 for the purposes of making arrangements for her daughter's guardianship, pursuant to article 57 of the Belgian Civil Code.

The child, who had been born out of wedlock on 16 October 1973, effectively did not have a legal mother until she was legally recognised by her mother's voluntary testimony on 29 October 1973, pursuant to article 334 of the Civil Code. During this period she had no inheritance rights on intestacy over her mother's estate, by virtue of article 756 of the Civil Code. Once the child was recognised she acquired the status of "exceptional heir" (*successeur irrégulier*), which gave a more restricted right than that enjoyed by the presumed heir (*héritière présomptive*) applied to a legitimate child. Only with Ms Marckx's adoption of her daughter on 30 October 1974, pursuant to article 349 of Civil Code, did the child acquire full inheritance rights (*héritière présomptive*) over her mother's estate. However even on adoption, Alexandra Marckx had no rights to inherit from any other member of her mother's family. During the period between recognition and adoption Ms Marckx had only limited capacity to make dispositions in her daughter's favour.

The applicants complained that a number of aspects of Belgian law in respect to illegitimacy were in violation of rights guaranteed by the European Convention on Human Rights: article 8 (right to respect for family life) taken alone and together with article 14 (rights to be secured without discrimination); and article 1 of Protocol No 1 (right to peaceful enjoyment of possessions) taken alone and together with article 14. They also complained that the requirement that a mother adopt her illegitimate child in order to secure him or her more favourable rights was itself in violation of Convention rights. In addition they alleged that there was a violation of the right to marry under article 12 and the right not to be subject to degrading treatment prohibited under article 3 of the Convention.

The European Commission of Human Rights found, by majority, that there had been violations of articles 8 and 14 of the Convention and article 1 of Protocol No 1, but not of articles 12 and 3 of the Convention. The case was referred to the European Court of Human Rights.

HELD (finding a violation of article 8 alone and in conjunction with article 14 of the convention)

Applicability of article 8

1   Article 8 made no distinction between the "legitimate" and "illegitimate" family. Article 8 thus applied to the "family life" of the "illegitimate family" as it did to that of the "legitimate family". (Para 31)

The manner of establishing the maternal affiliation of the second applicant (the child)

Article 8 taken alone

2   Paula Marckx was able to establish her daughter's affiliation only through the recognition procedure laid down in article 334 of the Belgian Civil Code, a procedure that presented few difficulties. Nevertheless, the need to resort to this procedure was the result of a refusal fully to acknowledge Paula Marckx's maternity from the moment of the birth of her child. Moreover, in Belgium an unmarried mother was faced with an alternative: if she recognised her child, she would at the same time prejudice it since her capacity to give or bequeath her property to it would be restricted; if she desired to retain the possibility of making such dispositions as she chose in her child's favour, she would be obliged to renounce establishing a family tie with the child in law. This dilemma was not consonant with "respect" for family life and amounted to a violation of article 8 taken alone. (Para 36)

3   Alexandra Marckx had only one method of establishing her maternal affiliation available to her under Belgian law, namely to take legal proceedings for that purpose. There was a risk that the establishment of affiliation would be time-consuming, and that in the interim, the child would remain separated in law from its mother. This system resulted in a lack of respect for the family life of Alexandra Marckx, who, in the eyes of the law, was motherless from 16 to 29 October 1973. Despite the brevity of this period, there was a violation of article 8. (Para 37)

Article 14 in conjunction with article 8

4   The interest of an "illegitimate" child in having a legal bond of affiliation established was no less than that of a "legitimate" child. The support and encouragement of the traditional family in itself was legitimate or even praiseworthy. However, in pursuing this goal, measures whose object or result was, as in the present case, to prejudice the "illegitimate" family were impermissible; members of an "illegitimate" family enjoyed the guarantees of article 8 equally with members of the traditional family. The manner of establishing Alexandra Marckx's maternal affiliation violated, with respect to both applicants, article 14 taken in conjunction with article 8. (Paras 39, 40 and 43)

The extent in law of the family relationships of the second applicant (the child)

5   "Family Life", within the meaning of article 8, included at least the ties between near relatives, for instance, those between grandparents and grandchildren. "Respect for family life" implied an obligation for the State to act in a manner calculated to allow family ties to develop normally. Yet the development of the family life of an unmarried mother and her child whom she has recognised may be hindered if the child does not become a member of the mother's family and if the establishment of affiliation has effects only as between the two of them. There was therefore in this connection a violation of article 8, taken alone, with respect to both applicants. (Para 45)

Patrimonial rights relied on by the second applicant (the child)

6   The restrictions which the Belgian Civil Code placed on Alexandra Marckx's inheritance rights on intestacy were not in themselves in conflict with the Convention. Nonetheless the distinction made between "legitimate" and "illegitimate" children lacked objective and reasonable justification, and was in violation of article 8 taken together with article 14. (Paras 52–56)

Patrimonial rights relied on by the first applicant (the mother)

Article 8, taken both on its own and in conjunction with article 14

7   Article 8 did not guarantee complete freedom to a mother to give or bequeath her property to her child. In principle it left to the Contracting States the choice of the means calculated to allow everyone to lead a formal family life, and such freedom was not indispensable in the pursuit of a normal family life. However, there was no objective and reasonable justification for the distinction made between unmarried and married mothers in this regard and this distinction was therefore contrary to article 14 taken in conjunction with article 8. (Paras 61 and 62)

Article 1 of Protocol No 1, taken both on its own and in conjunction with article 14

8   While there was no violation of article 1 of Protocol No 1 taken alone, there was no general interest or no objective and reasonable justification for a State to limit an unmarried mother's right to make gifts or legacies in favour of her child when at the same time a married woman was not subject to any similar restriction. Therefore there was a violation of Article 1 of Protocol No 1 taken in conjunction with Article 14. (paras 50 and 65)

Articles 3 and 12

9   While the legal rules at issue probably presented aspects which the applicants might feel to be humiliating, they did not constitute degrading treatment within the ambit of article 3. (Para 66)

10 The issue under consideration fell outside the scope of article 12 concerning the right to marry and to found a family. (Para 67)

Treaties and other international instruments referred to

Brussels Convention on the Establishment of Maternal Affiliation of Natural Children 1962

European Convention on the Legal Status of Children Born out of Wedlock 1975, arts 2 and 14(1)

European Convention for the Protection of Human Rights and Fundamental Freedoms 1950, arts 3, 8, 12, 14, 25 and 50

Protocol No 1 to the European Convention for the Protection of Human Rights and Fundamental Freedoms 1952, art 1

Committee of Ministers of the Council of Europe, Resolution (70) 15 of 15 May 1970 on the social protection of unmarried mothers and their children, paras I-10, II-15

National legislation referred to

Belgium

Civil Code, arts 57, 150, 159, 161–162, 203, 319–320, 326–334, 338, 339, 341a–341c, 345(2)(2), 350–356, 365, 368–370, 394, 396, 405, 724, 756–758, 760–761, 769–773, 908 and 913

Constitution, art 6

Cases referred to

Case "Relating to Certain Aspects of the Laws on the Use of Languages in Education in Belgium" v Belgium (Merits ("Belgian Linguistics Case (No 2)"), ECHR, judgment of 23 July 1968, Series A, No 6; 1 EHRR 252

De Becker v Belgium, ECHR, judgment of 27 March 1962, Series A, No 4; 1 EHRR 43

Defrenne v Sabena, ECJ Case C-43/75, [1981] 1 All ER 122; [1976] ECR 455; [1976] 2 CMLR 98; [1976] ICR 547

De Wilde, Ooms and Versyp v Belgium, ECHR, judgment of 10 March 1972, Series A, No 14; 1 EHRR 438

Engel v The Netherlands, ECHR, judgment of 8 June 1976, Series A, No 22; 1 EHRR 647

Golder v The United Kingdom, ECHR, judgment of 21 February 1975, Series A, No 18; 1 EHRR 524

Handyside v The United Kingdom, ECHR, judgment of 7 December 1976; Series A, No 24; 1 EHRR 737

Judgment of the Belgian Court of Cassation (Pasicrisie I, 1967, pp 78–79), 22 September 1966

Klass and Others v Germany, ECHR, judgment of 6 September 1978; Series A, No 28; 2 EHRR 214

National Union of Belgian Police v Belgium, ECHR, judgment of 27 October 1975, Series A, No 19; 1 EHRR 578

JUDGMENT

PROCEDURE

[...]*

AS TO THE FACTS

A   Particular circumstances of the case

8   Alexandra Marckx was born on 16 October 1973 at Wilrijk, near Antwerp; she is the daughter of Paula Marckx, a Belgian national, who is unmarried and a journalist by profession.

Paula Marckx duly reported Alexandra's birth to the Wilrijk registration officer who informed the District Judge (*juge de paix*) as is required by Article 57 *bis* of the Belgian Civil Code ("the Civil Code") in the case of "illegitimate" children.

9   On 26 October 1973, the District Judge of the first district of Antwerp summoned Paula Marckx to appear before him (Article 405) so as to obtain from her the information required to make arrangements for Alexandra's guardianship; at the same time, he informed her of the methods available for recognising her daughter and of the consequences in law of any such recognition (see para 14 below). He also drew her attention to certain provisions of the Civil Code, including Article 756 which concerns "exceptional" forms of inheritance (*successions "irrégulieres"*).

10   On 29 October 1973, Paula Marckx recognised her child in accordance with Article 334 of the Code. She thereby automatically became Alexandra's guardian (Article 396 *bis*); the family council, on which the sister and certain other relatives of Paula Marckx sat under the chairmanship of the District Judge, was empowered to take in Alexandra's interests various measures provided for by law.

11   On 30 October 1974, Paula Marckx adopted her daughter pursuant to Article 394 of the Civil Code. The procedure, which was that laid down by Articles 350 to 356, entailed certain enquiries and involved some expenses. It concluded on 18 April 1975 with a judgment confirming the adoption, the effect whereof was retroactive to the date of the instrument of adoption, namely, 30 October 1974.

12   At the time of her application to the Commission, Ms Paula Marckx's family included, besides Alexandra, her own mother, Mrs Victorine Libot, who died in August 1974, and a sister, Mrs Blanche Marckx.

---

*   **Eds:** paras 1-7, which relate to procedural matters, have not been included.

13 The applicants complain of the Civil Code provisions on the manner of establishing the maternal affiliation of an "illegitimate" child and on the effects of establishing such affiliation as regards both the extent of the child's family relationships and the patrimonial rights of the child and of its mother. The applicants also put in issue the necessity for the mother to adopt the child if she wishes to increase its rights.

B   Current law

(1)   Establishment of the maternal affiliation of an "illegitimate child"

14 Under Belgian law, no legal bond between an unmarried mother and her child results from the mere fact of birth: whilst the birth certificate recorded at the register office suffices to prove the maternal affiliation of the married woman's children (Article 319 of the Civil Code), the maternal affiliation of an "illegitimate" child is established by means either of a voluntary recognition by the mother or of legal proceedings taken for the purpose (*action en recherche de maternité*).

Nevertheless, an unrecognised "illegitimate" child bears its mother's name which must appear on the birth certificate (Article 57). The appointment of its guardian is a matter for the family council which is presided over by the District Judge.

Under Article 334, recognition, "if not inserted in the birth certificate, shall be effected by a formal deed". Recognition is declaratory and not attributive: it does not create but records the child's status and is retroactive to the date of birth. However, it does not necessarily follow that the person effecting recognition is actually the child's mother; on the contrary, any interested party may claim that the recognition does not correspond to the truth (Article 339). Many unmarried mothers – about 25% according to the Government, although the applicants consider this an exaggerated figure – do not recognise their child.

Proceedings to establish maternal affiliation (*action en recherche de maternité*) may be instituted by the child within five years from its attainment of majority or, whilst it is still a minor, by its legal representative with the consent of the family council (Articles 341a–341c of the Civil Code).

(2)   Effects of the establishment of maternal affiliation

15 The establishment of maternal affiliation of an "illegitimate" child has limited effects as regards both the extent of its family relationships and the rights of the child and its mother in the matter of inheritance on intestacy and voluntary dispositions.

(a)   The extent of family relationships

16 In the context of the maternal affiliation of an "illegitimate" child, Belgian legislation does not employ the concepts of "family" and "relative". Even once such affiliation has been established, it in principle creates a legal bond with the mother alone. The child does not become a member of its mother's family. The law excludes it from that family as regards inheritance rights on intestacy (see para 17 below). Furthermore, if the child's parents are dead or under an incapacity, it cannot marry, before attaining the age of 21, without consent, which has to be given by its guardian (Article 159 of the Civil Code) and not, as is the case for a "legitimate" child, by his grandparents (Article 150); the law does not expressly create any maintenance obligations, etc, between the child and its grandparents. However, certain texts make provision for exceptions, for example as regards the impediments to marriage (Articles 161 and 162). According to a judgment of the Belgian Court of Cassation (Pasicrisie I, 1967, pp 78–79 (22 September 1966)), these

texts "place the bonds existing between an illegitimate child and its grandparents on a legal footing based on the affection, respect and devotion that are the consequence of consanguinity ... [which] creates an obligation for the ascendants to take an interest in their descendants and, as a corollary, gives them the right, whenever this is not excluded by the law, to know and protect them and exercise over them the influence dictated by affection and devotion". The Court of Cassation deduced from this that grandparents were entitled to a right to access to the child.

(b)   Rights of a child born out of wedlock and of his mother in the matter of inheritance on intestacy and voluntary dispositions.

17 A recognised "illegitimate" child's rights of inheritance on intestacy are less than those of a "legitimate" child. As appears from Articles 338, 724, 756, 760, 761, 769 to 773 and 913 of the Civil Code, a recognised "illegitimate" child does not have, in the estate of its parent who dies intestate, the status of heir, but solely that of "exceptional heir" (*successeur irrégulier*): it has to seek a court order putting it in possession of the estate (*envoi en possession*). It is the sole beneficiary of its deceased mother's estate only if she leaves no relatives entitled to inherit (Article 758); otherwise, its maximum entitlement – which arises when its mother leaves no descendants, ascendants, brothers or sisters – is three-quarters of the share which it would have taken if "legitimate" (Article 757). Furthermore, its mother may, during her life-time, reduce that entitlement by one-half. Finally, Article 756 denies to the "illegitimate" child any rights on intestacy in the estate of its mother's relatives.

18 Recognised "illegitimate" children are also at a disadvantage as regards voluntary dispositions, since Article 908 provides that they "may receive by disposition *inter vivos* or by will no more than their entitlement under the title 'Inheritance on Intestacy'".

Conversely, the mother of such a child, unless she has no relatives entitled to inherit, may give in her lifetime or bequeath to it only part of her property. On the other hand, if the child's affiliation has not been established, the mother may so give or bequeath to it the whole of her property, provided that there are no heirs entitled to a reserved portion of her estate (*héritiers réservataires*). The mother is thus faced with the following alternative: either she recognises the child and loses the possibility of leaving all her estate to it; or she renounces establishing with it a family relationship in the eyes of the law, in order to retain the possibility of leaving all her estate to it just as she might to a stranger.

(3)   Adoption of "illegitimate" children by their mother

19 If the mother of a recognised "illegitimate" child remains unmarried, she has but one means of improving its status, namely, "simple" adoption. In such cases, the age requirements for this form of adoption are eased by Article 345(2)(2) of the Civil Code. The adopted child acquires over the adopter's estate the rights of a "legitimate" child but, unlike the latter, has no rights on intestacy in the estates of its mother's relatives (Article 365).

Only legitimation (Article 331–333) and legitimation by adoption (Articles 368–370) place an "illegitimate" child on exactly the same footing as a "legitimate" child; both of these measures presuppose the mother's marriage.

C   The Bill submitted to the Senate on 15 February 1978

20 Belgium has signed, but not yet ratified, the Brussels Convention of 12 September 1962 on the Establishment of Maternal Affiliation of Natural Children, which was

prepared by the International Commission on Civil Status and entered into force on 23 April 1964. Neither has Belgium yet ratified, nor even signed, the Convention of 15 October 1975 on the Legal Status of Children Born out of Wedlock, which was concluded within the Council of Europe and entered into force on 11 August 1978. Both of these instruments are based on the principle *mater semper certa est*; the second of them also regulates such questions as maintenance obligations, parental authority and rights of succession.

21 However, the Belgian Government submitted to the Senate on 15 February 1978 a Bill to which they referred the Court. The official statement of reasons accompanying the Bill, which mentions, *inter alia*, the Conventions of 1962 and 1975 cited above, states that the Bill "seeks to institute equality in law between all children". In particular, maternal affiliation would be established on the mother's name being entered on the birth certificate, which would introduce into Belgian law the principle *mater semper certa est*. Recognition by an unmarried mother would accordingly no longer be necessary, unless there were no such entry. Furthermore, the Civil Code would confer on children born out of wedlock rights identical to those presently enjoyed by children born in wedlock in the matter of inheritance on intestacy and voluntary dispositions.

PROCEEDINGS BEFORE THE COMMISSION

22 The essence of the applicants' allegations before the Commission was as follows:

– as an "illegitimate" child, Alexandra Marckx is the victim, as a result of certain provisions of the Belgian Civil Code, of a *capitis deminutio* incompatible with Articles 3 and 8 of the Convention;

– this *capitis deminutio* also violates the said articles with respect to Paula Marckx;

– there are instances of discrimination, contrary to Article 14 taken in conjunction with Article 8, between "legitimate" and "illegitimate" children and between unmarried and married mothers;

– the fact that an "illegitimate" child may be recognised by any man, even if he is not the father, violates Articles 3, 8 and 14;

– Article 1 of Protocol No 1 is violated by reason of the fact that an unmarried mother is not free to dispose of her property in favour of her child.

23 By partial decision of 16 March 1975, the Commission declared the penultimate complaint inadmissible. On 29 September 1975, it accepted the remainder of the application and also decided to take into consideration *ex officio* Article 12 of the Convention.

In its report of 10 December 1977, the Commission expresses the opinion:

– by ten votes to four, "that the situation" complained of "constitutes a violation of Article 8 of the Convention with respect to the illegitimate child" as far as, firstly, the "principle of recognition and the procedure for recognition" and, secondly, the "effects" of recognition are concerned;

– by nine votes to four with one abstention, that the "simple" adoption of Alexandra by her mother "has not remedied" the situation complained of in that "it maintains an improper restriction on the concept of family life", with the result that "the position complained of constitutes a violation of Article 8 with respect to the applicants";

– by twelve votes with two abstentions, "that the legislation as applied constitutes a violation of Article 8 in conjunction with Article 14 with respect to the applicants";

- by nine votes to six, that the "Belgian legislation as applied violates Article 1 of the First Protocol in conjunction with Article 14 of the Convention" with respect to the first, but not to the second, applicant;
- that it is not "necessary" to examine the case under Article 3 of the Convention; and
- unanimously, that "Article 12 is not relevant".

The report contains one separate opinion.

FINAL SUBMISSIONS MADE TO THE COURT

24 At the hearings on 24 October 1978, the Government confirmed the submission appearing in their memorial, namely:

> That the Court should decide that the facts related by the Commission in its report do not disclose a violation by the Belgian State, in the case of the applicants Paula and Alexandra Marckx, of the obligations imposed by the Convention.

The Delegates of the Commission, for their part, made the following submission at the hearings:

> May it please the Court to decide whether the Belgian legislation complained of violates, in the case of the applicants, the rights guaranteed to them by Article 8 of the Convention and Article 1 of Protocol No 1, taken alone or in conjunction with Article 14 of the Convention.

AS TO THE LAW

I   On the Government's preliminary plea

25 The application of the Civil Code provisions concerning children born out of wedlock and unmarried mothers is alleged by the applicants to contravene, with respect to them, Articles 3, 8, 12 and 14 of the Convention and Article 1 of Protocol No 1.

26 In reply, the Government first contends – if not by way of an objection of lack of jurisdiction or inadmissibility as such, at least by way of a preliminary plea – that the issues raised by the applicants are essentially theoretical in their case. The Government illustrate this by the following points: the child Alexandra Marckx did not suffer from the fact that her maternal affiliation was not established as soon as she was born (16 October 1973) but only thirteen days later, when she was recognised, since at the time she was unaware of the circumstances of her birth; her mother, Paula Marckx, was acting of her own accord, and not under duress, when she recognised Alexandra (29 October 1973) and when she adopted her (30 October 1974); there is nothing to indicate that, during the interval of a year and a day between these two latter dates, Paula Marckx had any wish to make, by will or by gift inter vivos, a provision for her daughter more generous than that stipulated by Article 908 of the Civil Code; a very substantial proportion of the expenses incurred by Paula Marckx for the adoption could have been avoided; since 30 October 1974, Alexandra's position *vis-à-vis* her mother has been the same as that of a "legitimate" child. Briefly, the applicants are overlooking, in the Government's submission, the fact that it is not the Court's function to rule *in abstracto* on the compatibility with the Convention of certain legal rules. (*Golder* judgment of 21 February 1975, Series A, No 18, para 39).

The Commission's response is that it did not examine the impugned legislation *in abstracto* since the applicants are relying on specific and concrete facts.

27 The Court does not share the Government's view. Article 25 of the Convention entitles individuals to contend that a law violates their rights by itself, in the absence of an individual measure of implementation, if they run the risk of being directly affected by it (see, *mutatis mutandis*, the *Klass and others* judgment of 6 September 1978, Series A, No 28, para 33). Such is indeed the standpoint of the applicants: they raise objections to several Articles of the Civil Code which applied or apply to them automatically. In submitting that these articles are contrary to the Convention and to Protocol No 1, the applicants are not inviting the Court to undertake an abstract review of rules which, as such, would be incompatible with Article 25 (see in addition to the two judgments cited above, the *De Becker* judgment of 27 March 1962, Series A, No 4 p 26 *in fine*, and the *De Wilde, Ooms and Versyp* judgment of 10 March 1972, Series A, No 14, para 22): they are challenging a legal position – that of unmarried mothers and of children born out of wedlock – which affects them personally.

The Government appear, in short, to consider that this position is not or is barely detrimental to the applicants. The Court recalls in this respect that the question of the existence of prejudice is not a matter for Article 25 which, in its use of the word "victim", denotes "the person directly affected by the act or omission which is in issue" (above-cited *De Wilde, Ooms and Versyp* judgment, paras 23–24; see also the *Engel and others* judgments of 8 June and 23 November 1976, Series A, No 22, para 89 and para 11).

Paula and Alexandra Marckx can therefore "claim" to be victims of the breaches of which they complain. In order to ascertain whether they are actually victims, the merits of each of their contentions have to be examined.

II   On the merits

28 The applicants rely basically on Articles 8 and 14 of the Convention. Without overlooking the other provisions which they invoke, the Court has accordingly turned primarily to these two articles in its consideration of the three aspects of the problem referred to it by the Commission: the manner of establishing affiliation, the extent of the child's family relationships, the patrimonial rights of the child and of her mother.

29 Article 8 of the Convention provides:

1   Everyone has the right to respect for his private and family life, his home and his correspondence.

2   There shall be no interference by a public authority with the exercise of this right except such as is in accordance with the law and is necessary in a democratic society in the interests of national security, public safety or the economic well-being of the country, for the prevention of disorder or crime, for the protection of health or morals, or for the protection of the rights and freedoms of others.

30 The Court is led in the present case to clarify the meaning and purport of the words "respect for ... private and family life", which it has scarcely had the occasion to do until now (judgment of 23 July 1968 in the *"Belgian Linguistic"* case, Series A, No 6, para 7; *Klass and others* judgment of 6 September 1978, Series A, No 21, para 41).

31 The first question for decision is whether the natural tie between Paula and Alexandra Marckx gave rise to a family life protected by Article 8.

By guaranteeing the right to respect for family life, Article 8 presupposes the existence of a family. The Court concurs entirely with the Commission's established case law on a crucial point, namely, that Article 8 makes no distinction between the "legitimate" and the "illegitimate" family. Such a distinction would not be consonant with the word "everyone", and this is confirmed by Article 14 with its prohibition, in the enjoyment of the rights and freedoms enshrined in the Convention, of discrimination grounded on "birth". In addition, the Court notes that the Committee of Ministers of the Council of Europe regards the single woman and her child as one form of family no less than others. (Resolution (70) 15 of 15 May 1970 on the social protection of unmarried mothers and their children, paras I-10, II-15, etc).

Article 8 thus applies to the "family life" of the "illegitimate" family as it does to that of the "legitimate" family. Besides, it is not disputed that Paula Marckx assumed responsibility for her daughter Alexandra from the moment of her birth and has continuously cared for her, with the result that a real family life existed and still exists between them.

It remains to be ascertained what the "respect" for this family life required of the Belgian legislature is in each of the areas covered by the application.

By proclaiming in para 1 the right to respect for family life, Article 8 signifies first that the State cannot interfere with the exercise of that right otherwise than in accordance with the strict conditions set out in para 2. As the Court stated in the *Belgian Linguistic* case, the object of the Article is "essentially" that of protecting the individual against arbitrary interference by the public authorities (judgment of 23 July 1968, Series A, No 6, para 7). Nevertheless it does not merely compel the State to abstain from such interference: in addition to this primarily negative undertaking, there may be positive obligations inherent in an effective "respect" for family life.

This means, amongst other things, that when the State determines in its domestic legal system the regime applicable to certain family ties such as those between an unmarried mother and her child, it must act in a manner calculated to allow those concerned to lead a normal family life. As envisaged by Article 8, respect for family life implies in particular, in the Court's view, the existence in domestic law of legal safeguards that render possible, as from the moment of birth, the child's integration in its family. In this connection, the State has a choice of various means, but a law that fails to satisfy this requirement violates para 1 of Article 8 without there being any call to examine it under para 2.

Article 8 being therefore relevant to the present case, the Court has to review in detail each of the applicants' complaints in the light of this provision.

32 Article 14 provides:

> The enjoyment of the rights and freedoms set forth in this Convention shall be secured without discrimination on any ground such as sex, race, colour, language, religion, political or other opinion, national or social origin, associated with a national minority, property, birth or other status.

The Court's case law shows that, although Article 14 has no independent existence, it may play an important autonomous role by complementing the other normative provisions of the Convention and the Protocols: Article 14 safeguards individuals, placed in similar situations, from any discrimination in the enjoyment of the rights and freedoms set forth in those other provisions. A measure which, although in itself in conformity with the requirements of the Article of the Convention or the Protocols enshrining a given right or freedom, is of a discriminatory nature incompatible with Article 14, therefore violates those two articles taken in conjunction. It is as though Article 14 formed an integral part of each of the provisions laying down rights and freedoms (judgment of 23 July 1968 in the *Belgian Linguistic* case, Series A, No 6, para 9; *National Union of Belgian Police* judgment of 27 October 1975, Series A, No 19, para 44).

Accordingly, and since Article 8 is relevant to the present case (see para 31 above), it is necessary also to take into account Article 14 in conjunction with Article 8.

33 According to the Court's established case law, a distinction is discriminatory if it "has no objective and reasonable justification", that is, if it does not pursue a "legitimate aim" or if there is not a "reasonable relationship of proportionality between the means employed and the aim sought to be realised" (see, *inter alia*, the above-cited *"Belgian Linguistic"* judgment of 23 July 1968, Series A, No 6, para 10).

34 In acting in a manner calculated to allow the family life of an unmarried mother and her child to develop normally (see para 31 above), the State must avoid any discrimination grounded on birth: this is dictated by Article 14 taken in conjunction with Article 8.

A   On the manner of establishing Alexandra Marckx's maternal affiliation

35 Under Belgian law, the maternal affiliation of an "illegitimate" child is established neither by its birth alone nor even by the entry – obligatory under Article 57 of the Civil Code – of the mother's name on the birth certificate; Articles 334 and 341a require either a voluntary recognition or a court declaration as to maternity. On the other hand, under Article 319, the affiliation of a married woman's child is proved simply by the birth certificate recorded at the registry office (see para 14 above).

The applicants see this system as violating, with respect to them, Article 8 of the Convention, taken both alone and in conjunction with Article 14. This is contested by the Government. The Commission, for its part, finds a breach of Article 8, taken both alone and in conjunction with Article 14, with respect to Alexandra, and a breach of Article 14, taken in conjunction with Article 8, with respect to Paula Marckx.

1   On the alleged violation of Article 8 of the Convention, taken alone

36 Paula Marckx was able to establish Alexandra's affiliation only by the means afforded by Article 334 of the Civil Code, namely, recognition. The effect of recognition is declaratory and not attributive: it does not create but records the child's status. It is irrevocable and retroactive to the date of birth. Furthermore, the procedure to be followed hardly presents difficulties: the declaration may take the form of a notarial deed, but it may also be added, at any time and without expense to the record of the birth at the registry office (see para 14 above).

Nevertheless, the necessity to have recourse to such an expedient derived from a refusal fully to acknowledge Paula Marckx's maternity from the moment of the birth. Moreover, in Belgium an unmarried mother is faced with an alternative: if she recognises her child (assuming she wishes to do so), she will at the same time prejudice it since her capacity to give or bequeath her property to it will be restricted; if she desires to retain the possibility of making such dispositions as she chooses in her child's favour, she will be obliged to renounce establishing a family tie with it in law (see para 18 above). Admittedly, that possibility, which is now open to her in the absence of recognition, would disappear entirely under the current Civil Code (Article 908) if, as is the applicants' wish, the mere mention of the mother's name on the birth certificate were to constitute proof of any "illegitimate" child's maternal affiliation. However, the dilemma which exists at present is not consonant with "respect" for family life; it thwarts and impedes the normal development of such life (see para 31 above). Furthermore, it appears from paras 60 to 65 below that the unfavourable consequences of recognition in the area of patrimonial rights are of themselves contrary to Article 14 of the Convention, taken in conjunction with Article 8 and with Article 1 of Protocol No 1.

The Court thus concludes that there has been a violation of Article 8, taken alone, with respect to the first applicant.

37 As regards Alexandra Marckx, only one method of establishing her maternal affiliation was available to her under Belgian law, namely, to take legal proceedings for the purpose (*recherche de maternité*). (Articles 341a–341c of the Civil Code). Although a judgment declaring the affiliation of an "illegitimate" child has the same effects as a voluntary recognition, the procedure applicable is, in the nature of things, far more complex. Quite apart from the conditions of proof that have to be satisfied, the legal representative of an infant needs the consent of the family council before he can bring, assuming he wishes to do so, an action for a declaration as to status; it is only after attaining majority that the child can bring such an action itself (see para 14 above). There is thus a risk that the establishment of affiliation will be time-consuming and that, in the interim, the child will remain separated in law from its mother. This system resulted in a lack of respect for the family life of Alexandra Marckx who, in the eyes of the law, was motherless from 16 to 29 October 1973. Despite the brevity of this period, there was thus also a violation of Article 8 with respect to the second applicant.

2 On the alleged violation of Article 14 of the Convention, taken in conjunction with Article 8

38 The Court also has to determine whether, as regards the manner of establishing Alexandra's maternal affiliation, one or both of the applicants have been victims of discrimination contrary to Article 14 taken in conjunction with Article 8.

39 The Government, relying on the difference between the situations of the unmarried and the married mother, advance the following arguments: whilst the married mother and her husband "mutually undertake ... the obligation to feed, keep and educate their children" (Article 203 of the Civil Code), there is no certainty that the unmarried mother will be willing to bear on her own the responsibilities of motherhood; by leaving the unmarried mother the choice between recognising her child or dissociating herself from it, the law is prompted by a concern for protection of the child, for it would be dangerous to entrust it to the custody and authority of someone who has shown no inclination to care for it; many unmarried mothers do not recognise their child (see para 14 above).

In the Court's judgment, the fact that some unmarried mothers, unlike Paula Marckx, do not wish to take care of their child cannot justify the rule of Belgian law whereby the establishment of their maternity is conditional on voluntary recognition or a court declaration. In fact, such an attitude is not a general feature of the relationship between unmarried mothers and their children; besides, this is neither claimed by the Government nor proved by the figures which they advance. As the Commission points out, it may happen that also a married mother might not wish to bring up her child, and yet, as far as she is concerned, the birth alone will have created the legal bond of affiliation.

Again, the interest of an "illegitimate" child in having such a bond established is no less than that of a "legitimate" child. However, the "illegitimate" child is likely to remain motherless in the eyes of Belgian law. If an "illegitimate" child is not recognised voluntarily, it has only one expedient, namely, an action to establish maternal affiliation (see para 14 above) (Articles 341a–341c of the Civil Code). A married woman's child also is entitled to institute such an action (Articles 326–330), but in the vast majority of cases the entries on the birth certificate (Article 319) or, failing that, the constant and factual enjoyment of the status of a legitimate child (*une possession d'état constante*, Article 320) render this unnecessary.

40 The Government do not deny that the present law favours the traditional family, but they maintain that the law aims at ensuring that family's full development and is thereby founded on objective and reasonable grounds relating to morals and public order (*ordre public*).

The Court recognises that support and encouragement of the traditional family is in itself legitimate or even praiseworthy. However, in the achievement of this end recourse must not be had to measures whose object or result is, as in the present case, to prejudice the "illegitimate" family; the members of the "illegitimate" family enjoy the guarantees of Article 8 on an equal footing with the members of the traditional family.

41 The Government concede that the law at issue may appear open to criticism but plead that the problem of reforming it arose only several years after the entry into force of the European Convention on Human Rights in respect of Belgium (14 June 1955), that is, with the adoption of the Brussels Convention of 12 September 1962 on the Establishment of Maternal Affiliation of Natural Children (see para 20 above).

It is true that, at the time when the Convention of 4 November 1950 was drafted, it was regarded as permissible and normal in many European countries to draw a distinction in this area between the "illegitimate" and the "legitimate" family. However, the Court recalls that this Convention must be interpreted in the light of present-day conditions (*Tyrer* judgment of 25 April 1978, Series A, No 26, para 31). In the instant case, the Court cannot but be struck by the fact that the domestic law of the great majority of the member States of the Council of Europe has evolved and is continuing to evolve, in company with the relevant international instruments, towards full juridical recognition of the maxim "*mater semper certa est*".

Admittedly, of the ten States that drew up the Brussels Convention, only eight have signed and only four have ratified it to date. The European Convention of 15 October 1975 on the Legal Status of Children Born out of Wedlock has at present been signed by only ten and ratified by only four members of the Council of Europe. Furthermore, Article 14 (1) of the latter Convention permits any State to make, at the most, three reservations, one of which could theoretically concern precisely the manner of establishing the maternal affiliation of a child born out of wedlock (Article 2). However, this state of affairs cannot be relied on in opposition to the evolution noted above. Both the relevant Conventions are in force and there is no reason to attribute the currently small number of Contracting States to a refusal to admit equality between "illegitimate" and "legitimate" children on the point under consideration. In fact, the existence of these two treaties denotes that there is a clear measure of common ground in this area amongst modern societies.

The official statement of reasons accompanying the Bill submitted by the Belgian Government to the Senate on 15 February 1978 (see para 21 above) provides an illustration of this evolution of rules and attitudes. Amongst other things, the statement points out that "in recent years several Western European countries, including the Federal Republic of Germany, Great Britain, the Netherlands, France, Italy and Switzerland have adopted new legislation radically altering the traditional structure of the law of affiliation and establishing almost complete equality between legitimate and illegitimate children". It is also noted that "the desire to put an end to all discrimination and abolish all inequalities based on birth is apparent in the work of various international institutions". As regards Belgium itself, the statement stresses that the difference of treatment between Belgian citizens, depending on whether their affiliation is established in or out of wedlock, amounts to a "flagrant exception" to the fundamental principle of the equality of everyone before the law (Art 6 of the Constitution). It adds that "lawyers and public opinion are becoming increasingly convinced that the discrimination against [illegitimate] children should be ended".

42 The Government maintain, finally, that the introduction of the rule *"mater semper certa est"* should be accompanied, as is contemplated in the 1978 Bill, by a reform of the provisions on the establishment of paternity, failing which there would be a considerable and one-sided increase in the responsibilities of the unmarried mother. Thus, for the Government, there is a comprehensive problem and any piecemeal solution would be dangerous.

The Court confines itself to noting that it is required to rule only on certain aspects of the maternal affiliation of "illegitimate" children under Belgian law. It does not exclude that a judgment finding a breach of the Convention on one of those aspects might render desirable or necessary a reform of the law on other matters not submitted for examination in the present proceedings. It is for the respondent State, and the respondent State alone, to take the measures it considers appropriate to ensure that its domestic law is coherent and consistent.

43 The distinction complained of therefore lacks objective and reasonable justification. Accordingly, the manner of establishing Alexandra Marckx's maternal affiliation violated, with respect to both applicants, Article 14 taken in conjunction with Article 8.

B   On the extent in law of Alexandra Marckx's family relationships

44 Under Belgian law, a "legitimate" child is fully integrated from the moment of its birth into the family of each of its parents, whereas a recognised "illegitimate" child, and even an adopted "illegitimate" child, remains in principle a stranger to its parents' families (see para 16 above). In fact, the legislation makes provision for some exceptions – and recent case law is tending to add more – but it denies a child born out of wedlock any rights over the estates of its father's or mother's relatives (Article 756 *in fine* of the Civil Code), it does not expressly create any maintenance obligations between it and those relatives, and it empowers its guardian rather than those relatives to give consent, where appropriate, to its marriage (Article 159, as compared with Article 150), etc.

It thus appears that in certain respects Alexandra never had a legal relationship with her mother's family, for example with her maternal grandmother, Mrs Victorine Libot, who died in August 1974, or with her aunt, Mrs Blanche Marckx (see para 12 above).

The applicants regard this situation as incompatible with Article 8 of the Convention, taken both alone and in conjunction with Article 14. This is contested by the Government. The Commission, for its part, finds a breach of the requirements of Article 8, taken both alone and in conjunction with Article 14, with respect to Alexandra, and a breach of Article 14 taken in conjunction with Article 8, with respect to Paula Marckx.

1   On the alleged violation of Article 8 of the Convention, taken alone

45 In the Court's opinion, "family life", within the meaning of Article 8, includes at least the ties between near relatives, for instance, those between grandparents and grandchildren, since such relatives may play a considerable part in family life.

"Respect" for a family life so understood implies an obligation for the State to act in a manner calculated to allow these ties to develop normally (see, *mutatis mutandis*, para 31 above). Yet the development of the family life of an unmarried mother and her child whom she has recognised may be hindered if the child does not become a member of the mother's family and if the establishment of affiliation has effects only as between the two of them.

46 It is objected by the Government that Alexandra's grandparents were not parties to the case and, furthermore, that there is no evidence before the Court as to the actual existence, now or in the past, of relations between Alexandra and her grandparents, the normal manifestations whereof were hampered by Belgian law.

The Court does not agree. The fact that Mrs Victorine Libot did not apply to the Commission in no way prevents the applicants from complaining, on their own account, of the exclusion of one of them from the other's family. Besides, there is nothing to prove the absence of actual relations between Alexandra and her grandmother before the latter's death; in addition, the information obtained at the hearings suggests that Alexandra apparently has such relations with an aunt.

47 There is thus in this connection violation of Article 8, taken alone, with respect to both applicants.

2   On the alleged violation of Article 14 of the Convention, taken in conjunction with Article 8

48 It remains for the Court to determine whether, as regards the extent in law of Alexandra's family relationships, one or both of the applicants have been victims of discrimination in breach of Article 14 taken in conjunction with Article 8. One of the differences of treatment found in this area between "illegitimate" and "legitimate" children concerns inheritance rights on intestacy (Article 756 in fine of the Civil Code); the Court's opinion on this aspect appears at paras 56 to 59 below. With respect to the other differences, the Government do not put forward any arguments beyond those they rely on in connection with the manner of establishing affiliation (see paras 39 to 42 above). The Court discerns no objective and reasonable justification for the differences of treatment now being considered. Admittedly, the "tranquillity" of "legitimate" families may sometimes be disturbed if an "illegitimate" child is included, in the eyes of the law, in his mother's family on the same footing as a child born in wedlock, but this is not a motive that justifies depriving the former child of fundamental rights. The Court also refers, *mutatis mutandis*, to the reasons set out in paras 40 and 41 of the present Judgment.

The distinction complained of therefore violates, with respect to both applicants, Article 14 taken in conjunction with Article 8.

C   On the patrimonial rights relied on by the applicants

49 The Civil Code limits, in varying degrees, the rights of an "illegitimate" child and its unmarried mother as regards both inheritance on intestacy and dispositions *inter vivos* or by will (see paras 17 and 18 above).

Until her recognition on 29 October 1973, the fourteenth day of her life, Alexandra had, by virtue of Article 756, no inheritance rights on intestacy over her mother's estate. On that date she did not acquire the status of presumed heir (*héritière présomptive*) of her mother, but merely that of "exceptional heir" (*successeur irrégulier*) (Articles 756–758, 760 and 773). It was only Alexandra's adoption, on 30 October 1974, that conferred on her the rights of a "legitimate" child over Paula Marckx's estate (Article 365). Moreover, Alexandra has never had any inheritance rights on intestacy as regards the estate of any member of her mother's family (Articles 756 and 365).

In the interval between her recognition and her adoption, Alexandra could receive from her mother by disposition *inter vivos* or by will no more than her entitlement under the Code under the title "Inheritance on Intestacy" (Article 908). This restriction on her capacity, like that on Paula Marckx's capacity to dispose of her property, did not exist before 29 October 1973 and disappeared on 30 October 1974.

On the other hand, the Belgian Civil Code confers on "legitimate" children, from the moment of their birth and even of their conception, all those patrimonial rights which it denied and denies Alexandra; the capacity of married women to dispose of their property is not restricted by the Code in the same way as that of Paula Marckx.

According to the applicants, this system contravenes in regard to them Article 8 of the Convention, taken both alone and in conjunction with Article 14, and also, in Paula Marckx's case, Article 1 of Protocol No 1, taken both alone and in conjunction with Article 14. This is contested by the Government. The Commission, for its part, finds only a breach of Article 14, taken in conjunction with Article 1 of Protocol No 1, with respect to Paula Marckx.

1   On the patrimonial rights relied on by Alexandra

50   As concerns the second applicant, the Court has taken its stand solely on Article 8 of the Convention, taken both alone and in conjunction with Article 14. The Court in fact excludes Article 1 of Protocol No 1: like the Commission and the Government, it notes that this Article does no more than enshrine the right of everyone to the peaceful enjoyment of "his" possessions, that consequently it applies only to a person's existing possessions and that it does not guarantee the right to acquire possessions whether on intestacy or through voluntary dispositions. Besides, the applicants do not appear to have relied on this provision in support of Alexandra's claims. Since Article 1 of the Protocol proves to be inapplicable, Article 14 of the Convention cannot be combined with it on the point now being considered.

51   The applicants regard the patrimonial rights they claim as forming part of family rights and, hence, as being a matter for Article 8. This reasoning is disputed by the Government. Neither does the majority of the Commission agree with the applicants, but, as the Principal Delegate indicated at the hearings, a minority of six members considers the right of succession between children and parents, and between grandchildren and grandparents, to be so closely related to family life that it comes within the sphere of Article 8.

52   The Court shares the view of the minority. Matters of intestate succession – and of disposition – between near relatives prove to be intimately connected with family life. Family life does not include only social, moral or cultural relations, for example in the sphere of children's education; it also comprises interests of a material kind, as is shown by, amongst other things, the obligations in respect of maintenance and the position occupied in the domestic legal systems of the majority of the Contracting States by the institution of the reserved portion of an estate (*réserve héréditaire*). Whilst inheritance rights are not normally exercised until the estate-owner's death, that is, at a time when family life undergoes a change or even comes to an end, this does not mean that no issue concerning such rights may arise before the death: the distribution of the estate may be settled, and in practice fairly often is settled, by the making of a will or of a gift on account of a future inheritance (*avance d'hoirie*); it therefore represents a feature of family life that cannot be disregarded.

53 Nevertheless, it is not a requirement of Article 8 that a child should be entitled to some share in the estates of his parents or even of other near relatives: in the matter of patrimonial rights also, Article 8 in principle leaves to the Contracting States the choice of the means calculated to allow everyone to lead a normal family life (see para 31 above) and such an entitlement is not indispensable in the pursuit of a normal family life. In consequence, the restrictions which the Belgian Civil Code places on Alexandra Marckx's inheritance rights on intestacy are not of themselves in conflict with the Convention, that is, if they are considered independently of the reason underlying them. Similar reasoning is to be applied to the question of voluntary dispositions.

54 On the other hand, the distinction made in these two respects between "illegitimate" and "legitimate" children does raise an issue under Articles 14 and 8 when they are taken in conjunction.

55 Until she was adopted (30 October 1974), Alexandra had only a capacity to receive property from Paula Marckx (see para 49 above) that was markedly less than that which a child born in wedlock would have enjoyed. The Court considers that this difference of treatment, in support of which the Government put forward no special argument, lacks objective and reasonable justification: reference is made, *mutatis mutandis*, to paras 40 and 41 above.

However, the Government plead that since 30 October 1974 the second applicant has had, *vis-à-vis* the first applicant, the patrimonial rights of a "legitimate" child; they therefore consider it superfluous to deal with the earlier period.

This argument represents, in essence, no more than one branch of the preliminary plea that has already been set aside (see paras 26 and 27 above). Moreover, in common with the Commission, the Court finds that the need to have recourse to adoption in order to eliminate the said difference of treatment involves of itself discrimination. As the applicants emphasised, the procedure employed for this purpose in the present case is one that usually serves to establish legal ties between one individual and another's child; to oblige in practice an unmarried mother to utilise such a procedure if she wishes to improve her own daughter's situation as regards patrimonial rights amounts to disregarding the tie of blood and to using the institution of adoption for an extraneous purpose. Besides, the procedure to be followed is somewhat lengthy and complicated. Above all, the child is left entirely at the mercy of his parent's initiative, for he is unable to apply to the courts for his adoption.

56 Unlike a "legitimate" child, Alexandra has at no time before or after 30 October 1974 had any entitlement on intestacy in the estates of members of Paula Marckx's family (see para 49 above). Here again, the Court fails to find any objective and reasonable justification.

In the Government's submission, the reason why adoption in principle confers on the adopted child no patrimonial rights as regards relatives of the adopter is that the relatives may not have approved of the adoption. The Court does not have to decide this point in the present proceedings since it considers discriminatory the need for a mother to adopt her child (see para 55 above).

57 As regards the sum total of the patrimonial rights claimed by the second applicant, the Court notes that the Bill submitted to the Senate on 15 February 1978 (see para 21 above) advocates, in the name of the principle of equality, "the abolition of the inferior status characterising, in matters of inheritance, the lot of illegitimate children" as compared with children born in wedlock.

58 The Government also state that they appreciate that an increase in the "illegitimate" child's inheritance rights is considered indispensable; however, in their view, reform should be effected by legislation and without retrospective effect. Their argument runs as follows: if the Court were to find certain rules of Belgian law to be incompatible with the Convention, this would mean that these rules had been contrary to the Convention since its entry into force in respect of Belgium (14 June 1955); the only way to escape such a conclusion would be to accept that the Convention's requirements had increased in the intervening period and to indicate the exact date of the change; failing this, the result of the judgment would be to render many subsequent distributions of estates irregular and open to challenge before the courts, since the limitation period on the two actions available under Belgian law in this connection is thirty years.

The Court is not required to undertake an examination *in abstracto* of the legislative provisions complained of: it is enquiring whether or not their application to Paula and Alexandra Marckx complies with the Convention (see para 27 above). Admittedly, it is inevitable that the Court's decision will have effects extending beyond the confines of this particular case, especially since the violations found stem directly from the contested provisions and not from individual measures of implementation, but the decision cannot of itself annul or repeal these provisions: the Court's judgment is essentially declaratory and leaves to the State the choice of the means to be utilised in its domestic legal system for performance of its obligation under Article 53.

Nonetheless, it remains true that the Government have an evident interest in knowing the temporal effect of the present judgment. On this question, reliance has to be placed on two general principles of law which were recently recalled by the Court of Justice of the European Communities: "the practical consequences of any judicial decision must be carefully taken into account", but "it would be impossible to go so far as to diminish the objectivity of the law and compromise its future application on the ground of the possible repercussions which might result, as regards the past, from such a judicial decision" (*Defrenne v Sabena* [1976] ECR 455, 480; [1976] 2 CMLR 98, 128). The European Court of Human Rights interprets the Convention in the light of present-day conditions but it is not unaware that differences of treatment between "illegitimate" and "legitimate" children, for example in the matter of patrimonial rights, were for many years regarded as permissible and normal in a large number of Contracting States (see, *mutatis mutandis*, para 41 above).

Evolution towards equality has been slow and reliance on the Convention to accelerate this evolution was apparently contemplated at a rather late state. As recently as 22 December 1967, the Commission rejected under Article 27(2) – and rejected *de plano* (Rule 45(3)(a) of its then Rules of Procedure) – another application (No 2775/67) which challenged Articles 757 and 908 of the Belgian Civil Code; the Commission does not seem to have been confronted with the issue again until 1974 (application no 6833/74 of *Paula and Alexandra Marckx*). Having regard to all these circumstances, the principle of legal certainty, which is necessarily inherent in the law of the Convention as in Community Law, dispenses the Belgian State from re-opening legal acts or situations that antedate the delivery of the present Judgment. Moreover, a similar solution is found in certain Contracting States having a constitutional court: their public law limits the retroactive effects of those decisions of that court that annul legislation.

59 To sum up, Alexandra Marckx was the victim of a breach of Article 14, taken in conjunction with Article 8, by reason both of the restrictions on her capacity to receive property from her mother and of her total lack of inheritance rights on intestacy over the estates of her near relatives on her mother's side.

2   On the patrimonial rights relied on by Paula Marckx

60   From 29 October 1973 (recognition) to 30 October 1974 (adoption), the first applicant had only limited capacity to make dispositions in her daughter's favour (see para 49 above). She complains of this situation, relying on Article 8 of the Convention and of Article 1 of Protocol No 1, taken in each case both alone and in conjunction with Article 14.

(a)   *On the alleged violation of Article 8 of the Convention, taken both alone and in conjunction with Article 14.*

61   As the Court has already noted, Article 8 of the Convention is relevant to the point now under consideration (see paras 51 and 52 above). However, Article 8 does not guarantee to a mother complete freedom to give or bequeath her property to her child: in principle it leaves to the Contracting States the choice of the means calculated to allow everyone to lead a normal family life (see para 31 above) and such freedom is not indispensable in the pursuit of a normal family life. In consequence, the restriction complained of by Paula Marckx is not of itself in conflict with the Convention, that is, if it is considered independently of the reason underlying it.

62   On the other hand, the distinction made in this area between unmarried and married mothers does raise an issue. The Government put forward no special argument to support this distinction and, in the opinion of the Court, which refers *mutatis mutandis* to paras 40 and 41 above, the distinction lacks objective and reasonable justification; it is therefore contrary to Article 14 taken in conjunction with Article 8.

(b)   *On the alleged violation of Article 1 of Protocol No 1, taken both alone and in conjunction with Article 14 of the Convention*

63   Article 1 of Protocol No 1 reads as follows:

> Every natural or legal person is entitled to the peaceful enjoyment of his possessions. No one shall be deprived of his possessions except in the public interest and subject to the conditions provided for by law and by the general principles of international law.
>
> The preceding provisions shall not, however, in any way impair the right of a State to enforce such laws as it deems necessary to control the use of property in accordance with the general interest or to secure the payment of taxes or other contributions or penalties.

In the applicants' submission, the patrimonial rights claimed by Paula Marckx fall within the ambit of, *inter alia*, this provision. This approach is shared by the Commission but contested by the Government.

The Court takes the same view as the Commission. By recognising that everyone has the right to the peaceful enjoyment of his possessions, Article 1 is in substance guaranteeing the right of property. This is the clear impression left by the words "possessions" and "use of property" (in French: *"biens"*, *"propriété"*, *"usage des biens"*); the *travaux préparatoires*, for their part, confirm this unequivocally: the drafters continually spoke of "right of property" or "right to property" to describe the subject-matter of the successive drafts which were the forerunners of the present Article 1. Indeed, the right to dispose of one's property constitutes a traditional and fundamental aspect of the right of property (see the *Handyside* judgment of 7 December 1976, Series A, No 24, para 62).

64   The second paragraph of Article 1 nevertheless authorises a Contracting State to "enforce such laws as it deems necessary to control the use of property in accordance with the general interest". This paragraph thus sets the Contracting States up as sole judges of the "necessity" for such a law (above-mentioned *Handyside* judgment, para 62).

As regards "the general interest", it may in certain cases induce a legislature to "control the use of property" in the area of dispositions *inter vivos* or by will. In consequence, the limitation complained of by the first applicant is not of itself in conflict with Protocol No 1.

65 However, the limitation applies only to unmarried and not to married mothers. Like the Commission, the Court considers this distinction, in support of which the Government put forward no special argument, to be discriminatory. In view of Article 14 of the Convention, the Court fails to see on what "general interest", or on what objective and reasonable justification, a State could rely to limit an unmarried mother's right to make gifts or legacies in favour of her child when at the same time a married woman is not subject to any similar restriction. In other respects, the Court refers, *mutatis mutandis*, to paras 40 and 41 above.

Accordingly, there was on this point breach of Article 14 of the Convention, taken in conjunction with Article 1 of Protocol No 1, with respect to Paula Marckx.

D   On the alleged violation of Articles 3 and 12 of the Convention

66 The applicants claim that the legislation they complain of entails an affront to their dignity as human beings; they contend that it subjects them to "degrading treatment" within the meaning of Article 3. The Government contest this. The Commission, for its part, did not consider that it had to examine the case under this Article.

In the Court's judgment, while the legal rules at issue probably present aspects which the applicants may feel to be humiliating, they do not constitute degrading treatment coming within the ambit of Article 3.

67 In its report of 10 December 1977, the Commission expresses the opinion that Article 12, which concerns "the right to marry and to found a family", is not relevant to the present case.

The applicants, on the other hand, maintain their view that the Belgian Civil Code fails to respect, in the person of Paula Marckx, the right not to marry which, in their submission, is inherent in the guarantee embodied in Article 12. They argue that in order to confer on Alexandra the status of a "legitimate" child, her mother would have to legitimate her and, hence, to contract marriage. The Court notes that there is no legal obstacle confronting the first applicant in the exercise of the freedom to marry or to remain single; consequently, the Court has no need to determine whether the Convention enshrines the right not to marry.

The fact that, in law, the parents of an "illegitimate" child do not have the same rights as a married couple also constitutes a breach of Article 12 in the opinion of the applicants; they thus appear to construe Article 12 as requiring that all the legal effects attaching to marriage should apply equally to situations that are in certain respects comparable to marriage. The Court cannot accept this reasoning; in company with the Commission, the Court finds that the issue under consideration falls outside the scope of Article 12.

Accordingly, Article 12 has not been infringed.

E   The application of Article 50 of the Convention

68 At the hearing on 24 October 1978, Mrs Van Look asked the Court to award each applicant, under Article 50 of the Convention, one Belgian franc as compensation for moral damage. The Government did not advert to the matter.

The Court regards the question as being ready for decision (Rules of Court, Rule 50(3), first sentence, read in conjunction with Rule 48(3)). In the particular circumstances of the case, the Court is of opinion that it is not necessary to afford Paula and Alexandra Marckx any just satisfaction other than that resulting from the finding of several violations of their rights.

For these reasons, **THE COURT HOLDS:**

I   *On the Government's preliminary plea*

    1   by fourteen votes to one that the applicants can claim to be "victims" within the meaning of Article 25 of the Convention;

II   *On the manner of establishing Alexandra Marckx's maternal affiliation*

    2   by ten votes to five that there has been breach of Article 8 of the Convention, taken alone, with respect to Paula Marckx;

    3   by eleven votes to four that there has also been breach of Article 14 of the Convention, taken in conjunction with Article 8, with respect to this applicant;

    4   by twelve votes to three that there has been breach of Article 8 of the Convention, taken alone, with respect to Alexandra Marckx;

    5   by thirteen votes to two that there has also been breach of Article 14 of the Convention, taken in conjunction with Article 8, with respect to this applicant;

III   *On the extent in law of Alexandra Marckx's family relationships*

    6   by twelve votes to three, that there is breach of Article 8 of the Convention, taken alone, with respect to both applicants;

    7   by thirteen votes to two, that there is also breach of Article 14 of the Convention, taken in conjunction with Article 8, with respect to both applicants;

IV   *On the patrimonial rights relied on by Alexandra Marckx*

    8   unanimously that Article 1 of Protocol No 1 is not applicable to Alexandra Marckx's claims;

    9   unanimously that there has been no breach of Article 8 of the Convention, taken alone, with respect to this applicant;

    10   by thirteen votes to two that there is breach of Article 14 of the Convention, taken in conjunction with Article 8, with respect to the same applicant;

V   *On the patrimonial rights relied on by Paula Marckx*

    11   unanimously that there has been no breach of Article 8 of the Convention, taken alone, with respect to Paula Marckx;

    12   by thirteen votes to two, that there has been breach of Article 14 of the Convention, taken in conjunction with Article 8 with respect to this applicant;

    13   by ten votes to five, that Article 1 of Protocol No 1 is applicable to Paula Marckx's claims;

    14   by nine votes to six, that there has been no breach of this Article, taken alone, with respect to the same applicant;

15 by ten votes to five, that there has been breach of Article 14 of the Convention, taken in conjunction with Article 1 of Protocol No 1, with respect to this applicant;

VI *On the alleged violation of Articles 3 and 12 of the Convention*

16 unanimously that there is no breach of Article 3 or of Article 12 of the Convention in the present case;

VII *On Article 50*

17 by nine votes to six that the preceding findings amount in themselves to adequate just satisfaction for the purposes of Article 50 of the Convention.

[*Eds:* the following separate opinions were given, but due to space constraints, have not been included:*

– joint dissenting opinion of Judges Balladore Pallieri, Pedersen, Ganshof van der Meersch, Evrigenis, Pinheiro Farinha and Garcia de Enterria on the application of Article 50 of the Convention;

– partly dissenting opinion of Judge O'Donoghue;

– partly dissenting opinion of Judge Thor Vilhjalmsson;

– dissenting opinion of Judge Sir Gerald Fitzmaurice;

– partly dissenting opinion of Judge Bindschedler-Robert;

– partly dissenting opinion of Judge Matscher; and

– partly dissenting opinion of Judge Pinheiro Farinha.

In addition, Judges Balladore Pallieri, Zekia, Pedersen, Ganshof van der Meersch, Evrigenis and Lagergren stated their dissent from the majority of the Court as regards item 14 of the operative provisions of the Judgment; they considered that there had been a breach of Article 1 of Protocol No 1, taken alone, with respect to Paula Marckx.]

---

* *Eds:* the full text of the judgment is available at the website of the European Court of Human Rights (see *On-Line Access to Human Rights Source Materials, supra* p xlv); ECHR Series A, No 31; 2 EHRR 330 and 58 ILR 561.

CASE NO 19

JOHNSTON AND OTHERS v IRELAND

EUROPEAN COURT OF HUMAN RIGHTS

Application No: 9697/82

Judgment: 18 December 1986

Panel: *Judges*: Ryssdal (*President*), Cremona, Thór Vilhjálmsson, Lagergren, Gölcücklü, Matscher, Pinheiro Farinha, Pettiti, Walsh, Sir Vincent Evans, Macdonald, Russo, Bernhardt, Gersing, Spielmann, De Meyer and Carrilo Salcedo

Human rights — Right to marry — Right to family life — Right to freedom of thought, conscience and religion — Divorce — Whether the absence of a right to divorce (and re-marry) under Irish Law violated Convention rights — Illegitimacy — Whether status of illegitimate children under Irish law violated the right to family life — Constitution of Ireland, art 41.3.2 — European Convention for the Protection of Human Rights and Fundamental Freedoms, arts 8, 9 and 12

Human rights — State obligations — Right to respect for family life — Divorce — Whether effective respect for family life imposed a positive obligation on Contracting States to introduce measures that permit divorce — Margin of appreciation — European Convention for the Protection of Human Rights and Fundamental Freedoms, art 8

BACKGROUND

The three applicants were all residents of the Republic of Ireland. Following the breakdown of his marriage, the first applicant, Mr Johnston, cohabited with the second applicant, Ms Williams-Johnston. The third applicant was their daughter. Since divorce was not permitted under article 43.3 of the Irish Constitution, the first and second applicants were unable to marry. Consequently, their daughter was considered illegitimate under Irish law. Although the three applicants lived together as a family, the third applicant could not be recognised in law as the child of both her parents with full rights of support and succession in relation to both of them, as a child born to parents who were married would have been. Furthermore, under Irish law it was not possible for her status to be legitimated by the marriage of her parents.

The applicants alleged violations of their rights under the European Convention on Human Rights, in particular article 8 (right to family life), article 9 (right to freedom of thought, conscience and religion), article 12 (right to marry) and article 14 (discrimination in relation to articles 8 and 12) of the Convention as regards their inability to marry, the legal status of cohabiting couples, and the legal status of illegitimate children. The European Commission of Human Rights found a breach of article 8 in respect of the third applicant's illegitimate status, and referred the case to the European Court of Human Rights.

HELD (finding a violation of article 8 in respect of all three applicants, due to the third applicant's status as an illegitimate child)

FIRST AND SECOND APPLICANTS

Inability to divorce and remarry

Articles 8 and 12

1   The ordinary meaning of the words "right to marry" in article 12 of the Convention was clear, in the sense that they covered the formation of marital relationships and not their dissolution. Prohibition on the right to divorce could not be regarded as injuring the substance of the right guaranteed by article 12. (Paras 52 and 53)

2   Article 8 applied to the "family life" of the "illegitimate" family as well as to that of the "legitimate" family. The applicants were entitled to the protection of article 8, notwithstanding that their relationship existed outside marriage. (Para 55)

3   The Convention had to be read as a whole. The right to divorce, which was excluded from article 12, could not be derived from article 8, a provision of more general purpose and scope. Although the protection of private or family life might sometimes necessitate means whereby spouses could be relieved from the duty to live together, this did not extend to a positive obligation under article 8 to introduce measures permitting divorce and remarriage. (Paras 57 and 58)

Article 14 in conjunction with article 8

4   Foreign divorces were recognised in Ireland only if they had been obtained by persons domiciled abroad. The situations of such persons and the applicants could not be regarded as analogous for the purposes of article 14. Accordingly, there was no discrimination under article 14. (Paras 60 and 61)

Article 9

5   Article 9, which guarantees the right to freedom of thought, conscience and religion, could not be taken to extend to the non-availability of divorce under Irish law. (Para 63)

Other matters

Article 8

6   It was not possible to derive from article 8 an obligation on the part of Contracting States to establish for unmarried couples a status analogous to that of married couples; nor a special regime for unmarried couples who, like the applicants, wished to marry but were legally incapable of marrying. (Paras 68 and 69)

THIRD APPLICANT

Article 8

7   "Respect" for family life, understood as including the ties between near relatives, implied an obligation for the State to act in a manner calculated to allow these ties to develop normally. In the present case, this required that the third applicant be placed, legally and socially, in a position akin to that of a legitimate child. Notwithstanding the wide margin of appreciation enjoyed by Ireland in this area, the absence of an

appropriate legal regime reflecting the third applicant's natural family ties amounted to a failure to respect her family life. (Paras 72, 74 and 75)

8   Because of the close relationship between the third applicant and her parents, there was also a failure to respect the family life of the parents. (Paras 75 and 76)

Treaties and other international instruments referred to

European Convention for the Protection of Human Rights and Fundamental Freedoms 1950, arts 8, 9, 12, 13, 14, 25, 26, 50 and 53

European Convention on the Legal Status of Children born out of Wedlock 1975, Preamble

Protocol No 7 to the European Convention for the Protection of Human Rights and Fundamental Freedoms 1983, art 5

Universal Declaration of Human Rights 1948, art 16(1)

Vienna Convention on the Law of Treaties 1969, art 31(1)

National legislation referred to

Republic of Ireland

Adoption Act 1952, as amended

Domicile and Recognition of Foreign Divorces Act 1986

Family Home Protection Act 1976

Family Law (Maintenance of Spouses and Children) Act 1976, as amended by Family Law (Protection of Spouses and Children) Act 1981

Guardianship of Infants Act 1964, ss 6(4) and 11(4)

Illegitimate Children (Affiliation Orders) Act 1930, as amended by the Family Law (Maintenance of Spouses and Children) Act 1976 and the Courts Act 1983

Legitimacy Act 1931, ss 1(1), 1(2), 9(1)

Registration of Births and Deaths (Ireland) Act 1863, as amended by the Births and Deaths Registration (Ireland) Act 1880

Succession Act 1965, s 117

The Constitution of the Republic of Ireland 1937, arts 40.3, 41.1, 41.3, 42.1 and 42.5

Cases referred to

Abdulaziz, Cabales and Balkandali v The United Kingdom, ECHR, judgment of 28 May 1985, Series A, No 94; 7 EHRR 471; below, p 618

Airey v Ireland, ECHR, judgment of 9 October 1979, Series A, No 32; 2 EHRR 305; *supra*, p 67

Case "Relating to Certain Aspects of the Laws on the Use of Languages in Education in Belgium" v Belgium (Merits) ("Belgian Linguistics Case (No 2)"), ECHR, judgment of 23 July 1968, Series A, No 6; 1 EHRR 252

Re Caffin [1971] IR 123

Campbell and Fell v The United Kingdom, ECHR, judgment of 28 June 1984, Series A, No 80; 7 EHRR 165

De Jong, Baljet and Van Den Brink v The Netherlands, ECHR, judgment of 22 May 1984, Series A, No 77; 8 EHRR 20

G v An Bord Uchtála [1980] IR 32

Gaffney v Gaffney [1975] IR 133

Golder v The United Kingdom, ECHR, judgment of 21 February 1975, Series A, No 18; 1 EHRR 524

Handyside v The United Kingdom, ECHR, judgment of 7 December 1976, Series A, No 24; 1 EHRR 737

James and Others v The United Kingdom, ECHR, judgment of 21 February 1986, Series A, No 98; 8 EHRR 123

Le Compte, Van Leuven and De Meyere v Belgium, ECHR, judgment of 23 June 1981, Series A, No 43; 4 EHRR 1

Lingens v Austria, ECHR, judgment of 8 July 1986, Series A, No 103; 8 EHRR 103

Lithgow v The United Kingdom, ECHR, judgment of 8 July 1986, Series A, No 102; 8 EHRR 329

Marckx v Belgium, ECHR, judgment of 13 June 1979, Series A, No 31; 2 EHRR 330; *supra*, p 273

O'B v S [1984] IR 316

Silver and Others v The United Kingdom, ECHR, judgment of 25 March 1983, Series A, No 61; 5 EHRR 347

The State (Nicolau) v An Bord Uchtála [1966] IR 567

Young, James and Webster v The United Kingdom, ECHR, judgment of 13 August 1981, Series A, No 44; 4 EHRR 38

Zimmermann and Steiner v Switzerland, ECHR, judgment of 13 July 1983, Series A, No 66; 6 EHRR 17

JUDGMENT

PROCEDURE

[...]*

AS TO THE FACTS

I   The particular circumstances of the case

10 The first applicant is Roy HW Johnston, who was born in 1930 and is a scientific research and development manager. He resides at Rathmines, Dublin, with the second

---

*   *Eds:* paras 1-9, which relate to procedural matters, have not been included.

applicant, Janice Williams-Johnston, who was born in 1938; she is a school-teacher by profession and used to work as director of a play-group in Dublin, but has been unemployed since 1985. The third applicant is their daughter, Nessa Doreen Williams-Johnston, who was born in 1978.

11   The first applicant married a Miss M in 1952 in a Church of Ireland ceremony. Three children were born of this marriage, in 1956, 1959 and 1965.

In 1965, it became clear to both parties that the marriage had irretrievably broken down and they decided to live separately at different levels in the family house. Several years later both of them with the other's knowledge and consent, formed relationships and began to live with third parties. By mutual agreement, the two couples resided in self-contained flats in the house until 1976, when Roy Johnston's wife moved elsewhere.

In 1978, the second applicant, with whom Roy Johnston had been living since 1971, gave birth to Nessa. He consented to his name being included in the Register of Births as the father (see para 26 below).

12   Under the Constitution of Ireland (see paras 16–17 below), the first applicant is unable to obtain in Ireland a dissolution of his marriage to enable him to marry the second applicant. He has taken the following steps to regularise his relationship with her and with his wife and to make proper provision for his dependents:

(a) With his wife's consent, he has consulted solicitors in Dublin and in London as to the possibility of obtaining a dissolution of the marriage outside Ireland. His London solicitors advised that, in the absence of residence within the jurisdiction of the English courts, he would not be able to do so in England, and the matter has therefore not been pursued (see also paras 19–21 below).

(b) On 19 September 1982, he concluded a formal separation agreement with his wife, recording an agreement implemented some years earlier. She received a lump-sum of IR£8,800 and provision was made for maintenance of the remaining dependent child of the marriage. The parties also mutually renounced their succession rights over each other's estates.

(c) He has made a will leaving his house to the second applicant for life with remainder over to his four children as tenants in common, one half of the residue of his estate to the second applicant, and the other half to his four children in equal shares.

(d) He has supported the third applicant throughout her life and has acted in all respects as a caring father.

(e) He contributed towards the maintenance of his wife until the conclusion of the aforementioned separation agreement and has supported the three children of his marriage during their dependency.

(f) The second applicant has been nominated as beneficiary under the pension scheme attached to his employment.

(g) He has taken out health insurance in the names of the second and third applicants, as members of his family.

13   The second applicant, who is largely dependent on the first applicant for her support and maintenance, is concerned at the lack of security provided by her present legal status, in particular the absence of any legal right to be maintained by him and of any potential rights of succession in the event of intestacy (see also para 23 below). As is permitted by law, she has adopted the first applicant's surname, which she uses amongst friends and neighbours, but for business purposes continues to use the name Williams. According to her, she has felt inhibited about telling employers of her domestic

circumstances and although she would like to become an Irish citizen by naturalisation, she has been reluctant to make an application, not wishing to put those circumstances in issue.

14 The third applicant has, under Irish law, the legal situation of an illegitimate child and her parents are concerned at the lack of any means by which she can, even with their consent, be recognised as their child with full rights of support and succession in relation to them (see paras 30–32 below). They are also concerned about the possibility of a stigma attaching to her by virtue of her legal situation, especially when she is attending school.

15 The first and second applicants state that although they have not practised any formal religion for some time, they have recently joined the Religious Society of Friends (the Quakers) in Dublin. This decision was influenced in part by their concern that the third applicant receive a Christian upbringing.

II   Relevant domestic law

A   *Constitutional provisions relating to the family*

16 The Constitution of Ireland, which came into force in 1937, includes the following provisions:

> 40.3.1 The State guarantees in its laws to respect, and, as far as practicable, by its laws to defend and vindicate the personal rights of the citizen.
>
> 40.3.2 The State shall, in particular, by its laws protect as best it may from unjust attack and, in the case of injustice done, vindicate the life, person, good name, and property rights of every citizen.
>
> 41.1.1 The State recognises the Family as the natural primary and fundamental unit group of Society, and as a moral institution possessing inalienable and imprescriptible rights, antecedent and superior to all positive law.
>
> 41.1.2 The State, therefore, guarantees to protect the Family in its constitution and authority, as the necessary basis of social order and as indispensable to the welfare of the Nation and the State.
>
> 41.3.1 The State pledges itself to guard with special care the institution of Marriage, on which the family is founded, and to protect it against attack.
>
> 41.3.2 No law shall be enacted providing for the grant of a dissolution of marriage.
>
> 42.1 The State acknowledges that the primary and natural educator of the child is the Family and guarantees to respect the inalienable right and duty of parents to provide, according to their means, for the religious and moral, intellectual, physical and social education of their children.
>
> 42.5 In exceptional cases, where the parents for physical or moral reasons fail in their duty towards their children, the State as guardian of the common good, by appropriate means shall endeavour to supply the place of the parents, but always with due regard for the natural and imprescriptible rights of the child.

17 As a result of Article 41.3.2 of the Constitution, divorce in the sense of dissolution of a marriage (divorce *a vinculo matrimonii*) is not available in Ireland. However, spouses may be relieved of the duty of cohabiting either by a legally binding deed of separation concluded between them or by a court decree of judicial separation (also known as a divorce *a mensa et thoro*); such a decree, which is obtainable only on proof of commission of adultery, cruelty or unnatural offences, does not dissolve the marriage. In the

remainder of the present judgment, the word divorce denotes a divorce *a vinculo matrimonii*.

It is also possible to obtain on various grounds a decree of nullity, that is a declaration by the High Court that a marriage was invalid and therefore null and void *ab initio*. A marriage may also be annulled by an ecclesiastical tribunal, but this does not affect the civil status of the parties.

18 The Irish courts have consistently held that the "Family" that is afforded protection by Article 41 of the Constitution is the family based on marriage. Thus, in *The State (Nicolaou) v An Bord Uchtála* [1966] IR 567, 643–644, the Supreme Court said:

> It is quite clear from the provisions of Article 41, and in particular section 3 thereof, that the family referred to in this Article is the family which is founded on the institution of marriage and, in the context of the Article, marriage means valid marriage under the law for the time being in force in the State.

> While it is quite true that unmarried persons cohabiting together and the children of their union may often be referred to as a family and have many, if not all, of the outward appearances of a family, and may indeed for the purposes of a particular law be regarded as such, nevertheless as far as Article 41 is concerned the guarantees therein contained are confined to families based upon marriage.

The Supreme Court has, however, held that an illegitimate child has unenumerated natural rights (as distinct from rights conferred by law) which will be protected under Article 40.3 of the Constitution, such as the right to be fed and to live, to be reared and educated, to have the opportunity of working and of realising his or her full personality and dignity as a human being, as well as the same natural rights under the Constitution as a legitimate child to "religious and moral, intellectual, physical and social education" (*G v An Bord Uchtála* [1980] IR 32).

B   Recognition of foreign divorces

19 Article 41.3.3 of the Constitution provides:

> No person whose marriage has been dissolved under the civil law of any other State but is a subsisting valid marriage under the law for the time being in force within the jurisdiction of the Government and Parliament established by this Constitution shall be capable of contracting a valid marriage within that jurisdiction during the lifetime of the other party to the marriage dissolved.

20 A series of judicial decisions has established that the foregoing provision does not prevent the recognition by Irish courts, under the general Irish rules of private international law, of certain decrees of divorce obtained, even by Irish nationals, in another State. Such recognition used to be granted only if the parties to the marriage were domiciled within the jurisdiction of the foreign court at the time of the relevant proceedings (*Re Caffin Deceased; Bank of Ireland v Caffin* [1971] IR 123; *Gaffney v Gaffney* [1975] IR 133); however, since 2 October 1986 a divorce will be recognised if granted in the country where either spouse is domiciled (Domicile and Recognition of Foreign Divorces Act 1986). To be regarded as domiciled in a foreign State, a person must not only be resident there but also have the intention of remaining there permanently and have lost the *animus revertendi*. Moreover, the foreign divorce will not be recognised if domicile has been fraudulently invoked before the foreign court for the purpose of obtaining the decree.

21 If notice is served for a civil marriage before a Registrar of Births, Marriages and Deaths in Ireland and he is aware that either of the parties has been divorced abroad, he

must, under the regulations in force, refer the matter to the Registrar-General. The latter will seek legal advice as to whether on the facts of the case the divorce would be recognised as effective to dissolve the marriage under Irish law and as to whether the intended marriage can consequently be permitted.

C   Legal status of persons in the situation of the first and second applicants

1   Marriage

22 Persons who, like the first and second applicants, are living together in a stable relationship after the breakdown of the marriage of one of them are unable, during the lifetime of the other party to that marriage, to marry each other in Ireland and are not recognised there as a family for the purposes of Article 41 of the Constitution (see paras 17 and 18 above).

2   Maintenance and succession

23 Such persons, unlike a married couple, have no legal duty to support or maintain one another and no mutual statutory rights of succession. However, there is no impediment under Irish law preventing them from living together and supporting each other and, in particular, from making wills or dispositions *inter vivos* in each other's favour. They can also enter into mutual maintenance agreements, although the Government and the applicants expressed different views as to whether these might be unenforceable as contrary to public policy.

In general, the married member of the couple remains, at least in theory, under a continuing legal obligation to maintain his or her spouse. In addition, testamentary dispositions by that member may be subject to the rights of his or her spouse or legitimate children under the Succession Act 1965.

3   Miscellaneous

24 As compared with married couples, persons in the situation of the first and second applicants:

(a) have no access, in the event of difficulties arising between them, to the system of barring orders instituted to provide remedies in respect of violence within the family (Family Law (Maintenance of Spouses and Children) Act 1976, as amended by the Family Law (Protection of Spouses and Children) Act 1981); they can, however, obtain analogous relief by seeking a court injunction or declaration;

(b) do not enjoy any of the rights conferred by the Family Home Protection Act 1976 in relation to the family home and its contents, notably the prohibition on sale by one spouse without the other's consent and the exemption from stamp duty and Land Registry fees in the event of transfer of title between them;

(c) as regards transfers of property between them are less favourably treated for the purposes of capital acquisition tax;

(d) enjoy different rights under the social welfare code, notably the benefits available to deserted wives;

(e) are unable jointly to adopt a child (see also para 29 below).

D Legal situation of illegitimate children

1 Affiliation

25 In Irish law, the principle *mater semper certa est* applies: the maternal affiliation of an illegitimate child, such as the third applicant, is established by the fact of birth, without any requirement of voluntary or judicial recognition.

The Illegitimate Children (Affiliation Orders) Act 1930, as amended by the Family Law (Maintenance of Spouses and Children) Act 1976 and the Courts Act 1983, provides procedures whereby the District Court of the Circuit Court may make an "affiliation order" against the putative father of a child directing him to make periodic payments in respect of the latter's maintenance and also whereby the court may approve a lump-sum maintenance agreement between a person who admits he is the father of an illegitimate child and the latter's mother. Neither of these procedures establishes the child's paternal affiliation for all purposes, any finding of parentage being effective solely for the purposes of the proceedings in question and binding only on the parties.

26 Under the Registration of Births and Deaths (Ireland) Act 1863, as amended by the Births and Deaths Registration (Ireland) Act 1880, the Registrar may enter in the register the name of a person as the father of an illegitimate child if he is so requested jointly by that person and the mother. The act of registration does not, however, establish paternal affiliation.

2 Guardianship

27 The mother of an illegitimate child is his sole guardian as from the moment of his birth (section 6(4) of the Guardianship of Infants Act 1964) and has the same rights of guardianship as are jointly enjoyed by the parents of a legitimate child. The natural father can apply to the court under section 11(4) of the same Act regarding the child's custody and the right of access thereto by either parent; however, he cannot seek the court's directions on other matters affecting the child's welfare, nor is there any means whereby he can be established as guardian of the child jointly with the mother, even if she consents.

3 Legitimation

28 An illegitimate child may be legitimated by the subsequent marriage of his parents, provided that, unlike the first and second applicants, they could have been lawfully married to one another at the time of the child's birth or at some time during the preceding 10 months (section 1(1) and (2) of the Legitimacy Act 1931).

4 Adoption

29 Under the Adoption Act 1952, as amended, an adoption order can only be made in favour of a married couple living together, a widow, a widower, or the mother or natural father or a relative of the child.

5 Maintenance

30 The effect of the Illegitimate Children (Affiliation Orders) Act 1930, as amended by the Family Law (Maintenance of Spouses and Children) Act 1976, is to impose on each of the parents of an illegitimate child an equal obligation to maintain him. This obligation cannot be enforced against the father until an "affiliation order" has been made against him (see para 25 above).

6   Succession

31   The devolution of estates on intestacy is governed by the Succession Act 1965 which provides, basically, that the estate is to be distributed in specified proportions between any spouse or "issue" who may survive the deceased. In *O'B v S* ([1984] IR 316), the Supreme Court held that the word "issue" did not include children who were not the issue of a lawful marriage and that accordingly an illegitimate child had, under the Act, no right to inheritance on the intestacy of his natural father. Whilst also holding that the resultant discrimination in favour of legitimate children was justifiable by reason of sections 1 and 3 of Article 41 of the Constitution (see para 16 above), the Supreme Court stated that the decision to change the existing rules of intestate succession and the extent to which they were to be changed were primarily matters for the legislature. The relevant rules in the Act formed part of a statute designed to strengthen the protection of the family in accordance with Article 41, an Article which created not merely a State interest but a State obligation to safeguard the family; accordingly, the said discrimination was not necessarily unjust, unreasonable or arbitrary and the rules were not invalid having regard to the provisions of the Constitution.

An illegitimate child may, on the other hand, in certain circumstances have a right to inheritance on the intestacy of his mother. A special rule (section 9(1) of the Legitimacy Act 1931) lays down that where the mother of an illegitimate child dies intestate leaving no legitimate issue, the child is entitled to take any interest in his mother's estate to which he would have been entitled if he had been born legitimate.

32   As regards testate succession, section 117 of the Succession Act 1965 empowers a court to make provision for a child for whom it considers that the testator has failed in his moral duty to make proper provision. An illegitimate child has no claim against his father's estate under this section, but may be able to claim against his mother's estate provided that she leaves no legitimate issue.

33   An illegitimate child inheriting property from his parents is potentially liable to pay capital acquisition tax on a basis less favourable than a child born in wedlock.

E   *Law reform proposals*

1   Divorce

34   In 1983, a Joint Committee of the *Dáil* (Chamber of Deputies) and the Seanad (Senate) was established, *inter alia*, to examine the problems which follow the breakdown of marriage. In its report of 1985, it referred to figures suggesting that approximately 6 per cent of marriages in Ireland had broken down to date, but noted the absence of accurate statistics. The Committee considered that the parties to stable relationships formed after marriage breakdown and the children of such relationships currently lacked adequate legal status and protection; however, it expressed no view on whether divorce legislation was at present necessary or desirable.

In a national referendum held on 26 June 1986, a majority voted against an amendment of the Constitution, which would have permitted legislation providing for divorce.

2   Illegitimacy

35   In September 1982, the Irish Law Reform Commission published a Report on Illegitimacy. Its basic recommendation was that legislation should remove the concept of illegitimacy from the law and equalise the rights of children born outside marriage with those of children born within marriage.

36 After considering the report, the Government announced in October 1983 that they had decided that the law should be reformed, and that reform should be concentrated on the elimination of discrimination against persons born outside marriage and on the rights and obligations of their fathers. However, the Government decided not to accept a proposal by the Law Reform Commission that the father be given automatic rights of guardianship in relation to a child so born.

36 In May 1985, the Minister of Justice laid before both Houses of Parliament a Memorandum entitled "The Status of Children", indicating the scope and nature of the main changes proposed by the Government. On 9 May 1986, the Status of Children Bill 1986, a draft of which had been annexed to the aforesaid Memorandum, was introduced into the Seanad. If enacted in its present form, the Bill – which has the stated purpose of removing as far as possible provisions in existing law which discriminate against children born outside marriage – would have, *inter alia*, the following effects:

(a) Where the name of a person was entered on the register of births as the father of a child born outside marriage, he would be presumed to be the father unless the contrary was shown (cf para 26 above).

(b) The father of a child born outside marriage would be able to seek a court order making him guardian of the child jointly with the mother (cf para 27 above). In that event, they would jointly have all the parental rights and responsibilities that are enjoyed and borne by married parents.

(c) The proviso qualifying the possibility of legitimation by subsequent marriage would be removed by the repeal of section 1(2) of the Legitimacy Act 1931 (see para 28 above).

(d) The legal provisions governing the obligation of both of the parents of a child born outside marriage to maintain him would be similar to those governing the corresponding obligation of married parents (see para 30 above).

(e) For succession purposes, no distinction would be made between persons based on whether or not their parents were married to each other. Thus, a child born outside marriage would be entitled to share on the intestacy of either parent and would have the same rights in relation to the estate of a parent who died leaving a will as would a child of a family based on marriage (cf paras 31 and 32 above).

The Explanatory Memorandum to the Bill states that any fiscal changes necessitated by the proposed new measures would be a matter for separate legislation promoted by the Minister for Finance.

3   Adoption

37 Work is also in progress on legislation reforming the law of adoption, following the publication in July 1984 of the Report of the Review Committee on Adoption Services. That Committee recommended that, as at present (see para 29 above), unmarried couples should not be eligible to adopt jointly even their own natural children.

PROCEEDINGS BEFORE THE COMMISSION

38 The application of Roy Johnston, Janice-Williams-Johnston and Nessa Williams-Johnston (no 9697/82) was lodged with the Commission on 16 February 1982. The applicants complained of the absence of provision in Ireland for divorce and for recognition of the family life of persons who, after the breakdown of the marriage of one of them, are living in a family relationship outside marriage. They alleged that on this

account they had been victims of violations of Articles 8, 9, 12 and 13 of the Convention and also of Article 14 (taken in conjunction with Articles 8 and 12).

39 The Commission declared the application admissible on 7 October 1983.

In its report adopted on 5 March 1985 (Article 31), the Commission expressed the opinion that:

- there was no breach of Articles 8 and 12 in that the right to divorce and subsequently to re-marry was not guaranteed by the Convention (unanimously);

- there was no breach of Article 8 in that Irish law did not confer a recognised family status on the first and second applicants (twelve votes to one);

- there was a breach of Article 8 in that the legal regime concerning the status of the third applicant under Irish law failed to respect the family life of all three applicants (unanimously);

- there was no breach of the first applicant's rights under Article 9 (unanimously):

- there was no breach of Article 14 in conjunction with Articles 8 and 12 in that the first and second applicants had not been discriminated against by Irish law (twelve votes to one);

- it was not necessary to examine the third applicant's separate complaint of discrimination;

- there was no breach of Article 13 (unanimously).

FINAL SUBMISSIONS MADE TO THE COURT

40 The applicants invoked before the Court the same Articles (Articles 8, 9 and 12) as they did before the Commission, other than Article 13.

At the hearings on 23–24 June 1986, the Government maintained in substance the submissions in their memorial of 28 November 1985, whereby they had requested the Court:

(1) *With regard to the preliminary submission*: to decide and declare that (a) the applicants cannot claim to be victims within the meaning of Article 25 of the Convention; (b) the applicants have not exhausted their domestic remedies.

(2) *With regard to Articles 8 and 12*: to decide and declare that there has been no breach of Articles 8 and 12 of the Convention in regard to the claim of the first and second-named applicants of a right to divorce and re-marry.

(3) *With regard to Article 8*: to decide and declare that there has been no breach of Article 8 of the Convention in respect of the family life of all three applicants or any of them.

(4) *With regard to Article 9*: to decide and declare that there has been no breach of Article 9 of the Convention.

(5) *With regard to Article 14 in conjunction with Articles 8 and 12*: to decide and declare that there has been no breach of Article 14 read in conjunction with Article 8 and Article 12 of the Convention.

(6) *With regard to Article 13 of the Convention*: to decide and declare that there has been no breach of Article 13 of the Convention.

(7) *With regard to Article 50*: (i) to decide and declare that an award of compensation is not justified or appropriate; (ii) alternatively, if and in so far as a breach of any Article of the Convention is found, to decide and declare that a finding of violation in itself constitutes sufficient just satisfaction.

The Government noted, however, that the claim of violation of Article 13 had been abandoned by the applicants; they also made some additional submissions regarding the admissibility of certain of the applicants' complaints (see para 47 below).

AS TO THE LAW

I   The Government's preliminary pleas

A   *Whether the applicants are entitled to claim to be "victims"*

41 The Government pleaded that the tranquil domestic circumstances of the applicants showed that they were not at risk of being directly affected by those aspects of Irish law of which they complained. In a dispute which was manufactured or contrived, they had raised problems that were purely hypothetical and could therefore not properly claim to be "victims", within the meaning of Article 25(1) of the Convention, which, so far as is relevant, provides:

> The Commission may receive petitions ... from any person, non-governmental organisation or group of individuals claiming to be the victim of a violation by one of the High Contracting Parties of the rights set forth in [the] Convention ...

42 The Government had already – unsuccessfully – made this plea at the admissibility stage before the Commission; accordingly, they are not estopped from raising it before the Court (*Campbell and Fell v The United Kingdom*, judgment of 28 June 1984, Series A, No 80, para 57).

However, the Court considers that the plea cannot be sustained. Article 25 entitles individuals to contend that a law violates their rights by itself, in the absence of an individual measure of implementation, if they run the risk of being directly affected by it (*Marckx v Belgium*, judgment of 22 May 1984, Series A, No 31, para 27). And, in fact, the applicants raise objections to the effects of the law on their own lives.

Furthermore, the question of the existence or absence of detriment is not a matter for Article 25 which, in its use of the word "victim", denotes "the person directly affected by the act or omission which is in issue" (see, amongst various authorities, *De Jong, Baljet and Van Den Brink v The Netherlands*, judgment of 22 May 1984, Series A, No 77, para 41).

The applicants are therefore entitled in the present case to claim to be victims of the breaches which they allege.

43 The Court does not consider that it should accede to the Government's invitation to defer judgment until after the enactment of the Status of Children Bill, which is designed to modify the relevant Irish law in a number of respects (see para 36 above). On several occasions the Court has proceeded with its examination of a case notwithstanding the existence of proposed or intervening reforms (see, for example, *Marckx v Belgium*, above; *Airey v Ireland*, judgment of 9 October 1979, Series A, No 32; *Silver v The United Kingdom* , judgment of 25 March 1983, Series A, No 61.

B   *Whether the applicants have failed to exhaust domestic remedies*

44 According to the Government – which had already raised a similar plea at the appropriate time before the Commission – the constitutionality of each of the provisions of Irish law complained of by the applicants could have been tested in the Irish courts. Since, however, they had failed to exhaust such domestic remedies as they might have been advised, the Commission had erred in declaring their application admissible.

45 The only remedies which Article 26 of the Convention requires to be exhausted are those that relate to the breaches alleged; the existence of such remedies must be sufficiently certain not only in theory but also in practice, failing which they will lack the requisite accessibility and effectiveness; and it falls to the respondent State, if it pleads non-exhaustion, to establish that these various conditions are satisfied (see, amongst many authorities, the above-mentioned *De Jong, Baljet and Van Den Bank* judgment, Series A, No 77, para 39).

46 In so far as the applicants' complaints relate to the prohibition of divorce under the Constitution of Ireland, no effective domestic remedy is available.

As regards the remaining issues, the Court, bearing particularly in mind the established case law of the Irish courts (see paras 18 and 31 above), does not consider that the Government have established with any degree of certainty the existence of any effective remedy.

C *Whether certain of the applicants' complaints are inadmissible on other grounds*

47 At the hearings on 23–24 June 1986, the Government maintained that since the Commission's admissibility decision in the present case the applicants had advanced, before both the Commission and the Court, a number of new complaints, relative to their status under Irish law, which had not been declared admissible in that decision. In the Government's view, these complaints – which concerned the availability of barring orders, the applicability of the Family Home Protection Act 1976, rights of intestate succession as between the first and second applicants, the incidence of taxation and stamp duty, entitlement under the social welfare code and alleged discrimination in employment – were "not properly before the Court".

48 The Commission's Delegate pointed out that these matters were relied upon by the applicants as illustrations of the general complaint submitted to and declared admissible by the Commission, namely that the applicants "are placed in a position whereby it is impossible to establish a recognised family status under Irish law or to ensure that their child becomes a fully integrated member of their family".

Likewise, the Court notes that the applicants' original application to the Commission states that they "complain that, by the manner in which their family relationships are treated under law, Ireland is in breach of Article 8 ...". Moreover, at the hearings before the Court the Government argued that the case presented to the Court and to which they had to respond was "a package".

In these circumstances, the matters in question do not fall outside the compass of the case brought before the Court, which compass is delimited by the Commission's admissibility decision. Besides, the Court has already found, at para 46 above, that none of them is inadmissible for non-exhaustion of domestic remedies (see *James and Others v The United Kingdom*, judgment of 21 February 1986, Series A, No 98, para 80).

II Situation of the first and second applicants

A *Inability to divorce and re-marry*

1 Articles 12 and 8

49 The first and second applicants alleged that because of the impossibility under Irish law of obtaining a dissolution of Roy Johnston's marriage and of his resultant inability to

marry Janice Williams-Johnston, they were victims of breaches of Articles 12 and 8 of the Convention. These provisions read as follows:

Article 12

Men and women of marriageable age have the right to marry and to found a family, according to the national laws governing the exercise of this right.

Article 8

1   Everyone has the right to respect of his private and family life, his home and his correspondence.

2   There shall be no interference by a public authority with the exercise of this right except such as is in accordance with the law and is necessary in a democratic society in the interests of national security, public safety or the economic well-being of the country, for the prevention of disorder or crime, for the protection of health or morals, or for the protection of the rights and freedoms of others.

This allegation was contested by the Government and rejected by the Commission.

50 The applicants stated that, as regards this part of the case, the central issue was not whether the Convention guaranteed the right to divorce but rather whether the fact that they were unable to marry each other was compatible with the right to marry or remarry and with the right to respect for the family life, enshrined in Articles 12 and 8.

The Court does not consider that the issues arising can be separated into watertight compartments in this way. In any society espousing the principle of monogamy, it is inconceivable that Roy Johnston should be able to marry as long as his marriage to Mrs Johnston has not been dissolved. The second applicant, for her part, is not complaining of a general inability to marry but rather of her inability to marry the first applicant, a situation that stems precisely from the fact that he cannot obtain a divorce. Consequently, their case cannot be examined in isolation from the problem of the non-availability of divorce.

(a)   Article 12

51 In order to determine whether the applicants can derive a right to divorce from Article 12, the Court will seek to ascertain the ordinary meaning to be given to the terms of this provision in their context and in the light of its object and purpose (see *Golder v The United Kingdom*, judgment of 21 February 1975, Series A, No 18, para 29 and Art 31(1) of the Vienna Convention of 23 May 1969 on the Law of Treaties).

52 The Court agrees with the Commission that the ordinary meaning of the words "right to marry" is clear, in the sense that they cover the formation of marital relationships but not their dissolution. Furthermore, these words are found in a context that includes an express reference to "national laws"; even if, as the applicants would have it, the prohibition on divorce is to be seen as a restriction on capacity to marry, the Court does not consider that, in a society adhering to the principle of monogamy, such a restriction can be regarded as injuring the substance of the right guaranteed by Article 12.

Moreover, the foregoing interpretation of Article 12 is consistent with its object and purpose as revealed by the *travaux préparatoires*. The text of Article 12 was based on that of Article 16 of the Universal Declaration of Human Rights, para 1 of which reads:

Men and women of full age, without any limitation due to race, nationality or religion, have the right to marry and to found a family. They are also entitled to equal rights as to marriage, during marriage and at its dissolution.

In explaining to the Consultative Assembly why the draft of the future Article 12 did not include the words found in the last sentence of the above-cited paragraph, Mr Teitgen, Rapporteur of the Committee on Legal and Administrative Questions, said:

> In mentioning the particular Article of the Universal Declaration, we have used only that part of the paragraph of the Article which affirms the right to marry and to found a family, but not the subsequent provisions of the Article concerning equal rights after marriage, since we only guarantee the right to marry (Collected Edition of the *Travaux Préparatoires*, vol 1, p 268).

In the Court's view, the *travaux préparatoires* disclose no intention to include in Article 12 any guarantee of a right to have the ties of marriage dissolved by divorce.

53   The applicants set considerable store on the social developments that have occurred since the Convention was drafted, notably an alleged substantial increase in marriage breakdown.

It is true that the Convention and its Protocols must be interpreted in the light of present-day conditions (see, amongst several authorities, the above mentioned Marckx judgment, Series A, No 31, para 58). However, the Court cannot, by means of an evolutive interpretation, derive from these instruments a right that was not included therein at the outset. This is particularly so here, where the omission was deliberate.

It should also be mentioned that the right to divorce is not included in Protocol No 7 to the Convention which was opened to signature on 22 November 1984. The opportunity was not taken to deal with this question in Article 5 of the Protocol, which guarantees certain additional rights to spouses, notably in the event of dissolution of marriage. Indeed, para 39 of the explanatory report to the Protocol states that the words "in the event of its dissolution" found in Article 5 "do not imply any obligation on a State to provide for dissolution of marriage or to provide any special forms of dissolution."

54   The Court thus concludes that the applicants cannot derive a right to divorce from Article 12. That provision is therefore inapplicable in the present case, either on its own or in conjunction with Article 14.

(b)   Article 8

55   The principles which emerge from the Court's case law on Article 8 include the following.

(a) By guaranteeing the right to respect for family life, Article 8 presupposes the existence of a family (see the above-mentioned *Marckx* judgment, Series A, No 31, para 31).

(b) Article 8 applies to the "family life" of the "illegitimate" family as well as to that of the "legitimate" family (*ibid*).

(c) Although the essential object of Article 8 is to protect the individual against arbitrary interference by the public authorities, there may in addition be positive obligations inherent in an effective "respect" for family life. However, especially as far as those positive obligations are concerned, the notion of "respect" is not clear-cut: having regard to the diversity of the practices followed and the situations obtaining in the Contracting States, the notion's requirements will vary considerably from case to case. Accordingly, this is an area in which the Contracting Parties enjoy a wide margin of appreciation in determining the steps to be taken to ensure compliance with the Convention with due regard to the needs and resources of the community and of individuals (*Abdulaziz, Cabales and Balkandali v The United Kingdom*, judgment of 28 May 1985, Series A, No 94, para 67).

56 In the present case, it is clear that the applicants, the first and second of whom have lived together for some fifteen years, constitute a "family" for the purposes of Article 8. They are thus entitled to its protection, notwithstanding the fact that their relationship exists outside marriage (see para 55(b) above).

The question that arises, as regards this part of the case, is whether an effective "respect" for the applicants' family life imposes on Ireland a positive obligation to introduce measures that would permit divorce.

57 It is true that, on this question, Article 8, with its reference to the somewhat vague notion of "respect" for family life, might appear to lend itself more readily to an evolutive interpretation than does Article 12. Nevertheless, the Convention must be read as a whole and the Court does not consider that a right to divorce, which it has found to be excluded from Article 12 (see paragraph 54 above), can, with consistency, be derived from Article 8, a provision of more general purpose and scope. The Court is not oblivious to the plight of the first and second applicants. However, it is of the opinion that, although the protection of private or family life may sometimes necessitate means whereby spouses can be relieved from the duty to live together (see the above-mentioned *Airey* judgment (1979), Series A, No 32, para 33), the engagements undertaken by Ireland under Article 8 cannot be regarded as extending to an obligation on its part to introduce measures permitting the divorce and the re-marriage which the applicants seek.

58 On the point, there is therefore no failure to respect the family life of the first and second applicants.

2   Article 14, taken in conjunction with Article 8

59 The first and second applicants complained of the fact that whereas Roy Johnston was unable to obtain a divorce in order subsequently to marry Janice Williams-Johnston, other persons resident in Ireland and having the necessary means could obtain abroad a divorce which would be recognised *de jure* or *de facto* in Ireland (see paras 19–21 above). They alleged that on this account they had been victims of discrimination, on the ground of financial means, in the enjoyment of the rights set forth in Article 8, contrary to Article 14, which reads as follows:

> The enjoyment of the rights and freedoms set forth in the Convention shall be secured without discrimination on any ground such as sex, race, colour, language, religion, political or other opinion, national or social origin, association with a national minority, property, birth or other status.

This allegation, contested by the Government, was rejected by the Commission.

60 Article 14 safeguards persons who are "placed in analogous situations" against discriminatory differences of treatment in the exercise of the rights and freedoms recognised by the Convention (see as the most recent authority, *Lithgow and Others v The United Kingdom*, judgment of 8 July 1986, Series A, No 102, para 177).

The Court notes that under the general Irish rules of private international law foreign divorces will be recognised in Ireland only if they have been obtained by persons domiciled abroad (see para 20 above). It does not find it to have been established that these rules are departed from in practice. In its view, the situations of such persons and of the first and second applicants cannot be regarded as analogous.

61 There is, accordingly, no discrimination, within the meaning of Article 14.

3   Article 9

62 The first applicant also alleged that his inability to live with the second applicant other than in an extra-marital relationship was contrary to his conscience and that on that account he was the victim of a violation of Article 9 of the Convention, which guarantees to everyone the "right to freedom of thought, conscience and religion."

The applicant supplemented this allegation, which was contested by the Government and rejected by the Commission, by a claim of discrimination in relation to conscience and religion, contrary to Article 14 taken in conjunction with Article 9.

63 It is clear that Roy Johnston's freedom to have and manifest his convictions is not in issue. His complaint derives, in essence, from the non-availability of divorce under Irish law, a matter to which, in the Court's view, Article 9 cannot, in its ordinary meaning, be taken to extend.

Accordingly, that provision, and hence Article 14 also, are not applicable.

4   Conclusion

64 The Court thus concludes that the complaints related to the inability to divorce and re-marry are not well-founded.

B   Matters other than the inability to divorce and re-marry

65 The first and second applicants further alleged that, in violation of Article 8, there had been an interference with, or lack of respect for, their family life on account of their status under Irish law. They cited, by way of illustration, the following matters:

(a) their non-recognition as a "family" for the purposes of Article 41 of the Constitution of Ireland (see para 18 above);

(b) the absence of mutual maintenance obligations and mutual succession rights (see para 23 above);

(c) their treatment for the purposes of capital acquisition tax, stamp duty and Land Registry fees (see paras 24 (b) and (c) above);

(d) the non-availability of the protection of barring orders (see para 24(a) above);

(e) the non-applicability of the Family Home Protection Act 1976 (see para 24(b) above);

(f) the differences, in the social welfare code, between married and unmarried persons (see para 24(d) above).

The Government contested this allegation. The Commission, for its part, considered that the fact that Irish law did not confer a recognised family status on the first and second applicants did not give rise to a breach of Article 8.

66 In the Court's view, there has been no interference by the public authorities with the family life of the first and second applicants: Ireland has done nothing to impede or prevent them from living together and continuing to do so and, indeed, they have been able to take a number of steps to regularise their situation as best they could (see para 2 above). Accordingly, the sole question that arises for decision is whether an effective "respect" for their family life imposes on Ireland a positive obligation to improve their status (see para 55(c) above).

67 The Court does not find it necessary to examine, item by item, the various aspects of Irish law relied on by the applicants and listed in para 65 above. They were put forward

as illustrations to support a general complaint concerning status (see para 48 above) and, whilst bearing them in mind, the Court will concentrate on this broader issue.

68 It is true that certain legislative provisions designed to support family life are not available to the first and second applicants. However, like the Commission, the Court does not consider that it is possible to derive from Article 8 an obligation on the part of Ireland to establish for unmarried couples a status analogous to that of married couples.

The applicants did, in fact, make it clear that their complaints concerned only couples who, like themselves, wished to marry but were legally incapable of marrying and not those who had chosen of their own volition to live together outside marriage. Nevertheless, even it is circumscribed in this way, the applicants' claim cannot, in the Court's opinion, be accepted. A number of the matters complained of are but consequences of the inability to obtain a dissolution of Roy Johnston's marriage, enabling him to marry Janice Williams-Johnston, a situation which the Court has found not to be incompatible with the Convention. As for the other matters, Article 8 cannot be interpreted as imposing an obligation to establish a special regime for a particular category of unmarried couples.

69 There is accordingly no violation of Article 8 under this head.

III   Situation of the third applicant

A   Article 8

70 The applicants alleged that, in violation of Article 8, there had been an interference with, or lack of respect for, their family life on account of the third applicant's situation under Irish law. In addition to the points mentioned at paras (d) and (e) of para 65 above, they cited, by way of illustration, the following matters:

(a) the position regarding the third applicant's paternal affiliation (see paras 25 and 26 above);

(b) the impossibility for the first applicant to be appointed joint guardian of the third applicant and his lack of parental rights in relation to her (see para 27 above);

(c) the impossibility for the third applicant to be legitimated even by her parents' subsequent marriage (see para 28 above);

(d) the impossibility for the third applicant to be jointly adopted by her parents (see para 29 above);

(e) the third applicant's succession rights *vis-à-vis* her parents (see paras 31 and 32 above);

(f) the third applicant's treatment for the purposes of capital acquisition tax (see para 33 above) and the repercussions on her of her parents' own treatment for fiscal purposes (see paras 24(b) and (c) above).

The Government contested this allegation. The Commission, on the other hand, expressed the opinion that there had been a breach of Article 8, in that the legal regime concerning the status of the third applicant under Irish law failed to respect the family life of all three applicants.

71 Roy Johnston and Janice Williams-Johnston have been able to take a number of steps to integrate their daughter in the family (see para 12 above). However, the question arises whether an effective "respect" for family life imposes on Ireland a positive obligation to improve her legal situation (see para 55(c) above).

72 Of particular relevance to this part of the case, in addition to the principles recalled in para 55 above, are the following passages from the Court's case law:

> ... when the State determines in its domestic legal system the regime applicable to certain family ties such as those between an unmarried mother and her child, it must act in a manner calculated to allow those concerned to lead a normal family life. As envisaged by Article 8, respect for family life implies in particular, in the Court's view, the existence in domestic law of legal safeguards that render possible as from the moment of birth the child's integration in his family. In this connection, the State has a choice of various means, but a law that fails to satisfy this requirement violates para 1 of Article 8 without there being any call to examine it under para 2. (Above-mentioned *Marckx* judgment, Series A, No 31, para 31).

> In determining whether or not a positive obligation exists, regard must be had to the fair balance that has to be struck between the general interest of the community and the interests of the individual, the search for which balance is inherent in the whole of the Convention ... In striking this balance the aims mentioned in the second paragraph of Article 8 may be of a certain relevance, although this provision refers in terms only to "interferences" with the right protected by the first paragraph – in other words is concerned with the negative obligations flowing therefrom ... (*Rees v The United Kingdom*, judgment of 17 October 1986, Series A, No 106, para 37)

As the Government emphasised, the *Marckx* case related solely to the relations between mother and child. However, the Court considers that its observations on the integration of a child within his family are equally applicable to a case such as the present, concerning as it does parents who have lived, with their daughter, in a family relationship over many years but are unable to marry on account of the indissolubility of the existing marriage of one of them.

73 In this context also, the Court will concentrate on the general complaint concerning the third applicant's legal situation (see, *mutatis mutandis*, para 67 above); it will bear in mind, but not examine separately, the various aspects of Irish law listed in para 70 above. It notes in any event that many of the aspects in question are interrelated in such a way that modification of the law on one of them might have repercussions on another.

74 As is recorded in the Preamble to the European Convention of 15 October 1975 on the Legal Status of Children Born Out of Wedlock, "in a great number of member States of the Council of Europe efforts have been, or are being, made to improve the legal status of children born out of wedlock by reducing the differences between their legal status and that of children born in wedlock which are to the legal or social disadvantage of the former". Furthermore, in Ireland itself this trend is reflected in the Status of Children Bill recently laid before Parliament (see para 36 above).

In its consideration of this part of the present case, the Court cannot but be influenced by these developments. As it observed in its above mentioned *Marckx* judgment, "respect" for family life, understood as including the ties between near relatives, implies an obligation for the State to act in a manner calculated to allow these ties to develop normally ((1979), Series A, No 31, para 45). And in the present case the normal development of the natural family ties between the first and second applicants and their daughter requires, in the Court's opinion, that she should be placed, legally and socially, in a position akin to that of a legitimate child.

75 Examination of the third applicant's present legal situation, seen as a whole, reveals, however, that it differs considerably from that of a legitimate child; in addition, it has not been shown that there are any means available to her or her parents to eliminate or reduce the differences. Having regard to the particular circumstances of this case and

notwithstanding the wide margin of appreciation enjoyed by Ireland in this area (see para 55(c) above), the absence of an appropriate legal regime reflecting the third applicant's natural family ties amounts to a failure to respect her family life.

Moreover, the close and intimate relationship between the third applicant and her parents is such that there is of necessity also a resultant failure to respect the family life of each of the latter. Contrary to the Government's suggestion, this finding does not amount, in an indirect way, to a conclusion that the first applicant should be entitled to divorce and re-marry; this is demonstrated by the fact that in Ireland itself it is proposed to improve the legal situation of illegitimate children, whilst maintaining the constitutional prohibition on divorce.

76 There is accordingly, as regards all three applicants, a breach of Article 8 under this head.

77 It is not the Court's function to indicate which measures Ireland should take in this connection; it is for the State concerned to choose the means to be utilised in its domestic law for performance of its obligation under Article 53 (see the above-mentioned *Airey* judgment, Series A, No 32, para 26; and the above-mentioned *Marckx* judgment, Series A, No 31, para 58). In making its choice, Ireland must ensure that the requisite fair balance is struck between the demands of the general interest of the community and the interests of the individual.

B   Article 14

78 The third applicant alleged that, by reason of the distinctions existing under Irish law between legitimate and illegitimate children in the matter of succession rights over the estates of their parents (see paras 31–32 above), she was the victim of discrimination contrary to Article 14, taken in conjunction with Article 8.

The Government contested this allegation.

79 Since succession rights were included amongst the aspects of Irish law which were taken into consideration in the examination of the general complaint concerning the third applicant's legal situation (see paras 70–76 above), the Court, like the Commission, does not consider it necessary to give a separate ruling on this allegation.

IV   The application of article 50

80 Under Article 50 of the Convention,

> If the Court finds that a decision or a measure taken by a legal authority or any other authority of a High Contracting Party is completely or partially in conflict with the obligations arising from the ... Convention, and if the internal law of the said Party allows only partial reparation to be made for the consequences of this decision or measure, the decision of the Court shall, if necessary, afford just satisfaction to the injured party.

The applicants sought under this provision just satisfaction in respect of material loss, non-pecuniary loss and legal costs and expenses.

A   Material loss

81 By way of compensation for material loss, the first applicant claimed specified amounts in respect of the potential loss of the tax allowance available to married persons and in respect of accountant's fees relative to this issue; the second applicant claimed

IR£2,000 for curtailment of job opportunities attributed to her lack of family status. The Government pleaded the absence of any supporting evidence.

82 The Court finds that these claims have to be rejected. They both stem from matters in respect of which it has found no violation of the Convention, namely the inability to divorce and re-marry and other aspects of the second applicant's status under Irish law (see paras 49 – 64 and 65 – 69 above).

B   Non-pecuniary loss

83 The applicants claimed IR£20,000 as compensation for non-pecuniary loss in the shape of the severe emotional strain and worry which they had endured as a direct result of the lack of recognition of their family relationship and the inability to marry. The Government submitted that it was not necessary to award just satisfaction under this head.

84 In support of their claim, the applicants listed a number of inconveniences or areas of concern affecting them. The Court notes, however, that several of those matters originate either in the inability of the first and second applicants to marry or in other aspects of their own status under Irish law. Since these issues have not given rise to any finding of violation of the Convention, they cannot ground an award of just satisfaction under Article 50.

If and in so far as the remaining matters are connected with the legal situation of the third applicant – a point which does not emerge clearly from the material before the Court – they could in principle form the object of such an award. Nevertheless, the Court considers that, in the particular circumstances of the case, its findings of violation on that issue (see paras 70–76 above) of themselves constitute sufficient just satisfaction.

The applicants' claim cannot therefore be accepted.

C   Legal costs and expenses

85 The applicants sought reimbursement of their costs and expenses referable to the proceedings before the Commission and the Court. Whilst particulars of their claim were incomplete in some respects, they indicated at the hearings before the Court that they could supply further information in writing if so requested. The Government confined themselves to submitting that details of the computation of the fees should have been furnished initially.

Notwithstanding the foregoing, the Court considers that this aspect of the question of the application of Article 50 can also be regarded as ready for decision.

86 The applicants had the benefit of legal aid before the Convention institutions. However, the Court sees no reason to doubt that they have incurred liability for costs additional to those covered by the legal aid or that the quantified items of their claim satisfy the Court's criteria in the matter (see, amongst many authorities, *Zimmermann and Steiner v Switzerland*, judgment of 13 July 1983, Series A, No 66, para 36).

Nevertheless, although the proceedings in Strasbourg have led to findings of violation as regards the legal situation of the third applicant, the applicants' remaining complaints were unsuccessful. In these circumstances, the Court considers that it would not be appropriate to award them the full amount (some IR£20,000) of the fees incurred (see *Le Compte, Van Leuven and De Meyere v Belgium*, judgment of 21 February 1986, Series A, No 43, para 21). Making an assessment on an equitable basis, as is required by Article 50, the

Court finds that the applicants should be awarded IR£12,000 in respect of their costs and expenses. This figure is to be increased by any value added tax that may be chargeable.

For these reasons, **THE COURT:**

1   *Rejects* unanimously the Government's preliminary pleas;

2   *Holds* by 16 votes to one that the absence of provision for divorce under Irish law and the resultant inability of the first and second applicants to marry each other does not give rise to a violation of Article 8 or 12 of the Convention;

3   *Holds* by 16 votes to one that the first and second applicants are not victims of discrimination, contrary to Article 14 taken in conjunction with Article 8, by reason of the fact that certain foreign divorces may be recognised by the law of Ireland;

4   *Holds* by 16 votes to one that Article 9 is not applicable in the present case;

5   *Holds* unanimously that, as regards the other aspects of their own status under Irish law complained of by the first and second applicants, there is no violation of Article 8;

6   *Holds* unanimously that the legal situation of the third applicant under Irish law gives rise to a violation of Article 8 as regards all three applicants;

7   *Holds* by 16 votes to one that it is not necessary to examine the third applicant's allegation that she is a victim of discrimination, contrary to Article 14 taken in conjunction with Article 8, by reason of the disabilities to which she is subject under Irish succession law;

8   *Holds* unanimously that Ireland is to pay to the three applicants together, in respect of legal costs and expenses referable to the proceedings before the Commission and the Court, the sum of twelve thousand Irish pounds (IR£12,000), together with any value added tax that may be chargeable.

9   *Rejects* unanimously the remainder of the claim for just satisfaction.

DECLARATION BY JUDGE PINHEIRO FARINHA

(Translation)

With great respect to my eminent colleagues, I consider that the following sentence should have been added to sub-para (b) of para 55 of the judgment: "The Court recognises that support and encouragement of the traditional family is in itself legitimate or even praiseworthy."

This is a citation from para 40 of the *Marckx* judgment of 13 June 1979, the omission of which might cause the present judgment to be interpreted – incorrectly – as meaning that the Court attaches no importance to the institution of marriage.

SEPARATE OPINION, PARTLY DISSENTING AND PARTLY CONCURING, OF JUDGE DE MEYER

(Translation)

I   The impossibility for the first applicant to seek the dissolution of his 1952 marriage and the resultant inability of the first and second applicants to marry each other

1   As the Court observes, in para 50 of the judgment, these two questions cannot be separated: in fact, they come down to a single question, namely the first.

The fact that the first and second applicants are unable to marry each other so long as the first applicant's 1952 marriage is not dissolved cannot, of itself, constitute a violation of their fundamental rights.

It is only the fact that the first applicant cannot seek the dissolution of his 1952 marriage that may constitute such a violation. It may, of itself, do so, as regards the first applicant, because he is a party to that marriage. It may also do so, as regards the second as well as the first applicant, because it necessarily means that neither of them can marry the other during the lifetime of the first applicant's wife.

2   In the present case, the facts found by the Commission are, basically, fairly simple.

The first applicant and the lady whom he married in 1952, in a Church of Ireland ceremony, separated by mutual consent in 1965, having recognised that their marriage had irretrievably broken down.[1] They entered into a separation agreement that regulated their own rights and also those of their three children,[2] who were born in 1956, 1959 and 1965.[3] They have complied with their obligations under that agreement.[4] Each of them, with the other's consent, entered into a new relationship with another partner:[5] in the first applicant's case, this relationship was established with the second applicant in 1971 and it led to the birth, in 1978, of the third applicant.[6]

Since divorce is forbidden in Ireland, the first applicant, apparently with his wife's consent, sought advice as to the possibility of obtaining a divorce elsewhere. For this purpose he consulted lawyers in Dublin and in London, but he has not pursued the matter since they indicated that he could not obtain a divorce in England unless he was resident within the jurisdiction of the English courts.[7]

3   These findings on the part of the Commission were not contested.

The respondent Government confined themselves to observing that the attitude of the first applicant's wife and of their children towards the divorce which he wishes to obtain was not known for certain.[8]

---

1   Commissioner's Report, para 34.
2   *Ibid*, para 38(b).
3   *Ibid*, para 34.
4   *Ibid*, para 38(e).
5   *Ibid*, para 35.
6   *Ibid*, paras 35 and 36.
7   *Ibid*, para 38(a).
8   Observations of Mr Gleeson at the hearing of 23-24 June 1986.

This point would have merited clarification, but it is not decisive for the issue raised in the present case. This is because the sole question is whether the fundamental rights of the first and second applicants have or have not been violated because, in the factual situation recalled above, the first applicant cannot request the dissolution of his 1952 marriage: if that were possible, his wife would of necessity have to participate in the proceedings, to the extent that she had not associated herself with the request, and the deciding authority would of necessity have to have regard to the interests of the children.

4   Of course, the issue raised in the present case concerns only the civil dissolution of the marriage, since the latter, being a religious marriage celebrated in a Church of Ireland ceremony, cannot fall within the respondent State's jurisdiction: it can only do so as a marriage recognised by that State as regards its civil effects.

5   We are thus faced with a situation in which, by mutual consent and a considerable time ago, two spouses separated, regulated their own and their children's rights in an apparently satisfactory fashion and embarked on a new life, each with a new partner.

In my view, the absence of any possibility of seeking, in such circumstances, the civil dissolution of the marriage constitutes, first and of itself, a violation, as regards each of the spouses, of the rights guaranteed in Articles 8, 9 and 12 of the Convention. Secondly, in that it perforce means that neither spouse can remarry in a civil ceremony so long as his wife or husband is alive, it constitutes a violation of the same rights as regards each of the spouses and each of the new partners.

The absence of the aforesaid possibility is consonant neither with the right of those concerned to respect for their private and family life, nor with their right to freedom of conscience and religion, nor with their right to marry and to found a family.

In fact, it seems to me that in cases like the present the effective exercise of these rights may require that the spouses be allowed to apply not only to be relieved of their duty to live together but also to be completely released in civil law from their marital ties, by means of legal recognition of their definitive separation.[9]

The prohibition, under the Constitution of the respondent State, of any legislation permitting the dissolution of marriage is, as seems already to have been recognised in 1967 by a Committee of that State's Parliament, "coercive in relation to all persons, Catholics and non-Catholics, whose religious rules do not absolutely prohibit divorce in all circumstances" and "at variance with the accepted principles of religious liberty as declared at the Vatican Council and elsewhere". Above all, it is, as that Committee stated, "unnecessarily harsh and rigid." [10]

In what the Convention, in several provisions and notably those concerning respect for private and family life and freedom of conscience and religion, calls "a democratic society", the prohibition cannot be justified.

---

9   See, *mutatis mutandis*, *Airey v Ireland*, ECHR, judgment of 9 October 1979, Series A, No 32, at para 33.

10   "It can be argued, therefore, that the existing constitutional provision is coercive in relation to all persons, Catholics and non-Catholics, whose religious rules do not absolutely prohibit divorce in all circumstances. It is unnecessarily harsh and rigid and could, in our view, be regarded as being at variance with the accepted principles of religious liberty as declared at the Vatican Council and elsewhere" (Report of the Informal Committee on the Constitution, 1967, para 126, cited in the Report of the Joint Committee on Marriage Breakdown, 1985, para 7.8.8, which document formed Annex 3 to the Respondent Government's Memorial of 28 November 1985).

On more than one occasion, the Court has pointed out that there can be no such society without pluralism, tolerance and broadmindedness:[11] these are hallmarks of a democratic society.[12]

In a society grounded on principles of this kind, it seems to me excessive to impose, in an inflexible and absolute manner, a rule that marriage is indissoluble, without even allowing consideration to be given to the possibility of exceptions in cases of the present kind.

For so draconian a system to be legitimate, it does not suffice that it corresponds to the desire or will of a substantial majority of the population: the Court has also stated that "although individual interests must on occasion be subordinated to those of a group, democracy does not simply mean that the views of a majority must always prevail: a balance must be achieved which ensures the fair and proper treatment of minorities and avoids any abuse of a dominant position."[13]

In my opinion, this statement must also be applicable in the area of marriage and divorce.

6   The foregoing considerations do not imply recognition of a right to divorce or that such a right, to the extent that it exists, can be classified as a fundamental right.

They simply mean that the complete exclusion of any possibility of seeking the civil dissolution of a marriage is not compatible with the right to respect for private and family life, with the right to freedom of conscience and religion and with the right to marry and to found a family.

7   I also find that there is discrimination as regards the exercise of the rights involved.

Although it totally prohibits divorce within Ireland itself, the respondent State recognises divorces obtained in other countries by persons domiciled there at the time of the divorce proceedings.[14]

Thus, Irish citizens who move abroad and stay there long enough for it to be accepted that they intend to remain there permanently escape their inability to obtain a divorce in Ireland.

This state of affairs is in unfortunate contradiction with the absolute character of the principle of indissolubility of marriage, in that the principle thus appears to warrant observance only in Ireland itself and not elsewhere.

The distinction so made between Irish citizens according to whether they are domiciled in Ireland itself or elsewhere appears to me to lack an objective and reasonable justification.[15]

---

11   See *Handyside v The United Kingdom*, ECHR, judgment of 7 December 1976, Series A, No 24, para 49, and *Lingens v Austria*, ECHR, judgment of 8 July 1986, Series A, No 103, para 41.
12   See *Young, James and Webster v The United Kingdom*, ECHR, judgment of 13 August 1981, Series A, No 44, para 63.
13   *Ibid, loc cit.*
14   See paras 19 – 21 of the judgment.
15   See *"Relating to Certain Aspects of the Laws on the Use of Languages in Education in Belgium" v Belgium* (Merits), ECHR, judgment of 23 July 1968, Series A, No 6, para 10.

8   Unlike the majority of the Court, I am therefore of the opinion that in the present case the first and second applicants rightly complain of a violation of their right to respect for their private and family life, of their right to freedom of conscience and religion and of their right to marry and to found a family, as well as of discrimination in the exercise of these rights.

II   The other aspects of the situation of the first and second applicants, independently of their relations with or concerning the third applicant

On this issue I consider, like the other members of the Court, that no fundamental right has been violated in the present case.

From the point of view of fundamental rights, the State has no positive obligation *vis-à-vis* couples who live together as husband and wife without being married: it is sufficient that the State abstains from any illegitimate interference.

It is only to the extent that children are born of unions of this kind, and of transient relationships also, that there may arise positive obligations on the part of the State concerning the situation of those children, including, of course, their relations with their parents[16] and with the latter's families.[17]

Such obligations may likewise arise, to the extent that the interests of those children so require, as regards the mutual relations of their parents or the latter's families.

In cases of this kind, it is therefore always a question solely of obligations concerning the situation of those children. This is particularly so in the present case.

III   The situation of the third applicant and the situation of the first and second applicants in their relations with or concerning the third applicant

1   On this issue, I agree almost entirely with what is said in the judgment concerning the violation, as regards the three applicants, of the right to respect for private and family life.

However, it seems to me that it is not sufficient to say that the third applicant should be placed "in a position akin to that of a legitimate child":[18] in my view, we ought to have stated more clearly and more simply that the legal situation of a child born out of wedlock must be identical to that of a child of a married couple and that, by the same token, there cannot be, as regards relations with or concerning a child, any difference between the legal situation of his parents and of their families that depends on whether he was the child of a married couple or a child born out of wedlock.

I also note that, as the daughter of the first applicant – who is still bound by his 1952 marriage – the third applicant is the child of an adulterous union: this does not exclude the applicability in her case, as well as in that of any other child born out of wedlock, of the principles enounced in both the present and the *Marckx* judgments.

---

16   See *Marckx v Belgium*, ECHR, judgment of 13 June 1979, Series A, No 31, para 31.
17   *Ibid*, paras 45-48.
18   Para 74 of the judgment.

2   I consider that in the present case the Court should, as in the *Marckx* case, have found not only a violation of the right to respect for private and family life but also a violation, as regards that right, of the principle of non-discrimination.

In my view, the latter violation arises from the very fact that, on the one hand, the legal situation of the third applicant, as a child born out of wedlock, is different from that of a child of a married couple and that, on the other hand, the legal situation of the first and second applicants in their relations with or concerning the third applicant is different from that of the parents of a child of a married couple in their relations with or concerning that child.

In this respect, the facts of the case thus disclose not only a violation of the right to respect for private and family life but also, at the same time, a violation, as regards that right, of the principle of non-discrimination.

I would observe, for the sake of completeness, that the principle of non-discrimination appears to me to have been so violated as regards the first and second applicants as well as the third applicant, and as regards those aspects of the legal situation of the persons concerned that do not relate to their succession rights as well as those aspects that do so relate.

IV   The just satisfaction claimed by the applicants

1   Although I dissent from the majority as regards points 2, 3, 4 and 7 of the operative provisions of the judgment, I agree, in principle, with the Court's decision on the applicants' claim for just satisfaction. However, my reasons are somewhat different.

The applicants are not the only victims of the situation complained of, a situation which affects, in a general and impersonal manner, everyone whose circumstances are similar to theirs.

In my view, the just satisfaction to be afforded to the applicants in such a case should normally be confined to reimbursement of the costs and expenses referable to the proceedings before the Commission and the Court and should not include compensation for material or non-pecuniary loss.

However, such compensation could be warranted if there were measures or decisions which, in the guise of provisions of general or impersonal application, had had the object or the result of affecting the applicants directly and individually. But that is not the situation here.

2   As regards the quantum of the reimbursement, I agree, having regard to the majority's decision on the merits of the case, with point 8 of the operative provisions of the judgment.

CASE NO 20

KROON AND OTHERS v THE NETHERLANDS

EUROPEAN COURT OF HUMAN RIGHTS

Application No: 18535/91

Judgment: 27 October 1994

Panel: *Judges*: Ryssdal (*President*), Gölcüklü, Martens, Foighel, Loizou, Morenilla, Baka, Mifsud Bonnici, Gotchev

Human rights — Right to respect for family life — Equality and non-discrimination — Sex discrimination — Meaning of "family life" — "De facto" family — Whether child born of an extramarital relationship has family ties with its biological father — Paternity — Whether inability of a mother to deny paternity violated right to respect for family life — Positive obligations of Contracting States — State's obligations to protect the development of family ties — Margin of appreciation — European Convention for the Protection of Human Rights and Fundamental Freedoms, arts 8 and 14

BACKGROUND

Ms Kroon, the first applicant, wished to register the paternity of her son born in October 1987 of her relationship with Mr Zerrouk. Under Netherlands law the child was registered as the son of her husband Mr M'Hallem-Driss, whom she had married in 1979. Ms Kroon's marriage to M'Hallem-Driss had broken down in 1980 and Mr M'Hallem-Driss had subsequently left Amsterdam in January 1986. His whereabouts was unknown. The applicants (Ms Kroon, Mr Zerrouk and the child Samir M'Hallem-Driss) alleged that the fact that Ms Kroon was unable to have a statement entered in the register of births that her husband, Mr M'Hallem-Driss, was not the father of her child, Samir, with the result that Mr Zerrouk was unable to recognise the child as his own, violated their right to respect for family life under article 8 of the European Convention on Human Rights. They also claimed discrimination on the grounds of sex in violation of article 8 in conjunction with article 14 of the European Convention in that Netherlands law permitted a married man to deny the paternity of a child born in wedlock, but did not permit a married woman to do so.

The Netherlands Government argued that the relationship between the applicants did not amount to one of "family life". As the child had been born of an extramarital relationship, there was no juridical family tie between the child and Mr Zerrouk. Furthermore, Ms Kroon and Mr Zerrouk had chosen not to marry, and Mr Zerrouk neither lived with Ms Kroon nor was he the child's "social father" under the Government definition. However, the European Commission of Human Rights found that the long-standing relationship between Ms Kroon and Mr Zerrouk, and the fact that the latter was the undisputed biological father of not only Samir but four other children by Ms Kroon, established the existence of a "family" for the purposes of the Convention.

The Commission expressed the opinion, by twelve votes to six, that there had been a violation of article 8 taken alone, but no violation of article 8 taken in conjunction with article 14. The case was referred to the European Court of Human Rights.

HELD (finding a violation of article 8 of the Convention)

Article 8 (right to respect for family life)

1 The notion of "family life" in article 8 was not confined solely to marriage-based relationships and might encompass other *de facto* "family ties" where parties were living together outside marriage. Although, as a rule, living together might be a requirement for such a relationship, exceptionally other factors might also serve to demonstrate that a relationship had sufficient constancy to create *de facto* family ties, such as children born of the relationship. A child born of such a relationship was *ipso jure* part of that "family unit" from the moment of its birth and by the very fact of it. There thus existed between Samir and Mr Zerrouk a bond amounting to family life, whatever the contribution made by Mr Zerrouk to his son's care and upbringing. Article 8 was therefore applicable. (Para 30)

2 The essential object of article 8 was to protect the individual against arbitrary action by the public authorities. There might in addition be positive obligations inherent in effective "respect" for family life. However, the boundaries between the State's positive and negative obligations under this provision did not lend themselves to precise definition. The applicable principles were nonetheless similar. In both contexts regard had to be had to the fair balance that has to be struck between the competing interests of the individual and of the community as a whole; and in both contexts the State enjoyed a certain margin of appreciation. (Para 31)

3 Where the existence of a family tie with a child had been established, the State had to act in a manner calculated to enable that tie to be developed, and legal safeguards had to be established that render possible as from the moment of birth or as soon as practicable thereafter the child's integration in his family. In this case it had been established that the relationship between the applicants qualified as family life. There was thus a positive obligation on the part of the competent authorities to allow complete legal family ties to be formed between Mr Zerrouk and his son Samir as expeditiously as possible. (Paras 32 and 36)

4 If Mr Zerrouk were to marry Ms Kroon, he could establish legal ties with his son through a step-parent adoption. Whether or not the applicants wished to marry, a solution which allowed a father to create a legal tie with his child only if he married the child's mother could not be regarded as compatible with the notion of respect for family life. Respect for family life demanded that biological and social reality prevail over a legal presumption which flies in the face of both established fact and the wishes of those concerned without actually benefiting anyone. Thus, joint custody was also not an acceptable solution since, even if Mr Zerrouk were granted joint custody of Samir, it would leave the legal ties between Samir and Mr Omar M'Hallem-Driss intact and would continue to preclude the formation of such ties between Samir and Mr Zerrouk. Accordingly, even having regard to the margin of appreciation left to the State, the Netherlands had failed to secure to the applicants the respect for their family life to which they were entitled under the Convention. There had accordingly been a violation of article 8. (Paras 38–40)

Article 14 in conjunction with Article 8

5 The complaint of violation of article 14 in conjunction with article 8 was essentially the same as the one under article 8. Having found a violation of article 8 taken alone,

there was no need to consider any separate issue under article 8 in conjunction with article 14. (para 42)

Treaties and other international instruments referred to

European Convention for the Protection of Human Rights and Fundamental Freedoms 1950, arts 8, 13, 14 and 50

National legislation referred to

The Netherlands

Civil Code (*Burgerlijk Wetboek*), ss 1:16(1)–(2), 1:17(1)(c), 1:197–200, 1:205, 1:221(1), 1:222–223, 1:225(3), 1:227–229(1)

Cases referred to

Abdulaziz, Cabales and Balkandali v The United Kingdom, ECHR, judgment of 28 May 1985, Series A, No 94; 7 EHRR 471; below, p 618

Handyside v The United Kingdom, ECHR, judgment of 7 December 1976, Series A, No 24; 1 EHRR 737

Johnston and others v Ireland, ECHR, judgment of 18 December 1986, Series A, No 112; 9 EHRR 203; *supra*, p 296

Keegan v Ireland, ECHR, judgment of 26 May 1994, Series A, No 290; 18 EHRR 342

Marckx v Belgium, ECHR, judgment of 13 June 1979, Series A, No 31; 2 EHRR 330; 58 ILR 561; *supra*, p 273

Netherlands Supreme Court, judgment of 16 November 1990, NJ 1991, 475

Netherlands Supreme Court, judgment of 17 September 1993, NJ 1994, 373

JUDGMENT

PROCEDURE

[...]*

AS TO THE FACTS

I   The particular circumstances of the case

7   The first applicant, Catharina Kroon, is a Netherlands national born in 1954. The second applicant, Ali Zerrouk, born in 1961, was a Moroccan national at the time of the events complained of; he subsequently obtained Netherlands nationality. Although they were not living together at the time, they had a stable relationship from which the third applicant, Samir M'Hallem-Driss, was born in 1987; he has both Moroccan and Netherlands nationality. All three applicants live in Amsterdam.

---

*   *Eds:* paras 1-6, which relate to procedural matters, have not been included.

8   In 1979, Mrs Kroon had married Mr Omar M'Hallem-Driss, a Moroccan national. The marriage broke down towards the end of 1980. Thereafter, Mrs Kroon lived apart from her husband and lost contact with him. It appears from official records that he left Amsterdam in January 1986 and his whereabouts have remained unknown ever since.

9   Samir was born on 18 October 1987. He was entered in the register of births as the son of Mrs Kroon and Mr M'Hallem-Driss.

Mrs Kroon instituted divorce proceedings in the Amsterdam Regional Court (*arrondissementsrechtbank*) one month after Samir's birth. The action was not defended and the divorce became final when the Regional Court's judgment was entered in the register of marriages on 4 July 1988.

10 On 13 October 1988, relying on section 1:198(1) of the Civil Code (*Burgerlijk Wetboek*, "CC" – see para 19 below), Mrs Kroom and Mr Zerrouk requested the Amsterdam registrar of births, deaths and marriages (*ambtenaar van de burgerlijke stand*) to allow Mrs Kroon to make a statement before him to the effect that Mr M'Hallem-Driss was not Samir's father and thus make it possible for Mr Zerrouk to recognise the child as his.

The registrar refused this request on 21 October 1988. While expressing sympathy, he noted that Samir had been born while Mrs Kroon was still married to Mr M'Hallem-Driss, so that unless the latter brought proceedings to deny paternity (see paras 18 and 21 below), recognition by another man was impossible under Netherlands law as it stood.

11 On 9 January 1989 Mrs Kroon and Mr Zerrouk applied to the Amsterdam Regional Court for an order directing the registrar to add to the register of births Mrs Kroon's statement that Mr M'Hallem-Driss was not Samir's father and Mr Zerrouk's recognition of Samir. They relied on Article 8 of the Convention, taken both alone and together with Article 14, pointing out that while it would have been possible for Mrs Kroon's former husband to deny the paternity of Samir, it was not possible for her to deny her former husband's paternity of the child.

The Regional Court refused this request on 13 June 1989. It held that in spite of the justified wish of Mrs Kroon and Mr Zerrouk to have biological realities officially recognised, their request had to be refused since, under the law as it stood, Samir was the legitimate child of Mr M'Hallem-Driss. There were only limited exceptions to the rule that the husband of the mother was presumed to be the father of a child born in wedlock. This was justified in the interests of legal certainty, which were of great importance in this field, and by the need to protect the rights and freedoms of others. The law as it stood was therefore not incompatible with Articles 8 and 14 of the Convention.

12 Relying again on Articles 8 and 14, Mrs Kroon and Mr Zerrouk appealed to the Amsterdam Court of Appeal (*Gerechtshof*).

The Court of Appeal rejected the appeal on 8 November 1989. It held that Article 8 was applicable but had not been violated. The restrictions imposed on the mother's right to deny the paternity of her husband satisfied the requirements of Article 8(2). There had, however, been a violation of Article 14 taken together with Article 8, since there was no sound reason for the difference of treatment which the law established between husband and wife by not granting the latter the possibility, available to the former, of denying the husband's paternity. Nevertheless the appeal could not be allowed; it was not open to the court to grant the applicants' request, as that would require the creation of new Netherlands law, including administrative procedure, and would therefore go beyond the limits of the judiciary's powers to develop the law. Only the legislature could decide how best to comply with Article 14 of the Convention as regards the possibility of denying paternity of a child born in wedlock.

13 Mrs Kroon and Mr Zerrouk then lodged an appeal on points of law with the Supreme Court (*Hoge Raad*).

They argued, first, that the Court of Appeal had violated Article 8 of the Convention by holding that the limitations imposed by section 1:198 CC on the mother's possibility of denying her husband's paternity – more particularly the fact that she might do so only in respect of a child born after the dissolution of the marriage – satisfied the requirements of Article 8(2). The Court of Appeal had not properly weighed up the interests involved. It ought to have considered the relative weight of, on the one hand, the interests of the biological father and his child and, on the other, the interests protected by the legislation. The Court of Appeal should have given priority to the former interests, which in the case before it were best served by severing the legal ties between Samir and Mr M'Hallem-Driss and establishing such ties between Samir and Mr Zerrouk, who were entitled, under Article 8 of the Convention, to have their family relationship recognised.

In addition, they suggested that it followed from the Court of Appeal's finding of a violation of Article 14 that the interference concerned could not under any circumstances be covered by Article 8(2).

Secondly, they argued that, by holding that it was not empowered to grant the applicants' request as that would require the creation of new Netherlands law, the Court of Appeal had violated Articles 14 and 8 taken together. In the applicants' submission, there was no reason to consider that only the legislature was able to remove the discrimination which the Court of Appeal had rightly found to exist; it was sufficient to disregard the requirement that the child must have been born after the dissolution of the mother's marriage.

14 Following the advisory opinion of the Advocate General, the Supreme Court rejected the appeal on 16 November 1990.

The Supreme Court did not rule on the question whether section 1:198 CC violated Article 8, or Article 14 taken together with Article 8. It considered that it was not necessary to do so, because it agreed with the Court of Appeal that, even if there had been such a violation, solving the problem of what should replace section 1:198 CC went beyond the limits of the judiciary's powers to develop the law. This finding was based on the following reasoning:

> In this connection, it should not be overlooked that if a possibility were to be created for the mother to deny [her husband's] paternity [of a child born] during marriage, the question would immediately arise as to what other limitations should apply in order not to jeopardise the child's interest in certainty regarding its descent from its legitimate parents, which interest the child generally has and which is part of the basis for the present system. Such limitations have therefore also been written into the Bill to Reform the Law of Descent (*Wetsvoorstel Herziening Afstammingsrecht; Bijlage bij de Handelingen van de Tweede Kamer der Staten-Generaal* – Annex to the Records of the Lower House of Parliament – 1987–88, 0626, sections 201 *et seq*), which is now before Parliament ... [I]t is not certain whether [these limitations] will be retained, added to or withdrawn in the course of the further parliamentary discussion, many variations being conceivable, regard also being had to the need to ensure equal treatment of the father and the mother, in so far, at any rate, that unequal treatment is not justified.

The judgment of the Supreme Court was reported in *Nederlandse Jurisprudentie* (Netherlands Law Reports ("NJ") 1991, 475.

15 Three more children were born to Mrs Kroon and Mr Zerrouk after the birth of Samir: a daughter, Nadia, in 1989 and twins, Jamal and Jamila, in 1992. They were all recognised by Mr Zerrouk.

Mrs Kroon and Mr Zerrouk do not cohabit. The applicants claim, however, that Mr Zerrouk contributes to the care and upbringing of their children.

II   Relevant domestic law and practice

A   *The register of births*

16 Every municipality has a separate register for births (section 1:16(1) CC); this is kept by one or more registrars of births, deaths and marriages (section 1:16(2)).

An entry in the register of births, or birth certificate, mentions the mother's husband as the father if the mother was married at the time of the birth or within a period of 306 days immediately preceding the birth; in all other cases, the name of the father is mentioned only if he recognises the child before or at the time the entry is made (section 1:17(1)(c) CC).

17 An interested party or the public prosecutor (*officier van justitie*) can apply to the Regional Court within the jurisdiction of which the register in question is located for an order to correct or add to the register of births. The Regional Court's decision is forwarded to the registrar of births, deaths and marriages; the correction or addition is made in the form of a note in the margin or at the foot of the certificate (section 1:29(1)-(3) CC).

B   *Establishment of paternity and recognition*

18 Section 1:197 CC reads as follows:

> The husband shall be the father of a child born in wedlock. Where a child is born before the 307th day following dissolution of the marriage, the former husband shall be its father, unless the mother has remarried.

Section 1:197 CC thus creates two legal presumptions. First, a child born during marriage is presumed to be the issue of the mother's husband; secondly, a child born before the 307th day following the dissolution of the mother's marriage is presumed to be the progeny of the mother's former husband. The first presumption may be rebutted only by the mother's husband, who to that end must provide proof to the contrary (sections 1:199-200 CC – see para 21 below). The second presumption may be rebutted by either the mother of her former husband; the mother's former husband will, however, have to adduce proof, whereas for the mother a statement is sufficient (section 1:198 CC – see following paragraph).

19 Section 1:198 CC reads as follows:

> 1   The mother may deny that a child born to her within 306 days following the dissolution of the marriage is the child of her former husband by making a statement to that effect before the registrar of births, deaths and marriages, provided that another man recognises the child by the instrument in which that statement is recorded ...
>
> 2   The mother's statement and the recognition must take place within one year of the child's birth.

3   The [mother's] statement and the recognition shall take effect only if the mother and
     the man who recognises the child marry each other within one year of the birth of the
     child ...

4   If a judgment annulling the recognition in an action brought by the former husband
     becomes final, the mother's statement shall also lose its force.

5   ...

20 In its judgment of 17 September 1993 (NJ 1994, 373), the Supreme Court deprived
section 1:198(3) CC of its effect.

In the case in question – in which a child had been born within 306 days of the
dissolution of its mother's marriage – it was established, firstly, that there was a
relationship between the child and its biological father which qualified as "family life"
for the purposes of Article 8 of the Convention and, secondly, that the mother and the
biological father, who did not wish to marry, wanted the paternity of the mother's
former husband to be denied and the child to be recognised by its biological father.

The Supreme Court found that section 1:198(3) CC constituted an "interference" within
the meaning of Article 8, since it obstructed the formation of legally recognised family
ties unless the mother and the biological father got married.

In deciding whether such interference was permissible under the terms of Article 8(2),
the Supreme Court noted that when section 1:198(3) CC had been enacted it was
considered more important to protect a child from being deprived of its "legitimate"
status than to enable it to establish ties with its biological father. Since then, however, the
relative importance of these two opposing interests had changed; in particular, following
the, judgment of the European Court in the *Marckx v Belgium* case (13 June 1979, Series
A, No 31), legal differences between "legitimate" and "illegitimate" children had to a
large extent disappeared. In view of these developments, it could no longer be said that
in cases where, for the purposes of Article 8 of the Convention, there was a relationship
between the child and its biological father amounting to "family life", the importance of
maintaining a child's "legitimate" status overrode the interest protected by section
1:198(3) CC.

21 Section 1:199 CC reads as follows:

The husband can only deny paternity of the child by bringing an action to this end against
the mother as well as against the child, which, unless it has come of age, shall be
represented in the proceedings by a guardian *ad litem* appointed for that purpose by the
District Court (*kantonrechter*).

Section 1:200 CC reads:

1   The court shall allow the action to deny paternity if the husband cannot be the father
     of the child.

2   If during the period in which the child was conceived the husband did not have
     intercourse with the mother, or if they lived apart during that time, the court shall also
     declare the action to deny paternity well-founded, unless facts are established which
     make it appear possible that the husband is the father of the child.

     Such proceedings must be brought within six months from the day on which the
     father became aware of the fact that the child had been born; however, if the mother
     has made a statement of the kind provided for in section 1:198 CC (see paragraph 19
     above), this time-limit does not expire until 18 months after the birth of the child
     (section 1:203 CC).

22 According to section 1:205 CC, legitimacy is proved by a person's parentage (*afstamming*) and the marriage of his or her parents. If there is no birth certificate, the parentage of a "legitimate" child is proved by the undisturbed possession of the status of "legitimate" child.

23 Section 1:221(1) CC reads as follows:

> An illegitimate child has the status of natural child (*natuurlijk kind*) of its mother. Upon recognition it acquires the status of natural child of its father.

> Section 1:222 CC reads as follows:

> An illegitimate child and its descendants have legally recognised family ties (*familierechtelijke betrekkingen*) with the child's mother and her blood relations and, after the child has been recognised, also with the father and his blood relations.

> Section 1:223 CC reads as follows:

> Recognition may be effected:
>
> (a) on the child's birth certificate;
>
> (b) by an instrument of recognition drawn up by a registrar of births, deaths and marriages;
>
> (c) by any notarial deed (*notariële akte*).

There is no requirement that the man recognising an "illegitimate" child should be the biological father. Moreover, it is not possible for a man to recognise a "legitimate" child, even if he is the biological father.

Recognition under section 1:198 CC (see para 19 above) may be annulled on application by the mother's former husband if the man who has recognised the child is not the child's biological father (section 1:225(3) CC).

C   *Adoption by a parent and a step-parent of the child (stiefouderadoptie)*

24 Section 1:227 CC reads as follows:

> 1   Adoption is effected by a decision of the Regional Court at the request of a married couple who wish to adopt a child.
>
> 2   The request can only be granted if the adoption is in the apparent best interests of the child, as regards both breaking the ties with the [natural] parents and reinforcing the ties with the adoptive parents, or – in the case of adoption of a legitimate or natural child of one of the adoptive parents – as regards both breaking the ties with the other parent and reinforcing the ties with the step-parent, and provided that the conditions laid down in the following section are satisfied.

> Section 1:228 CC reads as follows:

> 1   Adoption shall be subject to the following conditions:
>
> (a) ...
>
> (b) that the child is not the legitimate or natural child of a legitimate or natural child of one of its adoptive parents;
>
> (c) that neither adoptive parent is less then eighteen or more than fifty years older than the child;
>
> (d) that the request is not opposed by a parent or the parents with legally recognised family ties with the child. Nevertheless the court shall not be obliged to refuse a request opposed by a parent who was summoned more than two years

previously to be heard on the occasion of a similar request by the same couple that was refused, although the conditions laid down in paragraphs (e) to (g) below were satisfied;

(e) ...

(f) ...

(g) that the adoptive parents were married at least five years before the day the request was filed."

2 In the case of adoption of a legitimate or natural child of one of the adoptive parents, the conditions set forth in paragraphs c and g of the preceding subsection shall not apply. In the case of adoption of a legitimate child of one of the adoptive parents, the condition specified in paragraph (d) shall be replaced by the condition that the former spouse, whose marriage with the spouse of the step-parent has been terminated [by divorce or dissolution of the marriage after judicial separation] if he or she has legally recognised family ties with the child, does not oppose the request.

3 ...

Section 1:229(1) CC reads as follows:

By adoption the adopted person acquires the status of legitimate child of the adoptive parents. However, if the adopted person already had the status of legitimate child of one of the spouses who adopted him or her, he or she shall retain it and by adoption acquire the status of legitimate child of the other spouse.

PROCEEDINGS BEFORE THE COMMISSION

25 Mrs Kroon, Mr Zerrouk and Samir M'Hallem-Driss applied to the Commission on 15 May 1991. They complained that they were unable under Netherlands law to obtain recognition of Mr Zerrouk's paternity of Samir and that while a married man might deny the paternity of a child born in wedlock, it was not open to a married woman to do so; they relied on Article 8 of the Convention, both taken alone and in conjunction with Article 14. They further argued that by not accepting these claims the Supreme Court had denied them an effective remedy within the meaning of Article 13.

26 On 31 August 1992 the Commission declared the application (No 18535/91) admissible as to the complaints relating to Articles 8 and 14 of the Convention and inadmissible as to the remainder. In its report of 7 April 1993 (made under Art 31) it expressed the opinion, by 12 votes to six, that there had been a violation of Article 8 taken alone and, unanimously, that there had been no violation of Article 14 in conjunction with Article 8. The full text of the Commission's opinion is available in Series A, No 297-C.

FINAL SUBMISSIONS BEFORE THE COURT

27 In their memorial, the Government concluded:

that in the present case:

– Article 8 was not applicable, or

– Article 8(1) had not been violated, or

– the restriction of the rights referred to in Article 8(1) was justifiable in accordance with Article 8(2), and that

– Article 14 in conjunction with Article 8 had not been violated.

AS TO THE LAW

I Alleged violation of Article 8 of the Convention

28 The applicants complained that under Netherlands law it was not possible for Mrs Kroon to have entered in the register of births any statement that Mr M'Hallem-Driss was not Samir's father, with the result that Mr Zerrouk was not able to recognise Samir as his child. They relied on Article 8 of the Convention, which reads:

> 1 Everyone has the right to respect for his private and family life, his home and his correspondence.
>
> 2 There shall be no interference by a public authority with the exercise of this right except such as is in accordance with the law and is necessary in a democratic society in the interests of national security, public safety or the economic well-being of the country, for the prevention of disorder or crime, for the protection of health or morals, or for the protection of the rights and freedoms of others.

The Government denied that any violation had taken place, whereas the Commission agreed with the applicants.

A Applicability of Article 8

29 The Government argued that the relationship between Mr Zerrouk on the one hand and Mrs Kroon and Samir on the other did not amount to "family life". Since Samir had been born of an extramarital relationship, there was no family tie *ipso jure* between him and Mr Zerrouk. Moreover, Mrs Kroon and Mr Zerrouk had chosen not to marry and it was from choice that the latter did not reside with Mrs Kroon and Samir. In addition, the Government alleged that Mr Zerrouk did not contribute to Samir's care and upbringing in any way and that there was nothing to show that he fulfilled the role of Samir's "social father".

The Commission noted the long-standing relationship between Mrs Kroon and Mr Zerrouk and the fact that it was not disputed that not only was the latter the biological father of Samir but also three other children had been born of that relationship.

The applicants noted that Netherlands law did not require a man to live with a child and its mother in order to leave the right to recognise the child as his and thereby create legally recognised family ties. They also claimed that Mr Zerrouk did in fact spend half his time on Samir's care and upbringing and made financial contributions from his modest income.

30 Throughout the domestic proceedings it was assumed by all concerned, including the registrar of births, deaths and marriages, that the relationship in question constituted "family life" and that Article 8 was applicable; this was also accepted by the Netherlands courts.

In any case, the Court recalls that the notion of "family life" in Article 8 is not confined solely to marriage-based relationships and may encompass other *de facto* "family ties" where parties are living together outside marriage (see as the most recent authority, *Keegan v Ireland* judgment of 26 May 1994, Series A, No 290, para 44). Although, as a rule, living together may be a requirement for such a relationship, exceptionally other factors may also serve to demonstrate that a relationship has sufficient constancy to create *de facto* "family ties"; such is the case here, as since 1987 four children have been born to Mrs Kroon and Mr Zerrouk.

A child born of such a relationship is *ipso jure* part of that "family unit" from the moment of its birth and by the very fact of it (see the *Keegan* judgment, above). There thus exists between Samir and Mr Zerrouk a bond amounting to family life, whatever the contribution of the latter to his son's care and upbringing.

Article 8 is therefore applicable.

B General principles

31 The Court reiterates that the essential object of Article 8 is to protect the individual against arbitrary action by the public authorities. There may in addition be positive obligations inherent in effective "respect" for family life. However, the boundaries between the State's positive and negative obligations under this provision do not lend themselves to precise definition. The applicable principles are nonetheless similar. In both contexts regard must be had to the fair balance that has to be struck between the competing interests of the individual and of the community as a whole; and in both contexts the State enjoys a certain margin of appreciation.

32 According to the principles set out by the Court in its case law, where the existence of a family tie with a child has been established, the State must act in a manner calculated to enable that tie to be developed and legal safeguards must be established that render possible as from the moment of birth or as soon as practicable thereafter the child's integration in his family (see, *mutatis mutandis*, as the most recent authority, the above-mentioned *Keegan* judgment, para 50).

C Compliance with Article 8

33 The applicants argued that Article 8(1) placed the Netherlands under a positive obligation to enable Mr Zerrouk to recognise Samir as his child and so establish legally recognised family ties between the two.

In the alternative, the applicants suggested that the existence of legislation which made impossible such recognition constituted an "interference" with their right to respect for their family life and that such interference was not necessary in a democratic society.

34 The Government argued that, even assuming "family life" to exist, the Netherlands had complied fully with any positive obligations it might have as regards the applicants.

They pointed, first, to the possibility of "step-parent adoption" (see para 24 above), ie adoption of Samir by Mrs Kroon and Mr Zerrouk. It was true that this possibility was contingent on there being no opposition from Mr Omar M'Hallem-Driss and on Mrs Kroon and Mr Zerrouk marrying each other. However, the possibility of any objection on the part of Mr M'Hallem-Driss could be discounted; if, for reasons of their own, Mrs Kroon and Mr Zerrouk did not wish to marry, that was not a state of affairs for which the State could be held responsible, since it placed no obstacles in the way of their marriage.

Further, under legislation in the course of preparation, an unmarried parent who had previously exercised sole parental authority over his or her child would be allowed joint custody with his or her partner; this would give the partner complete legal authority, on an equal footing with the parent.

In the alternative, the Government argued that if there was an "interference" with the applicant's right to respect for their family life then this was "necessary in a democratic society" in the interests of legal certainty.

35 In the Commission's view the fact that it was impossible under Netherlands law for anyone but Mr Omar M'Hallem-Driss to deny his paternity and for Mr Zerrouk to recognise Samir as his child constituted a lack of respect for the applicants' private and family life, in breach of a positive obligation imposed by Article 8.

36 The Court recalls that in the instant case it has been established that the relationship between the applicants qualifies as "family life" (see para 30 above). There is thus a positive obligation on the part of the competent authorities to allow complete legal family ties to be formed between Mr Zerrouk and his son Samir as expeditiously as possible.

37 Under Netherlands law the ordinary instrument for creating family ties between Mr Zerrouk and Samir was recognition (see para 23 above). However, since Samir was the "legitimate" child of Mr Omar M'Hallem-Driss, Mr Zerrouk would only be in a position to recognise Samir after Mr M'Hallem-Driss's paternity had been successfully denied. Except for Mr M'Hallem-Driss himself, who was untraceable, only Mrs Kroon could deny Mr Omar M'Hallem-Driss's paternity. However, under section 1:198 CC the possibility for the mother of a "legitimate" child to deny the paternity of her husband was, and is, only open in respect of a child born within 306 days of dissolution of the marriage (see para 19 above). Mrs Kroon could not avail herself of that possibility since Samir was born when she was still married. Indeed, this was not contested by the Government.

38 The Government, however, suggested that there were other ways of achieving an equivalent result.

The first such alternative suggested by the Government, step-parent adoption, would make Samir the "legitimate" child of Mr Zerrouk and Mrs Kroon. However, it would require Mrs Kroon and Mr Zerrouk to marry each other. For whatever reason, they do not wish to do so.

A solution which only allows a father to create a legal tie with a child with whom he has a bond amounting to family life if he marries the child's mother cannot be regarded as compatible with the notion of "respect" for family life.

39 The second alternative suggested by the Government, namely that of joint custody, is not an acceptable solution either. Even if the legislation being prepared comes into force as the Government anticipate, joint custody will leave the legal ties between Samir and Mr Omar M'Hallem-Driss intact and will continue to preclude the formation of such ties between Samir and Mr Zerrouk.

40 In the Court's opinion, "respect" for "family life" requires that biological and social reality prevail over a legal presumption which, as in the present case, flies in the face of both established fact and the wishes of those concerned without actually benefiting anyone. Accordingly, the Court concludes that, even having regard to the margin of appreciation left to the State, the Netherlands has failed to secure to the applicants the "respect" for their family life to which they are entitled under the Convention.

There has accordingly been a violation of Article 8.

II   Alleged violation of Article 14 of the Convention in conjunction with Article 8

41 The applicants also complained that, while Netherlands law made it possible for the husband of a child's mother to deny being the father of the child, the mother's right to

challenge her husband's paternity was much more limited. They relied on Article 14 of the Convention, which reads:

> The enjoyment of the rights and freedoms set forth in this Convention shall be secured without discrimination on any ground such as sex, race, colour, language, religion, political or other opinion, national or social origin, association with a national minority, birth or other status.

42 The Court finds that this complaint is essentially the same as the one under Article 8. Having found a violation of that provision taken alone, the Court does not consider that any separate issue arises under the Article in conjunction with Article 14.

III   Application of Article 50 of the Convention

43 Under Article 50 of the Convention,

> If the Court finds that a decision or a measure taken by a legal authority or any other authority of a High Contracting Party is completely or partially in conflict with the obligations arising from the ... Convention, and if the internal law of the said Party allows only partial reparation to be made for the consequences of the decision or measure, the decision of the Court shall, if necessary, afford just satisfaction to the injured party.

A   Damage

44 The applicants maintained that they had suffered non-pecuniary damage as a result of the Netherlands' failure to allow the establishment of legal family ties according to their wishes. Since there was no possibility under Netherlands law of obtaining *restitutio in integrum*, they claimed compensation in the amount of 30,000 Netherlands guilders (NLG).

45 The Court considers it likely that the impossibility of obtaining legal recognition of their family ties has caused the applicants some frustration. However, this is sufficiently compensated by the finding of a violation of the Convention.

B   Costs and expenses

46 As to costs and expenses incurred in the Strasbourg proceedings, the applicants claimed NLG 26,000, plus value-added tax, for lawyer's fees (65 hours at NLG 400), NLG 250 for out-of-pocket expenses and an unspecified amount for travel and subsistence in connection with their representative's attendance at the Court's hearing.

47 The Court reiterates that it allows claims for costs and expenses only to the extent to which they were actually and necessarily incurred and reasonable as to quantum.

In the instant case the Court finds it reasonable to award NLG 20,000 for lawyer's fees, less 13,855.85 FF paid by the Council of Europe in legal aid; any value-added tax that may be due is to be added to the resulting figure. However, it rejects the claims for out-of-pocket expenses and Mr Willems's travel and subsistence, since these have been covered by the Council of Europe's legal aid scheme.

For these reasons, **THE COURT:**

1   *Holds* by eight votes to one that Article 8 of the Convention is applicable;
2   *Holds* by seven votes to two that there has been a violation of Article 8 of the Convention;

3 *Holds* unanimously that no separate issue arises under Article 14 of the Convention in conjunction with Article 8;

4 *Holds* unanimously as regards the claim for non-pecuniary damage that the finding of a violation constitutes, in itself, sufficient just satisfaction;

5 *Holds* by eight votes to one that the respondent State is to pay to the applicants, within three months, NLG 20,000 (twenty thousand Netherlands guilders), less FF 13,855.85 (thirteen thousand eight hundred and fifty-five French francs and eighty-five centimes) to be converted into Netherlands guilders in accordance with the rate of exchange applicable on the date of delivery of the present judgment, plus any value-added tax that may be payable on the resulting figure, in respect of legal costs and expenses;

6 *Dismisses* unanimously the remainder of the claim for just satisfaction.

In accordance with Article 51(2) of the Convention and Rule 53(2) of the Rules of Court, the following separate opinions are annexed to this judgment (a) dissenting opinion of Mr Morenilla; (b) dissenting opinion of Mr Mifsud Bonnici.[*]

DISSENTING OPINION OF JUDGE MORENILLA

I regret that I am not able to agree with my colleagues who have found a violation of Article 8 of the Convention in this case.

I can nevertheless agree with their conclusions that this Article is applicable to the Netherlands authorities' refusal to grant the request by Catharina Kroon and Ali Zerrouk for official recognition of the "biological reality" of Mr Zerrouk's paternity of Samir M'Hallem-Driss (the third applicant), who was registered as the matrimonial son of Mrs Kroon and Mr Omar M'Hallem-Driss notwithstanding that they were separated *de facto* although not yet divorced. However, my agreement is based only on the fact that this refusal, which was in conformity with the Netherlands Civil Code, gives rise to an "interference" in the personal sphere (family life) of the three applicants, since it affects the legal situation of the alleged progenitor, the son and the mother. It also affects Mr Omar M'Hallem-Driss, the legal father of Samir and former spouse of Catharina Kroon, who is not a party in this litigation and who has not been heard in the case since his whereabouts are unknown.

I dissent from my colleagues' finding of a violation because I think that the interference of the Netherlands authorities was justified under Article 8(2), which draws the dividing line between the right of the individual to respect for his private and family life and the right of the State to take necessary action to protect the general interest of the community or the equal rights or interests of other persons. Paras 1 and 2 of this Article form a "whole" (Luzius Wildhaber, "Kommentierung des Artikels 8", in *Internationaler Kommentar zur Europäischen Menschenrechtskonvention*, 1992, pp 11–12) and have to be considered as such when deciding whether or not the interference was arbitrary and, in consequence, whether the respondent State has denied the applicants' right to respect for their family life. The Court's task, in each case, is to strike the proper balance between the general interest of society and the protection of the rights of the alleged victim.

---

[*] **Eds:** due to space constraints, the dissenting opinion of Judge Misfud Bonnici has not been included. The full text of the judgment is available at the website of the European Court of Human Rights (see *On-line Access to Human Rights Source Materials, supra*, p xlv); ECHR, Series A, No 297-C; and 19 EHRR 263.

Following its *Marckx v Belgium* judgment of 13 June 1979 (Series A, No 31), the Court has been developing an expanding case law on the "positive obligations" of the Contracting States under Article 8(1) of the Convention, and this involves significant modifications in the content of the right secured by this provision. This principle of "evolutive and creative" interpretation (see Luzius Wildhaber, "Nouvelle jurisprudence concernant l'article 8 CEDH", in *Mélanges en l'honneur de Jacques-Michel Grossen*, 1992, p 106), which allows the Convention to be adapted to the changing circumstances of our democratic societies, thus making it "a living instrument", means however that in practice the Court is confronted with a difficult dilemma: that "of guarding against the risk of exceeding its given judicial role of interpretation by overruling policy decisions taken by elected, representative bodies who have the main responsibility in democratic societies for enacting important legislative changes, whilst not abdicating its own responsibility of independent review of governmental action" (see Paul Mahoney and Søren Prebensen, "The European Court of Human Rights", in *The European System for the Protection of Human Rights*, R StJ Macdonald, F Matscher, H Petzold, 1993, pp 638–40).

This dilemma is even greater in matters such as marriage, divorce, filiation or adoption, because they bring into play the existing religious, ideological or traditional conceptions of the family in each community. The majority of my colleagues have, however, considered there to be a "positive obligation" incumbent on the Netherlands to recognise the right of the natural father to challenge the presumption of the paternity of the legal father (the husband of the mother), thus giving priority to biological ties over the cohesion and harmony of the family and the paramount interest of the child. In my opinion, this conclusion involves a dangerous generalisation of the special circumstances of the instant case and one which imposes on the Contracting States an obligation not included in the text of Article 8, based on changeable moral criteria or opinions on social values.

The Court, citing the *Abdulaziz, Cabales and Balkandali v United Kingdom* judgment of 28 May 1985 (Series A, No 94), said in the *Johnston and Others v Ireland* judgment of 18 December 1986 (Series A, No 112, para 55):

> [Especially] as far as those positive obligations are concerned, the notion of "respect" is not clear-cut: having regard to the diversity of the practices followed and the situations obtaining in the Contracting States, the notion's requirements will vary considerably from case to case. Accordingly, this is an area in which the Contracting Parties enjoy a wide margin of appreciation in determining the steps to be taken to ensure compliance with the Convention with due regard to the needs and resources of the community and of individuals ...

The aim of the Council of Europe to harmonise the legislation of the Contracting States in the field of family law has been accomplished by the recommendations adopted by the Committee of Ministers over the last two decades and by specialised conventions available for ratification by the Member States. This has led to reforms in family law in many countries of Europe, from the 1970s onwards. These reforms have achieved a certain approximation of national laws but not their uniformity, particularly in regard to the regulation of procedures for denying legal paternity, which still take many different forms. On the other hand, there is a tendency in the regulation of the use of new techniques of human reproduction towards prohibiting challenges to paternity by anonymous sperm donors.

Account should also be taken of the importance of the family in many Contracting States, of the persistence in these countries of a social rejection of adultery and of the common belief that a united family facilitates the healthy development of the child. These factors provide justification for interference by the State, in accordance with

Article 8(2), with the applicants' exercise of their right to respect for family life, since its aim is the protection of "morals" or the protection of the interests of the child against the intrusion of an alleged biological father into his or her family circle or legal status.

The social consequences of denying legal paternity as regards the cohesion and harmony of the family, or in terms of legal certainty concerning affiliation and parental rights, are better assessed by the national authorities in the exercise of the extensive margin of appreciation conferred on them. As the Court said in *Handyside v United Kingdom* in relation to the requirements of morals:

> By reason of their direct and continuous contact with the vital forces of their countries, State authorities are in principle in a better position than the international judge to give an opinion on the exact content of these requirements ...

The Court, when determining the scope of the margin of appreciation enjoyed by the Netherlands authorities in this case, should also take into consideration Netherlands family law as a whole, particularly sections 1:199 and 1:200 of the Civil Code (para 21 of this judgment) and the possibility of adoption by a step-parent of the child (para 24). This legal framework provides an alternative to the applicants' claim whilst protecting the interests of the community.

CASE NO 21

NAWAKWI v ATTORNEY GENERAL OF ZAMBIA

HIGH COURT OF ZAMBIA

Judgment: 24 June 1991

Panel: Musumali J

Constitutional law — Interpretation — Whether general non-discrimination provision in the Constitution included prohibition of discrimination on the ground of sex — Locus standi — Whether mother had locus standi to bring legal proceedings on behalf of her child — Constitution of Zambia, arts 25 and 29

Human rights — Equality and non-discrimination — Sex discrimination — Issue of passport to female citizens with children — Whether rules requiring a mother to swear an affidavit of parentage, and/or requiring a letter of consent from the father of the child, to have her children endorsed on her passport discriminatory — Position of unmarried mothers — Freedom of movement — Right to a passport — Whether holding of, or indorsement on, a passport a right or privilege — Constitution of Zambia, arts 24 and 25

BACKGROUND

The petitioner, Ms Edith Zewelani Nawakwi, was a Zambian citizen and an unmarried mother of two children. After the birth of her first child, D, she had to swear an affidavit that she was D's mother and that D was born out of wedlock in order to obtain a birth certificate for D. In order to have D endorsed on her passport she had to swear an almost identical affidavit. On the birth of her second child, the child's father completed the relevant documents at the Zambian High Commission in London in order to register the birth of the child. On the expiry of her passport, the petitioner found that she was required to again swear affidavits as to motherhood and her unmarried status in order to have her children included on her passport. She was also informed that it was necessary to have the consent of the children's father in order to include the children on her passport. The petitioner complained that these procedures were lengthy, costly and discriminatory. She informed the authorities that they already possessed the information they sought based on her first passport and refused to swear new affidavits.

Ms Nawakwi sought declaratory relief before the High Court of Zambia that, *inter alia*, she was subject to unlawful discrimination on the grounds of sex and that the passport authorities should automatically endorse the children on her passport based on affidavits previously sworn. She also sought declarations that a single parent family headed by a female be recognised as a family unit in Zambian society and that upon the birth of a child to a single mother, the name of the father of the child should only be included on the birth certificate if he is physically present at the Registrar General's office on the day of the registration.

HELD (allowing the petition)

1   The facts revealed by this case showed that a mother of a child was not regarded by the government to be an equal parent to a father. The father had been made to have more say over the affairs of a child by the Government, through the institution of the practice of asking for a father's letter of consent when matters of passports and travel documents concerning children have had to be dealt with at passport offices, as well as when obtaining children's birth certificates. This practice was discriminatory against mothers on no other basis than the fact that they were females. While the definition of discrimination in article 25(3) does not include "sex" or "gender", the intention of the framers of the Constitution when they passed the Bill of Rights could never have been to discriminate between males and females in the way the passport office had been doing. That discrimination was unacceptable and untenable legally in these times of enlightenment. Accordingly, a mother of a child would not need to get the consent of the father to have her children included in her passport or for them to be eligible for obtaining passports or travel documents (pp 345, 347).

2   A single parent family headed by a male or female was a recognised family unit in Zambian society. Zambia had to accord every mother of a child, single or married, the same powers that the father enjoyed (pp 346, 347).

3   The holding of a passport was not a privilege, but a right, as the right to freedom of movement was enshrined in article 24 of the Constitution. Since a passport was required to travel outside Zambia, every citizen had a right to a passport, or to be endorsed on one, unless legal restrictions attaching to the freedom of movement imposed by the Constitution validly applied (p 346).

4   A mother had *locus standi* to sue the state on behalf of her children, if the children had not yet attained maturity to be able to sue on their own, when she felt that the interests of her children so dictate (p 347).

National legislation referred to:

Zambia

Constitution of Zambia 1973, arts 4, 13, 24, 25 and 29

JUDGMENT

MUSUMALI J: This is a petition filed by the applicant in which she is asking the court to make a number of declarations. Those declarations are, as summarised in para 12 of her said petition, that:

(1) she has been and continues to be unfairly discriminated against on the ground of sex;

(2) since she had previously furnished the Department of Passport and Citizenship with satisfactory documentary evidence as to the personal particulars and social status of the two children (ie David Kayiwvambile Siwakwi, born on 31 July 1983 in Lusaka, and Mbwiga Mlozi Siwakwi, born on 10 June 1988 in London) the officers of the said department are estopped by record and their past conduct from refusing the application to endorse on the petitioner's new passport the personal particulars of the said children of her single-parent family;

(3) a single parent family headed by a female be recognised as a family unit in the Zambian society;

(4) upon the birth of a child to a single mother, the name of the father shall only be included on the child's birth certificate if the father is physically present at the Registrar General's office on the day of the registration of the child's birth, otherwise, the single mother should be declared the sole guardian and custodian of the child without undue administrative impediments; and such other orders of directions or reliefs as shall to the court seem appropriate for the purpose of enforcing or securing the enforcement of arts 13 and 25 of the (Republican) Constitution in relation to the petitioner;

(5) a passport is a right which is incidental to and consequent upon the petitioner's citizenship; thus the inclusion of the petitioner's Zambian children's particulars on her passport is a matter which is a natural incidence and consequence of both the petitioner's and the children's Zambian citizenship; and

(6) consequently upon (5), the petitioner's said children have been, are being, and are likely in the future to be, hindered in their enjoyment of freedom of movement out of and back into Zambia, otherwise guaranteed them under article 24 of the Constitution.

She also prays for the costs of this action to be granted to her. The petition was based on the provisions of arts 13, 25 and 29 of the Republican Constitution.

Article 13 provides as follows:

It is recognised and declared that every person in Zambia has been and shall continue to be entitled to the fundamental rights and freedoms of the individual, that is to say, the right whatever his race, place of origin, political opinions, colour, creed or sex, but subject to the limitations contained in Article 4 [which has since been amended] and in this Part, to each and all of the following, namely:

(a) life, liberty, security of the person and the protection of the law;

(b) freedom of conscience, expression, assembly and association; and

(c) protection for the privacy of his home and other property and from deprivation of property without compensation;

and the provisions of this Part shall have effect for the purpose of affording protection to those rights and freedoms subject to such limitations of the protection as are contained in Article 4 and in those provisions, being limitations designed to ensure that the enjoyment of the said rights and freedoms by any individual does not prejudice the rights and freedoms of others or the public interest.

Article 25 provides as follows:

(1) Subject to the provisions of clauses (4), (5) and (7) no law shall make any provision that is discriminatory either of itself or in its effect.

(2) Subject to the provisions of clauses (6), (7) and (8), no person shall be treated in a discriminatory manner by any person acting by virtue of any written law or in the performance of the functions of any public office or any public authority.

(3) In this Article, the expression "discriminatory" means according different treatment to different persons attributable wholly or mainly to their respective descriptions by race, tribe, place of origin, political opinions, colour or creed whereby persons of one such description are subjected to disabilities or restrictions to which persons of another such description are not made subject or are accorded privileges or advantages which are not accorded to persons of another such description.

(4) Clause (1) shall not apply to any law so far as that law makes provision: ...

    (c) with respect to adoption, marriage, divorce, burial, devolution of property on death or other matters of personal law; ...

    (e) whereby persons of any such description as is mentioned in clause (3) may be subjected to any disability or restriction or may be accorded any privilege or advantage which, having regard to its nature and to special circumstances pertaining to those persons or to persons of any other such description, is reasonably justifiable in a democratic society ...

(6) Clause (2) shall not apply to anything which is expressly or by necessary implication authorised to be done by any such provision of law as is referred to in clause (4) or (5).

(7) Nothing contained in or done under the authority of any law shall be held to be inconsistent with or in contravention of this Article to the extent that it is shown that the law in question makes provision whereby persons of any such description as is mentioned in clause (3) may be subjected to any restriction on the rights and freedoms guaranteed by Articles ... and 24, being such a restriction as is authorised by Article ... and 24(3), as the case may be ...

Article 29 provides as follows:

(1) Subject to the provisions of clause (6), if any person alleges that any of the provisions of Articles 13 to 27 (inclusive) has been, is being or is likely to be contravened in relation to him, then, without prejudice to any other action with respect to the same matter which is lawfully available, that person may apply to the High Court for redress.

(2) The High Court shall have original jurisdiction:

    (a) to hear and determine any application made by any person in pursuance of clause (1) ...

and may, subject to the provisions of clause (8), make such orders, issue such writs and give such directions as it may consider appropriate for the purpose of enforcing or securing the enforcement of any of the provisions of Articles 13 to 27 (inclusive) ... *

In this case, I heard the evidence of the petitioner only. She told the court that she is not married; that she is a mother of two boys, Kayivwambile Siwakwi aged seven and Mbwiga Mlozi Siwakwi aged two and a half years; that Kayivwambile was born in the University Teaching Hospital, Lusaka, and the other child in the Westminster Hospital, London. She went on and said that she is a Zambian citizen. She had held Zambian passports. The first one, which is now expired was No ZB088728 (ID1). Her two children were endorsed in that passport, she said; although one of them, the younger one, was later deleted from it because he was issued with a travel document in London to enable him to travel alone from London to Lusaka. That travel document has since expired, she said.

Following the expiry of the first passport she applied for its renewal and the inclusion of her children in it. She got a new passport she said but her children were refused to be included in it.

She then explained that when she had the first child, in order to get his birth certificate she was made to swear an affidavit showing that (1) she was the mother of

---

* **Eds:** Article 24 of the Constitution of Zambia 1973 provides: "(1) No person shall be deprived of his freedom of movement, and for the purposes of this Article the said freedom means the right to move freely throughout Zambia, the right to reside in any part of Zambia, the right to enter Zambia and immunity from expulsion from Zambia."

that child and (2) he was born out of wedlock. After that she applied to the passport office for his inclusion in her passport.

Again she was asked to swear an affidavit similar to the one she had sworn to get the child's birth certificate. She swore that affidavit and had the child included in the passport, ie the first passport.

She went on and said that she did not have any problems to include the second child in her passport. This was because his father filled in all the relevant documents in London and they were handed in and processed by the Zambian High Commission. She attacked that practice because it recognises a foreign male, as was the case in this case as the father of her second child is a Tanzanian, but refuses to recognise a Zambian female, who is a parent of a child.

The petitioner then explained that when she was issued with the second passport, she was again asked to swear a fresh affidavit of the sort she had sworn and filed to get Kayivwambile's birth certificate and to have him included in the expired passport. She then drew the attention of the passport officer who was handling her application to the presence of the details he wanted to know about her and her children in those affidavits and in Mbwiga's expired travel documents, which were in the possession of that (passport) office. The officer told her that much as he appreciated that the regulations and procedures he was enforcing were unfair to women, there was nothing he could do about them, but to follow them. Explaining the implication of the application of those regulations and procedures to her second child it was that she had to get the consent of the Tanzanian father to the inclusion of that child in her Zambian passport. It meant also that she had to swear those affidavits every time she was renewing her passport and/or whenever she had a new child as a single parent. These procedures were lengthy, costly, discriminatory and demeaning to her, she said. She therefore decided to petition against these procedures.

Talking about the specific forms which are used by the passport office she said that Form D, which is the "Application of Children or Child Under the Age of Sixteen Years to be added to Passport of a Relative", is discriminatory because only the father is recognised as the legal custodian of a child. Yet the mother of a child is the only one who will really know who the father of the child is/was. Maternity is the only thing that no one will question, she said. She then said that the word "father" on Form D should have been used in a broader sense to indicate physical and emotional support for the child/children; at least in the case of a single parent family headed by a woman.

The respondent did not call any witnesses. They intimated that they would only be putting in written submissions. That was on 2 March 1991. No such submissions have been received from them by this court. Mrs Mushota for the applicant sent in hers at the beginning of May.

Upon consideration of the evidence and said submissions in this case I have found the following facts as proved; that:

(1) The petitioner is a Zambian.

(2) She is single.

(3) She is the mother of David Kayivwarnbile Siwakwi and Mbwiga Mlozi Siwakwi.

(4) David will be eight years old on 31 July 1991 and Mbwiga will be three years old on 10 June 1991.

(5) David's unknown father is/was a Zambian. Mbwiga's (known) father is/was a Tanzanian. I have used the words is/was because both or either of those men

may/could have died since 21 March 1991 when the petitioner last appeared and gave evidence before this court in this case.

(6) The plaintiff applied for and was issued with a Zambian passport number ZA 088728. This passport was issued on 24 June 1980.

(7) On 8 October 1985, David's personal particulars were indorsed in that passport. The procedure she went through before David's particulars were indorsed in the said passport will be explained later in this judgment. Mbwiga's particulars were indorsed in the passport in London. I will also explain how that was done in the course of this judgment.

(8) As time went on, that passport expired. The applicant then applied for new passport, and that her two children's particulars should also appear.

(9) She was issued the new passport No ZB10738, but her children were not indorsed on it.

(10)In order to have those children indorsed in the new passport she was asked to swear fresh affidavits in respect of them to show their parentage.

(11)She was not keen to swear fresh affidavits.

(12)Because of her refusal to comply with the fresh affidavits requirement her children were not and I think have not up to now been indorsed on her new passport.

In this matter it was not disputed that in order to get David's birth certificate the petitioner was asked by the office of the Registrar of Births, Deaths and Marriages to swear an affidavit showing David's parentage. That was done and the birth certificate Number LUS/67/84 was issued. She then took that certificate to the passport office and applied for the indorsing of David's particulars on her passport. She was again asked to swear an affidavit, identical to the one she had sworn for the birth certificate. The essence of those affidavits was that they showed that the petitioner was the mother of the child and that he was born out of wedlock. Upon production of that affidavit to the passport office, David's particulars were indorsed on the first passport, as already found.

As for Mbwiga, his indorsement was done in London at the Zambian High Commission with relative ease. This was because his Tanzanian father was in attendance and filled in all the relevant documents.

The facts revealed by this case show that a mother of a child is not regarded by the governmment to be an equal parent to a father. The father has been made to have more say over the affairs of a child at least in so far as the endorsement of the particulars of the child and the issuing to a child of a passport or a travel document are concerned. This has been done by the government of this country through the institution of the practice of asking for a father's letter of consent when matters of passports and travel documents concerning children have had to be dealt with at passport offices, as well as when obtaining children's birth certificates, at least during the lifetime of the others. This practice is discriminatory to mothers on no other basis than the fact that they are females. Yet the mother is the one who must have conceived and carried that child in her womb for nine months, more or less, and then gone to the maternity ward to deliver. Having delivered she is again the one with the responsibility of looking after that child through the tender stages, feeding it and doing all the motherly chores until it gets out of its infancy. Some fathers have had to do those chores mothers do for infants but those have been in cases where due to one reason or the other the mother is not able to do those herself. Such situations are exceptions to the general rule. The mother, in a normal situation, continues to perform some very essential roles in the upbringing of the children. The father also plays equally important roles, if he is a responsible father. In my considered view it is not at all justified, from whatever angle the issue is looked at, for a father to treat himself or to be treated by the institutions of society to be more entitled to authority over the affairs of his children than the mother of those children. The mother is as much an authority over the affairs of her children as the father is. There would of course be some cases where one of the parents may lose, temporarily or forever, his/her share of that entitlement. Such a situation may arise where a parent abandons a child or children or becomes so mentally sick that the best interests of the child or children would dictate his/her exclusion from him/her or them. Each such case would of course depend on its own facts.

The realities of these times have brought about another dimension to this problem of child male parentage. This case now before this court is one in point. Here the petitioner is in the position of both the father and mother of the two children. She is an unmarried mother. She is bringing up her two children without a husband. Now is it fair for this society to have to require of her to have been or to be married in order for certain things to be possible to be done for her children? The answer, in my considered view, is in the negative. It is in the negative because firstly the reality of her situation and of many others like her, is that she has illegitimate children, and secondly because discrimination based on gender only has to be eliminated from our society. Men and women are partners and not only partners but equal partners in most human endeavours. They must thus be treated equally.

I noticed at the bottom right side of Form D the words "October 1963", I interpreted this to mean that either that was the month and year when that form came into effect or that that was the month and year when the form was printed or reprinted as the case may be. It may then be argued that that form did not emanate from the Zambian government but was one of the colonial leftovers, which is still to be redressed by the Zambian government. My answer to this is that this country has been independent for more than a quarter of a century now, and it does not need such a long time to comb the public service of remnants of colonial discriminatory practices. It is my view that this form ought to have been rectified when the Zambian coat of arms which it carries were put on it. So there can be no excuse for its use in its form in independent Zambia.

Going back to the facts of this case Zambia has to accord every mother of a child, single or married, the same powers that the father enjoys. Anything less would not be justified. The fear that the mothers may be stealing children if they are allowed to include their young children in their passports is a very unreasonable argument because in all honesty they are entitled to have those children where they want them to go. One cannot steal what belongs to oneself. It should be a matter between the father and the mother of a child to resolve as to whether to allow a child to go to country A and not to B. If they cannot agree then one or both of them should be free to apply to court for a solution. Such a situation would not arise in the case of a single parent.

Talking about passports, I think it is opportune to say here that the holding of a passport by a Zambian is not a privilege. It is not a privilege because he/she has a right of movement enshrined in the Constitution: article 24 of the Constitution. In order to travel outside the country a Zambian citizen needs a valid Zambian passport or travel document. Just as they don't need to get permission from the authorities to travel from one part of the country to another, so they do not need to get permission to travel outside the country. Since they cannot travel outside the country without passports, they are entitled to have them, unless legal restrictions attaching to the freedom of movement imposed by the Constitution validly apply.

During cross-examination of the petitioner, the respondent raised the question of the *locus standi* of the petitioner in these proceedings. The argument appeared to have been that since she has been issued with the passport she applied for, she has no cause of action in this matter as the aggrieved parties are her children and not herself. To this argument I have to say that since the children in question have not yet attained maturity to be able to sue on their own and the petitioner is a Zambian citizen she has legal standing as a petitioner in this case. In other words she has the *locus standi* to sue the state or indeed any other person when she feels that the interests of her children so dictate.

It is imperative also to say one or two things about the offices of the Registrar of Births, Deaths and Marriages as well as the passport office and some of the procedures they have put in place there. The first issue is whether or not those offices are public offices which fall under article 25(2) of the Constitution. My answer is that they are public offices. They are public offices because they belong to the Zambian Civil Service ie they are offices of the government of the Republic of Zambia. Article 25, clause 3 defines the expression "discriminatory" as used in that article. That definition does not include "sex" or "gender". Be that as it may, it is my very considered view that the intentions of the framers of this Constitution when they passed the Bill of Rights (Part III of the Constitution) could never have been to discriminate between males and females in the way the passport office and its sister department have been doing. I have no doubt in my mind therefore that if these practices were to have been brought to the attention of those people who were passing this Constitution into law, they would have not sanctioned them. I am not sanctioning them either. Forms A and D of the passport office have not been issued on the basis of any legal provision. And even if they were so issued, that law would be unconstitutional as it would be discriminatory between mothers and fathers in matters relating to their children's inclusion in the mothers' passports or getting passports or travel documents, for no good other reason than the fact that one is female and the other male. That discrimination is unacceptable and untenable legally or otherwise in these times of enlightenment.

Further, this court did not appreciate the logic in the refusal by the passport office to transfer all details which were in the expired passport, in particular those relating to the children and asking the petitioner to start swearing all over again affidavits. It is my considered view, and I hold, that in a case such as the petitioner's, the practice of the passport office should from now onwards be to renew a passport of a Zambian female with all the details and/or indorsements which were on the expired one. Common sense dictates this approach as preferable to the one that has been in use over all these years. Thus when all is said and considered I find and hold that (1) the petitioner has been unfairly discriminated against on the ground of sex; (2) the petitioner's children's particulars be indorsed on her present passport without a requirement for her to furnish fresh affidavits or other fresh documents in respect of them; (3) a single parent family headed by a male or female is a recognised family unit in Zambian society; (4) a passport is part of the freedom of movement and as such it is a right of every Zambian to have one or be indorsed on one unless there is a valid legal excuse barring such possession or indorsement; and (5) a mother of a child does not need to get the consent of the father to have her children included in her passport or for them to be eligible for obtaining passports or travel documents. Either partner has the inalienable right to be a recommender, in whatever form the recommendation is required to be made, for the child or children. This applies to birth certificates and passports in this country as to other things.

I also award the costs of this action to the petitioner.

REPRODUCTIVE RIGHTS

CASE NO 22

PATON v UNITED KINGDOM

EUROPEAN COMMISSION OF HUMAN RIGHTS

Application No: 8416/78

Decision on admissibility: 13 May 1980

Panel: Nørgaard (*Acting President*); *Members*: Sperduti, Daver Opsahl, Polak, Frowein, Jörundsson, Dupuy, Tenekides, Trechsel, Kiernan, Klecker, Melchior and Carrillo

Human rights — Right to life — Right to respect for family and private life — Right to a fair hearing — Determination of rights and obligations — Right to freedom of religion — Whether right to life applies to foetus — Rights of potential father in case of proposed abortion — European Convention for the Protection of Human Rights and Fundamental Freedoms, arts 2, 6, 8 and 9

Human rights — Standing — Victim — Potential father of unborn children — Abortion — Whether a putative father is sufficiently closely affected by a proposed abortion which his wife intends to be performed on her to qualify as a victim — European Convention for the Protection of Human Rights and Fundamental Freedoms, art 25

BACKGROUND

The applicant, Mr Paton, a British citizen, applied for an injunction to prevent the termination of his wife's pregnancy. After the court refused his application, he complained to the European Commission of Human Rights that this refusal and the provision of the Abortion Act of 1967 under which the abortion was carried out violated various rights guaranteed to him and his unborn child under the European Convention on Human Rights. He claimed that the law of England and Wales, in allowing abortions and denying the foetus rights, violated the right to life (article 2) and/or the right to liberty and security of person (article 5). He also claimed that the 1967 Act denied the father of the unborn child, whether or not he was married to the mother, the right to a fair trial (article 6), the right to protection of his family and private life (article 8), and the right to freedom of thought (article 9). The complaints included the lack of a right to object to, be consulted or informed about a proposed abortion, to apply to a Court for an order to prevent or postpone a proposed abortion or a right to demand that the mother be examined by independent registered practitioners where such practitioners issue certificates under section 1 of the 1967 Act.

The applicant claimed that since the abortion had been carried out within hours of the rejection by the High Court of his application for an injunction, it was not legally possible to pursue the application further and that he had therefore exhausted domestic remedies as required by article 26 of the Convention.

HELD (declaring the application inadmissible)

Locus standi and exhaustion of domestic remedies

1   The applicant, as the potential father, was so closely affected by the termination of his wife's pregnancy that he might claim to be a "victim", within the meaning of article 25 of the Convention, of the legislation complained of, as applied in the present case. (Para 2 of "The Law")

2   The applicant, by his unsuccessful application to the High Court for an injunction, had exhausted the only available "domestic remedy" in the sense of article 26 of the Convention. (Para 3 of "The Law")

The rights of the unborn child under article 2 (right to life)

3   Article 2(1), first sentence, provides "Everyone's right to life shall be protected by the law". The term "everyone" is not defined in the Convention. However, both the general usage of the term "everyone" in the Convention and the context in which this term is employed in article 2 tended to support the view that it did not include the unborn. (Paras 6, 7 and 9 of "The Law")

4   Article 2 was not to be construed as recognising an absolute "right to life" of the foetus. (Paras 19 and 20)

5   The Commission was not called upon to decide whether article 2 does not cover the foetus at all, or whether it recognises a "right to life" of the foetus with implied limitations. The authorisation, by the United Kingdom authorities, of the abortion complained of was compatible with article 2(1), because, if one assumed that this provision applied at the initial stage of the pregnancy, the abortion was covered by an implied limitation, protecting the life and health of the woman at that stage, of the "right to life" of the foetus. (Para 23 of "The Law")

The right to protection of the family and privacy of the father under article 8

6   The pregnancy of the applicant's wife was terminated in accordance with her wish and in order to avert risk or injury to her physical or mental health. This decision, in so far as it interfered with the applicant's right to respect for his family life, was justified under article 8(2). (Para 26 of "The Law")

7   Any interpretation of the husband's and potential father's right under article 8 of the Convention, as regards an abortion which his wife intends to have performed on her, should first of all take into account the right of the pregnant woman, being the person primarily concerned in the pregnancy and its continuation or termination, to respect for her private life. Having regard to the right of the pregnant woman, the potential father's rights to respect for his private and family life could not be interpreted so widely as to embrace such procedural rights as claimed by the applicant, ie a right to be consulted, or a right to make applications, about an abortion which his wife intended to have performed on her. (Para 27 of "The Law")

The remaining complaints

8   Articles 5, 6 and 9 of the Convention were not relevant for the examination of the applicant's complaints. (Para 28 of "The Law")

Treaties and other international instruments referred to

American Convention on Human Rights, 1969 art 4(1)

European Convention for the Protection of Human Rights and Fundamental Freedoms, 1950, arts 1, 2, 3, 5, 6, 8, 9, 25, 26 and 27(2)

National legislation referred to

United Kingdom

Abortion Act 1967, s 1(1)

Cases referred to

Amekrane v United Kingdom, ECommHR, Application No 5961/72 (1973), 44 Coll 101; 16 Yearbook 356

Austrian Constitutional Court, decision of 11 October 1974, Erk Slg, No 7400; [1975] *Europäische Grundrechtezeitschrift* 74; 1975 JC 9; 1974 SLT (Notes) 61

Brüggemann and Scheuten v Germany, ECommHR, Application No 6959/75; (1978) 10 D&R 100; (1981) 3 EHRR 244; below, p 361

Paton v British Pregnancy Advisory Service [1979] QB 276; [1978] 3 WLR 687; [1978] 2 All ER 987

Planned Parenthood of Central Missouri v Danforth, 428 US 52; 96 S Ct 2831; 49 L Ed 2d 788 (1976)

Roe v Wade, 410 US 113 (1973)

X v Austria, ECommHR, Application No 7045/75, (1977) 7 D&R 87

X v Belgium, ECommHR, Application No 2758/66, (1970) 30 Coll 11; 12 Yearbook 175

X v Norway, ECommHR, Application No 867/60, (1961) 6 Coll 34; 4 Yearbook 270

DECISION AS TO ADMISSIBILITY

THE FACTS

1   The applicant is a citizen of the United Kingdom born in 1944. He is a steel worker by profession.

2   From his statement and the documents submitted by the applicant it appears that he was married to Joan Mary Paton on 10 October 1974. On 12 May 1978 he was told by his wife that she was eight weeks pregnant and intended to have an abortion. On 17 May 1978 the applicant applied to the High Court of Justice for an injunction to prevent the abortion from being carried out. The original defendants to the application were Dr Peter Frederick Knight, the manager of the Merseyside Nursing Home at which two doctors had given certificates in accordance with section 1 of the Abortion Act 1967 (hereinafter called the "1967 Act"), and the applicant's wife.

3   Section 1(1) of the 1967 Act permits the termination of a pregnancy by a registered medical practitioner if two registered medical practitioners find:

(a) that the continuance of the pregnancy would involve risk to the life of the pregnant woman, or of injury to the physical or mental health of the pregnant woman or any existing children of her family, greater than if the pregnancy were terminated; or

(b) that there is a substantial risk that if the child were born it would suffer from such physical or mental abnormalities as to be seriously handicapped.

The certificate in the present case was issued under para (a) (injury to the physical or mental health of the pregnant woman) (in an affidavit submitted to the High Court the applicant's wife stated *inter alia*: "My marriage was increasingly unhappy ... and ... has broken down irretrievably. I left the plaintiff on legal advice as I feared for my safety and we live apart ... and in future I will live as a single woman ... Because of the plaintiff's behaviour life with him became increasingly impossible and my health suffered and I am receiving treatment from my doctor ... I could not cope and I verily believe that for months I have been close to a nervous breakdown.").

4 The application was heard and decided by Sir George Baker, the President of the Family Division of the High Court of Justice, sitting at Liverpool on 24 May 1978. At the hearing leave was granted to amend the writ by deleting Dr Knight and by adding as defendants the trustees and director of the British Pregnancy Advisory Service, by which the Merseyside Nursing Home was owned and operated.

5 In his oral submissions counsel for the applicant conceded that the 1967 Act had been complied with.

6 As to the question whether, in English law, the unborn child has a right to life, which could be invoked by the father, reference was *inter alia* made, on one hand, to Roman law, where abortion without the father's consent was a crime, and, on the other, to the United States Supreme Court's decision in *Planned Parenthood of Central Missouri v Danforth* (428 US 52 (1976)) where the Court, by a majority, held that the State of Missouri "may not constitutionally require the consent of the spouse ... as a condition for an abortion ..."

Counsel for the applicant observed:

I do not pretend to be, by size of shape or feat, a "Foetal Advocate", but I have endeavoured, whilst I have been developing the submissions to your Lordship, to look at it in that context. If the foetus has some kind of right to have its life preserved it might be possible to spell out of that a derivative right in the father. Everything is against that particular notion. It comes to this: the Supreme Court's decision has got to be wrong, admittedly although they are in a different jurisdiction in dealing with different principles. The fact a man has got a right to father children, in the face of the Abortion Act does not entitle him to cause a wife whose health may be at risk to bear that risk and produce a child. The fact he has got some interest in the child has been urged by some of the authorities both in the Commonwealth and in America, but in this country they are against any such notion.

7 The President dismissed the application. He stated that an injunction could be granted only to restrain the infringement of a legal right; that in English law the foetus has no legal rights until it is born and has a separate existence from its mother, and that the father of a foetus, whether or not he is married to the mother, has no legal right to prevent the mother from having an abortion or to be consulted or informed about a proposed abortion, if the provisions of the 1967 Act have been complied with (see *Paton v British Pregnancy Advisory Service* [1979] QB 276.)

8 The abortion was carried out within hours of the dismissal of the application.

Complaints

The applicant contends that the law of England and Wales violates:

(1) Articles 2 and/or 5 of the Convention in that it allows abortion at all, and/or that it denies the foetus any legal rights;

(2) Articles 6 and/or 8 and/or 9 of the Convention in that, if the provisions of the 1967 Act are complied with, it denies the father of a foetus, whether or not he is married to the mother:

(a) a right to object to a proposed abortion of the foetus; and/or

(b) a right to apply to the Courts for an order to prevent or postpone the proposed abortion; and/or

(c) a right to be consulted about the proposed abortion; and/or

(d) a right to be informed about the proposed abortion; and/or

(e) a right to demand, in a case where registered medical practitioners have given certificates under section 1 of the 1967 Act, that the mother be examined by a different registered medical practitioner or practitioners appointed by the father or by and upon his application to a designated court, tribunal or other body; and/or

(f) a right to demand that the registered medical practitioners, who examine the mother to decide whether or not to give certificates under section 1 of the 1967 Act, should be independent of the institution or organisation at or by which the abortion will be carried out should such certificates be given.

The applicant states that it is the object of his petition "to obtain the opinion of the European Court and the Commission of Human Rights upon the (above) contentions" and "to secure such amendments of the law of England and Wales as may be necessary to remove such violations of the Convention that the Court and Commission may find presently exist".

The applicant finally submits with regard to Article 26 of the Convention (exhaustion of domestic remedies) that his application to the High Court "was for an injunction. An abortion having been carried out on Mrs Paton within hours of the dismissal of the application, it was not legally possible to pursue the application further. An injunction is an equitable remedy. It is a maxim of equity that equity does nothing in vain. Accordingly, the dismissal of the application on 24 May 1978 by the President of the Family Division of the High Court of Justice marked the exhaustion of the applicant's domestic remedies".

THE LAW

1   The applicant complains of the refusal, by the High Court of Justice, of his application for an injunction to prevent the termination of his wife's pregnancy. He submits that the Abortion Act 1967, under which this abortion was authorised and eventually carried out, violates Articles 2 and/or 5, 6, 8 and 9 of the Convention.

2   The Commission accepts that the applicant, as potential father, was so closely affected by the termination of his wife's pregnancy that he may claim to be a "victim", within the meaning of Article 25 of the Convention, of the legislation complained of, as applied in the present case. The Commission here refers to its decision on the admissibility of Application No 2758/66 (*X v Belgium* (1970) 30 Coll 11; 12 Yearbook 175). The applicant in that case, a widow, complained that her husband had been killed in

violation of Article 2 of the Convention, and the Commission assumed by implication that, for the purpose of that complaint, she fulfilled the "victim" condition of Article 25. The Commission further recalls that in Application No 5961/72 (*Amekrane v United Kingdom* (1973) 44 Coll 101; 16 Yearbook 356), it accepted, again by implication, that the widow and the children of Mohamed Amerkrane could claim to be "victims" – not only under Article 8, but also under Articles 3 and 5 of the Convention – of the measures taken against their late husband and father.

3   The Commission also accepts that the present applicant, by his unsuccessful application to the High Court for an injunction, has exhausted the only available "domestic remedy" in the sense of Article 26 of the Convention.

4   The Commission, therefore, has to examine whether this application discloses any appearance of a violation of the provisions of the Convention invoked by the applicant, in particular Articles 2 and 8. It here recalls that the abortion law of High Contracting Parties to the Convention has so far been the subject of several applications under Article 25. The applicants either alleged that the legislation concerned violated the (unborn child's) right to life (Article 2) or they claimed that it constituted an unjustified interference with the (parents') right to respect for private life (Article 8). Two applications invoking Article 2 were declared inadmissible by the Commission on the ground that the applicants – in the absence of any measure of abortion directly affecting them by reason of a close link with the foetus – could not claim to be "victims" of the abortion laws complained of (*X v Norway* (1961) 4 Yearbook 270; 6 Coll 34 (App No 867/60); and *X v Austria* (1977) 7 D & R 87 (App No 2045/75)). One application (*Brüggemann and Scheuten v Germany* (1978) 10 D & R 100 (App No 6959/75)), invoking Article 8, was declared admissible by the Commission, in so far as it had been brought by two women. The Commission, and subsequently the Committee of Ministers, concluded that there was no breach of Article 8 (*Brüggemann and Scheuten*, above, at p 122). That conclusion was based on an interpretation of Article 8 which, *inter alia*, took into account the High Contracting Parties' law on abortion as applied at the time when the Convention entered into force (*Brüggemann and Scheuten*, above, at p 117, para 64 of the Commission's Report).

5   The question whether the unborn child is covered by Article 2 was expressly left open in Application No 6959/75 ((1978) 10 D & R 100, 116, para 60) and has not yet been considered by the Commission in any other case. It has, however, been the subject of proceedings before the Constitutional Court of Austria, a High Contracting State in which the Convention has the rank of constitutional law. In those proceedings the Austrian Constitutional Court, noting the different view expressed on this question in legal writings, found that Article 2(1), first sentence, interpreted in the context of Article 2(1) and 2(2), does not cover the unborn life (decision of 11 October 1974, *Erk Slg* (Collection of Decisions) No 7400, [1975] *Europäische Grundrechtezeitschrift* 74).

6   Article 2(1), first sentence, provides: "Everyone's right to life shall be protected by law" (in the French text: "*Le droit de toute personne à la vie est protégé par la loi*"). The Commission, in its interpretation of this clause and, in particular, of the terms "everyone" and "life", has examined the ordinary meaning of the provision in the context both of Article 2 and of the Convention as a whole, taking into account the object and purpose of the Convention.

7   The Commission first notes that the term "everyone" ("*toute personne*") is not defined in the Convention. It appears in Article 1 and in Section I, apart from Article 2(1), in Articles 5, 6, 8 to 11 and 13. In nearly all these instances the use of the word is such that it

can apply only post-natally. None indicates clearly that it has any possible prenatal application, although such application in a rare case – eg under Article 6(1) – cannot be entirely excluded.

8   As regards, more particularly, Article 2, it contains the following limitations of "everyone's" right to life enounced in the first sentence of para (1):

–   a clause permitting the death penalty in para (1), second sentence: "No one shall be deprived of his life intentionally save in the execution of a sentence of a court following his conviction of a crime for which this penalty is provided by law"; and

–   the provision, in para (2), that deprivation of life shall not be regarded as inflicted in contravention of Article 2 when it results from "the use of force which is no more than absolutely necessary" in the following three cases: "In defence of any person from unlawful violence"; "in order to effect a lawful arrest or to prevent the escape of a person lawfully detained"; "in action lawfully taken for the purpose of quelling a riot or insurrection".

All the above limitations, by their nature, concern persons already born and cannot be applied to the foetus.

9   Thus both the general usage of the term "everyone" ("*toute personne*") of the Convention (para 7 above) and the context in which this term is employed in Article 2 (para 8 above) tend to support the view that it does not include the unborn.

10 The Commission has next examined, in the light of the above considerations, whether the term "life" in Article 2(1), first sentence, is to be interpreted as covering only the life of persons already born or also the "unborn life" of the foetus. The Commission notes that the term "life", too, is not defined in the Convention.

11 It further observes that another, more recent international instrument for the protection of human rights, the American Convention on Human Rights of 1969, contains in Article 4(1), first and second sentences, the following provisions expressly extending the right to life to the unborn:

> Every person has the right to have his life respected. This right shall be protected by law and, in general, from the moment of conception.

12 The Commission is aware of the wide divergence of thinking on the question of where life begins. While some believe that it starts already with conception others tend to focus upon the moment of nidation, upon the point that the foetus becomes "viable", or upon live birth.

13 The German Federal Constitutional Court, when interpreting the provision "everyone has a right to life" in Article 2(2) of the Basic Law, stated as follows (Judgment of 25 February 1975, Appendix VI to the Commissioner's Report in the *Brüggemann and Scheuten* case, CI 1 b of the grounds.):

> Life in the sense of the historical existence of a human individual exists according to established biological and physiological knowledge at least from the 14th day after conception (Nidation, Individuation) ... The process of development beginning from this point is a continuous one so that no sharp divisions or exact distinction between the various stages of development of human life can be made. It does not end at birth: for example, the particular type of consciousness peculiar to the human personality only appears a considerable time after the birth. The protection conferred by Article 2(2) first sentence of the Basic Law can therefore be limited neither to the "complete" person after birth nor to the foetus capable of independent existence prior to birth. The right to life is guaranteed to every one who "lives"; in this context no distinction can be made between

the various stages of developing life before birth or between born and unborn children. "Everyone" in the meaning of Article 2(2) of the Basic Law is "every living human being", in other words: every human individual possessing life; "everyone" therefore includes unborn human beings.

14 The Commission also notes that, in a case arising under the Constitution of the United States (*Roe v Wade*, 410 US 113 (1973)), the State of Texas argued before the Supreme Court that, in general life begins at conception and is present throughout pregnancy. The Court, while not resolving the difficult question where life begins, found that, "with respect to the State's important and legitimate interest in potential life, the 'compelling' point is at viability".

15 The Commission finally recalls the decision of the Austrian Constitutional Court mentioned in para 6 above which, while also given in the framework of constitutional litigation, had to apply, like the Commission in the present case, Article 2 of the European Convention on Human Rights.

16 The Commission considers with the Austrian Constitutional Court that, in interpreting the scope of the term "life" in Article 2(1), first sentence, of the Convention, particular regard must be had to the context of the Article as a whole. It also observes that the term "life" may be subject to different interpretations in different legal instruments, depending on the context in which it is used in the instrument concerned.

17 The Commission has already noted, when discussing the meaning of the term "everyone" in Article 2 (para 8 above), that the limitations, in paras (1) and (2) of the Article, of "everyone's" right to "life", by their nature, concern persons already born and cannot be applied to the foetus. The Commission must therefore examine whether Article 2, in the absence of any express limitation concerning the foetus, is to be interpreted:

– as not covering the foetus at all;

– as recognising a "right to life" of the foetus with certain implied limitations; or

– as recognising an absolute "right to life" of the foetus.

18 The Commission has first considered whether Article 2 is to be construed as recognising an absolute "right to life" of the foetus and has excluded such an interpretation on the following grounds.

19 The "life" of the foetus is intimately connected with, and cannot be regarded in isolation from, the life of the pregnant woman. If Article 2 were held to cover the foetus and its protection under this Article were, in the absence of any express limitation, seen as absolute, an abortion would have to be considered as prohibited even where the continuance of the pregnancy would involve a serious risk to the life of the pregnant woman. This would mean that the "unborn life" of the foetus would be regarded as being of a higher value than the life of the pregnant woman. The "right to life" of a person already born would thus be considered as subject not only to the express limitations mentioned in para 8 above but also to a further, implied limitation.

20 The Commission finds that such an interpretation would be contrary to the object and purpose of the Convention. It notes that, already at the time of the signature of the Convention (4 November 1950), all High Contracting Parties, with one possible exception, permitted abortion when necessary to save the life of the mother and that, in the meanwhile, the national law on termination of pregnancy has shown a tendency towards further liberalisation.

21 Having thus excluded, as being incompatible with the object and purpose of the Convention, one of the three different constructions of Article 2 mentioned in para 17 above, the Commission has next considered which of the two remaining interpretations is to be regarded as the correct one – ie whether Article 2 does not cover the foetus at all or whether it recognises a "right to life" of the foetus with certain implied limitations.

22 The Commission here notes that the abortion complained of was carried out at the initial stage of the pregnancy – the applicant's wife was ten weeks pregnant – under section 1(1)(a) of the Abortion Act 1967 in order to avert the risk of injury to the physical or mental health of the pregnant woman. It follows that, as regards the second of the two remaining interpretations, the Commission is in the present case not concerned with the broad question whether Article 2 recognises a "right to life" of the foetus during the whole period of the pregnancy but only with the narrower issue whether such a right is to be assumed for the initial stage of the pregnancy. Moreover, as regards implied limitations of a "right to life" of the foetus at the initial stage, only the limitation protecting the life and health of the pregnant woman, the so-called "medical indication", is relevant for the determination of the present case and the question of other possible limitations (ethic indication, eugenic indication, social indication, time limitation) does not arise.

23 The Commission considers that it is not in these circumstances called upon to decide whether Article 2 does not cover the foetus at all or whether it recognises a "right to life" of the foetus with implied limitations. It finds that the authorisation, by the United Kingdom authorities, of the abortion complained of is compatible with Article 2(1), first sentence because, if one assumes that this provision applies at the initial stage of the pregnancy, the abortion is covered by an implied limitation, protecting the life and health of the woman at that stage, of the "right to life" of the foetus.

24 The Commission concludes that the applicant's complaint under Article 2 is inadmissible as being manifestly ill-founded within the meaning of Article 27(2).

25 In its examination of the applicant's complaints, concerning the Abortion Act 1967 and its application in this case, the Commission has next had regard to Article 8 of the Convention which, in para (1), guarantees to everyone the right to respect for his family life. The Commission here notes, apart from his principal complaint concerning the permission of the abortion, the applicant's ancillary submission that the 1967 Act denies the father of the foetus a right to be consulted, and to make applications, about the proposed abortion.

The Commission also observes that the applicant, who under Article 2 claims to be the victim of a violation of the right to life of the foetus of which he was the potential father, under Article 8 invokes a right of his own.

26 As regards the principal complaint concerning the permission of the abortion, the Commission recalls that the pregnancy of the applicant's wife was terminated in accordance with her wish and in order to avert the risk of injury to her physical or mental health. The Commission therefore finds that this decision, in so far as it interfered in itself with the applicant's right to respect for his family life, was justified under para (2) of Article 8 as being necessary for the protection of the rights of another person. It follows that this complaint is also manifestly ill-founded within the meaning of Article 27(2).

27 The Commission has next considered the applicant's ancillary complaint that the Abortion Act 1967 denies the father of the foetus a right to be consulted, and to make

applications, about the proposed abortion. It observes that any interpretation of the husband's and potential father's right, under Article 8 of the Convention, to respect for his private and family life, as regards an abortion which his wife intends to have performed on her, must first of all take into account the right of the pregnant woman, being the person primarily concerned in the pregnancy and its continuation or termination, to respect for her private life. The pregnant woman's right to respect for her private life, as affected by the developing foetus, has been examined by the Commission in its Report in the *Brüggemann and Scheuten* case (above, paras 59 ff). In the present case the Commission, having regard to the right of the pregnant woman, does not find that the husband's and potential father's right to respect for his private and family life can be interpreted so widely as to embrace such procedural rights as claimed by the applicant, ie a right to be consulted, or a right to make applications, about an abortion which his wife intends to have performed on her. The Commission concludes that this complaint is incompatible *ratione materiae* with the provisions of the Convention within the meaning of Article 27(2).

28 The Commission does not find that any of the other provisions invoked by the applicant (Articles 5, 6 and 9 of the Convention) are relevant for the examination of his complaints.

For these reasons, **THE COMMISSION** declares this application inadmissible.

CASE NO 23
BRÜGGEMANN AND SCHEUTEN v
FEDERAL REPUBLIC OF GERMANY

EUROPEAN COMMISSION OF HUMAN RIGHTS

Application No: 6959/75

Report: 12 July 1977

Panel: Sperduti (*Acting President, First Vice-President*); *Members*: Nørgaard, Busuttil, Kellberg, Daver, Opsahl, Custers, Frowein, Dupuy, Tenekides, Trechsel, Kiernan and Klecker[1]

Human rights — Right to respect for private life — Legal restrictions on obtaining abortions — Whether German legal restrictions consistent with right to respect for private life — Relevance of the legal orders of the Contracting States at the time of signature and subsequent legal development — European Convention for the Protection of Human Rights and Fundamental Freedoms, art 8

BACKGROUND

Following a judgment of the German Federal Constitutional Court on 25 February 1975 and an amendment of the German Criminal Code in 1976, German law provided that in principle an abortion was a criminal offence. However, it also provided that where a woman was in a situation of distress and an abortion was performed by a doctor with her consent, following consultation, this was not punishable.

The applicants, Ms Brüggemann and Ms Sheuten, claimed that the German law restricting abortion interfered with their rights under the European Convention on Human Rights. In particular, they complained that as they would not be free to have an abortion in the case of an unwanted pregnancy, there was a violation of their right to respect for private life under article 8 of the Convention. They further alleged violations of articles 9, 11, 12, 14, 17 and 18 of the Convention. The European Commission of Human Rights held the application admissible in relation to article 8 only.

HELD (finding that there had been no violation of article 8)

1   The right to respect for private life was of such a scope as to secure to the individual a sphere within which he could freely pursue the development and fulfillment of his personality. To this effect, he also had to have the possibility of establishing relationships of various kinds, including sexual, with other persons. In principle, therefore, whenever a State set up rules for the behaviour of the individual within this sphere, it interfered with the respect for private life and such interference had to be justified in light of article 8(2). (Para 55)

---

1   Although not present when the final vote was taken, Mr Fawcett (*President*), was permitted to express his separate opinion.

2   Not every regulation of the termination of unwanted pregnancies constituted an interference with the right to respect for the private life of the mother. Article 8(1) could not be interpreted as meaning that pregnancy and its termination were, as a principle, solely a matter of the private life of the mother. (Para 60)

3   Whenever a woman became pregnant, her private life became closely connected with the developing foetus. It was not necessary to decide in this context whether the unborn child should be considered as "life" in the sense of article 2 of the Convention, or whether it could be regarded as an entity which under article 8(2) could justify an interference "for the protection of others". (Paras 59 and 61)

4   The German legal solutions following the Fifth Criminal Law Reform Act could not be said to ignore the private life aspect connected with the problem of abortion. Abortion was not punishable in certain circumstances. In particular, abortion was permitted if continuation of the pregnancy would create a danger to the life or health of the woman, if it had to be feared that the child might suffer from an incurable injury to its health or if the pregnancy was a result of a crime. The legal rules complained about by the applicants did not interfere with their right to respect for their private life. (Paras 62 and 63)

Treaties and other international instruments referred to

European Convention for the Protection of Human Rights and Fundamental Freedoms 1950, arts 1, 2, 8, 9, 11, 12, 14, 17 and 18

International Covenant on Civil and Political Rights 1966, art 6(5)

National legislation referred to

Germany

Act on the Federal Constitutional Court (*Gesetz über das Bundesverfassungsgericht*), arts 21, 31(2) and 32

Basic Law (*Grundgesetz*) 1949, arts 1(1) and 2

Criminal Code (*Strafgesetzbuch*) 1871 (as last amended in 1969), arts 218 and 218(a)

Fifth Criminal Law Reform Act (*Fünftes Gesetz zur Reform des Strafrechts*) 1974, Federal Gazette (*Bundesgesetzblatt*, 21 June 1974, I, 1297–1300), arts 12(1), 218, 218(a), 218(b), 219 and 219(a)

Fifteenth Criminal Law Reform Act (*Fünfzehntes Strafrechtsänderungsgesetz*), Federal Gazette (*Bundesgesetzblatt*) I, 21 May 1976, 1213, arts 6, 218, 218(a), 218(b), 219 and 219(a)

Genetic Health Act (*Erbgesundheitsgesetz*) 1933, s 14(1)

Cases referred to

Federal Constitutional Court, judgment of 21 June 1974, 37 *BVerfGE* 324

Federal Constitutional Court, judgment of 25 February 1975, 39 *BVerfGE* 1

2 *Entscheidungen des Bundesgerichtshofs in Strafsachen*, 111, 242

3 *Entscheidungen des Bundesgerichtshofs in Strafsachen*, 7

X v Iceland, ECommHR, Application No 6825/75, (1976) 5 D&R 86

X v UK, ECommHR, Application No 3868/68, (1970) 34 CD 10

X v UK, ECommHR, Application No 5877/72, (1974) 45 CD 90

REPORT

I   INTRODUCTION

1   The following is an outline of the case as submitted by the parties to the European Commission of Human Rights.

2   The applicants are German citizens living in Hamburg. The first applicant, Rose Marie Brüggemann, born in 1936 and single, is a clerk. The second applicant, Adelheid Scheuten, *née* Patzeld, born in 1939, divorced and mother of two children, is a telephone operator and housewife.

The substance of the applicants' complaints

3   The application concerns the criminal law on the termination of pregnancy in the Federal Republic of Germany. It was initially directed against the judgment of the Federal Constitutional Court of 25 February 1975. The Court ruled that the Fifth Criminal Law Reform Act adopted by the *Bundestag* on 26 April 1974 (providing for advice to be given to pregnant women and containing new provisions as to the interruption of pregnancy) was void in so far as it allowed the interruption of pregnancy during the first 12 weeks without requiring any particular reason of necessity (indication). This part of the Act therefore never entered into force.

4   Following the Federal Constitutional Court's judgment, the Fifteenth Criminal Law Reform Act entered into force in the Federal Republic of Germany on 21 June 1976. It maintains the principle that abortion is a criminal offence but provides that, in specific situations of distress of the woman concerned, an abortion performed by a doctor with her consent after consultation is not punishable.

5   The applicants submit that both the judgment of the Federal Constitutional Court and the Fifteenth Criminal Law Reform Act interfered in particular with their right to respect for their private life under Article 8(1) of the European Convention on Human Rights and they consider that this interference was not justified on any of the grounds enumerated in para (2) of that Article.

[...]*

II   FACTS

15   This application concerns the recent development of the criminal law on the termination of pregnancy in the Federal Republic of Germany (for a summary of the criminal law on abortion in States which are Parties to the Convention, see the Commission's Report, App V), which has been as follows:

---

*   *Eds:* paras 6-14, which relate to procedural matters, have not been included.

1   The situation before 21 June 1974

16 Under Article 218 of the Criminal Code (*Strafgesetzbuch*) of 1871, as last amended in 1969, and as applied in the light of special legislation (Genetic Health Act (*Erbgesundheitsgesetz*) 1933, s 14 (1)), and the case law of the Federal Court (*Bundesgerichtshof*) (see 2 *Entscheidungen des Bundesgerichtshofs in Strafsachen*, 111 at 113–114, 242 at 244; Vol 3, 7 at 8–9), any abortion, except one indicated on medical grounds, ie to save the mother's life or health, was punishable (see the commentary by (Schwarz-) Dreher, *Strafgesetzbuch* (32nd ed, 1970), pp 814–815).

2   The Fifth Criminal Law Reform Act

17 On 26 April 1974, the *Bundestag* adopted the Fifth Criminal Law Reform Act (*Fünftes Gesetz zur Reform des Strafrechts*). The Act was promulgated on 21 June 1974. It contained a revised version of the provisions on abortion and provided for advice to be given to pregnant women.

18 The new provisions, in so far as they are of interest in the present case, read as follows:

Art 218. Termination of Pregnancy.

(1) Whoever terminates a pregnancy later than on the thirteenth day after conception shall be punished by imprisonment for a term not exceeding three years or a fine.

(2) The penalty shall be imprisonment for a term of between six months and five years where the perpetrator:

1   acts against the will of the pregnant woman, or

2   frivolously causes the risk of death or of a serious injury to the health of the pregnant woman.

The court may order the supervision of conduct (Art 68(1)(2)).

(3) If the act is committed by the pregnant woman herself, the penalty shall be imprisonment for a term not exceeding one year or a fine.

(4) The attempt shall be punishable. The woman shall not be punished for attempt.

Art 218a. No punishment for termination of pregnancy within the first 12 weeks.

An abortion performed by a doctor with the pregnant woman's consent shall not be punishable under Article 218 if no more than 12 weeks have elapsed after conception.

Art 218b. Termination of pregnancy on specific grounds (indications) after 12 weeks.

An abortion performed by a doctor with the pregnant woman's consent after 12 weeks have elapsed after conception shall not be punishable under Article 218 if, according to the knowledge of medical science:

(1) the termination of pregnancy is advisable in order to avert from the pregnant woman a risk to her life or a risk of serious injury to her health, unless the risk can be averted in some other way that she can reasonably be expected to bear; or

(2) there are strong reasons for the assumption that, as a result of a genetic trait or harmful influence prior to birth, the child would suffer from an incurable injury to its health which is so serious that the pregnant woman cannot be expected to continue the pregnancy, provided that no more than 22 weeks have elapsed after conception.

Art 218c. Termination of pregnancy in the absence of information and advice being given to the pregnant woman.

(1) Whoever terminates a pregnancy although the pregnant woman

   1   did not prior thereto consult a doctor, or a consulting agency authorised thereto, regarding the question of termination of her pregnancy, and was not informed there about the public and private assistance available to pregnant women, mothers and children, in particular about such assistance as facilitates the continuance of pregnancy and the situation of mother and child, and

   2   did not obtain medical counselling

      shall be punished by imprisonment for a term not exceeding one year or by a fine, unless the act is punishable under Article 218.

(2) The woman on whom the operation has been performed shall not be subject to punishment under paragraph (1).

Art 219. Termination of pregnancy without a medical opinion.

(1) Whomever terminates a pregnancy after 12 weeks have elapsed after conception although no competent authority certified prior to the termination that the conditions of Art 218b (1) or (2) are fulfilled, shall be punished by imprisonment for a term not exceeding one year or by a fine, unless the act is punishable under Article 218.

(2) The woman on whom the operation has been performed shall not be subject to punishment under paragraph (1).

3   The decisions of the Federal Constitutional Court

19 On 20 June 1974, the Land Government of Baden-Württemberg requested the Federal Constitutional Court (*Bundesverfassungsgericht*) to suspend, by a provisional ruling under Article 32 of the Act on the Federal Constitutional Court (*Gesetz über das Bundesverfassungsgericht*), the entry into force of the Fifth Criminal Law Reform Act which had been signed by the Federal President on 18 June 1974.

20 On 21 June 1974, the Fifth Criminal Law Reform Act was promulgated in the Federal Gazette (*Bundesgesetzblatt*, Pt I, pp 1297–1300). According to Article 12(1) of the Act, its essential provisions would have entered into force on the following day.

21 Still on 21 June 1974, however, the Federal Constitutional Court made the following order, as a provisional ruling under Article 21 of the Act on the Federal Constitutional Court:

   1   Article 218(a) of the Criminal Code as amended by the Fifth Criminal Law Reform Act of 18 June 1974 ... shall not enter into force for the time being.

   2   Article 218(b) and 219 of the Criminal Code as amended by this Act shall be applied also to abortions performed within the first 12 weeks after conception.

      An abortion performed by a doctor with the pregnant woman's consent within the first 12 weeks after conception shall not be punishable under Article 218 of the Criminal Code if an unlawful act under Articles 176 (sexual abuse of children), 177 (rape) or 179 (1) (sexual abuse of persons unable to defend themselves) of the Criminal Code was committed on the pregnant woman and there are strong reasons to suggest that the pregnancy was a result of the offence.

22 After the promulgation of the Fifth Criminal Law Reform Act, 193 members of the Bundestag and the Governments of five *Länder* (Baden-Württemberg, Saarland, Bavaria, Schleswig-Holstein and Rhineland-Palatinate) instituted proceedings for a review of the

Act as to its conformity with the Basic Law (*Grundgesetz*). They invoked in particular Article 2 (37 *Entscheidungen des Bundersverfassungsgerichts (BVerfGE)* 324, 325), first sentence ("Everyone has the right to life ..."), in conjunction with Article 1(1) of the Basic Law ("The dignity of man is inviolable. To respect and protect it is the duty of all State authority.").

23 These proceedings were concluded by the judgment of the Federal Constitutional Court of 25 February 1975 (39 *BVerfGE* 1–95). The operative part of this decision, which had the same effect as a statute (according to Art 31(2) of the Act on the Federal Constitutional Court), read as follows:

I   Article 218a of the Criminal Code as amended by the Fifth Criminal Law Reform Act of 18 June 1974 ... is incompatible with Article 2(2), first sentence, read in conjunction with Article 1(1) of the Basic Law and void as far as it exempts abortion from punishment even if there are no reasons which – within the meaning of the reasons given for this decision – are justifiable under the system of values incorporated in the Basic Law.

II   Pending the coming into force of a new statute, the following order is made in accordance with Article 35 of the Federal Constitutional Court Act:

1   Articles 218b and 219 of the Criminal Code as amended by the Fifth Criminal Law Reform Act of 18 June 1974 ... shall be applied also to abortions performed within the first 12 weeks after conception.

2   An abortion performed by a doctor with the pregnant woman's consent within the first 12 weeks after conception shall not be punishable under Article 218 of the Criminal Code if an unlawful act under Articles 176 to 179 of the Criminal Code was committed on the pregnant woman and there are strong reasons to suggest that the pregnancy was a result of the offence.

3   Where the pregnancy was terminated by a doctor with the pregnant woman's consent within the first 12 weeks after conception in order to avert from the pregnant woman the risk of serious distress that cannot be averted in any other way she might reasonably be expected to bear, the Court may abstain from imposing punishment in accordance with Article 218 of the Criminal Code (39 *BVerfGE* 2–3).

24 The grounds for this decision were summarised by the Federal Constitutional Court as follows:

1   The life of the child developing in the mother's womb constitutes an independent legal interest protected by the Constitution (Articles 2 (2) first sentence and 1 (1) of the Basic Law). The State's duty of protection not only forbids direct State interference with the life of the developing child but also requires the State to protect and foster it.

2   The State's duty to protect the life of the developing child applies even as against the mother.

3   The protection of the life of the embryo enjoys in principle priority over the pregnant woman's right of self-determination throughout the period of pregnancy and may not be considered as subject to derogation during a certain period.

4   The legislator may express the legal disapproval of termination of pregnancy which is in principle required otherwise than by the imposition of criminal penalties. The essential point is that the totality of the measures designed to protect the unborn child in fact provides a degree of protection which corresponds with the significance of the interest to be protected. In an extreme case where the protection required by the Constitution cannot be attained in any other way, the legislator is bound to make use of the criminal law in order to protect the life of the developing child.

5 A woman cannot be required to continue her pregnancy if its termination is necessary in order to avert a danger to her life or of serious injury to her health. Furthermore, the legislator is free to decide that there exist other exceptional adverse circumstances of similar gravity affecting a pregnant woman which she cannot reasonably be expected to bear and that in such cases a termination of pregnancy shall not render her liable to punishment.

6 The Fifth Criminal Law Reform Act of 18 June 1974 ... does not comply in a sufficient degree with the constitutional obligation to protect the unborn child (39 *BVerfGE* 1 (translated by the Council of Europe)).

4 The Fifteenth Criminal Law Amendment Act

25 On 12 February 1976, the Bundestag adopted the Fifteenth Criminal Law Amendment Act (*Fünfzehntes Strafrechtsänderungsgesetz*). The Act was promulgated on 21 May 1976 (Federal Gazette I, 1213), and entered into force one month thereafter (according to Art 6 of the Act).

26 The relevant provisions of the Criminal Code, as amended by the Fifteenth Criminal Law Amendment Act, read as follows:

Art 218. Termination of Pregnancy.

(1) Whoever terminates a pregnancy shall be punished by imprisonment for a term not exceeding three years or a fine.

(2) In particularly serious cases the punishment shall be imprisonment for a term between six months and five years. As a rule, a case is particularly serious where the perpetrator:

    1 acts against the will of the pregnant woman, or

    2 frivolously causes the risk of death or of a serious injury to the health of the pregnant woman.

The court may order the supervision of conduct (Art 68 (1)(2)).

(3) If the act is committed by the pregnant woman herself, the penalty shall be imprisonment for a term not exceeding one year or a fine. The pregnant woman is not punishable under the first sentence if the pregnancy is interrupted by a doctor after consultation (Art 218b(1)(1)-(2)) and if not more than 22 weeks have elapsed since conception. The court may abstain from punishing the pregnant woman if at the time of the intervention she was in a situation of particular distress

(4) The attempt shall be punishable. The woman shall not be punished for attempt.

Art 218a. Indications for the termination of pregnancy.

(1) An abortion performed by a doctor shall not be punishable if:

    1 the pregnant woman consents, and

    2 in view of her present and future living conditions the termination of the pregnancy is advisable according to medical knowledge in order to avert a danger to her life or the danger of a serious prejudice to her physical or mental health, provided that the danger cannot be averted in any other way she can reasonably be expected to bear.

(2) The prerequisites of paragraph (1)(2) are also considered as fulfilled if, according to medical knowledge:

    1 there are strong reasons to suggest that, as a result of a genetic trait or harmful influence prior to birth, the child would suffer from an incurable injury to its

       health which is so serious that the pregnant woman cannot be required to continue the pregnancy;

2   an unlawful act under Articles 176 to 179 has been committed on the pregnant woman and there are strong reasons to suggest that the pregnancy is a result of that offence; or

3   the termination of the pregnancy is otherwise advisable in order to avert the danger of a distress which:

   (a)   is so serious that the pregnant woman cannot be required to continue the pregnancy, and

   (b)   cannot be averted in any other way she can reasonably be expected to bear;

(3)   Provided that, in the cases envisaged in paragraph (2)(1), not more than 22 weeks have elapsed since conception and, in the cases envisaged in paragraph (2)(2) and (3), not more than 12 weeks.

Art 218b. Termination of pregnancy in the absence of advice being given to the pregnant woman.

(1)   Whoever terminates a pregnancy although the pregnant woman:

1   did not at least three days before the intervention consult a counsellor (para 2), regarding the question of termination of her pregnancy, and was not informed there about the public and private assistance available to pregnant women, mothers and children, in particular about such assistance as facilitates the continuance of pregnancy and the situation of mother and child, and

2   was not advised by a doctor on the medically significant aspects, shall be punished by imprisonment for a term not exceeding one year or by a fine, unless the act is punishable under Article 218. The pregnant woman is not punishable under the first sentence.

(2)   Counsellor with the meaning of paragraph (1)(1) is:

1   an advisory board approved by a public authority or by a corporation, institution or foundation under public law;

2   a doctor who does not himself perform the abortion and who:

   (a)   as a member of an approved advisory board (sub-para (1)) is charged to give advice within the meaning of paragraph (1)(1);

   (b)   is approved as a counsellor by a public authority or by a corporation, institution or foundation under public law; or

   (c)   has – by consulting a member of an approved advisory board (sub-para (1)) who is charged with giving advice within the meaning of paragraph (1)(1), by consulting a social authority or in another appropriate way – obtained information about the assistance available in individual cases.

3   Paragraph 1(1) does not apply where termination of pregnancy is advisable in order to avert from the pregnant woman a danger to her life or health caused by a physical disease or physical injury.

Art 219. Termination of pregnancy without medical certificate.

(1)   Whoever terminates a pregnancy although no written certificate, by a doctor who does not himself perform the abortion, has been submitted to him on the question whether the conditions of Article 218a(1)(2), (2) and (3) are fulfilled, shall be punished by imprisonment for a term not exceeding one year or by a fine, unless the act is punishable under Article 218. The pregnant woman is not punishable under the first sentence.

(2)   A doctor may not give a certificate under paragraph (1) if the competent authority has forbidden him to do so, on the ground that he has been finally convicted of an unlawful act under paragraph (1), or under Articles 218, 218b, 219a or 219c, or of

another unlawful act which he committed in connection with an interruption of pregnancy. The competent authority may provisionally forbid a doctor to give certificates under paragraph (1) if he has been committed for trial on suspicion of having committed such an unlawful act.

Art 219a. False medical certificate.

(1) Whoever as a doctor knowingly gives a false certificate on the conditions of Article 218a(1)(2), (2) and (3), shall be punished by imprisonment for a term not exceeding two years or by a fine, unless the act is punishable under Article 218.

(2) The pregnant woman is not punishable under paragraph (1).

Art 219d. Definition.

Acts, the effects of which occur before the termination of the implantation of the fertilised egg in the uterus, are deemed not to be interruptions of pregnancy within the meaning of this Code.

[...]**

IV   OPINION OF COMMISSION

1   The point at issue

50 The applicants mainly allege a violation of Article 8 of the Convention by the Federal Republic of Germany in that they are not free to have an abortion carried out in case of an unwanted pregnancy. They state that, as a result, they either have to renounce sexual intercourse or to apply methods of contraception or to carry out a pregnancy against their will.

Article 8 of the Convention provides:

(1) Everyone has the right to respect for his private and family life, his home and his correspondence.

(2) There shall be no interference by a public authority with the exercise of this right except such as is in accordance with the law and is necessary in a democratic society in the interests of national security, public safety or the economic well-being of the country, for the prevention of disorder or crime, for the protection of health or morals, or for the protection of the rights and freedoms of others.

51 The applicants further allege a violation of Article 9 of the Convention in that the judgment of the Federal Constitutional Court was based on religious grounds, as well as violations of Articles 9 and 11 of the Convention on the ground that the Constitutional Court interfered with the separation of powers which they allege to be codified in the Convention. The second applicant further alleges a violation of Article 12 of the Convention in that illegitimate children reduce their mothers' chances to marry. Finally, Articles 14, 17 and 18 of the Convention have also been invoked.

52 In its decision on admissibility of 19 May 1976, the Commission found that the application raised issues under Article 8 of the Convention, but did not find it necessary to decide upon further allegations.

53 The Commission now finds unanimously that the legal provisions complained of do not in any way interfere with any of the other Convention rights invoked by the

---

** ***Eds:*** Part III, paras 27–49, summarising the parties' submissions have not been included.

applicants and that, consequently, the only issue arising under the Convention in the present case is the question whether or not the rules on abortion existing under German law since the judgment of the Federal Constitutional Court of 25 February 1975 violate the applicants' right under Article 8 of the Convention to respect for their private life.

2   The interference with the right to respect for one's private life

54 According to Article 8 of the Convention, "Everyone has the right to respect for his private ... life ...". In its decision on admissibility, the Commission has already found that legislation regulating the interruption of pregnancy touches upon the sphere of private life. The first question which must be answered is whether the legal rules governing abortion in the Federal Republic of Germany since the judgment of the Constitutional Court of 25 February 1975 constitute an interference with the right to respect for private life of the applicants.

55 The right to respect for private life is of such a scope as to secure to the individual a sphere within which he can freely pursue the development and fulfilment of his personality. To this effect, he must also have the possibility of establishing relationships of various kinds, including sexual, with other persons. In principle, therefore, whenever the State sets up rules for the behaviour of the individual within this sphere, it interferes with the respect for private life and such interference must be justified in the light of Article 8(2).

56 However, there are limits to the personal sphere. While a large proportion of the law existing in a given State has some immediate or remote effect on the individual's possibility of developing his personality by doing what he wants to do, not all of these can be considered to constitute an interference with private life in the sense of Article 8 of the Convention. In fact, as the earlier jurisprudence of the Commission has already shown, the claim to respect for private life is automatically reduced to the extent that the individual himself brings his private life into contact with public life or into close connection with other protected interests.

57 Thus, the Commission has held that the concept of private life in Article 8 was broader than the definition given by numerous Anglo-Saxon and French authors, namely, the "right to live as far as one wishes, protected from publicity", in that it also comprises, "*to a certain degree*, the right to establish and to develop relationships with other human beings, especially in the emotional field for the development and fulfilment of one's own personality". But it denied "that the protection afforded by Article 8 of the Convention extends to relationships of the individual with his entire immediate surroundings". It thus found that the right to keep a dog did not pertain to the sphere of private life of the owner because "the keeping of dogs is by the very nature of that animal necessarily associated with certain interferences with the life of others and even with public life" (App No 6825/75, *X v Iceland* (1976) 5 D&R 86, 87) (emphasis added).

58 In two further cases, the Commission has taken account of the element of public life in connection with Article 8 of the Convention. It held that subsequent communication of statements made in the course of public proceedings (App No 3868/68, *X v UK* (1970) 34 CD 10, 18) or the taking of photographs of a person participating in a public incident (App No 5877/72, *X v UK* (1974) 45 CD 90, 93) did not amount to interference with private life.

59 The termination of an unwanted pregnancy is not comparable with the situation in any of the above cases. However, pregnancy cannot be said to pertain uniquely to the

sphere of private life. Whenever a woman is pregnant, her private life becomes closely connected with the developing foetus.

60 The Commission does not find it necessary to decide, in this context, whether the unborn child is to be considered as "life" in the sense of Article 2 of the Convention, or whether it could be regarded as an entity which under Article 8(2) could justify an interference "for the protection of others". There can be no doubt that certain interests relating to pregnancy are legally protected, eg as shown by a survey of the legal order in 13 High Contracting Parties (see the Commission's Report, App VII). This survey reveals that, without exception, certain rights are attributed to the conceived but unborn child, in particular the right to inherit. The Commission also notes that Article 6(5) of the United Nations Covenant on Civil and Political Rights prohibits the execution of death sentences on pregnant women.

61 The Commission therefore finds that not every regulation of the termination of unwanted pregnancies constitutes an interference with the right to respect for the private life of the mother. Article 8(1) cannot be interpreted as meaning that pregnancy and its termination are, as a principle, solely a matter of the private life of the mother. In this respect the Commission notes that there is not one member State of the Convention which does not, in one way or another, set up legal rules in this matter. The applicants complain about the fact that the Constitutional Court declared null and void the Fifth Criminal Law Reform Act, but even this Act was not based on the assumption that abortion is entirely a matter of the private life of the pregnant woman. It only provided that an abortion performed by a physician with the pregnant woman's consent should not be punishable if no more than 12 weeks had elapsed after conception.

62 The legal solutions following the Fifth Criminal Law Reform Act cannot be said to disregard the private-life aspect connected with the problem of abortion. The judgment of the Federal Constitutional Court of 25 February 1975 not only recognised the medical, eugenic and ethical indications but also stated that, where the pregnancy was terminated by a doctor with the pregnant woman's consent within the first 12 weeks after conception "in order to avert from the pregnant woman the risk of serious distress that cannot be averted in any other way she might reasonably be expected to bear, the Court may abstain from imposing punishment" (see para 23 above).

According to Article 218a of the Criminal Code in the version of the Fifteenth Criminal Law Reform Act of 18 May 1976 (see para 26 above), an abortion performed by a physician is not punishable if the termination of pregnancy is advisable for any reason in order to avert from the pregnant woman the danger of a distress which is so serious that the pregnant woman cannot be required to continue the pregnancy and which cannot be averted in any other way the pregnant woman might reasonably be expected to bear. In particular, the abortion is admitted if continuation of the pregnancy would create a danger to the life or health of the woman, if it has to be feared that the child might suffer from an incurable injury to its health or if the pregnancy is the result of a crime. The woman is required also to seek advice on medically significant aspects of abortion as well as on the public and private assistance available for pregnant women, mothers and children.

In the absence of any of the above indications, the pregnant woman herself is nevertheless exempt from any punishment if the abortion was performed by a doctor within the first 22 weeks of pregnancy and if she made use of the medical and social counselling.

63 In view of this situation, the Commission does not find that the legal rules complained about by the applicants interfere with their right to respect for their private life.

64 Furthermore, the Commission has had regard to the fact that, when the European Convention of Human Rights entered into force, the law on abortion in all member States was at least as restrictive as the one now complained of by the applicants. In many European countries the problem of abortion is or has been the subject of heated debates on legal reform since. There is no evidence that it was the intention of the Parties to the Convention to bind themselves in favour of any particular solution under discussion – eg a solution of the kind set out in the Fifth Criminal Law Reform Act (*Fristenlösung* – time limitation) which was not yet under public discussion at the time the Convention was drafted and adopted.

65 The Commission finally notes that, since 21 June 1974, the relevant legal situation has gradually become more favourable to the applicants.

V   CONCLUSION

66 The Commission unanimously concludes that the present case does not disclose a breach of Article 8 of the Convention.*

DISSENTING OPINION OF FAWCETT

I do not agree with the reasoning or conclusion of the Commission on Article 8 which is in my opinion to be applied to the facts before us in the following way:

1   "Private life" in Article 8(1) must in my view cover pregnancy, its commencement and its termination: indeed, it would be hard to envisage more essentially private elements in life. But pregnancy has also responsibilities for the mother towards the unborn child, at least when it is capable of independent life, and towards the father of the child, and for the father too towards both. But pregnancy, its commencement and its termination, as so viewed is still part of private and family life, calling for respect under Article 8(1). I am not then able to follow the Commission in holding, if I understand its reasoning correctly, that there are certain inherent limits to treating pregnancy and its termination as part of private life. Such limits, beyond those mentioned, at least in the form of intervention by legislation, must be found and justified in Article 8(2): in the absence of such limits, the decision to terminate a pregnancy remains a free part of private life.

2   I find it necessary to distinguish here between intervention and interference. By intervention in the present context I mean regulation of the termination of pregnancy by law, ranging from prohibition to requirements that various conditions be met; by interference I mean forms of regulation which fail to respect private and family life in the sense of Article 8. Intervention may be justified under Article 8(2); only if it is not justified does it become interference. But it must be added that regulation of termination of pregnancy by law constitutes intervention in private and family life even before pregnancy has begun because it will influence or govern decisions about commencement and termination of pregnancy.

---

*   *Eds:* the Committee of Ministers, agreeing with the Commission's opinion, decided that there had been no violation of the Convention: Res DH (78) 1 (17 March 1978), available at the website of the European Court of Human Rights (see *On-Line Access to Human Rights Source Materials, supra,* p xlv).

3 The provisions of Article 218a of the Federal Act, which were declared by the Federal Constitutional Court to be contrary to Article 1 of the Basic Law (1949), themselves imposed limiting conditions on the termination of pregnancy, which could be justified under Article 8(2) as necessary for the protection of health. However, it is not clear to me upon what grounds in Article 8(2) the elimination of Article 218a, and the introduction of additional limiting conditions in the Act which replaces it, are in fact based. The only possible grounds appear to be "the economic well-being of the country"; "the prevention of crime"; "the protection of health or morals"; "the protection of the rights and freedoms of others".

4 No facts have been produced to the Commission to show that the new legislation is aimed in part at maintaining or increasing the birth-rate for the economic well-being of the country: indeed, its well-being might call for an opposite policy. Again, there is evidence in a number of countries that over-restrictive legislation not only fails to prevent "back-street abortions", incompetently and even criminally performed, but may even encourage recourse to them.

5 The new legislation, like Article 218a which it replaces, certainly secures the protection of health; but there is the further limitation that unacceptable distress to the mother from continuance of the pregnancy must be shown before it can be terminated simply at her wish. It may of course be said that this limitation will be generously interpreted, that in practice there will be little difference between the new provision and the original Article 218a, and that that additional limitation is a compromise gesture to the anti-abortionists. But even if this were correct – and practice might well vary over the country in applying the limitation – I do not think it renders to the new legislative provision "necessary" under Article 8(2).

6 The intervention of the legislator in sexual morality may here have the purpose of preventing abortion being often reduced simply to a form of contraception, or of inducing a sense of moral responsibility in the commencement of pregnancy, but it is not shown how the new legislation, as distinct from what it replaces, will achieve these purposes. On the contrary, the statistics and other evidence quoted in the minority judgment in the Federal Constitutional Court demonstrate the ineffectiveness of the earlier restrictive law in achieving these purpose or, for that matter, those considered in para 4 above. Even though the new legislation is less restrictive of termination of pregnancy that the old law, it has not in my view been shown, in relation to the earlier Article 218a, that it is "necessary" under Article 8(2) for the protection of morals.

7 There remains "the protection of the rights and freedoms of others" and the question how far this can cover the unborn child. The Convention does not expressly extend the right to life, protected by Article 2, to an unborn child; but that is not I think conclusive. However, it would serve no purpose for me to try to answer so controversial a question at any length here and I can only say that I am unable to attribute rights and freedoms under the convention to an unborn child not yet capable of independent life, that Article 218a did not extend the permitted termination of pregnancy beyond 12 weeks from conception, and that the elimination of that section of the Act was therefore not "necessary" for the protection of the rights and freedoms of others.

I can only conclude that the changes in the law on termination of pregnancy that have taken place in consequence of the decision of the Federal Constitutional Court are interventions in private and family life, which are not justified under Article 8(2), and are therefore an interference with it contrary to the Convention.

SEPARATE OPINION OF OPSAHL

(Nørgaard and Kellberg concurring)

1 The main claim of the applicants concerns the right to respect for private (and family) life and was to some extent clarified during the proceedings. As regards the argument that the State must provide for the performance of abortions as an unconditional right upon the woman's request, such an obligation could not easily be made an aspect of the right to respect for private life, on any interpretation of Article 8. If, however, the self-determination of the woman is the essential claim, the main obligation of the state would be not to interfere with her decision in particular by such punishment as the law of the Federal Republic makes possible if the conditions for abortion are not met. Such interference in the case of the applicants remains hypothetical, but the possibility is said to affect their private life in various ways.

2 Although we have reached the same conclusion as the majority of the Commission, we agree with many of the views expressed by Mr Fawcett in his dissenting opinion. And we take the view, personally, that laws regulating abortion ought to leave the decision to have it performed in the early stage of pregnancy to the woman concerned. We do not wish to imply that members of the Commission who have not found it necessary to express themselves on this point must be of a different opinion. But we say this because we consider that among the various possible solutions, this one – a "Fristenlösung" based on self-determination – is the one most consistent with what we think a right to respect for private life in this context ought to mean in our time.

3 Nevertheless, we must admit that such a view cannot easily be read into the terms of Article 8. The problem is not a new one and traditional views of the interpretation and application of this Article have to be taken into account notwithstanding the rapid development of views on abortion in many countries. We are aware that the reality behind these traditional views is that the scope of protection of private life has depended on the outlook which has been formed mainly by men, although it may have been shared by women as well.

4 Under the Convention, the legal argument against the claim of the applicants can be made in various ways. Mr Kellberg has come to the conclusion that there is an interference, but that it can be justified under Article 8(2), taking into account the way the conditions for such interference have traditionally been understood and the margin of appreciation allowed, the legal position in Germany being in fact relatively liberal. Mr Nørgaard and Mr Opsahl have noted the distinction between intervention and interference. One could, for instance, say that legislative intervention (even when backed by criminal sanctions) does not necessarily amount to interference in the sense of Article 8, although in various ways affecting private life. There are many examples of legislation intervening in private or family life in ways which do not represent interference with the right to respect for private or family life, eg by regulating relations between family members, and which therefore do not need to be justified within the limits set out in Article 8(2). Mr Nørgaard is of the opinion that in this case there is no interference in relation to the applicants within the meaning of Article 8. Mr Opsahl shares this opinion and in addition wishes to state, like Mr Fawcett, that punishment for unlawful abortion, or the threat of it, cannot generally be justified on any of the grounds set out in Article 8(2).

CASE NO 24

OPEN DOOR COUNSELLING LTD AND DUBLIN WELL WOMAN CENTRE LTD v IRELAND

EUROPEAN COURT OF HUMAN RIGHTS

Application No: 14234/88, 14235/88

Judgment: 29 October 1992

Panel: *Judges*: Ryssdal (*President*), Cremona, Vilhjalmsson, Gölcüklü, Matscher, Pettiti, Macdonald, Russo, Bernhardt, Spielmann, De Meyer, Valticos, Martens, Palm, Foighel, Pekkanen, Loizou, Moranilla, Bigi, Sir John Freeland, Baka, Lopes Rocha and Blayney (*ad hoc Judge*)

Human rights — Right to life — Abortion — Right to life of the unborn — Freedom of expression — Freedom to impart and receive information — Non-directive counselling — Women travelling from one jurisdiction where abortion is illegal to another jurisdiction in order to obtain abortions — Provision of information on abortion clinics abroad — Whether an injunction prohibiting information to pregnant women on the available options regarding abortions violated the freedom to impart and receive information — Constitution of Ireland, art 40 — Offences Against the Person Act 1861 — Censorship of Publications Act 1929, as amended by the Health (Family Planning) Act 1979 — Civil Liberty Act 1961 — European Convention for the Protection of Human Rights and Fundamental Freedoms, art 10

Human rights — Limitations and restrictions — Margin of appreciation — Wide margin of appreciation of national authorities in respect of issues of morality — Whether proportionality test applicable to issues of morality — Power of Convention institutions to review measures concerning issues of morality, including the right to life

BACKGROUND

The applicants were Open Door Counselling Ltd and Dublin Well Woman Centre Ltd, both companies incorporated under Irish law, which provided counselling to pregnant women in Ireland; Ms Bonnie Maher and Ms Ann Downes, who worked as trained counsellors for Dublin Well Woman; and Mrs X and Ms Meave Geraghty who joined the application as women of child-bearing age.

In June 1985, the Society for the Protection of Unborn Children (Ireland) Ltd commenced a private action before the High Court against Open Door and Dublin Well Woman. It sought a declaration that the activities of the applicants in counselling pregnant women to travel abroad to obtain an abortion were unlawful, having regard to the rights of the unborn child under article 40(3)(3) of the Constitution of Ireland, and an order restraining the applicants from such counselling or assistance.[*]

On 16 December 1986, the High Court found the activities of Open Door and Dublin Well Woman to be unlawful under article 40(3)(3) of the Constitution and granted an injunction against the applicants, their servants or agents, that they "be perpetually

---

[*] *Eds:* Article 40(3)(3) of the Constitution is reproduced at paragraph 28 of the Court's judgment.

restrained from counselling or assisting pregnant women within the jurisdiction of [the] Court to obtain further advice on abortion or to obtain an abortion".

Open Door and Dublin Well Woman appealed against the decision to the Supreme Court. In a unanimous decision on 16 March 1988, the Supreme Court rejected the appeal and upheld the injunction, although varying the terms of the restraint as follows:

> ... the defendants and each of them, their servants or agents be perpetually restrained from assisting pregnant women within the jurisdiction to travel abroad to obtain abortions by referral to a clinic, by making for them travel arrangements, or by informing them of the identity and location of and the method of communication with a specified clinic or clinics or otherwise.

Costs were awarded against the applicant companies. Open Door, having no assets, subsequently ceased its activities.

On 19 August and 22 September 1988, the applicants lodged applications with the European Commission on Human Rights, complaining that the Supreme Court injunction was an unjustified interference with their right to impart and receive information, as guaranteed by article 10 of the European Convention on Human Rights. Open Door, Mrs X and Ms Geraghty further complained of interference with their right to respect for private life under article 8; and Open Door of discrimination contrary to article 14 taken in conjunction with articles 8 and 10.

The Commission found the applications admissible on 15 May 1990. In its opinion of 7 March 1991, it stated (by eight votes to five) that there had been a violation of article 10 by the Supreme Court injunction, as it affected the applicant companies and their counsellors; (by seven votes to six) there had been a violation of article 10 by the Supreme Court injunction as it affected Mrs X and Ms Geraghty; (by seven votes to two) it was not necessary to examine further the complaints under article 8 in respect of Mrs X and Ms Geraghty; and (unanimously) there had been no violation of articles 14 and 8 in respect of Open Door. The application proceeded to the European Court of Human Rights.

HELD (finding a violation of article 10 of the Convention)

(Judge Matscher partly dissenting; Judges Pettiti, Russo, Lopes Rocha and Bigi dissenting; Judge de Meyer separate opinion;[*] Judge Morentilla concurring opinion):

1   It was accepted that the Supreme Court injunction interfered with the freedom of the corporate applicants to impart information. Having regard to the scope of the injunction which also restrained the "servants or agents" of the corporate applicants from assisting "pregnant women", there could be no doubt that there was also an interference with the rights of the applicant counsellors to impart information and with the rights of Mrs X and Ms Geraghty to receive information in the event of being pregnant. To determine whether such an interference entailed a violation of article 10, the Court had to examine whether or not it was justified under article 10(2) by reason of being a restriction "prescribed by law" which was necessary in a democratic society on one or other of the grounds specified in article 10. (Para 55)

---

[*]   *Eds:* due to space constraints, the separate opinion of Judge de Meyer has not been included. The full text of the judgment is available at the website of the European Court of Human Rights (see *On-Line Access to Human Rights Source Materials, supra,* p xlv); Series A, No 246; and 15 EHRR 244.]

2   Taking into consideration the high threshold of protection of the unborn provided under Irish law generally and the manner in which the courts had interpreted their role as guarantors of constitutional rights, the possibility that action might be taken against the corporate applicants must have been, with appropriate legal advice, reasonably foreseeable. This conclusion was reinforced by the legal advice that was actually given to Dublin Well Women that, in the light of article 40(3)(3) of the Constitution, an injunction could be sought against its counselling activities. The restriction contained in the injunction was accordingly "prescribed by law". (Para 59)

3   It was evident that the protection afforded under Irish law to the right to life of the unborn was based on profound moral values concerning the nature of life, which were reflected in the stance of the majority of the Irish people against abortion as expressed in the 1983 referendum. The restriction thus pursued the legitimate aim of the protection of morals of which the protection in Ireland of the right to life of the unborn was one aspect. It was not necessary in the light of this conclusion to decide whether the term "others" under article 10(2) extended to the unborn. (Para 63)

4   The Court was not called upon to examine whether a right to abortion was guaranteed in the Convention or whether the foetus was encompassed by the right to life as contained in article 2. (Para 66)

5   National authorities enjoy a wide margin of appreciation in matters of morals, particularly in an area such as the present which touched on matters of belief concerning the nature of human life. However, it was for the Court to supervise whether a restriction was compatible with the Convention and accordingly to examine the question of "necessity" in the light of principles developed in its case law, in particular whether the restriction complained of was "proportionate to the legitimate aim pursued". (Paras 68 and 70)

6   The absolute nature of the Supreme Court injunction, which imposed a "perpetual" restraint on the provision of information to pregnant women concerning abortion facilities abroad, regardless of age or state of health or their reasons for seeking counselling on the termination of pregnancy, by itself suggested that the restriction appeared overbroad and disproportionate. This assessment was confirmed by other factors (Paras 73 and 74).

7   The restraint imposed on the applicants from receiving or imparting information was disproportionate to the aims pursued. Accordingly there had been a breach of article 10. (Para 80)

Treaties and other international instruments referred to

European Convention for the Protection of Human Rights and Fundamental Freedoms 1950, arts 2, 8, 10 14, 17, 19, 25, 26, 32(1), 40 and 60

Treaty establishing the European Community, arts 59 (now, after amendment, article 49 EC), 60 (now article 50 EC) and 177 (now article 234 EC)

National legislation referred to

Ireland

Censorship of Publications Act 1929, s 16

Civil Liability Act 1961, s 58

Constitution of the Republic of Ireland 1937, art 40(3)(3)

Health (Family Planning) Act 1979, s 12

Offences against the Person Act 1861, ss 58 and 59

Cases referred to

Attorney General at the relation of the Society for the Protection of Unborn Children (Ireland) Ltd v Open Door Counselling Ltd and Dublin Well Woman Centre Ltd [1988] IR 593

AG (SPUC) v Open Door Counselling Ltd [1988] IR 593

Attorney General v X and Others [1992] 1 IR 1

Brogan and Others v The United Kingdom, ECHR, judgment of 29 November 1988, Series A, No 145-B; 11 EHRR 117

Dudgeon v The United Kingdom, ECHR, judgment of 22 October 1981, Series A, No 45; 4 EHRR 149

G v An Bord Uchtala [1980] IR 32

Groppera Radio AG and Others v Switzerland, ECHR, judgment of 28 March 1990, Series A, No 173; 12 EHRR 321

Handyside v The United Kingdom, ECHR, judgment of 7 December 1976, Series A, No 24; 1 EHRR 737

Johnston and Others v Ireland, ECHR, judgment of 18 December 1986, Series A, No 112; 9 EHRR 203, *supra*, p 296

Kolompar v Belgium, ECHR, judgment of 24 September 1992, Series A, No 235-C; 16 EHRR 197

Kruslin and Huvig v France, ECHR, judgment of 24 April 1990, Series A, No 176-A; 12 EHRR 547

Malone v The United Kingdom, ECHR, judgment of 2 August 1984, Series A, No 82; 7 EHRR 14

McGee v Attorney General [1974] IR 264

Meskell v CIE [1973] IR 121

Müller and Others v Switzerland, ECHR, judgment of 24 May 1988, Series A, No 133; 13 EHRR 212

Norris v Attorney General [1984] IR 36

Norris v Ireland, ECHR, judgment of 26 October 1998, Series A, No 142; 13 EHRR 186

Observer and Guardian v The United Kingdom, ECHR, judgment of 26 November 1991, Series A, No 216; 14 EHRR 153

Olsson v Sweden, ECHR, judgment of 24 March 1988, Series A, No 130, 28

The People v Shaw [1982] IR 1

Pine Valley Developments Ltd and Others v Ireland, ECHR, judgment of 29 November 1991, Series A, No 222; 14 EHRR 319

Silver and Others v The United Kingdom, ECHR, judgment of 25 March 1983, Series A, No 61; 5 EHRR 347

Society for the Protection of Unborn Children (Ireland) Ltd v Coogan and Others [1989] IR 734

Society for the Protection of Unborn Children (Ireland) Ltd v Stephen Grogan and Others [1989] IR 753

Society for the Protection of Unborn Children (Ireland) Ltd v Stephen Grogan and Others [1991] ECR I, 4733.

The State (Quinn) v Ryan [1965] IR 70

Sunday Times v The United Kingdom, ECHR, judgment of 26 April 1979, Series A, No 30; 2 EHRR 245

JUDGMENT

PROCEDURE

1   The case was referred to the Court by the European Commission of Human Rights (the "Commission") on 24 April 1991, and on 3 July 1991 by the Government of Ireland (the "Government"). ... It originated in two applications against Ireland lodged with the Commission under Article 25 on 10 August and 15 September 1988. The first (no 14234/88) was brought by Open Door Counselling Ltd, a company incorporated in Ireland; the second (no 14235/88) by another Irish company, Dublin Well Woman Centre Ltd, and one citizen of the United States of America, Ms Bonnie Maher, and three Irish citizens, Ms Ann Downes, Mrs X and Ms Maeve Geraghty.

[...]*

5   On 28 August 1991, the President had granted, under Rule 37(2), leave to the International Centre against Censorship to submit written comments on specific aspects of the case. Leave had been granted on the same date to the Society for the Protection of Unborn Children ("SPUC"). The respective comments were received on 28 November.

AS TO THE FACTS

I   Introduction

A   The applicants

9   The applicants in this case are (a) Open Door Counselling Ltd ("Open Door"), a company incorporated under Irish law, which was engaged, *inter alia*, in counselling pregnant women in Dublin and in other parts of Ireland; and (b) Dublin Well Woman Centre Ltd ("Dublin Well Woman"), a company also incorporated under Irish law which provided similar services at two clinics in Dublin; (c) Bonnie Maher and Ann Downes, who worked as trained counsellors for Dublin Well Woman; (d) Mrs X, born in 1950 and Ms Maeve Geraghty, born in 1970, who join in the Dublin Well Woman application as

---

*   *Eds:* paras 2, 3, 4, 6 and 7, which relate to procedural matters, have not been included.

women of child-bearing age. The applicants complained of an injunction imposed by the Irish courts on Open Door and Dublin Well Woman to restrain them from providing certain information to pregnant women concerning abortion facilities outside the jurisdiction of Ireland by way of non-directive counselling (see paras 13 and 20 below).

Open Door and Dublin Well Woman are both non-profit-making organisations. Open Door ceased to operate in 1988 (see para 21 below). Dublin Well Woman was established in 1977 and provides a broad range of services relating to counselling and marriage, family planning, procreation and health matters. The services offered by Dublin Well Woman relate to every aspect of women's health, ranging from smear tests to breast examinations, infertility, artificial insemination and the counselling of pregnant women.

10 In 1983, at the time of the referendum leading to the Eighth Amendment of the Constitution (see para 28 below), Dublin Well Woman issued a pamphlet stating *inter alia* that legal advice on the implications of the wording of the provision had been obtained and that "with this wording anybody could seek a court injunction to prevent us offering" the non-directive counselling service. The pamphlet also warned that "it would also be possible for an individual to seek a court injunction to prevent a woman travelling abroad if they believe she intends to have an abortion".

B   The injunction proceedings

1   Before the High Court

11 The applicant companies were the defendants in proceedings before the High Court which were commenced on 28 June 1985 as a private action brought by the Society for the Protection of Unborn Children (Ireland) Ltd ("SPUC"), which was converted into a relator action brought at the suit of the Attorney General by order of the High Court of 24 September 1986 (the *Attorney General at the relation of the Society for the Protection of Unborn Children (Ireland) Ltd v Open Door Counselling Ltd and Dublin Well Woman Centre Ltd* [1988] Irish Reports, pp 593–627).

12 SPUC sought a declaration that the activities of the applicant companies in counselling pregnant women within the jurisdiction of the court to travel abroad to obtain an abortion were unlawful having regard to Article 40(3)(3) of the Constitution which protects the right to life of the unborn (see para 28 below) and an order restraining the defendants from such counselling or assistance.

13 No evidence was adduced at the hearing of the action, which proceeded on the basis of certain agreed facts. The facts as agreed at that time by Dublin Well Woman may be summarised as follows:

(a) It counsels in a non-directive manner pregnant women resident in Ireland;

(b) Abortion or termination of pregnancy may be one of the options discussed within the said counselling;

(c) If a pregnant woman wants to consider the abortion option further, arrangements will be made by the applicant to refer her to a medical clinic in Great Britain;

(d) In certain circumstances, the applicant may arrange for the travel of such pregnant women;

(e) The applicant will inspect the medical clinic in Great Britain to ensure that it operates at the highest standards;

(f) At those medical clinics abortions have been performed on pregnant women who have been previously counselled by the applicant;

(g) Pregnant women resident in Ireland have been referred to medical clinics in Great Britain where abortions have been performed for many years including 1984.

The facts agreed by Open Door were the same as above with the exception of point (d).

14 The meaning of the concept of non-directive counselling was described in the following terms by Mr Justice Finlay CJ in the judgment of the Supreme Court in the case (judgment of 16 March 1988, [1988] Irish Reports 618 at 621):

> It was submitted on behalf of each of the Defendants that the meaning of non-directive counselling in these agreed sets of facts was that it was counselling which neither included advice nor was judgmental but that it was a service essentially directed to eliciting from the client her own appreciation of her problem and her own considered choice for its solution. This interpretation of the phrase "non-directive counselling" in the context of the activities of the Defendants was not disputed on behalf of the Respondent. It follows from this, of course, that non-directive counselling to pregnant women would never involve the actual advising of an abortion as the preferred option but neither, of course, could it permit the giving of advice for any reason to the pregnant women receiving such counselling against choosing to have an abortion.

15 On 19 December 1986, Mr Justice Hamilton, President of the High Court, found that the activities of Open Door and Dublin Well Woman in counselling pregnant women within the jurisdiction of the court to travel abroad to obtain an abortion or to obtain further advice on abortion within a foreign jurisdiction were unlawful having regard to the provisions of Article 40(3)(3) of the Constitution of Ireland.

He confirmed that Irish criminal law made it an offence to procure or attempt to procure an abortion, to administer an abortion or to assist in an abortion by supplying any noxious thing or instrument (ss 58 and 59 of the Offences against the Person Act 1861 – see para 29 below). Furthermore, Irish constitutional law also protected the right to life of the unborn from the moment of conception onwards.

An injunction was accordingly granted "... that the Defendants [Open Door and Dublin Well Woman] and each of them, their servants or agents, be perpetually restrained from counselling or assisting pregnant women within the jurisdiction of this Court to obtain further advice on abortion or to obtain an abortion". The High Court made no order relating to the costs of the proceedings, leaving each side to bear its own legal costs.

2   Before the Supreme Court

16 Open Door and Dublin Well Woman appealed against this decision to the Supreme Court which, in a unanimous judgment delivered on 16 March 1988 by Mr Justice Finlay CJ, rejected the appeal.

The Supreme Court noted that the appellants did not consider it essential to the service which they provided for pregnant women in Ireland that they should take any part in arranging the travel of women who wished to go abroad for the purpose of having an abortion or that they arranged bookings in clinics for such women. However, they did consider it essential to inform women who wished to have an abortion outside the jurisdiction of the court of the name, address, telephone number and method of communication with a specified clinic which they had examined and were satisfied was one which maintained a high standard.

17 On the question of whether the above activity should be restrained as being contrary to the Constitution, Mr Justice Finlay CJ stated:

... the essential issues in this case do not in any way depend upon the Plaintiff establishing that the Defendants were advising or encouraging the procuring of abortions. The essential issue in this case, having regard to the nature of the guarantees contained in Article 40, s.3, sub-s.3 of the Constitution, is the issue as to whether the Defendants' admitted activities were assisting pregnant women within the jurisdiction to travel outside that jurisdiction in order to have an abortion. To put the matter in another way, the issue and the question of fact to be determined is: were they thus assisting in the destruction of the life of the unborn?

I am satisfied beyond doubt that having regard to the admitted facts the Defendants were assisting in the ultimate destruction of the life of the unborn by abortion in that they were helping the pregnant woman who had decided upon that option to get in touch with a clinic in Great Britain which would provide the service of abortion. It seems to me an inescapable conclusion that if a woman was anxious to obtain an abortion and if she was able by availing of the counselling services of one or other of the Defendants to obtain the precise location, address and telephone number of, and method of communication with, a clinic in Great Britain which provided that service, put in plain language, that was knowingly helping her to attain her objective. I am, therefore, satisfied that the finding made by the learned trial Judge that the Defendants were assisting pregnant women to travel abroad to obtain further advice on abortion and to secure an abortion is well supported on the evidence.

The Court further noted that the phrase in Article 40(3)(3) "with due regard to the equal right to life of the mother" did not arise for interpretation in the case since the applicants were not claiming that the service they were providing for pregnant women was "in any way confined to or especially directed towards the due regard to the equal right to life of the mother ...".

18 Open Door and Dublin Well Woman had submitted that if they did not provide this counselling service it was likely that pregnant women would succeed nevertheless in obtaining an abortion in circumstances less advantageous to their health. The Court rejected this argument in the following terms:

Even if it could be established, however, it would not be a valid reason why the Court should not restrain the activities in which the defendants were engaged.

The function of the courts, which is not dependent on the existence of legislation, when their jurisdiction to defend and vindicate a constitutionally guaranteed right has been invoked, must be confined to the issues and to the parties before them.

If the Oireachtas enacts legislation to defend and vindicate a constitutionally guaranteed right it may well do so in wider terms than are necessary for the resolution of any individual case. The courts cannot take that wide approach. They are confined to dealing with the parties and issues before them. I am satisfied, therefore, that it is no answer to the making of an order restraining these defendants' activities that there may be other persons or the activities of other groups or bodies which will provide the same result as that assisted by these defendants' activities.

19 As to whether there was a constitutional right to information about the availability of abortion outside the State, the court stated as follows:

The performing of an abortion on a pregnant woman terminates the unborn life which she is carrying. Within the terms of Article 40(3)(3) it is a direct destruction of the constitutionally guaranteed right to life of that unborn child. It must follow from this that there could not be an implied and unenumerated constitutional right to information about the availability of a service of abortion outside the State which, if availed of, would have the direct consequence of destroying the expressly guaranteed constitutional right to life of the unborn.

As part of the submission on this issue it was further suggested that the right to receive and give information which, it was alleged, existed and was material to this case was, though not expressly granted, impliedly referred to or involved in the right of citizens to express freely their convictions and opinions provided by Article 40, s.6, sub-s.1 (i) of the Constitution, since, it was claimed, the right to express freely convictions and opinions may, under some circumstances, involve as an ancillary right the right to obtain information. I am satisfied that no right could constitutionally arise to obtain information the purpose of the obtaining of which was to defeat the constitutional right to life of the unborn child.

20 The court upheld the decision of the High Court to grant an injunction but varied the terms of the order as follows:

> ... that the defendants and each of them, their servants or agents be perpetually restrained from assisting pregnant women within the jurisdiction to travel abroad to obtain abortions by referral to a clinic, by the making for them of travel arrangements, or by informing them of the identity and location of and the method of communication with a specified clinic or clinics or otherwise.

The costs of the Supreme Court appeal were awarded against the applicant companies on 3 May 1988.

21 Following the judgment of the Supreme Court, Open Door, having no assets, ceased its activities.

C   Subsequent legal developments

22 On 25 September 1989, SPUC applied to the High Court for a declaration that the dissemination in certain student publications of information concerning the identity and location of abortion clinics outside the jurisdiction was unlawful and for an injunction restraining its distribution. Their standing to apply to the courts for measures to protect the right to life of the unborn had previously been recognised by the Supreme Court following a similar action in the case of *Society for the Protection of Unborn Children (Ireland) Ltd v Coogan and Others* ([1989] Irish Reports, pp 734–751).

By a judgment of 11 October 1989, the High Court decided to refer certain questions to the European Court of Justice for a preliminary ruling under Article 177 of the EEC Treaty concerning, *inter alia*, the question whether the right to information concerning abortion services outside Ireland was protected by Community law.

23 An appeal was brought against this decision and, on 19 December 1989, the Supreme Court granted an interlocutory injunction restraining the students from "publishing or distributing or assisting in the printing, publishing or distribution of any publication produced under their aegis providing information to persons (including pregnant women) of the identity and location of and the method of communication with a specified clinic or clinics where abortions are performed" (*Society for the Protection of Unborn Children (Ireland) Ltd v Stephen Grogan and Others*, [1989] Irish Reports, pp 753–771).

Mr Justice Finlay CJ (with whom Mr Justice Walsh, Mr Justice Griffin and Mr Justice Hederman concurred) considered that the reasoning of the court in the case brought against the applicant companies applied to the activities of the students:

> I reject as unsound the contention that the activity involved in this case of publishing in the students' manuals the name, address and telephone number, when telephoned from this State, of abortion clinics in the United Kingdom, and distributing such manuals in Ireland, can be distinguished from the activity condemned by this Court in [the Open

Door Counselling case] on the grounds that the facts of that case were that the information was conveyed during periods of one to one non-directive counselling. It is clearly the fact that such information is conveyed to pregnant women, and not the method of communication which creates the unconstitutional illegality, and the judgment of this Court in the Open Door Counselling case is not open to any other interpretation.

Mr Justice McCarthy also considered that an injunction should be issued and commented as follows:

> In the light of the availability of such information from a variety of sources, such as imported magazines, etc., I am far from satisfied that the granting of an injunction to restrain these defendants from publishing the material impugned would save the life of a single unborn child, but I am more than satisfied that if the courts fail to enforce, and enforce forthwith, that guarantee as construed in *A.G. (S.PU.C.) v Open Door Counselling Ltd* [1988] Irish Reports 593, then the rule of law will be set at nought.

24 In a judgment of 4 October 1991 on the questions referred under Article 177 of the EEC Treaty, following the Supreme Court's judgment, the Court of Justice of the European Communities ruled that the medical termination of pregnancy, performed in accordance with the law of the State in which it is carried out, constitutes a service within the meaning of Article 60 of the EEC Treaty. However it found that the link between the activity of the student associations and medical terminations of pregnancy carried out in clinics in another member State was too tenuous for the prohibition on the distribution of information to be capable of being regarded as a restriction on the freedom to supply services within the meaning of Article 59 of the EEC Treaty. The Court did not examine whether the prohibition was in breach of Article 10 of the Convention. In the light of its conclusions concerning the restriction on services it considered that it had no jurisdiction with regard to national legislation "lying outside the scope of Community law". Accordingly, the restrictions on the publication of information by student associations were not considered to be contrary to Community law (see paras 22–23 above, the *Society for the Protection of Unborn Children (Ireland) Ltd v Stephen Grogan and Others* [1991] European Court Reports I, pp 4733–4742).

25 The interpretation to be given to Article 40(3)(3) of the Constitution also arose before the Supreme Court in the case of *The Attorney General v X and Others* which concerned an application to the courts by the Attorney General for an injunction to prevent a 14-year-old girl who was pregnant from leaving the jurisdiction to have an abortion abroad. The girl alleged that she had been raped and had expressed the desire to commit suicide. The Supreme Court, in its judgment of 5 March 1992, found that termination of pregnancy was permissible under Article 40(3)(3) where it was established as a matter of probability that there was a real and substantial risk to the life of the mother if such termination was not effected. Finding that this test was satisfied on the facts of the case the Supreme Court discharged the injunction which had been granted by the High Court at first instance.

A majority of three judges of the Supreme Court (Finlay CJ, Hederman and Egan JJ) expressed the view that Article 40(3)(3) empowered the courts in proper cases to restrain by injunction a pregnant woman from leaving the jurisdiction to have an abortion so that the right to life of the unborn might be defended and vindicated.

During the oral hearing before the European Court of Human Rights, the Government made the following statement in the light of the Supreme Court's judgment in this case:

> ... persons who are deemed to be entitled under Irish law to avail themselves of termination of pregnancy in these circumstances must be regarded as being entitled to

have appropriate access to information in relation to the facilities for such operations, either in Ireland or abroad.

D   *Evidence presented by the applicants*

26 The applicants presented evidence to the Court that there had been no significant drop in the number of Irish women having abortions in Great Britain since the granting of the injunction, that number being well over 3,500 women per year. They also submitted an opinion from an expert in public health (Dr JR Ashton), which concludes that there are five possible adverse implications for the health of Irish women arising from the injunction in the present case:

1   An increase in the birth of unwanted and rejected children;

2   An increase in illegal and unsafe abortions;

3   A lack of adequate preparation of Irish women obtaining abortions;

4   Increases in delay in obtaining abortions with ensuing increased complication rates;

5   Poor aftercare with a failure to deal adequately with medical complications and a failure to provide adequate contraceptive advice.

In their written comments to the Court, SPUC claimed that the number of abortions obtained by Irish women in England, which had been rising rapidly prior to the enactment of Article 40(3)(3), had increased at a much reduced pace. They further submitted that the number of births to married women had increased at a "very substantial rate".

27 The applicants claimed that the impugned information was available in British newspapers and magazines which were imported into Ireland as well as in the yellow pages of the London telephone directory which could be purchased from the Irish telephone service. It was also available in publications such as the British Medical Journal which was obtainable in Ireland.

While not challenging the accuracy of the above information the Government observed that no newspaper or magazine had been produced in evidence to the Court.

II   Relevant domestic law and practice concerning protection of the unborn

A   *Constitutional protection*

28 Article 40(3)(3) of the Irish Constitution (the Eighth Amendment), which came into force in 1983 following a referendum, reads:

> The State acknowledges the right to life of the unborn and, with due regard to the equal right to life of the mother, guarantees in its laws to respect, and, as far as practicable, by its laws to defend and vindicate that right.

This provision has been interpreted by the Supreme Court in the present case, in the *Society for the Protection of Unborn Children (Ireland) Ltd v Grogan and Others* ([1989] Irish Reports, p 753) and in *The Attorney General v X and Others* (see paras 22–25 above).

B   *Statutory protection*

29 The statutory prohibition of abortion is contained in sections 58 and 59 of the Offences Against the Person Act 1861. Section 58 provides that:

Every woman, being with child, who, with intent to procure her own miscarriage, shall unlawfully administer to herself any poison or other noxious thing or shall unlawfully use any instrument or other means whatsoever with the like intent, and whosoever, with intent to procure the miscarriage of any woman, whether she be or not be with child, shall unlawfully administer to her or cause to betaken by her any poison or other noxious thing, or shall unlawfully use any instrument or other means whatsoever with the like intent, shall be guilty of a felony, and being convicted thereof shall be liable, [to imprisonment for life] ...

Section 59 states that:

Whoever shall unlawfully supply or procure any poison or other noxious thing, or any instrument or thing whatsoever, knowing that the same is intended to be unlawfully used or employed with intent to procure the miscarriage of any woman, whether she be or be not with child, shall be guilty of a misdemeanour, and being convicted thereof ...

30 Section 16 of the Censorship of Publications Act 1929 as amended by section 12 of the Health (Family Planning) Act 1979 provides that:

It shall not be lawful for any person, otherwise than under and in accordance with a permit in writing granted to him under this section

(a) to print or publish or cause or procure to be printed or published, or

(b) to sell or expose, offer or keep for sale, or

(c) to distribute, offer or keep for distribution,

any book or periodical publication (whether appearing on the register of prohibited publications or not) which advocates or which might reasonably be supposed to advocate the procurement of abortion or miscarriage or any method, treatment or appliance to be used for the purpose of such procurement.

31 Section 58 of the Civil Liability Act 1961 provides that "the law relating to wrongs shall apply to an unborn child for his protection in like manner as if the child were born, provided the child is subsequently born alive".

32 Section 10 of the Health (Family Planning) Act 1979 re-affirms the statutory prohibition of abortion and states as follows:

Nothing in this Act shall be construed as authorising –

(a) the procuring of abortion,

(b) the doing of any other thing the doing of which is prohibited by section 58 or 59 of the Offences Against the Person Act, 1861 (which sections prohibit the administering of drugs or the use of any instruments to procure abortion) or,

(c) the sale, importation into the State, manufacture, advertising or display of abortifacients.

C   Case law

33 Apart from the present case and subsequent developments (see paras 11–25 above), reference has been made to the right to life of the unborn in various decisions of the Supreme Court (see, for example, *McGee v Attorney General* [1974] Irish Reports, p 264, *G v An Bord Uchtala* [1980] Irish Reports, p 32 and *Norris v Attorney General* [1984] Irish Reports, p 36).

34 In the case of *G v An Bord Uchtala (loc cit)* Mr Justice Walsh stated as follows:

[A child] has the right to life itself and the right to be guarded against all threats directed to its existence, whether before or after birth ... The right to life necessarily implies the right to be born, the right to preserve and defend and to have preserved and defended that life ...

35 The Supreme Court has also stated that the courts are the custodians of the fundamental rights set out in the Constitution and that their powers in this regard are as ample as the defence of the Constitution requires (*The State (Quinn) v Ryan* [1965] Irish Reports 70). Moreover, an infringement of a constitutional right by an individual may be actionable in damages as a constitutional tort (*Meskell v CIE* [1973] Irish Reports, p 121).

In his judgment in *The People v Shaw* ([1982] Irish Reports, p 1), Mr Justice Kenny observed:

When the People enacted the Constitution of 1937, they provided (Article 40, s 3) that the State guaranteed in its laws to respect, and, as far as practicable, by its laws to defend and vindicate the personal rights of the citizen and that the State should, in particular, by its laws protect as best it might from unjust attack and in the case of injustice done, vindicate the life, person, good name and property rights of every citizen. I draw attention to the use of the words "the State". The obligation to implement this guarantee is imposed not on the Oireachtas only, but on each branch of the State which exercises the powers of legislating, executing and giving judgment on those laws: Article 6. The word "laws" in Article 40, s 3 is not confined to laws which have been enacted by the Oireachtas, but comprehends the laws made by judges and by ministers of State when they make statutory instruments or regulations.

PROCEEDINGS BEFORE THE COMMISSION

36 In their applications (nos 14234 and 14235/88) lodged with the Commission on 19 August and 22 September 1988 the applicants complained that the injunction in question constituted an unjustified interference with their right to impart or receive information contrary to Article 10 of the Convention. Open Door, Mrs X and Ms Geraghty further claimed that the restrictions amounted to an interference with their right to respect for private life in breach of Article 8 and, in the case of Open Door, discrimination contrary to Article 14 in conjunction with Articles 8 and 10.

37 The Commission joined the applications on 14 March 1989 and declared the case admissible on 15 May 1990. In its report of 7 March 1991 (Article 31), it expressed the opinion:

(a) by eight votes to five, that there had been a violation of Article 10 in respect of the Supreme Court injunction as it affected the applicant companies and counsellors;

(b) by seven votes to six, that there had been a violation of Article 10 in respect of the Supreme Court injunction as it affected Mrs X and Ms Geraghty;

(c) by seven votes to two, with four abstentions, that it was not necessary to examine further the complaints of Mrs X and Ms Geraghty under Article 8;

(d) unanimously, that there had been no violation of Articles 8 and 14 in respect of Open Door.

FINAL SUBMISSIONS MADE TO THE COURT BY THE GOVERNMENT

38 In the public hearing on 24 March 1992 the Government maintained in substance the arguments and submissions set out in their memorial whereby they invited the Court to find that there had been no breach of the Convention.

AS TO THE LAW

I   Scope of the Dublin Well Woman case

39 In their original application to the Commission Dublin Well Woman and the two counsellors, Ms Maher and Ms Downes, alleged that the Supreme Court injunction constituted an unjustified interference with their right to impart information, in breach of Article 10 of the Convention.

In their pleadings before the Court they further complained that there had also been a breach of Article 8. They had not raised this complaint before the Commission.

40 The scope of the Court's jurisdiction is determined by the Commission's decision declaring the originating application admissible (see, *inter alia, Brogan and Others v the United Kingdom*, European Court of Human Rights, judgment of 29 November 1988, Series A, No 145-B, p 27, para 46). The Court considers that the applicants are now seeking to raise before the Court a new and separate complaint. As such it has no jurisdiction to entertain it.

II   The government's preliminary objections

A   *Whether Ms Maher, Ms Downes, Mrs X and Ms Geraghty can claim to be "victims" of a violation of the Convention*

41 The Government submitted, as they had done before the Commission, that only the corporate applicants could claim to be "victims" of an infringement of their Convention rights. Ms Maher, Ms Downes, Mrs X and Ms Geraghty had not been involved in the proceedings before the Irish courts. Moreover the applicants had failed to identify a single pregnant woman who could claim to be a "victim" of the matters complained of. In this respect the case was in the nature of an *actio popularis*, particularly as regards Mrs X and Ms Geraghty.

1   Ms Maher and Ms Downes

42 The Delegate of the Commission pointed out that the Government's plea as regards the applicant counsellors (Ms Maher and Ms Downes) conflicted with their concession in the pleadings before the Commission that these applicants were subject to the restraint of the Supreme Court injunction and could therefore properly claim to have suffered an interference with their Article 10 rights.

43 The Court agrees with the Commission that Ms Maher and Ms Downes can properly claim to be "victims" of an interference with their rights since they were directly affected by the Supreme Court injunction. Moreover, it considers that the Government are precluded from making submissions as regards preliminary exceptions which are inconsistent with concessions previously made in their pleadings before the Commission (see, *mutatis mutandis, Pine Valley Developments Ltd and Others v Ireland*, European Court of Human Rights, judgment of 29 November 1991, Series A, No 222, pp 21–22, para 47, and *Kolompar v Belgium*, European Court of Human Rights, judgment of 24 September 1992, Series A, No 235-C, p 54, para 32).

2   Mrs X and Ms Geraghty

44   The Court recalls that Article 25 entitles individuals to contend that a law violates their rights by itself, in the absence of an individual measure of implementation, if they run the risk of being directly affected by it (see, *inter alia, Johnston and Others v Ireland* European Court of Human Rights, judgment of 18 December 1986, Series A, No 112, p 21, para 42).

In the present case the Supreme Court injunction restrained the corporate applicants and their servants and agents from providing certain information to pregnant women. Although it has not been asserted that Mrs X and Ms Geraghty are pregnant, it is not disputed that they belong to a class of women of child-bearing age which may be adversely affected by the restrictions imposed by the injunction. They are not seeking to challenge *in abstracto* the compatibility of Irish law with the Convention since they run a risk of being directly prejudiced by the measure complained of. They can thus claim to be "victims" within the meaning of Article 25(1).

B   *Whether the application complies with the six-month rule*

45   At the oral hearing the Government submitted that the application should be rejected under Article 26 for failure to comply with the six-month rule, on the grounds that the applicants were relying on case-law and arguments which were not raised before the domestic courts.

46   The Court observes that while this plea was made before the Commission (see Appendix II of the Commission's report) it was not re-iterated in the Government's memorial to the Court and was raised solely at the oral hearing. Rule 48(1) of the Rules of Court, however, required them to file it before the expiry of the time-limit laid down for the filing of their memorial, with the result that it must therefore be rejected as being out of time (see, *inter alia, Olsson v Sweden*, European Court of Human Rights, judgment of 24 March 1988, Series A, No 130, p 28, para 56).

C   *Whether the applicants had exhausted domestic remedies*

47   In their memorial the Government submitted – as they had also done before the Commission – that domestic remedies had not been exhausted, as required by Article 26, by:

1   Open Door as regards its complaints under Articles 8 and 14;

2   both Open Door and Dublin Well Woman in so far as they sought to introduce in their complaint under Article 10 evidence and submissions concerning abortion and the impact of the Supreme Court injunction on women's health that had not been raised before the Irish courts;

3   Ms Maher, Ms Downes, Mrs X and Ms Geraghty on the grounds that they had made no attempt to exhaust domestic remedies under Irish law and that they had not been involved in any capacity in the relevant proceedings before the Irish courts.

48   As regards (1) the Court observes that Open Door would have had no prospect of success in asserting these complaints having regard to the reasoning of the Supreme Court concerning the high level of protection afforded to the right to life of the unborn child under Irish law (see paras 16–25 above).

49   As regards (2) Open Door and Dublin Well Woman are not introducing a fresh complaint in respect of which they have not exhausted domestic remedies. They are merely developing their submissions in respect of complaints which have already been

examined by the Irish courts. Article 26 imposes no impediments to applicants in this regard. It is clear from the judgment of the Supreme Court that the applicants had in fact argued that an injunction would adversely affect women's health and that this submission was rejected (see para 18 above).

50 Finally, as regards (3) it emerges from the judgments of the Supreme Court in the present case and in subsequent cases (see paras 16–25 above) that any action brought by the four individual applicants would have had no prospects of success.

51 Accordingly, the Government's objection based on non-exhaustion of domestic remedies fails.

Conclusion

52 To sum up, the Court is able to take cognisance of the merits of the case as regards all of the applicants.

III Alleged violation of article 10

53 The applicants alleged that the Supreme Court injunction, restraining them from assisting pregnant women to travel abroad to obtain abortions, infringed the rights of the corporate applicants and the two counsellors to impart information, as well as the rights of Mrs X and Ms Geraghty to receive information. They confined their complaint to that part of the injunction which concerned the provision of information to pregnant women as opposed to the making of travel arrangements or referral to clinics (see para 20 above). They invoked Article 10 which provides:

1 Everyone has the right to freedom of expression. This right shall include freedom to hold opinions and to receive and impart information and ideas without interference by public authority and regardless of frontiers ...

2 The exercise of these freedoms, since it carries with it duties and responsibilities, may be subject to such formalities, conditions, restrictions or penalties as are prescribed by law and are necessary in a democratic society, in the interests of national security, territorial integrity or public safety, for the prevention of disorder or crime, for the protection of health or morals, for the protection of the reputation or rights of others, for preventing the disclosure of information received in confidence, or for maintaining the authority and impartiality of the judiciary.

54 In their submissions to the Court the Government contested these claims and also contended that Article 10 should be interpreted against the background of Articles 2, 17 and 60 of the Convention the relevant parts of which state:

Article 2

1 Everyone's right to life shall be protected by law. No one shall be deprived of his life intentionally save in the execution of a sentence of a court following his conviction of a crime for which this penalty is provided by law ...

Article 17

Nothing in [the] Convention may be interpreted as implying for any State, group or person any right to engage in any activity or perform any act aimed at the destruction of any of the rights and freedoms set forth herein or at their limitation to a greater extent than is provided for in the Convention.

Article 60

> Nothing in [the] Convention shall be construed as limiting or derogating from any of the human rights and fundamental freedoms which may be ensured under the laws of any High Contracting Party or under any other agreement to which it is a Party.

A   Was there an interference with the applicants' rights?

55 The Court notes that the Government accepted that the injunction interfered with the freedom of the corporate applicants to impart information. Having regard to the scope of the injunction which also restrains the "servants or agents" of the corporate applicants from assisting "pregnant women" (see para 20 above), there can be no doubt that there was also an interference with the rights of the applicant counsellors to impart information and with the rights of Mrs X and Ms Geraghty to receive information in the event of being pregnant.

To determine whether such an interference entails a violation of Article 10, the Court must examine whether or not it was justified under Article 10(2) by reason of being a restriction "prescribed by law" which was necessary in a democratic society on one or other of the grounds specified in Article 10(2).

B   Was the restriction "prescribed by law"?

1   Arguments presented by those appearing before the Court

56 Open Door and Dublin Well Woman submitted that the law was not formulated with sufficient precision to have enabled them to foresee that the non-directive counselling in which they were involved would be restrained by the courts. It was not clear from the wording of Article 40(3)(3) of the Constitution (the Eighth Amendment), which gave rise to many difficulties of interpretation and application, that those giving information to pregnant women would be in breach of this provision. In the same way, it was not clear whether it could have been used as a means of prohibiting access to foreign periodicals containing advertisements for abortion facilities abroad or of restricting other activities involving a "threat" to the life of the unborn such as travelling abroad to have an abortion.

In this respect the applicants pointed out that the provision had been criticised at the time of its enactment by both the Attorney General and the Director of Public Prosecutions on the grounds that it was ambiguous and uncertain. Furthermore, although there was an expectation that there would be legislation to clarify the meaning of the provision, none was in fact enacted.

They also maintained that on its face Article 40(3)(3) is addressed only to the State and not to private persons. Thus they had no way of knowing that it would apply to non-directive counselling by private agencies. Indeed, since none of Ireland's other laws concerning abortion forbids such counselling or travelling abroad to have an abortion they had good reason to believe that this activity was lawful.

Finally, the insufficient precision of the Eighth Amendment was well reflected in the recent judgment of the Supreme Court of 5 March 1992 in *The Attorney General v X and Others* which, as conceded by the Government, had the consequence that it would now be lawful to provide information concerning abortion services abroad in certain circumstances (see para 25 above).

In sum, given the uncertain scope of this provision and the considerable doubt as to its meaning and effect, even amongst the most authoritative opinion, the applicants could not have foreseen that such non-directive counselling was unlawful.

57 The Government submitted that the legal position was reasonably foreseeable with appropriate legal advice, within the meaning of the Court's case-law. The applicants ought to have known that an injunction could be obtained against them to protect or defend rights guaranteed by the Constitution, or recognised at common law, or under the principles of the law of equity. Indeed, evidence had now come to light subsequent to the publication of the Commission's report that Dublin Well Woman had actually received legal advice concerning the implications of the wording of the Amendment which warned that a court injunction to restrain their counselling activities was possible (see para 10 above). It was thus not open to the applicants, against this background, to argue that the injunction was unforeseeable.

58 For the Commission, the Eighth Amendment did not provide a clear basis for the applicants to have foreseen that providing information about lawful services abroad would be unlawful. A law restricting freedom of expression across frontiers in such a vital area required particular precision to enable individuals to regulate their conduct accordingly. Since it was not against the criminal law for women to travel abroad to have an abortion, lawyers could reasonably have concluded that the provision of information did not involve a criminal offence. In addition, the Government had been unable to show, with reference to case-law, that the applicant companies could have foreseen that their counselling service was a constitutional tort (see para 35 above). Moreover, the wording of the Amendment suggested that legislation was to have been enacted regulating the protection of the rights of the unborn.

2 Court's examination of the issue

59 This question must be approached by considering not merely the wording of Article 40(3)(3) in isolation but also the protection given under Irish law to the rights of the unborn in statute law and in case-law (see paras 28–35 above).

It is true that it is not a criminal offence to have an abortion outside Ireland and that the practice of non-directive counselling of pregnant women did not infringe the criminal law as such. Moreover, on its face the language of Article 40(3)(3) appears to enjoin only the State to protect the right to life of the unborn and suggests that regulatory legislation will be introduced at some future stage.

On the other hand, it is clear from Irish case-law, even prior to 1983, that infringement of constitutional rights by private individuals as well as by the State may be actionable (see para 35 above). Furthermore, the constitutional obligation that the State defend and vindicate personal rights "by its laws" has been interpreted by the courts as not being confined merely to "laws" which have been enacted by the Irish Parliament (Oireachtas) but as also comprehending judge-made "law". In this regard the Irish courts, as the custodians of fundamental rights, have emphasised that they are endowed with the necessary powers to ensure their protection.

60 Taking into consideration the high threshold of protection of the unborn provided under Irish law generally and the manner in which the courts have interpreted their role as the guarantors of constitutional rights, the possibility that action might be taken against the corporate applicants must have been, with appropriate legal advice, reasonably foreseeable (see *Sunday Times v The United Kingdom*, European Court of Human Rights, judgment of 26 April 1979, Series A, No 30, p 31, para 49). This

conclusion is reinforced by the legal advice that was actually given to Dublin Well Woman that, in the light of Article 40(3)(3), an injunction could be sought against its counselling activities (see para 10 above).

The restriction was accordingly "prescribed by law".

C   Did the restriction have aims that were legitimate under Article 10(2)?

61 The Government submitted that the relevant provisions of Irish law are intended for the protection of the rights of others – in this instance the unborn – for the protection of morals and, where appropriate, for the prevention of crime.

62 The applicants disagreed, contending *inter alia* that, in view of the use of the term "everyone" in Article 10(1) and throughout the Convention, it would be illogical to interpret the "rights of others" in Article 10(2) as encompassing the unborn.

63 The Court cannot accept that the restrictions at issue pursued the aim of the prevention of crime since, as noted above (para 59), neither the provision of the information in question nor the obtaining of an abortion outside the jurisdiction involved any criminal offence. However, it is evident that the protection afforded under Irish law to the right to life of the unborn is based on profound moral values concerning the nature of life which were reflected in the stance of the majority of the Irish people against abortion as expressed in the 1983 referendum (see para 28 above). The restriction thus pursued the legitimate aim of the protection of morals of which the protection in Ireland of the right to life of the unborn is one aspect. It is not necessary in the light of this conclusion to decide whether the term "others" under Article 10(2) extends to the unborn.

D   Was the restriction necessary in a democratic society?

64 The Government submitted that the Court's approach to the assessment of the "necessity" of the restraint should be guided by the fact that the protection of the rights of the unborn in Ireland could be derived from Articles 2, 17 and 60 of the Convention. They further contended that the "proportionality" test was inadequate where the rights of the unborn were at issue. The Court will examine these issues in turn.

1   Article 2

65 The Government maintained that the injunction was necessary in a democratic society for the protection of the right to life of the unborn and that Article 10 should be interpreted *inter alia* against the background of Article 2 of the Convention which, they argued, also protected unborn life. The view that abortion was morally wrong was the deeply held view of the majority of the people in Ireland and it was not the proper function of the Court to seek to impose a different viewpoint.

66 The Court observes at the outset that in the present case it is not called upon to examine whether a right to abortion is guaranteed under the Convention or whether the foetus is encompassed by the right to life as contained in Article 2. The applicants have not claimed that the Convention contains a right to abortion, as such, their complaint being limited to that part of the injunction which restricts their freedom to impart and receive information concerning abortion abroad (see para 20 above).

Thus the only issue to be addressed is whether the restrictions on the freedom to impart and receive information contained in the relevant part of the injunction are necessary in a democratic society for the legitimate aim of the protection of morals as explained above (see para 63). It follows from this approach that the Government's argument based on Article 2 of the Convention does not fall to be examined in the present case. On the other hand, the arguments based on Articles 17 and 60 fall to be considered below (see paras 78 and 79).

2 Proportionality

67 The Government stressed the limited nature of the Supreme Court's injunction which only restrained the provision of certain information (see para 20 above). There was no limitation on discussion in Ireland about abortion generally or the right of women to travel abroad to obtain one. They further contended that the Convention test as regards the proportionality of the restriction was inadequate where a question concerning the extinction of life was at stake. The right to life could not, like other rights, be measured according to a graduated scale. It was either respected or it was not. Accordingly, the traditional approach of weighing competing rights and interests in the balance was inappropriate where the destruction of unborn life was concerned. Since life was a primary value which was antecedent to and a prerequisite for the enjoyment of every other right, its protection might involve the infringement of other rights such as freedom of expression in a manner which might not be acceptable in the defence of rights of a lesser nature.

The Government also emphasised that, in granting the injunction, the Supreme Court was merely sustaining the logic of Article 40(3)(3) of the Constitution. The determination by the Irish courts that the provision of information by the relevant applicants assisted in the destruction of unborn life was not open to review by the Convention institutions.

68 The Court cannot agree that the State's discretion in the field of the protection of morals is unfettered and unreviewable (see, *mutatis mutandis*, for a similar argument, *Norris v Ireland*, European Court of Human Rights, judgment of 26 October 1988, Series A, No 142, p 20, para 45).

It acknowledges that the national authorities enjoy a wide margin of appreciation in matters of morals, particularly in an area such as the present which touches on matters of belief concerning the nature of human life. As the Court has observed before, it is not possible to find in the legal and social orders of the Contracting States a uniform European conception of morals, and the State authorities are, in principle, in a better position than the international judge to give an opinion on the exact content of the requirements of morals as well as on the "necessity" of a "restriction" or "penalty" intended to meet them (see, *inter alia*, *Handyside v The United Kingdom*, European Court of Human Rights, judgment of 7 December 1976, Series A, No 24, p 22, para 48, and *Müller and Others v Switzerland*, European Court of Human Rights, judgment of 24 May 1988, Series A, No 133, p 22, para 35).

However this power of appreciation is not unlimited. It is for the Court, in this field also, to supervise whether a restriction is compatible with the Convention.

69 As regards the application of the "proportionality" test, the logical consequence of the Government's argument is that measures taken by the national authorities to protect the right to life of the unborn or to uphold the constitutional guarantee on the subject would be automatically justified under the Convention where infringement of a right of a lesser stature was alleged. It is, in principle, open to the national authorities to take such action as they consider necessary to respect the rule of law or to give effect to constitutional rights. However, they must do so in a manner which is compatible with their obligations under the Convention and subject to review by the Convention

institutions. To accept the Government's pleading on this point would amount to an abdication of the Court's responsibility under Article 19 "to ensure the observance of the engagements undertaken by the High Contracting Parties ...".

70   Accordingly, the Court must examine the question of "necessity" in the light of the principles developed in its case-law (see, *inter alia, Observer and Guardian v The United Kingdom*, European Court of Human Rights, judgment of 26 November 1991, Series A, No 216, pp 29–30, para 59). It must determine whether there existed a pressing social need for the measures in question and, in particular, whether the restriction complained of was "proportionate to the legitimate aim pursued".

71   In this context, it is appropriate to recall that freedom of expression is also applicable to "information" or "ideas" that offend, shock or disturb the State or any sector of the population. Such are the demands of that pluralism, tolerance and broadmindedness without which there is no "democratic society" (see, *inter alia*, the *Handyside* judgment, above, Series A, No 24, p 23, para 49).

72   While the relevant restriction, as observed by the Government, is limited to the provision of information, it is recalled that it is not a criminal offence under Irish law for a pregnant woman to travel abroad in order to have an abortion. Furthermore, the injunction limited the freedom to receive and impart information with respect to services which are lawful in other Convention countries and may be crucial to a woman's health and well-being. Limitations on information concerning activities which, notwithstanding their moral implications, have been and continue to be tolerated by national authorities, call for careful scrutiny by the Convention institutions as to their conformity with the tenets of a democratic society.

73   The Court is first struck by the absolute nature of the Supreme Court injunction which imposed a "perpetual" restraint on the provision of information to pregnant women concerning abortion facilities abroad, regardless of age or state of health or their reasons for seeking counselling on the termination of pregnancy. The sweeping nature of this restriction has since been highlighted by the case of The *Attorney General v X and Others* and by the concession made by the Government at the oral hearing that the injunction no longer applied to women who, in the circumstances as defined in the Supreme Court's judgment in that case, were now free to have an abortion in Ireland or abroad (see para 25 above).

74   On that ground alone the restriction appears over broad and disproportionate. Moreover, this assessment is confirmed by other factors.

75   In the first place, it is to be noted that the corporate applicants were engaged in the counselling of pregnant women in the course of which counsellors neither advocated nor encouraged abortion, but confined themselves to an explanation of the available options (see paras 13 and 14 above). The decision as to whether or not to act on the information so provided was that of the woman concerned. There can be little doubt that following such counselling there were women who decided against a termination of pregnancy. Accordingly, the link between the provision of information and the destruction of unborn life is not as definite as contended. Such counselling had in fact been tolerated by the State authorities even after the passing of the Eighth Amendment in 1983 until the Supreme Court's judgment in the present case. Furthermore, the information that was provided by the relevant applicants concerning abortion facilities abroad was not made available to the public at large.

76 It has not been seriously contested by the Government that information concerning abortion facilities abroad can be obtained from other sources in Ireland such as magazines and telephone directories (see paras 23 and 27 above) or by persons with contacts in Great Britain. Accordingly, information that the injunction sought to restrict was already available elsewhere although in a manner which was not supervised by qualified personnel and thus less protective of women's health. Furthermore, the injunction appears to have been largely ineffective in protecting the right to life of the unborn since it did not prevent large numbers of Irish women from continuing to obtain abortions in Great Britain (see para 26 above).

77 In addition, the available evidence, which has not been disputed by the Government, suggests that the injunction has created a risk to the health of those women who are now seeking abortions at a later stage in their pregnancy, due to lack of proper counselling, and who are not availing themselves of customary medical supervision after the abortion has taken place (see para 26 above). Moreover, the injunction may have had more adverse effects on women who were not sufficiently resourceful or had not the necessary level of education to have access to alternative sources of information (see para 76 above). These are certainly legitimate factors to take into consideration in assessing the proportionality of the restriction.

3   Articles 17 and 60

78 The Government, invoking Articles 17 and 60 of the Convention, have submitted that Article 10 should not be interpreted in such a manner as to limit, destroy or derogate from the right to life of the unborn which enjoys special protection under Irish law.

79 Without calling into question under the Convention the regime of protection of unborn life that exists under Irish law, the Court recalls that the injunction did not prevent Irish women from having abortions abroad and that the information it sought to restrain was available from other sources (see para 76 above). Accordingly, it is not the interpretation of Article 10 but the position in Ireland as regards the implementation of the law that makes possible the continuance of the current level of abortions obtained by Irish women abroad.

4   Conclusion

80 In the light of the above, the Court concludes that the restraint imposed on the applicants from receiving or imparting information was disproportionate to the aims pursued. Accordingly there has been a breach of Article 10.

IV   Alleged violations of articles 8 and 14

81 Open Door also alleged a violation of the right to respect for private life contrary to Article 8 claiming that it should be open to it to complain of an interference with the privacy rights of its clients. Similarly, Mrs X and Ms Geraghty complained under this provision that the denial to them of access to information concerning abortion abroad constituted an unjustifiable interference with their right to respect for private life.

Open Door further claimed discrimination contrary to Article 14 in conjunction with Article 8 alleging that the injunction discriminated against women since men were not denied information "critical to their reproductive and health choices". It also invoked Article 14 in conjunction with Article 10 claiming discrimination on the grounds of political or other opinion since those who seek to counsel against abortion are permitted to express their views without restriction.

82 The applicants in the Dublin Well Woman case, in their memorial to the Court, similarly complained of discrimination contrary to Article 14, firstly, in conjunction with Article 8 on the same basis as Open Door, and secondly, in conjunction with Article 10 on the grounds that it followed from the decision of the Court of Justice of the European Communities in the *Grogan* case (see para 24 above) that, had Dublin Well Woman been an "economic operator", they would have been permitted to distribute and receive such information.

83 The Court notes that the complaints of discrimination made by the applicants in Dublin Well Woman were made for the first time in the proceedings before the Court and that consequently it may be questioned whether it has jurisdiction to examine them (see para 40 above). However, having regard to its finding that there had been a breach of Article 10 (see para 80 above) the Court considers that it is not necessary to examine either these complaints or those made by Open Door, Mrs X and Ms Geraghty.

V   Application of article 50

84 Article 50 provides as follows:

"If the Court finds that a decision or a measure taken by a legal authority or any other authority of a High Contracting Party is completely or partially in conflict with the obligations arising from the ... Convention, and if the internal law of the said Party allows only partial reparation to be made for the consequences of this decision or measure, the decision of the Court shall, if necessary, afford just satisfaction to the injured party."

A   Damage

85 Open Door made no claim for compensation for damage. Dublin Well Woman, on the other hand, claimed pecuniary damages amounting to IR£62,172 in respect of loss of income for the period January 1987 to June 1988 due to the discontinuance of the pregnancy counselling service.

86 The Government submitted that the claim should be rejected. In particular, they contended that it was made belatedly; that it was inconsistent with Dublin Well Woman's status as a non-profit-making company to claim pecuniary damage and was excessive.

87 The Court notes that the claim was made on 24 February 1992 and thus well in advance of the hearing of the case on 24 March 1992. Furthermore, it considers that even a non-profit-making company such as the applicant can incur losses for which it should be compensated.

The Government have submitted that it was unclear on what basis or in what manner the sum of IR£62,172 was computed and Dublin Well Woman has not indicated how these losses were calculated or sought to substantiate them. Nevertheless, the discontinuance of the counselling service must have resulted in a loss of income. Having regard to equitable considerations as required by Article 50, the Court awards IR£25,000 under this head.

B   Costs and expenses

1   Open Door

88 Open Door claimed the sum of IR£68,985.75 referable to both the national proceedings and to those before the Convention institutions. This sum did not take into account what had been received by way of legal aid from the Council of Europe in

respect of fees. On 1 May 1992 Mr Cole, a lawyer who had appeared on behalf of Open Door, filed a supplementary claim for US$24,300 on behalf of the Centre for Constitutional Rights.

89 The Government considered the claim made by Open Door to be reasonable.

90 The Court observes that the claim made by Open Door includes an amount for the services of Mr Cole of the Centre for Constitutional Rights. It rejects his supplementary claim on behalf of the Centre for Constitutional Rights which was not itself a party to the proceedings. However, it allows Open Door's uncontested claim less 6,900 French francs paid by way of legal aid in respect of fees.

2 Dublin Well Woman

91 Dublin Well Woman claimed a total sum of IR£63,302.84 for costs and expenses incurred in the national proceedings. They further claimed IR£21,084.95 and IR£27,116.30 in respect of proceedings before the Commission and the Court. These sums did not take into account what had been received by way of legal aid in respect of fees and expenses.

92 The Government accepted that the claims for domestic costs were reasonable. However they submitted that, in the light of the claim made by Open Door, IR£16,000 and IR£19,000 were more appropriate sums for the proceedings before the Commission and Court.

93 The Court also considers that the amount claimed in respect of the proceedings before the Commission and Court is excessive taking into account the fees claimed by Open Door and the differences between the two applications. It holds that Dublin Well Woman should be awarded IR£100,000 under this head less 52,577 French francs already paid by way of legal aid in respect of fees and expenses.

94 The amounts awarded in this judgment are to be increased by any value-added tax that may be chargeable.

For these reasons, THE COURT:

1   *Dismisses* by fifteen votes to eight the Government's plea that Mrs X and Ms Geraghty cannot claim to be victims of a violation of the Convention;

2   *Dismisses* unanimously the remainder of the Government's preliminary objections;

3   *Holds* by fifteen votes to eight that there has been a violation of Article 10;

4   *Holds* unanimously that it is not necessary to examine the remaining complaints;

5   *Holds* by seventeen votes to six that Ireland is to pay to Dublin Well Woman, within three months, IR£25,000 (twenty-five thousand Irish pounds) in respect of damages;

6   *Holds* unanimously that Ireland is to pay to Open Door and Dublin Well Woman, within three months, in respect of costs and expenses, the sums resulting from the calculation to be made in accordance with paras 90, 93 and 94 of the judgment;

7   *Dismisses* unanimously the remainder of the claims for just satisfaction.

DISSENTING OPINION OF JUDGE CREMONA

There are certain aspects in this case which merit special consideration in the context of the "necessary in a democratic society" requirement for the purposes of Article 10(2) of the Convention.

Firstly, there is the paramount place accorded to the protection of unborn life in the whole fabric of Irish public policy, as is abundantly manifest from repeated pronouncements of the highest judicial and other national authorities.

Secondly, this is in fact a fundamental principle of Irish public policy which has been enshrined in the constitution itself after being unequivocally affirmed by the direct will of a strong majority of the people by means of the eminently democratic process of a comparatively recent national referendum.

Thirdly, in a matter such as this touching on profound moral values considered fundamental in the national legal order, the margin of appreciation left to national authorities (which in this case the judgment itself describes as wide), though of course not exempt from supervision by the Strasbourg institutions, assumes a particular significance. As has been said by the Court on other occasions:

(a) "it is not possible to find in the legal and social orders of the Contracting States a uniform European conception of morals" so that "the view taken of the requirements of morals varies from time to time and from place to place, especially in our era, characterised as it is by a far-reaching evolution of opinions on the subject" (*Müller and Others v Switzerland*, judgment of 24 May 1988, Series A, No 133, p 22, para 35; and see also *Handyside v The United Kingdom* judgment of 7 December 1976, Series A, No 24, p 22, para 48); and

(b) by reason of their direct and continuous contact with the vital forces of their countries, State authorities are in principle in a better position than an international judge to give an opinion on the exact content of these requirements as well as on the necessity of a restriction or penalty intended to meet them (*ibid*).

I think this assumes particular importance in the present case in view of the popular expression in a national referendum. The interference in question is in fact a corollary of the constitutional protection accorded to those unable to defend themselves (ie the unborn) intended to avoid setting at nought a constitutional provision considered to be basic in the national legal order and indeed, as the Government put it, to sustain the logic of that provision.

Fourthly, there is also a certain proportionality in that the prohibition in question in no way affects the expression of opinion about the permissibility of abortion in general and does not extend to measures restricting freedom of movement of pregnant women or subjecting them to unsolicited examinations. It is true that, within its own limited scope the injunction was couched in somewhat absolute terms, but what it really sought to do was to reflect the general legal principle involved and the legal position as then generally understood.

I am convinced that any inconvenience or possible risk from the impugned injunction which has been represented as indirectly affecting women who may wish to seek abortions, or any practical limitation on the general effectiveness of such injunction cannot, in the context of the case as a whole, whether by themselves or in conjunction with other arguments, outweigh the above considerations in the overall assessment.

In conclusion, taking into account all relevant circumstances and in particular the margin of appreciation enjoyed by national authorities, I cannot find that the injunction in question was incompatible with Article 10 of the Convention. In my view it satisfied all the requirements of paragraph 2 thereof. There was thus no violation of that provision.

PARTLY DISSENTING OPINION OF JUDGE MATSCHER

(Translation)

1(a) Despite the Court's reference (at para 44 of the present judgment) to para 42 of the *Johnston and Others v Ireland* judgment (which incidentally does not appear to me to be to the point because it concerns a very different situation), I have my doubts about the status of "victims" of the applicants Mrs X and Ms Geraghty, who have in no way claimed that they wished to seek information of the type the disclosure of which the contested injunction restrained.

By according, in these circumstances, the status of victims to the two applicants, the Court has, to my mind, adopted too broad an interpretation of this requirement, which is an essential condition for any individual application; in so doing it is liable to destroy the distinction between such applications and applications of the *actio popularis* type, which are not permissible under the Convention.

This amounts to affirming that anyone could claim to be the victim of a violation of the right to receive information once there is a restriction in any Contracting State on the disclosure of certain information. In my opinion, to be the victim of an infringement of this right, an applicant must assert, at least plausibly, that he or she wished to obtain information whose disclosure had been restrained in breach of the requirements of Article 10.

1(b) It is also my view that, for the reasons set out under (a) above, there has been no interference with the right protected by Article 10 in respect of these two applicants.

2   I subscribe fully to the opinion of the majority that the interference in question was "prescribed by law".

3   On the other hand, I cannot follow the majority where it finds a violation of the Convention in this case on the ground that the interference in question was not "necessary in a democratic society". I shall try to explain my position:

  (a) The case under review highlights the tension which exists between two of the conditions provided for in the second paragraphs of Articles 8 to 11 (Art 8(2), Art 9(2), Art 10(2), Art 11(2)) of the Convention, which if satisfied may render permissible interferences with the rights guaranteed under those Articles, the conditions in issue here being that of a "legitimate aim" and that of "necessity in a democratic society".

According to my understanding of the position, the criterion of "necessity" relates exclusively to the measures which the State adopts in order to attain the (legitimate) "aim" pursued; it therefore concerns the appropriateness and proportionality of such measures, but it in no way empowers the European organs to "weigh up" or to call in question the legitimacy of the aim as such, in other words to inquire into whether it is "necessary" to seek to attain such an aim (see my opinion – in which I dissented on other grounds – attached to *Dudgeon v the United Kingdom*, judgment of 22 October 1981, Series A, No 45, p 33).

That is why I cannot accept the definition of the term "necessary" as "corresponding to a pressing social need", which in fact expresses the intention of the European Court to assess for itself whether it is "necessary" for a national legislature or a national court to seek to attain an aim which the Convention recognises as legitimate. (This definition is, moreover, wholly inappropriate for the assessment of the "necessity" of a measure which is designed only to protect the legal position or the interests of an individual; but that is not the situation here.)

(b) The aim which the Irish courts were pursuing by prohibiting all "institutionalised" activity for the provision of information concerning the possibilities of obtaining abortions in the United Kingdom (and the organisation of trips to and stays in British clinics carrying out abortions, although this was not in issue in the present application, see para 53; it was nevertheless, in my view, an inherent aspect of the activities at least of Dublin Well Woman and – in assessing the legitimacy of the aim pursued and the necessity of the alleged interference – it cannot be dissociated from the first aspect, as the contested decision of the Irish courts concerned both aspects jointly) undoubtedly falls under "the prevention of disorder" and "the protection of (according to Irish standards) ... morals". I would mention further "the protection ... of the rights of others" (of the unborn child and also of his father). Indeed I consider that to reduce the problem of the "legitimate aim" solely to the protection of morals is to take too narrow a view of the case (see in this connection the very relevant arguments put forward by the Irish Government, para 64 et *seq* of the present judgment).

[...]

(c) I shall refrain from expressing an opinion on whether, from the point of view of legislative policy, the prohibition of and the imposition of criminal sanctions for abortion in Ireland can still be regarded as reasonable and desirable, or indeed whether the consequences of such a policy may even be pernicious.

The choice was made by the legislature, following the 1983 referendum. The introduction of Article 40(3)(3) of the Constitution, protecting the life of unborn children and prohibiting abortion, is merely the legislature's response to the democratically expressed will of the Irish people. I also accept that recently a number of derogations from this absolute prohibition have been allowed. That choice must be respected and is in no way contrary to the requirements of the Convention, and it is not even necessary in this connection to have recourse to the notion of the margin of appreciation which the national legislature enjoys in respect of such measures.

(d) If the Convention recognises as legitimate the aim (or aims) which the Irish legislation seeks to attain, it is not for the European Court to call in question that aim simply because it may have different ideas in this regard.

It remains only to examine the "necessity", within the meaning of Article 10(2), of the measures adopted by the Irish authorities, necessity to be assessed as explained under (a).

In my view those measures can be regarded as appropriate and as consistent with the criterion of proportionality.

There is, however, one more argument which has to be refuted in this discussion: it has been said that, in view of the fact that the women interested in having an abortion abroad were free to obtain the information they required from publications, whose distribution in Ireland was not prohibited, the ban on information services of the kind offered by the two applicant associations must inevitably be an ineffective measure, and thus no longer "necessary".

Nevertheless I consider there to be a considerable difference between advertisements in the press, whose circulation in a free country it is virtually impossible to prohibit, and the setting up of specific advice and information services (together with the organisation of trips to and stays in appropriate clinics in the United Kingdom which carry out abortions), so that the contested interference cannot be regarded as ineffective. Indeed it constitutes an entirely appropriate means – although evidently not 100% effective – to attain the (legitimate) aim pursued; in any event, without such a measure there was a risk that the aim in question would not be attained.

In these circumstances I do not see how the "necessity" of the contested measure can be denied.

4   I agree with the unanimous opinion of the Court that it is not necessary to consider whether there has been a breach of other provisions of the Convention.

5   Even if I had accepted the position of the majority of the Court as regards the substance of the case, I could not agree with the award of any sum to Dublin Well Woman in respect of pecuniary damage (at the most it might have been possible to envisage the award of compensation for non-pecuniary damage, if such a claim had been submitted). If this applicant is an idealistic, non-profit-making association, as it gave the Court to understand, it is not entitled to claim compensation for loss of earnings; if, on the other hand, it also operates as a commercial undertaking – a specialised travel agency – the whole case should equally appear to the majority in a rather different light.

DISSENTING OPINION OF JUDGES PETTITI, RUSSO AND LOPES ROCHA, APPROVED BY JUDGE BIGI

(Translation)

We did not vote with the majority of the Court on two points: firstly we do not accept that the two individual applicants had the status of victims and we share Judge Matscher's view in this respect; secondly we considered that the majority had adopted a wrong approach to the issue brought before it, perhaps because underlying the analysis of the application from the point of view of Article 10 of the European Convention on Human Rights was the problem of abortion.

It is our opinion that the effect of the criminal provisions in question should have been examined as if it were a typical problem of criminal law. On a general level more account should have been taken of the basis and object of the Irish legislation on the protection of life.

Let us consider what would be the position if Ireland's neighbouring States were to adopt legislation decriminalising drugs, whilst in Ireland itself they remained prohibited under the criminal law. If associations or organisations which provided services promoting trips for Irish nationals abroad and their introduction to the use of drugs in the countries concerned were prosecuted, the Court's approach under the Convention would probably lead to a finding that, in view of the sovereignty of States in the field of the criminal law and the margin of appreciation, Ireland would not be infringing Article 10 by prohibiting this type of provision of service. Similar reasoning should apply to activities of the kind engaged in by Open Door. In its judgment in the *Grogan* case (ECR 1992 – see para 24 of the present judgment), the Court of Justice of the European Communities classified as the provision of services the medical interventions in question. The scope of the activities proposed by Open Door went beyond social welfare or medical advice and served the interests of agencies and practitioners.

It is worth recalling here the substance of the applicable Irish provisions.

The provision of the Constitution in issue (Article 40(3)(3)) (which was not in the original text adopted in 1937) was supported by the majority of the population and adopted in a national referendum in 1983. There was a substantial majority – 67% of the votes – opposed to abortion.

This new provision concerns solely the protection and preservation of human life and does not refer to sexual morality, or to public or private morality. The issues of freedom of expression are dealt with in general under Article 40(6)(1)(i) of the Constitution.

The judgments of the Irish courts examined only the question of the protection of human life as provided for in the Constitution. The Constitution applies without distinction to all children in their mother's womb, irrespective of whether they were conceived in or out of wedlock. It is not correct to regard the adoption of a position on the question of abortion as simply an expression of a view on morality and sexuality.

In our opinion the Court has failed to take sufficient account of the reference to "the rights of others" in Article 10 of the Convention and of Article 60 in relation to the provisions in the Irish legislation which afford a broader protection of rights than the Convention. The Court confines itself to an assessment of the moral issues without really replying to the reasoning invoked by the Government to explain why they had to conform to the Constitution.

The injunctions of the Irish courts concerned questions related to the protection of unborn children, mothers and embryos on Irish territory with a view to preventing transactions or services which in Ireland were designed to achieve the contrary by promoting operations abroad, for which preparations were made in Ireland. In the Government's opinion, these activities constituted the preparation in Ireland of an abortion carried out abroad. Under Irish law the constitutional obligation is to protect such life while the future mother is in Ireland, which in turn necessitates the adoption of measures that can be implemented on Irish territory; it in no way concerns sexual morality.

It is well known in Ireland that abortions are possible subject to various conditions in other countries and the State has not tried to conceal this information. It is important to remember that in several member States abortion remains in principle a criminal offence, albeit with numerous exceptions and derogations. What is at issue for the Irish State is the setting up in Ireland of links between private clients and clinics carrying out abortions and the doctors at such clinics in the United Kingdom. These links are established with the aim of performing an act which is contrary to the Constitution and to the decisions of the Irish courts which must conform thereto.

Had it been a question of providing persons consulting the organisations concerned with advice on important health matters, the Irish medical and hospital services could have answered the patients' queries and catered for their needs.

The majority accept that the restriction was "prescribed by law" and that it pursued the "legitimate aim" of protecting morals, an aspect of which was the protection in Ireland of the unborn child's right to life. They also accept that the latter protection, recognised under Irish law, is based on moral values relating to the nature of life which are reflected in the attitude adopted by the majority of the Irish people.

It was merely considerations relating to the necessity and the proportionality of the injunctions concerning the activity of the applicant agencies which led the majority to conclude that there had been a violation of Article 10 of the Convention; in other words they reached the conclusion that the restraints imposed are too broad and disproportionate.

In our view, the restrictions were justified and, in any event, did not overstep the bounds of what was permissible. It was by any standards a minimal interference with the right to freedom of expression – concerning the aspect of that freedom relating to the communication and receipt of information – aimed at securing the primacy of values such as the right to life of the unborn child in accordance with the principles of the Irish legal system, which cannot be criticised on the basis of different principles applied in other legal systems.

The fact that Ireland cannot effectively prevent the circulation of reviews or of English telephone directories containing information on clinics in the United Kingdom, so that anyone can obtain information on abortion clinics in that country and the possibility of having an abortion in such clinics, can only, in our view, confirm the necessity of a specific measure such as that taken by the Irish courts. Such reviews, the directories and the persons possessing information on abortion clinics in the United Kingdom are "passive" factors, which require a personal and spontaneous attitude on the part of the person seeking advice. The activity of agencies which organise trips and provide special services for their clients, thereby influencing the decisions of those clients, is something entirely different.

The partial ineffectiveness of a law or a principle of case-law is not a reason for deciding not to take specific measures designed to prevent the activities of organisations committed to seeking means of obtaining results which do not conform to the interests and values of the legal system.

Moreover the fragmentary nature of legislation is well known, particularly in the field of criminal law, which aims to ensure that values protected by the law are fully respected.

The fact that the Irish legal system opts not to punish certain criminal behaviour where it occurs abroad does not mean that such conduct is no longer unlawful. Such a policy is simply a limit imposed on extra-territorial jurisdiction because of the difficulties of obtaining the necessary evidence.

In other words, the absence of an objective condition for imposing sanctions does not affect the unlawful nature of the act carried out outside the territorial jurisdiction of the criminal law.

Finally, the doctrine of *la fraude à la loi* (evasion of the law) may be invoked. This notion provides a legal system with a valid justification for taking legitimate measures in order to prevent results which are undesirable according to its fundamental legal standards and principles (the doctrine of *fraus legis* commented on by, among others, Mr Santoro Passarelli in his general theory of civil law).

It follows that the right of the authorities of a country to adopt appropriate measures to forestall the perpetration of the act calculated to evade the law and the effects of that act cannot be contested.

In conclusion, we consider that the decisions of the Irish courts did not violate Article 10 of the Convention.

CONCURRING OPINION OF JUDGE MORENILLA

1 I agree with the conclusions of the majority in the present case but not with the reasoning leading to the finding of a violation of Article 10 of the Convention. In my opinion the interference resulting from the injunction of the Supreme Court of Ireland prohibiting the dissemination of information to pregnant women concerning abortion services in the United Kingdom was not "prescribed by law" as required by paragraph 2 of this Article, having regard to the interpretation given by the Court to Articles 8 to 11 of the Convention and Article 2(3) and (4) of Protocol No 4, where the same condition can be found. In consequence, I cannot accept paragraphs 59 and 60 of the judgment.

Having found that the interference did not satisfy this requirement, I do not think it necessary to follow the majority in its further examination of the question whether the restriction was justified under Article 10(2). Consequently, I cannot share the opinion of the majority as expressed in paragraphs 61 to 77 of the judgment.

2 In my view, the concept "prescribed by law" refers to the requirement of legality under the rule of law to impose restrictions on fundamental rights or freedoms. According to the jurisprudence of this Court this condition implies that there must be a measure of protection in national law against arbitrary interferences with the rights safeguarded by paragraph 1 (see, *inter alia, Silver and Others v The United Kingdom*, judgment of 25 March 1983, Series A, No 61, p 33, para 88; the *Malone v The United Kingdom* judgment of 2 August 1984, Series A, No 82, pp 32–33, paras 67–68; and the *Kruslin and Huvig v France* judgments of 24 April 1990, Series A, No 176-A, pp 22–23, para 30, and No 176-B, pp 54–55, para 29); and it "does not merely refer back to domestic law but also relates to the quality of law, requiring it to be compatible with the rule of law, which is expressly mentioned in the preamble of the Convention" (see the above-mentioned *Malone* judgment, *ibid.*). The Court had also declared that not only "the interference in question must have some basis in domestic law", but "firstly, the law must be adequately accessible: the citizen must be able to have an indication that is adequate in the circumstances of the legal rules applicable to a given case. Secondly, a norm cannot be regarded as 'law' unless it is formulated with sufficient precision to enable the citizen to regulate his conduct: he must be able – if need be with appropriate advice – to foresee, to a degree that is reasonable in the circumstances, the consequence which a given action may entail" (*Sunday Times v The United Kingdom* judgment of 26 April 1979, Series A, No 30, p 31, para 49). In the *Groppera Radio AG and Others v Switzerland* judgment of 28 March 1990 (Series A, No 173, p 26, para 68) the Court determined that "the scope of the concepts of foreseeability and accessibility depends to a considerable degree on the content of the instrument in issue, the field it is designed to cover and the number and status of those to whom it is addressed".

3 This Court has also consistently declared since the *Handyside v The United Kingdom* judgment of 7 December 1976 (Series A, No 24, p 23, paras 48–49) that Article 10(2) does not give the Contracting States an unlimited margin of appreciation when interpreting and applying the domestic laws in force, the Court being empowered to give a final ruling on whether the restriction is reconcilable with freedom of expression as protected by Article 10 and that the European supervision "covers not only the basic legislation but also the decision applying it, even one given by an independent court" (*ibid*, p 23, para 49; see also the *Sunday Times* judgment, *ibid*, p 36, para 59). Therefore the power of the national authorities to interpret and apply the internal law when imposing a restriction on the freedom to receive and to impart information and ideas "goes hand in hand with the European supervision" (see the above-mentioned *Handyside* judgment, p 23, para 59). Consequently the supervision at a European level may result in a more

extensive protection of the individual than at State level because the law must be restrictively interpreted in order to secure the observance of the international engagement undertaken by the States under Articles 1 and 19 of the Convention.

4   The injunction granted by the High Court on 19 December 1986 and upheld by the Supreme Court of Ireland (judgment of 16 March 1988) was based on Article 40(3)(3) of the Irish Constitution (see para 28 of the judgment).

5   On reading this provision it seems to impose primarily obligations upon the State, including the enactment of a law defining the scope of the protection of the right to life of the unborn – acknowledged, according to the provision, "with due regard to the equal right to life of the mother", both rights to be defended and vindicated by the State "as far as practicable". As Mr Justice Niall McCarthy said in a recent judgment delivered by the Supreme Court of Ireland on 5 March 1992 in the *Attorney General v X and Others* case (judgment of 5 March 1992):

> I think it reasonable, however to hold that the People when enacting the Amendment were entitled to believe that legislation would be introduced as to regulate the manner in which the right to life of the mother could be reconciled ... the failure by the legislature to enact the appropriate legislation is no longer just unfortunate; it is inexcusable.

6   In my view, in the absence of specific legislation, the new constitutional provision did not provide a clear basis for the individual to foresee that imparting reliable information about abortion clinics in Great Britain would be unlawful: the penal, administrative or civil legislation on abortion then in force (paras 29–32 of the judgment) or the case-law of the Irish courts presented in this case relating to the protection of the right to life of the unborn before the Eighth Amendment (see paras 33–35 of the judgment) did not give sufficient ground for such an assertion; moreover, until the present case, the Supreme Court did not have the opportunity to interpret this Amendment.

7   The above situation may explain why the two corporate applicants were peaceably imparting this information for several years before and after the introduction of the Eighth Amendment until the commencement of the proceedings at issue on 28 June 1985, as a private action, to be converted by the Attorney General into a relator action fourteen months later. It also explains why British and other foreign magazines containing such information were circulating freely in Ireland (see para 23 of the judgment), and that no prosecution or any civil action was instituted in Ireland against Irish women who had abortions abroad, as well as the Government's statement (para 25 of the judgment) that in certain circumstances, under Irish law, persons could be entitled to have appropriate access to such information.

8   In these circumstances, *de jure* and *de facto*, my conclusion is that the relevant domestic law restricting freedom of expression, in an area of information so important for a large sector of Irish women, lacked the necessary definition and certainty. Accordingly, the injunction imposed on the two applicant corporations and their counsellors was not justified under Article 10(2) of the Convention.

9   Taking into account the vague and uncertain relationship between the information given by the corporate applicants and protection of the unborn (see para 75), I also consider that none of the applicants could reasonably have foreseen that these activities were unlawful and that their freedom to impart and receive reliable information about abortion services in Great Britain could be restricted under the domestic law prevailing prior to the Supreme Court judgment in this case.

In consequence, the above-mentioned legal uncertainties could not have been clarified by "appropriate legal advice"; nor could the exercise of the right to receive such important confidential information have been elucidated by a previous consultation as to its lawfulness. The vagueness of both the constitutional provision and Irish case-law previous to the present case was, in itself, inconsistent with the legality of the measure required, under the rule of law, to justify the interference with freedom of expression under paragraph 2 of the Convention.

PARTLY DISSENTING OPINION OF JUDGE BAKA

While I fully agree with the Court in holding that the restriction was prescribed by law, I regret that I cannot follow the majority as far as the question of the necessity in a democratic society is concerned. I am also unable to accept that Mrs X and Ms Geraghty can be considered as "victims" in the present case.

In my view the scope of the injunction granted by the domestic courts involved more than the restraint of information; it restricted various kinds of activities which were considered to be unlawful. The injunction granted by the High Court stated that "the Defendants ... be perpetually restrained from counselling or assisting pregnant women within the jurisdiction of this Court to obtain further advice or to obtain abortion". Similarly, the Supreme Court ordered that the Defendants "... be perpetually restrained from assisting pregnant women within the jurisdiction to travel abroad to obtain abortions by referral to a clinic, by the making for them of travel arrangements, or by informing them of the identity and location of and the method of communication with a specified clinic or clinics or otherwise".

While we are only concerned with the freedom of information in this case, we have to take into account the fact that providing (and receiving) information had been only one – albeit vitally important – feature of the applicants' services. The main concern of the domestic courts was not so much to stop the dissemination of information but rather to terminate an illegal activity which inevitably gave rise to certain restrictions on freedom of information as well. Unlike the majority, I do not perceive this restriction to be "absolute" since, in reality, the information was readily available "... from other sources in Ireland such as magazines, telephone directories or by persons with contacts in Great Britain" (judgment, para 76).

Examining the proportionality of the restriction against this background, I consider that it was unavoidable, subsidiary and limited in nature and has been not only necessary to protect the constitutionally enshrined right to life of the unborn, but also to maintain and safeguard the integrity of the Irish legal system. In my opinion therefore the injunction was proportionate and necessary in a democratic society. Consequently, there has been no breach of Article 10 of the Convention.

Nor can I follow the majority view which accepts that Mrs X and Ms Gerahty are "victims" in this case. The above-mentioned domestic judgments refer only to the corporate applicants, their servants and agents. It is obvious that the clients of these companies would have been affected as well. On the one hand, it is undeniable that society as a whole is potentially a victim of an interference with freedom of information. On the other hand, an applicant should be required to show that there is a direct and immediate interference, or at least a possible risk of a direct, immediate interference with his or her individual rights before he or she can be considered to be a "victim" before the Court.

In my view, the rights of these individual applicants were not endangered by imposing restrictions on the activities of Open Door and Dublin Well Woman which counselled pregnant women only (see judgment, para 13). They were not stated to be either pregnant or clients of the corporate applicants. Since their rights were not directly affected by the injunction, they could not therefore claim to be "victims" within the meaning of Article 25(1) of the Convention. Their application falls into the category of *actio popularis*.

DISSENTING OPINION OF JUDGE BLAYNEY

I am unable to agree with two of the decisions of the majority of the Court:

Firstly, that there was a breach of Article 10, and secondly, that Mrs X and Ms Geraghty were victims. In this opinion I propose to deal solely with Article 10. As regards Mrs X and Ms Geraghty, I agree with the reasoning in the dissenting opinion of Judge Baka.

In my opinion the Supreme Court injunction was not disproportionate to the aims which it pursued. Having found that the activities of the applicants were unlawful having regard to Article 40(3)(3) of the Constitution, and having made a declaration to that effect, the injunction followed as a logical consequence. The source of the injunction was to be found in the Constitution itself. In granting it, the Court was simply fulfilling its obligation to uphold the Constitution and to defend the rights of the unborn guaranteed by the Article in question. It was not a case of the Court granting an injunction in exercise of a discretionary jurisdiction. Once the Court had found that the activities of the applicants were unlawful having regard to Article 40(3)(3), the injunction followed as a necessary consequence. It was not open to the Court to adopt any lesser measure.

In the circumstances, the injunction could not in my opinion be said to be disproportionate. It was the only measure possible to uphold Article 40(3)(3). There was no other course that the Court could have taken. It was inconceivable that it should refuse to grant an injunction since this would have amounted to an abdication of its duty to protect the rights of the unborn and would have fatally undermined the moral values enshrined in Article 40(3)(3).

I am also of the opinion that our Court is precluded by Article 60 of the Convention from finding that there has been a breach of Article 10.

Article 60 provides as follows:

Nothing in [the] Convention shall be construed as limiting or derogating from any of the human rights and fundamental freedoms which may be ensured under the laws of any High Contracting Party or under any other agreement to which it is a Party.

The right of the unborn to be born is clearly a human right and it is guaranteed in Ireland by Article 40(3)(3) of the Constitution. Under Article 60 nothing in the Convention is to be construed as limiting or derogating from that right. If Article 10 is to be construed as entitling the applicants to give information to pregnant women so as to assist them to have abortions in England, then in my opinion it is being construed so as to derogate from the human rights of the unborn. In his judgment in the Supreme Court in the case of *The Attorney General at the relation of the Society for the Protection of Unborn Children (Ireland) Limited v Open Door Counselling Limited and Dublin Well Woman Centre Limited* [1988] Irish Reports 593, Finlay CJ said at page 624:

I am satisfied beyond doubt that having regard to the admitted facts the Defendants were assisting in the ultimate destruction of the life of the unborn by abortion in that they were helping the pregnant woman who had decided upon that option to get in touch with a clinic in Great Britain which would provide the service of abortion.

The decision that the injunction constituted a breach of Article 10 amounts to interpreting that Article as permitting information to be given which clearly derogates from the rights of the unborn since it assists in their destruction. In my opinion Article 60 precludes such a construction.

The applicants in their submissions placed reliance on the fact that the information provided by them was available elsewhere, and that the injunction did not prevent Irish women from continuing to have abortions abroad. In my opinion neither of these matters has any relevance to whether or not Article 60 applies. The sole issue is whether a finding that the injunction constitutes a breach of Article 10 amounts to interpreting that Article as derogating from the human rights of the unborn as guaranteed by the Constitution, and in my opinion it does. For this reason also, I consider that it is not possible to conclude that there has been a breach of Article 10.

RIGHTS TO EQUALITY AND NON-DISCRIMINATION IN EMPLOYMENT

CASE NO 25

KREIL v BUNDESREPUBLIK DEUTSCHLAND

EUROPEAN COURT OF JUSTICE

Case No: C-285/98

Judgment: 11 January 2000

Panel: *Judges*: Rodríguez Iglesias (*President*), Moitinho de Almeida, Sevón, Kapteyn, Gulmann, Puissochet (*Rapporteur*), Hirsch, Ragnemalm and Wathelet

Human rights — Equality and non-discrimination — Sex discrimination — Equal treatment of men and women — Employment in the military — Whether a general policy that women were not to be employed in military positions involving the use of arms violated the principle of equal treatment of men and women — Exceptions to the principle of equal treatment — Whether combat readiness was a permitted exception to equal treatment — EC Treaty, art 224 (now art 297 EC) — EC Council Directive 76/207/EEC, art 2

BACKGROUND

In 1996 Ms Tanja Kreil, who was trained in electronics, applied for voluntary service in the *Bundeswehr* (German army) requesting duties in weapon electronics maintenance. Her application was rejected on the ground that women were barred by law from serving in military positions involving the use of arms. Under German law, women who enlisted as volunteers were permitted to be engaged only in medical and military-music services and not in armed service, in any circumstances.

Ms Kreil brought an action in the *Verwaltungsgericht* (Administrative Court), Hannover, claiming that the rejection of her application on grounds based solely on her sex was contrary to European Community law. The Administrative Court formed the view that the cases required an interpretation of European Community law, including article 2 of Directive 76/207/EEC on the implementation of the principle of equal treatment for men and women as regards access to employment, vocational training and promotion, and working conditions ("Equal Treatment Directive"). The Court referred the case to the European Court of Justice for a preliminary ruling on the question whether the provisions of German law which barred women from military posts which involved the use of arms and allowed them access only to posts in the medical and military-music services were contrary to EC law, in particular article 2(2) of the Equal Treatment Directive.

HELD

1   The principle of equal treatment of men and women was of general application to employment in public service and was not subject to any general reservation as regards measures taken for the organisation of the armed forces. (Paras 18 and 19)

2   Article 2(2) of the Equal Treatment Directive permitted Member States the discretion to exclude from its scope occupational activities for which, by their nature or context in

which they are carried out, sex constitutes a determining factor. However, as a derogation from an individual right laid down in the Directive, that provision had to be interpreted strictly. The fact that persons serving in the armed forces might be called on to use arms could not in itself justify the exclusion of women from access to military posts, especially since in the services of the Bundeswehr that were accessible to women (ie the medical and military-music services), basic training in the use of arms was given. The national authorities could not, without contravening the principle of proportionality, adopt the general position that the composition of all armed units in the *Bundeswehr* had to remain exclusively male. (Paras 20, 28 and 29)

3   Article 2(3) of the Equal Treatment Directive was intended to protect a woman's biological condition and the special relationship which exists between a woman and her child. It did not allow women to be excluded from a certain type of employment on the ground that they should be given greater protection than men against risks which were distinct from women's specific needs of protection. (Para 30)

Treaties and other international instruments referred to

Treaty establishing the European Community, arts 36 (now, after amendment, art 30 EC), 48 (now, after amendment, art 39 EC), 56 (now, after amendment, art 46 EC), 177 (art 234 EC), 223 (now, after amendment, art 296 EC), and 224 (now, art 297 EC)

European Community law referred to

Council Directive 76/207/EEC of 9 February 1976 on the implementation of the principle of equal treatment for men and women as regards access to employment, vocational training and promotion, and working conditions (OJ 1976 L 39, p 40), art 2

National legislation referred to

Germany

Grundgesetz für die Bundesrepublik Deutschland (Basic Law), art 12a

Soldatengesetz (Law on Soldiers), art 1(2), in the version of 15 December 1995 (*Bundesgesetzblatt* I, p 1737), as last amended by the Law of 4 December 1997 (*Bundesgesetzblatt* I)

Soldatenlaufbahnverordnung (Regulations on Soldiers' Careers), in the version published on 28 January 1998 (*Bundesgesetzblatt* I), art 3a

Cases referred to

Commission v France, ECJ Case C-381/86; [1988] ECR 3559

Commission v Germany, ECJ Case C-248/83; [1985] ECR 1459

Gerster v Freistaat Bayern, ECJ Case C-1/95; [1997] ECR I-5253

Johnston v Chief Constable of the Royal Ulster Constabulary, ECJ Case C-222/84; [1986] ECR 1651

Leifer and Others, ECJ Case C-83/94; [1995] ECR I-3231

Richardt and "Les Accessoires Scientifiques", ECJ Case C-367/89; [1991] ECR I-4621

Sirdar v Army Board and Another, ECJ Case C/273/97; [2000] IRLR 47

JUDGMENT

1 By order of 13 July 1998, received at the Court on 24 July 1998, the *Verwaltungsgericht* (Administrative Court), Hannover, referred to the Court for a preliminary ruling under Article 177 of the EC Treaty (now Article 234 EC) a question on the interpretation of Council Directive 76/207/EEC of 9 February 1976 on the implementation of the principle of equal treatment for men and women as regards access to employment, vocational training and promotion, and working conditions (OJ 1976 L 39, p 40, hereinafter "the Directive"), in particular Article 2 thereof.

2 The question has been raised in proceedings between Tanja Kreil and the Bundesrepublik Deutschland concerning the refusal to engage her in the maintenance (weapon electronics) branch of the *Bundeswehr*.

The law applicable

3 Article 2(1), (2) and (3) of the Directive provides:

1 For the purposes of the following provisions, the principle of equal treatment shall mean that there shall be no discrimination whatsoever on grounds of sex either directly or indirectly by reference in particular to marital or family status.

2 This Directive shall be without prejudice to the right of Member States to exclude from its field of application those occupational activities and, where appropriate, the training leading thereto, for which, by reason of their nature or the context in which they are carried out, the sex of the worker constitutes a determining factor.

3 This Directive shall be without prejudice to provisions concerning the protection of women, particularly as regards pregnancy and maternity.

4 Article 9(2) of the Directive provides: "Member States shall periodically assess the occupational activities referred to in Article 2(2) in order to decide, in the light of social developments, whether there is justification for maintaining the exclusions concerned. They shall notify the Commission of the results of this assessment."

5 Article 12a of the *Grundgesetz für die Bundesrepublik Deutschland* (Basic Law for the Federal Republic of Germany) provides:

(1) Men who have attained the age of eighteen years may be required to serve in the Armed Forces, in the Federal Border Guard, or in a Civil Defence organisation.

...

(4) If, while a state of defence exists, civilian service requirements in the civilian public health and medical system or in the stationary military hospital organisation cannot be met on a voluntary basis, women between eighteen and fifty-five years of age may be assigned to such services by or pursuant to a law. They may on no account render service involving the use of arms.

6 Access for women to military posts in the *Bundeswehr* are governed in particular by Article 1(2) of the *Soldatengesetz* (Law on Soldiers, hereinafter "the SG") and by Article 3a of the *Soldatenlaufbahnverordnung* (Regulation on Soldiers' Careers, hereinafter "the SLV"), according to which women may enlist only as volunteers and only in the medical and military-music services.

The main proceedings

7   In 1996, Tanja Kreil, who has been trained in electronics, applied for voluntary service in the *Bundeswehr*, requesting duties in weapon electronics maintenance. Her application was rejected by the *Bundeswehr's* recruitment centre and then by its head staff office on the ground that women are barred by law from serving in military positions involving the use of arms.

8   Tanja Kreil then brought an action in the *Verwaltungsgericht* (Administrative Court) Hannover claiming in particular that the rejection of her application on grounds based solely on her sex was contrary to Community law.

9   Considering that the case required an interpretation of the Directive, the *Verwaltungsgericht* Hannover decided to stay the proceedings and to refer the following question to the Court for a preliminary ruling:

> Is Council Directive 76/207/EEC of 9 February 1976, in particular Article 2(2) of that directive, infringed by the third sentence of Article 1(2) of the *Soldatengesetz* (Law on Soldiers) in the version of 15 December 1995 (*Bundesgesetzblatt* I, p. 1737), as last amended by the Law of 4 December 1997 (*Bundesgesetzblatt* I, p. 2846), and Article 3a of the *Soldatenlaufbahnverordnung* (Regulations on Soldiers' Careers), in the version published on 28 January 1998 (*Bundesgesetzblatt* I, p. 326), under which women who enlist as volunteers may be engaged only in the medical and military-music services and are excluded in any event from armed service?

The question referred for a preliminary ruling

10 By its question the national court is asking essentially whether the Directive precludes the application of national provisions, such as those of German law, which bar women from military posts involving the use of arms and which allow them access only to the medical and military-music services.

11 The applicant argues that this bar constitutes direct discrimination contrary to the Directive. She considers that, under Community law, a law or a regulation may not prohibit a woman from access to the occupation which she wishes to pursue.

12 The German Government, on the other hand, considers that Community law does not preclude the provisions of the SG and SLV in question, which are in accordance with the German constitutional rule prohibiting women from performing armed service. According to it, Community law does not in principle govern matters of defence, which form part of the field of common foreign and security policy and which remain within the Member States' sphere of sovereignty. Secondly, even if the Directive could apply to the armed forces, the national provisions in question, which limit access for women to certain posts in the *Bundeswehr*, are justifiable under Article 2(2) and (3) of the Directive.

13 The Italian and United Kingdom Governments, which presented oral argument, argue basically that decisions concerning the organisation and combat capacity of the armed forces do not fall within the scope of the Treaty. Alternatively, they submit that in certain circumstances Article 2(2) of the Directive allows women to be excluded from service in combat units.

14 The Commission considers that the Directive, which is applicable to employment in the public service, applies to employment in the armed forces. It considers that Article 2(3) of the Directive cannot justify greater protection for women against risks to which men and women are equally exposed. As regards the question whether the employment

sought by Tanja Kreil forms part of activities whose nature or the context in which they are carried out require, as a determining factor within the meaning of Article 2(2) of the Directive, that they be carried out by men and not by women, it is for the referring court to answer that question having due regard for the principle of proportionality and taking account both of the discretion which each Member State retains according to its own particular circumstances and of the progressive nature of the implementation of the principle of equal treatment for men and women.

15 The Court observes first of all that, as it held in paragraph 15 of its judgment of 26 October 1999 in Case C-273/97 *Sirdar* [1999] ECR I-0000, it is for the Member States, which have to adopt appropriate measures to ensure their internal and external security, to take decisions on the organisation of their armed forces. It does not follow, however, that such decisions are bound to fall entirely outside the scope of Community law.

16 As the Court has already held, the only articles in which the Treaty provides for derogations applicable in situations which may affect public security are Articles 36, 48, 56, 223 (now, after amendment, Articles 30 EC, 39 EC, 46 EC and 296 EC) and 224 (now Article 297 EC), which deal with exceptional and clearly defined cases. It is not possible to infer from those articles that there is inherent in the Treaty a general exception excluding from the scope of Community law all measures taken for reasons of public security. To recognise the existence of such an exception, regardless of the specific requirements laid down by the Treaty, might impair the binding nature of Community law and its uniform application (see, to that effect, Case 222/84 *Johnston v Chief Constable of the Royal Ulster Constabulary* [1986] ECR 1651, para 26, and Case C-273/97 *Sirdar*, cited above, para 16).

17 The concept of public security, within the meaning of the Treaty articles cited in the preceding paragraph, covers both a Member State's internal security, as in the *Johnston* case, and its external security, as in the *Sirdar* case (see, to this effect, Case C-367/89 *Richardt and "Les Accessoires Scientifiques"* [1991] ECR I-4621, para 22, Case C-83/94 *Leifer and Others* [1995] ECR I-3231, para 26, and *Sirdar*, cited above, para 17).

18 Furthermore, some of the derogations provided for by the Treaty concern only the rules relating to the free movement of goods, persons and services, and not the social provisions of the Treaty, of which the principle of equal treatment for men and women relied on by Tanja Kreil forms part. In accordance with settled case-law, this principle is of general application and the Directive applies to employment in the public service (Case 248/83 *Commission v Germany* [1985] ECR 1459, para 16, Case C-1/95 *Gerster v Freistaat Bayern* [1997] ECR I-5253, para 18, and *Sirdar*, cited above, para 18).

19 It follows that the Directive is applicable in a situation such as that in question in the main proceedings.

20 Under Article 2(2) of the Directive, Member States may exclude from the scope of the Directive occupational activities for which, by reason of their nature or the context in which they are carried out, sex constitutes a determining factor; it must be noted, however, that, as a derogation from an individual right laid down in the Directive, that provision must be interpreted strictly (*Johnston*, para 36, and *Sirdar*, para 23).

21 The Court has thus recognised, for example, that sex may be a determining factor for posts such as those of prison warders and head prison warders (Case 318/86 *Commission v France* [1988] ECR 3559, paras 11 to 18), for certain activities such as policing activities performed in situations where there are serious internal disturbances (*Johnston*, paras 36 and 37) or for service in certain special combat units (*Sirdar*, paras 29 to 31).

22 A Member State may restrict such activities and the relevant professional training to men or to women, as appropriate. In such a case, as is clear from Article 9(2) of the Directive, Member States have a duty to assess periodically the activities concerned in order to decide whether, in the light of social developments, the derogation from the general scheme of the Directive may still be maintained (*Johnston*, para 37, and *Sirdar*, para 25).

23 In determining the scope of any derogation from an individual right such as the equal treatment of men and women, the principle of proportionality, one of the general principles of Community law, must also be observed, as the Court pointed out in paragraph 38 of *Johnston* and paragraph 26 of *Sirdar*. That principle requires that derogations remain within the limits of what is appropriate and necessary in order to achieve the aim in view and requires the principle of equal treatment to be reconciled as far as possible with the requirements of public security which determine the context in which the activities in question are to be performed.

24 However, depending on the circumstances, national authorities have a certain degree of discretion when adopting measures which they consider to be necessary in order to guarantee public security in a Member State (*Leifer*, para 35, and *Sirdar*, para 27).

25 As the Court emphasised in paragraph 28 of its judgment in *Sirdar*, the question is therefore whether, in the circumstances of the present case, the measures taken by the national authorities, in the exercise of the discretion which they are recognised to enjoy, do in fact have the purpose of guaranteeing public security and whether they are appropriate and necessary to achieve that aim.

26 As was explained in paragraphs 5, 6 and 7 above, the refusal to engage the applicant in the main proceedings in the service of the *Bundeswehr* in which she wished to be employed was based on provisions of German law which bar women outright from military posts involving the use of arms and which allow women access only to the medical and military-music services.

27 In view of its scope, such an exclusion, which applies to almost all military posts in the *Bundeswehr*, cannot be regarded as a derogating measure justified by the specific nature of the posts in question or by the particular context in which the activities in question are carried out. However, the derogations provided for in Article 2(2) of the Directive can apply only to specific activities (see, to this effect, *Commission v France*, cited above, para 25).

28 Moreover, having regard to the very nature of armed forces, the fact that persons serving in those forces may be called on to use arms cannot in itself justify the exclusion of women from access to military posts. As the German Government explained, in the services of the *Bundeswehr* that are accessible to women, basic training in the use of arms, to enable personnel in those services to defend themselves and to assist others, is provided.

29 In those circumstances, even taking account of the discretion which they have as regards the possibility of maintaining the exclusion in question, the national authorities could not, without contravening the principle of proportionality, adopt the general position that the composition of all armed units in the *Bundeswehr* had to remain exclusively male.

30 Finally, as regards the possible application of Article 2(3) of the Directive, upon which the German Government also relies, this provision, as the Court held in paragraph 44 of its judgment in *Johnston*, is intended to protect a woman's biological

condition and the special relationship which exists between a woman and her child. It does not therefore allow women to be excluded from a certain type of employment on the ground that they should be given greater protection than men against risks which are distinct from women's specific needs of protection, such as those expressly mentioned.

31 It follows that the total exclusion of women from all military posts involving the use of arms is not one of the differences of treatment allowed by Article 2(3) of the Directive out of concern to protect women.

32 The answer to be given to the question must therefore be that the Directive precludes the application of national provisions, such as those of German law, which impose a general exclusion of women from military posts involving the use of arms and which allow them access only to the medical and military-music services.

Costs

33 The costs incurred by the German, Italian and United Kingdom Governments and by the Commission, which have submitted observations to the Court, are not recoverable. Since these proceedings are, for the parties to the main proceedings, a step in the action pending before the national court, the decision on costs is a matter for that court.

On those grounds, **THE COURT**, in answer to the question referred to it by the *Verwaltungsgericht* Hannover by order of 13 July 1998, **HEREBY RULES:**

Council Directive 76/207/EEC of 9 February 1976 on the implementation of the principle of equal treatment for men and women as regards access to employment, vocational training and promotion, and working conditions precludes the application of national provisions, such as those of German law, which impose a general exclusion of women from military posts involving the use of arms and which allow them access only to the medical and military-music services.

CASE NO 26

BROWN v RENTOKIL

EUROPEAN COURT OF JUSTICE

Case No: C-394/96

Judgment: 30 June 1998

Panel: *Judges*: Gulmann, (*President*), Ragnemalm, Wathelet, Schintgen, Mancini, Kapteyn (Rapporteur), Murray, Edward, Puissochet, Jann and Sevón

Human rights — Equality and non-discrimination — Sex discrimination — Employment — Pregnancy — Inability to report to work because of pregnancy-related disorders — Contractual provision for dismissal — Dismissal at time of pregnancy — Whether dismissal constituted discrimination on basis of sex — UK Employment Protection (Consolidation) Act 1978, s 33

BACKGROUND

The applicant, Ms Mary Brown, was employed by Rentokil as a driver. Her employment contract stipulated that if she was absent from work for more than 26 weeks continuously because of sickness, she would be dismissed. In August 1990, she informed her employer that she was pregnant. She subsequently developed pregnancy-related complications, which meant that she was absent for work for more than 26 weeks.

At the time when the applicant was dismissed, section 33 of the Employment Protection (Consolidation) Act 1978 provided that employees who had been absent from work wholly or partially because of pregnancy or confinement would be entitled to return to work if the employee had been in employment immediately before the start of the 11th week before her expected date of confinement, and at that time, she had been continuously employed for a period of not less that two years. However, Ms Brown had not been in employment for two years at this time.

Ms Brown brought an application to the Industrial Tribunal that her dismissal was contrary to the Sex Discrimination Act 1975. The Industrial Tribunal held that, where absence through pregnancy-related illness which began long before the statutory maternity provisions could apply and subsisted continuously thereafter, is followed by dismissal, that dismissal did not fall into the category of dismissals which must automatically be considered discriminatory because they are due to pregnancy. The Employment Appeal Tribunal also dismissed her appeal, on the basis that her dismissal was on account of illness, not pregnancy.

Ms Brown appealed to the House of Lords, which sought a preliminary ruling from the European Court of Justice on whether it would be contrary to articles 2(1) and 5(1) of Directive 76/207 of the Council of European Communities ("the Equal Treatment Directive") to dismiss a female employee at any time during her pregnancy, as a result of absence through illness arising from that pregnancy, in particular where a contractual provision, which applied irrespective of gender, entitled the employer to dismiss employees after a stipulated number of weeks of continued absence. The House of Lords also asked if it would be contrary to the Equal Treatment Directive if a female employee was dismissed as a result of absence through illness arising from pregnancy, if she did not qualify for the right to absent herself from work on account of pregnancy for the period specified under national law at the time of the dismissal.

HELD

1   The dismissal of a female worker on account of pregnancy, or essentially on account of pregnancy, could affect only women and therefore constituted direct discrimination on grounds of sex for the purposes of the Equal Treatment Directive. (Para 16)

2   Dismissal of a female worker during pregnancy for absences due to incapacity for work resulting from her pregnancy was linked to the occurrence of risks inherent in pregnancy and therefore had to be regarded as essentially based on the fact of pregnancy. Such a dismissal could affect only women and therefore constituted direct discrimination on grounds of sex. (Para 24)

3   Where a woman was absent owing to illness resulting from pregnancy or childbirth, and that illness arose during pregnancy and persisted during and after maternity leave, her absence not only during maternity leave but also during the period extending from the start of her pregnancy to the start of her maternity leave could not be taken into account for computation of the period justifying her dismissal under national law. (Para 27)

4   Discrimination involved the application of different rules to comparable situations or the application of the same rule to different situations. Where a contractual term was relied on to dismiss a pregnant worker because of absences due to incapacity for work resulting from her pregnancy, such contractual term, applying both to men and to women, was applied in the same way to different situations since the situation of a pregnant worker who was unfit to work as a result of disorders associated with her pregnancy could not be considered to be the same as that of a male worker who was ill and absent through incapacity for work for the same length of time. Consequently, application of that contractual term in circumstances such as the present constituted direct discrimination on grounds of sex. (Paras 30, 31 and 32)

European Community law referred to

Council Directive 76/207/EEC on the implementation of the principle of equal treatment for men and women as regards access to employment, vocational training and promotion, and working conditions (OJ 1976 L 39, p 40), arts 2(1), 2(3) and 5(1)

Council Directive 92/85/EEC of 19 October 1992 on the introduction of measures to encourage improvements in the safety and health at work of pregnant workers and workers who have recently given birth or are breastfeeding (OJ 1992 L 348, p 1), art 10

National legislation referred to

United Kingdom

Employment Protection (Consolidation) Act 1978, s 33

Social Security Act 1986, ss 46 and 48

Sex Discrimination Act 1975

Cases referred to

Dekker v Stichting Vormingscentrum voor Jong Volwassenen (VJV-Centrum) Plus, ECJ Case C-177/88; [1990] ECR I-3941

Gillespie and Others v Northern Health and Social Services Board and Others, ECJ Case C-342/93; [1996] ECR I-475

Habermann-Beltermann v Arbeitwohlfahrt Bezirksverband Ndb/Opf eV, ECJ Case C-421/92; [1994] ECR I-1657; [1994] 2 CMLR 681

Handels-og Kontorfunktionaerenes Forbund i Danmark v Dansk Arbejdsgiverforening ('Hertz'), ECJ Case C-1 79/88; [1990] ECR I-3979; [1992] ICR 332

Larsson v Føtex Supermarked, ECJ Case C-400/95; [1997] ECR I-2757

Webb v EMS Air Cargo, ECJ Case C-32/93; [1994] ECR I-3567; [1994] 3 WLR 941; [1994] QB 718; [1994] 4 All ER 115

JUDGMENT

1   By order of 28 November 1996, received at the Court Registry on 9 December 1996, the House of Lords referred to the Court for a preliminary ruling under Article 177 of the EC Treaty two questions on the interpretation of Articles 2(1) and 5(1) of Council Directive 76/207/EEC of 9 February 1976 on the implementation of the principle of equal treatment for men and women as regards access to employment, vocational training and promotion, and working conditions (OJ 1976 L 39, p 40).

2   Those questions have been raised in proceedings brought by Mary Brown against Rentokil Ltd ("Rentokil") in connection with her dismissal whilst pregnant.

3   According to the order for reference, Mrs Brown was employed by Rentokil as a driver. Her job was mainly to transport and change "Sanitact" units in shops and other centres. In her view, it was heavy work.

4   In August 1990, Mrs Brown informed Rentokil that she was pregnant. Thereafter she had difficulties associated with the pregnancy. From 16 August 1990 onwards, she submitted a succession of four-week certificates mentioning various pregnancy-related disorders. She did not work again after mid-August 1990.

5   Rentokil's contracts of employment included a clause stipulating that, if an employee was absent because of sickness for more than 26 weeks continuously, he or she would be dismissed.

6   On 9 November 1990, Rentokil's representatives told Mrs Brown that half of the 26-week period had run and that her employment would end on 8 February 1991 if, following an independent medical examination, she had not returned to work by then. A letter to the same effect was sent to her on that date.

7   Mrs Brown did not go back to work following that letter. The parties agree that there was never any question of her being able to return to work before the end of the 26-week period. By letter of 30 January 1991, which took effect on 8 February 1991, she was accordingly dismissed while pregnant. Her child was born on 22 March 1991.

8   At the time when Mrs Brown was dismissed, section 33 of the Employment Protection (Consolidation) Act 1978 provided that an employee who was absent from work wholly or partially because of pregnancy or confinement would, subject to certain conditions, be entitled to return to work. In particular, the employee had to have been in employment until immediately before the start of the 11th week before the expected date of confinement and, at the beginning of the 11th week, have been continuously employed for a period of not less than two years.

9   According to the order for reference, on the assumption that the date on which Mrs Brown's child was born was also the expected date of delivery, she was not entitled, because she had not been in employment for two years as at 30 December 1990, to absent herself from work from the beginning of the 11th week before delivery pursuant to section 33 of the Employment Protection (Consolidation) Act 1978, or to return to work at any time during the 29 weeks following delivery. She was, however, entitled to statutory maternity pay under sections 46 to 48 of the Social Security Act 1986.

10   By order dated 5 August 1991, the Industrial Tribunal dismissed Mrs Brown's application under the Sex Discrimination Act 1975 concerning her dismissal. The Tribunal held that, where absence through pregnancy-related illness, but which began long before the statutory maternity provisions could apply and subsisted continuously thereafter, is followed by dismissal, that dismissal does not fall into the category of dismissals which must automatically be considered discriminatory because they are due to pregnancy.

11   By order of 23 March 1992, the Employment Appeal Tribunal dismissed Mrs Brown's appeal.

12   By judgment of 18 January 1995, the Extra Division of the Court of Session reached the preliminary conclusion that in this case there was no discrimination within the meaning of the Sex Discrimination Act 1975. It pointed out that, since the Court of Justice had drawn a clear distinction between pregnancy and illness attributable to pregnancy (Case C-179/88 *Handels- og Kontorfunktionærenes Forbund i Danmark v Dansk Arbejdsgiverforening* [1990] ECR I-3979 ("Hertz")), Mrs Brown, whose absence was due to illness and who had been dismissed on account of that illness, could not succeed.

13   Mrs Brown appealed to the House of Lords, which referred the following questions to the Court for a preliminary ruling:

1(a) Is it contrary to Articles 2(1) and 5(1) of Directive 76/207 of the Council of the European Communities ("the Equal Treatment Directive") to dismiss a female employee, at any time during her pregnancy, as a result of absence through illness arising from that pregnancy?

1(b) Does it make any difference to the answer given to Question 1(a) that the employee was dismissed in pursuance of a contractual provision entitling the employer to dismiss employees, irrespective of gender, after a stipulated number of weeks of continued absence?

2(a) Is it contrary to Articles 2(1) and 5(1) of the Equal Treatment Directive to dismiss a female employee as a result of absence through illness arising from pregnancy who does not qualify for the right to absent herself from work on account of pregnancy or childbirth for the period specified by national law because she has not been employed for the period imposed by national law, where dismissal takes place during that period?

2(b) Does it make any difference to the answer given to Question 2(a) that the employee was dismissed in pursuance of a contractual provision entitling the employer to dismiss employees, irrespective of gender, after a stipulated number of weeks of continued absence?

The first part of the first question

14 It should be noted at the outset that the purpose of Directive 76/207, according to Article 1(1), is to put into effect in the Member States the principle of equal treatment for men and women as regards access to employment, vocational training and promotion, and working conditions.

15 Article 2(1) of the Directive provides that "... the principle of equal treatment shall mean that there shall be no discrimination whatsoever on grounds of sex either directly or indirectly by reference in particular to marital or family status". According to Article 5(1) of the Directive, "[a]pplication of the principle of equal treatment with regard to working conditions, including the conditions governing dismissal, means that men and women shall be guaranteed the same conditions without discrimination on grounds of sex".

16 According to settled case-law of the Court of Justice, the dismissal of a female worker on account of pregnancy, or essentially on account of pregnancy, can affect only women and therefore constitutes direct discrimination on grounds of sex (see Case C-177/88 *Dekker v Stichting Vormingscentrum voor Jong Volwassenen* (VJV-Centrum) Plus [1990] ECR I-3941, para 12; *Hertz*, cited above, para 13; Case C-421/92 *Habermann-Beltermann v Arbeiterwohlfahrt Bezirksverband* [1994] ECR I-1657, para 15; and Case C-32/93 *Webb v EMO Air Cargo* [1994] ECR I-3567, para 19).

17 As the Court pointed out in paragraph 20 of its judgment in *Webb*, cited above, by reserving to Member States the right to retain or introduce provisions which are intended to protect women in connection with "pregnancy and maternity", Article 2(3) of Directive 76/207 recognises the legitimacy, in terms of the principle of equal treatment, first, of protecting a woman's biological condition during and after pregnancy and, second, of protecting the special relationship between a woman and her child over the period which follows pregnancy and childbirth.

18 It was precisely in view of the harmful effects which the risk of dismissal may have on the physical and mental state of women who are pregnant, women who have recently given birth or women who are breastfeeding, including the particularly serious risk that pregnant women may be prompted voluntarily to terminate their pregnancy, that the Community legislature, pursuant to Article 10 of Council Directive 92/85/EEC of 19 October 1992 on the introduction of measures to encourage improvements in the safety and health at work of pregnant workers and workers who have recently given birth or are breastfeeding (tenth individual Directive adopted within the meaning of Article 16(1) of Directive 89/391/EEC) (OJ 1992 L 348, p 1), which was to be transposed into the laws of the Member States no later than two years after its adoption, provided for special protection to be given to women, by prohibiting dismissal during the period from the beginning of their pregnancy to the end of their maternity leave. Article 10 of Directive 92/85 provides that there is to be no exception to, or derogation from, the prohibition of dismissal of pregnant women during that period, save in exceptional cases not connected with their condition (see, in this regard, paras 21 and 22 of the judgment in *Webb*, cited above).

19 In replying to the first part of the first question, which concerns Directive 76/207, account must be taken of that general context.

20 At the outset, it is clear from the documents before the Court that the question concerns the dismissal of a female worker during her pregnancy as a result of absences through incapacity for work arising from her pregnant condition. As Rentokil points out, the cause of Mrs Brown's dismissal lies in the fact that she was ill during her pregnancy to such an extent that she was unfit for work for 26 weeks. It is common ground that her illness was attributable to her pregnancy.

21 However, dismissal of a woman during pregnancy cannot be based on her inability, as a result of her condition, to perform the duties which she is contractually bound to carry out. If such an interpretation were adopted, the protection afforded by Community law to a woman during pregnancy would be available only to pregnant women who were able to comply with the conditions of their employment contracts, with the result that the provisions of Directive 76/207 would be rendered ineffective (see *Webb*, cited above, para 26).

22 Although pregnancy is not in any way comparable to a pathological condition (*Webb*, cited above, para 25), the fact remains, as the Advocate General stresses in point 56 of his Opinion, that pregnancy is a period during which disorders and complications may arise compelling a woman to undergo strict medical supervision and, in some cases, to rest absolutely for all or part of her pregnancy. Those disorders and complications, which may cause incapacity for work, form part of the risks inherent in the condition of pregnancy and are thus a specific feature of that condition.

23 In paragraph 15 of its judgment in *Hertz*, cited above, the Court, on the basis of Article 2(3) of Directive 76/207, also pointed out that that directive admits of national provisions guaranteeing women specific rights on account of pregnancy and maternity. It concluded that, during the maternity leave accorded to her under national law, a woman is protected against dismissal on the grounds of her absence.

24 Although, under Article 2(3) of Directive 76/207, such protection against dismissal must be afforded to women during maternity leave (*Hertz*, cited above, para 15), the principle of non-discrimination, for its part, requires similar protection throughout the period of pregnancy. Finally, as is clear from paragraph 22 of this judgment, dismissal of a female worker during pregnancy for absences due to incapacity for work resulting from her pregnancy is linked to the occurrence of risks inherent in pregnancy and must therefore be regarded as essentially based on the fact of pregnancy. Such a dismissal can affect only women and therefore constitutes direct discrimination on grounds of sex.

25 It follows that Articles 2(1) and 5(1) of Directive 76/207 preclude dismissal of a female worker at any time during her pregnancy for absences due to incapacity for work caused by an illness resulting from that pregnancy.

26 However, where pathological conditions caused by pregnancy or childbirth arise after the end of maternity leave, they are covered by the general rules applicable in the event of illness (see, to that effect, *Hertz*, cited above, paras 16 and 17). In such circumstances, the sole question is whether a female worker's absences, following maternity leave, caused by her incapacity for work brought on by such disorders, are treated in the same way as a male worker's absences, of the same duration, caused by incapacity for work; if they are, there is no discrimination on grounds of sex.

27 It is also clear from all the foregoing considerations that, contrary to the Court's ruling in Case C-400/95 *Larsson v Føtex Supermarked* [1997] ECR I-2757, para 23), where a woman is absent owing to illness resulting from pregnancy or childbirth, and that illness arose during pregnancy and persisted during and after maternity leave, her absence not

only during maternity leave but also during the period extending from the start of her pregnancy to the start of her maternity leave cannot be taken into account for computation of the period justifying her dismissal under national law. As to her absence after maternity leave, this may be taken into account under the same conditions as a man's absence, of the same duration, through incapacity for work.

28 The answer to the first part of the first question must therefore be that Articles 2(1) and 5(1) of Directive 76/207 preclude dismissal of a female worker at any time during her pregnancy for absences due to incapacity for work caused by illness resulting from that pregnancy.

The second part of the first question

29 The second part of the first question concerns a contractual term providing that an employer may dismiss workers of either sex after a stipulated number of weeks of continuous absence.

30 It is well settled that discrimination involves the application of different rules to comparable situations or the application of the same rule to different situations (see, in particular, Case C-342/93 *Gillespie and Others v Northern Health and Social Services Board and Others* [1996] ECR I-475, para 16).

31 Where it is relied on to dismiss a pregnant worker because of absences due to incapacity for work resulting from her pregnancy, such a contractual term, applying both to men and to women, is applied in the same way to different situations since, as is clear from the answer given to the first part of the first question, the situation of a pregnant worker who is unfit for work as a result of disorders associated with her pregnancy cannot be considered to be the same as that of a male worker who is ill and absent through incapacity for work for the same length of time.

32 Consequently, application of that contractual term in circumstances such as the present constitutes direct discrimination on grounds of sex.

33 The answer to the second part of the first question must therefore be that the fact that a female worker has been dismissed during her pregnancy on the basis of a contractual term providing that the employer may dismiss employees of either sex after a stipulated number of weeks of continuous absence cannot affect the answer given to the first part of the first question.

The second question

34 In view of the answer given to the first question, it is unnecessary to answer the second question.

Costs

35 The costs incurred by the United Kingdom Government and by the Commission, which have submitted observations to the Court, are not recoverable. Since these proceedings are, for the parties to the main proceedings, a step in the proceedings pending before the national court, the decision on costs is a matter for that court.

On those grounds, **THE COURT**, in answer to the questions referred to it by the House of Lords by order of 28 November 1996, **HEREBY RULES**:

Articles 2(1) and 5(1) of Council Directive 76/207/EEC of 9 February 1976, on the implementation of the principle of equal treatment for men and women as regards access to employment, vocational training and promotion, and working conditions, preclude dismissal of a female worker at any time during her pregnancy for absences due to incapacity for work caused by illness resulting from that pregnancy.

The fact that a female worker has been dismissed during her pregnancy on the basis of a contractual term providing that the employer may dismiss employees of either sex after a stipulated number of weeks of continuous absence does not affect the answer given.

CASE NO 27

BROOKS AND OTHERS v CANADA SAFEWAY LIMITED

SUPREME COURT OF CANADA

Judgment: 4 May 1989

Panel: Dickson CJC, Beetz, McIntyre, Wilson, Le Dain,[1] La Forest and L'Heureux-Dubé JJ

Human rights — Equality and non-discrimination — Sex discrimination — Pregnancy — Whether discrimination on the ground of pregnancy constitutes discrimination on the ground of sex — Employer accident and sickness plan excluding pregnant women from benefits during 17-week period — Pregnancy as a valid health reason for absence from the workplace — Whether plan discriminatory — Human Rights Act of Manitoba 1974, s 6(1) — Human Rights Code (Canada) 1987

BACKGROUND

The appellants, Ms Brooks, Ms Allen and Ms Dixon, were employed as part-time cashiers by Canada Safeway Ltd. They all became pregnant during 1982. Safeway maintained a group insurance plan for employees who had worked for the company for three consecutive months, which included weekly benefits for loss of pay due to accident or sickness for a maximum period of 26 weeks for any continuous period of disability. Prior to 1 January 1981, pregnancy was not covered under the plan. When the appellants became pregnant, the plan excluded pregnant employees from receiving benefits for a total of 17 weeks, covering ten weeks before the birth, the week of the birth and six weeks after. The 17-week period applied even if a woman was suffering from a non-pregnancy-related disability. The pregnant employees were entitled to 15 weeks' statutory unemployment benefits.

The appellants were refused benefits under Safeway's insurance plan, but they all received the less generous benefits under the statutory scheme: for two weeks the appellants received no benefits and then they received lesser benefits than a male employee or non-pregnant woman would have been entitled to under the plan.

They complained to the Manitoba Human Rights Commission that the differential treatment of pregnant women under Safeway's insurance plan constituted sex discrimination contrary to section 6(1) of the Human Rights Act 1974. The Act did not expressly prohibit discrimination on the grounds of pregnancy. However, a new Human Rights Code introduced in 1987 specified that discrimination on the grounds of sex included pregnancy. The adjudicator appointed by the Human Rights Commission dismissed the complaints on the grounds that under the 1974 Act, discrimination on the basis of pregnancy did not constitute discrimination on the grounds of sex. The appellant's appeals to the Manitoba Court of Queen's Bench and the Court of Appeal were unsuccessful, and they appealed to the Supreme Court of Canada.

---

1   Le Dain J took no part in the judgment.

HELD (allowing the appeal)

1   The purpose of anti-discrimination legislation was to remove unfair disadvantages from individuals or groups in society, such as where the major costs of procreation were borne by pregnant women. Those who bear children and benefit society as a whole should not be economically or socially disadvantaged, as was the effect of the employer's plan (p 439).

2   Discrimination on the basis of pregnancy was discrimination on the basis of sex because of the basic biological fact that only women have the capacity to become pregnant. Some states had expressly included pregnancy as a prohibited ground in respect of discrimination because of problems with the restrictive definition of sex. This did not mean that discrimination on the grounds of sex excluded pregnancy-related discrimination (pp 442, 445).

3   Employee benefit plans were increasingly a part of the terms and conditions of employment. Once an employer provided a plan, it had to be applied in a non-discriminatory way. The employer's group insurance plan treated pregnant women significantly less favourably than other employees. It singled out pregnancy for disadvantageous treatment in comparison with any other health reason which might prevent an employee from reporting to work, even if during the stated 17-week period she was affected by a non-pregnancy related disability (p 436).

4   Although pregnancy was not properly characterised as a sickness or accident it was a valid health-related reason for absence from the workplace. Therefore its exclusion from the plan was discriminatory (p 438).

5   The absence of an intention to discriminate was irrelevant. The notion that the plan was not discriminatory but rather just did not include all of the potential risks that it could have was simply a backhanded way of permitting discrimination (pp 439, 440).

National legislation referred to

Canada

Act to Amend the Unemployment Insurance Act 1971 (No 3), SC 1980-81-82-83, c 150, s 4

Canadian Bill of Rights, RSC 1970, App III, s 1(b)

Human Rights Act of Manitoba, SM 1974, c. 65, ss 6(1), 7(2), 10 and 19

Human Rights Code, SM 1987-88, c 45, s 9(2)(f)

Unemployment Insurance Act 1971, SC 1970-71-72, c 48, ss 30 and 46

Unemployment Insurance Regulations, CRC 1978, c 1576, s 19(h)(vii)

USA

Civil Rights Act, 1964, Title VII

Cases referred to

Action Travail des Femmes v Canadian National Railway Company [1987] 1 SCR 1114; (1987) 40 DLR (4th) 193

Andrews v Law Society of BC [1989] 1 SCR 143; (1989) 56 DLR (4th) 1

Bliss v Attorney General of Canada [1979] 1 SCR 183; (1979) 92 DLR (3d) 417

Brossard (Ville) v Quebec (Canadian Human Rights Commission) [1988] 2 SCR 279; (1989) 53 DLR (4th) 609

Canadian National Railway Company v Canada (Canadian Human Rights Commission), 87 CLLC para 17,022; 8 CHRR D/4210

Century Oils (Canada) Inc. v Davies (1988) 47 DLR (4th) 422; 22 BCLR (2d) 358

Geduldig v Aiello, 417 US 484; 41 L Ed 2d 256; 94 SCt 2485 (1974)

General Electric Co v Gilbert, 429 US 125; 50 L Ed 2d 343; 97 S Ct 401 (1976)

Insurance Corp of BC v Heerspink [1982] 2 SCR 145; (1982) 137 DLR (3d) 219

Manitoba Human Rights Commission v Canada Safeway Ltd [1985] 1 SCR x (sic), 31 Man R (2d) 240n

Nashville Gas Co v Satty, 434 US 136; 54 L Ed 2d 356, 98

Re Canada Safeway Ltd and Steel [1985] 1 WWR 479 (Man CA)

Re Manitoba Food & Commercial Workers Union, Local 832 and Canada Safeway Ltd (1981), [1981] 2 SCR 180; (1981) 123 DLR (3d) 512n

Re Ontario Human Rights Commission v Simpson-Sears Ltd [1985] 2 SCR 536; (1985) 23 DLR (4th) 321

Robichaud v Canada (Treasury Board), 87 CLLC para 17,025; 8 CHRR D/4326; 75 NR 303

Robichaud v The Queen [1987] 2 SCR 84; (1988) 40 DLR (4th) 577

JUDGMENT

The judgment of the court was delivered by Dickson CJC

DICKSON CJC: The principal issue to be considered in these appeals is whether a company accident and sickness plan which exempts pregnant women from benefits during a 17-week period discriminates because of sex, as prohibited by the Human Rights Act of Manitoba, SM 1974, c 65.

In March of 1983, Susan Brooks, of Brandon, Manitoba, laid a complaint before the Manitoba Human Rights Commission against her employer, Canada Safeway Ltd. (Safeway), on the ground that Safeway's employee benefit plan contravened s 6(1) of the Human Rights Act of Manitoba. Mrs Brooks said the plan discriminated on the basis of sex and family status in denying certain benefits to pregnant women. At a later date Patricia Allen and Patricia Dixon laid similar complaints. The Attorney-General of Manitoba, the Honourable Roland Penner, QC, appointed JF Reeh Taylor, QC, a Board of Adjudication to hear and decide the three complaints. The adjudicator held against the complainants, as did the Court of Queen's Bench and the Court of Appeal for Manitoba. Leave was granted to appeal to this court.

I   FACTS

Susan Brooks, Patricia Allen and Patricia Dixon were part-time cashiers employed by Safeway. All three became pregnant during 1982. Safeway maintains a group insurance plan that, among other forms of coverage, provides weekly benefits for loss of pay due to accident or sickness. Safeway describes its benefit package to employees in a pamphlet entitled "Group Insurance Benefits For You and Your Dependents" as follows:

> Weekly benefits are payable in event of loss of earnings due to accident or sickness which prevents you from performing any and every duty pertaining to your employment or occupation. You need not be house-confined; however, you must be under the direct care of a physician.

To qualify for coverage under the plan, an employee must have worked for Safeway for three consecutive months. Benefits are payable to a maximum of 26 weeks during any continuous period of disability. Employees receive two-thirds of weekly salary up to a ceiling of $189 per week.

Prior to an amendment on 1 January 1981, pregnancy was exempted from coverage under the plan. At the time each of the appellants became pregnant the plan provided:

> Disability benefits will also be made available for pregnancy related illness. However, disability benefits will not be payable:
>
> a)   during the period commencing with the tenth week prior to the expected week of confinement and ending with the sixth week after the week of confinement;
>
> b)   during any period of formal maternity leave taken by the employee pursuant to provincial or federal law or pursuant to mutual agreement between the employee and the Company, or
>
> c)   during any period for which the employee is paid Unemployment Insurance maternity benefits.

There is no dispute that the Safeway plan treats pregnancy differently from other health-related causes of inability to work. Pregnant employees are excluded from receiving any benefits during what is referred to as the "10-1-6" period, namely, the ten weeks before the anticipated date of birth, the actual birth week, and six weeks after. During this 17-week period, the exemption from coverage is absolute regardless of the reason an employee is unable to report to work. Pregnant women suffering from non-pregnancy related afflictions are ineligible for benefits simply because they are pregnant. Women who are unable to work because of pregnancy-related complications are also not eligible to receive weekly benefits. The mere fact of pregnancy disentitles Safeway's female employees from receiving standard compensation for temporary disability during the "10-1-6" period.

For part of the period during which pregnant women are ineligible to receive disability benefits, some coverage is available under the Unemployment Insurance Act, 1971, SC 1970-71-72, c 48, as amended. At the relevant time s 30 of that Act provided for the payment of weekly benefits for unemployment resulting from pregnancy for a maximum of 15 weeks in the following periods:

> 30(2)   Benefits under this section are payable for each week of unemployment in the period:
>
> (a)   that begins:
>
> (i)   eight weeks before the week in which her confinement is expected, or
>
> (ii)   the week in which her confinement occurs,

whichever is the earlier, and

(b) that ends:

    (i)   seventeen weeks after the week in which her confinement occurs, or

    (ii) fourteen weeks after the first week for which benefits are claimed and payable in any benefit period under this section,

whichever is the earlier,

if such a week of unemployment is one of the first fifteen weeks for which benefits are claimed and payable in her benefit period.

Section 30 was substantially amended in An Act to Amend the Unemployment Insurance Act 1971 (No 3), SC 1980-81-82-83, c 150, s 4.

The maternity benefits available under the Unemployment Insurance Act 1971 did not constitute an exact substitute for the coverage that would be provided by the Safeway plan. Women were only entitled to a maximum of 15 weekly payments under the Unemployment Insurance Act 1971, but were deprived of 17 weeks of benefits under the Safeway plan. For two weeks Safeway employees unable to work by reason of pregnancy were without a source of unemployment benefits. Employees also received less money per week under the Unemployment Insurance Act 1971 provisions than they would have if they were entitled to recover under the Safeway plan. Benefits under the Unemployment Insurance Act 1971 were calculated on the basis of 60% of eligible income. The Safeway plan, in contrast, provided 66% of weekly earnings. The qualifying period for benefits under the Unemployment Insurance Act 1971 was also significantly longer than the qualifying period under the Safeway plan. During the relevant period, s 30(1) of the Unemployment Insurance Act 1971 required a woman to have ten weeks of insurable earnings in the 20-week period immediately preceding the 30th week before the expected date of childbirth, in other words, to have commenced work at least 40 weeks before the anticipated date of birth. The Safeway plan entitled employees to full coverage after only three months of employment.

All three appellants applied for weekly benefits under the Safeway plan for a period of pregnancy-related disability that included the 17-week disentitlement period. All three claims were refused. The appellants applied for, and received, pregnancy benefits under the Unemployment Insurance Act 1971. Each appellant received less money than she would have received had she been eligible under the Safeway plan. We were told, for example, that in the case of Mrs Brooks, Unemployment Insurance provided $133.47 weekly, compared to approximately $188 weekly she might have received under the Safeway plan.

Each of the appellants filed a complaint with the Manitoba Human Rights Commission alleging that the differential treatment of pregnancy in the Safeway plan constituted a discrimination on the basis of sex and on the basis of family status contrary to s 6(1) of the Human Rights Act of Manitoba.

II   LEGISLATION

At the time of the applications, the relevant sections of the Manitoba Human Rights Act provided:

Discrimination prohibited in employment

6(1) Every person has the right of equality of opportunity based upon *bona fide* qualifications in respect of his occupation or employment or in respect of training for employment or in respect of an intended occupation, employment, advancement or promotion, and in respect of his membership or intended membership in a trade union, employers' organization or occupational association; and, without limiting the generality of the foregoing:

(a) no employer or person acting on behalf of an employer, shall refuse to employ, or to continue to employ or to train the person for employment or to advance or to promote that person, or discriminate against that person in respect of employment or any term or condition of employment;

(b) no employment agency shall refuse to refer a person for employment, or for training for employment, and no trade union, employers' organization or occupational association shall refuse membership to, expel, suspend or otherwise discriminate against that person, or negotiate, on behalf of that person, an agreement that would discriminate against him because of race, nationality, religion, colour, sex, age, marital status, physical or mental handicap, ethnic or national origin, or political beliefs or family status of that person.

Exception

7(2) No provision of section 6 or subsection (1) shall prohibit a distinction on the basis of age, sex, family status, physical or mental handicap or marital status:

(a) of any employee benefit plan or in any contract which provides an employee benefit plan, if the Commission is satisfied on the basis of the guidelines set out in the regulations that the distinction is not discriminatory or that the employee benefit can be provided only if the distinction is permitted;

In 1987 the Manitoba Human Rights Act was repealed and replaced by the Human Rights Code, SM 1987-88, c 45 (CCSM, c H175). Section 6 of the former Act was replaced by s 9(2) which prohibits discrimination on a number of grounds including:

(f) sex, including pregnancy, the possibility of pregnancy, or circumstances related to pregnancy.

III   THE HUMAN RIGHTS TRIBUNAL

1   The complaint of Susan Brooks

The complaint of Mrs Brooks was heard before the complaints of the other two appellants (1984) 6 CHRR D/2560. Adjudicator Taylor concluded that the complaint of Mrs Brooks had been filed out of time. Section 19 of the Human Rights Act required a complaint to be filed with the commission "not later than 6 months after the date of the alleged contravention or, where a continuing contravention is alleged, after the date of the last alleged contravention". Mrs Brooks filed her complaint on 22 March 1983. The adjudicator found that the contravention, if any, occurred at the beginning of the disentitlement period, on or about 30 August 1982, when Safeway notified Mrs Brooks that she was denied benefits. Adjudicator Taylor did not regard Safeway's refusal to pay benefits throughout the 17-week period as a continuing contravention within the meaning of the statute.

In anticipation of the two other complaints, and in the event he had erred in holding the complaint by Mrs Brooks to be out of time, Adjudicator Taylor dealt with the merits of Mrs Brooks' complaint. He considered first the question whether the Safeway plan did in fact discriminate against pregnant employees. The adjudicator made the following remarks (at p D/2562):

It is a simple fact, undisputed by the Respondent, that the treatment accorded a pregnant employee under the Canada Safeway Limited accident and sickness plan is markedly different from that accorded any other employee. Indeed, it is not merely pregnancy-related problems that are not covered under the plan during the seventeen-week period referred to above; any accident or sickness, whether pregnancy-related or not, occurring during the same seventeen weeks is excluded from the Canada Safeway Limited plan, and the pregnant employee must, during that limited time, rely upon benefits obtainable from the Unemployment Insurance Commission. Even if she qualified to receive UIC benefits during the entire seventeen weeks, the pregnant employee will receive a lesser amount during that period than would a non-pregnant employee who was away from work by reason of some other physical disability.

Adjudicator Taylor had no difficulty in concluding that Safeway's plan, "while by all accounts a generous one, does in fact discriminate against pregnant employees".

Having established the existence of pregnancy-based discrimination, the adjudicator then focussed his attention on the question whether to discriminate against someone because of her pregnancy is to discriminate against her "because of (her) sex or family status". He was of the view that the concept of family status was inapplicable to pregnancy since in his view an unborn child is not yet a member of a "family" and therefore could not be considered as part of a complaint of discrimination because of family status.

Adjudicator Taylor then rejected the argument that discrimination on the basis of pregnancy is discrimination on the basis of sex. He relied on the decision of this court in *Bliss v Attorney General of Canada* [1979] 1 SCR 183. In *Bliss*, the court held that s 46 of the Unemployment Insurance Act 1971, which disentitled pregnant women from receiving basic unemployment benefits, restricting them to special maternity benefits during a portion of their pregnancy, did not deny women the right to equality free from discrimination on the basis of sex, guaranteed by s 1(b) of the Canadian Bill of Rights, RSC 1970, App III. Adjudicator Taylor noted that *Bliss* had been followed across the country and that courts in England and in the United States had also concluded that discrimination on the basis of pregnancy did not amount to sex discrimination. He observed that after the Supreme Court of the United States of America had held in *Geduldig v Aiello*, 417 US 484 (1974); *General Electric Co v Gilbert*, 429 US 125 (1976), and *Nashville Gas Co. v. Satty*, 434 US 136 (1977), that discrimination by reason of pregnancy was not synonymous with discrimination by reason of sex, the Congress of the United States enacted a bill amending Title VII of the Civil Rights Act of 1964 so as to include, within the meaning of discrimination on the basis of sex, discrimination based upon pregnancy, childbirth or related medical conditions. The adjudicator also pointed to the fact that some provinces had amended their human rights legislation in the wake of *Bliss* to add pregnancy as a prohibited ground of discrimination. Adjudicator Taylor interpreted these amendments as recognition that sex discrimination does not include discrimination on the basis of pregnancy. Absent a broadened definition, the adjudicator concluded he was bound by *Bliss* to hold that discrimination on the basis of pregnancy was not sex discrimination.

2   The complaints of Patricial Allen and Patricia Dixon

The complaints of the appellants Mrs Allen and Mrs Dixon were heard by Adjudicator Taylor one month after the decision in Mrs Brooks' complaint. For the reasons given in Brooks, the adjudicator held that the appellants had not suffered discrimination on the basis of sex or family status contrary to s 6(1) of the Manitoba Human Rights Act, 6 CHRR D/2840.

IV   THE MANITOBA COURT OF QUEEN'S BENCH

Mrs Brooks, Mrs Allen, Mrs Dixon and the Human Rights Commission of Manitoba appealed the decisions of Adjudicator Taylor. Simonsen J delivered brief reasons: 38 Man R (2d) 192, 86 CLLC para 17,010, 7 CHRR D/3185. He began by rejecting the adjudicator's conclusion that the complaint of Mrs Brooks was out of time. In Simonsen J's view, the refusal to pay benefits for 17 weeks amounted to continuing discrimination. There was nothing in the Manitoba Human Rights Act requiring the limitation period to commence during the first week for which benefits could have been claimed. Simonsen J took the view that the alleged 17 weeks of discrimination commenced on 21 August 1982 and ended on 22 December 1982, and that the limitation period would begin to run on the later date. Mrs Brooks' complaint, filed on 22 March 1983, was therefore timely, that is, within the six-month limitation period.

Simonsen J agreed with the adjudicator's finding, as well as his reasoning, that the Safeway plan discriminated against pregnant employees. He said [at p 195]:

> It must be recognized ... that no benefits were payable for accident or sickness to a pregnant employee during the 17 week exclusion period whether related to pregnancy or not. Coverage under the policy for a pregnant employee was suspended for 17 weeks.

He continued:

> Was it discrimination to have a group policy which suspended coverage to a pregnant employee for the 17 week period during which some alternate coverage in the form of unemployment insurance was available? There was no obligation on the pregnant employee to take leave for the 17 week period but when leave was taken unemployment insurance was the only option available.

The learned adjudicator found discrimination. I agree with his reasoning and conclusions.

Simonsen J then considered whether discrimination on the basis of pregnancy was prohibited by the Manitoba Human Rights Act. He agreed with the adjudicator's conclusion that pregnancy was not encompassed in "family status" and held that the Safeway plan could not be faulted for discriminating on the basis of family status. Simonsen J was also of the view, largely on the authority of *Bliss* and cases subsequent to that decision, that the adjudicator was correct in finding that discrimination on the basis of pregnancy was not included in the phrase "discrimination by reason of sex". In the absence of an expanded statutory definition of sex, Simonsen J felt he could reach no other conclusion.

V   THE COURT OF APPEAL OF MANITOBA

In the very brief reasons, the Manitoba Court of Appeal (O'Sullivan, Huband and Twaddle JJ A) unanimously dismissed the appeal: 42 Man R (2d) 27, 7 CHRR D/3475. The decision of the Manitoba Court of Appeal may be set out in full:

> The facts are amply canvassed by Simonsen, J, with whose reasons we substantially agree, but we go further and say we are not satisfied that in the context of this case there was any discrimination at all.
>
> It may be noted that the disability plan in question is only part of a health benefit package agreed to between employer and union. One questions why complaint was not made against the union as well as against the company.
>
> The appeal is dismissed with costs.

VI   ISSUES AND INTERVENTIONS

The appellants appealed the decision of the Manitoba Court of Appeal on the following issues:

1   Did the Court of Appeal for Manitoba err in concluding that the disability plan offered by the respondent to its employees was not discriminatory?

2   Did the Court of Appeal for Manitoba err in law in adopting the conclusion of the learned judge and adjudicator below that discrimination due to "pregnancy" does not constitute discrimination because of "sex", as prohibited by the Manitoba Human Rights Act ?

3   Did the Court of Appeal for Manitoba err in law in adopting the conclusion of the learned judge and adjudicator below that discrimination due to "pregnancy" did not constitute discrimination on "family status", as set out in the Manitoba Human Rights Act ?

The question of the timeliness of Mrs Brooks' complaint was not raised before this court.

The Women's Legal Education and Action Fund (LEAF) intervened in support of the appellants' position.

VII   WAS THE DISABILITY PLAN DISCRIMINATORY ?

What does discrimination mean? The most recent pronouncement on this point will be found in the judgment of my colleague, McIntyre J in *Andrews v Law Society of BC* [1989] 1 SCR 143 at 173-75:

> What does discrimination mean? The question has arisen most commonly in a consideration of the Human Rights Acts and the general concept of discrimination under those enactments has been fairly well settled. There is little difficulty, drawing upon the cases in this court, in isolating an acceptable definition. In *Re Ontario Human Rights Commission and Simpsons-Sears Ltd* [1985] 2 SCR 536, at p 551, discrimination (in that case adverse effect discrimination) was described in these terms:
>
> > "It arises where an employer ... adopts a rule or standard ... which has a discriminatory effect upon a prohibited ground on one employee or group of employees in that it imposes, because of some special characteristic of the employee or group, obligations, penalties, or restrictive conditions not imposed on other members of the work force."
>
> It was held in that case, as well, that no intent was required as an element of discrimination, for it is in essence the impact of the discriminatory act or provision upon the person affected which is decisive in considering any complaint. At p 547 this proposition was expressed in these terms:
>
> > "The Code aims at the removal of discrimination. This is to state the obvious. Its main approach, however, is not to punish the discriminator, but rather to provide relief for the victims of discrimination. It is the result or the effect of the action complained of which is significant. If it does, in fact, cause discrimination; if its effect is to impose on one person or group of persons obligations, penalties, or restrictive conditions not imposed on other members of the community, it is discriminatory."
>
> In *Canadian National Railway Co v Canada* [1987] 1 SCR 114, better known as the *Action Travail des Femmes* case, where it was alleged that the Canadian National Railway was guilty of discriminatory hiring and promotion practices contrary to s 10 of the Canadian Human Rights Act, SC 1976-77, c 33, in denying employment to women in certain unskilled positions, Dickson CJC, in giving the judgment of the court, said at pp 1138-9:

"A thorough study of "systemic discrimination" in Canada is to be found in the Abella Report on equality in employment. The terms of reference of the Royal Commission instructed it "to inquire into the most efficient, effective and equitable means of promoting employment opportunities, eliminating systemic discrimination and assisting individuals to compete for employment opportunities on an equal basis". (Order in Council, PC 1983-1924, 24 June 1983). Although Judge Abella chose not to offer a precise definition of systemic discrimination, the essentials may be gleaned from the following comments, found at p 2 of the Abella Report:

'Discrimination ... means practices or attitudes that have, whether by design or impact, the effect of limiting an individual's or a group's right to the opportunities generally available because of attributed rather than actual characteristics.

It is not a question of whether this discrimination is motivated by an intentional desire to obstruct someone's potential, or whether it is the accidental by-product of innocently motivated practices or systems. If the barrier is affecting certain groups in a disproportionately negative way, it is a signal that the practices that lead to this adverse impact may be discriminatory.'"

There are many other statements which have aimed at a short definition of the term discrimination. In general, they are in accord with the statements referred to above. I would say then that discrimination may be described as a distinction, whether intentional or not but based on grounds relating to personal characteristics of the individual or group, which has the effect of imposing burdens, obligations, or disadvantages on such individual or group not imposed upon others, or which withholds or limits access to opportunities, benefits, and advantages available to other members of society. Distinctions based on personal characteristics attributed to an individual solely on the basis of association with a group will rarely escape the charge of discrimination, while those based on an individual's merits and capacities will rarely be so classed.

The first issue in these appeals is whether the complete disentitlement of pregnant women during a 17-week period from receiving disability benefits under the Safeway plan constitutes discrimination by reason of pregnancy. In my view, this ground of appeal may be addressed briefly. I have no difficulty in concluding that the Safeway sickness and accident plan discriminates against pregnant women.

As I have indicated, Adjudicator Taylor found the treatment accorded a pregnant employee (at p D/2562):

... markedly different from that accorded to any other employee. Indeed, it is not merely pregnancy-related problems that are not covered under the plan during the seventeen week period ... any accident or sickness, whether pregnancy related or not, occurring during that same seventeen weeks is excluded ...

He also observed that even if the employee qualifies for maternity benefits from the Unemployment Insurance Commission, the pregnant employee would receive (at p D/2562):

a lesser amount during that period than would a non-pregnant employee who was away from work by reason of some other physical disability.

Simonsen J shared the view that the plan discriminated against pregnant women.

The Court of Appeal for Manitoba was not satisfied that in the context of the case there was any discrimination at all. Apart from noting that the disability plan in question was only part of a health benefit package agreed to between employer and union, the court gave no reason for finding an absence of discrimination.

In my view, it is beyond dispute that pregnant employees receive significantly less favourable treatment under the Safety plan than other employees. For a 17-week period, pregnant women are not entitled to any compensation under the plan, regardless of the reason they are unable to work. During those 17 weeks, even if a pregnant woman suffers from an ailment totally unrelated to pregnancy, she is ineligible for benefits simply because she is pregnant. The plan singles out pregnancy for disadvantageous treatment, in comparison with any other health reason which may prevent an employee from reporting to work. With the sole exception of pregnancy, eligibility for compensation under the plan is available on broad and general terms. It is indeed generous, save in respect of pregnant women. For any single continuous period during which an employee is incapable of performing at work for health reasons, 26 weeks of benefits are available. Employees may recover under the plan without being house-confined. No restrictions are placed on disability, with the solitary exception of pregnancy. It is difficult to conclude otherwise than that, as a result of the unfavourable treatment accorded to pregnancy *vis-à-vis* all other medical conditions, the Safeway plan discriminates on the basis of pregnancy.

Counsel for Safeway advanced a number of arguments in support of the proposition that the disability plan does not discriminate by reason of pregnancy. The submissions can be grouped into five main headings. First, it was argued that pregnancy is neither "a sickness [n]or an accident" and, therefore, it need not be covered by a sickness and accident plan; second, that pregnancy is a voluntary state and, like other forms of voluntary leave, it should not be compensated; third, the plan could not be discriminatory because there was no intention to discriminate; fourth, the plan was not discriminatory but was underinclusive in that it exempted certain disabilities from coverage; finally, on the basis of a rather novel interpretation of the relationship between regulations under the Unemployment Insurance Act 1971 and the Manitoba Human Rights Act it was claimed that the Human Rights Act implicitly permits employee benefit plans to exclude compensation for pregnancy. In my view, none of these arguments can assist Safeway in escaping the conclusion that its sickness and accident plan discriminates on the basis of pregnancy.

The first two claims, that pregnancy is neither an accident nor an illness and that it is voluntary, are closely related. I agree entirely that pregnancy is not characterized properly as a sickness or an accident. It is, however, a valid health-related reason for absence from the workplace and as such should not have been excluded from the Safeway plan. That the exclusion is discriminatory is evident when the true character, or underlying rationale, of the Safeway benefits plan is appreciated. The underlying rationale of this plan is the laudable desire to compensate persons who are unable to work for valid health-related reasons. Pregnancy is clearly such a reason. By distinguishing "accidents and illness" from pregnancy, Safeway is attempting to disguised an untenable distinction. It seems indisputable that in our society pregnancy is a valid health-related reason for being absent from work. It is to state the obvious to say that pregnancy is of fundamental importance in our society. Indeed, its importance makes description difficult. To equate pregnancy with, for instance, a decision to undergo medical treatment for cosmetic surgery – which sort of comparison the respondent's argument implicitly makes – is fallacious. If the medical condition associated with procreation does not provide a legitimate reason for absence from the workplace, it is hard to imagine what would provide such a reason. Viewed in its social context, pregnancy provides a perfectly legitimate health-related reason for not working and as such it should be compensated by the Safeway plan. In terms of the economic consequences to the employee resulting from the inability to perform employment duties, pregnancy is no different from any other health-related reason for absence from the workplace. Furthermore, to not view pregnancy in this way goes against one of the purposes of anti-discrimination legislation. This purpose, which was noted earlier in the quotation from *Andrews, supra,* is the removal of unfair disadvantages which have been imposed on individuals or groups in society. Such an unfair disadvantage may result when the costs of an activity from which all of society benefits are placed upon a single group of persons. This is the effect of the Safeway plan. It cannot be disputed that everyone in society benefits from procreation. The Safeway plan, however, places one of the major costs of procreation entirely upon one group in society: pregnant women. Thus, in distinguishing pregnancy from all other health-related reasons for not working, the plan imposes unfair disadvantages on pregnant women. In the second part of this judgment I state that this disadvantage can be viewed as a disadvantage suffered by women generally. That argument further emphasizes how a refusal to find the Safeway plan discriminatory would undermine one of the purposes of anti-discrimination legislation. It would do so by sanctioning one of the most significant ways in which women have been disadvantaged in our society. It would sanction imposing a disproportionate amount of the costs of pregnancy upon women. Removal of such unfair impositions upon women and other groups in society is a key purpose of anti-discrimination legislation. Finding that the Safeway plan is discriminatory furthers this purpose.

In sum, if an employer such as Safeway enters into the field of compensation for health conditions and then excludes pregnancy as a valid reason for compensation, the employer has acted in a discriminatory fashion. In view of this finding, it should be noted that the Safeway plan would be considered discriminatory even if it did not exclude coverage for non-pregnancy related illness and accidents. It is enough that the plan excludes compensation for pregnancy. That it makes a further exclusion for non-pregnancy related conditions compounds the discrimination and highlights how the plan's designers viewed pregnancy.

It is also noteworthy that the plan by its own terms, does not exclude pregnancy-related absence from compensation for the major part of the nine months of pregnancy. Although a normal pregnancy is somewhat less than 40 weeks in duration, pregnant women, under the plan, are not disentitled until ten weeks before the anticipated week of child birth. During the first 29 weeks of pregnancy, Safeway does not refuse to compensate pregnant employees on the ground that pregnancy is neither an accident nor an illness. It is not compelling to argue that pregnancy is not compensated after 29 weeks because it is a voluntary condition, when, to that point, pregnancy has been compensated under the sickness and disability plan.

The third argument, that the plan cannot be discriminatory because the respondent had no intention to discriminate, has little or no force in light of the decision of this court in *Re Ontario Human Rights Commission and O'Malley v Simpsons-Sears Ltd* [1985] 2 SCR 536. In that case, the court held that the effect of an impugned practice, not the underlying intent, was the governing factor in determining whether the practice gave rise to discrimination. Intent to discriminate is not a necessary element of discrimination.

The fourth argument is that the plan is not discriminatory but merely under-inclusive of the potential risks it could conceivably insure. Safeway alleges that the decision to exclude pregnancy from the scope of its plan is not a question of discrimination, but a question of deciding to compensate some risks and to exclude others. It seeks support for this argument from two American cases in which the Supreme Court of the United States held that the exclusion of pregnancy from compensation schemes did not constitute discrimination on the basis of sex. In *Geduldig v Aiello, supra*, the court held that a disability insurance system which did not provide compensation for pregnancy did not violate the equal protection clause of the Fourteenth Amendment. Two years later, in *General Electric Co v Gilbert, supra*, the court affirmed this conclusion in the context of Title VII of the Civil Rights Act of 1964. In both cases the court held the group insurance plans to be under-inclusive of the risks they chose to insure but held that under-inclusiveness did not necessarily amount to discrimination.

In my view, the reasoning in those two cases does not fit well within the Canadian approach to issues of discrimination. In both *General Electric* and *Geduldig* the United States Supreme Court held that distinctions involving pregnancy were constitutionally permissible if made on a reasonable basis, unless the distinctions were designed to effect invidious discrimination against members of one sex or another. In Canada, as I have noted, discrimination does not depend on a finding of invidious intent. A further consideration militating against the application of the concept of under-inclusiveness in this context stems, in my view, from the effects of so-called "under-inclusion". Under-inclusion may be simply a backhanded way of permitting discrimination. Increasingly, employee benefits plans have become part of the terms and conditions of employment. Once an employer decides to provide an employee benefit package, exclusions from such schemes may not be made in a discriminatory fashion. Selective compensation of this nature would clearly amount to sex discrimination. Benefits available through employment must be disbursed in a non-discriminatory manner.

Safeway's fifth argument derives from a creative interpretation of s 7(2) of the Manitoba Human Rights Act. Section 7(2)(a) provides for exceptions to the general prohibition of discrimination embodied in s 6 of the Act. The section explicitly permits employee benefits plans to draw distinctions on the basis of age, sex, marital status, physical or mental handicap, or family status where "the Commission is satisfied on the basis of the guidelines set out in the regulations that the distinction is not discriminatory or that the employee benefit can be provided only if the distinction is permitted ...". No regulations were ever prescribed pursuant to this section. Safeway attempts to "read in" regulations by pointing to regulations passed under the Unemployment Insurance Act 1971 dealing with employer-provided wage loss plans. Section 19(h)(vii) of the Unemployment Insurance Regulations, CRC 1978, c 1576, specifically discusses employer plans which do not compensate pregnant women during the 17-week "10-1-6" period. The presence of this regulation, the respondent asserts, indicates that exceptions of this nature must have been envisioned by the drafters of the Human Rights Act as constituting a permissible distinction pursuant to s 7(2).

I cannot agree with the respondent's interpretation. The Manitoba legislature clearly considered the issue of discrimination in benefits plans. Distinction along sex lines might have been permissible in employee benefit plans, had regulations been passed pursuant to s 7(2). The only conclusion to be reached from the absence of regulations under that provision is that discrimination in employee benefit packages is not permissible. It is not correct to attribute regulations to the Human Rights Act where no regulations have been passed under that Act.

For the foregoing reasons, I am of the view that the respondent's accident and sickness plan discriminates on the basis of pregnancy.

VIII IS DISCRIMINATION ON THE BASIS OF PREGNANCY SEX DISCRIMINATION?

Having found that the Safeway plan discriminates by reason of pregnancy, it is necessary to consider whether pregnancy-based discrimination is discrimination on the basis of sex. I venture to think that the response to that question by a non-legal person would be immediate and affirmative. In retrospect, one can only ask - how could pregnancy discrimination be anything other than sex discrimination? The disfavoured treatment accorded Mrs Brooks, Mrs Allen and Mrs Dixon flowed entirely from their state of pregnancy, a condition unique to women. They were pregnant because of their sex. Discrimination on the basis of pregnancy is a form of sex. Discrimination because of the basic biological fact that only women have the capacity to become pregnant.

As I have noted, the respondent relies primarily on the decision of this court in *Bliss v Attorney General of Canada*, *supra*, to argue that discrimination by reason of pregnancy is not discrimination on the basis of sex. In *Bliss*, the court was asked to decide whether s 46 of the Unemployment Insurance Act 1971, which restricted the eligibility of pregnant women to unemployment benefits, constituted sex discrimination contrary to s 1(b) of the Canadian Bill of Rights RSC 1970, App III. Section 1(b) provides that each individual is entitled to "equality before the law" without discrimination due to, amongst other things, sex. The court held that the complainant had not been deprived of the right to equality before the law. Section 30 of the Unemployment Insurance Act 1971 provided pregnancy benefits for the 15-week period commencing eight weeks before the anticipated date of childbirth. Section 46 limited the eligibility of pregnant women who were unable to work during this 15-week period to benefits under s 30. The qualifying conditions for benefits under s 30 were more onerous than those for other types of unemployment benefits. To receive benefits under s 30, a woman had to have accumulated ten or more weeks of insurable earnings in the 20 weeks immediately preceding the expected date of birth. Basic employment insurance benefits merely required eight weeks of insurable employment in the relevant qualifying period. Ritchie J, speaking for the court, acknowledged that the effect of ss 30 and 46 of the Act was to impose conditions on women from which men were excluded, but stated that "any inequality between the sexes in this area is not created by legislation but by nature". He continued by quoting with approval the following *obiter* passage from the reasons of Pratte J in the Federal Court of Appeal (at 190-91):

> The question to be determined in this case is, therefore, not whether the respondent had been the victim of discrimination by reason of sex but whether she has been deprived of "the right to equality before the law" declared by s 1(b) of the Canadian Bill of Rights. Having said this, I wish to add that I cannot share the view held by the umpire that the application of s 46 to the respondent constituted discrimination against her by reason of sex. Assuming the respondent to have been "discriminated against", it would not have been by reason of her sex. Section 46 applies to women, it has no application to women who are not pregnant, and it has no application, of course, to men. If s 46 treats unemployed pregnant women differently from other unemployed persons, be they male or female, it is, it seems to me, because they are pregnant and not because they are women.

On this reasoning, pregnancy discrimination was held not to be discrimination on the basis of sex.

Over ten years have elapsed since the decision in *Bliss*. During that time there have been profound changes in women's labour force participation. With the benefit of a decade of hindsight and ten years of experience with claims of human rights discrimination and jurisprudence arising therefrom, I am prepared to say that *Bliss* was wrongly decided or, in any event, that *Bliss* would not be decided now as it was decided then. Combining paid work with motherhood and accommodating the childbearing needs of working women are ever-increasing imperatives. That those who bear children and benefit society as a whole thereby should not be economically or socially disadvantaged seems to bespeak the obvious. It is only women who bear children; no man can become pregnant. As I argued earlier, it is unfair to impose all of the costs of pregnancy upon one-half of the population. It is difficult to conceive that distinctions or discriminations based upon pregnancy could ever be regarded as other than discrimination based upon sex, or that restrictive statutory conditions applicable only to pregnant women did not discriminate against them as women. It is difficult to accept that the inequality to which Stella Bliss was subject was created by nature and therefore there was no discrimination; the better view, I now venture to think, is that the inequality was created by legislation, more particularly, the Unemployment Insurance Act 1971. The capacity to become pregnant is unique to the female gender. As the appellants state in their factum:

> The capacity for pregnancy is an immutable characteristic, or incident of gender and a central distinguishing feature between men and women. A distinction based on pregnancy is not merely a distinction between those who are and are not pregnant, but also between the gender that has the capacity for pregnancy and the gender which does not.

Distinctions based on pregnancy can be nothing other than distinctions based on sex or, at least, strongly, "sex related". The Safeway plan was no doubt developed, as Brennan J noted in the *General Electric* case, at pp 149-50, "in an earlier era when women openly were presumed to play a minor and temporary role in the labor force".

The decision of this court in *Brossard (Town) v Quebec (Commission des droits de la personne)* [1988] 2 SCR 279 augured the demise of *Bliss*. Writing for the court, Beetz J. said, at p 301:

> For present purposes I note simply that the improbable distinction in *Bliss* between discrimination based on sex and discrimination based on pregnancy has been called into question and, even if it were to stand, the case might not be decided in the same manner today given this court's recent recognition of adverse effect discrimination in *Ontario Human Rights Commission and O'Malley v Simpsons-Sears Ltd* [1985] 2 SCR 536.

The approach to interpreting human rights legislation taken in *Bliss* is inconsistent with that enunciated by this court in a number of decisions since *Bliss*. I refer, for example, to *Re Ontario Human Rights Commission and Simpsons-Sears Ltd, supra; Canadian National Railway Co v Canada (Canadian Human Rights Commission)* [1987] 1 SCR 1114 and *Insurance Corp of BC v Heerspink* [1982] 2 SCR 145. La Forest J summed up the thrust of these more recent cases in *Robichaud v The Queen* [1987] 2 SCR 84, at pp 89-90:

> The purpose of the Act is set forth in s 2 as being to extend the laws of Canada to give effect to the principle that every individual should have an equal opportunity with other individuals to live his or her own life without being hindered by discriminatory practices based on certain prohibited grounds of discrimination, including discrimination on the ground of sex. As McIntyre J, speaking for this court, recently explained in *Re Ontario Human Rights Commission and O'Malley v Simpsons-Sears Ltd* [1985] 2 SCR 536 the Act must be so interpreted as to advance the broad policy considerations underlying it. That task should not be approached in a niggardly fashion but in a manner befitting the special nature of the legislation, which he described as "not quite constitutional"; see also *Insurance Corporation of British Columbia v Heerspink* [1982] 2 SCR 145 per Lamer J, at pp 157-8. By this expression, it is not suggested, of course, that the Act is somehow entrenched but rather that it incorporates certain basic goals of our society. More recently still, Dickson CJ in the *Action Travail des Femmes* case [1987] 1 SCR 1114 emphasized that the rights

enunciated in the Act must be given full recognition and effect consistent with the dictates of the Interpretation Act, RSC 1970, c I-23, that statutes must be given such fair, large and liberal interpretation as will best ensure the attainment of their objects.

In the case mentioned earlier, *Andrews v Law Society of British Columbia*, McIntyre J rejected a "similarly situated" test in an equality rights challenge under the Canadian Charter of Rights and Freedoms. *Bliss* was not a Charter case, nor is the case at bar, but the comment of McIntyre J respecting *Bliss* is of surpassing interest. He stated (at pp 12-3):

> Thus, mere equality of application to similarly situated groups or individuals does not afford a realistic test for violation of equality rights. For, as has been said, a bad law will not be saved merely because it operates equally upon those to whom it has application. Nor will a law necessarily be bad because it makes distinctions.
>
> A similarly situated test focussing on the equal application of the law to those to whom it has application could lead to results akin to those in *Bliss v Attorney General of Canada* [1979] 1 SCR 183. In *Bliss*, a pregnant woman was denied unemployment benefits to which she would have been entitled had she not been pregnant. She claimed that the Unemployment Insurance Act violated the equality guarantees of the Canadian Bill of Rights because it discriminated against her on the basis of her sex. Her claim was dismissed by this court on the grounds that there was no discrimination on the basis of sex, since the class into which she fell under the Act was that of pregnant persons, and within that class, all persons were treated equally.

Professor Peter Hogg in *Constitutional Law of Canada* (2nd ed 1985), speaking of the *Bliss* case, commented at p 791:

> Ritchie J, who wrote the unanimous opinion of the Court, denied that the discrimination in the Act was based on sex. He quoted with approval a dictum in the lower court to the effect that the disadvantaged class was defined by pregnancy rather than by sex, and Ritchie J concluded that "any inequality between the sexes in this area is not created by legislation but by nature". This part of the reasoning is open to criticism. Bliss was not claiming the special maternity benefits, for which a longer period of qualification might well have been justifiable. She was claiming the regular benefits, to which she would have been entitled if her employment had been interrupted by layoff, illness or any cause other than pregnancy. The denial of benefits was the result of her pregnancy. Since pregnancy is a condition to which only women are vulnerable, the denial should have been characterized as sexual discrimination. It is true that the Act did not discriminate against all women, only pregnant women, but discrimination against some women should not be treated any differently than discrimination against all women.

I am not persuaded by the argument that discrimination on the basis of pregnancy cannot amount to sex discrimination because not all women are pregnant at any one time. While pregnancy-based discrimination only affects parts of an identifiable group, it does not affect anyone who is not a member of the group. Many, if not most, claims of partial discrimination fit this pattern. As numerous decisions and authors have made clear, this fact does not make the impugned distinction any less discriminating. David Pannick, Barrister and Fellow of All Souls College, Oxford, observed in his work *Sex Discrimination Law* (Clarendon Press, Oxford, 1985), at pp 147-8, that:

> The EAT [Employment Appeals Tribunal] was, however, correct to assume that the less favourable treatment (if any) of the pregnant woman was on the ground of her sex. Because only women can become pregnant, the complainant who is dismissed because she is pregnant can argue that she would not have been less favourably treated but for her sex. It requires a very narrow construction of the statute to exclude less favourable treatment on the ground of a characteristic unique to one sex. It is quite true that not all women are (or become) pregnant. But it is important to note that direct discrimination exists not

merely where the defendant applies a criterion that less favourably treats all women. It also exists where special, less favourable, treatment is accorded to a class consisting only of women, albeit not all women. Suppose an employer announces that it will employ any man with stated qualifications but only a woman who has those qualifications and who is over six feet tall. Albeit not all women are excluded, the employer has directly discriminated against women because it has imposed a criterion which less favourably treats a class composed entirely of women.

I would make note also of the article "Sex Discrimination in Canada: Taking Stock at the Start of a New Decade" (1980), 1 CHRR c/7, at p c/11, by Professor James MacPherson:

In *Bliss v Attorney-General (Canada)* provisions of the federal Unemployment Insurance Act which treated pregnant women more harshly than all other applicants for unemployment insurance were held not to constitute sex discrimination. "Any inequality between the sexes in this area", wrote Mr. Justice Ritchie for a unanimous Court, "is not created by legislation but by nature".

The argument that can be advanced in support of this conclusion is that the unemployment insurance legislation treats all women, except pregnant women, on an equal footing with men with respect to eligibility for benefits, and that the differentiation based on pregnancy works against women not *qua* women, but rather on the basis of a physical condition. It follows, the argument runs, that the differentiation in the legislation is between two classes of women, not between women and men.

In my view, this argument is not valid. The fact that discrimination is only partial does not convert it into non-discrimination. For example, federal legislation that treated some, but not all, Indians more harshly than whites would be discriminatory. Equally, an employer's decision not to hire a particular black solely because of his blackness would run afoul of provincial human rights legislation even though the employer hired other blacks. Legislation or the practice of individuals cannot be saved because they work only a partial discrimination. The legislation in *Bliss* works such a partial discrimination. Although most women are treated equally with men, a certain class, namely those women who are pregnant, are treated more harshly because they are pregnant. Since pregnancy is a condition unique to women, the legislation denies these women their equality before the law. By not recognizing this, and by concluding that differentiation on the basis of pregnancy is not sex-related, the Supreme Court of Canada has decided not to strike against one of the most long-standing and serious obstacles facing women in Canada, namely legislation and employer practices directed against pregnant women.

Reference might also be made to the judgment of Oppal J of the Supreme Court of British Columbia in *Century Oils (Canada) Inc v Davies*, 22 BCLR (2d) 358 delivered 28 January 1988, in which the following appears (at p 364-365):

It may be unduly restrictive and somewhat artificial to argue that a distinction based on a characteristic such as pregnancy, which is shared only by some members of a group, is not discrimination against the whole group. It is no answer to say that, since pregnancy discrimination is not usually applicable to all women, it is not discrimination on the basis of sex, for discrimination which is aimed at or has its effect upon some people in a particular group as opposed to the whole of that group, is not any the less discriminatory. This point was made by a board of inquiry under the former Human Rights Code, RSBC 1979, c. 186, in the case of *Zarankin v Johnstone* (1984), 5 CHRR D/2274 at p D/2276, wherein the board stated:

"... an employer who selects only some of his female employees for sexual harassment and leaves other female employees alone is discriminating by reason of sex because the harassment affects only one group adversely."

It cannot be said that discrimination is not proven unless all members of a particular class are equally affected. The interpretation of sex discrimination which is suggested by the petitioner is unduly restrictive and probably runs contrary to contemporary societal expectations.

Finally, on this point, the respondent referred to *Re Manitoba Food & Commercial Workers Union, Local 832 and Canada Safeway Ltd* [1981] 2 SCR 180, in which this court restored an arbitration award which found Safeway's "no beards" rule to be a "reasonable" rule. Safeway argues that, by analogy, this court has already found that discrimination because of pregnancy is not discrimination because of sex. Reference was also made to *Manitoba Human Rights Commission v Canada Safeway Ltd* [1985] 1 SCR x (sic), in which a panel of this court dismissed the Human Rights Commission's application for leave to appeal the decision that Safeway's "no beards" rule was not discrimination because of sex. The Manitoba Court of Appeal in a unanimous decision stated that the "no beards" rule was "definitely not a matter of sexual discrimination" (*sub nom Re Canada Safeway Ltd and Steel* [1985] 1 WWR 479, 480). It is contended that there is an analogy between that case and the present situation; beards are peculiar to men as pregnancy is peculiar to women; however, not all men grow beards and not all women become pregnant. I do not find these cases helpful; I cannot find any useful analogy between a company rule denying men the right to wear beards and an accident and sickness insurance plan which discriminates against female employees who become pregnant. The attempt to draw an analogy at best trivializes the procreative and socially vital function of women and seeks to elevate the growing of facial hair to a constitutional right.

I am also not persuaded by the respondent's argument that legislative amendments to preclude pregnancy-based discrimination in the aftermath of *Bliss* indicate that the term "sex discrimination" does not include pregnancy. One cannot conclude from the fact that some provinces have added pregnancy as an express prohibited ground of discrimination in light of a restrictive definition of sex, that discrimination on the basis of sex does not encompass pregnancy based discrimination.

IX   DISCRIMINATION ON THE BASIS OF FAMILY STATUS

In addition to arguing that discrimination based on pregnancy is sex discrimination, the appellants allege that it is discrimination by reason of family status. As I have already found pregnancy discrimination to violate the prohibition on sex discrimination in the Manitoba Human Rights Act, it is not necessary to consider this issue and I refrain from doing so at this time.

X   DISPOSITION

I am of the view that the respondent's accident and sickness plan discriminates on the basis of sex by excluding compensation for pregnant women during a 17-week period. I would therefore allow these appeals, and set aside the judgment of the Court of Appeal for Manitoba, with costs of the proceedings before the Manitoba courts and this court. I would remit the complaints of the appellants to the adjudicator for determination of the appropriate remedy pursuant to the Manitoba Human Rights Act.

Appeals allowed.

CASE NO 28

ABDOULAYE AND OTHERS v RÉGIE NATIONALE DES USINES RENAULT SA

EUROPEAN COURT OF JUSTICE

Case No: C-218/98

Judgment: 16 September 1999

Panel: *Judges*: Puissochet (*President*), Jann, Moitinho de Almeida (*Rapporteur*), Gulmann, Edward

Human rights — Equality and non-discrimination — Sex discrimination — Principle of equal treatment for men and women — Equal pay — Whether payment of an allowance for women going on maternity leave violated principle of equal treatment for men and women — Whether male and female workers in a comparable situation — EC Treaty, Art 119 — French Code du Travail (Employment Code), Art L 140-2 — EC Directive 75/117/EEC of 10 February 1975 — EC Directive 76/207/EEC of 9 February 1976

BACKGROUND

Some 244 male employees of the French car manufacturer Renault (the "plaintiffs") brought proceedings before the Industrial Tribunal in Le Havre, claiming that a maternity payment provided for in their collective agreement was incompatible with the prohibition of discrimination laid down in article 119 of the EC Treaty, as implemented by the French Code du Travail. The agreement provided for a lump sum payment of FRF 7,500 to pregnant women when they commenced maternity leave (as well as providing that female employees would continue to receive their net salary, less daily allowances paid by social security, during maternity leave). The plaintiffs applied for an order requiring their employer, Renault, to make the same payment for each of their children. According to the plaintiffs, certain instances of discrimination, such as maternity leave granted exclusively to women, were justified because they related to the physiological characteristics of one sex. However, this was not the case with the payment in question, since although the birth of a child concerned women alone from a strictly physiological point of view, it was equally a social event which concerned the whole family, including the father. To deny a father the same allowance as a mother therefore amounted to discrimination between men and women on the basis of pay.

The Industrial Tribunal referred to the European Court of Justice for a preliminary ruling on whether the principle of equal pay laid down in article 119 of the EC Treaty precluded the making of a lump-sum payment exclusively to female employees who took maternity leave. Renault argued before the Court that the payment was made to female workers taking maternity leave in order to offset certain disadvantages in taking such leave, for example, a woman on maternity leave might not be proposed for promotion, on her return her period of service would be reduced by the length of her absence, she might not claim performance-related salary increases while absent or take part in training, and she might have difficulties adapting to changes in technology when she returned.

HELD

1   The term "pay" in article 119 and Directive 75/117 included all consideration which workers receive directly or indirectly from their employers in respect of their employment; it included the payment in question. (Paras 12 and 15)

2   The principle of equal pay presupposed that male and female workers were in comparable situations. It did not preclude the making of a lump sum payment exclusively to female workers who took maternity leave where that payment was designed to offset the occupational disadvantage which arose for those workers as a result of their being away from work. In this case, male and female workers were in different situations, which excluded any breach of the principle of equal pay laid down in article 119. It was a matter for the national court to determine whether this was the case. (Paras 20, 21 and 22)

Treaties and other international instruments referred to

Treaty establishing the European community art 119 (now art 141)

European Community law referred to

Council Directive 75/117/EEC of 10 February 1975 on the approximation of the laws of the Member States relating to the application of the principle of equal pay for men and women (OJ 1975 L 45, p 19)

Council Directive 76/207/EEC of 9 February 1976 on the implementation of the principle of equal treatment of men and women as regards access to employment, vocational training and promotion, and working conditions (OJ 1976 L39, p 40)

National legislation referred to

France

Code du Travail (Employment Code), Art L 140-2

Cases referred to

Arbeiterwohlfahrt der Stadt Berlin eV v Monika Bötel, ECJ Case C-360/90, [1992] ECR I-3589

Douglas Harvey Barber v Guardian Royal Exchange Assurance Group, ECJ Case C-262/88, [1990] ECR I-1889

Eileen Garland v British Rail Engineering Limited, ECJ Case C-12/81, [1982] ECR 359

Joan Gillespie and others v Northern Health and Social Sciences Boards and others, ECJ Case C-342/93; [1996] ECR I-475

Maria Kowalska v Freie und Hansestadt Hamburg, ECJ Case C-33/89; [1990] ECR I-2591

JUDGMENT

1   By judgment of 24 April 1998, received at the Court on 15 June 1998, the *Conseil de Prud'hommes* (Industrial Tribunal), Le Havre, referred to the Court for a preliminary ruling under Article 177 of the EC Treaty (now Article 234 EC) a question on the interpretation of Article 119 of the EC Treaty (Articles 117 to 120 of the EC Treaty have been replaced by Articles 136 EC and 143 EC), of Council Directive 75/117/EEC of 10 February 1975 on the approximation of the laws of the Member States relating to the application of the principle of equal pay for men and women (OJ 1975 L 45, p 19) and of Council Directive 76/207/EEC of 9 February 1976 on the implementation of the principle of equal treatment for men and women as regards access to employment, vocational training and promotion, and working conditions (OJ 1976 L 39, p 40).

2   The question has been raised in proceedings between Oumar Dabo Abdoulaye and other plaintiffs and the *Régie Nationale des Usines Renault SA* (hereinafter "Renault").

3   The plaintiffs in the main proceedings are male workers at Renault. They claim that Article 18 of the agreement on social benefits for Renault employees (hereinafter "the Agreement") is incompatible with the prohibition of discrimination laid down in Article 119 of the Treaty, which was implemented by Article L 140-2 of the French *Code du Travail* (Employment Code).

4   Article 18 of the Agreement provides that "when taking maternity leave, a female employee shall be granted a sum of FRF 7,500".

5   Article 19 of the Agreement provides that "during the duration of maternity leave paid as such by social security, a female employee shall receive 100% of her net salary, less the daily allowances paid by social security".

6   Finally, Article 20 of the Agreement provides that "on the adoption of a child, the father or the mother employed by the undertaking shall receive a sum of FRF 2,000. If both spouses work in the undertaking, that right may be exercised by only one of the spouses".

7   According to the plaintiffs in the main proceedings, whereas certain instances of discrimination, such as maternity leave granted exclusively to women, are justified because they are related to the physiological characteristics of one sex, this is not the case with regard to the payment in question, since, although the birth of a child concerns women alone from a strictly physiological point of view, it is, in at least equal measure, a social event which concerns the whole family, including the father, and to deny him the same allowance amounts to unlawful discrimination.

8   The national court found that the Court of Justice has never ruled on the question of the compatibility with Article 119 of the Treaty of an allowance of the kind in question in the main proceedings although in its judgment in Case C-342/93 *Gillespie and Others* [1996] ECR I-475 it did consider a relatively similar case.

9   In those circumstances, it decided to stay proceedings and to refer the following question to the Court for a preliminary ruling:

> Does the principle of equal pay for men and women laid down by Article 119 of the Treaty of Rome and by subsequent legislation authorise payment to a pregnant woman only, and not to the father of the child, of the sum of FRF 7,500 when she takes maternity leave, given that:

such payment is provided for by the last part of Article 18 of the collective agreement of 5 July 1991 on social benefits for Renault employees;

Article 19(2) of the agreement provides that employees' salaries are to continue to be paid during maternity leave?

10 By its question the national court is asking essentially whether the principle of equal pay laid down in Article 119 of the Treaty precludes the making of a lump-sum payment exclusively to female employees who take maternity leave.

11 Article 119 of the Treaty lays down the principle of equal pay for men and women for the same work. That provision is clarified by Article 1 of Directive 75/117.

12 According to the case-law of the Court, the definition contained in the second paragraph of Article 119 of the Treaty makes clear that the term "pay" used in the abovementioned provisions includes all consideration which workers receive directly or indirectly from their employers in respect of their employment. The legal nature of such consideration is not important for the purposes of the application of Article 119 of the Treaty provided that it is granted in respect of employment (see, in particular, *Gillespie and Others*, cited above, para 12).

13 Consideration classified as pay includes, *inter alia*, consideration paid by the employer by virtue of legislative provisions and under a contract of employment whose purpose is to ensure that workers receive income even where, in certain cases specified by the legislature, they are not performing any work provided for in their contracts of employment (Case C-360/90 *Bötel* [1992] ECR I-3589, paras 14 and 15; see also Case C-33/89 *Kowalska* [1990] ECR I-2591, para 11, and Case C-262/88 *Barber* [1990] ECR I-1889, para 12, and *Gillespie*, cited above, para 13).

14 Since the benefit paid by an employer to a female employee when she goes on maternity leave, such as the payment in question in the main proceedings, is based on the employment relationship, it constitutes pay within the meaning of Article 119 of the Treaty and Directive 75/117.

15 While such a payment is not made periodically and is not indexed on salary, its characteristics do not, contrary to what Renault contends, alter its nature of pay within the meaning of Article 119 of the Treaty (see Case 12/81 *Garland* [1982] ECR 359, para 9).

16 According to the case-law of the Court, the principle of equal pay, like the general principle of non-discrimination of which it is a particular expression, presupposes that male and female workers whom it covers are in comparable situations (see *Gillespie*, cited above, paras 16 to 18).

17 The compatibility with Article 119 of the Treaty of a payment such as that in question in the main proceedings thus depends on the question whether, with regard to that payment, female workers are in a situation comparable to that of male workers.

18 In its answer to a question put by the Court, Renault mentioned several occupational disadvantages, inherent in maternity leave, which arise for female workers as a result of being away from work.

19 First of all, a woman on maternity leave may not be proposed for promotion. On her return, her period of service will be reduced by the length of her absence; second, a pregnant woman may not claim performance-related salary increases; third, a female worker may not take part in training; lastly, since new technology is constantly changing the nature of jobs, the adaptation of a female worker returning from maternity leave becomes complicated.

20 As the United Kingdom Government and the Commission rightly point out, Article 119 of the Treaty does not preclude the making of a payment such as that in question in the main proceedings exclusively to female workers since it is designed to offset the occupational disadvantages, such as those mentioned by Renault. In this case, male and female workers are, in their view, in different situations, which excludes any breach of the principle of equal pay laid down in Article 119 of the Treaty.

21 It is for the national court to determine whether this is the case.

22 The answer to be given to the national court must therefore be that the principle of equal pay laid down in Article 119 of the Treaty does not preclude the making of a lump-sum payment exclusively to female workers who take maternity leave where that payment is designed to offset the occupational disadvantages which arise for those workers as a result of their being away from work.

Costs

23 The costs incurred by the United Kingdom Government and by the Commission, which have submitted observations to the Court, are not recoverable. Since these proceedings are, for the parties to the main proceedings, a step in the proceedings pending before the national court, the decision on costs is a matter for that court.

On those grounds,

THE COURT (Fifth Chamber), in answer to the question referred to it by the *Conseil de Prud'hommes*, Le Havre, by judgment of 24 April 1998, **HEREBY RULES:**

> The principle of equal pay laid down in Article 119 of the EC Treaty (Articles 117 to 120 of the EC Treaty have been replaced by Articles 136 EC to 143 EC) does not preclude the making of a lump-sum payment exclusively to female workers who take maternity leave where that payment is designed to offset the occupational disadvantages which arise for those workers as a result of their being away from work.

CASE NO 29

JANZEN AND GOVEREAU v PLATY ENTERPRISES LTD

SUPREME COURT OF CANADA

Judgment: 4 May 1989

Panel: Dickson CJC, Beetz, McIntyre, Le Dain,[1] La Forest and L'Heureux-Dubé JJ

Human rights — Equality and non-discrimination — Sex discrimination — Sexual harassment — Whether sexual harassment constituted discrimination on the ground of sex — Vicarious liability — Whether employer liable for employee's actions — Whether acts in course of employment — Human Rights Act 1974 (Manitoba), s 6(1)

BACKGROUND

The appellants, Ms Janzen and Ms Govereau, made separate complaints to the Human Rights Commission of Manitoba against their employer Platy Enterprises Ltd, its owners, agents and servants. They both alleged that they had been sexually harassed during their employment as waitresses at Pharos restaurant by a fellow employee. The Board of Adjudication appointed under the Human Rights Act 1974 (Manitoba) found that they had been victims of sexual harassment, as a form of discrimination on the basis of sex, contrary to section 6(1) of the Human Rights Act. The harasser, Mr Grammas, and the employer, Platy Enterprises Ltd, were held jointly and severally liable for damages.

On appeal by Platy Enterprises, the Manitoba Court of Queen's Beach reduced the amount of damages awarded, but otherwise upheld the decision of the Board of Adjudication. On further appeal, the Manitoba Court of Appeal allowed the appeal of Platy, holding that the sexual harassment did not amount to sexual discrimination under section 6(1) of the Human Rights Act. Furthermore, the Manitoba Court of Appeal rejected the lower court's finding that Platy was vicariously liable for the acts of sexual harassment committed by Mr Grammas, finding that there was not a sufficient connection between the employer and the allegedly discriminatory conduct. Ms Janzen and Ms Govereau appealed to the Supreme Court of Canada.

HELD (allowing the appeal)

1 Sexual harassment in the workplace might broadly be defined as unwelcome conduct of a sexual nature that detrimentally affects the work environment or leads to adverse job-related consequences for the victims of the harassment. When sexual harassment occured in the workplace, it was an abuse of both economic and sexual power. By requiring an employee to contend with unwelcome sexual actions or explicit sexual demands, sexual harassment in the workplace attacked the dignity and self-respect of the victim both as an employee and as a human being (pp 468, 469).

---

1   Le Dain J took no part in the judgment.

2   Sexual harassment constituted sex discrimination within s 6(1) of the Human Rights Act. The sexual harassment suffered by the appellants fitted the proposed definition of sex discrimination, namely "practices or attitudes which have the effect of limiting the conditions of employment of, or the employment opportunities available to, employees on the basis of a characteristic related to gender". To argue that the sole factor underlying the discriminatory action was the sexual attractiveness of the appellants and to say that their gender was irrelevant strained credulity. Sexual attractiveness could not be separated from gender. The crucial fact in this case was that it was only female employees who ran the risk of sexual harassment. No man would have been subjected to this treatment (pp 471, 472).

3   The belief that sex discrimination only exists where gender is the sole ingredient in the discriminatory action and where, therefore, all members of the affected gender are mistreated identically, was a fallacy. While the concept of discrimination was rooted in the notion of treating an individual as part of a group, rather than on the basis of the individual's personal characteristics, discrimination did not require uniform treatment of all members of a particular group. It was sufficient that ascribing to an individual a group characteristic was one factor in the treatment of that individual (p 471).

4   The respondent (the employer) should be held liable for the actions of the cook Grammas. His actions fell within the course of his employment, and were clearly work-related. His opportunity to harass the appellants sexually was directly related to his employment position as the next in line in authority to the respondent. It was the respondent's responsibility to ensure that this power was not abused. This it clearly did not do, even after the appellants made specific complaints about the harassment (p 473).

National legislation referred to

Canada

Canada Labour Code, RSC, 1985 C&L-2 (as amended), s 61.7

Human Rights Act of Manitoba, SM 1974, c 65 ss 6 and 28

Manitoba Human Rights Code, SM 1987 – 88, c 45 s 19

Newfoundland Human Rights Code, RSN 1970, c 262, s 10.1

Ontario Human Rights Code, SO 1981, c 53 ss 4 and 6

United States

Civil Rights Act 1964, Title VII

Cases referred to

Barnes v Costle, 561 F.2d 983 (1977)

Bell v Ladas (1980), 1 CHRR D/155

Bliss v Attorney-General of Canada [1979] 1 SCR 183; (1978) 92 DLR (3d) 417

Boehm v National System of Banking Ltd (1978) 8 CHRR D/4110

Brooks v Canada Safeway Ltd [1989] 1 SCR 1219; *supra*, p 428

Bundy v Jackson, 641 F2d 934 (1981)

Canadian National Railway Co v Canada (Canadian Human Rights Commission), [1987] 1 SCR 1114

Commodore Business Machines Ltd v Ontario Minister of Labour (1984) 6 CHRR D/2833

Coutroubis v Sklavos Printing (1981) 2 CHRR D/457

Cox and others v Cowell Jagbritte Inc et al (1982) 3 CHRR D/609

Deisting v Dollar Pizza (1978) Ltd (1982) 3 CHRR D/898

Doherty v Lodger's International Ltd (1981) 3 CHRR D/628

Foisy v Bell Canada (1984) 6 CHRR D/2817

Giouvanoudis v Golden Fleece Restaurant (1984) 5 CHRR D/1967

Henson v Dundee, 682 F2d 897 (1982)

Hufnagel v Osama Enterprises Ltd (1982) 3 CHRR D/922

Hughes v Dollar Snack Bar (1981) 3 CHRR D/1014

Johnstone v Zarankin (1985) 6 CHRR D/2651 (BCSC)

Kotyk v Canadian Employment and Immigration Commission (1983) 4 CHRR D/1416

McPherson et al v Mary's Donuts and Doschoian (1982) 3 CHRR D/961

Meritor Savings Bank v Vinson, 106 S Ct 2399 (1986)

Mitchell v Traveller Inn (Sudbury) Ltd (1981) 2 CHRR D/590

Olarte v DeFilippis (1983) 4 CHRR D/1705

Phillips v Hermiz (1984) 5 CHRR D/2450

Porcelli v Strathclyde Regional Council [1985] ICR 177

Re Dakota Ojibway Tribal Council and Bewza (1985) 24 DLR (4th) 374

Re Mehta and MacKinnon (1985) 19 DLR (4th) 198

Robichaud v Canada (Treasury Board) [1987] 2 SCR 84

Torres v Royalty Kitchenware Ltd (1982) 3 CHRR D/858

Zarankin v Johnstone (1984) 5 CHRR D/2274

JUDGMENT

The judgment of the Court was delivered by Dickson CJC.

DICKSON CJC: On 24 January 1983, Dianna Janzen made a complaint to the Human Rights Commission of Manitoba against Platy Enterprises Ltd, its owners, agents and servants, Pharos Restaurant. The complaint reads:

> I am a female resident of Manitoba.
>
> I was employed as a waitress at the Pharos Restaurant, located at 9 St. Mary's Road, from August to October, 1982. I was hired by Phillip Anastasiadis, who I believe is part owner of the restaurant.

During my period of employment at the restaurant, was continuously sexually harassed by Tommy, the cook. On many occasions Tommy grabbed my legs and touched my knee, bum and crotch area. When I resisted his sexual advances, he told me to shut up or he would fire me. He began to yell at me in front of staff and criticize my work.

During the second week of October 1982 I spoke to Phillip about Tommy's behaviour. He told me he couldn't do anything about it. Under the circumstances I felt I had no alternative but to quit my job effective October 31st, 1982.

I believe I have been subjected to discriminatory terms and conditions of employment and that I have been discriminated against because of my sex contrary to Section 6 of The Human Rights Act.

Five days later, on 29 January 1983, Tracy Govereau made a complaint of a similar nature against the same parties, alleging sexual harassment by "Tommy, the cook".

The main issue in this appeal is whether sexual harassment in the workplace is discrimination on the basis of sex, and therefore prohibited by s 6(1) of the Manitoba Human Rights Act, SM 1974, c 65.

I Facts

The appellants, Dianna Janzen and Tracy Govereau, were employed as waitresses at Pharos Restaurant in Winnipeg, during the fall of 1982. The restaurant and two others of like name were owned and operated by the corporate respondent Platy Enterprises Ltd. The president of the corporation, Eleftherois (also known as Phillip) Anastasiadis, was the manager of the restaurant and the cook at the restaurant on the first shift. The respondent, Tommy Grammas, was the cook during evening shifts. He did not have an ownership interest in the restaurant, nor was he an officer of the corporation. Although Grammas had no actual disciplinary authority over the waitresses, he was represented by himself and by Anastasiadis as having control over firing employees.

The appellant Janzen was employed at the restaurant from 21 August 1982 until 31 October 1982. Approximately two to three weeks after she commenced her employment, the respondent Grammas began engaging in unwelcome conduct of a sexual nature. He began to make sexual advances towards her. Often this touching occurred when Janzen was burdened with duties as a waitress and unable to defend herself. Despite Janzen's clear and repeated objections to Grammas' behaviour, this course of conduct persisted for over a month.

Dianna Janzen's troubles did not end when the overtly sexual conduct ceased. Grammas continued to make the work environment difficult for her by a pattern of uncooperative and threatening behaviour. He was unjustifiably critical of her work, refused to respond co-operatively to her food orders and generally treated her in an unpleasant manner. Towards the middle of October, Janzen endeavoured to speak to Anastasiadis about Grammas' behaviour. Anastasiadis was unable to talk to her at the time, but according to Janzen's testimony, he said "If it is about Tommy, I can't do anything about it". At a second meeting in late October, Janzen described to Anastasiadis in detail the conduct to which she had been subjected. His reaction was unsympathetic. Janzen's evidence was that Anastasiadis treated the matter lightly and insinuated she was responsible for Grammas' conduct. Anastasiadis admits to telling Janzen she was over-reacting. Anastasiadis made no attempt to put an end to the harassment and, shortly after her discussion with him, Janzen terminated her employment. She was out of work for one month before finding employment at another restaurant. She gave evidence, accepted by the adjudicator, that the physical and emotional consequences of the harassment she endured included insomnia, vomiting and inability to concentrate.

The appellant Govereau was a waitress at Pharos restaurant from 13 October 1982 to 11 December 1982. At the end of her first week of employment, Grammas approached her and kissed her on the mouth. From that point onwards, Grammas repeatedly grabbed Govereau and attempted to kiss her. He constantly touched various parts of her body, including her stomach and breasts. On one occasion, when Govereau was washing dishes in the kitchen, Grammas came up behind her, put his hands under her sweater and attempted to fondle her breasts. Grammas also harassed Govereau verbally, commenting frequently and inappropriately on her appearance. Grammas' conduct persisted despite forceful objections.

As a result of conversations with another waitress at the restaurant, Carol Enns, Govereau decided to raise the matter with Anastasiadis. In mid-November she met with Anastasiadis and discussed Grammas' behaviour for approximately fifteen minutes. According to Govereau's testimony, Anastasiadis did not seem particularly surprised or perturbed by the situation. At one point during the conversation he asked Govereau why she let Grammas treat her that way. After Govereau's discussion with Anastasiadis, the physical harassment of her by Grammas came to an end. It was replaced, however, by a general pattern of verbal abuse by both Grammas and Anastasiadis. Govereau maintained that she was unjustly criticized by the two men and that both of them would yell at her in front of the other staff for no reason. There had been no criticism of her work prior to her decision to complain about Grammas. Govereau's testimony was supported by Carol Enns. The harassment culminated with Anastasiadis terminating Govereau's employment on 8 December 1982, ostensibly as a result of a customer complaint. Govereau worked three additional days, until 11 December. She was unable to find alternative employment until August 1983. Govereau testified that as a result of the harassment by Grammas and Anastasiadis she "felt dirty, wasn't relaxed, couldn't sleep or concentrate in class".

As I have mentioned, both Janzen and Govereau filed complaints with the Manitoba Human Rights Commission alleging that they had been victims of discrimination on the basis of sex contrary to s 6(1) of the Human Rights Act.

Grammas' employment at Pharos Restaurant was terminated before the hearing of the complaints and he did not participate in any of the proceedings.

II   Legislation

The Human Rights Act, SM 1974, c 65, as amended, reads:

6(1) Every person has the right of equality of opportunity based upon *bona fide* qualifications in respect of his occupation or employment or in respect of training for employment, or in respect of an intended occupation, employment, advancement or promotion, and in respect of his membership or intended membership in a trade union, employers' organization or occupational association; and, without limiting the generality of the foregoing:

(a) no employer or person acting on behalf of an employer shall refuse to employ, or to continue to employ or to train the person for employment or to advance or promote that person, or discriminate against that person in respect of employment or any term or condition of employment;

(b) no employment agency shall refuse to refer a person for employment; or for training for employment; and

(c) no trade union, employers' organization or occupational association shall refuse membership to, expel, suspend or otherwise discriminate against that person; or negotiate, on behalf of that person, an agreement that would discriminate against him;

because of the race, nationality, religion, colour, sex, age, marital status, physical or mental handicap, ethnic or national origin, or political beliefs or family status of that person.

28(1) Where the board of adjudication decides that there has been no contravention of the Act by any party, it shall dismiss the complaint.

28(2) Where the board of adjudication decides that a party has contravened any provision of the Act, it may do one or more of the following things:

...

(b) Make an order requiring the party who contravened the Act to compensate the person discriminated against for all, or such part as a board may determine, of any wages or salary lost or expenses incurred by reason of the contravention of this Act;

(c) Order the person who contravened the Act to pay to the person discriminated against, a penalty or exemplary damages in such amount as the board may determine, if the board is of the opinion that the person discriminated against suffered damages in respect of his feelings, or self-respect.

In 1987, subsequent to the adjudication of the complaints of Janzen and Govereau, the Manitoba Human Rights Act was repealed and replaced with The Human Rights Code, SM 1987–88, c 45. Section 19 of the new Human Rights Code expressly prohibits sexual discrimination in the workplace:

19(1) No person who is responsible for an activity or undertaking to which this Code applies shall:

(a) harass any person who is participating in the activity or undertaking; or

(b) knowingly permit, or fail to take reasonable steps to terminate, harassment of one person who is participating in the activity or undertaking by another person who is participating in the activity or undertaking.

19(2) In this section "harassment" means:

(a) a course of abusive or unwelcome conduct or comment undertaken or made on the basis of any characteristic referred to in subsection 9(2); or

(b) a series of objectionable and unwelcome sexual solicitations or advances; or

(c) a sexual solicitation or advance made by a person who is in a position to confer any benefit on, or deny any benefit to, the recipient of the solicitation or advance, if the person making the solicitation or advance knows or ought reasonably to know that it is unwelcome; or

(d) a reprisal or threat of reprisal for rejecting a sexual solicitation or advance.

III   Judgments below

1   The Adjudication Board

The complaints were heard by Adjudicator Henteleff. In a comprehensive decision of some 144 pages, rendered April 26, 1985 and reported at (1985), 6 CHRR D/2735, the adjudicator found that both Janzen and Govereau had been victims of sex discrimination. Much of the decision is devoted to preliminary matters which are not at issue in this Court. Adjudicator Henteleff conducted a thorough review of the evidence and concluded that the appellants had been subjected to persistent and abusive sexual harassment. He made the following finding in respect of Janzen, at p D/2768:

Further, I find that the cumulative effect of the physical and mental harassment that she had been subjected to created an intolerable work environment for her. She was justified in coming to the conclusion, as she did following her conversation with Phillip immediately prior to her terminating her employment, that there was very little likelihood, if any, that the situation would be rectified. Accordingly, I further find that the cumulative effect of such acts of harassment, sexual as well as mental, and the attitude of the employer as above described amounted to constructive dismissal (see *Cox and Cowell v Jagbritte Inc. et al.* (1982) 3 C.H.R.R. D/609 (Peter A. Cumming) at paras 5593 and 5594).

and in respect of Govereau, at p D/2768:

Based on all of the evidence I have no doubt in concluding that the individual respondent, Tommy, was guilty of sexual harassment of Tracy Govereau. The specific acts, of which she complained, consisted of unwanted sexual acts of a persistent and abusive nature. Her evidence, which I accept, also clearly established that Tommy knew or ought to have known that such acts were unwanted. It is clear from the evidence that Tommy made a variety of sexual advances including touching the complainant for sexual reasons, and that he persisted in this conduct even though it is obvious from her evidence that she forcibly rejected his actions. She impressed me as a truthful witness. Moreover, her evidence was corroborated in all essential respects by her co-worker, Carol Elizabeth Enns. Furthermore, I find that there was additional corroboration of Ms Govereau's evidence as to Tommy by virtue of the similar acts committed by Tommy on the complainant, Dianna Janzen.

The question of whether sexual harassment could amount to sex discrimination prohibited by the Manitoba statute was not raised before the arbitrator by either counsel. As there was no dispute on the point, the adjudicator was content to cite six authorities for holding that sexual harassment is sex discrimination: *Hufnagel v Osama Enterprises Ltd* (1982), 3 CHRR D/922 (Man Bd.); *Torres v Royalty Kitchenware Ltd* (1982), 3 CHRR D/858 (Ont Bd); *Olarte v DeFilippis* (1983), 4 CHRR D/1705 (Ont Bd); *Giouvanoudis v Golden Fleece Restaurant* (1984), 5 CHRR D/1967 (Ont Bd); and *Robichaud v Brennan* (1982), 3 CHRR. D/977; Review Tribunal (1983), 4 CHRR D/1272, and on appeal to the Federal Court of Appeal which gave its judgment dated 18th day of February, 1985, [1984] 2 FC 799. The adjudicator accepted the definition of sexual harassment quoted by Professor Cumming in *Giouvanoudis v Golden Fleece Restaurant, supra,* at para 16819, as follows:

From a factual standpoint, sexual harassment can be considered to include:

Unwanted sexual attention of a persistent or abusive nature, made by a person who knows or ought reasonably to know that such attention is unwanted; ... or

Implied or expressed threat or reprisal, in the form either of actual reprisal or the denial of opportunity for refusal to comply with a sexually oriented required; ... or

Sexually oriented remarks and behaviour which may reasonably be perceived to create a negative psychological and emotional environment for work.

Adjudicator Henteleff concluded that Grammas' conduct violated s 6(1) of the Human Rights Act.

The adjudicator made a number of findings of fact with respect to the position and responsibilities of Grammas at the restaurant and to Anastasiadis' knowledge of the existence of the harassment. He found: (1) that Grammas decided which of the waitresses went home early or stayed at work depending on the amount of business in the restaurant; (2) that in the absence of Anastasiadis, Grammas handled any problems with food quality or service; (3) that the staff had the clear and justifiable impression that Grammas was next in line in authority to Anastasiadis, and that he was in charge when Anastasiadis was absent; (4) that Grammas could clear cash from the till; and (5) that

Grammas had advised both of the appellants that he could fire them and that even though this was not the case, his authority to terminate the appellants' employment was confirmed by Anastasiadis. Anastasiadis testified that he had told the waitresses Grammas had firing authority because (at p D/2758) "the girls had to have somebody to be kind of afraid of or respect or whatever". The adjudicator also found that Anastasiadis was aware of the harassment of the appellants, that he failed to take any reasonable steps to ensure that the workplace was free from sexual harassment, and that he actively participated in the verbal harassment of the appellant Govereau.

The adjudicator also considered the liability of the corporate respondent, Platy Enterprises Ltd, for breaches of the Human Rights Act committed by Grammas. Adjudicator Henteleff reviewed earlier decisions of human rights tribunals, as well as the decision of the Federal Court of Appeal in *Robichaud*, before concluding that the corporate respondent was liable for the violations. The adjudicator appears to have found Platy Enterprises Ltd liable both on the principle of vicarious liability and on the organic theory of corporate liability. He remarked (at p D/2753):

> The clear intent of s.6(1), in respect of areas of discrimination arising therefrom, is not only to make the employer liable for any acts of sexual harassment directly committed by such employer, but also to make him responsible for any such acts committed by a person in authority during the course of his employment.

The adjudicator stated at p D/2768:

> After consideration of all of the evidence, it is my conclusion that Tommy was a person in such authority that his acts became those of his employer, Platy. The complainant Janzen was made aware of this to the extent that Tommy was in such a preferred position, that if she subjected herself to sexual harassment, she was to blame for it. Accordingly such harassment had become a condition of her continued employment since Phillip either couldn't or wouldn't do anything about it. (See *McPherson et al v Mary's Donuts and Doschoian* (1982) 3 C.H.R.R. D/961 (Peter A. Cumming) and particularly at paras. 8549 to 8558, both inclusive.)

The adjudicator did not consider himself to be bound by the decision of the Federal Court of Appeal in Robichaud which restricted vicarious liability of a corporation to acts of sexual harassment committed by the corporation's directors or officers. Adjudicator Henteleff interpreted the majority judgment as dealing solely with the question of vicarious liability in a complaint against the Crown and as having no application to private employers. The decision of the Federal Court of Appeal on the issue of liability was later reversed on appeal to this Court (*Robichaud v Canada (Treasury Board)* [1987] 2 SCR 84).

Adjudicator Henteleff found Grammas and Platy Enterprises Ltd jointly and severally liable to the complainants. He awarded Janzen the sum of $480 for lost wages and $3,500 in exemplary damages, and Govereau the sum of $3,000 for lost wages and $3,000 exemplary damages. In arriving at the quantum of exemplary damages, the adjudicator noted that both Janzen and Govereau had been subjected to physical and mental harassment of a severe nature and that the harassment had had a substantial psychological impact on both women. With respect to Janzen he said, at p D/2771:

> I further find that she was subject to physical and mental harassment which was of a most severe nature. I further find that the harassment was close to being constant throughout her period of employment. I find also that by virtue of her age (21) and her particular situation (including trying to be self-supporting for the first time), she was particularly vulnerable with the result that the cumulative effect of the harassment had a very substantial psychological impact upon her, and she suffered damage in respect of feelings and self-respect.

and with respect to Govereau, also at p D/2771:

> I further find that she was subject to physical and mental harassment which although severe and frequent, was not of the same degree as that suffered by Ms. Janzen. I find that by virtue of her situation (including attending University and her particular need of this part-time job) that the cumulative effect of the harassment had a substantial psychological impact upon her and she suffered damages in respect of feelings and self-respect.

The award to Janzen was greater than the award to Govereau, as the harassment Janzen endured was more severe.

The decision concluded, at p D/2772 by directing Platy Enterprises Ltd:

> Further and under the direction of the Manitoba Human Rights Commission, and within such time as the Commission determines, to establish and maintain in all of its restaurant premises such program as will reasonably assure such restaurant premises will remain free of sexual harassment.

2   The Manitoba Court of Queen's Bench

Platy Enterprises Ltd appealed the decision of Adjudicator Henteleff. With the exception of the quantum of damages, Monnin J upheld the adjudicator's decision: (1985), 38 Man R (2d) 20, 24 DLR. (4th) 31, [1986] 2 WWR 273, 86 CLLC paragraph 16,009, 7 CHRR D/3309. Monnin J began by noting that the question whether Janzen and Govereau had been sexually harassed was not before the court, counsel for the appellant having admitted that Grammas was guilty of sexual harassment. He then turned to consider whether sexual harassment is a form of sex discrimination prohibited by s 6(1) of the Human Rights Act. Monnin J rejected Platy Enterprises Ltd's argument that the term sex discrimination as used in the Manitoba statute was not intended to apply to activities of an individual directed against a particular individual, rather than against an entire identifiable group. Instead, he accepted the result and the reasoning of Adjudicator Shime in *Bell v Ladas* (1980), 1 CHRR D/155 (Ont Bd), who held that sexual harassment did amount to discrimination on the basis of sex.

Monnin J also rejected Platy Enterprises Ltd's argument that the amendments enacted by some provinces to prohibit specifically sexual harassment in their human rights legislation was to be construed as an indication that the term sex discrimination did not encompass sexual harassment.

Monnin J next considered the liability of Platy Enterprises Ltd for the actions of its employee, Grammas. He began by absolving Anastasiadis from any participation in the sexual harassment of Janzen and Govereau and from condoning Grammas' behaviour. In spite of his conclusion that Anastasiadis was not personally responsible for Grammas' conduct, Monnin J continued to find Platy Enterprises Ltd liable for sexual harassment (CHRR, p D/3314):

> ... I have no hesitation in finding, as did the adjudicator, that whether or not, in reality, Grammas had any power over the staff of the restaurant, the staff was purposefully led to believe by Anastasiadis that he did. In point of fact, Grammas might well not have been a directing mind of respondents but the perception given to the employees is what must be a determining factor ...

> By the admission of Anastasiadis, respondents have placed Grammas in a position of authority over the staff and therefore the complainants. By seemingly proffering this authority upon Grammas, respondents must be and are bound by his actions. Liability for Grammas' sexual harassment of complainants therefore extends to respondents.

On the issue of damages, Monnin J said, at CHRR pp D/3314-15:

> Section 28(2) of the Act empowers a board of adjudication to compensate a person who has been discriminated against for any wages or salary lost as a result of a contravention of the Act as well as ordering payments of a penalty or exemplary damages if a person who has been discriminated against has suffered damages in respect of feelings or self-respect.
>
> In this particular case the board of adjudication found that complainant Janzen suffered a one month loss of income and awarded her $480.00 in lost wages. I have little difficulty in upholding this finding. As to complainant Govereau however, the board of adjudication found a loss of income of approximately 6 months and awarded damages in the amount of $3,000.00 for such loss. I am not satisfied that the evidence warrants this finding. There is little evidence of what if any attempts complainant Govereau made to secure other employment. There is evidence that she was embarrassed by her firing from Pharos and that this caused her some difficulties in seeking out employment. I do not question this, but an award of damages and not compensation for loss of wages is the proper remedy for this state of affairs. Even by giving complainant Govereau every benefit of the doubt, I cannot justify an award for loss of wages in excess of one month or $500.
>
> I am now left with the issue of punitive or exemplary damages. This is a difficult concept with which to deal because the court must attempt to quantify feelings or self-respect. The concept itself is difficult to rationalize and even more so when it is of a nature with which courts do not normally deal with. Notwithstanding that human rights legislation is a new and specialized area of law, awards of damages in one area of law must maintain a certain balance with fines meted out in criminal or quasi criminal matters and damages awarded in general civil cases. Not to maintain this general balance will too easily bring into question the principle of equal justice for all. I fully realize and accept that the conduct of Grammas was demeaning and traumatic for both complainants. What must be realized however is that victims of criminal acts or persons wrongfully dismissed from their employment or injured by the conduct of others also have their feelings and self-respect attacked. This type of loss is not the sole preserve and domain of persons who have suffered discrimination. A loss based on discrimination cannot be assessed in a vacuum. Such a loss must be looked at in the context of damages in law as a whole.
>
> Bearing those comments in mind, I find the complainant Janzen is entitled under s. 28(2)(c) of the Act to an award of $1,000.00 while complainant Govereau is entitled to an award of $1,500.00. I have awarded Govereau an amount greater than Janzen because the evidence has convinced me that her feelings and self-respect were dealt a more severe attack by the actions of Grammas than were the feelings and self-respect of Janzen.

Thus Monnin J reduced the award for lost wages to Govereau from $3,000 to $500 because of insufficient evidence of her efforts to secure alternative employment and reduced the exemplary damage awards to Janzen and Govereau to $1,000 and $1,500 respectively.

3   The Manitoba Court of Appeal

Platy Enterprises Ltd appealed the decision of Monnin J and Janzen and Govereau cross-appealed on the quantum of damages. The Manitoba Court of Appeal (Matas, Huband and Twaddle JJA) allowed the appeal: (1986), 43 Man R (2d) 293, 33 DLR (4th) 32, [1987] 1 WWR 385, 87 CLLC paragraph 17,014, 8 CHRR D/3831 (hereinafter cited to CHRR) Huband JA and Twaddle JA rendered comprehensive separate reasons which I will review at some length because, with the greatest respect, I do not agree with them. Both held that sexual harassment could not constitute discrimination on the basis of sex. Due to his untimely death, Matas JA did not participate in the reasons for judgment.

Huband JA began by expressing his amazement that sexual harassment had been equated with discrimination on the basis of sex, and that an employer could be held vicariously responsible for the harassing conduct of an employee. He stated (CHRR, p D/3832):

> I am amazed to think that sexual harassment has been equated with discrimination on the basis of sex. I think they are entirely different concepts. But adjudicators under human rights legislation, legal scholars and writers, and jurists have said that the one is included in the other.

> Assuming sexual harassment to be a form of sexual discrimination, I am amazed to think that an employer could be held vicariously responsible for that form of discrimination on the part of an employee, or that a corporate employer could be found "personally responsible" for a sexually malevolent employee, except under the rarest of circumstances. Yet adjudicators, legal scholars, and judges have said otherwise.

Huband JA noted the line of cases in which both judges and adjudicators had found sexual harassment to be a form of sex discrimination but stated that these decisions were wrong.

Huband JA adopted two of the three meanings assigned to the word "discriminate" in *The Shorter Oxford English Dictionary* (3rd ed.): "1. To make or constitute a difference in or between; to differentiate ... ; 3. To make a distinction"; and concluded, "In this Act discrimination is a violation of the law. The word 'discriminate' used in a pejorative sense, means an unjustified differentiation or distinction."

Sexual harassment, in the view of Huband JA, embraced an entirely different concept, stating (CHRR, p D/3834):

> The word "harass" is given several definitions in The Shorter Oxford English Dictionary, the most pertinent for our purposes being to harry, or to trouble or vex by repeated attacks. Sexual harassment involves vexing or troubling a person with respect to sexual matters such as repeatedly touching or making suggestions, or threats.

> Sexual harassment is not socially acceptable conduct. Depending on the nature of it, it might constitute a criminal offence or a civil wrong under the common law. But I cannot understand how it can be equated with sexual discrimination.

Although he recognized that sexual harassment was not socially acceptable conduct, Huband JA cited the following example to illustrate how it could not be viewed as sex discrimination (CHRR, p D/3834):

> When a schoolboy steals kisses from a female classmate, one might well say that he is harassing her. He is troubling her; vexing her; harrying her – but he surely is not discriminating against her.

Huband JA next examined the meaning of discrimination in s 6(1) of the Human Rights Act. He discussed each of the clauses of s 6(1) and concluded that the section as a whole was aimed at discrimination in a generic sense. He gave the following examples of generic discrimination: discriminating against Blacks as a group, Jehovah's Witnesses as a group, or women as a group. In Huband JA's view, discrimination in the generic sense could not include sexual harassment, presumably because not all women were the victims of sexual harassment.

Even though his finding on the issue of sex discrimination rendered consideration of corporate liability unnecessary, Huband JA examined this issue. He noted that he did not believe Grammas could be held liable under the Human Rights Act, as he interpreted the statute to apply only to employers and not to fellow employees. Unlike Adjudicator Henteleff, Huband JA considered himself bound by the decision of the Federal Court of Appeal in *Robichaud, supra*, where the court held that absent a provision in the relevant human rights statute for the imposition of vicarious or strict liability, an employer could not be held vicariously liable for the actions of an employee, except where an employee was acting on behalf of an employer. No such foundation for vicarious liability could be found in the Manitoba Human Rights Act. Huband JA was firmly of the view that Platy Enterprises Ltd could not be held liable for Grammas' conduct as Grammas was not acting on behalf of the employer corporation.

Huband JA proceeded to examine the second ground on which the adjudicator held Platy Enterprises Ltd liable, the organic theory of corporate responsibility. On this theory, a corporation could be liable for wrongful acts of an employee where the corporation adopts or approves of the employee's wrongful acts or where an officer or official of the corporation is given the authority to originate the corporation's policies and to implement them. Huband JA was of the view that liability could not be founded on the organic theory for two reasons. First, Grammas was not the directing mind of the corporation. Second, Grammas did not commit the acts of harassment in the course of employment. In Huband JA's view, an employer could only be held liable for the acts of negligent employees where the employees were acting within their authorized capacity. In the case of a cook, Huband JA explained that this authority would extend to the preparation of food and the maintenance of safe conditions in the kitchen, but would not encompass acts of sexual harassment (CHRR, p D/3841):

> If the cook dumped too much pepper in the soup, he would clearly be acting in the course of his employment, trying, albeit negligently, to prepare and present a decent meal. If the cook, contrary to instruction, was smoking on the job, and as a result negligently caused a gas explosion in the kitchen, it would be arguable that he was still acting in the course of his employment in the sense that he was trying to fulfil his responsibilities as a cook. But what has patting the buttocks of a waitress to do with fulfilling the responsibilities as a cook?

Huband JA concluded that even if Grammas' actions did violate the Human Rights Act, Platy Enterprises Ltd could not be held liable on either theory of corporate liability.

Finally, Huband JA briefly discussed the issue of damages. He stated that Monnin J was correct in reducing the damage awards of the adjudicator in keeping with the decision of the Manitoba Court of Appeal in *Re Dakota Ojibway Tribal Council and Bewza* (1985), 24 DLR (4th) 374.

Like Huband JA, Twaddle JA was emphatic in his view that sexual harassment was not sex discrimination. To assert a claim of discrimination by reason of sex under s 6(1) of the Human Rights Act, Twaddle JA held that three elements must be present: (1) discrimination; (2) because of sex; and (3) in respect of employment. He proceeded to examine each of these elements in turn. With respect to the element of discrimination, Twaddle JA held that the intent of the Manitoba legislature was to prohibit differentiation on the basis of categorical grouping. It was not to prevent differentiation between people on the basis of individual characteristics or qualifications. Twaddle JA explained his understanding of categorical grouping as (CHRR, p D/3844): "a distinction which results in people being dealt with on account of group characteristics, unrelated to merit, rather than individual ability and qualifications". In his view, harassment could not be seen to constitute differentiation on a categorical basis (CHRR, p D/3845):

> Harassment is as different from discrimination as assault is from random selection. The victim of assault may be chosen at random just as the victim of harassment may be chosen because of categorical distinction, but it is nonsense to say that assault is random selection just as it is nonsense to say that harassment is discrimination. The introduction of a sexual element, be it the nature of the conduct or the gender of the victim, does not alter the basic fact that harassment and assault are acts, whilst discrimination and random selection are methods of choice.

The fact that harassment is sexual in form does not determine the reason why the victim was chosen. Only if the woman was chosen on a categorical basis, without regard to individual characteristics, can the harassment be a manifestation of discrimination. (Emphasis added.)

Twaddle JA next considered the second element, whether sexual harassment was differentiation based on sex. He began by providing the following definition of the word "sex" in the Manitoba Human Rights Act (CHRR, p D/3845):

Gender, as distinct from the physical attraction of the victim or the manner in which the discrimination is carried out, is in my view the meaning to be given to "sex" as it is used in s. 6 of the Act. Only in that sense does it constitute a category of persons as distinct from a personal quality.

Twaddle JA contrasted this meaning of the word sex with a different definition concerned with physical attractiveness (CHRR, pp D/3845-46):

"Sex" can also refer to that aura which attracts one person to another, particularly a person of one gender to a person of the other. In this meaning the word is frequently used in combination with another word, as in "sex appeal" ... The word in this sense, however, is not categorical in that the degree to which a person has it is determinable on a decidedly subjective basis.

Twaddle JA concluded that sexual harassment based on the "sex appeal" of the victim could not constitute sex discrimination (CHRR, p D/3846):

Where the conduct of an employer is directed at some but not all persons of one category, it must not be assumed that membership in the category is the reason for the distinction having been made. The distinction may have been based on another factor. Thus in *Bliss v Attorney-General of Canada* (1978), 92 DLR (3d) 417 it was held that statutory conditions applicable only to pregnant women did not discriminate against them as women.

The gender of a woman is unquestionably a factor in most cases of sexual harassment. If she were not a woman, the harassment would not have occurred. That, however, is not decisive. Only a woman can become pregnant, but that does not mean that she becomes pregnant because she is a woman. We are concerned with the effective cause of the harassment, be it a random selection, the conduct, or a particular characteristic of the victim, a wish on the part of the aggressor to discourage women from seeking or continuing in a position of employment or a contempt for women generally. Only in the last two instances is the harassment a manifestation of discrimination.

Twaddle JA then turned to the final issue, whether the discrimination occurred in respect of employment. He was of the view that if discriminatory conduct occurred in a way that directly prejudiced the employment opportunity, the conduct would be said to arise in respect of employment. He was also of the view that the Manitoba Human Rights Act only prohibited actions perpetrated by or on behalf of an employer. Co-employment of the discriminator and the victim was not, in Twaddle JA's opinion, sufficient unless the discriminatory behaviour was authorized by the employer.

Applying these principles to the case, Twaddle JA concluded there had been no violation of s 6 of the Human Rights Act. He dismissed the argument that the sexual harassment that occurred amounted to sex discrimination (at p D/3847):

This is not a case in which an employer adopted a practice whereby women as a class were treated differently from men. Nor is it a case in which a rule of general application adversely affected the complainants because they were women. For the harassment to amount to discrimination, it must have occurred by reason of the categorical selection of the complainants because they were women.

Although not conclusive, the sex of the victims and the sexual nature of the harassment is some evidence of the basis of their selection. There is, on the other hand, no evidence that women as a class were not welcome as employees or were subject to adverse treatment. On the contrary, the evidence discloses that at the restaurant in question women were the only employees other than the cook and the corporate officer. Another female employee testified that the cook touched her a lot by putting his arm around her or touching her neck, but she interpreted that as him being friendly ... *This evidence suggests that the complainants were chosen for the harassment because of characteristics peculiar to them rather than because of their sex. That is not discrimination no matter how objectionable the conduct.* (Emphasis added.)

Twaddle JA also dismissed the argument that the discrimination, if any, occurred in respect of employment. In his view, there was not a sufficient connection between the employer and the allegedly discriminatory conduct (CHRR, p D/3847):

Finally, because of the personal nature of the conduct and the fact that the employer could not gain by it, even in the achievement of a discriminatory goal, I do not consider that the victims were affected directly in respect of their employment. The board held that the employer condoned the cook's conduct. That is not, in my view, enough. Adoption of his conduct by the employer, not forgiveness, would be required at the very least to bring the cook's conduct within the meaning of the words "on behalf of the employer".

Twaddle JA also concluded that the Manitoba Human Rights Act did not impose upon employers the duty to provide a workplace free from sexual harassment.

IV   Issues

In this Court the appellants raise four grounds of appeal. The first and central ground of appeal is that the Manitoba Court of Appeal erred in holding that sexual harassment of the type to which the appellants were subjected was not discrimination on the basis of sex. Second, the appellants challenge the appellate court's holding that the employer could not be held liable for the sexual harassment perpetrated by Grammas. The liability of an employer for harassment of this nature is no longer in issue following the decision of this Court in *Robichaud v Canada (Treasury Board), supra.* Third, the appellants allege that the Court of Appeal erred in confirming the decision of Monnin J to reduce the damages awarded by the adjudicator. Finally, the appellants submit that the Court of Appeal erred by ordering costs against the Human Rights Commission in respect of the hearing before the adjudication board.

The respondent, Platy Enterprises Ltd, did not participate in this appeal either through written submission or oral argument. As I noted earlier, Grammas did not participate in any of the proceedings.

V   Is Sexual Harassment Sex Discrimination?

It would appear that since the decision in 1980 in *Bell v Ladas, supra,* human rights adjudication boards and courts in Canada have been to all intents unanimous in the recognition that certain forms of sexual harassment constitute sex discrimination. In *Bell,* in the course of determining whether sexual harassment was included in the concept of sex discrimination in s 4 of the Ontario Human Rights Code, Adjudicator Shime, in *obiter,* made the following oft-quoted remarks (CHRR, p D/156):

In my view, the purpose of The Code is to establish uniform working conditions for employees and to remove those matters enumerated in Section 4 as relevant considerations in the work place. Consideration of matters such as "race, creed, colour, age, sex, marital status, nationality or place of origin" strikes at what the preamble of The

Code refers to as "the foundation of freedom, justice and peace", and infringes on the "freedom of equality and dignity in rights" which this province and society revere as commonly held values and have enshrined those in The Code. Thus, The Code prohibits these values from becoming negative factors in the employment relationship.

Subject to the exception provided in Section 4(6), discrimination based on sex is prohibited by The Code. Thus, the paying of a female person less than a male person for the same job is prohibited, or dismissing an employee on the basis of sex is also prohibited. *But what about sexual harassment? Clearly a person who is disadvantaged because of her sex, is being discriminated against in her employment when employer conduct denies her financial rewards because of her sex, or exacts some form of sexual compliance to improve or maintain her existing benefits.* The evil to be remedied is the utilization of economic power or authority so as to restrict a woman's guaranteed and equal access to the work-place, and all of its benefits, free from extraneous pressures having to do with the mere fact that she is a woman. Where a woman's equal access is denied or when terms or conditions differ when compared to male employees, the woman is being discriminated against.

The forms of prohibited conduct that, in my view, are discriminatory run the gamut from overt gender based activity, such as coerced intercourse to unsolicited physical contact to persistent propositions to more subtle conduct such as gender based insults and taunting, which may reasonably be perceived to create a negative psychological and emotional work environment ... (Emphasis added.)

As Huband JA acknowledged, Adjudicator Shime's view that certain forms of sexual harassment fall within the statutory prohibition on sex discrimination has been adopted by human rights adjudication boards and tribunals across the country. For example: *Kotyk v Canadian Employment and Immigration Commission* (1983), 4 CHRR D/1416 (Can); *Phillips v Hermiz* (1984), 5 CHRR D/2450 (Sask); *Doherty v Lodger's International Ltd* (1981), 3 CHRR D/628 (NB); *Coutroubis v Sklavos Printing* (1981), 2 CHRR D/457 (Ont); *Hughes v Dollar Snack Bar* (1981), 3 CHRR D/1014 (Ont); *Cox v Jagbritte Inc* (1981), 3 CHRR D/609 (Ont); *Mitchell v Traveller Inn (Sudbury) Ltd* (1981), 2 CHRR D/590 (Ont); *Torres v Royalty Kitchenware Ltd, supra; Deisting v Dollar Pizza* (1978) Ltd (1982), 3 CHRR D/898 (Alta); *Hufnagel v Osama Enterprises Ltd, supra;* and *McPherson v Mary's Donuts* (1982), 3 CHRR D/961 (Ont.)

With the exception of the Manitoba Court of Appeal in the case at bar, all of the courts in Canada which have considered the issue, including two appellate courts, have also found sexual harassment to be a form of sex discrimination: *Johnstone v Zarankin* (1985), 6 CHRR D/2651 (BCSC); *Foisy v Bell Canada* (1984), 6 CHRR D/2817 (Que Sup Ct); *Commodore Business Machines Ltd v Ontario Minister of Labour* (1984), 6 CHRR D/2833 (Ont SC); *Re Mehta and MacKinnon* (1985), 19 DLR (4th) 198 (NSCA); and *Robichaud* (FCA), *supra*.

Since the middle of the 1970's, courts in the United States, including the United States Supreme Court, to which reference will be made later, have also reached the conclusion that forms of sexual harassment constitute sex discrimination.

The Manitoba Court of Appeal departed radically from this apparently unbroken line of judicial opinion. To determine whether the Manitoba Court of Appeal was correct in rejecting the reasoning in these cases and in holding that sexual harassment of the sort to which the appellants were subjected could not amount to sex discrimination, it is necessary to consider what is meant by the terms "sex discrimination" and "sexual harassment". Both sex discrimination and sexual harassment are broad concepts, encompassing a wide range of behaviour. For the purposes of this appeal I will restrict my discussion of each of these terms to their manifestations in the workplace. In *Canadian National Railway Co v Canada (Canadian Human Rights Commission)*, [1987] 1 SCR

1114, a case raising a claim of systemic sex discrimination, the Court had occasion to consider the meaning of discrimination in the employment context. The Court adopted at pp 1138–39 the definition of discrimination found in the Abella Report on equality in employment (Abella, *Equality in Employment: Royal Commission Report* (1984), at p 2), which I quote in full below:

> Equality in employment means that no one is denied opportunities for reasons that have nothing to do with inherent ability. It means equal access free from arbitrary obstructions. Discrimination means that an arbitrary barrier stands between a person's ability and his or her opportunity to demonstrate it. If the access is genuinely available in a way that permits everyone who so wishes the opportunity to fully develop his or her potential, we have achieved a kind of equality. It is equality defined as equal freedom from discrimination.

> Discrimination in this context means practices or attitudes that have, whether by design or impact, the effect of limiting an individual's or a group's right to the opportunities generally available because of attributed rather than actual characteristics. What is impeding the full development of the potential is not the individual's capacity but an external barrier that artificially inhibits growth.

> It is not a question of whether this discrimination is motivated by an intentional desire to obstruct someone's potential, or whether it is the accidental by-product of innocently motivated practices or systems. If the barrier is affecting certain groups in a disproportionately negative way, it is a signal that the practices that lead to this adverse impact may be discriminatory.

In keeping with this general definition of employment discrimination, discrimination on the basis of sex may be defined as practices or attitudes which have the effect of limiting the conditions of employment of, or the employment opportunities available to, employees on the basis of a characteristic related to gender.

Numerous definitions of sexual harassment have been proposed. Professor Catharine MacKinnon describes sexual harassment, most broadly defined, as "the unwanted imposition of sexual requirements in the context of a relationship of unequal power" (*Sexual Harassment of Working Women: A Case of Sex Discrimination* (1979), at p 1). In *Sexual Harassment in the Workplace* (1987), Arjun P Aggarwal states that sexual harassment (at p 1) "is any sexually-oriented practice that endangers an individual's continued employment, negatively affects his/her work performance, or undermines his/her sense of personal dignity". As Aggarwal states, at p 1:

> Sexual harassment is a complex issue involving men and women, their perceptions and behaviour, and the social norms of the society. Sexual harassment is not confined to any one level, class, or profession. It can happen to executives as well as factory workers. It occurs not only in the workplace and in the classroom, but even in parliamentary chambers and churches. Sexual harassment may be an expression of power or desire or both. Whether it is from supervisors, co-workers, or customers, sexual harassment is an attempt to assert power over another person.

> Sexual harassment is any sexually-oriented practice that endangers an individual's continued employment, negatively affects his/her work performance, or undermines his/her sense of personal dignity. Harassment behaviour may manifest itself blatantly in forms such as leering, grabbing, and even sexual assault. More subtle forms of sexual harassment may include sexual innuendos, and propositions for dates or sexual favours.

Professors Constance Backhouse and Leah Cohen cite a number of definitions in *The Secret Oppression: Sexual Harassment of Working Women* (1978), including the following description proposed by the Alliance Against Sexual Coercion (at p 38) "[a]ny sexually oriented practice that endangers a woman's job – that undermines her job performance and threatens her economic livelihood". Backhouse and Cohen list a number of concrete illustrations of harassing behaviour (at p 38):

> Sexual harassment can manifest itself both physically and psychologically. In its milder forms it can involve verbal innuendo and inappropriate affectionate gestures. It can, however, escalate to extreme behaviour amounting to attempted rape and rape. Physically, the recipient may be the victim of pinching, grabbing, hugging, patting, leering, brushing against, and touching. Psychological harassment can involve a relentless proposal of physical intimacy, beginning with subtle hints which may lead to overt requests for dates and sexual favours.

Common to all of these descriptions of sexual harassment is the concept of using a position of power to import sexual requirements into the workplace thereby negatively altering the working conditions of employees who are forced to contend with sexual demands.

Legislative definitions of sexual harassment and guidelines promulgated by various organizations reflect this general view of sexual harassment. In 1980 the American Equal Employment Opportunity Commission produced one of the first set of guidelines dealing with sexual harassment (Equal Employment Opportunity Commission, "Guidelines on Discrimination Because of Sex", 29 CFR 1604 11(a) (1985)). The Commission took the position that sexual harassment was a violation of Title VII of the Civil Rights Act of 1964, the prohibition against sex discrimination:

> (a) harassment on the basis of sex is a violation of Sec. 703 of Title VII. Unwelcome sexual advances, requests for sexual favors, and other verbal or physical conduct of a sexual nature constitute sexual harassment, when (1) submission to such conduct is made either explicitly or implicitly a term or condition of an individual's employment, (2) submission to or rejection of such conduct by an individual is used as the basis for employment decisions affecting such individual, or (3) such conduct has the purpose or effect of unreasonably interfering with an individual's work performance or creating an intimidating, hostile, or offensive working environment.

These guidelines have been quoted with approval by courts and human rights tribunals in both the United States and Canada. The Canada Labour Code, RSC, 1985, c L-2, as amended by c. 9 (1st Supp), s 17, provides the following definition of "sexual harassment":

> 61.7 ... any conduct, comment, gesture or contact of a sexual nature:
>
> (a) that is likely to cause offence or humiliation to any employee; or
>
> (b) that might, on reasonable grounds, be perceived by that employee as placing a condition of a sexual nature on employment or on any opportunity for training or promotion.

The Manitoba Human Rights Code, quoted earlier, which repeals and replaces the Manitoba Human Rights Act in force at the time of the initiation of the proceedings in this appeal, also explicitly defines sexual harassment.

The human rights legislation of Ontario and Newfoundland, both of which expressly prohibit sexual harassment, contain similar definitions of "sexual solicitation": Ontario Human Rights Code, 1981, SO 1981, c 53, s 6; The Newfoundland Human Rights Code, RSN 1970, c 262, s 10.1.

Emerging from these various legislative proscriptions is the notion that sexual harassment may take a variety of forms. Sexual harassment is not limited to demands for sexual favours made under threats of adverse job consequences should the employee refuse to comply with the demands. Victims of harassment need not demonstrate that they were not hired, were denied a promotion or were dismissed from their employment as a result of their refusal to participate in sexual activity. This form of harassment, in which the victim suffers concrete economic loss for failing to submit to sexual demands, is simply one manifestation of sexual harassment, albeit a particularly blatant and ugly one. Sexual harassment also encompasses situations in which sexual demands are foisted upon unwilling employees or in which employees must endure sexual groping, propositions, and inappropriate comments, but where no tangible economic rewards are attached to involvement in the behaviour.

The Manitoba Court of Appeal judges rejected a series of United States decisions which, over the past decade, considered the question whether sexual harassment of the nature of that found here by Adjudicator Henteleff could constitute sex discrimination within the context of human rights legislation, namely, Title VII of the Civil Rights Act of 1964. Title VII states that it is an unlawful employment practice "... to discriminate against any individual with respect to his compensation, terms, conditions, or privileges of employment, because of such individual's race, color, religion, sex, or national origin".

The American courts have tended to divide sexual harassment into two categories: the "quid pro quo" variety in which tangible employment related benefits are made contingent upon participation in sexual activity, and conduct which creates a "hostile environment" by requiring employees to endure sexual gestures and posturing in the workplace. Both forms of sexual harassment have been recognized by the American Courts including the United States Supreme Court: *Barnes v Costle*, 561 F 2d 983 (DC Cir 1977); *Bundy v Jackson*, 641 F 2d 934 (DC Cir 1981); *Henson v Dundee*, 682 F 2d 897 (11th Cir 1982); and *Meritor Savings Bank v Vinson*, 106 S Ct 2399 (1986). Canadian human rights tribunals have also tended to rely on the *quid pro quo*/hostile work environment dichotomy. I do not find this categorization particularly helpful. While the distinction may have been important to illustrate forcefully the range of behaviour that constitutes harassment at a time before sexual harassment was widely viewed as actionable, in my view there is no longer any need to characterize harassment as one of these forms. The main point in allegations of sexual harassment is that unwelcome sexual conduct has invaded the workplace, irrespective of whether the consequences of the harassment included a denial of concrete employment rewards for refusing to participate in sexual activity.

I am in accord with the following dictum of the United States Court of Appeals for the Eleventh Circuit in *Henson v Dundee*, quoted with approval in the *Meritor Savings Bank* case:

> Sexual harassment which creates a hostile or offensive environment for members of one sex is every bit the arbitrary barrier to sexual equality at the workplace that racial harassment is to racial equality. Surely, a requirement that a man or woman run a gauntlet of sexual abuse in return for the privilege of being allowed to work and make a living can be as demeaning and disconcerting as the harshest of racial epithets.

Without seeking to provide an exhaustive definition of the term, I am of the view that sexual harassment in the workplace may be broadly defined as unwelcome conduct of a sexual nature that detrimentally affects the work environment or leads to adverse job-related consequences for the victims of the harassment. It is, as Adjudicator Shime observed in *Bell v Ladas, supra*, and as has been widely accepted by other adjudicators and academic commentators, an abuse of power. When sexual harassment occurs in the workplace, it is an abuse of both economic and sexual power. Sexual harassment is a demeaning practice, one that constitutes a profound affront to the dignity of the employees forced to endure it. By requiring an employee to contend with unwelcome sexual actions or explicit sexual demands, sexual harassment in the workplace attacks the dignity and self-respect of the victim both as an employee and as a human being.

Perpetrators of sexual harassment and victims of the conduct may be either male or female. However, in the present sex stratified labour market, those with the power to harass sexually will predominantly be male and those facing the greatest risk of harassment will tend to be female. Professor Hickling documents this situation in an article entitled "Employer's Liability for Sexual Harassment" (1988), 17 *Man LJ* 124, at p 127:

> Sexual harassment as a phenomenon of the workplace is not new. Nor is it confined to harassment of women by men, though this is by far the most prevalent and significant context. It may be committed by women against men, by homosexuals against members of the same sex. According to a Canadian survey published in 1983 [Canadian Human Rights Commission, Research and Special Studies Branch, *Unwanted Sexual Attention and Sexual Harassment: Result of a Survey of Canadians* (Ottawa: Minister of Supply and Services Canada (1983))], women reported far more exposure to all forms of unwanted sexual attention than did men. Forty-nine percent of women (as compared to 33% of men) stated that they had experienced at least one form of this kind of harassment. The frequency of sexual harassment directed against women was also significantly higher. In the case of sexual harassment experienced by women, most (93%) of the harassers were men, while men complained of harassment by women (62%) and men (24%). The victims of sexual harassment are not confined to any particular group, identifiable by age, sex, class, educational background, income or occupation, although younger single women (and interestingly, those at the lower end of the economic scale) tend to suffer the most. One characteristic that victims usually share in common is their vulnerability to economic sanctions both real and threatened.

Professor Hickling's exposition suggests that women may be at greater risk of being sexually harassed because they tend to occupy low status jobs in the employment hierarchy. Arjun Aggarwal, in his article quoted earlier, offers an additional explanation for the increased vulnerability of women to sexual harassment. Drawing an analogy to the practice of racial discrimination where racial slurs reinforce perceived racial inequality, Aggarwal argues that sexual harassment is used in a sexist society to (at pp 5–6) "underscore women's difference from, and by implication, inferiority with respect to the dominant male group" and to "remind women of their inferior ascribed status".

In the context of this understanding of sexual harassment and discrimination on the basis of sex, the reasons of the Court of Appeal of Manitoba may be evaluated. Let me say at the outset that, in my opinion, the Court of Appeal erred to the extent that it relied on legislation enacted by the Parliament of Canada and three of the provinces, defining and prohibiting sexual harassment, for the inference that in the absence of such express legislation a prohibition against sexual discrimination could not embrace sexual harassment. The amendments were no doubt intended to make express and explicit what had previously been implicit. As the appellants point out in their factum:

> It is worth noting, however, that in those jurisdictions [Ontario, Quebec, Newfoundland, Canada] the decisions given prior to those amendments unanimously came to the conclusion that sexual harassment of the type we are dealing with here constituted sex discrimination. Moreover, most jurisdictions (eg. B.C., Alberta, Saskatchewan, Nova Scotia, etc.) have continued to rely on the prohibition against "sex discrimination" in employment, as a sufficient vehicle to cope with sexual harassment.

The amendments were meant to clarify and educate, not to alter the interpretation of the legislation. As one Ontario Adjudicator, Prof Peter Cummings, has noted in a subsequent analysis of the Court of Appeal for Manitoba's reasoning:

The question before the Court of Appeal in *Janzen*, however, was not, of course, whether a prohibition against sexual harassment should be a part of Manitoba's human rights legislation but rather whether such a prohibition is in fact implicit in the existing general anti-discrimination provisions of the Act. This must be the question in every jurisdiction examining the place of harassing behaviour under a general anti-discriminatory provision. In some provinces (Quebec, Newfoundland and Ontario) and in the federal sphere the legislatures have decided to use express language where before an implicit prohibition had been sufficient. Given this obvious advantage of clarity and certainty which an express prohibition allows, these new provisions are to be applauded. It seems ironic, however, at the least, that in making its own progressive policies explicit a legislature may endanger equally progressive implicit assumptions about general legislation in another province.

The legislative history of the Ontario provision suggests that the government of the day viewed the explicit inclusions of harassment as a measure to clarify existing rights rather than to create new ones ...

In my view the more general language found in legislation without explicit provisions also prohibits sexual harassment in employment.

See *Boehm v National System of Banking Ltd* (1987), 8 C.H.R.R. D/4110 at D/419-20; and also *Zarankin, supra*, at D/2276-77.

There appear to be two principal reasons, closely related, for the decision of the Court of Appeal of Manitoba that the sexual harassment to which the appellants were subjected was not sex discrimination. First, the Court of Appeal drew a link between sexual harassment and sexual attraction. Sexual harassment, in the view of the Court, stemmed from personal characteristics of the victim, rather than from the victim's gender. Second, the appellate court was of the view that the prohibition of sex discrimination in s 6(1) of the Human Rights Act was designed to eradicate only generic or categorical discrimination. On this reasoning, a claim of sex discrimination could not be made out unless all women were subjected to a form of treatment to which all men were not. If only some female employees were sexually harassed in the workplace, the harasser could not be said to be discriminating on the basis of sex. At most the harasser could only be said to be distinguishing on the basis of some other characteristic.

The two arguments raised by the Manitoba Court of Appeal may in fact be seen as alternate formulations of the following argument. Discrimination implies treating one group differently from other groups, thus all members of the affected group must be subjected to the discriminatory treatment. Sexual harassment, however, involves treating some persons differently from others, usually on the basis of the sexual attractiveness of the victim. The harasser will typically choose one, or several, persons to harass but will not harass all members of one gender. As harassers select their targets on the basis of a personal characteristic, physical attractiveness, rather than on the basis of a group characteristic, gender, sexual harassment does not constitute discrimination on the basis of sex.

This line of reasoning has been considered in both Canada and the United States and, in my view, quite properly rejected. The reasons for the rejection were cogently expressed by Adjudicator Lynn Smith in *Zarankin v Johnstone* (1984) 5 CHRR D/2274 (BC Bd), at p 2276 (appeal to Supreme Court of British Columbia dismissed (1985), 6 CHRR D/2651):

Although it might be thought that sexual harassment would not amount to sex discrimination unless all employees of the same gender were equally recipients of it, that is fallacious. So long as gender provides a basis for differentiation, it matters not that further differentiation on another basis is made. An analogy would be a complaint of sex discrimination against an employer who decided to dismiss all of his married female employees but none of his male employees and none of his unmarried female employees. The decision would affect one group adversely – female employees – even though it would not affect every member of that group. Similarly, an employer who selects only some of his female employees for sexual harassment and leaves other female employees alone is discriminatory by reason of sex because the harassment affects only one group adversely.

The fallacy in the position advanced by the Court of Appeal is the belief that sex discrimination only exists where gender is the sole ingredient in the discriminatory action and where, therefore, all members of the affected gender are mistreated identically. While the concept of discrimination is rooted in the notion of treating an individual as part of a group rather than on the basis of the individual's personal characteristics, discrimination does not require uniform treatment of all members of a particular group. It is sufficient that ascribing to an individual a group characteristic is one factor in the treatment of that individual. If a finding of discrimination required that every individual in the affected group be treated identically, legislative protection against discrimination would be of little or no value. It is rare that a discriminatory action is so bluntly expressed as to treat all members of the relevant group identically. In nearly every instance of discrimination the discriminatory action is composed of various ingredients with the result that some members of the pertinent group are not adversely affected, at least in a direct sense, by the discriminatory action. To deny a finding of discrimination in the circumstances of this appeal is to deny the existence of discrimination in any situation where discriminatory practices are less than perfectly inclusive. It is to argue, for example, that an employer who will only hire a woman if she has twice the qualifications required of a man is not guilty of sex discrimination if, despite this policy, the employer nevertheless manages to hire some women.

The argument that discrimination requires identical treatment of all members of the affected group is firmly dismissed by this Court in *Brooks v Canada Safeway Ltd* [1989] 1 SCR 1219. In *Brooks* I stated that pregnancy related discrimination is sex discrimination. The argument that pregnancy related discrimination could not be sex discrimination because not all women become pregnant was dismissed for the reason that pregnancy cannot be separated from gender. All pregnant persons are women. Although, in *Brooks*, the impugned benefits plan of the employer, Safeway, did not mention women, it was held to discriminate on the basis of sex because the plan's discriminatory effects fell entirely upon women.

The reasoning in *Brooks* is applicable to the present appeal. Only a woman can become pregnant; only a woman could be subject to sexual harassment by a heterosexual male, such as the respondent Grammas. That some women do not become pregnant was no defence in *Brooks*, just as it is no defence in this appeal that not all female employees at the restaurant were subject to sexual harassment. The crucial fact is that it was only female employees who ran the risk of sexual harassment. No man would have been subjected to this treatment. The sexual harassment the appellants suffered fits the definition of sex discrimination offered earlier: "practices or attitudes which have the effect of limiting the conditions of employment of, or the employment opportunities available to, employees on the basis of a characteristic related to gender".

To argue that the sole factor underlying the discriminatory action was the sexual attractiveness of the appellants and to say that their gender was irrelevant strains credulity. Sexual attractiveness cannot be separated from gender. The similar gender of both appellants is not a mere coincidence, it is fundamental to understanding what they experienced. All female employees were potentially subject to sexual harassment by the respondent Grammas. That his discriminatory behaviour was pinpointed against two of the female employees would have been small comfort to other women contemplating entering such a workplace. Any female considering employment at the Pharos restaurant was a potential victim of Grammas and as such was disadvantaged because of her sex. A potential female employee would recognize that if she were a male employee she would not have to run the same risks of sexual harassment. In *Brooks*, in reference to a health benefits plan which imposed the costs of pregnancy upon women, I stated [at p 1238] that "[R]emoval of such unfair impositions upon women and other groups in society is a key purpose of anti-discrimination legislation". That statement is equally applicable to the sexual harassment that was suffered by the appellants in this appeal. Because they were women, the appellants were subject to a disadvantage to which no man at the restaurant would have been subject. As the LEAF factum puts it, "... sexual harassment is a form of sex discrimination because it denies women equality of opportunity in employment because of their sex." It is one of the purposes of anti-discrimination legislation to remove such denials of equality of opportunity.

As noted earlier, the argument that sexual harassment is sex discrimination has been recognized by a long line of Canadian, American and English (see *Porcelli v Strathclyde Regional Council* [1985] ICR 177 (EAT-Scot), aff'd [1986] ICR 564 (Ct of Session)) cases which have found sexual harassment to be sex discrimination.

In conclusion on this point, I offer a quotation from a leading American decision, *Bundy v Jackson, supra*, at p 942, which is equally applicable to the legislation at issue in this appeal:

> ... our task of statutory construction in *Barnes* was to determine whether the disparate treatment Barnes suffered was "based on ... sex". We heard arguments there that whatever harm Barnes suffered was not sex discrimination, since Barnes' supervisor terminated her job because she had refused sexual advances, not because she was a woman. We rejected those arguments as disingenuous in the extreme. The supervisor in that case made demands of Barnes that he would not have made of male employees. "But for her womanhood" ... [Barnes'] participation in sexual activity would never have been solicited. To say, then, that she was victimized in her employment simply because she declined the invitation is to ignore the asserted fact that she was invited only because she was a woman subordinate to the inviter in the hierarchy of agency personnel.
>
> We thus made it clear in *Barnes* that sex discrimination within the meaning of Title VII is not limited to disparate treatment founded solely or categorically on gender. Rather, discrimination is sex discrimination whenever sex is for no legitimate reason a substantial factor in the discrimination.

VI   Is the Respondent liable?

The liability of employers for the acts of their employees in situations such as in the present appeal has been settled by the recent decision of this Court in *Robichaud v Canada (Treasury Board), supra*. This decision, which reversed the judgment of the Federal Court of Appeal, was delivered subsequent to the decision of the Manitoba Court of Appeal in the present case. In *Robichaud*, La Forest J, writing for the Court, considered the liability of an employer for sexual harassment under the Canadian Human Rights Act, where the harassment was committed by an employee. His words are equally applicable to the Manitoba legislation; each Act has a similar purpose and structure.

La Forest J began by stating that human rights legislation (at p 92):

... is not aimed at determining fault or punishing conduct. It is remedial. Its aim is to identify and eliminate discrimination. If this is to be done, then the remedies must be effective, consistent with the "almost constitutional" nature of the rights protected.

He continued two pages later:

Indeed, if the Act is concerned with the *effects* of discrimination rather than its *causes* (or motivations), it must be admitted that only an employer can remedy undesirable effects; only an employer can provide the most important remedy – a healthy work environment.

La Forest J then concluded that the statute requires that employers be held liable for the discriminatory acts of their employees where those actions are work-related. He did not try to apply principles of vicarious liability, saying that this was unhelpful and, in any event, unnecessary since the employer's liability could be found within the statute (at p 95):

Hence, I would conclude that the statute contemplates the imposition of liability on employers for all acts of their employees "in the course of employment", interpreted in the purposive fashion outlined earlier as being in some way related or associated with the employment. It is unnecessary to attach any label to this type of liability; it is purely statutory.

Although the employer in the *Robichaud* case was the Crown, it is clear that La Forest J's words are meant to apply to all employment relationships. At no point in his judgment is any significance attached to the Crown status of the employer.

On the basis of La Forest J's decision, the respondent Platy Enterprises Ltd must be held liable for the actions of the cook Grammas. Grammas' actions fall within the "course of his employment" as defined by La Forest J's purposive interpretation. On page 92, La Forest J expanded on the meaning to be given to "course of employment", arguing that the term should not be interpreted as only referring to activities which fall narrowly within the employee's job description. To employ such a narrow definition, he said, would be wrongly to import tortious notions of vicarious liability into the field of discrimination law. He concluded that employers are liable for any action of their employees which is "work-related" (at p 92):

It would appear more sensible and more consonant with the purpose of the Act to interpret the phrase "in the course of employment" as meaning work- or job-related ...

The difference between the words of the Manitoba Act, "in respect of employment", and those of the Canadian Act, "course of employment", is not significant. La Forest J's words apply equally to both Acts.

In light of this interpretation it cannot be argued that Grammas was not acting in respect of his employment when he sexually harassed the appellants. His actions were clearly work related. Grammas' opportunity to harass the appellants sexually was directly related to his employment position as the next in line in authority to the employer. Grammas used his position of authority, a position accorded him by the respondent, to take advantage of the appellants. The authority granted to Grammas, both through his control in running the restaurant, including his control over food orders and work hours, and through his purported ability to fire waitresses, gave him power over the waitresses. It was the respondent's responsibility to ensure that this power was not abused. This it clearly did not do, even after the appellants made specific complaints about the harassment. So it is liable for the actions of Grammas.

VII   The damages award

I quoted earlier the remarks of Monnin J in reducing the award of damages to Janzen and Govereau. With great respect, no persuasive arguments were presented by Monnin J as to why Adjudicator Henteleff erred in his award. The amounts are not inordinate in light of the seriousness of the complaints.

VIII   Costs before the Board of Adjudication

The Court of Appeal awarded costs to the respondents and against the Commission not only before the Court of Queen's Bench and the Court of Appeal, but also before the Board of Adjudication itself. The order with respect to costs will be set aside because of this Court's decision on the respondent's liability. I wish however to comment briefly on the Court of Appeal's decision to award costs against the Commission in respect of the hearing before the Board of Adjudication. Even if the Court of Appeal's decision on liability had been upheld in this Court, I would see no justification for this award of costs against the Commission. Under the Act, the Board of Adjudication itself is given no authority to award costs. One reason for this is that the Commission has a duty under s 20 of the Act to bring complaints before the Board, unless those complaints are, *per* s 19(4), "without merit". Therefore, while appreciating that courts do have a discretion with respect to costs, I believe costs should only be ordered against the Manitoba Human Rights Commission in exceptional circumstances. There was no reason to exercise that discretion on the facts of this case, even as these facts were interpreted by the Court of Appeal. The complaint brought forth by the Commission was clearly with merit. It succeeded before the Board and the Court of Queen's Bench. For the Commission to have refused to have brought forth the complaint would have been a neglect of its statutory duty.

IX   Disposition

For the aforementioned reasons I would allow the appeal, set aside the judgment of the Court of Appeal of Manitoba and restore the judgment of Monnin J of the Court of Queen's Bench, except as to the award of damages which should be as stated by Adjudicator Henteleff. The appellants are entitled to costs at all levels, except before the Board of Adjudication.

Appeal allowed.

CASE NO 30

H v E

EQUAL OPPORTUNITIES TRIBUNAL, NEW ZEALAND

Judgment: 19 September 1985

Panel: Smellie QC (*Chairman*), Jefferies and Morris (*Members*)

Human rights — Equality and non-discrimination — Sex discrimination — Sexual harassment — Whether sexual harassment constitutes discrimination on the ground of sex — Employment — Constructive dismissal — Whether resignation due to sexual harassment constitutes constructive dismissal — Human Rights Commission Act 1977, s 15(1)

Statutes — Interpretation — International treaties — Relevance of international obligations to interpretation of domestic law — Purposive approach to interpretation to promote the advancement of human rights — Whether sexual harassment constitutes discrimination on the ground of sex — Obligations under the International Covenant on Economic, Social and Cultural Rights to provide women just and favourable work conditions and conditions of work not inferior to those enjoyed by men, arts 7 and 23 — Acts Interpretation Act 1924, s5(j)

BACKGROUND

The plaintiff, a resident of New Zealand, was employed part-time for a period of eight months in a shop owned by the defendant and his wife. She complained that during that time the defendant sexually harassed her to the point at which she had no alternative but to leave, claiming constructive dismissal. The defendant disputed her allegations of sexual harassment and stated that the defendant's wife had dismissed her from her job on the same day that she resigned because of poor work performance.

The plaintiff brought her complaint before the Human Rights Commission, which was unable to make a finding on the facts due to lack of evidence. The case proceeded before the Equal Opportunities Tribunal which, having considered the evidence more fully, accepted the plaintiff's allegations. The Tribunal also considered whether sexual harassment amounted to discrimination on the grounds of sex under the Human Rights Commission Act 1979, section 15(1)(c).[*]

HELD (finding for the plaintiff)

1   It was an implied term of any contract between an employer and employee that they would so conduct themselves that the necessary relationship of confidence and trust between them would not be disrupted or destroyed. The conduct of the defendant in this instance destroyed that relationship of confidence and trust and the breach of the agreement was so fundamental that it brought the relationship to an end. Accordingly, what occurred could correctly be described as a constructive dismissal of the plaintiff (p 480).

---

[*]   *Eds:* section 15(1)(c) is reproduced at p 479 below.

2   Parliament must be presumed to have intended that the unlawful discrimination sections of the Human Rights Commission Act 1977, as they relate to employment, should be in conformity with New Zealand's international obligations. Only if section 15 of the Act outlawed sexual harassment, along with other discriminatory practices based on sex, would women in the workplace be afforded "just and favourable conditions of work" (Universal Declaration of Human Rights, article 23) and "conditions of work not inferior to those enjoyed by men" (International Covenant on Economic, Social and Cultural Rights, article 7). Sexual harassment was therefore covered by section 15(1)(c) of the Human Rights Commission Act 1997 (p 490).

Treaties and other international instruments referred to

International Covenant on Economic, Social and Cultural Rights 1966, art 7

Universal Declaration of Human Rights 1948, art 23

National legislation referred to

Australia

Anti-Discrimination Act (NSW) 1977, s 25(2)

Canada

British Columbia Human Rights Code, s 8

Human Rights Act, s 3(1)

New Zealand

Acts Interpretation Act 1924, s 5(j)

Human Rights Commission Act 1977, ss 15(1)(c), 38(6)(a), 38(6)(b), 40(1)(c), 52, 55, 56 and 62

Industrial Relations Act, s 117

United States of America

Civil Rights Act 1964, Title VII

Cases referred to

Ashby v Minister of Immigration (1981) 1 NZLR 222

Barnes v Costle 561 F 2d 983 (DC Cir 1977)

Bundy v Jackson 641 F 2d 934 (DC Cir 1981)

Crockett v Canterbury Clerical Workers Union (1984) EOC ¶92-025; (1983) 3 NZAR 435

Department of Labour v Latailakepa (1982) 1 NZLR 632

Giouvanoudis v Golden Fleece Restaurant & Anor (1984) 5 CHRR D/348

Hill v Water Resources Commission (1985) EOC ¶92-127

Holien v Sears Roebuck & Co (1984) 35 EPD 35,467

King-Ansell v Police [1979] 2 NZLR 531

Kotyk v Canadian Employment and Immigration Commission (1983) 4 CHRR D/1416

O'Callaghan v Loder & Anor (1984) (NSW) EOC 92-023

Phillips v Martin Marietta Corp 400 US 542 (1971); 91 S Ct 496; 27 L Ed 2d 613; 3 Fair Empl Prac Cas (BNA) 40; 3 Empl Prac Dec P 8088

The Auckland and Gisborne Amalgamated Society of Shop Employees and Related Trades Industrial Union of Workers v Woolworths (New Zealand) Ltd CA 150/84 Judgment 3/4/85 [1985] 2 NZLR 372

Zarankin v Wessex Inn 5 CHRR D/387

DECISION*

Preliminary matters

By consent at the commencement of the proceedings an order was made pursuant to s 54(3)(b) prohibiting any publication of the whole of the evidence and any part of this Decision which could lead to the parties to this litigation being identified.

Details of claim – Details of defence

The plaintiff, in the details she filed ... said she was unable to say the precise number of times that she was sexually harassed but alleged there were a number of incidents from about 9 October 1983 until and including Friday 13 April 1984. She then set out particulars in ten sub-paragraphs which the Tribunal summarises as follows:

(1) She complained of the defendant's behaviour on the evening of Sunday 9 October 1983 in respect of what was called the "peeping Tom incident" during the hearing.

(2) In the four weeks preceding Christmas 1983, the defendant began to engage in sexual talk and pressed her to co-operate in sexual activity, such as peeping and touching, which she refused and as far as she was able she tried to avoid him.

(3) The week before Christmas 1983, the defendant tried to persuade her to drive him into a park rather than home, as had been arranged, and she refused.

(4) Shortly before Christmas 1983, the defendant asked the plaintiff to go to work early and when she turned up at the normal time the defendant told her that he took that as an indication that her answer was no.

(5) The defendant on several occasions made open sexual remarks and asked about her sexual habits, started telling her what he would like to do to her sexually and enquired regarding the colour of her underwear and suggested that she refrain from wearing a bra.

---

*   ***Eds:*** the following is an abridged version of the decision of the Equal Opportunities Tribunal. In particular, the first part of the decision, which sets out the full background to the case and the detailed evidence, has been edited substantially. The full decision is available at (1985) 5 NZAR 33, and an alternative abridged version at EOC 92-137.

(6) After Christmas 1983 the defendant became more insistent and frequently tried to touch the plaintiff and on one occasion pinned her to a work bench and pressed up against her.

(7) After Christmas 1983, when the plaintiff refused to join the defendant at the back of the shop he asked her what she would do if he "took her by force".

(8) On several occasions the defendant offered to waive payment of purchase made by the plaintiff if she would let him have "a peep".

(9) On Thursday 12 April 1984, the defendant tried to lift the plaintiff's skirt while she was working in the shop.

(10) On Friday 13 April 1984, the defendant again pinned the plaintiff to a work bench and she had to duck under his arms to get away and later in the day, when she was signing for her wages, he tried to kiss her and pull up her skirt and then exposed his erect penis and grabbed her hand, telling her to touch him and endeavouring to force her to do so.

The plaintiff alleged that she made a number of protests directly to the defendant and made it clear to him that she was not interested in him and she took steps to avoid him. She finally alleged that the incident on Friday 13 April 1984 indicated to her that the defendant was not going to leave her alone and she began to fear for her safety. She also alleged that towards the end of her employment, after she had made it abundantly clear that she was not interested in the defendant, he began "picking" on the plaintiff and withholding the opportunity for extra work when it was available.

In response to those relatively precise details the defendant acknowledges in substance the "peeping Tom" incident as follows:

> The defendant agrees that he telephoned the plaintiff because he had had an argument with his wife. He was depressed over custody matters that he was experiencing and also financial matters with respect to the shop and because he regarded the plaintiff as a friend and wanted to discuss things with her over a cup of coffee. He admits that he later went to her house and was going to knock on the door but thought better of it. Next day he admitted to the plaintiff that he had been at her house and said that he had come to apologise for telephoning her.

The defendant also admitted there had been discussions of a sexual nature but said they were in the company of his wife and that they were "of a joking banter (sic) which all staff indulge in".

For the rest, however, the allegations were denied and the defendant also denied that the plaintiff had complained to him and alleged that he had had to speak to her for chatting to male customers for too long and further alleged that his wife had told the plaintiff to look for another job. [...]

In the result then, in summary, on the facts, the plaintiff established to our satisfaction that over a period of some six months, between October 1983 and April 1984, she was sexually harassed by the defendant with increasing intensity. We accept that she complained to him and made it clear that his attentions were unwelcome. We believe the plaintiff when she says that because of her friendship with Mrs E even if the defendant's attentions had been welcome, she would not have entertained them. We accept that the defendant propositioned the plaintiff on a number of occasions and we specifically accept that he did try to kiss and lift her skirts on Friday 13 April and that on that day also he did expose his erect penis to her and tried to force her to touch it. We are satisfied that the plaintiff only put up with the treatment prior to 13 April because the job suited her and she did not want to lose it and that what happened on that last day at work left her no option but to resign. We specifically reject the evidence of Mrs E that she was effectively dismissed from her employment on 13 April, although we do accept that both Mrs E and the defendant had made some complaint to the plaintiff towards the end of her employment about her work but on balance we doubt that those complaints were justified and see them as an oblique retaliation by the defendant because his sexual advances were being rejected.

It follows from these findings that if what has occurred is something in respect of which damages can be awarded under the Act, then the plaintiff is entitled to compensation and other relief.

Legal aspects of case

We turn, therefore, to a consideration of the legal aspects of the case.

Section 15(1)(c)

15   Employment

(1)   It shall be unlawful for any person who is an employer...

   (c)   to dismiss any person, or subject any person to any detriment, in circumstances in which other persons employed by that employer on work of that description are not or would not be dismissed or are not or would not be subjected to such detriment

by reason of the sex ... of that person.

The above is the section under which the plaintiff brings her action. Primarily, she is seeking damages for what in law is called a constructive dismissal but her case was also argued on the basis that she had been subjected to "detriment" and that approach was supported by counsel for the Proceedings Commissioner.

For the plaintiff to succeed, therefore, she must establish the following:

(1)   That the defendant was her employer;

(2)   That she was dismissed or subjected to detriment;

(3)   That the dismissal or detriment occurred in circumstances in which other persons employed by the defendant in the shop would not have been dismissed or subjected to such detriment; and

(4)   That the dismissal or detriment occurred by reason of her sex.

There is no difficulty with the first point, although the defendant and Mrs E were joint owners of the business, the defendant falls clearly within the definition of employer under the section.

As to dismissal

We have found as a fact that the plaintiff was not dismissed in the ordinary sense of that word from her employment. We have also found, however, that the treatment she received from the defendant left her with no alternative but to resign.

In the case of *Crockett v Canterbury Clerical Workers Union* (1984) EOC paras 92-025; (1983) 3 NZAR 435, a differently constituted Tribunal had to consider a comparable case, although in the end, the plaintiff there failed to bring the fact situation within the Act. When dealing with the first of two applications under s 55 of the Act in that case, however, a number of the authorities from jurisdictions in North America were considered. In some of those cases the Courts appeared to accept that to succeed in such a case as this the plaintiff has to establish that effectively compliance with an employer's sexual demands has become a term of her employment. Others of the cases expressed the view that an employee who resigns rather than being dismissed faces a greater evidentiary burden. We are not attracted to that approach.

Following the lead given by the Court of Appeal in an, as yet, unreported judgment (*The Auckland and Gisborne Amalgamated Society of Shop Employees and Related Trades Industrial Union of Workers v Woolworths (New Zealand) Limited CA* 150/84 Judgment 3/4/85)* we would hold that it is an implied term of any contract between an employer and employee that they will so conduct themselves that the necessary relationship of confidence and trust between them will not be disrupted or destroyed. We would further hold, in line with the above authority, that the conduct of the defendant in this instance destroyed that relationship of confidence and trust and that that breach of the agreement was so fundamental that it brought the relationship to an end. Accordingly, what occurred can be correctly described as a constructive dismissal.

At p 4 of the Court of Appeal judgment, which was delivered by Cooke J, the Court commences with a discussion of s 117 of the Industrial Relations Act. By a parity of reasoning we are of the opinion that what the Court had to say about that section as it relates to implied terms and constructive dismissal, applies equally to s 15 of the Human Rights Commission Act and in the circumstances of this case, provides ample authority for our holding that the constructive dismissal that occurred here is covered by the word "dismiss" in s 15(1)(c) of the Act. In particular, we rely upon the sentence in the portion of the judgment quoted below, which reads:

> In the context of an Act aimed at good industrial relations (cf. The Human Rights Commission Act aimed at eliminating discrimination) it is right to assume that Parliament would have meant "dismissal" (cf. "dismiss") to cover cases where in substance the employer had dismissed a worker although technically there has been a resignation.

The full portion of the judgment we rely upon is set out below. It is lengthy but we think too important to abbreviate:

> Section 117 of the Industrial Relations Act uses several times the expression "unjustifiable dismissal" or "unjustifiably dismissed". The concept is not a simple one. It is not in everyday use in the English language. Its permissible scope in the context of this Act is a question of interpretation and so of law (compare *R v Robinson* [1978] 1 NZLR 709, 716-7; *United Fisheries Ltd v Commissioner of Inland Revenue* (1985) 8 TRNZ 364. Very broadly a dismissal may be said to be unjustifiable if it is unreasonable or procedurally unfair. But there is no need here to go into the question of justification more fully. The case stated is concerned, not with that question, but with the meaning of dismissal.

> Obviously there is a dismissal when an employer in fact "dismisses" a worker in the ordinary meaning of the word. But the Arbitration Court has held in a line of cases that the concept is wider and includes constructive dismissal. In our opinion that is the correct approach. In the context of an Act aimed at good industrial relations it is right to assume that Parliament would have meant "dismissal" to cover cases where in substance the employer has dismissed a worker although technically there has been a resignation.

> The comparable English legislation has an exhaustive definition of dismissal: Employment Protection (Consolidation) Act 1978, s 55. What the English courts call constructive dismissal appears there to depend entirely on the words "if .... the employee terminates that contract, with or without notice, in circumstances such that he is entitled to terminate it without notice by reason of the employer's conduct". In New Zealand the courts are not

---

*   *Eds:* subsequently reported at [1985] 2 NZLR 372.

tied to a statutory definition. It would be undesirable to try to visualise all the kinds of case which the Arbitration Court could properly treat as constructive dismissals, but it is not difficult to list some.

The concept is certainly capable of including cases where an employer gives a worker an option of resigning or being dismissed; or where an employer has followed a course of conduct with the deliberate and dominant purpose of coercing a worker to resign. On the argument in this Court, it was made clear that the union does not contend that the present case falls within either of those categories.

A third category consists of cases where a breach of duty by the employer leads a worker to resign. This is the category into which the union seeks to place the present case. And in considering the duty of the employer that is now relevant it is helpful to take note of recent English case law.

Before the case about to be mentioned there was a school of judicial thought in England in favour of treating the employee's right to terminate by reason of the employer's conduct as depending simply on unreasonableness. It was said that if the employer conducted himself or his affairs so unreasonably that the employee could not fairly be expected to put up with it any longer, the employee was justified in leaving. In *Western Excavating Ltd v Sharp* [1978] QB 761 the Court of Appeal rejected that test, Lord Denning MR describing it as "too indefinite by far". The test preferred was a common law test of repudiation: namely, whether the employer had been guilty of a significant breach going to the root of the contract or conduct showing that he no longer intended to be bound by one or more of its essential terms.

But difficulties emerged. What they were and how they were approached appears from the judgment of the Employment Appeal Tribunal, delivered by Browne-Wilkinson J, in *Woods v WM Car Services (Peterborough) Ltd* [1981] ICR 666, 670-2, from which the following extracts are taken:

"In our view it is clearly established that there is implied in a contract of employment a term that the employers will not, without reasonable and proper cause, conduct themselves in a manner calculated or likely to destroy or seriously damage the relationship of confidence and trust between employer and employee: *Courtaulds Northern Textiles Ltd v Andrew* [1979] IRLR 84. To constitute a breach of this implied term it is not necessary to show that the employer intended any repudiation of the contract: the tribunal's function is to look at the employer's conduct as a whole and determine whether it is such that its effect, judged reasonably and sensibly, is such that the employee cannot be expected to put up with it: see *British Aircraft Corporation Ltd v Austin* [1978] IRLR 322 and *Post Office v Roberts* [1980] IRLR 347. The conduct of the parties has to be looked at as a whole and its cumulative impact assessed: *Post Office v Roberts*.

We regard this implied term as one of great importance in good industrial relations. ...

Experience in this appeal tribunal has shown that one of the consequences of the decision in the *Western Excavating* case has been that employers who wish to get rid of an employee or alter the terms of his employment without becoming liable either to pay compensation for unfair dismissal or a redundancy payment have had to resort to methods of 'squeezing out' an employee. Stopping short of any major breach of contract, such an employer attempts to make the employee's life so uncomfortable that he resigns or accepts the revised terms. Such an employer, having behaved in a totally unreasonable manner, then claims that he has not repudiated the contract and therefore that the employee has no statutory right to claim either a redundancy payment or compensation for unfair dismissal.

It is for this reason that we regard the implied term we have referred to as being of such importance. In our view, an employer who persistently attempts to vary an employee's conditions of service (whether contractual or not) with a view to getting rid of the employee or varying the employee's terms of service does act in a manner calculated or likely to destroy the relationship of confidence and trust between employer and employee. Such an employer has therefore breached the implied term. Any breach of that implied term is a fundamental breach amounting to a repudiation since it necessarily goes to the root of the contract: see *Courtaulds Northern Textiles Ltd v Andrew* [1979] IRLR 84."

The *Woods* case went on appeal, [1982] ICR 693. On this occasion Lord Denning MR married the approaches by speaking at p 698 of a duty "to be good and considerate":

"Now under modern legislation we have the converse case. It is the duty of the employer to be good and considerate to his servants. Sometimes it is formulated as an implied term not to do anything likely to destroy the relationship of confidence between them: see *Courtaulds Northern Textiles Ltd v Andrew* [1979] IRLR 84. But I prefer to look at it in this way: the employer must be good and considerate to his servants. Just as a servant must be good and faithful, so an employer must be good and considerate. Just as in the old days an employee could be guilty of misconduct justifying his dismissal, so in modern times an employer can be guilty of misconduct justifying the employee in leaving at once without notice. In each case it depends on whether the misconduct amounted to a repudiatory breach as defined in *Western Excavating (ECC) Ltd v Sharp* [1978] ICR 221.

The circumstances are so infinitely various that there can be, and is, no rule of law saying what circumstances justify and what do not. It is a question of fact for the tribunal of fact – in this case the industrial tribunal. Once they come to their decision, the appeal tribunal should not interfere with it. Thus when the manager told a man: 'You can't do the bloody job anyway', that would ordinarily not be sufficient to justify the man in leaving at once. It would be on a par with the trenchant criticism which goes on every day. But if the manager used those words dishonestly and maliciously – with no belief in their truth – in order to get rid of him, then it might be sufficient, because it would evince an intention no longer to be bound by the contract. At any rate an industrial tribunal so held in *Courtaulds Northern Textiles Ltd v Andrew* [1979] IRLR 84 and the appeal tribunal did not interfere with it."

Of the other members of the Court of Appeal in the *Woods* case, Watkins LJ used as a test whether the employers had committed any breach of contract, express or implied, which justified the employee in resigning (pp 700–701). Fox LJ used the test of repudiation, adding that the contract 'includes any implied obligations of the parties not to conduct themselves in a manner likely to destroy confidence between them' (p 703).

It may well be that in New Zealand a term recognising that there ought to be a relationship of confidence and trust is implied as a normal incident of the relationship of employer and employee. It would be a corollary of the employee's duty of fidelity (see *Schilling v Kidd Garrett Ltd* [1977] 1 NZLR 243). No formulation of duties in general terms can relieve a tribunal from assessing the overall seriousness of the particular conduct about which a complaint is made. And the seriousness of any breach of an employer's duties will often be important in deciding whether a resignation was in substance a dismissal. But the term favoured by the Employment Appeal Tribunal in England is, with respect, at least somewhat less nebulous than Lord Denning's later wording. In this case, however, we do not have the benefit of the Arbitration Court's view on how best to define an implied term so as to serve the needs of industrial relations in New Zealand. Therefore it is preferable that we should not now state a final opinion on that general conclusion. (Emphasis added.)

On the facts of the case before us, and adopting the statements of the Court of Appeal in the *Woolworths* case (in particular the passages italicised in the last paragraph of the above quote), it cannot be doubted that the defendant's conduct constituted a serious breach of his duty to maintain a relationship of confidence and trust between himself and the plaintiff. In our opinion the circumstances show clearly that the plaintiff's resignation was in substance a dismissal.

We so hold and accordingly the plaintiff has satisfied the major part of the second of the four factors she must establish to succeed.

Discrimination by reason of the plaintiff's sex

Under this heading we propose to deal with the other two factors that have to be established and this, it will be seen, is the more difficult part of the case.

As earlier mentioned, two cases based on sexual harassment have already come before the Equal Opportunities Tribunal but in both instances the necessity to decide whether sexual harassment falls within s 15 did not arise because the factual allegations advanced by the plaintiffs in those cases were not made out. In the passages of the *Crockett* case already referred to, the argument of counsel for the defendant, to the effect that the section does not cover sexual harassment, was adopted by Mr Cutting before us. We quote the adopted argument as recorded in the case:

4   Mr. Milligan's primary submission in regard to the interpretation of sec 15(1)(c) was that it operates to protect members of any one of the particular defined classes from detriment arising by reason of the fact of their membership of that class, or obversely by reason of their non-membership of some other. This construction he contended was consistent with the canons of construction earlier discussed.

5   As a corollary to that primary submission he urged that sec 15 does not operate to protect members of other groups from detriment arising from such membership, nor does it operate to protect members of the protected group from detriment which arises from some other cause. In particular, he stressed that the section does not deal with detriment occasioned by individual or personal factors. In elaboration of that contention, he submitted that the detriment which Mr. Crockett alleges he suffered arose (on his allegation) not from the fact that he is of the male sex, but because (according to him) the parties were at odds on questions affecting their future relationship. He contended that to say that the detriment arose out of the failure of the relationship was insufficient to bring the facts within the purview of sec 15. That, he said, is not the same thing as saying that Mr Crockett suffered detriment by reason of the fact that he is a male, or of the male sex.

Before discussing the specific provisions of the New Zealand Act, it is instructive to look at what has happened in other jurisdictions. Legislation seeking to outlaw discrimination on the grounds of sex, marital status, religious belief, or ethnic origin, is a phenomenon which has emerged in the Western world in the last two decades. The wording of such Acts is frequently expressed as "on the grounds of sex" or "because of sex" or some other rubric which is relatively close to the words in the New Zealand section "by reason of the sex". It is true, of course, that decisions in other jurisdictions on differently worded Acts must be approached with caution. They are, of course, not binding upon us and the degree to which they should be regarded as persuasive must be carefully weighed. Nonetheless, in the Tribunal's view, the central issue to be faced in this case is in reality the same as that which has been faced and resolved in some of the other jurisdictions.

The American Courts have used the expression "gender-plus" or "sex-plus" criteria to identify the issue. As Dr Barton put it in his submissions to us, the problem arises where:

the employer had not applied one criterion to all women and another to all men – that would be the clearest case of discrimination. Rather, the employer had applied one criterion to all men and another criterion to some women only. All men with stated qualifications will be appointed, promoted or retain their jobs, but only certain women with those qualifications. The women who are excluded are those who do not respond in the manner desired by the employer to his sexual advances.

Bringing it down to the facts of this case, it was summed up by Mr Cutting, in his submissions to us, in these words, "If the sexual harassment occurred, which is denied, then it was because this particular person appealed sexually to the defendant and the fact that they were in a work situation is irrelevant". And so it followed, Mr Cutting argued, that it was not the sex of the plaintiff but the fact that she appealed sexually to the defendant (the gender-plus criteria) that resulted in her dismissal.

The American cases

The equivalent legislation in the United States is to be found in Title VII of the Civil Rights Act 1964. There it is declared unlawful for an employer to discharge or discriminate because of an individual's gender. Although there is no specific reference to sexual harassment, it is now well settled that such conduct is prohibited by the Act. The very recent reported case of *Holien v Sears Roebuck & Co* (1984) 35 EPD 35,467 is a good example. At p 35,471, having set out the provisions of the statute, the leading judgment before the entire Bench of the Supreme Court of Oregon reads:

> Although Title VII does not specifically speak of sexual harassment, it is now well settled that such conduct can amount to discrimination on the basis of sex under Title VII. See, *Henson v. City of Dundee* [29 E.P.D. 32,993], *Bundy v. Jackson* [24 E.P.D. 31,439], *Tomkins v. Public Service Electric & Gas Co.* [15 E.P.D. 7954], *Barnes v. Castle* [14 E.P.D. 7755] and *Garber v Saxon Business Products Inc.* [14 E.P.D. 7587].

Perhaps the leading case in America is *Bundy v Jackson* (*supra*) a decision of the United States Court of Appeals on appeal from the United States District Court, District of Columbia. The plaintiff in this case had suffered constant sexual harassment from several superiors and her complaints to the head of her department had not been seriously pursued. The specific provisions of Title VII are set out at p 18,531 and read as follows:

> The key provision of Title VII states:
>
> It shall be an unlawful employment practice for an employer:
>
> (1) to ... discharge any individual, or otherwise discriminate against any individual with respect to (her) compensation, terms, conditions, or privileges of employment, because of such individual's sex.

Having quoted that section the judgment moves on to discuss the case of *Barnes v Castle* which was decided under a differently worded section and referring to the *Barnes* case, at p 18,532, the judgment reads:

> We heard arguments there that whatever harm Barnes suffered was not sex discrimination, since Barnes' supervisor terminated her job because she had refused sexual advances, not because she was a woman. We rejected those arguments as disingenuous in the extreme. The supervisor in that case made demands of Barnes that he would not have made of male employees. But for her womanhood .... [Barnes] participation in sexual activity would never have been solicited. To say, then, that she was victimized in her employment simply because she declined the invitation is to ignore the asserted fact that she was invited only because she was a woman subordinate to the inviter in the hierarchy of agency personnel.
>
> We thus made clear in *Barnes* that sex discrimination within the meaning of Title VII is not limited to disparate treatment founded solely or categorically on gender. Rather, discrimination is sex discrimination whenever *sex* is for no legitimate reason a *substantial factor in the discrimination*. (Emphasis added)

The judgment then refers to the case of *Phillips v Martin Marietta Corp* [3 EPD 8088] 400 US 542 (1971), where it was held:

so long as sex is a factor in the application of [an employer's decision], such application involves a discrimination based on sex.

We have emphasised the Court's comments regarding the arguments that were advanced in the *Barnes* case because they are precisely the arguments that were advanced in the *Crockett* case and put forward again by Mr Cutting in this case on behalf of the defendant.

The Canadian cases

There is a plethora of authority on the subject of sexual harassment to be found in the Canadian Human Rights Reporter decisions. Some of the leading authorities were examined by the Equal Opportunities Tribunal in the *Crockett* case and we do not propose to repeat the survey in respect of those cases that was carried out in that decision.

In February to March of 1984 two cases were reported in Canada which are worthy of note. The first is the case of *Kotyk & Anor v The Canadian Employment & Immigration Commission* 5 CHRR Decision No 339. In the case, counsel for the defendant raised what the Review Tribunal set up under the Canadian Human Rights Act described as "the fundamental question as to whether sexual harassment is a prohibited ground of discrimination within the meaning of the word 'sex' in s 3(1) of the Act."

Paras 16,281 to 16,287 of that judgment are illuminating. At para 16,282 the Tribunal records that counsel had submitted:

… that sexual discrimination under the Act is only applicable where the employer or a person acting as his servant or agent differentiates adversely in relation to an employee because in the general sense that person is a male or female as the case may be and not because of sexual preferences.

Here again, in a slightly different form, is the proposition which Mr Cutting urges upon us. The judgment considers that proposition and demonstrates its fallaciousness, and at para 16,286 the judgment reads:

Accordingly, the crux of the matter is whether the basis for the specific discrimination was sex related. If so, there is discrimination by reason of sex even though other employees of the same gender are not subjected to the same conduct.

The other case appearing in the same volume of the Reporter is *Giouvanoudis v Golden Fleece Restaurant & Anor* 5 CHRR Decision No 348. This is an extremely lengthy decision based on relatively simple facts. Miss Giouvanoudis applied for work as a waitress and during the interview the prospective employer made sexual advances to her which she rebuffed. She did not get a job immediately but was invited to ring back in a few days' time and was then told that the job was no longer available. Not surprisingly, the Board of Inquiry found that she had been refused employment in fact because she rejected the proprietor's advances.

The case contains a lengthy review of the law on sexual harassment. … The holding was that Miss Giouvanoudis had been discriminated against on the ground of her sex.

The other Canadian authority we would refer to is the case of *Zarankin v Wessex Inn* 5 CHRR Decision 387, published in September 1984. This is a decision of the Board of Inquiry under the British Columbia Human Rights Code, and at para 19,168 of the judgment the following statement is made:

Although complaints regarding sexual harassment have come before tribunals in several other Canadian jurisdictions and in the United States, this is the first to be heard by a Board of Inquiry in British Columbia.

In the next paragraph the opening sentence reads:

Sexual harassment in the workplace is not a new phenomenon: legal recourse for its victims is new.

Having discussed the facts and general circumstances and found that the complainant, who was a chambermaid, has been sexually harassed by touching and patting, indulged in by one Ian Johnstone, the owner of the Wessex Inn, the Board of Inquiry went on to discuss the question of jurisdiction under the British Columbia legislation. The provisions of s 8 of the Human Rights Code are set out in para 19,177 of the Report and the discussion of the topic in para 19,178 to 19,185 inclusive, is extremely instructive for our purposes. In para 19,178 the judgment refers to the fact that some jurisdictions have enacted legislation dealing specifically with sexual harassment and goes on to say that it is not referring to cases decided under such specific legislation, but rather to cases decided under legislation which prohibits discrimination "because of" or "based on" sex. The judgment then goes on to discuss gender-based discrimination and at the commencement of para 19,182 it reads:

Although it might be thought that sexual harassment would not amount to sex discrimination unless all employees of the same gender were equally recipients of it, that is fallacious. So long as gender provides a basis for differentiation it matters not that further differentiation on another basis is made.

And in para 19,184 the holding is that sexual harassment is discrimination even under statutes which do not have special provisions and the statement is made "... numerous Canadian human rights tribunals have so found. No tribunal or court, to my knowledge has found to the contrary". The following para 19,185 is worthy of being quoted in full, it reads:

I think a fair summary of the reasoning in the Canadian tribunal decisions is that sexual harassment is discrimination based on sex when it puts up an obstacle to achievement in a job because of gender. An employee should not have to bear the extra burden of gratifying or tolerating her (or his) employer's need for sexual titillation as a term or condition of employment. I conclude that sexual harassment is discrimination because of sex whenever it comes within the definition I have adopted and is not imposed upon both genders equally.

The Australian cases

The first case reported in Australia dealing with sexual harassment is *O'Callaghan v Loder & Anor*, a decision of the Equal Opportunity Tribunal in New South Wales reported in (1984) EOC para 92-023. It was a claim brought by a female lift-attendant under the Anti-Discrimination Act 1977 of New South Wales. The plaintiff alleged that she had been sexually harassed and the defendant sought a ruling by the Equal Opportunity Tribunal of New South Wales on a point of law as to whether or not the allegations of the plaintiff were covered by the Act. Mathews J ruled on the point before the evidence was heard. This was the first case of sexual harassment to be heard and the point was fully argued and the subject of a careful judgment.

In the opening paragraphs of the judgment the fact that there is no reference in the Anti-Discrimination Act to sexual harassment and therefore no statutory definition of it, is noted. For the purposes of the decision the Court took a wide definition of sexual harassment saying that "a person is sexually harassed if he or she is subjected to unsolicited and unwelcome sexual conduct by a person who stands in a position of power in relation to him or her".

The provisions of the Act are set out in the judgment and s 25(2) provides that it is unlawful for an employer to discriminate against an employee on the grounds of sex by, *inter alia*, dismissing him. At p 75,449 of the Report, the judgment records that:

> A number of United States and Canadian decisions have determined that sexual harassment by an employer can amount to discriminatory behaviour. They have held that it is irrelevant that factors other than the employee's gender might have contributed to the employer's conduct, so long as gender was a substantial contributing factor.

The judgment then goes on to record that counsel sought to distinguish North American cases on the basis "that the North American legislation makes it unlawful for a person to discriminate against another because of the other's sex". The judgment continues:

> The New South Wales Act makes it unlawful to discriminate against another *on the ground* of that person's sex. He [counsel] urges that although the American legislation might cover situations where the other person's gender was but one of the motivating factors in the discriminatory process, the New South Wales Act requires that it be the only one.

> I cannot accede to that proposition. I can see no difference in principle between the requirement, in New South Wales, that the discrimination should be on the ground of a person's sex and the requirement, in North America, that it should be because of that person's sex.

Similarly, in grappling with this problem we would say that we see no difference in principle between the North American and New South Wales requirements and our own, which, as earlier mentioned, deal with the subject by using the words "by reason of the sex".

The judgment continues, in the second half of the right-hand column on p 75,499, as follows:

> The meaning to be ascribed to the words "on the ground of his sex" was also discussed by the Court of Appeal in the *Director-General of Education & Anor v. Breen & Ors* (1984) EOC para 92-015 in a judgment which was handed down on 24 May 1982. In particular, Street C.J. said at p. 75,429 of his judgment:

>> "To amount to discriminatory conduct prohibited by the Act the characteristic which will provide the ground must have a proximate bearing upon the act charged as discrimination. Moreover, the characteristic must have a causally operative effect upon the decision to commit or the committing of the act of discrimination."

> In applying that test, an affirmative answer must be given to two questions in order to satisfy this requirement. They are, first: does the gender of a female complainant have a proximate bearing on her being sexually harassed by her male employer? Secondly, does her gender have a causally operative effect upon the employer in his sexual conduct towards her? ... The fact that the complainant is female must, in my view have both a proximate bearing and a causally operative effect on the sexual conduct towards her of a male heterosexual employer.

> It follows that I find that the present complaint is capable of fulfilling the second requirement under s 24(1) of the Act, namely that the complainant was treated less favourably than comparable males on the ground of her sex.

The judgment then moves on to consider the question of terms or conditions of employment afforded and referring to American authority at p 75,502, the judgment reads:

Similar questions in relation to the North American legislation have arisen in a number of cases in the United States and Canada. Counsel for the respondents have urged that this Tribunal should exercise caution in applying those decisions, as they relate to different legislation in different legal systems amid different social structures. That may well be so, and it goes without saying that this Tribunal is not bound by them. Nevertheless it would be quite wrong to disregard a substantial body of law which has grown up over a number of years in countries which enacted anti-discrimination legislation well before our own.

The judgment then goes on to discuss a number of the leading authorities under Title VII of the US Civil Rights Act 1964, in particular, the *Barnes v Costle* and *Bundy v Jackson* decisions are examined. The Ontario cases are also considered and at the end of that survey, at p 75,505, the judgment reads:

Mr Barker Q.C. for the complainant, has urged that this Tribunal should not only take note of the developments in those countries [United States and Canada] but should, in effect, adopt them. He argues that there would be little point in the Tribunal following the more restrictive approaches which marked the earlier United States decisions, just so that the process of judicial evolution can be repeated from the beginning.

Mr Barker's submission is, in my view, a compelling one. There are valuable lessons to be learned from examining the development of anti-discrimination laws, albeit it in different jurisdictions, and it would be a great pity if we were not to gain from them.

The other New South Wales case is that of *Hill v Water Resources Commission*, the judgment in which was handed down on 10 May 1985, (1985) EOC para 92-127. At pp 76,288-76,289 the *O'Callaghan v Loder* case is discussed and followed. At p 76,290 the Tribunal comes to deal with an argument put up by Mr Menzies, counsel for the Water Resources Commission, which, in effect, is the argument that Mr Cutting puts up for the defendant in this case. The judgment reads, at p 76,290:

On the American cases and in principle we cannot accept Mr Menzies' argument that the employer's less favourable treatment which we have found occurred was not on the ground of sex. It was less favourable treatment on the ground of sex because a comparable man would not have been similarly harassed. To look at it another way the harassment would not have happened "but for" the complainant's sex.

The position in the United Kingdom

There has been no decision on sexual harassment in the United Kingdom to date.

[...]

Is sexual harassment covered by the New Zealand statute?

We are conscious that our decision in this area of the case can have far-reaching consequences for New Zealand society as a whole and women in the workforce in particular. The findings of fact that we have made mean that the issue that did not have to be resolved in the earlier cases that have come before the Equal Opportunities Tribunal, must now be confronted.

When we first began our deliberations, following the conclusion of the hearing of the evidence and submissions, we decided that if in due course we found ourselves in any degree of substantial doubt as to whether sexual harassment is covered by our Act, then we would find the facts and state a case for the High Court, pursuant to s 62 of the Human Rights Commission Act 1977. That, we thought, would be the safer, if somewhat less robust, approach.

In the end, however, we have not been left with any substantial degree of doubt and therefore see it as our duty as the body primarily responsible for the interpretation of the Act, to proceed and make a ruling.

In the absence of binding authority our task involves an interpretation of the Act, and in particular s 15(1)(c) of the same. Our primary duty must be to discern the intention of Parliament.

We bear in mind first, and give great weight to, the provisions of s 5(j) of the Acts Interpretation Act 1924, which provides:

> Every act, and every provision or enactment thereof, shall be deemed remedial, whether its immediate purpose is to direct the doing of anything Parliament deems to be for the public good, or to prevent or punish the doing of anything it deems contrary to the public good, and shall accordingly receive such fair, large and liberal construction and interpretation as will best ensure the attainment of the object of the act and of such provision or enactment according to its true intent, meaning and spirit.

We observe in passing that if any Act ever called for a liberal and enabling interpretation, the Human Rights Commission Act 1977 must be it.

We look next at the provisions of the Act, and in particular, we pay attention to the long title which reads: "An Act to establish a Human Rights Commission and to promote the advancement of human rights in New Zealand in general accordance with the United Nations International Covenants on Human Rights". Two of the covenants that have been ratified by New Zealand are the Universal Declaration of Human Rights and the International Covenant on Economic, Social and Cultural Rights. Article 23 of the Declaration reads:

> (1) Everyone has the right to work, to free choice of employment, *to just and favourable conditions of work* and to protection against unemployment.

And art 7 of the Covenant commences:

> The States Parties to the present Covenant recognize *the right of everyone to the enjoyment of just and favourable conditions of work* which ensure, in particular:
>
> (a) Remuneration which provides all workers, as a minimum, with:
>
>   (i) Fair wages and equal remuneration for work of equal value without distinction of any kind, *in particular women being guaranteed conditions of work not inferior to those enjoyed by men*, with equal pay for equal work; ... (Emphasis added)

In an erudite article entitled "Statutory Interpretation in New Zealand" published in (1984) 11 NZULR 1, p 1, Professor JF Burrows states, at p 12:

> There is evidence also of a widening of the legal context. Increasing numbers of statutes are the result of treaties, conventions and other resolutions of the international community, or are on topics which have been the subject of international agreement. Applying the presumption that New Zealand should not be deemed to legislate inconsistently with its international obligations, the courts have shown great readiness to refer to international materials, although they have stopped well short of holding that they are binding on domestic courts. Thus treaties have been referred to, to determine which of two statutes should prevail in the particular case, and to assist in the interpretation of ambiguous expressions. Even the Universal Declaration of Human Rights and certain resolutions of the United Nations have been referred to, even if their force may properly be described as moral rather than legal. This tendency to set the New Zealand state in its international context, coupled with an expressed desire to ensure uniform interpretation of uniform statutes, is one of the most significant developments in recent years.

The author quotes in support of his conclusions such cases in the Court of Appeal as *King-Ansell v Police* [1979] 2 NZLR 531, especially at p 536 *per* Woodhouse J and at p 541 *per* Richardson J; *Ashby v Minister of Immigration* [1981] 1 NZLR 222 and *Department of Labour v Latailakepa* [1982] 1 NZLR 632, especially at p 635 *per* Richardson J.

In our opinion, Parliament must be presumed to have intended that the unlawful discrimination sections of the Human Rights Commission Act 1977, as they relate to employment, should be in conformity with New Zealand's international obligations. As we see it, only if s 15 outlaws sexual harassment, along with other discriminatory practices based on sex, will women in the workforce be afforded "just and favourable conditions of work" and otherwise be "guaranteed conditions of work not inferior to those enjoyed by men". It is, of course, true that men can be discriminated against by reason of sex but as the Declaration and Covenant recognise, and as is confirmed by common experience, the generally disadvantaged position of women in the workplace makes them more vulnerable.

Next we look at the scheme of the Act and draw attention to the fact that the real substance of it is to be found in Pt II, which declares the matters which are unlawful discrimination. Parts III and IV provide the remedies for such discrimination and the Tribunal which is to hear claims in respect of them.

In all this we recognise that we are adopting the purposive approach to statutory interpretation, whereas, of course, we were urged by Mr Cutting to follow the more cautious, and at one time more orthodox, literal approach. Quite apart from the fact that it is now out of fashion, a literal approach to legislation enacted to promote the advancement of human rights is an unattractive prospect and one which we are not prepared to follow.

Our conclusion is that sexual harassment is covered by s 15(1)(c) of the Human Rights Commission Act 1977 and that the "gender-plus" approach to the subject is every bit as valid in New Zealand as it is in the United States, Canada and Australia.

Whether we would have had the courage to so interpret the statute without the lead given in North America and Australia, must remain a matter of conjecture. We would add, however, that in our view, the treatment of women in the workplace should be no less fair and enlightened in New Zealand than elsewhere in the common law world. Had we felt obliged to record a narrow and restrictive interpretation of this legislation, we would have regarded such a result as out of step with the temperament of modern society.

Award

In her claim the plaintiff sought a declaration pursuant to s 38(6)(a) of the Human Rights Commission Act 1977 that the defendant had committed a breach of the Act. We make that declaration.

The plaintiff also sought an order, pursuant to s 38(6)(b) of the Act restraining the defendant from repeating the breach or from engaging in conduct of the same kind or conduct of a similar kind. We think it unnecessary to make such an order in this litigation. We anticipate that our ruling will constitute a salutary experience for the defendant which should be sufficient to restrain him from similar conduct in the future.

The plaintiff sought damages to the maximum amount allowable under the Act, namely, $2,000 for humiliation, loss of dignity and injury to feelings, pursuant to s 40(1)(c) of the Act. The maximum allowable by way of damages must be kept, in our view, for the most serious of cases. Here the plaintiff is a mature, sexually-experienced woman who handled much of the harassment she was subjected to in a level-headed and even tolerant way. But we are satisfied that the crescendo to which it built on the day that she left, was the culmination of an experience which was humiliating, which caused her loss of dignity and injury to her feelings. In all the circumstances, we think an award of $750 will compensate the plaintiff adequately.

In addition, she will have judgment for the sum of $177.44, being the monetary loss that she suffered during the period of 14 weeks before she found alternative employment.

Costs

We now turn to the question of costs. The plaintiff is legally aided but we do not see that as a reason for refraining from obliging the defendant to contribute to her costs. It should be remembered that the defendant had ample opportunity during the investigation carried out by the Human Rights Commission prior to the proceedings being issued before the Tribunal, to acknowledge his conduct and make suitable amends. Instead of that, he persisted in denying his conducts and that led to a three-day hearing in which both the facts and the law were extensively canvassed and hotly disputed. We order the defendant to contribute to the plaintiff's costs in the sum of $500.

Conclusion

This has been a distressing case for the parties and, despite the findings of fact that we have made, we have great sympathy, not only for the plaintiff but also for Mr and Mrs E. We doubt that the defendant, up until the commencement of the Human Rights Commission's investigations, regarded his conduct in anything like the serious light that we do. Similarly, we doubt that he envisaged for a moment that it could lead him to such a traumatic, expensive and possibly personally damaging experience as the hearing and the recording of our decision may be for him. All we can say is that once the plaintiff decided to exercise her right to proceed with the claim (despite the conclusion of the Commission that it did not have any substance), then she was entitled to a full hearing and pursuant to s 56 of the Act the reasoned decision of this Tribunal.

We were advised during the hearing, by counsel for the Proceedings Commissioner, that the Human Rights Commission has been receiving a steady flow of complaints concerning sexual harassment in employment. Our attention was drawn to the fact that when the Commission presented its Annual Report for the year ended 31 March 1985, it was receiving at least one fresh complaint or enquiry each week on the subject. It appears, therefore, that this socially undesirable conduct, which is unfair, degrading and humiliating for women, may be more prevalent in the workplace than many would suspect. And it follows that when such harassment is proved before this Tribunal, as it has been on this occasion, it is our duty to make the appropriate findings and award the appropriate remedies. We regret that it has not been possible for us to discharge our obligations in that regard without adding to what clearly already has been a difficult and distressing experience for all concerned.

CASE NO 31

*RINA BAJRACHARYA AND OTHERS v HIS MAJESTY'S GOVERNMENT SECRETARIAT OF THE COUNCIL OF MINISTERS AND OTHERS**

SUPREME COURT OF NEPAL

Writ no: 2812/054 (1997-98)

Judgment: 8 June 2000

Panel: Aryal, Verma and Poudel, JJ

Human Rights — Equality and non-discrimination — Sex discrimination — Royal Nepal Airlines Corporation Regulations — Whether different retirement ages for male and female flight attendants contrary to the constitutional right to equality — Status of treaties under Nepalese law — Treaty Act 1991, s 9 — Constitution of the Kingdom of Nepal 1990, art 11

BACKGROUND

The applicants were female flight attendants with Royal Nepal Airlines Corporation ("RNAC"), Nepal's state-owned airline corporation. Under the RNAC Service Regulations 1974, the general retirement age for crew was 55. However, the retirement age for female flight attendants was 30 years of age or 10 years of service, whichever occurred earlier. After a 1995 amendment to the Regulations, female flight attendants could serve an additional three years at the discretion of the management and then only in ground jobs. The applicants challenged the differential retirement ages on the ground that they violated article 11 of Nepal's Constitution, which included a guarantee against discrimination on the ground of sex and a guarantee of equal pay for equal work.

The applicants also contended that the Regulations breached Nepal's international obligations, in particular those under the Convention on the Elimination of All Forms of Discrimination against Women. Under section 9 of Treaty Act 1991, international conventions to which Nepal is a party have the status of municipal law in Nepal and in case of inconsistency prevail over Acts of Parliament.

HELD (allowing the petition and holding the Regulations *ultra vires* Article 11 of the Constitution)

1   The Constitution embodied a clear commitment to values of equality, including gender equality, and it was the duty of the Court to translate the spirit of the Constitution into action, to work towards the protection of human rights which had the status of fundamental rights and to end social inequality and gender-based discrimination. The biggest hurdle to the realisation of equality was the fact that because

---

*   **Eds:** the original judgment is published in *Supreme Court Bulletin*, Year 9, No 10 at 3 (in Nepali); unofficial translation by Jogendra Ghimire, formerly of Forum for Women, Law and Development, Kathmandu, Nepal.

of the deep-rooted discriminatory culture, discriminatory laws were drafted unknowingly and continued to exist. Therefore, to ensure effective gender-based social justice, it was necessary to eradicate the roots of the society's discriminatory thinking and culture (p 496).

2   The challenged Regulations violated the Constitution's guarantees of gender equality, and were also inconsistent with the State policy in Article 26(7) to encourage the greater participation of women in national development. The possibility of the extension of a female flight attendant's service did not change the basic fact of unequal treatment, since such an extension was at the discretion of management and not every woman would be able to be benefit from the possibility of a ground-based job (p 498).

3   The argument that the petitioners contractually accepted the Regulations when accepting offers of employment with the RNAC and therefore could not challenge them was not tenable, since no matter how one enters service, once a person becomes a permanent employee, the rules of service will apply (p 498).

Treaties and other international instruments referred to

Convention on the Political Rights of Women 1952

Convention on the Elimination of All Forms of Discrimination against Women 1979, art 15

Universal Declaration of Human Rights 1948, arts 2, 7 and 23

National legislation referred to

Nepal

Constitution of the Kingdom of Nepal, 1990, arts 2, 7, 11 (1), (2), (3) and (5), 12 (2) (e), 17 (1), 23, 26 (7), 46 (1) (b), 88(1) and 131

Treaty Act 1991, s 9

Country Code 1963

Royal Nepal Airlines Corporation Services Regulations 1974, Rule 16.1.3

Cases referred to

Man Bahadur Biswakarma v His Majesty's Government (2049BS/1994) 12NKP1010

Meera Dhungana v Ministry of Law, Justice and Parliamentary Affairs (2052BS/1995) 6NKP68

Chanda Bajracharya v Parliament Secretariat and Others (2053BS/1996) 7NKP537

DECISION*

The present writ petition seeks resolution of the following questions.

(a)   Does Rule 16.1.3 of RNAC Service Regulations contradict Article 11 (1), (2) and (3) of the Constitution of the Kingdom of Nepal, 1990?

---

*   **Eds:** the following is an extract from the judgment only.

(b) Is an order of the type sought in the petition warranted?

There appears to be no difference of opinion about the fact that the petitioners are employees working for the respondent Royal Nepal Airlines Corporation ("RNAC").

The legal provisions which govern their services with the RNAC, and also those of stewards, are set out in RNAC Service Regulations 2031. Rule 1.2.8 (Chapter 1) defines "employees" as "any person at any level appointed in the service of the Corporation." Similarly, under Rule 1.2.15, the term "crew" is defined to include "pilot, co-pilot, flight engineer, radio officer, flight navigator, air hostess, cabin attendant and pursers." Rule 4.1.1 divides services into various categories, including crew service, while Rule 4.1.3 divides crew officers into categories based on their salaries: flight attendants and air hostesses are categorised under class 5 and senior flight attendants and senior air hostesses under class 6.

Under Chapter 8 ("Work Hours"), Rule 8.1.4 provides that crew will work 65 hours per month and 650 hours per year, while under Chapter 14, the provision for leave provides for equal treatment of all employees.

Under Chapter 16 ("Termination of Service: Retirement and Resignation"), Rule 16.1.1 (as amended), provides that employees other than crew retire from service after attaining the age of 60 years while crew retire after attaining the age of 55 years. Their service period can be extended by an additional three years if found fit based, among others, on a medical examination. Under Rule 16.1.3 of the same Chapter, air hostesses, who fall under "crew" have to retire from service either at the attainment of 30 years of age or after completion of 10 years of service, whichever occurs earlier, while providing for an extension of their services in ground jobs if: (a) there is a vacancy, and (b) they have the qualifications to perform the responsibilities required by the job. Between Chapters 17 and 20, there are similar provisions relating to facilities, provident fund, retirement benefits and other benefits for both air hostesses and stewards.

The present writ petition has been registered under Article 88(1) of the Constitution of the Kingdom of Nepal (1990) claiming that while all other provisions under the RNAC Service Regulations are equal, provisions under Rules 16.1.1 and 16.1.3 are unequal and against the spirit of the Constitution. Article 88(1) provides that a citizen can petition the Court alleging that a law is inconsistent with the Constitution by reason of unreasonable restriction on the enjoyment of fundamental rights granted by the Constitution or for any other reason, and if the Court so determines, it shall have extraordinary jurisdiction to declare the law under consideration or a part thereof void *ab initio* or from the date of the decision. Several laws have been declared *ultra vires* under the same Constitutional provision. In the context of the issue of human rights of equality of sexes, it is relevant to consider here in brief its evolution.

There can be no two opinions on the fact that both men and women are humans and are therefore eligible equally to all the rights available to humans. This is a fundamental and non-derogable rule. But different countries have in different times applied this principle in different ways. The countries and eras that have followed this fundamental principle have been those that have become civilized and humane. On the other hand, the countries and eras that discriminate between men and women tend to become those that stand out as uncivilized and underdeveloped. Therefore, the demands for women's liberation has kept pace with the evolution of modern civilization, and in particular the rise of democracy, because equality is at the heart of a democratic system.

The League of Nations and the United Nations declared as human rights the rights which were identified as generally acceptable rights among democratic countries, and also undertook the responsibility to realise those rights in the member countries. The

Universal Declaration of Human Rights, declared after the conclusion of the World War II, has been a generally accepted document of human rights. Besides identifying the rights and stating in the Preamble that it was essential to make commitments to respect and uphold the dignity of a human being and equality of the sexes and freedom, the document provides for rights under various articles, providing, respectively, under Articles 2, 7 and 23 that there shall be no discrimination on the grounds of caste, creed, sex and others, that everybody shall be equal before law and shall be eligible for equal protection of all laws without any discrimination, and that every person shall have the right to work, choose their profession, be protected from unemployment and receive equal pay for equal work. As this document was a collective declaration of human rights and as with the passage of time countries began imposing their sets of restrictions on the implementation of those rights, based on their political backgrounds, human rights have been regulated and protected through several treaties, conventions, protocols and agreements.

Since the present dispute relates to equality of women, it is pertinent to note that the first worldwide initiative on the issue was the Convention on the Political Rights of Women, 1952, adopted by the UN General Assembly, which provided for granting the franchise to women. Similarly, the Convention on the Elimination of All Forms of Discrimination against Women was adopted by the General Assembly on 18 December 1979, which defines as discrimination any distinction, exclusion or restriction made on the basis of sex, lists the way women have to be treated at different stages, and accepts under article 15 in clear terms that under the law women should be treated on a par with men.

In post-democracy Nepal, human rights were initially placed within the framework of fundamental rights and civil rights. In the constitutions after 2007 Falgun 7 (1951 AD)* equality of sexes was mentioned under the right to equality. However, the existing discriminatory provisions which relate to punishment, parental property and intestate property, came about as a result of the Country Code of 2020 BS (1963 AD),** which was aimed at social equality. Despite attempts to amend the Country Code provisions on women's property intestate property etc on the occasion of international women's year, the issue of gender equality has received little attention due to discriminatory social cultures.

The Constitution of the Kingdom of Nepal seems to be geared to take a great leap forward in the area of women's rights. That fact can be proved by reference to the proclamations in the Preamble of the Constitution that purport to ensure the human rights of the citizens and the signing of a number of international conventions related to human rights after the promulgation of the new Constitution. Among those documents, Nepal first ratified and acceded to the Convention on the Elimination of All Forms of Discrimination against Women on 22 April 1991. Under section 9 of the Treaty Act 2047, international conventions to which Nepal is a party are provided with a status higher than the existing laws of the land, making their implementation simple and efficient.

---

*   *Eds:* reference to this date is important in Nepalese political history, because it was as a result of a successful popular revolt against the then autocratic family rule of Rana Prime Ministers (which ended on that date with the commoners participating in the government) that Nepal began a constitutional system of government.

**   *Eds:* the first Country Code of Nepal was enacted by Jung Bahadur Rana (the first Rana Prime Minister and founder of the clan) in 1853. With its roots firmly embedded in Hindu religious thought and social norms, the Code provided for separate sets of rules for people based on their castes, sex etc.

Since the main duty of the Court is to translate the spirit of the Constitution into action, it has been working towards the protection of human rights which have the status of fundamental rights and to end social inequality and gender-based discrimination, as can be seen in the precedents established and judicial directives in *Man Bahadur Biswakarma* (NKP 2049, p 1010), *Meera Dhungana* (NKP 2051, p 68) and *Dr Chanda Bajracharya* (NKP 2053, p 537) cases.[*]

The biggest hurdle in the realisation of equality is the fact that because of the deep-rooted discriminatory culture, discriminatory laws are drafted unknowingly and continue to exist. Therefore, to ensure effective gender-based social justice, it is necessary to eradicate the roots of society's thinking and culture. The *Meera Dhungana* case[**] should be analyzed from the same perspective. Instead of examining the judgment in the case, it is necessary to examine what role the case played towards creating awareness about equality of sexes. As a consequence of the directive in the case, the debate on whether sons and daughters should be given equal right to parental property became a subject of discussion even in the countryside, turning the whole nation into a parliament. As a result of that, there is a great deal more in terms of awareness on the issue of equality of sexes now.

As our Constitution of the Kingdom of Nepal was drafted in 1990, based on the experiences of the ups and downs of constitutional experiments in various countries, and taking into consideration the notion of universalism, especially in the areas of human rights, the Constitution carries with it, directly or indirectly, the spirit to end all types of discrimination against women, as can be substantiated by the proviso in article 11(3), and articles 11(5) and 26(7).[***] When interpreting the Constitution, its spirit should be given greater consideration than its letters. Our Constitution has provided for the proviso in article 11(3) and article 26(7) taking into consideration also the (need for) development of the capacity among women to utilise equality. However, what is lacking is the urgency to make new laws or to amend existing laws to give real meaning to the spirit of the Constitution. It is necessary that the legislative initiatives keep pace with social conscience and gender justice.

Based on this analysis, since the basic human right of equality is vital to the development of overall national life, it must be ensured that not even a trace of gender-

---

[*]   *Eds:* NKP (*Nepal Kanoon Patrika* which translates as Nepal Law Paper) is the official Law Report incorporating all the decisions of the Supreme Court of Nepal. The official calendar used in Nepal is the Bikram Samvat (or Bikram Era, BS for short) which is 57 years ahead of the Gregorian calendar.

[**] *Eds:* this 1995 case ended at the Court with a "directive order" passed by the Supreme Court requiring the government to introduce suitable legislation to eliminate all discriminatory provisions against women in existing laws (in particular the law denying daughters the right to inherit their parental property until they have attained the age of 35 and then only if they remain unmarried, while sons had a right to inheritance from birth). As a result of the heightened public debate on the issue subsequent to the directive (helped also by the mood created by the 1995 Beijing World Conference and subsequent activities), discrimination with regard to inheritance rights has been reduced. Daughters are now eligible to inherit parental property at birth, but are still required to return their share to their male siblings when they get married.

[***] *Eds:* these three articles are as follows: 11(3) The State shall not discriminate among citizens on grounds of religion, race, sex, caste, tribe or ideological conviction or any of these: Provided that special provisions may be made by law for the protection and advancement of the interests of women, children, the aged or those who are physically or mentally incapacitated or those who belong to a class which is economically socially or educationally backward; 11(5) No discrimination in regard to remuneration shall be made between men and women for the same work; and 26(7) The state shall pursue a policy of making the female population participate, to a greater extent, in the task of national development by making special provisions for their education, health and employment.

based discrimination remains in the laws and actions based on the law, because the issue of gender equality is a subject of entire humanity. It is a matter for everybody's common duty and concern.

In the context of the above, before we attempt to answer whether Rule 16.1.3 of the RNAC Services Regulations breaches Articles 11(1), (2), (3) and (5) of the Constitution, which incorporates within itself the spirit of Article 15 of CEDAW, it is pertinent to analyze those articles and also the provisions of fundamental rights and also the Constitutional provisions related to women.

Under Article 11 (Right to Equality) of the Constitution, sub-article (1) provides that all citizens shall be equal before the law and no one shall be deprived of the equal protection of law. Sub-article (2) ensures that in the exercise of general laws, no citizen shall be discriminated against on the grounds of religion, caste, sex, tribe or ideological conviction or any of them. Sub-article (3) provides that the state shall not discriminate among citizens based on religion, caste, tribe, sex or ideological conviction or any of them, but a special legal provision can be made for the protection of women, children, old or physically or mentally incapacitated person or a an economically, socially or educationally backward class or section of the society. Article 11(5) provides that for similar work there shall be no discrimination in remuneration between men and women. The provision prohibiting differential pay for similar work by men and women seems to have attempted to translate the provision of the Convention into reality. Work and pay for that work are fundamental to workers. Contingent on the same fundamental factor are the issues of security and facilities. Once there is equality on the fundamental issue, it is self-evident that the matters contingent upon the issue, like hours of work and other facilities, also need to be equal. Thus, all employees and workers become party to equal facilities and security. The spirit of Article 11(5) of the Constitution of the Kingdom of Nepal appears to be the same.

Under the Right to Freedom in Article 12, sub-article 2(e) provides for freedom to practice any profession, or to carry on any occupation, industry or trade. Proviso (5) of the same sub-article 2 provides that nothing in sub-clause (e) shall be deemed to prevent the making of laws to impose restrictions on any act which may be contrary to public health or morality, to confer on the State the exclusive right to undertake specified industries, businesses or services; or to impose any condition or qualification for carrying on any industry, trade, profession or occupation. Similarly, Article 17(1) provides that all citizens shall, subject to the existing laws, have the right to acquire, own, sell and otherwise dispose of, property. Article 131, under the title "Existing Laws to Remain in Operation" provides that all laws in force at the commencement of the Constitution shall remain in operation until repealed or amended, provided that laws inconsistent with the Constitution shall, to the extent of inconsistency, *ipso facto* cease to operate one year after the commencement of this Constitution. Article 26, under State Policies, provides under sub-article (7) that the State shall pursue a policy of making the female population participate, to a greater extent, in the task of national development by making special provisions for their education, health and employment.

Thus, Articles 11(2) and (3) of the Constitution incorporate the spirit of gender equality and several subjects of human rights and equality contained in the conventions and declarations. In response to the respondents' contention that article 11(3) of the Constitution allows unequal treatment of sexes, made in response to the petitioners' contention that they were being treated unequally in violation of article 11, it must be noted that the proviso under article 11(3) allows *additional* measures under the law for the uplift of women, rather than restricting such measures. The provision is merely an exception to the general rule of equality. In other words, it is not a provision that allows unequal treatment of women. The contention of the respondents that the provision can be used to accord more privilege to men than to women is untenable since it is a provision to allow special protection to women. It is against the spirit of the proviso to assert that it allows for unequal provision providing for better protection of men than women.

Similarly, it is not proper to interpret article 26(7) as one that can be used for restrictive purposes against women. Rule 16.1.3 of the RNAC Service Regulations runs counter to the state policy contained in Article 26(7) that provides that the state shall pursue a policy of making the female population participate to a greater extent in the task of national development by making special provisions for the education, health and employment. Similarly, Article 12(2)(e)(5) provides that nothing in sub-clause (e) shall be deemed to prevent the making of laws to impose restrictions on any act which may be contrary to public health and morality. Use of the provision to justify Rule 16.1.3 is an untenable proposition since in the present case there is no context of public health or morality. The contention related to Article 46(1)(b) is also illogical since the provision has no relevance to the present dispute.[*]

The respondents contend that since the proviso under Rule 16.1.3 provides security of service to the air hostesses, the provision can not be considered discriminatory. However, the provision is not a matter of right for the air hostesses, but something dependent on the discretion of the Corporation. Since it is dependent on the discretion of the management, and requires one to prove one's competence for another job, it cannot be argued that their services can be used for other jobs. It cannot be said that the petitioners can be certain of continuation of their services with the Corporation, based on this provision. Besides, since not all air hostesses will be able to benefit from the opportunity for ground jobs, and the provision is not definite or mandatory, it cannot be argued that a law of discretionary nature can protect the right to equality. Similarly, the contention of respondents' lawyer that the petitioners contractually accepted the Regulations when they accepted offers of employment with the RNAC, and therefore cannot challenge the contract, is not tenable since no matter how one enters service, once a person becomes a permanent employee, the rules of service apply.

Further, in case of a legal provision, the doctrine of estoppel does not apply. As far as the respondents' contention regarding the applicability of the doctrine of laches[**] is concerned, since Rule 16.1.3 came into operation in 2031 BS (1974/75AD) and Rule 16.1.1 was amended in 2052 (1995/96AD), firstly, the doctrine of laches does not apply to questions of constitutionality since, under Article 131 of the Constitution, laws inconsistent with the Constitution cease to operate one year after the commencement of the Constitution. On the other hand, since the respondents have been claiming that they have not applied the discriminatory provision under Rule 16.1.3, the contention is untenable.

---

[*]   *Eds:* Article 46(1)(b) provides for election of 35 of the 60 members of the National Assembly, the upper chamber of the bicameral legislature of Nepal. It reads as follows: "thirty five members, including at least three women members, to be elected by the House of Representatives in accordance with the provisions of law, on the basis of the system of proportional representation by means of the single transferable vote". (The respondents in the case had submitted that the provisions which make special arrangements for women, including those contained in Article 11(3), 26(7) and 46(1)(b) make the provision in Rule 16.1.3 compatible with the Constitutional provisions).

[**]   *Eds:* the equitable doctrine holds that courts may deny remedy to parties that bring a claim after an unreasonable delay or negligence in a way that might prejudice the party against whom relief is sought.

RIGHT TO EQUALITY IN THE ENJOYMENT OF OTHER ECONOMIC AND SOCIAL RIGHTS AND ACCESS TO ECONOMIC RESOURCES

CASE NO 32

ZWAAN DE VRIES v THE NETHERLANDS

UNITED NATIONS HUMAN RIGHTS COMMITTEE

Communication No: 182/1984

Views adopted: 9 April 1987

Human rights — Equality and non-discrimination — Sex discrimination — Social security — Legislation governing unemployment benefits — Benefits available for family breadwinner — Whether assumption that a married woman is not a breadwinner discriminatory — International Covenant on Civil and Political Rights, art 26

International law — Human rights treaties — Individual communication procedures — Admissibility — Individual communication under the Optional Protocol to the International Covenant on Civil and Political Rights — Whether examination of State reports submitted under art 16 of the International Covenant on Economic, Social and Cultural Rights constituted examination of same subject-matter by another international investigation procedure — Remedies — Whether remedy necessary where the national law has subsequently been reformed — Optional Protocol to the International Covenant on Civil and Political Rights, art 5(2)(a)

Treaties — Interpretation — Travaux préparatoires — Same subject matter in different international instruments — Vienna Convention on the Law of Treaties, arts 31 and 32 — International Covenant on Civil and Political Rights, art 26 — International Covenant on Economic, Social and Cultural Rights, art 9

BACKGROUND

The author of the communication, Ms Zwaan-de Vries, was a citizen of the Netherlands and was married. She became unemployed on 9 February 1979. She was granted unemployment benefits ("WWV benefits") for the maximum period of six months until 10 October 1979 pursuant to the Unemployment Benefit Act (the "Act") and then applied for continued support under the Act for WWV benefits. The Municipality of Amsterdam rejected her application on the grounds that as a married woman she did not qualify as a "breadwinner" under section 13(1)(1) of the Act and therefore was not entitled to benefits. Whether or not married women were breadwinners was calculated with reference to the income of the household. However, this provision did not apply to married men.

Ms Zwaan-de Vries appealed before the competent domestic authorities, each of which found her complaint unfounded and confirmed the decision of the Municipality. On 28 September 1984, she complained to the UN Human Rights Committee that she was a victim of a violation by the Netherlands of article 26 of the International Covenant on Civil and Political Rights ("ICCPR"), since she had been denied unemployment benefits on the basis of her sex and marital status.

HELD (finding for the author of the complaint)

Admissibility

1   The examination of state reports submitted under article 16 of the International Covenant on Economic and Social Rights ("ICESCR") did not constitute an examination of the "same matter" as a claim by an individual submitted to the Human Rights Committee under the Optional Protocol within the meaning of Article 5(2)(a); the Committee could therefore entertain the communication. (Para 6.2)

Scope of Article 26

2   The ICCPR would still apply even if a particular subject matter was referred to or covered in other international instruments – in the present case, the ICESCR. Notwithstanding the interrelated drafting history of the two Covenants, it remained necessary for the Committee to apply fully the terms of the ICCPR. In this connection, the provisions of article 2 of ICESCR did not detract from the full application of article 26 of the ICCPR. (Para 12.1)

3   Article 26 of the ICCPR is concerned with the obligations imposed on States in regard to their legislation and the application thereof. Although article 26 did not impose any obligation on a State to provide specific legislation, such as for social security, it did impose an obligation that any legislation which does exist must be implemented to all persons with equal and effective protection against discrimination. (Paras 12.3 and 12.4)

The complaint

4   Under the Unemployment Benefits Act, a married woman, in order to receive WWV benefits, had to prove that she was a "breadwinner" – a condition that did not apply to married men. Thus a differentiation which appeared on one level to be one of status was in fact one of sex, placing married women at a disadvantage compared with married men. Such a differentiation was not reasonable. (Para 14)

5   The author was a victim of a violation based on sex, of article 26 of the ICCPR, because she was denied social security benefits on an equal footing with men. Although the State party had taken the necessary measures to put an end to the kind of discrimination suffered by Ms Zwaan-de Vries at the time complained of (by subsequently reforming the law), the State party should offer the author an appropriate remedy. (Paras 15 and 16)

Treaties and other international instruments referred to

Convention on the Elimination of All Forms of Discrimination against Women 1979

Human Rights Committee, Rules of Procedure, r 87

International Convention on the Elimination of All Forms of Racial Discrimination 1965

International Covenant on Civil and Political Rights 1966, arts 2(2) and 26

International Covenant on Economic, Social and Cultural Rights 1966, arts 2, 3, 9 and 16

(First) Optional Protocol to the International Covenant on Civil and Political Rights 1966, arts 1, 2, 3, 4(2), 5(2)(a) and 5(2)(b)

Universal Declaration of Human Rights 1948, art 7

Vienna Convention on the Law of Treaties 1969, arts 31 and 32

European community law referred to

Council Directive 79/7/EEC of 19 December 1978 on the progressive implementation of the principle of equal treatment for men and women in matters of social security (OJ 1979 L6, p 24)

National legislation referred to

The Netherlands

Civil Code, arts 84 and 85

Unemployment Benefits Act (WWV), as amended 1985, s 13(1)(1)

Other material referred to

Annotations on the Text of the Draft International Covenants on Human Rights, 10 UN GAOR Annexes (Agenda item 28), UN Doc A/2929 (1955)

VIEWS UNDER ARTICLE 5(4) OF THE OPTIONAL PROTOCOL

1   The author of the communication (initial letter dated 28 September 1984 and subsequent letters of 2 July 1985, 4 and 23 April 1986) is Mrs F H Zwaan-de Vries, a Netherlands national residing in Amsterdam, the Netherlands, who is represented before the Committee by Mr DJ van der Vos, head of the Legal Aid Department (*Rechtskundige Dienst FNV*), Amsterdam.

2.1 The author was born in 1943 and is married to Mr C Zwaan. She was employed from early 1977 to 9 February 1979 as a computer operator. Since then she has been unemployed. Under the Unemployment Act, she was granted unemployment benefits until 10 October 1979. She subsequently applied for continued support on the basis of the Unemployment Benefits Act ("WWV"). The Municipality of Amsterdam rejected her application on the ground that she did not meet the requirements because she was a married woman; the refusal was based on section 13(1)(1) of WWV, which did not apply to married men.

2.2 Thus, the author claims to be a victim of a violation by the State party of article 26 of the International Covenant on Civil and Political Rights, which provides that all persons are equal before the law and are entitled without any discrimination to the equal protection of the law. The author claims that the only reasons she was denied unemployment benefits are her sex and marital status and contends that this constitutes discrimination within the scope of article 26 of the Covenant.

2.3 The author pursued the matter before the competent domestic instances. By decision of 9 May 1980, the Municipality of Amsterdam confirmed its earlier decision of 12 November 1979. The author appealed against the decision of 9 May 1980 to the Board of Appeal in Amsterdam, which, by an undated decision sent to her on 27 November 1981, declared her appeal to be unfounded. The author then appealed to the Central Board of Appeal, which confirmed the decision of the Board of Appeal on November 1983. Thus, it is claimed that the author has exhausted all national legal remedies.

2.4 The same matter has not been submitted for examination to any other procedure of international investigation or settlement.

3   By its decision of 16 October 1984, the Working Group of the Human Rights Committee transmitted the communication under rule 91 of the provisional rules of procedure, to the State party concerned, requesting information and observations relevant to the question of admissibility of the communication.

4.1   In its submission dated 29 May 1985, the State party underlined, *inter alia*, that:

(a) The principle that elements of discrimination in the realization of the right to social security are to be eliminated is embodied in article 9 in conjunction with articles 2 and 3 of the International Covenant on Economic, Social and Cultural Rights;

(b) The Government of the Kingdom of the Netherlands has accepted to implement this principle under the terms of the International Covenant on Economic, Social and Cultural Rights. Under these terms, States parties have undertaken to take steps to the maximum of their available resources with a view to achieving progressively the full realization of the rights recognized in that Covenant (art 2(1));

(c) The process of gradual realization to the maximum of available resources is well on its way in the Netherlands. Remaining elements of discrimination in the realization of the rights are being and will be gradually eliminated;

(d) The International Covenant on Economic, Social and Cultural Rights has established its own system for international control of the way in which States parties are fulfilling their obligations. To this end States parties have undertaken to submit to the Economic and Social Council reports on the measures they have adopted and the progress they are making. The Government of the Kingdom of the Netherlands to this end submitted its first report in 1983.

4.2   The State party then posed the question whether the way in which the Netherlands was fulfilling its obligations under article 9 in conjunction with articles 2 and 3 of the International Covenant on Economic, Social and Cultural Rights could become, by way of article 26 of the International Covenant on Civil and Political Rights, the object of an examination by the Human Rights Committee. The State party submitted that that question was relevant for the decision whether the communication was admissible.

4.3   The State party stressed that it would greatly benefit from receiving an answer from the Human Rights Committee to the question mentioned in paragraph 4.2 above. "Since such an answer could hardly be given without going into one aspect of the merits of the case – ie the question of the scope of article 26 of the International Covenant on Civil and Political Rights – the Government would respectfully request the Committee to join the question of admissibility to an examination of the merits of the case."

4.4   In case the Committee did not grant the request and declared the communication admissible, the State party reserved the right to submit, in the course of the proceedings, observations which might have an effect on the question of admissibility.

4.5   The State party also indicated that a change of legislation had been adopted recently in the Netherlands eliminating section 13(1)(1) of the Unemployment Benefits Act (WWV), which was the subject of the author's claim. This is the Act of 29 April 1985, S 230, having a retroactive effect to 23 December 1984.

4.6   The State party confirmed that the author had exhausted domestic remedies.

5.1   Commenting on the State party's submission under rule 91, the author, in a letter dated 2 July 1985, contended that the State party's question to the Committee as well as the answer to it were completely irrelevant with regard to the admissibility of the communication, because the author's complaint "pertains to the failure of the Netherlands to respect article 26 of the International Covenant on Civil and Political

Rights. As the Netherlands signed and ratified the Optional Protocol to that Covenant, the complainant is by virtue of articles 1 and 2 of the Optional Protocol, entitled to file a complaint with your Committee pertaining to the non-respect of article 26. Therefore her complaint is admissible."

5.2 The author further pointed out that, although section 13(1)(1) of WWV had been eliminated, her complaint concerned legislation in force in 1979.[1]

6.1 Before considering any claims contained in a communication, the Human Rights Committee must, in accordance with rule 87 of its provisional rules of procedure, decide whether or not it is admissible under the Optional Protocol to the Covenant.

6.2 Article 5(2)(a) of the Optional Protocol precludes the Committee from considering a communication if the same matter is being examined under another procedure of international investigation or settlement. In this connection the Committee observes that the examination of State reports, submitted under article 16 of the International Covenant on Economic, Social and Cultural Rights, does not, within the meaning of article 5(2)(a) constitute an examination of the "same matter" as a claim by an individual submitted to the Human Rights Committee under the Optional Protocol.

6.3 The Committee further observes that a claim submitted under the Optional Protocol concerning an alleged breach of a provision of the International Covenant on Civil and Political Rights is not necessarily incompatible with the provisions of that Covenant (see article 3 of the Optional Protocol), because the facts also related to a right protected by the International Covenant on Economic, Social and Cultural Rights or any other international instrument. It still had to be tested whether the alleged breach of a right protected by the International Covenant on Civil and Political Rights was borne out by the facts.

6.4 Article 5(2)(b) of the Optional Protocol precludes the Committee from considering a communication unless domestic remedies have been exhausted. The parties to the present communication agree that domestic remedies have been exhausted.

6.5 With regard to the State party's inquiry concerning the scope of article 26 of the International Covenant on Civil and Political Rights, the Committee did not consider it necessary to pronounce on its scope prior to deciding on the admissibility of the communication. However, having regard to the State party's statement (para 4.4 above) that it reserved the right to submit further observations which might have an effect on the question of the admissibility of the case, the Committee pointed out that it would take into account any further observations received on the matter.

7   On 23 July 1985, the Human Rights Committee therefore decided that the communication was admissible. In accordance with article 4(2) of the Optional Protocol, the State party was requested to submit to the Committee, within six months of the date of transmittal to it of the decision on admissibility, written explanations or statements clarifying the matter and the measures, if any, that might have been taken by it.

8.1 In its submission under article 4(2) of the Optional Protocol, dated 14 January 1986, the State party again objected to the admissibility of the communication, reiterating the arguments advanced in its submission of 29 May 1985.

---

1   The Covenant and the Optional Protocol entered into force on 11 March 1979 in respect of the Netherlands.

8.2 In discussing the merits of the case, the State party first elucidates the factual background as follows:

When Mrs. Zwaan applied for WWV benefits in October 1979, section 13(1)(1) was still applicable. This section laid down that WWV benefits could not be claimed by those married women who were neither breadwinners nor permanently separated from their husbands. The concept of 'breadwinner' as referred to in section 13(1)(1) of WWV was of particular significance, and was further amplified in statutory instruments based on the Act (the last relevant instrument being the ministerial decree of 5 April 1976, Netherlands Government Gazette 1976, 72). Whether a married woman was deemed to be a breadwinner depended, *inter alia*, on the absolute amount of the family's total income and on what proportion of it was contributed by the wife. That the conditions for granting benefits laid down in section 13(1)(1) of WWV applied solely to married women and not to married men is due to the fact that the provision in question corresponded to the then prevailing views in society in general concerning the roles of men and women within marriage and society. Virtually all married men who had jobs could be regarded as their family's breadwinner, so that it was unnecessary to check whether they met this criterion for the granting of benefits upon becoming unemployed. These views have gradually changed in later years. This aspect will be further discussed below (see para 8.4).

The Netherlands is a member State of the European Economic Community (EEC). On 19 December 1978, the Council of the European Communities issued a directive on the progressive implementation of the principle of equal treatment for men and women in matters of social security (79/7/EEC), giving member States a period of six years, until 23 December 1984, within which to make any amendments to legislation which might be necessary in order to bring it into line with the directive. Pursuant to this directive the Netherlands Government examined the criteria for the granting of benefits laid down in section 13(1)(1) of WWV in the light of the principle of equal treatment of men and women and in the light of the changing role patterns of sexes in the years since about 1960.

Since it could no longer be assumed as a matter of course in the early 1980s that married men with jobs should always be regarded as "breadwinners", the Netherlands amended section 13(1)(1) of WWV to meet its obligations under the EEC directive. The amendment consisted of the deletion of section 13(1)(1) with the result that it became possible for married women who were not breadwinners to claim WWV benefits, while the duration of the benefits, which had previously been two years, was reduced for people aged under 35.

In view of changes in the status of women – and particularly married women – in recent decades, the failure to award Mrs. Zwaan WWV benefits in 1979 is explicable in historical terms. If she were to apply for such benefits now, the result would be different.

8.3 With regard to the scope of article 26 of the Covenant, the State party argues, *inter alia*, as follows:

The Netherlands Government takes the view that article 26 of the Covenant does entail an obligation to avoid discrimination, but that this article can only be invoked under the Optional Protocol to the Covenant in the sphere of civil and political rights. Civil and political rights are to be distinguished from economic, social and cultural rights which are the object of a separate United Nations Covenant, the International Covenant on Economic, Social and Cultural Rights.

The complaint made in the present case relates to obligations in the sphere of social security, which fall under the International Covenant on Economic, Social and Cultural Rights. Articles 2, 3 and 9 of that Covenant are of particular relevance here. That Covenant has its own specific system and its own specific organ for international monitoring of how States parties meet their obligations and deliberately does not provide for an individual complaints procedure.

The Government considers it incompatible with the aims of both the Covenants and the optional Protocol that an individual complaint with respect to the right of social security as referred to in article 9 of the International Covenant on Economic, Social and Cultural Rights, could be dealt with by the Human Rights Committee by way of an individual complaint under the Optional Protocol based on article 26 of the International Covenant on Civil and Political Rights.

The Netherlands Government reports to the Economic and Social Council on matters concerning the way it is fulfilling its obligations with respect to the right to social security in accordance with the relevant rules of the International Covenant on Economic Social and Cultural Rights.

Should the Human Rights Committee take the view that article 26 of the International Covenant on Civil and Political Rights ought to be interpreted more broadly, thus that this article is applicable to complaints concerning discrimination in the field of social security, the Government would observe that in that case article 26 must also be interpreted in the light of other comparable United Nations conventions laying down obligations to combat and eliminate discrimination in the field of economic, social and cultural rights. The Government would particularly point to the International Convention on the Elimination of All Forms of Racial Discrimination and the Convention on the Elimination of All Forms of Discrimination against Women.

If article 26 of the International Covenant on Civil and Political Rights were deemed applicable to complaints concerning discriminatory elements in national legislation in the field of those conventions, this could surely not be taken to mean that a State party would be required to have eliminated all possible discriminatory elements from its legislation in those fields at the time of ratification of the Covenant. Years of work are required in order to examine the whole complex of national legislation in search of discriminatory elements. The search can never be completed, either, as distinctions in legislation which are justifiable in the light of social views and conditions prevailing when they are first made may become disputable as changes occur in the views held in society.

If the Human Rights Committee should decide that article 26 of the International Covenant on Civil and Political Rights entails obligations with regard to legislation in the economic, social and cultural field, such obligations could, in the Government's view, not comprise more than an obligation of States to subject national legislation to periodic examination after ratification of the Covenant with a view to seeking out discriminatory elements and, if they are found, to progressively taking measures to eliminate them to the maximum of the State's available resources. Such examinations are under way in the Netherlands with regard to various aspects of discrimination, including discrimination between men and women.

8.4 With regard to the principle of equality laid down in article 26 of the Covenant in relation to section 13(1)(1), of WWV in its unamended form, the State party explains the legislative history of WWV and in particular the social justification of the "breadwinner" concept at the time the law was drafted. The State party contends that with the "breadwinner" concept a proper balance was achieved between the limited availability of public funds (which makes it necessary to put them to limited, well-considered and selective use) on the one hand and the Government's obligation to provide social security on the other. The Government does not accept that the "breadwinner" concept as such was "discriminatory" in the sense that equal cases were treated in an unequal way by law. Moreover, it is argued that the provisions of WWV "are based on reasonable social and economic considerations which are not discriminatory in origin. The restriction making the provision in question inapplicable to men was inspired not by any desire to discriminate in favour of men and against women but by the *de facto* social and economic situation which existed at the time when the Act was passed and which would have made it pointless to declare the provision applicable to men. At the time when Mrs

Zwaan-de Vries applied for unemployment benefits, the *de facto* situation was not essentially different. There was therefore no violation of article 26 of the Covenant. This is not altered by the fact that a new social trend has been growing in recent years, which has made it undesirable for the provision to remain in force in the present social context."

8.5　With reference to the decision of the Central Board of Appeal of 1 November 1983, which the author criticizes, the State party contends that "the observation of the Central Board of Appeal that the Covenants employ different international control systems is highly relevant. Not only do parties to the Covenants report to different United Nations agencies but, above all, there is a major difference between the Covenants as regards the possibility of complaints by States or individuals, which exists only under the International Covenant on Civil and Political Rights. The contracting parties deliberately chose to make this difference in international monitoring systems, because the nature and substance of social, economic and cultural rights make them unsuitable for judicial review of a complaint lodged by a State party or an individual."

9.1　In her comments, dated 4 and 23 April 1986, the author reiterates that "article 13(1)(1) contains the requirement of being breadwinner for married women only, and not for married men. This distinction runs counter to article 26 of the Covenant ... The observations of the Netherlands Government on views in society concerning traditional roles of men and women are completely irrelevant to the present case. The question ... is in fact not whether those roles could justify the existence of article 13(1)(l) of WWV, but ... whether this article in 1979 constituted an infraction of article 26 of the Covenant . . . The State of the Netherlands is wrong when it takes the view that the complainant's view could imply that all discriminatory elements ought to have been eliminated from its national legislation at the time of ratification of the Covenant ... The complainant's view does imply, however, that ratification enables all Netherlands citizens to invoke article 26 of the Covenant directly ... if they believe that they are being discriminated against. This does not imply that the International Covenant on Economic, Social and Cultural Rights and the Convention on the Elimination of All Forms of Discrimination against Women have become meaningless. Those treaties in fact compel the Netherlands to eliminate discriminatory provisions from more specific parts of national legislation."

9.2　With respect to the State party's contention that article 26 of the Covenant can only be invoked in the sphere of civil and political rights, the author claims that this view is not shared by Netherlands courts and that it also "runs counter to the stand taken by the Government itself during parliamentary approval. It then stated that article 26 – as opposed to article 2(1) 'also applied to areas otherwise not covered by the Covenant'".

9.3　The author also disputes the State party's contention that applicability of article 26 with regard to the right of social security, as referred to in article 9 of the International Covenant on Economic, Social and Cultural Rights would be incompatible with the aims of both Covenants. The author claims that article 26 would apply "to one well-defined aspect of article 9 only, which is equal treatment before the law, leaving other important aspects such as the level of social security aside."

9.4　With regard to the State party's argument that, even if article 26 were to be considered applicable, the State party would have a delay of several years from the time of ratification of the Covenant to adjust its legislation, the author contends that this argument runs counter to the observations made by the Government at the time of [parliamentary] approval with regard to article 2(2) of the International Covenant on Civil and Political Rights stating that such a *terme de grâce* would be applicable only with respect to provisions that are not self-executing, whereas article 26 is in fact recognized by the Government and court rulings as self-executing. The author adds that "it can, in fact, be concluded from the *travaux préparatoires* of the International Covenant on Civil and Political Rights that according to the majority of the delegates 'it was essential to permit a certain degree of elasticity to the obligations imposed on States by the Covenant, since all States would not be in a position immediately to take the necessary legislative or other measures for the implementation of its provisions'."[2]

10   The Human Rights Committee has considered the present communication in the light of all information made available to it by the parties, as provided in article 5(1) of the Optional Protocol. The facts of the case are not in dispute.

11   Article 26 of the International Covenant on Civil and Political Rights provides:

All persons are equal before the law and are entitled without any discrimination to the equal protection of the law. In this respect, the law shall prohibit any discrimination and guarantee to all persons equal and effective protection against discrimination on any ground such as race, colour, sex, language, religion, political or other opinion, national or social origin, property, birth or other status.

12.1 The State party contends that there is considerable overlapping of the provisions of article 26 with the provisions of article 2 of the International Covenant on Economic, Social and Cultural Rights. The Committee is of the view that the International Covenant on Civil and Political Rights would still apply even if a particular subject-matter is referred to or covered in other international instruments, for example the International Convention on the Elimination of All Forms of Racial Discrimination, the Convention on the Elimination of All Forms of Discrimination against Women, or, as in the present case, the International Covenant on Economic, Social and Cultural Rights. Notwithstanding the interrelated drafting history of the two Covenants, it remains necessary for the Committee to apply fully the terms of the International Covenant on Civil and Political Rights. The Committee observes in this connection that the provisions of article 2 of the International Covenant on Economic, Social and Cultural Rights do not detract from the full application of article 26 of the International Covenant on Civil and Political Rights.

12.2 The Committee has also examined the contention of the State party that article 26 of the International Covenant on Civil and Political Rights cannot be invoked in respect of a right which is specifically provided for under article 9 of the International Covenant on Economic, Social and Cultural Rights (social security, including social insurance). In so doing, the Committee has perused the relevant *travaux préparatoires* of the International Covenant on Civil and Political Rights, namely the summary records of the discussions that took place in the Commission on Human Rights in 1948, 1949, 1950 and 1952 and in the Third Committee of the General Assembly in 1961, which provide a "supplementary means of interpretation" (article 32 of the Vienna Convention on the Law of Treaties).[3] The discussions, at the time of drafting, concerning the question whether the scope of article 26 extended to rights not otherwise guaranteed by the Covenant, were inconclusive and cannot alter the conclusion arrived at by the ordinary means of interpretation referred to in paragraph 12.3 below.

12.3 For the purpose of determining the scope of article 26, the Committee has taken into account the "ordinary meaning" of each element of the article in its context and in the

---

2   Official Records of the General Assembly, Tenth Session, Annexes, Agenda Item 28 (Part 11), Document A/2929, chapter V, para 8.
3   United Nations, Judicial Yearbook 1969 (United Nations publication, Sales No E 71, V 4), p 140.

light of its object and purpose (article 31 of the Vienna Convention on the Law of Treaties). The Committee begins by noting that article 26 does not merely duplicate the guarantees already provided for in article 2. It derives from the principle of equal protection of the law without discrimination, as contained in article 7 of the Universal Declaration of Human Rights, which prohibits discrimination in law or in practice in any field regulated and protected by public authorities. Article 26 is thus concerned with the obligations imposed on States in regard to their legislation and the application thereof.

12.4 Although article 26 requires that legislation should prohibit discrimination, it does not of itself contain any obligation with respect to the matters that may be provided for by legislation. Thus it does not, for example, require any State to enact legislation to provide for social security. However, when such legislation is adopted in the exercise of a State's sovereign power, then such legislation must comply with article 26 of the Covenant.

12.5 The Committee observes in this connection that what is at issue is not whether or not social security should be progressively established in the Netherlands but whether the legislation providing for social security violates the prohibition against discrimination contained in article 26 of the International Covenant on Civil and Political Rights and the guarantee given therein to all persons regarding equal and effective protection against discrimination.

13   The right to equality before the law and to equal protection of the law without any discrimination does not make all differences of treatment discriminatory. A differentiation based on reasonable and objective criteria does not amount to prohibited discrimination within the meaning of article 26.

14   It therefore remains for the Committee to determine whether the differentiation in Netherlands law at the time in question and as applied to Mrs Zwaan-de Vries constituted discrimination within the meaning of article 26. The Committee notes that in Netherlands law the provisions of articles 84 and 85 of the Netherlands Civil Code impose equal rights and obligations on both spouses with regard to their joint income. Under section 13(1)(1) of the Unemployment Benefits Act (WWV) a married woman, in order to receive WWV benefits had to prove that she was a "breadwinner" – a condition that did not apply to married men. Thus a differentiation which appears on one level to be one of status is in fact one of sex, placing married women at a disadvantage compared with married men. Such a differentiation is not reasonable, and this seems to have been effectively acknowledged even by the State party by the enactment of a change in the law on 29 April 1985, with retroactive effect to 23 December 1984 (see para 4.5 above).

15   The circumstances in which Mrs Zwaan-de Vries found herself at the material time and the application of the then valid Netherlands law made her a victim of a violation based on sex, of article 26 of the International Covenant on Civil and Political Rights, because she was denied a social security benefit on an equal footing with men.

16   The Committee notes that the State party had not intended to discriminate against women and further notes with appreciation that the discriminatory provisions in the law applied to Mrs Zwaan-de Vries have, subsequently, been eliminated. Although the State party has thus taken the necessary measures to put an end to the kind of discrimination suffered by Mrs Zwaan-de Vries at the time complained of, the Committee is of the view that the State party should offer Mrs Zwaan-de Vries an appropriate remedy.

CASE NO 33

VOS v THE NETHERLANDS

UNITED NATIONS HUMAN RIGHTS COMMITTEE

Communication No: 218/1986

Views adopted: 29 March 1989

Human Rights — Equality and Non-Discrimination — Sex Discrimination — Discrimination on the ground of marital status — Social security — National insurance schemes — Disability allowance — Whether cessation of a disabled woman's payment of disability allowance on the death of her husband (divorced or otherwise), when a disabled man retained his entitlement to disability benefit on the death of his wife (divorced or otherwise) constituted discrimination on the grounds of sex and marital status — Widows' allowance — General Disablement Benefits Act — General Widows and Orphans Act — International Covenant on Civil and Political Rights, art 26

Treaties — Interpretation — Same subject matter in different international instruments — International Covenant on Civil and Political Rights, art 26 — International Covenant on Economic, Social and Cultural Rights

BACKGROUND

The author of the communication, Ms Vos, was a citizen of the Netherlands, who received an allowance under the General Disablement Benefits Act ("AAW") from 1 October 1976. In May 1979, following the death of her ex-husband, whom she divorced in 1957, the payment of her disability allowance was discontinued in accordance with article 32(1)(b) of the General Disablement Benefits Act because she had become entitled to payment of a widow's allowance under the General Widows and Orphans Act ("AWW"). Under the new allowance, she received about 90 guilders less per month.

Ms Vos complained to the Arnhem Appeals Court that she was a victim of discrimination. On 10 March 1980, the Court rejected her appeal as being unfounded. She then further appealed to the Central Appeals Court where she claimed that article 26 of the International Covenant on Civil and Political Rights ("ICCPR") was directly applicable. She argued that whereas a disabled man whose former wife died retained his right to disability allowance, a disabled women whose former husband died did not, and so article 32 of the AAW made a distinction according to sex which was contrary to article 26 of the ICCPR. Furthermore the application of article 32 was particularly unfair in her case since she had been divorced from her husband for 22 years and had been supporting herself when she became disabled. Her appeal was dismissed on 1 November 1983. The Court stated, *inter alia*, that article 26 of the ICCPR was not applicable to the social security right in dispute. It was of the view that social security rights belong to the group of rights covered by the International Covenant on Economic, Social and Cultural Rights ("ICESCR"), which could only be reformed gradually by means of legislation. Moreover the fact that the two Conventions were concluded at the same time and provided distinctive implementation methods underlined the assertion that it was the intention of the drafters that economic, social and cultural rights, such as social security rights, which belong to the ICESCR did not come within the scope of article 26 of the ICCPR.

Having exhausted domestic remedies, Ms Vos complained to the United Nations Human Rights Committee that the Central Appeals Court had wrongly interpreted the scope of article 26 of the ICCPR and that the cessation of payments of her AAW allowance was a form of discrimination based on sex and marital status in violation of article 26.

HELD (Messrs Aguilar Urbina and Wennergren dissenting)

1   The ICCPR still applied even if a particular subject-matter was referred to or covered in other international instruments – in the present case, the ICESCR. Notwithstanding the interrelated drafting history of the ICCPR and the ICESCR, it remained necessary for the Human Rights Committee to apply fully the terms of the ICCPR. (Para 11.2)

2   The right to equality before the law and to equal protection of the law without any discrimination did not make all differences of treatment discriminatory. A differentiation based on reasonable and objective criteria did not amount to prohibited discrimination within the meaning of article 26 of the ICCPR. The unfavourable result complained of by Ms Vos followed from the application of a uniform rule to avoid overlapping in the allocation of social security benefits. This rule was based on objective and reasonable criteria, especially bearing in mind that both statutes under which the author qualified for benefits aimed at ensuring to all persons falling thereunder subsistence level income. Thus, the author had not been a victim of discrimination within the meaning of article 26 of the ICCPR. (Paras 11.3 and 12)

Treaties and other international instruments referred to

Convention on the Elimination of All Forms of Discrimination against Women 1979

International Convention on the Elimination of All Forms of Racial Discrimination 1965

International Covenant on Civil and Political Rights 1966, art 26

International Covenant on Economic, Social and Cultural Rights 1966, art 2

(First) Optional Protocol to the International Covenant on Civil and Political Rights 1966, arts 4(2), 5(1), 5(2)(a) and 5(2)(b)

European Community law referred to

Council Directive 79/7/EEC of 19 December 1978 on the progressive implementation of the principle of equal treatment for men and women in matters of social security (OJ 1979 L6, p 24)

National legislation referred to

The Netherlands

General Disablement Benefits Act 1975, art 32(1)(b)

General Widows and Orphans Act 1986

National Assistance Act

Supplements Act

Cases referred to

Brooks v The Netherlands, UN Human Rights Committee, Communication No 172/1984, views adopted on 9 April 1987, UN Doc CCPR/C/29/D/172/1984; UN Doc Supp No 40 (A/42/40) at 139

Danning v The Netherlands, UN Human Rights Committee, Communication No 180/1984, views adopted 9 April 1987, CCPR/C/29/D/180/1984; UN Doc Supp No 40 (A/42/40) at 151

PPC v The Netherlands, UN Human Rights Committee, Communication No 12/1986, Inadmissibility Decision adopted on 24 March 1988, UN Doc: CCPR/C/32/D/212/1986; UN Doc CCPR/C/OP/2 at 70

Zwaan-de-Vries v The Netherlands, UN Human Rights Committee, Communication No 182/1984, views adopted 9 April 1987, UN Doc CCPR/C/29/D/182/1984; UN Doc Supp No 40 (A/42/40) at 160; *supra*, p 501

VIEWS UNDER ARTICLE 5(4) OF THE OPTIONAL PROTOCOL

1 The author of the communication (initial letter dated 23 December 1986 and subsequent letters dated 5 and 26 March 1987 and 3 January 1989) is Hendrika Vos, a citizen of the Netherlands, residing in that country. She claims to be a victim of a violation of article 26 of the International Covenant on Civil and Political Rights by the Government of the Netherlands. She is represented by counsel.

2.1 The author states that since 1 October 1976 she had received an allowance from the New General Trade Association under the General Disablement Benefits Act ("AAW"), but that in May 1979, following the death of her ex-husband (from whom she had been divorced in 1957), payment of the disability allowance was discontinued, in accordance with article 32(1)(b) of AAW, because she then became entitled to a payment under the General Widows and Orphans Act ("AWW"). Under the latter, she receives some 90 guilders per month less than she had been receiving under AAW.

2.2 The author states that she first challenged the decision of the New General Trade Association before the Arnhem Appeals Court, but her claim of being a victim of discrimination was rejected on 10 March 1980. Thereupon, she lodged an objection with the same Appeals Court, which rejected it as unfounded by decision of 23 June 1981. A further appeal was taken to the Central Appeals Court in which the author invoked the direct application of article 26 of the Covenant. The court decided against her claim on 1 November 1983. Thus domestic remedies are said to be exhausted.

2.3 The author had argued before the Netherlands Courts that, whereas a disabled man whose (former) wife dies retains the right to a disability allowance, article 32 of AAW makes an improper distinction according to sex, in that a disabled woman whose (former) husband dies does not retain the right to a disability allowance. Subsection 1(b) of this article provides:

1   The employment disability benefit will be withdrawn when:

   ...

   (b) a woman, to whom this benefit has been granted, becomes entitled to a widow's
        pension or a temporary widow's benefit in compliance with the General Widows
        and Orphans Law.

In her specific case she claimed that the application of the law was particularly unjust
because she had been divorced from her husband for 22 years and had been providing
for her own support when she became disabled. Thus she claims that she should be
treated primarily as a disabled person and not as a widow.

2.4 In rejecting the author's claim that she is a victim of discrimination under article 26
of the Covenant, the Central Appeals Court, in its decision of 1 November 1983, stated:

   From the wording of these two articles (articles 26 and 2(1) of the Covenant), taken
   conjointly, it is apparent that article 26 is not solely applicable to the civil and political
   rights that are recognized by the Covenant. In answer to the question whether this article
   is also of significance in connection with a social security right, as in dispute here, the
   Court expresses the following consideration:

   In addition to the Covenant on Civil and Political Rights, the International Covenant on
   Economic, Social and Cultural Rights was concluded at the same time and place. The
   Court is of the opinion that the text and the import of the two Covenants under
   consideration here, and the intentions of the States involved therein, must be taken
   conjointly, because from the history of the conclusion of these Covenants it is apparent that
   the initial plan to conclude a single covenant was abandoned on the grounds that
   economic, social and cultural rights – in contrast to civil and political rights – can generally
   speaking only gradually be realized by means of legislation and other executive measures.
   That the States involved in those Covenants proceed from this distinction is also apparent
   from the fact that the Covenant on Economic, Social and Cultural Rights merely provides
   for a so-called reporting system with respect to the fulfilment of the rights recognized
   therein whereas the Covenant on Civil and Political Rights also includes an inter-State
   complaints system (regulated in article 41 *et seq* of the Covenant) and an individual
   complaints system (regulated in the Optional Protocol to the Covenant). Distinguishing
   criteria connected with existing social structures which appear also in social security
   regulations and which are possibly to be regarded as discriminatory, such as man/woman
   and married/single, can only gradually be done away with by means of legislation ... On
   the basis of the foregoing, the significance of article 26 of the International Covenant on
   Civil and Political Rights in connection with a social security right as in dispute here must
   be denied.

2.5 The author claims that the Central Appeals Court incorrectly interpreted the scope
of article 26 of the International Covenant on Civil and Political Rights and asks the
Committee to find that the cessation of the payment to her of an AAW allowance was a
form of discrimination based on sex and marital status in contravention of article 26 of
the Covenant.

3   By its decision of 18 March 1987, the Working Group of the Human Rights
Committee transmitted the communication under rule 91 of the provisional rules of
procedure to the State party concerned, requesting information and observations
relevant to the question of the admissibility of the communication.

4   In its submission dated 25 June 1987, the State party reserved the right to submit
observations on the merits of the communication which might turn out to have an effect
on the question of admissibility. For this reason the State party suggested that the
Committee might decide to join the question of the admissibility to the examination of
the merits of the communication.

5   The author's deadline for comments on the State party's submission expired on 4 September 1987. No comments were received from the author.

6.1 Before considering any claims in a communication, the Human Rights Committee must, in accordance with rule 87 of its provisional rules of procedure, decide whether or not it is admissible under the Optional Protocol to the Covenant.

6.2 Article 5(2)(a) of the Optional Protocol precludes the Committee from considering a communication if the same matter is being examined under another procedure of international investigation or settlement. In this connection the Committee ascertained that the same matter was not being examined under another procedure of international investigation or settlement.

6.3 Article 5(2)(b) of the Optional Protocol precludes the Committee from considering a communication unless domestic remedies have been exhausted. In this connection the Committee noted that the author's statement that domestic remedies had been exhausted remained uncontested.

7   On 24 March 1988, the Human Rights Committee therefore decided that the communication was admissible. In accordance with article 4(2) of the Optional Protocol, the State party was requested to submit to the Committee, within six months of the date of transmittal to it of the decision on admissibility, written explanations or statements clarifying the matter and the measures, if any, that may have been taken by it.

8.1 In its submission under article 4(2) of the Optional Protocol, dated 28 October 1988, the State party, before discussing the merits of the case, points out that it has taken note of the views of the Committee in communications CCPR/C/29/D/172/1984, CCPR/C/29/D/180/1984 and CCPR/C/29/D/182/1984 with respect to the applicability of article 26 of the Covenant in the field of social security rights and that it reserves its position, notwithstanding the fact that this aspect is not addressed in its submission.

8.2 In discussing the merits of the case, the State party elucidates first the relevant Netherlands legislation as follows:

8.3 "Netherlands social security legislation consists of employee insurance schemes and national insurance schemes: as employee insurance schemes are not of relevance to the present case, they will be disregarded. The aim of national insurance schemes is to insure all residents of the Netherlands against the financial consequences of certain contingencies. The national insurance schemes concerning survivors, old age and long-term disability guarantee payment of a benefit related to the statutory minimum wage. The entitlements concerned are gross benefits. They are set at such a level that, after tax and social insurance premiums have been deducted from them, net benefits are sufficient to enable the beneficiary to subsist."

8.4 "The AAW of 11 December 1975 created a national insurance scheme concerning long-term disability: under the terms of the Act, anybody who has been disabled for longer than one year is entitled to a basic benefit. If the beneficiary was employed full-time before becoming unfit for work, full benefit is paid (equivalent to the subsistence minimum). If the beneficiary is only partially disabled, the benefit is reduced proportionately: the amount of benefit payable is also based on the number of hours per week worked before the beneficiary became disabled. If the amount of AAW benefit payable is less than the subsistence minimum, as will often be the case if the claimant is only partially disabled or was working part-time before becoming disabled, supplementary benefit can be paid under the National Assistance Act (ABW) or Supplements Act (TW)."

8.5 "The AWW of 9 April 1986 created a national insurance scheme which entitles widows and orphans to receive benefit related to the statutory minimum wage if their husband or father dies. The rationale underlying the Act is that after a married man dies his widow may well have insufficient means of subsistence. At the time when the Act was passed, it was felt that, if there were good reasons why the widow should not be expected to earn her own living (for example, because she still had children to look after or because she was too old), it was desirable to pay her benefit. In some cases, women are eligible for the AWW benefit even if they have been divorced from the deceased."

8.6 "At the time when the General Widows and Orphan Act was passed, it was customary for husbands to act as bread-winners for their families, and it was therefore desirable to make financial provision for dependants in the event of the bread-winner's premature death. In recent years more married women have been going out to work and households consisting of unmarried people have increasingly been granted the same status as traditional families. This being so, the Government has been studying since the early 1980s ways of amending the AWW: one of the questions being examined is whether the privileged position enjoyed by women under the Act is still justified nowadays."

8.7 "It is too early to say what provisions the future Surviving Dependants Act will contain. As the Netherlands is a member of the European Community, it will in all events comply with the obligations arising from a European Community directive which is currently in preparation concerning sexual equality with regard to provision for survivors; it is expected to be many years before the directive enters into force. However, it is possible that the Netherlands Government may make proposals for new legislation on survivors before the European Community directive is finalized."

8.8 "In a social security system, it is necessary to ensure that individuals do not qualify for more than one benefit simultaneously under different social insurance acts, when each such benefit is intended to provide a full income at subsistence level. The various relevant acts therefore contain provisions governing entitlements for the eventuality of overlapping entitlements. The clause of which Mrs Vos complains – article 32(1)(b) of the AAW – falls into this category. The legislature had to decide whether claimants who were entitled to benefits under both the AAW and the AWW should receive benefits under the one or the other, and it was decided that in such cases the AWW benefit should be paid. The decision to opt for a rule on concurrence as laid down in article 32(1)(b) of the AAW is based, *inter alia*, on practical considerations with a view to the implementation of the legislation. It is necessary, for example, to avoid the necessity of entering the person concerned in the records of two different bodies responsible for paying benefits and to avoid having to levy income tax in arrears on income from two separate sources."

8.9 "From the point of view of widows, it is, generally speaking, more advantageous to receive AWW than AAW; if the legislature had decided that the AAW benefit should have precedence over the AWW benefit, many widows would have been worse off, because in most cases the AWW benefit exceeds the AAW benefit payable to married women. This is because most married women have worked part-time and therefore receive only a partial AAW benefit in the event of long-term disability. This is not to say that the rule on concurrence which gives procedure to the AWW is always advantageous to all widows: it merely benefits the majority of them. Cases are conceivable in which the award of the AWW benefit instead of the AAW benefit leads to a slight fall in income. This is evidently so in the case of Mrs Vos."

8.10 "However, the fact that, in a particular case, the application of article 32(1)(b) of AAW leads to a disadvantageous result for a particular individual is irrelevant for purposes of assessing whether a form of discrimination has occurred which is prohibited by article 26 of the International Covenant on Civil and Political Rights. In this connection, reference may be made to the Committee's decision in case No 212/1986 (*PPC v The Netherlands*), in which it was found, *inter alia*, that the scope of article 26 does not extend to differences of results in the application of common rules in the allocation of benefits."[1]

8.11 Lastly, the Netherlands Government observe that in the course of the review of the AWW (paras 8.6 and 8.7), explicit consideration was given to the problem of overlapping entitlements under AAW and AWW.

9.1 With regard to the author's specific complaint in relation to article 26 of the Covenant, the State party contests the contention of Mrs Vos "that article 32(1)(b) of AAW discriminates unjustifiably between the sexes, because a disabled man whose wife (divorced or otherwise) dies retains his right to disablement benefit whereas a disabled woman whose husband (divorced or otherwise) dies forfeits hers. The difference in position between a disabled widow and a disabled widower can be explained as follows. The provision which is made for survivors is not available to men, and the problem of overlapping of benefits therefore does not arise. Precisely on account of the fact that a disabled man cannot be eligible for AWW benefit and that the death of his wife therefore does not affect his AAW benefit, it is impossible to compare the rules of concurrence."

9.2 "By way of illustration of the relative discrimination in favour of women, which is inherent in the AWW rules, the Netherlands Government would observe that the favourable treatment which women receive in the Netherlands under AWW has led some people to suggest that the Act discriminates against men. This is one of the reasons why a review of AWW is under consideration. Be that as it may, this is not the point of Mrs Vos's complaint. In any case, it should be concluded that the cases to which the applicant refers are not cases which require equal treatment on the basis of article 26 of the Covenant."

10.1 In her comments, dated 3 January 1989, the author reiterates her view that the application of article 32(1)(b) of the General Disablement Act (AAW) violates article 26 of the Covenant. She also argues that, provided article 26 is found relevant, then it must be accepted that it has direct effect from the moment the International Covenant on Civil and Political Rights came into force. Although she acknowledges that not every inequality constitutes unlawful discrimination, she contends that since 1979 any existing inequality in the field of social security can be examined on the basis of article 26 of the Covenant.

10.2 Contesting the interpretation of article 26 of the Covenant by the Central Appeals Court, the author argues that it would be incompatible with article 26 to grant the Government additional time to eliminate unlawful discrimination, and that what is at issue in the communication under consideration is whether the distinction is acceptable or unacceptable, it being irrelevant whether the Government after 1979 needed some time to eliminate the alleged distinction.

---

1   *PPC v The Netherlands*, UN Doc CCPR/C/32/D/212/1986, para 6.2.

11.1 The Human Rights Committee has considered the present communication in the light of all the information made available to it by the parties, as provided in article 5(1) of the Optional Protocol.

11.2 The Committee notes that the State party in its submission under article 4(2) of the Optional Protocol has reserved its position with respect to the applicability of article 26 of the Covenant in the field of social security rights (para 8.1 above). In this connection, the Committee has already expressed the view in its case law[2] that the International Covenant on Civil and Political Rights would still apply even if a particular subject-matter is referred to or covered in other international instruments, eg the International Convention on the Elimination of All Forms of Racial Discrimination, the Convention on the Elimination of All Forms of Discrimination Against Women or, as in the present case, the International Covenant on Economic, Social and Cultural Rights. Notwithstanding the interrelated drafting history of the two covenants, it remains necessary for the Committee to apply fully the terms of the International Covenant on Civil and Political Rights. The Committee observes in this connection that the provisions of article 2 of the International Covenant Economic, Social and Cultural Rights do not detract from the full application of article 26 of the International Covenant on Civil and Political Rights.

11.3 The Committee further observes that what is at issue is not whether the State party is required to enact legislation such as the General Disablement Benefits Act or the General Widows and Orphans Act, but whether this legislation violates the author's rights contained in article 26 of the International Covenant on Civil and Political Rights. The right to equality before the law and to equal protection of the law without any discrimination does not make all differences of treatment discriminatory. A differentiation based on reasonable and objective criteria does not amount to prohibited discrimination within the meaning of article 26. Further differences in result of the uniform application of laws do not *per se* constitute prohibited discrimination.

12   It remains for the Committee to determine whether the disadvantageous treatment complained of by the author resulted from the application of a discriminatory statute and thus violated her rights under article 26 of the Covenant. In the light of the explanations given by the State party with respect to the legislative history, the purpose and application of the General Disablement Benefits Act and the General Widows and Orphans Act (paras 8.3-8.10 above), the Committee is of the view that the unfavourable result complained of by Mrs Vos follows from the application of a uniform rule to avoid overlapping in the allocation of social security benefits. This rule is based on objective and reasonable criteria, especially bearing in mind that both statutes under which Mrs Vos qualified for benefits aim at ensuring to all persons falling thereunder subsistence level income. Thus the Committee cannot conclude that Mrs Vos has been a victim of discrimination within the meaning of article 26 of the Covenant.

13   The Human Rights Committee, acting under article 5(4) of the Optional Protocol to the International Covenant on Civil and Political Rights, is of the view that the facts as submitted do not disclose a violation of any article of the International Covenant on Civil and Political Rights.

---

2   *Brooks v The Netherlands*, UN Doc CCPR/C/29/D/172/1984; *Danning v The Netherlands*, UN Doc CCPR/C/29/D/180/1984; and *Zwaan-de-Vries v The Netherlands*, UN Doc CCPR/C/29/D/182/1984.

APPENDIX

Individual opinion submitted by Urbina and Wennergren pursuant to rule 94(3) of the Committee's provisional rules of procedure

1   Article 26 of the Covenant has been interpreted as providing protection against discrimination whenever laws differentiating among groups or categories of individuals do not correspond to objective criteria. It has also been interpreted in the sense that whenever a difference in treatment does not affect a group of people but only separate individuals, a provision cannot be deemed discriminatory as such; negative effects on one individual cannot then be considered to be discrimination within the scope of article 26.

2   It is self-evident that, as the State party has stressed, in any social security system it is necessary to ensure that individuals do not qualify for more than one benefit simultaneously under different social insurance laws. The State party has admitted that the rule on concurrence which gives precedence to the General Widows and Orphans Act (AWW) is not always advantageous to *all* widows. It might merely benefit a majority of them. Cases are conceivable in which the award of AWW benefits leads to a decrease in income after cessation of payments under the General Disablement Benefits Act (AAW); this is evidently what happened in the case of Mrs Vos. The State party has also mentioned that in most cases AWW benefits exceed AAW benefits payable to married women, and that this is attributable to the fact that most married women have worked only part-time and therefore receive only partial AAW benefit in the event of long-term disability. It follows that disabled women with full AAW benefits enjoy higher benefits than women, disabled or not, who receive full AWW benefits because of their status as widows.

3   In cases where women receive full pensions under the AAW (being disabled and having worked full-time previously), if the husband dies, they will be given the AWW pension instead. This may reduce the level of pension which their physical needs as disabled persons require and which the General Disablement Benefits Act had recognised.

4   Article 32 of AAW provides in its subsection 1(b) that the employment disability benefit will be withdrawn when a woman to whom this benefit has been granted becomes entitled to a widow's pension or a temporary widow's benefit pursuant to the AWW. The State party contends that the legislature had to decide whether claimants who were entitled to benefits under both the AAW and the AWW should receive benefits under the one or the other. This is conceivable, but it is not justifiable that this necessarily should be solved by the introduction of a clause which does not allow for a modicum of flexibility in its implementation. An exception should, in our opinion, be made with regard to women who enjoy full AAW benefits, if such benefits exceed full AWW benefits. By failing to make such an exception the legislature has created a situation in which disabled women with full AAW benefits who become widows can no longer be treated on a par with other disabled women who enjoy full AAW benefits. The case cannot be considered as affecting only Mrs Vos, but rather an indeterminate group of persons who fall in the category of disabled women entitled to full disability pensions. Moreover, the intention of the legislator to grant maximum protection to those in need would be violated every time the law is applied in the strict formal sense as it has been applied in Mrs Vos's case. The increasing number of cases such as this one can be inferred from the assertion made by the State party that it has seen the need to change the legislation since the early 1980s.

5   A differentiation with regard to full AAW benefits among disabled women on the sole ground of marital status as a widow cannot be said to be based on reasonable and objective criteria. It therefore constitutes prohibited discrimination within the meaning of article 26. We note that a review of AWW is under consideration and hope that the discriminatory elements will be eliminated and compensation given to those who have been the victims of unequal treatment.

CASE NO 34

SCHULER-ZGRAGGEN v SWITZERLAND

EUROPEAN COURT OF HUMAN RIGHTS

Application No: 14518/89

Judgment: 24 June 1993

Panel: *Judges*: Bernhardt (*President*), Gölcüklü, Walsh, Russo, Spielmann, Foighel, Loizou, Lopes Rocha and Wildhaber

Human rights — Equality and non-discrimination — Sex discrimination — Whether discrimination to assume that applicant would have stopped working to look after her child regardless of health — European Convention for the Protection of Human Rights and Fundamental Freedoms, arts 6(1) and 14

Human rights — Right to a fair trial — Right to public and oral hearing — Whether lack of public hearing in breach of right to a fair trial — Discrimination in enjoyment of right — Sex-stereotypical assumptions made by tribunal — Right to access file — Whether denial of request to make copies of file, and lack of availability of one medical report, in breach of right to a fair trial — European Convention for the Protection of Human Rights and Fundamental Freedoms, arts 6(1) and 14

BACKGROUND

The applicant, Ms Schuler-Zgraggen, a Swiss national, received a full state invalidity pension as a result of an illness which incapacitated her for work. After the birth of her child and a medical examination by the Invalidity Insurance Board, the applicant's pension was stopped on the basis that she was 60-70 per cent able to look after her home and child, although she was still deemed wholly unfit for clerical work.

The applicant appealed against this decision to the Canton of Uri Appeals Board for Old Age, Survivors' and Invalidity Insurance ("Appeals Board"). She requested access to her file and the right to take copies of documents. The request to make copies of the file was initially refused, but on further appeal allowed, although one medical report was missing from the file. The Appeals Board dismissed her appeal. It assumed that, even if the applicant had not had health problems, after the birth of her child she would not have gone out to work, but rather would have would have been occupied as a housewife and mother.

On 20 August 1987, the applicant lodged an appeal with the Federal Insurance Court. The Court did not examine whether the applicant was fit to work in her previous employment, but determined the case solely on the extent to which (if any) she had been restricted in her activities as a housewife and mother, adopting the same assumptions as the Appeals Board. On 21 June 1988, the Court held that since the applicant was 33.33% incapacitated in this regard, she was eligible for a half-pension if she was in financial difficulties, and referred the case to the Compensation Office to determine this point. The Compensation Office subsequently decided that she could not claim a half-pension since she was not in financial difficulties.

The applicant lodged a complaint with the European Commission on Human Rights on 29 December 1988 that she had been denied the right to a fair trial in civil proceedings within the meaning of article 6(1) of the European Convention on Human Rights in that she had had insufficient access to her file held by the Appeals Board and there had been no hearing in the Federal Insurance Court. She also claimed that the assumption made by that court that she would have given up working even if she had not had health problems amounted to discrimination on the ground of sex within the meaning of article 14 taken together with article 6(1) of the Convention. The Commission rejected both claims and referred the case to the European Court of Human Rights.[*]

HELD (finding a violation of article 14 taken together with article 6(1))

Article 6(1) (right to fair and public hearing in determination of civil rights)

1   The general rule was that article 6(1) did apply in the field of social insurance, including welfare assistance. There was no convincing reason to distinguish between Ms Schuler-Zgraggen's right to an invalidity pension and the rights to social insurance benefits allowed in the earlier cases of *Feldbrugge v Netherlands* and *Deumeland v Germany*. (Para 46)

2   The proceedings before the Appeals Board did not enable the applicant to have a complete, detailed picture of the particulars supplied to the Board. However, the Federal Insurance Court remedied this shortcoming by requesting the Board to make all the documents available to the applicant – who was able to make copies – and then forwarding the file to the applicant's lawyer. Since, taken as a whole, the impugned proceedings were fair, there had not been a breach of article 6(1). (Para 52)

3   The public character of court hearings constituted a fundamental principle enshrined in article 6(1). However, neither the letter nor the spirit of this provision prevented a person from waiving of his own free will, either expressly or tacitly, the entitlement to have his case heard in public, provided such waiver was made in an unequivocal manner and did not run counter to any important public interest. In the present case, the Federal Insurance Court's Rules of Procedure provided in express terms for the possibility of a hearing on application by one of the parties. The applicant had not applied for such a hearing. It might reasonably be considered, therefore, that she had unequivocally waived her right to a public hearing in the Federal Insurance Court. There had been no breach of article 6(1) in respect of the oral and public nature of the proceedings. (Para 58)

Article 14 taken with Article 6(1) (discrimination in court's proceedings)

4   Whilst the admissibility of evidence was governed primarily by domestic law, and it was normally for the national courts to assess the evidence before them, it was the Court's task to ascertain whether the proceedings as a whole, including the way

---

[*]   *Eds:* between the report of the European Commission of Human Rights and the judgment of the European Court of Human Rights, in a decision of 22 August 1992, "the Federal Insurance Court changed its case-law so as to avoid discrimination in relation to the taking of evidence … Under Articles 139a and 141, para 1(c), of the Federal Act on the Organisation of the Judiciary, as amended on 15 February 1992, the applicant requested a revision of the Federal Insurance Court's judgment [in her case]. In a judgment of 24 March 1994, the [Federal Insurance] Court quashed the former decision [in Schuler-Zgraggen's case] and awarded the applicant an invalidity pension with retroactive effect (Resolution DH (95) 95 of 7 June 1995)": http://www.echr.coe.int/Eng/EDocs/EffectsOfJudgments.html.

evidence was submitted, were fair. The Federal Insurance Court had adopted in its entirety the Appeal Board's assumption that women give up work when they gave birth to a child, without attempting to probe the validity of that assumption itself by weighing arguments to the contrary. The assumption constituted the sole basis for the Court's reasoning, and introduced a difference of treatment based on the ground of sex only. The advancement of the equality of the sexes was today a major goal in the Member States of the Council of Europe and very weighty reasons would have to be put forward before such a difference of treatment could be regarded as compatible with the Convention. The Court discerned no such reason in this case. For want of any reasonable and objective justification, there had been a breach of article 14 taken together with article 6(1). (Paras 66 and 67)

Treaties and other international instruments referred to

European Convention for the Protection of Human Rights and Fundamental Freedoms 1950, arts 6(1), 14 and 50

National legislation referred to

Switzerland

Federal Old Age and Survivors' Insurance Act of 20 December 1949, ss 1, 3, 15–16, 49–73 and 85(2)

Federal Invalidity Insurance Act of 19 June 1959, ss 2, 3, 28 and 53–67

Federal Insurance Court's Rules of Procedure, rule 14(2)

Federal Constitution, art 4

Cases referred to

Abdulaziz, Cabales and Balkandali v The United Kingdom, ECHR, judgment of 28 May 1985, Series A, No 94; 7 EHRR 471; 81 ILR 139; below p 618

Boddaert v Belgium, ECHR, judgment of 12 October 1992, Series A, No 235-D; 16 EHRR 242

Deumeland v Germany, ECHR, judgment of 29 May 1986, Series A, No 100; 8 EHRR 448

Edwards v The United Kingdom, ECHR, judgment of 16 December 1992, Series A, No 247-B; 15 EHRR 417

Feldbrugge v The Netherlands, ECHR, judgment of 29 May 1986, Series A, No 99; 8 EHRR 425

Håkansson and Sturesson v Sweden, ECHR, judgment of 21 February 1990, Series A, No 171-A; 13 EHRR 1

Le Compte, Van Leuven and De Meyere v Belgium, ECHR, judgment of 23 June 1981, Series A, No 43; 4 EHRR 1; [1982] ECC 240; 62 ILR 318

Lüdi v Switzerland, ECHR, judgment of 15 June 1992, Series A, No 238; 15 EHRR 173

Olsson v Sweden (No 2), ECHR, judgment of 27 November 1992, Series A, No 250; 17 EHRR 134

Pine Valley Developments Ltd v Ireland, ECHR, judgment of 29 November 1991, Series A, No 222; 14 EHRR 319

Salesi v Italy, ECHR, judgment of 26 February 1993, Series A, No 257-E; 26 EHRR 187

Swiss Federal Court judgment of 31 March 1982, Judgments of the Swiss Federal Court ATF, vol 108, part Ia, 5–9

Swiss Federal Court judgment of 4 September 1986, Judgments of the Swiss Federal Court ATF, vol 112, part Ia, 377–381

JUDGMENT

PROCEDURE

[...]*

AS TO THE FACTS

The circumstances of the case

7   Mrs Margrit Schuler-Zgraggen, a Swiss national born in 1948, was married in 1972. She lives at Schattdorf in the Canton of Uri.

A   Granting of an invalidity pension

8   In 1973 she began to work for the industrial firm of D at Altdorf (Canton of Uri). Her employer regularly deducted contributions to the federal invalidity-insurance scheme from her wages (see para 33 below).

9   In the spring of 1975 she contracted open pulmonary tuberculosis.

On 29 April 1976 she applied for a pension on the grounds of incapacity for work due to her illness.

The Compensation Office (*Ausgleichskasse*) of the Swiss Machine and Metal Industry (*Schweizerische Maschinen- und Metallindustrie*) decided on 24 September 1976 to grant her half an invalidity pension for the period from 1 April to 31 October 1976.

10   On 28 September 1978 the D company dismissed the applicant with effect from 1 January 1979 on account of her illness.

11   After Mrs Schuler-Zgraggen had made a further application for a pension, the Compensation Office determined on 25 March 1980 that she was physically and mentally unfit for work and decided to pay her a full pension with effect from 1 May 1978.

In 1981 and 1982 the invalidity-insurance authorities reviewed her case and confirmed the award of a pension.

12   On 4 May 1984 the applicant gave birth to a son.

---

*   *Eds:* paras 1–8, which relate to procedural matters, have not been included.

B The proceedings before the Invalidity Insurance Board of the Canton of Uri

1 The medical examinations

13 In 1985, the Invalidity Insurance Board (*IV-Kommission*) of the Canton of Uri asked Mrs Schuler-Zgraggen to undergo an examination at the invalidity-insurance authorities' medical centre (*Medizinische Abklarungsstelle der Invalidenversicherung*) in Lucerne.

14 The medical centre asked Drs F and B for two reports (*Konsilien*) on the applicant's health – one on the state of her lungs and the other a psychiatric report – and these were sent in on 10 and 24 December 1985 respectively. The centre prepared a summary on 14 January 1986, to which it attached Dr B's report; it concluded that the applicant was wholly unfit for clerical work and assessed her fitness for household work at 60-70%.

2 The decision of 21 March 1986

15 On 21 March 1986, the Invalidity Insurance Board cancelled, with effect from 1 May 1986, Mrs Schuler-Zgraggen's pension, then amounting to 2,016 Swiss francs (CHF) a month, as her family circumstances had radically changed with the birth of her child, her health had improved, and she was 60-70% able to look after her home and her child.

C The proceedings before the Canton of Uri Appeals Board for Old Age, Survivors' and Invalidity Insurance

1 The appeal and the applications for access to and handing over of documents

16 On 21 April 1986 Mrs Schuler-Zgraggen lodged an appeal (*Beschwerde*) with the Canton of Uri Appeals Board for Old Age, Survivors' and Invalidity Insurance (*Rekurskommission für die Alters-, Hinterlassenen- und Invalidenversicherung* – "the Appeals Board"). She claimed a full invalidity pension or, failing that, a half-pension, arguing, in particular, that the Federal Invalidity Insurance Act conferred on her the right to a pension so long as she was at least 66.66% incapacitated. So as to continue receiving her pension, she also asked the Board to order that her appeal should have suspensive effect.

17 The Board dismissed the latter application on 7 May.

18 On 22 May Mrs Schuler-Zgraggen dispensed with the services of her counsel.

19 On 26 May she went to the Invalidity Insurance Board's headquarters to inspect her medical file, which had been sent there by the Appeals Board, but she was not allowed to see it. On the same day she wrote to the Invalidity Insurance Board to complain about this and to demand to be able to see the file or at least a photocopy of certain important documents.

In a letter of 28 July 1986 to the same board she again sought permission to inspect the file, in particular "all the medical reports, records of examinations and results of laboratory tests from 1975 to 1986," and the handing over of vital documents.

2 The decision of 8 May 1987

20 The Appeals Board dismissed the appeal on 8 May 1987.

In the first place, the right to inspect the file did not imply a right to take documents away or to have photocopies made of them. It sufficed that the appellant had had an opportunity to study her file at the Appeals Board registry; she had not availed herself of that opportunity, despite numerous invitations to do so.

In the second place, it could not be discounted that even if the appellant had been fit, she would have been content with looking after her home once her child had been born. At all events, having regard in particular to the examinations carried out by the medical centre, the invalidity in question was not enough, in the case of a mother and housewife, to make her eligible for a pension. Mrs Schuler-Zgraggen was in a position to be more active if she really wished to work despite her new family circumstances. The refusal to pay a pension could help her recover from her neurotic obsession with being unable to work.

3   The subsequent proceedings

21 On 11 August 1987 Mrs Schuler-Zgraggen wrote to the Appeals Board. She said she needed all the documents and expert reports in order to assess the prospects of succeeding in her legal action. She referred to a perfusion scintigram, a lung-function test, blood-gas analyses and a plethysmogram.

22 In a letter of 13 August the Appeals Board replied as follows:

> ... [T]hese documents provided the basis for the various medical reports. They are in our file only because of the right of inspection granted to you. We are therefore unable to make further documents available to you.

D   The proceedings in the Federal Insurance Court

1   The administrative law appeal

23 On 20 August 1987, Mrs Schuler-Zgraggen lodged an administrative law appeal with the Federal Insurance Court against the decision of the Appeals Board. She applied for a full pension or, in the alternative, an order remitting the case to the authority of first instance. She also sought leave to inspect the whole of her file (*vollumfängliches Akteneinsichtsrecht*).

24 The Federal Insurance Court received observations from the Compensation Office's invalidity insurance department on 20 October 1987 and from the Federal Social Insurance Office on 9 November. The Compensation Office submitted that the invalidity pension should cease; the Federal Social Insurance Office argued that the appeal should be dismissed, relying on a report by its own medical service, which referred in particular to the examination carried out by the medical centre.

25 In a letter of 23 November 1987 the Federal Court informed the applicant that her complete file had been sent to the Appeals Board, which "within the next fourteen days [would] make all the documents available [to her] for inspection". She would then have a further 10 days in which to supplement her administrative law appeal submissions.

26 On 30 November 1987, Mrs Schuler-Zgraggen inspected her file and photocopied a number of documents. On 1 December the file was returned to the Federal Insurance Court.

27 Mr Schleifer, a lawyer, wrote to the Federal Court on 7 December to inform it that he would henceforth be representing the applicant and to ask for the case file to be forwarded to him; this was done on 11 December.

28 On 11 January 1988, Mrs Schuler-Zgraggen filed supplementary pleadings in support of her appeal. They included a complaint that the medical centre took it for granted in its expert opinion that her lungs functioned normally, relying on the report of Dr F, which was not in the file however. She also criticised the arbitrariness of the

Appeals Board's opinion that even if she had been fit, she would have devoted herself to household tasks because of the birth of her child.

2   The judgment of 21 June 1988

29 The Federal Insurance Court gave judgment on 21 June 1988, holding that since 1 May, Mrs Schuler-Zgraggen had been 33.33% incapacitated and was therefore eligible for a half-pension if she was in financial difficulties, and that as there was no evidence before it on this point, the case should be remitted to the Compensation Office.

In such a case, the court's function was not limited to reviewing compliance with federal law and ascertaining that judicial discretion had not been exceeded or misused; it could also review the appropriateness of the impugned decision, and was bound neither by the facts found by the court below nor by the parties' claims.

The applicant had succeeded in her complaint that the Appeals Board had failed to produce all the documents for inspection; she had been able to argue her case in the Federal Court, whose file she had had an opportunity to examine and which had considered the facts and the law with complete freedom.

As to the pension claim, the court said:

> Regard must ... be had to the fact that many married women go out to work until their first child is born, but give up their jobs for as long as the children need full-time care and upbringing. This assumption based on experience of everyday life – experience which must be duly taken into account in determining the method to be applied for assessing incapacity ... – must be the starting-point in the present case. At the time the contested decision was taken, on 21 March 1986 ... the child, who was born on 4 May 1984, was just under two years old, and accordingly, on the balance of probabilities (*nach dem Beweisgrad der überwiegenden Wahrscheinlichkeit*) ..., it must be assumed that the applicant, even if her health had not been impaired, would have been occupied only as a housewife and mother.

In the court's view, this made it unnecessary to examine whether Mrs Schuler-Zgraggen was fit to work in her previous employment; the question was rather one of determining to what extent, if at all, she had been restricted in her activities as a mother and housewife. Here it was sufficient to rely on the expert opinion produced by the medical centre. The fact that the lung specialist's report was missing from her file was a defect (*ein gewisser Mangel*), but the examination carried out by the specialist in internal medicine made it possible to answer the question whether after 1980 there had been any change in the state of the applicant's lungs. After that date the applicant had no longer been treated for tuberculosis and in that respect was perfectly fit to work. As to her neurosis, it had much diminished in the meantime; and a handicap resulting from her back problems could in theory be assessed at 25% at most.

30 On 17 July 1989, the Compensation Office decided that Mrs Schuler-Zgraggen could not claim a half-pension since her income in 1986, 1987 and 1988 had greatly exceeded the maxima applicable in those years to "cases of hardship" (see para 35 below).

The applicant did not appeal.

II   Relevant domestic law and practice

A   Invalidity insurance

31 Invalidity insurance is governed by two federal statutes – the Old Age and Survivors' Insurance Act of 20 December 1949 ("OASIA") and the Invalidity Insurance Act of 19 June 1959 ("IIA").

1   The insured

32 Invalidity insurance is compulsory for all persons resident in Switzerland (OASIA, section 1). Certain other people may contribute on a voluntary basis, notably Swiss nationals living abroad (IIA, section 2).

2   Administration

33 Invalidity insurance is managed by cantonal and occupational associations under the supervision of the Confederation (OASIA, sections 49–73 and IIA, sections 53–67).

3   Financing

34 At the present time invalidity insurance is financed partly from employers' and insured persons' contributions and partly from contributions by the State, in roughly equal proportions.

There is no ceiling on contributions. Those paid by the insured are automatically deducted from earnings. Children, wives and widows of insured persons are exempted if not working, whereas others not gainfully employed pay from CHF43 to 1,200 a year (IIA, section 3 and OASIA, section 3).

4   The pensions

35 Section 28 IIA deals with the assessment of incapacity.

Provision is made in subsection 1 for pensions to be graduated in proportion to the degree of incapacity: a full pension is granted where incapacity is at least 66.66% and a half-pension where it is less than 50%. At the material time, 33.33% incapacity entitled a person to a half-pension only "in cases of hardship"; today incapacity must be at least 40% for a person to be eligible for a quarter-pension.

Subsection 2 provides:

> For the assessment of incapacity, the income which the insured person could earn after becoming incapacitated and after taking any appropriate rehabilitation measures from work that could reasonably be expected of him in a stable labour market is compared with the income he could have earned if he had not been incapacitated.

The amount of the pension is based on the insured's annual average income, which is calculated by dividing the total income taken as a basis for assessing contributions by the number of contribution years (IIA, sections 36 *et seq*, taken together with OASIA, sections 29 *et seq*). For full ordinary pensions the maximum amount is double the minimum amount.

Contributions are enforceable and the right to claim them is subject to a limitation period of five years (OASIA, sections 15 and 16).

B   Appeal procedure

1   Access to the file

36 The Federal Court has derived from Article 4 of the Federal Constitution, which enshrines the principle of equality, an individual's right to inspect his case file lodged with a judicial body.

The right in question means being given an opportunity to have access to the official documents and to take notes but not to take the file away or to demand that copies should be made and handed over (judgment of 31 March 1982, Judgments of the Swiss Federal Court ATF, vol 108, part Ia, pp 5–9).

On this last point the Federal Court has, however, accepted that individuals may ask for copies, provided that this does not entail an excessive amount of work or substantial expense for the authority concerned (judgment of 4 September 1986, Judgments of the Swiss Federal Court ATF, vol 112, part Ia, pp 377–381).

2   Hearings

(a)   Before appellate bodies

37   Section 85(2)(e) of OASIA, first sentence, provides: "If the circumstances so warrant, the parties shall be summoned to a hearing."

(b)   In the Federal Insurance Court

38   Under Rule 14(2) of the Federal Insurance Court's Rules of Procedure,

> The parties shall not have a right to demand a hearing in appeal proceedings. By agreement with the division, the presiding judge may order a hearing to be held, on an application by one of the parties or of his own motion. The parties may inspect the file before the hearing ...

PROCEEDINGS BEFORE THE COMMISSION

39   Mrs Schuler-Zgraggen applied to the Commission on 29 December 1988. She complained, first, that her right to a fair trial (Article 6(1) of the Convention) had been infringed in that she had had insufficient access to the file of the Appeals Board and there had been no hearing in the Federal Insurance Court. She also claimed that the assumption made by that court, that she would have given up working even if she had not had health problems, amounted to discrimination on the ground of sex (Article 14 taken together with Article 6(1).)

40   The Commission declared the application (No 14518/89) admissible on 30 May 1991. In its report of 7 April 1992 (made under Article 31), the Commission expressed the opinion that:

(a)   there had been no breach of Article 6(1) either on account of the failure to hold a hearing (by 10 votes to five) or in respect of access to the file (by 13 votes to two); and

(b)   there had been no breach of Article 14 taken together with Article 6(1) (by nine votes to six).

FINAL SUBMISSIONS TO THE COURT

41   In their memorial to the Government requested the Court to:

> hold that in the present case (in so far as Article 6(1) of the Convention is applicable and the applicant, with reference to a specific complaint, is a victim and, with reference to another complaint, has exhausted domestic remedies) there has not been a violation of Article 6(1) of the Convention or of any other of its provisions.

42   Counsel for the applicant asked the Court to:

(a)   continue along the path it took in the *Feldbrugge* and *Deumeland* cases and to rule that the rights claimed by the applicant in the present case likewise are mainly civil ones falling within the ambit of Article 6(1) of the Convention;

(b)   hold that there has been a breach of Article 6(1) with respect to the right to an adversarial hearing; and

(c) hold that there has been a breach by the Federal Insurance Court of Article 14 taken together with Article 6(1) of the Convention.

AS TO THE LAW

I   Alleged violation of Article 6(1)

43 Mrs Schuler-Zgraggen claimed to be the victim of breaches of Article 6(1), which provides:

> In the determination of his civil rights and obligations ..., everyone is entitled to a fair and public hearing ... by [a] ... tribunal ...

A   *Applicability of Article 6(1)*

44 It was common ground between the applicant and the Commission that this provision applied in the instant case.

45 The Government maintained the contrary as, in its submission, the case had public law features which clearly predominated. First, the claimed right did not derive from a contract of employment, since affiliation was compulsory for the self-employed and the unemployed too. Secondly, award of the pension depended exclusively on the degree of incapacity, no account being taken either of the insured's income or wealth or of the payment of contributions. Thirdly, the Swiss system was strikingly distinctive, in particular in that the financing of it was based on the principles of pay as you go, solidarity and partly drawing on tax revenues.

46 The Court is here once again confronted with the issue of the applicability of Article 6(1) to social security disputes. The question arose earlier in the cases of *Feldbrugge v Netherlands* and *Deumeland v Germany*, in which it gave judgment on 29 May 1986 (Series A, Nos 99 and 100). At that time the Court notes that there was great diversity in the legislation and practice of the member States of the Council of Europe as regards the nature of the entitlement to insurance benefits under social security schemes. Nevertheless, the development in the law that was initiated by those judgments and the principle of equality of treatment warrant taking the view that today the general rule is that Article 6(1) does apply in the field of social insurance, including even welfare assistance (see the *Salesi v Italy* judgment of 26 February 1993, Series A, No 257-E, para 19).

As in the two cases decided in 1986, the State intervention is not sufficient to establish that Article 6(1) is inapplicable; other considerations argue in favour of the applicability of Article 6(1) in the instant case. The most important of these lies in the fact that despite the public law features pointed out by the Government, the applicant was not only affected in her relations with the administrative authorities as such but also suffered an interference with her means of subsistence; she was claiming an individual economic right flowing from specific rules laid down in a federal statute (see para 35 above).

In sum, the Court sees no convincing reason to distinguish between Mrs Schuler-Zgraggen's right to an invalidity pension and the rights to social insurance benefits asserted by Mrs Feldbrugge and Mr Deumeland.

Article 6(1) therefore applies in the instant case.

B   Compliance with Article 6(1)

1   Access to the Appeals Board's file

47 Mrs Schuler-Zgraggen complained in the first place of insufficient access to the Appeals Board's file.

(a)   The Government's preliminary objection

48 As it had done before the Commission, the Government raised an objection of inadmissibility based on lack of victim status, arguing that the applicant had not availed herself of the opportunity of examining the file at the Appeals Board registry.

49 The Court notes that the applicant's complaint relates not so much to inspecting the file as to having the documents in it handed over or, at any rate, securing photocopies of them. The objection must therefore be dismissed.

(b)   Merits of the complaint

50 In Mrs Schuler-Zgraggen's submission, the facts of her case – as often in the social security field – were complex, and this made it necessary for her to submit documents to specialists. She should therefore have been granted the same facilities as the administrative departments, on whose premises the file was permanently held. Furthermore, she had never had access to Dr F's report on her lungs, so that she had been unable to submit it to her own expert.

51 The Government disputed this submission. In the proceedings before the Appeals Board the applicant had not availed herself of the opportunity to inspect part of the file and take notes. In the Federal Insurance Court she had had access to all the documents – as had her lawyer, who had received them not long afterwards – and had photocopied some of them. As to Dr F's report, it was not strictly speaking part of the file, as the Federal Insurance Court moreover noted in its judgment of 21 June 1988; in addition, it was summarised in the medical centre's report of 14 January 1986, which the applicant had seen. In short, the principle of equality of arms had not been contravened in any way.

52 The Court finds that the proceedings before the Appeals Board did not enable Mrs Schuler-Zgraggen to have a complete, detailed picture of the particulars supplied to the Board. It considers, however, that the Federal Insurance Court remedied this shortcoming by requesting the Board to make all the documents available to the applicant – who was able, among other things, to make copies – and then forwarding the file to the applicant's lawyer (see, as the most recent authority, *mutatis mutandis*, the *Edwards v The United Kingdom* judgment of 16 December 1992, Series A, No 247-B, paras 34–39). It also notes that neither the Appeals Board nor the Federal Insurance Court had Dr F's report before it.

Since, taken as a whole, the impugned proceedings were therefore fair, there has not been a breach of Article 6(1) in this respect.

2   Federal Insurance Court hearing

53 Mrs Schuler-Zgraggen also complained that there had been no hearing before the Federal Insurance Court.

(a)   The Government's preliminary objection

54 In the Government's submission, the applicant had not exhausted domestic remedies, as she had failed to apply to the Federal Insurance Court for the proceedings

to be oral and public. Admittedly, that court rarely held hearings, but it did not follow that such an application would have been bound to fail.

55 In respect of this preliminary objection there is an estoppel, as the Government only raised it before the Commission after the decision on admissibility, whereas nothing prevented them from doing so earlier (see, as the most recent authority, *mutatis mutandis*, the *Pine Valley Developments Ltd v Ireland* judgment of 29 November 1991, Series A, No 222, para 45).

(b) Merits of the complaint

56 Mrs Schuler-Zgraggen submitted that the Federal Insurance Court should have ordered a hearing so as to form its own opinion of her and ensure that she had a fair trial.

57 The Government considered, on the contrary, that in certain fields purely written court proceedings did not in any way prejudice the interests of the litigant. They emphasised a number of aspects. First, the traditional characteristics of social security disputes made oral presentation of arguments in which technical points and numerous figures were adduced difficult. Secondly, in the cases brought before it, the Federal Insurance Court was free to review the facts and the law, and this made it more akin to an ordinary court of appeal. This was particularly so in administrative law appeals, as here the Federal Court could rule on the appropriateness of the impugned decision and was not bound either by the cantonal authority's findings of fact or by the submissions of the parties. Thirdly, the number of judgments – approximately 1,200 a year – would drop dramatically if public, oral proceedings were to be the rule; in such an event, the lengthening of the proceedings would seriously jeopardise access to the supreme court.

58 The Court reiterates that the public character of court hearings constitutes a fundamental principle enshrined in Article 6(1). Admittedly, neither the letter nor the spirit of this provision prevents a person from waiving of his own free will, either expressly or tacitly, the entitlement to have his case heard in public, but any such waiver must be made in an unequivocal manner and must not run counter to any important public interest (see, among other authorities, the *Håkansson And Sturesson v Sweden* judgment of 21 February 1990, Series A, No 171-A, para 66).

In the instant case the Federal Insurance Court's Rules of Procedure provided in express terms for the possibility of a hearing "on an application by one of the parties or of the [presiding judge's] own motion" (Rule 14(2) – see para 38 above.) As the proceedings in that court generally take place without a public hearing, Mrs Schuler-Zgraggen could be expected to apply for one if she attached importance to it. She did not do so, however. It may reasonably be considered, therefore, that she unequivocally waived her right to a public hearing in the Federal Insurance Court.

Above all, it does not appear that the dispute raised issues of public importance such as to make a hearing necessary. Since it was highly technical, it was better dealt with in writing than in oral argument; furthermore, its private, medical nature would no doubt have deterred the applicant from seeking to have the public present.

Lastly, it is understandable that in this sphere the national authorities should have regard to the demands of efficiency and economy. Systematically holding hearings could be an obstacle to "the particular diligence required in social security cases," (see *Deumeland v Germany*, cited above, para 90) and could ultimately prevent compliance with the "reasonable time" requirement of Article 6(1) (see, *mutatis mutandis*, *Boddaert v Belgium* judgment of 12 October 1992, Series A, No 235-D, para 39).

There has accordingly been no breach of Article 6(1) in respect of the oral and public nature of the proceedings.

3 Independence of the medical experts

59 At the hearing before the Court, counsel for Mrs Schuler-Zgraggen called in question the independence of doctors bound by a long-term contract to a social security institution, on the ground that they received from that institution the greater part of their income.

60 This was a new complaint; it had not been raised before the Commission and does not relate to the facts the Commission found within the limits of its decision on admissibility. That being so, the Court has no jurisdiction to consider it (see, as the most recent authority and *mutatis mutandis, Olsson v Sweden* (No 2), judgment of 27 November 1992, Series A, No 250, para 75.)

II Alleged violation of Article 14 taken together with Article 6(1)

61 Mrs Schuler-Zgraggen said, lastly, that in the exercise of her right to a fair trial she had suffered discrimination on the ground of sex. She relied on Article 14, which provides:

> The enjoyment of the rights and freedoms set forth in [the] Convention shall be secured without discrimination on any ground such as sex, race, colour, language, religion, political or other opinion, national or social origin, association with a national minority, property, birth or other status.

A The Government's preliminary objection

62 As it had done before the Commission, the Government raised an objection of inadmissibility based on failure to exhaust domestic remedies. The applicant, it submitted, had done no more than characterise the wording used by the Appeals Board as "arbitrary" and had therefore not made to the Federal Insurance Court a precise complaint relating to discrimination in the exercise of a right secured by the Convention.

63 The Court adopts the Commission's reasoning. First, Mrs Schuler-Zgraggen objected to the terms of the Federal Insurance Court's judgment of 21 June 1988, against which no appeal lay. Secondly, in her administrative law appeal she had already criticised the (similar) assumption made by the Appeals Board in its decision of 8 May 1987. The objection is therefore unfounded.

B Merits of the complaint

64 According to the applicant, the Federal Insurance Court based its judgment on an "assumption based on experience of everyday life", namely that many married women give up their jobs when their first child is born and resume it only later. It inferred from this that Mrs Schuler-Zgraggen would have given up work even if she had not had health problems. The applicant considered that if she had been a man, the Federal Insurance Court would never have made such an assumption, which was contradicted by numerous scientific studies.

65 The Government argued that Article 6(1) and thus, indirectly, Article 14 were not applicable, as the complaint was concerned with the taking of evidence, a sphere which essentially came within the State authorities' competence.

66 The Court reiterates that the admissibility of evidence is governed primarily by the rules of domestic law, and that it is normally for the national courts to assess the evidence before them. The Court's task under the Convention is to ascertain whether the proceedings, considered as a whole, including the way in which the evidence was submitted, were fair (see, as the most recent authority and *mutatis mutandis*, the *Lüdi v Switzerland* judgment of 15 June 1992, Series A, No 238, para 43; and the *Edwards v The United Kingdom* judgment previously cited, para 34).

67 In this instance, the Federal Insurance Court adopted in its entirety the Appeals Board's assumption that women gave up work when they gave birth to a child. It did not attempt to probe the validity of that assumption itself by weighing arguments to the contrary.

As worded in the Federal Court's judgment, the assumption cannot be regarded – as asserted by the Government – as an incidental remark, clumsily drafted but of negligible effect. On the contrary, it constitutes the sole basis for the reasoning, thus being decisive, and introduces a difference of treatment based on the ground of sex only.

The advancement of the equality of the sexes is today a major goal in the member-States of the Council of Europe and very weighty reasons would have to be put forward before such a difference of treatment could be regarded as compatible with the Convention (see, *mutatis mutandis*, the *Abdulaziz, Cabales And Balkandali v The United Kingdom* judgment of 28 May 1985, Series A, No 94, para 78). The Court discerns no such reason in the instant case. It therefore concludes that for want of any reasonable and objective justification, there has been a breach of Article 14 taken together with Article 6(1).

III   Application of Article 50

68 Under Article 50,

> If the Court finds that a decision or a measure taken by a legal authority or any other authority of a High Contracting Party is completely or partially in conflict with the obligations arising from the ... Convention, and if the internal law of the said Party allows only partial reparation to be made for the consequences of this decision or measure, the decision of the Court shall, if necessary, afford just satisfaction to the injured party.

A   *Damage*

1   Non-pecuniary damage

69 Mrs Schuler-Zgraggen claimed that she had sustained non-pecuniary damage, which she did not quantify, and sought payment of a provisional sum of CHF22,500 for the length of the proceedings before the Convention institutions.

70 The Government submitted that the publication of a judgment in which a violation was found would satisfy the requirements of Article 50. The Delegate of the Commission did not express any view.

71 The Court considers that the applicant may have suffered non-pecuniary damage but that this judgment provides her with sufficient satisfaction for it.

2   Pecuniary damage

72 Mrs Schuler-Zgraggen also complained that she had lost the benefit of a full invalidity pension on account of proceedings incompatible with Articles 6(1) and 14. She did not, however, claim any specific sum.

73 The Government pointed out that since 15 February 1992, Swiss law had enabled a victim of a violation found by the Court, or by the Committee of Ministers of the Council of Europe, to apply for a reopening of the impugned proceedings. They therefore considered that the question was not ready for decision.

74 This is also the view of the Court. The question must accordingly be reserved and the further procedure must be fixed, due regard being had to the possibility of an agreement between the respondent State and the applicant (Rule 54(1) and (4) of the Rules of the Court).

B Costs and expenses

75 Mrs Schuler-Zgraggen sought CHF 7,130.90 in respect of costs and expenses for the proceedings before the national judicial bodies. (Mr Derrer: CHF 300; Mr Stockli: CHF 2,694.20; Mr Wehrli: CHF 2,936.70; own expenses: CHF 1,200.) She also claimed CHF 14,285.70 for the proceedings before the Convention institutions, not including the expenses incurred by attending two hearings before the European Court, the one on 26 January 1993 and the one for delivery of the judgment.

The Government found the claim excessive. The applicant had not incurred any legal costs before the cantonal authorities or the Federal Insurance Court, and before the Invalidity Insurance Board – at which stage she was assisted by three lawyers – she had not raised any complaint based on the Convention. A lump sum of CHF 5,000 would amply cover all the costs and expenses incurred in Switzerland and at Strasbourg.

The Delegate of the Commission considered that the expenses incurred in the proceedings before the Appeals Board were not concerned with remedying a breach of the Convention and he invited the Court to apply its case law on expenses incurred in the proceedings before the Strasbourg institutions.

76 Making its assessment on an equitable basis as required by Article 50 and having regard to the criteria which it applies in this field, the Court awards the applicant CHF 7,500 under this head as matters stand.

For these reasons, **THE COURT:**

1   *Holds* unanimously that Article 6(1) applied in the case;

2   *Dismisses* unanimously the Government's preliminary objections;

3   *Holds* unanimously that it has no jurisdiction to entertain the complaint concerning the independence of the medical experts;

4   *Holds* by eight votes to one that there has been no breach of Article 6(1);

5   *Holds* by eight votes to one that there has been a breach of Article 14 taken together with Article 6(1);

6   *Holds* unanimously that this judgment in itself constitutes sufficient just satisfaction as to the alleged non-pecuniary damage;

7   *Holds* as matters stand, by eight votes to one, that the Confederation is to pay the applicant, within three months, 7,500 (seven thousand five hundred) Swiss francs in respect of costs and expenses;

8   *Holds* by eight votes to one that the question of the application of Article 50 is not ready for decision as regards pecuniary damage; accordingly,

(a) reserves the said question in that respect;

(b) invites the Government and the applicant to submit, within the forthcoming six months, their written observations on the matter and, in particular, to notify the Court of any agreement they may reach;

(c) reserves the further procedure and delegates to the President of the Chamber the power to fix the same if need be.

DISSENTING OPINION OF JUDGE GÖLCÜKLÜ CONCERNING ARTICLE 14 TAKEN TOGETHER WITH ARTICLE 6(1)

(Translation)

To my great regret, I cannot share the majority's opinion as to the application of Article 14 taken together with Article 6(1) of the Convention. On this particular point the applicant criticised the Federal Insurance Court's ruling on the decisive issue, namely for having reached the conclusion – based, according to the reasons it gave, on experience of life – that during the period in question (after the birth of her child) her activities would very probably have been limited to the role of mother in the matrimonial home if her health had been good.

This complaint of discrimination against her on the ground of sex, directed at a point of fact, is an issue of substance, whereas Article 6(1) establishing the principle of a fair trial, being procedural in nature, relates only to formal issues.

In sum, what the applicant was challenging in the instant case was the reasons put forward by the Federal Insurance Court when it ruled on her appeal and not the fact of having suffered discrimination in the course of the proceedings in the national courts on account of belonging to the female sex; nor was any principle or standard of a fair trial infringed in regard to her.

I therefore conclude that there has been no breach of Article 14 taken together with Article 6(1) on the ground of sex discrimination against the applicant.

PARTLY DISSENTING OPINION OF JUDGE WALSH

1 In my opinion there has been a breach of Article 6(1) of the Convention, concerning access to the Appeals Board's file. That must necessarily include documents which should have been in it – namely, the pulmological report, which in fact was not in the file. That document was within the procurement of the Appeals Board and its non-availability to the applicant put her at a disadvantage.

2 I am also of the opinion that there was a breach of Article 6(1) by reason of the absence of an oral hearing in accordance with that Article. The Rules of Procedure of the Federal Insurance Court provide for an oral hearing either on the application of the party or on the motion of the presiding judge. The Convention requires such a hearing unless the parties agree to waive it. The position is similar with regard to the public nature of the hearing: see *Le Compte, Van Leuven and De Meyere v Belgium*, judgment of 23 June 1981, Series A, No 43). No such agreement was secured from the applicant. Indeed, it is not established that she was ever made aware of the possibility. I do not agree with the view of the majority of the Court (at paragraph 58 of the judgment) that because the applicant did not request an oral and public hearing she had "unequivocally waived her right ...". Article 6 throws no burden on an applicant to request a public hearing. Her

civil rights were in issue. I cannot agree with the inference contained in the third sub-paragraph of paragraph 58 of the Court's judgment. The fact that a matter that is highly technical, even if this was so, which is questionable, may induce the parties to agree to avoid the type of hearing envisaged by Article 6(1) is not a ground for denying such a hearing, particularly when the applicant had not so agreed.

Furthermore, the fact that the dispute does not appear to raise "issues of public importance" is not a condition precedent to the operation of Article 6(1). The dispute was undeniably important to the applicant and she is the party whose protection was envisaged by that provision of the Convention. The private citizen is thus enabled to pierce the bureaucratic veil or curtain. The fact that her private right was created by public law made the application of Article 6(1) all the more important. That such application may be thought to be inconvenient for the "demands of efficiency" by the bureaucracy can scarcely be regarded as a justification for ignoring the requirements of the Article.

3   I agree with the Court's findings in respect of Article 6 taken with Article 14.

CASE NO 35

EPHRAHIM v PASTORY AND KAIZILEGE

HIGH COURT OF TANZANIA

Judgment: 22 February 1990

Panel: Mwalusanya J

Human rights — Equality and non-discrimination — Sex discrimination — Rights of women to inherit and sell land — Customary law — Whether denying women the right to sell clan land under Tanzanian Haya customary law contrary to Tanzania's Bill of Rights and international obligations — Rules of Inheritance GN No 436/1963 of the Declaration of Customary Law, s 20 — Rules Governing the Inheritance of Holdings by Female Heirs (1994) made by the Bukoba Native Authority — Constitution of Tanzania, Bill of Rights, art 13(4) — Universal Declaration of Human Rights, art 7, incorporated into Constitution by virtue of art 9(1)(f) — Convention on the Elimination of All Forms of Discrimination against Women — African Charter on Human and Peoples' Rights, art 18(3) — International Covenant on Civil and Political Rights, art 26

Constitutional law — Bill of Rights — Interpretation of existing law — Obligation of courts to construe existing law, including customary law, with such modifications and qualifications as necessary to bring into conformity with the Bill of Rights — Rules of Inheritance GN No 436/1963 of the Declaration of Customary Law, s 20 — Rules Governing the Inheritance of Holdings by Female Heirs (1994) made by the Bukoba Native Authority — Constitution of Tanzania, Bill of Rights, art 13(4) — Constitution (Consequential, Transitional and Temporary Provisions) Act (No 16 of 1984), s 5(1)

BACKGROUND

The first respondent, Ms Holario d/o Pastory, inherited clan land from her father by a valid will. On 24 August 1988 she sold the land to Gervaz s/o Kaizilege, a man who was not a member of her clan. The next day the appellant, Bernard s/o Ephrahim, a nephew of the first respondent, Ms Pastory, filed a suit in the Kashasha Primary Court seeking a declaration that the sale of the clan land by Ms Pastory to Mr Kaizilege was void under Haya customary law, as stated in section 20 of the Rules of Inheritance GN No 436/1963 of the Declaration of Customary Law ("1963 Rules of Inheritance"). Under Haya customary law a woman has no power to sell clan land. In general a woman can inherit clan land only in usufruct, that is to say she cannot inherit full ownership of clan land, but only the right to use it during her lifetime according to the Rules Governing the Inheritance of Holdings by Female Heirs (1994) made by the Bukoba Native Authority ("Bukoba Inheritance Rules"). Only if there is no male clan member can she inherit full ownership rights. The Primary Court held that the sale was void and ordered Ms Pastory to refund the purchase price to Mr Kaizilege. The District Court overturned this decision on appeal, holding that the Bill of Rights 1987, which prohibits discrimination on the grounds of sex, grants equal rights to female and male clan members. The nephew, Mr Ephrahim, appealed to the High Court.

HELD (dismissing the appeal)

1   The Constitution of Tanzania, which incorporates the Tanzanian Bill of Rights and the Universal Declaration on Human Rights, prohibits discrimination on the ground of sex. Tanzania had also ratified the Convention on the Elimination of All Forms of Discrimination against Women, the African Charter on Human and Peoples' Rights and the International Covenant on Civil and Political Rights, all of which prohibit discrimination on the ground of sex. Haya customary law relating to women's property rights to clan land clearly discriminated against women on the ground of sex. This flew in the face of the Bill of Rights as well as the international conventions to which Tanzania was signatory (p 543).

2   Section 5(1) of the Constitution (Consequential, Transitional and Temporary Provisions) Act 1984, provides that with effect from March 1988, the courts will construe the existing law, including customary law "with such modifications, adoptions, qualifications and exceptions as may be necessary to bring it into conformity with the [Bill of Rights]". In enacting this provision, there could be no doubt that Parliament wanted to do away with all oppressive and unjust laws of the past. It wanted the courts to modify by construction those existing laws which were inconsistent with the Bill of Rights such that they were in line with the new era. This included the discriminatory customary laws under discussion (pp 545, 546).

3   Section 20 of the 1963 Rules of Inheritance barring women from selling clan land was inconsistent with article 13(4) of the Bill of Rights of the Constitution which bars discrimination on account of sex. In accordance with section 5(1) of the Constitution (Consequential, Transitional and Temporary Provisions) Act 1984, this provision was now taken to be modified and qualified such that males and females would have equal rights to inherit and sell clan land. Likewise the rules under the Bukoba Inheritance Rules entitling a woman to only usufructuary rights with no power to sell inherited clan land were equally void and of no effect (p 549).

Treaties and other international instruments referred to

African Charter on Human and Peoples' Rights 1980, art 18(3)

Convention on the Elimination of All Forms of Discrimination against Women 1979

International Covenant on Civil and Political Rights 1966, art 26

Universal Declaration of Human Rights 1948, art 7

National legislation referred to

Tanzania

Bill of Rights, incorporated into Constitution by Fifth Constitutional Amendment Act (No 15 of 1984), art 13(4)

Constitution 1977, arts 9(1)(f), 13(4), 30(3) and (4)

Constitution (Consequential, Transitional & Temporary Provisions) Act (No 16 of 1984), s 5(1)

Declaration of Customary Law Rules of Inheritance (GN No 436/1963), para 20

Law Reform (Fatal Accidents & Miscellaneous Provisions) Ordinance (Cap 360) (as amended by Act No 55 of 1968), s 18(1)

Rules (made by Bukoba Native Authority) Governing the Inheritance of Holdings by Female Heirs (1944), rr 4–8

Jamaica

Constitution

Sri Lanka

Constitution 1972, art 18(3)

Trinidad and Tobago

Constitution 1976, art 6(1)

Rent Restriction (Dwelling Houses) Act 1981

Zimbabwe

Constitution, art 13

Criminal Procedure and Evidence Act (Cap 59)

Zimbabwe Constitution (Transitional, Supplementary and Consequential Provisions) Order 1980, s 4(1)

Cases referred to

Abdul-Rahman Bin Mohamed v R [1963] EA 188

Alai v Uganda [1967] EA 596

A-G v Morgan [1985] LRC (Const) 770, T&T CA, affd [1988] LRC (Const) 468; [1988] 1 WLR 297, PC

Bi Hawa Mohamed v All Sefu (unreported), Tan CA (Civ App No 9 of 1983)

Bi Verdiana Kyabujo v Kyabuje [1968] HCD n 499

Buchanan (James) & Co Ltd v Babco Forwarding & Shipping (UK) Ltd [1977] 1 All ER 518; [1977] QB 208; [1977] 2 WLR 107, CA

Bull v Minister of Home Affairs [1987] LRC (Const) 547, Zim HC

Clarke v Karika [1985] LRC (Const) 732, Cook Is CA

De Freitas v Benny [1976] AC 239; [1975] 3 WLR 388, PC

Deocres Lutabana v Deus Kashaga (unreported) Tan CA (Civ App No 1 of 1981)

DPP v Nasralla [1967] 2 All ER 161; [1967] 2 AC 238; [1967] 3 WLR 13, PC

General Marketing Co Ltd v Shariff [1980] TLR 612

Gunaratne v People's Bank [1987] LRC (Const) 383, Sri Lan SC

Haji Athumani Isaa v Rwentama Mututa (unreported), Tanzania CA (Civ App No 9 of 1988)

Hdeamtzo v Malasi [1968] HCD n 127

Heydon's Case (1584) 3 Co Rep 7a

Kammins Ballrooms Co Ltd v Zenith Investments (Torquay) Ltd [1970] 2 All ER 871; [1971] AC 850; [1970] 3 WLR 287, HL

Kariapper v Wijesinha [1967] 3 All ER 485; [1968] AC 716; [1967] 3 WLR 1460, PC

Maharaj v A-G of Trinidad and Tobago (No 2) [1978] 2 All ER 670; [1979] AC 385; [1978] 2 WLR 902, PC

Noordally v A-G [1987] LRC (Const) 599, Maur SC

Nothman v Barnet London Borough Council [1978] 1 All ER 1243; [1978] 1 WLR 220, CA

Nyali Ltd v A-G [1955] 1 All ER 646; [1955] 1 QB 1; [1955] 2 WLR 649, CA

R v Amkeyo (1917) 7 EALR 14

Riley v A-G of Jamaica [1982] 3 All ER 469; [1983] 1 AC 719; [1982] 3 WLR 557, PC

Rukuba Nteme v Bi Jalia Hassani and Geryaz Baruti (unreported) Tan CA (Civ App No 19 of 1986)

Seaford Court Estate Ltd v Asher [1949] 2 All ER 155; [1949] 2 KB 481, CA

Vallet v Ramgoolam (1973) MR 29

JUDGMENT

MWALUSANYA J: This appeal is about women's rights under our Bill of Rights. Women's liberation is high on the agenda in this appeal. Women do not want to be discriminated on account of their sex. What happened is that a woman, one Holaria Pastory, who is the first respondent in this appeal, inherited some clan land from her father by a valid will. Finding that she was getting old and senile and no one to take care of her, she sold the clan land on 24 August 1988 to the second respondent, Gervaz Kaizilege, for Shs 300,000. This second respondent is a stranger and not a clan member. Then on 25 August 1988 the present appellant, Bernardo Ephrahim, filed a suit at Kashasha Primary Court in Muleba District, Kagera Region, praying for a declaration that the sale of the clan land by his aunt, the first respondent, to the second respondent was void as females under Haya customary law have no power to sell clan land. The primary court agreed with the appellant and the sale was declared void and the first respondent was ordered to refund the Shs 300,000 to the purchaser.

Indeed the Haya customary law is clear on the point. It is contained in the Laws of Inheritance of the Declaration of Customary Law (GN No 436 of 1963), which in para 20 provides:

> Women can inherit, except for clan land, which they may receive in usufruct but may not sell. However, if there is not male of that clan, women may inherit such land in full ownership.

In short that means that females can inherit clan land which they can use it in usufruct ie for their life time. But they have no power to sell it, otherwise the sale is null and void. As for male members of the clan the position is different. Cory and Hartnoll in their book on *Customary Law of the Haya Tribe*, tell us in paras 561 and 562 that a male member of the clan can sell clan land but, if he sells it without consent of the clan members, other clan members can *redeem* that clan land. The land returns to the clan and becomes the property of the man who repays the purchase price. It will be seen that the law discriminates against women and Hamlyn J was heard to say in the case of *Bi Verdiana Kyabuje v Gregory Kyabuje* (1968) HCD n 499 that:

> Now however much this court may sympathize with these very natural sentiments, it is in cases of this nature bound by the customary law applicable to these matters. It has frequently been said that it is not for courts to overrule customary law. Any variations in such law as take place must be variations initiated by the altering customs of the community where they originate. Thus, if a customary law draws a distinction in a matter of this nature between males and females, it does not fall to this court to decide that such law is inappropriate to modern development and conditions. That must be done elsewhere than in the courts of law.

The Tanzania Court of Appeal some 13 years later nodded in agreement with the above observations in the case of *Deocres Lutabana v Deus Kashaga* (unreported, Civ App No 1 of 1981) *per* Mwakasendo JA. The rule that females in the Bahaya community do not have the right to sell clan land was affirmed by the Tanzania Court of Appeal in *Rukuba Nteme v Bi Jalia Hassani and Geryaz Baruti* (unreported Civ App No 19 of 1986) *per* Nyalali CJ and later in *Haji Athumani Isaa v Rwentama Mututa* (unreported Civ App No 9 of 1988) *per* Kisanga JA. It appeared then that the fate of women as far as sale of clan land was concerned was sealed. The position was as an English novelist Sir Thomas Browne (1605–1682) had pointed out in his book *Religio Medici* where he said:

> The whole world was made for man; but the twelfth part of man for woman: man is the whole world, and the breath of God; woman the rib and crooked piece of man. I could be content that we might procreate like trees, without conjunction or that there were any way to perpetuate the world without the trivial and vulgar way of union.

However, the Senior District Magistrate of Muleba, Mr L S Ngonyani, did not think the courts were helpless or impotent to help women. He took a different stand in favour of women. He said in his judgment:

> What I can say here is that the respondent's claim is to bar female clan members from clan holdings in respect of inheritance and sale. That female clan members are only to benefit or enjoy the fruits from the clan holdings only. I may say that this was the old proposition. With the Bill of Rights of 1987 (sic) female clan members have same rights as male clan members.

And so he held that the first respondent had the right under the Constitution to sell clan land and that the appellant was at liberty to redeem that clan land on payment of the purchase price of Shs 300,000. That has spurred the appellant to appeal to this court, arguing that the decision of the district court was contrary to the law.

Is the doctrine that women should not be discriminated against because of their sex part of our law?

Since this country adopted the doctrine of "Ujamaa and Self-Reliance", discrimination against women was rejected as a crime. In his booklet *Socialism and Rural Development*, Mwalimu J K Nyerere states:

> Although every individual was joined to his fellow by human respect, there was in most parts of Tanzania an acceptance of one human inequality. Although we try to hide the fact and despite the exaggeration which our critics have frequently indulged in, it is true that the women in traditional society were regarded as having a place in the community which was not only different, but was also to some extent inferior ... This is certainly inconsistent

with our socialist conception of the equality of all human beings and the right of all to live in such security and freedom as is consistent with equal security and freedom from all other. If we want our country to make full and quick progress now, it is essential that our women live in terms of full equality with their fellow citizens who are men.

And as long ago as in 1968, Saidi J (as he then was) pointed out the inherent wrong in this discriminatory customary law. It was in the case of *Ndewawiosia Heamtzo v Imanuel Malasi* [1968] HCD n 127. He said:

Now it is abundantly clear that this custom, which bars daughters from inheriting clan land and sometimes their own father's estate, has left a loophole for undeserving clansmen to flourish within the tribe. Lazy clan members anxiously await the death of their prosperous clansman who happens to have no male issue and as soon as death occurs they immediately grab the estate and mercilessly mess up things in the dead man's household, putting the widow and daughters into terrible confusion, fear, and misery ... It is quite clear that this traditional custom has outlived its usefulness. The age of discrimination based on sex is long gone and the world is now in the stage of full equality of all human beings irrespective of their sex, creed, race or colour.

But the customary law in question has not been changed up to this day. The women are still suffering at the hands of selfish clan members.

What is more is that since the Bill of Rights was incorporated in our 1977 Constitution (*vide* Act No 15 of 1984) by art 13(4), discrimination against women has been prohibited. But some people say that that is a dead letter. And the Universal Declaration of Human Rights (1948), which is part of our Constitution by virtue of art 9(1)(f), prohibits discrimination based on sex as *per* art 7. Moreover, Tanzania has ratified the Convention on the Elimination of All Forms of Discrimination against Women. That is not all. Tanzania has also ratified the African Charter on Human and Peoples' Rights which in art 18(3) prohibits discrimination on account of sex. And finally, Tanzania has ratified the International Covenant on Civil and Political Rights which in art 26 prohibits discrimination based on sex. The principles enunciated in the above-named documents are a standard below which any civilised nation will be ashamed to fall. It is clear from what I have discussed that the customary law under discussion flies in the face of our Bill of Rights as well as the international conventions to which we are signatories.

Petitions under art 30(3) of the Constitution to invalidate discriminatory laws

Courts are not impotent to invalidate laws which are discriminatory and unconstitutional. The Tanzania Court of Appeal both in the cases of *Rukuba Nteme* and *Haji Athumani Issa* agreed that the discriminatory laws can be declared void for being unconstitutional by filing a petition in the High Court under art 30(3) of the Constitution.

In the case of *Haji Athumani Issa*, Kisanga JA pointed out that the constitutionality of a statute or any law could not be challenged in a course of an appeal by an appellate court. He said that the proper procedure was for the aggrieved party to file a petition in the High Court under art 30(3) of our Constitution. Equally here, as there is no petition under art 30(3) of the Constitution, and so the question of deciding any constitutionality of a statute or any law does not arise. When the issue of a basic right under the Constitution is raised or becomes apparent only after the commencement of proceedings in a subordinate court, it seems that the proper thing to do is for the subordinate court concerned to adjourn the proceedings and advise the party concerned to file petition in the High Court under art 30(3) of the Constitution for the vindication of his or her right.

One more observation before I leave this topic. In the *Haji Athumani Issa Kisanga* JA seems to suggest that "rules of the court" must first be enacted under art 30(4) of the Constitution before a citizen can file a petition under art 30(3) of the Constitution. However, that was just an *obiter dictum* as the decision of the case did not turn on that point. I wish to make certain observations on the point. It will be recalled that art 30(4) states that the authority "may" make rules of the court and does not say it *must* make them. That appears to envisage a situation whereby petitions may be filed without rules of the court made for the purpose. That is not a new phenomenon. Under s 18(1) of the Law Reform (Fatal Accidents and Misc Provisions) Ordinance (Cap 360) (as amended by Act No 55 of 1968) it is provided that:

> The Chief Justice *may* make rules of the court prescribing the procedure and the fees payable or documents filed or issued in cases where an order of mandamus, prohibition or certiorari is sought.

It is now 22 years since that provision was made and yet the successive Chief Justices have yet to make rules of the court for the purpose. But that has not prevented nor deterred litigants from filing the necessary applications under that law. By parity of reasoning, when art 30(4) of the court states that the authority may make rules of the court for filing petitions in the absence of those rules of the courts it does not mean the courts are impotent to act. The High Court will invoke its inherent powers and use the available rules of the court. After all, the rules of procedure are the handmaidens of justice and should not be used to defeat substantive justice – see Biron J in *General Marketing Co Ltd v Shariff* [1980] TLR 612 at 65. Therefore, failure to invoke the correct rules of the court cannot defeat the course of justice, particularly when human rights are at stake. In other words, wrong rules of the court may only render the proceedings a nullity when they result in a miscarriage of justice. That was a conclusion reached by the Supreme Court of Mauritius in *Noordally v Attorney General* [1987] LRC (Const) 599, which was a petition under the Constitution. What happened is that the applicant did not apply in person as required by the Constitution, and the proper respondent was not cited and the application was not made according to the correct procedure as prescribed. Delivering the judgment of the court Moollan CJ held that, notwithstanding all those procedural irregularities, the court would disregard the errors since the case raised matters of great public interest and no useful purpose would be served by insistence on form other than to delay a decision on the merits. The court cited the decision of their earlier case in *Vallet v Ramgoolam* (1973) MR 29 at 33–35 where they had said:

> It is the court's *duty* to determine the validity of any statute which is alleged to be unconstitutional, because no law that contravenes the Constitution can be suffered to survive, and the authority to determine whether the legislature has acted within the powers conferred upon it by the Constitution is vested in the court. The court's primary concern, therefore, in any case where a contravention of the constitution is invoked, is to ensure that it be redressed as conveniently and speedily as possible …

That approach was also made by the Privy Council in the case of *Kariapper v Wijesinha* [1967] 3 All ER 485. It is a commendable approach which I hope will be adopted by the High Court of Tanzania as well as the Tanzania Court of Appeal. The primary concern of the court should not be as to whether the correct rules of the court have been invoked but rather to redress the wrong as speedily as possible.

If the Tanzania Court of Appeal is to regard the decision in *Haji Athumani Issa* as the last word on the matter then it is only hoped that their conscience will be tempered by what the former Chief Justice of Botswana Aguda CJ had said in the article "The Role of the Judge with Special Reference to Civil Liberties" in (1974) *EALJ*, vol X No 2 at 158:

> If the Constitution entrenches fundamental rights, these must be regarded as the basic norm of the whole legal system. Therefore all laws and statutes which are applicable to the State ... must be subjected, as the occasion arises, to rigorous tests and meticulous scrutiny to make sure that they are in consonance with the declared basic norm of the Constitution ... It is clear from this that there is no room here, for a rigid application of the common law doctrine of *stare decisis*. It is submitted therefore that a court can refuse to follow the judgment of a higher court which was given before the enactment of a Constitution if such a judgment is in conflict with a provision of the Constitution. Also the final court of the land must regard itself absolutely bound only by the Constitution and not by any previous decision of the same court.

If *Haji Athumani Issa* is to be regarded as binding authority and not just *obiter dicta* then the hopes of the masses of Tanzania that they would be saved by the Bill of Rights have been dashed. This is because the rules of the court may not be enacted for years on end.

The reception clause of s 5(1) of Act No 16 of 1984

It has been provided by s 5(1) of the Constitution (Consequential, Transitional and Temporary Provisions) Act (No 16 of 1984) that with effect from March 1988 *the courts* will construe the existing law, including customary law:

> with such modifications, adaptations, qualifications and exceptions as may be necessary to bring it into conformity with the provisions of the [Fifth Constitutional Amendment Act (No 15 of 1984) ie Bill of Rights].

All courts in Tanzania have been enjoined to interpret that section in the course of their duties. And I think it is the section which the Senior District Magistrate of Muleba had invoked in hearing this appeal. In the book *Law and its Administration in a One-Party State* by R W James and F M Kassam (East African Literature Bureau, 1973), the former Chief Justice of Tanzania, Mr T Georges, says at 49:

> Apart from judicial review, the courts can usually be depended upon to be astute in finding interpretations for enactments which will promote rather than destroy the rights of the individual and this is quite apart from declaring them bad or good.

The shape in which a statute is imposed on the community as a guide for conduct is that statute as interpreted by the courts. The courts put life into the dead words of the statute. By statutory interpretation courts make judge-made law affecting the fundamental rights of a citizen.

Professor B A Rwezaura of the Faculty of Law of University of Dar es Salaam, in his article the "Reflections on the Relationship between State Law and Customary Law in Contemporary Tanzania: Need for Legislative Action?" in *Tanz Law Reform Bull* vol 2 no 1 (July 1988), holds the view that courts in Tanzania can modify discriminatory customary law in the course of statutory interpretation. He says at 19:

> It is also anticipated by s 5(1) of the Constitution (Consequential, Transitional and Temporary Provisions) Act (No 16 of 1984) with effect from March 1988 that courts will construe existing law, including customary law, "with such modifications, adaptations, qualifications and exceptions as may be necessary to bring it into conformity with the provisions of the Constitution".

Now how should s 5(1) of Act 16 of 1984 be interpreted by the courts? That is the big question.

Lord Denning MR in the case of *Seaford Court Estate Ltd v Asher* [1949] 2 KB 481 tells us what a judge should do whenever a statute comes up for construction. He says at 499:

He must set to work on the constructive task of finding the intention of Parliament, and he must do this not only from the language of the statute, but also from a consideration of the social conditions which gave rise to it, and of the *mischief* which it was passed to remedy and then he must supplement the written word so as to give "force and life" to the intention of the legislature. That was clearly laid down by the resolution of the judges in *Heydon's case* (1584) 3 Co Rep 7a, and it is the safest guide today. Good practical advice on the subject was given about the same time by Plowden ... (Emphasis added).

In two more cases Lord Denning MR had to repeat his warnings as regards the use for the courts to invoke a *purposive approach of interpretation* which is sometimes referred to as the *schematic and teleological method of interpretation*. The two cases are *James Buchanan & Co v Babco Forward Shipping (UK) Ltd* [1977] QB 208 and *Nothman v Barnet Council* [1978] 1 WLR 220. In the latter case he emphasised that the days of strict literal and grammatical construction of the words of a statute were gone. He continued at 228:

The literal method is now completely out of date. It has been replaced by the approach which Lord Diplock described as the "purposive approach" [in *Kammins Ballrooms Co Ltd v Zenith Investments (Torquay) Ltd* [1971] AC 850, 881]. In all cases now in the interpretation of statutes we adopt such a construction as will "promote the general legislative purpose" underlying the provision.

The Tanzania Court of Appeal has adopted the above *purposive approach* as shown in the case of *Bi Hawa Mohamed v Ali Sefu* (unreported, Civ App No 9 of 1983) *per* Nyalali CJ. There the High Court took a narrow view of a statutory provision with the result that the meaning attributed to the relevant part of the statute excluded the wife's domestic services in computing her contribution in building her husband's house. By applying the purposive approach the Court of Appeal of Tanzania arrived at a different conclusion. And *ex cathedra* in a paper delivered to the First Commonwealth Africa Judicial Conference in The Gambia on 6 May 1986 entitled "The Challenges of Development to Law in Developing Countries Viewed from the Perspective of Human Rights", Nyalali CJ cited with approval the purposive approach of interpretation enunciated by Lord Denning MR in *Buchanan & Co v Babco Ltd* and stated at p 19:

By failing to give due weight to the reasons and objectives of a statute, this methodology (the literal construction), commonly used in common law countries, misdirects the courts into a position where they end up applying the intention of the parliamentary legal draftsman instead of the presumed intention of Parliament concerned.

Now what was the intention of the Parliament of Tanzania in passing s 5(1) of Act 16 of 1984, and what was the mischief that it intended to remedy?

There can be no doubt that Parliament wanted to do away with all oppressive and unjust laws of the past. It wanted all existing laws (as they existed in 1984) which were inconsistent with the Bill of Rights to be inapplicable in the new era or be treated as modified so that they are in line with the Bill of Rights. It wanted the courts to modify by construction those existing laws which were inconsistent with the Bill of Rights such that they were in line with the new era. We had a new *grundnorm* since 1984, and so Parliament wanted the country to start with a clean slate. That is clear from the express words of s 5(1) of Act 16 of 1984. The mischief it intended to remedy is all the unjust existing laws, such as the discriminatory customary law now under discussion. I think the message the Parliament wanted to impart to the courts under s 5(1) is loud and clear and needs no interpolations.

If Parliament meant otherwise it could have said so in clear words. Many countries in the Commonwealth which had to incorporate Bill of Rights in their constitutions have expressly indicated what they wanted to be the position of the existing law after the introduction of the Bill of Rights in their constitutions. For example in Sri Lanka, art 18(3) of their 1972 Constitution clearly states that: "all existing law shall operate notwithstanding any inconsistency with the provisions of the Bill of Rights": see the case of *Gunaratne v People's Bank* [1987] LRC (Const) 383 at 398. In Trinidad and Tobago their 1976 Constitution in art 6(1) clearly states: "nothing in the Bill of Rights shall invalidate the existing law" – and so in *A-G v Morgan* [1985] LRC (Const) 770 at 783-784 Kelsick CJ held that the Rent Restriction (Dwelling House) Act 1981 was protected from challenge by the above section. Other cases from Trinidad and Tobago on the same point are *De Freitas v Benny* [1976] AC 239 (PC) and *Maharaj v A-G* [1979] AC 385 (PC). The Constitution of Jamaica states: "nothing contained in any law in force immediately before the commencement of the Constitution shall be held inconsistent with the human rights provisions in the said Constitution". And so the then existing law even if it was oppressive was saved as indicated in the two cases from Jamaica, *DPP v Nasralla* [1967] 2 AC 238 (PC) and *Riley v A-G of Jamaica* [1982] 3 All ER 469. And from the Cook Islands in *Clarke v Karika* [1985] LRC (Const) 732, Speight CJ of the Court of Appeal held that the human rights provisions in their Constitution only declared rights already afforded by the existing statutory and common law, and so all the existing law had been saved intact.

But we in Tanzania did not want to adopt the above provisions which "saved" the existing law operating prior to the introduction of the Bill of Rights. We wanted to start with a clean slate, a new *grundnorm*. That was nice for the people. The people of Zimbabwe did the same when their Constitution came into effect on 18 April 1980. And they had a similar provision like our s 5(1) of Act 16 of 1984 and theirs is s 4(1) of the Zimbabwe Constitution (Transitional, Supplementary and Consequential Provision) Order 1980 and provides:

> That existing laws must be so construed with such modifications, adaptations, qualifications and exceptions as may be necessary to bring them into conformity with the Constitution.

In Zimbabwe in 1987 a certain provision in the Criminal Procedure and Evidence Act (Cap 59) restricting the right to bail came into question as to whether it should not be *construed as modified* for being inconsistent with the right to liberty in the Bill of Rights. The case is *Bull v Minister of Home Affairs* [1987] LRC (Const) 547. In the High Court Sansole J agreed with the applicant that if indeed that provision in the Criminal Procedure Act restricting bail was inconsistent with the right to liberty prescribed in the Bill of Rights then it would be taken to be *modified* such that it did not exist but was void. But the judge found as a fact that the section in question was not inconsistent with any provision in the Bill of Rights as art 13 of the Constitution allowed pre-trial detention without bail subject to the limitation that the period of detention was reasonable. And so the question of construing the section in the Criminal Procedure Act as modified did not arise. The Supreme Court of Zimbabwe (as *per* Beck JA) agreed with that reasoning at pp 555–6.

The above case from Zimbabwe is persuasive authority for the proposition of law that any existing law that is inconsistent with the Bill of Rights should be regarded as modified such that the offending part of that statute or law is void.

Parallel with the reception clause of the common law

The reception clause of s 5(1) of Act 16 of 1984 has its parallel in the reception clause of the English common law introduced by the Tanganyika Order in Council of 1920. Both clauses give the mandate to the courts to construe the received law with some modifications and qualifications. The reception clause of the English common law said:

"the received law was subject to the qualification that it be applied so far as the circumstances of the territory and its inhabitants permit and subject to such qualifications as local circumstances may render necessary". Mfalila J very correctly lamented in his paper "The Challenges of Dispensing Justice in Africa According to Common Law" of the second Commonwealth Africa Judicial Conference in Arusha, Tanzania, 8–12 August 1988, where he said at p 10:

> If these colonial judges had wished they could have developed over the years a version of the common law relevant to Africa as the reception statutes themselves stated. They could have done this by construing the reception statutes strictly, for instance in East Africa where only "the substance" of the common law and equity was received, the colonial judges had even greater scope of creativity. They could have proceeded to create a body of laws responsive to the emergent demands of each territory. As one writer put it, "the colonial judges never approached the problem as one calling essentially for the exercise of a policy-making legislative power". This was a pity because in West Africa they had the power to determine whether the limits of the local jurisdiction and local circumstances permitted the application of the received rules and to what extent. In East Africa they had the further power to decide whether a specific rule of English law was part of the "substance" of the common law and in all the territories they had the power to determine whether the statutes were of general application.

It is for this reason that the colonial judges in criminal trials held that, a customary law spouse was not regarded as a wife or husband for the purposes of the rules of evidence and as a result she or he could be compelled to testify against her or his spouse whereas the common law counterpart could not be so compelled. That was so in *R v Amkeyo* (1917) 7 EALR 14 (*per* Hamilton CJ) and *Abdul-Rahman Bin Mohamed v R* [1963] EA 188 by Sir Ronald Sinclair P at 192–193.

But even under the reception clause of the English common law there were judges who liberally construed the provision under discussion. For example Sir Udo Udoma then Chief Justice of Uganda, in *Alai v Uganda* [1967] EA 596 interpreted the phrase "any married woman" from the reception clause to include a wife of common law marriage as well as a wife of a customary law marriage, contrary to the stand of the previous judges discussed above. But the hero of the construction of the reception clause of the English common law is Lord Denning MR who in *Nyali Ltd v A-G of Kenya* [1955] 1 All ER 649 said at 653:

> This wise provision should, I think be liberally construed. It is a recognition that the common law cannot be applied in a foreign land without considerable qualification ... It has many principles of manifest justice and good sense which can be applied with advantages to peoples of every race and colour all the world over, but it also has many refinements, subtleties and technicalities which are not suited to other folk. These offshoots must be cut away. In these far off lands the people must have a law which they understand and which they will respect. The common law cannot fulfil this role except with considerable qualifications. The task of making these qualifications is entrusted to the judges of these lands. It is a great task. I trust that they will not fail therein.

The issue in the above case was that by the English common law applicable to Kenya, the Kenya Government should be exempt from payment of a bridge toll at Mombasa. Lord Denning MR rejected that argument, holding that the common law rule that the Crown had a prerogative not to pay tax was not applicable to Kenya as local circumstances did not permit.

I am inclined to think that if Lord Denning MR was confronted with the present problem now at hand he would have unhesitatingly said:

This wide provision should, I think, be liberally construed. It is a recognition that the law existing before the introduction of the Bill of Rights cannot be applied in the new era without considerable qualification. It has many principles of manifest justice and good sense which can be applied with advantages to the people of Tanzania. But it also has many provisions which are not suited to a country with a Bill of Rights. These offshoots must be cut away. The people must have a law which they understand and which they will respect. The law existing prior to the introduction of the Bill of Rights cannot fulfil this role except with considerable qualifications. The task of making these qualifications is entrusted to the judges of Tanzania. It is a great task. I trust that they will not fail therein.

Therefore Lord Denning MR will wriggle in his Chair (not in the grave for he is still alive) to hear that some judges interpret the reception clause in s 5(1) of Act 16 of 1984 as *not to affect the content and the quality of the law* existing prior to the enactment of the Bill of Rights. But it should be noted that the reception clause in s 5(1) affects only statutes and customary law existing prior to 1984 but does not affect any later law. And the position is understandable because for three years from March 1985 to March 1988 the government was given a period of grace to put its house in order, ie to amend all laws that were inconsistent with the Bill of Rights. And so the statutory interpretation that we have adopted here need not raise any eye-brows.

Women's liberation

I have found as a fact that s 20 of the Rules of Inheritance (GN No 436 of 1963) of the Declaration of Customary Law is discriminatory of females in that unlike their male counterparts they are barred from selling clan land. That is inconsistent with art 13(4) of the Bill of Rights of our Constitution which bars discrimination on account of sex. Therefore under s 5(1) of Act No 16 of 1984 I take s 20 of the Rules of Inheritance to be *now modified and qualified* such that males and females now have equal rights to inherit and sell clan land. Likewise the Rules Governing the Inheritance of Holdings by Female Heirs (1944) made by the Bukoba Native Authority which in rr 4 to 8 entitle a female who inherits self-acquired land of her father to have usufructuary rights only (rights to use for their lifetime only) with no power to sell that land is equally void and of no effect. Females just like males can now and onwards inherit clan land or self-acquired land of their fathers and dispose of the same when and as they like. The disposal of the clan land to strangers without the consent of the clansmen is subject to the fiat that any other clan member can *redeem* that clan land on payment of the purchase price to the purchaser. That now applies to both males and females. Therefore the District Court of Muleba was right to take judicial notice of the provisions of s 5(1) of Act 16 of 1984, and to have acted on them the way it did.

From now on, females all over Tanzania can at least hold their heads high and claim to be equal to men as far as inheritance of clan land and self-acquired land of their father's is concerned. It is part of the long road to women's liberation. But there is no cause for euphoria as there is much more to do in other spheres. One thing which surprises me is that it has taken a simple, old rural woman to champion the cause of women in this field but not the elite women in town who chant jejune slogans years on end on women's lib but without delivering the goods. To the male chauvinists, they should remember what that English writer John Gay (1685–1732) had said in *The Beggar's Opera*:

Fill every glass, for wine inspires us,

And fires us, with courage, love and joy,

Women and wine should life employ.

Is there aught else on earth desirous?

If the heart of a man is depressed with cares,

The mist is dispelled when a woman appears.

It is hoped that, from the time the woman has been elevated to the same plane as the man, at least in respect of inheritance of clan land, then the mist will be dispelled.

Conclusion

At the hearing of this appeal Mr Jacob Iazaro Mbasa, who held the special power of attorney of the appellant, argued that the district court was wrong to hold that the purchase price was Shs 300,000 and not Shs 30,000. However, on perusal of the evidence on record I find that the district court was right. The record of the primary court shows that, besides the vendor and the purchaser, there were two independent witnesses who witnessed the sale and these were Mr Abeli Byalwasha and Mr Elizeus Balongo. Both these witnesses testified that the purchaser paid out Shs 300,000. The evidence of the only other witness who witnessed the sale, that of Mr Francis Joseph, was very suspect. He conceded at the trial that he belonged to the clan of the appellant and that he was not happy with the sale of their clan land by the first respondent. When pressed to state what amount was paid by the purchaser he said it was Shs 30,000. You will note that Francis Joseph as a clan member had an axe to grind as he was not happy with the sale of their clan land. Therefore his evidence concerning the amount of the purchase price paid was suspect and was rightly ignored by the district court. Like the district court I hold that the clan land in question was sold for Shs 300,000.

Like the District Court I hold that the sale was valid. The appellant can redeem that clan land on payment of Shs 300,000. I give the appellant six months from today to redeem the clan land, otherwise if he fails the land becomes the property of the purchaser – the second respondent. The appeal is dismissed with costs.

Order accordingly.

EQUALITY AND NON-DISCRIMINATION IN RELATION TO CITIZENSHIP, NATIONALITY AND IMMIGRATION

CASE NO 36

PROPOSED AMENDMENTS TO THE NATURALIZATION PROVISIONS OF THE CONSTITUTION OF COSTA RICA

INTER-AMERICAN COMMISSION OF HUMAN RIGHTS

Advisory Opinion: 19 January 1984

Panel: Nikken (*President*); Buergenthal (*Vice-President*); Cisneros, Reina, Piza, Nieto Navia (*Judges*); also present: Moyer (*Secretary*), Ventura (*Deputy Secretary*)

Human rights — Nationality — Naturalisation — Whether proposed amendments to the Constitution of Costa Rica regarding naturalisation contrary to the right to nationality — Constitution of Costa Rica, arts 14 and 15 — American Convention on Human Rights, art 20

Human rights — Nationality — Naturalisation — Equality and non-discrimination — Whether proposed amendment to the Constitution granting preferential treatment in the acquisition of Costa Rican nationality through naturalisation to native born Central Americans, Ibero-Americans and Spaniards over non-native born nationals of these countries and other aliens discriminatory — Constitution of Costa Rica, art 14(2) and 14(3) — American Convention on Human Rights, art 24

Human rights — Nationality — Naturalisation — Equality and non-discrimination — Sex discrimination — Whether proposed amendment to the Constitution granting preferential treatment in the acquisition of Costa Rican nationality through naturalisation to foreign wife over foreign husband of Costa Rican national discriminatory — Constitution of Costa Rica, art 14(4) — American Convention on Human Rights, arts 1, 17(4) and 24

International Tribunals — Competence — Inter-American Court of Human Rights — Jurisdiction of Court to give advisory opinion regarding compatibility of national laws with Convention — Whether includes provisions of constitution — Whether includes proposed legislation — Vienna Convention on the Law of Treaties, art 31(1) — American Convention on Human Rights, arts 29 and 64(2)

BACKGROUND

The Government of Costa Rica sought an advisory opinion of the Inter-American Court of Human Rights on its proposed amendments to articles 14 and 15 of the Constitution of Costa Rica. The effect of these amendments would have been to make it more difficult to acquire Costa Rican nationality by introducing longer residency requirements and additional qualifying standards and examinations. In particular, the amendments would have given preferential treatment to Central Americans, Ibero-Americans or Spaniards who acquired their nationality by birth over those who obtained it by naturalisation; to applicants who were Central Americans, Ibero-Americans or Spaniards over other aliens; and to foreign women who married Costa Rican nationals, over foreign men who married Costa Rican nationals. The Government asked the Court to consider whether the proposed amendments were compatible with the American Convention on Human

Rights, in particular, the right to nationality under article 20(1), the right of equality between spouses under article 17(4) and the right to equal protection of the law under article 24.

The Court first had to determine whether its jurisdiction to provide an advisory opinion in relation to the compatibility of "domestic laws" with the Convention under Article 64(2) of the Convention included constitutional provisions and proposed laws (as opposed to laws in force).

HELD (finding a violation of the Convention as regards the different treatment of spouses of Costa Ricans)

Right to nationality

1   Whilst the conferral and regulation of nationality were matters for each state to decide, the powers of states were circumscribed by their obligations to ensure the full protection of human rights. However, the proposed amendments would not violate the right to nationality under article 20 of the Convention since no Costa Ricans would lose their nationality (article 20(1)), nor would the proposed amendments affect the right of anyone born in Costa Rica to nationality of Costa Rica (article 20(2)) or interfere with the rights of Costa Ricans to acquire a new nationality under the new provisions (article 20(3)). (Paras 32 and 42)

Right to equality and non-discrimination

2   It was within the sovereign power of Costa Rica to decide what standards should determine the granting or denial of nationality to aliens which sought it, and to establish certain reasonable differentiations based on factual differences, which viewed objectively, recognised that some applicants might have a closer affinity than others to Costa Rica's value system and interests. It would not appear to be inconsistent with the purpose and grant of nationality to expedite the naturalisation procedures for those who, viewed objectively, shared closer historical, cultural and spiritual bonds with Costa Rica, here Central Americans, Ibero-Americans and Spaniards. Less obvious was the basis for the distinction, made in article 14(2) and 14(3) of the proposed amendment, between those Central Americans, Ibero-Americans and Spaniards who acquired their nationality by birth and those who obtained it by naturalisation. However, it could not be concluded that the proposed amendment was clearly discriminatory in character. (Paras 59, 60 and 61)

3   Draft article 14(4) accorded a foreign woman who marries a Costa Rican special consideration for obtaining Costa Rican nationality (compared to a foreign man). In doing so, it followed the formula adopted in the current Constitution, which gives women but not men who marry Costa Ricans a special status for purposes of naturalisation. This system was based on the principle of family unity, including the assumption that all members of a family should have the same nationality, and notions about paternal authority. In the 1930s, a movement developed opposing these traditional notions, which was reflected in various international instruments, including article 17(4) of the Convention, which guarantees equality of rights of spouses in marriage. The different treatment envisaged for spouses by article 14(4) of the proposed amendment could not be justified and had to be considered discriminatory. It was therefore incompatible with articles 17(4) and 24 of the Convention. (Paras 64 and 66)

Jurisdiction

4   If the Court were to decline to hear a government's request for an advisory opinion because it concerned "proposed laws" and not laws duly promulgated and in force, this might in some cases have the consequence of forcing a government desiring the Court's opinion to violate the Convention by the formal adoption and possibly even application of the legislative measure, which steps would then be deemed to permit the appeal to the Court. Such a requirement would not "give effect" to the objectives of the Convention, for it would not advance the protection of the individual's basic human rights and freedoms. A restrictive reading of article 64(2), which would permit states to request advisory opinions under that provision only in relation to laws already in force, would unduly limit the advisory function of the Court. (Paras 26 and 28)

Treaties and other international instruments referred to

American Convention on Human Rights 1969, arts 1(1), 2, 17(1), 17(2), 17(4), 20, 24, 26, 29 and 64

American Declaration of the Rights and Duties of Man 1948, arts 2 and 19

Charter of the Organization of American States 1948, art 3(j)

Charter of the United Nations 1948, art 1(3)

Montevideo Convention on the Nationality of Women 1933, art 1

Montevideo Convention on Nationality 1933, art 6

Rules of Procedure of the Inter-American Court of Human Rights, art 52

United Nations Convention on the Elimination of All Forms of Discrimination against Women 1979, art 9

United Nations Convention on the Nationality of Married Women 1957, art 3

Universal Declaration of Human Rights 1948, art 15

Vienna Convention on the Law of the Treaties 1969, art 31(1)

National legislation referred to

Costa Rica

Constitution of Costa Rica 1949, arts 14 and 15

Cases referred to

Case "Relating to Certain Aspects of the Laws on the Use of Languages in Education in Belgium" v Belgium (Merits), ECHR, judgment of 23 July 1968, Series A, No 6; 1 EHRR 252; 45 ILR 114

Competence of the General Assembly for the Admission of a State to the United Nations, ICJ, Advisory Opinion of 3 March 1950, ICJ Reports 1950, p 4; 17 ILR 326

The Effect of Reservations on the Entry into Force of the American Convention on Human Rights (Arts 74 and 75), IACHR, Advisory Opinion OC-2/82 of 24 September 1982, Series A, No 2 (1982); 67 ILR 558; 22 ILM 37 (1983)

In the matter of Viviana Gallardo et al, IACHR, Decision No G101/81 of 13 November 1981; 67 ILR 577; 20 ILM 1424 (1981)

Nottebohm Case (Liechtenstein v Guatemala) (second phase), ICJ, judgment of 6 April 1955; ICJ Reports 1955, p 4; 22 ILR 349

"Other treaties" subject to the Advisory Jurisdiction of the Court (Art 64 American Convention on Human Rights), IACHR, Advisory Opinion OC-1/82 of 24 September 1982, Series, A No 1 (1982); 67 ILR 594; 22 ILM 51

Restrictions to the Death Penalty (Arts 4(2) and 4(4) American Convention on Human Rights), IACHR, Advisory Opinion OC-3/83 of 8 September 1983, Series A, No 3 (1983); 70 ILR 449; 23 ILM 320

ADVISORY OPINION

[STATEMENT OF THE ISSUES]*

[...]**

7   The relevant parts of the Government's request for an advisory opinion read as follows:

II Provisions to be analyzed in the determination of compatibility

(a) Domestic legislation:

1) PRESENT TEXT of Articles 14 and 15 of the Constitution of Costa Rica:

Article 14

By Naturalization

The following are Costa Ricans by naturalization:

1   Those who have acquired this status by virtue of former laws;

2   Nationals of the other countries of Central America, who are of good conduct, who have resided at least one year in the republic, and who declare before the civil registrar their intention to be Costa Ricans;

3   Native-born Spaniards and Ibero-Americans who obtain the appropriate certificate from the civil registrar, provided they have been domiciled in the country during the two years prior to application;

4   Central Americans, Spaniards and Ibero-Americans who are not native-born, and other foreigners who have been domiciled in Costa Rica for a minimum period of five years immediately preceding their application for naturalization, in accordance with the requirements of the law;

5   A foreign woman who by marriage to a Costa Rican loses her nationality or who indicates her desire to become a Costa Rican; and

---

*   **Eds:** additional headings (in square brackets) have been included for the convenience of readers.

**   **Eds:** paras 1–6, which relate to procedural issues, have not been included.

6   Anyone who receives honorary nationality from the Legislative Assembly.

Article 15

Requirements for Naturalization; the Concept of Domicile

Anyone who applies for naturalization must give evidence in advance of good conduct, must show that he has a known occupation or means of livelihood, and must promise to reside in the Republic regularly.

For purposes of naturalization, domicile implies residence and stable and effective connection with the national community, in accordance with regulations established by law.

2)   AMENDMENTS PROPOSED by the Special Committee of the Legislative Assembly in its Report of June 22, 1983:

Article 14

The following are Costa Ricans by naturalization:

1   Those who have acquired this status by virtue of previous laws;

2   Native-born nationals of the other countries of Central America, Spaniards and Ibero-Americans with five years official residence in the country and who fulfill the other requirements of the law;

3   Central Americans, Spaniards and Ibero-Americans, who are not native-born, and other foreigners who have held official residence for a minimum period of seven years and who fulfill the other requirements of the law;

4   A foreign woman who, by marriage to a Costa Rican loses her nationality or who after two years of marriage to a Costa Rican and the same period of residence in the country, indicates her desire to take on our nationality; and

5   Anyone who receives honorary nationality from the Legislative Assembly.

Article 15

Anyone who applies for naturalization must give evidence of good conduct, must show that he has a known occupation or means of livelihood, and must know how to speak, write and read the Spanish language. The applicant shall submit to a comprehensive examination on the history of the country and its values and shall, at the same time, promise to reside within the national territory regularly and swear to respect the constitutional order of the Republic.

The requirements and procedures for applications of naturalization shall be established by law.

3)   MOTION OF AMENDMENT to Article 14(4) of the Constitution presented by the Deputies of the Special Committee:

A foreigner, who by marriage to a Costa Rican loses his or her nationality and who after two years of marriage to a Costa Rican and the same period of residence in the country, indicates his or her desire to take on the nationality of the spouse.

(b)   Articles of the Convention

The above-mentioned legal texts should be compared to the following articles of the American Convention on Human Rights in order to determine their compatibility:

Article 17

Rights of the Family

Paragraph 4. The States Parties shall take appropriate steps to ensure the equality of rights and the adequate balancing of responsibilities of the spouses as to marriage, during marriage, and in the event of its dissolution. In case of dissolution, provision shall be made for the necessary protection of any children solely on the basis of their own best interests.

Article 20

Right to Nationality

1   Every person has the right to a nationality.

2   Every person has the right to the nationality of the state in whose territory he was born if he does not have the right to any other nationality.

3   No one shall be arbitrarily deprived of his nationality or of the right to change it.

Article 24

Right to Equal Protection

All persons are equal before the law. Consequently, they are entitled, without discrimination, to equal protection of the law.

III   Specific questions on which the opinion of the Court is sought

In accordance with the request originally made by the Special Committee to study amendments to Articles 14 and 15 of the Constitution, the Government of Costa Rica requests that the Court determine:

(a) Whether the proposed amendments are compatible with the aforementioned provisions of the American Convention on Human Rights.

Specifically, within the context of the preceding question, the following questions should be answered:

(b) Is the right of every person to a nationality, stipulated in Article 20(1) of the Convention, affected in any way by the proposed amendments to Articles 14 and 15 of the Constitution?

(c) Is the proposed amendment to Article 14(4), according to the text proposed in the Report of the Special Committee, compatible with Article 17(4) of the Convention with respect to equality between spouses?

(d) Is the text of the motion of the Deputies found in their opinion to amend this same paragraph compatible with Article 20(1) of the Convention?

[ADMISSIBILITY]

8   This advisory opinion has been requested by the Government pursuant to Article 64(2) of the American Convention on Human Rights (hereinafter "the Convention"). The Court's opinion is sought concerning the compatibility of certain proposed amendments to the Constitution with various provisions of the Convention.

9   Article 64 of the Convention reads as follows:

1   The member states of the Organization may consult the Court regarding the interpretation of this Convention or of other treaties concerning the protection of human rights in the American states. Within their spheres of competence, the organs

listed in Chapter X of the Charter of the Organization of American States, as amended by the Protocol of Buenos Aires, may in a like manner consult the Court.

2   The Court, at the request of a member state of the Organization, may provide that state with opinions regarding the compatibility of any of its domestic laws with the aforesaid international instruments.

10   Costa Rica, being a Member State of the Organization of American States (hereinafter "the OAS"), has standing to request an advisory opinion under Article 64(2) of the Convention.

11   It should be noted that the instant request was initially referred to the Court by a Committee of the Legislative Assembly, which is not one of the governmental entities empowered to speak for Costa Rica on the international plane. Only when the Minister of Foreign Affairs formally filed the request, followed by the communication of the Minister of Justice supplying relevant information bearing on it, did the Court become seized of the matter now before it.

12   The instant request, being the first to be referred to the Court under Article 64(2), raises a number of issues bearing on its admissibility that have not been previously considered by the Court.

13   Since the instant request does not relate as such to laws in force but deals instead with proposed amendments to the Constitution, it should be asked whether the reference in Article 64(2) to "domestic laws" includes constitutional provisions and whether the proposed legislation comes within the scope of the Court's advisory jurisdiction under that article of the Convention.

14   The answer to the first question admits of no doubt: whenever an international agreement speaks of "domestic laws" without in any way qualifying that phrase, either expressly or by virtue of its context, the reference must be deemed to be to all national legislation and legal norms of whatsoever nature, including provisions of the national constitution.

15   The answer to the second question is more difficult. The request does not seek an advisory opinion referring to a domestic law in force; it involves a legislative proposal for a constitutional amendment which has not as yet been adopted by the Legislative Assembly, although it has been admitted for debate by the latter and was approved by the appropriate Committee.

16   It should be borne in mind that under Article 64(1) the Court would have jurisdiction to render an advisory opinion requested by a Member State of the OAS on the question of whether a proposed law is compatible with the Convention. Although it is true that in this context the request would be formulated in a different manner, it could nevertheless involve an issue identical in character to the one that is envisaged under Article 64(2).

17   The only major difference between opinions dealt with under Article 64(1) and those falling under Article 64(2) is one of procedure. Under Article 52 of the Rules of Procedure, advisory opinions filed under Article 64(2) of the Convention are not *ipso facto* subject to the system of notices that applies to Article 64(1) opinions. Instead, in dealing with requests under Article 64(2), the Court enjoys broad discretion to fix, on a case by case basis, the procedures to be followed, it being quite likely that the requested opinion, by its very nature, can properly be resolved without seeking views other than those of the applicant state.

18 Any attempt to interpret Article 64(2) as referring exclusively to laws in force, that is, to laws that have passed through all the required stages resulting in their enactment, would have the effect of preventing states from seeking advisory opinions from the Court relating to draft legislation. This would mean that states would be compelled to complete all steps prescribed by domestic law for the enactment of a law before being able to seek the opinion of the Court regarding the compatibility of that law with the Convention or with other treaties concerning the protection of human rights in the American states.

19 It should also be kept in mind that the advisory jurisdiction of the Court was established by Article 64 to enable it "to perform a service for all of the members of the inter-American system and is designed to assist them in fulfilling their international human rights obligations". [Inter-Am Ct HR *"Other treaties" Subject to the Advisory Jurisdiction of the Court (Art 64 American Convention on Human Rights)*; Advisory Opinion OC-1/82 of 24 September 1982, Series A No 1, para 39.] Moreover, as the Court noted elsewhere, its advisory jurisdiction "is designed to assist states and organs to comply with and to apply human rights treaties without subjecting them to the formalism and the sanctions associated with the contentious judicial process." [Inter-Am Ct HR *Restrictions to the Death Penalty (Arts 4(2) and 4(4) American Convention on Human Rights)*; Advisory Opinion OC-3/83 of 8 September 1983, Series A No 3, para 43.]

20 Article 29 of the Convention contains the following specific rules applicable to questions of interpretation:

Article 29

Restrictions Regarding Interpretation

No provision of this Convention shall be interpreted as:

(a) permitting any State Party, group, or person to suppress the enjoyment or exercise of the rights and freedoms recognized in this Convention or to restrict them to a greater extent than is provided for herein;

(b) restricting the enjoyment or exercise of any right or freedom recognized by virtue of the laws of any State Party or by virtue of another convention to which one of the said states is a party;

(c) precluding other rights or guarantees that are inherent in the human personality or derived from representative democracy as a form of government; or

(d) excluding or limiting the effect that the American Declaration of the Rights and Duties of Man and other international acts of the same nature may have.

This provision was designed specifically to ensure that it would in no case be interpreted to permit the denial or restriction of fundamental human rights and liberties, particularly those rights that have already been recognized by the State.

21 This Court has determined, moreover, that "the rules of interpretation set out in the Vienna Convention [on the Law of Treaties] ... may be deemed to state the relevant international law principles applicable to this subject." [*Restrictions to the Death Penalty, supra* 19, para 48.]

22 In determining whether the proposed legislation to which the request relates may form the basis of an advisory opinion under Article 64(2), the Court must therefore interpret the Convention "in good faith in accordance with the ordinary meaning to be given to the terms of the treaty in their context and in the light of its object and purpose."

[Vienna Convention on the Law of Treaties, Article 31(1); *Restrictions to the Death Penalty, supra* 19, para 49.]

23   It follows that the "ordinary meaning" of terms cannot of itself become the sole rule, for it must always be considered within its context and, in particular, in the light of the object and purpose of the treaty. In its Advisory Opinion on the Competence of the General Assembly for the Admission of a State to the United Nations, the International Court of Justice declared that "the first duty of a tribunal which is called upon to interpret and apply the provisions of a treaty, is to endeavour to give effect to them in their natural and ordinary meaning in the context in which they occur" [*Competence of the General Assembly for the Admission of a State to the United Nations*, Advisory Opinion, ICJ Reports 1950, p 8], which of necessity includes the object and purpose as expressed in some way in the context.

24   The Court has held [*Restrictions to the Death Penalty, supra* 19, para 47] in dealing with reservations, but this argument is equally valid when applied to the articles of the Convention, that the interpretation to be adopted may not lead to a result that "weakens the system of protection established by [the Convention]", bearing in mind the fact that the purpose and aim of that instrument is "the protection of the basic rights of individual human beings". [Int-Am Ct HR, *The Effect of Reservations on the Entry into Force of the American Convention on Human Rights* (Arts 74 and 75), Advisory Opinion OC-2/82 of 24 September 1982, Series A No 2, para 29.]

25   In this context, the Court concludes that its advisory function, as embodied in the system for the protection of basic rights, is as extensive as may be required to safeguard such rights, limited only by the restrictions that the Convention itself imposes. That is to say, just as Article 2 of the Convention requires the States Parties to "adopt ... such legislative or other measures as may be necessary to give effect to [the] rights and freedoms" of the individual, the Court's advisory function must also be viewed as being broad enough in scope to give effect to these rights and freedoms.

26   Thus, if the Court were to decline to hear a government's request for an advisory opinion because it concerned "proposed laws" and not laws duly promulgated and in force, this might in some cases have the consequence of forcing a government desiring the Court's opinion to violate the Convention by the formal adoption and possibly even application of the legislative measure, which steps would then be deemed to permit the appeal to the Court. Such a requirement would not "give effect" to the objectives of the Convention, for it does not advance the protection of the individual's basic human rights and freedoms.

27   Experience indicates, moreover, that once a law has been promulgated, a very substantial amount of time is likely to elapse before it can be repealed or annulled, even when it has been determined to violate the state's international obligations.

28   Keeping the above considerations in mind, the Court concludes that a restrictive reading of Article 64(2), which would permit states to request advisory opinions under that provision only in relation to laws already in force, would unduly limit the advisory function of the Court.

29   The foregoing conclusion is not to be understood to mean that the Court has to assume jurisdiction to deal with any and all draft laws or proposals for legislative action. It only means that the mere fact that a legislative proposal is not as yet in force does not *ipso facto* deprive the Court of jurisdiction to deal with a request for an advisory opinion relating to it. As the Court has already had occasion to note, "its advisory jurisdiction is

permissive in character [and] ... empowers the Court to decide whether the circumstances of a request for an advisory opinion justify a decision rejecting the request." ["*Other treaties*", *supra* 19, para 28. See also *Restrictions to the Death Penalty*, *supra* 19, para 36.]

30 In deciding whether to admit or reject advisory opinion requests relating to legislative proposals as distinguished from laws in force, the Court must carefully scrutinize the request to determine, *inter alia*, whether its purpose is to assist the requesting state to better comply with its international human rights obligations. To this end, the Court will have to exercise great care to ensure that its advisory jurisdiction in such instances is not resorted to in order to affect the outcome of the domestic legislative process for narrow partisan political ends. The Court, in other words, must avoid becoming embroiled in domestic political squabbles, which could affect the role which the Convention assigns to it. In the instant case which, moreover, is without precedent in that it involves a government's request for the review by an international court of a proposed constitutional amendment, the Court finds no reason whatsoever to decline complying with the advisory opinion request.

[ISSUES RELATING TO THE RIGHT TO NATIONALITY]

31 The questions posed by the Government involve two sets of general legal problems which the Court will examine separately. There is, first, an issue related to the right to nationality established by Article 20 of the Convention. A second set of questions involves issues of possible discrimination prohibited by the Convention.

32 It is generally accepted today that nationality is an inherent right of all human beings. Not only is nationality the basic requirement for the exercise of political rights, it also has an important bearing on the individual's legal capacity.

Thus, despite the fact that it is traditionally accepted that the conferral and regulation of nationality are matters for each state to decide, contemporary developments indicate that international law does impose certain limits on the broad powers enjoyed by the states in that area, and that the manners in which states regulate matters bearing on nationality cannot today be deemed within their sole jurisdiction; those powers of the state are also circumscribed by their obligations to ensure the full protection of human rights.

33 The classic doctrinal position, which viewed nationality as an attribute granted by the state to its subjects, has gradually evolved to the point that nationality is today perceived as involving the jurisdiction of the state as well as human rights issues. This has been recognized in a regional instrument, the American Declaration of the Rights and Duties of Man of 2 May, 1948 (hereinafter "the American Declaration"), whose Article 19 reads as follows:

> Every person has the right to the nationality to which he is entitled by law and to change it, if he so wishes, for the nationality of any other country that is willing to grant it to him.

Another instrument, the Universal Declaration of Human Rights (hereinafter "the Universal Declaration"), approved by the United Nations on 10 December, 1948, provides the following in its Article 15:

> 1   Everyone has the right to a nationality.
>
> 2   No one shall be arbitrarily deprived of his nationality nor denied the right to change his nationality.

34 The right of every human being to a nationality has been recognized as such by international law. Two aspects of this right are reflected in Article 20 of the Convention: first, the right to a nationality established therein provides the individual with a minimal measure of legal protection in international relations through the link his nationality establishes between him and the state in question; and, second, the protection therein accorded the individual against the arbitrary deprivation of his nationality, without which he would be deprived for all practical purposes of all of his political rights as well as of those civil rights that are tied to the nationality of the individual.

35 Nationality can be deemed to be the political and legal bond that links a person to a given state and binds him to it with ties of loyalty and fidelity, entitling him to diplomatic protection from that state. In different ways, most states have offered individuals who did not originally possess their nationality the opportunity to acquire it at a later date, usually through a declaration of intention made after complying with certain conditions. In these cases, nationality no longer depends on the fortuity of birth in a given territory or on parents having that nationality; it is based rather on a voluntary act aimed at establishing a relationship with a given political society, its culture, its way of life and its values.

36 Since it is the state that offers the possibility of acquiring its nationality to persons who were originally aliens, it is natural that the conditions and procedures for its acquisition should be governed primarily by the domestic law of that state. As long as such rules do not conflict with superior norms, it is the state conferring nationality which is best able to judge what conditions to impose to ensure that an effective link exists between the applicant for naturalization and the systems of values and interests of the society with which he seeks to fully associate himself. That state is also best able to decide whether these conditions have been complied with. Within these same limits, it is equally logical that the perceived needs of each state should determine the decision whether to facilitate naturalization to a greater or lesser degree; and since a state's perceived needs do not remain static, it is quite natural that the conditions for naturalization might be liberalized or restricted with the changed circumstances. It is therefore not surprising that at a given moment new conditions might be imposed to ensure that a change of nationality not be effected to solve some temporary problems encountered by the applicants when these have not established real and lasting ties with the country, which would justify an act as serious and far-reaching as the change of nationality.

37 In the *"Nottebohm Case"*, the International Court of Justice voiced certain ideas which are consistent with the views of this Court, expressed in the foregoing paragraph. The International Court declared:

> Naturalization is not a matter to be taken lightly. To seek and to obtain it is not something that happens frequently in the life of a human being. It involves his breaking of a bond of allegiance and his establishment of a new bond of allegiance. It may have far-reaching consequences and involve profound changes in destiny of the individual who obtains it. It concerns him personally, and to consider it only from the point of view of its repercussions with regard to his property would be to misunderstand its profound significance. [*Nottebohm Case* (second phase), judgment of 6 April 1955, ICJ Reports 1955, p 24.]

38 It follows from what has been said above that in order to arrive at a satisfactory interpretation of the right to nationality, as embodied in Article 20 of the Convention, it will be necessary to reconcile the principle that the conferral and regulation of nationality fall within the jurisdiction of the state, that is, they are matters to be determined by the domestic law of the state, with the further principle that international

law imposes certain limits on the state's power, which limits are linked to the demands imposed by the international system for the protection of human rights.

39 An examination of the provisions of the proposed amendment submitted to this Court by the Government makes clear that the amendment as a whole seeks to restrict the conditions under which an alien may acquire Costa Rican nationality. Some of the problems dealt with by the proposed amendment are not of a legal nature; others, although legal in character, are not for this Court to consider, either because they are of little consequence from the point of view of human rights or because, although tangentially important thereto, they fall within the category of issues within the exclusive domain of Costa Rica's domestic laws.

40 The Court will consequently not address certain issues that were raised during the public hearing, despite the fact that many of these issues reveal the overall purpose sought to be achieved by the amendment and expose differences of opinion on that subject. Here one might note, among other things, the doubts that were expressed at the hearing regarding the following questions: whether the spirit underlying the proposed amendments as a whole reflects, in a general way, a negative nationalistic reaction prompted by specific circumstances relating to the problem of refugees, particularly Central American refugees, who seek the protection of Costa Rica in their flight from the convulsion engulfing other countries in the region; whether that spirit reveals a tendency of retrogression from the traditional humanitarianism of Costa Rica; whether the proposed amendment, in eliminating the privileged naturalization status enjoyed by Central Americans under the current Constitution of Costa Rica, is indicative of a position rejecting the unity and solidarity that has historically characterized the peoples of Central America who achieved independence as a single nation.

41 Mindful of the foregoing considerations, the Court is now in a position to examine the question whether the proposed amendments affect the right to nationality guaranteed in Article 20 of the Convention, which reads as follows:

Article 20

Right to Nationality

1   Every person has the right to a nationality.

2   Every person has the right to the nationality of the state in whose territory he was born if he does not have the right to any other nationality.

3   No one shall be arbitrarily deprived of his nationality or of the right to change it.

42 Since the proposed amendments are designed, in general, to impose stricter requirements for the acquisition of Costa Rican nationality by naturalization, but since they do not purport to withdraw that nationality from any citizen currently holding it, nor to deny the right to change that nationality, the Court concludes that the proposals do not in any formal sense contravene Article 20 of the Convention. Although Article 20 remains to be more fully analyzed and is capable of development, it is clear in this case that since no Costa Ricans would lose their nationality if the proposed amendments entered into force, no violation of paragraph 1 can be deemed to take place. Neither is there a violation of paragraph 2 of that same Article, for the right of any person born in Costa Rica to the nationality of that country is in no way affected. Finally, considering that the proposed amendments are not intended to deprive any Costa Rican nationals of their nationality nor to prohibit or restrict their right to acquire a new nationality, the Court concludes that no contradiction exists between the proposed amendments and paragraph 3 of Article 20.

43   Among the proposed amendments there is one that, although it does not violate Article 20 as such, does raise some issues bearing on the right to nationality. It involves the amendment motion to Article 14, paragraph 4, of the proposal presented by the Members of the Special Legislative Committee. Under that provision, Costa Rican nationality would be acquired by:

> A foreigner who, by marriage to a Costa Rican loses his or her nationality and who after two years of marriage to a Costa Rican and the same period of residence in the country, indicates his or her desire to take on the nationality of the spouse.

44   Without entering into an examination of all aspects of the present text that touch on the subject of discrimination – a topic which will be considered later on this opinion [cf *infra* Chapter IV] some related problems raised by the wording of the proposal need to be addressed. As a matter of fact, the above wording differs in more than one respect from the text of Article 14, para 5, of the present Constitution and from the text of Article 14, para 4, of the proposed amendment as originally presented. The two latter texts read as follows:

> *Article 14*
>
> *By Naturalization*
>
> The following are Costa Ricans by naturalization:
>
> 5   A foreign woman who by marriage to a Costa Rican loses her nationality or who indicates her desire to become a Costa Rican;
>
> *Article 14*
>
> The following are Costa Ricans by naturalization:
>
> 4   A foreign woman who, by marriage to a Costa Rican loses her nationality or who after two years of marriage to a Costa Rican and the same period of residence in the country, indicates her desire to take on our nationality.

The above provisions indicate that a foreign woman who loses her nationality upon marrying a Costa Rican would automatically acquire Costa Rican nationality. They prescribe additional specific requirements only for cases where no automatic loss of the previous nationality occurs.

45   It is clear, on the other hand, that the text proposed by the Members of the Special Legislative Committee effects a substantial change in the here relevant provision, for it imposes additional conditions which must all be complied with in order for a person to become eligible for naturalization.

46   One consequence of the amendment as drafted is that foreigners who lose their nationality upon marrying a Costa Rican would have to remain stateless for at least two years because they cannot comply with one of the obligatory requirements for naturalization unless they have been married for that period of time. It should also be noted that it is by no means certain that statelessness would be limited to a period of two years only. This uncertainty results from the fact that the other concurrent requirement mandates a two-year period of residence in the country. Foreigners forced to leave the country temporarily due to unforeseen circumstances would continue to be stateless for an indefinite length of time until they will have completed all the concurrent requirements established under this proposed amendment.

47   Furthermore, whereas in the text here under consideration the automatic loss of nationality is one of the concurrent conditions for naturalization by reason of marriage,

no special provisions are made to regulate the status of foreigners who do not lose their nationality upon marriage to Costa Ricans.

48 The amendment proposed by the Members of the Special Legislative Committee would not as such create statelessness. This status would in fact be brought about by the laws of the country whose nationals, upon marrying a Costa Rican, lose their nationality. It follows that this amendment cannot therefore be deemed to be directly violative of Article 20 of the Convention.

49 The Court nevertheless considers it relevant, for the sole purpose of providing some guidance to the Costa Rican authorities in charge of this subject and without doing so *in extenso* and with lengthy citations, to call attention to the stipulations contained in two other treaties bearing on the subject. The Court refers to these treaties, without enquiring whether they have been ratified by Costa Rica, to the extent that they may reflect current trends in international law.

50 Thus, the Convention on the Nationality of Married Women provides in its Article 3:

1   Each Contracting State agrees that the alien wife of one of its nationals may, at her request, acquire the nationality of her husband through specially privileged naturalization procedures; the grant of such nationality may be subject to such limitations as may be imposed in the interests of national security or public policy.

2   Each Contracting State agrees that the present Convention shall not be construed as affecting any legislation or judicial practice by which the alien wife of one of its nationals may, at her request, acquire her husband's nationality as a matter of right.

51 The Convention on the Elimination of all Forms of Discrimination against Women provides in its Article 9:

States Parties shall grant women equal rights with men to acquire, change or retain their nationality. They shall ensure in particular that neither marriage to an alien nor change of nationality by the husband during the marriage shall automatically change the nationality of the wife, render her stateless or force upon her the nationality of the husband.

[ISSUES RELATING TO DISCRIMINATION]

52 The provisions of the proposed amendments that have been brought before the Court for interpretation as well as the text of the Constitution that is now in force establish different classifications as far as the conditions for the acquisition of Costa Rican nationality through naturalization are concerned. Thus, under paragraphs 2 and 3 of Article 14 of the proposed amendment, the periods of official residence in the country required as a condition for the acquisition of nationality differ, depending on whether the applicants qualify as native-born nationals of "other countries of Central America, Spaniards and Ibero-Americans" or whether they acquired the nationality of those countries by naturalization. Paragraph 4 of that same Article in turn lays down special conditions applicable to the naturalization of "a foreign woman" who marries a Costa Rican. Article 14 of the Constitution now in force makes similar distinctions which, even though they may not have the same purpose and meaning, suggest the question whether they do not constitute discriminatory classifications incompatible with the relevant texts of the Convention.

53 Article 1(1) of the Convention, a rule general in scope which applies to all the provisions of the treaty, imposes on the States Parties the obligation to respect and guarantee the free and full exercise of the rights and freedoms recognized therein "without any discrimination." In other words, regardless of its origin or the form it may

assume, any treatment that can be considered to be discriminatory with regard to the exercise of any of the rights guaranteed under the Convention is *per se* incompatible with that instrument.

54 Article 24 of the Convention, in turn, reads as follows:

> *Article 24*
>
> *Right to Equal Protection*
>
> All persons are equal before the law. Consequently, they are entitled, without discrimination, to equal protection of the law.

Although Articles 24 and 1(1) are conceptually not identical – the Court may perhaps have occasion at some future date to articulate the differences – Article 24 restates to a certain degree the principle established in Article 1(1). In recognizing equality before the law, it prohibits all discriminatory treatment originating in a legal prescription. The prohibition against discrimination so broadly proclaimed in Article 1(1) with regard to the rights and guarantees enumerated in the Convention thus extends to the domestic law of the States Parties, permitting the conclusion that in these provisions the States Parties, by acceding to the Convention, have undertaken to maintain their laws free of discriminatory regulations.

55 The notion of equality springs directly from the oneness of the human family and is linked to the essential dignity of the individual. That principle cannot be reconciled with the notion that a given group has the right to privileged treatment because of its perceived superiority. It is equally irreconcilable with that notion to characterize a group as inferior and treat it with hostility or otherwise subject it to discrimination in the enjoyment of rights which are accorded to others not so classified. It is impermissible to subject human beings to differences in treatment that are inconsistent with their unique and congenerous character.

56 Precisely because equality and nondiscrimination are inherent in the idea of the oneness in dignity and worth of all human beings, it follows that not all differences in legal treatment are discriminatory as such, for not all differences in treatment are in themselves offensive to human dignity. The European Court of Human Rights, "following the principles which may be extracted from the legal practice of a large number of democratic States," has held that a difference in treatment is only discriminatory when it "has no objective and reasonable justification." [Eur Court HR, Case *"Relating to Certain Aspects of the Laws on the Use of Languages in Education in Belgium" (Merits)*, judgment of 23 July 1968, p 34.] There may well exist certain factual inequalities that might legitimately give rise to inequalities in legal treatment that do not violate principles of justice. They may in fact be instrumental in achieving justice or in protecting those who find themselves in a weak legal position. For example, it cannot be deemed discrimination on the grounds of age or social status for the law to impose limits on the legal capacity of minors or mentally incompetent persons who lack the capacity to protect their interests.

57 Accordingly, no discrimination exists if the difference in treatment has a legitimate purpose and if it does not lead to situations which are contrary to justice, to reason or to the nature of things. It follows that there would be no discrimination in differences in treatment of individuals by a state when the classifications selected are based on substantial factual differences and there exists a reasonable relationship of proportionality between these differences and the aims of the legal rule under review.

These aims may not be unjust or unreasonable, that is, they may not be arbitrary, capricious, despotic or in conflict with the essential oneness and dignity of humankind.

58 Although it cannot be denied that a given factual context may make it more or less difficult to determine whether or not one has encountered the situation described in the foregoing paragraph, it is equally true that, starting with the notion of the essential oneness and dignity of the human family, it is possible to identify circumstances in which considerations of public welfare may justify departures to a greater or lesser degree from the standards articulated above. One is here dealing with values which take on concrete dimensions in the face of those real situations in which they have to be applied and which permit in each case a certain margin of appreciation in giving expression to them.

59 With this approach in mind, the Court repeats its prior observation that as far as the granting of naturalization is concerned, it is for the granting state to determine whether and to what extent applicants for naturalization have complied with the conditions deemed to ensure an effective link between them and the value system and interests of the society to which they wish to belong. To this extent there exists no doubt that it is within the sovereign power of Costa Rica to decide what standards should determine the granting or denial of nationality to aliens who seek it, and to establish certain reasonable differentiations based on factual differences which, viewed objectively, recognize that some applicants have a closer affinity than others to Costa Rica's value system and interests.

60 Given the above considerations, one example of a non-discriminatory differentiation would be the establishment of less stringent residency requirements for Central Americans, Ibero-Americans and Spaniards than for other foreigners seeking to acquire Costa Rican nationality. It would not appear to be inconsistent with the nature and purpose of the grant of nationality to expedite the naturalization procedures for those who, viewed objectively, share much closer historical, cultural and spiritual bonds with the people of Costa Rica. The existence of these bonds permits the assumption that these individuals will be more easily and more rapidly assimilated within the national community and identify more readily with the traditional beliefs, values and institutions of Costa Rica, which the state has the right and duty to preserve.

61 Less obvious is the basis for the distinction, made in paragraphs 2 and 3 of Article 14 of the proposed amendment, between those Central Americans, Ibero-Americans and Spaniards who acquired their nationality by birth and those who obtained it by naturalization. Since nationality is a bond that exists equally for the one group as for the other, the proposed classification appears to be based on the place of birth and not on the culture of the applicant for naturalization. The provisions in question may, however, have been prompted by certain doubts about the strictness of the conditions that were applied by those states which conferred their nationality on the individuals now seeking to obtain that of Costa Rica, the assumption being that the previously acquired nationality – be it Spanish, Ibero-American or that of some other Central American country – does not constitute an adequate guarantee of affinity with the value system and interests of the Costa Rican society. Although the distinctions being made are debatable on various grounds, the Court will not consider those issues now. Notwithstanding the fact that the classification resorted to is more difficult to understand given the additional requirements that an applicant would have to meet under Article 15 of the proposed amendment, the Court cannot conclude that the proposed amendment is clearly discriminatory in character.

62   In reaching this conclusion, the Court is fully mindful of the margin of appreciation which is reserved to states when it comes to the establishment of requirements for the acquisition of nationality and the determination whether they have been complied with. But the Court's conclusion should not be viewed as approval of the practice which prevails in some areas to limit to an exaggerated and unjustified degree the political rights of naturalized individuals. Most of these situations involve cases not now before the Court that do, however, constitute clear instances of discrimination on the basis of origin or place of birth, unjustly creating two distinct hierarchies of nationals in one single country.

63   Consistent with its clearly restrictive approach, the proposed amendment also provides for new conditions which must be complied with by those applying for naturalization. Draft Article 15 requires, among other things, proof of the ability to "speak, write and read" the Spanish language; it also prescribes a "comprehensive examination on the history of the country and its values." These conditions can be deemed, *prima facie*, to fall within the margin of appreciation reserved to the state as far as concerns the enactment and assessment of the requirements designed to ensure the existence of real and effective links upon which to base the acquisition of the new nationality. So viewed, it cannot be said to be unreasonable and unjustified to require proof of the ability to communicate in the language of the country or, although this is less clear, to require the applicant to "speak, write and read" the language. The same can be said of the requirement of a "comprehensive examination on the history of the country and its values." The Court feels compelled to emphasize, however, that in practice, and given the broad discretion with which tests such as those mandated by the draft amendment tend to be administered, there exists the risk that these requirements will become the vehicle for subjective and arbitrary judgments as well as instruments for the effectuation of discriminatory policies which, although not directly apparent on the face of the law, could well be the consequence of its application.

64   The fourth paragraph of draft Article 14 accords "a foreign woman who [marries] a Costa Rican" special consideration for obtaining Costa Rican nationality. In doing so, it follows the formula adopted in the current Constitution, which gives women but not men who marry Costa Ricans a special status for purposes of naturalization. This approach or system was based on the so-called principle of family unity and is traceable to two assumptions. One has to do with the proposition that all members of a family should have the same nationality. The other derives from notions about paternal authority and the fact that authority over minor children was as a rule vested in the father and that it was the husband on whom the law conferred a privileged status of power, giving him authority, for example, to fix the marital domicile and to administer the marital property. Viewed in this light, the right accorded to women to acquire the nationality of their husbands was an outgrowth of conjugal inequality.

65   In the early 1930's, there developed a movement opposing these traditional notions. It had its roots in the acquisition of legal capacity by women and the more widespread acceptance of equality among the sexes based on the principle of nondiscrimination. These developments, which can be documented by means of a comparative law analysis, received a decisive impulse on the international plane. In the Americas, the Contracting Parties to the Montevideo Convention on the Nationality of Women of 26 December 1933 declared in Article 1 of that treaty that "There shall be no distinction based on sex as regards nationality, in their legislation or in their practice." [Adopted at the Seventh International Conference of American States, Montevideo, 3–26 December 1933. The Convention is reproduced in International Conferences of American States –

Supplement 1933–1940. Washington, Carnegie Endowment for International Peace, 1940, p 106.] And the Convention on Nationality, signed also in Montevideo on that same date, provided in Article 6 that "Neither matrimony nor its dissolution affects the nationality of the husband or wife or of their children." [*Ibid*, at 108.] The American Declaration, in turn, declares in Article 2 that "All persons are equal before the law and have the rights and duties established in this declaration, without distinction as to race, sex, language, creed or any other factor." These same principles have been embodied in Article 1(3) of the United Nations Charter and in Article 3(j) of the OAS Charter.

66   The same idea is reflected in Article 17(4) of the Convention, which reads as follows:

> The States Parties shall take appropriate steps to ensure the equality of rights and the adequate balancing of responsibilities of the spouses as to marriage, during marriage, and in the event of its dissolution. In case of dissolution, provision shall be made for the necessary protection of any children solely on the basis of their own best interests.

Since this provision is consistent with the general rule enunciated in Article 24, which provides for equality before the law, and with the prohibition of discrimination based on sex contained in Article 1(1), Article 17(4) can be said to constitute the concrete application of these general principles to marriage.

67   The Court consequently concludes that the different treatment envisaged for spouses by paragraph 4 of Article 14 of the proposed amendment, which applies to the acquisition of Costa Rican nationality in cases involving special circumstances brought about by marriage, cannot be justified and must be considered to be discriminatory. The Court notes in this connection and without prejudice to its other observations applicable to the amendment proposed by the members of the Special Legislative Committee [cf *supra*, para 45 *et seq*] that their proposal is based on the principle of equality between the spouses and, therefore, is more consistent with the Convention. The requirements spelled out in that amendment would be applicable not only to "a foreign woman" but to any "foreigner" who marries a Costa Rican national.

68   For the foregoing reasons, responding to the questions submitted by the Government of Costa Rica regarding the compatibility of the proposed amendments to Articles 14 and 15 of its Constitution with Articles 17(4), 20 and 24 of the Convention,

THE COURT IS OF THE OPINION

As regards Article 20 of the Convention

By five votes to one

1   That the proposed amendment to the Constitution, which is the subject of this request for an advisory opinion, does not affect the right to nationality guaranteed by Article 20 of the Convention.

As regards Articles 24 and 17(4) of the Convention

By unanimous vote

2   That the provision stipulating preferential treatment in the acquisition of Costa Rican nationality through naturalization, which favors Central Americans, Ibero-Americans and Spaniards over other aliens, does not constitute discrimination contrary to the Convention.

By five votes to one

3   That it does not constitute discrimination contrary to the Convention to grant such preferential treatment only to those who are Central Americans, Ibero-Americans and Spaniards by birth.

By five votes to one

4   That the further requirements added by Article 15 of the proposed amendment for the acquisition of Costa Rican nationality through naturalization do not as such constitute discrimination contrary to the Convention.

By unanimous vote

5   That the provision stipulating preferential treatment in cases of naturalization applicable to marriage contained in Article 14(4) of the proposed amendment, which favors only one of the spouses, does constitute discrimination incompatible with Articles 17(4) and 24 of the Convention.

DISSENTING:*

JUDGE BUERGENTHAL with regard to point 3.

JUDGE PIZA ESCALANTE with regard to points 1 and 4.

---

*   *Eds:* due to space constraints, the dissenting opinion of Judge Buergenthal and separate opinion of Judge Piza Escalante have not been included. The full text of the advisory opinion is available at the IACHR website and the University of Minnesota Human Rights Library website (see *On-Line Access to Human Rights Source Material, supra,* p xlv).

CASE NO 37

ATTORNEY GENERAL OF BOTSWANA
v UNITY DOW

COURT OF APPEAL, BOTSWANA

Judgment: 3 July 1992

Panel: Amissah JP, Aguda, Bizos, Schreiner and Puckrin JJA

Human rights — Equality and non-discrimination — Right to freedom of movement — Citizenship — Nationality of children — Denial of citizenship of Botswana to children born to citizen mother married to non-citizen father — Whether discrimination on the ground of sex or violation of mother's freedom of movement — Citizenship Act 1984, ss 4 and 5 — Constitution of Botswana, ss 3, 14, 15 and 18

Constitutional interpretation — International obligations — Whether Constitution to be interpreted in line with international conventions — African Charter on Human and People's Rights, Art 2 — Universal Declaration on Human Rights, art 2 — Constitution of Botswana, s 15 — Interpretation Act 1984, s 24

Locus standi — Citizenship — Nationality of children — Denial of citizenship of Botswana to children born to citizen mother married to non-citizen father — Whether constitutional rights of mother adversely affected — Whether mother had locus standi — Citizenship Act 1984, ss 4 and 5 — Constitution of Botswana, s 14

BACKGROUND

The respondent, Ms Unity Dow, was a citizen of Botswana. On 7 March 1984, she married Mr Peter Nathan Dow, a citizen of the United States of America who had been resident in Botswana for nearly 14 years. Prior to their marriage one child was born to them on 29 October 1979 and after their marriage two more children were born, on 26 March 1985 and 26 November 1987 respectively. All three children were born in Botswana. The first child was a citizen of Botswana by virtue of section 21 of the Constitution, whereas the two children born during the marriage were not citizens of Botswana pursuant to section 4(1) of the Citizenship Act 1984, which provides as follows:

> (1) A person born in Botswana shall be a citizen of Botswana by birth and descent if, at the time of his birth: (a) his father was a citizen of Botswana; or (b) in the case of a person born out of wedlock, his mother was a citizen of Botswana.

Therefore, by virtue of section 4 of the Citizenship Act, a child who is born to a citizen mother, who is married to a non-citizen father, cannot be a citizen of Botswana. Similarly, section 5(1), which relates to the citizenship of children born outside Botswana, provides as follows:

> 5(1) A person born outside Botswana shall be a citizen of Botswana by descent if, at the time of his birth: (a) his father was a citizen of Botswana; or (b) in the case of a person born out of wedlock, his mother was a citizen of Botswana.

On 11 June 1991, Ms Dow made an application to the High Court of Botswana, contending that sections 4 and 5 of the Citizenship Act violated her constitutional rights and freedoms, including the right to equal protection of the law irrespective of sex (section 3), personal liberty (section 5), protection from being subjected to degrading treatment (section 7), freedom of movement (section 14) and protection from discrimination on the basis of sex (section 15). Horwitz Ag J granted Ms Dow's application, declaring both sections 4 and 5 of the Citizenship Act *ultra vires* the Constitution on the grounds that they were discriminatory against women (see [1991] LRC (Const) 574).

The Attorney General appealed to the Court of Appeal, contending that neither s 4 nor section 5 denied the respondent any of the rights or protections mentioned above. Particular grounds for appeal included that Horwitz Ag J had erred in holding that section 15 of the Constitution prohibited discrimination on the grounds of sex, when the definition of discrimination in section 15(3) did not refer to sex, and in holding that the respondent had *locus standi* to bring the action.

HELD (dismissing the appeal, subject to a variation of the declaration of the High Court)

1   The very nature of a Constitution required that a broad and generous approach be adopted in the interpretation of its provisions; that all the relevant provisions bearing on the subject for interpretation be considered together as a whole in order to effect the objective of the Constitution; and that where rights and freedoms were conferred on persons by the Constitution, derogations from such rights and freedoms should be narrowly or strictly construed (p 582).

2   Section 3 of the Constitution of Botswana, which guarantees equal protection of the law irrespective of sex, was not only a substantive provision, but was the key or umbrella provision in Chapter II under which all rights and freedoms protected under the chapter must be subsumed. The rest of the provisions of Chapter II, including s 15, should be construed as expanding on or placing limitations on s 3, and should be construed within the context of that section. A fundamental right or freedom once conferred by the Constitution could only be taken away or circumscribed by an express and unambiguous statement in that Constitution or by a valid amendment of it. It could not be inferred from the omission of the word "sex" in the definition of discrimination in s 15(3) that the right to equal protection of the law given in s 3 of the Constitution to all persons (irrespective of sex) had, in the case of sex-based differentation in equality of treatment, been taken away. The classes or groups mentioned in the definition in s 15(3) were more by way of example than an exclusive itemisation (pp 584, 593, 594).

3   As provided by s 24 of the Interpretation Act 1984, relevant international treaties and conventions might be referred to as an aid to interpretation. Unless it was impossible to do otherwise, it would be wrong for Botswana's courts to interpret its legislation in a manner which conflicted with the international obligations Botswana had undertaken. This principle added reinforcement to the view that the intention of the framers of the Constitution could not have been to permit discrimination purely on the basis of sex (p 597).

4   Custom and tradition should *a fortiori* yield to the Constitution of Botswana. A constitutional guarantee could not be overridden by custom. Custom would as far as possible be read so as to conform with the Constitution, but where this was impossible, it was custom not the Constitution which had to go (p 587).

5   The respondent had *locus standi* with respect to her challenge of s 4 of the Citizenship Act 1984. She had substantiated her allegation that the Act circumscribed her freedom of movement given by s 14 of the Constitution, having made a case that as a mother her movements are determined by what happens to her children. However, she did not have *locus standi* with respect to s 5 of the Act, as the situation which that section provided for, namely, the citizenship of children born outside Botswana, did not apply to the respondent in any of the cases of her children, and the possibility of the respondent giving birth at some future date to children abroad was too remote to form a basis for such a challenge (pp 600, 601).

6   Section 4 of the Citizenship Act 1984 infringed the fundamental rights and freedoms of the respondent conferred by s 3 (fundamental rights and freedoms of the individual), s 14 (protection of freedom of movement) and s 15 of the Constitution (protection from discrimination) and was *ultra vires* (p 601).

Per Shreiner and Puckrin JJA (dissenting)

1   Discrimination on the ground of sex was not prohibited by s 15 of the Constitution. The idea that the list of descriptions of persons in s 15(3) was not exhaustive had to be rejected. Section 3 was an introductory or explanatory section which did not, by itself, create substantive rights and freedoms, but was in the nature of a preamble or a recital. Section 3 would only become relevant in interpreting s 15(3) if it could be shown that there was some vagueness or ambiguity in s 15(3). The mere absence of mention of sexual discrimination in s 15(3) did not create any such vagueness or ambiguity and a reference to s 3 in order to create one was not permissible.

2   The general injunctions regarding the interpretation of constitutional statutes should not be relied upon as a licence to a court, even when dealing with rights and freedoms, in effect, to alter a provision to avoid a consequence which it considers is not, in view of its assessment of the position in existing society, socially or morally desirable, if the meaning is clear. The special approach to interpretation of a constitution applied only where there is an ambiguity or obscurity. If a human rights code did not outlaw discrimination on the ground of sex, the court had no right to declare that it did because, in its view, such a provision was desirable in the atmosphere of the time; it had to be satisfied from the wording of the provision that the legislature intended to prevent such discrimination.

Treaties and other international instruments referred to

African Charter on Human and People's Rights 1980, arts 2, 3, 12 and 18(3)

Convention on the Elimination of All Forms of Discrimination against Women 1979, arts 2, 3, 9(1) and 9(2)

Organisation of African Unity Convention on Non-Discrimination

Declaration on the Elimination of Discrimination against Women 1967, art 2

Declaration on the Rights of the Child 1959

Universal Declaration of Human Rights 1948, art 2

National legislation referred to

Bermuda

Constitution of Bermuda, s 11

Botswana

Citizenship Act 1984 (Cap 01:01), ss 4, 5, 13 and 15

Common Law and Customary Law Act (Cap 16:10), s 7

Constitution of Botswana, ss 1–25, 27, 33, 39, 42, 61, 62, 67, 86 and 89

Immigration Act

Interpretation Act 1984 (Cap 01:04) ss 2, 24, 26 and 33

Namibia

Constitution, art 140(3)

United States

Constitution of the United States of America, 5th Amendment (1791)

Constitution of the United States of America, 14th Amendment (1868)

Cases referred to

Abdiel Caban v Kazim Mohammed & Maria Mohammed 441 US 380 (1979); 60 L Ed 2d 297; 99 S Ct 1760

A-G for New South Wales v Brewery Employees Union of New South Wales (1908) 6 CLR 469

A-G of Namibia, ex parte Re Corporal Punishment by Organs of State [1992] LRC (Const) 515; 1991 (3) SA 76 (Nam SC)

A-G v British Broadcasting Corporation [1981] AC 303; [1980] 3 WLR 109; [1980] 3 All ER 161

A-G v Moagi [1981] BLR 1

A-G v Prince Ernest Augustus of Hanover [1957] AC 436; [1957] 2 WLR 1; [1957] 1 All ER 49

Birds Galore Ltd v A-G [1989] LRC (Const) 928

Boyd v United States 116 US 616 (1986); 29 L Ed 746; 6 S Ct 524

Cabinet of the Transitional Government of South West Africa v Eins 1988 (3) SA 369 (A)

Colonial Treasurer v Rand Water Board [1907] TS 479

Craig v Boren, Governor of Oklahoma 429 US 190 (1976); 50 L Ed 2d 397

Darymple v Colonial Treasurer [1910] TS 372

Docksteader v Clark (1903) 11 BCR 37

Dow v Attorney-General of Botswana [1991] LRC (Const) 574

Dred Scott v Sanford 60 US 393 (1857); 15 L Ed 691; 19 How 393

Eton College v Minister of Agriculture Fisheries and Foods [1962] 3 WLR 726; [1962] 3 All ER 290; [1964] Ch 274

Frontiero v Richardson 411 US 677 (1973); 36 L Ed 2d 583

Harris v Minister of Interior 1952 (2) SA 428 (A)

Hewlett v Minister of Finance 1982 (1) SA 490

Ifezu v Mbadugha [1984] 1 SC NLR 427; 5 SC 79

James v Commonwealth of Australia [1936] AC 578

Law Union and Rock Insurance Co Ltd v Carmichael's Executor [1917] AD 593

Metropolitan Railway Co v Fowler [1892] 1 QB 165

Minister of Home Affairs v Bickle [1985] LRC (Const) 755; 1984 (2) SA 439

Minister of Home Affairs v Fisher [1980] AC 319; [1979] 2 WLR 889; [1979] 3 All ER 21

Mwandingi v Minister of Defence, Namibia 1991 (1) SA 851 (Nam HC); aff'd 1992 (2) SA 355 (Nam SC)

Petrus v State [1985] LRC (Const) 699; [1984] BLR 14 (Bot CA)

R v Big M Drug Mart Ltd [1986] LRC (Const) 332; [1985] 1 SCR 295

R v Morgentaler [1990] LRC (Const) 242; [1988] 1 SCR 30

Rafiu Rabiu v State (1981) 2 NCLR 293

Reed v Reed 404 US 71 (1971); 30 L Ed 2d 225

Schering Chemicals Ltd v Falkman Ltd [1982] QB 18; [1981] 2 WLR 848; [1981] 2 All ER 321

South Dakota v North Carolina 192 US 286 (1904); 48 L Ed 448; 24 S Ct 269

State v Ncube [1988] LRC (Const) 442; 1988 (2) SA 702 (Zim SC)

Taff Vale Railway Co v Cardiff Railway Co [1917] 1 Ch 199

Trop v Dulles 35 US 86 (1958); 2 L Ed 2d 630

Veriava v President of South African Medical and Dental Council 1985 (2) SA 293 (T)

Weinberger, Secretary of Health, Education and Welfare v Wiesenfeld 420 US 636 (1975); 43 L Ed 2d 514; 95 S Ct 1225; 9 Empl Prac Dec P 9998

Wood & Others v Ondangwa Tribal Authority & Another 1975 (2) SA 294 (A)

JUDGMENT*

AMISSAH JP: This appeal is brought by the Attorney General against the judgment given by Horwitz Ag J in favour of Unity Dow in her claim that her constitutional rights had been infringed by certain specified provisions of the Citizenship Act 1984 (Cap 01:01).

[Facts]**

The facts of the case which gave cause for the respondent's complaint were well summarised by the learned judge *a quo*, and for convenience and with due apologies I will repeat that summary. As he said ([1991] LRC (Const) 574 at 577):

---

*   *Eds:* the following is an abridged version of the judgment. The full text is available at [1992] LRC (Const) 623; 1994 (6) BCLR 1 (Botswana).

**   *Eds:* headings (in square brackets) have been added for the convenience of readers.

The applicant Unity Dow is a citizen of Botswana having been born in Botswana of parents who are members of one of the indigenous tribes of Botswana. She is married to Peter Nathan Dow who, although he has been in residence in Botswana for nearly 14 years, is not a citizen of Botswana but a citizen of the United States of America.

Prior to their marriage on 7 March 1984 a child was born to them on 29 October 1979 named Cheshe Maitumelo Dow and after the marriage two more children were born, Tumisang Ted Dow born on 26 March 1985 and Natasha Selemo Dow born on 26 November 1987. She states further in her founding affidavit that "my family and I have established our home in Raserura Ward in Mochudi and all the children regard that place and no other as their home".

In terms of the laws in force prior to the Citizenship Act 1984 the daughter born before the marriage is a Botswana citizen and therefore a Botswana, whereas in terms of the Citizenship Act 1984 the children born during the marriage are not citizens of Botswana (although children of the same parents), and are therefore aliens in the land of their birth.

The respondent claimed that the provisions of the Citizenship Act 1984 which denied citizenship to her two younger children were s 4 and 5. Those sections read as follows:

4(1) A person born in Botswana shall be a citizen of Botswana by birth and descent if, at the time of his birth: (a) his father was a citizen of Botswana; or (b) in the case of a person born out of wedlock, his mother was a citizen of Botswana. 4(2) A person born before commencement of this Act shall not be a citizen by virtue of this section unless he was a citizen at the time of such commencement.

5(1) A person born outside Botswana shall be a citizen of Botswana by descent if, at the time of his birth: (a) his father was a citizen of Botswana; (b) in the case of a person born out of wedlock, his mother was a citizen of Botswana. 5(2) A person born before the commencement of this Act shall not be a citizen by virtue of this section unless he was a citizen as the time of such commencement.

I should here add that the respondent's case before the court *a quo* also embraced discriminatory treatment which she claimed the Act of 1984 gave to alien men married to Botswana women on the one hand and alien women married to Botswana men on the other. The section of the Citizenship Act 1984 which, according to the respondent, perpetrated this distinction was s 15. But as the judgment of the court *a quo* did not refer to that aspect of the case in its determination of the injustice suffered by the respondent from the Citizenship Act 1984, I shall refrain from going further into that aspect of the case.

[Complaint]

The case which the respondent sought to establish and which was accepted by the court *a quo* was captured by paras 13 to 15, 18, 19, 21 and 22 of her founding affidavit. They read as follows:

13 I am prejudiced by section 4(1) of the Citizenship Act by reason of my being female from passing citizenship to my two children Tumisang and Natasha.

14 I am precluded by the discriminatory effect of the said law in that my said children are aliens in the land of mine and their birth and thus enjoy limited rights and legal protections.

15 I verily believe that the discriminatory effect of the said sections, (4 and 5 *supra*) offend against section 3(a) of the Constitution of the Republic of Botswana...

18 I am desirous of being afforded the same protection of law as a male Botswana citizen and in this regard I am desirous that my children be accorded with Botswana citizenship.

19 As set out above, I verily believe and state that the provisions of section 3 of the Constitution have been contravened in relation to myself...

21 As a citizen of the Republic of Botswana, I am guaranteed under the Constitution immunity from expulsion from Botswana and verily believe that such immunity is interfered with and limited by the practical implications of sections 4, 5 and 13 of the said Citizenship Act.

22 I verily believe that the provisions of the Constitution have been contravened in relation to myself.

The sections of the Constitution of the Republic which the Respondent prayed in aid in this regard, therefore, are ss 3 and 14. Section 3 is the section which deals with the fundamental rights and freedoms of the individual. Section 14 deals with the protection of freedom of movement. I shall have occasion to recite them and to refer to them in some detail in the course of this judgment.

[High Court judgment]

After hearing the respondent, then the applicant in the case, and the Attorney General in opposition, the learned judge *a quo* found in favour of the former. The relevant parts of his judgment are as follows ([1991] LRC (Const) 574 at 588–589):

I therefore find that s 4 [of the Citizenship Act] is discriminatory in its effect on women in that, as a matter of policy:

(i) It may compel them to live and bear children outside wedlock.

(ii) Since her children are only entitled to remain in Botswana if they are in possession of a residence permit and since they are not granted permits in their own right, their right to remain in Botswana is dependent upon their forming part of their father's residence permit.

(iii) The residence permits are granted for no more than two years at a time, and if the applicant's husband's permit were not to be renewed both he and the applicant's minor children would be obliged to leave Botswana.

(iv) In addition the applicant is jointly responsible with her husband for the education of their children. Citizens of Botswana qualify for financial assistance in the form of bursaries to meet the costs of university education. This is a benefit which is not available to a non-citizen. In the result the applicant is financially prejudiced by the fact that her children are not Botswana citizens.

(v) Since the children would be obliged to travel on their father's passport the applicant will not be entitled to return to Botswana with her children in the absence of their father.

What I have therefore set out at length inhibits women in Botswana from marrying the man whom they love. It is no answer to say that there are laws against marrying close blood relations – that is a reasonable exclusion...

It seems to me that the effect of s 4 is to punish a citizen female for marrying a non-citizen male. For this she is put in the unfavourable position in which she finds herself *vis-à-vis* her children and her country.

The fact that according to the Citizenship Act a child born to a marriage between a citizen female and non-citizen male follows the citizenship of its father may not in fact have that result. It depends on the law of the foreign country. The result may be that the child may be rendered stateless unless its parents emigrate. If they are forced to emigrate then the unfortunate consequences which I have set out earlier in this judgment may ensue.

I have therefore come to the conclusion that the application succeeds. I have also come to the conclusion that s 5 of the Act must join the fate of s 4.

[Grounds of appeal]

The appellant has appealed against this decision on several grounds. He complains that the court *a quo* erred in holding that the applicant had sufficiently shown that any of the provisions of ss 3-16 (inclusive) of the Constitution had been, was being, or was likely to be contravened in relation to her by reason of the provisions of s 4 or s 5 of the Citizenship Act 1984 so as to confer on her *locus standi* to apply to the High Court for redress pursuant to s 18 of the Constitution. After holding that the provisions of the Constitution should be given a "generous interpretation", the court *a quo* erred in failing to give any or any adequate effect to other principles of construction, in particular, the principle that an Act of the national assembly must be presumed to be *intra vires* the Constitution; the principle that an Act or instrument, including the Constitution should be construed as a whole; and with regard to s 15(3) of the Constitution, the principle of *"inclusio unius exclusio alterius"*, to which effect is given in s 33 of the Interpretation Act 1984 (Cap 01:04). The Court *a quo* also erred, in that instead of holding that the word "sex" had been intentionally omitted from s 15(3) of the Constitution so as to accommodate, subject to the fundamental rights protected by s 3 thereof, the patrilineal structure of Botswana society, in terms of the common law, the customary law, and statute law, it held that s 15(3) of the Constitution merely listed examples of different grounds of discrimination and was to be interpreted as including discrimination on the grounds of "sex", and that s 4 and/or s 5 of the Citizenship Act denied to the respondent by reason of sex her rights under the Constitution. The rights mentioned in the appellants' grounds on his appeal being the respondent's: her right to liberty and/or her right to the protection of the law under s 3 of the Constitution, her right to freedom of movement and immunity from expulsion from Botswana under s 14 of the Constitution, and her protection from subjection to degrading punishment or treatment under s 7 of the Constitution. According to the complaint neither s 4 nor s 5 in fact denied the respondent any of the rights and protections mentioned. Further, the complaint went on, the court *a quo*, having extended the definition of discrimination in s 15(3) of the Constitution, also erred in failing to consider and apply the limitations to the rights and freedoms protected by s 15 of the Constitution which are contained in sub-s 48 (the law of citizenship being a branch of personal law), sub-s (4)(e) and sub-s (9) (to the extent that the Citizenship Act 1984 re-enacts prior laws), or to advert its mind to the special nature of citizenship legislation, and the fact that citizenship was not a right protected under Chapter II of the Constitution, nor was any right "to pass on citizenship" there created or protected. Finally, the complaint stated, the court *a quo* erred in holding that s 4 and s 5 of the Citizenship Act 1984 were discriminatory in their effect or contravened s 15 of the Constitution.

Argument was offered before us on most of the grounds stated above, but rearranged to follow a somewhat different format. Apart from the *locus standi* point, the basic question was whether upon a proper interpretation of Chapter II of the Constitution, the chapter on protection of fundamental rights and freedoms of the individual, especially ss 3, 14, 15 and 18, the constitutional right which the respondent claimed to have been infringed had actually not been infringed with respect to her by ss 4 or 5 of the Citizenship Act 1984. The other submissions were formulated as argument around that central theme.

[Principles of constitutional interpretation]

It will be recalled from her founding affidavit which has been recited above that the respondent complained in the court below that she was prejudiced by s 4(1) of the Citizenship Act 1984 by reason of her being female from passing citizenship to her two children Tumisang and Natasha; that the law in question had discriminatory effect in that her children named were aliens in her own land and the land of their birth, and they thus enjoyed limited rights and legal protections therein; that she believed that the discriminatory effect of specified sections of the Citizenship Act 1984 offended against s 3(a) of the Constitution; and that she believed that the provisions of s 3 had been contravened in relation to herself.

We are here faced with some difficult questions of constitutional interpretation. But our problems are to some extent eased by the fact that not all matters for our consideration were in dispute between the parties: neither party maintained that the Constitution had to be construed narrowly or restrictively. Both parties agreed that a generous approach had to be taken in constitutional interpretation. Both sides also agreed that s 3 of the Constitution was a substantive section conferring rights on the individual. This, in my view, put an end to any possible argument about whether the section was a preamble or not. It also, in my view, totally undermines any judgment based on the premise that s 3 is only a preamble. The sections of the Constitution which arose for construction were also, more or less, agreed.

With regard to the approach to the interpretation of the Constitution, learned counsel for the appellant further drew our attention to the Interpretation Act 1984 which in s 26 provides that:

> 26   Every enactment shall be deemed remedial and for the public good and shall receive
>   such fair and liberal construction as will best attain its object according to its true
>   intent and spirit.

He then submitted that by s 2 of the Act, each provision of the Act applied to every enactment, whether made before, on or after the commencement of the Act, including the Constitution. This section, he submitted, therefore, must be the section which has to be applied to the present case. I agree that the provisions of the Interpretation Act 1984 apply to the interpretation of the Constitution. The section cited, however, is not inconsistent with viewing the Constitution as a special enactment which in many ways differs from the ordinary legislation designed, for example, to establish some public utility or to remedy some identified defect in the body politic.

A written constitution is the legislation or compact which establishes the state itself. It paints in broad strokes on a large canvas the institutions of that state; allocating powers, defining relationships between such institutions and between the institutions and the people within the jurisdiction of the state, and between the people themselves. A Constitution often provides for the protection of the rights and freedoms of the people, which rights and freedoms have thus to be respected in all future state action. The existence and powers of the institutions of state, therefore, depend on its terms. The rights and freedoms, where given by it, also depend on it. No institution can claim to be above the Constitution; no person can make any such claim. The Constitution contains not only the design and disposition of the powers of the state which is being established but embodies the hopes and aspirations of the people. It is a document of immense dimensions, portraying, as it does, the vision of the people's future. The makers of a

Constitution do not intend that it be amended as often as other legislation; indeed, it is not unusual for provisions of the Constitution to be made amendable only by special procedures imposing more difficult forms and heavier majorities of the members of the legislature. By nature and definition, even when using ordinary prescriptions of statutory construction, it is impossible to consider a Constitution of this nature on the same footing as any other legislation passed by a legislature which is itself established, with powers circumscribed, by the Constitution. The object it is designed to achieve evolves with the evolving development and aspirations of its people. In terms of the Interpretation Act 1984, the remedial objective is to chart a future for the people, a liberal interpretation of that objective brings into focus considerations which cannot apply to ordinary legislation designed to fit a specific situation. As Lord Wright put it when dealing with the Australian case of *James v Commonwealth of Australia* [1936] AC 578 at 614:

> It is true that a Constitution must not be construed in any narrow and pedantic sense. The words used are necessarily general, and their full import and true meaning can often only be appreciated when considered, as the years go on, in relation to the vicissitudes of fact which from time to time emerge. It is not that the meaning of the words changes, but the changing circumstances illustrate and illuminate the full import of that meaning.

We in this court, however, are not bereft of previous authority of our own to guide us in our deliberations on the meaning of the Botswana Constitution. The present case does not present us with a first opportunity to explore uncharted waters and to interpret the Constitution free from all judicial authority. We do have some guidance from previous pronouncements of this court as to the approach which we should follow in this matter. In *Attorney General v Moagi* 1981 BLR 1 at 32 Kentridge JA said:

> ... a constitution such as the Constitution of Botswana, embodying fundamental rights, should as far as its language permits be given a broad construction. Constitutional rights conferred without express limitation should not be cut down by reading implicit restrictions into them, so as to bring them into line with the common law.

In *Petrus and Another v The State* [1985] LRC (Const) 699 at 719, [1984] BLR 14 at 34 my brother Aguda JA had occasion to review the courts' approach to constitutional construction. In that review he said at 34:

> It was once thought that there should be no difference in approach to constitutional construction from other statutory interpretation. Given the British system of government and the British judicial set-up, that was understandable, it being remembered that whatever statutes that might have the look of constitutional enactment in Britain, such statutes are nevertheless mere statutes like any others and can be amended or repealed at the will of Parliament. But the position where there is a written Constitution is different.

Aguda JA then cited in support the view of Higgins J in the Australian High Court in *Attorney General for New South Wales v Brewery Employees Union of New South Wales* (1908) 6 CLR 469 at 611–612 that:

> ... although we interpret the words of the Constitution on the same principles of interpretation as we apply to any ordinary law, these very principles of interpretation compel us to take into account the nature and scope of the Act that we are interpreting — to remember that *it is a Constitution, a mechanism under which laws are to be made, and not a mere Act which declares what the law is to be.*

He also cited Sr Udo Uodma of the Supreme Court of Nigeria in *Rafiu Rabiu v State* (1981) 2 NCLR 293 at 326 where that learned judge said:

... the Supreme Law of the Land; that it is a written, organic instrument meant to serve not only the present generation, but also several generations yet unborn ... that the function of the Constitution is to establish a framework and principles of government, broad and general in terms, intended to apply to the varying conditions which the development of our several communities, must involve, ours being a plural, dynamic society, and therefore, more technical rules of interpretation of statues are to some extent inadmissible in a way as to defeat the principles of government enshrined in the Constitution.

Finally, he cited Justice White of the Supreme Court of the United States in *South Dakota v North Carolina* (1940) 192 US 286, 48 L Ed 448 at 465, where the learned judge said:

I take it to be an elementary rule of constitutional construction that no one provision of the Constitution is to be segregated from all others, and to be considered alone, but that all the provisions bearing upon a particular subject are to be brought into view and to be so interpreted as to effectuate the great purpose of the instrument.

Aguda JA concludes his review in the *Petrus* case by saying:[*]

... it is another well known principle of construction that exceptions contained in constitutions are ordinarily to be given strict and narrow, rather than broad, construction. See *Corey v Knight* (1957) Cal App. 2d. 671; 310 p. 2d. 673 at p. 679.

With such pronouncements from our own court as guide, we do not really need to seek outside support for the views we express. But just to show that we are not alone in the approach we have adopted in this country towards constitutional interpretation, I refer to similar *dicta* of judges from various jurisdictions such as Lord Wilberforce in *Minister of Home Affairs and Another v Fisher and Another* [1980] AC 319 at 328–329; Dickson CJ in the Canadian case of *R v Big M Drug Mart Ltd* [1985] 1 SCR 295 at 344; the Namibian case of *Mwandingi v Minister of Defence, Namibia* 1991 (1) SA 851 at 857858; and the Zimbabwe cases of *Hewlett v Minister of Finance and Another* 1982 (1) SA 490 at 495–496 and *Ministry of Home Affairs v Bickle and Others* 1984 (2) SA 439 *per* Georges CJ at 447; United States cases such as *Boyd v United States* 116 US 616 at 635 and *Trop v Dulles* 356 US 86.

In my view these statements of learned judges who have had occasion to grapple with the problem of constitutional interpretation capture the spirit of the document they had to interpret, and I find them apposite in considering the provisions of the Botswana Constitution which we are now asked to construe. The lessons they teach are that the very nature of a Constitution requires that a broad and generous approach be adopted in the interpretation of its provisions; that all the relevant provisions bearing on the subject for interpretation be considered together as a whole in order to effect the objective of the Constitution; and that where rights and freedoms are conferred on persons by the Constitution, derogations from such rights and freedoms should be narrowly or strictly construed.

[Status of section 3 of the Constitution]

It is now necessary to examine the constitutional provision giving rise to the dispute in this case.

Section 3 states that:

Whereas every person in Botswana is entitled to the fundamental rights and freedoms of the individual, that is to say, the right, whatever his race, place of origin, political opinions, colour, creed or sex, but subject to respect for the rights and freedoms of others and for the public interest to each and all of the following, namely:

---

*   *Eds:* see [1985] LRC (Const) 699, at 720.

    (a)   life, liberty, security of the person and the protection of law;

    (b)   freedom of conscience, of expression and of assembly and association; and

    (c)   protection for the privacy of his home and other property and from deprivation of property without compensation,

the provisions of this Chapter shall have effect for the purpose of affording protection to those rights and freedoms subject to such limitations of that protection as are contained in those provisions, being limitations designed to ensure that the enjoyment of the said rights and freedoms by any individual does not prejudice the rights and freedoms of others or the public interest.

The first impression gained from the opening with "whereas" is that s 3 is a preamble. If it were so, different consequences might arise from it when compared with the consequences arising from it being a substantive provision conferring rights on the individual. In section 272 of Bennion on *Statutory Interpretation* the effect of a preamble is given as follows:

The preamble is an optional feature in public general Acts, though compulsory in private Acts. It appears immediately after long title, and states the reason for passing the Act. It may include a recital of the mischief to which the Act is directed. When present, it is thus a useful guide to the legislative intention.

Obviously s 3 is not a preamble to the whole of the Constitution. An argument made that it is a preamble, therefore, would have to limit its operative effect as such, if any, to Chapter II on the Protection of Fundamental Rights and Freedoms of the Individual. Were it a preamble, it would have to be taken as a guide to the intention of the framers of the Constitution in enacting the provisions of that chapter.

    A careful look as the section, however, shows that it was not intended merely as a preamble indicating the legislative intent for the provisions of Chapter II at all. The internal evidence from the structure of the section is against such a interpretation. Although the section begins with "whereas", it accepts that "every person in Botswana is entitled to the fundamental rights and freedoms of the individual ... whatever his race, place of origin, political opinions, colour, creed or sex" is, and continues to enact positively that "the provisions of this Chapter shall have effect for the purpose of affording protection to those rights and freedoms [ie the rights and freedoms itemised in s 3(a), (b) and (c)], subject to such limitations ... as are contained in those provisions [ie the provisions in the whole of Chapter II], being limitations designed to ensure that the enjoyment of the said rights and freedoms by any individual does not prejudice the rights and freedoms of others or the public interest." That positively enacted part of s 3 alone should be sufficient to refute a suggestion that it is a mere preamble. But s 18(1) of the Constitution which finds itself in the same Chapter II put the matter beyond doubt. It provides that:

18(1) Subject to the provisions of subsection (5) of this section, if any person alleges that any of the provisions of sections 3 to 16 (inclusive) of this Constitution has been, is being or is likely to be contravened in relation to him, without prejudice to any other action with respect to the same matter which is lawfully available, that person may apply to the High Court for redress.

If a preamble confers no right but merely provides an aid to the discovery of legislative intention, it is impossible to hold otherwise than that it is clear from s 18(1) that contravention of s 3 leads to enforcement by legal action.

    From the wording of s 3, it seems to me that the section is not only a substantive provision, but that it is the key or umbrella provision in Chapter II under which all rights and freedoms protected under the chapter must be subsumed. Under the section, every person is entitled to the stated fundamental rights and freedoms. Those rights and freedoms are subject to limitations only on two grounds, that is to say, in the first place, "limitations designed to ensure that the enjoyment of the said rights and freedoms by any individual does not prejudice the rights and freedoms of others", and secondly on the ground of "public interest". Those limitations are provided in the provisions of Chapter II itself, which is constituted by ss 3 (but effectively s 4) to 19 of the Constitution.

[Relationship between sections 3 and 5 of the Constitution]

The argument has been advanced that even if rights and freedoms are conferred by s 3, that section makes no mention of discrimination, and therefore, that section does not deal with the question of discrimination at all. Discrimination is mentioned only in s 15 of the Constitution; it is, therefore, that section only which we ought to look at in a case which basically alleges discrimination. But that argument assumes that s 15 is an independent section standing alone in Chapter II of the Constitution. It is only if s 15 is considered as standing on its own, separate and distinct, and conferring new rights unconnected with the rights and freedoms in s 3 that it can be said that s 15 has no connection with s 3. As I have tried to demonstrate by the examination of the wording used in s 3, that assumption cannot be right. The wording is such that the rest of the provisions of Chapter II, other than those dealing with derogations under the general powers exercisable in times of war and emergency in ss 17 and 18, and the interpretation of s 19 of the Constitution, have to be read conjunction with s 3. They must be construed as expanding on or placing limitations on s 3, and be construed within the context of that section. As pointed out before, the wording of s 3 itself shows clearly that whatever exposition, elaboration or limitation is found in ss 4 to 19, must be exposition, elaboration or limitation of the basic fundamental rights and freedoms conferred by s 3. Section 3 encapsulates the sum total of the individual's rights and freedoms under the Constitution in general terms, which may be expanded upon in the expository, elaborating and limiting sections ensuing in the chapter. We are reminded of the lesson that all the provisions of a constitution which have a bearing on a particular interpretation have to be read together. If that is the case then s 15 cannot be taken in isolation as requiring separate treatment from the other relevant provisions of Chapter II, or indeed from those of the rest, of the Constitution.

Support is given to this view by a look at other provisions of Chapter II. A number of rights and freedoms dealt with in s 3 are not specifically referred to in the express terms in which they are later dealt with in the succeeding sections of Chapter II.

Take, for example, s 6 of Chapter II which details the protection against slavery, servitude or forced labour. Section 3 does not specifically mention the words "slavery", "servitude" or "forced labour". But clearly these words can, and in the structure of the Constitution must, be subsumed under some general expression or term in s 3. That section confers the right and freedom to "liberty" and "security of the person". A person who is put in slavery or servitude or made to do forced labour cannot be said to enjoy a right to liberty or security of his person. Infringing s 6 will automatically infringe s 3. Take s 7 of the same Chapter II which gives protection against torture or inhuman or degrading treatment. Section 3 does not specifically mention "torture", "inhuman treatment" or "degrading treatment". But s 3(a) confers the rights to "life, liberty, security of the person and the protection of the law". It would be strange to propound the argument that a person who has been subjected to torture, inhuman or degrading treatment has only his right under s 7 infringed, but that his right to life, liberty, security of the person and the protection of the law remains intact because torture, inhuman or degrading treatment are not specifically mentioned in s 3. The same applies to s 14 which deals with freedom of movement. Again freedom of movement is not mentioned in s 3 although the person deprived of such freedom cannot be said to be enjoying his "liberty" or "security of the person" which are mentioned in s 3.

The United States Constitution makes no specific reference to discrimination as such. Yet several statutes have been held to be in contravention of the Constitution on the ground of discrimination. These cases have been decided on the basis of the 14th Amendment of the Constitution passed in 1868 which forbids any state to "deny to any person within its jurisdiction the equal protection of the laws" (see, for example, *Reed v Reed* 404 US 71, *Craig v Boren, Governor of Oklahoma* 429 US 190, *Abdiel Caba v Kazim Mohammend and Maria Mohammend* 441 US 380) or on the equally wide due process clause in the 5th Amendment passed in 1791 (for example, *Frontiero v Richardson, Secretary of Defence* 411 US 677, *Weinberger, Secretary of Health, Education and Welfare v Wiesenfeld* 420 US 636), or sometimes on both Amendments. In Botswana, when the Constitution, in s 3, provides that "every person … is entitled to the fundamental right and freedoms of the individual", and counts among these rights and freedoms "the protection of the law", that fact must mean that, with all enjoying the rights and freedoms, the protection of the law given by the Constitution must be equal protection. Indeed, the appellant generously agreed that the provision in s 3 should be taken as conferring equal protection of the law on individuals. I see s 3 in that same light. That the word "discrimination" is not mentioned in s 3, therefore, does not mean that discrimination, in the sense of unequal treatment, is not proscribed under the section.

I also conclude from the foregoing that the fact that discrimination is not mentioned in s 3, does not detract from s 3 being the key or umbrella provision conferring rights and freedoms under the Constitution under and in relation to which the other sections in Chapter II merely expound further, elaborate or limit those rights and freedoms. Section 15, which specifically mentions and deals with discrimination, therefore does not, in my view, confer an independent right standing on its own.

[Limitations on the rights and freedoms conferred by section 3 of the Constitution]

One other possible argument may be advanced against s 3 as the section of the Constitution conferring rights and freedoms: it arises from the question whether the proposition can seriously be maintained that the section gives the same right to every person in Botswana. What, it may be asked in this connection, about children? Do they have the same rights and freedoms as adults? What about aliens? Can they claim the same rights and freedoms at citizens? The answer to both questions is, while under the jurisdiction of the State of Botswana, yes, but subject to whatever derogations or limitations may have been placed by specific provisions of the Constitution with respect to them. With regard to a child, s 5 which gives protection against deprivation of personal liberty, for example, makes in sub-s 1(f) an exception by restriction imposed on him "with the consent of his parent or guardian, for his education or welfare during any period ending not later than the date when he attains the age of eighteen years." Section 10(11)(b) places a limitation on the right of persons under the age of eighteen to free access to proceedings in court. The qualifications for the office of President (s 33) places a minimum age of 35 on the capacity to be elected President, and a minimum age limit of 21 years is placed on the capacity for election of a member of Parliament. These are all limitations to his freedoms under the Constitution.

Aliens, on the other hand, have their rights and freedoms curtailed by, for example, s 14(3)(b) which permits "the imposition of restrictions on the freedom of movement of any person who is not a citizen of Botswana"; and by s 15(4)(b) which permits discrimination "with respect to persons who are not citizens of Botswana".

Where other derogations or limitations are made to the general rights and freedoms conferred by s 3 of the Constitution, they are made in ss 4 to 16 or through specific provisions of the Constitution which are inconsistent with the rights or freedoms conferred.

[Extent to which section 15 derogates from section 3]

If my reading of ss 3 to 16 of the Constitution is correct, and if s 3 provides, as I think, equal treatment to all save in so far as derogated from or limited by other sections, the question in this particular case is whether and how s 15 derogates from the rights and freedoms conferred by s 3(a) which requires equal protection of the law to all persons irrespective of sex.

The case made for the appellant in this respect is, to put it succinctly, that s 15 is the section of the Constitution which deals with discrimination; that, significantly, whereas s 3 confers rights and freedoms irrespective of sex, the word "sex" is not mentioned among the identified categories in the definition of "discriminatory" treatment in s 15(3); that the omission of sex is intentional and is made in order to permit legislation in Botswana which is discriminatory on grounds of sex; that discrimination on grounds of sex must be permitted in Botswana society as the society is patrilineal and, therefore, male oriented. The appellant accepts that the Citizenship Act 1984 is discriminatory, but this was intentionally made so in order to preserve the male orientation of the society; that Act, though discriminatory, was not actually intended to be so, its real objective being to promote the male orientation of society and to avoid dual citizenship, the medium for achieving these ends being to make citizenship follow the descent of the child; and that even if the Act were as a result discriminatory, it was not unconstitutional.

[Legislative powers of parliament under a Constitution]

Before I attempt to answer the question whether any of the sections of the Citizenship Act infringe the rights and freedoms conferred by s 3(a), as the respondent has complained that they do, it is necessary that one or two incidental matters put forward in support of the central theme described be disposed of. It was submitted by the appellant that Parliament could enact any law for the peace, order and good government of Botswana, and that the Citizenship Act 1984 was a law based on descent which was required to ensure that the male orientation imperative of Botswana society and the need to avoid dual citizenship be advanced. There is no doubt that the Citizenship Act 1984 is an Act of Parliament. I also accept that an Act of Parliament is presumed to be *intra vires* the Constitution. But it must be added that that presumption is not irrebuttable. The power of Parliament to legislate in the terms propounded is found in s 86 of the Constitution. It is a provision which, I dare say, is found in the constitution of all former colonies and protectorates of Britain, and which gives the legislature the amplitude of power to legislate on all matters necessary for the proper governance of a country. In Britain, the power of Parliament to legislate is uncircumscribed. That fact was what led Philip Herbert, fourth Earl of Pembroke and Montgomery, in a speech at Oxford on 11 April 1648 to say that, "My father said, that a Parliament could do any thing but make a man a woman, and a woman a man". But as we know, when in the 19th century Kay LJ gave a property and mathematical rendition of the same sentiment by saying in *Metropolitan Railway Co v Fowler* [1892] 1 QB 165 at 183 that "Even an Act of Parliament cannot make a freehold estate in land an easement, any more than it could make two plus two equal five", Scrutton LJ *in Taff Vale Railway Co v Cardiff Railway Co* [1917] 1 Ch 199 at 317 countered by saying, "I respectfully disagree with him, and think that "for the purposes of the Act" it can effect both statutory results" (see Megarry *A Second Miscellany-at-Law*). Scrutton LJ's statement is correct because Britain does not live under a written constitution; no piece of legislation by Parliament has primacy over others and Parliament cannot legislate to bind future Parliaments. We, therefore, speak of the supremacy of Parliament in Britain. What the British Parliament has done or is capable of doing is no sure guide to us trying to understand a written constitution. The American revolution which started off the era of written constitutions changed all that. With a written constitution, under which the existence and powers of the legislature are made dependent on the constitution, the power to legislate is circumscribed by the constitution. As s 86 of the Botswana Constitution put it, the power of Parliament "to make laws for the peace, order and good government of Botswana" is "subject to the provisions of the Constitution". Parliament cannot, therefore, legislate to take away or restrict the fundamental rights and freedoms of the individual, unless it is on a subject on which the Constitution has made an exception by giving Parliament power to do so, or the Constitution itself is properly amended. Instead of the supremacy of Parliament, we have, if anything, the supremacy of the Constitution.

As the legislative powers of Parliament in Botswana are limited by the provisions of the Constitution, where the Constitution lays down matters on which Parliament cannot legislate in ordinary form, as it does in Chapter II for example, or guarantees to the people certain rights and freedoms, Parliament has no power to legislate by its normal procedures in contravention or derogation of these prescriptions. This view of a Constitution is, of course, contrary to the law and practice of the British Constitution under which the normal canons of construction of Acts of Parliament are formulated.

Scope of legislative powers to preserve customs and traditions[*]

Our attention has been drawn to the patrilineal customs and traditions of the Botswana people to show, I believe, that it was proper for Parliament to legislate to preserve or advance such customs and traditions. Custom and tradition have never been static. Even then, they have always yielded to express legislation. Custom and tradition must *a fortiori*, and from what I have already said about the pre-eminence of the Constitution, yield to the Constitution of Botswana. A constitutional guarantee cannot be overridden by custom. Of course, the custom will as far as possible be read so as to conform with the Constitution. But where this is impossible, it is custom not the Constitution which must go.

[...]

It seems to me that the argument of the appellant was to some extent influenced by a premise that citizenship must necessarily follow the customary or traditional systems of the people. I do not think that view is supported by the development of the law relating to citizenship.

[...]

---

[*]   *Eds:* this section of the judgment, which deals with the development of the concept of citizenship generally and in the context of Botswana, has been abridged.

Although it is possible that citizenship should by municipal law be based on descent or guardianship, there is no historical reason for compelling any state to so base it citizenship laws, especially where there is some serious obstacle like a constitutional guarantee in the way. ... I find, therefore, no necessary nexus mandating that citizenship should be based on traditional or customary ideas of descent or guardianship.

[...]

Of course in modern states, it is the municipal law which determines the citizenship of the individual. The legislature may choose which prescription to follow. The basis may be birth to parents who are themselves citizens irrespective of where the child is born, or may be birth with the territorial jurisdiction, while yet a third course may have a mixture of both. There may be other prescriptions. It is all a matter for the state legislature. But whatever course municipal law adopts must comply with two prerequisites: it must, in the first place, conform to the Constitution of the state in question, and secondly it must conform to international law. For as Oppenheim points out, at pp 643–644, "while it is for each State to determine under its law who are nationals, such law must be recognised by other States only in so far as it is consistent with international conventions, international custom, and the principles of law generally recognised with regard to nationality". As he points out by way of example, a state which imposes its nationality upon aliens residing for a brief period in its territory or upon persons resident abroad, may not have the privilege so conferred accepted by other members of the international community.

[...]

As far as the present case is concerned, the more important prerequisite which each legislation must comply with is the requirement that the legislative formula chosen must not infringe the provisions of the Constitution. It cannot be correct that because the legislature is entitled to lay down the principles of citizenship, it should, in doing so, flout the provisions of the constitution under which it operates. Where legislature is confronted with passing a law on citizenship, its only course is to adopt a prescription which complies with the imperatives of the Constitution, especially those which confer fundamental rights on individuals in the State.

[Discrimination on the grounds of sex: scope of section 15 of the Constitution]

With those considerations in mind, I come now to deal with the central question, namely, whether s 15 of the Constitution allows discrimination on the ground of sex. The provisions of the section which are for the moment relevant to this issue are sub-ss (1), (2), (3) and (4). They state as follows:

15(1) Subject to the provision of subsections 4, 5 and 7 of this section, no law shall make any provision that is discriminatory either of itself or in its effect.

(2) Subject to the provisions of subsections 6, 7 and 8 of this section, no person shall be treated in a discriminatory manner by any person acting by virtue of any written law or in the performance of the functions of any public office or any public authority.

(3) In this section, the expression "discriminatory" means affording different treatment to different persons, attributable wholly or mainly to their respective descriptions by race, tribe, place of origin, political opinions, colour or creed whereby persons of one such description are subjected to disabilities or restrictions to which persons of another such description are not made subject or accorded privileges or advantages which are not accorded to persons of another such description.

(4) Subsection 1 of this section shall not apply to any law so far as that law makes provision:

    (a) for the appropriation of public revenues or other public funds;

    (b) with respect to persons who are not citizens of Botswana;

    (c) with respect to adoption, marriage, divorce, burial, devolution of property on death or other matters of personal law;

    (d) for the application in the case of members of a particular race, community or tribe of customary law with respect to any matter whether to the exclusion of any law in respect to that matter which is applicable in the case of other persons or not;

    (e) whereby persons of any such description as it mentioned in subsection 3 of this section may be subjected to any disability or restriction or may be accorded any privilege or advantage which, having regard to its nature and to special circumstances pertaining to these persons or to persons of any other such description, is reasonably justifiable in a democratic society.

Subsection (1) mandates that "no law shall make any provision that is discriminatory either of itself or in its effect." Subsection (2) mandates that "no person shall be treated in a discriminatory manner by any person acting by virtue of any written law or in the performance of the functions of any public office or any public authority." Subsection (3) then defines what discriminatory means in this section. It is:

> ... affording different treatment to different persons, attributable wholly or mainly to their respective descriptions by race, tribe, place of origin, political opinions, colour or creed whereby persons of one such description are subjected to disabilities or restrictions to which persons of another such description are not made subject or accorded privileges or advantages which are not accorded to persons of another such description.

The word "sex" is not included in the categories mentioned. According to the appellant, therefore, "sex" had been intentionally omitted from the definition in s 15(3) of the Constitution so as to accommodate, subject to the fundamental rights protected by s 3 thereof, the patrilineal structure of Botswana society, in terms of the common law, the customary law, and statute law.

If that is so, the next question is whether the definition in s 15(3) in any way affects anything stated in s 3 of the Constitution. We must always bear in mind that s 3 confers on the individual the right to equal treatment of the law. That right is conferred irrespective of the person's sex. The definition in s 15(3) on the other hand is expressly stated to be valid "in this section". In that case, how can it be said that the right which is expressly conferred is abridged by a provision which in a definition for the purposes of another section of the Constitution merely omits to mention sex? I know of no principle of construction in law which says that a fundamental right conferred by the Constitution on an individual can be circumscribed by a definition in another section for the purposes of that other section. Giving the matter the most generous interpretation that I can muster, I find it surprising that such a limitation could be made, especially where the manner of limitation claimed is the omission of a word in a definition in that other section which is valid only for that section. What the legal position, however, is, is not that the courts should give the matter a generous interpretation but that they should regard limitations to fundamental rights and freedoms strictly.

If one comes imploring the court for a declaration that his or her right under s 3 of the Constitution has been infringed on the ground that, as a male or female, unequal protection of the law has been accorded to him or her as compared to members of the other gender, the court cannot drive that person away empty-handed with the answer that a definition in s 15 of the Constitution does not mention sex so his or her right conferred under s 3 has not been infringed. How can the right to equal protection of the law under s 3 be amended or qualified by an omission in a definition for the purposes of s 15? We are told that the answer lies in an application of the rule of construction *expressio unius exclusio alterius*.

Before testing the validity of that maxim in this case, I think we should examine further the manner in which limitations on the fundamental rights and freedoms of Chapter II of the Constitution are set out in the Constitution itself. A number of sections in the chapter make exceptions or place limitations on the rights and freedoms conferred. A close reading of the provisions of the chapter discloses that whenever a provision wishes to state an exception or limitation to a described right or freedom, it does so expressly in a form which is bold and clear. In some cases the form of words used occurs so frequently that it can even be characterised as a formula. In s 4(2) the protection of the right to life is limited by:

> 4(2) A person shall not be regarded as having been deprived of his life in contravention to subsection (1) of this section if he dies as the result of the use, to such extent and in such circumstances as are permitted by law, of such force as is reasonably justified:
>
> (a) for the defence of any person from violence or for the defence of property ...

In s 6(3) the protection from slavery, servitude and forced labour is limited by:

> 6(3) For the purposes of this section, the expression "forced labour" does not include:
>
> (b) any labour required in consequence of the sentence or order of a court ...

In s 7(2) the protection from inhuman treatment is limited by:

> 7(2) Nothing contained in or done under the authority of any law shall be held to be inconsistent with or in contravention of this section to the extent that the law in question authorizes the infliction of any description of punishment that was lawful in the former Protectorate of Bechuanaland immediately before the coming into operation of this Constitution.

The expression "Nothing contained in or done under the authority of any law shall be held to be inconsistent with or in contravention ... of this section to the extent that the law authorizes or makes provision for", in particular, is often used to create the required exceptions. It is again used in s 8(5) with respect to the protection from deprivation of property; in s 9(2) with respect to the limitations on the protection for privacy of home and other property; in s 10(12) with respect to limitations to the provisions to secure protection of law; in s 11(5) with respect to limitations on the protection of freedom of conscience; in s 12(2) with respect to limitations on the protection of freedom of expression; in s 13(2) with respect to the limitation to the protection of freedom of assembly and association; and in s 14(3) with respect to the limitation on the protection of freedom of movement. Section 16(1), which gives a general and comprehensive power to derogate from fundamental rights and freedoms in time of war or where a state of emergency has been declared under s 17, uses a variation of the formula.

Even s 15 follows that pattern. As we have seen, sub-s (1) proscribes laws which make any provision which is discriminatory either of itself or in its effect, and sub-s (2) proscribes discriminatory treatment in actions under any law or public office or authority. Then sub-s (4) places the limitations on that proscription. It opens by saying "Subsection (1) of this section shall not apply to any law so far as that law makes provision" and proceeds to itemise the provisions which are exempted from the application of sub-ss 15(1) and (2). Then in sub-s (5) a limitation is placed on the protection from discrimination with respect to qualifications for service as a public officer etc by the use of what has been described before as the formula "Nothing contained in any law shall be held to be inconsistent with or in contravention of subsection (1) of this section." And in sub-s (9), where savings are made from the protection with respect to laws in force immediately before the coming into force of the Constitution or to written laws repealed and re-enacted, a variation of the same formula is used.

If the makers of the Constitution had intended that equal treatment of males and females be excepted from the application of sub-ss 15(1) or (2), I feel confident, after the examination of these provisions, that they would have adopted one of the express exclusion forms of words that they had used in this very same section and in the sister sections referred to. I would expect that, just as s 3 boldly states that every person is entitled to the protection of the law irrespective of sex, in other words giving a guarantee of equal protection, s 15 in some part would also say, again equally expressly, that for the purposes of maintaining the patrilineal structure of the society, or for whatever reason the framers of the Constitution thought necessary, discriminatory laws or treatment may be passed for or meted to men or women. Nowhere in the Constitution is this done. Nowhere is it mentioned that its objective is the preservation of the patrilineal structure of the society. But I am left to surmise that the Constitution intended sex-based legislation by the omission of the word "sex" from s 15(3) and that the reason for the word's omission was to preserve the patrilineal structure of the society. I find it a startling proposition. If that were so, is it not extraordinary that equal protection is conferred irrespective of sex at all by s 3? What is even more serious is that s 15 would then, under sub-s (1), permit not only the making of laws which are discriminatory on the basis of sex, but under sub-s (2) it would permit the treatment of people in a discriminatory manner by "any person acting by virtue of any written law or in the performance of the functions of any public office or any public authority." Does this mean that differential treatment is permissible under the Constitution by any person in the performance of any public office or any public authority depending on whether the person being dealt with is a man or a woman? That interpretation boggles the mind.

Faced with the remarkable consistency in the manner in which the Constitution makes exceptions to or places limitations on the protections that it grants, I have the greatest difficulty in accepting that the Constitution chose only the all important question of sex discrimination to make its desired exception by omission in a definition. Why did the framers of the Constitution choose, in this most crucial issue of sex-based discrimination, required to preserve the male orientation of traditional society, to leave the matter to this method? Why did they make the discovery of their intention on this vital question dependent on an aid to construction, an aid which is not conclusive in its application, when in other cases desired exclusions had been so boldly and expressly stated? I can find no satisfactory answers to these questions. My difficulty is further compounded when I consider that this omission in the definition is expected not only to exclude "sex" from a protection conferred in s 15 but also to actually limit or qualify a right expressly conferred by s 3, the basic and umbrella provision for the protection of fundamental rights and freedoms under the Constitution.

The application of the *expressio unius* principle to statutory interpretation in Botswana, which has to compete for supremacy in this case with conclusions derived from the positive internal evidence of the Constitution itself as to how it makes exceptions when desired, is, according to the argument of the appellant, provided for by s 33 of the Interpretation Act 1984 which states that:

33 Where an enactment qualifies a general expression by providing that it shall include a number of particular matters or things, any matter of thing which is not expressly included is by implication excluded from the meaning of the general expression.

It is true that "sex" is omitted from the categories mentioned in the definition in s 15(3) of the Constitution. But even if that definition through the omission qualifies any general expression found in the subsection, it appears to me that it does not qualify any general expression in s 3, which is the section under which the respondent complained. Nevertheless, as the appellant submits that the respondent could challenge the provisions of the Citizenship Act, if at all, only on the ground that her rights under s 15 of the Constitution have been contravened, the *expression unius* principle calls for examination. In any event, s 24(2) of the Interpretation Act 1984 admits all aids to the construction of an enactment in dispute when it provides that:

> 24(2) The aids to construction referred to in this section [i.e. those dealing with what material could be used by a court as an aid to construction] are in addition to any other accepted aid.

The occasions on which the *expressio unius* principle applies are summarised in *Bennion on Statutory Interpretation* at p 844 as:

> ... it is applied where a statutory proposition might have covered a number of matters but in fact mentions only some of them. Unless these are mentioned merely as examples, or *ex abundanti cautela*, or for some other sufficient reason, the rest are taken to be excluded from the proposition ... it also applied where a formula which in itself may or may not include a certain class is accompanied by words of *extension* naming only some members of that class. The remaining members of the class are then taken to be excluded. Again the principle may apply where an item is mentioned in relation to one matter but not in relation to another equally eligible.

The competing claims in this case are that the omission was deliberate and intended to exclude sex-based discrimination, the alternative being that the omission was neither intentional nor made with the object of excluding sex-based discrimination. I have already shown how exclusions from the protections in the fundamental rights chapter of the Constitution have in other cases been made. The method is wholly against the argument based on the application of the *exclusio unius* principle. Further, when the categories mentioned in ss 3 and 15(3) of the Constitution are compared, it will be seen that they do not exactly match. Not only is "sex" omitted from the definition in s 15(3) although it appears in s 3, but "tribe" is added to the definition in s 15(3) so that it reads, "race, tribe, place of origin, political opinions, colour or creed", although "tribe" does not appear in s 3. The appellant explained the addition of "tribe" on the ground that it was specifically included because of the concern that the framers of the Constitution had for possible discrimination on that ground. That indicates that the classes were mentioned in order to highlight some vulnerable groups or classes that might be affected by discriminatory treatment. I find this conforming more to mention of the class or group being *ex abundanti cautela* rather than with the intention to exclude from cover under s 15 a class upon which rights had been conferred by s 3. Here, as Bennion points out at p 850, the ruling is *abundans cautela non nocet* (abundance of caution does not harm) (see the Canadian case of *Docksteader v Clark* (1903) 11 BCR 37, cited by E A Driedger in *The Construction of Statutes*). I do not think that the framers of the Constitution intended to declare in 1966 that all potentially vulnerable groups or classes who would be affected for all time by discriminatory treatment have been identified and mentioned in the definition in s 15(3). I do not think that they intended to declare that the categories mentioned in that definition were forever closed. In the nature of things, as far-sighted people trying to look into the future, they would have contemplated that with the passage of time not only the groups of classes which had caused concern at the time of writing the Constitution but other groups or classes needing protection would arise. The categories might grow or change. In that sense, the classes or groups itemised in the definition would be, and in my opinion, are by way of example of what the framers of the Constitution thought worth mentioning as potentially some of the most likely areas of possible discrimination.

I am fortified in this view by the fact that other classes or groups with respect to which discrimination would be unjust and inhuman and which, therefore, should have been included in the definition were not. A typical example is the disabled. Discrimination wholly or mainly attributable to them as a group as such would, in my view, offend as much against s 15 as discrimination against any group or class. Discrimination based wholly or mainly on language or geographical divisions within Botswana would similarly be offensive, although not mentioned. Arguably religion is different from creed, but although creed is mentioned, religion is not. Incidentally, it should also be noticed, that although the definition mentions "race" and "tribe", it does not mention "community", yet the limitation placed on s 15(1) by s 15(4) refers to "a particular race, community or tribe." All these lead me to the conclusion that the words included in the definition are more by way of example than as an exclusive itemisation. The main thrust of that definition in s 15(3) is that discrimination means affording different treatment to different persons wholly or mainly attributable to their respective characteristic groups. Then, of course, s 15(4) comes in to state the exceptions when such differential treatment is acceptable under the Constitution. I am, therefore, in agreement with the learned judge *a quo* when he says that the classes or groups mentioned in s 15(3) are by way of example.

On the basis of the appellant's argument, the legislature relying on the omission of "sex" in s 15(3), could, for example legislate that the women of Botswana shall have no vote. Legislation in Botswana may also provide in that case that no woman shall be President or be a member of Parliament. The appellant states that the legislature will not do that because there will be no rational basis for it, and in any case it will not, under s 15(4)(e), be reasonably justifiable in a democratic society. But is not the basis for such legislation the same as the preservation of the patrilineal structure of the society which, as has been urged, led to the deliberate omission of "sex" in the definition of discrimination? In any case, the appellant cannot, for this purpose, take advantage of the exception provided in s 15(4)(e) which permits discrimination which is reasonably justifiable in a democratic society to support his argument on the rationality of the basis of the legislation, because in the first place that would be using the exception for purposes directly opposite to what was intended, and secondly, on his own argument, if "sex" is deliberately left out of the definition of discrimination in sub-s (3) in order to perpetuate the patrilineal society, it is left out for all purposes of s 15, including the provisions of sub-s (4)(e). That provision in s 15(4)(e) expressly refers to "persons of any description as is mentioned in subsection (3) of this section ...". That, by the argument of the appellant, cannot include anything done on the basis of the sex of the person.

Fundamental rights are conferred on individuals by Constitutions, not on the basis of the track records of governments of a state. If that were the criterion, fundamental rights need not be put in the Constitution of a state which is known for the benevolent actions of its government. In any event, if the Constitution is the basic or founding document of the particular state, that state would have no track record for anyone to go by. In the best of all possible worlds, entrenchment of fundamental rights in a Constitution should not be necessary. All that these rights require in such state would be accorded as a matter of course by the government. Fundamental rights are conferred on the basis that, irrespective of the government's nature or predilections, the individual should be able to assert his rights and freedoms without reliance on its goodwill or courtesy. It is protection against possible tyranny, oppression or deprivations of those self same rights. A fundamental right or freedom once conferred by the Constitution can only be taken away or circumscribed by an express and unambiguous statement in that Constitution or by a valid amendment of it. It cannot be taken away or circumscribed by inference. It is for these reasons that I find it difficult to accept the argument of the appellant which asks us to infer from the omission of the word "sex" in the definition of discrimination in s 15(3) that the right to equal protection of the law given in s 3 of the Constitution to all persons has, in the case of sex-based differentiation in equality of treatment, been taken away.

Questions as to whether every act of differentiation between classes or group amounts to discrimination and what categories of persons are protected under s 15 may arise. If the categories of groups or classes mentioned in s 15(3) are but examples, where does one draw the line as to the categories to be included? Of course, treatment of different sexes based on biological differences cannot be taken as discrimination in the sense that s 15(3) proscribes. With regard to the classes which are protected, it would be wrong to lay down any hard and fast rules. The vulnerable classes identified in ss 3 and 15 are well known. I would add that not only the classes mentioned in the definition in s 15(3), but, for example, the class also mentioned in sub-s (4)(d), where it speaks of "community" in addition to "race" and "tribe" has to be taken as vulnerable. Civilised society requires that different treatment should not be given to people wholly or mainly on the ground of membership of the designated classes or groups. But as has been shown with respect to race and gender based discrimination the development of thought and conduct on these matters may take years. One feels a sense of outrage that there was a time when a Chief Justice of the United States would say, as did Taney CJ in *Dred Scott v Sanford* 19 How 393 (1857):

> The question then arises, whether the provisions of the Constitution, in relation to personal rights and privileges to which the citizen of a state should be entitled, embraced the negro African race, at that time in this country ... In the opinion of the court, the legislation and histories of the times, and the language used in the Declaration of Independence, show, that neither the class of persons who had been imported as slaves, nor their descendants, whether they had become free or not, were then acknowledged as part of the people, nor intended to be included in the general words used in that memorable instrument ... They had for more than a century before been regarded as beings of an inferior order; and altogether unfit to associate with the white race, either in social or political relations; and so far inferior, that they had no rights which the white man was bound to respect; and that the negro might justly and lawfully be reduced to slavery for his benefit ... This opinion was at that time fixed and universal in the civilised portion of the white race. It was regarded as an axiom in morals as well as in politics, which no one thought of disputing, or supposed to be open to dispute; and men in every grade and position in society daily and habitually acted upon it in their private pursuits, as well as in matters of public concern, without doubting for a moment the correctness of this opinion.

Today, it is universally accepted that discrimination on the ground of race is an evil. It is within the memory of men still living today in some countries that women were without a vote and could not acquire degrees from institutions of higher learning, and were otherwise discriminated against in a number of ways. Yet today the comity of nations speaks clearly against discrimination against women. Changes occur. The only general criterion which could be put forward to identify the classes or groups is what to the right-thinking man is outrageous treatment only or mainly because of membership of that class or group and what the comity of nations has come to adopt as unacceptable behaviour.

[...]*

[Relevance of international treaties as an aid to interpretation]

The learned judge *a quo* referred to the international obligations of Botswana in his judgment in support of his decision that sex-based discrimination was forbidden under the Constitution. That was objected to by the appellant. But by the law of Botswana, relevant international treaties and conventions, may be referred to as an aid to interpretation. We noticed this in our earlier citation of s 24 of the Interpretation Act 1984 which stated that, "as an aid to the construction of the enactment a court may have regard to ... any relevant international treaty, agreement or convention ...". The appellant conceded that international treaties and conventions may be used as an aid to interpretation. His objection to the use by the learned judge *a quo* of the African Charter on Human and People's Rights, the Convention for the Protection of Human Rights and Freedoms, and the Declaration on the Elimination of Discrimination against Women, was founded on two grounds. In the first place, he argued that none of them had been incorporated into the domestic law by legislation, although international treaties became part of the law only when so incorporated. According to this argument, of the treaties referred to by the learned judge *a quo*, Botswana had ratified only the African Charter on Human and People's Rights, but had not incorporated it into domestic law. That, the appellant admitted, however, did not deny that particular charter the status of an aid to interpretation. The appellant's second objection was that treaties were only of assistance in interpretation when the language of the statute under consideration was unclear. But the meaning of both s 15(3) of the Constitution and ss 4 and 5 of the Citizenship Act 1984 was quite clear, and, therefore, no interpretative aids were required.

I agree that the meaning of the questioned provisions of the Citizenship Act 1984 is clear. But from the strenuous efforts that the appellant has made in justification of his interpretation of s 15(3) of the Constitution his claim that the meaning of that subsection is clear seems more doubtful. The problem before us is one of discrimination on the basis of sex under the Constitution. Why, one may ask, do ss 3 and 15 of the Constitution apparently say contradictory things? It is the provisions of the Constitution itself which give rise to the difficulty of interpretation, if any, not the Citizenship Act 1984. What we have to look at when trying to determine the intentions of the framers of the Constitution, the ethos, the environment, which the framers thought Botswana was entering into by its acquisition of statehood, and what, if anything, can be found likely to have contributed to the formulation of their intentions in the Constitution that they made. Botswana was, at the time the Constitution was promulgated, about to enter the comity of nations. What could have been the intentions and expectations of the framers of its Constitution? It is to be recalled that Maisels P in the *Petrus* case, referred to earlier, at 714–715 said in this connection that:

> ... Botswana is a member of a comity of civilised nations and the rights and freedoms of its citizens are entrenched in its constitution which is binding on the legislature.

The comity of civilised nations was the international society into which Botswana was about to enter at the time its Constitution was drawn up. Lord Wilberforce in the case of

---

* **Eds:** the text which has been omitted relates to a number of peripheral points taken by the appellant in his grounds of appeal, but not developed before the Court.

Minister of Home Affairs (Bermuda) and Another v Fisher and Another [1980] AC 319 at
328–329 spoke of this international environment acting as one of the contributory
influences which fashioned and informed the approach of the framers of the
Constitution of Bermuda in words which could, with slight modification, have been
written equally for Botswana. He said:

> Here, however, we are concerned with a Constitution, brought in force certainly by Act of
> Parliament, the Bermuda Constitution Act 1967 of the United Kingdom, but established by
> a self-contained document ... It can be seen that this instrument has certain special
> characteristics. 1. It is, particularly in Chapter I, drafted in a broad and ample style which
> lays down principles of width and generality. 2. Chapter I is headed "Protection of
> Fundamental Rights and Freedoms of the Individual". It is known that this chapter, as
> similar portions of other constitutional instruments drafted in the post-colonial period,
> starting with the Constitution of Nigeria, and including the constitutions of most
> Caribbean territories, was greatly influenced by the European Convention for the
> Protection of Human Rights and Fundamental Freedoms (1953) ... That Convention was
> signed and ratified by the United Kingdom and applied to dependent territories including
> Bermuda. It was in turn influenced by the United Nations Universal Declaration of
> Human Rights of 1948. These antecedents, and the form of Chapter I itself, call for a
> generous interpretation, avoiding what has been called "the austerity of tabulated
> legalism," suitable to give to individuals the full measure of the fundamental rights and
> freedoms referred to.

The antecedents of the Constitution of Botswana with regard to the imperatives of the
international community could not have been any different from the antecedents found
by Lord Wilberforce in the case of Bermuda. Article 2 of the Universal Declaration of
Human Rights of 1948 states that:

> Everyone is entitled to all the rights and freedoms set forth in this Declaration, without
> distinction of any kind, such as race, colour, sex, language, religion, political or other
> opinion, national or social origin, property, birth or other status.

The British government must have subscribed to this Declaration on behalf of itself and
all dependent territories, including Bechuanaland, long before Botswana became a state.
And it must have formed part of the backdrop of aspirations and desires against which
the framers of the Constitution of Botswana formulated its provisions.

Article 2 of the African Charter on Human and People's Rights provide that:

> Every individual shall be entitled to the enjoyment of the rights and freedoms recognized
> and guaranteed in the present Charter without distinction of any kind such as race, ethnic
> group, colour, sex, language, religion, political or any other opinion, national and social
> origin, fortune, birth or other status.

Then paras 1 and 2 of art 12 state that:

1 Every individual shall have the right to freedom of movement and residence within
   the borders of a State provided he abides by the law.

2 Every individual shall have the right to leave any country including his own, and
   return to his country. This right may only be subject to restriction, provided for by law
   for the protection of national security, law and order, public health and morality.

Botswana is a signatory to this Charter. Indeed it would appear that Botswana is one of
the credible prime movers behind the promotion and supervision of the Charter. The
learned judge *a quo* made reference to Botswana's obligations under such treaties and
conventions. Even if it is accepted that those treaties and conventions do not confer
enforceable rights on individuals within the state until Parliament has legislated its
provisions into the law of the land, in so far as such relevant international treaties and

conventions may be referred to as an aid to construction of enactments, including the Constitution, I find myself at a loss to understand the complaint made against their use in that manner in the interpretation of what no doubt are some difficult provisions of the Constitution. The reference made by the learned judge *a quo* to these materials amounted to nothing more than that. What he had said was ([1991] LRC (Const) 574 at 586):

> I am strengthened in my view by the fact that Botswana is a signatory to the OAU Convention on Non-Discrimination. I bear in mind that signing the Convention does not give it the power of law in Botswana but the effect of the adherence by Botswana to the Convention must show that a construction of the section which does not do violence to the language but is consistent with and in harmony with the Convention must be preferable to a narrow construction which results in a finding that s 15 of the Constitution permits unrestricted discrimination on the basis of sex.

That does not seem to me to be saying that the OAU Convention, or by its proper name the African Charter of Human and People's Rights, is binding within Botswana as is legislation passed by its Parliament. The learned judge said that we should so far as is possible so interpret domestic legislation so as not to conflict with Botswana's obligations under the charter or other international obligations. Indeed, my brother Aguda JA referred in his judgment to the Charter and other international conventions in a similar light in the *Petrus* case [1985] LRC (Const) 699 at 721–722, [1984] BLR 14 at 27. I am in agreement that Botswana is a member of the community of civilised states which has undertaken to abide by certain standards of conduct, and, unless it is impossible to do otherwise, it would be wrong for its courts to interpret its legislation in a manner which conflicts with the international obligations Botswana has undertaken. This principle, used as an aid to construction as is quite permissible under s 24 of the Interpretation Act 1984, adds reinforcement to the view that the intention of the framers of the Constitution could not have been to permit discrimination purely on the basis of sex.

[Locus Standi]

I now come to the submission on *locus standi*. I have left the point until the end because like the appellant who himself admitted in his submissions that, "This is a case where in view of the 'circularity' of some of the arguments, it may be necessary for the court to consider the merits before coming to a conclusion on the *locus standi*", I feel that it could not have been determined without first going into the merits. With respect to the point, the appellant argued that the court *a quo* erred in holding that the respondent had *locus standi* to ask it to pass on either ss 4 or 5 of the Citizenship Act 1984. The appellant, it was submitted, is a practising lawyer, who on marrying on 7 March 1984, freely married into an existing citizenship regime carrying with it all the consequences referred to by the judge *a quo*, namely, that not only her husband but her children by the marriage were liable to be expelled from Botswana, and that if her husband were to decide to leave both Botswana and herself, the children, assuming that they were left behind, could only continue to live in Botswana if granted residence permits. She was, went on the argument, at the time of her marriage exercising her right to liberty, and could not now be heard to complain of a consequence which she had consciously invited. Nor could she rely on the choice she freely made as an infringement of her rights which should confer jurisdiction under s 18 of the Constitution. In any event, the appellant argued, there was no threat or likelihood of it alleged by the respondent of expulsion of her husband, who had been in Botswana for 15 or more years, and potential adverse consequences of a speculative nature were not sufficient to confer *locus standi* under s 18. Section 5 of the Citizenship Act 1984, the appellant argued, had no relevance at all to the respondent; the argument advanced that she was still of child-bearing age and might choose to have another child outside Botswana was too remote for consideration.

And in the case of her present children, it was submitted that there were strong reasons for holding that she was not sufficiently closely affected by any action taken against them as a result of s 4 of the Act of 1984 to enable her to claim that the provisions of the Constitution were being or likely to be contravened in relation to her by such action as required by s 18.

I do not think a person should be prejudiced in the enjoyment of his or her constitutional rights just because that person is a lawyer.

On the *locus* point, the appellant further argued that the *popularis actio* of Roman law, which gave an individual a right of action in matters of public interest, was not a part of Roman-Dutch common law. The principle of our law being that a private individual must sue on his own behalf; the right he sought to enforce must be available to him personally, or the injury for which he or she claimed redress must be sustained or apprehended by himself. The cases of *Darymple v Colonial Treasurer* 1910 TS 372, *Director of Education, TVL v McCagie and others* 1918 AD 616 at 621, *Veriava v President of SA Medical and Dental Council* 1985 (2) SA 293 at 315 and *Cabinet of the Transitional Government of SWA v Eins* 1988 (3) SA 369 were cited as authorities to show that s 18 of the Constitution reflected this principle when it provided that the wrong (ie the actual threatened contravention of the relevant sections) must be in relation to the applicant. But the point made by those authorities has been distinguished in cases affecting the liberty of the subject by the South African Appellate Division in *Wood and Others v Ondangwa Tribal Authority and Another* 1975 (2) SA 294 at 310 where Rumpff CJ, after analysing the proposition that the *actio popularis* did not apply in Roman-Dutch law, said:

> Nevertheless, I think it follows from what I have said above, that although the *actiones populares* generally have become obsolete in the sense that a person is not entitled "to protect the rights of the public", or "champion the cause of the people" it does not mean that when the liberty of a person is to stake, the interest of the person who applies for the interdict *de libero homine exhibendo* should be narrowly construed. On the contrary, in my view it should be widely construed because illegal deprivation of liberty is a threat to the very foundation of a society based on law and order.

I need not, however, go into these cases in detail. Section 18 speaks for itself. I have recited the relevant provisions in sub-s (1) earlier on in this judgment. It says that "if any person alleges that any of the provisions of sections 3 to 16 (inclusive) of this Constitution has been, is being or is likely to be contravened in relation to him", that person may apply to the High Court for redress. The section shows that the applicant must "allege" that one of the named sections of the Constitution has been, is being or is likely to be infringed in respect of him. He must therefore sue only for acts or threats to himself. But the section does not say that the applicant must establish as a matter of proof that any of these things has or is likely to happen to him. The meaning of "allege" is "declare to be the case, especially without proof" or "advance as an argument or excuse" (see *Concise Oxford Dictionary* (8th edn, 1990)). I believe that in the context of s 18(1), it is the earlier of the two meanings that the word has. Of course, the allegation to enable the applicant to seek the aid of the courts must not be frivolous or without some foundation. But that is not the same thing as a requirement to establish positively. In my opinion, we here see an example of a case where constitutional rights should not be whittled down by principles derived from the common law, whether Roman-Dutch, English or Botswana. Under s 18 (1), an applicant has the right to come before the courts for redress if he declares with some foundation of fact that the breach he complains of has, is in the process of being or is likely to be committed in respect of him. Where a person comes requesting the aid of the courts to enforce a constitutional right, therefore, the question which has to be asked in order that the courts might listen to the merits of his case is whether he makes the required allegation with reasonable foundation. If that is shown the courts ought to hear him. Any more rigid test would deny persons their rights on some purely technical grounds. In this connection I refer to a parallel situation in the case of *Craig v Boren* (*supra*) in which the United States Supreme Court at 194 demonstrated, on the point of *locus*, to bring a constitutional challenge on the ground of discrimination, that persons not directly affected within the class discriminated against could bring the action if they could show that they were or could be adversely affected by the application of the law. In that case, the question was whether a law prohibiting the sale of "non-intoxicating" 3.2% beer to males under the age of twenty-one and to females under the age of eighteen constituted gender-based discrimination that denied males between eighteen and twenty years of age the equal protection of the laws. The court held that a licensed vendor of the beer had standing to challenge the law.

Did the applicant allege that her constitutional right had been, was being, or was likely to be infringed? That question I now proceed to answer in the case of the respondent. We recall from the paragraphs of her founding affidavit which are recited in the earlier part of this judgment that after setting out what she believed to be the constitutional provisions which had been infringed, she continued in para 19 thereof to state that as set out above she verily believed that "the provisions of section 3 of the Constitution had been contravened in relation to myself". I do not think the allegation could be clearer.

Has the allegation some basis of truth? No doubt due to a mixture of some adventitious claims made by her with respect to her husband, who is without doubt an alien and could under the Constitution be placed under some disabilities, her case seems to have been misunderstood. It was, for example, argued by the appellant that the Citizenship Act 1984 laid down how citizenship should be acquired and taken away, and therefore, for a person to attack the Act of 1984 he or she must be shown to be a person who did not enjoy the rights of citizenship, not one, like respondent who was enjoying full rights of citizenship. In this case, the respondent's children might, according to the argument, have been affected by the Citizenship Act 1984, not herself. But the Citizenship Act 1984, although defining who should be a citizen, had consequences which affect a person's right to come into, live in and go out of this country, when he likes. Such consequences may primarily affect the person declared not to be a citizen. But there could be circumstances where such consequences would extend to others. In such circumstances, the courts are not entitled to look at life in a compartmentalised form, with the misfortunes and disabilities of one always kept separate and sanitised from the misfortunes and disabilities of others.

The case which I understand the respondent to make is that due to the disabilities under which her children were likely to be placed in her own country of birth by the provisions of the Citizenship Act 1984, her own freedom of movement protected by s 14 of the Constitution was correspondingly likely to be infringed and that gave her the right under s 18(1) to come to court to test the validity of the Act. What she says is that it is her freedom which has been circumscribed by the disabilities placed on her children. If there is any substance to the allegation, the courts ought to hear her. The argument that a mother's relationship to her children is entirely emotional and that an emotional feeling cannot found a legal right does not sound right to me. Nor am I impressed by the argument that a mother has no responsibility towards a child because it is only the guardian who has a responsibility recognised by law, and in Botswana, that guardian is the father. The very Constitution which all in Botswana must revere recognises a parent's, as distinct from the guardian's, responsibility towards the child. Recall that s 5(1)(f) states that:

> 5(1) No person shall be deprived of his personal liberty save as may be authorised by law in any of the following cases, that is to say ...
>
>   (f)   under order of a court or with the consent of his parent or guardian, for his education or welfare during any period ending not later than the date when he attains the age of 18 years.

This provision assumes that before the child is eighteen years of age, the parents, a term which we all must agree includes a mother, also has some responsibility towards the child's education and welfare. In any case he or she can control what happens to the child. During that period, especially at the younger end of the infant's life span, the parents', especially the mother's, movements are to a large extent determined by the child's. At about this same time, the welfare of a child in a broken home is generally considered better protected in the custody of the mother than that of the father. It is totally unrealistic to think that you could permanently keep the child out of Botswana and yet by that not interfere with the freedom of movement of the mother.

But, then, the argument goes, the respondent has not shown that there was any likelihood of her non-Botswana children being kept out of Botswana. The answer to that is that governments with a discretion to exercise do not always give advance notice of how they intend to exercise that discretion. It is not unknown for a government which decides to deport or expel an alien to do so without prior notice of its intention. Must the person who is subject to, or may directly be affected by, such expulsion wait until the expulsion order is made before he or she can bring legal proceedings? When is he or she threatened with the likelihood that an order could be made? To the question whether the immigration officers in Botswana had a discretion to turn away an alien from entering the country, the appellant's reply was that they had.

[...]

The mother's concern for permission for her children to stay cannot be lightly dismissed on the ground that it was no business of hers, the responsibility being the children's father's. Well-knit families do not compartmentalise responsibilities that way. As long as the discretion lies with the governmental authorities to decide whether or not to extend further the residence permit of the husband, on whose stay in Botswana the stay of the respondent's children depend, the likelihood of the children's sudden exhaustion of their welcome in the country of their mother's birth and citizenship is real. Those with the power to grant the permission have the power to refuse. Were they to be refused continued stay, not only the children's position but the mother's enjoyment of life and her freedom of movement would be prejudiced. It does seem to me not unreasonable that a citizen of Botswana should feel resentful and aggrieved by a law which puts her in this invidious position as a woman when that same law is not made to apply in the same manner to other citizens, just because they are men. Equal treatment by the law irrespective of sex has been denied her.

The respondent has, in my view, substantiated her allegation that the Citizenship Act 1984 circumscribes her freedom of movement given by s 14 of the Constitution. She has made a case that as a mother her movements are determined by what happens to her children. If her children are liable to be barred from entry into or thrown out of her native country as aliens, her right to live in Botswana would be limited. As a mother of young children she would have to follow them. Her allegation of infringement of her rights under s 14 of the Constitution by s 4 of the Citizenship Act 1984 seems to me to have substance. The court a quo, therefore, had no alternative but to hear her on the merits.

The appellant has argued that if even the respondent had *locus standi* with respect to a challenge to s 4 of the Citizenship Act of 1984, she certainly did not have locus with respect to s 5, as the situation which that section provides for, namely, the citizenship of children born outside Botswana, does not apply to the respondent in any of the cases of her children. The possibility of the respondent giving birth at some future date to children abroad was too remote to form a basis for a challenge to s 5. With this submission I agree. But I must point out that the objections to s 4 may well apply to s 5. I, however, make no final judgment on that.

The appellant has argued that because of the manner in which the repeal and re-enactment of the laws on citizenship was done, declaring that s 4 was unconstitutional would create a vacuum. On that I would like to adopt the words of Centlivres CJ in the case of *Harris and Others v Minister of Interior and Another* 1952 (2) SA 428 at 456 where he says:

> The Court in declaring that such Statute is invalid is exercising a duty which it owes to persons whose rights are entrenched by Statute; its duty is simply to declare and apply the law and it would be inaccurate to say that the Court in discharging that is controlling the Legislature. See Bryce's *American Constitution* (3rd ed., Vol 1 p. 582). It is hardly necessary to add that Courts of law are not concerned with the question whether an Act of Parliament is reasonable, politic or impolitic. See *Swart N.O. and Nicol N.O. v de Kock and Garner and Others* 1951 (3) S.A. 589 at p. 606 (A.D.).

I expect if there is indeed a vacuum, Parliament would advise itself as to how to meet the situation.

The upshot of this discourse is that in my judgment the court *a quo* was right in holding that s 4 of the Citizenship Act 1984 infringes the fundamental rights and freedoms of the respondent conferred by ss 3 (on fundamental rights and freedoms of the individual), 14 (on protection of freedom of movement) and 15 (on protection from discrimination) of the Constitution. The respondent has, however, not given satisfactory basis for *locus standi* with respect to s 5 of the Act. And I therefore make no pronouncement in that regard. The learned judge *a quo* in the course of his judgment accepted the argument of counsel for the respondent that ss 4 and 5 of the Act denied the respondent protection from subjection to degrading treatment. I do not think it necessary to go into that question for the purposes of this decision. The declaration of the courts *a quo* that ss 4 and 5 of the Citizenship Act 1984 (Cap 01:01) are *ultra vires* the Constitution, is, accordingly, varied by deleting the reference to s 5. Otherwise the appeal is dismissed.

It remains for me to thank counsel for the very able and painstaking manner in which they have researched and presented their cases. I think here I speak for all my brothers if I say that we have indeed profited from, and enjoyed the manner of presentation of, their arguments.

AGUDA JA:*

Introduction

I have had the privilege of reading in draft the judgment of the Judge President just delivered, and I agree with the conclusions reached in that judgment together with the reasons upon which he based the conclusions. I also agree on the orders made. However

---

* **Eds:** the following is an abridged version of the judgment of Aguda JA.

because of the importance to which this case is entitled I feel constrained to add my own words to those of the Judge President.

[...]

Canons of constitutional construction

At the outset let me say that I have had no reasons to change my mind as regards the principles to be followed in the construction of the Constitution which I stated in *Petrus v State* [1984] BLR 14 at 35–35. Here I wish to refer in particular to what White J of the Supreme Court of the United States said in *South Dakota v North Carolina* 192 US 268 (1904), 48 L Ed 448 at 465 thus:

> I take it to be an elementary rule of constitutional construction that no one provision of the Constitution is to be segregated from all others, and to be considered alone, but that all the provisions bearing upon a particular subject are to be brought into view to be so interpreted as to effectuate the great purpose of the instrument.

I would also wish to refer once again to what Sir Udo Udoma of the Supreme Court of Nigeria said in *Rafiu Rabiu v The State* [1981] 2 NCLR 293 at 326 thus:

> I do not conceive it to be the duty of this Court so to construe any of the provisions of the Constitution as to defeat the obvious ends the Constitution was designed to serve where another construction equally in accord and consistent with the words and sense of such provisions will serve to enforce and protect such ends.

And in *Ifezu v Mbadugha* [1984] 1 SC NLR 427, 5 SC 79, Bello JSC put the matter thus:

> The fundamental principle is that such interpretation as would serve the interest of the Constitution and would best carry out its object and purpose should be preferred. To achieve this goal its relevant provisions must be read together and not disjointly ... where the provisions of the Constitution are capable of two meanings the Court must choose the meaning that would give force and effect to the Constitution and promote its purpose.

To these I would like to add the very important voice of Lord Diplock in Attorney General of the *Gambia v Jobe* [1985] LRC (Const) 556 at 565 thus:

> A constitution, and in particular that part of it which protects and entrenches fundamental rights and freedoms to which all persons in the State are to be entitled, is to be given a generous and purposive construction.

Generous construction means in my own understanding that you must interpret the provisions of the Constitution in such a way as not to whittle down any of the rights and freedoms unless by very clear and unambiguous words such interpretation is compelling. The construction can only be purposive when it reflects the deeper inspiration and aspiration of the basic concepts which the Constitution must for ever ensure, in our case the fundamental rights and freedoms entrenched in s 3.

The Constitution is the supreme law of the land and it is meant to serve not only this generation but also generations yet unborn. It cannot be allowed to be a lifeless museum piece; on the other hand the courts must continue to breathe life into it from time to time as the occasion may arise to ensure the healthy growth and development of the state through it. In my view the first task of a court when called upon to construe any of provisions of the Constitution is to have a sober and objective appraisal of the general canvas upon which the details of the constitutional picture are painted. It will be doing violence to the Constitution to take a particular provision and interpret it one way which will destroy or mutilate the whole basis of the Constitution when by a different construction the beauty, cohesion, integrity and healthy development of the state through the Constitution will be maintained. We must not shy away from a basic fact that whilst a particular construction of a constitutional provision may be able to meet the demands of the society of a certain age such construction may not meet those of a later age. In my view the overriding principle must be an adherence to the general picture presented by the Constitution into which each individual provision must fit in order to maintain in essential details the picture of which the framers could have painted had they been faced with circumstances of today. To hold otherwise would be to stultify the living constitution in its growth. It seems to me that a stultification of the Constitution must be prevented if this is possible without doing extreme violence to the language of the Constitution. I conceive it that the primary duty of the judges is to make the Constitution grow and develop in order to meet the just demands and aspirations of an ever developing society which is part of the wider and larger human society governed by some acceptable concepts of human dignity.

Status of customary law and the common law

The learned Deputy Attorney General did all his possible best to inform this court of the rules of customary law and of the common law under which women are seriously discriminated against, and that this provided the background which informed the enactment of the Citizenship Act in 1984. This may well be so, but what we are called upon to do is to consider s 4 of the Act in the light of the Constitution and see how that Constitution must be construed today bearing in mind the changed circumstances of our society. It is clear of course, and I have not the slightest doubt on the issue, that if any rule of customary law or of the common law is inconsistent with any of the provisions of the Constitution, but especially of the entrenched provisions, such rule of customary law or/and of the common law must be held to have been abrogated by the provisions of the Constitution to the extent of such inconsistency. ... Kentridge JA made this ... point in *Attorney General v Moagi* 1982 BLR 124 when he said at p 184:

> Constitutional rights conferred without express limitation should not be cut down by reading implicit restrictions into them so as to bring them into line with the common law.

Status of s 3 of the Constitution

There was some suggestion that s 3 of the Constitution is a mere preamble to the other sections which follow merely because it begins with the words "whereas". However, that that cannot be so has been exhaustively and adequately dealt with by my brother the learned Judge President in the judgment which he has just delivered and I do not feel that I should traverse the same route again. But I must express, as strongly as I can, that by no stretch of the imagination can such a basic overriding provision of the Constitution be regarded as a mere preamble and the learned Deputy Attorney General conceded this during argument. There can be no iota of doubt as regards the status of s 3, namely that it is a substantive provision of the Constitution. This conclusion is very much compelling when it is noted that the Constitution itself (s 18) gives power to any person to institute an action in court to test if the right entrenched in ss 3 to 16 has been, is being or is likely to be contravened in relation to him.

[...]

Status of international treaties, agreements, conventions, protocols, resolutions, etc

In considering whether this court can interpret s 15 of the Constitution in such a way as to authorise legislation which in its term and intent meant to discriminate on grounds of sex, in this case the female sex, it appears to me that now more than ever before, the whole world has realised that discrimination on grounds of sex, like that institution which was in times gone by permissible both by most religions and the conscience of men of those times, namely, slavery, can no longer be permitted or even tolerated, more so by the law.

At this juncture I wish to take judicial notice of that which is known the world over that Botswana is one of the few countries in Africa where liberal democracy has taken root. It seems clear to me that all the three arms of the government – the legislative, the executive and the judiciary – must strive to make it remain so except to any extent as may be prohibited by the Constitution in clear terms. It seems to me that in so striving we cannot afford to be immuned from the progressive movements going on around us in other liberal and not so liberal democracies such movements manifesting themselves in international agreements, treaties, resolutions, protocols and other similar understandings as well as in the respectable and respected voices of our other learned brethren in the performance of their adjudicatory roles in other jurisdictions. Mr. Browde SC, counsel for the respondent, referred us to the words of Earl Warren, Chief Justice of the United States, when he said in *Trop v Dulles* 356 US 86 (1958) that:

> The provisions of the Constitution are not time-worn adages or hollow shibboleths. They are vital, living principles that authorise and limit government powers in our nation.

My learned counsel also pointed out what Mohamed AJA of the Supreme Court of Namibia said in *ex parte Attorney-General, Namibia: In re Corporal Punishment by Organs of State* [1992] LRC (Const) 515, 1991(3) SA 76 as regards the question of corporal punishment, thus:

> What may have been accepted as a just form of punishment some decades ago, may appear to be manifestly inhuman or degrading today. Yesterday's orthodoxy might appear to be today's heresy.

Now in the report of a judicial colloquium held in Bangalore, Pakistan on 24 to 26 February 1988 (*Developing Human Rights Jurisprudence*, Commonwealth Secretariat, London, September 1988) the Hon Justice Michael Kirby, CMG, President of the Court of Appeal, Supreme Court of New South Wales, Australia, said (at 78):

> ... in the function of Courts in giving meaning to a written Constitution, to legislation on human rights expressed in general terms or even to old precedents inherited from judges of an earlier time, there is often plenty of room for judicial choice. In that opportunity for that choice lies the scope for drawing upon each judge's own notions of the content and requirements of human rights. In doing so, the judge should normally seek to ensure compliance by the Court with the international obligations of the jurisdiction in which he or she operates. An increasing number of judges in all countries are therefore looking to international developments and drawing upon them in the course of developing the solutions which they offer in particular cases that come before them.

At the same colloquium the Chief Justice of Pakistan, Muhammad Heleen CJ, voiced his own opinion thus (at 101–103):

> A State has an obligation to make its municipal law conform to its undertakings under treaties to which it is a party. With regard to interpretation, however, it is a principle

generally recognised in national legal systems that, in the event of doubt, the national rule is to be interpreted in accordance with the State's international obligations ...

The domestic application of human rights norms is now regarded as a basis for implementing constitutional values beyond the minimum requirements of the Constitution. The international human rights norms are in fact part of the constitutional expression of liberties guaranteed at the national level. The domestic courts can assume the task of expanding these liberties.

I am prepared to accept and embrace the views of these two great judges and hold them as the light to guide my feet through the dark path to the ultimate construction of the provisions of our Constitution now in dispute.

However, whatever the views of judges within the Commonwealth must have been in the past as regards the position of a state's international obligation and other undertakings *vis-à-vis* their domestic laws, many of them have since the past two decades or so begun to have a re-think. They have started to express the opinion that they have an obligation to ensure that the domestic laws of their countries conform to the international obligations of those countries. Lord Scarman in *Attorney General v British Broadcasting Corp* [1981] AC 303 at 354 said:

Yet there is a presumption, albeit rebuttable, that our municipal law will be consistent with our international obligations.

And in *Schering Chemicals Ltd v Falkman Ltd* [1982] QB 18, [1981] 2 All ER 321, Lord Denning MR said of the law of England that:

I take it that our law should conform so far as possible with the provisions of the European Convention on Human Rights.

England has no written Constitution and the rather cautious but clearly progressive approach of these great judges of that country must be understood in that light. We have a written Constitution, and if there are two possible ways of interpreting that Constitution or any of the laws enacted under it, one of which obliges our country to act contrary to its international undertakings and the other obliges our country to conform with such undertakings, then the courts should give their authority to the latter.

I would wish to call attention to two documents which were placed before us. The first is the Convention on the Elimination of All Forms of Discrimination against Women which was adopted by the General Assembly of the United Nations GA Res 34/180 on 18 December 1979 by a vote of 130–0, and which came into effect on 3 December 1981. Article 2 of the convention says that States Parties to it "condemn discrimination against women in all its forms", and that they would take all appropriate measures, including legislation for "the purpose of guaranteeing women the exercise and enjoyment of human rights and fundamental freedom on a basis of equality with men" (art 3). Article 9(1) says that "States Parties shall grant women equal rights with men to acquire, change or retain their nationality. They shall ensure in particular that neither marriage to an alien nor change of nationality by the husband during marriage shall automatically change the nationality of the wife" whilst art 9(2) says that "States Parties shall grant women equal rights with men with respect to the nationality of their children".

By the end of February 1990, 100 states had ratified or acceded to this convention. There is no evidence that Botswana is one of the 100 states that have ratified or acceded to the convention but I take it that a court in this country is obliged to look at the convention of this nature which has created an international regime when called upon to interpret a provision of the Constitution which is so much in doubt to see whether that Constitution permits discrimination against women as has been canvassed in this case.

I take judicial notice that Botswana is an important member of the Organisation of African Unity (the "OAU"). We were informed by the Deputy Attorney General that she has ratified the African Charter on Human and People's Rights which were adopted on 27 June 1981 by members of the OAU. Indeed the published document itself shows that Botswana was among the 35 states that had ratified it by 1 January 1988. I need quote only two of its 68 articles. Article 2 says that:

> Every individual shall be entitled to the enjoyment of the rights and freedoms recognised and guaranteed in the present Charter without distinction of any kind such as race, ethnic group, colour, sex language, religion, political opinion.

I take the view that in all these circumstances a court in this country, faced with the difficulty of interpretation as to whether or not some legislation breached any of the provisions entrenched in Chapter II of our Constitution which deal with fundamental rights and freedoms of individual, is entitled to look at the international agreements, treaties and obligations entered into before or after the legislation was enacted to ensure that such domestic legislation does not breach any of the international conventions, agreements, treaties and obligations binding upon this country save upon clear and unambiguous language.

In my view this must be so whether or not such international conventions, agreements, treaties, protocols or obligations have been specifically incorporated into our domestic law. In this respect I wish to make reference to what Barker J said in *Bird's Galore Ltd v A-G* [1989] LRC (Const) 928 at 939 thus:

> An international treaty, even one not acceded to by New Zealand, can be looked at by the court on the basis that in the absence of express words Parliament would not have wanted a decision-maker to act contrary to such a treaty. See for example *Van Gorkom v A-G* [1977] 1 NZLR 535 where the treaty in question had not been acceded to by New Zealand.

If an international convention, agreement, treaty, protocol, or obligation has been incorporated into domestic law, there seems to me to be no problem since such convention, agreement, and so on will be treated as part of the domestic law for purposes of adjudication in a domestic court. If it has merely been signed but not incorporated into domestic law, a domestic court must accept the position that the legislature or the executive will not act contrary to the undertaking given on behalf of the country by the Executive in the convention, agreement, treaty, protocol or other obligation. However where the country has not in terms become party to an international convention, agreement, treaty, protocol or obligation it may only serve as an aid to the interpretation of a domestic law, or the construction of the Constitution if such international convention agreement, treaty, protocol, etc purports to or by necessary implication, creates an international regime within international law recognised by the vast majority of states. One can cite some of such conventions, agreements, treaties, protocols which have created regimes which no member of the community of nations can or should neglect with impunity. Take for example the United Nations Declaration on the Rights of the Child adopted by resolution 1286 on 29 November 1959 which says that the child shall:

> Wherever possible grow in the care and under the responsibility of his parents ...

and that:

> a child of tender years shall not, save in exceptional circumstances, be separated from the mother.

Another example is United Nations General Assembly Declaration on the Elimination of Discrimination against Women passed on 7 September 1967 to the effect that:

> The State shall ensure the elimination of every discrimination against women and also ensure the protection of the rights of the women and the child as stipulated in international declarations and conventions.

In my view there is clear obligation on this country like on all other African states signatories to the Charter to ensure the elimination of every discrimination against their womenfolk. In my view it is the clear duty of this court when faced with the difficult task of the construction of provisions of the Constitution to keep in mind the international obligation. If the constitutional provisions are such as can be construed to ensure the compliance of the state with its international obligations then they must be so construed. It may be otherwise, if fully aware of its international obligations under a regime creating treaty, convention, agreement or protocol, a state deliberately and in clear language enacts a law in contravention of such treaty, convention, agreement or protocol. However in this case before this court the clear provisions of s 3 of the Constitution accords with the international obligations of the state whilst construing s 15 in the manner canvassed by the appellant will lead to the inevitable failure of the state to conform with its international obligation under international regimes created by the United Nations and the OAU. In this regard I am bound to accept the position that this country will not deliberately enact laws in contravention of its international undertakings and obligations under those regimes. Therefore the courts must interpret domestic statutory laws in a way as is compatible with the state's responsibility not to be in breach of international law as laid down by law creating treaties, conventions, agreements and protocols within the United Nations and the Organisation of African Unity.

In the light of all the foregoing therefore the Constitution must be held not to permit discrimination on grounds of sex which will be a breach of international law. Therefore s 4 of the Citizenship Act 1984 must be held to be *ultra vires* the Constitution and must therefore be and it is hereby declared null and void.

BIZOSJA: I concur in the judgment of the Judge President and the proposed orders to be made dismissing the appeal from the judgment of Horwitz Ag J (1991] LRC (Const) 574). I agree with the reasons advanced by the Judge President. ...

SCHREINER and PUCKRIN JAA dissented.[*]

---

[*]   *Eds:* due to space constraints, the dissenting judgments of Schreiner JA and Puckrin JA have not been included, although their main findings are included in the headnote.

CASE NO 38

AUMEERUDDY-CZIFFRA AND OTHERS v MAURITIUS

UNITED NATIONS HUMAN RIGHTS COMMITTEE

Communication No: 35/1978

Views adopted: 9 April 1981

Human rights — Immigration — Right to protection against arbitrary or unlawful interference with family life — Right to protection of family by State — Right to take part in public affairs — Equal protection of the law — Whether immigration laws restricting the residence in Mauritius of foreign husbands of Mauritian women, but not the residence of foreign wives of Mauritian men violated Covenant rights — Mauritius Immigration (Amendment) Act 1977 — Mauritius Deportation (Amendment) Act 1977 — International Covenant on Civil and Political Rights, arts 2(1), 3, 17(1), 23(1), 25 and 26

International human rights law — Individual complaint procedures — Standing — Meaning of "victim" — Whether an individual not personally affected entitled to challenge a law allegedly contrary to the Covenant — Optional Protocol to International Covenant on Civil and Political Rights, art 1

BACKGROUND

In 1997, the legislature of Mauritius enacted the Immigration (Amendment) Act 1977 and the Deportation (Amendment) Act 1977. Before the enactment of these two laws, a foreign spouse of a Mauritian citizen had the right to reside in Mauritius with his or her Mauritian spouse. Under the new laws, a foreign husband of a Mauritian woman was required to apply to the Minister of the Interior for a residence permit and could be deported with no right to judicial review, although this did not apply to a foreign wife of a Mauritian man.

Twenty Mauritian women, seventeen of whom were unmarried and three of whom were married to foreign nationals, brought a complaint to the United Nations Human Rights Committee against Mauritius, arguing *inter alia* that the 1977 Acts were discriminatory on the grounds of sex, in that they constituted an unlawful or arbitrary interference with the family life of Mauritian women (article 17) and restricted their right to choose whom to marry and found a family with (article 23) under the International Covenant on Civil and Political Rights.

Ms Aumeeruddy-Cziffra was one of the women married to a foreign national. She was a leading figure in the opposition party *Mouvement Militant Mauricien* and an elected member of the legislative assembly. Since the statutes had retrospective effect, her husband had lost his residence status in Mauritius and had had to apply for a residence permit. Three years after he had applied for a permit he had not yet had a response. Mrs Aumerruddy-Cziffra also alleged interference with her right to take part in public affairs (article 25), arguing that the Government had deliberately made her husband's residence insecure in order to force her to abandon her political career.

HELD (finding various violations of the Covenant)

1   A person could only claim to be a victim in the sense of article 1 of the Optional Protocol if he or she was actually affected. No individual could in the abstract, by way of an *actio popularis*, challenge a law or practice claimed to be contrary to the Covenant. In the case of the 17 unmarried co-authors there had been no actual interference with their rights nor was there evidence that any of them were facing a personal risk of being affected in the enjoyment of their rights. (Paras 9.2 and 9.2 (a))

2   The relationships of the three married co-authors to their husbands clearly belonged to the area of "family" as used in article 17(1) of the Covenant. They were therefore protected against "arbitrary and unlawful interference" in this area. The exclusion of a person from a country where his close family members were living could amount to interference within the meaning of article 17(1). In the present cases, not only the future possibility of deportation, but the existing precarious residence situation of foreign husbands in Mauritius represented an interference by the authorities with the family life of the Mauritian wives and their husbands. Whenever restrictions were placed on a right guaranteed by the Covenant, this had to be done without discrimination on the ground of sex. In the present case, an adverse distinction based on sex was made, affecting the alleged victims in the enjoyment of their rights. No sufficient justification for this difference had been given. There was therefore a violation of articles 2(1) and 3, in conjunction with article 17(1). (Paras 9.2 (b) 2, 9.2 (b) 2(i)1 – 2 and 8)

3   Each of the three married co-authors and their husbands also constituted a "family" within the meaning of article 23 of the Covenant and was therefore entitled to "protection by society and the State". The protection of the family could not vary with the sex of the one or the other spouse. There was therefore a violation of articles 2(1), 3 and 26 in conjunction with article 23(1). (Paras 9.2 (b) 2(ii)1 – 4)

4   The right to take part in the conduct of public affairs guaranteed under article 25 of the Covenant had not been violated. Ms Aumeeruddy-Cziffra was actively participating in political life and had neither in fact nor in law been prevented from doing so. (Paras 9.2 (c) 3)

Treaties and other international instruments referred to

International Covenant on Civil and Political Rights 1966, arts 2(1), 2(2), 3, 4, 13, 17(1), 23(1), 23(2), 23(4), 25 and 26

Optional Protocol to the International Covenant on Civil and Political Rights 1966, arts 1, 4(2), 5(4)

National legislation referred to

Mauritius

Constitution of Mauritius, s 16

Deportation (Amendment) Act 1977

Immigration (Amendment) Act 1977, s 9

VIEWS UNDER ARTICLE 5(4) OF THE OPTIONAL PROTOCOL[1]

1.1   The authors of this communication (initial letter dated 2 May 1978 and a further letter dated 9 March 1980) are 20 Mauritian women, who have requested that their identity should not be disclosed to the State party.[2] They claim that the enactment of the Immigration (Amendment) Act 1977, and the Deportation (Amendment) Act 1977, by Mauritius constitutes discrimination based on sex against Mauritian women, violation of the right to found a family and home, and removal of the protection of the courts of law, in breach of articles 2, 3, 4, 17, 23, 25 and 26 of the International Covenant on Civil and Political Rights. The authors claim to be victims of the alleged violations. They submit that all domestic remedies have been exhausted.

1.2   The authors state that prior to the enactment of the laws in question, alien men and women married to Mauritian nationals enjoyed the same residence status, that is to say, by virtue of their marriage, foreign spouses of both sexes had the right, protected by law, to reside in the country with their Mauritian husbands or wives. The authors contend that, under the new laws, alien husbands of Mauritian women lost their residence status in Mauritius and must now apply for a "residence permit" which may be refused or removed at any time by the Minister of Interior. The new laws, however, do not affect the status of alien women married to Mauritian husbands who retain their legal right to residence in the country. The authors further contend that under the new laws alien husbands of Mauritian women may be deported under a ministerial order, which is not subject to judicial review.

2   On 27 October 1978, the Human Rights Committee decided to transmit the communication to the State party, under rule 91 of the provisional rules of procedure, requesting information and observations relevant to the question of admissibility.

3   The State party, in its reply of 17 January 1979, informed the Committee that it had no objection to formulate against the admissibility of the communication.

4   On 24 April 1979, the Human Rights Committee,

(a) Concluding that the communication, as presented by the authors, should be declared admissible;

(b) Considering, however, that it might review this decision in the light of all the information which would be before it when it considered the communication on the merits;

Therefore decided:

(a) That the communication was admissible;

(b) That in accordance with article 4(2) of the Optional Protocol, the State party be requested to submit to the Committee, within six months of the date of the transmittal to it of this decision, written explanations or statements on the substance of the matter under consideration;

(c) That the State party be requested, in this connection, to transmit copies of any relevant legislation and any relevant judicial decisions.

---

1   Pursuant to rule 85 of the provisional rules of procedure, Mr Rajsoomer Lallah did not participate in the consideration of this communication or in the adoption of the views of the Committee under article 5(4) of the Optional Protocol in this matter.

2   Subsequently one of the authors agreed to the disclosure of her name.

[State party's submissions]*

5.1   In its submission dated 17 December 1979, the State party explains the laws of Mauritius on the acquisition of citizenship and, in particular on the naturalization of aliens. The State party further elaborates on the deportation laws, including a historical synopsis of these laws. It is admitted that it was the effect of the Immigration (Amendment) Act 1977 and of the Deportation (Amendment) Act 1977 to limit the right of free access to Mauritius and immunity from deportation to the wives of Mauritian citizens only, whereas this right had previously been enjoyed by all spouses of citizens of Mauritius, irrespective of their sex. Both Acts were passed following certain events in connection with which some foreigners (spouses of Mauritian women) were suspected of subversive activities. The State party claims, however, that the authors of the communication do not allege that any particular individual has in fact been the victim of any specific act in breach of the provisions of the Covenant. The State party claims that the communication is aimed at obtaining a declaration by the Human Rights Committee that the Deportation Act and the Immigration Act, as amended, are capable of being administered in a discriminatory manner in violation of articles 2, 3, 4, 17, 23, 25 and 26 of the Covenant.

5.2   The State party admits that the two statutes in question do not guarantee similar rights of access to residence in Mauritius to all foreigners who have married Mauritian nationals, and it is stated that the "discrimination", if there is any, is based on the sex of the spouse. The State party further admits that foreign husbands of Mauritian citizens no longer have the right to free access to Mauritius and immunity from deportation therefrom, whereas prior to 12 April 1977, this group of persons had the right to be considered, *de facto*, as residents of Mauritius. They now must apply to the Minister of the Interior for a residence permit and in case of refusal of the permit they have no possibility to seek redress before a court of law.

5.3   The State party, however, considers that this situation does not amount to a violation of the provisions of the Covenant which – in the State party's view – does not guarantee a general right to enter, to reside in and not to be expelled from a particular country or a certain part of it and that the exclusion or restriction upon entry or residence of some individuals and not others cannot constitute discrimination in respect of a right or freedom guaranteed by the Covenant. The State party concludes that if the right "to enter, reside in and not to be expelled from" Mauritius is not one guaranteed by the Covenant, the authors cannot claim that there has been any violation of articles 2(1), 2(2), 3, 4 or 26 of the Covenant on the grounds that admission to Mauritius may be denied to the authors' husbands or prospective husbands or that these husbands or prospective husbands may be expelled from Mauritius, and that such exclusion of their husbands or prospective husbands may be an interference in their private and family life.

5.4   As far as the allegation of a violation of article 25 of the Covenant is concerned, the State party argues that if a citizen of Mauritius chooses to go and live abroad with her husband because the latter is not entitled to stay in Mauritius, she cannot be heard to say that she is thus denied the right to take part in the conduct of public affairs and to have access on general terms of equality to public service in her country. The State party claims that nothing in the law prevents the woman, as such, from exercising the rights guaranteed by article 25, although she may not be in a position to exercise the said rights as a consequence of her marriage and of her decision to live with her husband abroad.

---

*   *Eds:* headings (in square brackets) have been added for the convenience of readers.

The State party mentions, as an example of a woman who has married a foreign husband and who is still playing a prominent role in the conduct of public affairs in Mauritius, the case of Mrs Aumeeruddy-Cziffra, one of the leading figures of the *Mouvement Militant Mauricien* opposition party.

5.5   The State party further argues that nothing in the laws of Mauritius denies any citizen the right to marry whomever he may choose and to found a family. Any violation of articles 17 and 23 is denied by the State party, which argues that this allegation is based on the assumption that "husband and wife are given the right to reside together in their own countries and that this right of residence should be secure". The State party reiterates that the right to stay in Mauritius is not one of the rights guaranteed by the provisions of the Covenant, but it admits that the exclusion of a person from a country where close members of his family are living can amount to an infringement of the person's right under article 17 of the Covenant, ie that no one should be subjected to arbitrary and unlawful interference with his family. The State party argues, however, that each case must be decided on its own merits.

5.6   The State party recalls that the Mauritian Constitution guarantees to every person the right to leave the country, and that the foreign husband of a Mauritian citizen may apply for a residence permit or even naturalization.

5.7   The State party is of the opinion that if the exclusion of a non-citizen is lawful (the right to stay in a country not being one of the rights guaranteed by the provisions of the Covenant), then such an exclusion (based on grounds of security or public interest) cannot be said to be an arbitrary or unlawful interference with the family life of its nationals in breach of article 17 of the Covenant.

[Authors' submissions]

6.1   In their additional information and observations dated 19 March 1980, the authors argue that the two Acts in question (Immigration (Amendment) Act 1977 and Deportation (Amendment) Act 1977) are discriminatory in themselves in that the equal rights of women are no longer guaranteed. The authors emphasize that they are not so much concerned with the unequal status of the spouses of Mauritian citizens – to which the State party seems to refer – but they allege that Mauritian women who marry foreigners are themselves discriminated against on the basis of sex, and they add that the application of the laws in question may amount to discrimination based on other factors such as race or political opinions. The authors further state that they do not claim "immunity from deportation" for foreign husbands of Mauritian women but they object that the Deportation (Amendment) Act, 1977 gives the Minister of the Interior an absolute discretion in the matter. They argue that, according to article 13 of the Covenant, the alien who is lawfully in the country has the right not to be arbitrarily expelled and that, therefore, a new law should not deprive him of his right of hearing.

6.2   As has been stated, the authors maintain that they are not concerned primarily with the rights of non-citizens (foreign husbands) but of Mauritian citizens (wives). They allege:

(a) That female citizens do not have an unrestricted right to married life in their country if they marry a foreigner, whereas male citizens have an unrestricted right to do so;

(b) That the law, being retroactive, had the effect of withdrawing from the female citizens the opportunity to take part in public life and restricted, in particular, the right of one of the authors in this respect;

(c) That the "choice" to join the foreign spouse abroad is only imposed on Mauritian women and that only they are under an obligation to "choose" between exercising their political rights guaranteed under article 25 of the Covenant, or to live with their foreign husbands abroad;

(d) That the female citizen concerned may not be able to leave Mauritius and join her husband in his country of origin for innumerable reasons (health, long-term contracts of work, political mandate, incapacity to stay in the husband's country of origin because of racial problems, as, for example, in South Africa);

(e) That by rendering the right of residence of foreign husbands insecure, the State party is tampering with the female citizens' right to freely marry whom they choose and to found a family.

The authors do not contest that a foreign husband may apply for a residence permit, as the State party has pointed out in its submission; but they maintain that foreign husbands should be granted the rights to residence and naturalization. The authors allege that in many cases foreign husbands have applied in vain for both and they claim that such a decision amounts to an arbitrary and unlawful interference by the State party with the family life of its female citizens in breach of article 17 of the Covenant, as the decision is placed in the hands of the Minister of the Interior and not of a court of law, and as no appeal against this decision is possible.

6.3   The authors enclose as an annex to their submission a statement by one of the co-authors, Mrs Shirin Aumeeruddy-Cziffra, to whose case the State party had referred (see para 5.4 above). She states *inter alia* that on 21 April 1977, in accordance with the new laws, her foreign husband applied for a residence permit and later for naturalization. She alleges that during 1977 her husband was twice granted a one-month visa and that an application for a temporary work permit was refused. She states that when returning to Mauritius, after a one week stay abroad, her husband was allowed to enter the country on 24 October 1978 without question and that he has been staying there since without a residence or work permit. She remarks that her husband is slowly and gradually giving up all hope of ever being naturalized or obtaining a residence permit. The author, an elected member of the legislative assembly, points out that this situation is a cause of frustration for herself and she alleges that the insecurity has been deliberately created by the Government to force her to abandon politics in view of the forthcoming elections in December 1981. She stresses that she does not want to leave Mauritius, but that she intends, after the expiry of her present mandate, to be again a candidate for her party.

[Views of Human Rights Committee]

7.1   The Human Rights Committee bases its view on the following facts, which are not in dispute:

7.2   Up to 1977, spouses (husbands and wives) of Mauritian citizens had the right of free access to Mauritius and enjoyed immunity from deportation. They had the right to be considered *de facto* as residents of Mauritius. The coming into force of the Immigration (Amendment) Act 1977, and of the Deportation (Amendment) Act 1977, limited these rights to the wives of Mauritius citizens only. Foreign husbands must apply to the Minister of the Interior for a residence permit and in case of refusal of the permit they have no possibility to seek redress before a court of law.

7.3   Seventeen of the co-authors are unmarried. Three of the co-authors were married to foreign husbands when, owing to the coming into force of the Immigration

(Amendment) Act 1977, their husbands lost the residence status in Mauritius which they had enjoyed before. Their further residence together with their spouses in Mauritius is based under the statute on a limited, temporary residence permit to be issued in accordance with section 9 of the Immigration (Amendment) Act 1977. This residence permit is subject to specified conditions which might at any time be varied or cancelled by a decision of the Minister of the Interior, against which no remedy is available. In addition, the Deportation (Amendment) Act, 1977 subjects foreign husbands to a permanent risk of being deported from Mauritius.

7.4   In the case of Mrs Aumeeruddy-Cziffra, one of the three married co-authors, more than three years have elapsed since her husband applied to the Mauritian authorities for a residence permit, but so far no formal decision has been taken. If her husband's application were to receive a negative decision, she would be obliged to choose between either living with her husband abroad and giving up her political career, or living separated from her husband in Mauritius and there continuing to participate in the conduct of public affairs of that country.

8.1   The Committee has to consider, in the light of these facts, whether any of the rights set forth in the Covenant on Civil and Political Rights have been violated with respect to the authors by Mauritius when enacting and applying the two statutes in question. The Committee has to decide whether these two statutes, by subjecting only the foreign husband of a Mauritian woman – but not the foreign wife of a Mauritian man – to the obligation to apply for a residence permit in order to enjoy the same rights as before the enactment of the statutes, and by subjecting only the foreign husband to the possibility of deportation, violate any of the rights set forth under the Covenant, and whether the authors of the communication may claim to be victims of such a violation.

8.2   Pursuant to article 1 of the Optional Protocol to the International Covenant on Civil and Political Rights, the Committee only has a mandate to consider communications concerning individuals who are alleged to be themselves victims of a violation of any of the rights set forth in the Covenant.

9.1   The Human Rights Committee bases its views on the following considerations:

9.2   In the first place, a distinction has to be made between the different groups of the authors of the present communication. A person can only claim to be a victim in the sense of article 1 of the Optional Protocol if he or she is actually affected. It is a matter of degree how concretely this requirement should be taken. However, no individual can in the abstract, by way of an *actio popularis*, challenge a law or practice claimed to be contrary to the Covenant. If the law or practice has not already been concretely applied to the detriment of that individual, it must in any event be applicable in such a way that the alleged victim's risk of being affected is more than a theoretical possibility.

9.2 (a) In this respect the Committee notes that in the case of the 17 unmarried co-authors there is no question of actual interference with, or failure to ensure equal protection by the law to any family. Furthermore there is no evidence that any of them is actually facing a personal risk of being thus affected in the enjoyment of this or any other rights set forth in the Covenant by the laws complained against. In particular it cannot be said that their right to marry under article 23(2) or the right to equality of spouses under article 23(4) are affected by such laws.

9.2 (b) 1 The Committee will next examine that part of the communication which relates to the effect of the laws of 1977 on the family life of the three married women.

9.2 (b) 2 The Committee notes that several provisions of the Covenant are applicable in this respect. For reasons which will appear below, there is no doubt that they are actually affected by these laws, even in the absence of any individual measure of implementation (for instance, by way of a denial of residence, or an order of deportation, concerning one of the husbands). Their claim to be "victims" within the meaning of the Optional Protocol has to be examined.

9.2 (b) 2 (i) 1 First, their relationships to their husbands clearly belong to the area of "family" as used in article 17(1) of the Covenant. They are therefore protected against what that article calls "arbitrary or unlawful interference" in this area.

9.2 (b) 2 (i) 2 The Committee takes the view that the common residence of husband and wife has to be considered as the normal behaviour of a family. Hence, and as the State party has admitted, the exclusion of a person from a country where close members of his family are living can amount to an interference within the meaning of article 17. In principle, article 17(1) applies also when one of the spouses is an alien. Whether the existence and application of immigration laws affecting the residence of a family member is compatible with the Covenant depends on whether such interference is either "arbitrary or unlawful" as stated in article 17(1), or conflicts in any other way with the State party's obligations under the Covenant.

9.2 (b) 2 (i) 3 In the present cases, not only the future possibility of deportation, but the existing precarious residence situation of foreign husbands in Mauritius represents, in the opinion of the Committee, an interference by the authorities of the State party with the family life of the Mauritian wives and their husbands. The statutes in question have rendered it uncertain for the families concerned whether and for how long it will be possible for them to continue their family life by residing together in Mauritius. Moreover, as described above (para 7.4) in one of the cases, even the delay for years, and the absence of a positive decision granting a residence permit, must be seen as a considerable inconvenience, among other reasons because the granting of a work permit, and hence the possibility of the husband to contribute to supporting the family, depends on the residence permit, and because deportation without judicial review is possible at any time.

9.2 (b) 2 (i) 4 Since, however, this situation results from the legislation itself, there can be no question of regarding this interference as "unlawful" within the meaning of article 17(1) in the present cases. It remains to be considered whether it is "arbitrary" or conflicts in any other way with the Covenant.

9.2 (b) 2 (i) 5 The protection owed to individuals in this respect is subject to the principle of equal treatment of the sexes which follows from several provisions of the Covenant. It is an obligation of the State parties under article 2(1) generally to respect and ensure the rights of the Covenant "without distinction of any kind, such as ... (*inter alia*) sex", and more particularly under article 3 "to ensure the equal right of men and women to the enjoyment" of all these rights, as well as under article 26 to provide "without any discrimination" for "the equal protection of the law".

9.2 (b) 2 (i) 6 The authors who are married to foreign nationals are suffering from the adverse consequences of the statutes discussed above only because they are women. The precarious residence status of their husbands, affecting their family life as described, results from the 1977 laws which do not apply the same measures of control to foreign wives. In this connection the Committee has noted that under section 16 of the Constitution of Mauritius sex is not one of the grounds on which discrimination is prohibited.

9.2 (b) 2 (i) 7   In these circumstances, it is not necessary for the Committee to decide in the present cases how far such or other restrictions on the residence of foreign spouses might conflict with the Covenant if applied without discrimination of any kind.

9.2 (b) 2 (i) 8   The Committee considers that it is also unnecessary to say whether the existing discrimination should be called an "arbitrary" interference with the family within the meaning of article 17. Whether or not the particular interference could as such be justified if it were applied without discrimination does not matter here. Whenever restrictions are placed on a right guaranteed by the Covenant, this has to be done without discrimination on the ground of sex. Whether the restriction in itself would be in breach of that right regarded in isolation, is not decisive in this respect. It is the enjoyment of the rights which must be secured without discrimination. Here it is sufficient, therefore, to note that in the present position an adverse distinction based on sex is made, affecting the alleged victims in their enjoyment of one of their rights. No sufficient justification for this difference has been given. The Committee must then find that there is a violation of articles 2(1) and 3 of the Covenant, in conjunction with article 17(1).

9.2 (b) 2 (ii) 1   At the same time each of the couples concerned constitutes also a "family" within the meaning of article 23(1) of the Covenant, in one case at least – that of Mrs Aumeeruddy-Cziffra – also with a child. They are therefore as such "entitled to protection by society and the State" as required by that article, which does not further describe that protection. The Committee is of the opinion that the legal protection or measures a society or a State can afford to the family may vary from country to country and depend on different social, economic, political and cultural conditions and traditions.

9.2 (b) 2 (ii) 2   Again, however, the principle of equal treatment of the sexes applies by virtue of articles 2(1), 3 and 26, of which the latter is also relevant because it refers particularly to the "equal protection of the law". Where the Covenant requires a substantial protection as in article 23, it follows from those provisions that such protection must be equal, that is to say not discriminatory, for example on the basis of sex.

9.2 (b) 2 (ii) 3   It follows that also in this line of argument the Covenant must lead to the result that the protection of a family cannot vary with the sex of the one or the other spouse. Though it might be justified for Mauritius to restrict the access of aliens to their territory and to expel them therefrom for security reasons, the Committee is of the view that the legislation which only subjects foreign spouses of Mauritian women to those restrictions, but not foreign spouses of Mauritian men, is discriminatory with respect to Mauritian women and cannot be justified by security requirements.

9.2 (b) 2 (ii) 4   The Committee therefore finds that there is also a violation of articles 2(1), 3 and 26 of the Covenant in conjunction with the right of the three married co-authors under article 23(1).

9.2 (c) 1   It remains to consider the allegation of a violation of article 25 of the Covenant, which provides that every citizen shall have the right and the opportunity without any of the distinctions mentioned in article 2 (*inter alia* as to sex) and without unreasonable restrictions, to take part in the conduct of public affairs, as further described in this article. The Committee is not called upon in this case to examine any restrictions on a citizen's right under article 25. Rather, the question is whether the opportunity also referred to there, ie a *de facto* possibility of exercising this right, is affected contrary to the Covenant.

9.2 (c) 2 The Committee considers that restrictions established by law in various areas may prevent citizens in practice from exercising their political rights, ie deprive them of the opportunity to do so, in ways which might in certain circumstances be contrary to the purpose of article 25 or to the provisions of the Covenant against discrimination, for example if such interference with opportunity should infringe the principle of sexual equality.

9.2 (c) 3 However, there is no information before the Committee to the effect that any of this has actually happened in the present cases. As regards Mrs. Aumeeruddy-Cziffra, who is actively participating in political life as an elected member of the legislative assembly of Mauritius, she has neither in fact nor in law been prevented from doing so. It is true that on the hypothesis that if she were to leave the country as a result of interference with her family situation, she might lose this opportunity as well as other benefits which are in fact connected with residence in the country. The relevant aspects of such interference with a family situation have already been considered, however, in connection with article 17 and related provisions above. The hypothetical side-effects just suggested do not warrant any finding of a separate violation of article 25 at the present stage, where no particular element requiring additional consideration under that article seems to be present.

10.1 Accordingly, the Human Rights Committee acting under article 5(4) of the Optional Protocol to the International Covenant on Civil and Political Rights, is of the view that the facts, as outlined in paragraph 7 above, disclose violations of the Covenant, in particular of articles 2(1), 3 and 26 in relation to articles 17(1) and 23(1) with respect to the three co-authors who are married to foreign husbands, because the coming into force of the Immigration (Amendment) Act 1977, and the Deportation (Amendment) Act 1977, resulted in discrimination against them on the ground of sex.

10.2 The Committee further is of the view that there has not been any violation of the Covenant in respect of the other provisions invoked.

10.3 For the reasons given above, in para 9(2)(a), the Committee finds that the 17 unmarried coauthors cannot presently claim to be victims of any breach of their rights under the Covenant.

11 The Committee, accordingly, is of the view that the State party should adjust the provisions of the Immigration (Amendment) Act 1977 and of the Deportation (Amendment) Act 1977 in order to implement its obligations under the Covenant, and should provide immediate remedies for the victims of the violations found above.

CASE NO 39

ABDULAZIZ, CABALES AND BALKANDALI v UNITED KINGDOM

EUROPEAN COURT OF HUMAN RIGHTS

Application Nos: 9214/80; 9473/81; 9474/81

Judgment: 28 May 1985

Panel: *Judges*: Wiarda (*President*), Ryssdal, Cremona, Vilhjâlmsson, Ganshof van der Meersch, Evrigenis, Gölcüklü, Matscher, Pettiti, Walsh, Sir Vincent Evans, Russo and Bernhardt Gersing

Human rights — Right to respect for family life — Whether right to respect for family life includes the right to establish a matrimonial home in the country of one's residence — Whether denial of residence to non-national husbands of lawfully resident wives contravened the rights of the wives to respect for family life — Equality and non-discrimination — Discrimination on the grounds of sex, birth and race — Whether such denial of residence contravened the rights of the wives to respect for family life without discrimination — European Convention for the Protection of Human Rights and Fundamental Freedoms, arts 8 and 14 — Immigration Act 1971 and immigration practice rules

Human rights — Right to respect for family life — Definition of "family" — Whether relationship arising from marriage sufficient to constitute "family" — Whether "family" means established family — Whether intended family life excluded — European Convention for the Protection of Human Rights and Fundamental Freedoms, art 8

Human rights — Right to respect for family life — Immigration — Positive obligation on Contracting States to protect the right respect for family life — Margin of appreciation in relation to immigration control — European Convention for the Protection of Human Rights and Fundamental Freedoms, art 8

BACKGROUND

The three applicants, Ms Abdulaziz, Ms Cabales and Ms Balkandali, were all immigrants residing permanently and lawfully in the United Kingdom with the right to remain indefinitely. Their husbands, who were non-nationals, had been refused entry to the United Kingdom to remain with or join their wives on the basis of immigration rules promulgated under the Immigration Act 1971. The new rules, amended in the early 1980s, reformed the regime governing the entry into and residence in the United Kingdom of husbands and fiancés of residents but not wives and fiancées of residents. The main purpose of these rules was to curtail "primary immigration", that is immigration by someone who could be expected to seek full-time work in order to support a family, so as to protect the labour market at a time of high unemployment.

The applicants lodged an application under the European Convention on Human Rights, claiming that the immigration practice of the United Kingdom violated their right to respect for family life under article 8 of the Convention. They contended that the right to respect for family life encompasses the right to establish one's family home in the country of one's nationality or lawful residence. They also claimed that they had been victims of discrimination on the grounds of sex and race contrary to article 14 in conjunction with article 8, and that such discrimination constituted degrading treatment contrary to article 3. Mrs Balkandali further claimed that she had been a victim of discrimination on the ground of birth as her husband's application had been refused under the United Kingdom's immigration rules on the basis that neither she nor either of her parents had been born in the United Kingdom and Colonies. Finally, the applicants alleged that there had been no effective remedy for their complaints, in breach of article 13 of the Convention.

The European Commission held that the United Kingdom was in violation of article 14 in conjunction with article 8 on the grounds of sex and birth, but not on the ground of race, and also in violation of article 13. The case was referred to the European Court of Human Rights.

HELD (finding a violation of article 14 in conjunction with article 8, and a violation of article 13 of the Convention)

Article 8 (right to respect for family life)

1   By guaranteeing the right to respect for family life, article 8 presupposed the existence of a family. However, this did not mean that all *intended* family life fell entirely outside its ambit. Whatever else the word "family" might mean, it should at any rate include the relationship that arose from a lawful and genuine marriage, such as that contracted by the applicants. Each of the applicants had to a sufficient degree entered upon "family life" for the purposes of article 8 and that provision was therefore applicable to the present case. (Paras 62 and 65)

2   The expression "family life", in the case of a married couple, normally comprised cohabitation. This was reinforced by the existence of article 12, for it was scarcely conceivable that the right to found a family should not encompass the right to live together. (Para 62).

3   There might be positive obligations inherent in an effective "respect" for family life under article 8. However, as far as those positive obligations were concerned, the notion of "respect" was not clear cut and this was an area in which the Contracting States enjoyed a wide margin of appreciation. In particular, the extent of a State's obligation to admit to its territory relatives of settled immigrants would vary according to the particular circumstances of the persons involved. None of the three applicants already had a family which they left behind in another country. It was only after becoming settled in the United Kingdom, as single persons, that the applicants contracted marriage. The duty imposed by article 8 could not be considered as extending a general obligation on the part of a Contracting State to respect the choice by married couples of the country of their matrimonial residence and to accept the non-national spouses for settlement in that country. There was accordingly no lack of respect for family life and hence no breach of article 8 taken alone. (Paras 67, 68 and 69).

Article 14 taken together with Article 8 (discrimination in right to respect for family life)

4   In response to the argument that the difference of treatment between immigrant wives and immigrant husbands was justified by the need to protect the domestic labour

market at a time of high unemployment, the Court was not convinced that there was in fact such a difference between the respective impact on the United Kingdom labour market of immigrant wives and of immigrant husbands. In any event, even if such a difference did exist, it was not sufficiently important to justify the difference in treatment complained of by the applicants, as to the possibility for a person settled in the United Kingdom to be joined by, as the case may be, his wife or her husband. The applicants had therefore been victims of discrimination on the ground of sex in violation of article 14 taken together with article 8. (Paras 79 and 83)

5   The immigration rules in question, which were applicable in general to all "non-patrials" wanting to enter and settle in the United Kingdom, did not contain regulations differentiating between persons or groups on the ground of their race or ethnic origin; they were grounded not on objections regarding the origin of the non-nationals wanting to enter the country, but on the need to stem the flow of immigrants at the relevant time. The applicants had not been victims of discrimination on the ground of race. (Para 85)

6   There were in general persuasive social reasons for giving special treatment to those whose link with a country stemmed from birth within it. The rule that, as between women citizens of the United Kingdom and Colonies settled in the United Kingdom, only those born or having a parent born in that country could have their non-national husband accepted for settlement there, should be regarded as having had an objective and reasonable justification and, in particular, its results had not been shown to transgress the principle of proportionality. Ms Balkandali was not the victim of discrimination on the ground of birth. (Paras 88 and 89)

Article 3 (right not to be subjected to degrading treatment)

7   The difference of treatment complained of by the applicants did not denote any contempt or lack of respect for the personality of the applicants, and it was not designed to, and did not, humiliate or debase. It could not be regarded as "degrading" and there was no violation of article 3. (Para 91)

Article 13 (right to effective remedy)

8   Since the United Kingdom had not incorporated the Convention into domestic law, there could be no "effective remedy" as required by article 13. Recourse to the available channels of complaint could have been effective only if the complainant had alleged that the discrimination resulted from a misapplication of the immigration rules. No such allegation was made nor was it suggested that the discrimination in any other way contravened domestic law. Hence there had been a violation of article 13. (Para 93)

Treaties and other international instruments referred to

European Convention for the Protection of Human Rights and Fundamental Freedoms 1950, arts 3, 8, 12, 13, 14 and 50

Optional Protocol No 4 to the European Convention for the Protection of Human Rights and Freedoms 1968

National legislation referred to

United Kingdom

British Nationality Act 1948

British Nationality Act 1981, ss 6, 11, 39; Schedule 1

Commonwealth Immigrants Act 1962

Commonwealth Immigrants Act 1968

Immigration Act 1971, ss 1(2), 1(4), 2, 3(1), 3(2), 3(3), 3(5)(a), 3(6), 4(1), 5, 6, 7, 13, 14, 15, 19(1), 19(2), 19(3), 20(1), 20(2) and 24(1)(b)

Immigration Appeals Act 1969

Immigration Appeals (Procedure) Rules 1972, rule 14

Statement of Changes in Immigration Rules (HC 384) 1980, paras 1, 2, 13, 42, 43, 44, 50, 51, 52, 53, 55, 88, 114, 115, 116 and 117

Statement of Changes in Immigration Rules (HC 66) 1982, paras 41, 54 and 126

Statement of Changes in Immigration Rules (HC 169) 1983, paras 54 and 177

Philippines

Civil Code, arts 53, 76 and 80

Cases referred to

Airey v Ireland, ECHR, judgment of 9 October 1979, Series A, No 32; 2 EHRR 305; 58 ILR 624; *supra* p 67

Albert and Le Compte v Belgium, ECHR, judgment of 10 February 1983, Series A, No 58; 5 EHRR 553

Case "Relating to Certain Aspects of the Laws on the Use of Languages in Education in Belgium" v Belgium (Merits), ECHR, judgment of 23 July 1968, Series A, No 6; 1 EHRR 252

Campbell and Fell v The United Kingdom, ECHR, judgment of 28 June 1984, Series A, No 80; 7 EHRR 165

Marckx v Belgium, ECHR, judgment of 13 June 1979, Series A, No 31; 2 EHRR 330; 58 ILR 561; *supra* p 273

National Union of Belgian Police v Belgium, ECHR, judgment of 27 October 1975, Series A, No 19; 1 EHRR 578

R v Secretary of State for the Home Dept ex parte Hosenball [1977] 1 WLR 766; [1977] 3 All ER 452

Rasmussen v Denmark, ECHR, judgment of 28 November 1984, Series A, No 87; 7 EHRR 371

Silver v The United Kingdom, ECHR, judgment of 25 March 1983, Series A, No 61; 5 EHRR 347

Young, James and Webster v The United Kingdom, ECHR, judgment of 13 August 1981, Series A, No 44; 3 EHRR 20

JUDGMENT

PROCEDURE

[...]*

AS TO THE FACTS

10 The applicants are lawfully and permanently settled in the United Kingdom. In accordance with the immigration rules in force at the material time, Mr Abdulaziz, Mr Cabales and Mr Balkandali were refused permission to remain with or join them in the United Kingdom as their husbands. The applicants maintained that, on this account, they had been victims of a practice of discrimination on the grounds of sex, race and also, in the case of Mrs Balkandali, birth, and that there had been violations of Article 3 of the Convention and of Article 8, taken alone or in conjunction with Article 14. They further alleged that, contrary to Article 13, no effective domestic remedy existed for the aforesaid claims.

I Domestic law and practice

A History and background

11 The evolution of immigration controls in the United Kingdom has to be seen in the light of the history of the British Empire and the corresponding developments in nationality laws. Originally all persons born within or having a specified connection with the United Kingdom or the dominions owed allegiance to the Crown and were British subjects. A common British nationality was, however, difficult to reconcile with the independence of the self-governing countries of the Commonwealth into which the Empire was transformed. As the various territories concerned became independent, they introduced their own citizenship laws but, for the purposes of United Kingdom law, persons having a citizenship of an independent Commonwealth country retained a special status, known as "British subject" or "Commonwealth citizen" (these terms being synonymous). This status was also held by "citizens of the United Kingdom and Colonies". Prior to 1 January 1973, the latter citizenship was, briefly, acquired by birth within the United Kingdom or one of its remaining dependencies, by descent from a father having that citizenship, by naturalisation or by registration (British Nationality Act 1948).

12 Whereas aliens have been subject to continuing strict immigration controls over a long period, the same is not true of Commonwealth citizens. Until 1962, Commonwealth citizens, irrespective of their local citizenship, all had freedom to enter the United Kingdom for work and permanent residence, without any restriction. A rapid rise in the influx of immigrants, especially in 1960 and 1961, and the consequent danger of the rate of immigration exceeding the country's capacity to absorb them led to a radical change in this situation. The Commonwealth Immigrants Act 1962, and then the Commonwealth Immigrants Act 1968, restricted the right of entry of, and imposed immigration controls on, certain classes of Commonwealth citizens, including citizens of the United Kingdom and Colonies, who did not have close links to Britain.

---

* *Eds:* paras 1 to 9, which relate to procedural matters, have not been included.

B   The Immigration Act 1971

13   The existing immigration laws were amended and replaced by the Immigration Act 1971 ("the 1971 Act"), which came into force on 1 January 1973. One of its main purposes was to assimilate immigration controls over incoming Commonwealth citizens having no close links to Britain to the corresponding rules of aliens. The Act created two new categories of persons for immigration purposes, namely those having the right of abode in the United Kingdom ("patrials") and those not having the right ("non-patrials").

14   "Patrials" were to be free from immigration controls. The status of "patrial" was intended to designate Commonwealth citizens who "belonged" to the United Kingdom and, in summary, was conferred (by section 2 of the 1971 Act) on:

(a) citizens of the United Kingdom and Colonies who had acquired that citizenship by birth, adoption, naturalisation or registration in British Islands (that is, the United Kingdom, the Channel Islands and the Isle of Man), or were the children or grandchildren of any such persons;

(b) citizens of the United Kingdom and Colonies who had at any time been settled in the British Islands for at least five years;

(c) other Commonwealth citizens who were the children of a person having citizenship of the United Kingdom and Colonies by virtue of birth in the British Islands;

(d) women, being Commonwealth citizens, who were or had been married to a man falling within any of the preceding categories.

15   Under section 1(2) of the 1971 Act, "non-patrials" (whether Commonwealth citizens or aliens) "may live, work and settle in the United Kingdom by permission and subject to such regulation and control of their entry into, stay in, and departure from the United Kingdom as is imposed" by the Act.

Subject to certain exceptions not relevant to the present case, a "non-patrial" shall not enter the United Kingdom unless given leave to do so (section 3(1)). He may be given such leave (or, if he is already in the country, leave to remain) either for a limited or for an indefinite period; in the former case, the leave may be subject to conditions restricting employment or requiring registration with the police or both (section 3(1)). Where limited leave to enter or remain is granted, it may subsequently be varied, either as regards its duration or the conditions attaching thereto but, if the limit on duration is removed, any conditions attached to the leave cease to apply (section 3(3)). The power to give or refuse leave to enter is exercised by immigration officers but the power to give or vary leave to remain can be exercised only by the Home Secretary (section 4(1)).

C   The Immigration Rules

16   Under section 3(2) of the 1971 Act, the Home Secretary is obliged from time to time to lay before Parliament statements of the rules, or of any changes therein, laid down by him as to the practice to be followed in the administration of the Act for regulating entry into, and stay in, the United Kingdom. These rules contain instructions to immigration officers as to how they shall exercise the statutory discretions given to them by the Act and statements of the manner in which the Home Secretary will exercise his own powers of control after entry. The rules are required to provide for the admission of persons coming for the purpose of taking employment, or for the purpose of study, or as visitors, or as dependants of persons lawfully in or entering the United Kingdom, but uniform provision does not have to be made for these categories and, in particular, account may be taken of citizenship or nationality (sections 1(4) and 3(2)). Thus, different rules can be

and are made for nationals of the member States of the European Economic Community under community law, and Irish citizens are in a special position.

17 The rules are subject to a negative resolution procedure whereby, if a resolution disapproving the Home Secretary's statement is passed by either House of Parliament within 40 days of its being laid, the Home Secretary is required as soon as may be possible to make such changes as appear to him to be required in the circumstances and to lay the rules as amended before Parliament within 40 days of the passing of the resolution (section 3(2)). The statement of rules thus amended is subject to the same procedure as the original statement. Because of the continuous nature of decision-making by immigration officers, the statement originally laid is not abrogated by any negative resolution; it will come into operation when made or on the date therein provided and will remain in force until replaced.

18 The exact legal status of the rules is of some complexity. This question was considered by the Court of Appeal in *R v Secretary of State for the Home Department, ex parte Hosenball* [1977] 3 All ER 452 when Lord Denning MR said [at p 459]

> [The Home Secretary's rules] are not rules of law. They are rules of practice laid down for the guidance of immigration officers and tribunals who are entrusted with the administration of the [1971 Act]. They can be, and often are, prayed in aid by applicants before the courts in immigration cases. To some extent the courts must have regard to them because there are provisions in the Act itself, particularly in section 19, which show that in appeals to an adjudicator, if the immigration rules have not been complied with, then the appeal is to be allowed. In addition the courts always have regard to those rules, not only in matters where there is a right of appeal; but also in cases under prerogative writs where there is a question whether officers have acted fairly. But they are not rules in the nature of delegated legislation so as to amount to strict rules of law.

Geoffrey Lane LJ also doubted whether the rules constituted delegated legislation. He observed [at p 463]: "These rules are very difficult to categorise or classify. They are in a class of their own. They are certainly a practical guide for ... immigration officers ... Indeed they are, as to large parts, ... little more than explanatory notes of the [1971 Act] itself." However, he noted that if Parliament disapproved of the rules, they were not thereby abrogated. Furthermore, at least as far as an adjudicator dealing with appeals was concerned, the rules had the force of law, although it seemed that they could be departed from with the consent of the applicant himself.

Cumming-Bruce LJ said [at pp 465–466]

> [The rules] are a totally different kind of publication from the rules that usually come into being under the authority delegated to Ministers under Acts of Parliament; ... they are not in my view in any sense of themselves of legislative force. It is true that ... the rules are given legal effect in the field of the appellate process to the adjudicator or the tribunal ... But the legal effect that the rules have in that limited field flows not from the fact that they have been published by the Minister and laid before Parliament, but because by section 19(2) of the [1971] Act the rules are given an effect which is in a certain field clearly legally enforceable, and that is a quite different matter.

19 Notwithstanding that an application for entry clearance (see para 22(b) below) or leave to enter or remain may fall to be refused under the relevant immigration rules, the Home Secretary has a discretion, deriving from historic prerogative powers, to authorise in exceptional circumstances the grant of entry clearance or of leave to enter, or to allow a person to remain in the United Kingdom. Where the applicant is a husband seeking to join or remain with his wife settled in the United Kingdom, factors which the Home Secretary will consider include the extent of her ties with that country and of the

hardship she might suffer by going to live abroad, and any recommendations by the immigration appellate authorities.

D   *Position at the time of the events giving rise to the present case*

1   Introduction

20 The rules in force at the time of the events giving rise to the present case were contained in the "Statement of Changes in Immigration Rules" (HC 384) laid before Parliament on 20 February 1980 ("the 1980 Rules"); they applied to all decisions taken on or after 1 March 1980, except those relating to applications made on or before 14 November 1979. A draft of the rules had previously been included in a White Paper published in November 1979.

The 1980 Rules, which in para 2 instructed immigration officers to carry out their duties without regard to the race, colour or religion of the intending entrant, detailed firstly the controls to be exercised on the entry into the United Kingdom of "non-patrials" and then those to be exercised after entry. The former [ie controls on entry] depended on whether the individual concerned was coming for temporary purposes (for example, visitors or students), for employment of business or as a person of independent means, or for settlement. As under the rules previously in force, visitors were normally to be prohibited from taking employment and persons wishing to come for employment were subject to strict regulations as to work permits. The work permit requirements, however, did not apply to nationals of other Member States of the European Economic Community nor to persons covered by the "United Kingdom ancestry rule"; under the latter rule, which had been in force since the 1971 Act came into operation, a Commonwealth citizen having a grandparent born in the British Islands and wishing to take or seek employment in the United Kingdom could obtain indefinite leave to enter even without a work permit. A further exception was to be found in the "working holiday rule", whereby young Commonwealth citizens could, without a permit, take employment incidental to an extended holiday being spent in the United Kingdom; however, the period of their stay could, under the 1980 Rules, not exceed two years. All these exceptions have been maintained in subsequent immigration rules.

21 A particular feature of the changes introduced by the 1980 Rules was the inclusion of a number of provisions directed towards implementing a policy of protecting the domestic labour market at a time of high unemployment by curtailing "primary immigration", that is immigration by someone who could be expected to seek full-time work in order to support a family. In taking these measures, the Government was concerned also to advance public tranquility and, by exercising firm and fair immigration control, to assist in securing good community relations.

To these ends, among the changes effected was the introduction of stricter conditions or the grant of leave to a "non-patrial" husband or fiancé seeking to join or remain with his wife or fiancée settled in the United Kingdom. Previously, any such husband or fiancé would normally have been allowed to settle after a qualifying period, provided that the primary purpose of the marriage was not to obtain settlement in that country. These new measures were not extended to the wives or fiancées of settled men, a fact attributed by the Government to long-standing commitments (based allegedly on humanitarian, social and ethical reasons) to the reunification of the families of male immigrants. Nor did the new measures apply to nationals of other Member States of the European Economic Community.

22 The relevant provisions of the 1980 Rules – and of their successors – are summarised below in terms of the following expressions:

(a) A person is "settled in the United Kingdom" when he or she is ordinarily resident there without having entered or remained in breach of the immigration laws, and is free from any restriction on the period for which he or she may remain (para 1).

(b) An "entry clearance" is a document (either a visa, an entry certificate or a Home Office letter of consent, depending on the nationality of the person concerned) which is to be taken by an immigration officer as evidence that the holder, although a "non-patrial", is eligible under the immigration rules for entry to the United Kingdom. It is obtained at British missions abroad or from the Home Office prior to arrival in the United Kingdom.

(c) A marriage or intended marriage is "non-qualifying" if there is reason to believe that:

 – its primary purpose is to obtain admission to or settlement in the United Kingdom; or

 – the parties do not intend to live together permanently as man and wife; or

 – the parties have not met (paras 50, 52, 117).

(d) There is "potential evasion of the rules" if there is reason to believe that a husband has remained in the United Kingdom in breach of the immigration rules before the marriage, that the marriage has taken place after a decision or recommendation that he be deported or that the marriage has terminated (para 117).

(e) The "financial requirement" is a requirement that varies according the circumstances of the particular case: basically it means that adequate maintenance and accommodation must be available to the person concerned without the need for recourse to public funds (paras 42, 52 and 55).

2 "Non-patrials" seeking to join a spouse or intended spouse settled in the United Kingdom

23 Where a "non-patrial" whose spouse or intended spouse was "settled in the United Kingdom" came to that country for settlement, he or she would be admitted for that purpose provided that he or she held a current "entry clearance" and unless the circumstances specified in para 13 of the 1980 Rules obtained (for example, false representations, medical grounds, criminal record, exclusion would be conductive to the public good).

(a) Where the intending entrant was a *husband* or *fiancé*,[*] he could, under paras 50 and 52, obtain an "entry clearance":

 (i) unless the marriage or intended marriage was "non-qualifying";

 (ii) if his wife or fiancée was a citizen of the United Kingdom and Colonies who or one of whose parents had been born in the United Kingdom; and

 (iii) if, in the cases of fiancés only, the "financial requirement" was satisfied.

(b) Where the intending entrant was a *wife* or *fiancée*[*] she could, under paras 42, 43 and 55, obtain an "entry clearance" irrespective of the nationality of her husband or fiancé or of his own or his parents' place of birth. Here, there was no provision as to "non-qualifying" marriages, but the "financial requirement" had generally to be satisfied.

---

[*]   *Eds:* emphasis added.

(c) Wives admitted under these rules would be given indefinite leave to enter; husbands would be initially admitted for twelve months and fiancés or fiancées for three months, with the possibility, subject to certain safeguards, of applying subsequently to the Home Office for indefinite leave (paras 44, 51, 53, 55, 114, 116).

3 "Non-patrials" seeking to remain in the United Kingdom with a spouse settled there.

24 "Non-patrials" already admitted to the United Kingdom in a temporary capacity who subsequently married a person "settled in the United Kingdom" could also obtain permission to stay:

(a) Where the "non-patrial" seeking permission was a *man,** the basic conditions (para 117) were that:

    (i) his wife was a citizen of the United Kingdom and Colonies who, or one of whose parents, had been born in the United Kingdom; and

    (ii) the marriage was not "non-qualifying" and there was not "potential evasion of the rules".

(b) Where the "non-patrial" seeking permission was a *woman,** she would normally be granted leave to remain on application (para 115).

(c) Leave to remain granted under these rules would be, for wives, indefinite and, for husbands, for an initial period of 12 months with the possibility, subject again to the conditions referred to in sub-para (a)(ii) above, of subsequent removal of the time limit (paras 115 and 117).

4 General considerations regarding leave to remain

25 Decisions on applications for leave to remain were taken in the light of all relevant facts; thus, even where the individual satisfied the formal requirements, permission would normally be refused if the circumstances specified in para 88 of the 1980 Rules obtained (for example, false representations, non-compliance with the time limit or conditions subject to which he or she had been admitted or given leave to remain, undesirable character, danger to national security).

E Subsequent developments

1 Introduction

26 One result of the 1971 Act was that the right of abode in the United Kingdom became divorced from nationality: thus, a number of citizens of the United Kingdom and Colonies did not have that right (for example, because they had not been born in the British Islands), whereas it was enjoyed by a number of persons who were not such citizens (for example, Commonwealth citizens having an ancestral link with the United Kingdom). With a view to bringing citizenship and immigration laws into line, the position was substantially amended by the British Nationality Act 1981, which came into force on 1 January 1983. So far as is relevant for the present purposes, that Act:

(a) replaced citizenship of the United Kingdom and Colonies (see para 11 in fine above) with three separate citizenships, "British", "British Dependent Territories" and "British Overseas";

(b) provided, in section 11(1), that on 1 January 1983 "British citizenship" was to be acquired by persons who were then citizens of the United Kingdom and Colonies and

---

*   *Eds:* emphasis added.

had the right of abode in the United Kingdom under the 1971 Act; this category could include a person who was neither born nor had a parent born in the United Kingdom;

(c) laid down detailed provisions on the acquisition of British citizenship by persons born after 1 January 1983;

(d) contained, in section 6 and Schedule 1, detailed provisions on naturalisation as a British citizen on the basis of residence in the United Kingdom, the grant of a certificate of naturalisation being at the discretion of the Home Secretary;

(e) amended the 1971 Act by providing in section 39 that the right of abode in the United Kingdom – use of the expressions "patrial" and "non-patrial" was abandoned – and the consequential freedom from immigration controls were in future to be enjoyed only by British citizens and by such Commonwealth citizens as on 31 December 1972 had the right of abode under the 1971 Act.

2 The 1982 immigration rules

27 On 6 December 1982, after debates in the House of Commons and the House of Lords, the Home Secretary laid before Parliament a Statement of Changes in Immigration Rules (HC 66, "the 1982 Rules"), intended to harmonise the immigration rules with the British Nationality Act 1981 and expressed to come into force on 1 January 1983. However, on 15 December 1982 the House of Commons passed a resolution disapproving the Statement, some Members finding the changes too lax and others, insufficient. Since by 1 January 1983 no further changes had been laid before Parliament, the 1982 rules came into force on that date, notwithstanding the negative resolution.

28 The 1982 Rules made no changes to the regime governing wives and fiancées, described in paras 23–25 above. The regime governing a husband or fiancé was modified in the following main respects:

(a) The requirement that, for him to be eligible for leave to enter or remain, his wife or fiancée had to be a citizen of the United Kingdom and Colonies born or having a parent born in the United Kingdom was, under paras 41, 54 and 126, replaced by a requirement that she be a British citizen. The place of her own or her parents' birth ceased to be material since British citizens could include persons without the territorial birth link (for example, a woman born in a former Colony but having the right of abode in the United Kingdom by virtue of long residence there; see paras 14(b) and 26(b) above).

(b) By virtue of paras 41, 54 and 126, the onus of proof was reversed, so that it became for the man seeking leave to enter or remain to show that the marriage was not "non-qualifying" or, in cases to which para 126 applied, that there was not "potential evasion of the rules".

(c) Leave to remain for settlement following marriage, granted to a man admitted in a temporary capacity (see para 24(c) above), would be for an initial period of 12 months, followed by a further period of 12 months and then by the possibility, subject again to the conditions referred to in sub-para (b) above, of subsequent removal of the time limit (para 126).

29 No provision was made in the 1982 Rules for women settled in the United Kingdom who were not British citizens to be joined by their husbands, although leave could be granted by the Home Secretary in the exercise of his extra-statutory discretion (see para 19 above). These women could also apply for naturalization as British citizens on the basis of residence, under section 6 of the British Nationality Act 1981 (see para 26(d) above).

3 The 1983 immigration rules

30 On 9 February 1983, a further Statement of Changes in Immigration Rules (HC 169; "the 1983 Rules") was laid before Parliament. A motion disapproving these rules was defeated in the House of Commons and they came into force on 16 February 1983.

31 The 1983 rules again did not modify the regime governing wives and fiancées. The regime governing husbands was amended, so far as is material to the present case, in that, under para 126, the position concerning the length of leave to remain granted to a man already in the United Kingdom reverted to that obtaining under the 1980 Rules (that is, initial leave of 12 months, followed by the possibility of indefinite leave, see para 24(c) above). This change was coupled with a transitional provision (para 177) concerning men who, whilst the 1982 Rules were in force (see para 28(c) above), had been granted thereunder an extension of stay for a second period of 12 months: they were entitled to apply immediately for indefinite leave without awaiting the expiry of that period.

32 There was no change in the position concerning women settled in the United Kingdom who were not British citizens, described in para 29 above.

F Sanctions

33 Under section 3(5)(a), 3(6), 5, 6, 7 and 24(1)(b) of the 1971 Act, a person not having the right of abode in the United Kingdom and having only limited leave to enter or remain in that country who overstays the period of leave or fails to observe a condition attached thereto:

(a) commits a criminal offence punishable with a fine of not more than £200 or imprisonment of not more than six months or both, to which penalties the court may, with certain exceptions, add a recommendation for deportation; and

(b) is, with certain exceptions, liable to deportation, although he cannot be compelled to leave unless the Home Secretary decides to make a deportation order against him.

G Appeals

34 Appellate authorities in immigration matters were established by the Immigration Appeals Act 1969. They consist of:

(a) adjudicators, who sit alone and are appointed by the Home Secretary;

(b) the Immigration Appeal Tribunal which sits in divisions of at least three members; the members are appointed by the Lord Chancellor and a certain number must be lawyers.

There is no further right of appeal as such to the ordinary courts, but decisions of the appellate authorities are susceptible to judicial review by the High Court on the ground of such matters as error of law or unreasonableness. Judicial review of immigration decisions may also cover questions of an abuse or excess of power by the Home Secretary or whether an immigration officer acted impartially and fairly.

35 Under sections 13, 14 and 15 of the 1971 Act, an appeal may, subject to certain exceptions, be made to an adjudicator against, *inter alia*:

(a) refusal of leave to enter the United Kingdom or of an entry clearance;

(b) variation of, or refusal to vary, a limited leave to remain in the United Kingdom;

(c) a decision to make a deportation order.

An appellant shall not be required to leave the United Kingdom by reason of the expiration of his leave so long as his appeal is pending against a refusal to enlarge or remove the limit on the duration of the leave. However, no appeal lies against refusal of an extension of leave to remain if application therefor was made after expiry of the existing leave.

36 Except as otherwise provided by the 1971 Act, an adjudicator is, under section 19(1), to allow an appeal only if he considers:

(a) that the decision or action in question was not in accordance with the law or any immigration rules applicable to the case; or

(b) that, where the decision or action involved the exercise of a discretion by the Home Secretary or an officer, that discretion should have been exercised differently.

If, however, the decision or action is in accordance with the rules, the adjudicator may not review a refusal by the Home Secretary of a request, by the person concerned, that he should depart from the rules (section 19(2)).

Where an appeal is allowed, the adjudicator must give such directions for giving effect to his decision as he thinks requisite and may also make further recommendations; the directions are binding on the Home Secretary except so long as an appeal to the Immigration Appeal Tribunal can be brought or is pending (sections 19(3) and 20(2)).

37 Any party to an appeal to an adjudicator may appeal against his decision to the Immigration Appeal Tribunal, which may affirm that decision or make any other decision which the adjudicator could have made; it also had similar duties and powers in the matter of directions and recommendations. As the law stood at the relevant time, leave to appeal had generally to be obtained; it had to be granted, *inter alia*, if determination of the appeal turned upon an arguable point of law (section 20(1) of the 1971 Act and Rule 14 of the Immigration Appeals (Procedure) Rules 1972)

H   Statistics

38(a) The Government estimated total immigration into the United Kingdom from the New Commonwealth (that is, the Commonwealth except Australia, Canada and New Zealand) at 500,000 in the period from 1955 to mid-1962. It was thought that by the latter date some 600 million people had the right of abode in the United Kingdom. Between mid-1962 and the end of 1981, a further 900,000 people were estimated to have settled in that country from the New Commonwealth and Pakistan, some 420,000 from non-Commonwealth countries other than Pakistan and some 94,000 from the Old Commonwealth (Australia, Canada and New Zealand); relatively few countries were said to have accounted for most of this immigration.

The official estimates for 1981 show that the population of the United Kingdom (53.7 million) included 2.2 million persons of New Commonwealth and Pakistan origin (of whom about 1 million were in the Greater London area) and 1.2 million other persons not born in the United Kingdom (including those born in the Old Commonwealth but not those born in the Republic of Ireland). It is estimated that the population of New Commonwealth and Pakistan origin could rise to 2.5 million by 1986 and 3 million (5% of the projected total population) by 1991.

38(b) According to the Government, some 3,500 persons entered the United Kingdom annually under the "United Kingdom ancestry rule", but many of them emigrated after a few years.

38(c) In 1980–1983, there was an average net annual emigration from the United Kingdom of about 44,000 but the population density in 1981 – 229 persons per square kilometer or 355 persons per square kilometer for England alone – was higher than that of any other Member State of the European Communities.

38(d) Statistics supplied by the Government showed that in Great Britain in 1981 90% of all men of working age and 63% of all women of working age were "economically active" (that is, either in employment, or self-employed, or unemployed). The corresponding figures for persons coming from the Indian sub-continent were 86% for men and 41% for women and, for persons coming from the West Indies or Guyana, 90% for men and 70% for women. The statistics also disclosed that a considerably higher proportion of "economically active" women (particularly married women) than men were in part-time employment only – 47% of married women, compared with 2.3% of men.

Recent years have seen a high level of unemployment in the United Kingdom. In 1983, 15.3% of "economically active" men and 8.4% of "economically active" women were unemployed, as measured by official figures based on persons claiming unemployment benefit. There was a marked increase between 1980 and 1981, when the figures rose from 7.9 to 12.6% and from 4.3 to 6.4%, respectively.

38(e) The Government also produced to the court detailed statistics in support of their claim that the overall effect of the 1980 Rules had been to lead to an annual reduction of up to 5,700 (rather than 2,000, as they had estimated before the Commission) in the number of husbands either accepted for settlement or applying successfully to come for settlement from all parts of the world. They recognised, however, that part – though not a major part – of this figure might represent a decrease attributable to economic conditions. In their submission, this reduction was of a considerable scale when viewed in relation to the figures for the total number of persons accepted for settlement into the United Kingdom. The latter figures (about one-half of which were in each year accounted for by wives and children of men already settled in the country) were: over 80,000 in 1975 and 1976; around 70,000 in each year from 1977 to 1980; 59,100 in 1981; 53,900 in 1982; and 53,500 in 1983. The number of men accepted for settlement by reason of marriage was 11,190 in 1975; 11,060 in 1976; 5,610 in 1977; 9,330 in 1978; 9,900 in 1979; 9,160 in 1980; 6,690 in 1981; 6,070 in 1982; and 5,210 in 1983. The number of women so accepted was 19,890 in 1977; 18,950 in 1978; 19,708 in 1979; 15,430; in 1980; 16,760 in 1981; 15,490 in 1982; and 16,900 in 1983.

The claimed reduction of 5,700 per annum was questioned by the applicants on the following grounds: it was based on a comparison with the figures for 1979, a year in which the number of applications from the Indian sub-continent was artificially high; in order to take account of the delays in processing applications and the 12-month waiting period before indefinite leave to remain between the 1981 and the 1983 figures; no account was taken of the natural decline in applications; and no account was taken of persons properly excluded (for example, on the ground that the marriage was not genuine).

II   The particular circumstances of the case

A   Mrs Abdulaziz

39 Mrs Nargis Abdulaziz is permanently and lawfully resident in the United Kingdom with the right to remain indefinitely. She was born in Malawi in 1948 and brought up in

that country. Her parents were also born there. According to her, she was a citizen of Malawi at birth but, being of Indian origin, was subsequently deprived of that citizenship and is now stateless. She holds a Malawian travel document.

This applicant went to the United Kingdom on 23 December 1977. She was given leave, as a "non-patrial", to enter as a visitor, leave which was subsequently extended on three occasions. Since special vouchers had been allocated to members of her family enabling them to settle in the United Kingdom, an application was made on her behalf for indefinite leave to remain. On 16 May 1979, as an act of discretion outside the immigration rules, she was given such leave, essentially on the ground that she was an unmarried woman with little prospect of marriage who formed part of a close family, including her father and mother, settled in the United Kingdom.

40 Mr Ibramobai Abdulaziz is a Portuguese national who was born in Daman, a former Portuguese territory in India, in 1951. He emigrated to Portugal in 1978. On 4 October 1979, he was admitted, as a "non-patrial", to the United Kingdom for six months as a visitor. He met the applicant six days later and they became engaged to be married on 27 November. They were married on 8 December 1979 and, during the following week, Mrs Abdulaziz applied for leave for her husband to remain permanently in the United Kingdom. Shortly afterwards, the Joint Council for the Welfare of Immigrants also applied for leave for him to remain, for a period of twelve months.

41 After Mr and Mrs Abdulaziz had been interviewed at the Home Office on 6 June 1980, her application was refused, on 1 July, on the ground that she was not a citizen of the United Kingdom and Colonies who, or one of whose parents, had been born in the United Kingdom (para 117 of the 1980 Rules; see para 24(a)(1) above).

Mr Abdulaziz appealed to an adjudicator against this decision but the appeal was dismissed on 6 October 1981 as he did not qualify for leave to remain under the 1980 Rules. The adjudicator pointed out that, had the application been made before 14 November 1979 or the decision taken before 1 March 1980, Mr Abdulaziz would have been admitted, under the previous rules (see paras 20 and 21 above). Leave to appeal to the Immigration Appeal Tribunal was refused by the Tribunal on 9 December 1981 on the ground that the determination of the appeal did not turn on any arguable point of law and that leave to appeal was not otherwise merited (see para 37 above).

42 Subsequently Mr Abdulaziz remained, and still remains, in the United Kingdom, without leave. He is currently employed as a chef in a restaurant; his wife does not work. A son was born to the couple in October 1982. Representations through Members of Parliament to the Home Office have been rejected, basically on the ground that the couple could live together in Portugal and that the circumstances of the case were not such as to warrant exceptional treatment. In a letter of 24 February 1982 to one Member, the Minister of State at the Home Office indicated that the authorities would shortly be advising Mr Abdulaziz to depart without delay, adding that if he did not, "consideration will have to be given to enforcing his departure"; however, a letter of 29 November 1982 to another Member stated that "[the Minister did] not propose for the time being to take any action regarding [Mr Abdulaziz's] removal". In fact, the authorities have not to date instituted any criminal or deportation proceedings against him; their decision, according to the Government, was taken in the light of all the circumstances, including the Commission's decision on the admissibility of Mrs Abdulaziz's application (see para 55 below).

The couple's situation has not until now been changed by the 1982 or the 1983 Rules since Mrs Abdulaziz, although settled in the United Kingdom, is not a British citizen (see paras 27 to 32 above). She has, however, applied, on 16 August 1984, for naturalisation as such a citizen, under section 6 of the British Nationality Act 1981 (see para 26(d) above).

43 At the Home Office interview, Mr Abdulaziz said that his wife could not be expected to live in Portugal because she had always been close to her family and because her sick father – who in fact died in September 1980 – needed her company. Before the Commission and the Court, she claimed that her health was under strain because of her husband's settlement problems and that humanitarian considerations prevented her going to Portugal, a country where she had no family and whose language she did not speak. The Government maintain that there is no obstacle whatever to her going with her husband to live in Portugal.

B   Mrs Cabales

44 Mrs Arcely Cabales is permanently and lawfully resident in the United Kingdom with the right to remain indefinitely. She was born in the Philippines in 1939 and was brought up there, and is of Asian origin. She had the nationality of that country until 1984 (see para 47 below). Her parents were born and live in the Philippines.

This applicant went to the United Kingdom in 1967 with a work permit for employment as a nursing assistant and was admitted, as a "non-patrial" (see paras 13–15 above) for 12 months. She remained in approved work thereafter and, on 10 June 1971, the conditions attached to her stay were removed and she was allowed to remain in the United Kingdom indefinitely. She is now employed, and has an established career, as a state enrolled nurse.

45 Mr Ludovico Cabales is a citizen of the Philippines, born in that country in 1937. He met the applicant in Manila in 1977 when she was on holiday and again in 1979 when she was there for one or two months. During the latter period, the couple became engaged. On 23 April 1980, they went through a ceremony of marriage in the Philippines. The applicant returned to the United Kingdom shortly afterwards to take up her job again. In May 1980, she informed the Home Office of the marriage and applied for leave for Mr Cabales to enter the United Kingdom, a request which she repeated in August. On 27 November, he, being a "non-patrial", applied to the British Embassy in Manila for a visa to join his wife for settlement in the United Kingdom.

46 After Mrs Cabales had supplied certain further information requested by it, the Home Office wrote to her on 23 February 1981 to advise her that the visa application had been refused on the ground that she was not a citizen of the United Kingdom and Colonies who, or one of whose parents, had been born in the United Kingdom (para 50 of the 1980 Rules; see para 23(a)(ii) above). Notice of the decision was not handed to Mr Cabales until 12 November 1981 as he had failed to respond to an invitation of March 1981 to attend at the Manila Embassy for that purpose.

On 20 August 1981, the Joint Council for the Welfare of Immigrants wrote to the Home Office Immigration and Nationality Department, seeking a review of this decision. However, on 13 January 1982, the Department, having considered the circumstances, informed the Council of its decision to maintain the refusal. Mr Cabales had on 8 December 1981 lodged an appeal with an adjudicator (see paras 34–36 above) against the decision but the appeal was dismissed on 25 July 1983 on the ground that the visa officer's decision was in accordance with the law and the immigration rules. The adjudicator, who noted that Mrs Cabales had not taken legal advice but had thought at the time of the marriage ceremony that a forthcoming change in the law would allow Mr Cabales to be admitted, expressed the hope that the authorities would look at the case sympathetically. This was not initially recognised by the authorities as a recommendation, but the Home Secretary subsequently concluded that there were not sufficient grounds for acting outside the immigration rules. There is no record of an application for leave to appeal to the Immigration Appeal Tribunal. Representations to the Home Office were also rejected, basically on the ground that the couple could live together in the Philippines and that there were not sufficient reasons for the Home Secretary to exercise his extra-statutory discretion.

47 Between April 1980 and December 1984, Mr Cabales continued to live in the Philippines and the couple were separated, apart from a short period in 1983 when Mrs Cabales visited that country. However, following an application made by her in November 1982 under section 6 of the British Nationality Act 1981 (see paras 34–36 above), Mrs Cabales obtained naturalisation as a British citizen with effect from 18 April 1984; she thereby lost her Philippine citizenship. On 10 July 1984, Mr Cabales applied for entry clearance for permanent settlement as the husband of a British citizen, under para 54 of the 1983 Rules (see paras 30–31 above). For the reasons and in the circumstances indicated in the following paragraph this application was refused on 1 October 1984 but, on the following day, Mr Cabales applied for and was granted a visa entitling him to enter the United Kingdom for three months for the purposes of marriage. He arrived in that country on 19 December 1984 and the parties were married there on 26 January 1985. On 4 February, he was granted leave to remain as a husband for the next twelve months; on the expiry of that period, he will be eligible to apply for indefinite leave.

48 In a memorial filed with the Court on 27 July 1984, the government questioned the validity of the 1980 marriage (see para 45 above). Under Articles 53 and 80 of the Philippine Civil Code, a marriage solemnised without a licence was to be considered void, save in the case of a "marriage of exceptional character", that is one between persons who have lived together as husband and wife for at least five years (Article 76). The Cabales marriage contract recited that the ceremony the couple went through in 1980 had been performed, without a licence, under Article 76. The parties had stated in a contemporaneous affidavit that they had previously cohabited for at least five years, but according to Mrs Cabales' version of the facts this could not be so since she had not met Mr Cabales until 1977 (see para 45 above). According to the Government, the requirements of Article 76 were therefore not satisfied and the marriage thus had to be considered void.

At the hearings on 25 September 1984, the applicant's counsel expressed the view that, assuming a defect existed, it was purely formal and the status of Mr and Mrs Cabales could be regarded as akin to that of the parties to a common law marriage. Her representative subsequently filed with the Court details of the advice he had received from Philippine lawyers, to the effect that under the law of that country the marriage was to be presumed valid unless and until it was declared void by a court. The Government replied that they had been advised that the marriage was void *ab initio* and that no judicial decree was necessary to establish its invalidity. This opinion was contradicted in further advice obtained on behalf of Mrs Cabales.

Mr and Mrs Cabales were interviewed by the United Kingdom authorities in August and September 1984. They adduced no evidence to alter the Government's conclusion that the marriage was void. However, Mrs Cabales stated that if Mr Cabales were admitted to the United Kingdom, the couple would go through a ceremony of marriage in that country. It was in these circumstances that in October 1984 Mr Cabales was refused leave to settle as a husband but was regarded as eligible, under the 1983 Rules, for leave to enter the United Kingdom temporarily as the fiancé of a British citizen.

49 Before the Commission and the Court, Mrs Cabales submitted that there would have been real obstacles to her returning to live in the Philippines: she was too old, her qualifications were not recognised there and, by working in the United Kingdom, she was able to support financially her parents and other members of her family. These claims were contested by the Government, in particular on the ground that it was unrealistic to suppose that her nursing skills could not be put to good use in the Philippines.

C   Mrs Balkandali

50 Mrs Sohair Balkandali is permanently and lawfully resident in the United Kingdom with the right to remain indefinitely. She was born in Egypt in 1946 or 1948. Her parents were born and live in that country.

This applicant first went to the United Kingdom in November 1973 and was given leave, as a "non-patrial" (see paras 13–15 above), to enter as a visitor for one month. Subsequently, she obtained several further leaves to remain, as a visitor or a student, the last being until August 1976. She has a high level of university education. In 1978, she married a Mr Corbett, a citizen of the United Kingdom and Colonies, and, five days later, was given indefinite leave to remain in the United Kingdom, by virtue of her marriage, under the provisions then in force. On 26 October 1979, again by virtue of her marriage, she obtained registration as a citizen of the United Kingdom and Colonies under the British Nationality Act 1948, as a result of which she became a "patrial" (see paras 11 *in fine* and 14(a) above). At that time, she was already separated from Mr Corbett and the marriage was dissolved in October 1980.

51 Mr Bekir Balkandali is a Turkish national born in Turkey on 9 April 1946. In January 1979, he was granted leave, as a "non-patrial" (see paras 13–15 above), to enter the United Kingdom, apparently as a visitor, for one month. Subsequently, he obtained leave to remain as a student until 31 March 1980. His application of 2 April for an extension of this leave was refused on 23 September 1980 because he had not attended his course of studies and the Home Secretary was not satisfied that he was a genuine student who intended to leave the country on their conclusion. Since his application for an extension had been made after his leave had expired, he had no right of appeal under the 1971 Act (see para 35 above); he was advised to leave the United Kingdom and warned of the risk of criminal or deportation proceedings (see para 33 above) if he did not.

52 Since the autumn of 1979, the applicant had been living with Mr Balkandali. In April 1980 they had a son, who has the right of abode in the United Kingdom. On 14 October 1980, an application was made by the Joint Council for the Welfare of Immigrants for leave for Mr Balkandali to remain in the United Kingdom until he married his fiancée, the applicant. They were interviewed together by Home Office officials on 30 March 1981 and produced evidence of their marriage, which had been celebrated in January 1981. The application was therefore treated as one to remain as the husband of a woman settled in the United Kingdom.

Leave was refused on 14 May 1981 on the ground that Mrs Balkandali was not a citizen of the United Kingdom and Colonies who, or one of whose parents, had been born in the United Kingdom (para 117 of the 1980 Rules; see para 24(a)(i) above). There was no right of appeal against this decision as Mr Balkandali had no current leave to remain at the time when his application was made (see para 35 above). Representations through a

Member of Parliament to the Home Office were rejected, basically on the ground that the couple could live together in Turkey and that there were not sufficient compelling compassionate circumstances to warrant exceptional treatment outside the immigration rules. In a letter of 18 December 1981 to the Member, the Minister of State at the Home Office wrote that "Mr Balkandali should now make arrangements to leave the United Kingdom forthwith, otherwise arrangements will be made to enforce his departure"; however, a letter of 3 December 1982 to the Member stated that "[the Minister did] not propose for the time being to take any action against [Mr Balkandali]". In fact, the authorities did not at any time institute criminal or deportation proceedings against him; their decision, according to the Government, was taken in the light of all the circumstances, including the Commission's decision on the admissibility of Mrs Balkandali's application (see para 55 below).

53 On 20 January 1983, as the husband of a British citizen, Mr Balkandali was given 12 months' leave to remain in the United Kingdom in accordance with para 126 of the 1982 Rules (see para 28(a) above); this was possible because, on 1 January 1983, Mrs Balkandali had automatically acquired British citizenship by virtue of the British Nationality Act 1981 (see para 26(b) above). Mr Balkandali subsequently applied for indefinite leave to remain and this was granted on 18 January 1984 under para 177 of the 1983 Rules (see para 31 above). In September 1984, he was working in the catering business and planned shortly to open a restaurant; his wife was working two days a week in a crèche.

54 Before the Commission and the Court, Mrs Balkandali submitted that there would have been real obstacles to her going with her husband to live in Turkey: she cited her strong ties to the United Kingdom and alleged that as an educated woman and the mother of an illegitimate child she would have been treated as a social outcast in Turkey. The Government maintain that there were no real obstacles.

PROCEEDINGS BEFORE THE COMMISSION

55 The application of Mrs Abdulaziz (App No 9214/80) was lodged with the Commission on 11 December 1980 and those of Mrs Cabales (App No 9473/81) and Mrs Balkandali (App No 9474/81) on 10 August 1981. Each applicant claimed to be the victim of a practice authorised by parliament and contained in the 1980 Rules, which practice was incompatible with the Convention, and alleged violations of Article 3, Article 8 (taken alone and in conjunction with Article 14) and Article 13.

56 On 11 May 1982, the Commission declared the three applications admissible and ordered their joinder in pursuance of Rule 29 of its Rules and Procedure.

In its report adopted on 12 May 1983 (Article 31), the Commission expressed the opinion:

- that there had been a violation of Article 14, in conjunction with Article 8, on the ground of sexual discrimination (unanimously);

- that there had been no violation of the same Articles on the ground of racial discrimination (nine votes to three);

- that the original application of the 1980 Rules in the case of Mrs Balkandali constituted discrimination on the ground of birth, contrary to Article 14 in conjunction with Article 8 (eleven votes with one abstention);

- that the absence of effective domestic remedies for the applicants' claims under Articles 3, 8 and 14 constituted a violation of Article 13 (eleven votes to one);

    –   that it was not necessary to pursue a further examination of the matter in the light of Articles 3 and 8.

FINAL SUBMISSIONS MADE TO THE COURT BY THE GOVERNMENT AND BY THE APPLICANTS

57   At the hearings on 25 September 1984, the Government submitted that Mrs Cabales' application was inadmissible *ratione materiae*. In other respects, they maintained in substance the submissions set out in their memorial of 12 March 1984, whereby they had requested the Court:

1   With regard to Articles 8 and 14,

   (a) to decide and declare that matters of immigration control lie outside the scope of Article 8, so that no complaints based on the application of immigration control can succeed under Article 8, or under Article 14 taken together with Article 8;

   (b) to decide and declare that upon an examination of the facts of these cases, the matters complained of lie outside the scope of Article 8, with the consequence mentioned above;

   (c) to decide and declare, if necessary, that any discrimination under Article 14 is objectively and reasonably justified and not disproportionate to the aims of the measures in question;

   (d) to decide and declare, if necessary, that if there has been any interference with the exercise of rights arising under Article 8 in these applications, it is in accordance with the law and necessary in a democratic society in the interests of the economic well-being of the country, the prevention of disorder, and the protection of the rights and freedoms of others;

2   With regard to Article 3, to decide and declare that the facts of these cases are not capable of amounting, alternatively do not amount, to inhuman or degrading treatment under that Article

3   To decide and declare that Article 13 has no application to these cases, since the complaints fall outside the scope of Articles 3, 8 and 14; in any event to hold that as regards the immigration rules there is no obligation to provide a domestic remedy under that Article; alternatively to hold that insofar as Article 13 does impose, on the facts, any obligation to provide a domestic remedy in relation to any of the matters complained of, that obligation is fulfilled.

The applicants, for their part, maintained in substance the submissions set out in their memorial of 30 March 1984, whereby they had requested the Court to decide and declare:

1   that the applicants are victims of a practice in violation of their right to respect for family life, contrary to Article 8 of the Convention;

2   that they are further victims of a practice of discrimination in the securement of their said right:

   (a) in respect of all three applicants, on the grounds of sex and race; and

   (b) in respect of Mrs Balkandali, on the ground of birth, contrary to Article 14 in conjunction with Article 8 of the Convention;

3   that such discrimination constituted degrading treatment contrary to Article 3 of the Convention;

4   that the absence of effective remedies for the applicant's claims under Articles 3, 8 and 14 constituted a violation of Article 13 of the Convention;

5 that the United Kingdom Government should pay appropriate compensation, including costs, to the applicants by way of just satisfaction.

AS TO THE LAW

I   Alleged violation of Article 8

58 The applicants claimed to be victims of a practice in violation of their right to respect for family life, guaranteed by Article 8 of the Convention, which reads as follows:

1   Everyone has the right to respect for his private and family life, his home and his correspondence.

2   There shall be no interference by a public authority with the exercise of this right except such as is in accordance with the law and is necessary in a democratic society in the interests of national security, public safety or the economic well-being of the country, for the prevention of disorder or crime, for the protection of health or morals, or for the protection of the rights and freedom of others.

A   Applicability of Article 8

59 The Government's principal submission was that neither Article 8 nor any other Article of the Convention applied to immigration control, for which Protocol No 4 was the only appropriate text. In their opinion, the fact that that Protocol was, as stated in its preamble, designed to afford rights additional to those protected by section I of the Convention conclusively demonstrated that rights in the field of immigration were not already accorded by the Convention itself, and in particular by Article 8 thereof. Furthermore, the applicants were claiming a right which was not secured to aliens, even by the Protocol, an instrument that in any event had not been ratified by the United Kingdom.

The Commission rejected this argument at the admissibility stage. In doing so, it confirmed – and the applicants now relied on – its established case law: the right of a foreigner to enter or remain in a country was not as such guaranteed by the Convention, but immigration controls had to be exercised consistently with Convention obligations, and the exclusion of a person from a State where members of his family were living might raise an issue under Article 8.

60 The Court is unable to accept the Government's submission. The applicants are not the husbands but the wives, and they are complaining not of being refused leave to enter or remain in the United Kingdom but, as persons lawfully settled in that country, of being deprived (Mrs Cabales), or threatened with deprivation (Mrs Abdulaziz and Mrs Balkandali), of the society of their spouses there.

Above all, the Court recalls that the Convention and its Protocols must be read as a whole; consequently a matter dealt with mainly by one of their provisions may also, in some of its aspects, be subject to other provisions thereof (see the "Belgian Linguistic" judgment of 23 July 1968, Series A, No 6, para 7). Thus, although some aspects of the right to enter a country are governed by Protocol No 4 as regards States bound by that instrument, it is not to be excluded that measures taken in the field of immigration may affect the right to respect for family life under Article 8. The Court accordingly agrees on this point with the Commission.

61 In the alternative, the Government advanced two further arguments to support their contention that Article 8 was not applicable.

Firstly, the Article was said to guarantee respect solely for existing family life, whereas here the couples concerned had not, at the time when the request was made for permission for the man to enter or remain in the United Kingdom, established any such life with the legitimate expectation of the enjoyment of it in that country.

Secondly, since there was no obstacle to the couples living together in, respectively, Portugal, the Philippines or Turkey, they were in reality claiming a right to choose their country of residence, something that was not guaranteed by Article 8.

These arguments were contested by the applicants. Whilst the Commission did not examine the applications under Article 8 taken alone, it considered that they did not lie outside its scope.

62 The Court recalls that, by guaranteeing the right to respect for family life, Article 8 "presupposes the existence of a family" (see the *Marckx* judgment of 13 June 1979, Series A, No 31, para 31). However, this does not mean that all intended family life falls entirely outside its ambit. Whatever else the word "family" may mean, it must at any rate include the relationship that arises from a lawful and genuine marriage, such as that contracted by Mr and Mrs Abdulaziz and Mr and Mrs Balkandali, even if a family life of the kind referred to by the Government has not yet been fully established. Those marriages must be considered sufficient to attract such respect as may be due under Article 8.

Furthermore, the expression "family life", in the case of a married couple, normally comprises cohabitation. The latter proposition is reinforced by the existence of Article 12, for it is scarcely conceivable that the right to found a family should not encompass the right to live together. The Court further notes that Mr and Mrs Abdulaziz had not only contracted marriage but had also cohabited for a certain period before Mr Abdulaziz was refused leave to remain in the United Kingdom (see paras 40–41 above). Mr and Mrs Balkandali had also cohabited and had a son, although they were not married until after Mr Balkandali's leave to remain as a student had expired and an extension been refused; their cohabitation was continuing when his application for leave to remain as a husband was rejected (see paras 51–52 above).

63 The case of Mrs Cabales has to be considered separately, having regard to the question raised as to the validity of her marriage (see para 48 above). The Government argued that, in the circumstances, her application was inadmissible *ratione materiae* and thus did not have to be examined by the Court.

Although this plea was framed in terms of admissibility, the Court is of the opinion that it goes to the merits of the application and is therefore preferably dealt with on that basis (see, *mutatis mutandis*, the *Airey* judgment of 9 October 1979, Series A, No 32, para 18).

The Court does not consider that it has to resolve the difference of opinion that has arisen concerning the effect of Philippine law. Mr and Mrs Cabales had gone through a ceremony of marriage (see para 45 above) and the evidence before the Court confirms that they believed themselves to be married and that they genuinely wished to cohabit and lead a normal family life. And indeed they subsequently did so. In the circumstances, the committed relationship thus established was sufficient to attract the application of Article 8.

64 There remains the Government's argument concerning choice of country of residence. The Court considers that this goes more to the degree of respect for family life, which must be afforded and will therefore examine it in that context (see para 68 below).

65 To sum up, each of the applicants had to a sufficient degree entered upon "family life" for the purposes of Article 8; that provision is therefore applicable to the present case. In view of the importance of the issues involved, the Court, unlike the Commission, considers that it has to determine whether there has been a violation of Article 8 taken alone.

B   Compliance with Article 8

66 The applicants contended that respect for family life – which in their cases the United Kingdom had to secure within its own jurisdiction – encompassed the right to establish one's home in the State of one's nationality or lawful residence; subject only to the provisions of para 2 of Article 8, the dilemma either of moving abroad or of being separated from one's spouse was inconsistent with this principle. Furthermore, hindrance in fact was just as relevant as hindrance in law: for the couples to live in, respectively, Portugal, the Philippines or Turkey would involve or would have involved them in serious difficulties, although there was no legal impediment to their doing so.

67 The Court recalls that, although the essential object of Article 8 is to protect the individual against arbitrary interference by the public authorities, there may in addition be positive obligations inherent in an effective "respect" for family life (see the above-mentioned *Marckx* judgment, Series A, No 31, para 31). However, especially as far as those positive obligations are concerned, the notion of "respect" is not clear cut: having regard to the diversity of the practices followed and the situations obtaining in the Contracting States, the notion's requirements will vary considerably from case to case. Accordingly, this is an area in which the Contracting Parties enjoy a wide margin of appreciation in determining the steps to be taken to ensure compliance with the Convention with due regard to the needs and resources of the community and of individuals (see amongst other authorities, *mutatis mutandis*, the above-mentioned *"Belgian Linguistic"* judgment, Series A, No 6, para 5; the *National Union of Belgian Police* judgment of 27 October 1975, Series A, No 19, para 39; the above-mentioned *Marckx* judgment, Series A, No 31, para 31 and the *Rasmussen* judgment of 28 November 1984, Series A, No 87, para 40). In particular, in the area now under consideration, the extent of a State's obligation to admit to its territory relatives of settled immigrants will vary according to the particular circumstances of the persons involved. Moreover, the Court cannot ignore that the present case is concerned not only with family life but also with immigration and that, as a matter of well-established international law and subject to its treaty obligations, a State has the right to control the entry of non-nationals into its territory.

68 The Court observes that the present proceedings do not relate to immigrants who already had a family which they left behind in another country until they had achieved settled status in the United Kingdom. It was only after becoming settled in the United Kingdom, as single persons, that the applicants contracted marriage. The duty imposed by Article 8 cannot be considered as extending to a general obligation on the part of a Contracting State to respect the choice by married couples of the country of their matrimonial residence and to accept the non-national spouses for settlement in that country.

In the present case, the applicants have not shown that there were obstacles to establishing family life in their own or their husbands' home countries or that there were special reasons why that could not be expected of them.

In addition, at the time of their marriage:

(i) Mrs Abdulaziz knew that her husband had been admitted to the United Kingdom for a limited period as a visitor only and that it would be necessary for him to make an application to remain permanently, and she could have known, in the light of draft provisions already published (see para 20 above), that this would probably be refused;

(ii) Mrs Balkandali must have been aware that her husband's leave to remain temporarily as a student had already expired, that his residence in the United Kingdom was therefore unlawful and that under the 1980 Rules, which were then in force, his acceptance for settlement could not be expected.

In the case of Mrs Cabales, who had never cohabited with Mr Cabales in the United Kingdom, she should have known that he would require leave to enter and that under the rules then in force this would be refused.

69 There was accordingly no "lack of respect" for family life and, hence, no breach of Article 8 taken alone.

II   Alleged violation of Article 14 taken together with Article 8

A   *Introduction*

70 The applicants claimed that, as a result of unjustified differences of treatment in securing the right to respect for their family life, based on sex, race and also – in the case of Mrs Balkandali – birth, they had been victims of a violation of Article 14 of the Convention, taken together with Article 8. The former Article reads as follows:

> The enjoyment of the rights and freedoms set forth in [the] Convention shall be secured without discrimination on any ground such as sex, race, colour, language, religion, political or other opinion, national or social origin, association with a national minority, property, birth or other status.

In the event that the Court should find Article 8 to be applicable in the present case, the Government denied that there was any difference of treatment on the ground of race and submitted that since the differences of treatment on the ground of sex and of birth had objective and reasonable justification and were proportionate to the aims pursued, they were compatible with Article 14.

71 According to the Court's established case law, Article 14 complements the other substantive provisions of the Convention and the Protocols. It has no independent existence since it has effect solely in relation to "the enjoyment of the rights and freedoms" safeguarded by those provisions. Although the application of Article 14 does not necessarily presuppose a breach of those provisions – and to this extent it is autonomous – there can be no room for its application unless the facts at issue fall within the ambit of one or more of the latter (see, *inter alia*, the above-mentioned *Rasmussen* judgment, Series A, No 87, para 29).

The Court has found Article 8 to be applicable (see para 65 above). Although the United Kingdom was not obliged to accept Mr Abdulaziz, Mr Cabales and Mr Balkandali for settlement and the Court therefore did not find a violation of Article 8 taken alone, the facts at issue nevertheless fall within the ambit of that Article. In this respect, a parallel may be drawn, *mutatis mutandis*, with the *National Union of Belgian Police* case (see the judgment of 27 October 1975, Series A, No 19, para 45). Article 14 also is therefore applicable.

72 For the purposes of Article 14, a difference of treatment is discriminatory if it "has no objective and reasonable justification", that is, if it does not pursue a "legitimate aim" or

if there is not a "reasonable relationship of proportionality between the means employed and the aim sought to be realised" (see, *inter alia*, the above-mentioned "*Belgian Linguistic*" judgment, Series A, No 6, para 10; the above-mentioned *Marckx* judgment, Series A, No 31, para 33 and the above-mentioned *Rasmussen* judgment, Series A, No 87, para 38).

The Contracting States enjoy a certain margin of appreciation in assessing whether and to what extent differences in otherwise similar situations justify a different treatment in law (see the above-mentioned *Rasmussen* judgment, *ibid*, para 40), but it is for the Court to give the final ruling in this respect.

73 In the particular circumstances of the case, the Court considers that it must examine in turn the three grounds on which it was alleged that a discriminatory difference of treatment was based.

B   Alleged discrimination on the ground of sex

74 As regards the alleged discrimination on the grounds of sex, it was not disputed that under the 1980 Rules it was easier for a man settled in the United Kingdom than for a woman so settled to obtain permission for his or her non-national spouse to enter or remain in the country for settlement (see paras 23–25 above). Argument centred on the question whether this difference had an objective and reasonable justification.

75 According to the Government, the difference of treatment complained of had the aim of limiting "primary immigration" (see para 21 above) and was justified by the need to protect the domestic labour market at a time of high unemployment. They placed strong reliance on the margin of appreciation enjoyed by the Contracting States in this area and laid particular stress on what they described as a statistical fact: men were more likely to seek work than women, with the result that male immigrants would have a greater impact than female immigrants on the said market. Furthermore, the reduction, attributed by the Government to the 1980 Rules, of approximately 5,700 *per annum* in the number of husbands accepted for settlement in the United Kingdom was claimed to be significant. This was said to be so especially when the reduction was viewed in relation to its cumulative effect over the years and to the total number of acceptances for settlement.

This view was contested by the applicants. For them, the Government's plea ignored the modern role of women and the fact that men may be self-employed and also, as was exemplified by the case of Mr Balkandali (see para 53 above), create rather than seek jobs. Furthermore, the Government's figure of 5,700 was said to be insignificant and, for a number of reasons, in any event unreliable (see para 38(e) *in fine* above).

76 The Government further contended that the measures in question were justified by the need to maintain effective immigration control, which benefited settled immigrants as well as the indigenous population. Immigration caused strains on society; the Government's aim was to advance public tranquility, and a firm and fair control secured good relations between the different communities living in the United Kingdom.

To this, the applicants replied that the racial prejudice of the United Kingdom population could not be advanced as a justification for the measures.

77 In its report, the Commission considered that, when seen in the context of the immigration of other groups, annual emigration and unemployment and economic activity rates, the impact on the domestic labour market of an annual reduction of 2,000 (as then estimated by the Government) in the number of husbands accepted for

settlement in the United Kingdom (see para 38(e) above) was not of a size or importance to justify a difference of treatment on the ground of sex and the detrimental consequences thereof on the family life of the women concerned. Furthermore, the longstanding commitment to the reunification of the families of male immigrants, to which the Government had referred as a reason for accepting wives whilst excluding husbands, no longer corresponded to modern requirements as to the equal treatment of the sexes. N[or] was it established that race relations or immigration controls were enhanced by the rules: they might create resentment in part of the immigrant population and it had not been shown that it was more difficult to limit abuses by non-national husbands than by other immigrant groups. The Commission unanimously concluded that there had been discrimination on the ground of sex, contrary to Article 14, in securing the applicants' right to respect for family life, the application of the relevant rules being disproportionate to the purported aims.

At the hearings before the Court, the Commission's Delegate stated that this conclusion was not affected by the Government's revised figure (about 5,700) for the annual reduction in the number of husbands accepted for settlement.

78 The Court accepts that the 1980 Rules had the aim of protecting the domestic labour market. The fact that, as was suggested by the applicants, this aim might have been further advanced by the abolition of the "United Kingdom ancestry" and the "working holiday" rules (see para 20 above) in no way alters this finding. N[or] does the Court perceive any conclusive evidence to contradict it in the Parliamentary debates, on which the applicants also relied. It is true, as they pointed out, that unemployment in the United Kingdom in 1980 was lower than in subsequent years, but it had nevertheless already attained a significant level and there was a considerable increase as compared with previous years (see para 38(d) above).

Whilst the aforesaid aim was without doubt legitimate, this does not in itself establish the legitimacy of the difference made in the 1980 Rules as to the possibility for male and female immigrants settled in the United Kingdom to obtain permission for, on the one hand, their non-national wives or fiancées and, on the other hand, their non-national husbands or fiancés to enter or remain in the country.

Although the Contracting States enjoy a certain "margin of appreciation" in assessing whether and to what extent differences in otherwise similar situations justify a different treatment, the scope of this margin will vary according to the circumstances, the subject matter and its background (see the above-mentioned *Rasmussen* judgment, Series A, No 87, para 40).

As to the present matter, it can be said that the advancement of the equality of the sexes is today a major goal in the Member States of the Council of Europe. This means that very weighty reasons would have to be advanced before a difference of treatment on the ground of sex could be regarded as compatible with the Convention.

79 In the Court's opinion, the Government's arguments summarised in para 75 are not convincing.

It may be correct that on average there is a greater percentage of men of working age than of women of working age who are "economically active" (for Great Britain 90% of the men and 63% of the women) and that comparable figures hold good for immigrants (according to the statistics, 86% for men and 41% for women for immigrants of the Indian sub-continent and 90% for men and 70% for women for immigrants from the West Indies and Guyana) (see para 38(d) above).

Nevertheless, this does not show that similar differences in fact exist – or would but for the effect of the 1980 Rules have existed – as regards the respective impact on the United Kingdom labour market of immigrant wives and of immigrant husbands. In this connection, other factors must also be taken into account. Being "economically active" does not always mean that one is seeking to be employed by someone else. Moreover, although a greater number of men and women may be inclined to seek employment, immigrant husbands were already by far outnumbered, before the introduction of the 1980 Rules, by immigrant wives (see para 38(e) above), many of whom were also "economically active". Whilst a considerable proportion of those wives, in so far as they were "economically active", were engaged in part-time work, the impact on the domestic labour market of women immigrants as compared with men ought not to be underestimated.

In any event, the Court is not convinced that the difference that may nevertheless exist between the respective impact of men and of women on the domestic labour market is sufficiently important to justify the difference of treatment complained of by the applicants, as to the possibility for a person settled in the United Kingdom to be joined by, as the case may be, his wife or her husband.

80 In this context the Government stressed the importance of the effect on the immigration of husbands of the restrictions contained in the 1980 Rules, which had led, according to their estimate, to an annual reduction of 5,700 (rather than 2,000, as mentioned in the Commission's report) in the number of husbands accepted for settlement.

Without expressing a conclusion on the correctness of the figure of 5,700, the Court notes that in point of time the claimed reduction coincided with a significant increase in unemployment in the United Kingdom and that the Government accepted that some part of the reduction was due to economic conditions rather than to the 1980 Rules themselves (see paras 38(d) and (e) above).

In any event, for the reasons stated in para 79 above, the reduction achieved does not justify the difference in treatment between men and women.

81 The Court accepts that the 1980 Rules also had, as the Government stated, the aim of advancing public tranquility. However, it is not persuaded that this aim was served by the distinction drawn in those rules between husbands and wives.

82 There remains a more general argument advanced by the Government, namely that the United Kingdom was not in violation of Article 14 by reason of the fact that it acted more generously in some respects – that is, as regards the admission of non-national wives and fiancées of men settled in the country – than the Convention required.

The Court cannot accept this argument. It would point out that Article 14 is concerned with the avoidance of discrimination in the enjoyment of the Convention rights in so far as the requirements of the Convention as to those rights can be complied with in different ways. The notion of discrimination within the meaning of Article 14 includes in general cases where a person or group is treated, without proper justification, less favourably than another, even though the more favourable treatment is not called for by the Convention.

83 The Court thus concludes that the applicants have been victims of discrimination on the ground of sex, in violation of Article 14 taken together with Article 8.

C   Alleged discrimination on the ground of race

84 As regards the alleged discrimination on the ground of race, the applicants relied on the opinion of a minority of the Commission. They referred, *inter alia*, to the whole history of and background to the United Kingdom immigration legislation (see paras 11–15 above) and to the Parliamentary debates on the immigration rules.

In contesting this claim, the Government submitted that the 1980 Rules were not racially motivated, their aim being to limit "primary immigration" (see para 21 above).

A majority of the Commission concluded that there had been no violation of Article 14 under this head. Most immigration policies – restricting, as they do, free entry – differentiated on the basis of people's nationality, and indirectly their race, ethnic origin and possibly their colour. Whilst a Contracting State could not implement "policies of a purely racist nature", to give preferential treatment to its nationals or to persons from countries with which it had the closest links did not constitute "racial discrimination". The effect in practice of the United Kingdom rules did not mean that they were abhorrent on the grounds of racial discrimination, there being no evidence of an actual difference of treatment on grounds of race.

A minority of the Commission, on the other hand, noted that the main effect of the rules was to prevent immigration from the New Commonwealth and Pakistan. This was not coincidental: the legislative history showed that the intention was to "lower the number of coloured immigrants". By their effect and purpose, the rules were indirectly racist and there had thus been a violation of Article 14 under this head in the cases of Mrs Abdulaziz and Mrs Cabales.

85 The Court agrees in this respect with the majority of the Commission.

The 1980 Rules, which were applicable in general to all "non-patrials" wanting to enter and settle in the United Kingdom, did not contain regulations differentiating between persons or groups on the ground of their race or ethnic origin. The rules included in para 2 a specific instruction to immigration officers to carry out their duties without regard to the race, colour or religion of the intending entrant (see para 20 above), and they were applicable across the board to intending immigrants from all parts of the world, irrespective of their race or origin.

As the Court has already accepted, the main and essential purpose of the 1980 Rules was to curtail "primary immigration" in order to protect the labour market at a time of high unemployment. This means that their reinforcement of the restrictions on immigration was grounded not on objections regarding the origin of the non-nationals wanting to enter the country but on the need to stem the flow of immigrants at the relevant time.

That the mass immigration against which the rules were directed consisted mainly of would-be immigrants from the New Commonwealth and Pakistan, and that as a result they affected at the material time fewer white people than others, is not a sufficient reason to consider them as racist in character: it is an effect which derives not from the content of the 1980 Rules but from the fact that, among those wishing to immigrate, some ethnic groups outnumbered others.

The Court concludes from the foregoing that the 1980 Rules made no distinction on the ground of race and were therefore not discriminatory on that account. This conclusion is not altered by the following two arguments on which the applicants relied:

(a) The requirement that the wife or fiancée of the intending entrant be born or have a parent born in the United Kingdom and also the "United Kingdom ancestry rule" (see paras 23, 24 and 20 above) were said to favour persons of a particular ethnic origin. However, the Court regards these provisions as being exceptions designed for the benefit of persons having close links with the United Kingdom, which do not affect the general tenor of the rules.

(b) The requirement that the parties to the marriage or intended marriage must have met (see paras 22–24 above) was said to operate to the disadvantage of individuals from the Indian sub-continent, where the practice of arranged marriages is customary. In the Court's view, however, such a requirement cannot be taken as an indication of racial discrimination: its main purpose was to prevent evasion of the rules by means of bogus marriages or engagements. It is, besides, a requirement that has nothing to do with the present cases.

86 The Court accordingly holds that the applicants have not been victims of discrimination on the ground of race.

D   Alleged discrimination on the ground of birth

87 Mrs Balkandali claimed that she had also been the victim of discrimination on the ground of birth, in that, as between women citizens of the United Kingdom and Colonies settled in the United Kingdom, only those born or having a parent born in that country could, under the 1980 Rules, have their non-national husband accepted for settlement there (see paras 23–24 above).

It was not disputed that the 1980 Rules established a difference of treatment on the ground of birth, argument being centred on the question whether it had an objective and reasonable justification.

In addition to relying on the Commission's report, Mrs Balkandali submitted that the elimination of this distinction from subsequent immigration rules demonstrated that it was not previously justified (see para 28(a) above).

The Government maintained that the difference in question was justified by the concern to avoid the hardship which women having close ties to the United Kingdom would encounter if, on marriage, they were obliged to move abroad in order to remain with their husbands.

The Commission considered that, notwithstanding the subsequent elimination of this difference, the general interest and the possibly temporary nature of immigration rules required it to express an opinion. It took the view that a difference of treatment based on the mere accident of birth, without regard to the individual's personal circumstances or merits, constituted discrimination in violation of Article 14.

88 The Court is unable to share the Commission's opinion. The aim cited by the Government is unquestionably legitimate, for the purposes of Article 14. It is true that a person who, like Mrs Balkandali, has been settled in a country for several years may also have formed close ties with it, even if he or she was not born there. Nevertheless, there are in general persuasive social reasons for giving special treatment to those whose link with a country stems from birth within it. The difference of treatment must therefore be regarded as having had an objective and reasonable justification and, in particular, its results have not been shown to transgress the principle of proportionality. This conclusion is not altered by the fact that the immigration rules were subsequently amended on this point.

89 The Court thus holds that Mrs Balkandali was not the victim of discrimination on the ground of birth.

III   Alleged violation of Article 3

90 The applicants claimed to have been subjected to degrading treatment, in violation of Article 3, which reads:

> No one shall be subjected to torture or to inhuman or degrading treatment or punishment.

In their view, the discrimination against them constituted an affront to human dignity. They also referred to Mr and Mrs Cabales' lengthy separation and to the anxiety and stress undergone by Mrs Abdulaziz and Mrs Balkandali.

The Government contested this claim on various grounds. According to the Commission, Article 14 incorporated a condemnation of the degrading aspects of sexual and other forms of discrimination and no separate issues arose under Article 3.

91 The Court observes that the difference of treatment complained of did not denote any contempt or lack of respect for the personality of the applicants and that it was not designed to, and did not, humiliate or debase but was intended solely to achieve the aims referred to in paras 75, 76, 78 and 81 above (see the *Albert and Le Compte* judgment of 10 February 1983, Series A, No 58, para 22). It cannot therefore be regarded as "degrading".

There was accordingly no violation of Article 3.

IV   Alleged violation of Article 13

92 The applicants alleged that they had had no effective remedy for their complaints under Articles 3, 8 and 14 and that there had accordingly been a breach of Article 13, which reads:

> Everyone whose rights and freedoms as set forth in [the] Convention are violated shall have an effective remedy before a national authority notwithstanding that the violation has been committed by persons acting in an official capacity.

In the event that the Court should find Articles 3, 8 and 14 to be applicable, the Government contended that the immigration rules, though not constituting delegated legislation, fell within the principle enunciated by the Commission in its report in the case of *Young, James and Webster* ((1981), Series B, No 39), namely that Article 13 does not require that a remedy be provided for controlling the conformity of a law with the Convention. In the alternative, they submitted that the remedies that were available to the applicants were "effective".

The Commission considered the immigration rules fell outside the aforementioned principle. Having reviewed the available channels of complaint, it concluded that there had been a violation of Article 13.

93 The Court has found that the discrimination on the ground of sex of which Mrs Abdulaziz, Mrs Cabales and Mrs Balkandali were victims was the result of norms that were in this respect incompatible with the Convention. In this regard, since the United Kingdom has not incorporated the Convention into its domestic law, there could be no "effective remedy" as required by Article 13 (see the *Silver and Others* judgment of 25 March 1983, Series A, No 61, paras 111–119, and the *Campbell & Fell* judgment of 28 June 1984, Series A, No 80, para 127). Recourse to the available channels of complaint (the immigration appeals system, representations to the Home Secretary, application for judicial review) could have been effective only if the complainant alleged that the

discrimination resulted from a misapplication of the 1980 Rules. Yet here no such allegation was made nor was it suggested that that discrimination in any other way contravened domestic law.

The Court accordingly concludes that there has been a violation of Article 13.

V   Application of Article 50

94 Mrs Abdulaziz, Mrs Cabales and Mrs Balkandali claimed, for "moral damage" and costs and expenses, just satisfaction under Article 50, which reads:

> If the Court finds that a decision or a measure taken by a legal authority or any other authority of a High Contracting Party is completely or partially in conflict with the obligations arising from the ... Convention, and if the internal law of the said Party allows only partial reparation to be made for the consequences of this decision or measure, the decision of the Court shall, if necessary, afford just satisfaction to the injured party.

All the applicants, including Mrs Cabales, have been victims of a breach of Article 14 taken in conjunction with Article 8 (see paras 63 and 83 above) with the result that Article 50 is applicable as regards each of them.

A   Damages

95 The applicants sought "substantial", but unquantified, compensation for non-pecuniary damage in the form of distress, humiliation and anxiety. They stated that the interference complained of concerned a vital element in society, namely family life; that sexual discrimination was universally condemned; and that the existence of a practice in breach of the Convention was an aggravating factor. They also cited, *inter alia*, the adverse effects on the development of family ties and on the making of long-term plans; the threat of criminal or deportation proceedings against Mr Abdulaziz and Mr Balkandali (see para 33 above); the lengthy separation of Mr and Mrs Cabales; and the fact that Mr Abdulaziz would have been accepted for settlement in the United Kingdom under the rules in force at the dates of his marriage and of his application for leave to remain (see para 41 above). Mrs Balkandali added that the subsequent grant to her husband of leave to remain (see para 53 above) had afforded no reparation for her previous distress.

The Government contended firstly that an award of just satisfaction to Mrs Abdulaziz and Mrs Balkandali was not "necessary": there was no evidence of the alleged damage nor had it been proved that any damage was the result of the violations that might be found by the Court. In the alternative, they submitted that a finding of violation would of itself constitute sufficient just satisfaction: at the time of their marriage, the couples concerned knew that they were not entitled to live together in the United Kingdom; in fact, they had not been prevented from doing so; and since they could have lived in Portugal or Turkey, family ties and long-term plans had not been adversely affected. Similar pleas were advanced concerning Mrs Cabales.

96 By reason of its very nature, non-pecuniary damage of the kind alleged cannot always be the object of concrete proof. However, it is reasonable to assume that persons who, like the applicants, find themselves faced with problems relating to the continuation or inception of their married life may suffer distress and anxiety. Nevertheless, having regard in particular to the factors relied on by the Government in their alternative submission, the Court considers that in the circumstances of these cases its findings of violation of themselves constitute sufficient just satisfaction. The applicants' claim for monetary compensation cannot therefore be accepted.

[...]*

For these reasons, **THE COURT** unanimously: **

1   *Holds* that Article 8 was applicable in the present case but that, taken alone, it has not been violated;

2   *Holds* that Article 14 was applicable in the present case;

3   *Holds* that Article 14 taken together with Article 8 has been violated by reasons of discrimination against each of the applicants on the ground of sex;

4   *Holds* that there has been no other violation of Article 14 taken together with Article 8;

5   *Holds* that there has been no breach of Article 3;

6   *Holds* that there has been a violation of Article 13 in regard to the complaint of discrimination on the ground of sex; and

7   *Holds* that the United Kingdom is to pay to the applicants jointly, for costs and expenses, the sums resulting from the calculations to be made in accordance with para 100 of the judgment.

---

*   **Eds:** paras 97 to 100, which relate to costs and expenses, have not been included.

**   **Eds:** due to space constraints, the concurring opinions, which were given by Judges Thor Viljálmsson, Bernhardt, Pettiti and Gersing, have not been included. The full text of the judgment is available at the website of the European Court of Human Rights (see *On-line Access to Human Rights Source Materials, supra*, p xlv); (1985) ECHR Series A, No 94; 7 EHRR 471 and 81 ILR 139.

CASE NO 40

RATTIGAN AND OTHERS v
THE CHIEF IMMIGRATION OFFICER AND OTHERS

SUPREME COURT OF ZIMBABWE

Judgment: 13 June 1994

Panel: Gubbay CJ; McNally, Korsah, Ebrahim and Muchechetere, JJA

Human rights — Freedom of movement — Right to protection for the privacy of one's home — Whether denial of residence permits to non-citizen husbands married to citizen wives contravened the wives' freedom of movement — Constitution of Zimbabwe, ss 11 and 22(1)

Human rights — Constitutional law — Purposive interpretation of constitutional rights in context of international human rights law — Constitution of Zimbabwe, ss 11 and 22(1) — International Covenant on Civil and Political Rights, art 17 — European Convention for the Protection of Human Rights and Fundamental Freedoms, art 8(1)

BACKGROUND

The three applicants were female citizens of Zimbabwe, who were married to non-citizens of Zimbabwe. They all wished to reside in Zimbabwe and to establish matrimonial homes there. However, the husbands of all three applicants had been refused permanent residence permits entitling them to reside in Zimbabwe, on the grounds that they failed to offer any scarce skills or qualify under any other category normally required for the issue of a family residence permit based on the application of a foreign husband. The applicants claimed that the refusal to grant their husbands residence permits violated their rights as citizens to freedom of movement guaranteed by section 22(1) of the Constitution of Zimbabwe, and that it also infringed section 11 of the Constitution, which they argued, having been upgraded from a preamble in earlier constitutions, conferred substantive rights on the individual, including the right to life, liberty, security of the person and protection of the law, and protection for the privacy of one's home.

The respondents, the Chief Immigration Officer, the Minister for Home Affairs and the Attorney-General, contended that the applicants' right to freedom of movement was not restricted. They remained free to move in and out of the country as often as they wished and reside in Zimbabwe for as long as they wished. The fact that they must decide to either reside in Zimbabwe without their husbands or to accompany their husbands to the countries of their citizenship and live together there in order to establish a matrimonial home was no more than an inconvenience, which did not remove or infringe their constitutional right to freedom of movement.

HELD (allowing the application)

1 Section 11 of the Constitution should be regarded as conferring substantive rights on the individual, and not merely as a guide to the intention of the framers in enacting

Chapter 3. Thus under section 11, every person in Zimbabwe was guaranteed, *inter alia*, the right to life, liberty, security of the person and the protection of the law, and protection for the privacy of his home, subject to their enjoyment and exercise not prejudicing the rights and freedoms of others or the public interest (pp 654, 655).

2   The claim by the wives to an infringement of their fundamental right to freedom of movement under section 22(1) of the Constitution should be adjudged in the light of the institution of marriage, which embodied the obligations to found a home, to cohabit, to have children and to live together as a family unit (p 656).

3   Article 17 of the International Covenant on Civil and Political Rights and article 8(1) of the European Convention on Human Rights both afford protection against interference with family life and lay emphasis on the importance of preserving well-established family ties. Although there was no provision in the Constitution of Zimbabwe which equated directly with these provisions, section 11 of the Constitution guarantees every person "protection for the privacy of his home". Taken in conjunction with section 22(1) and interpreting the whole Constitution generously and purposively, to prohibit the husbands from residing in Zimbabwe and to so disable them from living with their wives in the country of which they were citizens and to which they owed allegiance, was in effect to undermine and devalue the protection of freedom of movement accorded to each of the wives as a member of a family unit (pp 657, 658).

Treaties and other international instruments referred to

International Covenant on Civil and Political Rights 1966, art 17

European Convention for the Protection of Human Rights and Fundamental Freedoms 1950, art 8

National Legislation referred to

Zimbabwe

Constitution of Zimbabwe, ss 11, 24(1) and 113(1)

Immigration Regulations of 1979 (RGN 373/79), ss 17(1)(a) and 38(1)

Cases referred to

Abdulaziz, Cabales and Balkandali v The United Kingdom, ECHR, judgment of 28 May 1985, Series A, No 94; 7 EHRR 471; *supra* p 618

Application Number 9773/82 v The United Kingdom, ECommHR, Application No 9773/82; 5 EHRR 296

Aumeeruddy-Cziffra and others v Mauritius, Communication No 35/1978, Views adopted 9 April 1981, UN Doc CCPR/C/OP/1 at 67 (1984); *Selected Decisions under the Optional Protocol* (second to sixteenth sessions) (New York: United Nations, 1985), Vol 1, 67; *supra*, p 608

Berrehab v Netherlands, ECHR, judgment of 21 June 1988, Series A, No 138; 11 EHRR 322

Beldjoudi v France, ECHR, judgment of 26 March 1992, Series A, No 234-A; 14 EHRR 801

Bull v Minister of Home Affairs 1986 (1) ZLR 202 (ZS); 1986 (3) SA 870 (ZSC)

Dow v Attorney-General (1992) LRC (Const) 623 (Botswana Court of Appeal); 1994 (6) BCLR 1 (Botswana); *supra* p 572

Excell v Douglas 1924 CPD 472

Government of the Republic of Namibia v Cultura 2000 1994 (1) SA 407 (NmSC)

Hunter et al v Southam Inc [1984] 2 SCR 145; (1985) 11 DLR (4th) 641

Loving v Virginia 388 US 1 (1967); 18 L Ed 2d 1010

MacNaught v Caledonian Hotel 1938 TPD 577

Maynard v Hill 125 US 190 (1888); 31 L Ed 654

Minister of Home Affairs v Dabengwa 1982 (1) ZLR 236 (SC); 1982 (4) SA 301 (ZSC)

Moustaquim v Belgium, ECHR, judgment of 18 February 1991, Series A, No 193; 13 EHRR 802

Nkomo v Attorney-General, Zimbabwe 1994 (1) SACR 302 (ZS); 1994 (3) SA 34 (ZSC)

Platt v Platt 1965 (2) PH B 15 (N)

Re Munhumeso SC 221/93 1995 (1) SA 551 (ZSC); 1995 (2) BCLR 125 (ZS)

T v T 1968 (2) RLR 178 (GD); 1968 (3) SA 554 (R)

Van Oosten v Van Oosten 1923 CPD 409

Webber v Webber 1915 AD 239

JUDGMENT

GUBBAY CJ:

Introduction

The short and undisputed facts of this joint application conceal a problem of considerable constitutional significance and no little difficulty. It concerns the pervasive issue of whether a female citizen of Zimbabwe married to a man who is an alien, being a citizen of a foreign country, is entitled to the right to reside permanently with her husband in Zimbabwe.

The factual background

The first applicant, Devagi Rattigan, *née* Naidoo, was born in Bulawayo on 25 July 1960, and is a citizen of Zimbabwe. She married John David Rattigan, at Harare, on 18 January 1992. He was born in Hamilton, Scotland, on 4 April 1950 and is a British subject. He entered Zimbabwe on 1 June 1991, for a three month holiday and shortly thereafter met and fell in love with the first applicant. He was denied a permit to work or reside in Zimbabwe as, in the opinion of the immigration authorities, he has no scarce skill to offer. In consequence of being issued with a notice to leave Zimbabwe, he and the first applicant departed for England where they presently reside. Both are anxious to return and set up their matrimonial home in Zimbabwe. They have no children.

The second applicant, Marchelle Caroline Butler-Rees, *née* Morta, was born in Bulawayo, on 2 February 1959, and is a citizen of Zimbabwe. She married Steven James

Butler-Rees on 4 January 1992. He was born on 27 November 1961, in Dublin, Ireland, and is a citizen of that country. He first entered Zimbabwe on 7 June 1993, and thereafter made numerous visits to the country. He too was denied a permit to work or reside in Zimbabwe as he possessed no scarce skill. The last refusal was on 16 August 1993. He is presently in the country on an extended visitor's permit and lives with the second applicant in a house in Bulawayo. She is pregnant with his child. Both ardently desire to establish a matrimonial abode permanently in Zimbabwe.

The third applicant, Edith May Caules, *née* Stroud, was born in Bulawayo on 17 May 1942, and is a citizen of Zimbabwe. She married Frank Caules on 29 February 1972. He was born on 8 August 1928, in Dublin, Ireland, and is a citizen of that country. Twin children were born of the marriage on 13 April 1973. Since May 1980, the third applicant and the children have been living in Bulawayo and from the latter part of 1988, Mr Caules has resided continuously with them. He was initially allowed entry on a visitor's permit but subsequently was granted a two year residence permit. This was extended for a further three year period, expiring on 29 September 1993. His application for a permanent residence permit was refused on 24 August 1993, on the ground that he has absolutely nothing to offer the country. On 4 December 1993, an interdict was granted by the High Court prohibiting the deportation of Mr Caules pending the determination of this application. Both he and the third applicant wish to remain living in their home in Bulawayo, together with the children, who have been granted permanent residence permits and have applied to become citizens of Zimbabwe.

I shall henceforth refer to the applicants as "the wives".

The respondents' stance

It is not contended by the first respondent, who is the Chief Immigration Officer, that the marriages in question were contracted in an effort to evade the immigration laws of the country or in order to persuade the immigration authorities to allow the alien husbands to remain living unimpeded in the country of their wives. In other words, these were not marriages of convenience. They were genuinely entered into by the respective couples with the intention of establishing a common home and consortium between them "for better or for worse".

The policy adopted by the Chief Immigration Officer, who speaks, as well, for the second and third respondents, being the Minister of Home Affairs and the Attorney-General, is outlined in his opposing affidavit. It is to the following effect:

> ... the principal applicant for a family residence permit should always be the husband unless the wife is a highly qualified professional, that is medical practitioner, offering a scarce skill in her own right, in which case the husband may be treated as dependant.

> Where a foreign husband applies to come and settle here, a residence permit may only be issued if he fulfils one of the following requirements:

> (a) possesses a skill considered to be in a critical skills shortage area;

> (b) invests substantial capital in a project approved by the Zimbabwe Investment Centre;

> (c) be retired with sufficient financial means to sustain himself and family without resort to public funds during his stay in the country.

> None of the husbands concerned could meet the basic requirements for issuance of residence permits at the time of application.

It is firmly disputed that the disability thereby imposed on the husbands in any way circumscribes the constitutional rights of the wives.

The rule of constitutional construction

This Court has on several occasions in the past pronounced upon the proper approach to constitutional construction embodying fundamental rights and protections. What is to be avoided is the imparting of a narrow, artificial, rigid and pedantic interpretation; to be preferred is one which serves the interest of the Constitution and best carries out its objects and promotes its purpose. All relevant provisions are to be considered as a whole and where rights and freedoms are conferred on persons, derogations therefrom, as far as the language permits, should be narrowly or strictly construed: see *Minister of Home Affairs v Dabengwa* 1982 (1) ZLR 236 (SC) at 243G–244A, 1982 (4) SA 301 (ZS) at 306E–H; *Bull v Minister of Home Affairs* 1986 (1) ZLR 202 (ZS) at 210E–211C, 1986 (3) SA 870 (ZS) at 880J-881D: *Nkomo v Attorney-General, Zimbabwe* 1994 (3) SA 34 (ZS), 1994 (1) SACR 302 (ZS) at 309e–f. A recent reminder that courts cannot allow a constitution to be "a lifeless museum piece" but must continue to breathe life into it from time to time when opportune to do so, was graphically expressed by Aguda JA in *Dow v Attorney-General* (1992) LRC (Const) 623 (Botswana Court of Appeal) at 668f–h:

> ... the overriding principle must be an adherence to the general picture presented by the Constitution into which each individual provision must fit in order to maintain in essential details the picture of which the framers could have painted had they been faced with circumstances of today. To hold otherwise would be to stultify the living Constitution in its growth. It seems to me that a stultification of the Constitution must be prevented if this is possible without doing extreme violence to the language of the Constitution. I conceive it that the primary duty of the judges is to make the Constitution grow and develop in order to meet the just demands and aspirations of an ever developing society which is part of the wider and larger human society governed by some acceptable concepts of human dignity.

See, too, *Hunter et al v Southam Inc* (1984) 9 CRR 355 at 364 (Supreme Court of Canada); *Government of the Republic of Namibia v Cultura 2000* 1994 (1) SA 407 (NmSC) at 418F-G.

The status of section 11 of the Constitution

Considerable argument was addressed by counsel as to whether section 11 in the Declaration of Rights, which forms Chapter 3 of the Constitution, is a mere preamble to the other sections which follow or a substantive provision. It reads:

> Whereas every person in Zimbabwe is entitled to the fundamental rights and freedoms of the individual, that is to say, the right whatever his race, tribe, place of origin, political opinions, colour, creed or sex, but subject to respect for the rights and freedoms of others and for the public interest, to each and all of the following, namely:
>
> (a) life, liberty, security of the person and the protection of the law;
>
> (b) freedom of conscience, of expression and of assembly and association; and
>
> (c) protection for the privacy of his home and other property and from deprivation of property without compensation,
>
> and whereas it is the duty of every person to respect and abide by the Constitution and the Laws of Zimbabwe, the provisions of this Chapter shall have effect for the purpose of affording protection to those rights and freedoms subject to such limitations of that protection as are contained herein, being limitations designed to ensure that the enjoyment of the said rights and freedoms by any individual does not prejudice the rights and freedoms of others or the public interest.

In *Re Munhumeso* SC 221/93 1995 (1) SA 551 (ZS), this Court was of the view that the upgraded status of the provision from a preamble in each of the four earlier constitutions, to a numbered section, signified that it is to be regarded as conferring substantive rights on the individual, and not merely a guide to the intention of the framers in enacting Chapter 3. It was accepted to be "the key or umbrella provision" in the Declaration of Rights under which all rights and freedoms must be subsumed, and that it encapsulates the sum total of the individual's rights and freedoms in general terms, which may be expanded upon in the expository, elaborating or limiting ensuing sections 12 to 23.

I can perceive of no warrant to differ from that analysis and reiterate my respectful concurrence with the reasoning of Amissah JP and Aguda JA in *Dow v Attorney-General* (*supra*) in the passages of their respective judgments at 636e-637c and 669i-670c. I would simply add that their conclusion is much supported by the meaning given to "Declaration of Rights" in section 113(1) as "the Declaration of Rights set out in Chapter 3". That chapter comprises sections 11 to 26 (not sections 12 to 26) and it is in relation to an alleged contravention or likely contravention of the Declaration of Rights as so defined that section 24(1) gives the right to any person to apply to the Supreme Court for redress.

Thus under section 11 every person in Zimbabwe is guaranteed, *inter alia*, the right to life, liberty, security of the person and the protection of the law, and protection for the privacy of his home, subject to their enjoyment and exercise not prejudicing the rights and freedoms of others or the public interest.

The alleged violation of section 22(1) of the Declaration of Rights

Subsection (1) of section 22 mandates that "no person shall be deprived of his freedom of movement". Embodied in such protection are: (i) the right to move freely throughout Zimbabwe; (ii) the right to reside in any part of Zimbabwe; (iii) the right to enter and leave Zimbabwe; and (iv) immunity from expulsion from Zimbabwe. Under subsection (2) any restriction on the person's freedom of movement that is involved in his lawful detention shall not be held to be a contravention of subsection (1). The further derogations specified in subsection (3) fall outside the issue debated, in particular, paragraph (d) only permits the imposition of restrictions on the movement or residence within Zimbabwe, or the exclusion or expulsion from Zimbabwe, of persons who are neither citizens of Zimbabwe nor regarded by virtue of a written law as permanently resident in Zimbabwe. Subsection (4), as read with subsection (3)(a), provides that, although in the interests of defence, public safety, public order, public morality or public health, it is lawful to restrict the freedom of movement of persons, such right is not to be construed as authorising a law preventing a citizen from leaving Zimbabwe or excluding or expelling him from the country. In the present context subsections (3)(d) and (4) are significant only to the extent that they underscore the importance placed by the Constitution, which is the supreme law of Zimbabwe, upon the protection of the right of a citizen to freedom of movement in the manner that phrase is particularised.

The case made by the wives is that the refusal of the Chief Immigration Officer to issue a residence permit to each husband in terms of section 17(1)(a) of the Immigration Regulations of 1979 (RGN 373/79), or an alien's permit pursuant to section 38(1) thereof, and the consequent requirement that they leave the country, circumscribe their fundamental and unqualified right as citizens to freedom of movement. If the husbands are compelled to depart (an actuality in respect of Mr Rattigan) the right of the wives to reside in Zimbabwe is directly affected. In essence, the freedom of movement of the wives is determined by what happens to their husbands, for in order to secure and maintain the marital relationship they would have to accompany them.

The respondents' answer is that the freedom of movement of the wives is not restricted by the refusal to permit the husbands to reside in Zimbabwe. They may move in and out of the country as often as they wish and remain for indefinite periods of time.

But so far as establishing the matrimonial home in Zimbabwe is concerned they must decide either to exercise their constitutional right to reside in Zimbabwe without their husbands or accompany them to the countries of their citizenship and live together there. This may cause inconvenience but no more. Their right of freedom of movement in any of its aspects has not been removed from them or indeed infringed.

The predicament of each wife has not been caused by the decision of the husband, as head of the family, to establish the common household in a country other than Zimbabwe. If that were so then, provided the decision was not unreasonable, the wife, if she wished the marriage to survive, would be obliged to accept it and leave Zimbabwe: see *Webber v Webber* 1915 AD 239 at 246; *MacNaught v Caledonian Hotel* 1938 TPD 577 at 579; *Platt v Platt* 1965 (2) PH B 15 (N) at 73. To the contrary, the husbands share the desire of the wives that the matrimonial abode be located in Zimbabwe. The impediment is the alien status of the husbands and the refusal of the immigration authorities to permit them to remain in Zimbabwe.

Marriage is a juristic act *sui generis*. It gives rise to a physical, moral and spiritual community of life – a *consortium omnis vitae*. It obliges the husband and wife to live together for life (more realistically, for as long as the marriage endures) and to confer sexual privileges exclusively upon each other. Conjugal love embraces three components: (i) *eros* (passion); (ii) *philia* (companionship); and (iii) *agape* (self-giving brotherly love). See *T v T* 1968 (2) RLR 178 (GD) at 180G-H, 1968 (3) SA 554 (R) at 555E. The duties of cohabitation, loyalty, fidelity and mutual assistance and support, flow from the marital relationship. To live together as spouses in community of life, to afford each other marital privileges and to be ever faithful, are the inherent commands which lie at the very heart of marriage. See *Van Oosten v Van Oosten* 1923 CPD 409 at 411; *Excell v Douglas* 1924 CPD 472 at 476 *in fine*, and, generally, Schafer, Family Law Service, section A3 at 2. "Marriage", as observed by Warren CJ in *Loving v Virginia* 388 US 1 (1967) at 12, "is one of the basic rights of man, fundamental to our very existence and survival". Eighty years earlier in *Maynard v Hill* 125 US 190 (1887) at 211-2 Field J spoke eloquently of marriage as:

> ... an institution, in the maintenance of which in its purity the public is deeply interested, for it is the foundation of the family and of society, without which there would be neither civilisation nor progress ... It is ... a social relation, like that of parent and child, the obligations of which arise not from the consent of concurring minds, but are the creation of the law itself, a relation the most important, as affecting the happiness of individuals, the first step from barbarism to incipient civilisation, the purest tie of social life, and the true basis of human progress ... In strictness, though formed by contract, it signifies the relation of husband and wife, deriving both its rights and duties from a source higher than any contract of which the parties are capable, and as to these uncontrollable by any contract which they can make. When formed, this relation is no more a contract than "fatherhood" or "sonship" is a contract.

These sentiments hold as firm today as they did then.

It is in the light of the institution of marriage as I have ventured to portray it that the claim by the wives to an infringement of their fundamental right to freedom of movement has to be adjudged.

In support of the wives' contention, counsel relied strongly on the second aspect of the Dow case (*supra*). It was there argued by the Attorney-General that Mrs Dow had no *locus standi* to have brought the application in the court *a quo* since at issue was the right of her two young children to citizenship of their birth, their father being an alien. Amissah JP at 659g-h summed up Mrs Dow's answer to this submission in these words:

The case which I understand the respondent to make is that due to the disabilities under which her children were likely to be placed in her own country of birth by the provisions of the Citizenship Act, her own freedom of movement protected by section 14 of the Constitution was correspondingly likely to be infringed and that gave her the right under section 18(1) to come to court to test the validity of the Act. What she says is that it is her freedom which has been circumscribed by the disabilities placed on her children.

The learned Judge President then proceeded to rule in favour of Mrs Dow. He said at 660c-e:

> It is totally unrealistic to think that you could permanently keep the child out of Botswana and yet by that not interfere with the freedom of movement of the mother. When the freedom of the mother to enter Botswana to live and to leave when she wishes is indirectly controlled by the location of the child, excluding the child from Botswana is in effect excluding the mother from Botswana. If the exclusion is the result of a determination of the child's citizenship which is wrong, surely this would amount to an interference with, and therefore an infringement of, the mother's freedom of movement.

To like effect Aguda JA remarked at 678d-e:

> In my view it is too artificial and unnatural to hold that in these circumstances [the two children being subject to expulsion from Botswana away from the mother and away from the only place they regarded as their home] the respondent's ... right to free movement within and into and out of Botswana [has] not been breached.

Bizos JA, the third member of the majority of the court, at 684e, stressed the strength of the bond between a mother and her children as the determinative factor.

> Mrs Dow's situation seems to me analogous to that which pertains to the wives. The bond between husband and wife may be equally as strong as that between mother and child. Marriages are almost invariably entered into by parties who have deep affection for one another and who intend to devote the remainder of their lives together. Although the condition of matrimony does not, as a concept of law, make the spouses one flesh – *una caro* – it nonetheless embodies the obligations to found a home, to cohabit, to have children and to live together as a family unit. It is the most fundamental institution known to mankind "the first step from barbarism" and "the true basis of human progress".
>
> Decisions concerning article 17 of the International Covenant on Civil and Political Rights, and article 8(1) of the European Convention on Human Rights, both provisions of which afford protection against interference with family life, lay emphasis upon the importance of preserving well established family ties.

In *Aumeeruddy-Cziffra v Mauritius* (1981) 62 ILR 285, the United Nations Human Rights Committee examined the effect of a law passed by the government of Mauritius which removed the right of alien husbands of Mauritian women citizens to the right of residence and immunity from deportation, and found that it infringed article 17 of the Covenant. It was stated at 293–4:

> The Committee takes the view that the common residence of husband and wife has to be considered as the normal behaviour of a family. Hence, and as the State party has admitted, the exclusion of a person from a country where close members of his family are living can amount to an interference within the meaning of article 17. In principle, article 17(1) applies also when one of the spouses is an alien. Whether the existence and application of immigration laws affecting the residence of a family member is compatible with the covenant depends on whether such interference is either "arbitrary or unlawful" as stated in article 17(1), or conflicts in any other way with the State party's obligations under the covenant.

In the present cases, not only the future possibility of deportation, but the existing precarious residence situation of foreign husbands in Mauritius represents, in the opinion of the Committee, an interference by the authorities of the State party with the family life of the Mauritian wives and their husbands. The statutes in question have rendered it uncertain for the families concerned whether and for how long it will be possible for them to continue their family life by residing together in Mauritius.

The European Court of Human Rights in Abdulaziz Cabales and *Balkandali v United Kingdom* (1985) 7 EHRR 471 at 62 and *Berrehab v Netherlands* (1989) 11 EHRR 322 at 21, indicated that the relationship created between two spouses to a lawful and genuine marriage had to be regarded as "family life" within the meaning of article 8 of the Convention, and was sufficient to attract such respect as may be due under that article.

In *Moustaquim v Belgium* (1991) 13 EHRR 802 at 36 and *Beldjoudi v France* (1992) 14 EHRR 801 at 56–7, the same Court held in each instance that, notwithstanding the fairly formidable criminal records possessed by the applicant, the deportation order issued against him was, in the particular circumstances of his close family ties in the country, likely to compromise the continuation of his family life and accordingly amounted to an interference with the right to respect for family life.

I must also mention the judgment of the European Commission of Human Rights in *Application Number 9773/82 v United Kingdom* 5 EHRR 296, for reliance was placed upon it by the respondents' counsel. Alluded to was the statement that: "a right to marry and found a family does not, in principle, include the right to choose the geographical location of the marriage". In the context of the particular facts of that case the observation was probably justifiable, for the applicant was seeking to establish a new relationship by marrying a foreign woman whom he had never actually met, who had been refused entry into the United Kingdom and, if admitted, would be dependent, in all probability, on public funds. The action taken, therefore, caused no actual interference with family life.

Although there is no provision in the Constitution of Zimbabwe which equates directly to article 17 of the Covenant or article 8(1) of the Convention, section 11 guarantees every person "protection for the privacy of his home". Taken in conjunction with section 22(1) and interpreting the whole generously and purposively so as to eschew the "austerity of tabulated legalism", I reach the conclusion that to prohibit the husbands from residing in Zimbabwe and so disable them from living with their wives in the country of which they are citizens and to which they owe allegiance, is in effect to undermine and devalue the protection of freedom of movement accorded to each of the wives as a member of a family unit.

Order

In the result:

1   The application is allowed, with costs to be paid by the second respondent, save for such costs as were occasioned in the preparation of pages 27 to 46 (inclusive) in the affidavit of Edith May Caules.

2   It is hereby declared that the right of the applicants under section 22(1) of the constitution of Zimbabwe to freedom of movement, that is to say, the right to move freely throughout Zimbabwe, the right to reside in any part of Zimbabwe, and the right to enter and to leave Zimbabwe, has been contravened by the decision of the first respondent not to permit their alien husbands to reside with them in Zimbabwe.

CASE NO 41

SALEM v CHIEF IMMIGRATION OFFICER AND ANOTHER

SUPREME COURT OF ZIMBABWE

Judgment: 8 November 1994

Panel: Gubbay CJ, Korsah and Ebrahim JJA

Human rights — Freedom of movement — Immigration — Husband and wife — Whether a wife's freedom of movement and right to reside in Zimbabwe was violated by her foreign national husband being denied the right to engage in gainful employment in Zimbabwe — Constitution of Zimbabwe, s 22(1)

BACKGROUND

The applicant, Ms Patricia Salem, was a citizen of Zimbabwe and a permanent resident there. On 16 April 1994, she married Mr Charles Salem, a British national, in Zimbabwe. They both wished to reside in Zimbabwe. On 2 June 1994, Mr Salem applied to the Chief Immigration Officer (the first respondent) for a residence permit, but was later informed by an immigration officer (the second respondent) that he would have to leave the country in order to await the outcome of his application.

Mr and Ms Salem immediately queried the reason for imposing this requirement, given that the Supreme Court had recently held in *Rattigan v Chief Immigration Officer*, (*supra*, p 650) that a female citizen of Zimbabwe, married to a national of a foreign country, is entitled by virtue of the protection of freedom of movement under section 22(1) of the Constitution of Zimbabwe to reside permanently with her husband in Zimbabwe. In response, the second respondent informed them that the Supreme Court judgment in *Rattigan* "does not state that foreign husbands shall not be required to apply for permits; neither does it say that the granting of such permits should be automatic" and that "what we are talking about … is purely an immigration requirement which has nothing to do with the Supreme Court judgment".

Mrs Salem applied to the Supreme Court for enforcement of her right to freedom of movement under section 22(1) of the Constitution of Zimbabwe and to have the ruling in *Rattigan* extended to include the right of her husband to lawfully engage in employment or other gainful activity in Zimbabwe. She argued that as she was pregnant she would not be able to continue in employment, and would need her husband to support her and their child. If her husband was not permitted to do so, then she would be forced to leave Zimbabwe, which, she argued, was against the spirit of the judgment in *Rattigan*.

HELD (allowing the application)

1   In absence of a stated suspicion that the marriage was one of convenience, the second respondent, by his insistence that the applicant's husband was to leave the

country, knowingly acted in defiance of the applicant's constitutional right to have her husband living with her in Zimbabwe (as established in *Rattigan v Chief Immigration Officer*). Such disdainful disregard for a judgment of this court by a government official was deserving of censure. To ensure the rights contained in the *Rattigan* judgment were given effect, it was necessary to issue a directive to the Chief Immigration Officer, rather than adopt the preferred expedient of merely declaring their existence under the Constitution (p 661).

2   A generous and purposive interpretation should be given to the protection of the freedom of movement expressed in s 22(1) of the Constitution. Unless the protection guaranteed under section 22(1) of the Constitution embraced the entitlement of a citizen wife, residing permanently with her alien husband in Zimbabwe, to look to him for partial or total support, depending upon her circumstances, the exercise of her unqualified right to remain residing in Zimbabwe as a member of a family unit was put in jeopardy (p 662).

National legislation referred to

Zimbabwe

Constitution of Zimbabwe 1980, s 22(1)

Cases referred to

Breull, Ex p, In re Bowie (1880) 16 Ch D 484; [1874–80] All ER Rep 646, UK CA

Edelstein v Edelstein NO 1952 (3) SA 1, AD

Gammon v McClure 1925 CPD 137

Karim v Karim 1962 (1) PH B 4

McKelvey v Cowan, NO 1980 ZLR 235, 1980 (4) SA 525

Miller v Miller 1940 CPD 466

Pyke, Ex p 1948 (1) SA 526

Rattigan v Chief Immigration Officer [1994] 1 LRC 343, Zim SC; 1995 (2) SA 182 (ZSC); 1995 (1) BCLR 1 (ZS); *supra* p 650

State v Naicker 1967 (4) SA 214

Witham v Minister of Home Affairs 1987 (2) ZLR 143; 1989 (1) SA 117

Woodhead v Woodhead 1955 SR 70; 1955 (3) SA 138

JUDGMENT

GUBBAY CJ: In the recent decision in *Rattigan v Chief Immigration Officer* [1994] 1 LRC 343 this court declared that a female citizen of Zimbabwe, married to an alien, being a national of another country, is entitled by virtue of the protection of freedom of movement under s 22(1) of the Constitution of Zimbabwe to reside permanently with her husband in any part of Zimbabwe. For to prohibit the husband of a marriage, genuinely entered into with the mutual intention of establishing a consortium *omnis vitae*, from residing in Zimbabwe would undermine and devalue the exercise of the fundamental and unqualified right of the wife, as a citizen and member of a family unit, to live here.

The present application brought by Patricia Ann Salem, *née* Campbell, a citizen of Zimbabwe by birth and a permanent resident of the country, seeks to extend the ruling in *Rattigan* to embrace within her own mobility rights the right of her husband, Charles Christopher John Salem, to lawfully engage in employment or other gainful activity in Zimbabwe.

The applicant met her husband, a British subject, in early April 1992 while on a working holiday in South Africa. They fell in love and were married in Harare on 16 April 1994. Both desire to establish a fixed abode in Zimbabwe. It is here that the applicant's parents and siblings reside.

On 2 June 1994, Mr Salem applied to the first respondent, the Chief Immigration Officer, for the issue of a residence permit. He was advised in a letter written on 23 August 1994, by the second respondent, an immigration officer, that it was necessary that he leave the country in order to await the outcome of the application. An immediate query as to the reason for imposing the requirement elicited the following response from the second respondent:

> I wish to advise that the Supreme Court judgment does not state that foreign husbands shall not be required to apply for permits; neither does it say the granting of such permits should be automatic. What we are talking about in this case is purely an immigration requirement, which has nothing to do with the Supreme Court judgment. I wish to advise once again that your client must leave the country and await the outcome of his application outside the country, and his departure must be confirmed.

In the absence of a stated suspicion that the marriage was one of convenience, the second respondent, by his insistence that Mr Salem was to leave the country, knowingly acted in defiance of the applicant's constitutional right to have her husband living with her in Zimbabwe. He disdainfully disregarded a judgment of this court that clearly enunciated the rights of three citizen wives whose situation was indistinguishable from that of the applicant. Such an attitude by a government official is deserving of censure. It enjoins this court, so as to ensure that such rights are given effect to, to issue directives to the Chief Immigration Officer, rather than adopt the preferred expedient of merely declaring their existence under the Constitution.

The applicant deposed that she is pregnant and due to give birth some time in March 1995. With the advancement of her pregnant condition and after the birth of the child she will not be able to continue in employment; she will need her husband to support first her and then herself and their child. Her founding affidavit ends with these words:

> If my husband cannot work to support me and my unborn child then I will be forced to leave Zimbabwe, which surely is against the spirit of the order (*sic*). If he leaves and is denied entry whilst his application is being considered at such future date as suits the Department, the result will be the same.

Although the application was served on both the respondents, neither filed an opposing affidavit. Service was also effected upon the Civil Division of the Attorney General's Office. Thereafter, notice of set down was served upon the Civil Division, as were the heads of argument prepared by the applicant's counsel. No response was forthcoming. At the hearing both the respondents were in default of appearance.

It was submitted by Mr de Bourbon, who appeared for the applicant, that to construe the phrase "the right to reside in any part of Zimbabwe" in s 22(1) of the Constitution as merely entitling a citizen wife to have her alien husband living with her in the country, without affording him the ability to engage in gainful employment, would be unduly restrictive of that fundamental right. Frequently it would lead to the dilemma cited by the applicant. One in which, notwithstanding a common desire to locate the matrimonial home in Zimbabwe, a citizen wife, through inability adequately to support her alien husband and children, is compelled by necessity to forego her right to remain living in the country and accompany her husband to a land where he is not prohibited from earning a livelihood.

I agree that a generous and purposive interpretation is to be given to the protection expressed in s 22(1). This was so held in *Rattigan v Chief Immigration Officer* [1994] 1 LRC 343.

The word "reside" is ambiguous. It may have a variety of meanings in accordance with the intent and object of the enactment in which it appears: see *Ex p Breull, In re Bowie* (1880) 16 Ch D 484 at 487, [1874–80] All ER Rep 646 at 647; *Ex p Pyke* 1948 (1) SA 526 at 527; *State v Naicker* 1967 (4) SA 214 at 222. To ascribe it the strict meaning of the place where an individual eats and sleeps after the work of the day is done, would be to diminish the guaranteed right of the citizen wife who, through such causes as old age, poverty, illiteracy, redundancy, physical or mental disability is unable sufficiently to provide for her alien husband and children in Zimbabwe. And so in order to secure and maintain the marital relationship she is left no option but to depart with her husband to a country where he is in a position to assume the role and responsibility of breadwinner. Put otherwise, to impart the normally narrow meaning to "the right to reside in any part of Zimbabwe" would be to differentiate between the affluent wife, who is not dependent upon the support of her husband for herself and children, and she who is impoverished or destitute, and partly or wholly dependent upon him.

It has long been recognised that there is a reciprocal duty of support as between husband and wife: see, eg, *Woodhead v Woodhead* 1955 SR 70 at 72, 1955 (3) SA 138 at 139–140; *McKelvey v Cowan*, NO 1980 ZLR 235 at 236,1980 (4) SA 525 at 526; *Witham v Minister of Home Affairs* 1987 (2) ZLR 143 at 164, 1989 (1) SA 117 at 131. The duty, of course, endures *stante matrimonio*. It depends on the one spouse's need for support and the other's ability to provide it.

In practice, however, the primary duty of maintaining the household rests upon the husband: see *Miller v Miller* 1940 CPD 466 at 469; *Edelstein v Elelstein*, NO 1952 (3) SA 1 at 15; Hahlo, *The South African Law of Husband and Wife* (5th edn, 1985) at p 135; Boberg, *The Law of Persons and the Family* (1977) at p 252. It is he who has to provide the matrimonial home as well as food, clothing medical and dental care, and whatever else is reasonably required. He must do so on a scale commensurate with the social position, financial means and standard of living of the spouses. He cannot evade that responsibility by showing that his wife is receiving assistance from blood relations, friends or charitable institutions: see *Gammon v McClure* 1925 CPD 137 at 139; *Karim v Karim* 1962(1) PH B 4.

It follows, in my view, that unless the protection guaranteed under s 22(1) of the Constitution embraces the entitlement of a citizen wife, residing permanently with her alien husband in Zimbabwe, to look to him for partial or total support, depending upon her circumstances, the exercise of her unqualified right to remain residing in this country, as a member of a family unit, is put in jeopardy.

Accordingly, the applicant is due the relief claimed. In the result:

(1) The application is allowed, with costs to be paid by the first respondent.

(2) It is hereby declared that the right of the applicant under s 22(1) of the Constitution of Zimbabwe to freedom of movement, that is to say, the right to reside in any part of Zimbabwe, has been contravened by the actions of the first and second respondents.

(3) By virtue of the applicant's right under the aforementioned s 22(1) to have her husband residing with her in any part of Zimbabwe, it is hereby ordered that:

    (a) the first respondent issue to Charles Christopher John Salem, within thirty days hereof, such written authority as is necessary to enable him to remain in Zimbabwe on the same standing as any other alien who is a permanent resident;

    (b) the said Charles Christopher John Salem be accorded the same rights as are enjoyed by all permanent residents of Zimbabwe, including the right to engage in employment or other gainful activity in any part of Zimbabwe, and that the first respondent impose no restriction upon such right.

CASE NO 42

ISLAM v SECRETARY OF STATE FOR THE HOME DEPARTMENT; R v IMMIGRATION APPEAL TRIBUNAL AND ANOTHER, EX PARTE SHAH (CONSOLIDATED APPEALS)

HOUSE OF LORDS

Judgment: 25 March 1999

Panel: Lord Steyn, Lord Hoffmann, Lord Hope of Craighead, Lord Hutton and Lord Millett

Human rights — Asylum — Refugee status — State sanctioning and tolerating discrimination against women — Whether Pakistani women were members of a "particular social group" — Alternatively whether Pakistani women accused of adultery were members of a "particular social group" — Whether social group requires degree of cohesiveness, cooperation and independence – Whether Pakistani women persecuted on basis of membership of social group — Geneva Convention relating to Status of Refugees 1951 as amended by Protocol 1967, art 1A(2)

BACKGROUND

The appellants, Ms Islam and Ms Shah, were both citizens of Pakistan, but otherwise unconnected to each other. The women had both been victims of domestic violence, had been forced by their husbands to leave their homes and risked being falsely accused of adultery in Pakistan. They both fled to the United Kingdom where they were granted limited leave to enter as visitors. They subsequently applied for asylum, claiming that that they were unprotected by the state and were at risk of criminal proceedings for sexual immorality and, if found guilty, to flogging or death by stoning. They both claimed refugee status on the ground that they had a well-founded fear of being persecuted for reasons of "membership of a particular social group" within the meaning article 1A(2) of the Geneva Convention relating to the Status of Refugees 1951.*

The Secretary of State for the Home Department refused the applications on the basis that the applicants were not members of a "particular social group" within the meaning of article 1A(2) of the Convention, which decision was later affirmed by special adjudicators. The Immigration Appeals Tribunal refused Ms Shah leave to appeal and dismissed Ms Islam's appeal. Ms Shah was granted an application for judicial review of the Tribunal's decision, with the judge ruling that she was capable of bringing herself within the definition of a particular social group for the purposes of article 1A(2) of the Convention. The Court of Appeal allowed an appeal by the Secretary of State in Ms Shah's case, and dismissed Ms Islam's appeal against the Tribunal's decision, on the ground that Ms Islam and Ms Shah were not members of a particular social group since they had no common uniting attribute which existed independently of their fear of persecution. Ms Islam and Ms Shah appealed to the House of Lords.

---

* *Eds:* the text of article 1A(2) is reproduced at p 669.

HELD (allowing the appeals (Lord Millet dissenting))

1   The Convention was concerned with persecution based on discrimination on specified grounds, including membership of a "particular social group". This was not an all-encompassing residual category; there was a limitation involved in the words "particular social group". However, what was not justified was to introduce into that formulation an additional restriction of cohesiveness, since this would be contrary to the *ejusdem generis* rule and would be at variance with the principle that a treaty ought to be construed in a purposive sense. Whilst cohesiveness might prove the existence of a particular social group, a requirement of cohesiveness foisted an impermissible restrictive requirement on the words of article 1A(2). The phrase should extend to what was fairly and contextually inherent in it, which included women in Pakistan. Further, the fact that some Pakistani women were able to avoid the impact of persecution did not mean that women in Pakistan could not be treated as a relevant social group, or that the persecution of a few could not be on grounds of membership of that class. To treat this factor as negativing a Convention ground under article 1A(2) would drive a juggernaut through the Convention (pp 673, 674, 675 and 682).

2   The concept of a social group was perfectly adequate to accommodate women as a group in a society that discriminates on the ground of sex, that is, that perceives women as not being entitled to the same fundamental rights as men. However, there was no suggestion that a woman was entitled to refugee status merely because she lived in a society which, for religious or any other reason, discriminated against women. The Convention was about persecution, a well-founded fear of serious harm, which was a very different matter. The distinguishing feature of the present case was the evidence of institutionalised discrimination against women. What made it persecution, was that women were unprotected by the state; indeed the state tolerated and sanctioned the discrimination against them (pp 681, 683).

Treaties and other international instruments referred to

Charter of the United Nations 1945

Convention on the Elimination of All Forms of Discrimination against Women 1979

Geneva Convention Relating to the Status of Refugees 1951 (as amended by the Protocol Relating to Status of Refugees 1967), arts 1A(2), 1(F), 32 and 33

Universal Declaration of Human Rights 1948, first preamble, arts 1 and 2

Vienna Convention on the Law of Treaties 1969, art 31

National legislation referred to

United Kingdom

Asylum and Immigration Appeals Act 1993, s 8(2)

Domestic Violence and Matrimonial Proceedings Act 1976

Pakistan

Evidence Act

Hudood Ordinances (promulgated in 1979)

Zina Ordinance

Cases referred to

A v Minister for Immigration and Ethnic Affairs (1997) 142 ALR 331; (1997) 2 BHRC 143

Attorney-General of Canada v Ward [1993] 2 SCR 689; (1993) 103 DLR (4th) 1

Bastanipour v Immigration and Naturalization Service (1992) 980 F2d 1129

Canada (Minister of Employment and Immigration) v Mayers [1993] 1 FC 154; (1992) 97 DLR (4th) 729

Chan v Minister of Employment and Immigration [1995] 3 SCR 593; (1996) 128 DLR (4th) 213

De Valle v Immigration and Naturalization Service (1990) 901 F2d 787

Environment Agency (formerly National Rivers Authority) v Empress Car Co (Abertillery) Ltd [1999] 2 AC 22

Fatin v Immigration and Naturalization Service (1993) 12 F3d 1233

Gomez v Immigration and Naturalization Service (1990) 947 F2d 660

In re Acosta (1985) 19 I & N 211

James v Eastleigh Borough Council [1990] 2 AC 751

Matter of Kasinga 13 June 1996, Interim Decision 3278, (1997, Special Issue Autumn) *International Journal of Refugee Law* 213

Matter of Toboso-Alfonso, (unreported) 12 March 1990, Interim Decision

Re GJ [1998] INLR 387

R v Immigration Appeal Tribunal and Secretary of State for the Home Department, Ex parte Shah [1998] 1 WLR 74; reversing [1997] Imm AR 145

Sanchez-Trujillo v Immigration and Naturalization Service (1986) 801 F2d 1571

Savchenko v Secretary of State for the Home Department [1996] Imm AR 28

JUDGMENT

LORD STEYN: My Lords, the two appeals before the House raise important questions about the interpretation of article 1A(2) of the Convention Relating to the Status of Refugees 1951, and in particular the meaning of the words "membership of a particular social group". Section 8(2) of the Asylum and Immigration Appeals Act 1993 provides that a person who has limited leave to enter the United Kingdom may appeal to a special adjudicator against a refusal to vary leave "on the ground that it would be contrary to the United Kingdom's obligations under the Convention for him to be required to leave the United Kingdom after the time limited by the leave". The common features of the two appeals are as follows. Both appeals involve married Pakistani women, who were forced by their husbands to leave their homes. They are at risk of being falsely accused of adultery in Pakistan. They are presently in England. They seek asylum in this country as refugees. They contend that if they are forced to return to Pakistan, they would be unprotected by the state and would be subject to a risk of criminal proceedings for sexual immorality. If found guilty the punishment may be flogging or stoning to death. In these circumstances both women claim refugee status on a ground specified in article 1A(2) of the Convention, namely that they have a well founded fear of being persecuted for reasons of "membership of a particular social group". The Court of Appeal rejected these claims: *R v Immigration Appeal Tribunal, Ex-parte Shah* [1998] 1 WLR 74. Both women have been granted exceptional leave to remain in the United Kingdom. But both women still seek refugee status. The principal question of law is whether the appellants are members of a particular social group within the meaning of article 1A(2) of the Convention. This question can only be considered against a close and particular focus on the facts of the case.

Women in the Islamic Republic of Pakistan

Generalisations about the position of women in particular countries are out of place in regard to issues of refugee status. Everything depends on the evidence and findings of fact in the particular case. On the findings of fact and unchallenged evidence in the present case, the position of women in Pakistan is as follows. Notwithstanding a constitutional guarantee against discrimination on the grounds of sex a woman's place in society in Pakistan is low. Domestic abuse of women and violence towards women is prevalent in Pakistan. That is also true of many other countries and by itself it does not give rise to a claim to refugee status. The distinctive feature of this case is that in Pakistan women are unprotected by the state: discrimination against women in Pakistan is partly tolerated by the state and partly sanctioned by the state. Married women are subordinate to the will of their husbands. There is strong discrimination against married women, who have been forced to leave the matrimonial home or have simply decided to leave. Husbands and others frequently bring charges of adultery against such wives. Faced with such a charge the woman is in a perilous position. Similarly, a woman who makes an accusation of rape is at great risk. Even Pakistan statute law discriminates against such women. The position is described in a report of Amnesty International dated 6 December 1995 on *Women in Pakistan*. The report states, at pp 5–7:

> ... several Pakistani laws explicitly discriminate against women. In some cases they allow only the evidence of men to be heard, not of women. In particular, the Evidence Act and the *Zina* Ordinance, one of four *Hudood* Ordinances promulgated in 1979, have eroded women's rights and denied them equal protection by the law.

> Women are also disadvantaged generally in the criminal justice system because of their position in society. ... Women are particularly liable to be punished under the *Zina* Ordinance which deals with extramarital sexual intercourse. ... Offences under this law attract different punishments according to the evidence on which the conviction is based. In cases where the most severe (*hadd*) punishments may be imposed, the evidence of women is not admissible.

> In a rape case the onus of proof falls on the victim. If a woman fails to prove that she did not give her consent to intercourse, the court may convict her of illicit sexual intercourse. ...

> The majority of cases tried under the *Hudood* laws result in convictions carrying the less severe (*ta'zir*) punishments, but there are also some acquittals and a few convictions involving the most severe (*hadd*) punishments. ...

> About half the women prisoners in Pakistan are held on charges of *Zina*; ... Arrests under the *Zina* Ordinance can be made without a magistrate first investigating whether there is any basis for the charge and issuing a warrant. As a result, women in Pakistan are often held under the *Zina* Ordinance for years although no evidence has ever been produced that they have committed any offence. Men frequently bring charges against their former wives, their daughters or their sisters in order to prevent them marrying or remarrying against the man's wishes. ...

> Most women remain in jail for two to three years before their cases are decided, often on the basis of no evidence of any offence.

For what may be a small minority who are convicted of sexual immorality, there is the spectre of 100 lashes in public or stoning to death in public. This brief description of the discrimination against women, which is tolerated and sanctioned by the state in Pakistan, is the defining factual framework of this case.

The Shah case

The appellant is 43. Her husband turned her out of the marital home in Pakistan. She arrived in the United Kingdom in 1992 and gave birth to a child shortly thereafter. In June 1993 she claimed asylum. She is afraid that her violent husband may accuse her of adultery and may assault her or denounce her under Sharia law for the offence of sexual immorality. In her case the evidence of state toleration and sanctioning of discrimination against women was sketchy.

This claim was rejected on the ground that the appellant does not come within "a particular social group" under article 1A(2). The appellant appealed to the special adjudicator. On 25 July 1995 the special adjudicator found that the appellant's fear of persecution was well founded. But she concluded that the appellant does not fall within "a particular social group", being the only conceivable ground for her Convention claim. On 7 August 1995 the Immigration Appeal Tribunal refused leave to appeal on the ground "that the adjudicator gave clear adverse findings of fact, after giving to each element on the evidence the weight she considered appropriate". The appellant sought judicial review of the refusal of leave. The substantive hearing took place before Sedley J (now Sedley LJ). The Secretary of State conceded that the IAT had misdirected itself but contended that relief should be denied because the claim to refugee status is as a matter of law unsustainable. Sedley J held that the appellant's case is arguable. He granted an order directing the IAT to grant leave and to hear and determine the appeal: *R v Immigration Appeal Tribunal and Secretary of State for the Home Department, Ex parte Shah* [1997] ImmAR 145.

The Islam case

The appellant is 45 and has two children. She arrived with her children in the United Kingdom in 1991. In the same year she claimed asylum. She is a teacher. She married her husband in 1971. He was often violent towards her. But the marriage endured. In 1990 a fight broke out in the school where she was teaching. The fight was between young supporters of two rival political factions. She intervened. One faction became hostile towards her. They made allegations of infidelity against her. These allegations were made, *inter alia*, to her husband who was a supporter of the same faction. Her husband assaulted her and she was twice admitted to hospital. She left her husband. She stayed briefly at her brother's house. Unknown men threatened her brother. She could not remain with him. After a brief stay in a temporary refuge she came to the United Kingdom. In claiming asylum she relied on two Convention grounds under article 1A(2), namely a well founded fear of persecution for reasons of (1) membership of a particular social group and (2) political opinion.

The claim was rejected. By a determination dated 7 December 1995 the special adjudicator accepted the evidence of the appellant. She found that the appellant had been persecuted in Pakistan. She also found that the authorities in Pakistan are both unable and unwilling to protect the appellant. But she held that as a matter of law the appellant was not a member of a "particular social group" because the group could not exist independently of the feared persecution. Moreover, she found that on the facts neither the particular political faction nor the appellant's husband persecuted her because of an actual or perceived political opinion. By a determination of 2 October 1996 the IAT dismissed the appeal. The IAT found that the appellant cannot be said to belong to a particular social group because the "sub-group does not ... have any innate or unchangeable characteristic, nor is it a cohesive homogeneous group whose members are in close voluntary association". The IAT further concluded that on the facts the appellant's persecution was motivated neither by an actual nor attributed political opinion.

The decision of the Court of Appeal

Both women appealed to the Court of Appeal. The appeals were held together. In separate and careful judgments the Court of Appeal dismissed both appeals: *R v Immigration Appeal Tribunal and Another, Ex parte Shah* [1998] 1 WLR 74. Given that those judgments are reported, it will be sufficient to state in outline effect the judgments. All three members of the Court of Appeal found that the appeal in the case of Islam, so far as it was based on persecution on the ground of political opinion, failed on the facts. The principal issue revolved round the question of law whether appellants could claim to be members of the "particular social group" under article 1A(2). Waite LJ based his decision on the ground that independently of the feared persecution there was no common uniting attribute which could entitle the appellants to the status of "membership of a particular social group" under article 1A(2): 86A-87B. Staughton LJ went further. He held that that what is required is a number of people "joined together with some degree of cohesiveness, co-operation and interdependence": at 93D. And this requirement was not satisfied. Henry LJ agreed with the ground on which Waite LJ decided the matter. It is not clear whether there was a second ground for his decision. Henry LJ agreed with Waite LJ that "cohesion" was "not necessary in every case": p 91H. Henry LJ added that "it is not necessary where the particular social group is recognised as such by the public, though is not organised ...". It would seem that Henry LJ contemplated that cohesiveness is sometimes a requirement.

Article 1A(2) in the scheme of the Convention

The critical and operative provision of the Convention is article 1A(2). It provides as follows:

> For the purposes of the present Convention, the term "refugee" shall apply to any person who: ... (2) ... owing to well founded fear of being persecuted for reasons of race, religion, nationality, membership of a particular social group or political opinion, is outside the country of his nationality and is unable or, owing to such fear, is unwilling to avail himself of the protection of that country.

In order to qualify as a refugee the asylum seeker (assumed to be a woman) must therefore prove: (1) That she has a well founded fear of persecution. (2) That the persecution would be for reasons of race, religion, nationality, membership of a particular social group, or political opinion. (3) That she is outside the country of her nationality. (4) That she is unable, or owing to fear, unwilling to avail herself of the protection of that country.

[...]*

---

*   *Eds:* one paragraph, which summarises articles 1F, 1C, 32 and 33 of the Convention (not directly relevant to the present case) has not been included.

In the search for the correct interpretation of the words "membership of a particular social group" the *travaux préparatoires* of the Convention are uninformative. The words in question were introduced at a late stage of the process leading to the finalisation of the Convention. That fact tells one nothing about their contextual meaning. But the preambles to the Convention are significant. I set out the relevant preambles:

> *Considering* that the Charter of the United Nations and the Universal Declaration of Human Rights approved on 10 December 1948 by the General Assembly have affirmed the principle that human beings shall enjoy fundamental rights and freedoms without discrimination,

> *Considering* that the United Nations has, on various occasions, manifested its profound concern for refugees and endeavoured to assure refugees the widest possible exercise of these fundamental rights and freedoms,

> *Considering* that it is desirable to revise and consolidate previous international agreements relating to the status of refugees and to extend the scope of and the protection accorded by such instruments by means of a new agreement,

> *Considering* that the grant of asylum may place unduly heavy burdens on certain countries, and that a satisfactory solution of a problem of which the United Nations has recognized the international scope and nature cannot therefore be achieved without international co-operation.

The relevance of the preambles is twofold. First, they expressly show that a premise of the Convention was that all human beings shall enjoy fundamental rights and freedoms. Secondly, and more pertinently, they show that counteracting discrimination, which is referred to in the first preamble, was a fundamental purpose of the Convention. That is reinforced by the reference in the first preamble to the Universal Declaration of Human Rights, 1948, which proclaimed the principle of the equality of all human beings and specifically provided that the entitlement to equality means equality "without distinction of any kind, such as race, colour, sex, language, religion, political or other opinion, national or social origin, property, birth or other status", see articles 1 and 2.

Narrowing the issue

Putting to one side the separate question whether the appellant in the Islam case can rely on the Convention ground of political opinion, the principal issue before the House is the meaning and application of the words "membership of a particular social group". It is accepted that each appellant has a well founded fear of persecution in Pakistan if she is returned to that country. The appellants are outside the country of their nationality. And they are unable to avail themselves of the protection of Pakistan. On the contrary, it is an unchallenged fact that the authorities in Pakistan are unwilling to afford protection for women circumstanced as the appellants are. Except for the requirements inherent in the words "persecution *for reasons* of ... membership of a particular social group" in article 1A(2) all the conditions of that provision are satisfied. Two issues remain: (1) Do the women satisfy the requirement of "membership of a particular social group"?: (2) If so, a question of causation arises, namely whether their fear of persecution is "for reasons of" membership of a particular social group. I will now concentrate on the first question. It is common ground that there is a general principle that there can only be a "particular social group" if the group exists independently of the persecution. In *A v Minister for Immigration and Ethnic Affairs and Another* (1997) 142 ALR 331, 358 McHugh J neatly explained the point as follows:

> ... If it were otherwise, Art. 1(A)(2) would be rendered illogical and nonsensical. It would mean that persons who had a well founded fear of persecution were members of a

particular social group because they feared persecution. The only persecution that is relevant is persecution for reasons of membership of a group which means that the group must exist independently of, and not be defined by, the persecution ...

In other words relying on persecution to prove the existence of the group would involve circular reasoning. It is therefore unsurprising that counsel for the appellants and counsel for the United Nations High Commissioner for Refugees (UNHCR) accept the general principle that there can only be a "particular social group" if it exists independently of the persecution.

The first issue: is cohesiveness a requirement for the existence of a particular social group?

Before the Court of Appeal [1998] 1 WLR 74 counsel for the Secretary of State submitted that "there is a need for the group to be homogeneous and cohesive". On that occasion counsel said that the adjective "social" refers to persons who are "interdependent or co-operative": at p 85. This argument persuaded Staughton LJ to rule that as a matter of law a particular social group can only exist if there is "some degree of cohesiveness, co-operation or interdependence": at 93D. If this ruling is right, the arguments of the appellants fail at the first hurdle. There is some authority for this view. The origin of the idea appears to be the decision of the United States Court of Appeals, Ninth Circuit, in *Sanchez-Trujillo v Immigration and Naturalization Service* (1986) 801 F2d 1571. This case involved young, working class Salvadoran males, who failed to do military service in El Salvador. They claimed that if they were repatriated to El Salvador they would be persecuted. They contended that they were members of a particular social group. The court held that "particular social group" implies a collection of people closely affiliated with each other: at 1576. The claimants to refugee status did not meet this standard and failed on this ground. But they also failed on the anterior ground that they were unable to demonstrate that the government of El Salvador had singled the alleged group out for persecution. On the contrary, the court found that the risk of persecution related to the existence of actual or imputed political opinion, which was found to turn on individual circumstances. This decision has been followed on the same Circuit in *De Valle v Immigration and Naturalization Service* (1990) 901 F2d 787, 793. Counsel for the Secretary of State suggested that the Court of Appeals for the Second Circuit followed Sanchez-Trujillo in *Gomez v Immigration and Naturalization Service* (1990) 947 F2d 660, 664. For my part I found the passage relied on equivocal.

In any event, on circuits other than the Ninth Circuit, a less restrictive interpretation of the words "particular social group" has been adopted. The foundation of the contrary view is the earlier decision of the Board of Immigration Appeals in *In re Acosta* (1985) 19 I & N 211. This decision was not mentioned in *Sanchez-Trujillo*. In *Acosta* the Board dismissed the claim of a collection of Salvadoran taxi drivers who allegedly feared persecution from an organised group of taxi drivers in El Salvador. The reasoning is important. The Board observed:

We find the well-established doctrine of *ejusdem generis*, meaning literally, "of the same kind", to be most helpful in construing the phrase "membership in a particular social group". That doctrine holds that general words used in an enumeration with specific words should be construed in a manner consistent with the specific words. ... The other grounds of persecution in the Act and the Protocol listed in association with 'membership in a particular social group' are persecution on account of "race", "religion", "nationality" and "political opinion". Each of these grounds describes persecution aimed at an immutable characteristic: a characteristic that either is beyond the power of an individual to change or is so fundamental to individual identity or conscience that it ought not be required to be changed. ... Thus, the other four grounds of persecution enumerated in the Act and the Protocol restrict refugee status to individuals who are either unable by their own actions, or as a matter of conscience should not be required, to avoid persecution.

Applying the doctrine of *ejusdem generis*, we interpret the phrase "persecution on account of membership in a particular social group" to mean persecution that is directed toward an individual who is a member of a group of persons all of whom share a common, immutable characteristic. The shared characteristic might be an innate one such as sex, color, or kinship ties, or in some circumstances it might be a shared past experience such as former military leadership or land ownership. The particular kind of group characteristic that will qualify under this construction remains to be determined on a case-by-case basis. ... By construing "persecution on account of membership in a particular social group" in this manner, we preserve the concept that refuge is restricted to individuals who are either unable by their own actions, or as a matter of conscience should not be required, to avoid persecution.

Support for this approach is to be found in a number of United States decisions: see *Matter of Toboso-Alfonso*, (unreported) 12 March 1990, Interim Decision, cited in *Re: GJ* [1998] INLR 387, 418; *Bastanipour v Immigration and Naturalization Service* (1992) 980 F2d 1129; *Fatin v Immigration and Naturalization Service* (1993) 12 F3d 1233; *Matter of Kasinga* 13 June 1996, Interim Decision 3278, reported in International Journal of Refugee Law 1997, at 213–234. It is therefore clear that there are divergent streams of authority in the United States. And it may be right to say that the preponderance of US case law does not support *Sanchez-Trujillo*.

Counsel for the Secretary of State also tried to rely on *dicta* by two members of the majority in the High Court of Australia in *A v Minister of Immigration and Ethnic Affairs* (1997) 142 ALR 331. This case involved a claim to refugee status by a husband and wife who had come from China to Australia. They said that they feared sterilisation under the "one child policy" of China if they were returned. The majority (Dawson, McHugh and Gummow JJ) rejected the argument that the appellants were members of a particular social group. Brennan CJ and Kirby J dissented. Contrary to counsel's submission I consider it clear that Dawson J did not accept the *Sanchez-Trujillo* theory. On the contrary, he said that *Sanchez-Trujillo* is unpersuasive so far as it suggested that "the uniting particular must be voluntary": at 341. Gummow J may have adopted the *Sanchez-Trujillo* principle. And McHugh J and the dissenting judges took a broader view. In any event, in a case such as *A v Minister of Immigration and Ethnic Affairs* a significant difficulty in the way of claimants to refugee status is the fact that the one child policy is apparently applied uniformly in China. There is no obvious element of discrimination. That may be the true basis of the decision of the Australian High Court. Far from assisting the argument of the Secretary of State the trend of the *dicta* in *A's* case (except for the observations of Gummow J) is against a requirement of cohesiveness. Moreover, in Canada the Supreme Court has adopted a broader approach which depends on the reasoning in Acosta and is inconsistent with *Sanchez-Trujillo*: see *Attorney-General of Canada v Ward* (1993) 103 DLR (4th) 1; see also *Chan v Minister of Employment and Immigration* 128 DLR (4th) 213, 247. This is made explicit by La Forest J in Ward. He said, at 34 that "social group" could include individuals fearing persecution on "such bases as gender, linguistic background and sexual orientation".

Apart from the judgment of Staughton LJ in the present case, there is no English authority for the view that cohesiveness is an indispensable requirement for the existence of a "particular social group". Counsel for the Secretary of State cited the decision of the Court of Appeal in *Savchenko v Secretary of State for the Home Department* [1996] Imm AR 28. The judgments in that case contain references to *Sanchez-Trujillo* but no adoption of its reasoning on the element of cohesiveness. The ratio of *Savchenko* is that the alleged group (Russian security guards at a hotel who feared victimisation by the mafia) did not exist independently of the persecution. But MacCowan LJ recorded, at 34:

> The Secretary of State submits, we were told by Mr Pannick, that the concept of membership of a particular social group covers persecution in three types of case: (1) membership of a group defined by some innate or unchangeable characteristic of its members analogous to race, religion, nationality or political opinion, for example, their sex, linguistic background, tribe, family or class; (2) membership of a cohesive, homogeneous group whose members are in a close voluntary association for reasons which are fundamental to their rights, for example, a trade union activist; (3) former membership of a group covered by (2).

Para (1) is in line with *Acosta's* case (1985) 19 I & N 211 and inconsistent with *Sanchez-Trujillo's* case (1986) 801 F2d 1571. It was not explicitly adopted by the Court of Appeal but it was also not rejected. In these circumstances *Savchenko's* case [1996] ImmAR 28 cannot assist the argument of the Secretary of State. Counsel for the Secretary of State informed the House that the Secretary of State no longer supports his submission in para (1). That is understandable: his earlier submission weakens his case on the present appeals.

The support in the case law for the *Sanchez-Trujillo* view is slender. In the literature on the subject there is no support: see the criticism in Hathaway, *The Law of Refugee Status*, (1991), at 161 (n 182). Considering that view on its merits I am satisfied that for the reasons given in *Acosta's* case the restrictive interpretation of "particular social group" by reference to an element of cohesiveness is not justified. In 1951 the draftsmen of article 1A(2) of the Convention explicitly listed the most apparent forms of discrimination then known, namely the large groups covered by race, religion, and political opinion. It would have been remarkable if the draftsmen had overlooked other forms of discrimination. After all, in 1948 the Universal Declaration had condemned discrimination on the grounds of colour and sex. Accordingly, the draftsmen of the Convention provided that membership of a particular social group would be a further category. It is not "an all-encompassing residual category": Hathaway, *The Law of Refugee Status*, 1991, at p 159. Loyalty to the text requires that one should take into account that there is a limitation involved in the words "particular social group". What is not justified is to introduce into that formulation an additional restriction of cohesiveness. To do so would be contrary to the *ejusdem generis* approach so cogently stated in *Acosta*. The potential reach of the *Acosta* reasoning may be illustrated by the case of homosexuals in countries where they are persecuted. In some countries homosexuals are subjected to severe punishments including the death sentence. In *Re GJ* [1998] INLR 387 the New Zealand Refugee Status Authority faced this question. Drawing on the case law and practice in Germany, The Netherlands, Sweden, Denmark, Canada, Australia and the USA, the Refugee Status Authority concluded in an impressive judgment that depending on the evidence homosexuals are capable of constituting a particular social group with the meaning of article 1A(2): see 412–422. This view is consistent with the language and purpose of article 1A(2). Subject to the qualification that everything depends on the state of the evidence in regard to the position of homosexuals in a particular country I would in principle accept the reasoning in *Re GJ* as correct. But homosexuals are, of course, not a cohesive group. This is a telling point against the restrictive view in *Sanchez-Trujillo's* case. Finally, the restrictive interpretation is at variance with the principle that a treaty ought to be construed in a purposive sense: see article 31 of the Vienna Convention on the Law of Treaties.

Given the unequivocal acceptance by Staughton LJ of the restrictive theory of the interpretation of article 1A(2) I have thought it right to explain at some length why in my view his conclusion was not justified. In oral argument counsel for the Secretary of State expressly conceded that Staughton LJ erred in ruling that cohesiveness is an indispensable requirement. Instead counsel submitted that "particular social group" normally requires cohesiveness. What the practical implications of this qualification are I do not know. For my part the position is as follows. Cohesiveness may prove the existence of a particular social group. But the meaning of "particular social group" should not be so limited: the phrase extends to what is fairly and contextually inherent in that phrase.

The second issue: the different theories of "particular social group"

In oral argument different foundations for treating the two appellants as members of a particular social group were explored and tested. First, counsel for the appellants argued that three characteristics set the appellants apart from the rest of society *viz* gender, the suspicion of adultery, and their unprotected status in Pakistan. He submitted that this combination of characteristic exists independently of persecution. Secondly, while counsel for the UNHCR made no submissions on the merits of the cases of the appellants he placed before the House general submissions as to the meaning of "particular social group". He submitted that individuals who believe in or are perceived to believe in values and standards which are at odds with the social mores of the society in which they live may, in principle, constitute "a particular social group" within the meaning of article 1A(2). Women who reject those mores – or are perceived to reject them – are capable of constituting "a particular social group". The third way of approaching the matter was suggested in argument by my noble and learned friend Lord Hoffmann. It involves the proposition that women in Pakistan are a particular social group. Counsel for the Secretary of State pointed out that this way of approaching the case is a new development. But it was thoroughly explored and tested in oral argument in the House. In these circumstances it must be considered on its merits. Indeed as the wider theory it seems right and convenient to examine it first.

Women in Pakistan as a group

The idea so incisively put forward by Lord Hoffmann is neither novel nor heterodox. It is simply a logical application of the seminal reasoning in *Acosta's* case 19 I & N 211. Relying on an *ejusdem generis* interpretation the Board interpreted the words "persecution on account of membership in a particular social group" to mean persecution "that is directed toward an individual who is a member of a group of persons all of whom share a common immutable characteristic". The Board went on to say that the shared characteristic might be an innate one "such as sex, color, or kinship ties". This reasoning covers Pakistani women because they are discriminated against and as a group they are unprotected by the state. Indeed the state tolerates and sanctions the discrimination. The analogy of discrimination against homosexuals who may in some countries be a "particular social group" supports this reasoning. What is the answer to this reasoning? It avoids any objection based on the principle that the group must exist *dehors* the persecution. The objection based on a requirement of cohesiveness foists an impermissible restrictive requirement on the words of article 1A(2). What then is left by way of counter-argument? Counsel for the Secretary of State said that there is a clear answer to this line of reasoning. That turned out to be the fact that some Pakistani women are able to avoid the impact of persecution, eg because their circumstances enable them to receive protection. In such cases there will be no well founded fear of persecution and the claim to refugee status must fail. But this is no answer to treating women in Pakistan as a relevant social group. After all, following the New Zealand judgment in *Re GJ* [1998] INLR 387 I regard it as established that depending on the evidence homosexuals may in some countries qualify as members of a particular social group. Yet some homosexuals may be able to escape persecution because of their relatively privileged circumstances. By itself that circumstance does not mean that the social group of homosexuals cannot exist. Historically, under even the most brutal and repressive regimes some individuals in targeted groups have been able to avoid persecution. Nazi Germany, Stalinist Russia and other examples spring to mind. To treat this factor as negativing a Convention ground under article 1A(2) would drive a juggernaut through the Convention. My Lords, on careful reflection there is no satisfactory answer to the argument that the social group is women in Pakistan.

The narrower group

If I had not accepted that women in Pakistan are a "particular social group", I would have held that the appellants are members of a more narrowly circumscribed group as defined by counsel for the appellants. I will explain the basis of this reasoning briefly. It depends on the coincidence of three factors: the gender of the appellants, the suspicion of adultery, and their unprotected position in Pakistan. The Court of Appeal held (and counsel for the Secretary of State argued) that this argument falls foul of the principle that the group must exist independently of the persecution. In my view this reasoning is not valid. The unifying characteristics of gender, suspicion of adultery, and lack of protection, do not involve an assertion of persecution. The cases under consideration can be compared with a more narrowly defined group of homosexuals, namely practising homosexuals who are unprotected by a state. Conceptually such a group does not in a relevant sense depend for its existence on persecution. The principle that the group must exist independently of the persecution has an important role to play. But counsel for the Secretary of State is giving it a reach which neither logic nor good sense demands. In *A v Minister for Immigration and Ethnic Affairs* 142 ALR 331, 359 McHugh J explained the limits of the principle. He said:

> Nevertheless, while persecutory conduct cannot define the social group, the actions of the persecutors may serve to identify or even cause the creation of a particular social group in society. Left-handed men are not a particular social group. But, if they were persecuted because they were left-handed, they would no doubt quickly become recognisable in their society as a particular social group. Their persecution for being left-handed would create a public perception that they were a particular social group. But it would be the attribute of being left-handed and not the persecutory acts that would identify them as a particular social group.

The same view is articulated by Goodwin-Gill, *The Refugee in International Law*, 2nd ed, (1996) at 362. I am in respectful agreement with this qualification of the general principle. I would hold that the general principle does not defeat the argument of counsel for the appellants.

My Lords, it is unchallenged that the women in Pakistan are unprotected by state and public authorities if a suspicion of adultery falls on them. The reasoning in *Acosta*, which has been followed in Canada and Australia, is applicable. There are unifying characteristics which justify the conclusion that women such as the appellants are members of a relevant social group. On this additional ground I would hold that the women fall within the scope of the words "particular social group".

The third issue: the causation test

Having concluded on a two-fold basis that the appellants are within the scope of the words "particular social group", it is necessary to consider whether they have a well founded fear of being persecuted "for reasons of" their membership of the group in question. A question of causation is involved. Here a further legal issue arose. Counsel for the appellants argued that a "but for" test is applicable. He relied on the adoption of such a test in the sex discrimination field: see *James v Eastleigh Borough Council* [1990] 2 AC 751; and compare Hathaway, *The Law of Refugee Status*, 1991, at 140. Counsel for the Secretary of State challenged this submission. He argued that in the different context of issues of refugee status the test of effective cause – and there may be more than one effective cause – is the correct one. In the present case it makes no difference which test is applied. It matters not whether causation is approached from the vantage point of the wider or narrower social group I have identified. In either event it is plain that the admitted well founded fear of the two women is "for reasons" of their membership of the social group. Given the central feature of state-tolerated and state-sanctioned gender discrimination, the argument that the appellants fear persecution not because of membership of a social group but because of the hostility of their husbands is unrealistic. And that is so irrespective whether a "but for" test, or an effective cause test, is adopted. In these circumstances the legal issue regarding the test of causation, which did not loom large on this appeal, need not be decided.

The view of UNHCR

My Lords, Mr Peter Duffy QC, counsel for the UNHCR, placed before the House all the relevant background materials and produced a valuable written review supplemented by helpful oral argument. Except to point out that the UNHCR view is wider than the grounds upon which I have reached my conclusion I do not propose to express a concluded view on the UNHCR position. My diffidence on this point is reinforced by an observation by Sedley J in *Shah*. Commenting on the unique complexity of such issues Sedley J said [1997] ImmAR 145, 153:

> Its adjudication is not a conventional lawyer's exercise of applying a legal litmus test to ascertain facts; it is a global appraisal of an individual's past and prospective situation in a particular cultural, social, political and legal milieu, judged by a test which, though it has legal and linguistic limits, has a broad humanitarian purpose.

Political opinion

In the *Islam* case there was also a discrete issue as to whether the appellant can rely on the Convention ground of political opinion. Given my conclusions this issue falls away. Nevertheless, I must make clear that I was not attracted by this argument. The special adjudicator and the IAT decided this issue against the appellant. The findings of fact were open on the evidence. There were no misdirections. In agreement with all members of the Court of Appeal I regard this ground of appeal as unsustainable.

Conclusion

In the *Islam* case I would allow the appeal and make a declaration in accordance with section 8(2) of the Asylum and Immigration Appeals Act 1993 that it would be contrary to the United Kingdom's obligations for her to be required to leave the United Kingdom. In the *Shah* appeal I would allow the appeal to the extent of setting aside the order of the

Court of Appeal and restoring the order of Sedley J remitting her case to the Immigration Appeal Tribunal.

LORD HOFFMANN: My Lords, in Pakistan there is widespread discrimination against women. Despite the fact that the constitution prohibits discrimination on grounds of sex, an investigation by Amnesty International at the end of 1995 reported that government attempts to improve the position of women had made little headway against strongly entrenched cultural and religious attitudes. Women who were victims of rape or domestic violence often found it difficult to obtain protection from the police or a fair hearing in the courts. In matters of sexual conduct, laws which discriminated against women and carried severe penalties remained upon the statute book. The International Bar Association reported in December 1998 that its mission to Pakistan earlier in the year "heard and saw much evidence that women in Pakistan are discriminated against and have particular problems in gaining access to justice". (*Report on Aspects of the Rule of Law and Human Rights in the Legal System of Pakistan*, 29).

These appeals concern two women who became victims of domestic violence in Pakistan, came to the United Kingdom and claimed asylum as refugees. Shahanna Islam is a graduate school teacher from Karachi. In 1990 she became involved in a playground dispute between rival gangs of politically motivated boys. Those supporting the Mohaijur Quami Movement or "MQM" told her husband, who belonged to the same party, that she had been unfaithful to him. As a result he gave her severe beatings which eventually drove her out of the house. The other woman, Syeda Shah is simple and uneducated. She was frequently beaten by her husband and eventually, when pregnant, turned out of the house. She too came to the United Kingdom, where her child was born.

Both women were given limited leave to enter the United Kingdom as visitors. Afterwards they claimed the right to remain as refugees under the 1951 Geneva Convention Relating to the Status of Refugees as amended by the 1967 Protocol. The United Kingdom is a party to this Convention, which has been incorporated into domestic law by section 8 of the Asylum and Immigration Appeals Act 1993. Subsection (2) provides that a person who has limited leave to enter the United Kingdom may appeal to a special adjudicator against a refusal to vary the leave "on the ground it would be contrary to the United Kingdom's obligations under the Convention for him to be required to leave the United Kingdom after the time limited by the leave". Both accordingly appealed to a special adjudicator.

The Convention defines a refugee in article 1A(2) as a person who:

> ... owing to well founded fear of being persecuted for reasons of race, religion, nationality, membership of a particular social group or political opinion, is outside the country of his nationality and is unable, or owing to such fear is unwilling, to avail himself of the protection of that country ...

The question for the special adjudicators was whether Mrs Islam and Mrs Shah came within this definition.

Domestic violence such as was suffered by Mrs Islam and Mrs Shah in Pakistan is regrettably by no means unknown in the United Kingdom. It would not however be regarded as persecution within the meaning of the Convention. This is because the victims of violence would be entitled to the protection of the state. The perpetrators could be prosecuted in the criminal courts and the women could obtain orders restraining further molestation or excluding their husbands from the home under the Domestic Violence and Matrimonial Proceedings Act 1976. What makes it persecution in Pakistan is the fact that according to evidence which was accepted by the special adjudicator in Mrs Islam's case and formed the basis of findings which have not been challenged, the State was unwilling or unable to offer her any protection. The adjudicator found it was useless for Mrs Islam, as a woman, to complain to the police or the courts about her husband's conduct. On the contrary, the police were likely to accept her husband's allegations of infidelity and arrest her instead. The evidence of men was always deemed more credible than that of women. If she was convicted of infidelity, the penalties could be severe. Even if she was not prosecuted, as a woman separated from her husband she would be socially ostracised and vulnerable to attack, even murder, at the instigation of her husband or his political associates. The special adjudicator said:

> On the evidence, the agents of persecution are the MQM boys who made false allegations against her to her husband, and/or her husband who had subjected her to violence. In order for them to be regarded as agents of persecution the appellant has to show that the authorities in Pakistan were unable or unwilling to offer her protection. It is the appellant's case that in her particular circumstances, given the structure of society and the attitude of the authorities towards domestic violence and given the impunity with which MQM members have acted and still act in Pakistan, that the authorities in Pakistan are both unable and unwilling to offer her protection. I find on the evidence that this is indeed the case.

The Immigration Appeal Tribunal summed up her position as follows:

> She cannot return to her husband. She cannot live anywhere in Pakistan without male protection. She cannot seek assistance from the authorities because in Pakistan society women are not believed or they are treated with contempt by the police. If she returns she will be abused and possibly killed.

In the case of Mrs Shah, the evidence of the legal and institutional background was much more sketchy. She said that she was afraid that if she returned to Pakistan her husband would deny paternity of the child to which she had given birth in England and either assault her himself or charge her with immorality before a religious tribunal. In her case, the special adjudicator found that she was simply a battered wife. Although as a matter of ordinary language her husband might be said to have persecuted her, it was not persecution within the meaning of the Convention.

The question in both cases was therefore whether the women had a well founded fear of persecution within the meaning of the Convention and, critically, whether such persecution was for one of the five enumerated reasons, namely, "race, religion, nationality, membership of a particular social group or political opinion". Of these, the only serious candidate for consideration was that they feared persecution because they were members of a "particular social group". There was an attempt to argue that Mrs Islam was being persecuted by the MQM and her husband for her political opinions, but I agree with my noble and learned friend Lord Steyn that this was not made out on the evidence.

The problem for both women was to specify the "social group" of which they claimed their membership had given rise to persecution. Mrs Shah's counsel seems to have tried to persuade the special adjudicator that "women who had suffered domestic violence" were a social group. This submission was rejected and the application dismissed. Her application to the Immigration Appeal Tribunal for leave to appeal was refused on the ground that the special adjudicator had found against her on the facts. She moved for judicial review before Sedley J, where counsel for the Home Office conceded that this reason was a bad one: [1997] ImmAR 145. The special adjudicator had entirely accepted her version of the facts but ruled that the reason for her apprehended persecution was not her membership of anything which could as a matter of law qualify as a "social group". Sedley J then proceeded to consider whether she had any reasonable prospect of satisfying the tribunal that she was being persecuted for such a reason. Her counsel made several attempts to define the group: one was "women who are perceived to have transgressed Islamic mores" and another was "women rejected by their husbands on the ground of alleged adultery". Sedley J was sceptical of both these formulations but said that there was nevertheless a sufficiently arguable case to go before the Tribunal, which would be entitled to hear evidence about the social and legal background which had not been before the special adjudicator. "Its adjudication", said the judge, at 153:

> is not a conventional lawyer's exercise of applying a legal litmus test to ascertained facts; it is a global appraisal of an individual's past and prospective situation in a particular cultural, social, political and legal milieu, judged by a test which, though it has legal and linguistic limits, has a broad humanitarian purpose.

He therefore granted *mandamus* ordering the Tribunal to hear and determine the appeal. Mrs Islam also argued before the special adjudicator that she feared persecution because she belonged to a social group defined as "Pakistani women subject to domestic violence, namely wife abuse". The special adjudicator found that such a group, defined by reference to its fear of persecution, could not constitute a social group for the purposes of the Convention. The argument was a circular one: if one belonged to a group because one shared a common fear of persecution, one could not be said to be persecuted because one belonged to that group. This decision was upheld by the Immigration Appeal Tribunal.

The Secretary of State appealed against the decision of Sedley J and Mrs Islam appealed against the decision of the Immigration Appeal Tribunal. The Court of Appeal (Staughton, Waite and Henry LJJ) heard both appeals together. By this time, the definition of the social group had been greatly elaborated. Mr Blake QC who appeared, as he did before your Lordships, for the women, defined it as "Pakistani women ... accused of transgressing social mores (in the instant case, adultery, disobedience to husbands) ... who are unprotected by their husbands or other male relatives". This, he submitted, was not a group defined by its common fear of persecution. It had objective distinguishing features in its sex, isolation (being abandoned by the husband and having no male relative to turn to) and being ostracised because perceived to be deserving of condemnation by the community for infringement of the sexual code for woman. But the Court of Appeal [1998] 1 WLR 74 held that these features (apart from sex) were all the product of the persecution itself. If one took away the persecution, then, as Waite LJ said, at 87G, "the stigma and the isolation necessarily depart with them. They are not the independent attributes of a particular group". Staughton and Henry LJJ agreed but Staughton LJ, at 93D and possibly also Henry LJ (the judgment is not altogether free from ambiguity on this point) also rejected the alleged social group on the additional ground that it lacked "cohesiveness, co-operation or interdependence". Its members were solitary individuals having no contact with each other. The Court of Appeal therefore allowed the appeal against the judgment of Sedley J in favour of Mrs Shah and dismissed Mrs Islam's appeal from the Immigration Appeal Tribunal. Against those decisions, Mrs Shah and Mrs Islam appeal to your Lordship's House. In hearing the appeal, the House has been greatly assisted by the intervention of the United Nations High Commissioner for Refugees, who was represented by Mr Peter Duffy QC, whose untimely death since the hearing in this appeal has deprived the Bar and the cause of human rights of one of its brightest talents. The *travaux préparatoires* for the Geneva Convention shed little light on the meaning of "particular social group". It appears to have been added to the draft at the suggestion of the Swedish delegate, who said that "experience had shown that certain refugees had been persecuted because they belonged to particular social groups". It seems to me, however, that the general intention is clear enough. The preamble to the Convention begins with the words:

> *Considering* that the Charter of the United Nations and the Universal Declaration of Human Rights approved on 10 December 1948 by the General Assembly have affirmed the principle that human beings shall enjoy fundamental rights and freedoms without discrimination.

In my opinion, the concept of discrimination in matters affecting fundamental rights and freedoms is central to an understanding of the Convention. It is concerned not with all cases of persecution, even if they involve denials of human rights, but with persecution which is based on discrimination. And in the context of a human rights instrument, discrimination means making distinctions which principles of fundamental human rights regard as inconsistent with the right of every human being to equal treatment and respect. The obvious examples, based on the experience of the persecutions in Europe which would have been in the minds of the delegates in 1951, were race, religion, nationality and political opinion. But the inclusion of "particular social group" recognised that there might be different criteria for discrimination, in *pari materiae* with discrimination on the other grounds, which would be equally offensive to principles of human rights. It is plausibly suggested that the delegates may have had in mind persecutions in Communist countries of people who were stigmatised as members of the *bourgeoisie*. But the concept of a social group is a general one and its meaning cannot be confined to those social groups which the framers of the Convention may have had in mind. In choosing to use the general term "particular social group" rather than an enumeration of specific social groups, the framers of the Convention were in my opinion intending to include whatever groups might be regarded as coming within the anti-discriminatory objectives of the Convention.

The notion that the Convention is concerned with discrimination on grounds inconsistent with principles of human rights is reflected in the influential decision of the US Board of Immigration Appeals in *In re Acosta* (1985) 19 I & N 211 where it was said that a social group for the purposes of the Convention was one distinguished by:

> an immutable characteristic ... [a characteristic] that either is beyond the power of an individual to change or that is so fundamental to his identity or conscience that it ought not to be required to be changed.

This was true of the other four grounds enumerated in the Convention. It is because they are either immutable or part of an individual's fundamental right to choose for himself that discrimination on such grounds is contrary to principles of human rights.

It follows that I cannot accept that the term "particular social group" implies an additional element of cohesiveness, co-operation or interdependence. The fact that members of a group may or may not have some form of organisation or interdependence seems to me irrelevant to the question of whether it would be contrary to principles of human rights to discriminate against its members. Among the other four categories, "race" and "nationality" do not imply any idea of co-operation; "religion" and "political opinion" might, although it could be minimal. In the context of the Convention it seems to me a contingent rather than essential characteristic of a social group. In the opinion of Judge Beezer for the US Court of Appeals in *Sanchez Trujillo v Immigration and Naturalization Service* (9th Cir 1986) 801 F2nd 1571) it was said that "'particular social group' implies a collection of people closely affiliated with each other, who are actuated by some common impulse or interest". This remark has been taken up in some (but not all) other US cases. It has however been rejected by the Supreme Court of Canada in *Attorney-General of Canada v Ward* (1993) 103 DLR (4th) 1 and the High

Court of Australia in *A v Minister for Immigration and Ethnic Affairs* [1998] INLR 1. I would reject it also. I agree with La Forest J in the *Ward* case when he said (at 34) that "social group" could include individuals fearing persecution on "such bases as gender, linguistic background and sexual orientation". None of these implies any form of interdependence or co-operation.

To what social group, if any, did the appellants belong? To identify a social group, one must first identify the society of which it forms a part. In this case, the society is plainly that of Pakistan. Within that society, it seems to me that women form a social group of the kind contemplated by the Convention. Discrimination against women in matters of fundamental human rights on the ground that they are women is plainly in *pari materiae* with discrimination on grounds of race. It offends against their rights as human beings to equal treatment and respect. It may seem strange that sex (or gender) was not specifically enumerated in the Convention when it is mentioned in article 2 of the Universal Declaration of Human Rights. But the Convention was originally limited to persons who had become refugees as a result of events occurring before 1 January 1951. One can only suppose that the delegates could not think of cases before that date in which women had been persecuted because they were women. But the time limit was removed by the 1967 New York Protocol and the concept of a social group is in my view perfectly adequate to accommodate women as a group in a society that discriminates on grounds of sex, that is to say, that perceives women as not being entitled to the same fundamental rights as men. As we have seen, La Forest J in the *Ward* case had no difficulty in saying that persecution on grounds of gender would be persecution on account of membership of a social group. I therefore think that women in Pakistan are a social group.

As we have seen, however, the appellants in the Court of Appeal did not say that they feared persecution simply on the ground that they were women. They produced a much more restricted and complicated definition of the social group to which they claimed to belong and membership of which was said to be the ground for their persecution. In so doing, they introduced into the definition elements which the Court of Appeal regarded as arbitrary except by reference to the persecution they feared. Thus they found that the parts of the definition which restricted the group to anything narrower than the entire sex were essentially circular and incapable of defining a group for the purposes of the Convention.

The reason why the appellants chose to put forward this restricted and artificial definition of their social group was to pre-empt the question of whether their feared persecution was "for reasons of" their membership of the wider group of women. It was argued for the Secretary of State that they could not fear persecution simply for the reason that they were women. The vast majority of women in Pakistan conformed to the customs of their society, did not chafe against discrimination or have bullying husbands, and were not persecuted. Being a woman could not therefore be a reason for persecution. The question is essentially one of causation. Being a woman does not necessarily result in persecution and therefore cannot be the reason for those cases in which women are persecuted. The appellants' argument in the Court of Appeal accepted this reasoning and tried to confess and avoid by opting for a sub-category of women.

I do not need to express a view about whether this strategy should have succeeded because, as I shall explain in a moment, I think that the argument on causation which it was designed to meet is fallacious. The question is therefore capable of being given a much simpler answer. The strategy probably derives from conclusion 39 "Refugees, Women and International Protection" adopted by the Executive Committee of the United Nations High Commission for Refugees in 1985, which read as follows:

[S]tates in the exercise of their sovereignty, are free to adopt the interpretation that women asylum seekers who face harsh or inhuman treatment due to their having transgressed social mores of the society in which they live may be regarded as a "particular social group" within the meaning of article 1 A(2) of the 1951 United Nations Refugee Convention.

This was a well-meaning attempt to encourage a more liberal treatment of women refugees, who frequently did not conform to the standard characteristics of the male refugees, fleeing for racial or political reasons, with which national authorities were familiar. But I think that, whether right or wrong, it unnecessarily overcomplicates the matter.

I turn, therefore, to the question of causation. What is the reason for the persecution which the appellants fear? Here it is important to notice that it is made up of two elements. First, there is the threat of violence to Mrs Islam by her husband and his political friends and to Mrs Shah by her husband. This is a personal affair, directed against them as individuals. Secondly, there is the inability or unwillingness of the State to do anything to protect them. There is nothing personal about this. The evidence was that the State would not assist them because they were women. It denied them a protection against violence which it would have given to men. These two elements have to be combined to constitute persecution within the meaning of the Convention. As the *Gender Guidelines for the Determination of Asylum Claims in the UK* (published by the Refugee Women's Legal Group in July 1988) succinctly puts it (at 5): "Persecution = Serious Harm + The Failure of State Protection".

Answers to questions about causation will often differ according to the context in which the question is asked. (See *Environment Agency (formerly National Rivers Authority) v Empress Car Co (Abertillery) Ltd.* [1998] 2 WLR 350). Suppose oneself in Germany in 1935. There is discrimination against Jews in general, but not all Jews are persecuted. Those who conform to the discriminatory laws, wear yellow stars out of doors and so forth can go about their ordinary business. But those who contravene the racial laws are persecuted. Are they being persecuted on grounds of race? In my opinion, they plainly are. It is therefore a fallacy to say that because not all members of a class are being persecuted, it follows that persecution of a few cannot be on grounds of membership of that class. Or to come nearer to the facts of the present case, suppose that the Nazi government in those early days did not actively organise violence against Jews, but pursued a policy of not giving any protection to Jews subjected to violence by neighbours. A Jewish shopkeeper is attacked by a gang organised by an Aryan competitor who smash his shop, beat him up and threaten to do it again if he remains in business. The competitor and his gang are motivated by business rivalry and a desire to settle old personal scores, but they would not have done what they did unless they knew that the authorities would allow them to act with impunity. And the ground upon which they enjoyed impunity was that the victim was a Jew. Is he being persecuted on grounds of race? Again, in my opinion, he is. An essential element in the persecution, the failure of the authorities to provide protection, is based upon race. It is true that one answer to the question "Why was he attacked?" would be "because a competitor wanted to drive him out of business". But another answer, and in my view the right answer in the context of the Convention, would be "he was attacked by a competitor who knew that he would receive no protection because he was a Jew".

In the case of Mrs Islam, the legal and social conditions which according to the evidence existed in Pakistan and which left her unprotected against violence by men were discriminatory against women. For the purposes of the Convention, this discrimination was the critical element in the persecution. In my opinion, this means that she feared persecution because she was a woman. There was no need to construct a more restricted social group simply for the purpose of satisfying the causal connection which the Convention requires.

Mr Blake, in supporting this argument, suggested that the requirement of causation could be satisfied by applying a "but for" test. If they would not have feared persecution but for the fact that they were women, then they feared persecution for reason of being women. I think that this goes from overcomplication to oversimplification. Once one has established the context in which a causal question is being asked, the answer involves the application of common sense notions rather than mechanical rules. I can think of cases in which a "but for" test would be satisfied but common sense would reject the conclusion that the persecution was for reasons of sex. Assume that during a time of civil unrest, women are particularly vulnerable to attack by marauding men, because the attacks are sexually motivated or because they are thought weaker and less able to defend themselves. The government is unable to protect them, not because of any discrimination but simply because its writ does not run in that part of the country. It is unable to protect men either. It may be true to say women would not fear attack but for the fact that they were women. But I do not think that they would be regarded as subject to persecution within the meaning of the Convention. The necessary element of discrimination is lacking. (Compare *Gomez v Immigration and Naturalization Service* (1991) 947 F2d 660).

I am conscious, as the example which I have just given will suggest, that there are much more difficult cases in which the officers of the State neither act as the agents of discriminatory persecution nor, on the basis of a discriminatory policy, allow individuals to inflict persecution with impunity. In countries in which the power of the State is weak, there may be intermediate cases in which groups of people have power in particular areas to persecute others on a discriminatory basis and the State, on account of lack of resources or political will and without its agents applying any discriminatory policy of their own, is unable or unwilling to protect them. I do not intend to lay down any rule for such cases. They have to be considered by adjudicators on a case by case basis as they arise. The distinguishing feature of the present case is the evidence of institutionalised discrimination against women by the police, the courts and the legal system, the central organs of the State.

Finally, I must say something about the general implications of this case. The Chairman of the Immigration Appeal Tribunal which heard Mrs Islam's case was dismissive about the evidence of discrimination against women in Pakistan. He said that it contained:

> overt and implicit criticisms of Pakistani society and the position of women in that and other Islamic states. We do not think that the purpose of the Convention is to award refugee status because of a disapproval of social mores or conventions in non-western societies.

There was in my view no suggestion that a woman was entitled to refugee status merely because she lived in a society which, for religious or any other reason, discriminated against women. Although such discrimination is contrary not merely to western notions but to the constitution of Pakistan and a number of international human rights instruments, including the Convention on the Elimination of All Forms of Discrimination Against Women, which Pakistan ratified in 1996, it does not in itself found a claim under the Convention. The Convention is about persecution, a well founded fear of serious harm, which is a very different matter. The discrimination against women in Pakistan found by the special adjudicator to exist there is relevant to show that the fear of persecution is on a Convention ground but is not in itself enough.

Furthermore, the findings of fact as to discrimination have not been challenged. They cannot be ignored merely on the ground that this would imply criticism of the legal or social arrangements in another country. The whole purpose of the Convention is to give protection to certain classes of people who have fled from countries in which their human rights have not been respected. It does not by any means follow that there is similar persecution in other Islamic countries or even that it exists everywhere in Pakistan. Each case must depend upon the evidence.

I would therefore allow the appeals. In the case of Mrs Islam, I would make a declaration in accordance with section 8(2) of the Asylum and Immigration Appeals Act 1993 that it would be contrary to the United Kingdom's obligations under the Convention for her to be required to leave the United Kingdom. In the case of Mrs Shah, I would restore the order of Sedley J remitting her case to the Immigration Appeal Tribunal.

LORD HOPE OF CRAIGHEAD: My Lords, I have had the advantage of reading in draft the speeches which have been prepared by my noble and learned friends Lord Steyn and Lord Hoffmann. I agree with them that these appeals should be allowed, and I would make the same orders as they have proposed. I also agree with what they have said on the questions of causation and political opinion. I should like to make these observations on the question of "particular social group".

Article 1A(2) of the United Nations Convention Relating to the Status of Refugees, 1951 defines the term "refugee" for the purposes of the Convention. The relevant part of that definition, as amended by the 1967 Protocol, states that "refugee" means any person who:

> ... owing to well founded fear of being prosecuted for reasons of race, religion, nationality, membership of a particular social group or political opinion, is outside the country of his nationality and is unable or, owing to such fear, is unwilling to avail himself of the protection of that country.

The issue which is common to these appeals is whether the appellants, who are both married women of Pakistani nationality, are members of a "particular social group". The "particular social group" to which they claim to belong is said to comprise women in Pakistan accused of transgressing social mores who are unprotected by their husbands or other male relatives.

I would make three general points about the definition before I examine the phrase "particular social group". The first is that the characteristics, commonly referred to as the Convention reasons, which are set out in paragraph (2) of article 1A are designed to provide an inclusive list of the reasons for which the person who is seeking refugee status must claim that he has a well founded fear of being prosecuted. The list is not, as one finds in some human rights instruments, an illustrative one. This means that it is necessary for the person to be able to show that his fear is of persecution for a Convention reason, not just that he has a fear of being persecuted.

The second relates to a feature which is common to all five of the Convention reasons which are set out in the paragraph. The first preamble to the Convention explains that one of its purposes was to give effect to the principle that human beings shall enjoy fundamental rights and freedoms without discrimination. This principle was affirmed in the Charter of the United Nations and in the Universal Declaration of Human Rights approved by the General Assembly of the United Nations on 10 December 1948. If one is looking for a genus, in order to apply the eiusdem generis rule of construction to the phrase "particular social group", it is to be found in the fact that the other Convention reasons are all grounds on which a person may be discriminated against by society.

The third point is that, while the risk of discrimination by society is common to all five of the Convention reasons, the persecution which is feared cannot be used to define a particular social group. The rule is that the Convention reasons must exist independently of, and not be defined by, the persecution. To define the social group by reference to the fear of being persecuted would be to resort to circular reasoning: *A and Another v Minister for Immigration and Ethnic Affairs and Another* (1997) 142 ALR 331, 358, *per* McHugh J. But persecution is not the same thing as discrimination. Discrimination involves the making of unfair or unjust distinctions to the disadvantage of one group or class of people as compared with others. It may lead to persecution or it may not. And persons may be persecuted who have not been discriminated against. If so, they are simply persons who are being persecuted. So it would be wrong to extend the rule that the Convention reasons must exist independently of, and not be defined by, the persecution so as to exclude discrimination as a means of defining the social group where people with common characteristics are being discriminated against. That would conflict with the application of the *eiusdem generis* rule, and it would ignore the statement of principle which is set out in the first preamble to the Convention.

I turn now to the phrase "particular social group". As a general rule it is desirable that international treaties should be interpreted by the courts of all the states parties uniformly. So, if it could be said that a uniform interpretation of this phrase was to be found in the authorities, I would regard it as appropriate that we should follow it. But, as my noble and learned friend Lord Steyn has demonstrated in his review of the United States, Australian and Canadian case law, no uniform interpretation of it has emerged. The only clear rule which can be said to have been generally recognised is that the persecution must exist independently of, and not be used to define, the social group. I agree that the *traveaux préparatoires* of the Convention are uninformative. But it is more important to have regard to the evolutionary approach which must be taken to international agreements of this kind. This enables account to be taken of changes in society and of discriminatory circumstances which may not have been obvious to the delegates when the Convention was being framed.

In general terms a social group may be said to exist when a group of people with a particular characteristic is recognised as a distinct group by society. The concept of a group means that we dealing here with people who are grouped together because they share a characteristic not shared by others, not with individuals. The word "social" means that we are being asked to identify a group of people which is recognised as a particular group by society. As social customs and social attitudes differ from one country to another, the context for this inquiry is the country of the person's nationality. The phrase can thus accommodate particular social groups which may be recognisable as such in one country but not in others or which, in any given country, have not previously been recognised.

Mr Pannick QC said that a social group normally required cohesion between its members, and that if it lacked cohesion this was a very strong indication that it was not a group. But I think that this cannot be so in all cases. There are various ways in which a social group may be formed. It may be voluntary and self-generating. In that event it makes good sense to say, as Staughton LJ said in the Court of Appeal at 93D, that it must have some degree of cohesiveness, co-operation or interdependence among its members. But, in the context of article 1A(2) of the Convention, I do not think that it needs to be self-generating. It may have been created, quite contrary to the wishes of the persons who are comprised in it, by society. Those persons may have been set apart by the norms or customs of that society, so that all people who have their particular characteristic are recognised as being different from all others in that society. This will almost certainly be because they are being discriminated against by the society in which they live as they have that characteristic. I do not think that the fact that it is discrimination which identifies the group to which these people belong as a "particular social group" within that society offends against the rule that the group must exist independently of, and not be defined by, the persecution. As I said earlier, people can be and often are discriminated against without being persecuted.

The rule that the group must exist independently of the persecution is useful, because persecution alone cannot be used to define the group. But it must not be applied outside its proper context. This point has been well made by Guy S. Goodwin-Gill, *The Refugee in International Law*, 2nd ed (1996). At 47–48 he observes that the importance, and therefore the identity, of a social group may well be in direct proportion to the notice taken of it by others. Thus the notion of social group is an open-ended one, which can be expanded in favour of a variety of different classes susceptible to persecution. In a footnote at p 361, under reference to the analysis in *Ward v Attorney-General of Canada* (1993) 103 DLR (4th) 1, he notes that the "grouping" will often be independent of will, so that the requirement of voluntary association relationship, if adopted in all cases, would introduce an unjustified, additional evidential burden on the person who seeks protection under the Convention. At p 362, after further discussion, he concludes that to treat persecution as the sole factor which results in the identification of the particular social group is too simple. Persecution may be but one facet of broader policies and perspectives, all of which contribute to the group and add to its pre-existing characteristics.

The unchallenged evidence in this case shows that women are discriminated against in Pakistan. I think that the nature and scale of the discrimination is such that it can properly be said the women in Pakistan are discriminated against by the society in which they live. The reason why the appellants fear persecution is not just because they are women. It is because they are women in a society which discriminates against women. In the context of that society I would regard women as a particular social group within the meaning of article 1A(2) of the Convention.

In the decision of the US Board of Immigration Appeals in *In re Acosta* (1985) 19 I & N 2H, it was recognised that, on the application of the *eiusdem generis* principle, the shared common, immutable characteristic which would qualify to form a particular social group could include the person's sex. La Forest J in *Attorney-General v Ward* (1993) 103 DLR (4th) 1, 34 accepted that a particular social group could include persons who feared persecution because they were being discriminated against on the basis of gender. So to hold that the appellants were members of a particular social group in Pakistan because they are women and because women are discriminated against in that country would be consistent with previous authority. I do not think that it is necessary in this case to define the social group more narrowly. As the particular social group must be identified in each case in the light of the evidence, the fact that women in Pakistan belong to a particular social group because of the way people of their gender are treated in their society does not mean that the same result will be reached in every other country where women are discriminated against. In other cases the evidence may show that the discrimination is based on some other characteristic as well as gender. If so, some other definition will be needed to identify the group. But that problem does not arise in this case.

LORD HUTTON: concurred with the judgment of Lord Steyn.[*]

LORD MILLET: dissented.[*]

---

[*]   ***Eds:*** due to space constraints, the concurring judgment of Lord Hutton and the dissenting judgment of Lord Millett have not been included. Lord Hutton concurred with the judgment of Lord Steyn, though he left open the question of whether women in Pakistan constitute "a particular social group" within the meaning of article 1A(2) of the Convention. Lord Millet, dissenting, was of the view that persecution was not merely an aggravated form of discrimination and even if women constituted a particular social group, it was not accurate to say that those women in Pakistan who were persecuted were persecuted because they were members of it. They were persecuted because they were thought to have transgressed social norms, not because they were women. There was no evidence that men who transgressed the different social norms which applied to them were treated more favourably. The full text of the judgment is available at [1999] 2 AC 629; [1999] 2 WLR 1015; [1999] 2 All ER 545; (1999) 6 BHRC 356; [1999] Imm AR 283.

RIGHT NOT TO BE SUBJECTED TO VIOLENCE

CASE NO 43

R v R (RAPE: MARITAL EXEMPTION)

HOUSE OF LORDS

Judgment: 23 October 1991

Panel: Lord Keith of Kinkel, Lord Brandon of Oakbrook, Lord Griffiths, Lord Ackner and Lord Lowry

Human rights — Right not to be subjected to violence — Criminal law — Rape — Marital rape exemption — Whether husband could be convicted of rape if he had sexual intercourse with his wife without her consent — Whether marital rape exemption continued to apply after introduction of statutory definition of rape — Meaning of "unlawful" sexual intercourse in statutory definition of rape — Sexual Offences (Amendment) Act 1976, s 1(1)

BACKGROUND

This case involved a husband (the appellant) and wife who had separated. Before divorce proceedings had commenced, the husband forced his way into the house of his wife's parents, where his wife was living at the time, and found her alone. He then attempted to have sexual intercourse with her against her will, during which he assaulted her by squeezing her neck with both hands. The husband was arrested and charged with rape and assault occasioning actual bodily harm.

At first instance, the husband claimed that he could not be criminally liable for raping his own wife on the basis of the so-called marital rape exemption, which provides that, on marriage, a wife should be taken to have consented to sexual intercourse with her husband for the duration of the marriage. The judge at first instance rejected this claim. The Court of Appeal dismissed the husband's appeal, but granted him leave to appeal to the House of Lords on the question of the continued existence of the marital exemption to rape.

HELD (dismissing the appeal)

1   Hale's proposition that a husband could not be guilty of raping his wife was, for some 150 years, generally regarded as an accurate statement of the common law of England. The common law was, however, capable of evolving in the light of changing social, economic and cultural developments. Hale's proposition reflected the state of affairs in these respects at the time it was enunciated. Since then, the status of women, and particularly of married women, had changed out of all recognition. Today, husbands and wives were equals, wives did not in law consent at marriage to sexual intercourse in all circumstances, including by force. On grounds of principle, there was no justification for the marital exemption to rape (p 694, 695).

2   Section 1(1)(a) of the Sexual Offences (Amendment) Act 1976 presented no obstacle to declaring that in modern times the supposed marital exemption in rape forms no part of the law of England. The term "unlawful" in the definition of the offence as "unlawful sexual intercourse with a woman who at the time of intercourse does not consent to it"

should not be viewed as meaning "illicit" or outside of marriage, but should be treated as mere surplusage (p 699).

3   Affirming the statement of the Court of Appeal, it was appropriate for the court to make such a declaration and not to leave the matter to the parliamentary process, since the court was not creating a new criminal offence, but was rather removing a common law fiction which had become anachronistic and offensive (p 699).

National legislation referred to

United Kingdom

Offences against the Person Act 1861, ss 47 and 20

Domestic Proceedings and Magistrates' Courts Act 1978, s 16

Local Government (Miscellaneous Provisions) Act 1982, para 3A of Sch 3

Sexual Offences Act 1956, ss 1, 17, 18 and 19

Sexual Offences (Amendment) Act 1976, s 1(1)

Cases referred to

HM Advocate v Duffy 1983 SLT 7

HM Advocate v Paxton 1984 JC 105

McMonagle v Westminster City Council [1990] 1 All ER 993; [1990] 2 AC 716

R v C (rape: marital exemption) [1991] 1 All ER 755

R v Caswell [1984] Crim LR 111

R v Chapman [1958] 3 All ER 143; [1959] 1 QB 100

R v Clarence (1888) 22 QBD 23; [1886–90] All ER Rep 133

R v Clarke [1949] 2 All ER 448

R v H (5 October 1990, unreported)

R v J (rape: marital exemption) [1991] 1 All ER 759

R v Jackson [1891] 1 QB 671; [1891–4] All ER Rep 61

R v Kowalski (1987) 86 Cr App R 339

R v Miller [1954] 2 All ER 529; [1954] 2 QB 282

R v O'Brien [1974] 3 All ER 663

R v R [1991] 2 All ER 257; [1991] 2 WLR 1065

R v R [1991] 1 All ER 747

R v Roberts [1986] Crim LR 188

R v S (15 January 1991, unreported)

R v Sharples [1990] Crim LR 198

R v Steele (1976) 65 Cr App R 22

S v HM Advocate 1989 SLT 469

JUDGMENT

LORD KEITH OF KINKEL: My Lords, in this appeal to the House with leave of the Court of Appeal, Criminal Division that court has certified the following point of law of general public importance as being involved in its decision, namely: "Is a husband criminally liable for raping his wife?"

The appeal arises out of the appellant's conviction in the Crown Court at Leicester on 30 July 1990, upon his pleas of guilty, of attempted rape and of assault occasioning actual bodily harm. The alleged victim in respect of each offence was the appellant's wife. The circumstances of the case were these. The appellant married his wife in August 1984 and they had one son born in 1985. On 11 November 1987 the couple separated for about two weeks but resumed cohabitation at the end of that period. On 21 October 1989 the wife left the matrimonial home with the son and went to live with her parents. She had previously consulted solicitors about matrimonial problems, and she left at the matrimonial home a letter for the appellant informing him that she intended to petition for divorce. On 23 October 1989 the appellant spoke to his wife on the telephone indicating that it was his intention also to see about a divorce. No divorce proceedings had, however, been instituted before the events which gave rise to the charges against the appellant. About 9 pm on 12 November 1989 the appellant forced his way into the house of his wife's parents, who were out at the time, and attempted to have sexual intercourse with her against her will. In the course of doing so he assaulted her by squeezing her neck with both hands. The appellant was arrested and interviewed by police officers. He admitted responsibility for what had happened. On 3 May 1990 a decree *nisi* of divorce was made absolute.

The appellant was charged on an indictment containing two counts, the first being rape and the second being assault occasioning actual bodily harm. When he appeared before Owen J in the Crown Court at Leicester on 30 July 1990, it was submitted to the judge on his behalf that a husband could not in law be guilty as a principal of the offence of raping his own wife (see [1991] 1 All ER 747). Owen J rejected that proposition as being capable of exonerating the appellant in the circumstances of the case. His ground for doing so was that, assuming an implicit general consent to sexual intercourse by a wife on marriage to her husband, that consent was capable of being withdrawn by agreement of the parties or by the wife unilaterally removing herself from cohabitation and clearly indicating that consent to sexual intercourse had been terminated. On the facts appearing from the depositions either the first or the second of these sets of circumstances prevailed. Following the judge's ruling the appellant pleaded guilty to attempted rape and to the assault charged. He was sentenced to three years' imprisonment on the former count and to 18 months' imprisonment on the latter.

The appellant appealed to the Court of Appeal, Criminal Division on the ground that Owen J:

> made a wrong decision in law in ruling that a man may rape his wife when the consent to intercourse which his wife gives in entering the contract of marriage has been revoked neither by order of a Court nor by agreement between the parties.

On 14 March 1990 that court (Lord Lane CJ, Sir Stephen Brown P, Watkins, Neill and Russell LJJ) ([1991] 2 All ER 257, [1991] 2 WLR 1065) delivered a reserved judgment dismissing the appeal but certifying the question of general public importance set out above and granting leave to appeal to your Lordships' House, which the appellant now does.

Sir Matthew Hale in his *History of the Pleas of the Crown* wrote (1 Hale PC (1736) 629):

But the husband cannot be guilty of rape committed by himself upon his lawful wife, for by their mutual matrimonial consent and contract the wife hath given herself up this kind unto her husband which she cannot retract.

There is no similar statement in the works of any earlier English commentator. In 1803 East in his *Treatise of the Pleas of the Crown* wrote (1 East PC 446):

... a husband cannot by law be guilty of ravishing his wife, on account of the matrimonial consent which she cannot retract.

In the first edition of Archbold *A Summary of the Law Relative to Pleading and Evidence in Criminal Cases* (1822) p 259 it was stated, after a reference to Hale: "A husband also cannot be guilty of a rape upon his wife".

For over 150 years after the publication of Hale's work there appears to have been no reported case in which judicial consideration was given to his proposition. The first such case was *R v Clarence* (1888) 22 QBD 23, [1886–90] All ER Rep 133, to which I shall refer later. It may be taken that the proposition was generally regarded as an accurate statement of the common law of England. The common law is, however, capable of evolving in the light of changing social, economic and cultural developments. Hale's proposition reflected the state of affairs in these respects at the time it was enunciated. Since then the status of women, and particularly of married women, has changed out of all recognition in various ways which are very familiar and upon which it is unnecessary to go into detail. Apart from property matters and the availability of matrimonial remedies, one of the most important changes is that marriage is in modern times regarded as a partnership of equals, and no longer one in which the wife must be the subservient chattel of the husband. Hale's proposition involves that by marriage a wife gives her irrevocable consent to sexual intercourse with her husband under all circumstances and irrespective of the state of her health or how she happens to be feeling at the time. In modern times any reasonable person must regard that conception as quite unacceptable.

In *S v HM Advocate* 1989 SLT 469 the High Court of Justiciary in Scotland recently considered the supposed marital exemption in rape in that country. In two earlier cases, *HM Advocate v Duffy* 1983 SLT 7 and *HM Advocate v Paxton* 1984 JC 105, it had been held by single judges that the exemption did not apply where the parties to the marriage were not cohabiting. The High Court held that the exemption, if it had ever been part of the law of Scotland, was no longer so. The principal authority for the exemption was to be found in Hume *Commentaries on the Law of Scotland Respecting the Description and Punishment of Crimes*, first published in 1797. The same statement appeared in each edition up to the fourth, by Bell, in 1844. In that edition, dealing with art and part guilt of abduction and rape, it was said (vol 1, p 306):

This is true without exception even of the husband of the woman; who, though he cannot himself commit a rape on his own wife, who has surrendered her person to him in that sort, may however be accessory to that crime ... committed on her by another.

It seems likely that his pronouncement consciously followed Hale.

The Lord Justice General (Lord Emslie), who delivered the judgment of the court, expressed doubt whether Hume's view accurately represented the law of Scotland even at the time when it was expressed and continued (1989 SLT 469 at 473):

We say no more on this matter which was not the subject of debate before us, because we are satisfied that the Solicitor-General was well-founded in his contention that whether or not the reason for the husband's immunity given by Hume was a good one in the 18th and early 19th centuries, it has since disappeared altogether. Whatever Hume meant to encompass in the concept of a wife's "surrender of her person" to her husband "in that sort" the concept is to be understood against the background of the status of women and the position of a married woman at the time when he wrote. Then, no doubt, a married woman could be said to have subjected herself to her husband's dominion in all things. She was required to obey him in all things. Leaving out of account the absence of rights of property, a wife's freedoms were virtually non-existent, and she had in particular no right whatever to interfere in her husband's control over the lives and upbringing of any children of the marriage. By the second half of the 20th century, however, the status of women, and the status of a married woman, in our law have chanced quite dramatically. A husband and wife are now for all practical purposes equal partners in marriage and both husband and wife are tutors and curators of their children. A wife is not obliged to obey her husband in all things nor to suffer excessive sexual demands on the part of her husband. She may rely on such demands as evidence of unreasonable behaviour for the purposes of divorce. A live system of law will always have regard to changing circumstances to test the justification for any exception to the application of a general rule. Nowadays it cannot seriously be maintained that by marriage a wife submits herself irrevocably to sexual intercourse in all circumstances. It cannot be affirmed nowadays, whatever the position may have been in earlier centuries, that it is an incident of modern marriage that a wife consents to intercourse in all circumstances, including sexual intercourse obtained only by force. There is no doubt that a wife does not consent to assault upon her person and there is no plausible justification for saying today that she nevertheless is to be taken to consent to intercourse by assault. The modern cases of *HM Advocate v Duffy* and *HM Advocate v Paxton* show that any supposed implied consent to intercourse is not irrevocable, that separation may demonstrate that such consent has been withdrawn, and that in these circumstances a relevant charge of rape may lie against a husband. This development of the law since Hume's time immediately prompts the question: is revocation of a wife's implied consent to intercourse, which is revocable, only capable of being established by the act of separation? In our opinion the answer to that question must be no. Revocation of a consent which is revocable must depend on the circumstances. Where there is no separation this may be harder to prove but the critical question in any case must simply be whether or not consent has been withheld. The fiction of implied consent has no useful purpose to serve today in the law of rape in Scotland. The reason given by Hume for the husband's immunity from prosecution upon a charge of rape of his wife, if it ever was a good reason, no longer applies today. There is now, accordingly, no justification for the supposed immunity of a husband. Logically the only question is whether or not as matter of fact the wife consented to the acts complained of, and we affirm the decision of the trial judge that charge 2(b) is a relevant charge against the appellant to go to trial.

I consider the substance of that reasoning to be no less valid in England than in Scotland. On grounds of principle there is now no justification for the marital exemption in rape.

It is now necessary to review how the matter stands in English case law. In *R v Clarence* (1888) 22 QBD 23, [1886–90] All ER Rep 133 a husband who knew that he suffered from a venereal disease communicated it to his wife through sexual intercourse. He was convicted on charges of unlawfully inflicting grievous bodily harm contrary to s 20 of the Offences against the Person Act 1861 and of assault occasioning actual bodily harm contrary to s 47 of the same Act. The convictions were quashed by a court of 13 judges for Crown Cases Reserved, with four dissents. Consideration was given to Hale's proposition, and it appears to have been accepted as sound by a majority of the judges. However, Wills J said that he was not prepared to assent to the proposition that rape between married persons was impossible (see 22 QBD 23 at 33, [1886–90] All ER Rep 133 at 139). Field J (in whose judgment Charles J concurred) said that he should hesitate before he adopted Hale's proposition, and that he thought there might be many cases in which a wife might lawfully refuse intercourse and in which, if the husband imposed it by violence, he might be held guilty of a crime (see 22 QBD 23 at 57, [1886–90] All ER Rep 133 at 152).

In *R v Clarke* [1949] 2 All ER 448 a husband was charged with rape upon his wife in circumstances where justices had made an order providing that the wife should no longer be bound to cohabit with the husband. Byrne J refused to quash the charge. He accepted Hale's proposition as generally sound, but said (at 449):

> The position, therefore, was that the wife, by process of law, namely, by marriage, had given consent to the husband to exercise the marital right during such time as the ordinary relations created by the marriage contract subsisted between them, but by a further process of law, namely, the justices' order, her consent to marital intercourse was revoked. Thus, in my opinion, the husband was not entitled to have intercourse with her without her consent.

In *R v Miller* [1954] 2 All ER 529, [1954] 2 QB 282 the husband was charged with rape of his wife after she had left him and filed a petition for divorce. He was also charged with assault upon her occasioning actual bodily harm. Lynskey J quashed the charge of rape but refused to quash that of assault. He proceeded on the basis that Hale's proposition was correct, and also that *R v Clarke* [1949] 2 All ER 448 had been rightly decided, but took the view that there was no evidence which entitled him to say that the wife's implied consent to marital intercourse had been revoked by an act of the parties or by an act of the court (see [1954] 2 All ER 529 at 533, [1954] 2 QB 282 at 290). As regards the count of assault, having referred to *R v Jackson* [1891] 1 QB 671, [1891–4] All ER Rep 61, where it was held that a husband had no right to confine his wife in order to enforce a decree for restitution of conjugal rights, he said ([1954] 2 All ER 529 at 533–534, [1954] 2 QB 282 at 291–292):

> It seems to me, on the reasoning of that case, that, although the husband has a right to marital intercourse, and the wife cannot refuse her consent, and although if he does have intercourse against her actual will, it is not rape, nevertheless he is not entitled to use force or violence for the purpose of exercising that right. If he does so, he may make himself liable to the criminal law, not for the offence of rape, but for whatever other offence the facts of the particular case warrant. If he should wound her, he might be charged with wounding or causing actual bodily harm, or he may be liable to be convicted of common assault. The result is that in the present case I am satisfied that the second count is a valid one and must be left to the jury for their decision.

So the case had the strange result that although the use of force to achieve sexual intercourse was criminal the actual achievement of it was not. Logically, it might be thought that if a wife be held to have by marriage given her implied consent to sexual intercourse she is not entitled to refuse her husband's advances, and that if she resists then he is entitled to use reasonable force to overcome that resistance. This indicates the absurdity of the fiction of implied consent. In the law of Scotland, as Lord Emslie observed in *S v HM Advocate* 1989 SLT 469 at 473, rape is regarded as an aggravated assault, of which the achievement of sexual intercourse is the worst aggravating feature. It is unrealistic to sort out the sexual intercourse from the other acts involved in the assault and to allow the wife to complain of the minor acts but not of the major and most unpleasant one.

The next case is *R v O'Brien* [1974] 3 All ER 663, when Park J held that a decree *nisi* effectively terminated a marriage and revoked the wife's implied consent to marital intercourse, so that subsequent intercourse by the husband without her consent constituted rape. There was a similar holding by the Criminal Division of the Court of Appeal in *R v Steele* (1976) 65 Cr App R 22 as regards a situation where the spouses were living apart and the husband had given an undertaking to the court not to molest his wife. A decision to the like effect was given by the same court in *R v Roberts* [1986] Crim LR 188, where the spouses had entered into a formal separation agreement. In *R v Sharples* [1990] Crim LR 198, however, it was ruled by Judge Fawcus that a husband could not be convicted of rape upon his wife in circumstances where there was in force a family protection order in her favour and he had had sexual intercourse with her against her will. The order was made under s 16 of the Domestic Proceedings and Magistrates' Courts Act 1978 in the terms that "the respondent shall not use or threaten to use violence against the person of the applicant". Judge Fawcus took the view that it was not to be inferred that by obtaining an order in these terms the wife had withdrawn her consent to sexual intercourse.

There should be mentioned next a trio of cases which were concerned with the question whether acts done by a husband preliminary to sexual intercourse with an estranged wife against her will could properly be charged as indecent assaults: see *R v Caswell* [1984] Crim LR 111, *R v Kowalski* (1987) 86 Cr App R 339 and *R v H* (5 October 1990, unreported), Auld J. The effect of these decisions appears to be that in general acts which would ordinarily be indecent but which are preliminary to an act of normal sexual intercourse are deemed to be covered by the wife's implied consent to the latter, but that certain acts, such as fellatio, are not to be so deemed. Those cases illustrate the contortions to which judges have found it necessary to resort in face of the fiction of implied consent to sexual intercourse.

The foregoing represent all the decisions in the field prior to the ruling by Owen J in the present case. In all of them lip service, at least, was paid to Hale's proposition. Since then there have been three further decisions by single judges. The first of them is *R v C – (rape: marital exemption)* [1991] 1 All ER 755. There were nine counts in an indictment against a husband and a co-accused charging various offences of a sexual nature against an estranged wife. One of these was of rape as a principal. Simon Brown J followed the decision in *S v HM Advocate* 1989 SLT 469 and held that the whole concept of a marital exemption in rape was misconceived. He said (at 758):

> Were it not for the deeply unsatisfactory consequences of reaching any other conclusion on the point, I would shrink, if sadly, from adopting this radical view of true position in law. But adopt it I do. Logically, I regard it as the only defensible stance, certainly now as the law has developed and arrived in the late twentieth century. In my judgment, the position in law today is, as already declared in Scotland, that there is no marital exemption to the law of rape. That is the ruling I give. Count seven accordingly remains and will be left to the jury without any specific direction founded on the concept of marital exemption.

A different view was taken in the other two cases, by reason principally of the terms in which rape is defined in s 1(1) of the Sexual Offences (Amendment) Act 1976, *viz*:

> For the purposes of section 1 of the Sexual Offences Act 1956 (which relates to rape) a man commits rape if – (a) he has unlawful sexual intercourse with a woman who at the time of the intercourse does not consent to it; and (b) at the time he knows that she does not consent to the intercourse or he is reckless as to whether she consents to it ...

In *R v J – (rape: marital exemption)* [1991] 1 All ER 759 a husband was charged with having raped his wife, from whom he was living apart at the time. Rougier J ruled that the charge was bad, holding that the effect of s 1(1)(a) of the 1976 Act was that the marital exemption embodied in Hale's proposition was preserved, subject to those exceptions established by cases decided before the Act was passed. He took the view that the word "unlawful" in the subsection meant "illicit", ie outside marriage, that being the meaning which in *R v Chapman* [1958] 3 All ER 143, [1959] 1 QB 100 it had been held to bear in s 19 of the Sexual Offences Act 1956. Then in *R v S* (15 January 1991, unreported), Swinton Thomas J followed Rougier J in holding that s 1(1) of the 1976 Act preserved the marital exemption subject to the established common law exceptions. Differing, however, from Rougier J, he took the view that it remained open to judges to define further exceptions. In the case before him the wife had obtained a family protection order in similar terms to that in *R v Sharples* [1990] Crim LR 198. Differing from Judge Fawcus in that case, Swinton Thomas J held that the existence of the family protection order created an exception to the marital exemption. It is noteworthy that both Rougier and Swinton Thomas JJ expressed themselves as being regretful that s 1(1) of the 1976 Act precluded them from taking the same line as Simon Brown J in *R v C —* (rape: marital exemption) [1991] 1 All ER 755.

The position then is that that part of Hale's proposition which asserts that a wife cannot retract the consent to sexual intercourse which she gives on marriage has been departed from in a series of decided cases. On grounds of principle there is no good reason why the whole proposition should not be held inapplicable in modern times. The only question is whether s 1(1) of the 1976 Act presents an insuperable obstacle to that sensible course. The argument is that "unlawful" in the subsection means outside the bond of marriage. That is not the most natural meaning of the word, which normally describes something which is contrary to some law or enactment or is done without lawful justification or excuse. Certainly in modern times sexual intercourse outside marriage would not ordinarily be described as unlawful. If the subsection proceeds on the basis that a woman on marriage gives a general consent to sexual intercourse, there can never be any question of intercourse with her by her husband being without her consent. There would thus be no point in enacting that only intercourse without consent outside marriage is to constitute rape.

R v Chapman [1958] 3 All ER 143, [1959] 1 QB 100 is founded on in support of the favoured construction. That was a case under s 19 of the Sexual Offences Act 1956, which provides:

(1) It is an offence, subject to the exception mentioned in this section, for a person to take an unmarried girl under the age of eighteen out of the possession of her parent or guardian against his will, if she is so taken with the intention that she shall have unlawful sexual intercourse with men or with a particular man.

(2) A person is not guilty of an offence under this section because he takes such a girl out of the possession of her parent or guardian as mentioned above, if he believes her to be of the age of eighteen or over and has reasonable cause for the belief ...

It was argued for the defendant that "unlawful" in that section connoted either intercourse contrary to some positive enactment or intercourse in a brothel or something of that kind. Donovan J, giving the judgment of the Court of Criminal Appeal, rejected both interpretations and continued ([1958] 3 All ER 143 at 145, [1959] 1 QB 100 at 105):

If the two interpretations suggested for the appellant are rejected, as we think they must be, then the word "unlawful" in s 19 is either surplusage or means "illicit". We do not think it is surplusage, because otherwise a man who took such a girl out of her parents' possession against their will with the honest and *bona fide* intention of marrying her might have no defence, even if he carried out that intention. In our view the word simply means "illicit", ie, outside the bond of marriage. In other words, we take the same view as the trial judge. We think this interpretation accords with the common sense of the matter, and with what we think was the obvious intention of Parliament. It is also reinforced by the alternatives specifically mentioned in s 17 and s 18 of the Act of 1956, ie, "with the intention that she shall marry or have unlawful intercourse" ...

In that case there was a context to the word "unlawful" which by cogent reasoning led the court to the conclusion that it meant outside the bond of marriage. However, even though it is appropriate to read the 1976 Act along with that of 1956, so that the provisions of the latter Act form part of the context of the former, there is another important context to s 1(1) of the 1976 Act, namely the existence of the exceptions to the marital exemption contained in the decided cases. Sexual intercourse in any of the cases covered by the exceptions still takes place within the bond of marriage. So if "unlawful" in the subsection means "outside the bond of marriage" it follows that sexual intercourse in a case which falls within the exceptions is not covered by the definition of rape, notwithstanding that it is not consented to by the wife. That involves that the exceptions have been impliedly abolished. If the intention of Parliament was to abolish the exceptions it would have been expected to do so expressly, and it is in fact inconceivable that Parliament should have had such an intention. In order that the exceptions might be preserved, it would be necessary to construe "unlawfully" as meaning "outside marriage or within marriage in a situation covered by one of the exceptions to the marital exemption". Some slight support for that construction is perhaps to be gathered from the presence of the words "who at the time of the intercourse does not consent to it", considering that a woman in a case covered by one of the exceptions is treated as having withdrawn the general consent to intercourse given on marriage but may nevertheless have given her consent to it on the particular occasion. However, the gloss which the suggested construction would place on the word "unlawfully" would give it a meaning unique to this particular subsection, and if the mind of the draftsman had been directed to the existence of the exceptions he would surely have dealt with them specifically and not in such an oblique fashion. In *R v Chapman* [1958] 3 All ER 143 at 144, [1959] 1 QB 100 at 102 Donovan J accepted that the word "unlawfully" in relation to carnal knowledge had in many early statutes not been used with any degree of precision, and he referred to a number of enactments making it a felony unlawfully and carnally to know any woman-child under the age of 10. He said ([1958] 3 All ER 143 at 144, [1959] 1 QB 100 at 103): "One would think that all intercourse with a child under ten would be unlawful; and on that footing the word would be mere surplusage". The fact is that it is clearly unlawful to have sexual intercourse with any woman without her consent, and that the use of the word in the subsection adds nothing. In my opinion there are no rational grounds for putting the suggested gloss on the word, and it should be treated as being mere surplusage in this enactment, as it clearly fell to be in those referred to by Donovan J. That was the view taken of it by this House in *McMonagle v Westminster City Council* [1990] 1 All ER 993, [1990] 2 AC 716 in relation to para 3A of Sch 3 to the Local Government (Miscellaneous Provisions) Act 1982.

I am therefore of the opinion that s 1(1) of the 1976 Act presents no obstacle to this House declaring that in modern times the supposed marital exemption in rape forms no part of the law of England. The Court of Appeal, Criminal Division took a similar view. Towards the end of the judgment of that court Lord Lane CJ said ([1991] 2 All ER 257 at 266, [1991] 2 WLR 1065 at 1074):

> The remaining and no less difficult question is whether, despite that view, this is an area where the court should step aside to leave the matter to the parliamentary process. This is not the creation of a new offence, it is the removal of a common law fiction which has become anachronistic and offensive and we consider that it is our duty having reached that conclusion to act upon it.

I respectfully agree.

My Lords, for these reasons I would dismiss this appeal, and answer the certified question in the affirmative.

LORD BRANDON OF OAKBOOK: My Lords, for the reasons given in the speech of my noble and learned friend Lord Keith of Kinkel, I would answer the certified question in the affirmative and dismiss the appeal.

LORD GRIFFITHS: My Lords, for the reasons given by my noble and learned friend Lord Keith of Kinkel, I would dismiss this appeal and answer the certified question in the affirmative.

LORD ACKNER: My Lords, for the reasons given in the speech of my noble and learned friend Lord Keith of Kinkel, I, too, would answer the certified question in the affirmative and dismiss the appeal.

LORD LOWRY: My Lords, for the reasons given by my noble and learned friend Lord Keith of Kinkel, I would dismiss this appeal and answer the certified question in the affirmative.

*Appeal dismissed**

---

*   *Eds:* The appellant subsequently lodged an application with the European Commission of Human Rights. He claimed that the decisions of the English courts declaring the marital rape exception to be no longer in existence amounted to the imposition of a retrospective criminal penalty contrary to article 7(1) of the European Convention on Human Rights, since at the time of the acts in question there was no criminal liability and the decisions of the courts had involved the reversal of existing law rather than just clarification of it. Article 7 provides in relevant part:

1   No one shall be held guilty of any criminal offence on account of any act or omission which did not constitute a criminal offence under national or international law at the time when it was committed.

In its report of 27 June 1994, the Commission rejected the claim by 12 votes to 3, and referred the case to the European Court of Human Rights. In its judgment of 22 November 1995, the Court unanimously held that there had been no violation of article 7(1): *C R v United Kingdom*, Series A No 335-C. See also the companion case *S W v United Kingdom*, European Court of Human Rights, Series A, No 335-B, judgment of 22 November 1995. The reports of the Commission and the judgments of the Court are available at www.echr.coe.int (see *On-Line Access to Human Rights Source Materials, supra*, p xlv).

CASE NO 44

STATE v D AND ANOTHER

HIGH COURT OF NAMIBIA

Judgment: 4 October 1991

Panel: Strydom JP and Frank J

Human rights — Equality and non-discrimination — Sex discrimination — Rape — Sexual assault — Criminal procedure — Evidence — Woman alleging rape only witness to rape — Cautionary rule — Whether cautionary rule discriminated against women — Constitution of Namibia, art 10

BACKGROUND

The defendants were alleged to have taken the two complainants to a burnt-out building, where in separate rooms they had each raped one of the complainants. Apart from the evidence relating to the approach by the defendants to the complainants, the complainants were the only witnesses in respect of the actual rapes. The two defendants were convicted of rape and sentenced to three years' imprisonment.

The defendants appealed to the High Court against their convictions and sentences. The High Court considered whether, in each instance, the State had proved a case of rape beyond reasonable doubt and in particular, considered the validity of the cautionary rule in relation to sexual offences. Under this rule, if a complainant alleges a sexual offence and there is no independent corroborative evidence, the complainant's evidence is to be treated with special caution.

HELD (allowing the appeal of the first appellant only)

1   The cautionary rule which had evolved in cases of rape had no rational basis. There was no reason why cases of sexual assault which were "easily laid and difficult ... to disprove" should be treated on a different basis than any other type of crime. While it was true that different motives might exist for laying false charges, this applied to any offence and not only to offences of a sexual nature. There was no evidence that false charges in cases of rape were any more likely than in other offences, in fact the evidence that was available indicated the contrary. Thus only one test should apply, namely was the accused's guilt proved beyond reasonable doubt; and this test should be the same whether the crime was theft or rape (pp 704, 705).

2   Whilst it had been said that the cautionary rule applies to all cases of this nature irrespective of the sex of the complainant, in the overwhelming majority of cases the complainants were female. The cautionary rule had no purpose other than to discriminate against women complainants and was probably contrary to article 10 of the Constitution of Namibia which provides for the equality of all before the law regardless of sex. It should not form part of Namibian law and was probably contrary to the provisions of the Namibian Constitution (p 705).

3   In respect of the first appellant, the State had not proved its case beyond reasonable doubt. The first complainant was a single witness and where one would have expected corroboration there was contradiction. Whilst it was not suggested that the complainant was untruthful, in the light of the discrepancies in the surrounding circumstances of the case, the State could not be said to have discharged its onus of proof. The appeal of the first appellant was therefore allowed (p 703).

4   In the case of the second appellant, the State had proved its case beyond reasonable doubt, even considering the evidence of the second complainant in the light of the cautionary rule. The appeal of the second appellant was therefore dismissed (p 704).

National legislation referred to

Namibia

Constitution of Namibia, art 10

Cases referred to

R v Difford 1937 AD 370

R v F 1966 (1) SA 88 (SR)

R v W 1949 (3) SA 772 (A)

S v Balhuber 1987 (1) PH H22 (A)

S v C 1965 (3) SA 105 (N)

S v F 1989 (3) SA 847 (A)

JUDGMENT

FRANK J: This is an appeal. Both appellants were convicted of rape and sentenced to three years' imprisonment. Eighteen months of the imprisonment were suspended on the usual conditions.

Briefly stated, the two complainants testified that they were called by the two appellants and then taken to a burnt-out building. There they were raped. Each complainant was raped by one of the appellants. Although this happened more or less simultaneously, the respective rapes did not occur in the same locality. Thus, apart from the evidence relating to the initial approach from the appellants, the complainants were single witnesses insofar as the actual rapes were concerned. The appellants admitted intercourse but averred that they had consented thereto.

First complainant testified, *inter alia*:

(a) That she heard second complainant screaming although she could not see where second complainant was. This is not corroborated by second complainant, who specifically stated that she did not scream because of the nature of the threats directed to her.

(b) That the appellants were confronted with the alleged rape by the headboy of their school in the complainants' presence. This is denied by second complainant and by the headboy.

(c) That she immediately reported the matter to her room-mates. This is not corroborated by one of the room-mates called as a witness. According to the room-mate first complainant entered the room with nothing wrong with her clothing, took a wash-cloth and went to the bathroom. It was only after second complainant arrived on the scene and complained that first complainant also indicated that she had been raped.

(d) That they, ie the two complainants, with others reported the matter to the matron. The matron confirms that girls did approach her with allegations that boys had pulled off clothing from some girls but she did not notice first complainant in this group, but only second complainant.

In view of the aforegoing, the fact that no medical evidence was presented and the nature of the case, I am not satisfied that the State proved a case of rape beyond reasonable doubt. As pointed out, as far as the absence of consent was concerned, the first complainant was a single witness and where one would have expected corroboration one finds contradiction.

I must point out that, by criticising the evidence of the complainant, I am not suggesting that she was untruthful. She may well have told the truth, but in view of the discrepancies seen in the light of the surrounding circumstances the State cannot be said to have discharged the onus resting upon it. It is apposite to refer to the *locus classicus* in this regard where it was stated:

> It is equally clear that no onus rests on the accused to convince the Court of the truth of any explanation he gives.

> If he gives an explanation, even if that explanation be improbable, the Court is not entitled to convict unless it is satisfied, not only that the explanation is improbable, but that beyond any reasonable doubt it is false.

(*R v Difford* 1937 AD 370 at 373)

The second complainant gave evidence that second appellant threatened her and removed her skirt and panties. He commenced to have intercourse with her while she was still standing. He then tripped her so that she fell onto the floor and told her to move somewhere else. In this process she managed to escape and she ran back to the hostel where she reported the rape to her room-mates whereupon they also reported it to the matron. The second appellant admitted the sequence of events immediately prior to second complainant running away, but averred that up to that stage everything was done with the consent of second complainant. When second complainant ran away she left her skirt and panties behind. This is common cause. She, furthermore, in this state of undress, immediately made a report to her room-mates and to the matron. This was confirmed by one of her room-mates as well as the matron. The fact that her clothes and head were dirty was also confirmed by the room-mate. I find the fact that she ran away in the state of undress she was in, and in the middle of intercourse she consented to, highly improbable. The fact that she did not corroborate first complainant's allegation about the discussion between the headboy, themselves and the accused is also significant in my view. It is a further indicator that she was a truthful witness.

The cautionary rule relating to sexual cases as espoused in the case law can briefly be stated as follows:

(a) In rape cases, for instance, the established and proper practice is not to require that the complainant's evidence be corroborated before a conviction is competent. But what is required is that the trier of fact should have clearly in mind that these cases of sexual assault require special treatment, that charges of this kind are generally difficult to disprove, and that various considerations may lead to their being falsely laid ...

Had the charge against the appellant been, for instance, one of theft, requiring no more than the ordinary high but not exceptional standard of careful scrutiny ..., the verdict of guilty must have stood.

(*R v W* 1949 (3) SA 772 (A) at 780 and 783)

(b) In the case of all females alleging sexual assaults the need for similar caution, in the absence of corroboration, flows from the fact that such charges are easily laid and difficult for the accused to disprove, and a multiplicity of motives may exist for their being falsely laid. This has been recognised since time immemorial, and a classic example of such a false charge can be found in the Biblical story of Potiphar's wife and Joseph.

Apart from the danger of maliciously false charges, it is also recognised that, even with adults, one may encounter cases of unfounded allegations of sexual assault which owe their origin to flights of fancy.

(*R v F* 1966 (1) SA 88 (SR) at 92A-C)

(c) In the present case, a number of possible motives for the complainant to have acted as the appellant alleged she did, suggest themselves. She may have been overcome by shame, disgust or remorse (perhaps even alcoholic remorse) at the fact that she had consented to intercourse with the appellant; she may have been sexually frustrated because of the appellant's drunken state (he may not have realised that they both did not enjoy the act); she may have been filled with revulsion at the unusual sexual acts to which the appellant had wanted her to submit, whether or not she was a willing party to such acts (as distinct from the act of intercourse); or she may simply have become afraid, with the coming of the morning, that her male friend would arrive at the flat. It is true that these possibilities are speculative and that a court is not usually required to speculate on possibilities having no foundation in the evidence placed before it ..., but if the appellant was telling the truth there was no way in which he could have offered any explanation in evidence for the complainant's conduct, and possibilities of the kind I have mentioned are inherently present in the circumstances of a case such as the present. It is precisely because of the difficulty of discerning hidden motives that cases of this nature require special treatment.

(*Per* Botha JA in *S v Balhuber* 1987 (1) PH H22 (A) quoted with approval – *S v F* 1989 (3) SA 847 (A) at 854H-855A)

Considering the evidence relating to the incident involving the second complainant in view of the said cautionary rule and even taking the stunningly imaginative approach adopted in the *Balhuber* case into consideration, I am of the view that the State did prove its case beyond reasonable doubt against the second appellant.

Why cases of sexual assaults which are "easily laid and difficult ... to disprove" should be treated on a different footing is not clear. There is no empirical data to support the contention that in cases of this nature more false charges are laid than in any other category of crimes. Indeed, the evidence that is available indicates the contrary. D Hubbard "A Critical Discussion of the Law of Rape in Namibia" states at p 34 of her discussion that "(a) US study found that the incidence of false reports for rape is exactly the same as that for other felonies – about two per cent". Why should the Court not speculate as to possible defences in other cases as well? Why is the ordinary burden of proof applicable to all other criminal offences not applicable to cases such as the present? Surely, whatever the offence, the trial court must take the nature of the evidence into account, ie reliance upon the evidence of a single witness, an accomplice or a child. The trial court must, of course, consider the nature and circumstances of the particular offence, but why must a different ultimate test be applied as suggested in *R v W (supra)*?

While it is true that different motives may exist for laying false charges, this surely applies to any offence and not only to offences of a sexual nature. Of what relevance is the reference to the Biblical story of Potiphar's wife except to indicate male bias? If the wife laid a false charge against Joseph, so what? False charges are laid in respect of all types of offences. I would have thought that the moral of this particular story was that one should stand by one's principles irrespective of the consequences. It would appear, however, that the reasoning in this regard is as follows. As the story appears in the Bible it is the truth. As it is the gospel truth it does not relate to a single incident but is of universal application. Thus all women are *prima facie* deceitful and act with hidden motives and all men are *prima facie* incorruptible and act without hidden motives. Hence one can speculate about motives of complainants in cases such as rape even without any evidence to suggest hidden motives. The question whether such hidden motive will be found by the trial court would depend, it seems to me, to a very large extent upon the fecundity of the presiding officer's imagination.

The cautionary rule relating to cases of sexual assault applies to all cases of this nature irrespective of the sex of the complainant (*S v C* 1965 (3) SA 105 (N)).

This, however, does not alter the fact that in the overwhelming majority of cases the complainants are female. Given the social fabric of society in Namibia this state of affairs is hardly likely to change. In this Court, for example, there were 31 cases involving sexual assault during 1990 with not a single one involving a male complainant. In my view one can safely assume that in at least 95% of the cases of this nature the complainants are female. Taking this factual situation into consideration, I am of the view that the so-called cautionary rule has no other purpose than to discriminate against women complainants. This rule thus probably also is contrary to art 10 of the Namibian Constitution which provides for the equality of all persons before the law regardless of sex.

To sum up, in my view, the cautionary rule evolved in cases of rape has no rational basis for its existence and should therefore not form part of our law and is probably contrary to the provisions of the Namibian Constitution.

In conclusion, I must emphasise, however, that this does not mean that the nature and circumstances of the alleged offence need not be considered carefully. Where the complainant is a single witness the cautionary rule relating to single witnesses will obviously apply. Where any motive for a false charge is suggested by the accused or appears from the evidence this must carefully be considered. In the end, however, only one test applies, namely was the accused's guilt proved beyond reasonable doubt, and this test must be the same whether the crime is theft or rape.

As indicated above, the appellants were each sentenced to three years' imprisonment of which 18 months were suspended for five years on the usual conditions. I find nothing wrong with this sentence. A totally suspended sentence, as was suggested on behalf of the appellants, due primarily to their youthfulness coupled with the fact that they were first offenders, would not have been apposite. Rape is a serious infringement upon the dignity and person of the victim and only in rare and exceptional cases would a totally suspended sentence be appropriate.

The sentence is not shockingly inappropriate. Indeed, taking all the relevant factors into account, I would also have imposed a sentence of a similar nature in this matter and the question of misdirections vitiating the sentence therefore do not arise.

In the result:

(a) The appeal is upheld in respect of the first appellant and his conviction and sentence is set aside.

(b) The appeal against conviction and sentence by second appellant is dismissed.

STRYDOM JP concurred.

CASE NO 45

SAFIA BIBI v STATE

FEDERAL SHARIAT COURT OF PAKISTAN

Judgment: 13 December 1983

Panel: Hussain CJ

Human rights — Violence against women — Extra-marital sex — Offence of Zina — Burden of proof — Whether woman could be convicted of zina (extra-marital sex) on the basis of her pregnancy and self-exculpatory statement alleging rape by co-accused — Islamic jurisprudence — Offence of Zina (Enforcement of Hudood Ordinance (VII of 1979)

Human rights — Violence against women — Rape — Offence of Zina-bil-Jabr — Law of evidence — Whether statement of accused (woman) sufficient to convict co-accused (male) of zina-bil-jabr (rape) without independent corroborating evidence — Islamic jurisprudence — Offence of Zina (Enforcement of Hudood Ordinance (VII of 1979), s 10(2); Evidence Act 1872, s 30

BACKGROUND

The appellant, Ms Safia Bibi, a 20-year woman who was almost blind, carried out domestic work in the house of Maqsood Ahmad, her co-accused. She was taken to the house to work by his grandmother. There, she claimed, he committed *Zina-bil-Jabr* with her, that is raped her. She left and returned home, reporting the rape to her mother. Later the grandmother again took her back to the house to work. She claimed that she was then raped by Muhammad Ali, Maqsood Ahmed's father. She became pregnant and gave birth to a child who died shortly after its birth. On 15 July 1982, Safia Bibi's father filed a report with the police, claiming that his daughter had been raped by Maqsood Ahmad and subsequently given birth to a child. Both Safia Bibi and Maqsood Ahmed were medically examined and then arrested.

At trial Safia Bibi's pregnancy was taken as evidence of her culpability of having had extra-marital relations. Her own statement was held to be self-exculpatory and therefore entirely excluded from consideration. On 24 July 1983, she was convicted of *Zina* (extra-marital relations) under section 10(2) of the Offence of *Zina* (Enforcement of Hudood) Ordinance 1979, despite the fact that there was no evidence of her having consented to sexual intercourse. She was sentenced to three years' imprisonment, whipping and a fine of Rs 1,000, in default of payment of which she was ordered to undergo an additional six months' imprisonment. Her co-accused, Maqsood Ahmend, was acquitted of *Zina-bil-Jabr* (rape), since Safia Bibi's statement against him (as that of a co-accused) was not sufficient evidence without independent corroborative evidence.

HELD (allowing the appeal)

1   The appellant should not have been found guilty of *Zina* by consent under section 10(2) of the Ordinance. The trial judge had departed from the well-known principle of criminal law that it is the duty of the prosecution to establish by evidence the offence of the accused beyond reasonable doubt. It was also settled law that a confession should be

read as a whole and the self-exculpatory portions could not be excluded from consideration unless those portions were proved to be incorrect. There was no evidence that Safia Bibi and Maqsood Ahmad were on intimate terms; thus the appellant should not have been found guilty of *Zina* by consent. (Para 13)

2   Even under Shariah, if a woman makes such a statement as that made in the present case, she could not be convicted of *Zina* (para 18). According to the Hanafis and the Shafis, if an unmarried woman delivering a child pleads that the birth was the result of commission of the offence of rape on her, she cannot be punished. Her statement, including the self-exculpatory part thereof, is sufficient to absolve her of the charge. However, according to Iman Malik she would be subject to punishment unless she showed a lack of consent on her part by raising alarm or by complaining later. Thus she would have the burden of proving the self-exculpatory evidence, which she could do by producing circumstantial evidence (paras 19 and 20). The fact that the appellant soon after the first occurrence had informed her mother, and had also refused to visit the house of Maquood Ahmad for many days was sufficient evidence to confirm her statement. (Para 17)

3   *Per curiam.* It was not strange that there may be cases in which only the woman who has given birth to a child may be convicted of *Zina*, and the co-accused who is blamed for committing *Zina* with her is acquitted (para 14). Section 30 of the Evidence Act allowed the court to take into consideration a confession of one accused against a co-accused. But it was settled law that conviction of a co-accused could not be based on such a confession unless it was corroborated by independent evidence (para 15). The position was the same under the Shariah. (Para 29)

National legislation referred to

Pakistan

Evidence Act, s 30

Offence of Zina (Enforcement of Hudood) Ordinance, 1979, s 10(2)

Cases referred to

State v Zulfiqar Ali Bhutto PLD 1978 Lah 523

JUDGMENT

1   This is an unfortunate case which received considerable publicity in the national and international press. In view of the circumstances and facts which were apparent from the reporting it was considered reasonable to issue a notice to the State in exercise of the Revisional Jurisdiction of this Court to show cause why the judgment be not set aside. Thereafter Criminal Appeal No. 123/I of 1983 was filed on behalf of Mst Safia Bibi, through Mr Muhammad Ajran Sheikh, who out of sympathy offered to act *gratis* as her counsel, a gesture which ought to be appreciated. The matter evoked such emotional compassion and pity that one counsel from Karachi, namely Mr Hasan Rizvi, and another from Lahore namely Miss Hina Jilani have come to appear as *amicus curiae*.

2   Mst Safia Bibi, aged 20 years, who suffered from acute myopia, and is now said to be blind, was convicted by Ch Muhammad Aslam, Additional Sessions Judge II, Sahiwal, on 24 July 1983, under section 10(2) of the Offence of Zina (Enforcement of Hudood)

Ordinance, 1979 and sentenced to 3 years' rigorous imprisonment, whipping numbering 15 stripes and a fine of Rs1,000, in default of payment of which she was directed to undergo further rigorous imprisonment for a period of 6 months. Her co-accused Maqsood Ahmad was, however, acquitted for want of evidence.

3   On 15 July 1982, Dilawar Khan, father of the appellant, gave a first information report in Police Station Chak Bedi, complaining that his daughter Mst Safia Bibi who worked in the house of Maqsood Ahmad was subjected by him to *Zina-bil-Jabr* (rape) as a result of which she gave birth to a child.

4   The police arrested Maqsood Ahmad and got him medically examined by Doctor Sajid Latif, who was of the opinion that there was nothing to show that he was not able to perform sexual intercourse. Mst Safia Bibi, appellant was also medically examined by Lady Doctor Zubaida Khatoon, PW 2, on 19 July 1982. She found that the appellant had given birth to a child about 15 or 20 days before her examination. Thereafter the police arrested her also and challenged both the accused persons.

5   The prosecution examined on facts Dilawar Khan, complainant, PW 3, Abdul Wahid, PW 4, Siraj, PW 5 and Muhammad Ibrahim, PW 6. Ghulam Farid, SI appeared as Investigating Officer.

6   Dilawar Khan reiterated his statement which had been made in the first information report and also stated that after the commission of *Zina-bil-Jabr* by Maqsood Ahmad about which information had been given by Mst Safia Bibi to her mother, she refused to go to his house. However, she agreed when subsequently Mst Rashida Bibi, wife of Muhammad Ali (mother of Maqsood Ahmad) came to his house and took her away in the absence of her parents.

7   The other three witnesses (PWs 4, 5 and 6) did not support the prosecution case and were declared hostile.

8   Mst Safia Bibi, in her own statement under section 342, Cr PC stated that she was taken by the grandmother of Maqsood Ahmad to her house for domestic work and there Maqsood Ahmad committed *Zina-bil Jabr* with her. After about 10 days, Mst Rashida Bibi, mother of Maqsood Ahmad again took her to her house for some domestic work and at that time Muhammad Ali, father of Maqsood Ahmad, committed the same offence with her. She conceived from this *Zina* and gave birth to an illegitimate child, who died in the DHQ Hospital, Schiwai.

9   She produced three defence witnesses namely, Muhammad Din, DW1, Dulla DW 2, and Dina, DW 3, but their evidence is not at all helpful since they did not throw any light on the occurrence.

10 It is clear from this evidence that no offence was proved against Maqsood Ahmad as the bare statement of his co-accused was not sufficient for his conviction. Moreover, the statement was clearly self-exculpatory in nature and did not fall under the provisions of section 30 of the Evidence Act.

11 There is also no evidence against Mst Safia Bibi. It is unfortunate that though a victim of *Zina-bil-Jabr*, the natural phenomena of her pregnancy and motherhood betrayed her and she had to suffer the humiliation of a trial, conviction and sentence in addition to the disgrace and dishonour suffered by her at the hands of her fellow human beings in the society.

12 The trial Court took her pregnancy as evidence of culpability. He held that her statement was self-exculpatory and could not be called a confession. Despite this, he

entered the realm of conjecture, and convicted her simply on the ground that there was no evidence that she had ever complained about the commission of the offence by Maqsood Ahmad, and had kept quiet for almost 10 months.

13 This is a clear departure from the well-known principles of criminal law that it is the duty of the prosecution to establish by evidence the offence of an accused person beyond any shadow of doubt. It is settled law that a confession should be read as a whole and the self-exculpatory portions therein cannot be excluded from consideration unless there be evidence on record to prove those portions to be incorrect. The learned Additional Sessions Judge could not hold Mst Safia Bibi guilty of *Zina* by consent under section 10(2) of the Ordinance, in the absence of any evidence to establish that she and Maqsood Ahmad had any sentimental attachment for and were on intimate terms with one another. No such evidence is forthcoming on the record.

14 I may, however, take note of some comments that it was strange that the person who had committed the offence of *Zina* was acquitted, but the girl was convicted. I do not think that this comment is at all reasonable. There may be cases in which only the girl, who has given birth to a child may be convicted and the co-accused who is blamed for committing *Zina* with her, be acquitted. If there is no evidence of eye-witnesses and the only evidence is for example, a confessional statement made by the girl involving the male accused, then in the absence of any other evidence against the male accused, he cannot be convicted but the girl can be convicted on her confession.

15 Section 30, Evidence Act allows the Court to take into consideration a confession of one accused made in the Court in a joint trial of more persons than one, against a co-accused. But it is settled law that conviction of the co-accused cannot be based on such confession unless it is corroborated by independent evidence (*State v Zulfiqar Ali Bhutto*). This may be one category of cases in which the girl may be convicted while the male may be acquitted.

16 Another category may be, in which a self-exculpatory statement is made by the girl, as in this case, putting the entire blame for committing rape with her on the male accused. If there is evidence on the record showing that both of them had been seen in amorous position off and on, and that their relationship was of close and intimate lovers negating the possibility of rape, it may be sufficient to hold that the statement of the girl to the extent of self-exculpation, is not correct. In such a case she may be convicted. But her statement would not be evidence against her paramour under section 30 and in the absence of any other evidence, he may be acquitted.

17 In the present case, it is clear that except for the self-exculpatory statement of the girl and the statement of her father, who also maintained that she had been subjected to *Zina-bil-Jabr*, there is no other evidence. The learned Additional Sessions Judge has obviously ignored, for technical reasons, that portion of the evidence of Dilawar Khan, complainant, PW 3, in which he stated that Mst Safia Bibi soon after the first occurrence, had informed her mother of the commission of *Zina-bil-Jabr* with her by Maqsood Ahmad, and also that thereafter she refused to visit the house of Maqsood Ahmad for many a day till Mst Rashida Bibi came to fetch her. This is sufficient evidence to confirm her statement under section 342, Cr PC.

18 Even under Shariah if a girl makes such a statement as made in the present case, she cannot be convicted of *Zina*. The principle of *Fiqh* is that she will be asked about the cause of pregnancy, if she says that she was forced to commit adultery or someone had committed sexual intercourse with her under suspicion about her identity, her statement will be accepted and she will not be convicted. This is based on the tradition of Hazrat

Ali that when Shuraha came to him and said, "I have committed adultery", Hazrat Ali said to her, "You might have been forced or someone might have committed sexual intercourse with you while you were sleeping" (Kitabul Fiqh alal Mazahibil Arabaa (Urdu translation), Vol V pp 166, 167).

19 If an unmarried woman delivering a child pleads that the birth was the result of commission of the offence of rape on her, she cannot be punished. This is the view of the Hanafis and the Shafis. But Imam Malik said she shall be subjected to *Hadd* punishment unless she manifested the want of consent on her part by raising alarm or by complaining against it later, (Ela ul Sunnan, Vol XI, p 666, Bidayat ul Mujtahid, Vol II, p 329, Fathul Qadeer, Vol V, p 52, Al Mughni by Ibn-e-Qudama, Vol VIII, p 186, Badaius Sanai by Kashani, Vol VII, p 62, Mabahis fil Tashri il Janaiyyil Islami by Dr Muhammad Farooq Nabhan, pp 225, 226. Altashri-il-Janaiyyal Islami by Abdul Qadir Auda, Vol II, p 364, Al-Tashriul-Janaiyyul Islami, Vol II, pp 434, 435, Tabyinul Haqaiq by Zailai, Vol III, p 184). Ibne Qudama said that it is generally held that there is no *Hadd* on one who is raped. This view was held by Omar, Alzahri, Qatada, Shafei and the people of opinion (*inter alia* Hanafis). He did not know of any contrary view. This view is based upon the Hadith from the Holy Prophet who said "my people are excused for mistakes, forgetfulness and for anything done under compulsion" [translation]. It is reported from Abdul Jabbar on the authority of his father that a woman was raped and the Prophet (SAW) acquitted her of the charge punishable with Hadd (Al Mughni, Vol VIII, p 186).

20 There is little difference between the view of Imam Malik and others on the point of law that rape with a woman absolves her of criminal liability. The only difference is on the point of the evidentiary value of the self-exculpatory statement. Iman Malik places the burden of proving the self-exculpatory evidence on the woman, and this burden case be discharged by her by proving that she raised alarm or complained against it. She can discharge her burden by production of circumstantial evidence.

21 The others, however, consider her statement including the self-exculpatory portion thereof, as sufficient for absolving her of the charge.

22 These views, however, do not deal with a matter in which there is evidence negating the possibility of rape. In that case the woman obviously cannot be let off on the basis of her self-exculpatory statement.

23 The question whether the confession of one accused is sufficient for conviction of the co-accused is determinable on the basis of the traditions of the Holy Prophet.

24 Abu Daud reported on the authority of Saad ul Saaidi that a man came to the Prophet (SAW) and confessed that he had committed adultery with such woman. He named the woman. The Prophet (SAW) sent for the woman and enquired from her about it. She denied the allegation. The Prophet (SAW) punished the male but acquitted the female (Al Mughni by Ibn-e-Qudama, Vol VIII, p 193).

25 Another tradition is of Aseef. A rustic came with another person to the Prophet (SAW) and said that his son had committed adultery with the wife of the person accompanying him. It is unnecessary to reproduce the full tradition. But it is important to note that the Prophet (SAW) announced the sentence for the male culprit and ordered Onaid to go to the woman and punish her if she confessed (Muslim, English Translation, Vol IV, pp 917, 918). Obviously the punishment of the woman was dependent on her confession.

26 There are other cases also in which a female and at another time a male confessed the offence of adultery but the other person was not punished.

27 The view of Imam Abu Hanifa was that in a case where one party confesses and the other party denies the charge, both of them should be acquitted since the confession of one is disproved by the denial of the other. According to one version Abu Yousaf was also of the same view. Muhammad Al Shaibani held that the person confessing should be punished. According to another version Abu Yousaf was also of the same view. Muhammad Al Shaibani held that the person confessing should be punished. According to another version Abu Yousaf agreed with Muhammad. However, others did not agree with the view of Imam Abu Hanifa including Imam Shafei because the person confessing is to be punished on the basis of his own confession. The person denying is let off on account of absence of proof of his/her own confession. He/she is not absolved because of mere denial by the other. The confession is conclusive evidence against the confessor only and the denial of the other cannot throw any doubt on the confession of the confessor, *Al Tashriil Janai ul Islami* by Abdul Qair Audah, Vol II, pp 434, 435. See also Al Mughni, Vol VIII, p 193, Badai-us-Sanai, Vol VII, pp 61, 62 and *Mabahis fil Tashriil Islami* by Dr Muhammad Farooq Nabhan, p 266.

28 It has also been related from Hazrat Umar that once a woman came to him and said that a man committed sexual intercourse with her while she was sleeping. He then ran away and she could not identify him. Hazrat Umar accepted her excuse and acquitted her. (*Ela-us-Sunnan* by Maulana Zafar Ahmad Usmani, Vol XI, pp 666–667.)

29 It would be clear that even in Shariah the confession of one accused against the co-accused is not sufficient for the conviction of the latter. Views differ only on the point whether only the person denying should be acquitted or the person confessing should also be absolved of the charge. There is no difference on the main point between *Fiqh*, the Common Law of England or the Law in Pakistan, that the appellant also cannot be convicted on the evidence on record.

30 Even if the view of Imam Malik be treated to be preferable the appellant cannot be punished since there is evidence of her complaining to her mother. However, the opinion of other jurists on the point of burden of proof is preferable, and is in conformity with the modern law.

31 This being a case of no evidence, the appeal is accepted and the appellant is acquitted. Her bail bond is discharged. The notice for exercise of revisional jurisdiction has been rendered infructuous by the filing of appeal and is discharged.

CASE NO 46

MEJÍA AND ANOTHER v PERU

INTER-AMERICAN COMMISSION ON HUMAN RIGHTS

Report No: 5/96

Case No: 10.970

Decision: 1 March 1996

Panel: Tirado Mejía (*Chairman*), Ayala Corao, Donaldson, Exume, Luján Fappiano, Goldman, Grossman[i]

Human rights — Violence against women — Right to humane treatment — Torture — Rape by member of security forces — Whether rape could constitute an act of torture — Elements required — American Convention on Human Rights, art 5

Human rights — Violence against women — Right to privacy — Sexual abuse as deliberate outrage of a person's dignity — American Convention on Human Rights, art 11

Human rights — Right to judicial protection — Whether petitioner had access to effective domestic judicial recourse — American Convention on Human Rights, art 25

BACKGROUND

Ms Raquel Martín de Mejía and her husband, Dr Fernando Mejía Egocheaga, lived in Oxapampa, Peru where the latter was a local opposition politician as well as a lawyer and journalist. In June 1989, after some soldiers had been killed by a terrorist group in the town, around one hundred soldiers were billeted there to conduct a counter-insurgency campaign and the area was placed under state of emergency legislation. On 15 June 1989, a group of masked men, allegedly soldiers wearing Peruvian army fatigues, assaulted and forcibly abducted Dr Mejía from his home at gunpoint and the same night Ms Mejía was raped. She later learnt that her husband had been severely beaten and killed.

Ms Mejía filed a criminal charge with the office of the Attorney-General of the Republic in respect of the abduction and subsequent killing of her husband. She did not report the rapes as she feared for her safety. A judicial inquiry was initiated, but due to various delays and obstructions by the parties involved, no progress was made. Meanwhile Ms Mejía continued to receive threatening telephone calls warning her to cease her complaints.

In August 1989, Ms Mejía fled Peru and was subsequently granted political asylum in Sweden. After the Peruvian government identified her as a member of a subversive organisation supporting terrorists in Peru while living abroad, criminal charges were filed against her under Peruvian anti-terrorist legislation. Although no formal evidence was submitted, an indictment was issued against her and she was sentenced to twenty years' imprisonment, whereupon the Peruvian government sought her extradition.

---

i   Commission President Grossman and Commission Member Goldman did not participate in the consideration and voting on this Report, in accordance with article 19 of the IAComm HR's Regulations.

On 17 October 1991, Ms Mejía lodged a petition with the Inter-American Commission on Human Rights on behalf of herself and her deceased husband. As regards her own case, Ms Mejía requested that the Commission declare the Peruvian Government responsible for violations of articles 5 (right to humane treatment), 8 (right to fair trial), 11 (right to privacy) and 25 (right to judicial protection) of the American Convention on Human Rights, in connection with article 1, which obliges States parties to respect and guarantee the exercise of these rights.

HELD (finding various violations of the Convention)

Presumption of the acceptance of the facts of the petitioner

1   Under principles of general international law, when the State does not provide information concerning the facts alleged to an international organ whose competence it recognises, or its responses are evasive and/or ambiguous, a presumption of the acceptance of the facts of the petition arises. The Peruvian government had not addressed the facts presented by the petitioners (which met the criteria of consistency, credibility and specificity). The Commission, in order to make a decision, therefore had to limit itself to the arguments and the proofs offered by the petitioner and other elements available to it that would enable it to decide the matter, such as the reports of the UN Special Rapporteur against Torture and non-governmental agencies (pp 724, 725).

Torture (article 5 of the Convention)

2   For the purpose of article 5 of the Convention, torture is an intentional act through which physical or mental pain and suffering is inflicted on a person; is committed with a purpose (including the purpose of affecting the victim's personality or diminishing her mental or physical capacity, even if it does not cause physical pain or mental anguish) and is committed by or at the instigation of a public official. The three elements of the definition of torture were present in the instant case: Ms Mejía was a victim of rape, and in consequence a victim of an intentional act of violence that caused her "physical and mental pain and suffering", was raped with the aim of punishing her personally and intimidating her, and the man who raped her was member of the security forces. Accordingly, the State was responsible for a violation of article 5 of the Convention (pp 733, 734).

Right to privacy (article 11 of the Convention)

3   Article 11 of the Convention specifies that a State must guarantee the protection of the honour and dignity of individuals within the framework of the broader right to privacy. Sexual abuse implied a deliberate outrage of a person's dignity in violation of article 11 and since the violations of articles 5 and 11 had been carried out by an agent of a public authority of the State, the State itself was in violation of article 1(1) (p 734).

Right to judicial protection (article 25 of the Convention)

4   The right to effective judicial remedy under article 25 required that there be effective recourses to victims of human rights violations. The formal existence of such recourses was not sufficient to demonstrate their effectiveness; to be effective, a recourse had to be adequate (appropriate for protecting the juridical situation affected) and efficacious (capable of producing the result for which it was designed). There were not in Peru any

effective domestic remedies through which a victim of sexual abuse by members of the security forces could obtain an impartial investigation of the events and punishment of those guilty. Further, the State's failure to provide for a thorough investigation in the case of Fernando Mejía affected his wife's right to an effective recourse, as under Peruvian law, the fact that the existence of the rape was not established through criminal proceedings made it materially impossible, in practice, for Ms Mejía to exercise her right to obtain compensation. The State of Peru was in violation of articles 25 of the Convention (p 737).

Treaties and other international instruments referred to

American Convention on Human Rights 1969, arts 1(1), 4, 5, 7, 11, 25 and 50

Geneva Convention for the Amelioration of the Condition of the Wounded and Sick in Armed Forces in the Field of 12 August 1949 (First Geneva Convention), art 3

Geneva Convention for the Amelioration of the Condition of Wounded, Sick and Shipwrecked Members of Armed Forces at Sea of 12 August 1949 (Second Geneva Convention), art 3

Geneva Convention Relative to the Treatment of Prisoners of War of 12 August 1949 (Third Geneva Convention), art 3

Geneva Convention Relative to the Protection of Civilian Persons in Time of War of 12 August 1949 (Fourth Geneva Convention), arts 3, 27 and 147

Inter-American Convention to Prevent and Punish Torture 1985, arts 2 and 3

Protocol Additional to the Geneva Conventions of 12 August 1949 and relating to the Protection of Victims of International Armed Conflicts (Protocol I), of 8 June 1977, arts 76 and 85(4)

Protocol Additional to the Geneva Conventions of 12 August 1949 and relating to the Protection of Victims of Non-International Armed Conflicts (Protocol II) of 8 June 1977, art 4(2)

Regulations made under the American Convention on Human Rights, arts 32, 42 11, 25 and 50

Statute of the International Tribunal established for investigating the serious violations of international humanitarian law committed in the territory of the former Yugoslavia, UN Doc S/RES/827 (1993), art 5

National legislation referred to

Peru

Code of Criminal Procedure, arts 3, 5, 77 and 170

Decree Law 25.475

Cases referred to

Consuelo et al v Argentina, IACommHR, Annual Report 1993, Cases 10.147, 10.181, 10.240, 10.262, 10.309, 10.311, Report No 28/92, IACHR, OEA/Ser.L/V/II.83 Doc 14 at 41 (1993)

Corfu Channel Case (Assessment of Compensation) [1949] ICJ 248

Fanali v Italy, UN Human Rights Committee, Communication No 75/1980, Selected Decisions of the Human Rights Committee under the Optional Protocol, vol 2 (New York: United Nations, 1990)

Golder v United Kingdom, ECHR, judgment of 21 February 1975, Series A, No 18; 1 EHRR 524

Judicial Guarantees in States of Emergency (Articles 27(2), 25 and 8 of the American Convention on Human Rights), IACHR, Advisory Opinion OC-9/87 of 6 October 1987, Series A, No 9 (1987)

Mendoza et al v Uruguay, IACommHR, Annual Report 1993, Cases 10.029, 10.036, 10.145, 10.305, 10.372 10.373, 10.374 and 10.375, Report No 29/92, IACHR, OEA/Ser.L/V/II.83 Doc 14 at 154 (1993)

Restrictions to the Death Penalty (Arts 4(2) and 4(4) of the American Convention on Human Rights), IACHR, Advisory Opinion OC-3/83 of 8 September 1983, Series A, No 3 (1983); 70 ILR 449; 23 ILM 320

Velásquez Rodríguez v Honduras (Preliminary exceptions), IACHR, judgment of 26 July 1987, Series C, No 1 (1987)

X and Y v The Netherlands, ECHR, judgment of 26 March 1985, Series A, No 167; 8 EHRR 235; *supra* p 81

REPORT

On 17 October 1991, the Inter-American Commission on Human Rights (hereinafter the Commission) received a petition reporting violation of the human rights of Fernando Mejía Egocheaga and of his wife Raquel Martín de Mejía. This petition requested that Peru be declared responsible for violation of the following rights recognized in the American Convention on Human Rights (hereinafter the Convention):

1   In regard to Fernando Mejía, right to personal liberty (Article 7), right to humane treatment (Article 5), and right to life (Article 4), all in connection with Article 1(1) of the Convention.

2   In regard to Raquel Mejía, right to humane treatment and right to privacy (Article 11), both in connection with Article 1(1) of the Convention.

3   In regard to both petitioners, the right of everyone to an effective domestic remedy that protects him against acts that violate his fundamental rights (Article 25).

I   BACKGROUND

Fernando Mejía Egocheaga and his wife Raquel were living in Oxapampa, in the Department of Pasco, at the time the events reported to the Commission took place.

Dr Mejía Egocheaga was a lawyer, journalist and political activist. At the time of his death he was President of the Oxapampa Bar Association and also Chairman of the Provincial Committee of Izquierda Unida (United Left), a Peruvian political party. He was also a member of the Peruvian Journalists' Association and worked as a journalist on the paper "Campanaria Oxapampa", which he had founded and of which he was editor. As a lawyer, Dr Mejía Egocheaga concentrated mainly on defending the rights to land of the most disadvantaged groups in Peru. Between 1982 and 1986 he was legal adviser to the "Pichis Palcazu" special project, a rural development initiative launched under the auspices of the Presidency of the Republic. In 1986 he represented the indigenous peoples of the Amuesha Community in a land conflict with the Catholic Church. In his political activity, Dr Mejía Egocheaga planned to run for mayor of Oxapampa and later possibly to make a bid for a seat in Congress.

Mrs Raquel Martín de Mejía was a teacher and worked as principal of a school for the handicapped in Oxapampa. She is presently living in Sweden, where she obtained political asylum in 1989.

In June 1989 some soldiers were killed by *Sendero Luminoso* (Shining Path) terrorists in Posuzo, a town not far from Oxapampa. A few days afterwards, about 100 military personnel from the "Batallón Nueve de Diciembre", based in Huancayo, were helicoptered into Oxapampa to conduct counterinsurgency operations in the region. These soldiers were billeted in the local Municipal Library.

II   FACTS REPORTED

According to the information provided by the petitioners to the Commission, the facts reported as violations of human rights protected by the Convention are stated to be those described in the following:

In the night of 15 June 1989, Oxapampa residents saw a yellow pickup truck belonging to the "Pichis Palcazu" government project parked in front of the bar. In it were Julio Arias Dorregaray, Subprefect of Oxapampa, Army officers and four soldiers. A witness who was there reported hearing Mr Arias Dorregaray say to his companions: "it's time to go look for the lawyer".

The same night, at 10.05 pm, a number of military personnel with their faces covered by ski masks and carrying submachine guns violently entered the home of Professor Aladino Melgarejo, who was the Secretary General of the *Sindicato Unico de Trabajadores de la Educación Peruana* (SUTEP – Peruvian Education Workers' Union) in Oxapampa and a member of *Izquierda Unida*. The soldiers made him leave the house, beat him and finally pushed him into a government-owned yellow pickup truck used for the "Pichis Palcazu" special project. The abduction of Professor Melgarejo was witnessed by his wife, Haydeé Verde, by his sister-in-law, Mrs Nancy Verde de Nano and by the latter's husband, Mr Hugo Nano.

According to the petitioners, the Army personnel in charge of the operation ordered Professor Melgarejo to drive them to the home of Dr Fernando Mejía Egocheaga.

At 11.15 that night (15 June 1989), a group of persons with their faces covered by ski masks and carrying submachine guns suddenly turned up at the Mejías' home and demanded to see Dr Fernando Mejía Egocheaga. When he opened the door, six individuals wearing military uniforms went in and one of them struck Dr Mejía with his weapon; then the one in charge of the operation ordered him into a yellow government-owned pickup. The events described were witnessed by his wife, Raquel Martín de Mejía.

That same night, about 15 minutes after the above-described events, a group of between six and ten military personnel with their faces concealed by black ski masks showed up at the Mejías' house again. One of them – the one who had been in charge of the abduction of Fernando Mejía – went into the house, apparently to ask Mrs Mejía for her husband's identity documents.

While she was looking for them he followed her into the room and told her she was also considered a subversive. He then showed her a list containing a number of names and said that they were people who were members of the *Movimiento Revolucionario*

Tupac Amaru (MRTA – Tupac Amaru Revolutionary Movement). When Mrs Mejía moved closer to read it, he covered it so that she could only see two names: those of Fernando Mejía and Aladino Melgarejo.

Mrs Mejía tried to explain to him that neither she nor her husband belonged to any subversive movements; however, without listening to her he began to spray himself with her perfumes and finally raped her. He then took her outside the house to see the man who had denounced her husband; this man was lying face down in the back of the same pickup that had been used to abduct Fernando Mejía. Finally, the individual who had abused her sexually got into the pickup and drove off.

About twenty minutes later the same person returned to the Mejías' home, apparently with the intention of telling Mrs Mejía that her husband might possibly be taken to Lima by helicopter the next day. He then dragged her into the room and raped her again. Raquel Mejía spent the rest of the night in a state of terror that the one who had assaulted her would come back and fearing for her safety and for her husband's life.

The next morning Mrs Mejía went to the police station in Oxapampa to report the disappearance of her husband. The duty corporal told her that a person could not be reported as missing until after four days had elapsed. The station chief then suggested that she ask for information at the offices of the Republican Police, where she went and was advised to go to the Municipal Library where the troops of the "Batallón Nueve de Diciembre" had been billeted since their arrival in Oxampapa some days earlier.

When she got to the Municipal Library she saw a large number of soldiers lined up in front of the building and noted that they were wearing the same uniforms as the men who had abducted her husband and the man who had abused her sexually.

Also there was Professor Melgarejo's wife Haydeé, accompanied by a local lawyer, trying to find out about the disappearance of her husband. The two women talked with some soldiers who told them they were members of the "Batallón Nueve de Diciembre" and said that their commander was known as "Chito". Another soldier then came up and abruptly ordered them to go away. Mrs Mejía recognized him as one of her husband's abductors. Raquel Mejía and Haydeé Verde requested the assistance of the Mayor of Oxapampa, Mr Eduardo Koch Muller, and of the Provincial Prosecutor of Oxapampa, Dr Abraham Lino Obregón, but neither of them did anything to help the two women.

As a last resort, Mrs Mejía went to the Bar Association, where Dr Lora, a lawyer belonging to the association, prepared petitions for protection of civil rights and *habeas corpus*, which were immediately lodged with the examining magistrate, Dr Johnny Macetas. Despite having received and sealed them, Dr Macetas stated that he was busy with other cases and did not have time to investigate the disappearance of Fernando Mejía Egocheaga. On 16 June 1989, members of the Permanent Congressional Commission sent a letter to the Minister of the Interior requesting information concerning Fernando Mejía and asking that he be freed. The Minister of the Interior never responded to that letter.

On 17 June, César Barrera Bazán, a Member of Congress and a friend of Professor Melgarejo, went to Oxapampa to investigate the disappearances. The Army troops there refused to cooperate or to provide any information as to the fate of Mejía and Melgarejo.

In the morning of 18 June, Raquel Mejía learned that Professor Melgarejo's body had been found on the bank of the Santa Clara River with another half-buried body alongside it. Raquel Mejía, together with the acting judge and the secretary of the court with responsibility for the case, then went to the place in question and found there, at the foot of the column supporting the bridge, the beheaded corpse of Aladino Melgarejo and, alongside it, the body of her husband, Dr Fernando Mejía. The latter showed clear signs of torture, cuts in the legs and arms and an open wound in the head apparently caused by a bullet. He had been severely beaten and the body was extensively swollen.

The body was taken to the municipal hospital where the requisite autopsy was performed. This confirmed that Fernando Mejía had been severely tortured and had died from a bullet in the head. It was also determined that he had died between 48 and 72 hours earlier. On 20 June 1989, Raquel Mejía filed a deposition with the local police concerning the abduction and subsequent killing of her husband. Then, accompanied by Deputy César Barrera Bazán, she moved her husband's body from Oxapampa to Lima for burial there.

At the request of APRODEH (*Asociación Pro Derechos Humanos* – Human Rights Association) and of Raquel Mejía, on 21 June 1989, the Provincial Prosecutor of Oxapampa, Dr Lino Obregón, ordered the local police to investigate the homicides of Fernando Mejía and Aladino Melgarejo.

On 22 June 1989, Dr Lino Obregón inspected the area where the bodies of Mejía and Melgarejo had been found and discovered cartridges from bullets similar to those used by the Peruvian Army. He then immediately asked the Military Political Chief of the region to identify the officers of the "Batallón Nueve de Diciembre".

On three occasions, between 28 and 30 June 1989, Raquel Mejía received anonymous phone calls threatening her with death if she persisted with the investigation of the homicide of her husband.

On 11 July 1989, APRODEH and Raquel Mejía filed a criminal charge with the Office of the Attorney General of the Republic in respect of the crimes of homicide and abuse of authority against Fernando Mejía and Aladino Melgarejo, requesting that the Attorney General's office as the authority responsible for initiating criminal action would take the necessary steps to clear up the cases.

Two days later, the Office of the Attorney General forwarded the documents to Dr Ramón Pinto Bastidas, Provincial Prosecutor of the Senior Prosecutor's Office in Junín, who ordered the Provincial Prosecutor in Oxapampa to investigate the homicides and submit an opinion to the investigating judge for the case.

Because she feared for her safety, Raquel Mejía left Peru in August 1989, going first to the United States and then to Sweden, where she was granted political asylum.

In November 1989, the Oxapampa Provincial Prosecutor, for reasons that are unknown, transferred jurisdiction for investigating the abduction and subsequent homicide of Fernando Mejía and Aladino Melgarejo to the Technical Police in La Merced, a city 200 km from Oxapampa.

On 30 January 1990, the Huancayo Permanent Military Court declared itself competent concerning the case and ordered the civil criminal judge in Oxapampa to halt any action on it. However, the military court did not draw up any charges or make any sort of investigation aimed at clearing up the matter.

One year later, in January 1991, the Head Provincial Prosecutor of Oxapampa filed a formal charge with the local criminal judge against Julio Arias Dorregaray, the former subprefect of the locality, and against unidentified members of the "Batallón Nueve de Diciembre" to the effect that they had committed the crime of homicide against Fernando Mejía and Aladino Melgarejo. Dorregaray fled from Oxapampa and his present whereabouts are unknown.

On two occasions, on 6 May and 2 July 1991, the Oxapampa criminal judge requested the Military Political Chief of Mantaro-Junín, General Luis Pérez, to identify the officers who took part in the "antisubversive campaign" in Oxapampa between 13 and 17 June 1989. According to the petitioners, the Army never responded to these requests. The criminal court handling the case extended the investigation period to 26 August 1991 in order to ascertain the occurrence of the crimes detailed in the charge. According to the petitioners, the court has not taken any further action since then.

As a last resort, the petitioners reported that the Peruvian Government had published a list of Peruvians living abroad that included Raquel Mejía and had described those named in the list as subversives. The persons listed were in fact accused of supporting *Sendero Luminoso* (Shining Path) from their places of residence. The Government was accordingly calling for their extradition; if they did not return to Peru, the Government stated it would revoke their nationality.

In the particular case of Raquel Mejía, the list claimed that she was a member of an organization called "Movimiento Popular", from which she supported *Sendero Luminoso*. The Government had consequently filed criminal charges against her under the antiterrorist legislation in effect in Peru. After being formally charged, Mrs Mejía could be brought before a "faceless court".

The petitioners allege that the charges against Raquel Mejía are absolutely unfounded. In support of their arguments, the petitioners attach copies of the opinions of the Lima Provincial Prosecutor and of the Senior Prosecutor for Terrorism which show there is no evidence to substantiate the charges against Raquel Mejía.

III   PROCESSING OF THE PETITION BEFORE THE COMMISSION

[...]*

IV   OBSERVATIONS OF THE PARTIES

A   Position of the Government

The Government observed that the present petition was a repetition of Case 10.466 in which the Commission had condemned the Peruvian State for violation of the human rights of Fernando Mejía Egocheaga and Aladino Ponce Melgarejo. It added that the report in question had been published in the Commission's Annual Report for the period May 1990 - February 1991.

Based on this argument, the Peruvian Government requested the Commission to declare the present case inadmissible in accordance with Article 39(1)(b) of its Regulations.

The Government failed to refute the petitioners' allegations as to the alleged repeated violation of Mrs Raquel Martín de Mejía, the alleged failure to perform the obligation set forth in Article 1(1) of the Convention and to provide an effective remedy and judicial protection as referred to in Article 25 of the Convention. The Peruvian Government moreover also failed to present any argument in connection with the existence of criminal proceedings instituted against Mrs Raquel Martín de Mejía on grounds of alleged commission of the crime of terrorism.

---

*   **Eds:** this section, which deals with procedural issues, has not been included. The full text of the judgment is available at I BHRC 229, 4 IHRR 609 and the websites of the IACHR and University of Minnesota Human Rights Library (see *On-Line Access to Human Rights Source Materials, supra,* p xlv).

B   Position of the petitioners

Regarding admissibility of the case, the petitioners note that a petition in favor of Fernando Mejía and Aladino Melgarejo was in fact submitted to the Commission on 25 September 1989. However, they point out that Mrs Mejía, her lawyer and the human rights organizations that were helping her never gave their consent to the submission of said petition. They add that since the Peruvian Government did not respond to the Commission's requests for information, the Commission, on the basis of Article 42 of its Regulations, presumed that the facts reported were correct and in its 83/90 Report declared the Peruvian State responsible.

The petitioners consider that the case should be declared admissible for two reasons:

1   Article 44 of the Convention must not be interpreted in such a way as to prevent victims of human rights violations from making a full presentation of the questions of fact and law underlying their case, especially when a petition filed earlier was submitted without their consent or, in case of death, without the consent of their surviving relatives and when the report prepared by the Commission is based on presumptions that do not include a detailed account of the events that took place and of the persons responsible for them.

2   The present petition sets out human rights violations that were not considered in Case 10.466. In point of fact, the petitioners note that the Report 83/90 does not include violation of the right to an effective remedy in connection with Fernando Mejía Egocheaga nor the violations of the rights to humane treatment, privacy and an effective domestic remedy of Raquel Mejía.

For the reasons set forth, the petitioners request the Commission to reject the arguments used by the Peruvian Government and to declare the case admissible.

Regarding the alleged human rights violations, the petitioners request the Commission to declare Peru's international responsibility for the violation of the rights to personal liberty (Article 7), to humane treatment (Article 5) and to life (Article 4) of Fernando Mejía, in connection with the obligation assumed under Article 1(1), all of which rights are protected by the American Convention on Human Rights. They further call upon the Commission to establish that the repeated sexual abuse to which Raquel Martín de Mejía was subjected violated the provisions of Articles 5 (right to humane treatment) and 11 (right to privacy) in connection with Article 1(1) of the said international Convention and that Peru is internationally responsible.

Finally, the petitioners allege that the Peruvian State failed to respect and guarantee the right of Fernando and Raquel Mejía to an effective domestic recourse for protection against acts that violated their fundamental rights (Articles 1 and 25 of the Convention).

The petitioners base the Peruvian State's international responsibility for violation of human rights protected by the American Convention on the following points:

1   The existence of proof by witnesses and circumstantial evidence that demonstrate the involvement of members of the Peruvian Army in commission of the crimes denounced. These proofs also indicate that the crimes in question were not committed by guerrillas.

2   The facts reported fit in perfectly with the pattern of abuses committed by the Peruvian military and their *modus operandi* in previous situations. The petitioners indicate that the following pieces of evidence serve to fully demonstrate the responsibility of members of the Peruvian Army in the abduction, torture and death of Fernando Mejía and in the repeated violation of his wife Raquel Martín de Mejía:

(a) Members of the "Batallón Nueve de Diciembre" arrived in Oxapampa a few days before the events denounced took place, for the purpose of carrying out an anti-subversive campaign. They were in that city on the night that Fernando Mejía was abducted and Raquel Mejía was raped more than once. They were in the area where the bodies of Mejía and Melgarejo were found.

(b) Raquel Mejía identified the vehicle that was used in the abduction of her husband as a yellow pickup truck belonging to the Government that was normally used for the activities of the "Pichis Palcazu" special project. This truck was seen on the night of the abductions in front of the Oxapampa bar with military personnel in the back. Both Hugo Nano and his wife Nancy Verde, who were there when Professor Melgarejo was abducted, recognized that the yellow pickup belonged to the government project. In addition, the way in which the two men were abducted and the similarity of their abductors indicate that the disappearances were part of a coordinated plan in which the same government-owned vehicle was used.

(c) The FAL 7.62-mm cartridges found near the bodies of Mejía and Melgarejo link the Peruvian military with the commission of the crimes in question. These are the type of bullets normally fired by assault rifles used by the Peruvian Army.

(d) The men who abducted Fernando Mejía and the one who repeatedly raped his wife Raquel were wearing military uniforms. Although they kept their faces concealed with ski masks, at no time did these men attempt to hide that they belonged to the Peruvian Army. When Raquel Mejía went to the Municipal Library the next day she observed that the uniform worn by the soldiers billeted there was the same as that worn by the men who forced their way into her house, abducted her husband and sexually abused her.

(e) The abductors operated at night with total impunity. They moved around in a large group of over six persons, openly seized Fernando Mejía and put him in a truck that was parked in a public street without hiding their presence or their actions. The individual who sexually abused Raquel Mejía forced his way into her house on two occasions, accompanied each time by a number of soldiers. Only Army personnel could have acted with such freedom and impunity in those days, especially bearing in mind that there was a sizable military presence in Oxapampa then.

Secondly, the petitioners point out that the abduction and subsequent homicide of Fernando Mejía and the repeated sexual abuse to which Raquel Mejía was subjected are consistent with the *modus operandi* of Peruvian Army personnel in the commission of other serious human rights crimes. The general characteristics of the methods employed are as follows:

(a) the abductions are carried out at night in the victims' own homes;

(b) the persons heading up the operations usually abduct more than one person at a time. In this case, Fernando Mejía and Aladino Melgarejo were taken on the same night, with only minutes between the two abductions;

(c) the abductors wear military uniforms with ski masks to conceal their features;

(d) the victims are taken, tortured and finally executed without any trial or due process.

As their concluding point, the petitioners note that the Peruvian Government has published a list of Peruvians living abroad that includes Raquel Mejía, and has classified the persons on the list as subversives. In Raquel Mejía's case, the list names her as a member of an organization known as "Movimiento Popular", from which she is alleged to support *Sendero Luminoso*. On these grounds the Government has instituted criminal proceedings against her for alleged commission of the crime of terrorism. After the formal charge, Mrs Mejía can be tried before a "faceless court".

The petitioners allege that the charges against Raquel Mejía are absolutely unfounded since there is no evidence that demonstrates her criminal liability.

V   GENERAL CONSIDERATIONS

A   Competence of the Commission and formal requirements for admissibility

1   *Duplication of Proceedings*

[...]*

The present petition includes, besides the violations of Fernando Mejía's human rights, alleged violations of Convention-protected rights of his wife, Mrs Raquel Martín de Mejía. Regarding the latter, contrary to the Peruvian Government's assertion, the Commission is competent to pronounce on this occasion.

Accordingly, and as regards the admissibility requirement stipulated in Articles 47 of the Convention and 39(1) of the Regulations, the Commission considers that it lacks competence to reassess the human rights violations suffered by Fernando Mejía. It does not, however, consider itself blocked from pronouncing on the alleged violation of Articles 25 (right to effective domestic recourse), 5 (right to humane treatment), 11 (right to privacy) and 8 (right to due process), in respect of Raquel Martín de Mejía.

2   *Exhaustion of local remedies*

Article 46(1)(a) of the Convention specifies that for a petition or communication submitted to the Commission in accordance with Articles 44 or 45 of the Convention to be admissible, the remedies under domestic law must have been pursued and exhausted in accordance with generally recognized principles of international law.

The Inter-American Court of Human Rights, concerning the exhaustion of domestic remedies rule has stated that:

> Generally recognized principles of international law indicate, in the first place, that this is a rule whose invocation may be expressly or tacitly renounced by a State entitled to invoke it, a point that has already been recognized by the Court on an earlier occasion (see *Viviana Gallardo et al* case, Decision of November 13, 1981, No. G 101/81. Series A para 26). Secondly, the exception of non-exhaustion of domestic remedies, to be timely, must be filed

---

*   *Eds:* due to space constraints, this section has not been included. In summary, having declared itself competent to consider the case, the Commission turned to the formal requirements for admissibility of the petition. It noted that, like other international bodies, the Inter-American Commission cannot consider a petition which concerns the same facts and the same individual dealt with in a prior petition (Article 47 of the Convention and Article 39 of the Commission's Regulations). The Commission therefore held that it lacked competence to consider the grounds of human rights violations concerning Dr Fernando Mejía Egocheaga which had been previously considered by the Commission in Report 83/90, Case 10.466. It further held that although the earlier petition had been brought without the consent of Fernando Mejía's family, this was irrelevant as, unlike other international instruments, the Convention permits a petition to be lodged by a non-governmental organisation, a group of persons, or individuals who have no connection with the alleged victim (Article 44 of the Convention and Article 26(1) of the Commission's Regulations) and, as a corollary, the victim's consent is not required to a petition.

in the initial stages of the proceedings; if this is not done, tacit renunciation of use of same by the State concerned can be presumed.[1]

On applying these principles to the present case, the Commission observes that the Peruvian State omitted to file the exception to exhaustion of domestic remedies. The fact is that after 25 January 1992, when the Commission began the processing of the petition, the Peruvian State had various opportunities to indicate whether the petitioners had met the said admissibility requirement. This being so, the Commission assumes that the Peruvian State renounced filing of the exception and accordingly concludes that it is not obliged to give a ruling on this question.

B   Considerations on the substance of the case

1   Presumption of facts

The Peruvian State had various opportunities to provide information to the Commission concerning the facts denounced. However, in all its communications it limited itself to maintaining the inadmissibility of the case without in any instance discussing the detailed arguments submitted to the Commission by the petitioners, and which were transmitted by the Commission to the Government in due form, in compliance with the rules of its Regulations.

Article 42 of the Commission's Regulations specifies that:

> The facts reported in the petition whose pertinent parts have been transmitted to the government of the State in reference shall be presumed to be true if, during the maximum period set by the Commission under the provisions of Article 34, paragraph 5, the government has not provided the pertinent information, as long as other evidence does not lead to a different conclusion.

Reaffirming the provisions of the said article, the Inter-American Court of Human Rights has stated that: "... the silence of the accused or elusive or ambiguous answers on its part may be interpreted as an acknowledgment of the truth of the allegations, so long as the contrary is not indicated by the record or is not compelled as a matter of law." [2]

Accordingly the presumption of acceptance of the facts of a petition derives not only from the assumption that a State which fails to appear before an international organ whose competence it recognizes accepts such facts, but also from the tacit message conveyed when, having appeared, said State does not provide the information required or its responses are evasive and/or ambiguous.

The principles of general international law under which a State cannot evade the jurisdiction of an international agency that it has accepted, have been incorporated into the Statute of the International Court of Justice, Article 53 of which reads:

> 1   When one of the parties does not appear before the Court, or abstains from defending its case, the other party may request the Court to decide in its favor.
>
> 2   Before handing down its decision, the Court must ensure not only that it possesses jurisdiction in accordance with the provisions of Articles 36 and 37, but also that the petition is well founded in terms of facts and law.

---

1   Inter-American Court of Human Rights, *Velásquez Rodríguez* case, Preliminary Exceptions, judgment of July 26, 1987, Series C No 1, para 88.
2   Inter-American Court of Human Rights, *Velásquez Rodríguez* case, judgment of 29 July 1988, Series C No 4, para 138.

According to the above article, the ICJ must seek to preserve the interests of the parties in dispute. Within the sphere of the American Convention, however, Article 42 of the Regulations must be interpreted in light of the basic purpose of the Convention, ie protection of human rights.[3]

The Commission considers that the petitioner must provide sufficient information to enable it, firstly, to make the admissibility assessment referred to in Articles 46 and 47 of the Convention and in the pertinent articles of its Regulations and secondly, to assess the version of the facts presented in accordance with the provisions of Article 32 of its Regulations.

As a result, the Commission can only declare inadmissible a petition in which the Government has omitted to provide information when the petitioner has manifestly and evidently failed to meet the requirements for admissibility, unless additional new information provides sufficient evidence to confirm admissibility.

Regarding the substance of a case brought before the Commission, the Commission considers that a simple failure to appear on the part of a State or failure by it to supply information do not in and of themselves transform the facts denounced into truth. Rather, they need to be analyzed in light of certain criteria that make it possible to establish whether, in terms of Article 42 of the Commission's Regulations, there is "other evidence" that might lead to "a different conclusion" from that presented by the petitioner. These evaluation criteria are consistency, credibility and specificity.[4]

The ICJ, regarding the provisions of Article 53 of its Statute, has specified that in analyzing a matter submitted for its consideration the Court must assure itself, by whatever means it deems appropriate, that the facts alleged by the petitioners are well founded.[5]

The Commission considers that in determining, in a concrete case, whether the facts alleged are well founded, failure to appear on the part of the State cannot oblige the petitioners to satisfy a standard of proof equivalent to that which would have been initially required if the State had appeared. If this were to be so, the petitioner would be in the position of being able to bring additional proofs and/or to contest the Government's response. As a result, when the State does not appear or omits to provide information concerning the alleged facts, the Commission, in order to make a decision must limit itself to the arguments and proofs offered by the petitioner and other elements available to it that will enable it to decide the matter.

In the present case, since the Peruvian Government has not discussed the facts presented by the petitioners, the Commission has considered the version presented by them and, after establishing that it meets the criteria of consistency, credibility and specificity, has decided:

(a) To presume the facts relating to the repeated violation of Raquel Mejía by Peruvian Army personnel to be true

---

3   Inter-American Court of Human Rights, Restrictions to the Death Penalty (Arts 4(2) and 4(4) of the American Convention on Human Rights), Consultative Opinion C-3/83 of 8 September 1983, Series A, No 3 para 50.

4   These criteria were set implicitly by the Inter-American Court of Human Rights in the *Velásquez Rodríguez* case. Examination of consistency is the logical and rational exercise of scrutinizing the basic information provided by the petitioner in order to establish that there is no contradiction between the facts and/or the evidence submitted. The credibility of the facts is determined by assessing the version submitted, including its consistency and specificity, in the evaluation of the proofs submitted and taking into account public or well-known facts and other information that the Commission considers pertinent. Specificity, for its part, is deduced as a corollary of the preceding two criteria.

5   *Corfu Channel* case [Assessment of Compensation] [1949] ICJ 248.

The petitioners have presented a detailed and consistent version in which they state the date on which and place in which the events occurred, noting that the individual responsible was wearing Peruvian Army fatigues and was accompanied by a large number of soldiers. Another point alleged is that, at the time the acts denounced occurred, Raquel Mejía was living in an area under state of emergency legislation. In such areas the military customarily assume control of the population and set themselves up as the supreme authority, even above the duly elected and constituted civil authorities. As a consequence, they commonly perpetrate numerous human rights violations in these areas.

The credibility of the version presented by the petitioner is corroborated, in the Commission's views, by various reports of intergovernmental and nongovernmental bodies that document numerous rapes of women in Peru by members of the security forces in emergency areas and in which the specific case of Raquel Mejía is mentioned and described as representative of this situation.

In fact the Special Rapporteur against Torture appointed by the United Nations Human Rights Commission,[6] in his report for 1992, noted that in Peru, in the areas under the state of emergency, military personnel frequently resorted to sexual abuse.[7] Similarly, in the section on Peru in his 1993 report, he stated that:

> ... abundant information was also received about the practice of rape and sexual aggression frequently undergone by women in the context of the security forces' campaign against the insurgent groups ... In the areas under state of emergency ... rape seems to be used as a form of intimidation or punishment against groups of civilians suspected of collaborating with the insurgent groups ... Sexual abuse and rape appear ... to be customary in the areas under state of emergency. [8]

Amnesty International, for its part, has stated that in Peru the military personnel who operate in conflict areas have broad powers and their actions are not usually subject to any type of authorization. Back in 1986 Amnesty International had already received information on different cases of sexual abuse against women in emergency areas. In this connection, government spokesmen commented that rapes are to be expected when troops are operating in rural areas, so criminal proceedings should not be instituted to punish this type of abuse.[9] It is not therefore surprising that women living in areas subject to emergency legislation report being victims of sexual abuse by soldiers, who generally act with absolute impunity.[10] In another report on Peru, Amnesty International denounced the existence of an extended practice of rapes committed by military personnel in different incursions into rural communities.[11]

In addition, Human Rights Watch, in a study on sexual abuse against women in Peru, has reported that rape is a common practice in that country.[12] Since the start of the

---

6　At its 41st Session, the Human Rights Commission approved Resolution 1985/33, by which it resolved to appoint a Special Rapporteur to examine the questions relating to torture.

7　UN Doc. E/CN.4/1993/26, para 355.

8　*Ibid*, paras 429, 431and 432.

9　Amnesty International, *Women in the Front Line: Human Rights Violations against Women* (March 1991), p 20.

10　*Ibid*, p 20.

11　Amnesty International, *Peru: Human Rights in a Climate of Terror* (London, 1991), p 7.

12　Citing the reports on the Practice of Human Rights in different countries published by the US Department of State in 1990 and 1991. The 1990 report refers to reliable information documenting sexual abuses committed by military personnel in Peru. It further notes that the number of rapes committed by the security forces in the emergency zones is so large that it can be stated to be common practice, supported – or at least winked at – by the military chiefs. The report for 1991 also indicates that cases are continuing of sexual abuses by the security forces in the emergency zones.

counterinsurgency campaign against the armed groups, rape has become a terrible reality for women. According to this report, soldiers use sexual abuse as a weapon for punishing, intimidating, coercing, humiliating and degrading women. For a woman, living in a certain area implies running the risk of being raped, commonly for being suspected of belonging to one or the other insurgent movement. While there are no statistics on the number of rapes attributable to the security forces, Human Rights Watch reports that local groups say the number is very high.[13]

The above-mentioned report documents more than 40 cases of sexual abuse against women in Peru between 1989 and 1992. Among these, the case of Raquel Martín de Mejía is described as a classic instance.[14] In addition, the 11 March 1993 number of "Caretas" magazine, in an article on sexual violence in Peru, includes a detailed description of Mrs Mejía's case. This article also states that in a letter dated 2 March 1993, sent to President Alberto Fujimori of Peru, a group of 23 United States senators expressed their concern about the rapes committed by the security forces and the police. "The case... specifically mentioned by the U.S. senators in their letter... is that of Raquel Mejía. Her husband was killed by military personnel, who also raped her, according to her report."[15]

The petitioners have furnished circumstantial evidence that makes it possible to establish the responsibility of military personnel in the abduction, torture and killing of Fernando Mejía. They have also established the close relationship between the human rights violations committed against Dr Mejía and the indignities suffered by his wife Raquel. As the Commission has been informed, at the time the events reported took place, members of the "Batallón Nueve de Diciembre" were in Oxapampa conducting a counterinsurgency campaign. Both Professor Melgarejo's family and Raquel Mejía herself have repeatedly stated that the persons who came to their homes were wearing military uniforms and had their faces concealed by ski masks. When Mrs Mejía went to the Municipal Library the day after the events, she observed that the uniform of the soldiers billeted there was the same as that worn by the individuals who forced their way into her house.

In addition, the petitioner and the members of the Melgarejo family have all reported that the military personnel used a yellow government-owned pickup for transportation that was normally assigned to the "Pichis Palcazu" special project. Moreover, the FAL 7.62-mm cartridges found near the bodies of Mejía and Melgarejo point to the Peruvian Army, since they are the bullets normally used in the Army's assault rifles. Finally, as a result of the investigations performed in January 1991 the Head Provincial Prosecutor of Oxapampa filed a formal charge in the local criminal court against Julio Arias Dorregaray, the former subprefect of the locality, and against unidentified members of the "Batallón Nueve de Diciembre" in respect of commission of the crime of homicide against Fernando Mejía and Aladino Melgarejo.

The Commission considers that the acts against the husband of Raquel Mejía are closely connected with the sexual abuse that she underwent since they took place the same night and were perpetrated by the same individuals. On these grounds, the circumstantial evidence provided, while not directly pertaining to the case in question, is sufficient, in the Commission's view, to presume the responsibility of troops of the Peruvian Army in the commission of the abuses against Raquel Mejía.

---

13 Human Rights Watch, Americas Watch and the Women's Rights Project, *Untold Terror: Violence Against Women in Peru's Armed Conflict*, pp 2 and 3.

14 *Ibid*, pp 41ff.

15 Caretas, *Violencia Sexual* (11 March 1993), pp 26ff.

(b)   To presume the nonexistence of effective domestic recourses that would permit remedies for the human rights violations suffered by Fernando and Raquel Mejía

The petitioners have provided the Commission with a detailed and concise version of the judicial remedies pursued to obtain redress for the human rights violations undergone by Fernando Mejía. The affirmations made in the petition have been sufficiently documented by submission of copies of the different legal proceedings instituted. It is important to note that in Peru the opening of criminal proceedings and of investigations to clarify commission of a crime of a criminal nature are an exclusive monopoly of the Government Attorney's office. Private individuals may only have a limited involvement in the instituting – filing of a petition – and initiating of a criminal trial because Peruvian criminal procedure does not include provision for a private plaintiff, as found in other Latin American legislations.

As noted in the petition, the Peruvian State has failed to properly investigate the abduction and subsequent homicide of Dr Mejía. Notwithstanding the opening of criminal proceedings by the Oxapampa Provincial Prosecutor, the chief individual involved had fled the area. To this circumstance was added the difficulties created by the Army itself, which refused to identify the officers who took part in the counterinsurgency actions between 13 and 17 June 1989, in the locality.

The credibility of the petitioners' petition is supported by the Commission's own assessments, the Commission having repeatedly raised the problem of impunity in Peru through inclusion of recommendations in reports on individual cases[16] or in its special reports. In this respect it is apposite to cite certain of the Commission's observations:

> One element that has been particularly disturbing to the Commission is that, up till 1990, no member of the security forces had been tried and punished for involvement in human rights violations. The fact that no one had been sanctioned was an indictment not only of the authors of very serious human rights violations, but also of the Peruvian State organs charged with enforcing the law. Not only do those guilty of serious human rights violations go unpunished, but there are no effective measures taken to defend the rights of the affected parties.[17]

Moreover:

> in cases of human rights violations by National Police and Armed Forces personnel, the question of competent jurisdiction for trying and punishing those alleged responsible has frequently been raised. The military courts have always claimed authority to try military and police personnel, on the grounds that such acts committed in the performance of their official duties. As a result, there have been very few cases in which the guilty parties were determined, and even fewer in which police or military personnel whose guilt has been established by a military court have actually been punished.[18]

Raquel Mejía informed the Commission that when, on 20 June 1989, she filed her declaration with the Oxapampa police concerning the abduction and subsequent homicide of her husband, she did not report the sexual abuse to which she had been subjected because:

---

16   In 1988, the Commission adopted fourteen individual cases in which the Peruvian State's responsibility for serious human rights violations was established. In 1989 it adopted two such cases, and in 1990 and 1991 fifty-one, and then a further five in the course of 1992 and 1993.

17   Report on the Situation of Human Rights in Peru, OEA/Ser.L/V/II.83, doc 31 (12 March 1993), para 26.

18   Annual Report of the Inter-American Commission on Human Rights, 1993, OEA/Ser.L/V/II.85, doc 8 (11 February 1994), p 545.

[I was] fearful that the violations committed against my person would have caused me to be ostracized and exposed me to greater danger or physical harm ...

Furthermore, it has been noted that there are not in Peru any effective domestic remedies through which a victim of sexual abuse by members of the security forces can obtain an impartial investigation of the events and punishment of those guilty. This situation is aggravated in the emergency zones since the exercise of authority in them is under the control of the same individuals who perpetrate serious human rights violations and because the military courts assume jurisdiction in cases where a member of the security forces is the accused party. As a result, in virtually no case are individuals accused of sexual abuse and other serious human rights violations convicted.

The Commission observes that the reasons given by the petitioner for not submitting a petition in the domestic courts are supported by different documents published by intergovernmental bodies and nongovernmental organizations which expressly note that women who have been victims of sexual abuse by members of the security forces or police have no means open to them for obtaining a remedy for the violations of their rights.

The UN Special Rapporteur against Torture observes in this connection that:

it is reported ... that those guilty of [rape and other sexual abuses] were rarely brought to trial even in those cases where complaints were filed with competent authorities. The military courts took no action in these cases and failed to place the accused at the disposal of the civil courts, as they were required to do by law. This situation of impunity together with other factors such as the difficulty of submitting evidence or society's attitude to the victims meant that a large percentage of these cases were never even reported.[19]

Amnesty International has stated that despite the existence of a large number of cases of sexual violations in emergency areas, to date no member of the security forces operating in those areas has been tried for rape; neither have effective investigations been made following complaints submitted by women who have been victims of sexual abuse by soldiers.[20]

Human Rights Watch, for its part, has observed that despite the widespread incidence of sexual abuse in Peru, very few police and even fewer members of the security forces have been tried for this abuse, even in cases where complaints were filed with the appropriate authorities. On the contrary, the evidence gathered demonstrates that the police and armed forces protect those guilty of these violations and grant them promotions, thereby implicitly tolerating the commission of these crimes.[21]

Human Rights Watch also maintains that it is practically impossible to prove a charge of rape against a member of the security forces. The emergency legislation specifies that crimes committed in the "performance of duty" fall under military jurisdiction, in accordance with the Code of Military Justice. Although sexual abuse is a common crime – and not one of the so-called "duty crimes" – there have been no rape cases in which the ordinary courts have exercised jurisdiction.[22]

Women who have been raped by members of the security forces do not report these assaults for two reasons: public humiliation and the perception that those responsible

---

19 UN Doc E/CN.4/1994/31, para 433.
20 Amnesty International, *supra* (note 9), p 22.
21 Human Rights Watch, *supra* (note 13), p 3.
22 *Ibid*, p 4.

will never be punished. In addition, they are usually threatened with reprisals against themselves or their families if they do report them.[23]

Finally, the response given by President Fujimori himself when questioned about the many sexual abuses perpetrated by military personnel in the emergency zones is of particular importance: "In cases where women have been raped, I hope investigations are being carried out. There is a regrettable tradition of impunity in Peru."[24]

(c)　To presume that the Peruvian Government had no grounds for instituting criminal proceedings against Raquel Mejía charging her with committing the crime of terrorism

The petitioners have submitted to the Commission various pieces of evidence to the effect that criminal proceedings have been opened against Raquel Mejía for alleged commission of the crime of terrorism. This evidence includes a copy of a list published by the Government of various Peruvian nationals residing abroad and who, allegedly, contribute from their places of residence to supporting the activities of *Sendero Luminoso* in Peru. This list, headed "The Organizations and their Leaders", includes the name of Raquel Mejía and states that she belongs to an organization called "Movimiento Popular" through which she collaborates with *Sendero Luminoso* from Sweden.

In addition, the petitioners have provided the Commission with a copy of an opinion issued by the Lima Provincial Prosecutor in which the Prosecutor, besides stating that proceedings have been instituted against Mrs Mejía and that a warrant has been issued for her arrest, states that "[r]egarding those accused of proselytizing in favor of the PCP-SL (*Partido Comunista Peruano-Sendero Luminoso* (Peruvian Communist Party – Shining Path), notwithstanding the large number of people involved and the time that has elapsed, our Diplomatic Mission has not been able to send us a report on the activities that the accused have carried out or are presently carrying out ..."

Recording those listed, who include Raquel Mejía, the Prosecutor stated: "... the evidence that would provide the basis for formulation of the charge *has not to date been assembled*, which means that their participation in the events under examination cannot for the moment be established."

Notwithstanding the Provincial Prosecutor's opinion, the Lima Senior Prosecutor for Terrorism filed a formal indictment against Raquel Mejía for belonging to an organization abroad – identified as *Movimiento Popular* – that provides support to the Shining Path group. The indictment charges her with alleged commission of the crime of terrorism against the State and recommends that she be condemned to 20 years' imprisonment plus payment of a sum of money as civil reparation for the State.

The Commission does not have information on the final verdict in this case; however, in accordance with the Peruvian antiterrorist legislation, the accused should in this instance be tried by means of oral proceedings by a "faceless court".

2　Questions raised

Once the Commission has established the facts of the present petition, it must proceed to ascertain whether they amount to violations of any of the rights protected by the American Convention. In particular, the Commission must establish:

1　Whether the sexual abuses to which Raquel Mejía was subjected constitute violation of the rights to humane treatment (Article 5) and to privacy (Article 11), in connection with the obligation set forth in Article 1(1);

23　*Ibid*, p 5.
24　"Rapists in Uniform: Peru Looks the Other Way", *The New York Times*, 29 April 1993.

2   Whether the impossibility of effective domestic recourse to remedy the violations of Fernando and Raquel Mejía's human rights constitutes a violation of the right to due process (Article 8) and to judicial protection (Article 25), all in connection with the obligation contained in Article 1(1); and

3   Whether the groundless instituting of criminal proceedings for terrorism in the absence of the accused constitutes a violation of the right to due process (Article 8), in connection with the obligation contained in Article 1(1).

3   Analysis

(a)   The repeated sexual abuse to which Raquel Mejía was subjected constitutes a violation of Article 5 and Article 11 of the American Convention on Human Rights

Current international law establishes that sexual abuse committed by members of security forces, whether as a result of a deliberate practice promoted by the State or as a result of failure by the State to prevent the occurrence of this crime, constitutes a violation of the victims' human rights, especially the right to physical and mental integrity.

In the context of international humanitarian law, Article 27[25] of the Fourth Geneva Convention of 1949 concerning the protection due to civilians in times of war explicitly prohibits sexual abuse.[26] Article 147[27] of that Convention which lists acts considered as "serious offenses" or "war crimes" includes rape in that it constitutes "torture or inhuman treatment".[28] The International Committee of the Red Cross (ICRC) has declared that the "serious offense" of "deliberately causing great suffering or seriously harming physical integrity or health" includes sexual abuse.[29]

Moreover, Article 76[30] of Additional Protocol I to the 1949 Geneva Conventions expressly prohibits rape or other types of sexual abuse. Article 85(4),[31] for its part, states that when these practices are based on racial discrimination they constitute "serious offenses". As established in the Fourth Convention and Protocol I, any act of rape committed individually constitutes a war crime.[32]

---

25   Article 27, insofar as it concerns us, reads: "Protected persons are entitled, in all circumstances, to respect for their persons, their honour, their family rights, their religious convictions and practices, and their manners and customs. They shall at all times be humanely treated, and shall be protected especially against all acts of violence or threats, thereof and against insults and public curiosity. Women shall be especially protected against any attack on their honour, in particular, against rape, enforced prostitution or any form of indecent assault."

26   Final Report of the Commission of Experts established pursuant to Security Council Resolution 780/1992 (5 May 1994), p 17.

27   Article 147 reads: "Serious offenses are those that involve one or more of the following acts, 'if committed against persons or property protected by the present Convention: ... *torture or inhuman treatment, including ... wilfully fact of causing great suffering or serious injury to body or health ...'*"

28   Final Report of the Commission of Experts, *supra* (note 26), p 17.

29   ICRC, Aide Mémoire (3 Dec 1992) cited in T Meron, *Rape as a Crime under International Humanitarian Law*, 87 AJIL 426.

30   Article 76, entitled "Protection of Women", specifies that: "1. Women shall be afforded special respect and protected in particular against rape, forced prostitution and any other form of indecent assault."

31   Article 85(4) states that: ... "The following acts will be considered serious offenses under the present Protocol when committed intentionally and in violation of the Conventions or the Protocol: ... (c) The practices of apartheid and other inhuman and degrading practices, based on racial discrimination, that entail an outrage against personal dignity."

32   Final Report of the Commission of Experts, *supra* (note 26), p 17.

In the case of non-international conflicts, both Article 3[33] common to the four Geneva Conventions and Article 4(2)[34] of Protocol II additional to the Conventions, include the prohibition against rape and other sexual abuse insofar as they are the outcome of harm deliberately influenced on a person.[35] The ICRC has stated that the prohibition laid down in Protocol II reaffirms and complements the common Article 3 since it was necessary to strengthen the protection of women, who can be victims of rape, forced prostitution or other types of abuse.[36]

Article 5 of the Statute of the International Tribunal established for investigating the serious violations of international humanitarian law committed in the territory of the former Yugoslavia, considers rape practiced on a systematic and large scale a crime against humanity.[37]

In the context of international human rights law, the American Convention on Human Rights stipulates in its Article 5 that:

1   Every person has the right to have his physical, mental and moral integrity respected.

2   No one shall be subjected to torture or to cruel, inhuman or degrading punishment or treatment ...

The letter of the Convention does not specify what is to be understood by torture. However, in the inter-American sphere, acts constituting torture are established in the Inter-American Convention to Prevent and Punish Torture, which states:

> ... torture will be understood to be any act performed intentionally by which physical and mental pain or suffering is inflicted on a person for purposes of criminal investigation, as a means of intimidation, as a personal punishment, as a preventive measure, as a penalty or for any other purpose. Torture will also be understood to be application to a person of methods designed to efface the victim's personality or to diminish his physical or mental capacity, even if they do not cause physical pain or mental anguish.[38]

The following will be guilty of the crime of torture:

(a) Public employees or officials who are acting in that capacity order, instigate, induce its commission, commit it directly or, when in a position to prevent it, do not do so.

---

33   Article 3 states: "The following are prohibited, at any time and in any place..."(a) Attacks against life and bodily integrity, especially homicide in all its forms, mutilations, cruel treatment, torture and ordeals; ... (c) Attacks against personal dignity ..."

34   Article 4(2) of Protocol II, for its part, states: "1. All persons who are not participating directly in the hostilities, or have ceased to participate in them, whether or not deprived of their liberty, shall be entitled to respect of their persons, their honor, their religious convictions and practices.... 2. The following shall be prohibited at all times and in all places with respect to the persons referred to in paragraph 1: (a) Attacks against the life, health and physical and mental integrity of persons, in particular homicide and cruel treatments such as torture ... (e) Attacks against personal dignity, especially humiliating and degrading treatment, rape, forced prostitution and any form of indecent assault;..."

35   Final Report of the Commission of Experts, *supra* (note 26), p 18

36   Yves Sandoz, Christophe Swinarski, Bruno Zimmerman, eds, *ICRC Commentary on the Additional Protocols of 8 June 1977 to the Geneva Conventions of 12 August 1949* (Geneva: Martinus Nijhoff Publishers, 1987), p 1375.

37   United Nations: Secretary General Report on aspects of establishing an international tribunal for the prosecutions of persons responsible for serious violations of International Humanitarian Law committed in the territory of the former Yugoslavia, 32 ILM, 1159, 1173, 1174 (1993).

38   *See* Article 2 of the Convention.

(b) Persons who, at the instigation of the public officials or employees referred to in paragraph 1, order, instigate or induce its commission, commit it directly or are accomplices in its commission.[39]

Accordingly, for torture to exist three elements have to be combined:

1   it must be an intentional act through which physical and mental pain and suffering is inflicted on a person;

2   it must be committed with a purpose;

3   it must be committed by a public official or by a private person acting at the instigation of the former.

Regarding the first element, the Commission considers that rape is a physical and mental abuse that is perpetrated as a result of an act of violence. The definition of rape contained in Article 170 of the Peruvian Criminal Code confirms this by using the phrasing "[h]e who, *with violence* or serious threat, obliges a person to practice the sex act ...". The Special Rapporteur against Torture has noted that sexual abuse is one of the various methods of physical torture.[40] Moreover, rape is considered to be a method of psychological torture because its objective, in many cases, is not just to humiliate the victim but also her family or community.[41] In this connection, the above-mentioned Special Rapporteur has stated that, particularly in Peru, "... rape would appear to be a weapon used to punish, intimidate and humiliate."[42]

Rape causes physical and mental suffering in the victim. In addition to the violence suffered at the time it is committed, the victims are commonly hurt or, in some cases, are even made pregnant. The fact of being made the subject of abuse of this nature also causes a psychological trauma that results, on the one hand, from having been humiliated and victimized, and on the other, from suffering the condemnation of the members of their community if they report what has been done to them.[43]

Raquel Mejía was a victim of rape, and in consequence of an act of violence that caused her "physical and mental pain and suffering". As she states in her testimony, after having been raped she "was in a state of shock, sitting there alone in her room". She was in no hurry to file the appropriate complaint for fear of suffering "public ostracism". "The victims of sexual abuse do not report the matter because they feel humiliated. In addition, no woman wants to publicly announce that she has been raped. She does not know how her husband will react. [Moreover], the integrity of the family is at stake, the children might feel humiliated if they know what has happened to their mother".*

The second element establishes that for an act to be torture it must have been committed intentionally, ie to produce a certain result in the victim. The Inter-American Convention to Prevent and Punish Torture includes, among other purposes, personal punishment and intimidation.

Raquel Mejía was raped with the aim of punishing her personally and intimidating her. According to her testimony, the man who raped her told her that she, too, was wanted as a subversive, like her husband. He also told her that her name was on a list of persons connected with terrorism and, finally, warned her that her friendship with a

---

39   *See* Article 3 of the Convention.

40   UN Doc E/CN.4/1986/15, para 119.

41   D Blatt, *Recognizing Rape as a Method of Torture*, 19 NYU RevL & Soc Change 821, 854.

42   UN Doc E/CN.4/1994/31, para 431.

43   D Blatt, *supra* (note 41), p 855.

*   *Eds:* no source is given for this quote in the original text.

former official in the previous government would not serve to protect her. On the second occasion, before leaving he threatened to come back and rape her again. Raquel Mejía felt terrorized not only for her own safety but also for that of her daughter who was sleeping in another room and for the life of her husband.

The third requirement of the definition of torture is that the act must have been perpetrated by a public official or by a private individual at the instigation of the former.

As concluded in the foregoing, the man who raped Raquel Mejía was member of the security forces who had himself [been] accompanied by a large group of soldiers.

Accordingly, the Commission, having established that the three elements of the definition of torture are present in the case under consideration, concludes that the Peruvian State is responsible for violation of Article 5 of the American Convention.

The petitioners have also asserted that the sexual abuse suffered by Raquel Mejía violates the provisions of Article 11 of the Convention.

Said article specifies that a State must guarantee everybody protection of their honor and dignity, within the framework of a broader right, namely the right to privacy.

The relevant parts of paragraphs 1 and 2 of this article read as follows:

1   Everyone has the right to have his honor respected and his dignity respected.

2   No one may be the object of arbitrary or abusive interference with his private life ...

The Special Rapporteur against Torture has stated that "Rape is a particularly base attack against human dignity. Women are affected in the most sensitive part of their personality and the long-term effects are perforce extremely harmful, since in the majority of cases the necessary psychological treatment and care will not and cannot be provided."[44]

The Commission considers that sexual abuse, besides being a violation of the victim's physical and mental integrity, implies a deliberate outrage to their dignity. In this respect, it becomes a question that is included in the concept of "private life". The European Court of Human Rights has observed that the concept of private life extends to a person's physical and moral integrity, and consequently includes his sex life.[45]

For the Commission, therefore, the rapes suffered by Raquel Mejía, in that they affected both her physical and her moral integrity, including her personal dignity, constituted a violation of Article 11 of the Convention, responsibility for which is attributable to the Peruvian State.

Article 1(1) of the Convention states:

The State Parties to this Convention undertake to respect the rights and freedoms recognized herein and to ensure to all persons subject to their jurisdiction the free and full exercise of those rights and freedoms.

The Inter-American Court of Human Rights has interpreted this article as establishing two obligations for the States Parties to the Convention: that of *respecting* the rights and freedoms recognized in it and that of *ensuring* their free and full exercise to individuals under their jurisdiction.[46] According to the Court, any form of exercise of public power

44   UN Doc E/CN.4/1994/31, para 580.

45   *See X and Y v The Netherlands,* Application No 8978/80, Series A No 167.

that violates the rights protected by the Convention is unlawful. Thus, when an organ or agent of the public authority violates any of these rights, this is a violation of the obligation to "respect", and consequently a violation of Article 1(1).[47]

On the basis of these considerations, the Commission concludes that since the Peruvian State omitted to respect the rights to humane treatment and to protection of her honor and dignity of Raquel Mejía, the State is in violation of the obligation contained in Article 1(1).

(b) The impossibility for Raquel Mejía to access domestic recourses for remedying the violations of her husband's human rights and of her own constitutes a violation of Article 25 and 8(1), in relation to Article 1(1) of the Convention

Article 25 and 8(1) of the Convention respectively provide as follows:

Article 25

1 Everyone has the right to simple and prompt recourse, or any other effective recourse, to a competent court or tribunal for protection against acts that violate his fundamental rights recognized by the constitution or laws of the state concerned or by this Convention...

2 The States Parties undertake:

(a) to ensure that any person claiming such remedy shall have his rights determined by the competent authority provided for by the legal system of the State;

(b) to develop the possibilities of judicial remedy; and

(c) to ensure that the competent authorities shall enforce such remedies when granted.

Article 8

1 Every person has the right to a hearing, with due guarantees and within a reasonable time, by a competent, independent, and impartial tribunal, previously established by law, in the substantiation of any accusation of a criminal nature made against him or for the determination of his rights and obligations of a civil, labor, fiscal, or any other nature.

The Commission has had opportunity to pronounce on the interpretation of these articles in previous cases in which the scope of the right to effective recourse in the context of the provisions of the American Convention was established.[48]

Concerning Article 1(1), the Commission, citing the Inter-American Court of Human Rights in the *Velásquez Rodríguez* case, has stated:

the second obligation of the States Parties is that of "ensuring" the free and full exercise of the rights recognized in the Convention to all persons subject to their jurisdiction ... Consequently, the States must *prevent, investigate and punish any violation* of the rights recognized by the Convention ... The Court expanded this concept in various subsequent paragraphs of the same judgment, for example: "The decisive factor is to determine whether a particular violation of the rights recognized by the Convention has taken place with the *support or the tolerance of the public authorities* or whether the latter have acted in such a way that the violation has occurred without any prevention or *with impunity*". "The State has the *juridical duty* to prevent, to the extent it reasonably can, human rights

---

46 *Velásquez Rodríguez* case, *supra* (note 2), paras 165 and 166.

47 *Ibid*, para 169.

48 *See* in particular Reports 28/92 (Argentina) and 29/92 (Uruguay), Report of the IACHR 1992-1993, OEA/Ser.L/V/II.83, Doc 14 (12 March 1993).

violations, to *purposefully investigate* with the means at its disposal, such violations as may be committed within the sphere of its jurisdiction in order to identify those responsible, *apply to them the appropriate penalties* and ensure adequate compensation for the victim"; ... "if *the State apparatus* acts in such a way that *the violation remains unpunished* and the victim's full rights are not restored to him to the extent possible, *it can be affirmed that the State has failed to perform its duty to ensure free and full exercise of said rights to all persons* under its jurisdiction". Regarding the obligation to investigate, the Commission notes that this must be "... for a purpose and *be assumed by the State as a specific juridical duty and not as a simple matter of management of private interests* that depends on the initiative of the victim or his family in bringing suit or on the provision of evidence by private sources, without *the public authority effectively seeking to establish the truth*" ...[49]

The obligation contained in Article 1(1) is a necessary corollary of the right of every individual to recourse to a tribunal to obtain judicial protection when he believes he has been a victim of violation of any of his human rights. If this were not so, the right to obtain effective recourse set forth in Article 25 would be absolutely without content.

In this connection, the Inter-American Court of Human Rights has observed as follows:

[In the terms of the Convention] the States Parties undertake to make effective judicial recourses available to human rights violations victims (Article 25), recourses that must be substantiated in accordance with the rules of due process (Article 8(1)), all within the general obligation on the same States to ensure the free and full exercise of the rights recognized in the Convention to all persons under their jurisdiction (Article 1(1)).[50]

The Commission considers that the right to a recourse set forth in Article 25, interpreted in conjunction with the obligation in Article 1(1) and the provisions of Article 8(1), must be understood as the right of every individual to go to a tribunal when any of his rights have been violated (whether a right protected by the Convention, the constitution or the domestic laws of the State concerned), to obtain a judicial investigation conducted by a competent, impartial and independent tribunal that will establish whether or not a violation has taken place and will set, when appropriate, adequate compensation.

In this way, when a human rights violation is the outcome of an act classified as criminal, the victim is entitled to obtain from the State a judicial investigation that is conducted "purposefully with the means at its disposal ... in order to identify those responsible [and] apply to them the appropriate penalties ..."

Purposeful investigation, in the Commission's view, implies that the competent State authority "will develop the possibilities of judicial remedy",[51] ie that it will undertake the investigation "as a specific juridical duty and not as a simple matter of management of private interests that depends on the initiative of the victim or of his family in bringing suit or on the provision of evidence by private sources, without the public authority effectively seeking to establish the truth ...". Thus, the obligation to investigate purposefully means in practice that the State will act with due diligence, ie with the existing means at its disposal, and will endeavor to arrive at a decision.[52] However, when the State has performed its obligation to diligently investigate the matter, the fact that the investigation does not produce a positive result or the decision is not favorable to the petitioner does not *per se* demonstrate that the latter has not had access to a

---

49   *Ibid*, Report No 28/92 (Argentina), 40.
50   *Velásquez Rodríguez case, supra* (note 2), para 91.
51   *See* Article 25(2) (b).
52   *See* Article 25(2)(a).

recourse.[53] According to Article 25 of the Convention, the right to judicial protection includes the obligation of the State to guarantee the enforcement of any remedy when granted.[54]

In this way, within the context of the Convention the term "recourse" must be understood in a broad sense and not be limited to the meaning that this word has in the legal terminology of the States' procedural legislation.

The American Convention requires the States to offer effective recourses to human rights violations victims. The formal existence of such recourses is not sufficient to demonstrate their effectiveness; to be effective, a recourse must be adequate and efficacious. Adequate means that the function of the recourse in a State's domestic legal system must be appropriate for protecting the juridical situation affected. A recourse is efficacious when it is capable of producing the result for which it was designed.[55]

Whether the existence or not of an effective recourse is established in a concrete case and taking into consideration the special features of each legislation, the Commission understands that, in those States where determination of the civil reparation of injury caused by an unlawful act is subject to establishment of same in a criminal trial, the instituting of criminal action and the subsequent furthering of the proceedings by the State is the adequate recourse required by the victim.

In the case under analysis, the Commission, on the basis of the facts reported, presumed that Raquel Mejía had not had access to an effective recourse that would have remedied the human rights violations suffered by her. As established, Raquel Mejía did not file a complaint with the domestic courts since practice in Peru is that this type of act involving State agents is not investigated while moreover those who report them run the risk of reprisals.

The Peruvian State's failure to give the victim access to a judicial investigation conducted by an independent and impartial tribunal made it, in practice, materially impossible for her to exercise her right to obtain compensation. The fact is that, in Peruvian law, the obtaining of civil compensation for injuries resulting from an unlawful act in the criminal category is subject to establishment of the crime by means of criminal proceedings.[56]

For this reason, in the concrete case of Raquel Mejía, the Peruvian State's failure to guarantee her right to an effective recourse, besides constituting a violation of her right to judicial protection, also constituted a violation of her right to go to a tribunal that would determine whether she was entitled to compensation for injuries suffered as a result of the sexual abuse to which she was subjected.[57]

---

53 *Velásquez Rodríguez* case, *supra* (note 2), paras 177 and 67.
54 *See* Article 25(2)(c).
55 *Velásquez Rodríguez* case, *supra* (note 2), paras 63, 64 and 66.
56 Article 3 of the Peruvian Code of Criminal Procedure specifies that: "When in the course of civil proceedings reasonable indications are brought to light of commission of a crime calling for official prosecution, the judge shall inform the representative of the Government Attorney's office so that the pertinent criminal proceedings may be instituted. In this case, the judge shall suspend the civil proceedings, if he considers that the criminal judgment may influence the decision to be handed down in the civil case."
57 Article 8 of the Convention provides, in this connection, that "Every person has the right to a hearing ... by a competent tribunal ... for the determination of his rights ... of a civil ... nature".

The American Convention establishes a distinction between the petitioner and the victim. While the term "petitioner" refers to the person with active legitimation to file a petition with the system, the word "victim" refers to individuals who have been impacted by violation of their rights. The Commission understands that, in cases where the right to life is violated, omission by the State to provide effective recourses affects the family of the dead person and, therefore, makes them into indirect "victims" of the violation of the right to judicial protection defined in a broad sense, ie including the right to compensation.

The Commission has presumed that the Peruvian State omitted to guarantee the right to an effective recourse in the case of Fernando Mejía. In his case, adequate recourse was judicial investigation by the State through initiation of criminal proceedings and, once the existence of an unlawful act was established, determination of compensation for the injuries caused to the victim. While the pertinent criminal proceedings were instituted, the behavior of the State organs, namely the Government Attorney's office, the judge assigned to the case and the Peruvian Armed Forces in delaying or obstructing the investigation, rendered the recourse inefficacious in practice.

The State's failure to provide for a thorough investigation in the case of Fernando Mejía affected his wife's right to an effective recourse and, according to Peruvian law, the fact that the existence of an unlawful act was not established through criminal proceedings prevented Raquel Mejía's access to a tribunal to determine whether compensation was due to her.

On the basis of the analysis made above, the Commission concludes that the Peruvian State, in not offering effective recourses to Raquel Mejía in both the case of the homicide of her husband and in connection with the violations of her own rights, constituted violation of the rights set forth in Articles 1(1), 8(1) and 25 of the Convention.

(c)   The groundless instituting of criminal proceedings for terrorism against Raquel Mejía constitutes a violation of the right to due process (Article 8), in conjunction with the obligation contained in Article 1(1)

[...]*

VI   CONCLUSIONS

The Commission, on the basis of the considerations analyzed in this report, formulates the following conclusions:

1   In application of Articles 47 of the Convention and 39 of its Regulations:

(a) it declares the petitions concerning the human rights violations suffered by Fernando Mejía inadmissible;

(b) it declares the petitions concerning the human rights violations suffered by Raquel Mejía admissible.

2   In regard to the petitions considered admissible it concludes that:

(a) the Peruvian State is responsible for the violation of the right to humane treatment (Article 5) and the right to protection of honor and dignity (Article 11)

---

*   *Eds:* due to space constraints, this section has not been included. The Commission went on to examine the provisions of Decree Law 25.475, which set out various procedures for the investigation and trial of crimes of terrorism, as well as stipulating the penalty for those offences. It concluded that the law itself and the use made of it against Ms Mejía violated the right to a fair trial guaranteed by articles 8 and 1(1) of the American Convention.

of Raquel Mejía and of the general obligation to respect and guarantee the exercise of these rights contained in the Convention (Article 1(1)).

(b) the Peruvian State is responsible for the violation of the right to an effective recourse (Article 25), the right to due process (Article 8) and of the general obligation to respect and guarantee the exercise of these rights contained in the Convention (Article 1(1)).

(c) Article 13 of Decree Law 25.475 is incompatible with the right to a fair trial protected by Article 8 of the Convention and, in consequence, constitutes a violation of the general obligation contained in Article 1(1) of same.

(d) the application of the said article in the specific case of Raquel Mejía constitutes a violation of her right to presumption of innocence and to be heard by an impartial tribunal (Article 8(1) and (2)).

VII   RECOMMENDATIONS

Therefore, the **COMMISSION**, in consideration of its analysis and of the law, **HEREBY AGREES**:

1   *To declare* that the Peruvian State is responsible for violating the right to humane treatment, the right to protection of one's honor and dignity, the right to a fair trial and the right to judicial protection guaranteed, respectively, in Articles 5, 11, 8 and 25 of the American Convention, and its general obligation to respect and guarantee the exercise of those rights, under Article 1.1 of the Convention.

2   *To recommend* to the Peruvian State that it conduct a thorough, rapid and impartial investigation into the events in the kidnapping, torture and subsequent murder of Fernando Mejía, in order to identify those responsible and, where appropriate, impose the appropriate punishment.

3   *To recommend* to the Peruvian State that it conduct a thorough, rapid and impartial investigation of the sexual abuse of which Raquel Mejía was the victim, in order to identify the perpetrators so that they may be punished in accordance with the law, and that it pay the injured party a fair compensation.

4   *To recommend* to the Peruvian State that it abolish or amend Article 13 of Decree Law 25.475, so that it guarantees everyone's right to a fair trial.

5   *To recommend* to the Peruvian State that it drop the criminal proceedings against Raquel Mejía for the alleged crime of terrorism, inasmuch as it has failed to guarantee her right to a fair trial.

6   *To publish* this Report in the Annual Report to the General Assembly.

CASE NO 47

FERNANDES v BRAZIL

INTER-AMERICAN COMMISSION ON HUMAN RIGHTS

Report No: 54/01

Case No: 12.051

Decision: 16 April 2001

Panel: Grossman (*Chairman*); Méndez, Altolaguirre; Goldman, Laurie and Prado Vallejo.

Human rights — Violence against women — Obligation of the State to prevent, investigate and punish violations of rights by private actors — American Convention on Human Rights, arts 1(1), 8, 24, 25 and 28 — American Declaration of the Rights and Duties of Man, arts II and XVIII — Inter-American Convention on the Prevention, Punishment, and Eradication of Violence against Women (Convention of Belém do Pará), arts 2, 3, 4, 5, 7 and 12

BACKGROUND

The petitioner, Ms Maria da Penha Maia Fernandes, was married to Mr Heredia Viveiros, who had engaged in physical violence against her and their daughters over many years. In May 1983, her husband shot her while she was sleeping, in an attempt to murder her. Although she survived, she sustained serious injuries, including paraplegia. Two weeks later, her husband again attempted to murder her, on this occasion allegedly trying to electrocute her while she was bathing. At that stage, Ms Fernandes decided to seek a legal separation from him.

A criminal judicial investigation was initiated in June 1983, a few days after the second assault, and in September 1984 criminal charges were laid against Mr Viveiros. However, the trial proceedings were not completed until May 1991, when the jury found Mr Viveiros guilty; he was sentenced to 15 years' imprisonment. Mr Viveiros appealed against this decision, and three years later the Appeal Court overturned the decision of the jury. A second trial by jury took place in March 1996, which resulted in Mr Viveiros being convicted again and sentenced to 10½ years' imprisonment. An appeal against that decision, lodged in April 1997, was still pending at the time the matter came before the Inter-American Commission on Human Rights in August 1998, more than 15 years after the original events. Under the Brazilian statute of limitations, this lengthy delay in handing down a final decision on the case risked it being time-barred as in 2002, 20 years would have elapsed since the commission of the offence, preventing the accused from being held accountable for the crime committed.

Ms Fernandes and a number of non-governmental organisations filed a petition with the Commission, claiming that the delays in dealing with the cases against Mr Viveiros had led to effective impunity for him and that this situation violated a number of Ms Fernandes' human rights, including under article XVIII (right to justice) of the American Declaration of the Rights and Duties of Man; articles 8 (right to fair trial) and 25 (right to judicial protection) of the American Convention on Human Rights, in conjunction with article 1(1), which obliges States parties to respect and guarantee the exercise of these rights; as well as article 24 of the Convention and articles II and XVIII of the Declaration (right to equality before the law). It was also argued that the State had breached its duties to refrain from, prevent and punish violence against women under article 7 of the Inter-American Convention on the Prevention, Punishment, and Eradication of Violence against Women (Convention of Belém do Pará), since the failure by the authorities to prosecute diligently in this case was allegedly not an isolated incident, but an example of a pattern of impunity in cases of domestic violence against women in Brazil.

HELD (finding various violations of the Convention, the Declaration and the Convention of Belém do Pará)

1 The obligation of the State to ensure the free and full exercise of the rights in the Convention to every person subject to its jurisdiction involved a duty of the State to organise the governmental apparatus and the structure through which public power was exercised so that they were capable of juridically ensuring the enjoyment of those rights. (Para 43)

2 In this case the failure of the Brazilian court to hand down a final ruling in the prosecution against Mr Viveiros seventeen years after the events in question was the result of inefficiency, negligence, and failure to act on the part of the Brazilian judicial authorities and unjustified delay by the prosecution. These failures stood in the way of punishment of the accused, and raised the spectre of impunity and failure to compensate the victim as a result of the possibility that prosecution for the offence would become time-barred. They demonstrated that the State had not been capable of organizing its entities in a manner that guarantees those rights. As a whole, this situation represented a separate violation of articles 8 and 25 of the Convention in relation to article 1(1) thereof and the corresponding articles of the Declaration. (Para 44)

3 In Brazil, compared to the numbers of men affected, women were the victims of domestic violence in disproportionate numbers. The treatment of cases of domestic violence by the Brazilian justice system involved clear discrimination against women, resulting from the inefficiency of the Brazilian judicial system and the inadequate application of national and international rules, including those arising from the case law of the Brazilian Supreme Court. Accordingly, Brazil was in violation of article 24 of the Convention and articles II and XVIII of the Declaration. This was so despite the various initiatives that had been taken to address the problem, which had not had any impact on the present case nor any significant impact on the pattern of State tolerance of violence against women. (Paras 47–50, 60)

4 Brazil had failed to prosecute and convict the perpetrator in this case and it was clear that this was part of a broader pattern. The condoning of this situation by the entire system only served to perpetuate the psychological, social, and historical roots and factors that sustained and encouraged violence against women. Given that the violence suffered by Ms Fernandes was part of a general pattern of negligence and lack of effective action by the State in prosecuting and convicting aggressors, Brazil had also failed in its obligation to prevent violence against women. Such general and discriminatory judicial ineffectiveness created a climate that was conducive to domestic violence, since society saw no evidence of willingness by the State, as the representative of the society, to take effective action to sanction such acts. Accordingly, Brazil was liable for failing to perform its duties set forth in articles 7(b), (d), (e), (f), and (g) of the Convention of Belém do Pará in relation to rights protected therein, among them, the

right to a life free of violence (article 3), the right of a woman to have her life, her physical, mental, and moral integrity, her personal safety, and personal dignity respected, to equal protection before and of the law, and to simple and prompt recourse to a competent court for protection against acts that violate her rights (articles 4(a), (b), (c), (d), (e), (f), and (g)). (Paras 55–58)

Treaties and other international instruments referred to

American Convention on Human Rights 1969, arts 1(1), 8, 24, 25, 28, 44, 46, 47 and 48

American Declaration of the Rights and Duties of Man 1948, arts II and XVIII

Inter-American Convention on the Prevention, Punishment, and Eradication of Violence against Women 1994 (Convention of Belém do Pará), arts 2, 3, 4, 5, 7 and 12

Regulations of the Inter-American Commission on Human Rights, art 42 and 45

Cases referred to

Blake Case, IACHR, judgment on Preliminary Objections of 2 July 1996, Series C, No 27 (1996)

Viviana Gallardo et al, IACHR, judgment of 13 November, 1981, Series A, No G 101/81

Genie Lacayo Case, IACHR, judgment of 29 January 1997, Series C, No 30 (1997)

Godínez Cruz Case (Preliminary Objections), IACHR, judgment of 26 June 1987, Series C, No 3 (1987)

Godínez Cruz Case, IACHR, judgment of 20 January 1989, Series C, No 5 (1989)

Newton Coutinho Mendes et al v Brazil, IACommHR, Annual Report 1998, Case 11.405, Report No 59/99, IACHR, OEA/Ser.L/V/II.95 Doc 7 rev at 399 (1998)

João Canuto de Oliveira v Brazil, IACommHR, Annual Report 1997, Case 11.287, Report No 24/98, IACHR, OEA/Ser.L/V/II.95 Doc 7 rev at 379 (1997)

Ovelario Tames v Brazil, IACommHR, Annual Report 1998, Case 11.516, Report No 60/99, IACHR, OEA/Ser.L/V/II.95 Doc 7 rev at 424 (1998)

Alonso Eugenio da Silva v Brazil, IACommHR, Annual Report 1999, Case 11.598, Report Nº 9/00, IACHR, OEA/Ser.L/V/II.106 Doc 3 rev at 399 (1999)

Velásquez Rodríguez v Honduras, IACHR, judgment of 29 July 1988, Series C, No 4 (1988); *supra* p 91

REPORT

I   SUMMARY

1   On 20 August 1998, the Inter-American Commission on Human Rights (hereinafter "the Commission") received a petition filed by Mrs Maria da Penha Maia Fernandes, the Center for Justice and International Law (CEJIL), and the Latin American and Caribbean Committee for the Defense of Women's Rights (CLADEM) (hereinafter "the petitioners"), as provided for in Articles 44 and 46 of the American Convention on Human Rights (hereinafter "the Convention" or "the American Convention") and

Article 12 of the Inter-American Convention on the Prevention, Punishment, and Eradication of Violence against Women ("Convention of Belém do Pará").

2   The petition alleges that the Federative Republic of Brazil (hereinafter "Brazil" or "the State") condoned, for years during their marital cohabitation, domestic violence perpetrated in the city of Fortaleza, Ceará State, by Marco Antônio Heredia Viveiros against his wife at the time, Maria da Penha Maia Fernandes, culminating in attempted murder and further aggression in May and June 1983. As a result of this aggression, Maria da Penha has suffered from irreversible paraplegia and other ailments since 1983. The petition maintains that the State has condoned this situation, since, for more than 15 years, it has failed to take the effective measures required to prosecute and punish the aggressor, despite repeated complaints. The petition alleges violation of Article 1(1) (obligation to respect rights), 8 (a fair trial), 24 (equal protection), and 25 (judicial protection) of the American Convention, in relation to Articles II and XVIII of the American Declaration of the Rights and Duties of Man ("the Declaration"), as well as Articles 3, 4(a), (b), (c), (d), (e), (f), and (g), and 5 and 7 of the Convention of Belém do Pará. The Commission processed the petition in accordance with the regulations. In view of the fact that the State failed to provide comments on the petition despite the repeated requests of the Commission, the petitioners asked that the events related in the petition be presumed to be true and that Article 42 of the Regulations of the Commission be applied.

3   In this report, the Commission analyzes admissibility requirements and considers the petition admissible pursuant to Articles 46(2)(c) and 47 of the American Convention, and 12 of the Convention of Belém do Pará. With respect to the merits of the case, the Commission concludes that the State violated the right of Mrs Maria da Penha Maia Fernandes to a fair trial and judicial protection, guaranteed in Articles 8 and 25 of the American Convention, in relation to the general obligation to respect and guarantee rights set forth in Article 1(1) of that instrument and Articles II and XVIII of the Declaration, as well as Article 7 of the Convention of Belém do Pará. It also concludes that this violation forms a pattern of discrimination evidenced by the condoning of domestic violence against women in Brazil through ineffective judicial action. The Commission recommends that the State conduct a serious, impartial, and exhaustive investigation in order to establish the criminal liability of the perpetrator for the attempted murder of Mrs Fernandes and to determine whether there are any other events or actions of State agents that have prevented the rapid and effective prosecution of the perpetrator. It also recommends prompt and effective compensation for the victim, and the adoption of measures at the national level to eliminate tolerance by the State of domestic violence against women.

II   PROCESSING BY THE COMMISSION AND FRIENDLY SETTLEMENT OFFER

4   On 20 August 1998, the Inter-American Commission received the petition related to this case and on 1 September of that year, it forwarded a communication to the petitioners acknowledging receipt of their petition and informing them that it had begun to process the case. On 19 October 1998, the Inter-American Commission forwarded the petition to the State and requested information from it on the matter.

5   In light of the failure on the part of the State to respond, on 2 August 1999, the petitioners requested application of Article 42 of the Regulations of the Commission, so that the events related in the petition could be presumed to be true, in view of the fact

that more than 250 days had elapsed since the forwarding of the petition to Brazil and no comments had been received from the latter on the case.

6   On 4 August 1999, the Inter-American Commission again asked the State to submit the information that it deemed pertinent, and warned of the possible application of Article 42 of its Regulations.

7   On 7 August 2000, the Commission made itself available to the parties for 30 days to begin the friendly settlement process pursuant to Articles 48(1)(f) of the Convention and 45 of the Regulations of the Commission. To date it has not received a positive response from either party, and, for this reason, the Commission holds the view that during this processing phase, the matter cannot be resolved through these channels.

III   POSITIONS OF THE PARTIES

A   The petitioners

8   The petition states that on 29 May 1983, Mrs María da Penha Maia Fernandes, a pharmacist, was the victim of attempted murder by her then husband, Marco Antônio Heredia Viveiros, an economist, at her home in Fortaleza, Ceará State. He shot her while she was asleep, bringing to a climax a series of acts of aggression carried out over the course of their married life. As a result of this aggression of her spouse, Mrs Fernandes sustained serious injuries, had to undergo numerous operations, and suffered irreversible paraplegia and other physical and psychological trauma.[1]

9   The petitioners state that Mr Heredia Viveiros was an aggressive and violent person, and that he would assault his wife and three daughters during his marriage. According to the victim, the situation became unbearable but she was too afraid to take steps to obtain a separation. They maintain that the husband tried to cover up the attack by reporting it as an attempted robbery and the work of thieves who had fled. Two weeks after Mrs Fernandes returned from the hospital and was recovering from the attempt on her life on May 29, 1983, Mr Heredia Viveiros again attempted to kill her by allegedly trying to electrocute her while she was bathing. At that point, she decided to seek a legal separation from him.[2]

---

1   According to the petition and documents enclosed by the petitioners, Mr Viveiros shot his wife while she was asleep. Fearful and in order to avoid being shot a second time, Mrs Fernandes lay prostrate in the bed pretending to be dead. However, when she was admitted to the hospital she was in shock, with tetraplegia resulting from injury to her third and fourth vertebrae, in addition to other injuries that became apparent later on. Correspondence from the petitioners of 13 August 1998, received by the IACHR Secretariat on 20 August 1998, p 2; and Fernandes (Maria da Penha Maida), Sobrevivi Posso Contar, Fortaleza, 1994, pp 28–30 (Enclosure 1 of the petition).

2   According to statements provided by the victim, the second weekend after she returned from Brasilia, Mr Viveiros asked her whether she wanted to take a bath and when she went in the shower, she felt an electric shock that came from the water. Mrs Fernandes panicked and tried to get out of the shower, but her husband told her that a small electrical shock was not going to kill her. She stated that at that moment she understood why, from the time of her return, Mr Viveiros showered only in his children's bathroom. Correspondence of the petitioners dated 13 August 1998, p 5, and enclosure 2 of that document.

10 They maintain that Mr Viveiros acted with premeditation, since the week before the attack he had tried to convince his wife to make him the beneficiary of a life insurance policy, and five days before attacking her, he tried to force her to sign a document for the sale of her car that provided no indication of the name of the purchaser. They state that Mrs Fernandes learned subsequently that Mr Viveiros had a criminal record, that he was bigamous, and that he had a child in Colombia, information that he had concealed from her.

11 They add that because of the resulting paraplegia, the victim had to undergo extensive physical therapy, and, because of her loss of independence, required constant assistance from nurses in order to move around. The ongoing need for medication and physical therapy is expensive and Mrs Maria da Penha receives no financial assistance from her ex-husband to cover her expenses. Also, he is not paying the alimony stipulated in the separation order.

12 The petitioners maintain that during the judicial investigation, which was launched a few days after the 6 June 1983 assault, statements were taken establishing that Mr Heredia Viveiros was responsible for the assault, and that despite this, he maintained that it was the work of thieves who were trying to enter their home. During the judicial proceedings, evidence was presented demonstrating that Mr Heredia Viveiros intended to kill her, and a rifle owned by him was found in the house, contradicting his claim that he did not own any firearms. Subsequent analyses indicated that this was the weapon used in the assault. Based on all of the above, the Office of the Public Prosecutor filed charges against Mr Heredia Viveiros on 28 September 1984, leading to public criminal proceedings in the First District Court of Fortaleza, in Ceara State.

13 The petitioners indicate that despite the clear nature of the charges and preponderance of the evidence,[3] the case languished for eight years before the jury found Mr Viveiros guilty on 4 May 1991, sentencing him to 15 years in prison for assault and attempted murder, which was reduced to ten years because he had no prior convictions.

14 They state that on that same day, that is, 4 May 1991, the defense filed an appeal against the decision handed down by the Jury. According to Article 479 of the Brazilian Code of Criminal Procedure, this appeal was time-barred, since it could only be filed during rather than after the proceedings, a matter that has been borne out repeatedly by Brazilian case law and, in the case at hand, by the Office of the Public Prosecutor.

15 Another three years went by. On 4 May 1994, the Appeal Court ruled on the appeal. In that decision, it accepted the time-barred appeal, and, using as a basis the argument of the defense that the formulation of questions to the jury was flawed, threw out its decision.

16 They allege that at the same time, other legal action was being taken to appeal the indictment [*pronuncia*] (first judicial decision by means of which the judge identifies signs pointing to a perpetrator that warrant a trial by jury). This appeal was also time-

---

3 The petition states that "a great deal of evidence was collected showing that the former husband of Maria da Penha intended to kill her and pass it off as a robbery of his home". They include a copy of the decision of the Technical Police and the sworn statements of the maids who provided a detailed description of events that point to the guilt of Mr Heredia Viveiros. Among the elements described is the defendant's denial; that he had a shotgun (*espingarda*), which was later proved to be in his possession; the constant physical attacks on his wife; and serious contradictions in his version of the events.

barred and the judge handed down a ruling to that effect. That decision was also appealed in the Ceará State court, which agreed to hear the appeal and issued an unfavorable ruling, upholding the indictment on 3 April 1995, maintaining once more that there was sufficient evidence pointing to a perpetrator.

17 In the petition providing an account of legal ineptitude and delays, it is further stated that two years after the guilty sentence of the first jury was thrown out, a second trial by jury took place on 15 March 1996, in which Mr Viveiros was condemned to ten years and six months in prison.

18 The petitioners claim that the Court again agreed to hear a second appeal filed by the defense, in which it was maintained that the accused was convicted without consideration being given to the evidence contained in the court file. Since 22 April 1997, a decision has been pending in the second instance appeal to the Ceará State Court. As of the date of submission of the petition to the Commission, no decision had been handed down regarding the appeal.

19 The petitioners maintain that as of the date of the petition, the Brazilian justice system had dragged its feet for more than 15 years without handing down a final ruling against the ex-husband of Mrs Fernandes, who has been free during that entire period, despite the serious nature of the charges, the mountain of evidence against him, and the serious nature of the crime committed against Mrs Fernandes. The judicial system of Ceará and the Brazilian State have thus been ineffective, as seen in their failure to conduct proceedings in a prompt and efficient manner, thereby creating a great risk of impunity, since punishment in this case will be barred by the statute of limitations twenty years after the occurrence of these events, a date that is approaching. They maintain that the primary aim of the Brazilian State ought to have been to ensure compensation for the suffering of Maria da Penha, by guaranteeing her a fair trial within a reasonable time period.[4]

20 They maintain that this complaint does not represent an isolated situation in Brazil; rather, it is an example of a pattern of impunity in cases of domestic violence against women in Brazil, since the majority of complaints filed do not lead to criminal prosecution and in the few cases where they do, the perpetrators are convicted in only a small number of cases. We note the comments of this Commission in its report on Brazil:

> The crimes which fall within the heading of violence against women constitute human rights violations under the American Convention, as well as under the more specific terms of the Convention of Belém do Pará. When committed by state agents, the use of violence against the physical and/or mental integrity of an individual gives rise to the direct responsibility of the State. Additionally, the State has an obligation under Article 1(1) of the American Convention and Article 7.b of the Convention of Belém do Pará to exercise due diligence to prevent human rights violations. This means that, even where conduct may not initially be directly imputable to a state (for example, because the actor is unidentified or not a state agent), a violative act may lead to state responsibility "not because of the act itself, but because of the lack of due diligence to prevent the violation or respond to it as the Convention requires".[5]

---

4   This same court noted the overwhelming guilt of the accused and his dangerous personality, as revealed by the crime committed, and its serious consequences, when he was convicted to 15 years in prison in the first trial. FERNANDES (Maria da Penha Maia), Sobrevivi Posso Contar, Fortaleza, 1994, p 74.

5   Report on the Situation of Human Rights in Brazil, 1997, Chapter VIII

21 They allege that the State has not taken effective measures to prevent and punish, from a legal standpoint, domestic violence in Brazil, despite its international obligation to prevent and sanction this violence. They also note that statistics on homicide and sexual violence against women show that in most instances, these acts are perpetrated by their companions or persons whom they know.[6]

22 They maintain that the State of Brazil should take preventive action, in accordance with its international commitments, to reduce the incidence of domestic violence, and to investigate, prosecute, and punish the aggressors within a reasonable time period, in compliance with its obligations assumed internationally to protect human rights, something that it has failed to do. In the case of Mrs Fernandes, the primary aim of action by the Brazilian Government should have been to ensure compensation for the wrongs suffered and the guarantee of fair proceedings against the aggressor within a reasonable time period.

23 In their view, it has been demonstrated that domestic resources have not been effective in providing redress for the human rights violations suffered by Maria da Penha Maia Fernandes, and this situation is further aggravated by the fact that the delay on the part of the Brazilian justice system in handing down a final decision may lead, in 2002, to the barring of the punishment of the offense by the statute of limitations, inasmuch as 20 years would have elapsed since its commission, thereby preventing the State from exercising *jus punendi* and the accused from being held accountable for the crime committed. This inaction of the State is also leading to the inability on the part of the victim to obtain appropriate civil reparations.

24 Finally, the petitioners are seeking application of Article 42 of the Regulations of the Commission so that the acts alleged in the petition may be presumed to be true, since the State has failed to respond, despite the fact that more than 250 days have elapsed since the forwarding of the petition to Brazil.

B   The State

25 The Brazilian State has not provided the Commission with a response regarding the admissibility or the merits of the petition, despite the requests of the Commission to the State on 19 October 1998, 4 August 1999, and 7 August 2000.

IV   ANALYSIS OF COMPETENCE AND ADMISSIBILITY

A   Competence of the Commission

26 The petitioners maintain that the State has violated the rights of the victims pursuant to Articles 1(1), 8, 24 (in relation to Articles II and XVIII of the American Declaration), and Article 25 of the American Convention (ratified by Brazil on November 25, 1992), and Articles 3, 4, 5, and 7 of the Convention of Belém do Pará (ratified on November 27, 1995), as a result of the events that occurred from 29 May 1983, on an ongoing basis, to the present. They maintain that the lack of effective action and the tolerant attitude of the State continued after the entry into force of these two inter-American Conventions.

---

6   The petitioners state that this situation has also been recognized by the United Nations and have submitted newspaper articles with their petition. They note that 70% of the cases of violence against women occur in their homes (Human Rights Watch, *Report on Brazil*, 1991, p 351), and that a police officer in Río de Janeiro stated that of the more than 2,000 cases of rape or beatings reported at his police station, he did not know of any that resulted in the punishment of the perpetrator (HRW Report, p 367).

27   In the view of the Commission, it has *ratione materiae, ratione loci,* and *ratione temporis* competence since the petition pertains to rights originally protected by the American Declaration on the Rights and Duties of Man; and by the American Convention and the Convention of Belém do Pará when they became binding with respect to the Federative Republic of Brazil. Despite the fact that the original assault occurred in 1983, while the American Declaration was in effect, the Commission holds the view, with regard to the alleged failure to guarantee due process that, inasmuch as it is an ongoing violation, it would also be covered under the American Convention and the Convention of Belém do Pará, which took effect later on, since the alleged tolerant attitude of the State constituted an ongoing denial of justice, to the detriment of Mrs Fernandes, which could make it impossible to convict the perpetrator and compensate the victim. Consequently, the State allegedly tolerated a situation of impunity and defenselessness, the effects of which were felt even after the date on which Brazil acceded to the American Convention and the Convention of Belém do Pará.[7]

28   The Commission has general competence with respect to application of the Inter-American Convention on the Prevention, Punishment, and Eradication of Violence against Women (Convention of Belém do Pará or CMV), since it is an inter-American human rights instrument, and because of the competence assigned to it specifically by States in Article 12 of the Convention, which stipulates:

> Any person or group of persons, or any non-governmental entity legally recognized in one or more member states of the Organization, may lodge petitions with the Inter-American Commission on Human Rights containing denunciations or complaints of violations of Article 7 of this Convention by a State Party, and the Commission shall consider such claims in accordance with the norms and procedures established by the American Convention on Human Rights and the Statutes and Regulations of the Inter-American Commission on Human Rights for lodging and considering petitions.

29   With respect to *ratione personae* competence, the petition was filed jointly by Mrs Maria da Penha Maia Fernandes, the Center for Justice and International Law (CEJIL), and the Latin American and Caribbean Committee for the Defense of Women's Rights (CLADEM), all of whom have legal authority to file a petition with the Commission pursuant to Article 44 of the American Convention. In addition, insofar as the State is concerned, Article 28 of the American Convention states that when a federative State is involved, as is the case with Brazil, the national Government is answerable in the international sphere for its own acts and for those taken by the agents of the entities that compose the Federation.

---

7   In this regard, the Commission has abundant case law. See IACHR Case 11.516, *Ovelario Tames,* Annual Report 1998, (Brazil) para. 26 and 27; Case 11.405 *Newton Coutinho Mendes et al,* Annual Report 1998 (Brazil); Case 11.598 *Alonso Eugenio da Silva,* Annual Report 1999 (Brazil), paras 19 and 20; Case 11.287 *João Canuto de Oliveira,* Annual Report 1997 (Brazil). The Inter-American Court of Human Rights has addressed the concept of the ongoing violation of rights on many occasions, particularly in the context of forced disappearances, and in this regard, it has stated the following:

> "forced disappearance implies the violation of various human rights recognized in international human rights treaties, including the American Convention, and that the effects of such infringements - even though some may have been completed, as in the instant case - may be prolonged continuously or permanently until such time as the victim's fate or whereabouts are established.

> In the light of the above, as Mr Blake's fate or whereabouts were not known to his family until 14 June 1992, that is, after the date on which Guatemala accepted the contentious jurisdiction of this Court, the preliminary objection raised by the ...

B Requirement for admissibility of a petition

(a) Exhaustion of domestic remedies

30 Article 46(1)(a) of the Convention states that domestic remedies must be exhausted if a petition is to be considered admissible by the Commission. However, Article 46(2)(c) also states that where there has been unwarranted delay in obtaining a decision in the domestic sphere, that provision shall not apply. As the Inter-American Court has stated, this is a rule which, when cited, may be explicitly or implicitly waived by the State, and, to be timely, must be invoked during the initial stages of proceedings, failing which the State in question will be considered to have tacitly waived its right in this regard.[8]

31 The Brazilian State has not responded to numerous communications forwarded with this petition; consequently, it has not raised this objection. It is the view of the Commission in this case that the silence of the State constitutes tacit waiver of the right to invoke this requirement, and, for this reason, the Commission is not required to consider fulfillment thereof later on.

32 Furthermore, the Commission considers it necessary to point to the uncontested fact that after 15 years, the Brazilian justice system has not handed down a final ruling in this case, and, since 1997, a decision has been pending at the second instance level of appeal in the Ceará State Court. The Commission also thinks that there has been an unwarranted delay in the processing of the complaint, which is exacerbated by the fact that this delay can lead to barring of the offense by the statute of limitations and, as a result, definitive impunity of the perpetrator and the inability of the victim to receive compensation. Consequently, the exception provided for in Article 46(2)(c) of the Convention can also be applied.

(b) Time period for submission

33 In accordance with Article 46(1)(b) of the American Convention, acceptance of a petition is subject to the submission thereof in a timely manner, within six months of the date of notification of the petitioner of the final ruling in the domestic sphere. Since there has not been a final ruling, the Commission holds the view that the petition was submitted within a reasonable time frame, based on analysis of the information

---

7 ... Government must be deemed to be without merit insofar as it relates to effects and actions subsequent to its acceptance. The Court is therefore competent to examine the possible violations which the Commission imputes to the Government in connection with those effects and actions."

Inter-American Court, *Blake* case, Judgment on Preliminary Objections of 2 July 1996, paras 39 and 40. In that regard, see also Inter-American Court, *Velásquez Rodríguez* case, Judgment of 29 July 1988, para 155; and *Godínez Cruz* case, Judgment of 20 January 1989, para 163. Also in the *Genie Lacayo* case (paras 21 and 24 Excep Preliminaries), the Court agreed to consider violation of Articles 2, 8, 24, and 25, involving the denial of justice that started prior to the non-retroactive acceptance of the competence of the Court but continued after acceptance thereof.

In addition, the notion of an ongoing situation has also been accepted by the European Court of Human Rights in decisions on cases pertaining to arrests dating back to the 1960s, and by the Human Rights Commission, the practices of which, under the United Nations International Covenant on Civil and Political Rights and its first Optional Protocol, from the early 1980s, contains examples of ongoing situations that led to events that occurred or persisted after the entry into force of the Covenant and Protocol with respect to the State in question, and thus violated rights enshrined in the Covenant.

8 Inter-American Court, *Godínez Cruz* case, Preliminary Objections, Judgment of 26 June 1987. Series C. N° 3. Paras 90 and 91 state: "Generally recognized principles of international law indicate, first, that this is a rule that may be waived, either expressly or by implication, by the State having the right to invoke it, as this Court has already recognized (see *Viviana Gallardo et.al.*, Judgment of 13 November 1981, N° G 101/81. Series A, para 26). Second, the objection...

submitted by the petitioners, and that the exception with regard to the six-month period set forth in Article 46(2)(c) and Article 37(2) (c) of the Regulations of the Commission is applicable. The Commission notes that it holds the same view regarding its competence with respect to the Convention of Belém do Pará, as stipulated in the final part of Article 12 thereof.

(c)   Duplication of proceedings

34 With regard to the duplication of proceedings, it does not seem that this case has been referred to another entity and the State has not made any claim to that effect. Consequently, the Commission considers the petition admissible pursuant to Article 46(c) and 47(d) of the American Convention.

(d)   Conclusions related to competence and admissibility

35 In light of the foregoing, the Commission considers itself competent to make a decision on the case, and holds the view that this petition fulfills the requirements of admissibility set forth in the American Convention on Human Rights and the Convention of Belém do Pará.

V   ANALYSIS OF THE MERITS OF THE CASE

The silence of the State with respect to the case outlined in this petition is at odds with its obligation assumed upon ratification of the American Convention, pertaining to the authority of the Commission "to act on petitions and other communications, pursuant to the provisions of Articles 44 to 51 of the Convention". The Commission has analyzed the case on the basis of the documents provided by the petitioners and other materials obtained, taking into account Article 42 of its Regulations.

[...]*

In the view of the Commission, an analysis of all the evidence available does not lead to conclusions that are different from those presented below, with respect to the matters analyzed.[9] The Commission will analyze first the right to justice in accordance with the Declaration and the American Convention, and then complete the analysis by applying the Convention of Belém do Pará.

---

8   ... asserting the non-exhaustion of domestic remedies, to be timely, must be made at an early stage of the proceedings by the State entitled to make it, lest a waiver of the requirement be presumed. Third, the State claiming non-exhaustion has an obligation to prove that domestic remedies remain to be exhausted and that they are effective". In applying the foregoing principles to this case, the Court notes that the case file reveals that the Government did not file an objection in a timely manner when the Commission began hearings related to the complaint brought before it, nor did it even do so later on during the entire period that the case was being examined by the Commission.

9   In this analysis, the Commission used the documents submitted by the petitioners as the main source of information for its review, in addition to other instruments available such as: IACHR, Report of the Inter-American Commission on Human Rights on the status of women in the Americas. 13 October 1998, p 91; IACHR, Report on the Situation of Human Rights in Brazil, 29 September 1997, p 164. United Nations Development Programme, Human Development Report 2000 (Oxford University Press, 2000), p 290, as well as the different sources of case-law of the inter-American and international system.

*   Eds: due to space constraints, the list of documents provided by the petitioners and reviewed by the Commission has not been included.

A   **Right to Justice (Article XVIII of the Declaration); and to a Fair Trial (Article 8) and Judicial Protection (Article 25), in relation to the Obligation to Respect and Guarantee Rights (Article 1(1) of the Convention**

37 Articles XVIII of the Declaration and 8 and 25 of the American Convention on Human Rights stipulate that all persons are entitled to access to judicial remedies and to be heard by a competent authority or court when they think that their rights have been violated, which is reaffirmed in Article XVIII (right to justice) of the Declaration, all in relation to the obligation set forth in Article 1(1) of the Convention. Article 25(1) of the Convention states:

> Everyone has the right to simple and prompt recourse, or any other effective recourse, to a competent court or tribunal for protection against acts that violate his fundamental rights recognized by the constitution or laws of the state concerned or by this Convention, even though such violation may have been committed by persons acting in the course of their official duties.

38 More than 17 years have elapsed since the launching of the investigation into the attack on the victim Maria da Penha Maia Fernandes and to date, based on the information received, the case against the accused remains open, a final ruling has not been handed down, and remedies have not been provided for the consequences of the attempted murderer of Mrs Fernandes.[10] The Inter-American Court of Human Rights has stated that the term "reasonable time" established in Article 8(1) of the Convention is not a concept that can be defined easily and has referred to the decisions of the European Court of Human Rights for guidance in this regard. These decisions state that the following elements must be evaluated in determining whether the time period within which proceedings take place is reasonable: the complexity of the case, the procedural activity of the interested party, and the conduct of the judicial authorities.[11]

39 In that regard, the determination of the meaning of the term "within a reasonable time" must be made taking into account the specific facts surrounding each case. In this case, the Commission took into account the claims of the petitioners and the silence of the State.[12] The Commission concludes that the police investigation completed in 1984 provided clear and decisive evidence for concluding the trial and that the proceedings were delayed time and time again by long waits for decisions, acceptance of appeals that were time-barred, and unwarranted delays. Moreover, in the view of the Commission, the victim/petitioner in this case has fulfilled the requirement related to procedural activity with respect to the Brazilian courts, which is being handled by the Office of the Public Prosecutor and the pertinent courts, with which the victim/complainant has cooperated at all times. In the view of the Commission therefore, the characteristics of the case, the personal situation of persons involved in the proceedings, the level of

---

10 During almost half of that period, since 25 September 1992, this situation has existed while the American Convention has been in effect for Brazil. The Convention of Belém do Pará has been in effect since 27 November 1995.

11 Inter-American Court of Human Rights *Genie Lacayo* case, Judgment of 29 January 1997, para 77.

12 In this regard, the Commission deems it important to point out that the Inter-American Court stated that: "The State controls the means to verify acts occurring within its territory. Although the Commission has investigative powers, it can exercise them within a State's jurisdiction only with the cooperation and resources offered by that State." Inter-American Court of Human Rights, *Velásquez Rodríguez*, Judgment of 29 July 1988, para 136.

complexity, and the procedural action of the interested party cannot explain the unwarranted delay in the administration of justice in this case.

40   Eight years elapsed between the time that Mrs Fernandes was the victim of attempted murder in 1983, allegedly by her then husband, and the launching of the appropriate investigations, given the fact that the first trial of the accused did not take place until 1991. The defendants filed a time-barred appeal that was accepted despite its procedural irregularity and, after more than three years, the court decided to declare the proceedings and conviction null and void.[13]

41   The new proceedings were delayed by a special appeal against the 1985 indictment (an appeal that was also alleged to be time-barred), and a decision was handed down recently, after a long delay, on 3 April 1995. The Ceará State Court upheld, ten years later, the 1985 decision of the court that there were signs pointing to commission of the crime by the accused. One year later, on 15 March 1996, another jury condemned Mr. Viveiros to ten years, six months in prison, that is, five years after a ruling was first handed down with respect to this case. Finally, proceedings have not yet ended inasmuch as an appeal against this conviction has been pending since 22 April 1997. In that regard, the Inter-American Commission notes that the judicial delay and long wait for decisions on appeals reveal conduct on the part of the judicial authorities that violates the right to the prompt and effective remedies provided for in the Declaration and the Convention. Throughout these 17-year proceedings, the individual accused of attempting to kill his wife on two occasions has been and continues to be free.

42   As the Inter-American Court of Human Rights has stated:

> What is decisive is whether a violation of the rights recognized by the Convention has occurred with the support or the acquiescence of the government, or whether the State has allowed the act to take place without taking measures to prevent it or to punish those responsible. Thus, the Court's task is to determine whether the violation is the result of a State's failure to fulfill its duty to respect and guarantee those rights, as required by Article 1(1) of the Convention.[14]

Also, the Court has stated the following:

> The State is obligated to investigate every situation involving a violation of the rights protected by the Convention. If the State apparatus acts in such a way that the violation goes unpunished and the victim's full enjoyment of such rights is not restored as soon as possible, the State has failed to comply with its duty to ensure the free and full exercise of those rights to the persons within its jurisdiction. The same is true when the State allows private persons or groups to act freely and with impunity to the detriment of the rights recognized by the Convention.[15]

43   With regard to the obligations of the State in situations where action has not been taken to guarantee the victim the ability to exercise his rights, the Inter-American Court has stated the following:

> The second obligation of the States Parties is to "ensure" the free and full exercise of the rights recognized by the Convention to every person subject to its jurisdiction. This

---

13   The petitioners maintain that this appeal was inadmissible based on Article 479 of the Code of Criminal Procedure of Brazil. The Commission is considering this aspect pursuant to the authority conferred on it under Article XVIII of the American Declaration.

14   Inter-American Court of Human Rights, *Velásquez Rodríguez* case, Judgment of 29 July 1988, para 173.

15   Inter-American Court of Human Rights, *Velásquez Rodríguez* case, Judgment of 29 July 1988, para 176; and Inter-American Court of Human Rights, *Godínez Cruz* case, Judgment of 20 January 1989, para 187.

obligation implies the duty of the States Parties to organize the governmental apparatus and, in general, all the structures through which public power is exercised, so that they are capable of juridically ensuring the free and full enjoyment of human rights. As a consequence of this obligation, the States must prevent, investigate and punish any violation of the rights recognized by the Convention and, moreover, if possible attempt to restore the right violated and provide compensation as warranted for damages resulting from the violation.[16]

44 In this case, the Brazilian courts have failed to hand down a final ruling after seventeen years and this delay is leading to the distinct possibility of definitive impunity because of barring of the offense by the statute of limitations, thereby precluding receipt of compensation which, in any event, would be very late. The Commission holds the view that the domestic judicial decisions in this case reveal inefficiency, negligence, and failure to act on the part of the Brazilian judicial authorities and unjustified delay in the prosecution of the accused. These decisions are standing in the way of punishment of the accused and are raising the specter of impunity and failure to compensate the victim as a result of barring of the offense by the statute of limitations. They demonstrate that the State has not been capable of organizing its entities in a manner that guarantees those rights. As a whole, this situation represents a separate violation of Articles 8 and 25 of the American Convention on Human Rights in relation to Article 1(1) thereof and the corresponding Articles of the Declaration.

B   Equality before the Law (Article 24 of the Convention) and Articles II and XVIII of the Declaration

45 The petitioners also allege violation of Article 24 of the American Convention in relation to the right to equality before the law and the right to justice enshrined in the American Declaration on the Rights and Duties of Man (Articles II and XVIII).

46 In that regard, the Inter-American Commission notes that it has followed with special interest developments related to respect for the rights of women, particularly those related to domestic violence. The Commission has received information on the high number of domestic attacks of women in Brazil. In Ceará alone (the place where the events related to this case took place), there were 1,183 death threats reported to special police stations handling women's affairs in 1993, out of a total of 4,755 complaints.[17]

47 Compared to men, women are the victims of domestic violence in disproportionate numbers. A study done by the National Movement for Human Rights in Brazil compares the incidence of domestic violence against women and men and shows that in terms of murders, women are 30 times more likely to be killed by their husbands than husbands by their wives. In its special report on Brazil in 1997, the Commission found that there was clear discrimination against women who were attacked, resulting from the inefficiency of the Brazilian judicial system and inadequate application of national and international rules, including those arising from the case law of the Brazilian Supreme Court. In its 1997 Report on the Situation of Human Rights, the Commission stated:

> Moreover, even where these specialized stations exist, it remains frequently the case that complaints are not fully investigated or prosecuted. In some cases, resource limitations

---

16 Inter-American Court of Human Rights, *Godínez Cruz* case, Judgment of 20 January 1988, para 175.
17 Maia Fernandes, Maria da Penha "Sobrevivi Posso Contar" Fortaleza 1994, p 150; data based on information received from police stations.

hinder efforts to respond to these crimes. In other cases, women refrain from pressing formal charges. In practice, legal and other limitations often expose women to situations where they feel constrained to act. By law, women have to register their complaint at a police station, and explain what happened so the delegate can write up an "incident report." Delegates who have not received sufficient training may be unable to provide the required services, and some reportedly continue to respond to victims in ways that make them feel shame and humiliation. For certain crimes, such as rape, victims must present themselves at an Institute of Forensic Medicine (*Instituto Médico Legal*), which has the exclusive competence to perform the examinations required by law to process a charge. Some women are not aware of this requirement, or do not have access to such a facility in the timely manner necessary to obtain the required evidence. These Institutes tend to be located in urban areas, and, where available, are often understaffed. Moreover, even when women take the steps necessary to denounce the use of criminal violence, there is no guarantee that the crime will be investigated and prosecuted.

Although the Supreme Court of Brazil struck down the archaic "honor defense" as a justification for wife-killing in 1991, many courts remain reluctant to prosecute and punish the perpetrators of domestic violence. In some areas of the country, use of the "honor defense" persists, and in some areas the conduct of the victim continues to be a focal point within the judicial process to prosecute a sexual crime. Rather than focusing on the existence of the legal elements of the crime in question, the practices of some defense lawyers-sustained in turn by some courts-have the effect of requiring the victim to demonstrate the sanctity of her reputation and her moral blamelessness in order to exercise the remedies legally required to be available to her. The initiatives taken by the public and private sector to confront violence against women have begun to combat the silence which customarily has concealed it, but have yet to surmount the social, legal and other barriers which contribute to the impunity in which these crimes too often languish.

48 That report also makes reference to various studies that demonstrate that in cases where statistics have been kept, they have shown that only one percent of the offenses reported to specialized stations are actually investigated. (Unido de Mulheres de Sao Paulo, *A Violencia Contra a Mulher e a Impunidade: Una Questão Política* (1995), In 1994, of 86,815 complaints filed by women who were assaulted in the home, only 24,103 led to police investigations, according to that report.

49 Other reports indicate that 70% of the criminal complaints pertaining to domestic violence are put on hold without any conclusion being reached. Only 2% of the criminal complaints for domestic violence against women lead to conviction of the aggressor. (Report of the San Pablo Catholic University, 1998).

50 In this analysis examining the pattern shown by the State in responding to this kind of violation, the Commission also notes that positive measures have been taken in the legislative, judicial, and administrative spheres.[18] The Commission points to three

---

18   As a result of joint action taken by the Government and the CNDM [National Council for Women's Rights], the 1988 Brazilian Constitution has been amended in a manner that reflects significant progress in women's rights. In the context of the National Program on Human Rights, the initiatives proposed by the Government aimed at strengthening the rights of women include: support for the National Council for Women's Rights and the National Program to Prevent Violence against Women; efforts to support and prevent sexual and domestic violence against women, to provide comprehensive assistance to women who are at risk, and to educate the public about discrimination and violence against women and safeguards that are available; repeal of certain discriminatory provisions in the Penal and Civil Code on parental authority; support for efforts to develop gender-specific approaches in the training of State agents and in the establishment of curriculum guidelines at the primary and secondary education levels; and support for statistical studies related to the status of women in the labor sphere. The program also recommends that the Government implement the decisions contained in the Inter-American Convention on the Prevention, Punishment, and Eradication of Violence against Women.

initiatives that are directly related to the situation seen in this case: (1) the establishment of special police stations to handle reports on violence against women; (2) the establishment of shelters for battered women; and (3) the 1991 decision of the Supreme Court to strike down the archaic concept of "honor defense " as a justification for crimes against wives. These positive and other similar initiatives have been implemented on a limited basis in relation to the scope and urgency of the problem, as indicated earlier. In this case, which stands as a symbol, these initiatives have not had any effect whatsoever.

C   Article 7 of the Convention of Belém do Pará

51 On 27 November 1995, Brazil deposited its ratification of the Convention of Belém do Pará, the inter-American instrument by means of which American States acknowledge the extent of this problem, establish guidelines to be followed, make commitments to address it, and establish the possibility for any individual or organization to file petitions and take action on a matter before the Inter-American Commission on Human Rights and through its proceedings. The petitioners are seeking a finding of violation by the State of Articles 3, 4, 5, and 7 of this Inter-American Convention on the Prevention, Punishment, and Eradication of Violence against Women, and are alleging that this case must be analyzed in a context of gender-based discrimination by Brazilian State organs, which serves to reinforce the systematic pattern of violence against women and impunity in Brazil.

52 As indicated earlier, the Commission has *ratione materiae* and *ratione temporis* competence to hear the case pursuant to the provisions of the Convention of Belém do Pará with respect to acts that occurred subsequent to ratification thereof by Brazil, that is, the alleged ongoing violation of the right to effective legal procedures, and, consequently, the tolerance that this would imply of violence against women.

53 The Convention of Belém do Pará is an essential instrument that reflects the great effort made to identify specific measures to protect the right of women to a life free of aggression and violence, both outside and within the family circle. The CVM provides the following definition of violence against women:

Article 2

Violence against women shall be understood to include physical, sexual, and psychological violence:

(a) that occurs within the family or domestic unit or within any other interpersonal relationship, whether or not the perpetrator shares or has shared the same residence with the woman, including, among others, rape, battery and sexual abuse;

(b) that occurs in the community and is perpetrated by any person, including, among others, rape, sexual abuse, torture, trafficking in persons, forced prostitution, kidnapping and sexual harassment in the workplace, as well as in educational institutions, health facilities or any other place; and

(c) that is perpetrated or condoned by the state or its agents regardless of where it occurs.

54 Within the scope of application of the CMV, reference is made to situations defined by two conditions: first, violence against women as described in sections (a) and (b); and, second, violence perpetrated or condoned by the State. The CMV protects, *inter alia*, the following rights of women when they have been violated by acts of violence: the right to a life free of violence (Article 3), the right to have her life, her physical, mental, and moral integrity, her personal safety, and personal dignity respected, to equal protection

before and of the law; and to simple and prompt recourse to a competent court for protection against acts that violate her rights (Articles 4 (a), (b), (c), (d), (e), (f), and (g)) and the resulting duty of the State set forth in Article 7 of that instrument. Article 7 of the Inter-American Convention on the Prevention, Punishment, and Eradication of Violence against Women states:

DUTIES OF THE STATES

Article 7

The States Parties condemn all forms of violence against women and agree to pursue, by all appropriate means and without delay, policies to prevent, punish and eradicate such violence and undertake to:

(a) refrain from engaging in any act or practice of violence against women and to ensure that their authorities, officials, personnel, agents, and institutions act in conformity with this obligation;

(b) apply due diligence to prevent, investigate and impose penalties for violence against women;

(c) include in their domestic legislation penal, civil, administrative and any other type of provisions that may be needed to prevent, punish and eradicate violence against women and to adopt appropriate administrative measures where necessary;

(d) adopt legal measures to require the perpetrator to refrain from harassing, intimidating or threatening the woman or using any method that harms or endangers her life or integrity, or damages her property;

(e) take all appropriate measures, including legislative measures, to amend or repeal existing laws and regulations or to modify legal or customary practices which sustain the persistence and tolerance of violence against women;

(f) establish fair and effective legal procedures for women who have been subjected to violence which include, among others, protective measures, a timely hearing and effective access to such procedures;

(g) establish the necessary legal and administrative mechanisms to ensure that women subjected to violence have effective access to restitution, reparations or other just and effective remedies; and

(h) adopt such legislative or other measures as may be necessary to give effect to this Convention.

55 The impunity that the ex-husband of Mrs Fernandes has enjoyed and continues to enjoy is at odds with the international commitment voluntarily assumed by the State when it ratified the Convention of Belém do Pará. The failure to prosecute and convict the perpetrator under these circumstances is an indication that the State condones the violence suffered by Maria da Penha, and this failure by the Brazilian courts to take action is exacerbating the direct consequences of the aggression by her ex-husband. Furthermore, as has been demonstrated earlier, that tolerance by the State organs is not limited to this case; rather, it is a pattern. The condoning of this situation by the entire system only serves to perpetuate the psychological, social, and historical roots and factors that sustain and encourage violence against women.

56 Given the fact that the violence suffered by Maria da Penha is part of a general pattern of negligence and lack of effective action by the State in prosecuting and convicting aggressors, it is the view of the Commission that this case involves not only failure to fulfill the obligation to prosecute and convict, but also the obligation to prevent these degrading practices. That general and discriminatory judicial ineffectiveness also

creates a climate that is conducive to domestic violence, since society sees no evidence of willingness by the State, as the representative of the society, to take effective action to sanction such acts.

57 The Commission must consider, in relation to Articles 7(c) and (h), the measures taken by the State to eliminate the condoning of domestic violence. The Commission notes the positive measures taken by the current administration towards that objective, in particular the establishment of special police stations, shelters for battered women, and others.[19] However, in this case, which represents the tip of the iceberg, ineffective judicial action, impunity, and the inability of victims to obtain compensation provide an example of the lack of commitment to take appropriate action to address domestic violence. Article 7 of the Convention of Belém do Pará seems to represent a list of commitments that the Brazilian State has failed to meet in such cases.

58 In light of the foregoing, the Commission holds the view that this case meets the conditions for domestic violence and tolerance on the part of the State, defined in the Convention of Belém do Pará, and that the State is liable for failing to perform its duties set forth in Articles 7(b), (d), (e), (f), and (g) of that Convention in relation to rights protected therein, among them, the right to a life free of violence (Article 3), the right of a woman to have her life, her physical, mental, and moral integrity, her personal safety, and personal dignity respected, to equal protection before and of the law, and to simple and prompt recourse to a competent court for protection against acts that violate her rights (Articles 4(a), (b), (c), (d), (e), (f), and (g)).

VI   PROCEEDINGS SUBSEQUENT TO REPORT N° 105/00

59 The Commission approved Report N° 105/00 pertaining to this case on 19 October 2000, at its 108th session. This report was transmitted to the State on 1 November 2000, and it was granted a period of two months to implement the recommendations made. The Commission informed the petitioners of the approval of a report in accordance with Article 50 of the Convention. Inasmuch as the period granted has expired and the Commission has not received a response from the State regarding these recommendations, the IACHR adopts the view that these recommendations have not been implemented.

VII   CONCLUSIONS

THE INTER-AMERICAN COMMISSION ON HUMAN RIGHTS DECIDES THAT:

60 The Inter-American Commission on Human Rights reiterates to the State the following conclusions:

1   It is competent to hear this case and that the petition is admissible pursuant to Articles 46(2)(c) and 47 of the American Convention and in accordance with Article 12 of the Convention of Belém do Pará, with respect to violation of the rights and duties established in Articles 1(1) (Obligation to Respect Rights); 8 (a Fair Trial); 24 (Equal Protection); and 25 (Judicial Protection) of the American Convention, in relation to Articles II and XVIII of the American Declaration (the Declaration); as well as Article 7 of the Convention of Belém do Pará.

---

19   See the chapter pertaining to the rights of Brazilian women in the 1997 IACHR Special Report on the Situation of Human Rights in Brazil.

2   Based on the facts, which have not been disputed, and the foregoing analysis, the Federative Republic of Brazil is responsible for violation of the right to a fair trial and judicial protection, guaranteed in Articles 8 and 25 of the American Convention, in accordance with the general obligation to respect and guarantee rights set forth in Article 1(1) of this instrument, because of the unwarranted delay and negligent processing of this case of domestic violence in Brazil.

3   The State has adopted a number of measures intended to reduce the scope of domestic violence and tolerance by the State thereof, although these measures have not yet had a significant impact on the pattern of State tolerance of violence against women, in particular as a result of ineffective police and judicial action in Brazil.

4   The State has violated the rights of Mrs Fernandes and failed to carry out its duty assumed under Article 7 of the Convention of Belém do Pará and Articles 8 and 25 of the American Convention; both in relation to Article 1(1) of the Convention, as a result of its own failure to act and tolerance of the violence inflicted.

VIII   RECOMMENDATIONS

61   Based on the foregoing analysis and conclusions, the Inter-American Commission on Human Rights recommends once more that the Brazilian State:

1   Complete, rapidly and effectively, criminal proceedings against the person responsible for the assault and attempted murder of Mrs Maria da Penha Fernandes Maia.

2   In addition, conduct a serious, impartial, and exhaustive investigation to determine responsibility for the irregularities or unwarranted delays that prevented rapid and effective prosecution of the perpetrator, and implement the appropriate administrative, legislative, and judicial measures.

3   Adopt, without prejudice to possible civil proceedings against the perpetrator, the measures necessary for the State to grant the victim appropriate symbolic and actual compensation for the violence established herein, in particular for its failure to provide rapid and effective remedies, for the impunity that has surrounded the case for more than 15 years, and for making it impossible, as a result of that delay, to institute timely proceedings for redress and compensation in the civil sphere.

4   Continue and expand the reform process that will put an end to the condoning by the State of domestic violence against women in Brazil and discrimination in the handling thereof. In particular, the Commission recommends:

(a) Measures to train and raise the awareness of officials of the judiciary and specialized police so that they may understand the importance of not condoning domestic violence.

(b) The simplification of criminal judicial proceedings so that the time taken for proceedings can be reduced, without affecting the rights and guarantees related to due process.

(c) The establishment of mechanisms that serve as alternatives to judicial mechanisms, which resolve domestic conflict in a prompt and effective manner and create awareness regarding its serious nature and associated criminal consequences.

(d) An increase in the number of special police stations to address the rights of women and to provide them with the special resources needed for the effective processing and investigation of all complaints related to domestic violence, as well as resources and assistance from the Office of the Public Prosecutor in preparing their judicial reports.

(e) The inclusion in teaching curriculums of units aimed at providing an understanding of the importance of respecting women and their rights recognized in the Convention of Belém do Pará, as well as the handling of domestic conflict.

(f) The provision of information to the Inter-American Commission on Human Rights within sixty days of transmission of this report to the State, and of a report on steps taken to implement these recommendations, for the purposes set forth in Article 51(1) of the American Convention.

IX   PUBLICATION

62 The Commission transmitted the report adopted pursuant to Article 51 of the American Convention to the State and to the petitioner on 13 March 2001, and gave the State one month to submit information on the measures adopted to comply with the Commission's recommendations. The State failed to present a response within the time limit.

63 Pursuant to the foregoing considerations, and in conformity with Article 51(3) of the American Convention and Article 48 of its Regulations, the Commission decides to reiterate the conclusions and recommendations of paragraphs 1 and 2, to make this Report public, and to include it in its Annual Report to the General Assembly of the OAS. The Commission, pursuant to its mandate, shall continue evaluating the measures taken by the Brazilian State with respect to the recommendations at issue, until they have been fully fulfilled.

SUBJECT-MATTER INDEX

ABORTION (see under REPRODUCTIVE RIGHTS)

CHILD, RIGHTS OF

Rights of the child – Immigration – Parent's application for permanent residence denied although child permanent resident – Judicial review – Unincorporated treaties – Doctrine of legitimate expectation – Whether legitimate expectation that best interests of child would be primary consideration of administrative decision-maker in reviewing parent's application for permanent residence

CONSTITUTIONAL LAW (see also under STATUTES)

INTERPRETATION

Equality and non-discrimination – Whether general non-discrimination provision in the Constitution included prohibition of discrimination on the ground of sex – *Locus standi* – Whether mother had *locus standi* to bring legal proceedings on behalf of her child

International law – Purposive interpretation of constitutional rights in context of international human rights law

International law – International obligations – Whether Constitution to be interpreted in line with international conventions

International law – Human rights guarantees – Relevance of international human rights instruments and governments' commitments in international *fora*

International law – Human rights guarantees – Relevance of international human rights instruments – Freedom of movement guaranteed to child belonging to Bermuda – Whether "child" included illegitimate child

Scope of application of constitutional guarantees – Acts of private persons – Freedom of movement

PRACTICE AND PROCEDURE

Locus standi – Citizenship – Nationality of children – Denial of citizenship of Botswana to children born to citizen mother married to non-citizen father – Whether constitutional rights of mother adversely affected – Whether mother had *locus standi*

CRIMINAL LAW AND PROCEDURE

Criminal law – Offences – Rape – Marital rape exemption – Whether husband could be convicted of rape if he had sexual intercourse with his wife without her consent – Whether marital rape exemption continued to apply after introduction of statutory definition of rape – Meaning of "unlawful" sexual intercourse in statutory definition of rape

Criminal procedure – Rape – Sexual assault – Evidence – Woman alleging rape only witness to rape – Cautionary rule – Whether cautionary rule discriminated against women

Criminal procedure – Rape – Evidence – Whether statement of accused (woman) sufficient to convict co-accused (male) of *zina-bil-jabr* (rape) without independent corroborating evidence – Islamic jurisprudence

DUE DILIGENCE, DUTY OF (*see under* INTERNATIONAL LAW – STATE RESPONSIBILITY)

EQUALITY AND NON-DISCRIMINATION

CONCEPTS OF EQUALITY AND DISCRIMINATION

Concept of equality – "Similarly situated" v "substantive disadvantage" approaches – Whether persons similarly situated should be similarly treated – Differential treatment of citizens and non-citizens

Sexual harassment – Whether sexual harassment constitutes discrimination on the ground of sex – Employment – Constructive dismissal – Whether resignation due to sexual harassment constitutes constructive dismissal

Sexual harassment – Whether sexual harassment constitutes discrimination on the ground of sex – Vicarious liability – Whether employer liable for employee's actions – Whether acts in course of employment

Sexual harassment – Constitutional guarantees of gender equality and right to life and liberty – Lack of domestic legislative measures against sexual harassment – Appropriateness of court guidelines to fill legislative gap and prevent continued violations of constitutional rights

AFFIRMATIVE ACTION

Affirmative action – Sex discrimination – Positive discrimination – Whether union rules reserving certain executive positions for women, and limiting elections for such positions to women, discriminatory – Whether rules covered by exception for positive discrimination

Affirmative action – Sex discrimination – Positive discrimination – Whether a national law which guaranteed women absolute and unconditional priority over equally qualified men for appointment or promotion in certain sectors where women were under-represented was compatible with principle of equal treatment for men and women under European Community law

BIRTH, DISCRIMINATION BASED ON (see under ILLEGITIMACY, DISCRIMINATION BASED ON)

CITIZENSHIP, DISCRIMINATION BASED ON

Citizenship – Discrimination against non-citizens – Proportionality – Citizenship required for admission to the practice of law – Whether the requirement was discriminatory with respect to qualified Canadian residents who were not citizens – Whether discriminatory requirement justified

Citizenship – Nationality of children – Denial of citizenship of Botswana to children born to citizen mother married to non-citizen father – Whether discrimination on the ground of sex

DISABILITY, DISCRIMINATION BASED ON

Discrimination on grounds of disability – Whether legal impossibility of victim of sexual assault who had an intellectual disability, or of non-victim, to bring criminal proceedings against perpetrator violated European Convention rights

ILLEGITIMACY, DISCRIMINATION BASED ON

Illegitimacy – Discrimination on grounds of birth (legitimacy) – Whether illegitimate child deemed to belong to Bermuda

Illegitimacy – Discrimination on ground of being unmarried mother – Whether requirement that the maternal affiliation of an illegitimate child could only be established in Belgian law by a formal act of recognition, which then had effect only as between mother and child, and not between the mother's family and child, was consistent with European Convention rights

Marckx v Belgium ECtHR 273

Illegitimacy – Whether status of illegitimate children under Irish law violated the right to respect for family life

Johnston v Ireland ECtHR 296

INTERSECTIONALITY (*see under* MULTIPLE FORMS OF DISCRIMINATION)

LEGITIMACY, DISCRIMINATION BASED ON (*see under* ILLEGITIMACY)

MARITAL STATUS, DISCRIMINATION BASED ON

Discrimination on the basis of marital status – Social security – National insurance schemes – Disability allowance – Whether cessation of a disabled woman's payment of disability allowance on the death of her husband (divorced or otherwise), when a disabled man retained his entitlement to disability benefit on the death of his wife (divorced or otherwise) was discrimination on the grounds of sex and marital status – Widow's allowance

Vos v The Netherlands UNHRC 511

MULTIPLE FORMS OF DISCRIMINATION

Discrimination on the grounds of sex, birth and race – Whether such denial of residence contravened the rights of wives of husbands with citizenship or permanent residence violated right to respect for family life without discrimination

Abdulaziz, Cabales v Balkandali v UK ECtHR 618

Sex discrimination – Marital status discrimination – Disability pension – Social security – National insurance schemes – Disability allowance – Whether cessation of a disabled woman's payment of disability allowance on the death of her husband (divorced or otherwise), when a disabled man retained his entitlement to disability benefit on the death of his wife (divorced or otherwise) was discrimination on the grounds of sex and marital status – Widow's allowance

Vos v The Netherlands UNHRC 511

NATIONAL ORIGIN, DISCRIMINATION BASED ON

National origin – Citizenship – Whether proposed amendment to the Constitution granting preferential treatment in the acquisition of Costa Rican nationality through naturalisation to native born Central Americans, Ibero-Americans and Spaniards over non-native born nationals of these countries and other aliens discriminatory

*Proposed Amendments to the Naturalization
Provisions of the Constitution of Costa Rica* IACtHR 553

PREGNANCY, DISCRIMINATION BASED ON

Pregnancy discrimination – Employment – Inability to report to work because of pregnancy-related disorders – Contractual provision for dismissal – Dismissal at time of pregnancy – Whether dismissal discrimination on the ground of sex

Pregnancy discrimination – Employment – Whether discrimination on the ground of pregnancy constitutes discrimination on the ground of sex – Employer accident and sickness plan excluding pregnant women from benefits during 17-week period – Pregnancy as a valid health reason for absence from the workplace – Whether plan discriminatory

PROPERTY OR WEALTH, DISCRIMINATION BASED ON

Property – Judicial separation – Lack of legal aid – Whether discrimination in favour of those with means to pay for legal representation

RACE, DISCRIMINATION BASED ON

Discrimination on the grounds of sex, birth and race – Whether such denial of residence contravened the rights of wives of husbands with citizenship or permanent residence violated right to respect for family life without discrimination

RELIGION, DISCRIMINATION BASED ON

Discrimination on the ground of religion – Spouses of different religions – Lawful marriage in country in which it took place (Lebanon) – Whether prosecution of spouses in United Arab Emirates for having contracted illegal marriage, and declaration that marriage was null and void under domestic law, was discriminatory on the ground of religion

SEX, DISCRIMINATION BASED ON

Sex discrimination – Intersectionality – Discrimination on the grounds of sex, birth and race – Whether denial of residence violated the rights of a wife of a husband with citizenship or permanent residence to respect for family life without discrimination

Sex discrimination – Citizenship – Nationality of children – Denial of citizenship of Botswana to children born to citizen mother married to non-citizen father – Whether discrimination on the ground of sex

Sex discrimination – Criminal law and procedure – Rape – Sexual assault – Criminal procedure – Evidence – Woman alleging rape only witness to rape – Cautionary rule – Whether cautionary rule discriminated against women

Sex discrimination – Employment – Equal treatment of men and women – Employment in the military – Whether a general policy that women were not be employed in military positions involving the use of arms violated the principle of equal treatment of men and women – Exceptions to the principle of equal treatment – Whether combat readiness was a permitted exception to equal treatment

Sex discrimination – Employment – Equal pay – Principle of equal treatment for men and women – Equal pay – Whether payment of an allowance for women going on maternity leave violates principle of equal treatment for men and women – Whether male and female workers in a comparable situation

Sex discrimination – Employment – Pregnancy – Inability to report to work because of pregnancy-related disorders – Contractual provision for dismissal – Dismissal at time of pregnancy – Whether dismissal discrimination on the ground of sex

Sex discrimination – Employment – Pregnancy – Whether discrimination on the ground of pregnancy constitutes discrimination on grounds of sex – Employer accident and sickness plan excluding pregnant women from benefits during 17-week period – Pregnancy as a valid health reason for absence from the workplace

Sex discrimination – Employment – Sexual harassment – Whether sexual harassment constitutes sex discrimination on the ground of sex – Employment – Constructive dismissal – Whether resignation due to sexual harassment constitutes constructive dismissal

Sex discrimination – Employment – Sexual harassment – Whether sexual harassment constitutes discrimination on the ground of sex – Vicarious liability – Whether employer liable for employee's actions – Whether acts in course of employment

Sex discrimination – Employment – Sexual harassment – Constitutional guarantees of gender equality and right to life and liberty – Lack of domestic legislative measures against sexual harassment – Appropriateness of court guidelines to fill legislative gap and prevent continued violations of constitutional rights

Sex discrimination – Employment – Retirement – Differential retirement ages – Whether different retirement ages for male and female flight attendants was contrary to the constitutional right to equality – Status of treaties under Nepalese law

Sex discrimination – Freedom of movement – Freedom of association – Whether rule barring unaccompanied women from a public place a violation of freedom of movement or association – Obligations under international human rights instruments

FAMILY AND PRIVATE LIFE, RIGHT TO RESPECT FOR

STATE RESPONSIBILITY

MARRIAGE AND DIVORCE, RIGHTS RELATING TO

Marriage – Equality of rights and responsibilities in marriage – Legal capacity of wife – Whether laws reflecting traditional divisions of roles in marriage consistent with human rights

Marriage – Right to marry – Right freely to choose a spouse and to enter into marriage only with free and full consent – Validity of marriage (*Nikah*) – Need for consent – Meaning of consent – Determination of validity of marriage in case of conflicting marriage certificates (*Nikah Namas*)

Marriage – Right to marry — Spouses of different religions – Lawful marriage in country in which it took place (Lebanon) – Whether prosecution of spouses in United Arab Emirates for having contracted illegal marriage, and declaration that marriage was null and void under domestic law, was discriminatory on the ground of religion

Marriage – Right to marry and found a family – Discrimination on grounds of illegitimacy – Whether the requirement that the maternal affiliation of an illegitimate child could only be established in Belgian law by a formal act of recognition, which then had effect only as between mother and child and not between the mother's family and child, was consistent with European Convention rights – Whether "family" includes "illegitimate" family – Whether bond between a mother and child is sufficient to establish a "family" – Whether "family" extends to family of mother, including grandparents

Marriage and divorce – Right to marry and right to protection of family life and children – Right to choose one's residence – Right to enjoy cultural life – Preservation of Indian reserve and ethnic group — Indian women married to non-Indian men denied right to live on Indian reserve – Whether different treatment of Indian women married to non-Indian men vis-à-vis Indian men married to non-Indian women amounted to discrimination on the ground of sex – Whether woman who had lost her legal status as an Indian through marriage to a non-Indian was still a "person belonging" to a minority

Marriage and divorce – Divorce – Maintenance – Muslim Personal Law – Duty of husband to pay maintenance after the period of *iddat* to a divorced wife who is unable to maintain herself – Whether a conflict between Muslim Personal Law and right to maintenance – Payment of *Mahr* (dowry) – Whether *Mahr* is an amount payable on the occurrence of divorce, so as to cancel the husband's obligation to pay maintenance

Marriage and divorce – Right to marry – Divorce – Whether the absence of a right to divorce (and re-marry) under Irish Law violated European Convention rights

MINORITIES, RIGHTS OF MEMBERS OF

Minorities – Right to enjoy cultural life – Preservation of Indian reserve and ethnic group – Indian women married to non-Indian men denied right to live on Indian reserve – Whether different treatment of Indian women married to non-Indian men vis-à-vis Indian men married to non-Indian women amounted to discrimination on the ground of sex – Whether woman who had lost her legal status as an Indian through marriage to a non-Indian was still a "person belonging" to a minority

Lovelace v Canada   **UNHRC**   **261**

NATIONALITY, RIGHT TO

Nationality – Naturalisation – Whether proposed amendments to the Constitution of Costa Rica regarding naturalisation contrary to the right to nationality

Proposed Amendments to the Naturalization
Provisions of the Constitution of Costa Rica   **IACtHR**   **553**

PEACEFUL ENJOYMENT OF ONE'S POSSESSIONS, RIGHT TO (*see under* PROPERTY, RIGHT TO)

POSITIVE OBLIGATIONS OF THE STATE (*see under* INTERNATIONAL LAW – STATE RESPONSIBILITY)

PRIVATE ACTORS (*see under* INTERNATIONAL LAW – STATE RESPONSIBILITY)

PROPERTY, RIGHT TO

Right to property – Rights of women to inherit and sell land – Sex discrimination – Customary law – Constitutional law – Bill of Rights – Interpretation of reception clause –Interpretation of existing law

Ephrahim v Pastory   **HCt Tanzania**   **538**

Right to peaceful enjoyment of possessions – Inheritance – Property – Successions "irrégulières" – Right to respect for family life – Whether restrictions on illegitimate child's rights of inheritance regarding mother's and mother's family's property violated Convention rights

Marckx v Belgium   **ECtHR**   **273**

PARTICIPATION IN CULTURAL LIFE, RIGHT TO

Minorities – Right to enjoy cultural life – Preservation of Indian reserve and ethnic group – Indian women married to non-Indian men denied right to live on Indian reserve – Whether different treatment of Indian women married to non-Indian men vis-à-vis Indian men married to non-Indian women amounted to discrimination on the ground of sex – Whether woman who had lost her legal status as an Indian through marriage to a non-Indian was still a "person belonging" to a minority

Lovelace v Canada   **UNHRC**   **261**

PARTICIPATION IN POLITICAL AND PUBLIC LIFE, RIGHT TO

PRIVATE LIFE, RIGHT TO RESPECT FOR

REFUGEES

Interpretation – Relationship between international law and domestic law (law of Australia) – Unincorporated treaties – Whether administrative decision-makers required to take unincorporated treaties into account in interpreting domestic law – Doctrine of legitimate expectation – Immigration – Application by parent for permanent resident status

TORTURE OR CRUEL, INHUMAN OR DEGRADING TREATMENT , RIGHT NOT TO BE SUBJECTED TO

Right not to be subjected to inhuman or degrading treatment – Right to effective remedy – Whether legal impossibility of victim of sexual assault who had an intellectual disability, or non-victim, bringing criminal proceedings against perpetrator violated European Convention rights

Right not to be subjected to torture – Duty of state not to expel or return person to another state where substantial grounds exist for believing person would be in danger of being subjected to torture – Evidentiary requirements – Burden of proof – Right to choose one's spouse – Forced marriage – Subsequent relationship with person of one's own choosing – Whether substantial grounds existed for believing person would be in danger of being subjected to torture (stoning to death for adultery) if returned

Right not to be subjected to torture or cruel, inhuman or degrading treatment – Violence against women – Rape by member of security forces – Whether rape can constitute an act of torture – Elements required

Right not to be subjected to violence – Criminal law – Rape – Marital rape exemption – Whether husband could be convicted of rape if he had sexual intercourse with his wife without her consent – Whether marital rape exemption continued to apply after introduction of statutory definition of rape – Meaning of "unlawful" sexual intercourse in statutory definition of rape

VIOLENCE AGAINST WOMEN

Violence against women – Extra-marital sex – Offence of *Zina* (extra-marital sex) – Burden of proof – whether woman could be convicted of *Zina* on the basis of her pregnancy and self-exculpatory statement alleging rape by co-accused – Islamic jurisprudence

Violence against women – Right to humane treatment – Torture – Rape by member of security forces – Whether rape can constitute an act of torture – Elements required